INTEGRATED OPERATIONS MANAGEMENT
A Supply Chain Perspective

Mark D. Hanna •
Georgia Southern University

W. Rocky Newman •
Miami University

THOMSON

SOUTH-WESTERN

Australia · Brazil · Canada · Mexico · Singapore · Spain · United Kingdom · United States

THOMSON

SOUTH-WESTERN

Integrated Operations Management: A Supply Chain Perspective, Second Edition
Mark D. Hanna, W. Rocky Newman

VP/Editorial Director:
Jack W. Calhoun

VP/Editor-in-Chief:
Alex von Rosenberg

Sr. Acquisitions Editor:
Charles E. McCormick, Jr.

Sr. Developmental Editor:
Taney H. Wilkins

Sr. Marketing Manager:
Larry Qualls

Sr. Content Project Manager:
Heather Mann

Manager of Technology, Editorial:
Vicky True

Technology Project Editor:
John Rich

Sr. Manufacturing Coordinator:
Diane Lohman

Production House:
Interactive Composition
Corporation

Printer:
Courier Corporation
Westford, MA

Art Director:
Stacy Jenkins Shirley

Internal Design:
Trish Knapke

Cover Design:
Paul Neff

Cover Images:
© Getty Images

Photography Manager:
Deanna Ettinger

Photo Researcher:
Robin Samper

Library of Congress Control Number:
2006926973

For more information about our
products, contact us at:

Thomson Learning Academic
Resource Center
1-800-423-0563

Thomson Higher Education
5191 Natorp Boulevard
Mason, OH 45040
USA

With gratitude to our wives,
Beth and Lisa,
And our children,
Bonnie, Lainey, Rhys, and Marshall.
We appreciate your love and support.

About the Authors

Mark D. Hanna

Mark Hanna is a Professor of Operations Management and Director of the Center for Global Business at Georgia Southern University. Originally from Sonapurhat, West Bengal, India, he earned his B.A. in Mathematics from LeTourneau University (Longview, Texas). His M.S. in Management and Ph.D. in Industrial Management (1989) were earned at Clemson University. The bulk of his academic career has been spent at Miami University and Georgia Southern University—where he has previously served as Associate Dean of the College of Business Administration and Chair of the Department of Information Systems and Logistics.

Dr. Hanna's research has mainly focused on Operations Strategy, Quality Management and Environmental Issues in OM. It has been published in *The Journal of Operations Management, Production and Operations Management, The International Journal of Operations and Production Management, The International Journal of Production Economics* and other journals. He is a lifetime member of the Production and Operations Management Society (POMS) and is active in the Decision Sciences Institute.

W. Rocky Newman

W. Rocky Newman is a Professor of Supply Chain Management at Miami University. He has a Ph.D. from The University of Iowa (1988) and both an MBA (1981) and a B.S. in Business Administration (1980) from Bowling Green State University. Professor Newman teaches in the areas of operations management, supply chain management, and manufacturing strategy. His research interests include manufacturing strategy, environmental issues in manufacturing, supply chain management as well as the implementation of advanced manufacturing technologies. His work has been published in several journals including: the *International Journal of Production Research, The Journal of Production and Inventory Management, The Journal of Manufacturing Systems, The International Journal of Flexible Manufacturing Systems,* the *Mid American Journal of Business, The International Journal of Operations and Production Management, The International Journal of Production Economics, The International Journal of Forecasting, Integrated Manufacturing Systems, The International Journal of Quality and Reliability Management,* and others.

He is the past editor of the *Mid American Journal of Business* and still serves on the editorial advisory board it as well as for the *Journal of Operations Management, The International Journal of Services and Operation Management,* and the *Quality Management Journal.* He is an active member of the DSI, CSCMP, ISM, and APICS.

Contents

Preface   xv

1

Developing a Customer Orientation   1

Operations Managers at the Recreation Center   *2*

Introduction   4

What Is Operations Management?   5

Satisfying Customers with OM   6

The Scope of Operations and SCM   9

Integrating OM Across Business Functions   10

Measuring the Effectiveness of OM   14

Productivity   14

Customer Satisfaction   15

Integrating OM: American Airlines Goes On Time to Better Satisfy Customers   *16*

Brand Equity   17

History and Trends in Operations Management   18

The History   18

Trends in OM   22

Integrating OM: Careers in OM   *25*

Summary   26

Key Terms   26

Discussion Questions   27

Case 1: Mitchellace: Managing a Manufacturing Transformation Process   *27*

2

Operations Strategy: Aligning Operations within the Firm   31

. . . Back at the Rec Center   *32*

Introduction   34

Integrating Operations Management Across the Functions   35

What Is a Strategy?   36

The Strategic Decision Hierarchy   38

Integrating OM: Satisfying Customers with Business Strategy   *43*

Effective Alignment of Operational Decisions   46

Decision Auditing   56

Strategic Integration of Operational Decisions   57

Integrating OM: Satisfying Customers at Rogue Ales   *58*

Environmental Excellence and Operations Strategy   59

Summary   60

Key Terms   61

Discussion Questions   61

Case 2: Goodyear and Michelin Cash in on Firestone's Problems   *62*

References   63

3

Supply Chain Strategy: Aligning Operations with Customer Expectations and Supplier Processes   65

. . . Back at the Rec Center   *66*

Introduction   68

Integrating Operations Management Across the Functions   69

Supply Chain Management: From Henry Ford to E-Commerce   69

Supply Chain Management Decisions   73

   SCM in the Automobile Industry   76

   Integrating OM: I'm Majoring in Supply Chain Management   77

   Supply Chain Configuration Strategies   80

   Integrating OM: Ford Suppliers Move Next Door   83

   The Supply Chain Operating Reference (SCOR) Model   86

Supply Chain Coordination Strategies   90

   Relationship Management   90

   E-Commerce   91

   Improving Supply Chains: Seven Principles   93

   Integrating OM: Satisfying Customers at Toshiba Toner Products Division   94

   Integrating OM: Smart Tags Let Our Inventory Talk   96

   The Stock Price Impact of Supply Chain Savings   98

Summary   102

Key Terms   102

Solved Problems   102

Discussion Questions   104

Problems   105

Challenge Problems   106

Case 3: Your Everyday $2 Billion Supply Chain Blunder—and a Solution   107

References   109

4

Quality Management and Statistical Process Control   111

... Back at the Rec Center   112

Introduction   113

Cross-Functionally Integrating Operations Management   115

Quality Management Processes   115

   Commitment 1: A Commitment to the Customer and Total Customer Satisfaction   117

   Commitment 2: A Commitment to Understanding and Improving the Firm's Process   118

   Commitment 3: A Commitment to the Firm's Employees and to Total Employee Involvement   119

   Commitment 4: A Commitment to Data-Based Decision Making   119

   Shifting Paradigms of Management   119

   Leaders of the Quality Movement in the United States   124

Quality System Effectiveness Measurement Processes   130

   The Baldrige Award   130

   ISO 9000 Certification   130

   Integrating OM: Satisfying Customers at Intel Corporation   132

Quality Detection, Prevention, and Improvement Processes   132

   Detection Processes   132

   Integrating OM: Satisfying Customers at Ritz-Carlton Hotels   134

   Prevention Processes   155

   Improvement Processes   161

Summary   170

Key Terms   171

Solved Problems   172

Discussion Questions   176

Problems   178

Challenge Problems   183

Case 4: NASA's Problems with Mars Probes Linked to Communication Failure   185

References   186

5

The Project Management Process   187

. . . Back at the Rec Center   188

Introduction   190

Integrating Operations Management Across the Functions   191

Building the Project Management Organization   194

Integrating OM: Project Management Outsourcing Gains in Popularity   198

The Project Management Body of Knowledge   199

Managing through the Project Life Cycle   199

Integrating OM: The Human Genome Project   204

Project Planning, Scheduling, and Control   205

Detailed Scheduling Using Network Modeling   206

Analyzing PERT/CPM Networks   209

Time-Cost Trade-offs or Project Crashing   218

Summary   226

Key Terms   227

Solved Problems   227

Discussion Questions   233

Problems   235

Challenge Problems   241

Case 5: Project Scope: To See the Birth of the Universe (and More)   244

References   245

6

The Product-Service Bundle Design Process   247

. . . Back at the Rec Center   248

Introduction   250

Integrating Operations Management Across the Functions   252

Product-Service Bundle Design Tasks   253

Designing Product-Service Bundles Using Cross-Functional Teams   257

Integrating OM: Designing the Jet Propelled Surfboard to Make Its Own Waves   262

Concurrent Engineering versus Sequential/ Hierarchical Engineering   262

Group Technology, Modular Design, Product Simplification, and E-Commerce   264

Tools Used in Design Processes   266

The Kano Model   266

Integrating OM: "I Don't Want No Satisfaction, I Want . . . LOYALTY!"   268

Quality Function Deployment   271

Computer-Aided Design   275

Service Blueprinting   276

Product Costing Methods   278

Summary   280

Key Terms   280

Solved Problems   280

Discussion Questions   282

Problems   285

Challenge Problems   287

Case 6: What's Bright Yellow, Takes a Beating Every Time It Comes Out, Yet Has Good Hair?   288

References   289

7

Transformation Process Design Processes   291

. . . Back at the Rec Center   292

Introduction   293

Integrating Operations Management Across the Functions   294

Matching Process Characteristics to Customer
Requirements   295

   Process Design Factors   297

   *Integrating OM: Getting More Flexible
but Not More Expensive at
DaimlerChrysler   301*

   Process Choice   316

Business Process Reengineering   320

   A Reengineering Algorithm   322

   *Integrating OM: Satisfying Customers
at Toyota's Manufacturing Plants   323*

   Reengineering Principles   329

Summary   330

Key Terms   330

Solved Problems   330

Discussion Questions   333

Problems   334

Challenge Problems   335

*Case 7: Hey, Where'd the Ticket
Agent Go?   337*

References   338

8

Building the Global Supply Chain: Capacity and Location Decision-Making Processes   339

. . . Back at the Rec Center   340

Introduction   342

Integrating Operations Management Across
the Functions   342

Capacity Decision-Making Issues   343

   Capacity Strategy   345

   Capacity Utilization   348

   Long-Term Forecasting   350

   Learning Curves and Capacity Requirements   352

   The Economics of Capacity Decisions   353

Location Decisions   363

   The Location Decision Hierarchy   363

   *Integrating OM: Boeing Looks
to the Windy City and Beyond   366*

   Locating Near Suppliers or Customers   367

   *Integrating OM: Fire and Water Provide
an Unusual Combination   370*

   Supply Chain Management and Collocation   371

   Decision-Making Tools for Locating Facilities   371

Summary   386

Key Terms   386

Solved Problems   387

Discussion Questions   392

Problems   394

Challenge Problems   397

*Case 8: Capacity and Location Issues in a
Yacht Building and Repair Business?   398*

Reference   399

9

Facility Layout Design Processes   401

. . . Back at the Rec Center   402

Introduction   404

Integrating Operations Management Across
the Functions   405

General Layout Types   406

   Fixed-Position Layouts   406

   Product Layouts   408

   Process Layouts   410

   Cellular Layouts   410

   Hybrid Layouts   411

Layout Decisions and Competitiveness   412

   *Integrating OM: Chrysler Group's Windsor
Assembly Plant Launches Next Phase of
Flexible Manufacturing   415*

Considerations That Drive Layout Decisions   416

Tools to Help with Process-Oriented Layout Decisions   417

Integrating OM: Fantastic Food Facts from the "Fun Ship" Fleet   418

Summary   443

Key Terms   444

Solved Problems   444

Discussion Questions   447

Problems   448

Challenge Problems   450

Case 9.1: Intel's "Seedy" Plant Cloning Process   453

References   454

10

Job Design Processes   455

. . . Back at the Rec Center   456

Introduction   458

Integrating Operations Management Across the Functions   459

Job Design with a Focus on Work Standards   461

Standard Times   462

Standard Procedure   464

Task Familiarity in Job Design   464

Job Specialization and Skill Set Stratification   465

Designing Jobs with a Focus on Their Motivating Potential   465

Integrating OM: Things Get Dicey When the Job Description Includes the "Look"   466

The Motivating Potential Score   468

Improving a Job's Motivating Potential   469

Designing Jobs Including Socio-Technical Systems Perspectives   469

Integrating OM: The Cost of Addiction   470

Designing Jobs for Employee Involvement and the High-Performance Workplace   472

Encouraging Teamwork   472

Rewarding Employee Involvement   474

The Service Profit Chain   475

Job Design and Competitive Priorities   477

Summary   479

Key Terms   480

Discussion Questions   480

Case 10: Southwest Airlines Feels the Pain of Growing Older   481

References   483

11

The Demand Forecasting Process   485

. . . Back at the Rec Center   486

Introduction   488

Integrating Operations Management Across the Functions   488

Using Forecasts for Planning and Control   489

Integrating OM: True Value Hardware Improves Forecasting with CPFR   492

Choosing a Forecasting Method   494

Forecasting Model Types   494

Time-Series Components   495

Short-Term Forecasting   498

Measuring Forecast Accuracy   503

Estimating Trend   506

Estimating and Using Seasonal Indexes   507

Summary   515

Key Terms   515

Solved Problems   516

Discussion Questions   519

Problems   520

Challenge Problems   523

Case 11: Data: How Much Is Enough?   525

13

Supply Chain Coordination: Master Scheduling and Inventory Management Processes   569

. . . Back at the Rec Center   570

Introduction   572

Integrating Operations Management Across the Functions   572

Master Scheduling: Supply Chain Coordination Decisions   573

   Building the Master Schedule   577

   The Supply Chain Perspective: Fitting the Master Schedule to Competitive Priorities   580

Rough-Cut Capacity Planning   581

Independent Demand Inventory: Competitive Considerations   582

   Negative Aspects of Inventory   582

   Positive Aspects of Inventory   583

   Finding the Right Inventory Level   584

Integrating OM: Improving Video and DVD Rental Inventory Management   585

Independent Demand Inventory Models   587

   ABC Inventory Analysis   587

   The Basic Fixed Order Quantity Model   589

   Fixed Order Quantity with Price Discounts   592

   Fixed Order Quantity with Variable Demand and Lead Times   595

Integrating OM: Satisfying Customers Requiring Financial Advice   596

   Fixed Order Quantity with Non-Instantaneous Replenishment   602

   Fixed Interval or Periodic Review Models   603

   Periodic Review Systems When Demand Is Probabilistic   605

   Supply Chain Management—Based Improvements to Master Scheduling and Inventory Management   606

   Enterprise Resources Planning Systems   606

   Improving on "Optimal" Order Quantities   609

Summary   611

12

Aggregate Sales and Operations Planning Processes   527

. . . Back at the Rec Center   528

Introduction   530

Integrating Operations Management Across the Functions   531

Planning for the Intermediate Term   533

   Integrating OM: Planning Milk Production the New Zealand Way   537

Aggregate Planning Variables   538

   Special Aggregate Planning Considerations in Service Environments   540

General Aggregate Planning Strategies   542

   The Level Production Strategy   543

   The Chase Demand Strategy   545

   The Peak Demand Strategy   546

   Mixed Strategies   548

Aggregate Planning Methods   551

   Optimizing Methods   551

   Methods that Model Manager Decisions   554

   The Cut-and-Try Method   554

E-Commerce, Supply Chain Management, and Aggregate Planning   555

Summary   555

Key Terms   556

Solved Problems   556

Discussion Questions   560

Problems   561

Challenge Problems   563

Case 12: Resizing the Workforce in the Netherlands and the U.S.   567

Key Terms   612

Solved Problems   612

Discussion Questions   616

Problems   617

Challenge Problems   620

Case 13: Inventory Tracking with RFID Chips   621

Reference   622

14

Detailed Scheduling and Control Processes with Lean Thinking and the JIT System   623

. . . Back at the Rec Center   624

Introduction   626

Integrating Operations Management Across the Functions   627

Overview of JIT Systems   630

Integrating OM: Satisfying Customers at General Motors   631

JIT, Toyota Production System, and Lean Systems   632

The Enormous Impact of JIT and Lean Systems   632

The Applicability of Lean Thinking and JIT   633

Scheduling and Capacity Management in JIT Systems   635

Level Scheduling   636

JIT Perspectives on Inventory   637

Supply Chain and E-Commerce Considerations in JIT   644

Integrating OM: Coke Cuts Inventory through Better Planning   645

Material Planning   648

Lot Sizes and Setup Time   648

Outside Suppliers and Logistical Issues   651

Integrating OM: Quick-Change Artists   652

Kanban Systems   654

Controlling Inventory Levels with Kanbans   656

Lean Systems in Services   660

Summary   662

Key Terms   662

Solved Problems   663

Discussion Questions   665

Problems   666

Challenge Problems   668

Case 14: J. C. Penney "Tailors" Its Inventory Management to the Twenty-first Century   669

15

Detailed Scheduling and Control Processes in Synchronous Environments with TOC   673

. . . Back at the Rec Center   674

Introduction   676

Integrating Operations Management Across the Functions   677

Optimizing Revenues in a Simple Synchronous Value-Adding System   681

Applicability of Synchronous Planning and Control   690

Integrating OM: The World's Highest Bottleneck—The Hillary Step   691

Overview of TOC   694

Performance Measures and Capacity Issues   695

Cost Accounting   697

The Management Process   698

Integrating OM: Enhancing the Capacity of a Bottleneck to Global Trade   699

Supply Chain Impact of Synchronous Planning and Control   700

Detailed Scheduling: The Drum-Buffer-Rope System   702

Summary   710

Key Terms   710

Solved Problems   711

Discussion Questions   713

Problems   715

Challenge Problems   719

Case 15: The Advanced Regional Traffic Interactive Management and Information System—ARTIMIS   721

References   722

16

Detailed Scheduling and Control Processes in Complex Environments with MRP   723

. . . Back at the Rec Center   724

Introduction   726

Integrating Operations Management Across the Functions   727

Where to Use MRP Planning and Control   731

Overview of a Material Requirements Planning System   733

MRP System Logic   735

An MRP Application   737

    The Product Structure   737

    From Master Schedule to Material Plan   739

    Reducing Lumpiness and Lead Time   742

Managing MRP Systems   743

    Choosing a System   748

    Expediting Orders   748

    Combining MRP with JIT and TOC   748

    Applying MRP in Service Operations   749

    Yield Management Systems   750

Integrating OM: Satisfying Customers at United Airlines   751

Supply Chain Impact of an MRP System   752

Detailed Scheduling in an MRP Environment   753

    Local Priority Rules   754

    Local Priority Rules: An Application   756

    Gantt Charts   759

Summary   763

Key Terms   764

Solved Problems   764

Discussion Questions   772

Problems   773

Challenge Problems   777

Case 16: To Varian Semiconductor, Speed Is the Key to Success   780

References   781

Appendix   783

Supplement A   785

Supplement B   809

Supplement C   852

Glossary   853

Index   863

Preface

Why Did We Write This Book?

Since our first course in operations management (OM), a lot has changed in business and in OM. Many firms have adopted the just-in-time system. Total quality management has changed the way we think about employees, customers, suppliers, business processes, and quality. Business process re-engineering has helped firms achieve revolutionary process improvements. The practice of the theory of constraints has allowed firms to better manage facilities containing capacity-constrained resources. Effective delivery of services has become a more important success factor for every business. Even firms that are perceived to be manufacturers now have to consider the service required to enhance the value of their products from a customer perspective. For example, services such as OnStar and financing or lease packages make a big difference to buyers of luxury automobiles.

Many businesses are now managed from a cross-functional perspective, which emphasizes how operations issues affect—and are affected by—*all* the areas of a firm. The result of this is that business activities can now be managed to improve the value-adding processes to which they contribute rather than being managed from a functional perspective alone. Accompanying all of these developments is the computer revolution. E-commerce and supply chain management—the most recent products of this new computer infrastructure—are central to state-of-the-art OM.

Over the years, we have noticed that OM textbooks have generally kept up with the changes by adding a chapter about the latest developments in OM to the traditional content. Failure to integrate these changes throughout the text has created some problems for instructors. For example, a chapter on total quality management would suggest the importance of customer-focused operations, as well as of cross-training workers and including them in improvement efforts. Later chapters on location and scheduling issues would ignore these concepts and present cost-centered local optimization models, while job design content would focus heavily on job specialization through traditional work standards approaches. Similarly, a chapter on just-in-time systems would present suggestions for customer and supplier relationship management, but would not explain how those concepts fit (or did not fit) other operational environments. Further, service operations were usually treated as separate from manufacturing operations, even though most customers expect (and most businesses provide) a combination of service and manufactured value. The service content seemed to always follow the manufacturing content as an obligatory end-of-chapter appendix.

As a result of this add-on approach, we became increasingly frustrated in our efforts to teach a current, state-of-the-art OM course to non-operations majors. We needed a book that integrated the changes of the last twenty years into each topic area, and we wanted the book to be relevant to business students with majors other than OM. We needed a book that helped business majors integrate their knowledge of other functional areas with what they were learning in OM. We did not think any of the available texts met these needs, so we developed such a book—and this is the result.

How Is the Second Edition Different from the First?

▶ We have developed a new process model of OM in the context of supply chain management to effectively illustrate and link supply chain management (SCM), business process management, cross-functional understanding, and customer satisfaction with the traditional input-process-output model of OM (see page 9). We also use this new model as a means to integrate these issues in each chapter. Our text now has greater appeal to instructors who seek to effectively portray the traditional model of OM in the context of a broader model of supply chain management.

▶ We have emphasized the process nature of a modern approach to OM and extended it to include the broader perspective of supply chain management throughout the book. In short, we have taken the traditional view of OM that focuses on the value added from the receiving dock to the shipping dock (where the unit of analysis is the individual transformation process) and extended it to include the value added from the shipping dock to the receiving dock (where the unit of analysis is the greater supply chain and the relationships between supply chain players). While the transformation process is our primary focus within a supply chain, we make clear that supply chain relationships heavily affect such processes.

▶ We have supplemented our conversational approach to explaining quantitative problem solving situations in the body of the text with boxed examples. In addition, we doubled the number of solved and unsolved problems at the end of each chapter. We also added a "Challenge" level to the problems. This allows us to identify the problems that ask students to go beyond a basic understanding of the material and to extrapolate and apply the concepts to more challenging issues.

▶ We have identified managerial "dilemmas" in each chapter that have cross-functional and, in most cases, cross-organizational (i.e., supply chain) implications. These dilemmas ask the student to think about the OM issues from the perspective of a different functional area or even a supplier or customer's perspective.

▶ In the first edition, project management coverage was located near the end of the book, but because it is closely aligned with the subject of Chapter 6, the product-service bundle design process, we have relocated it to Chapter 5. Many students will go to work in project management environments, but many more will work for organizations that hire other firms to provide project management services ad hoc (e.g., buy and have new capital equipment installed, have an IT firm install and implement new software, have an accounting firm perform an audit, or even have someone build a house for them). Given this fact, this material fits more closely with the chapters in which we cover structural issues in OM (Chapters 6 through 10).

▶ We have combined the chapters on TQM and SPC into one chapter. A separate chapter on TQM made more sense when it was a new approach and not yet integrated into the managerial culture of many firms. Many of the managerial philosophies and underpinnings of TQM are now commonplace, however, so we have integrated these throughout the book.

▶ While we discuss the application of demand forecasting techniques within the context of many decision processes throughout the book, we have increased our emphasis on forecasting tools by adding Chapter 11, The Demand Forecasting Process. We feel this topic is worthy of its own chapter because many business programs include this topic only in their OM course. Additionally, many instructors feel that understanding forecasting processes is essential to effective operational decision making.

▶ A major strength of the first edition—cross-functional thinking—has been enhanced in this edition. This enhancement occurs throughout the chapters, through examples and perspectives woven into the text and a new table for each chapter. (For examples, consider Claudio's story on pages 12–14 and see Table 5.1 on page 192.) These tables illustrate the impact of key issues in Chapter 5 on the various business functions.

Pedagogical Features in the Book

In writing this fully integrated OM text, which is focused on approaches that provide the value required to satisfy customers, we offer pedagogical features that reinforce the book's uniqueness. Among these features are:

▶ **. . . Back at the Rec Center:** These chapter-opening vignettes feature conversations among four fictional managers that provides practical insight into the issues presented in each chapter. The managers' businesses also provide an efficient way to illustrate theoretical concepts—because these industries are already familiar to readers, examples referencing this feature do not require a long description of the operational setting.

▶ **Integrating OM across the Functions:** A table in each chapter highlights the relevance of the chapter's material to professionals in other functional areas and vice versa. Because most students taking an OM course are not OM majors, this feature helps students approach the material from the perspective of other functional areas of their major. It also helps instructors reduce their natural tendency to view the topics from an OM perspective alone.

▶ **E-commerce perspectives:** Throughout the text, where relevant, we seek to provide an e-commerce perspective on the OM topic under consideration. For example, Chapter 12, which focuses on inventory management and master scheduling issues, contains significant content on enterprise resources planning (ERP) systems and electronic data interchange (EDI). Similarly, Chapter 8 provides meaningful exposure to Geographic Information Systems (GIS) in the context of location decisions.

▶ **Real-world examples woven into the text:** Examples come from both service-intensive and manufacturing-intensive businesses. For example, Chapter 16, on material planning and scheduling in complex environments contains information about the yield management practices of major airlines.

▶ **Integrated Operations Management boxed inserts:** These succinct illustrations of current companies' integrated operations practices are found in each chapter. These features help instructors and students relate the topic under consideration to actual managerial practice.

▶ **Boxed quantitative examples in the text.** These problems are similar to end-of-chapter exercises and provide step-by-step methods to solve the problems. They benefit students and instructors by providing an additional reference to draw on when seeking to master the quantitative techniques covered in the book.

▶ **End-of-chapter materials, including Key Words, Solved Problems, Discussion Questions, Problems, and Cases:** These elements are designed to highlight the integrated nature of the chapter's coverage as well as reinforce the OM concepts covered within each chapter.

Ancillaries

Instructor's Resource CD-ROM

This invaluable resource available to adopting professors contains a comprehensive set of PowerPoint© slides created by Jake Simons of Georgia Southern University. The slides are a valuable classroom resource, an aid in lecture preparation, and an excellent study tool. The Test Bank, thoroughly revised by Robert Donnelly of Goldey-Beacom College and verified by Mark Ferguson of George Institute of Technology, is available in Word® and ExamView. These prepared tests make assessing your students' progress effortless. The Test Bank includes true/false, multiple-choice, fill-in-the-blank, short answer, and quantitative problems. Additionally, an author-prepared Solutions Manual includes answers to end-of-chapter discussion questions, case questions, and, where appropriate, solutions to problems. Faculty using this text in their classes may request the IRCD (0-324-37791-6) by contacting their local Thomson sales rep or by contacting the Academic Resource Center at 800-423-0563 or review@thomsonlearning.com. Selected student resources are available at the book support website: www.thomsonedu.com/decisionsciences/hanna.

Acknowledgments

We would like to extend special thanks to our colleagues whose valuable suggestions and thoughtful consideration added significantly to this edition. Special thanks to the following second edition reviewers:

E. Powell Robinson Jr., Texas A&M University

Gyu C. Kim, Northern Illinois University

Shrikant S. Panwalkar, Purdue University

Rex Cutshall, Indiana University

Edward C. Rosenthal, Temple University

Frank C. Barnes, University of North Carolina–Charlotte

Mark Ferguson, Georgia Institute of Technology

Craig A. Hill, Georgia State University

Renato de Matta, University of Iowa

Additionally, we would like to thank the dedicated and hard working members of our team at Thomson/South-Western, including Senior Acquisitions Editor, Charles McCormick Jr.; Senior Marketing Manager, Larry Qualls; Senior Developmental Editor, Taney Wilkins; Senior Content Project Manager, Heather Mann; Art Director, Stacy Shirley; Senior Editorial Assistant, Julie Klooster; and countless others without whom our book would not be the success it is today.

1

Developing a Customer Orientation

Chapter Outline

Introduction   4

What Is Operations Management?   5

Satisfying Customers with OM   6

The Scope of Operations and SCM   9

Integrating OM Across Business Functions   10

Measuring the Effectiveness of OM   14

Productivity   14

Customer Satisfaction   15

Brand Equity   17

History and Trends in Operations Management   18

The History   18

Trends in OM   22

Summary   26

Key Terms   26

Discussion Questions   27

Case 1: Mitchellace: Managing a Manufacturing Transformation Process   27

Learning Objectives

After studying this chapter, you should be able to

▶ Define and describe operations management within a broader context of supply chain management

▶ Argue the need for integration of operations management and other functional areas

▶ Summarize the historical development and current trends in operations management

▶ Summarize the enabling impact that e-commerce has had on operations management

▶ State the similarities and differences between manufacturing and service intensive operations

▶ Describe the value-adding role operations management plays in organizations and their supply chains

▶ Demonstrate your understanding of the role operations management plays in satisfying customers both internal and external to the firm

Operations Managers at the Recreation Center

Four operations managers—Tom Jackson, Cheryl Sanders, Luis Flores, and Fred Silverton—work out every morning at a local recreation center before heading off to their respective jobs in diverse industries. Because all are operations managers and because they see each other every morning, the four have formed a friendship and share their thoughts on numerous OM issues, despite their different functional backgrounds and operations management (OM) roles, and despite being at different stages in their careers.

The companies at which the four managers work represent the variety of settings available in operations management. The group includes small and large businesses. Two of the companies are service firms, and two are manufacturing firms. Two businesses customize their offerings, while two have standardized offerings.

As we proceed through the chapters of this book, we hope that, by listening in on these managers' casual conversations, you will gain a broader understanding of the real-world issues related to the concepts presented in each chapter.

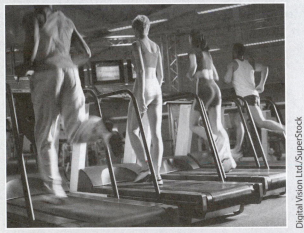

Here's a view of the Rec Center where managers discuss the Operations Management issues covered in each chapter of this book. As you read the "Back at the Rec Center" section at the beginning of each chapter you'll "hear" their conversation and get a feel for what the chapter covers.

Digital Vision Ltd./SuperStock

Tom Jackson

Tom Jackson, 48, is chief of operations for a small but growing airline. He has an undergraduate degree in engineering and earned an MBA by attending night school while serving full-time as an Air Force officer. Tom has spent the last eighteen years in the reserves and will retire in about three years. He

Chabruken/Getty Images Inc.

has worked with two airlines during his civilian career: he left a larger company three years ago when an old Air Force friend offered him a chance to get in at the ground level of a start-up business, the airline for which he now works. The new airline is a regional carrier that offers frequent flights on selected routes. It is always looking to cut costs and pass the savings on to customers. Minimizing frills on frequent flights along high-traffic routes has made the service both inexpensive (by industry standards) and highly reliable—points that the airline exploits in its advertising. But the company is less flexible than other airlines on certain services: it requires that passengers check in earlier than for other airlines; it offers only one class of service on its flights; and it is more restrictive about carry-on luggage than most of its competitors. However, the airline's scheduling approach and other business processes have made it easier for the company to implement the increased security precautions in effect since 9/11. And, the company's lower cost structure is especially beneficial during economic downturns.

Cheryl Sanders

Cheryl Sanders, 32, is an administrator at a small general hospital located in the suburbs. The hospital is one of many operated by a large chain of hospitals and allied health care facilities based in the Southwest. Cheryl has a master's degree in health care administration from a well-known eastern school, and an undergraduate degree in business administration. She began her career with the chain seven years ago and transferred to the hospital where she now works after receiving a major promotion.

Ernst Grasser/Getty Images Inc.

Cheryl is considered to be a rising star in her corporation. She does not have the seniority some of her contemporaries possess, but her ability to think across functional boundaries, or "outside the box," has been noted by senior managers. Since assuming her new position, Cheryl has begun to feel more and more pressure to control costs while maintaining excellence in the delivery of a wide range of services. She sees the hospital's mission as providing high-quality health care for common health problems, and when necessary, transferring more complicated cases to specialist hospitals.

Fred Silverton

Fred Silverton, 40, is very wrapped up in his job as the marketing manager for a division of a large electronics firm. Fred has an undergraduate degree in engineering and an Ivy League MBA, which he occasionally mentions to those he works with. Fred looks younger than he is, which he fears may put him at a disadvantage when dealing with coworkers.

Wide Group/Getty Images Inc.

Fred's division manufactures low-end versions of two cellular communication products for the cost-conscious segment of the consumer electronics market. Model changeovers are few and far between; production volumes are high. Because the manufacture of both products requires similar steps—circuit board preparation, insertion of purchased electronic components, flow soldering, and final assembly—the production process has been largely automated.

Two years ago, before he joined this division, Fred worked for a division that manufactured a greater variety of cutting-edge time management and communication products, such as high-end PDAs. Innovation was not only rewarded, but expected. He found the pace of product development and the variety of customers and products both challenging and exhilarating. Adjusting to the new job has been difficult, because the product designs rarely change, and changes are made only to squeeze pennies from product cost by enhancing the manufacturing process. While Fred understands the cost-conscious strategy of this market segment, he begrudges the change in attitude he feels he must make in order to succeed in the new division.

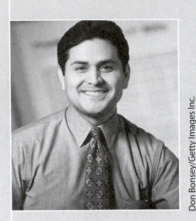

Don Bonsey/Getty Images Inc.

He has always been a self-starter with a great work ethic. Luis is in his eighth year with the business. He spent his first six years with the company as a machine operator on the factory floor, and then moved into a supervisory position after completing his degree in business administration at night. An accounting major in college, Luis realized early that he wanted to be close to "where the padding meets the frame," as he likes to put it; thus his decision to stay on the factory floor after graduation.

Luis's company manufactures a wide variety of products, primarily of upholstered wood. The company is known for the quality and contemporary styling of its furniture. But in the last few years, discount-priced competitors, whose products have traditionally been limited in quality and styling, have been able to expand their product lines and increase quality without raising their prices significantly. So, the company's owners have looked into other lines of furniture to appeal to what they see as an increasingly cost-conscious market for their products. At least for now, Luis feels that the superior styling and variety of his company's products will protect the firm's market share, but no one can predict how long this will be the case.

Luis Flores

Luis Flores is a 27-year-old production supervisor for a small, privately owned furniture manufacturer with annual revenues of about $8 million.

Operations management (OM)

The administration of processes that transform inputs of labor, capital, and materials into output bundles of products and services that are valued by customers.

Introduction

You cannot live a day without benefiting in some way from operations management, because businesses cannot exist without it. And now, after years of schooling and college you are finally in a class where you can learn about this topic In this chapter you will learn what **operations management (OM)** is, the scope of OM within a broader context of supply chain management (SCM), its history, and current and future trends in the field. You will learn that OM and SCM underlie your standard of living, are critical to business success, and impact your life daily in many ways.

What Is Operations Management?

Figure 1.1 illustrates the concept of OM in its simplest and most traditional form. It suggests that companies have transformation processes that convert inputs of labor, capital, and materials into outputs of products and services. A **transformation process,** also called a **conversion process,** is the core set of operations used by a company to provide the primary goods and services that they sell to customers. Table 1.1 on page 6 illustrates the concept of a transformation process for several organizations.

OM is the administration of transformation processes. As such, OM is not just about how people manage factories; it is just as much about how you run a radio station, municipal park, or special fundraiser. It is about managing any transformation process—whether that process is a manufacturing process or a service delivery system. OM is also about realizing that this is done within a context of suppliers and customers who, in turn, often have suppliers and customers of their own. Successfully managing the transformation process of a firm, as well as the other processes that support it, now requires this broader perspective.

It is important that companies think about their transformation processes in terms of what value they can deliver to customers and not just in terms of "outputs," such as those mentioned in Table 1.1. This is known as identifying the primary customer value. For instance, if all that Hummer's transformation process delivered was "automotive vehicles," there wouldn't be many people spending several times the price of a Scion xB for an H1 or H2. (It is hard to say one's more boxy than the other!) So, Hummer must identify its primary customer value, and then manage its transformation processes differently than Scion does so as to create products that reflect its primary customer value—i.e., Hummer must think

transformation (conversion) process

The core set of operations used by a company to provide the primary goods and services that they sell to customers.

REC CENTER DILEMMA

Luis has a hard time seeing "service" in his role

Luis has worked his entire adult life for his current company—first as a machine operator and now as a shop supervisor—so he takes much of what his company does for granted. In the past, he has said his company makes furniture and that's all they do. He is having a hard time seeing how service is relevant to his job. He also sees his job as independent of other functional areas within the company and assumes that "people higher up than me can connect the dots—I don't have to think about marketing or finance, just making furniture." Luis further believes that his company is so different from the others he joins at the club that cross-functional interaction and understanding is not as important to him as it is to Tom, Cheryl, and Fred. What would you advise him?

Figure 1.1

The *transformation process* is the set of operations used by a company to convert the inputs they buy into the outputs that they sell.

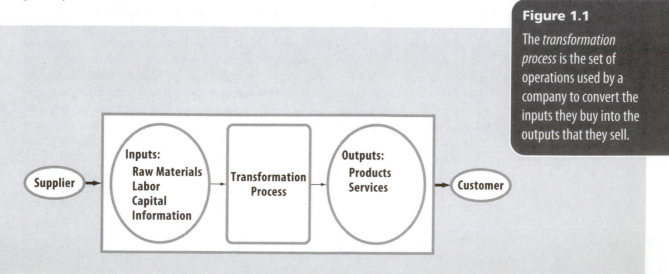

Table 1.1

Transformation Process
Examples

Company or Organization	Main Inputs	Transformation Process	Outputs
Hummer	• Raw materials inventories • Labor • Capital equipment	Auto assembly line	Automotive vehicles (big ones!), owner self image, transportation
Marriott	• Resorts and hotels • Labor	Hotel and resort management system	Hospitality services
Beta Gamma Sigma Business Honor Society	• Labor • Information	Student recognition process	Scholarships and honors for business students
NASA	• Labor • Capital • Intellectual property • Raw materials • Equipment • Facilities	Scientific experimentation process (aka the scientific method)	Knowledge, technology, and space services

about operations in a different way than Scion does. When thinking about the primary value delivered by the firm's operations, it is helpful to consider alternatives such as those listed below in Table 1.2. Once the primary customer value has been identified, operations managers can administer their conversion process accordingly.

Satisfying Customers with OM

When examining Table 1.2, you will notice that OM is about both *manufacturing* and *services*. Manufacturing operations transform physical (or tangible) materials into physical goods. The primary value added by manufacturing can be either stored or transported as long as the physical good can be stored or transported. In contrast, the primary value added by service operations is not as tangible. Services are not physical entities, so they cannot be stored or transported, meaning that the value created by those service operations is generally consumed as the operations are conducted.

Notice, in Table 1.2, that some value-adding activities are better suited to manufacturing operations, such as storage and distribution, while others better fit service operations, such as information and exchange. In most cases, customers require more than one of these forms of value, and they usually do not distinguish between them. Customers simply expect the value provider to bundle the required elements in one package, because customers generally prefer to purchase their service value and manufactured value from a single source. Whether or not the driver delivering our new refrigerator works for the store or is an independent contractor does not much matter to us as long as we do not have to bring the appliance home in our compact car. This

Table 1.2

Value-Adding Activities

Value-Adding Activity	Definition	For Instance
Physical Change	Physically changing the shape or form of input materials.	• Sawing trees into dimensional lumber • Baking flour, yeast, and salt into bread • Cosmetic surgery • Photo film developing
Transportation	Transporting material or customers from where they are to where they need to be.	• Commuting on the local mass transit system • UPS delivering packages • Flying on an airline • Shipping coal or grain via the railroad • Transporting cars from the assembly plant to the local dealership
Storage/ Distribution	Stocking quantities of material until needed by a customer.	• Storing gas at the corner filling station • Warehousing toys until Christmas • A vending machine keeping soda cold until you want to buy a can • Managing the inventory at any retail store
Inspection	Stratifying, comparing, or verifying some characteristic to a predetermined standard or specification.	• The IRS monitoring the income tax system • An audit performed by a public accounting firm • The USDA grading meat before it gets to the grocery store • Administering the SAT, ACT, MCAT, LCAT, GMAT, or GRE tests
Exchange	Facilitating the interchange of product-service bundles.	• The New York Stock Exchange • The classified ads of a local newspaper • Operating an employment agency or real estate agency • Operating a consignment shop
Information	Transferring or disseminating valuable information.	• Advertising • The class for which you are reading this (we hope!) • Swimming lessons • Watching CNN • Calling 1-800-555-1212 • The doctor's office
Physiological	Improving the customer's physical or mental state.	• Working out at the health club • Disneyland • Going to church • Seeing an eating disorders therapist

BananaStock/SuperStock

When this student signed up for a cell plan, what did she think she was buying? What good is the phone without a plan (minutes)? What good is a plan (minutes) without a phone?

Product-service bundle

The total value of the purchase, usually including a "bundle" of goods and services.

Facilitating services

Services that allow the customer to enjoy the benefits of the good's intended use.

Facilitating goods

Goods that allow for the transfer of a service's value to the customer.

Business process

An administrative decision-making process that is used to help an organization to leverage its resources toward accomplishing its objectives.

synergistic combination of service and manufactured value is called the **product-service bundle.**

In order to satisfy their customers, most service companies have to bundle tangible goods with their services, and most manufacturers have to bundle services with their manufactured products. An example of bundling goods with a service is when Sprint gives away or sells at a discount the phones needed to utilize their wireless communication services. Bundling a physical product with their service allows the customers to retain the value of Sprint's system literally in their pockets. On the other hand, General Electric's Aircraft Engine division, which makes jet engines, provides an example of a manufacturer bundling services with a product. The company maintains a database that tracks the vital signs of every engine they make—and keeps it up to date on a real-time basis by accepting input directly from airplanes all over the world. Services such as financing, warranties, after-sales service, information management, and network services are so prevalent in our society that most customers have come to expect businesses to package services with their products and vice versa. We expect convenience, so we also expect the businesses we patronize to bundle manufactured value with service value for us.

Customers expect to receive a product-service bundle with every purchase. In practice, almost all purchases of manufactured products also include purchases of what we will call **facilitating services**—those services that allow the customer to enjoy the benefits of the good's intended use. What does a customer purchase when she hands the auto dealer a cashier's check? If all she really purchases is steel, plastic, and rubber, then she should not care whether she drives her purchase home or carries it in a large number of boxes ("Some assembly required"). Obviously, when a customer purchases a car, she is also buying the facilitating services of the workers who assembled the car, the trucker who delivered it to the dealer, and the mechanic who prepared it for final delivery. Most dealers are more than happy to bundle a host of other services with the purchase of a new vehicle, such as a maintenance contract, automatic roadside assistance, routing assistance, etc.

Similarly, almost all purchases of services include bundled purchases of **facilitating goods**—those goods that allow for the transfer of a service's value to the customer. Let's say you just bought a pair of athletic shoes endorsed by all three of your favorite professional athletes. Chances are you bought these shoes at a store, which charged you more than it paid the distributor for the shoes. You also paid the store for various services, which probably included a convenient location, on-site storage, and maybe even a guaranteed return policy. In other words, you were seeking a value far greater than the physical value of the rubber, cloth, laces, and binding you received. The store, in turn, paid the distributor more than the physical value of the rubber, cloth, laces, and binding. It paid for the national promotion campaign (the professional endorsements), the availability of an adequate supply of shoes at the beginning of the athletic season, shipping and handling, and the privilege of returning unsold or damaged goods. Finally, the distributor paid the manufacturer more for the shoes than the cost of the materials. It paid for the assembly service, as well as the coordination of work-force schedules and material procurement. In most cases, whether a customer purchases a good or a service, the total value of the purchase usually includes a "bundle" of goods and services: the product-service bundle.

Because virtually all purchases encompass a bundle of goods and services, focusing solely on the productivity segment of the transformation process may result in poor customer service. For instance, the cost of the physical production of a daily newspaper might be minimized (and productivity of the conversion process maximized) if the publisher were to print one month's supply at a time. The publisher might thereby take advantage of quantity discounts on paper and delivery. But in so doing, the publisher would utterly compromise the effectiveness of the service component of the bundle; the idea of a monthly publication of daily news is absurd.

Managing service operations without considering the linkages to the physical processes that support the service's delivery is equally inadvisable. For instance, a digital satellite TV service provider might contract an entertainment distribution company to provide excellent entertainment content (how about 56 new-release movie channels) to be delivered via their network. If the distributor's disks are back ordered for months, however, making it impossible for the satellite provider to supply its customers with the promised new releases, the satellite provider will not be in business long.

To satisfy customers, therefore, most operations managers must focus on both service operations and manufacturing operations. Product-service bundles are rarely a fifty-fifty mix of manufacturing and service, however. Operations at a pediatrician's office, for example, are clearly service intensive, with a very small percentage of value, if any, derived from facilitating goods. Service-intensive businesses—e.g., fitness training, auditing, consulting, and medical practice—dominate the economy in many areas of the United States. In the product-service bundles of manufacturing-intensive businesses, most of the value you are paying for is manufactured, whether the product is a refrigerator, washing machine, car, or wrench. The service component of these bundles is primarily related to the distribution and storage of the product that makes it available to the customer.

Figure 1.2 illustrates what it takes to satisfy customers: a **value-adding system**. The figure shows that the role of the product-service bundle is to provide the value that satisfies customers. The transformation process supports the bundling of products and services by providing the relevant products and services to be bundled. Operations managers administer (or support) the transformation process by executing business processes. A **business process** is an administrative decision-making process that is used to help an organization to leverage its resources toward accomplishing its objectives.

The Scope of Operations and SCM

Figure 1.3 lists the business processes covered in this book that fall within the scope of OM and the broader context of SCM. These decision-making processes involve many of the various functions of the firm and support the ability of OM to create value for the firm's customers. These processes generally fall into three categories:

▶ Business processes that provide strategic direction and context for other operational decisions (Chapters 2–5). Topics covered include operations and supply chain strategy, forecasting, project management, and the management and statistical control of quality.

Wolfgang Spunbarg/PhotoEdit

The manufacturing of a newspaper is a relatively small part of the total package. Newsgathering and editing consume more resources and time, and they are what makes the customer willing to pay for the paper. Providing value for customers usually requires a combination of service and manufacturing operations.

Value-adding system

An organized group of interrelated activities and/or processes that creates the product-service bundle and thereby adds the value required by customers. It includes an organization's managerial infrastructure and the physical processes it uses; traditionally referred to as the service delivery system in service organizations and in manufacturing as the manufacturing process.

Figure 1.2

The *value-adding system* results in a product-service bundle that creates customer satisfaction.

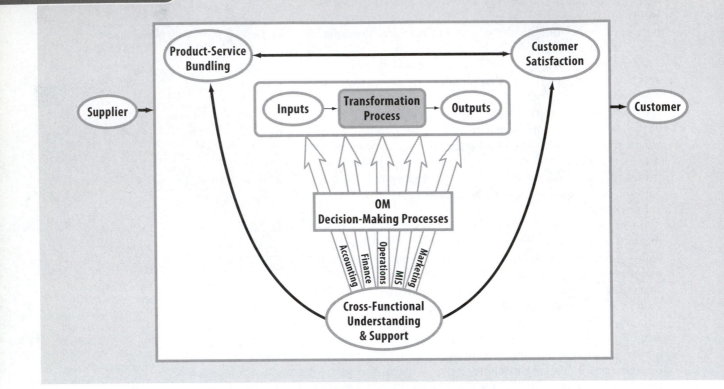

▶ Business processes that determine the operating structure (Chapters 6–10). These decisions deal with the physical design of the transformation process. They have long-term implications because they cannot quickly be changed once a facility is built and equipped and personnel are in place.

▶ Business processes that execute the operating structure (Chapters 11–16). These include planning and control decisions about how the transformation process will be utilized. Obviously, they are constrained by previous structural decisions and have more of a short-term focus.

Integrating OM Across Business Functions

Business processes usually require a lot of interaction among a company's functional areas. This is certainly true of the business processes that form the discipline of OM. This is why Figure 1.2 shows "cross-functional understanding and support" as a foundation for "OM Decision-Making Processes."

It has been said that the basic functional areas in any organization are marketing, finance, and operations. While these three functions form the core of a business,

Figure 1.3

The Scope of OM includes processess that span multiple functions and (perhaps) the supply chain.

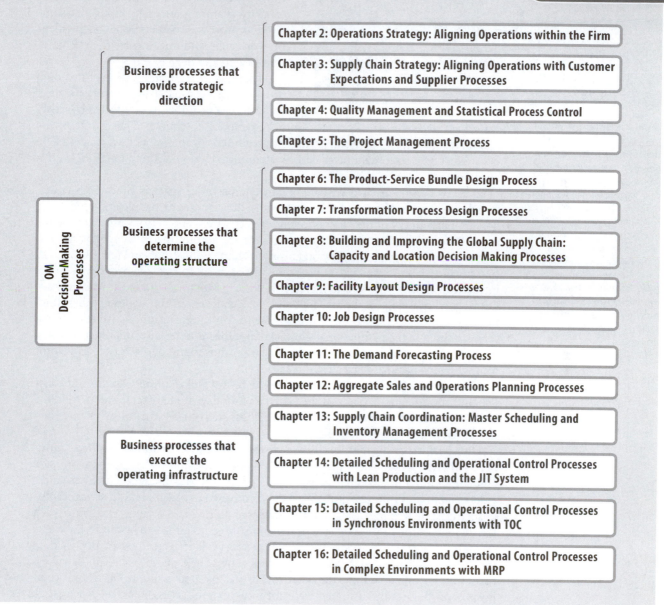

OM Decision-Making Processes

Business processes that provide strategic direction

- Chapter 2: Operations Strategy: Aligning Operations within the Firm
- Chapter 3: Supply Chain Strategy: Aligning Operations with Customer Expectations and Supplier Processes
- Chapter 4: Quality Management and Statistical Process Control
- Chapter 5: The Project Management Process

Business processes that determine the operating structure

- Chapter 6: The Product-Service Bundle Design Process
- Chapter 7: Transformation Process Design Processes
- Chapter 8: Building and Improving the Global Supply Chain: Capacity and Location Decision Making Processes
- Chapter 9: Facility Layout Design Processes
- Chapter 10: Job Design Processes

Business processes that execute the operating infrastructure

- Chapter 11: The Demand Forecasting Process
- Chapter 12: Aggregate Sales and Operations Planning Processes
- Chapter 13: Supply Chain Coordination: Master Scheduling and Inventory Management Processes
- Chapter 14: Detailed Scheduling and Operational Control Processes with Lean Production and the JIT System
- Chapter 15: Detailed Scheduling and Operational Control Processes in Synchronous Environments with TOC
- Chapter 16: Detailed Scheduling and Operational Control Processes in Complex Environments with MRP

functions such as accounting, human resources (HR), engineering, and management information systems (MIS) are important support functions. When it comes to executing a business process, it's hard to think of any situation where managers would be more effective without cross-functional perspectives and support. Depending on the particular business process, interaction with one function may be more critical

Susan Van Etten/PhotoEdit

Grain storage elevators illustrate what is meant by functional silos. Just as grain can only be transferred from one silo to another by pumping it over the tops of the silos, information is only shared between functional areas at the highest levels of many organizations. Modern organizations are using information systems, cross-functional teams, and other techniques described in this book to break down their functional silos and manage their cross-functional business processes.

than with another. For example, because companies need to understand customer preferences to succeed, the product-service bundle design process necessarily requires significant interaction between the production and marketing functions but less interaction between the production and HR functions. By contrast, the production function's capacity planning and scheduling decision-making processes may be heavily dependent on work rules and thus involve the HR function to a greater degree.

When people from the various functional areas within a company do not work together well, it is very difficult to effectively satisfy customers or even to make minor improvements in operations. That is one of the major reasons why most business students, regardless of their major, take a course in OM. Satisfying customers takes coordinated effort across all functional areas of a business.

In many companies, workers are organized and office space is allocated by functional area. The marketing people work with other marketing people and report to a boss in marketing, but they do not often interact with workers from other functional areas. The same holds true for employees in finance, accounting, HR, engineering, and operations. The typical company organization chart, as illustrated in Figure 1.4, shows that functional areas are linked only at the top of the corporate hierarchy. This limits interaction among functions to high levels of the company, so that most workers have little or no knowledge of the activities and work concerns of colleagues in other functional areas. What is more, they have no way to communicate among functions, as if they are stuck in their "functional silos." (We use this term because the functions on a traditional organization chart resemble the grain silos found in the agricultural communities; look again at Figure 1.4.)

Consider the following example of a welder—we will call him Claudio—at Cast-Fab, Inc., in Cincinnati, Ohio. At the Cast-Fab foundry, molten metal is poured into a mold and cast into various parts. These casings, and other forms of metal, are then fabricated into a variety of applications.

One machine casing that Cast-Fab made for an industrial customer required a number of internal welds. The casing was a rectangular cube, completely open on one side and containing three compartments separated by internal dividers. The internal dividers had to be reinforced once they had been riveted in place, a task that was accomplished by spot-welding the joints on both sides of the dividers. To allow welders to reach the dividers through a closed side of the cube, three holes had to be cut in the metal casing opposite the open side of the cube. When the welders were finished spot-welding the dividers, they welded the three access holes shut. Later on, the welds on the access holes were ground down, and the entire casing was "painted" using an electrolytic coating process. As a result, customers were not aware that the access holes had ever existed.

However, because he and the other welders could more easily climb into the casing through the open side to do the spot welding, they usually chose not to use the access holes. The holes existed only because the product engineer who designed the casing had put them on the blueprint, quite possibly before a subsequent engineering change resulted in the opposite-side wall being open.

Claudio had a great money-saving idea: Because nobody used the holes, he suggested to his boss that the fabrication department stop cutting them into the casing.

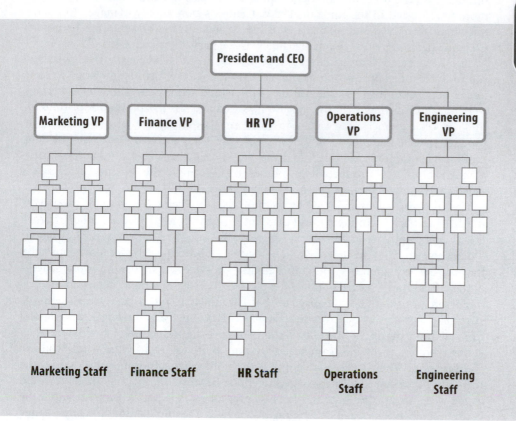

Figure 1.4

Organization chart for a typical company

Cutting the holes wasted the fabricators' time; welding them shut wasted the welders' time; and prepping the holes for coating wasted the painters' time.

Cast-Fab was organized traditionally, by function. Not only were finishing, welding, and fabrication workers housed in separate departments; those departments were physically separate from each other. Engineering occupied an office space that was well removed from the plant floor. To complicate matters further, any design change required the approval of all affected departments.

Claudio's boss thought Claudio's suggestion was a great idea, and he promised to pass it on. The welding coordinator was on vacation, however, and by the time he came back to work, Claudio's boss had forgotten to call him back about the new idea. A couple of weeks later, Claudio worked on a new casing and saw that his idea had not been implemented. Claudio did not give up easily; he reminded his boss of his suggestion. This time his boss's message got through to the welding coordinator, and eventually the information made it to the engineering supervisor's desk. The engineering supervisor simply needed to tell a product design engineer to have a drafter change the master blueprint on the computerized drafting system, and then ask the process engineer to change the work standards (the time required for cutting, welding, and finishing of the casing) used in scheduling the production of the casing. The whole set of changes could have been completed in less than 15 minutes.

Unfortunately, the engineering supervisor happened to be very busy with a new design project that was running late, and he forgot to make these simple requests. After several more attempts, Claudio's boss's boss managed to get the part diagram changed—but nobody told the fabrication coordinator. After another casing came through with the usual access holes, another adventure in communication, and a lot more time wasted in the functional silos, Claudio's boss finally managed to get the information on the design change to the folding and cutting workers. Only because of Claudio's persistence was the change finally made part of the process.

But the story does not end there. Once the engineering change was made, the person who scheduled production did not get the message that because the holes were no longer being cut, the next order of the casing would require less time in the cutting, welding, and finishing departments. So he scheduled the usual amount of time for these processes, which now was more time than needed for the job. The result? The production scheduler got an unwelcome surprise: the plant had more idle time, utilization of equipment dropped, and the Vice President (VP) for operations complained about low productivity! Another trip through the functional silos was required to straighten out that aspect of the matter.

Cast-Fab's president and CEO was new on the job when Claudio made his suggestion. He had been encouraging workers to make suggestions that would either improve the company's process or enhance the employees' work life. Maybe that is why Claudio did not give up. The CEO tells Claudio's story in public frequently, because it illustrates the problems companies encounter when their processes cut across the "white spaces" of their organization chart, but their people and decision-making systems cannot.

Fortunately, things have changed at Cast-Fab. Today, Claudio can make suggestions at regular meetings of his cross-functional work group. The group includes workers from all of the pertinent functional areas—engineers, production planners, and marketing representatives. His team has full responsibility for a particular set of products and processes. The whole team works at the same physical location because all the members have been collocated to the shop floor. Because all functions are represented at the work group meetings and because everyone works at the same location, the group members can readily see and understand the implications of any change request. Today, Claudio's suggestions can be implemented immediately.

Like Claudio, workers in many companies are stuck in functional silos. Although the transformation processes may proceed through several functional areas, such as fabrication, welding, and painting, the traditional organization chart (Figure 1.4) includes no direct lines between employees of one function and employees of another. For a company to satisfy customers and remain competitive, it must be able to manage processes that cut across the so-called "white spaces," or empty spaces, of the organizational chart, and its employees must be able to interact across functional silos.

As you learn about OM in this book, you will also be learning how operations interacts with other functional areas of business. Whether you are planning a career in accounting, marketing, HR, or some other function, this course will help you to effectively interact with operations managers, so that you can integrate your functional area with OM and better manage your company's "white spaces."

Measuring the Effectiveness of OM

Productivity

Productivity

The relationship between output and input for any process.

Both manufacturing and service industries measure the efficiency of their transformation processes by evaluating **productivity,** the relationship between output and input for any process. This is determined using a simple ratio:

Productivity = Output/Input

Based on the traditional view of OM, as presented in Figure 1.1, improvements to the transformation process increase one aspect of productivity. Increased productivity, in turn, leads to a higher standard of living for those who have a stake in the process—which motivates companies to focus attention on OM to ensure that their practices are not wasteful. Excessive focus on productivity, however, can be detrimental. Training employees or buying new equipment may increase input (the denominator in the ratio) without immediately increasing output (the numerator), which leads to decreased productivity in the short term. As a result, managers who are rewarded for maintaining or improving productivity levels on a short-term basis often choose to forego investing in training, new equipment, product-service bundle redesign, or other ways to improve the value they deliver to customers over the long term. Operations managers who focus too heavily on improving productivity may sacrifice the long-term benefits of improving customer service, such as greater market share and improved operating margins.

Measuring productivity is fairly straightforward in manufacturing, but it can be challenge in the services sector, where it is harder to measure inputs and outputs as discrete units. For example, how does one measure the fitness a customer gains from a workout in a gym? As a result, productivity measures in services are usually geared more toward the availability and utilization of resources. For example, a gym can use the number of visits to the weight room per day as an indicator of the value generated by that facility.

Customer Satisfaction

Every operation has a customer or customers, and every customer has expectations regarding the product-service bundles she purchases. This truism holds whether the transformation process produces a tangible good (such as cars) or provides an intangible service (such as health care), and whether or not it seeks a profit. If a manager believes that the business exists for the customers first, productivity and profitability will not be overlooked because these facets of a business are needed to remain competitive in the global marketplace, stay in business, and continue to satisfy customers. If, however, a manager is driven solely to maximize productivity, customer satisfaction may be sacrificed over the short or long term. Thus, a second important measure of operational performance is customer satisfaction.

The primary determinant of value is the customer, but that term can take on several different nuances. A **customer** may be defined as any individual or group that uses the output of a process. Most people would probably define a customer as the target of the service provided by an organization. What they are really thinking of is only the **external customer,** such as a patient who receives medical services in a hospital. Organizations also have **internal customers,** customers who exist within the organization. A doctor at a hospital may send biological specimens to a lab for analysis, which may require several procedures performed in sequence by a team of technicians. This process creates a set of internal customers within the hospital. To the lab technicians, the doctor is an external customer. But lab technicians are customers, too, in that they must use the paperwork the doctor creates in order to provide the desired service. To the hospital administrator who seeks to measure the effectiveness of patient services, the doctor and the lab are both internal customers.

As a customer, you can probably think of numerous times when you were dissatisfied with your purchase. It might have been that the great food and service you expected in a restaurant was ruined by a rude server or an unexpected wait. At other times, you may have been delighted by your purchase because received some unexpected value—such as the first time you took a picture with your cell phone and someone asked you if you would e-mail it to them, and you said, "Wow, I didn't know

Customer

Any individual or group that uses the output of a process.

External customer

A customer who exists outside of the organization.

Internal customers

Customers who exist within the organization.

INTEGRATING OM:

American Airlines Goes On-Time to Better Satisfy Customers

For several years passengers have been increasingly observant of the extent to which airlines hold to their published schedules. A flight is considered late if it misses a 14-minute window around its scheduled departure or arrival time. During much of the 1990s the world's largest airline, American, was stuck at the bottom of the on-time standings. These rankings are very important to the airlines, because more and more customers consider them when making travel plans.

After targeting this area for improvement, in the second quarter of 2002 American made it to the top of the on-time rankings among the six big hub-and-spoke players, trailing only Continental Airlines overall. In addition, baggage was getting to passengers on time. Passengers noticed, and complaints were down. "I've been on time a lot more on American recently," said one American passenger who had been an elite-level frequent flyer for more than a decade. "I assume they are doing it because they are seeing pressure from competitors, Southwest and others, that run on time."

Improving on-time performance has had benefits beyond customer satisfaction, because running late is also expensive. Burning extra fuel, wasting crew time, reducing the time in a day that a plane can be earning revenue, and even securing hotel rooms for stranded passengers added up to significant financial costs while providing no additional income.

Getting a carrier that makes in excess of 2,500 take-offs a day to run on time requires more than padding extra minutes into its schedules and herding passengers more quickly into their seats. At American, it took a huge philosophical shift. The airline had to accept that outside factors such as weather, air traffic control, and scheduling are not the only reasons that planes are late. Decisions the airline makes when it purchases planes, assigns mechanics at airports, or even decides the number of first-class seats for a plane can also be the root cause of many delays. "We studied every departure delay and cancellation by city, by time, and we didn't find any one thing that was causing the problems. It was tough to figure out," said Ralph Richardi, the company's VP of operations planning and performance.

American's underlying problem was its own complexity. Flights were often delayed by hundreds of things that intertwined and bogged down operations. Rivals such as Southwest saved money by running a simpler operation—flying one type of plane, having simpler routes, etc. American went the opposite direction. It had prided itself on its complexity, and the company complicated matters by trying to customize the airline to suit its key markets and passengers.

For example, American divided its fleet into fourteen different jets with 30 different "sub-fleets" of different seating configurations and design. The company could buy 757s cheaper without life rafts, so it bought planes equipped with life rafts only for the over-water routes. This action saved money and created room for additional first-class seats in the planes that didn't contain life rafts, but it effectively land-locked the rest of the fleet. If a life raft–equipped 757 broke down, another 757, though idle, might not be capable of replacing the first plane if the replacement plane was not also equipped with rafts. And, when an MD-80 used on the New York route and equipped with twenty first-class seats was replaced by one with only fourteen first-class seats, "we'd have six first-class passengers that we'd have to have the 'big conversation' with," said Dan Garton, executive VP of customer service. Similarly, American installed bunks for pilots only on planes used to fly to Asia, so a plane normally scheduled for use in Europe might not be capable of flying to Tokyo in a pinch. Complexity was costly from a maintenance perspective, too. Mechanics might routinely have to maintain four or five different types of planes, thus never becoming wholly familiar with any one type.

Former CEO Robert Crandall believed American could be a better airline by being smarter about its operations, and American now admits that the costs of complexity were never figured into their number-crunching analysis. "In this environment, the cost of complexity isn't offset by what you can charge," said American's president, Gerhard Arpey, who led the operational overhaul. He added, "Complexity creates opportunities for you to fail your customer."

In its attempt to simplify operations, American reduced its plane types from fourteen to seven. Half of the thirty "sub-fleet" configurations were eliminated. Basic changes in the communications process were made, such as creating a way to allow pilots to send messages to mechanics. Fundamental procedural changes were made, as well. For instance, instead of trying to close doors within five minutes of the scheduled departure, the doors are now shut only two minutes prior to departure in an attempt to get planes off the gate on time more often. And, to speed up repairs at major airports, American now staffs each cluster of gates with its own team of mechanics instead of using one team for the whole airport.

Employees say they are under more pressure to gets flights out on time, especially the early morning flights. When these flights are late, they can mess up an entire day's schedule. But employees also say their jobs are easier when the airline runs on schedule, because there are fewer angry customers and their supervisors are not barking at them. "The numbers show that it is working," said one mechanic in Chicago, who now works on a smaller number of planes.

"If an airline runs reliably and on time, everything is better from the customer perspective. The food is better, the flight attendants are friendlier; it drives everything," said Arpey. "The converse is also true: If you don't run on time, it's a miserable experience."

Source: Adapted from: "American Airlines Improves On-Time Record," *Wall Street Journal*, Sept. 17, 2002 pg. D3, reporter Scott McCartney

this thing could do that!" Repeat business and customer referrals increase when customers are satisfied and decrease when customers are dissatisfied—and that is what makes customer satisfaction such an important measure of operational performance.

Operations managers who focus solely on improving the productivity of the transformation process are in danger of becoming too concerned with the technical characteristics and cost of their product or service. They can easily lose sight of what customers expect to receive in the product-service bundle. Henry Ford revolutionized the world by making his Model-T automobile both reliable and affordable. He famously offered his customers cars in "any color you want as long as it's black." That approach could not work today. Innovative features, personalized choices, and bundled services, such as OnStar, GPS systems, and 24-hour roadside assistance, define customer satisfaction today, along with low prices.

Brand Equity

In the mid-1980s, Xerox had a remarkable insight on the measurement of customer satisfaction. In conducting customer surveys, Xerox provided customers with a five-point scale to use to report their level of satisfaction. Customers gave four points if they were "satisfied" with Xerox products and services, and five points if they were "very satisfied." Comparing individual customer survey responses with data indicating whether those customers decided to purchase more Xerox products showed that those who gave Xerox 5s ("very satisfied") for

REC CENTER DILEMMA

Cheryl wonders about ER productivity

Cheryl has begun to look at the level of activity in her hospital's Emergency Room (ER) over the past few months. She is noticing that many of the treatment areas are empty most of the time. Concerned about productivity, she is considering approaching a few local health insurance companies to see whether they would consider offering after-hours, nonemergency appointments to their policy holders for a fee just slightly higher than their customers pay for daytime office visits to a general practitioner. Cheryl sees this as a way to keep the ER staff busy during the slow times. What do you think of this idea?

performance were six times more likely to repurchase than customers who gave the company 4s ("satisfied"). Since making this discovery, Xerox has fine-tuned its performance measurement system to use 5s as the only meaningful measure of customer satisfaction.

Brand equity

The general perception of value associated with an organization's product service bundle.

One indicator of customer satisfaction levels is **brand equity,** the general perception of value associated with an organization's product-service bundle. For example, brand equity explains why someone will pay more for a pair of Nike's than for another, equally sophisticated brand of athletic shoe. Similarly, the concept of brand equity explains why Coca-Cola can charge more for its soft drinks than a manufacturer of generic soft drinks. Brand equity can be measured. In the Coca-Cola example, it is the difference between the price customers will pay for Coke and the price they will pay for generic drinks.

Brand equity is constituted of both the customer's perception and the delivery system used to back up that perception. Brand equity is not merely the name of a product or service. Indeed, a successful brand will quickly be perceived by customers as being less desirable if the product's delivery system changes and no longer supports the brand's image. A common mistake made by businesses is to focus on the cosmetic part of brand equity, the customer perception, at the expense of the whole, the combination of customer perception and delivery system. Cadillac, for example, experienced a serious loss of brand equity in the mid-1980s because of problems with quality and changes in the product line. The marketing program remained as aggressive as ever, but could not stem the decline of the company's brand.

An organization may seek to add value for customers directly or indirectly, through physical alterations, transportation, storage, inspection, exchange, the facilitation of physiological change, the provision of informational services, or other such activities. From the customer's perspective, however, the value created exists only because it is customer, time, or place specific. Customer-specific value implies the creation of value for a particular individual or group. Examples of goods or services with customer-specific value include tailor-made suits, prescription eyeglasses, team uniforms, health care, and haircuts. Time specificity is most relevant to product-service bundles whose value declines rapidly, such as an issue of a daily newspaper, a fresh-cut Christmas tree, and last-minute tax advice. Many service industries may, by definition, place a relatively high level of importance on the place where a service is provided. From large civil engineering projects to the delivery of a single pizza, services provide satisfactory customer value only when they are delivered at the exact location the customer specifies.

History and Trends in Operations Management

The History

THE INDUSTRIAL REVOLUTION: THE BIRTH OF MASS PRODUCTION

While people have managed transformation processes from the beginning of time, we trace the roots of OM to the birth of mass production during the Industrial Revolution.

Adam Smith popularized the concept of division of Labor in England in the late 1700s. He illustrated this concept with the example of pin makers. Working alone, a worker could produce 20 pins a day. When repeatedly performing a limited portion of the work involved in making a pin, a small group of workers could produce 48,000 pins

Figure 1.5

Operations management
time line

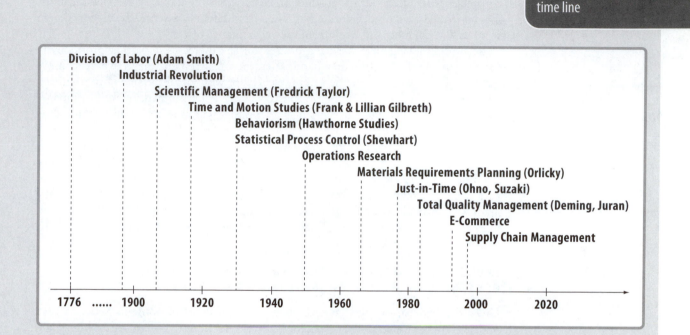

a day. Along with this specialization of labor came the concerns of industrialization, in-cluding worker motivation and development, worker welfare, the organization of work, tracking inventory, product design for mass production, and questions regarding the limits of economies of scale (including how many units should be produced at a given time and appropriate rationale for the mechanization of human work).

It was the Industrial Revolution that made common the mass production of stan-dardized products. At that time, a host of operational complexities and problems were encountered for the first time. As a result, a number of individuals attempted to solve problems related to the methods used and the organization of work, while others fo-cused on the human problems associated with mass production in factories. It soon became clear that piecemeal organization, varied approaches to communication, and nonstandardized information handling were not adequate to meet the needs of busi-ness; rather, a structured system of management was needed in order to effectively administer large scale enterprises.

SCIENTIFIC MANAGEMENT: DEVELOPING A TECHNICAL UNDERSTANDING OF WORK

The term "scientific management" refers to the system of management introduced by Frederick W. Taylor in the late 1800s. In fact, scientific management has also been called the Taylor system (or Taylorism). Time study, a technique used to precisely de-fine an activity or job as a detailed set of repeatable tasks and determine the time in which these are to be done, was the foundation of the Taylor system. By using time study, management could set work standards "scientifically," rather than relying on past performance of workers to set work standards. Given the ability to independently analyze work, management gained the opportunity to use a piece-rate incentive plan, to select workers best suited to particular jobs, to train workers in the ideal way to complete a task, and to track production costs according to particular classifications for reporting based on deviations from those standards. In essence, the Taylor System separated the planning of work from the performance of work.

Scientific management has been praised for the increases in worker productivity that it generated. On the other hand, scientific management may have been more suited to a time when a great deal of physical labor was not automated or mechanized and the level of education in the workforce was extremely limited. Scientific management has been criticized for developing work settings that were boring and not fulfilling from a human perspective.

As a result of Taylor and others who worked to promote scientific management, this system became widely used in the industrialized world. Because Taylor and many of his disciples were engineers, the ongoing development of scientific management let to a field of engineering now known as industrial engineering. Additionally, the analytic approach to defining work standards and pay resulted in perceptions of worker exploitation and contributed to the strength of the union movement in the early twentieth century.

INDUSTRIAL PSYCHOLOGY AND INDUSTRIAL SOCIOLOGY: DEVELOPING A HUMAN UNDERSTANDING OF WORK

Given the criticisms of the Taylor System, many of the developments between 1910 and 1940 were related to the psychology of workers. In 1913, Hugo Münsterberg laid the foundation for the field of industrial psychology with the publication of his work *Psychology and Industrial Efficiency*. In 1912, Lillian Gilbreth completed a dissertation that was later published as *The Psychology of Management: The Function of Mind in Determining, Teaching, and Installing Methods of Least Waste*. To be sure, these efforts were presented in the context of the Taylor System and were used to point out the value of understanding human mental processes when designing work. It was suggested that considering human factors in the design of work would allow for the development of systems in which workers were both better off and more productive.

As a result of interest in the human behavioral dimensions of work, Elton Mayo performed a series of experiments at the Hawthorne plant of the Western Electric Company in the late 1920s and early 1930s. Initially designed to identify optimal environmental conditions for worker productivity, these well-known experiments actually led to a greater understanding of the implications of social factors for worker productivity. In fact, the very understanding that work systems are also social systems (and that social factors profoundly influence individual work behavior) can be attributed to these "Hawthorne Studies." The Hawthorne Studies are frequently credited with providing a foundation for the study of human behavior in organizations, which continues today in the field of organizational behavior.

STATISTICAL CONTROL OF QUALITY

Control charts

Statistical tools that allow decision makers to distinguish processes that are in control from those that are out of control.

Walter Shewhart, was the first to develop and use statistical methods to control quality. As early as 1924, he was promoting the use of **control charts**. (A control chart plots the behavior of some system variable to determine whether there are unusual causes of variation in the system.) By 1931 Shewhart had published *Economic Control of Quality of Manufactured Product*. Following this, in the 1930s and 1940s, there were a number of statisticians who contributed methods of sampling, analysis, and control that were useful to managers attempting to maintain and improve in product quality.

Statistical quality control techniques provide an interesting counterpoint to the job design techniques of the Taylor System. The time study, job assignment, and training techniques of scientific management were used to design variability out of a job. They allowed managers to set a standard production rate, or quota, for workers. By contrast, statistical quality control techniques recognize that there is inherent variation in any system. A worker cannot reasonably be expected to produce the very same amount of quality product every hour of every day—there are good days and bad days. Based on the ability to estimate the natural variation in the system, quality control techniques are designed to alert managers to unusual variation from system standards.

MANAGEMENT SCIENCE: OPTIMIZING THE USE OF LIMITED RESOURCES

During World War II, the U.S. industrial sector was faced with the challenge of supplying geographically distant troops with supplies that were available in only limited amounts. In short, the demand for products from the industrial sector exceeded the production capacity, transportation capacity, and the capacity of the resource supply base. Coordinated decisions had to be made about the use of resources, production capacity, and transportation capacity. The military relied on mathematicians to develop solutions to their resource allocation problems, and the field of mathematics referred to as **operations research (OR)** was developed. Much of the early development of OR involved refining the operation of radar, estimating war losses, and forecasting enemy strength. In short, the practice of building mathematical decision models took root at this time. (Today, operations research is also known as **management science (MS).**)

Mathematical modeling moved from wartime applications to peacetime business applications during the 1950s. The tools were particularly useful at that time because of the large backlog of demand for household products that resulted from wartime austerity and postwar economic prosperity. In general, these mathematical decision-modeling tools are useful to any business whose attainment of objectives is limited by one or more constraints. It is easy to see the value of these tools to business because virtually all business managers try to maximize profits or minimize costs in the context of such limitations as budgets, plant capacity, market size, and supply of raw materials.

FUNCTIONALIZATION OF OM: BRINGING IT ALL TOGETHER IN ONE DISCIPLINE

In the late 1950s, it became clear that factory managers were applying techniques from all of the areas discussed in the above: the Taylor System, industrial psychology, statistical quality control, and management science. These managers were referred to as production managers, and the field of production management gained a foothold in business schools.

When many of the tools of production management were applied to service sectors in the 1970s, the field came to be known as production/operations management (POM). Since the 1980s, the field has simply called operations management (OM). OM is widely recognized as one of the core business functions and is critical to the success of any organization.

THE MRP CRUSADES: COMPUTERIZING OPERATIONAL DECISION MAKING

The 1960s and 1970s represented a period of significant progress in the application of computing technologies in OM. Many transformation processes were automated. Decision models began to be computerized. The most widely applied computerized production management planning program, called **material requirements planning (MRP),**

Operations research (OR)

Much of the early development of OR involved refining the operation of radar, estimating war losses, and forecasting enemy strength. Today, operations research is also known as management science (MS).

Management science (MS)

The current term for operations research.

Material requirements planning (MRP)

A system needed to identify the quantity and timing of materials required for individual orders and track the progress of those offers through each part of the value-adding system. This is the most-widely-applied computerized production management planning.

helped managers by providing detailed advice about the timing and quantity of orders to place for parts in complex manufacturing environments. The drive to promote MRP has been referred to as the MRP crusades. As a result of the MRP crusades, widespread application of automation technologies, and subsequent development of computerized decision support systems, operations managers now rely heavily on state-of-the-art information systems.

JIT AND THE QUALITY REVOLUTION

Just-in-time (JIT)

A system largely developed to enhance productivity and reduce cost by removing waste from production.

Lean production

An approach to managing operations without massive buffers of inventory which is becoming much more common.

Total quality management (TQM)

A system of management based on a commitment to the customer's total satisfaction, understanding and improving the organization's processes, employee involvement, and data-based decision making.

Also during the post-war period, significant developments were taking place in Japan. **Just-in-time (JIT)**, or **lean production**, is a manufacturing system developed by Toyota to enhance productivity and reduce cost by removing waste from production. This system has gained widespread global acceptance and is widely credited as a major factor in the global competitiveness of Japanese manufacturers from the 1970s on.

Poor quality is a major source of waste targeted by the JIT system. Application of JIT concepts and quality management techniques promoted by Americans such as W. Edwards Deming, Joseph Juran, and Armand Feigenbaum allowed Japanese companies to produce goods of better quality at a lower cost than their American counterparts. In the 1980s, often out of painful necessity, American businesses flocked to **total quality management (TQM)**, a method of involving the entire workforce in the pursuit of customer satisfaction through process improvement.

Observing the practices of Japanese managers has led to an American rediscovery of many of the roots of OM. In fact, the Japanese formula for global competitiveness through effective OM has become a way of life the world over.

Trends in OM

GROWTH AND DOMINANCE OF SERVICES

At one time, the primary employment sector in the U.S. economy was agriculture. With the industrial revolution, that changed, and manufacturing became the primary economic sector. Today, it is services. This is true of other advanced nations as well. A 1993 sampling showed that the percentage of employment in the service sector broke down accordingly for the following countries: Canada 75%, U.S. 74%, Belgium 71%, Israel 68%, France 66%, Italy 60%, and Japan 60%. For most of these countries today, the percentage of workers employed by service businesses is even higher.

GLOBALIZATION

Globalization

The expanding geographic scope of a firm's value-adding system beyond regional, national, and international levels toward a worldwide multinational scale.

Globalization refers to the expanding geographic scope of a firm's value-adding system beyond regional, national, and international levels toward a worldwide multinational scale. The growing global scope of investment and outsourcing has created new opportunities and challenges in the design of value-adding systems, including improvements in logistical systems, communication technologies, and opportunities for international trade. Improved logistical systems allow for greater coordination of geographically distributed operations and reduce the need for large inventories of materials that are transported from one plant to another. Today, it is much easier to tie together the work of several manufacturing and service facilities to create the firm's product-service bundle. At the same time, reliable communications networks allow information to be shared widely, allowing decision making to be decentralized without a significant loss in coordination. The challenges of greater diversity of customers and suppliers, made possible by the elimination of trade restrictions, means today's operations face increasing pressure to be "world class," because product-service bundles must meet the expectations of a diverse set of customers.

ENVIRONMENTAL QUALITY

Environmental concerns have traditionally not been the focus of operations managers. That has changed, however, because of increased regulation, public scrutiny, customer expectations, and the concern of employees for their communities. A new and expanded emphasis on quality that includes environmental concerns and issues has changed the way in which firms view both the product-service bundle's design and production. Operations managers are learning that effectiveness of operations can be as important to environmental management as it is to managing product quality and cost. As a result, environmental concerns are a growing aspect of operational decisions.

CROSS-FUNCTIONAL MANAGEMENT

On traditional organization charts, black lines connect functional areas of responsibility, illustrating the decision-making and communication hierarchies of functional silos. Between the functional areas are white spaces. Most value-adding processes occur in the white spaces of the organization chart and span several functional areas. To manage within those white spaces, managers and teams are being given responsibility for processes instead of, or in addition to, their functional responsibilities. This cross-functional management requires integrating the work and decisions of all functions in the value-adding system. Information systems are being redesigned to support cross-functional decision making and communication. Workers are being collocated, in order that their decisions are more likely to support the process and less likely to be dominated by functional turf rivalries. All of these changes suggest that, in contrast to the dominance of functional hierarchies in the twentieth century, integrative management that spans the white spaces will become the central business paradigm of the twenty-first century.

Business processes that evolved in the context of functional silos are often inefficient and complex. Modifying the mechanisms and interactions of functional silos, however, sometimes requires radical, system-wide changes. **Business process reengineering (BPR),** a frequently used technique, helps redesign processes that are weak because they span functional boundaries in hierarchical organizational charts but are not coordinated across these boundaries. Because BPR completely reinvents the process, it can be used to implement radical changes based on new and cross-functional business models.

E-COMMERCE

Less than 25 years ago, most industrial computer applications ran off mainframes or minicomputers; the Internet was virtually unknown outside of large-scale research environments, and personal computers (PCs) were not much more than toys. Most businesses today are either running sophisticated business software on PCs or using client-server technology to enhance their decision-making processes. The Internet has connected businesses with their suppliers and customers across the world with instantaneous communication.

E-commerce refers to the integrated set of computer technologies that enable consumers and businesses to conduct business over electronic networks. Today that means doing business on the Internet. Whereas companies once used Electronic Data Interchange (EDI) across their own networks with suppliers and/or customers, today's

---

Business process reengineering (BPR)

A "blow it up and start over from scratch" improvement technique frequently used to reinvent processes that are weak because they span functional boundaries in hierarchical organization charts but aren't coordinated across these boundaries.

E-commerce

The integrated set of computer technologies that enable consumers and businesses to conduct business over electronic networks.

web applications have replaced many of the internal systems that companies once used for EDI. Companies once had to spend their own money to create private EDI networks, but the Internet boom drastically altered these business functions. E-commerce pervades nearly every aspect of business, with benefits that include reduced paperwork, improved decision making, reduced inventory requirements, and more rapid response to customer requirements.

E-commerce activities generally fall into two categories: business to business (B2B) and business to consumer (B2C). B2B e-commerce involves using the Internet to communicate between businesses that are related in a chain of suppliers and customers. Online information can be used to make operational decisions in the individual businesses, and, as a result, the entire chain can be more coordinated. For example, e-commerce allows a vendor company to determine what it needs to supply to its business customers by simply accessing the production schedules of those companies—no purchase orders are needed, and no time is required for a decision makers to prepare purchase orders. Vendors may also be able to forecast customer needs based on sales information provided by its customers. A paper pulp supplier to Procter & Gamble's tissue-making operation, for example, could predict upcoming demand for their pulp by tracking sales information gathered at Wal-Mart's cash registers. With this improved coordination, less time elapses between the demand and supply of those items. Consequently, businesses have less need for carrying extra inventory or excess capacity in case they need to respond to unforeseen surges in demand.

B2C e-commerce involves using the Internet to market a firm's value offerings to customers and gather information regarding customer preferences and opinion. Electronic marketplaces, such as the eBay online auction site, have become very popular ways to facilitate trade. Companies may also design their websites to:

- promote themselves to investors

- attract prospective employees and recruit applicants

- collect market feedback

- advertise the superior aspects of their product-service bundle directly to customers enable customers to purchase products directly from the company

Enterprise Resources Planning (ERP)

Systems Software packages that integrate decision support programs for the various functional areas with a common database. They allow companies to access the schedules of their downstream suppliers and schedule their own operations so that they are making what will be needed rather than what they think will be needed.

The advent of e-commerce has also made business decision making more integrated and less functionally oriented. **Enterprise resources planning (ERP) systems** are software packages that integrate decision support programs for the various functional areas that share a common database. The ability to easily gather and immediately transfer information anywhere in the world at any time has allowed companies to coordinate marketing, operations, and financial decisions based on the same information. They can therefore coordinate their functional areas on a global basis without the delays previously required for the exchange of information. For example, sales information can immediately influence financial and operational decisions. Operational information—such as capacity, schedules, and inventory levels—can immediately affect marketing and financial decisions. Financial information—such as the cost of capital, production costs, and so on—can be used immediately to inform the decisions of other functional areas. Consequently, OM has become much more integrated with the other functional areas of business, and operational decision makers can no longer afford to take a functional perspective when they make decisions. Rather, they have to take a business perspective and make sure that their decision fits with the decisions that are being made by others in the organization.

INTEGRATING OM:

Careers in OM

As you might have guessed from our description of the development of OM, the job of the operations manager is a professional position of increasing significance to a firm's competitive future. It is no longer the blue-collar factory job that fails to tax the capabilities of today's business school graduate. The connotation of a grimy sweatshop is far removed from the reality of a career in OM. Operations professionals are just as likely to apply their knowledge in the most prestigious management consulting firms, financial institutions, airlines, or hospitals as they are to apply it in a manufacturing company.

Many operations professionals belong to APICS— the Educational Society for Resource Professionals, formerly known as the American Production and Inventory Control Society (APICS). APICS is currently the largest professional organization dedicated only to operations managers. This international organization, founded in the United States in 1957, boasts more than 50,000 members and has administered examinations for certification in production and inventory management (CPIM) since 1972. More than 10,000 APICS members have earned the CPIM. The existence of such a certification program suggests that there is clear consensus among industry members regarding the body of knowledge in which operations professionals should be competent. In turn, the existence of a large number of certified professionals attests to a high level of professionalism in the field. Other organizations, such as The Council for Supply Chain Management Professionals and the Institute for Supply Management, play similar roles in education and professional development.

Recently, a number of articles have recommended OM as one of the top fields for career opportunities, offering graduates excellent job prospects, salaries, and growth potential. Common entry-level opportunities for OM majors include coordinating the value-adding processes in banks, purchasing materials for manufacturing organizations, scheduling or supervising value-adding activities in any service or manufacturing context, coordinating logistics to ensure that information and materials are available when needed, quality assurance, process improvement consulting, and supply chain management. The typical company has most of its capital invested in the value-adding processes that are managed by operations managers. As a result, entry-level positions in OM are especially appealing to individuals who want visibility early in their career. In fact, it is not uncommon for entry-level operations personnel to coordinate and supervise value-adding activities that use tens of millions of dollars of capital investment and annual purchases of many millions of dollars of materials to create millions of dollars' worth of profit. If these entry-level professionals perform well, they can positively influence their firm's performance, which can open doors to advancement.

Working in the area of OM is an effective way to move up in a corporation. One study by an executive recruiting firm, showed that of seventy-four individuals promoted to top positions, sixty came up through operations. Many companies have formally defined vice-presidential positions in OM. Operational concerns are very important to senior managers in every organization. In sum, opportunity for rewarding work and professional advancement is abundant within the functional area of operations management.

SUPPLY CHAIN MANAGEMENT

Supply chain management (SCM) refers to managing the relationships between firms beginning with the extraction of natural resources and extending to the ultimate disposal of the leftover material in landfills, smokestacks, or drains. In the past, companies within

Supply-chain management (SCM)

The configuration, coordination, and improvement of a sequentially-related set of operations.

a supply chain would compete vigorously for the profit in the chain. A firm would negotiate lower prices with a supplier in order to lower their cost, increase their profits, and price products based on some profit maximization criteria. For example, part suppliers would haggle with auto assembly companies over pricing. Today, businesses are concerned with the competitiveness of the entire chain of value-adding activities used to satisfy their customers. To remain competitive in the long run, the entire value chain needs to be competitive. Thus, today you will find more cooperation between part suppliers and auto assemblers who recognize that they are mutually dependent on the others' success.

At Toyota, which is currently considered to be one of the world's most efficient companies, less than half of the cost accumulated in their supply chain can be traced directly to the car that benefits their customers. Unnecessary transportation, rework, scrap, wasted time, redundancy, etc. all increase cost through the supply chain without adding value for the eventual customer. No company can make 100% of their supply chain costs beneficial to customers, but this example illustrates that there is plenty of room for improvement. By focusing on supply chain improvements—especially the coordination of value-adding activities of different companies in the chain—a company can make tremendous improvements in the value provided to customers.

SUMMARY

OM is responsible for the administration of transformation processes that convert inputs into outputs that are of value to customers. Traditionally, operations managers had a narrow focus on the firm's technical core and an emphasis on productivity rather than the firm's broader value-adding system and customer satisfaction. Today, OM is recognized as a business function that plays a critical role in any company's success by providing the means to satisfy customers.

Today, most customers expect more than a product or service. They are not satisfied unless the whole product-service bundle meets their expectations. Together with a company's transformation process, its OM decision-making processes (or business processes) form a value-adding system that ensures customer satisfaction by providing the appropriate product-service bundle. But OM is only one of several vital business functions.

Effectively managing the cross-functional linkages between operations and other functional areas is critical in the effectiveness of business processes in accomplishing customer satisfaction and competitive advantage.

OM traces its roots to several different fields including scientific management, industrial psychology, industrial sociology, statistical quality control, and operations research. It is a field that is heavily dependent on quantitative modeling and computing technologies. Currently, trends such as growth in the service economy, globalization of business, demands environmental stewardship, cross-functional integration of business decision-making approaches, supply chain management, and the rapid rise of e-commerce continue to reshape the field.

KEY TERMS

Brand equity, 18
Business process, 9
Business process reengineering (BPR), 23
Control charts, 20

Conversion process, 5
Customer, 15
E-commerce, 23
Enterprise resources planning (ERP) systems, 24

External customer, 15
Facilitating goods, 8
Facilitating service, 8
Globalization, 22
Internal customer, 15

Just-in-time (JIT), 22

Lean production, 22

Manufacturing resource planning
    (MRP), 21

Management science, 21

Operations management (OM), 4

Operations research, 21

Product-service bundle, 8

Productivity, 14

Supply chain management (SCM), 24

Total quality management (TQM), 22

Transformation process, 5

Value-adding system, 9

DISCUSSION QUESTIONS

1. In the Cast-Fab, Inc. example, what made Claudio's simple redesign suggestion so difficult to accomplish?

2. What did Cast-Fab do to more effectively manage the "white spaces" in their firm?

3. What is a transformation process? How is this different from a business process?

4. Compare and contrast the traditional input-process-output model of operations management (Figure 1.1) with the view in which OM is responsible for satisfying customers (Figure 1.2). How is a value-adding system different from a transformation process?

5. What is a product-service bundle? Explain the role of facilitating goods and facilitating services in meeting customer expectations.

6. Describe the alternative product-service bundles sold by most cellular phone companies in your region. What are the facilitating goods? What are the facilitating services?

7. Describe the product-service bundles that are available in common personal computer sales packages. What does this product-service bundle design imply for the measurement of customer satisfaction?

8. Is it possible for a firm to consistently satisfy customers without an effectively managed operations function? Why or why not?

9. Is it possible for a firm to consistently satisfy customers without effectively integrating operational decisions with those made in other functional areas? Why or why not?

10. Four managers were introduced at the beginning of this chapter. How do their companies' value-adding systems differ? What do you think is the greatest OM challenge for each of these managers? Why?

Case 1: Mitchellace: Managing a Manufacturing Transformation Process

They are practical, fashionable, and worn by millions of people around the world every day. You usually do not even notice that you are wearing them—unless they break. Yet to more than 300 employees of Mitchellace, Inc. of Portsmouth (Ohio), they are the tie to the future. Mitchellace is the world's largest manufacturer of shoelaces, producing four to five million pairs per week.

"When you really think about it, we're in the fashion business in a lot of ways," said Kerry Keating, chairman and chief executive officer of the company. "Shoes change, colors change, styles change. For example, round laces are big now in athletic and hiking shoes. It is a fast-paced business, and the only thing constant is change."

In addition to shoelaces, Mitchellace produces shoe care products such as brushes, shine clothes, heel tips, and Shine-Rite Shoe Polish. The company also manufactures narrow fabrics, which are used as straps and pull cords for clothes, ear plugs cords, blinds, bracelets, and other products. The company is expanding into the production of straps for luggage, camera, and other items, where it can apply the weaving technology used in producing shoelaces.

"We have a diverse operation," said Keating. "For example, in the shoe polish business, we compete with Kiwi, who has about 93 percent of the market. Still, the demand for our shoe polish products is growing. At the same time, Kiwi is also our largest customer. We supply them with all their shoelaces."

Manufacturing shoelaces in such quantities is an equipment-intensive effort. Shoelaces are made primarily from synthetic fibers, including nylon, polyester, polypropylene, rayon, and various combinations of those fibers, as well as from cotton. The yarn comes to Mitchellace in various colors on large cones and is transferred to various kinds of braider bobbins, according to the type of shoelace or braid required. Shoelaces are then manufactured on braider or weaver machines.

Mitchellace operates more than 3,000 braiding machines—a process that Keating described as similar to "dancing the Maypole." Many of the braiding machines used by Mitchellace are up to 80 years old. "Nobody makes braiding machines anymore," he said. "We take the old ones and rebuild them here. Obviously, we have a large maintenance staff to maintain that number of machines."

In the 1980s, needle looms were introduced to the industry. The needle loom weaves laces and other narrow fabrics faster than the braider, uses less labor, and manufactures a superior product. Rather than winding yarn onto bobbins, as in the braiding machine process, yarn is woven from beams or creels.

"We employ one operator for every 50 braiders," said Keating. "But one needle loom produces what 50 braiders can produce. And we employ one operator for every 10 to 15 looms. Still, looms haven't replaced braiders. There are many operations that looms simply cannot perform."

After the shoelace has been braided or woven, tips are applied to the shoelaces by automatic machines that apply a solvent and heat to the ends of each shoelace. The tips are made of cellulose acetate that is formed in a tipping die.

Once produced, shoelaces can be shipped in bulk or are paired and branded by automatic pairing machines. Mitchellace also operates its own in-house printing shop, where blister card packaging, labels, hangtags, and other materials are produced.

Mitchellace produces shoelaces for three primary markets:

▶ The self-service trade, including department stores, discount chain stores, and grocery stores

▶ The wholesale market, with shoe repair shops and shoeshine operators offering the product for sale

▶ Shoe manufacturers

"There has been a problem with the shoe manufacturers since the early 1980s, with factories in the United States closing at a rapid rate," Keating said. "Right now, 85 to 90% of the shoes sold in the United States are imported. So, we also export shoelaces. For example, we ship shoelaces to Taiwan, to be used in FootJoy golf shoes that are manufactured there and sent back here to be sold. We also export shoelaces to Japan, Europe, South America, and Canada. Canada is our biggest foreign market, and we are the dominant supplier of shoelaces in Canada."

While Mitchellace is enjoying success, Keating points out that market pressures continue to mount.

"We are under constant pressure from our customers for lower prices," Keating said. "And depending upon our ability to respond, that pressure could mean some developments that aren't good for Portsmouth or the state of Ohio."

Overall, Keating cites Ohio and the Portsmouth area as a great location for manufacturing. "We have a good labor force here," he said. "We buy most of our fabric from North Carolina. We get our printed blister board from Illinois. It's a good location for business."

Still, Keating says Ohio has its competitive disadvantages. One that he cites prominently is worker's compensation. Rates to insure Ohio workers are many times those paid by Mitchellace's competitors in North Carolina.

"We've seen some improvement from the Bureau of Worker's Compensation," he said. "Rates are better, and we've made some big improvements in safety. Still, worker's compensation rates are much higher here than what our competitors pay in other states. That can be a big factor when you are manufacturing a product with the margins we get on shoelaces."

SOME QUESTIONS TO THINK ABOUT:

1. What are the inputs to Mitchellace's value-adding system?

2. How does Mitchellace add value? What is their value-adding system?

3. Who are Mitchellace's customers? Describe Mitchellace's product-service bundle for each customer. Does the bundle vary across the three different customer types?

4. What impact has the globalization of business had on Mitchellace's business? What impact does their location have on their business?

5. What other issues do you think Mitchellace will face in the future? How would operations play a role in these issues?

Source: Adapted from *Ohio Manufacturing Association News* 2, no. 7 (July 1996).

2

Operations Strategy: Aligning Operations within the Firm

Chapter Outline

Introduction   34

Integrating Operations Management Across the Functions   35

What Is a Strategy?   36

The Strategic Decision Hierarchy   38

Effective Alignment of Operational Decisions   46

Decision Auditing   56

Strategic Integration of Operational Decisions   57

Environmental Excellence and Operations Strategy   59

Summary   60

Key Terms   61

Discussion Questions   61

Case 2: Goodyear and Michelin Cash in on Firestone's Problems   62

References   63

Learning Objectives

After studying this chapter you should be able to

▶ Describe strategy as it applies a business within the broader context of a supply chain

▶ Describe the strategic decisions made at various levels of the business hierarchy

▶ Describe the strategic decisions within the function of operations management

▶ Describe the role that operations management can play in creating strategic advantages for a company when effectively integrated across the supporting processes within a business and across the supply chain

▶ Describe the relationship between environmental excellence and operations strategy

. . . Back at the Rec Center

The four managers have arrived early at the rec center and are in the exercise room. They are well into their workout when Fred cuts his stay short, saying, "I'm off to another mind-numbing sales meeting. Those sales people all want to bring home that big commission. They'll promise the moon if it gets them the order!" Fred puffs as he climbs off the stepper.

Fred has complained before that his staff is always trying to promise some new phone color or some other special feature to prospective customers. Many of those promises create problems for the manufacturing people, who must keep costs low for the division to be profitable. "The little favors a salesperson might sneak in for a customer in order to make a bigger sale can be very problematic for production," Fred adds. He knows the production people want to keep the schedule simple and easy to plan, and to create the schedule well in advance of actual production. "They want plain vanilla with no surprises. I think it's kind of boring, you know, no bells or whistles, but that's what works in this market. I keep hearing that our customers buy from us because we're the cheapest. The way we squeeze pennies, we must be pretty darn good," he sighs.

"Yeah, our agents deal with a similar situation when they're confronted with passengers who want some slack with check-in time or schedule changes," Tom responds. Like Fred's company, Tom's airline makes its bread and butter on being less expensive than the competition. Last-minute changes and special requests are just the sort of thing that adds to the cost of a ticket. Tom knows that an airline like his, or any other business that focuses on low-cost operation, cannot turn a profit on special orders.

"We go by the book; if we don't, we lose money. If we do, we keep costs down, make a little money on each seat, and make a profit by filling more seats over the long run," continues Tom. "Plain old vanilla might not be too exciting. If they want thirty-three flavors, well, they'd be going someplace else," Tom says.

Fred nods in agreement. "I know what you're saying."

"This division seems a little different from your last job, doesn't it?" asks Cheryl, almost rhetorically.

"Yeah, it's different all right, but what's the same is that when the customer is in your face, you want to make him happy!" Fred replied. "It's frustrating; we make some things in house that my other division used to buy from a supplier, we automate things that used to be done by hand, and we buy in huge truckloads as opposed to buying a box or two at my other job, all to save money."

"But that only works when you keep your numbers high," comments Tom. "We have to watch that too." He knows that low costs are the key to his business.

"Right," Tom responds. "In my old job, we made smaller numbers of more custom products. We did what we needed to suit our customers to a tee. We weren't stupid about costs, we just passed on whatever costs we felt were justified. Nobody complained as long as we got the product right."

Fred knows he cannot do that in his new job. Like Tom's airline, his division is selling only plain vanilla, but Fred is gradually starting to see the challenge of cooperating with operations and his supply chain as a whole in order to keep production costs down and his sales up. "It'll take some time, but I can learn," Fred concludes, as he reaches for a towel and wipes the sweat from his eyes.

Luis and Cheryl are listening from across the room as they take turns doing sets on a weight machine.

"At the hospital, we're more like your old division," Cheryl offers. "People want exactly what they need, they want it now, and they want it to be the best technology can offer. Everybody in our business, from the drug companies to the HMOs, knows that's not easy, and it certainly isn't cheap. We feel we're winning when we keep costs down to what is reasonable and customary for our type of hospital, and focus on health care to fit the individual. If cost were a big issue, we couldn't always do what is expected of us. But then, maybe you and I ought to trade jobs for a while. It sounds as if we both like the grass on the other side of the fence."

"Compared to what we deal with, plain vanilla sounds like a vacation!" Luis adds in as he walks over to where the rest are talking.

"Wait a minute, I've seen your prices," laughs Fred, as Tom and Cheryl nod in agreement.

"Okay, we're definitely not the cheapest sofa maker in town," Luis admits. "To be the cheapest, we'd have to cut a lot of the services that our customers ask of us. All kidding aside, though, I know we could try and get more work based on price, maybe land a deal with one of the big discount chains, but that wouldn't be us. What we do for the small mom-and-pop furniture store sets us apart from the other guys. Being good, always. Giving them what they want, always. Being cheapest, no, that's not what we're in business for. Our problem is getting everybody, from sales to manufacturing, to work together. It's as if we all look at the same picture and then go off into our little silos and describe something different to our people. Eventually we work it out, but it takes time, and it isn't cheap."

Top managers in Luis's company have expressed concern about this same issue in the past. They sometimes feel that marketing, finance, and operations aren't always in sync. What's more, workers on the shop floor often feel confused about priorities and sense they are being pulled in different directions. Middle managers such as Luis sometimes doubt that the issue of what kind of company the firm wants to be has ever been settled. He knows how much time the designers spend creating new styles and fresh fabrics, and how hard the sales staff works to ensure a good fit between the product line and each customer's needs. He knows his company does a lot of things that add value to the product but that customers don't see. But he isn't sure that the company always takes the best path to reach its objectives. With everyone interpreting their functional goals independently, the results can be wasteful and frustrating. Ironically, the company is small and closely held by just a few owners. If any company should be able to get it together, Luis thinks, it should be his.

Fred is nodding again, but this time he is more comfortable with what he is hearing. "Yes, I guess it's sort of like what we want out of this club. Tom and I are here to lose some pounds, keep the ticker in shape, and maybe extend what we have a little longer. We pay the same membership fees as you two, yet you and Cheryl are after something else. You want to add something with those weights. We don't get what we want with the weights, but I doubt you'd leave the weight machine and the mirror long enough to use this stepper! The more I think about it, the more I realize that our goals are different in this new division. I guess that means that the strategy for meeting those goals has to be different, too."

Fred is beginning to see that the priorities a firm chooses help to shape its strategies: Different priorities require different strategies. Listening to Luis and thinking about his upcoming meeting, he realizes that regardless of the priorities a company chooses, the better they are understood across functional lines, the more competitive the firm will be. "You know me, I'm used to giving customers what they want. Add the features, bells, and whistles—newer, neater, cutting edge. But cost? Now they tell me to be the cheapest?" After a pause, Fred concludes, "I need to adjust my thinking."

Introduction

For a company to provide consistent value for its customers and gain a competitive advantage as a result, its decisions must be made according to a clearly defined operational strategy. If the decisions are not consistent, the company is not implementing a clear strategy.

Decisions are made at every level of an organization and across the supply chain, therefore, decisions fit within a hierarchy. At the corporate level, decisions generally answer the question, What business are we in? Where do we fit within the supply chain? At the business level, they indicate how a firm will compete against others that offer the same kind of products and services from a comparable supply chain position. This involves deciding what type of competitive advantage the company will seek in the marketplace and allocating resources in light of that decision. Within the various functions, decision makers have to figure out how they will use their resources to support the pursuit of competitive advantage.

Operations management involves both structural and infrastructural decisions. Structural decisions include those made about facilities, product and service designs, technology, and how responsibilities will be divided among the various companies involved in a sequence of value-adding activities. These "bricks and mortar" decisions have long-term implications. Infrastructural decisions pertain to scheduling, quality assurance,

REC CENTER DILEMMA

How does fred explain "plain vanilla" to his sales force?

Fred is certain that his sales people will have promised, or want to promise, things to their customers that go way beyond the "plain vanilla" products the company offers. Help him explain why that is not consistent with the goals and focus of their division. Given that the salespeople are working on commission, what should be their sales pitch?

employee supervision, and maintenance of the system, and any other decisions that focus on the use of existing operational resources over the short and intermediate terms.

Companies vary in the degree to which they integrate their operational decisions into the broader strategy of their company and across the supply chain. A company may

- ▶ Treat operations as an independent function, the only expectation being that operations not create problems

- ▶ Expect operations to at least match what positioned comparably competitors are doing

- ▶ Expect operations to provide some source of competitive advantage in support of the business strategy

- ▶ Expect the operations function to drive the business strategy by developing unique sources of competitive advantage within the current supply chain context or beyond

The more decisions within operations are integrated and the more operational decisions are integrated with those of the other business functions, the more likely it is that the firm will gain the competitive advantages it seeks within its supply chain and the marketplace.

One contemporary area of interest to many companies and their customers is the environmental impact of their ongoing operations. This is one area where we can clearly illustrate the importance of integrating operational decisions with those of other functions. In fact, the last section of this chapter suggests that the more effectively a company integrates its operational decisions with those of other functions, the more likely it is to attain environmental excellence.

Integrating Operations Management Across the Functions

Can you imagine how frustrating it would be for a salesperson whose marketing department has advertised a new product based on its unequaled design quality to find out that the operations function had tried to make the item as inexpensively as possible? Or what if a service is advertised as the fastest but the operations managers are always delaying jobs to save money and avoid paying overtime? What if a product is marketed as being low cost and inexpensively built, but the finance department tries to charge consumers unusually high interest rates? How do you think a human resources professional, whose job is to recruit engineers and scientists at the cutting edge of their profession, would react when asked by a cost-conscious controller to save money by advertising positions in the local paper instead of a scientific journal? What about the engineer whose research and development budget is cut because of the same cost-conscious controller—just as a technological breakthrough is within reach?

Conflicting situations between different functional areas are not the least bit uncommon. Conflicting priorities also occur at different levels of the corporate hierarchy, even within the same function. It is a real challenge for companies to get decision makers—who have different educational backgrounds, different performance measures, different pay scales, and different jobs—to make all of their decisions mutually reinforcing. Strategic planning is one way that companies attempt to do this. Through the strategic planning process, companies get managers in every area to figure out how

Table 2.1

Cross-Functionally
Integrating Operations
Management

Integration Perspective \ Functional Area	Finance	Accounting
Why Cross-Functional Integration Matters to Operations Strategy	Financial structure of a company and resource requirements will be determined by operations strategy.	Audit strategies and the specifics of fiscal accountability will be determined by operations strategy.
Key Issues	What financial policies should be applied to operations? For example, how will capital expenditures be justified?	What cost accounting and inventory valuation policies should be applied?
	What performance expectations should be used to evaluate operations? For example, are average industry financial ratios appropriate?	How, where and when should asset, cost, and revenue data be gathered?

they can contribute to a common mission and vision of their firm. Then, when strategic plans are implemented, the hope is that the frustrating conflicts between functional areas will not arise. Table 2.1 highlights some of the major relationships between this chapter's content and various functional areas in business.

What Is a Strategy?

Most successful businesses have a clear mission. They set long-term goals that reflect that mission and then set more specific short-term objectives that reflect those goals. Frequently, mission statements, key organizational goals, and specific objectives are published and given to all employees, as well as to other interested parties. These resources are supposed to inform employees about their firm's strategy. Using these formal statements to establish a strategic direction acceptable to most employees helps to keep a company's decisions consistent over time.

In contrast to these formal statements, a **strategy** is the set of actual decisions made by an organization over time. A strategy may not reflect the beliefs and attitudes of all employees, but if the decisions are consistent or follow a defined pattern, the

Strategy

A set of actual decisions made by an organization over time.

Human Resources	Marketing	Engineering	Management Information Systems
Worker skill, labor relations, and other workforce characteristics will be determined by the operations strategy.	Target customer demographics and the operations strategy must be consistent.	Technological choices and operational process requirements will be determined by the operations strategy.	Software, hardware, support, and systems compatibility requirements will be determined by the operations strategy.
What compensation and benefits plans will best support the HR needs of the firm? What recruiting and succession strategies will ensure the ongoing HR needs of the firm will be met? What approach to union relations is best suited?	What are the product and service characteristics that will best satisfy our key customer demographics (i.e., win orders)? What does it take to simply gain the consideration of our potential customers (i.e., qualify for orders)? What competitive advantage is most sustainable for our firm?	To what extent can our processes rely on equipment rather than workers? Can internally developed technologies provide desirable competitive advantages over purchased equipment? What equipment and process technology, selection, maintenance, and support policies are needed?	What information is needed and by whom? Thus, what system requirements must be satisfied? Can internally developed systems provide better solutions than software from vendors? What security, maintenance, and user support systems and policies are needed?

organization is more likely to accomplish its long-term goals. Not all organizations have similar goals or make similar decisions, even when they are in the same industry. Decisions made by the manufacturer of the disposable pen you use to take notes, for example, may differ from those of the manufacturer of the fountain pen you received as a high school graduation gift.

One purpose of a company's strategy is to ensure that everyone pulls together to achieve shared objectives. When employees make decisions that are not consistent, their decisions do not reinforce the work of others, and the organization's progress suffers, as illustrated in Figure 2.1. The large arrow in Figure 2.1a represents organizational progress, while the small arrows represent the separate directions in which various decisions pull the organization. As Figure 2.1b suggests, consistent individual decisions work together to enhance the organization's progress, because the alignment of the small arrows is consistent with the direction of the large arrow. Often, consistent decisions reinforce each other to create **synergy**, which is a condition that makes a combined total worth more than the sum of its individual parts.

As suggested in Chapter 1, several business processes support the value-adding system's ability to create a product-service bundle that meets the needs of the customer. Specifically, Figure 2.2 highlights the strategic formulation process that is the central theme of this chapter. It is important that a company's OM function identifies and

Synergy

A condition that makes a combined total worth more than the sum of its individual parts.

Figure 2.1

Organizational decision making: inconsistent vs. consistent

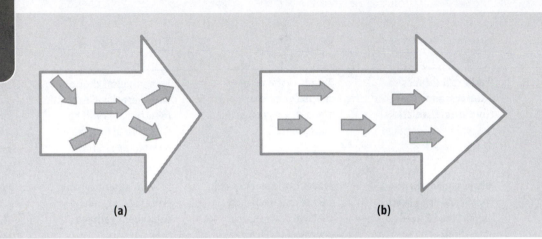

(a)   (b)

Figure 2.2

Strategy formulation process needs to support the transformation process from a cross-functional and supply chain perspective

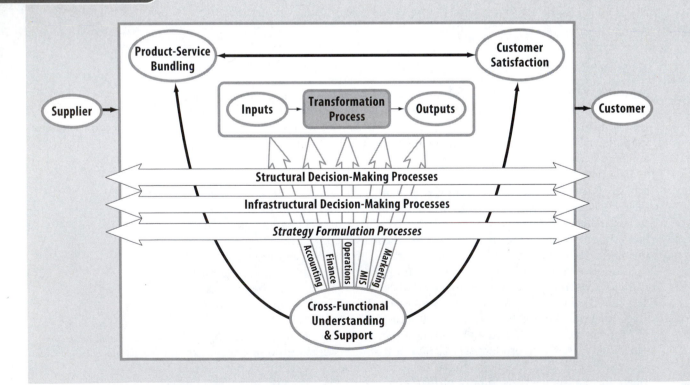

formulates a clear transformation-process strategy that is consistent with the strategies of the other functional areas so that all functions are working in concert. Having such strategies in place enables lower-level decision makers to prioritize activities that support the firm's value-adding system. Figure 2.2 goes beyond the context of the firm, however, to include the formulation of strategy for positioning a company within its supply chain. Formulating a successful strategy not only provides direction for the firm within its supply chain (think of the big arrows in Figure 2.1) but also to individual functions within the firm that are consistent with each other (think of the small arrows in Figure 2.1).

The Strategic Decision Hierarchy

Strategic decisions are made on several levels of a business. This strategic decision hierarchy includes corporate decisions, business decisions, and functional decisions. This decision structure is called a *hierarchy* because functions are found within businesses, and businesses within corporations. Figure 2.3 describes this hierarchy of decisions that managers make. Using this figure as a road map, we will discuss each level of the strategic decision hierarchy.

CORPORATE STRATEGY: WHAT BUSINESS ARE WE IN?

Every day, newspapers' business sections report on businesses being started, bought, sold, merged, shut down under bankruptcy protection laws, or reorganized or downsized in order to allocate corporate resources to higher-priority projects. Newspapers also cover new and developmental products, and new markets. The decisions, made by senior corporate executives, to take any of the above actions comprise what is frequently referred to as corporate strategy. As Figure 2.3 illustrates, a **corporate strategy** is the set of decisions made by senior corporate executives that answer the question: What business are we in?

Two common decision-making patterns exist at the corporate level. One is **conglomerate (or unrelated) diversification**. Organizations that pursue conglomerate diversification end up owning a wide variety of unrelated business ventures. They may simply be financial amalgamations, or holding companies, that make no attempt to coordinate the strategies of their individual member companies. General Electric (GE) is one example of such a company: It runs a broad portfolio of businesses, including companies that make light bulbs, appliances, jet engines, industrial diamonds, and power turbines. GE also owns a broadcasting company. In conglomerates, the strategies of the corporation's various businesses do not need to be related, and decision making can be fully decentralized.

In **related diversification**, corporate decision-making activities seek to coordinate the activities of the companies they own. Companies may be related in a variety of ways, including common product technologies, process technologies, resource requirements, or markets. Procter & Gamble is a very large corporation, but it sells only consumer products such as soaps, detergents, shampoos, diapers, and pharmaceuticals.

A third approach provides a compromise between conglomerate diversification and related diversification. For example, some large conglomerates may seek to coordinate the activities of certain groups of companies, or divisions, within their portfolios. This approach to organizing corporate resources is called *divisionalization*.

Under related diversification or divisionalization, corporate policies frequently limit the freedom of business managers to act independently of other companies in

Corporate strategy

A set of decisions that answer the question, "What business are we in?"

Conglomerate (or unrelated) diversification

Decision-making pattern in which an organization owns a wide variety of unrelated business ventures.

Related diversification

Decision-making pattern in which an organization seeks to coordinate the activities of the companies they own.

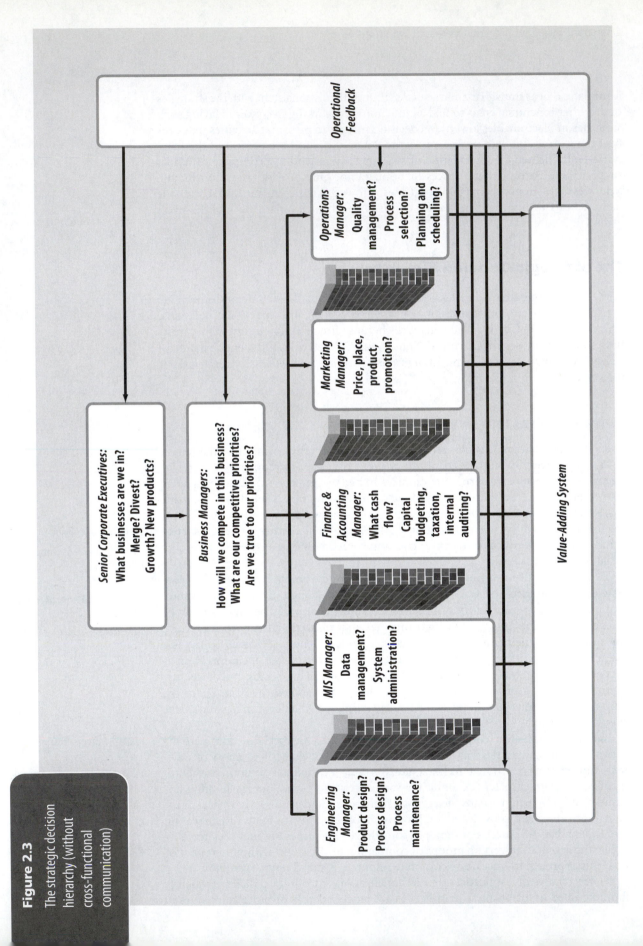

Figure 2.3

The strategic decision hierarchy (without cross-functional communication)

Senior Corporate Executives:
What businesses are we in?
Merge? Divest?
Growth? New products?

Business Managers:
How will we compete in this business?
What are our competitive priorities?
Are we true to our priorities?

Engineering Manager:
Product design?
Process design?
Process maintenance?

MIS Manager:
Data management?
System administration?

Finance & Accounting Manager:
What cash flow?
Capital budgeting, taxation, internal auditing?

Marketing Manager:
Price, place, product, promotion?

Operations Manager:
Quality management? Process selection? Planning and scheduling?

Operational Feedback

Value-Adding System

the organization. For example, a corporation that has constructed a diversified portfolio of new businesses, growing businesses, and mature businesses may manage those businesses differently, treating the mature businesses as cash cows and giving the newer businesses preference for developmental funding. Other such corporate policies might include the use of formal financial hurdles for investment decisions and the establishment of a centralized corporate staff to deal with technology, compliance, and other complex issues.

Louie Psihoyos/Corbis

When a standard product service bundle meets the needs of the customer and a quality design is established, using automation to lower production cost is key to successful strategy

BUSINESS STRATEGY: HOW WILL WE COMPETE IN THIS BUSINESS?

The development of strategy is a top-down activity. Large corporations develop strategies for achieving long-term objectives that may include growth, stability, or long-term return on assets and investments. Shown at the second level of the strategic decision hierarchy in Figure 2.3, a **business strategy** is the set of decisions that answer the question, How will we compete in this business? (Keep in mind that for many organizations, the corporation and the business unit are the same, in which case the corporate- and business-level strategies are the same.) The business strategy should be designed to create some sustainable competitive advantage by providing unique value in the markets the business serves.

To determine how to compete in a given industry, companies need to analyze their external environments. Five forces play a critical role in determining the opportunities and threats to which a firm's business strategy must respond:[1]

1. The competitiveness that results from interfirm rivalry (e.g., Chevrolet versus Ford)

2. The threat of new entrants (e.g., could a new business open up next door and sell essentially the same product-service bundle to essentially the same customers?)

3. The threat of substitute products (e.g., satellite dish versus cable)

4. The relative power of suppliers (e.g., Intel's power as a supplier of microprocessors to computer manufacturers versus the power of a small company that supplies metal screws used in assembling the computers)

Business strategy

The set of decisions that answer the question, "How will we compete in this business?"

[1]Michael J. Porter, *Competitive Strategy* (New York: Free Press, 1980).

5. The relative power of customers (e.g., the customer's power in dealing with Wal-Mart versus Wal-Mart's power in dealing with suppliers)

Companies need to consider their internal strengths and weaknesses, as well as their external threats and opportunities, in order to target a sustainable competitive position. Typically, executives think there are several ways to do so, including (1) setting aside time specifically to review long-term objectives, strategies, and tactics; (2) developing a formal written plan that outlines the strategies and tactics to be used in achieving business objectives; (3) rethinking how products are made, with the idea of completely changing the process; and (4) maintaining a written mission statement. Recently, e-commerce has created an entirely new set of opportunities for many businesses and has at the same time threatened the established competitive position of many others. E-commerce systems can be used to enhance interaction and facilitate cooperation with customers and suppliers. An effective business strategy develops and uses internal strengths to capitalize on existing and future opportunities, while preventing the development of internal weaknesses that expose a company to current and anticipated external threats.

Business unit goals frequently address issues of profitability, market share, and service to other business units within the corporation. Individual business units need to pursue these goals in a way that is consistent with the policies and expectations of the parent corporation. For example, treating customer firms within a conglomerate differently from customer firms outside such a company would make little sense. But in a firm that has pursued related diversification, giving preference to other divisions in terms of service schedules, inside information on new designs, and other collaborative benefits often makes sense. In general, the corporate strategy will constrain the business strategy, limiting the strategic options available to a division manager.

The challenge in devising a business strategy is to gain a sustainable competitive advantage in the marketplace. To do so, managers must understand their specific markets' **order-qualifying criteria**, which must be met to gain the consideration of targeted customers. They must also know their **order-winning criteria**, which must be met to actually win customers' business. Order-qualifying criteria may include a competitive product warranty, a product design that is legally acceptable for customer use, an acceptable price range, a certain set of features, or reliability at or above a specified level. In the case of a pizza parlor in a small college town, order-qualifying criteria might include convenient location (in other words, close to the campus), rapid order fulfillment, sufficient seating availability, menu variety, decent quality, and a lively atmosphere.

Though business managers cannot afford to overlook order-qualifying criteria, in and of themselves these criteria do not provide a sustainable competitive advantage. Competitive advantage is gained by including order-winning criteria in the product-service bundle. In the case of the pizza parlor, order-winning criteria are probably related to the cost of the product-service bundle.

Rather than trying to be all things to all people, managers must use their order-winning criteria to set competitive priorities at the business level, and each functional area must stick to them. A **competitive priority** is a defined emphasis that a business chooses to pursue and that should be supported by the decisions it makes. By setting competitive priorities and clearly communicating them to all employees, companies tell decision makers what they should be achieving with their decisions. If the decisions a company makes consistently emphasize the same set of competitive priorities, the business has a good chance of gaining a competitive advantage in those priorities. For example, if on every day and in every way, a company's employees all make decisions that help the company to keep costs down, that company is likely to become a cost leader and thus win the business of cost-conscious customers.

Order-qualifying criteria

The process of devising a business strategy to gain a sustainable competitive advantage in the marketplace.

Order-winning criteria

Gaining the consideration to win their business.

Competitive priority

A defined emphasis that a business chooses to pursue and which should be supported by the decisions it makes.

Satisfying Customers with Business Strategy

Three steps any company can follow to create a customer-focused business strategy are discussed below.

1. **Establish performance criteria based on customer needs.** Collect information on the present and future needs of customers. The goal is to understand the performance criteria that customers consider most important to meeting their needs. These criteria include one or more of the following:

   ◗ The level of customization required
   ◗ The importance of speed, reliability, and convenience of delivery
   ◗ The price of the product-service bundle
   ◗ The quality of the product-serviced bundle
   ◗ Once the key criteria for customer satisfaction are identified, they become the performance priorities for the organization and form the basis from which the organization will compete.

2. **Design the product-service bundle based on the selected performance criteria.** The goal is a design that will lead to superior performance built on these criteria:

   ◗ *Facilities.* What physical resources, such as buildings and equipment, are needed to fulfill customer needs? Where should they be located? How much should they cost? What technologies should be employed?
   ◗ *Goods.* What role do the tangible goods play in satisfying the customer? What are the design and cost implications?
   ◗ *Explicit services.* These are the readily observable elements of the service. For example, a heart bypass surgery, a haircut, and a flight to Hawaii are explicit services. In manufacturing organizations, explicit services can include on-time delivery to a customer's door, attractive financing arrangements, and custom packaging or labeling arrangements. Decisions must be made to ensure that the service meets customer expectations in regard to quality, cost, speed, and customization.
   ◗ *Implicit services.* These are the less observable, psychological benefits that the customer enjoys and may in fact be the most important reason why the customer chooses one firm over another. For example, although the vast majority of physicians are competent to perform health care services, patients often prefer to carefully choose their own doctors because of the high importance they place on trust and comfort in this relationship. Psychological benefits should not be overlooked in the manufacturing sector. How many automobile advertisements have you seen that promote the safety features of the vehicle?

3. **Develop the core competencies that enable achievement of performance priorities.** Processes, resources, systems, and employees must be developed to build competitive advantage.

EXAMPLE:

1. Taco Bell conducted extensive marketing research and identified the following performance priorities of its customers (summarized by the acronym FACT): fast-food fast, accuracy of orders, cleanliness, and temperature control.

2. Equipped with these performance priorities, Taco Bell set out to redesign the product-service bundle. Restaurants were redesigned to include more than double the original table space for customers, from 30% of the facility's square footage to 70%. Basic food preparation activities (chopping, slicing, and cooking) were de-emphasized and shifted to centralized suppliers.

3. Employees and managers were trained to spend less time preparing food and more time serving customers. Information technology was installed to reduce administrative work and to ensure speed and accuracy in filling customer orders. The new strategy was a smashing success, as food quality and customer service increased while costs and prices decreased. The result was an upheaval in the fast-food industry, as giants such as McDonald's were left scrambling to match Taco Bell's "value price meals" strategy. These other companies also began looking not just at goods and facilities but at the entire product-service bundle—including implicit and explicit services.

When a business has a clearly focused set of competitive priorities, managers of that business understand better what the business is and what it is not. Quality, flexibility, timeliness, and low cost form a reasonably complete set of competitive priorities, although each of these could be pursued in a variety of ways by different companies. For example, quality could be pursued through improved product reliability, improved customer service, or improved conformance to design specifications. Similarly, flexibility could be pursued through value-adding systems that provide a wide range of offerings or a limited range of offerings in a variety of volumes. Timeliness could be pursued through improved product development speed, improved on-time delivery performance, or reduced service response times. Formulating a business strategy involves choosing to emphasize a limited combination of low cost, flexibility, quality, and timeliness in making business decisions. Because of the trade-offs inherent in implementing these competitive priorities, a firm can seldom focus on all of them to the same degree.

FUNCTIONAL STRATEGIES: HOW CAN WE FUNCTION WITHIN THE WHOLE?

Because each functional and support area in a business is responsible for a particular set of decisions, managers need to develop functional objectives that are consistent with and supportive of the business unit's goals to guide decision makers in each function. From an operational perspective, this task entails making decisions about the value-adding system (the business's processes and decision-making infrastructures) that will create value for the business's internal and external customers.

Often, such decisions are made independently of their impact on other functions. As organizations evolve, the walls that separate thinking and decision making in one function from thinking and decision making in other functions can become rigid. As managers in a given function work within the guidelines of a defined business-level strategy, they frequently do so without using cross-functional thinking and communication, as illustrated in Figure 2.3. Physical barriers may impede communication between and among the functions. Marketing might be housed in regional sales centers, finance in the corporate headquarters, and operations at centralized facilities. Even when the functions are combined under one roof, they may be housed on separate floors or wings of the building. In their own office suites, employees relate only to people from their own function. In such settings, cross-functional communication happens only at the highest executive levels. As a result, managers and workers do not know what is happening in other areas, so they cannot collaborate with those areas. This phenomenon, in which organizational barriers prohibit communication among functions, is commonly called the **silo effect**. When a company suffers from the silo effect, the only way to communicate is from the top down.

Silo effect

The phenomenon in which organizational barriers prohibit communication among functions.

Today, though many companies are mired in the silo syndrome, many progressive firms appear to be moving toward the cross-functional thinking illustrated by Figure 2.4. They are finding ways to break down the barriers between functions. One simple way is to collocate workers from different functions. Why not put the office of a salesperson close to the office of the operations manager who schedules the service being sold? Why not let the members of a cross-functional team share the same office suite?

Another approach to managing across the "white spaces" is to build a formal matrix structure that gives members of management teams responsibility for an entire product-service bundle in addition to their functional responsibility. Because business processes (such as designing, building, marketing, and servicing a product-service bundle) span the functions of the typical organizational chart, a focus on processes is a good way to create teamwork across functional barriers.

At the Chrysler division of Daimler-Chrysler Corporation, in addition to the traditional hierarchy, "platform teams" are responsible for specific vehicle types. Thus, a

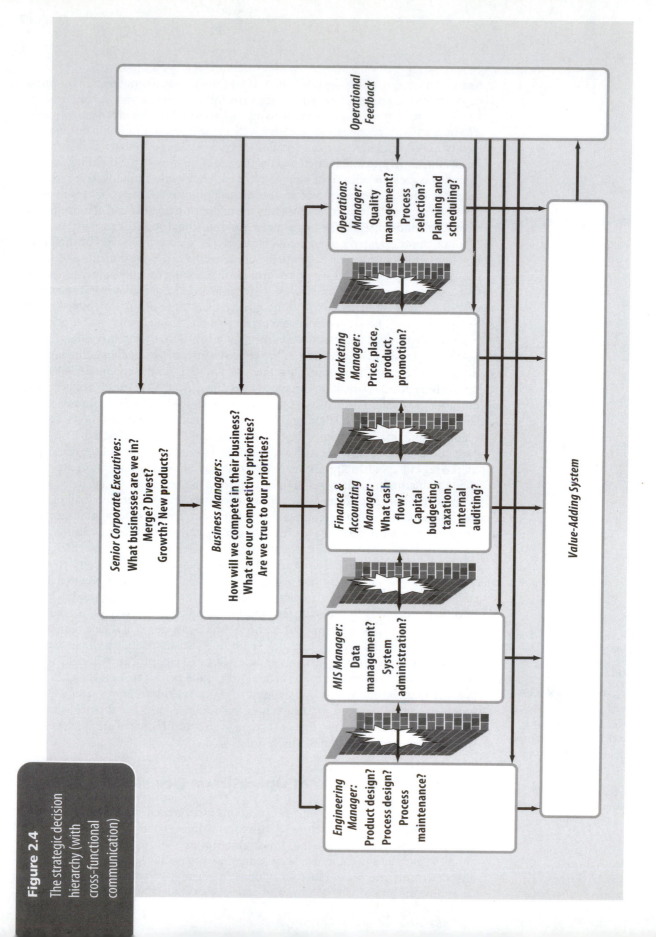

Figure 2.4

The strategic decision hierarchy (with cross-functional communication)

Senior Corporate Executives:
What businesses are we in?
Merge? Divest?
Growth? New products?

Business Managers:
How will we compete in their business?
What are our competitive priorities?
Are we true to our priorities?

Engineering Manager:
Product design?
Process design?
Process maintenance?

MIS Manager: **Data management? System administration?**

Finance & Accounting Manager:
What cash flow?
Capital budgeting, taxation, internal auditing?

Marketing Manager:
Price, place, product, promotion?

Operations Manager:
Quality management?
Process selection?
Planning and scheduling?

Operational Feedback

Value-Adding System

financial manager at Chrysler would have at least two bosses: a supervisor in the finance department and a supervisor on the platform team. When the company created this matrix structure, they were so committed to managing cross-functional processes that they also built a new corporate headquarters to reflect their new way of doing business. The facility in Auburn Hills, Michigan (called Chrysler Technical Center), is built around hubs. Functional areas are located together on the same wing of the building, and platform teams are generally on the same floor. At each hub of the building, there are many meeting rooms; teams need not reserve a meeting room—one is always available. Because the physical barriers to cross-functional decision making and communication have been removed, it is easier to manage across functional boundaries at Chrysler.

To obtain the desired mix of competitive priorities, decision makers in the various functions must pull together rather than oppose each other. Cross-functional decisions can generate a positive and synergistic relationship among functional areas. Decisions that do not cut across functions may create a negative relationship, however, because they may cause trade-offs between functional goals and outcomes. Trade-offs between functional preferences need to be evaluated in terms of the business' competitive priorities.

Thinking through the relationships using a matrix such as the one in Figure 2.5 can help managers overcome differences between the functions by enabling them to identify areas where they are working together well and thus reach agreement. Review the matrix in Figure 2.5, which was prepared with Luis's business in mind; notice that key decision areas within each of the functions are identified. Note the columns headed "low cost," "flexibility," "quality," and "timeliness," which indicate that most of the decisions within this firm enhance the company's flexibility and timeliness. If Luis's company had completed a matrix such as this one and found that many of the decisions in marketing enhanced and promoted a low-cost position while decisions in other areas were driving toward other competitive priorities, the company would be in a good position to clarify its priorities and improve the consistency of decision making across the functional areas. To be competitive in the twenty-first century, managers need to make functional decisions with a full understanding of those decisions' cross-functional impact on the entire organization.

Visuals such as Figure 2.5 also can help decision makers think through why a business change might not make sense. Say Luis's top sales executive is trying to make the case that the company's sofas are not cost competitive and that prices need to be lowered. To maintain the appropriate level of profitability, this would require a reduction in the company's cost structure. What change will be made? Will it be a reduction in the product range? Then the firm has excess operational flexibility, design capacity, and staffing flexibility, but perhaps too little dedicated equipment. Will reductions in all of these areas be made? Or is it better for the sales personnel to leverage the wide product range to more effectively appeal to a market that requires distinctive and unique furniture? Using a matrix such as the one in Figure 2.5, the firm can work across all functions to ensure that changes made in one functional area are consistent with the commonly held competitive priorities.

Effective Alignment of Operational Decisions

The set of decisions made in a firm's operations management function is its **operations strategy**, which includes structural decisions and infrastructural decisions. **Structural decisions** establish the design—the "bricks and mortar"—of the value-adding system, and have long-term significance because they are not easily changed. Their outcomes also determine the firm's range of options in making **infrastructural decisions**, which determine the procedures, systems, and policies that coordinate the firm's operations.

Operations strategy

The set of decisions made in a firm's operations management.

Structural decisions

Choices which establish the design, or "bricks and mortar," of the value-adding system. They typically have long-term significance, because they are not easily changed.

Infrastructural decisions

Choices which determine the procedures, systems, and policies that coordinate the firm's operations. These decisions are more easily reversed or changed than "bricks and mortar" decisions.

Figure 2.5

Impact of functional areas on competitive priorities

FUNCTION / Decision area	Low Cost	Flexibility	Quality	Timeliness	Comments
Marketing					
Product Range		+			Wide range is sold
Selling Price	−				Product is priced higher than most competitors
Promotion				+	Large budget ads emphasize timeliness
Availability/Delivery Time				−	Wide range requires make to order lead times
Finance					
Cash Flow				+	Customer terms require payment on delivery (COD)
Capital Investment		+			General purpose equipment is used - low capital
Accounting					
Costing Accuracy		−			Costing complicated by general purpose equipment
Taxation Burden				+	Rapid product turnover reduces inventory tax
Internal Auditing		−			Auditing complicated by general purpose equipment
Engineering					
Product Design and Change		+			Rapid design capability with digitized tools
Process Design and Change		+			Rapid changeover capability
Operations Management					
Make/Buy Mix		+			Make all parts/buy only commodity stocks to enhance flexibility
Facility Capacity and Location		+			Multiple facilities with capacity buffer close to customers
Technology Mix		+			General purpose/low tech equipment used
Process Layout		+			Functional layout to support flexibility
Planning and Scheduling		+			MRP system, batch sequencing by workstation
Quality Assurance		+			Worker administered conformance inspections
Supervisory Policies		+			Supervision by empowered work area teams
Maintenance Management				+	Preventive maintenance system in place
Human Resources					
Staffing		+			Cross-trained work area teams
Employee Relations		+			Teams, non-unionized, flexible work rules
Compensation/Benefits		+			Skill- and training-based hourly rates
Management Information Systems					
Information System Design		+			Client/Server ERP system with central data warehouse
Information System Operations		+			Extensive, need-based user services and training

These are more easily reversed or changed than "bricks and mortar" decisions. Because, on average, the operations function controls roughly 70% of a business's assets, it is important to make operational decisions that are consistent with the business's strategy.

STRUCTURAL DECISIONS

Structural decisions may be divided into four major categories: (1) the "make or buy" question, (2) facility capacity and location choices, (3) the technological mix decision, and (4) process type and layout choices.

Make or Buy Choices So-called "make or buy" decisions answer questions such as the following: When there is a choice, should the firm make a component or subassembly in house or buy it from a supplier? How does this decision influence the firm's cost structure, product quality, flexibility, profitability in times of recession and economic expansion, risk of excess capacity, and overall level of profitability? Do the firm's make or buy choices support its competitive priorities?

Make or buy decisions extend to service environments where managers must decide whether to use outside services as part of the overall package. For example, many organizations outsource food services and janitorial services to organizations that have developed expertise in these areas. While a hospital or school may manage these services in house, they often find that companies like Aramark (food service) and ServiceMaster (janitorial services) deliver superior performance at reasonable cost. Outsourcing in such cases permits the hospital to focus on health care and the school to focus on education—their respective areas of primary competency.

Facility Capacity and Location Choices These decisions relate to questions such as the following: Can the firm satisfy the demand for its products and services? Has its ability to do so changed over time? Has increased globalization of demand for the product-service bundle or the supply of raw material, labor, or other necessary inputs to the value-adding system changed over time? Will these factors change in the future? Does the firm purposely keep its capacity low or high? If so, what does that choice imply about its cost structure, profitability, service level, flexibility, workforce policies, and product quality? In light of the firm's competitive priorities, is the firm making the correct capacity decisions?

Firms must decide how many facilities they need, how big those facilities should be, and where they should be located. To make such decisions, managers need to think about the focus of specific facilities and how they are organized into groups or divisions. Facilities may be grouped by process similarities, product-service bundle commonalities, technology, or scale. A hospital might choose to put all its lab facilities in one area, because of process similarities, but to keep its emergency room separate from the surgical and long-term care areas, because of product-service bundle differences. These decisions will have clear implications for cost, service level, workforce policy, production planning and control, and quality, and therefore should be evaluated in light of the firm's competitive priorities.

Technological Mix Choices Given the wide array of available technologies, managers must select those that are most supportive of the organization's competitive priorities. The choices are not limited only to technologies that have been tested and are immediately available. In fact, many technological choices set a standard that influences the compatibility of a firm's products, services, and processes with yet-to-be-developed, cutting-edge technologies. Thus, a technological choice must be viewed as having long-term implications for the firm's competitiveness.

As such, a technological choice cannot be made effectively without first establishing some guiding standards and principles in an overall technology strategy. Obviously, decision makers must weigh the trade-offs between new and mature technologies, between slowly changing and rapidly expanding technologies, and between predictable technologies and those whose future is uncertain. Other factors an organization should consider include:

▶ the degree to which work should be mechanized

▶ the degree to which equipment should be automated

▶ the desired extent of specialization of equipment

▶ the choice between in-house technology and that of outside vendors

▶ setup and changeover requirements

▶ the skills required to use a new technology versus those available in house

▶ maintenance requirements

The implications of new technology for a firm's investment, service levels, production planning, product quality, risk, cost structure, and break-even levels are critical to the firm's future competitiveness.

Service Process Type Choices

Figure 2.6 presents a model for categorizing service organizations called the service process matrix. The model uses two dimensions to characterize different service delivery processes. The first dimension is the degree of labor intensity, which is the ratio of labor cost to capital cost. Service-intensive processes with high labor intensity include universities, dental offices, and law firms. Services with low labor intensity include airlines, railways, and hospitals.

The second dimension is the degree of interaction and customization, which measures the degree of individual attention required by the customer. While doctors and auto repair businesses must customize their diagnoses and prescriptions for individual clients, airlines and schools can package and deliver standardized services for large groups of customers.

When combined, the two dimensions of the service process matrix create four categories of service environments: the service factory, the service shop, mass service, and

Figure 2.6

The service process matrix

Degree of Customer Interaction and Customization

	Low	High
Low	**Service Factory:** • Airlines • Trucking/Railroads • Film Processing • Radio/TV Stations	**Service Shop:** • Hospitals • Printing Shop • Auto Repair Shop • Other Repair Shops
High	**Mass Service:** • Retailing • K–12 Schools • Dry Cleaners • Postal Services	**Professional Service:** • Doctors • Lawyers • Accountants • Financial Planners

Degree of Labor Intensity (vertical axis label)

Source: Adapted from "How Can Service Businesses Survive and Prosper?" by Roger Schmenner, *Sloan Management Review*, Vol. 27, n. 3, 1986, p. 25

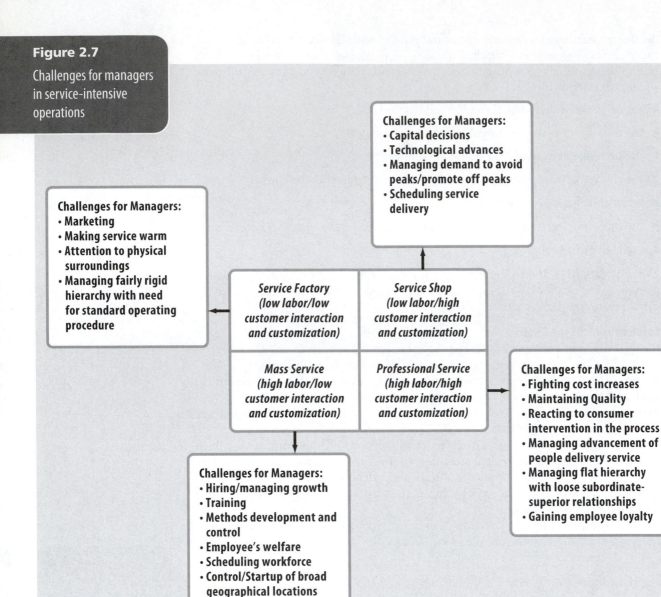

Figure 2.7
Challenges for managers in service-intensive operations

Challenges for Managers:
- **Capital decisions**
- **Technological advances**
- **Managing demand to avoid peaks/promote off peaks**
- **Scheduling service delivery**

Challenges for Managers:
- **Marketing**
- **Making service warm**
- **Attention to physical surroundings**
- **Managing fairly rigid hierarchy with need for standard operating procedure**

Service Factory (low labor/low customer interaction and customization)

Service Shop (low labor/high customer interaction and customization)

Mass Service (high labor/low customer interaction and customization)

Professional Service (high labor/high customer interaction and customization)

Challenges for Managers:
- **Fighting cost increases**
- **Maintaining Quality**
- **Reacting to consumer intervention in the process**
- **Managing advancement of people delivery service**
- **Managing flat hierarchy with loose subordinate-superior relationships**
- **Gaining employee loyalty**

Challenges for Managers:
- **Hiring/managing growth**
- **Training**
- **Methods development and control**
- **Employee's welfare**
- **Scheduling workforce**
- **Control/Startup of broad geographical locations**

Source: Adapted from "How Can Service Businesses Survive and Prosper?" by Roger Schmenner, *Sloan Management Review*, V. 27, n. 3, 1986, p. 25

Service factory

A service-intensive process with low labor intensity and low customization.

professional service. Each has its own set of management challenges, as detailed in Figure 2.7. For example, an airline is categorized as a **service factory** (service-intensive processes with low labor intensity and low customization) because it routinely flies hundreds of passengers at a time on a Boeing 747 between Chicago and Tokyo nonstop. The airline managers must pay special attention to the timing and selection of new aircraft purchases, the planning of promotions to fill plane capacity during off-peak periods, the scheduling of flights, the need for standard operating procedures to reduce uncertainty, and the need to make customers feel comfortable despite the standardized nature of the environment.

Service shops (service-intensive processes with low labor intensity and high customization), such as hospitals, present managers with concerns about capital expenditures, such as MRI equipment. Other challenges include managing hospital capacity by emphasizing outpatient services instead of building more hospital rooms, scheduling elective surgeries during times of low demand, pushing decision-making power down to lower levels of the hierarchy to satisfy individual patient needs, and seeking ways to keep costs down while maintaining quality care.

Mass services (service-intensive processes with high labor intensity and low customization), such as universities, present administrators with challenges such as ensuring a qualified and motivated faculty, scheduling classes to match student needs with classroom availability, developing new programs while dropping others to keep services relevant and costs low, and promoting the unique aspects of the university despite its overall standard design.

In **professional services** (service-intensive processes with high labor intensity and high customization), such as law offices, managers must nurture the expertise of the partners, associates, and staff; maintain a flat hierarchy to be responsive to individual clients; and devote attention to hiring, training, and motivating personnel, while developing procedures and schedules that make efficient use of personnel.

By identifying their service environment as one of the four types in the service process matrix, managers can develop a strategy that supports the decision areas critical to success. Other service-intensive processes in the same category can be studied for innovative ideas, which managers can apply to their own company. For example, bank managers can study the customer relations approach of Wal-Mart and adopt a new customer-friendly image.

Hybrid Service Processes

In hybrid operations, managers have to balance the competitive requirements of two (or more) different kinds of processes. The university student recreation center where our four managers work out can be called a hybrid service operation, because it operates as both a service shop and a mass service. As a service shop, the center offers a wide variety of choices for individual recreation and social interaction with the option of a personal trainer for an additional fee. As a mass service, it offers a number of classes oriented to physical and mental development and provides the venue for major aquatic sports competitions. Considering its service shop functions, center administrators are concerned with making the best choices for equipment purchases, managing capacity and demand by establishing variable time limits at different times of the day, scheduling competitive major events during university holidays and weekends, training the staff to quickly respond to customer needs, and seeking ways to keep costs down while maintaining a wide variety of recreational opportunities. Considering its mass service functions, administrators are concerned with ensuring a qualified and motivated staff, scheduling recreational events and competitions to match demand and facility availability, developing new programs while dropping others to keep the offerings current and costs low, and promoting the unique aspects of the facility.

In hybrid service operations, the multiple service types sometimes conflict. At the rec center, from the mass service perspective, the ideal time to schedule swimming competitions is during university breaks. From the service shop perspective, however, there are a number of local residents—including some faculty and students—for whom the best time to get a workout is when the university is on a break. Similarly, the best time to have an intramural competition is in the late afternoon and evening, but that is also the time that many students are looking for pickup games. Balancing the

Service shops

A service-intensive process with low labor intensity and high customization.

Mass services

A service-intensive process with high labor intensity and low customization.

Professional services

A service-intensive process with high labor intensity and high customization.

service shop and mass service aspects of the rec center's operations is one of the biggest challenges its managers face.

Process Type and Process Layout Choices Operational processes may be classified along a continuum ranging from project, job shop, and batch processes to repetitive manufacturing and continuous-flow production. The choice of manufacturing process is a basic structural decision, and it must be consistent with a firm's competitive priorities and with other structural decisions so as to produce a synergistic pursuit of the firm's strategic objectives. Because these structural decisions cannot be reversed quickly, they have long-term implications. They establish the set of options available to the decision makers who must run the firm day to day.

Project

A set of tasks that is completed only once.

Projects are operations that complete "one-of-a-kind" goods and services. These may be major research and development initiatives, large construction projects, or the design and implementation of a computer system. Projects are usually costly, time-consuming, and of vital strategic importance to the customer. Because projects are often unique, there is frequently a great deal of uncertainty in managing them. Often, a project represents work that has not been done before and will not need to be done again. Predicting exactly how long a project will take and what it will cost is extremely difficult. Thus, projects are frequently completed late and over budget. Furthermore, the workers assigned to a project are in some cases under pressure to "work themselves out of a job." Thus, workforce considerations are also unique in project management.

Fixed-position layout

Layout in which a project produces large deliverables, so the material, equipment, and other resources are brought to a central location.

Most of the time, the resources used to complete a project are organized around a **fixed-position layout**. That is, since most projects produce large, one-of-a-kind deliverables, the material, equipment, and other resources for the project are brought to a central location, rather than passing through a factory. Building construction sites are a common example of a fixed-position layout. Ships, airplanes, and many large machines are also produced in permanent facilities using a fixed-position layout.

Job shop

A production process that is designed to produce small volumes of highly customized products.

A **job shop** is a process designed to produce small volumes of highly customized products. The job shop uses general-purpose equipment and skilled workers to produce specialized items, such as prototypes, in very small volume. This type of process is the natural choice for firms seeking to provide flexibility, customization, and low fixed cost, possibly at the expense of conformance quality, delivery speed, and unit (or variable) cost.

Batch process

A manufacturing system that produces groups of items that are essentially identical, called production lots or batches.

Batch processes produce groups of items that are essentially identical, called production lots or batches. The size of a production lot is usually a function of the time required to ready the equipment for production and the near-term demand for the item. For example, when a family makes cookies, it usually bakes them in batches large enough to be worth the expense and effort, but not so large that they will go stale and be wasted. Batch production may be required by technical factors such as fermentation (in wine making), color uniformity (in fabric printing), or customer demand (for group tours). Items such as clothing, furniture, and many food products are commonly manufactured in batches. In a batch process, flexibility, fixed costs, and product customization are lower than they are in the job shop. On the other hand, consistency, unit (variable) cost, and delivery speed are improved.

Process-oriented (functional) layout

Layout in which all equipment of similar function or type is grouped together in departments or sections.

Job shop and batch manufacturing processes usually employ a **process-oriented**, or **functional**, **layout**. In this type of layout, all equipment of similar function or type is grouped together in departments or sections. Products move from department to department along a route dictated by the item's processing requirements. Because general-purpose equipment is used, skilled workers are needed to meet the specific requirements of each customer's order.

The functional layout provides a great deal of flexibility and enhances the development of function-specific skills. On the other hand, functional layouts are not as efficient as other types of layout. If you have ever been to an amusement park, you may remember how much time you had to spend waiting in line. The same is true for parts moving through a facility using a functional layout. As much as 90% of a part's production time may be spent waiting in queue to be processed. To simplify what can be a logistical nightmare, entire batches are generally completed at a single work center before being moved, all together, to the next work center. Although slow and inefficient, the functional layout provides flexibility and easy process tracking. (Imagine how long it would take a group of 55 children, a typical busload, to go through all the rides in an amusement park if no one in the group could go on to the next ride until the last person finished the previous ride! Slow, yes; efficient, no. But think how easily the chaperones could monitor group progress and how quickly they could change their plans.)

When most people think of mass production, they think of a **repetitive process**, which is a system used to make large volumes of standardized products. The traditional assembly line, whether worker paced or machine paced, is the most common example of repetitive manufacturing or processing. In this type of process, low-skilled workers use dedicated equipment installed at a high fixed cost. In the age of mass production and global consumer marketing, repetitive manufacturing provides a large volume of highly standardized products of consistent quality, at a very low unit cost.

The assembly line is actually a repetitive discrete manufacturing process. **Discrete processes** produce products that are counted in integer units and are functional only in their completed form, such as cars and appliances. In contrast, nondiscrete manufacturing processes produce items that can be counted in noninteger units, such as chemicals and most agricultural commodities, such as flour and sugar which are counted by volume. Repetitive nondiscrete manufacturing systems are called **continuous-flow processes** and are used to make these types of products. While most are eventually packaged in discrete (countable) units that can be bought off the shelf, during production they are handled in nondiscrete form.

Repetitive and continuous-flow manufacturing generally employ a **product- oriented layout**. In these cases, the demand for a single product or family of similar products is sufficient to warrant the use of a dedicated process. Equipment is laid out according to the processing sequence required for a particular product or product family. The logistics for a single flow-through process are simple compared to those for a process-oriented layout. The level of automation and other economies of scale usually found in product-oriented layouts provide extremely low unit cost and high conformance quality. But these capabilities are achieved at the expense of product flexibility and require a high commitment of capital up front (in other words, a high fixed cost).

Figure 2.8 illustrates the relationships among order-winning criteria, order-qualifying criteria, and process choice. Order-winning criteria for job shops are high flexibility, a wide range of design capabilities, and fast delivery. A common order-qualifying criterion in job shops is reasonably low cost. As one moves to the other end of the spectrum of process types, demand for product volume increases and the ability to provide product variety decreases. Thus, low cost is a common order-winning criterion in the continuous-flow process, while order qualifiers include sufficient flexibility, established design capability, and reasonable delivery speed. (Note that Figure 2.8 does not include the project process choice, because each project has unique order winners and order qualifiers.)

INFRASTRUCTURAL DECISIONS

Infrastructural decisions include matters such as policies, procedures, information support systems, and definitions of responsibility. Because infrastructural decisions often pertain to issues that are less tangible than the "bricks and mortar" of structural

Repetitive process

A process that produces standardized outputs from standardized inputs using dedicated equipment.

Discrete processes

A method of producing products that can be counted in integer units and are functional only in their completed form.

Continuous-flow processes

Repetitive non-discrete manufacturing systems.

Product-oriented layout

Layout employed by repetitive and continuous-flow manufacturing.

Figure 2.8

Order-winning/-qualifying criteria, market demand, and process type

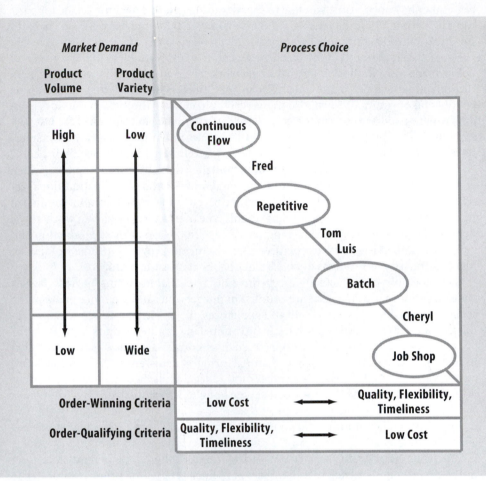

decisions, their impact is usually less permanent. In operations, infrastructural decisions cover production planning and control, quality assurance, supervision policy, and maintenance management.

Production Planning and Control Choices Most organizations use a planning system to buy materials and deploy process resources in order to meet customer demand. Such systems allow decision makers to check the availability of resources and schedule the resources that are needed to satisfy customer orders, forecasted demand, or some combination of the two. Control systems must be used to monitor actual production performance against planned schedules.

A wide variety of demands is placed on firms using project, job shop, and batch processes. As a result, it is very difficult to forecast the demand for such a range of customized products far enough in advance to have them ready and waiting on store shelves when a customer needs them. Consequently, many firms apply a **make-to-order** policy for such products—that is, they do not actually start the production process until the customer places an order. Maintaining the proper balance of competitive priorities in such an environment can be a challenge. With a large number of customer orders sharing the firm's process resources simultaneously, devising a suitable production planning and control system is a key factor in achieving successful operations.

Make-to-order

A policy where managers have purchase orders in hand when they are planning, so they know the demand for products and services at least as far forward as their processing lead times. They do not actually start the production process until the customer places an order.

In contrast, a company that wants to allow for immediate product availability by building inventories of finished product based on forecasted customer demand is using a **make-to-stock** policy. This approach usually makes sense for companies that produce a narrow range of products and services repetitively or continuously using a product-oriented layout. In such setups, production planning and control is less challenging, so a simpler system may be used.

Today, given the competitive challenges of a changing marketplace, a growing number of companies are considering hybrid versions of the make-to-order and make-to-stock policies called **assemble-to-order** policies. When a pizzeria readies the ingredients of a pizza in advance of the customer's call (mixing the dough, letting it rise, and preparing the other ingredients), but waits until the a customer's order has been placed before adding the toppings and baking the pizza, it is following an assemble-to-order policy. An oft-publicized example of a company that uses a hybrid system is Dell computer, which processes online orders for new PCs. The assemble-to-order policy is a compromise between the competitive priorities of delivery speed and product variety. While this approach may require increased flexibility in process design, it also helps a company maintain a wide variety of product offerings. By simplifying much of the production planning and control, it also keeps delivery time to the customer within competitive ranges.

Quality Assurance Choices Quality assurance guarantees that an organization's processes create products that meet customers' needs and expectations for design, quality conformance, reliability, and value. Traditionally, approaches to quality focused on the inspection of process output in order to sort out nonconforming units. But in contemporary business, quality assurance has become a pervasive issue whose ramifications affect decision making throughout the organization at every level. Operationally speaking, a system must be in place to address quality concerns proactively and to respond to problems detected during production or service or from a complaint by a customer.

Supervisory Policy Choices Today's workforce is more educated than that of the past. As a result, highly structured, centralized decision making, where a front line manager tells workers what to do and when, is being questioned at many firms. Policies and organization structures that decentralize decision making and push decisions to the lowest possible level in the organization are becoming more common. For instance, team-based management has replaced employee supervisors with autonomous work teams in many organizations. **Employee involvement (EI)** programs, which allow employee teams to make improvements in their own workplaces, and cross-functional problem-solving teams are also finding their way into the managerial infrastructure of most organizations.

Maintenance Management Choices Inadequate maintenance of equipment creates numerous operational problems, including unplanned downtime, long setups, reduced operating speed and efficiency, poor employee morale, increased numbers of defects, and accelerated aging of equipment. Yet maintenance is often conducted by an outside department or vendor and is therefore viewed by many managers as an intrusive activity. Balancing the intrusiveness of regularly scheduled preventive maintenance against the inconvenience and potential disaster of process failures is an important aspect of a company's infrastructure. While no one wants to tighten the availability of important resources to allow for scheduled "tune-ups," developing a systematic approach to preventive maintenance has been very beneficial to many companies. As a rule, companies that stress preventive maintenance are moving away from a policy of "If it's not broke, don't fix it" and toward a policy of "A stitch in time saves nine."

Make-to-stock

A policy where a company wants to allow for immediate product availability by building inventories of finished product based on forecasted customer demand. The entire schedule is based on forecasted demand figures.

Assemble-to-order

A combination of the make-to-stock and make-to-order approaches. The production of customer orders are scheduled using components and sub-assemblies that have been made to stock.

Employee involvement (EI)

A formal approach to creating a spirit of teamwork that will lead to widespread process improvements.

Total productive maintenance (TPM)

An approach that stresses the idea that workers should maintain their own equipment.

Total productive maintenance (TPM) recognizes that machine operators frequently "know" their equipment better than any outside maintenance staff ever could. Thus, the TPM approach stresses that workers should help to maintain their own equipment. In such a program, specialists in the maintenance department are responsible for advising the firm on equipment purchases, training workers to perform routine maintenance, and performing major equipment overhauls. The idea is to ensure that equipment is always in peak performance condition, rather than to focus only on preventing or correcting breakdowns.

Decision Auditing

Wickham Skinner, a leader in the development of the field of operations strategy, once wrote:

> *The most typical serious condition in most manufacturing plants is that of inconsistencies existing within the infrastructure. Different sectors of manufacturing policy are implicitly set up to accomplish conflicting objectives. It is as if an automobile engine were designed for Indy racing, the transmission for fuel economy, the tires for comfort, the suspension for road race maneuverability and the trunk space for camping. (Skinner 1985, 96)*

Skinner encouraged companies to regularly conduct a manufacturing strategy audit in which manufacturing managers detail the strategic priorities and biases suggested by the way decisions are made in each of the structural and infrastructural decision categories. The managers then share the information with top management, who might ask why a certain approach has been used and what its alternatives are. A manufacturing strategy audit may reveal a less-than-optimal alignment of decision-making priorities, perhaps caused by organizational change, growth, customer pressure, or new technologies. It may also reveal a need for a change in operations or suggest new organizational possibilities based on the development of new operational capabilities.

Integration of strategy starts with top management "getting on the same page." A clear understanding (and agreement) on the firm's competitive priorities is essential.

Triangle Images/Digital Vision/Getty Images Inc

Strategic Integration of Operational Decisions

Most firms move through four distinct stages as they develop their ability to manage operations strategically (Hayes and Wheelwright 1984). Beginning with the (1) internally neutral stage, they progress through an (2) externally neutral stage, then to an (3) internally supportive stage, and finally to the (4) externally supportive stage.

1. The motto of an *internally neutral* firm might be "We want to be as good as we have been in the past." Such organizations manage their operations reactively, failing to see the proactive strategic contribution operations can make. They tend to stress goals and measures that emphasize the avoidance of surprises. The general attitude is that operations can have a significant negative impact on the firm through its mistakes—but little positive impact. Thus, the management of operations is left to functional experts who receive little strategic direction.

2. Occasionally, firms in the internally neutral stage will realize that their competitors have managed to gain a competitive edge based on the advancement of their operational capabilities. Having awakened to the threat, the firm's strategic managers recognize that operations can play a strategic role—at least to the extent that it controls costs. At this point, decision makers will set goals for operations: namely, that the firm should follow industry practice and achieve industry standards. Essentially, the focus has moved from internal neutrality to external neutrality. The motto of the *externally neutral* firm might be "We want to be as good as the competition." When external neutrality is the firm's focus, managers more readily approve the capital investments needed to make significant changes in infrastructure or process technology, provided that the investments will put the firm on a par with the competition.

3. In organizations that have attained external neutrality, managers may eventually realize that the firm's strategy is different from that of other firms; hence, following industry practice will not provide any lasting competitive advantages. In such firms, managers may begin to align their operational decisions with the organization's competitive priorities and strategic goals. These firms have moved from a focus on external neutrality to a focus on *internally supportive* operations. In this stage, managers realize that a proactive OM strategy can play a synergistic role in the firm's overall strategy. Their motto might be "We want operational decisions to match up with and play a forward-thinking role in our business strategy, so that we don't waste time and energy on the wrong questions."

4. The final stage in the integration of operations strategy is the *externally supportive* stage. This stage differs from the internally supportive stage in that operations becomes a full-fledged, proactive partner in setting the firm's strategic direction. Whereas in the prior stage, operational decisions had to conform to corporate

REC CENTER DILEMMA

Luis is asked to make a recommendation

The family owners of Luis's company have asked senior management to make recommendations for capital improvement. In turn, the VP of Operations has asked Luis to evaluate one of the recommendations.

The VP of Operations has asked for a new high-tech painting system. The demand for painted products makes the painting department one of the two or three busiest areas on the shop floor in the current system. The new system would add capacity and would reduce painting costs due to more efficient use of paint and energy, and quicker changeovers from one color to the next. The CFO feels a new $600,000 painting machine will pay for itself in 4 years at current production levels. He also points out that the company has an ROI policy requiring no more than a 3-year payback. The VP of operations feels that the company is getting most of the business it can expect from the markets they currently target. He has checked with marketing and they tell him there is enough "price sensitive" business available with some of the bigger discount chains to increase overall sales of painted products by 33%. The increased volume through the paint department would allow the machine to pay for itself in the required 3-year window.

What should Luis recommend? Why? Given the framework for the strategic integration of operations decision making presented above, what level do you think Luis's firm operates at? How might that be a problem?

Satisfying Customers at Rogue Ales

The mission of Newport, Oregon's Rogue Ales is

▶ to brew the finest varietal ales in the world with an uncompromising devotion to quality and the art of brewing

▶ to present the finished work with a touch of educational, entertaining mischief

▶ to be dedicated to the rogue in each of us

▶ to remember it is not simply a matter of profit but a highly personal work of art

▶ to build relationships, not just ales

▶ to be like great friends and remember that it's what's inside that counts

This mission has grown out of Rogue Ales's success. Rogue Ales was established as a small brewery and brewpub in 1989. From its local beginnings, the company has become an operation that now sells limited editions of its varietals in more than 30 states. How does the company's mission statement influence its operations?

Rogue Ales has no designs on becoming a less-expensive, large-batch, simple-formation, mass-market, push-button macro operation. Instead, it is happily focused on producing small batches of high-quality beer and operating the Rogue Public House at the original brewery site, as well as running tasting rooms at both the brewery and at the International Association of Rogues offices nearby. The complex depth of Rogue Ales's distinctively flavored products are a result of using proprietary yeasts, the blending of multiple varieties of the finest available hops, and malt. The company believes its beer's high hop and barley quotient ensures the creation of unique, fresh, fragrant beer. Each 30-barrel batch is a distinct micro-piece, handmade in a labor-intensive process by renowned brewer John Maier and his dedicated crew of experts. Each of the brewery's products is then packaged to provide a colorful, entertaining selling

presence, whether in a retail, tap, or shelf-space environment. Rogue Ales is confident that its beers are worthy of special-occasion purchase, enjoyment, and collection. These operational decisions demonstrate that Rogue Ales is committed to providing a diversity of products in all shapes and sizes and is willing to continually change to survive.

Rogue's numerous accolades prove that customers do, in fact, choose Rogue beer based upon taste. The brewery has been awarded dozens of medals at the Great American Beer Festival over recent years, and Microbrew Appreciation Society members have selected it in as the Northwest's Best Brewery several times since the mid 1990s. Many of the company's beers stand out individually, as well—for example, its Rogue Chocolate Stout took Top Honours at the 2005 Great British Beer Fest.

Perhaps most importantly, Rogue Ales has gained the recognition of retailers and their customers who demand unique taste and excellent beer. Rogue's marketing effort does not compare with larger regional or contract mass-market micros, but is consistent with the company's size and its preference for putting its money into the product. Rogue's marketing approach exemplifies the notion that brand equity is not just a marketing concept but can be built from a firm's operations.

Rogue Ales is a good example of a company whose operations strategy fits its mission. The brewery's broad array of varietal offerings symbolizes its refusal to slip into sameness, but also complicates the production process. The potential downside of this effect is offset, however, by the company's value-adding system, which allows their marketing people and retailers the opportunity to offer a wide range of choices. Customers may select from an array of traditional ale styles (Rauch, Belgium, fruit, and spiced Americanized varietals), all within a brand that has earned critical acclaim and the trust of customers for the integrity and value of its products.

Source: http://www.rogue.com

strategy, in this stage they can influence and set the direction for corporate strategy. Thus, an operations-based competitive advantage that could not have been envisioned in an earlier stage may be targeted and gained in this final stage. For example, operations may discover a unique approach to providing a service that allows the organization to bundle other services at no additional cost. If the organization is focused on the development of a competitive advantage through such innovations, it has reached the externally supportive stage.

Hayes and Wheelwright suggest that a firm cannot move directly from the first to the fourth stage in this evolution. Organizations must move from one stage to the next, learning at each stage. Changes in decision-making procedures, changes in corporate structures and infrastructures, and even changes in personnel may be necessary to prepare for movement to a more advanced stage. Failure to lay the groundwork for the process of evolving to a higher level of integration can produce only the well-meant goal of externally supportive operational decision making, without the people, perspectives, and systems necessary to support the expectations and requirements of this stage.

Environmental Excellence and Operations Strategy

In recent years, society has made increasing demands for social responsibility on the part of business. Today, companies must comply with a host of local, state, national, and international regulations, many of them dealing with the preservation of the natural environment. In the United States over the past 30 years, concern for the health of the environment has led to the creation of the Environmental Protection Agency and a large body of environmental legislation that affects business. At the national level, these legal requirements include the reporting of toxic releases that result from the manufacture, use, or transportation of any of more than 300 chemicals named in Title III of the Superfund Amendments and Reauthorization Act (SARA), also called the Emergency Planning and Community Right to Know Act. In addition, the Comprehensive Environmental Response, Compensation, and Liability Act (CERCLA), which created the Superfund, established joint and several liability for the cleanup of environmental problems created in the past (meaning that you are responsible if you ever owned the property in question, whether or not you did the damage). U.S. businesses are also required to comply with the Clean Air Act, the Clean Water Act, the Toxic Substances Control Act, and the Resource Conservation and Recovery Act, in addition to many other national, state, and local statutes.

Beyond these legislative hurdles, companies must respond to customer, employee, community, and shareholder pressure for environmental excellence. One critical

Stockbyte/SuperStock

Functional integration is essential at all levels. How the server (i.e. sales) takes the order greatly affects the way in which the cooks (i.e. operations) will prepare the meal. How would this step in the process be different at a fast food restaurant?

incident, such as the chemical plant disaster in Bhopal, India, or the grounding of the oil-cargo supertanker Exxon *Valdez*, can have significant implications both for the environment and for the long-term profitability of a business organization. Given the risks and the potential impact of environmental issues on profitability, environmental issues now play a significant role in the corporate- and business-level strategies of many firms. Because operations is directly responsible for the creation of the goods and services that customers value, it is also directly responsible for the creation of the wastes they abhor. As a result, it is imperative that companies integrate the requirement for environmental excellence into their operations strategies.

Effective operations management can have a significant impact on a firm's environmental performance. In a recent survey (Newman and Hanna 1996), firms were asked questions about their environmental awareness and the degree to which operations had been strategically integrated in the firms' strategies. Firms in the early stages of strategic integration did not report high levels of environmental awareness. Only those firms in the later stages of strategic integration reported high levels of environmental awareness. Based on the results of this survey, on the research of others who have studied the relationship between operational performance and environmental excellence, and on what is known about how organizations develop capabilities over time, it seems likely that operational excellence is a necessary prerequisite to environmental excellence.

SUMMARY

Decisions are made at every level of an organization, and the pattern of these decisions forms a company's strategy. Companies must implement a strategic decision hierarchy to ensure that the various decisions within the pattern are aligned to keep all functions of a firm moving in the same direction. Decisions made by top corporate managers (the corporate strategy) determine what businesses a company will pursue. These decision makers allocate resources based on the potential they see for shareholder rewards. With those allocated resources, business managers have to determine how they will seek to satisfy customers and create competitive advantages (the business strategy). Finally, managers in the functional areas make the decisions that actually create the value envisioned by the business strategy.

An operations strategy is a pattern of decisions made in the operations function. When the decision pattern is consistent and is well aligned with a business's competitive priorities, operations is likely to be in tune with customer expectations and to make significant contributions that place the firm in a position of competitive advantage.

Operations strategy includes both structural and infrastructural decisions. Structural decisions establish the system that is used to add value for customers. These decisions, which have long-term significance, constrain the firm's infrastructural decisions, which determine how the value-adding system will be run on an ongoing basis. Though infrastructural decisions generally have only short-term significance, the pattern of infrastructural decisions that develops over time can influence the firm's structural requirements.

Any OM decision should be consistent with other OM decisions, as well as with the decisions made in other functions to support the business strategy. Some firms treat the operations function as an independent decision-making entity and do not effectively integrate the area with the rest of the business. Other firms use their operational strengths to drive the company's pursuit of competitive advantage. The degree to which operational decisions are integrated with the business strategy plays a significant role in building customer satisfaction and competitive advantage.

Significant benefits arise from consistent decision making between operations and other functional areas. For this reason, it is important that firms determine how they can break down communication barriers among functions so that managers and employees can work together across functional boundaries.

Today, society is increasingly concerned with business' effect on the environment, and companies are under pressure to comply with federal, state, and local statutes designed to curb pollution. The development of operations management capabilities can positively affect a firm's environmental record: When operations are more efficient they waste less and therefore pollute less. Operations managers who can effectively manage a firm's resources to create competitive advantages in terms of cost, quality, flexibility, or speed, are also likely to be able to address environmental concerns. This is one area that illustrates the importance of operational excellence and cross-functional cooperation as a basis for the pursuit of company objectives.

KEY TERMS

Assemble-to-order, 55
Batch process, 52
Business strategy, 41
Competitive priority, 42
Conglomerate (nonrelated)
  diversification, 39
Continuous-flow process, 53
Corporate strategy, 39
Discrete process, 53
Employee Involvement (EI), 55
Fixed-position layout, 52
Infrastructural decisions, 46

Job shop, 52
Make-to-order, 54
Make-to-stock, 55
Mass service, 51
Operations strategy, 46
Order-qualifying criteria, 42
Order-winning criteria, 42
Process-oriented (functional)
  layout, 52
Product-oriented layout, 53
Professional service, 51

Projects, 52
Related diversification, 39
Repetitive process, 53
Service factory, 50
Service shop, 51
Silo effect, 44
Strategy, 36
Structural decisions, 46
Synergy, 37
Total productive maintenance
  (TPM), 56

DISCUSSION QUESTIONS

1. Compare and contrast the different types of corporate diversification. How is corporate-level strategy related to business-level strategy? Consider the college or university you attend. What type of diversification best describes it?

2. How does Southwest's business strategy of differ Delta's?

3. Using the terms *quality*, *timeliness*, *low cost*, and *flexibility*, describe the competitive priorities of McDonald's, Mercedes, a one-hour photo shop, Subway (the sandwich shop chain), your university, and a dentist's office. How might the competitive priorities you have identified set these businesses apart from other competitors?

4. Compare the companies in the previous question to their competition. What are some of the implied operational differences? How might those operational differences affect the other functions in these companies?

5. Assume this is your first day as manager of a small cabinet-making business. Your predecessor erased all the computer files, account histories, records, manuals, and other operating information relating to the business. All that remains is the machines, the employees, and a crowd of anxious customers at the front desk. Is this a structural or an infrastructural problem? If you still have all the "bricks and mortar," why do you have a problem?

6. Assume this is your first day as the new director of a city youth sports league. Your predecessor cleaned out the office when he left, taking the league's information, rules, sign-up forms, records, and schedules. All you have left is the balls, bats, ball fields, swimming pool, and staff, as well as

some anxious parents. Is this a structural or an infrastructural problem? If you still have all the "bricks and mortar," why do you have a problem?

7. Compare "make-to-stock," "make-to-order," and "assemble-to-order" policies. How do the differences between them relate to the choice of a business' competitive priorities?

8. Compare the choice of a production process type (project, job shop, batch, repetitive, or continuous flow) to that of a process layout (fixed position, process layout, or product layout). How are the two choices related?

9. Compare the choice of process type (project, job shop, batch, repetitive, or continuous flow) to the concepts of "make to stock," "make to order," or "assemble to order."

10. What is the advantage of an "externally supportive" operations strategy? Identify an organization with which you are familiar and state the stage of strategic integration it has achieved. Justify your answer.

11. Can a business be both profitable and environmentally benign at the same time? Is this combination of priorities a likely one? Are environmental excellence and operational excellence negatively or positively correlated? Illustrate your answer with examples of real companies.

12. It has been suggested that firms whose OM functions are "externally supportive" may be more likely to reach environmental success than those who are "internally neutral." Why do you think this is true?

Case 2: Goodyear and Michelin Cash in on Firestone's Problems

If you are reading this case on the North American continent, you probably remember the extremely negative publicity Ford Motor Company and the Bridgestone/Firestone tire company suffered during the late 1990s as a result of tire failures on sport utility vehicles (SUV) made by Ford and bearing Bridgestone/Firestone tires. Each company continues to wage significant public relations and legal battles in light of consumer lawsuits. The firms have blamed each other as well as the SUV owners, arguing that the latter may have overloaded their vehicles or driven with under-inflated tires. Making a long, tragic, and costly story short, the tire failures have been blamed for thousands of accidents, many of which included fatalities and significant injuries, and have prompted one of the most expensive product recalls in corporate history.

Goodyear Tire & Rubber Co. and France's Groupe Michelin chose to leverage their powerful brand names during this time of heightened concern about tire quality by demanding that some of the major car makers pay more for Goodyear and Michelin tires. Edouard Michelin, chief executive of the French tire maker, credited his company's success in boosting prices partly to a "flight to quality" in the wake of the Firestone recall. Goodyear spokesman Chuck Sinclair said, "We have made it known that we're evaluating and exploring all possibilities to improve our profitability and service to the [car makers]." That included, in some cases, raising the prices paid by the vehicle manufacturers.

Car companies (often called original equipment manufacturers, or OEMs), which have been asking their suppliers to lower prices, admit to feeling pressure from the tire makers to pay higher prices. While car manufacturers are always working to lower prices, they do not supply information about costs for specific purchased items. In the recent past, selling to OEMs has become even less profitable for tire makers because car companies are also demanding bigger and more highly engineered tires, even as they try to drive down the prices they pay for those tires. This conflict between OEMs and tire makers will not improve soon, because federal regulators are implementing plans for much tougher tire standards that will force tire makers to build sturdier and more expensive tires. Still, tire makers are trying to boost profitability without implementing outright price increases by working with car manufacturers to make slight alterations in the construction of or materials used for tires to shave costs without harming performance.

Tire makers have more clout with automakers than companies that supply other parts, such as fan belts and bucket seats, because the tire makers have more consumer brand-name recognition and because they do not depend on the original-equipment market. In fact, more than three-quarters of the passenger tires produced in the U.S. are sold as replacements. Because the same tire can easily cost twice as much in the replacement market as it does when it is supplied to an OEM for a new car, the replacement market is a much more profitable one for tire manufacturers than the OEM market.

Until recently, tire makers fought to place their products on as many new vehicles as possible because car owners typically replace tires with the same brand that came with the vehicle. "In the old days when you sold tires to [car makers], you broke even, but you made a lot of money when they were replaced three or four times," said David Bradley, an analyst with J. P. Morgan Securities. But with tires lasting far longer than before, original owners may buy only one set of replacements or even none at all before they trade the car in or their lease expires. The vehicle's second owner is far less likely to stick with the original brand. Instead, replacement consumers generally shop for the best combination of price, quality, and value. Often, replacement decisions are driven by promotions, availability, and service offerings at retailers such as Wal-Mart and Sears Auto Center. Pricing pressure from large retailers can also significantly influence tire company profit margins in the replacement market.

Ultimately, tire makers court risk when they pressure OEMs to pay higher prices for tires. If certain tire makers play too hard during pricing negotiations with OEMs, the latter can shift their business to other tire manufacturers. For example, when Michelin announced that it would stop supplying tires to General Motors in Europe after the two firms clashed over prices, Germany's Continental AG was ready to take GM's business. Therefore, a hard stand on pricing by Goodyear and Michelin could benefit Firestone, and Continental as well as smaller companies such as Kumho Industrial Co. and Hankook Tire, two Korean tire producers that recently landed new business with GM.

SOME QUESTIONS TO THINK ABOUT:

1. What are the two main customer groups for the tire companies described in this case?

2. What appears to be the order-qualifying criteria and order-winning criteria for each company described in this case?

3. What do the competitive priorities appear to be for Goodyear, Michelin, and Bridgestone?

4. Do you think it is right for the tire companies to charge such radically different prices to OEMs and the replacement market for the very same item? Why?

5. Do any of the companies have a competitive advantage? Explain?

Source: Adapted from the *Wall Street Journal*, Sept. 16, 2002, staff reporter Timothy Aeppel

REFERENCES

Buchholz, R. A. Principles of Environmental Management: The Greening of Business. Englewood Cliffs, NJ: Prentice Hall, 1993.

Hayes, R., and S. Wheelwright. *Restoring Our Competitive Edge.* New York: Wiley & Sons, 1984.

Hayes, R., S. Wheelwright, and K. Clark. *Dynamic Manufacturing.* New York: The Free Press, 1988.

Hill, T. *Manufacturing Strategy, 3e.* Burr Ridge, IL: R. D. Irwin Publishing, 1999.

Kim, J. S. Search for New Manufacturing Paradigm: Executive Summary of the 1996 U.S. Manufacturing Futures Survey. Boston: Boston University School of Management Manufacturing Roundtable, October 1996.

McKinsey & Company. "The Corporate Response to the Environmental Challenge." Internal report. Amsterdam, 1991.

Newman, R. W., and M. D. Hanna. "An Empirical Exploration of the Relationship between Manufacturing Strategy and Environmental Management: Two Complementary Models." *International Journal of Operations and Production Management* 16, no. 4 (1996): 69–87.

Skinner, W. Manufacturing: The Formidable Competitive Weapon. New York: John Wiley & Sons, 1985.

Ward, P., K. Leong, and K. Boyer. "Manufacturing Proactiveness and Performance." *Decision Sciences* 25, no. 3 (May–June 1994): 337–358.

Wheelwright, S. C., and R. H. Hayes. "Competing through Manufacturing." *Harvard Business Review* (January–February, 1985): 99–109.

3

Supply Chain Strategy: Aligning Operations with Customer Expectations and Supplier Processes

Chapter Outline

Introduction   68

Integrating Operations Management Across the Functions   69

Supply Chain Management: From Henry Ford to E-Commerce   69

Supply Chain Management Decisions   73

SCM in the Automobile Industry   76

Supply Chain Configuration Strategies   80

The Supply Chain Operating Reference (SCOR) Model   86

Supply Chain Coordination Strategies   90

Relationship Management   90

E-Commerce   91

Improving Supply Chains: Seven Principles   93

The Stock Price Impact of Supply Chain Savings   98

Summary   102

Key Terms   102

Solved Problems   102

Discussion Questions   104

Problems   105

Challange Problems   106

Case 3: Your Everyday $2 Billion Supply Chain Blunder—and a Solution   107

References   109

Learning Objectives

After studying this chapter, you should be able to

▶ Demonstrate your understanding of the linkages between supply chain management and the various functional areas of business

▶ Describe the historical development of supply chain management

▶ Describe supply chain management decisions

▶ Describe supply chain management configuration strategies

▶ Describe the Supply Chain Operating Reference Model and its use

▶ Describe supply chain management coordination strategies

▶ Describe supply chain management improvement strategies

▶ Compute the stock price impact of supply chain savings

. . . Back at the Rec Center

It's 6 a.m., and the rec center has just opened. Early risers who want to get in a workout before heading off to face the day are starting to arrive. Fred is the first to arrive again. On this day he seems to be in a world of his own.

"What is it that has your head somewhere else this morning?" asked Tom from a stepper.

"I guess I'm a little preoccupied," Fred admits, sitting down on a bench in between Tom's stepper and the dumbbells Luis and Cheryl were using. "Some stuff going on, you know; I'm still getting used to this new position." Fred had recently moved from a division that manufactures a wide array of customized electronics for a variety of customers to become marketing manager for a company that produces a couple of standardized products for a small number of big volume customers. He still wasn't sure he liked the switch. "We used to sit and wait for the phone to ring, take an order, somebody made it, and we shipped it! I never even knew how it was made, just what it could do and how to sell it!" he says.

"So what's the big deal?" asks Luis, as he finishes a set of bicep curls and puts the dumbbell back on the rack. "I thought you said your life was simpler now. You've got that 'plain vanilla' thing going, one model, one line, just a handful of happy customers—shoot, I'll bet you're even going home by 5 most nights!" he jokes.

"You're right in most ways," Fred replies. "In other ways, though, it's making life difficult! Might only be a couple but the accounts I deal with now, these people think they own you!" He went on to describe to the group how he was to meet outside experts and a team from one of his bigger accounts today to go through his process. "I've got to meet them at the plant this morning. They want to check us out. We told them we're working on ISO certification, but they still want to see our process. Why should they care?" he asks, annoyed.

"I've read about that 'ISO' thing," says Luis. "It's some sort of deal for doing business in Europe, isn't it? We don't export much, so it's not an issue for us right now. But, Tom, weren't you talking about it last week?" he asks.

"Yeah, it doesn't mean you're really good, it just means you're really as good as you say you are and you've got a system in place to manage and improve your quality," replies Tom.

"That's it!" says Fred. "We have 'em coming in to look us over, mostly people from our customers, and the others are some sort of judges or something like that."

"You mean 'registrars'?" asks Cheryl. She had finished her last set of curls and is now listening.

"A hospital worries about ISO certification?" asks Luis.

"Sure, we went through it already. We had to in order to work with some of the bigger health insurance companies," she adds. She explained that some of the major insurers were becoming more selective in how they managed health care, and that steering more patients to fewer hospitals was a form of "putting all their eggs in one basket." It simplified things for the insurance companies by giving them economies of scale and allowing them to offload some of the administrative side of their business to the hospital. ISO certification was a way of ensuring a business had the systems in place to help it live up to its end of an agreement with another company.

"I guess that explains some of the other things these customers are asking for," adds Fred, responding to Cheryl's explanation. He talks about how some of his company's larger accounts also wanted the firm to take over a larger share of their business relationship. In fact, he says, one of the accounts wanted Fred's company to handle all the logistics of moving materials between them. Another account even wants Fred's people to manage the inventory of his cell phones in their warehouses. Fred adds that most of his current customers used his company as the primary or only source for the product categories he handled. "I guess they're willing to pay a little more when they ask us to do this stuff, and we get some guarantees," he says, as he began to realize that the situation might hold some benefits for his company. As Fred talks, Tom is nodding. They understand what Cheryl is saying about companies wanting to have "all of their eggs in a basket."

"That's it," Cheryl says. "We can add those other services when we have that kind of a relationship with an insurance company." She suggests it was the same with a hospital as it was with making cell phones. "Fred, when they buy a basic cell phone from you, your customers are paying you to manage their inventory too," she adds.

"They couldn't do that unless we were their only supplier, could they?" asks Fred as his understanding grew.

"You know," says Luis, looking puzzled, "I always thought that was what you weren't supposed to do, you know, the 'all the eggs in one basket' thing?" He was thinking, for instance, that he might get a higher return from his retirement fund by putting the same amount of money into a single stock, assuming he picked a good one, but he also knew the risk involved—what if he picked a bad one? In other words, Cheryl and Fred's discussion seemed to contradict the idea that diversification minimizes risk.

"I think what Fred's customers, the insurance companies, my hospital, and all of our suppliers are doing to get on the same page is called supply chain management," Cheryl adds. She explains that the more you simplify and ensure what you do, how you do it, and with whom you do it, then the more you can view the relationships between business partners with certainty, which lessens the need to spread the risk. She argued that what all of them were working toward—what is now called supply chain management—is about knowing and not guessing or playing the odds. She said it's about knowing what your customer and your customer's customer is going to want from you, and knowing what your supplier and your supplier's supplier will do for you, rather than trying to guess what these variables are. She also points out that you eliminate uncertainty by working with supply chain partners or ISO-certified firms and that you benefit by dealing exclusively with them.

Fred and Luis nod in agreement as they finish their workouts.

"Yup," says Tom, getting off the stepper and heading for the showers. "Just like getting on a 737—if you're going to put all your eggs in one basket, make darn sure it's a good basket!" he laughs.

"But Tom, didn't your son call the other morning to say he ran out of gas driving your car to school?" asks Luis, grinning.

"Yes," Tom answers, looking confused. "So?"

"Well, next time I fly on your airline, can you get somebody else to check the gas?"

Introduction

Supply chain management (SCM)

The configuration, coordination, and improvement of a sequentially-related set of operations.

Supply chain management (SCM) may be defined as the configuration, coordination, and improvement of a sequentially related set of operations. The Supply Chain Council, a professional organization for supply chain management professionals, offers a more comprehensive definition:

> *The supply chain—a term now commonly used internationally—encompasses every effort involved in producing and delivering a final product or service, from the supplier's supplier to the customer's customer. Supply Chain Management includes managing supply and demand, sourcing raw materials and parts, manufacturing and assembly, warehousing and inventory tracking, order entry and order management, distribution across all channels, and delivery to the customer.*

Our discussion of supply chain management is, therefore, an extension of the focus on customer service that was introduced in Chapter 1. With SCM, the idea of satisfying an entire chain of customers (and competing with suppliers to win the business of the ultimate customer) becomes reality.

This chapter

▶ Links supply chain management with other functional areas of business

▶ Describes the historic development of supply chain management, showing that coordinating sequentially related activities is not really anything new. What is new is our ability to do this in complex environments where customers are given significant choices in regard to the product-service bundle

▶ Provides a general overview of the decisions that comprise supply chain management

▶ Discusses "bricks and mortar" issues in supply chain configuration, such as which technology to use, what

REC CENTER DILEMMA

Fred makes the case for being a sole supplier

One of Fred's main customers has played Fred against another supplier for years by dividing its business between Fred's company and the other company to keep them both looking for ways to reduce costs or cut profit margins to win a bigger share of the customer's business. If Fred's company could reliably have a bigger share of that business, or even all of it, Fred felt sure that there were technologies and other initiatives his company could invest in so as to do a better job for this customer. Help Fred formulate an argument to the customer for making his company their sole supplier.

to make and what to buy, how many vendors to use, where to locate certain types of capacity, and what types of product-service bundles to provide

▶ Illustrates how coordination of the supply chain can help firms more effectively communicate and interact with their upstream suppliers and downstream customers

▶ Addresses the of improving supply chains, an ongoing process of continual improvement to existing configurations and coordination processes

Integrating Operations Management Across the Functions

Historically, the idea of greater product customization led from a divide-and-conquer approach to issues of coordination across entire supply chains. Giving customers choices, however, has increased business complexity in the form of product variety, demand uncertainty, and the resulting variable capacity requirements. Today, there is more opportunity to coordinate activities across the supply chain—even in the presence of complexity—because of the enabling information systems and communication technologies. The result: Supply chain management has become a critical aspect of business success and mass customization has replaced mass production in many industries.

Table 3.1 highlights some of the key links among the various functional areas of business and the SCM. All functions are involved in SCM decisions:

▶ SCM has direct implications for estimating financial performance for equity markets and for capital allocation decisions.

▶ Accounting plays a significant role in SCM through providing cost estimates that drive SCM configuration and coordination issues.

▶ Human Resource issues are common in SCM configuration and coordination, whether through questions of labor cost and workforce skill in global sourcing decisions or capacity and scheduling issues in SCM coordination.

▶ Marketing plays a key part through its role in coordinating logistical systems, product-service bundle design, and transferring customer intelligence to the organization.

▶ Engineering provides significant input to SCM configuration through its involvement in design of both the product-service bundle and the value-adding system.

▶ Finally, MIS is responsible for the enabling information system technologies that play such a significant role in coordinating and improving supply chains.

Supply Chain Management: From Henry Ford to E-Commerce

Until quite recently, the ownership of business supply chains was always highly concentrated. Craftspeople generally handled all stages of a process, from the conversion of natural resources to providing customers with products. Musicians designed and

Table 3.1

Integrating Operations Management with Other Functions

Integration Perspective / Functional Area	Finance	Accounting
Why Cross-Functional Integration Matters in supply chain management	Financial performance forecasts and long-term capital requirements depend on supply chain configuration and coordination respectively.	Measurement of costs and revenues are largely related to transactions with supply chain partners (i.e., supply chain coordination).
Key Issues	What long-term requirements for fixed and operating capital are anticipated due to the firm's supply chain strategy? What cost and revenue streams should result from supply chain operations and thus, be used in financial forecasts? What financing should be extended to customers? What financial terms should be granted to suppliers?	Are purchase and sales transactions being captured and accurately reflected in financial statements? How will channel inventory be valued? How will long-term sales and purchase contracts be reported? What liabilities and risks related to supply chain partners should be reported to stockholders?

built their own instruments, carpenters hewed lumber from beams and built their products, metalworkers smelted their own materials and made products from these. Even in the early twentieth century, after the Industrial Revolution, capitalists tended to control large vertically integrated empires, such as Henry Ford's company, which did everything from mining to final assembly of its Model T vehicles in the early 1900s. This one-company-does-all approach allowed Ford to coordinate all of the business' sequentially related activities and gain very large efficiencies. Every part of the chain became extremely efficient at doing one thing. The weakness of this system was that it was difficult to accommodate product variety or make model changes. When the company switched from manufacturing the Model A to making the Model T, Ford spent about $200 million to change all of the process tools and systems. The result, however, was that Ford could still make only one car. This lack of flexibility in Ford's system during the 1920s allowed General Motors (GM) to gain the upper hand in the automobile business at the time by offering a variety of products. Ford attempted to regain his lead in the market by offering a variety of colors, engines, and interiors within one model of car, and by expanding his product line to include multiple models

Human Resources	Marketing	Engineering	Management Information Systems
Supply chain configuration decisions will determine Human Resource needs and strategies.	Supply chain coordination and improvement decisions impact product placement and distribution plans. Supply chain configuration will drive customer relationships.	Supply chain configuration will drive engineering design decisions regarding both processes and product-service bundles.	Supply chain coordination and improvement requirements directly impact information system requirements.
How will vertical integration or outsourcing decisions impact our organization's human resource needs, costs and strategies?	From a logistical perspective how should we structure our product distribution network? How will supply chain partnerships impact our brand image? What supply chain improvements do our customers seek? Do we manage our customer relationships effectively?	Are our processes effectively designed to utilize supplier materials and satisfy customers? Can we improve the design of our product–service bundle?	What are the current and future information system requirements imposed by our supply chain partners? What are our own current and future information system requirements associated with supply chain coordination? What Enterprise Resources Planning (ERP) system should be adopted?

produced in varying quantities. The company also began frequently redesigning models. But Ford lost the ability to control his now more complex supply chain.

As a result of the coordination problems eventually faced by Ford, the typical industrial supply chain has been broken into many pieces which are managed separately. This is the divide-and-conquer solution referred to above. In addition to complexity, factors leading to the division of supply chains include:

1. *Technology*. It is common to manage high-tech operations and low-tech operations separately. Capital-intensive operations are often separated from labor-intensive operations.

2. *Scale*. It is common to manage operations that produce standardized products or services in large quantities separately from those that produce a greater variety of customized products in smaller volumes.

3. *The need for focus in operations*. It is desirable for a business in a supply chain to have a homogeneous mix of products and customers. Where there are mismatches in the product line or customer set, it is common to divide up businesses.

Figure 3.1

SCM as a river

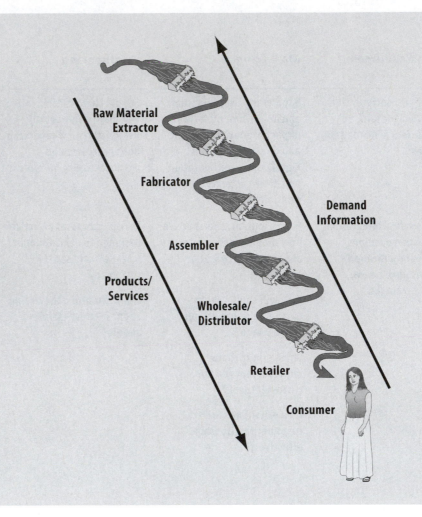

Raw Material Extractor

Fabricator

Demand Information

Assembler

Products/ Services

Wholesale/ Distributor

Retailer

Consumer

Figure 3.1 describes a supply chain using the metaphor of a river with dams. Each dam represents the interface between one company and another, while the river represents material flowing through the supply chain. (The figure is much simpler than a real-world supply chain, of course, because there is only one material flow in the figure. A more accurate analogy is a picture of a river with many tributaries and many channels at its delta.) Notice the pools behind each dam. These are needed to ensure that the company can respond quickly to the exact material needs of their customer and also protect the company from problems with their suppliers. Having an extra stock of raw materials, work-in-process inventory, and finished goods helps buffer the operations of individual companies from the demand-and-supply uncertainty they face. However, these buffers are expensive to maintain, both in terms of out-of-pocket expense and opportunity costs. In a real way, they represent the cost of the uncertainty. Effective supply chain management reduces these costs by reducing uncertainty.

One of the weaknesses of a supply chain that has been divided up between multiple businesses is that the businesses are likely to act in their own interests to optimize their own profit. In this situation, the goal of satisfying an ultimate customer is easily lost, as are opportunities that could arise from partial coordination of decisions across stages of the supply chain. Many companies recognized this with the advent of just-in-time manufacturing during the 1970s and 1980s. These firms' efforts to reduce waste in internal operations led them to begin working more closely with suppliers and customers. If suppliers could be made more reliable, there was less need for inventories of raw materials, quality inspection systems, rework, and other non-value-adding activities. Similarly, if customer demand could be leveled and customer needs better understood, there was need for finished goods inventory, sales incentives, and so on. Thus, companies began to realize how high the cost of maintaining the buffers actually was. (The inventory buffers are represented by the pools behind the dams in Figure 3.1.) Instead, the practice of **lean production**, which is an approach to managing operations without massive buffers of inventory, became much more common. By removing the pools of inventory, companies were able to cut costs, improve quality feedback, shorten production lead times, and reduce the time required to introduce new products or services. Today, recent advances in information systems technology allow many firms to go one step further by looking upstream beyond their suppliers and downstream beyond their customers to make their supply chain even leaner.

EPA/Mike Nelson/Landov

Efficient technology and methods applied to logistics are key to improving supply chain management.

Supply Chain Management Decisions

As we define supply chain management, it involves three types of activity: configuration, coordination, and improvement.

In Chapter 2, we discussed the importance of strategy to an organization. Strategy gives direction to the organization and allows lower level managers the security to perform their roles and make decisions with confidence that other managers are also making consistent decisions that move the organization toward its goals. We argued that strategy provides a cross-functional basis for structural decision making as well as infrastructural decision making. Table 3.2 extends this discussion to SCM strategy. SCM strategy extends decision-making input to include external enterprise-wide considerations. Configuration decision-making processes result in structural decisions that determine "who does what" in the supply chain. Coordination decision-making processes lead to infrastructural decisions that direct the production and movement of material through the supply chain. Improvement processes are the systems that guide efforts to make a supply chain more effective in satisfying the customer expectations strategically targeted by the firms of the supply chain. As Figure 3.2 illustrates, for these decision-making processes to have a supply chain perspective they need to draw in considerations of importance to stakeholders including such groups as suppliers, suppliers' suppliers, customers and customers' customers.

Two functional areas of business that are central to SCM are logistics and purchasing. **Logistics** is a function responsible for managing the flow and storage of materials. From a supply chain perspective it is important from the original source of raw materials to the end user, and it is critical to customer satisfaction. In the past this meant

Lean production

An approach to managing operations without massive buffers of inventory which is becoming much more common.

Logistics

A function responsible for managing the flow and storage of materials.

Table 3.2

Supply Chain Management Activity

Configuration of the supply chain, from the perspective of individual companies, involves determining:	• What the product-service bundle will include • What portion of the bundle's value will be provided by the company and what part will be bought from others • Where facilities will be located and what their capabilities will be • What technologies will be used • How communication between customers and suppliers will be handled • The expectations to which suppliers and customers will be held
Coordination of the supply chain, from the perspective of individual companies, involves:	• Determining when to provide products and services in the bundle and in what quantities • Ensuring that suppliers are able to effectively provide the value required of them in the appropriate levels of quality, cost, and timeliness • Setting appropriate levels for capacity, inventory, and lead time in light of supply-and-demand uncertainty • Communicating demand, performance expectations, and performance results with suppliers and customers
Improvement of the supply chain from the perspective of individual companies involves changing the configuration and/or the approach to coordination in order to enhance the overall performance of the chain. As such, it can involve:	• Installing enterprise resources planning (ERP) systems or other information technologies such as bar coding, automated data collection in point-of-sale (POS) systems, geographic positioning and material tracking systems in logistical systems, and other communication and decision-supporting information technologies • Streamlining the channels of supply by working with suppliers and/or customers to eliminate capacity imbalances between their processes and yours, weeding out under-performing suppliers, creating more effective logistical systems, and so on • Changing technologies or planning systems to improve quality, lead time, cost, or service • Redesigning the product-service bundle to make it easier to provide or be of greater value to the customer

arranging for the use of trucks, trains, planes, boats, and warehouses to move and store inventory in response to contractual obligations. Most logistical analysis involved time and cost trade-offs between these modes of transportation. Also, many supplies and products were sold "free on board" (FOB), which meant that once they left the supplier's loading dock the buyer owned them and was responsible for any damages.

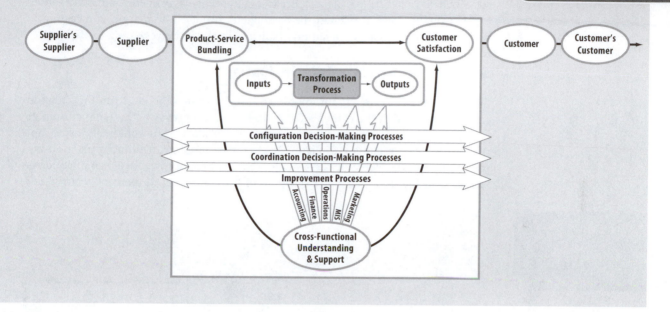

Little information was available regarding the whereabouts of these FOB shipments other than they had left the loading dock.

Changes in logistics have changed the world of business. Technologies that enable real-time tracking of inventory have reduced the uncertainty in supply chains and also the impact of the time-cost trade-off. Having (1) a great product in the wrong place, (2) an insufficient supply of the product, or (3) imprecise or erroneous information about product location and quantities are not formulas for business success. Rather, the keys to success are (1) having a great product, in the right quantity, at the right place, at the right time; (2) knowing that it is there; and (3) enabling the customer to see that information. All of this is possible in today's world of information-enabled, agile supply chains. This shift in the field of logistics has led to the creation of numerous firms that may not provide transportation or warehousing at all—as most logistics firms once did—but simply provide management of logistical functions. (Firms that provide outsourcing opportunities for logistical services, whether they provide warehousing and transportation or just logistics management, are called "third-party logistics" providers are referred to as 3PLs.)

Purchasing, or procurement, is the business function responsible for managing the acquisition of the materials used by an organization. Historically, purchasing departments were created to ensure that firms obtained price advantages through effective negotiation with suppliers, elimination of conflicts of interest (such as nepotism), and leveraging of opportunities to purchase in volume. A common strategy was to place large orders on bid and award business to the supplier whose price was lowest.

Purchasing

The business function responsible for managing the acquisition of the materials used by an organization.

Generally, a purchaser's tactic was to have at least two suppliers that could be played against each other, even when the purchaser made recurring purchases from custom suppliers. Currently, however, more purchasing departments are seeking to cooperate with their suppliers to create a more efficient total supply chain. Purchasers are looking for ways to make suppliers more healthy and effective so that the latter's company also benefits from the relationship. Indeed, rather than competing for margins within the supply chain, it makes more sense to enhance the competitiveness of the shared supply chain (make the pie bigger). Because supply chains compete against each other, companies that have weakened their suppliers through low margin contracting in many cases only weaken their supply chain and hurt themselves.

SCM in the Automobile Industry

Today's supply chain in the automobile industry is quite different from the situation Henry Ford faced in the early 1900s, when he could get away with saying customers could have "any color they wanted as long as it was black." Automobile industry supply chains are characterized in Figure 3.3. In the automobile manufacturing industry, the companies that assemble cars—such as Ford, GM, Chrysler, Toyota, and Honda—usually bear the largest capital investment of the companies in the supply chain. For

Figure 3.3

SCM in the automobile industry

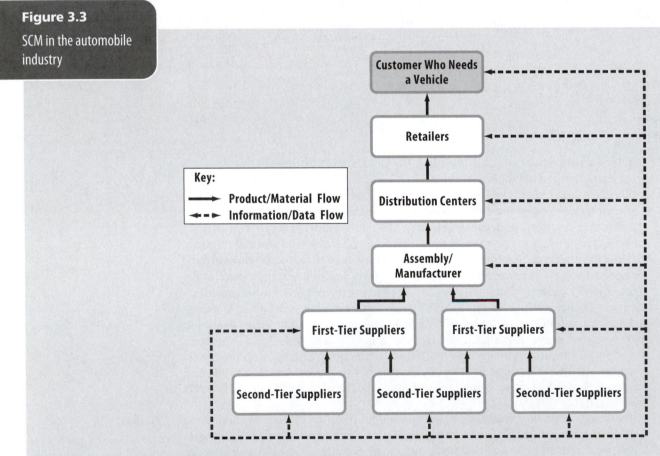

Source: Adapted from Handfield & Nichols, Prentice Hall, 1999, p. 15

I'm Majoring in Supply Chain Management

"You're majoring in what?!" was the response your roommate or parent might have given just a few years ago when you told them you were studying supply chain management (SCM). In the past, SCM lacked the name recognition of fields such as finance, marketing, or accounting, so announcing a major in SCM often drew puzzled responses. But not anymore: SCM has entered the mainstream at several first-rate B-schools, and the employers who recruit at your school have certainly heard of it. These days, supply chain managers take a broad perspective and look across multiple functions as they span the links among trading partners. They often make the difference between pleased customers and dissatisfied ones. And in today's cost-conscious times, they're especially valuable. "Firms are under tremendous pressure to cut costs," said Jack Nevin, executive director of the Grainger Center for Supply Chain Management at the University of Wisconsin-Madison School of Business. "And most of those costs are just sitting there in the supply chain."

Business schools that have SCM programs—Wisconsin, Michigan State, Miami University, Bowling Green State University, Arizona State, and Penn State,

to name a few—have seen student interest skyrocket. At ASU, one-third of the class of 2003 specialized in supply chain management, up from 9% in 1995. And average salaries for supply chain grads at ASU increased 25% over the past five years; at MSU they're up almost 50% since 1995. While the clunky economy has put hiring plans on hold at many companies, supply chain opportunities still exist. "Supply chain is the most recession-proof of the majors here," said Robert Nason, chair of MSU's Marketing and Supply Chain Management department.

Don't expect to sleep through class and get a plum SCM job. David Wieber, a senior materials manager at Cisco, said competition is fierce and that snagging the right internship is critical. Top recruiters include IBM, Motorola, Rubbermaid, DaimlerChrysler, Ford, and Solectron, and an ASU rep says the school has even gotten inquiries from E. & J. Gallo Winery. So, if you're looking to study in one of today's hottest majors and to work in a rapidly growing field, think about supply chain management.

Source: Adapted from "Supply Chains Get Sexy," *Fortune*, December 2001, Matthew Boyle reporter

this reason, and because of the amount of materials they buy, automobile assemblers have tremendous leverage within, and exert a huge influence on, the supply chain. The decisions the car companies make in designing the product-service bundle, designing the value-adding system, and operating the value-adding system have a major impact both on the level of satisfaction experienced by the ultimate customer and on the competitiveness of the supply chain.

Looking upstream, the companies most directly affected by the assemblers' influence are the assemblers' first-tier suppliers, which sell items such as radios, seats, headlamps, and paint to the car companies. First-tier suppliers are generally held accountable for the quality and timeliness of the materials that they provide.

Through their first-tier suppliers, assemblers influence their second-tier suppliers. Examples of second-tier suppliers include fabric producers who sell to the companies that make car seats, electronic component manufacturers who sell electronics to the firms that produce dashboard parts and radios, and so on. Though Figure 3.3 shows only two levels of supply, in fact there often are several. The influence of the large car assemblers on other companies in the supply chain diminishes, however, in proportion to the other companies' distance from the assemblers in the supply chain. For example, you could say that the company making the thread that goes into car seat fabric is a third-tier supplier, the cotton broker that sells to the thread maker is a fourth-tier supplier, the farmer that sells to the cotton broker is a fifth-tier supplier, and so on. Because cotton is a commodity and thread is a standardized product with multiple applications, the auto assemblers would have limited ability and little reason to attempt to influence the activities of the firms supplying these materials.

Looking downstream, automobile assemblers also significantly influence the distribution and retail practices in their supply chain. Distributors transport cars from the factory to the retailers and often use a regional distribution center where they may hold a large inventory of finished cars. If you have bought a car in the United States, the dealer probably added a "destination charge" to the price of the car. This distribution cost varies for different kinds of cars on the dealer's lot because not every automobile assembler uses the same logistics companies and distribution network. As a result, some companies may have much more inventory in the pipeline than others, some may incur much greater distribution costs, and some may gain competitive advantage from their distribution systems. When the vehicles are distributed to car dealers (in other words, the retailers), the assemblers control many of the dealers' practices. Because the assembly companies can decide what cars a dealer gets and when—as well as the difference between Manufacturer's Suggested Retail Price (MSRP) and dealer's invoice cost—it is in the best interests of the retailers to adhere to the guidelines set forth by the assemblers.

In today's world of almost unlimited customer choice, it takes many companies, each with its own expertise, to convert materials such as plastic, metal, glass, and fabric into the car you drive away from a retail showroom. Supply chain management is the configuring, coordinating, and improving of the activities of all of these firms. This implies establishing and managing the flow of materials, money, and information. Material flows are shown in Figure 3.3 as solid lines. Notice in the figure that material flows in only one direction—downstream. In reality, however, material can flow upstream as well. For example, unused or damaged materials can be returned from any stage of the supply chain to earlier stages if they are recyclable, reusable, repairable, or remanufacturable.

Money flows in the opposite direction of the material. Financial managers, accountants, and auditors oversee cash flows, monitoring the value of inventory, and predicting earnings, so they are quite concerned with managing the same links in the supply chain as those who manage the material and information flows.

Notice that information flows from any stage of the supply chain to any other stage. This was not the case in the past, because information regarding demand and customer requirements was passed upstream through the supply chain one stage at a time. Let's continue using the automobile industry as an example: Customers told retailers what they wanted, retailers ordered vehicles, distributors told the assemblers what was in short supply, assemblers bought what they needed to fulfill the demand for that supply, and so on. The exchange of demand information generally relied on purchase orders, and financial information was exchanged via paper invoice. Because this form of communication was so inefficient, manufacturers at each stage of the chain simply forecasted demand, scheduled their facilities based on this expected customer demand, and then met the demand from stock. If the forecast was wrong, they found ways to liquidate their excess inventories through incentives and other demand management practices.

Today, information is frequently exchanged via **Electronic Data Interchange (EDI)**, which is a method of transferring business information such as demand, price, available

Electronic data interchange (EDI)

A method of transferring business information such as demand, price, available capacity, and the anticipated delivery date between suppliers and customers via a predetermined protocol.

capacity, and anticipated delivery date between suppliers and customers via a predetermined protocol. In fact, material flows and financial transactions need not rely on paper documents, such as purchase orders. Often, companies provide passwords to suppliers so they can access assembly schedules on their web site and deliver material when needed. **Enterprise resources planning (ERP)** systems are information systems that allow companies to access the schedules of their downstream suppliers and schedule their own operations so that they are making what actually will be needed rather than what they think will be needed. Information technologies such as EDI and ERP systems are key enablers of supply chain management.

Each of the major auto assembly companies employs its own strategy in its dealings with upstream suppliers. These strategies even vary within a company depending on the particular vehicle being built. In one strategy, the design and assembly of some vehicles is completely outsourced. For example, Magna Steyr engineered and assembles low-volume specialty vehicles for a number of companies, including BMW and Saab. Volkswagen, perhaps suggesting that it sees itself more as an auto design and marketing company than as a manufacturer, developed a truck assembly facility in Brazil where suppliers assemble their own part of the car on the assembly line. (For example, Bosch employees, not VW employees, put the Bosch brakes and fuel injection systems on the truck.) DaimlerChrysler buys more of the parts that go into their Chrysler vehicles than many other auto assembly companies, including 100% of the parts that go into the Dodge Viper. On the other hand, they make most of the critical components that go into the Jeep Wrangler. On average, it is estimated that 70% of the parts in Chrysler cars were bought by DaimlerChrysler. This allows the company to focus on what it wants to be good at—designing and assembling cars—and on leveraging the technological expertise of its suppliers by managing the supply chain. When Honda and Toyota began making automobiles in North America, many of their Japanese suppliers opened facilities in North America. One of the distinctive features of Honda and Toyota's supply chain strategies is their loyalty to their suppliers. GM, on the other hand, has historically owned many of its first-tier suppliers. Delphi, for instance, is a collection of what once were GM divisions that produced electronic components for GM vehicles.

This discussion of SCM in the auto industry provides a fairly representative picture of supply chains for most durable goods. The picture is quite different for consumer goods, where large retailers such as Wal-Mart generally dictate the delivery requirements and terms of purchase for both large and small suppliers. In a consumer goods situation, suppliers generally are expected to keep the shelves stocked based on point-of-sale (POS) information uploaded into Wal-Mart's computer system when items are scanned at cash registers. Wal-Mart suppliers often are not paid for their merchandise until after it has been sold. Also, where product-service bundles are less customized, SCM requires greater coordination of design- and technical-information exchanges and is less oriented toward cost savings. Regardless of the situation, the point of supply chain management is to configure operational resources so that the needs of the ultimate customer can be competitively satisfied.

In any industrial supply chain, service-intensive operations play a key role. Logistics—including transportation, warehousing, and material tracking services—account for a large portion of most product-service bundles. This is especially true when you consider international or global supply chains. Additionally, information systems provide the critical data-processing services needed to coordinate industrial supply chains. Without these two key services, the concept of supply chain management could never become a reality. In fact, it may be the integration of information systems and logistics across functional silos and then between companies in the supply chain that has enabled much of what has come to be known as SCM.

Enterprise Resources Planning (ERP)

Systems Software packages that integrate decision support programs for the various functional areas with a common database. They allow companies to access the schedules of their downstream suppliers and schedule their own operations so that they are making what will be needed rather than what they think will be needed.

Supply Chain Configuration Strategies

Supply chain configuration involves establishing the parameters and boundaries that govern a firm's relationships within its chain of suppliers and customers.

VERTICAL INTEGRATION

Vertical integration

The decision to expand a firm's value-adding process ownership into activities provided by suppliers or customers.

Vertical integration is the decision to expand a firm's value-adding process ownership into activities provided by suppliers or customers, and it defines what the firm will do in house and what it will contract out. Backward vertical integration decisions determine what a firm will make and what it will buy; forward vertical integration decisions determine what a firm will keep for use in subsequent operations and what it will sell. These decisions set the boundaries of the firm's value-adding system. Vertical integration is more frequently pursued in situations in which production volumes are high and firms have the needed expertise to run the supplying process (backward integration) or the customer involvement process (forward integration). Such high-volume operations depend on a reliable supply of materials and dependable channels of distribution.

Table 3.3 indicates when vertical integration makes sense and when it does not. If input materials are not related to the current focus of a company's business, nor are they unique or exclusive, vertical integration does not make sense. (Why would General Motors make paper for its photocopiers?) If producing the input material is consistent with the company's current focus, then vertical integration would be worthwhile only if internal suppliers are more competitive than external suppliers. For example, General Motors might make ball bearings or radios or any number of automotive components and subassemblies, but only if its internal suppliers are competitive with external suppliers. If a company holds the exclusive rights to an input, or needs to maintain the uniqueness of an offering on the basis of the uniqueness of that material, then vertical integration is worth considering. For example, Brush Wellman

Table 3.3

Guidelines for Vertical Integration Decisions

Exclusivity of Use	Consistency with Current Business Focus	
	Low	**High**
High	Make the decision based on the long-term economics of the "supplier" business—e.g., should McDonald's make their own Happy Meal toys?	This is an obvious candidate for vertical integration—e.g., should Kentucky Fried Chicken make their own "special blend of spices" for their "original recipe" fried chicken?
Low	This is an obvious situation for purchasing material from an outside supplier—e.g., should your university make paper for its photocopying and printing needs?	Make the decision based on the competitiveness of the internal supplier—e.g., should General Motors make car radios?

makes engineered products from alloys of beryllium. The company is vertically integrated backward to the mining of beryllium—it controls the only mine for this metal outside of China and the Commonwealth of Independent States. Thus, vertical integration gives Brush Wellman a significant competitive advantage in the market for engineered products of Beryllium alloys.

When a material does not fit a firm's focus, the option of vertical integration may still be considered, based on the long-term economic question of the value of the supplier's business. For example, McDonald's might get into the toy-making business in order to stock its Happy Meals with toys, but only if the toy-making business promises to be profitable over the long-term. Obviously, an item that is both required by a business and consistent with the business' focus provides the strongest incentive for vertical integration.

The terms *basic producer, converter, fabricator,* and *assembler* have been used to distinguish common steps in the creation of value among manufacturers. Common relationships among these steps are illustrated by the network seen in Figure 3.4. **Basic producers** use natural resources, such as iron ore, oil, wheat, and minerals as inputs. Their outputs include basic materials, such as rolled steel, flour, and plastic powders. **Converters** use basic materials as their inputs and add value by cutting and blending them in various ways. For example, a steel converter purchases rolls of steel in standard widths and thicknesses from steel mills. These rolls of steel are too heavy and too big to be used (or even handled) by the equipment in most manufacturing plants. Thus the converter provides a valuable service by cutting the rolls into sheets and slitting them into smaller rolls on smaller spools, so that the steel will be suitable for processing. **Fabricators** use the material that is provided by converters to create parts for

Basic producers

Producers which use natural resources such as iron ore, oil, wheat, and minerals as inputs. Their outputs are basic materials such as rolled steel, flour and plastic powders.

Converters

Devices which use basic materials as their inputs and add value by cutting and blending them in various ways.

Fabricators

Tools which use the material that is provided by converters to create parts for assembly operations.

Figure 3.4

Common interrelationships between supply-chain stages

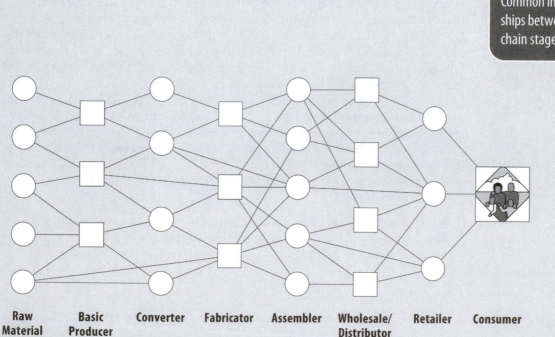

| Raw Material Extractor | Basic Producer | Converter | Fabricator | Assembler | Wholesale/ Distributor | Retailer | Consumer |

Assemblers

Anything that brings together a variety of different parts, resulting in converging material flows.

Hollow corporation

A company that does not actually add value to the items it sells, but interacts with a network of supplying companies to sell their products.

Original equipment manufacturers

Companies that manufacture components and/or products for sale under some other company's name.

assembly operations. For example, folding a sheet of steel to make the metal part of a refrigerator door is a fabrication operation. Because basic producers, converters, and fabricators tend to make a variety of outputs from standardized inputs, they are said to have diverging material flows. By contrast, **assemblers** bring together a variety of different parts; thus they have converging material flows.

The range of possibilities in vertical integration runs from the hollow corporation at one end of the spectrum to full vertical integration at the other end of the spectrum. A **hollow corporation** is a company that does not actually add value to the items it sells, but interacts with a network of supplying companies to sell those companies' products. No material conversions take place in a hollow corporation. Mail-order companies are often hollow corporations. These operations—whose only working assets are a phone bank, a web page, or a mailbox with which to take orders—place items in their catalogs if they believe the supply to be adequate. Ordered goods are then sent directly from the supplier to the customer. In contrast, **original equipment manufacturers (OEMs)** are companies that manufacture components and/or products for sale under some other company's name.

For example, RCA was the first company to introduce digital satellite systems (DSS) for home television, though it does not make the systems. Thomson Consumer Electronics is RCA's OEM; it manufactures the DSS systems sold under RCA's label. This arrangement allows Thomson to benefit from RCA's name recognition, while enabling RCA to avoid the expense of developing its own process for manufacturing the complex systems. By integrating backward, companies can create subsidiary suppliers. Similarly, by integrating forward, they can create subsidiary distributors. For example, Universal Studios is a subsidiary supplier of films for Disney.

Fully integrated companies own all the value-adding steps related to providing their product-service bundles. These firms are engaged in everything from raw material extraction to post-sale service activities. During the early part of the 1900s, Henry Ford's manufacturing operations were fully integrated. Ford owned rubber plantations, farms, and mines; made the metal, rubber, concrete, and other basic materials; fabricated parts and subassemblies of every type; assembled cars and trucks; and distributed all of these. A modern example is large paper companies, many of which are fully integrated: They own and manage forest land, harvest timber, operate lumber mills, make paper pulp, and manufacture paper products.

For vertically integrated firms, the entire value chain eventually ends up on one consolidated income statement, which has its downside: increased exposure to financial risk associated with the business cycle of recession and growth. When companies control more of the assets in a supply chain, they bear more of the economic problems during slow sales periods. When many companies share the supply chain, the economic problems can be spread across these companies. Other drawbacks of vertical integration include:

1. A loss of expertise resulting from the consolidation of management and operations (supplies and expertise from companies specializing in one area are generally lost with vertical integration)

2. Failure to recognize external market opportunities because of the secure internal market

3. A loss of competitiveness because of the secure internal market

For example, GM might be very good at assembling cars, but that does not mean that it would be good at making tires. If GM were to integrate backward and buy Michelin, managers would find that many issues relevant to tire making are not relevant to car assembly. If GM were to replace Michelin's management with auto executives or even

Ford Suppliers Move Next Door

Nine suppliers joined Ford Motor Company at its renovated Chicago Assembly Plant to be part of the first U.S. supplier manufacturing campus. Announced in May of 2002, the company's "brownfield" site employs up to 1,000 people plus those employed by the nine suppliers.

A brownfield site is a former manufacturing site, often found in urban areas. A brownfield can be used only for certain industrial purposes, because it does not require the expensive environmental cleanup necessary to reclaim and sell the land as a "greenfield," in other words, a site on which a school or housing development could be built. Many communities see brownfields as win-win solutions to a tough real-estate problem: manufacturers who use brownfields receive tax breaks, and cities that own brownfields earn property taxes on viable land instead of bearing costs for an eyesore.

Ford's reclaimed 155-acre park is a collaboration among Ford, Chicago-based CenterPoint (a civic development group), and local and state officials. The group invested more than $250 million in the campus and related infrastructure improvements during the first four years, revitalizing a brownfield site that had been vacant for 40 years. This supplier manufacturing campus, which includes six buildings totaling 1.5 million square feet, is Ford's first such venture in the United States, and it is the first one anywhere that started with a mature assembly plant. The plant's configuration is designed to increase flexibility, allow for quicker response to customer preferences, lower inventory costs, and help control shipping and capital costs.

The plant is being renovated to handle the assembly of two new models, the Ford CrossTrainer and the Ford Five Hundred. In doing so, the plant's body shop has become cleaner and more flexible to allow for a quicker changeover, and the plant's paint processes are cleaner. While the new vehicles produced at the plant have a larger painted surface than the Ford Taurus, the number of tons of volatile organic compounds produced annually have dropped because less paint is wasted due to overspray—so there is less paint to clean up and, thus, fewer cleaning chemicals need to be used. In addition, new production concepts and tooling that greatly enhance the plant's flexibility and quality efforts are being implemented. One example is an electrified monorail system and flexible tooling that allow rapid changeovers—even if production switches from small car building to SUV building. The plant also uses laser welding to attach car roofs to the bodies to provide the vehicles with greater structural integrity—another industry first in the United States. Dimensional pallets carry the product through the underbody and framing tools, adding improved fit and finish to the final product.

The biggest advantages of the new campus configuration, however, are evident from a supply chain perspective, because the configuration allows for cross-tier supplier relationships. For example, one supplier, SY Systems, ships main-body wire harnesses for cars directly into the plant. At the same time, they deliver wire harnesses to other campus suppliers such as ZF Lemforder (suspensions), Visteon (instrument panels, fuel tanks, and engine coolant components [bolsters]), and Summit Polymers (consoles [injected plastics]) for use in the new models. These cross-tier relationships add significant value and create synergistic opportunities among suppliers because market changes can be addressed more quickly when suppliers are in close proximity. Further, quality is enhanced when suppliers can integrate the design of the parts with the assembly process. Other benefits include reductions in inventory-carrying costs. Today, materials travel an average of 450 miles to the Chicago Assembly Plant. Bringing key suppliers together reduces the average trip to just 125 miles, and more than half of Chicago Assembly's external buy will come from the supplier campus. Some of the nine suppliers, which include Sanderson (stampings), Tower Automotive (stampings), Plastech (injected and blow-molded plastics), Brose (door components), and Pico (manufacturing equipment) in addition to the ones already mentioned, share a single building; others are housed next door.

Source: Adapted from "Ford Welcomes Nine Suppliers to First U.S. Supplier Manufacturing Campus," http://media.ford.com/newsroom/release_display.cfm? release=12001, May 16, 2002

to consolidate the management of the two firms, the company would lose key expertise in regard to tire making. Michelin would have less need to compete for GM's
orders and might not even pursue outside sales opportunities because it had adequate
demand from GM. Thus, Michelin would become less competitive and less attuned to
consumer needs. Finally, if the car market were to take a downturn, GM would suffer
in two areas (assembly and tire making) instead of one (assembly).

The benefits of vertical integration include greater control over product quality,
greater coordination of operations across the value chain, access to new technologies
and other intelligence of strategic importance, and the potential for larger aggregate
profit margins. Ultimately, by weighing what is to be gained against what is to be lost,
a company must determine its ideal degree of vertical integration. Firms that choose
not to integrate vertically may attempt to gain some of the benefits of vertical integration by devoting significant resources and energy to developing trusting long-term
relationships with their suppliers and customers.

OUTSOURCING

Outsourcing

The process of contracting with a third party to provide some aspect of the product-service bundle.

In contrast to vertical integration, **outsourcing** is contracting with a third party to provide some aspect of the product-service bundle. The practice of outsourcing is rapidly
growing because of the increased ability to communicate electronically and the availability of modern cost-accounting tools that can be used to compare in-house and
supplier costs. In fact, as early as 1999 a study published in *Purchasing* magazine indicated that 54% of the companies surveyed had outsourced manufacturing or service
activities in the prior two to three years and 46% indicated they were intending to increase their outsourcing activity. By contrast only 38% had done no outsourcing and
only 4% intended to reduce their outsourcing activity. Other findings of this study
were that most companies are satisfied with their outsourcing arrangements,
rigorous supplier qualification and monitoring are central to successful outsourcing,
and outsourcing decisions are most commonly made by cross-functional teams.
Specifically, one respondent indicated that outsourcing decisions were "completely
cross-functional" and based on input from "purchasing, technology, quality, marketing, finance, manufacturing, etc."[1]

Outsourcing allows a company to focus on what it does best: its core competencies.
It adds capacity without adding significant fixed costs and overhead. It is often more
cost effective, because suppliers may be better at the outsourced activity, and they may
gain economies of scale by providing the same service or manufacturing value to multiple customers. Finally, outsourcing supports corporate growth and market agility by
allowing companies to grow without making large capital investments that would hurt
their income levels in the case of an economic downturn.

Many domestic and international companies have emerged as contract manufacturers. The emerging industrial economies of the Pacific Rim have become common
locations for contract manufacturers. Singapore, with excellent port facilities, a highly
educated and disciplined workforce, and outstanding communications and technological infrastructure, has become a major player for electronics contract manufacturing.
Singapore-based firms such as NatSteel Electronics Ltd. and Venture Manufacturing
Ltd. manufacture products for HP, IBM, Apple, Seagate Technologies, Lockheed Martin,
Motorola, Iomega, and others from production facilities located around the world.
SCI Systems, Solectron Corporation, and Jabil Circuit, Inc. are among the largest con-
tract manufacturers in the United States. Jabil's customer list includes Cisco Systems,

[1]Anne Millen Porter, "Outsourcing Gains Popularity," *Purchasing Online: The Magazine of Supply Chain Management,*
March 11, 1999.

Dell, HP, 3Com, Gateway 2000, Nortel Networks, and Ascend Communications. In fact, although Cisco dominates the market for Internet routers, it makes almost no products itself. The company's vice president was quoted as saying: "We've cleaned up the supply chain . . . . You don't add value by having multiple people touch a product."[2]

Contract manufacturers often describe themselves as manufacturing services and are classified as service providers. Manufacturers may consider employing service providers not only when they are short on capacity, but to improve quality and supply chain performance by working with top-notch providers. A good example of such a provider is Solectron, which has been ranked consistently among the top performing Information Technology companies by the business media and has won the highly prestigious Malcolm Baldrige National Quality Award twice. The company's press releases suggest that "by partnering with Solectron, OEMs can achieve better asset utilization, faster time-to-market and time-to-volume, and the lowest total product costs."

Trends in outsourcing suggest that many well known companies that once manufactured their own brand-name products may someday exit manufacturing entirely and busy themselves with other business activities such as design and marketing.[3]

Channel assembly and vendor-managed inventory are value-added services being offered by many logistics companies, which allow companies to outsource activities that would have been unthinkable in the past. Now, rather than transporting a fully assembled product, a number of trucking firms have trained their drivers to assemble products that they frequently transport. This is one example of channel assembly. In this case, the strategy significantly reduces transportation costs and the risk of damage during transportation. **Vendor managed inventory** is a similar concept, whereby the logistics provider or material supplier keeps track of the materials that are bought by a customer on a regular basis. Instead of responding to a purchase order, they just make sure the customer has what they need when it's needed and bill them for what is used.

If a logistics provider is managing the inventory, this allows them to decide when to transport the materials on the basis of other shipments that they have to handle and can result in significant savings in shipping costs. If a supplier is managing the inventory, this allows them to see usage patterns and schedule production based on what is best for them instead of waiting for a purchase order to schedule production. Stockless purchasing is frequently associated with vendor managed inventory. In this case, a supplier manages inventory that is physically housed in the customer's facility but owned by the supplier. Thus, the inventory is available to the customer but not owned by the customer. From the customer's accountant's perspective, they are stockless. Only when the customer actually uses the inventory does a transaction occur that is recognized as a sale.

So what should a company outsource? In general, as the various business and operational processes that make up the value-adding system become more standardized—even become commodities in and of themselves—it is possible that they may be outsourced to give the business more resources to focus on those key competencies that differentiate them in the market place. Charles Fine, in the *Clock Speed Chronicles,* suggests that as the pace of innovation and change picks up over time, knowing what processes

Vendor managed inventory

A concept whereby the logistics provider or material supplier keeps track of the materials that are bought by a customer on a regular basis.

REC CENTER DILEMMA

Cheryl wonders about outsourcing some business processes

At a recent health-care industry trade show, Cheryl noticed a booth for a company that could take over most of her hospital's insurance processing and interface it with the hospital's accounting system. She had always found the processing of insurance claims, pre-certifications, and the miles of related red tape to be a major source of problems. Is hiring this company a good way to get rid of the headaches she feels are thrust upon her by insurance companies? How does it fit the long-range strategy of the hospital where she works?

[2]Neil Weinberg, "Bill Morean's $1.2 Billion Haircut," *Forbes*, June 14, 1999.
[3]Ibid.

you have an advantage with and outsourcing the rest may be the key to success in the future. For example, a car company could decide that they are really better at designing certain types of cars than building them and then outsource the actual assembly of their cars to a firm that specializes in assembly processes. That would allow the two firms to focus their resources on design and assembly processes respectively and could accelerate the rate of product innovation in that supply chain. There are myriad possibilities, and barring any unusual circumstance (such as trade secrets) it seems reasonable to outsource anything that can be done more effectively by another provider.

The Supply Chain Operating Reference (SCOR) Model

The Supply Chain Council is a professional organization for supply chain management professionals. Major industrial, logistics, and software companies from around the globe are the primary membership base of this organization. Supply Chain Council members worked together to develop a standard way to communicate supply chain management practices and concerns among companies. This method is called the Supply Chain Operating Reference (SCOR) Model. As a process reference model, SCOR provides a common framework, language, and measures for describing processes and enables their coordinated improvement. SCOR provides a standardized framework, terminology, and measures for supply chains. This allows companies to compare their supply chain performance with benchmarks and best practices, which helps them to discover better ways of structuring and coordinating their supply chains, target improvement areas, and set improvement goals.

As summarized in Table 3.4, SCOR models are representations of industrial supply chains made up of some combination of five core management processes, plan,

Table 3.4

Management Processes in the SCOR Model

SCOR Process	SCOR Model Definition
Plan	Processes that balance aggregate demand and supply to develop a course of action which best meets sourcing, production, and delivery requirements.
Source	Processes that procure goods and services to meet planned or actual demand.
Make	Processes that transform product to a finished state to meet planned or actual demand.
Deliver	Processes that provide finished goods and services to meet planned or actual demand, typically including order management, transportation management, and distribution management.
Return	Processes associated with returning or receiving returned products for any reason. These processes extend into post-delivery customer support.

Source: The Supply Chain Council. Used with permission.

source, make, deliver, and return:

1. Plan is the process of managing and planning demand and supply. This includes balancing availability of resources with requirements and establishing strategies for the other four processes and communicating these to supply chain partners. Also included in planning are alignment of supply chain units with financial plans, and management of business rules and such matters as data collection, capital assets, regulatory compliance, and so on.

2. Source is the process for procuring materials purchased for stock, made to order by vendors, or engineered to order by vendors. This involves such activities as scheduling deliveries, verifying receipt of product, and authorizing supplier payment. Also involved is the maintenance of supplier capability and performance data along with management of business rules.

3. Make is the process by which materials are produced to satisfy customer orders or stocking requirements. Thus production scheduling, actual production, testing, packaging, and releasing of product for shipping are typical activities within this process. Management of business rules and maintenance of data, work in process inventories, equipment, and regulatory compliance are also involved.

4. Deliver is the process involving management of customer orders and finished goods warehousing, transportation, and (possibly) installation, along with customer billing. As with other processes, management of business rules and maintenance of data is an important aspect of the deliver process and includes inventory levels, transportation regulations, import/export requirements, capital assets, and the like.

5. Return is the process by which excess or defective materials or maintenance items are returned to suppliers or received from customers. Here, too, business rules must be managed, and data collection and regulatory compliance must be assured.

Whether it is simple, complex, global, regional, or local, any supply chain can be modeled as a combination of the five processes described above. Once constructed, the model describes the business activities associated with every step involved in satisfying an ultimate customer's demand. As Figure 3.5 illustrates, SCOR models stretch from supplier's supplier to customer's customer. It should be obvious that these models typically span multiple industries and not only describe supply chains but also provide a basis for supply chain improvement.

The process of modeling a supply chain often begins with a visual picture of the chain on a map representing the geographic flow of materials. This mapping of the chain is helpful in determining the boundaries of the model—in other words, what to include and what to leave out. SCOR models are generally developed without explicit geographic representation and are built in a hierarchical way by adding more business detail as lower levels of the model are built. At the top level (Level 1), the scope and content of the model are established by identifying entities involved in the supply chain. Thus the Level 1 SCOR model is the combination of plan, source, make, deliver, and return processes interacting to form the chain. The model simply indicates what process types are performed and by which supply chain partners. Much like a business strategy answers the question, "What business are we in?" the Level 1 model establishes who intends to do what in the supply

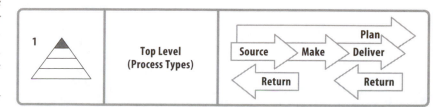

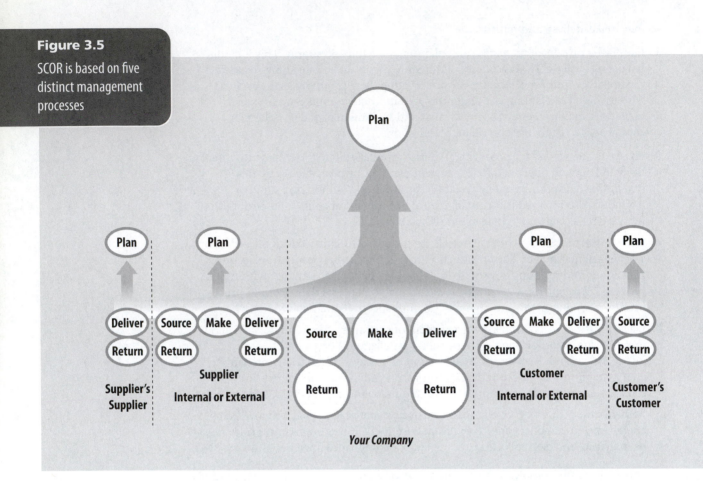

Figure 3.5

SCOR is based on five distinct management processes

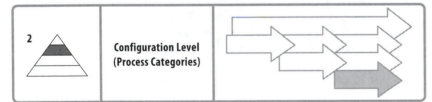

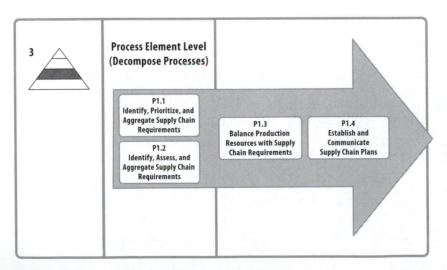

| 2 | Configuration Level (Process Categories) | |
| 3 | Process Element Level (Decompose Processes) | |

P1.1 Identify, Prioritize, and Aggregate Supply Chain Requirements

P1.2 Identify, Assess, and Aggregate Supply Chain Requirements

P1.3 Balance Production Resources with Supply Chain Requirements

P1.4 Establish and Communicate Supply Chain Plans

chain. Thus, this level sets the basis of competition and the areas in which competitive performance targets will be set.

At Level 2, called the Configuration Level, the SCOR model is configured using standardized process categories. Think of these process categories as being like Lego® blocks: If you have the full set of Legos, you can erect a building in any shape you like. Similarly, with the full set of process categories, you can describe virtually any supply chain process. Figure 3.6 illustrates the process categories commonly used in the five process areas. While the Level 1 model was descriptive of the business strategy, the Level 2 model is more descriptive of the structural aspects of the operations strategy. Thus, the

Figure 3.6

SCOR model can represent different types of business relationships

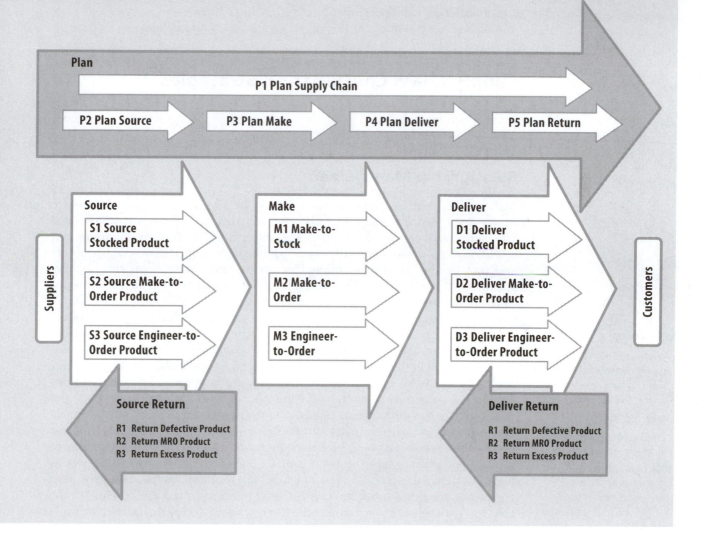

longer-term decisions that a company makes in regard to its operations are reflected in the Level 2 model.

At Level 3, called the Process Element Level, the SCOR model provides a standardized set of process elements that help flesh out the generic process categories from Level 2. At this point the model will represent information about required inputs and outputs for each process category, how performance will be measured, what the best practices are (information provided by the Supply Chain Council through its involvement with members), and what system capabilities are required to adopt the best practices. At this point, the model is descriptive of the infrastructural aspects of a company's operations strategy. Thus, the model describes the decisions about how the company will utilize its resources, and, in turn, can be used to fine tune the operations strategy.

Beyond the Level 3 process elements, the SCOR model does not provide a standardized set of building blocks. Nevertheless, at Level 4 companies may further detail their Level 3 model with a flowchart of the company's supply chain, which can be developed using a computer simulation or modeling language. At this level of detail the model clearly defines a company's specific practices and indicates the methods by which they are pursuing their desired competitive advantage. Additionally, the Level 4 model can be used to identify specific ways that the company must change to adapt to shifting business conditions or to improve their business performance.

Supply Chain Coordination Strategies

Supply chain coordination requires a firm to integrate its strategy decisions with those made within its chain of suppliers and customers.

Relationship Management

Both supplier relations and customer relations are key to effective coordination of supply chains. In the past, the interaction between suppliers and their customers was often adversarial and based on negotiated contracts that spelled out the terms and conditions with which both parties were required to comply. This may still be a suitable way for large companies to buy commodities that would be of equal quality regardless of the supplier. However, many supplier-customer relationships do not work like that any more. Instead, companies are creating long-term strategic relationships with their suppliers and expecting them to provide much more than a product at a particular price. **Sole sourcing** is a practice whereby a company commits to buy all of a particular type of its services or goods from one vendor. In exchange, the vendor becomes a partner in the design of new product-service bundles. Vendor expertise and knowledge can be shared and leveraged for product and process improvement; this reduces the costs of negotiating and administering contracts and allows planning decisions to be coordinated more closely. **Integrated supply** is one approach to sole sourcing now being promoted by many distributing companies. With integrated supply, a distributor offers to provide a high level of service on an entire line of products at agreed-upon prices in exchange for a guarantee that they will receive all of the distribution business in that product line. Ultimately, such relationships require supply chain partners to trust each other and conduct their business with integrity. Without the ability to trust supply chain partners, the strategies described in this chapter are difficult to implement and manage.

Many companies are becoming more aggressive in their attempts to manage their suppliers. One way to do this is through **supplier certification**, which is a practice of requiring suppliers to document certain characteristics in order to obtain business. A company may require its suppliers to maintain certain standards for quality and on-time delivery, have a certain level of financial strength, use a particular approach for electronic exchange of data, use certain workforce management practices, follow certain ethical guidelines, and so on. Many companies do not set their own supplier certification standards but instead rely on universal quality standards called ISO 9000 standards, which were introduced in the late 1980s and updated in 2000. Thousands of facilities were certified under these standards during the 1990s. By requiring suppliers

Sole sourcing

A practice whereby a company commits to buy all of a particular type of services or goods from one vendor.

Integrated supply

A distributor offers to provide a high level of service on an entire line of products at agreed-upon prices in exchange for a guarantee that they will receive all of the distribution business in that product line.

Supplier certification

A practice of requiring suppliers to document certain characteristics in order to obtain business.

to be ISO 9000 certified, a company could ensure that the practices of the supplier were consistent. This allowed a company to base their planning decisions on a known level of supplier quality—and also to eliminate suppliers that provided inconsistent quality. Certain industries have specialized standards. For example, the U.S. automobile industry requires suppliers to comply with an expanded version of ISO 9000. Another set of standards, called ISO 14000 standards, allows companies to gain certification for their environmental management systems.

Beyond certification, many customers are working to help suppliers improve their processes. During the 1990s, the Chrysler side of DaimlerChrysler spent considerable resources to reduce the costs of its purchased materials through its Supplier Cost Reduction (SCORE) program. In this program, Chrysler set cost-reduction goals and suppliers made cost-reduction proposals to achieve those goals. Chrysler and its suppliers shared the savings, which are estimated to exceed $1 billion.

Relationship management is not only a matter of customers dictating requirements for suppliers; it is a two-way street. Certainly, suppliers can benefit from the preferential treatment they receive. But relationship management also helps them rethink their approach to the marketplace. Rather than following a sales-intensive strategy, for instance, suppliers may benefit from relationship marketing techniques. Instead of focusing on negotiating the optimal conditions for individual orders, suppliers can demonstrate their strengths and capabilities to gain the trust of their customers. Further, by investing their money, time, and effort to gain a clear understanding of their customers' needs and satisfying these, they gain the preferential treatment they desire from a company.

E-Commerce

Information technology is a key enabler of supply chain coordination, and e-commerce has become a major component of business-to-business relationships across most manufacturing supply chains. Table 3.5 illustrates the role of information in making coordination possible without relying heavily on inventory buffers between steps of the supply chain. Essentially, effective use of information technologies allows firms to turn the supply chain management process upside down. Upstream planning decisions can be based on downstream demand. In the past, these decisions would be based on forecasts, and material availability would be used to influence demand.

Without collecting and sharing information regarding demand, inventory, capacity, and schedules, it is not possible to make coordinated decisions even within one company, let alone across an entire supply chain. As a consequence, **Automated Data Collection (ADC)** devices are critical components of the SCM coordination picture. ADC can be accomplished through point-of-sale systems and other types of bar code scanners. More sophisticated technologies are available, however, including **radio frequency identification (RFID)** systems, and real-time locator systems. RFID work by placing small microchip-based tags and transponders on items, so their location and quantities can be immediately verified. In the past, RFID was economically viable only when the tags and transponders were reused. Today, however, disposable and ultrathin transponders are beginning to be used in a variety of applications. It is likely that RFID systems will eventually replace many bar code-based inventory tracking systems. In the meantime, real-time locator systems are becoming available; they use wall-mounted readers to monitor the movement of materials in a facility based on information from the data tags.

The security benefits of tracking inventory using RFID tags are obvious. Airlines that tag passenger luggage will be able to tell exactly what has been loaded on a particular plane, check the actual contents of a cargo hold against a freight manifest, and

Automated Data Collection (ADC)

Critical components of SCM coordination, accomplished through point-of-sale systems and other types of bar code scanners.

radio frequency identification (RFID)

Devices that work by placing small microchip-based tags and transponders on items, so their location and quantities can be immediately verified.

Table 3.5

Supply Chain Information Reverses Coordination Approach

Old Supply Chain Coordination Approach (information used)	E-Commerce–Based Supply Chain Coordination Approach (shared information)
Step 1: Buy raw materials and schedule capacity. Buy extra inventory or reserve extra capacity in case the forecast is wrong. (Forecasted use of the materials.)	**Step 1: Provide a customized product in response to a known customer requirement. (Customer specifications for desired product-service bundle.)**
Step 2: Make a finished product or service. Make a little extra and put it in inventory in case the forecast is wrong. (Product/Service standards fixed by design. Quantities based on demand forecasts.)	**Step 2: Deliver products/service based on their consumption. (Customer sales information collected through POS system. Logistics and distribution system responds to actual consumption.)**
Step 3: Distribute goods to market. Make sure to have some channel inventory or expediting systems in case the demand does not match availability. (Established logistical/distribution system.)	**Step 3: Provide no more of the product-service bundles than is justified by known demand. (Value-adding system responds to known consumption.)**
Step 4: Sell through retailers. Offer incentives such as rebates or promotional pricing if inventories are too large. (Actual sales information may not be shared with the product-service bundle provider.)	**Step 4: Buy materials and schedule capacity based on known demand. (Suppliers respond in the same way and may use POS information rather than requiring purchase orders and demand forecasts.)**

Source: Adapted from "Managing the Demand Chain through Managing the Information Flow: Capturing 'Moments of Information.'" *Production and Inventory Management Journal* 40, no. 1 (1999): 17, Rhonda R. Lummus and Robert J. Vokura

immediately identify the location of suspect materials. Freight carriers such as railroads and trucking firms will no longer need to use the FAK (Freight All Kinds) shipment designation for their loads, but instead will be able to prepare an exact load manifest with a simple RFID scan of the vehicle. Put simply, RFID systems will allow companies to have a better understanding of what they are holding in storage and transit.

Once data has been collected, it is necessary to provide access- and decision-support systems to enhance its usefulness. Enterprise resources planning (ERP) systems that allow companies to communicate demand, inventory, and scheduling decisions with one another can have a big impact on the level of coordination across the supply chain. Where ERP systems are successfully implemented, their value is difficult to understate. Yet, not all companies have been pleased with their ERP systems. Large ERP systems are expensive, and their implementation usually takes on a high profile in a company and often requires the use of outside consulting agencies that may be perceived as being unfamiliar with existing company concerns. The effectiveness of ERP systems may be significantly influenced by a company's inability or unwillingness to change existing systems and processes to make way for the system. Ultimately, some companies have invested a great deal of money on an ERP system, but obtained only mediocre or even dismal results. Consequently, when such systems fail, it is a big deal.

Like data collection, e-commerce has had a large impact on the structure of supply chains. In the e-commerce process, middlemen, the historic channels for trade of materials and information, are less influential—or not even needed—in the supply chain. By contrast, logistics providers and experts on materials processing, warehousing, and transfers (such as UPS, Federal Express, DHL) have grown in importance, particularly with the globalization of business. Similarly, the channel power of retailers has extended backward through entire supply chains. As an example, Wal-Mart has pioneered such innovations as data sharing, business partnerships that allow suppliers to ensure that their merchandise is fully stocked on the retail shelves, and direct connections via the Internet to those who schedule their vendors' processes.

Finally, the Internet has enabled supply chain coordination by providing an information umbrella in materials auction systems that allow buyers to pool their orders to obtain volume pricing, while at the same time allowing a wider range of suppliers the opportunity to bid for such orders.

Improving Supply Chains: Seven Principles

Figure 3.7 shows that—despite supply chain configuration and functioning coordination mechanisms—there is always room for improvement. In some cases, the ideal configuration changes over time with changes in technology and customer preferences. In other cases, technology allows different mechanisms for coordination across the supply chain. At any rate, it is generally advisable for companies to view their

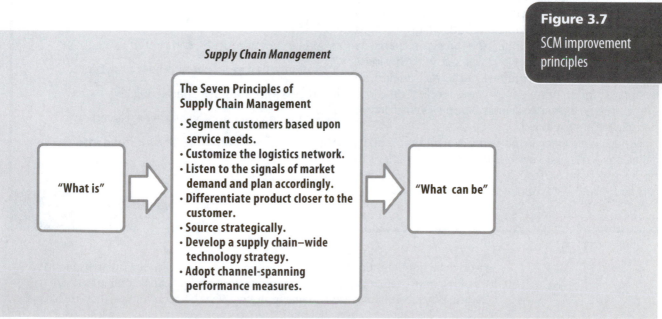

Figure 3.7

SCM improvement principles

Supply Chain Management

"What is"

The Seven Principles of Supply Chain Management
- Segment customers based upon service needs.
- Customize the logistics network.
- Listen to the signals of market demand and plan accordingly.
- Differentiate product closer to the customer.
- Source strategically.
- Develop a supply chain–wide technology strategy.
- Adopt channel-spanning performance measures.

"What can be"

INTEGRATING OM:

Satisfying Customers at Toshiba Toner Products Division

In the 1990s, Toshiba Toner Products Division (TPD) buyers believed it was time to move away from adversarial relationships with its suppliers. Pressuring suppliers to cut prices "did not improve the system or promote healthy relationships," says Mona Ward, a Toshiba buyer. "We needed a long-range plan to reduce costs and improve the purchasing process."

In response to this need, Toshiba created the Partners Plus + program, which works with suppliers to make improvements in such areas as design, process/manufacturing, inventory, volume, business practices, materials handling, transportation/logistics, and tier-two secondary supply networks. The program promotes integration between supply chain partners and increases value for the ultimate consumer. TPD is targeting twenty-one priority suppliers that are either based in the United States or operating U.S. distribution centers. The program, introduced in 1998, was developed after evaluating similar programs and borrowing ideas and best practices from other purchasing operations.

The buyers created a program that would work with the company's supplier base to help suppliers meet cost-reduction goals. For example, the program has resulted in two competing transportation companies working with TPD to help reduce freight charges and improve service. Under the program, partners who meet targets can be rewarded with business guarantees, increased volumes, public recognition, an honors banquet, preference in new product development, and performance awards. Suppliers who do not participate are excluded.

For each supplier involved in the program, goals called for a 6% first-year reduction, 5% reductions in both the second and third years, a 4% fourth-year cost reduction, and a 3% reduction in the fifth year. Beyond the fifth year, suppliers are asked to generate 3% per year bottom-line reductions.

The program uses several different measures including a mix of quantifiable (cost reduction) and nonquantifiable (relating to quality) criteria. Quantifiable criteria are added directly to the bottom-line reduction. Nonquantifiable criteria are awarded points based on a matrix of items weighted for value.

The process consists of an on-site supplier survey in which TPD documents and reports current status. A Business Partners Assessment committee conducts periodic reviews and reports progress to the supplier. Once an implementation is made, the committee collects data on the effects of a suggestion and awards the appropriate amount of points based on the matrix; thus, TPD and the supplier share the rewards. As suppliers who do not participate receive less business, the size of the rewards to the suppliers who do increases. TPD suggests that Partners Plus + and similar programs should be based on the following:

Requirements of a "win-win" program:

◗ Dollar benefits are shared

◗ Corporate objectives are known by partners

◗ Margins/profits must not erode for either partner

◗ Management must be committed to "win-win"

◗ Nothing is sacred—everything is analyzed

◗ Process information is shared quickly

◗ E-commerce technologies are employed

◗ Follow-up and communication is frequent

Source: Adapted from "Toshiba TPD," http://www.purchasing.com/article/CA146270.html, May 20, 1999, reporter Susan Avery

supply chain configuration and coordination systems as worthy of regular evaluation. By making improvements over time, competitive advantages can be gained in the marketplace. When companies think their supply chain has been optimized, they are likely to become resistant to changes that might lead to improvement. This can lead, over the long range, to a loss of competitive advantage or even to competitive disadvantage. The seven principles for SCM improvement are discussed in further detail below.

1. SEGMENT CUSTOMERS BASED UPON SERVICE NEEDS

Different customers have unique service requirements, and meeting their requirements necessitates different approaches to supply chain configuration and coordination. Henry Ford's "one size fits all" approach is clearly not what supply chain management is all about. Instead, performance can be improved (from the customer's perspective and eventually from a competitive perspective) by more effectively matching specific customer requirements to what is provided, when it is provided, and the quantities in which it is provided. Building a system that allows customers to specify just what their product and service preferences are sounds great, but this does require a certain level of marketing research skill, operational flexibility, and cost accounting sophistication. Companies need to have a good handle on what specific customer groups want; be able to accurately estimate what that will cost and justify the cost to the customer; and be good enough to follow through on promises to satisfy those preferences.

Jason Homa/Getty Images Inc.

2. CUSTOMIZE THE LOGISTICS NETWORK

Logistics is a big part of the supply chain. It is not enough just to make what a customer wants or provide the desired level of service: It is equally important to distribute the product-service bundle within the quantity and timing requirements determined by the customer. Again, one size does not fit all. For example, the logistics network used to provide replacement parts to a trucking company that maintains its own large fleet of vehicles would be quite different from the network used to provide parts to the many independent vehicle repair shops. From the customer's perspective, improvement of the supply chain often implies customization of the logistics network based on the segmentation described in the first step above.

Communication technology that we may take for granted, such as this cell phone, can greatly improve the relationship between links in the supply chain. The ability to track, trace, and even change destination of material in transit can have a great impact on how those links do business.

3. LISTEN TO THE SIGNALS OF THE MARKETPLACE AND PLAN ACCORDINGLY

Traditionally, firms have listened to demand forecasts created independently by various functions of the business, as well as various businesses across the supply chain, and then planned according to these forecasts. As a result, capacity and material imbalances occurred across the supply chain—a phenomenon referred to as the **bullwhip effect**. The bullwhip effect is the tendency of small variations in demand to become larger as their implications are transmitted backward through a supply chain. Handfield and Nichols (1999) describe the findings of a study on this phenomenon[4] as a result of "distorted information from one end of the supply chain

Bullwhip effect

The tendency of small variations in demand to become larger as their implications are transmitted backward through a supply chain.

[4]Hau Lee, V. Padmanabhan, and Seungjin Whang, "The Bullwhip Effect in Supply Chains," *Sloan Management Review*, Spring 1997: 93–102.

INTEGRATING OM:

Smart Tags Let Our Inventory Talk

In a few years, a new generation of electronic sensors called RFID tags will track your inventory, stock your shelves—and even (perhaps) choose the washer settings when you do your laundry. Truckloads of consumer products will announce their arrival to workers on the loading dock. Boxes will record each time they are moved, and missing items will reveal their location by emitting a distinctive electronic shout. Empty store shelves will signal when they need to be restocked, and when inventories run low, vendors will receive an automated request to ship more product.

All of this will be made possible by an emerging technology called radio frequency identification, or RFID. RFID relies on memory chips equipped with tiny radio antennas—RFID tags—that can be attached to objects to transmit streams of data about those objects. That data need not be encyclopedic (an advanced chip's capacity is 2 kilobytes, enough to encode a serial number, information about where and when the product was manufactured, and a bit more) but the RFID tag obviates the need for bar-code scanning—even the need for visual contact. That opens up worlds of possibilities. Supply chain specialists see RFID as the backbone of an infrastructure designed to identify and track billions of individual objects all over the world, all in real time.

Wal-Mart is investing heavily in RFID tags with an eye toward dramatically reducing supply chain management expenses, trimming inventories, cutting theft, and eliminating misdirected shipments. At the same time, by pumping information from RFID tags into Wal-Mart's 101-terabyte sales-transaction

database, the company hopes to give suppliers a real-time view of what is happening on store shelves—now becoming "smart shelves"—enabling retailers and suppliers alike to monitor stocks in danger of running low or identify stock as being stolen.

RFID applications are not limited to the supply chain. The military is developing RFID-enabled sensors to detect toxins such as anthrax. Similar sensors could appear inside bottle caps to alert consumers if foods are unfit for consumption. In the home, RFID tags could warn consumers when medications reach their expiration date. It has been suggested that RFID chips be inserted into passports to speed up immigration lines and onto credit cards to speed up checkout lines. And in a few years, tiny sensors in car engines could provide early indication of worn bearings.

Up to now, cost and privacy concerns have been the major stumbling blocks to widespread RFID implementation. Right now, tags cost pennies per chip, but with increasing demand and mass production, costs will fall dramatically. RFID spending for the U.S. retail supply chain is likely to grow from $91.5 millon in 2003 to nearly $1.3 billon in 2008, according to IT research firm IDC. By that time, chip makers estimate the cost to be less than 1 cent per chip. But while cost concerns are likely to diminish quickly, issues surrounding your right to privacy and security are more complicated and much less easily resolved.

Source: Adapted from "Your Inventory Wants to Talk to You," *Business 2.0*, May 2002, reporter Mark Roberti; and Indiatimes News Network, "RFID: Unraveling the Future of Supply Chain," April 21, 2005

to the other" and describe Procter & Gamble's (somewhat funny) experience as follows:

P&G began to explore this phenomenon after a series of particularly erratic shifts in ordering up and down the supply chain for one of its most popular products, Pampers disposable diapers. After determining that it was highly unlikely that the infants and toddlers at the ultimate user level for Pampers were creating extreme swings in demand for the product, the examination began to work back through the supply chain. It was found that distributors' orders showed far more variability than the level of demand represented at retail stores themselves. Continuing through the supply chain, P&G's orders to its supplier, 3M, indicated the most variability of all.[5]

The variability was found to come from updates and changes in demand forecasts, batching orders together to reduce transportation and other costs associated with producing and stocking the diapers, price fluctuations that occurred to move inventory close to the end of accounting reporting periods, or quantity discounts and other means of rationing supply across the supply chain.[6] Studies have indicated that stockpiling inventory across the supply chain can result in companies having to warehouse inventory for hundreds of days. Eliminating such inefficiencies can result in significant savings and improve the responsiveness of supply chains.

Ken Davies/Masterfile

4. DIFFERENTIATE PRODUCTS CLOSER TO THE CONSUMER

Postponement is a strategy that delays customization of the product-service bundle as long as possible. For example, a drug manufacturer could postpone customization by distributing drugs in powder form to pharmacies and allowing the pharmacies to create tablets of various sizes depending on customer dosages (e.g., 500 mg and 1000 mg). Similarly, creating modular product and service designs supports a postponement strategy. One diesel engine manufacturer, for example, produces both V6 and V12 engines from the same V6 engine blocks. The V12 is made of two V6 engine blocks bolted together. Contract manufacturers that assemble computers based on customer orders also provide a good example of the customization made available through postponement.

5. SOURCE STRATEGICALLY

Strategic sourcing suggests that suppliers who have demonstrated superior performance deserve customer loyalty and preferential treatment. Clearly, one way to improve the supply chain is to select an excellent set of suppliers—particularly for critical or strategic elements of the product-service bundle—and invest money, time, and effort in making them even better. This also allows the developments and improvements pursued by suppliers to be targeted to the needs of the downstream stages of the supply chain. However, safeguards need to be in place to prevent complacency. The same assumptions and conditions that lead to the establishment of long-term relationships must be reviewed on a regular basis to prevent strategic alliances from becoming too stable.

6. DEVELOP A SUPPLY CHAIN–WIDE TECHNOLOGY STRATEGY

One of the difficulties in implementing mechanisms and tools for supply chain coordination is that companies make technology decisions independently of one another.

Technology like Radio Frequency Identification (RFID) chips will soon make it possible to know exactly what is in each of these boxes instantly and automatically. Reader units within the warehouse will not only tell managers and the forklift driver what is in the warehouse but where it is located.

Postponement

A strategy that delays the customization of the product service bundle as long as possible.

---

[5]Robert B. Handfield and Ernest L. Nichols Jr., *Introduction to Supply Chain Management* (Upper Saddle River, NJ: Prentice-Hall, 1999), 17–18.

[6]Ibid.

This results in information systems that may not share information easily. Because the flow of information is just as important to supply chain coordination as the logistical system is to the supply chain configuration, when information systems are not compatible, companies are likely to spend a great deal of time, money, and energy in building managerial and software interfaces that span the systems. When technology investments across the supply chain result in compatible information systems, readily available data can be transformed into useful information that leads to coordinated decision making. Even with compatible interfaces, it is sometimes difficult to get access to the information that enables coordinated decision making.

7. ADOPT CHANNEL-SPANNING PERFORMANCE MEASURES

One of the biggest difficulties faced by those who are trying to make improvements in supply chains is that individual companies pay decision makers. Their rewards are generally based on functional performance measures and to some extent on the financial performance of their company. Improving the performance of the whole chain may not result in improvements of narrow functional measures, especially in the short term, so those decision makers may have no incentive to contribute to channel-spanning improvements. For example, if we are studying local performance measures for a logistics provider (such as average shipment weight or dollars billed per mile), it might not look good for a logistics provider to carry special shipments for a valued customer on a less-than-truckload basis. On the other hand, if we are looking at a global performance measure (such as days of inventory in the supply chain), this customized treatment would work better.

Even in one business, it is difficult to establish agreed-upon performance measures that lead to cross-functional coordination but do not result in sacrifices of long-term performance for short-term results and do not create undesired incentives. Of course, expanding the development of performance measures to consider an entire supply chain is even more difficult. Nevertheless, if there is no measurement of supply chain–wide performance, there will be little incentive for supply chain improvement. Localized decision making will be perpetuated, and the inefficiencies associated with it will persist. Generally, it requires a strong party—such as a company like Wal-Mart in the consumer goods supply chain, a large auto company in the automobile supply chain, or a large insurance company in the health-care supply chain—to force the adoption of chain-spanning performance measures and objectives.

The SCOR model, introduced earlier in this chapter, shows the standard approach to describing supply chains is very helpful in choosing performance measures and assessing supply chain effectiveness. In fact, as shown in Table 3.6, the Supply Chain Council (SCC) has specific suggested performance measures to monitor for firms with various competitive agendas. In addition to defining these performance measures, the SCC maintains performance data from member companies that have modeled their processes using the SCOR model. These performance metrics allow SCC to identify the best-in-class companies from a variety of perspectives. Member companies, in turn, can use the data to benchmark the performance of their supply chain against the best supply chains of similar structure and purpose. Benchmarking performance in this way is very helpful to improvement efforts because it enables a company to set improvement goals that are both challenging and objectively known to be feasible.

The Stock Price Impact of Supply Chain Savings

One reason SCM has become such a mainstream business is the value of cost reductions to business owners. Cost reductions do not just increase profit in a given period—once

Table 3.6

Relevant Performance Measures for Various Competitive Agendas

Competitive Agenda	Relevant Performance Measures
Reliability	• Delivery Performance • Fill Rate • Perfect Order Fulfillment
Responsiveness	• Order Fulfillment Lead Time
Flexibility	• Supply Chain Response Time • Production Flexibility
Cost	• Total Supply Chain Management Cost • Cost of Goods Sold • Value-Added Productivity • Warranty Cost or Returns Processing Cost
Asset Utilization	• Cash-to-Cash Cycle Time • Inventory Days of Supply • Asset Turns

cost is taken out of a supply chain, it can generally be kept out. As a result, supply chain cost reductions impact corporate income projections and cause positive changes in the value of the firm. In other words, supply chain cost reductions can drive stock prices upward.

Table 3.7 illustrates the impact of supply chain cost reductions on stock price for firms with varying levels of dependence on outside suppliers. The first row represents a company that buys virtually all of the materials they sell (90%) and adds very little value to these materials (10%). An example of such a company would be a distributor that buys in bulk and adds value only by packaging the material. At the other end of the spectrum, as represented by the last row of the table, a company can buy a small percentage of materials (30%) but add significant value to them (70%). This might be a company that buys raw materials and packaging but does its own basic material production, parts fabrication, and production. In the automotive industry, for example, General Motors (GM) buys only 40% of the value in their vehicles and is considered to be at the low end of the spectrum. In contrast, the Chrysler division of DaimlerChrysler claims to buy 80% of the value in their vehicles, putting the firm at the high end of the spectrum.

A small percentage reduction in the cost of purchased materials has a large impact on stock price for firms that purchase the lion's share of their product-service bundle. As the table shows, a firm that buys 90% of the value of their sales could realize a 180% increase in the value of their stock from a mere 2% reduction in their purchase costs. This, of course, assumes that all other factors—market sentiment, revenue outlook, etc.—remain constant. Chrysler, with 80% of their sales value coming from purchased material, would recognize an 80% increase in stock price. Perhaps Chrysler's stock appreciation during the 1990s, when shares increased from $10 to $100, was largely caused by their famous success in reducing supply costs by billions of dollars. GM, with less exposure to suppliers and more internal value added, might be expected to focus more of its resources on reducing internal costs. Nevertheless, even a more integrated company such as GM could get double-digit stock price gains (13%) from a mere 2% reduction in purchased costs.

Purchased Material as a Percent of Revenue	Incremental Value Added as a Percent of Revenue**	Earnings as a Percent of Revenue	Earnings**	Stock Price*	Savings from the 2% Reduction in Purchased Material Cost*	Earnings After Reduction in Cost*	Stock Price After Reduction in Cost*	Improvement in Stock Price Resulting from the 2% Reduction in Purchased Material Cost*
90.00%	10.00%	1.00%	$1.00	$25.00	$1.80	$2.80	$70.00	180.00%
80.00%	20.00%	2.00%	$2.00	$50.00	$1.60	$3.60	$90.00	80.00%
70.00%	30.00%	3.00%	$3.00	$75.00	$1.40	$4.40	$110.00	46.67%
60.00%	40.00%	4.00%	$4.00	$100.00	$1.20	$5.20	$130.00	30.00%
50.00%	50.00%	5.00%	$5.00	$125.00	$1.00	$6.00	$150.00	20.00%
40.00%	60.00%	6.00%	$6.00	$150.00	$0.80	$6.80	$170.00	13.33%
30.00%	70.00%	7.00%	$7.00	$175.00	$0.60	$7.60	$190.00	8.57%

*per $100 in revenue
**assumes P/E = 25

It is worth noting that many companies focus heavily on increasing sales revenues and contribute significant resources to that effort. This may not, however, be the most effective allocation of resources if a company's primary objective is to raise its stock price. Let's work through an example: Managers of a company with the cost structure assumed in Table 3.7 and at the 80% purchased value level will expect their stock price to increase by 80% if their sales revenue increases by 80% (all other factors remaining constant).

To gain the 80% increase in stock price, earnings must increase by $1.60 per $100 of revenue. (This can be seen in the second row of Table 3.7.)

If earnings increase $1.6 per $100 of revenue, and

Earnings represent 2% of sales, then

The sales increase must = $1.6/2%= $1.6/(0.02) = $80 per $100 of revenue, or 80%

To summarize, in this example we have seen that a 2% reduction in the cost of purchased material would have about the same impact on earnings as an 80% increase in sales. This information could help a manager decide whether to expend resources on efforts to reduce the cost of materials purchased via supply chain improvements or spend to support efforts directed at increasing sales (through promotions, advertising, etc.).

Clearly, there are other long-term benefits to increasing sales if it results in enhanced market-share and customer loyalty. Yet the immediate leverage of revenue increases on stock price is often not as significant as supply chain cost reductions, especially for companies that purchase a large share of the value in their product-service bundles.

Example 3.1

Fred has just come back from a meeting where a new corporate supply chain management effort was described to some top managers from a variety of functional areas. For every $100 in sales Fred's company has, they buy $70 worth of material and add $30 in value. From that, they earn a before-tax return of $3 (E). The company's stock is trading at $75 per share (P), resulting in a price-over-earnings ratio ("P/E ratio") of about 25. A manager from finance and a sales director from marketing were questioning the significance of a 2% reduction in purchased material costs. Even in a cost-conscious market such as theirs, neither manager could fully appreciate the significance of such a small decrease. "It's not like it would have a big impact on our stock price or anything!" the finance manager suggested. "Wouldn't affect sales revenues that much!" the sales director laughed.

Help Fred set the record straight by determining (1) the stock price impact of the cost reduction and (2) the amount by which revenue would have to increased to generate the same stock price impact.

Step 1: Determine the impact of the cost reduction on earnings.

A 2% reduction in material cost would be applied to the 70% of value allocated to purchased material cost. Therefore, per $100 in sales, the reduction in cost would be $70 × .02 = $1.40. Before-tax earnings would increase by $1.40 per $100 in sales.

Step 2: Determine the percentage increase in earnings.

Earnings would jump from $3 to $4.40 before taxes, a 47% increase.

Step 3: Determine the stock price increase.

Given a constant P/E ratio of 25 and what economists call an "efficient market," the new stock price would be 25 × $4.40 = $110, also a 47% increase.

Step 4: Determine the required revenue increase to generate the same earnings increase and stock price impact.

Fred's company earns $3 per every $100 in sales, an operating margin of 3%. Divide the earnings increase by the operating margin: $1.40/0.03 = $46.67. This means the 2% reduction in material costs on current sales would require a 46.7% increase in sales using current material costs to result in the same earnings and stock price impact.

SUMMARY

Supply chain management (SCM) deals with the configuration, coordination, and improvement of sequentially related operations. It is a cross-functional, cross-business, integrative process that has gained attention in recent years because of coordination opportunities available as a result of advances in information systems technology and because of the operational benefits observed through lean production methods.

Supply chains vary from industry to industry. In the automobile industry, for example, powerful companies with large operational volumes and significant capital drive supply chain management configuration and coordination approaches. In health care, service providers drive the configuration of the supply chain and all coordination goes through them.

Supply chain configuration involves design decisions and strategic alignment of an organization's resources with those of other product or service providers in the chain. Companies need to decide what their core competencies will be, become the best in the chain at executing those competencies, and find ways to get the other members of the chain to effectively provide the

other aspects of the product-service bundle. Thus, configuration choices may involve either vertical integration or outsourcing.

Supply chain coordination involves scheduling resources, information exchange, and material flows across the extended enterprise. Relationship management activities, such as supplier development and relationship marketing, are key enablers of supply chain coordination. Information technologies, such as ADC and ERP systems, are also key enablers of coordinated decision making across the chain.

Typical supply chains present many opportunities for system-wide improvement, and we have described seven of them in this chapter: (1) Segmenting customers based on their unique service needs, (2) customizing the logistics network for each customer segment, (3) listening to the signals of the marketplace and planning according to these rather than to independent forecasts, (4) differentiating products closer to the customer through the postponement strategy, (5) sourcing strategically, (6) developing supply-chain-wide technology strategies, and (7) adopting channel-spanning performance measurement strategies.

KEY TERMS

Assembler, 82

Automated Data Collection (ADC), 91

Basic producer, 81

Bullwhip effect, 95

Converter, 81

Electronic Data Interchange (EDI), 78

Enterprise resources planning (ERP), 79

Fabricator, 81

Hollow corporation, 82

Integrated supply, 90

Lean production, 73

Logistics, 73

Original equipment manufacturer (OEM), 82

Outsourcing, 84

Postponement, 97

Purchasing, 75

Radio frequency identification (RFID), 91

Sole sourcing, 90

Supplier certification, 90

Supply chain management (SCM), 68

Vendor managed inventory, 85

Vertical integration, 80

SOLVED PROBLEMS

1. Orange Computers, manufacturer of Personal Computers used in most K–12 schools wants to increase earnings. They currently earn 4% on every dollar of revenue. If they want to double their current earnings, one way is to double sales (i.e., increase sales by 100%). With purchased components accounting for 60% of their revenue, they feel

it may also be possible to work with suppliers to reduce the cost of meeting their needs.

a) How much would the cost of purchased components need to be reduced to double earnings?

b) Five years from now, they expect purchased component costs to be a bigger part of their revenue. If the cost of purchased parts were 80% of revenue, how would your answer to part a) be different?

Answer:

a) Doubling earnings would mean increasing earnings from $4 to $8 per $100 in revenue. Given that purchase components account for $60 out of every $100 in revenue, it would mean that reducing the cost of purchased components by $4/$60 or 6.67% would result in the same benefit to earnings.

b) It would change as the percentage of revenue spent of purchased components increased. It would take a small increase of a larger proportion of revenue to have the same impact. At 80%, it would only take a 5% ($4/$80) decrease in the cost of purchased components to double earnings.

2. The president of Sunshine Foods, a large interstate chain of grocery supermarkets, has challenged his staff to examine their supply chain in an effort to reduce the cost of their annual purchases by 1% this year and every year for the next three after that. They currently spend about $95 dollars for every $100 they generate in revenue and earn a before tax margin of 0.5% of revenue.

a) What impact would that savings have on earnings over the next four years?

b) Assuming the reduction in costs from the prior year, determine the required sales increase in each of the 4 years that would result in the same increase in earnings as a 1% reduction in sales.

c) Though both are related to food, would you think Sunshine Foods to be more or less interested in such a challenge than a statewide chain of restaurants? Why?

Answer (a and b):

	Current Year	Second Year	Third Year	Fourth Year
Earnings Before Improvement*	$100 × 0.5% = $.50	Last year's improved earnings = $1.45	Last year's improved earnings = $2.39	Last year's improved earnings = $3.32
1% Improvement in Purchase Costs*	$95 × 1% = $.95	$94.05 × 1% = $.94	$93.11 × 1% = $.93	$92.18 × 1% = $.92
Improved Earnings*	$0.50 + $0.95 = $1.45	$1.45 + $.94 = $2.39	$2.39 + $.93 = $3.32	$3.32 + $.92 = $4.24
New Purchase Cost	$95 × 99% = $94.05	$94.05 × 99% = $93.11	$93.11 × 99% = $92.18	92.18 × 99% = $91.26
Increase in Sales Required to Match Improved Earning from (a)	$.95/ $.50 = 190%	$.94/$1.45 = 65%	$.93/$2.39 = 39%	$.92/$3.32 = 28%

* per $100 in revenue

c) Sunshine Foods will have a larger proportion of revenue in purchased products and less incremental value added than a typical restaurant chain that actually prepares the food and serves it. This would typically mean a tighter margin for earnings at Sunshine Foods and even a small decrease in the costs of purchased products would have a bigger impact on earnings improvement.

3. Redhawk Motor Company's common stock currently trades on the open market at $50 per share with a P/E ratio of 22. They currently earn 3% on

revenue yet they spend 80% of revenue on outside purchases of components. It has been suggested by certain senior executive staff that by working more closely with first- and second-tier suppliers they can reduce the cost of purchased components by 2% in the coming year. Executives from marketing and finance are skeptical.

a) Given current earnings, what would be the stock price per $100 in revenue?

b) How much would earnings improve with the improved supply chain initiative?

c) How much would you expect stock prices to change per $100 in revenue? Per share of common stock?

d) How much would sales have to improve at the current earnings rate to equal the stock price appreciation from the supply chain management related improvements of part (c) above?

Answer:

a) Earning $3 per $100 in revenue gives an earning to revenue ratio of 0.03. With a P/E ratio of 22, the stock price per $100 in revenue would be $66. Arithmetically:
$[(\$22/\$1) \times (.03 \times \$100)] = \$66$

b) Reducing the roughly $80 spent on purchased components per $100 in revenue by 2% would increase earnings by $0.02 \times \$80 = \$1.60$. (That's a 53.3% improvement to a $3.00 earnings figure.) Total earnings increase from $3 to $4.60 per $100 in revenue.

c) Earning $4.60 per $100 in revenue and having a P/E ratio of 22, the stock price per $100 in revenue would be $ 101.20. (Also, a 53.3 % gain relative to the $66.00 derived in part (a) above.)

Arithmetically: $[(\$22/\$1) \times (.046 \times \$100)] = \$101.20$

The price per share of common stock would go up 53.3% as well to $76.65 per share.

Arithmetically: $\$50.00 \times 1.533 = \$76.65$

d) Currently earning 3% of revenue, sales would also have to increase 53.3% to match the incremental earnings made possible by improved supply chain management.

Arithmetically: $\$4.60/0.03 = \$153.33$ and $153.33 in revenue is 53.33 percent more than the $100.00 required to generate the earnings of $4.60 with the supply chain improvement.

DISCUSSION QUESTIONS

1. What was the undoing of Henry Ford's idea concerning vertical integration? Would his approach be more or less feasible given the nature of business and technology today?

2. What is the role of communication in SCM? How does information technology fit into this new role? Can you describe how things might have changed in Tom's airline over the last few years?

3. What role has technology played in recent changes in logistics? How does it relate to the last question about communication?

4. Does your university outsource its food service? Should they? How would a residential school be different than a commuter school in this regard?

5. Fred is not happy about his company's decision to buy all their microchips from one supplier. With no immediate competition, he feels that giving all the business to one company will reduce their willingness to keep prices low. What would you tell him?

6. What is enterprise resource planning (ERP)? Is it only for manufacturing firms? Could Tom's airline

or Cheryl's hospital have a need for something like it?

7. How do you balance long-term business relationships with direct competition between multiple suppliers vying for your business? What are some of the new ethical issues that emerge?

8. Can you make an argument linking downsizing within a supply chain to growth of the supply chain in the aggregate? How might that work? Is this a good thing? Why? Why not?

9. A lot of people use home delivery service for the bulk of their grocery shopping needs. How would you sell this service to someone? What are the negative issues that someone might logically argue? What is its future potential?

10. What is "integrated supply"? What is actually being outsourced in these situations? How would this work in Fred's cell phone factory or Luis's furniture factory?

11. Assume a contract electronics manufacturer (i.e., Solectron Inc.) approaches Fred. They want him to

consider outsourcing his printed circuit board operations to them. What value would they then add? What would be left for Fred's company? What do you think of the idea?

12. Fred is interested in comparing the efforts his sales force must put forward to increase sales with the benefits arising from cost reductions negotiated with suppliers and other supply-chain partners. The following table indicates the impact of cost reductions and increases in sales on net profits before taxes. (Of course, an added dollar of sales will not lead to an added dollar of profits because of the costs required to satisfy the sale.)

Gross Margin	Incremental Sales Required to Increase Pretax Profit by $1	Reduction in Operating/ Material Costs Required to Increase Pretax Profit by $1
5%	$20	$1
10%	$10	$1
15%	$6.66	$1
20%	$5	$1
25%	$4	$1

Assume Fred only has the managerial time to pursue one significant improvement project this year. He projects that a marketing investment of $400,000 will yield a two-million dollar sales increase for the year. Likewise, a supplier cost reduction program modeled after the SCORE program used by Chrysler in the 1990s would require an investment of $500,000 and yield first year savings of $650,000.

a) If Fred's best estimate of his gross margin is 5%, which project would you advise him to pursue?

b) What would his gross margin need to be for the answer to change?

c) What considerations in addition to "the numbers" would you advise Fred to consider in this decision?

13. Given that a typical grocery store has a 3–4% gross margin on sales, how would you explain their interest in streamlining their SCM relative to increasing sales?

14. A $20,000 car may generate a $1000–$1500 profit margin to the manufacturer. How does improving the supply chain compare to increasing sales in this situation?

15. How would Fred model his business using the SCOR model? Assume Fred outsources the printing of his company logo onto the cell phone covers to a small industrial screen printer who works on a make to order basis. How would SCOR help him (and the printer) understand their business relationship?

16. How might RFID chips help Cheryl's hospital? What might be some of the first applications?

17. How would you describe Fred's supply chain? Should he be more concerned with physical efficiency or market responsiveness?

18. How would you describe Luis's supply chain? Should he be more concerned with physical efficiency or market responsiveness?

19. How does the service nature of Tom and Cheryl's supply chains complicate their environments?

PROBLEMS

1. Acme Manufacturing has a 4% earning on sales before taxes. They are looking at improved supply chain management. For every $1 they reduce material cost and everything else equal, how much would sales have to increase to earn a comparable amount?

2. Tucker Toys has a PE ratio of 22 and wants to increase earnings as a way to increase their market capitalization. They are looking to increase earning by reducing material costs. With everything else equal, how much would each $1 in cost reductions affect their market capitalization?

3. Tucker Toys (see above) also estimates they earn 5% before taxes and spends 65% of their revenue on purchased material. If their common stock

currently trades for $64 per share, what impact would a 3% reduction in the cost of materials have on the earnings and subsequent trading price of their stock?

4. Marshall's Manufacturing outsources a large portion of the component parts needed to make their advanced robotic equipment. With revenues of more than $100 million last year, they purchased almost $70 million in parts with a network of suppliers with a 5% earnings before taxes. Marshall's major suppliers argue that better demand information from Marshall's would help them reduce the costs of over and under production of the highly specialized materials they sell to Marshall's. This, they argue, would result in a 3% reduction in the cost of purchased materials.

   a) What would be the increase in Marshall's earning attributed to this saving?

   b) Would it have an impact on their stock price? How much?

5. Bonnie's Bicycles has had a hard time dealing with competition from inexpensive imports. They currently earn just over 2% on revenues and spend about 70% of the revenue on purchased material. By increasing the amount of material outsourced to other companies another 10%, the purchasing, operations, and accounting people tell Bonnie (the CEO) that she could cut material costs by 1% of the increased total. Finance and marketing people argue for the current system and insist that they can increase sales by enough to equal the savings projected by the increased outsourcing.

   a) If the purchasing, operations, and accounting staff are correct, what would be the effect on earnings?

   b) How much would sales have to increase to equal that effect?

6. Redhawk Motors, a large automotive manufacturer, has a current PE ratio of 32 for their common stock that currently trades at $45 per share. They buy most of their components and spend 80% of their revenue on them. They earn 2% on sales before taxes. A consultant has analyzed their supply chain and feels investing in "e-business" through the supply chain could result in 5% reduction in the cost of purchased material.

   a) If the consultant is correct, what impact will that have on material costs?

   b) What would be the resulting impact on earnings?

   c) What effect should that earnings change have on the price of common stock for Redhawk Motors?

   d) What if it is only a 1% earnings instead of a 5% earnings?

7. GASOU, a petroleum company with more than 1500 gasoline stations in twelve states, spends almost 90% of its revenue on gasoline from a network of refineries. They earn an industry leading 2% on their operations before taxes. By installing computerized systems that use satellite links to their suppliers' distribution systems, they feel they can meet demand for gas at their stations with less inventory yet avoid expensive rush deliveries. All in all, they feel it will reduce the cost of gasoline by 1%.

   a) What impact will this small decrease in gasoline stock have on their earnings?

   b) How much would their sales have to increase to have the same effect on earning under the previous circumstances?

   c) What other areas might they look to improve operations in order to have a similar effect?

CHALLENGE PROBLEMS

1. Construct a spreadsheet, identical in form to Table 3.7, describing the impact of a 5% reduction in sales for a firm with a P/E ratio of 15 and a 5% operating margin. Use the $100.00 revenue unit of analysis.

2. For a publicly traded company in your community, use available sources, such as Edgar Online, which

provides SEC filings of publicly traded firms, or the business press, to determine a) the company's P/E ratio, b) their operating margin, and c) an estimate of the percentage of their product-service bundle that is purchased material cost. (You will have to look at an income statement to estimate the latter two items.)

a) Build a spreadsheet comparable in form to Table 3.7, which describes the stock price impact of supply chain savings.

b) Adapt your spreadsheet such that any company could use it by simply entering their values for P/E ratio, operating margin, and percentage of revenue attributable to purchases.

Case 3: Your Everyday $2 Billion Supply Chain Blunder—and a Solution

In May 2001, Cisco Systems announced the largest inventory write-down in history: $2.2 billion erased from its balance sheet for components it ordered but could not use. The mistake was especially embarrassing because of publicity about Cisco's brilliant integration of its vast information systems and supply chain. Cisco CEO John Chambers was known to have widely boasted that the company could close its books in 24 hours, any day of the year. Despite its sophisticated system, however, Cisco had billions of dollars' worth of stuff nobody wanted.

Cisco tried to pin the blame on a bad market for technology companies. If company forecasters had only been able to see this coming, Cisco implied, the supply chain system would have worked perfectly. But, as Paul Harvey might say, that was not "the rest of the story." In reality, the problem came largely from a bad supply management system. Since the write-down, a group of Cisco executives and engineers has been working to prevent a recurrence of the problem by creating a program they call eHub.

So, what is the rest of the story? It comes down to Cisco's supply chain management practices. During the late 1990s, Cisco was known as a virtual hardware company. Instead of manufacturing their own equipment, Cisco used contract manufacturers. This arrangement had two advantages. First, it allowed Cisco to concentrate on marketing and product innovation. Second, it liberated Cisco from much of the hassle and expense of maintaining inventory, as Cisco's information systems make it possible to ship fully assembled machines directly from the contract manufacturer's factory to Cisco's customers, more or less on demand.

The contract manufacturing arrangement also had disadvantages. Cisco's (and its competitors') supply chains were structured as a pyramid, with Cisco at the top. On the second tier were a group of contract manufacturers—including Celestica (CLS), Flextronics (FLEX), and Solectron (SLR)—who handled final assembly. These contract manufacturers were supplied by a larger sub-tier providing components such as processor chips (Intel and Xilinx) and fiber optic gear (JDS Uniphase and Corning). Those companies, in turn, drew on an even larger base of commodity suppliers scattered all over the globe.

To lock in supplies of scarce components during the boom, Cisco ordered large quantities well in advance, based on demand projections from the company's sales force. What Cisco's forecasters did not notice, however, was that many of their projections were too high. Also, with network gear hard to come by, many customers double and triple ordered by procuring similar equipment from Cisco's competitors, knowing that they would ultimately make just one purchase—from whoever could deliver the goods first.

The double and triple ordering bloated contract manufacturer demand forecasts and because of the bullwhip effect, became magnified in their suppliers' schedules. Suppose Cisco projected sales of 10,000 units of a particular router. Each of the company's contract manufacturers would compete to fill the entire order, and to gain an edge, they often tried to lock up supplies of scarce components.

Component suppliers would be swamped with orders, but Cisco's supply chain system could not show that the spike in demand represented overlapping orders. If three manufacturers were competing to build those 10,000 routers, to chipmakers it looked like a sudden demand for 30,000 machines. The cycle of sales forecasts that were too high and artificially inflated demand for scarce components increased costs and hampered communication and trust throughout the supply chain.

Cisco's inventory woes highlighted the shortcomings of a supply-chain communication system that stopped only partway down the pyramid. That is where eHub comes in. The project was originally intended as a private exchange to help eliminate bidding wars for then-scarce components. (Private exchanges that link members of a supply chain were not a new idea. In the past, companies such as Dell and General Motors have created electronic hubs that feed supply chain data to outsource manufacturers and suppliers, and vice versa. These exchanges typically provide a web interface where vendors manually type in factors such as sales forecasts, purchase orders, and shipping schedules. The systems are not real time, and they are plagued by data-entry errors.)

eHub overcame many of the problems with previous private exchanges by automating the flow of information between Cisco, its contract manufacturers, and its component suppliers. The key was an XML technology called Partner Interface Process, or PIP. eHub's dozen or so PIPs indicate whether a document requires a response, and if so, how quickly. For example, a PIP purchase order might stipulate that the recipient's system must send a confirmation two hours after receipt and a confirmed acceptance within 24 hours. If the recipient's system fails to meet these deadlines, the purchase order is considered null and void.

Under eHub, Cisco's production cycle begins when a demand forecast PIP is sent out, showing cumulative orders. That forecast goes not only to contract manufacturers but also to second-tier suppliers, such as the chip makers. Thus, if three contract manufacturers bidding on the same Cisco order came to a chip maker at the same time, and each said they wanted 10,000 of a certain chip, the chip maker could see from eHub that the total demand was for 10,000 chips and not for 30,000. By requiring all the systems in the supply network to talk to each other, eHub prevented inventory shortfalls, production blackouts, and other scheduling mistakes almost as fast as they occurred.

Complexity and cost put eHub a bit behind schedule. Cisco originally planned to connect 250 contractors and suppliers by the end of 2001. Instead it linked roughly 60, including Agilent Technologies (A), Hitachi, IBM (IBM), Intel (INTC), LSI Logic (LSI), Motorola (MOT), and Xilinx (XLNX). Cisco's ultimate goal is to integrate as many as 650 supply chain participants. Furthermore, eHub is only the first stage of Cisco's plans. Ultimately, Cisco hopes to automate the whole supply-management process. When a customer purchases a product online, that order will go into both Cisco's financial database and supply chain system simultaneously. When the next tech boom comes, Cisco expects eHub to provide the parts it needs in the right quantity, at the right location, and at the right time. As a result, when the next bust follows the boom, eHub might keep Cisco and its supply-chain partners from getting stuck with so much unwanted stuff.

SOME QUESTIONS TO THINK ABOUT:

1. How would the orders of Cisco's competitors have made the original problem worse?

2. Which advantage of eHub is most applicable here? Are there others?

3. As Cisco automates "the whole enchilada," how do they add value to justify their profit margin?

Source: Adapted from *Business 2.0*, March 2002, reporter Paul Kaihla

REFERENCES

Handfield, R. B., and E. L. Nichols Jr. *Introduction to Supply Chain Management.* Upper Saddle River, NJ: Prentice-Hall, Inc., 1999.

Anderson, D. L., F. E. Britt, and D. J. Favre. "The Seven Principles of Supply Chain Management." *Supply Chain Management Review,* accessed on the World Wide Web at http://www.manufacturing.net/scm/. Accessed on April 17, 2006.

Lummus, R. R., and R. J. Vokurka. "Managing the Demand Chain Through Managing the Information Flow: Capturing 'Moments of Information'." *Production and Inventory Management,* 40, no. 1 (1999): 16–20.

Forger, G. "Top Trends in ADC Hardware That You Need to Track." *ADC News and Solutions Online,* January 1, 1999.

Fine, C. *The Clockspeed Chronicles.* Reading, MA: Perseus Books, 1998.

Davenport, T. H., "The Coming Commoditization of Processes" *Harvard Business Review,* June 2005: 100–111.

Vigoroso, M. "Buyers Pare Down Supplier Rosters." *Purchasing Online: The Magazine of Supply Chain Management.* October 22, 199, accessed on April 14, 2006.

Ernst, D., and J, Bamford, "Best Practice: Your Alliances Are Too Stable." *Harvard Business Review,* June 2005: 133–146.

Weinberg, N. "Bill Morean's $1.2 Billion Haircut." *Forbes,* June 14, 1999: online version.

Tanzer, A. "Singapore Fling." *Forbes,* June 14, 1999: online version.

Porter, A. M. "Outsourcing Gains Popularity." *Purchasing Online: The Magazine of Supply Chain Management.* March 11, 1999, accessed on April 14, 2006.

4

Quality Management and Statistical Process Control

Chapter Outline

Introduction   113

Cross-Functionally Integrating Operations Management   115

Quality Management Processes   115

    Commitment 1: A Commitment to the Customer and Total Customer Satisfaction   117

    Commitment 2: A Commitment to Understanding and Improving the Firm's Process   118

    Commitment 3: A Commitment to the Firm's Employees and to Total Employee Involvement   119

    Commitment 4: A Commitment to Data-Based Decision Making   119

    Shifting Paradigms of Management   119

    Leaders of the Quality Movement in the United States   124

Quality System Effectiveness Measurement Processes   130

    The Baldrige Award   130

    ISO 9000 Certification   130

Quality Detection, Prevention, and Improvement Processes   132

    Detection Processes   132

    Prevention Processes   155

    Improvement Processes   161

Summary   170

Key Terms   171

Solved Problems   172

Discussion Questions   176

Problems   178

Challenge Problems   183

Case 4: NASA's Problems with Mars Probes Linked to Communication Failure   185

References   186

Learning Objectives

After studying this chapter you should be able to

▶ Demonstrate your understanding of the linkages between quality management processes and the various functional areas of business

▶ Describe the primary commitments that characterize total quality management

▶ Describe differences between the total quality management paradigm and traditional management paradigms

▶ Describe the primary contributions of Deming, Juran, and Crosby

▶ Describe key quality awards and certifications and what competitive benefits can accompany their attainment

▶ Describe acceptance sampling methods and risks

▶ Use attribute and variables based control charting methods

▶ Compute and interpret process capability indices

▶ Describe fail proofing tools

▶ Describe improvement methods such as Kaizen workshops, the quality improvement story, six-sigma projects, and cross-functional teams

... Back at the Rec Center

It's about 6:30 on Friday morning, near the end of another work week, and our managers are at the rec center and working up an early sweat.

"You're pumping pretty hard, going to a fire?" Luis asks, seeing a heavily breathing Fred on an elliptical strider. "The pulse meter is going to go off the chart in a second!"

"Nah, just thinking about my meetings this morning!" snarls Fred. "I just got my price down to where my customers are okay with it, and now my biggest account is beefing about our defect rate!" he adds. Obviously frustrated, Fred had spent several years marketing a premium-priced product made with all the bells and whistles. Now, just as he was finally getting used to making a low-end, standardized cell phone where price was everything, his customers want quality, too! The representative for his biggest account had just told him that if Fred's company couldn't cut its defect rate by 10% per year, she could no longer do business with Fred.

"We just undercut our competition to grab all of this account's business, and then, BOOM, she hit us with the defect rate. She can't be serious!" Fred objects, getting off the elliptical. For almost a year, his division had been cutting its costs to the bone to keep the delivered price to this account competitive. Fred felt the defect rate was reasonable. In fact, they had shipped fewer defective pagers than the competition and at a better price, too! Inspectors always checked the products as they went out and scrapped a fair share of them, he thought, but nobody can catch everything.

"Consumer electronics is a tough business, Fred. Maybe you need to think about what your customers want from you—not your old ones, but your new ones," Tom responds. He recalled that his company brought in some quality management consultants who helped them identify their customers and how the company could serve them better at less cost.

Tom also remembered how strange it had seemed to him the first time he heard the consultants' plan. But the consultants argued that even an airline could do better by customers and lower costs at the same time, if marketers really knew what the customers wanted. Fortunately, as a relatively new carrier, Tom's outfit didn't have to unlearn as much as other airlines might have to. The consultants told Tom that his people needed to define their customers' needs, identify a market niche of customers whose needs they could satisfy, and focus on continually improving their ability to meet those needs.

It wasn't easy. "We took a look at what we do, who we are, and who our customers are," Tom explains. "We figured our customers were travellers who need on-time service to places where the only alternative to our service is driving. Those customers wanted service without frills, at a low cost," he adds. "We collected data on our customers' needs, how well our process meets those needs, and how we compared to the competition. Then, we used all that information to improve our performance."

"For example," Tom went on, "we always fly the same type of plane, avoid crowded airports, and keep frills down. We don't even handle interline baggage. Do you know how much a plane can earn per hour flying? A lot more than it can earn sitting on the ground!

"We also realized that flying to older, smaller, less-crowded urban airports is usually cheaper, allowing us to keep costs down and avoid long, irritating delays on arrival or departure." He says they also realized that on short flights, serving food or offering reserved seating is unnecessary. "Guess how much it costs to take a can of soda to 30,000 feet, serve it, and collect the empty cup?"

"Well, I know you get what you pay for, and you pay for what you need!" replies Luis, as he takes off his sweats.

"Come on, guys, it may be 6:30 in the morning, but I can see that all three of you are right. It's just that you're in different businesses," Cheryl notes, after listening patiently as the other three blew off steam. "Fred, you and Tom sell the low-cost, off-the-shelf, no-frills basic model. Luis, you sell high-end stuff with all the extras, and you tailor it to the customer's specifications. That's different," Cheryl says, understanding that her hospital is more like Luis's furniture factory, in that each patient, like a customer looking to buy a custom-tailored table or chair, has different needs. Cheryl knows that if managers at the hospital, like those at the furniture factory, can accurately determine what patients truly need and what they don't, then they can still keep costs reasonable.

"But in a lot of ways, our businesses are the same," Cheryl continues. "We're all concerned with getting waste out of the system. In our case, and I'm sure the same goes for Luis, we balance flexibility and effective treatment with efficiency," she says. Hospitals may reorganize doctors', nurses', and technicians' duties to increase the productivity of all concerned, but they won't do this at the expense of safe and effective patient care. "A key for us would be to improve communication between our processes and our patients," Cheryl explains. "But the automated phone-answering system that works for Tom's airline won't cut it in ER."

Introduction

In a 1956 article in the *Harvard Business Review*, Armand Feigenbaum identified three new trends that would have significant implications for the management of quality. First, customer expectations for quality were rising sharply. The post-World War II era of high demand and low capacity was sure to end, and with it the day when providers of goods and services could specify their own levels of quality. Customers would

Total quality control (TQC)

An approach to ensuring that products conform to specifications that utilizes employees from all functional areas in addition to support from a quality control department.

Figure 4.1

Quality management and statistical process control

eventually be able to hold out for their preferred levels of quality. Second, quality practices and techniques, which had been in use since the early days of the industrial revolution, were outmoded. They required large inspection departments and emphasized standards for the quantity rather than the quality of output. Third, costs arising from poor quality had become very high, limiting the competitive strength of American companies. Taken together, these three trends suggested that firms would have to improve the quality of their output at the same time that they reduced the costs of creating that output.

Feigenbaum proposed a solution to these problematic trends, which he called **total quality control (TQC)**. The major difference between TQC and prior practice was that in TQC, quality was everyone's job. Feigenbaum's proposal was based on a thorough acquaintance with the production process. In most organizations, the marketing personnel are in close contact with customers; they understand customer requirements better than others in the organization. But to effectively satisfy customers' expectations, operations personnel must understand the quality standards customers require. Likewise, to set appropriate technical parameters for products and services, design engineers must rely on information provided by marketing and operations. All functions within the system, including but not limited to marketing, design, and operations, must interact effectively in a coordinated effort to satisfy the customer. Clearly, quality *is* everyone's job.

Figure 4.1 illustrates the major decision processes and concepts presented in this chapter as they integrate with other functions and the supply chain in general. They include

▸ Today's "quality management processes" as they have evolved from the total quality management (TQM) systems of the 1990s, including a historical perspective on the leaders of the quality movement in the United States

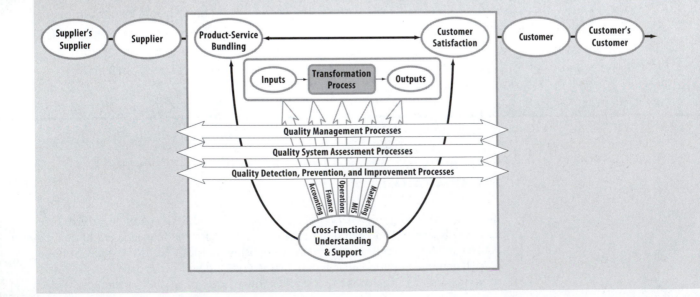

◗ "Quality system assessment processes," a discussion of ways that companies can validate their quality systems based on external review, such as the Malcolm Baldrige National Quality Award and the ISO 9000 certification

◗ "Quality detection, prevention, and improvement processes," statistically grounded approaches used to detect quality problems, prevent them, and improve processes, including acceptance sampling, control charting, the quality improvement story, and six-sigma programs

Cross-Functionally Integrating Operations Management

As Table 4.1 illustrates, the importance of quality is reflected in all areas of business. From a financial and cost accounting perspective, it is important to recognize the implications of quality management decisions. Making prudent investments to improve quality requires knowledge of the costs of quality, reliability of quality improvement methods and financial justification techniques.

From a human resources perspective, it is important to recognize that personnel management and motivation systems are a key element in any quality enhancement program. Whereas traditional management systems relied on specialists, such as engineers, inspectors, statisticians, and quality managers, modern systems engage all employees in quality improvement. Personnel measurement and reward schemes, job descriptions, availability of training, and selection systems can be radically different depending on a firm's approach to quality management.

Because marketing is usually the business function that most directly interacts with customers, its importance to quality management is difficult to overstate. The means by which market intelligence regarding customer preferences and satisfaction is gathered and built into organizational decisions must be clearly laid out if this information is to have any impact on a company's competitiveness.

Engineering plays a significant role in the design of the product-service bundle and the value-adding system. It is also critical to any significant product or process enhancements, as well as testing and inspection methods. In fact, there is a large enough body of engineering knowledge tied to the area of quality that engineers may specialize in this area and gain the credential of Certified Quality Engineer (CQE).

Management information systems (MIS) provide such critical support to companies that they pervade virtually all business decisions in the modern corporation. Quality decisions are no exception because they must be based on data regarding customer satisfaction, customer preferences, process capability, product performance, quality costs, and so on. The MIS function is critical to effective quality management in that it provides data collection, storage, analysis, and reporting solutions to decision makers.

Quality Management Processes

Today's quality management processes have evolved from **total quality management (TQM)** systems that were at the heart of the quality revolution of the 1990's in the United States. TQM is a management approach based on four fundamental commitments:

1. Commitment to the customer's total satisfaction

Total quality management (TQM)

A system of management based on a commitment to the customer's total satisfaction, understanding and improving the organization's processes, employee involvement, and data-based decision making.

Table 4.1

Cross-Functionally
Integrating Operations
Management

Integration Perspective / Functional Area	Finance	Accounting
Why Cross-Functional Integration Matters in Quality Management	Managers need to financially justify investments that are required to improve quality. This requires an understanding of quality costs and quality improvement methods, in addition to knowledge of financial tools.	Measurement of quality costs and reconciliation of financial statements in light of quality losses is an important accounting activity.
Key Issues	What is the relationship among customer satisfaction, quality, and financial performance? How should investments in quality improvement be financially justified?	How should quality costs be measured? When and how should quality losses be reflected on financial statements?

2. Commitment to understanding and improving the organization's processes

3. Commitment to employee involvement

4. Commitment to data-based decision making

While the first two commitments represent outcomes; the third and fourth represent methods that provide a foundation for achieving the desired outcomes.

A firm's shared vision and values provide the basis for making these commitments. Without these values, individuals would find it difficult to agree to any commitment, much less act on it. Implementing the four commitments often requires behavior that is not customary to managers. In most organizations, unusual steps must be taken to ensure that workers and customers do not perceive the commitments as hollow promises. In addition to verbal commitments, financial resources must be allocated, appropriate reward systems established, human resource management practices

Human Resources	Marketing	Engineering	Management Information Systems
Providing a meaningful role in improvement efforts for all workers requires installation and maintenance of appropriate motivational and training systems.	Information regarding customer preferences and perceptions of a product-service bundle (i.e., quality data) originates in the marketplace and must be transferred to the organization by the marketing function.	Engineering expertise plays a critical role in quality of design and in efforts to improve process capability. Engineering also may be involved in establishing test and inspection methods.	Data regarding product quality and process performance must be maintained and accessible for managers to make quality management and improvement decisions. Information systems provide this capability.
How should worker involvement in quality improvement be reflected in employee job descriptions, selection, reward systems, and training programs?	How will the marketing function gather customer and competitor intelligence on quality? What systems can be used to transfer quality information to other functional areas—particularly operations?	What role will quality play in design decisions (relative to other factors such as cost, features, and performance)? What are the appropriate specifications for components, subassemblies, and product-service bundles? How will quality be measured and tested? How may processes be improved?	What data must be captured and how? Who will have access to quality-related information and with what system capabilities and interfaces? How will quality related data be maintained?

altered, and training provided. Finally, once the new system has been put in place, it must be given time to produce results.

Commitment 1: A Commitment to the Customer and Total Customer Satisfaction

The very purpose of organizations is to meet customer needs and satisfy their expectations. Whether the customer is internal or external, making a true commitment to customer satisfaction requires managers to follow through with the commitments in at least three ways:

1. They must establish an ongoing process that effectively measures the level of satisfaction customers are receiving from the firm's product-service bundle.

2. They must maintain excellent communication between employees and the customers they serve.

Knowing the needs of the customer will help the steel company determine what their definition of quality needs to be.

Masterfile Royalty Free

3. They must design processes and product-service bundles that delight customers, both by responding to customers' concerns and by anticipating customers' needs and expectations.

Commitment 2: A Commitment to Understanding and Improving the Firm's Process

All value is added through some kind of process. Every worker has a direct supplier and a direct customer, whether that worker has a clerical, manufacturing, service, or managerial job. Unfortunately, not all workers understand the relationships between processes. Few have the opportunity to discuss their work requirements with their suppliers and customers, and fewer still have the opportunity to improve their processes.

Thus, the second major commitment of TQM is to develop an understanding of the operations system as a whole, one that is shared by all employees within that system. Firms committed to TQM recognize that, in an ever-changing business environment, no process can be perfect. They continually stress process improvement, even when there is no danger of producing defective items, because process improvement is the foundation on which customer satisfaction is built.

Firms that are committed to understanding and improving their processes train all their employees to use a wide variety of techniques to analyze data and make informed decisions about the processes where they work. Unlocking the creativity of the workforce, the third commitment in TQM, is a critical foundation of the ongoing improvement of a process.

Commitment 3: A Commitment to the Firm's Employees and to Total Employee Involvement

There is a subtle distinction between the traditional view of the worker and the perspective promoted by TQM. Traditionally, a worker was viewed as a person who completed a task. In that context, it was easy for workers to "check their brains at the door" when they arrived at work. But in TQM, the worker is viewed as the source of process improvements. Rather than seeing this week's production quota in the workers' hands, managers see the company's future in the workers' minds. For many firms seeking to pursue total quality, this kind of mental adjustment may require considerable change on the part of managers as well as employees.

Employees, in fact, are as much a part of a business process as are the machines they use and the work procedures they follow. Thus, a focus on improving the process must include improvements in the skills and knowledge of employees. Furthermore, the cooperation of all employees is essential to the effective implementation of positive change. Because the people who work in the system every day are the ones best equipped to understand and improve the system, they must be empowered to do so.

Employee involvement (EI) is a management approach to stimulating worker participation and creating a spirit of teamwork in order to gain widespread process improvements. Typically, workers are encouraged to make suggestions that will produce improvements in their workplace, including reduced costs, higher quality, greater safety, better ergonomics, more effective environmental safeguards, enhanced decision making, and more efficient use of space. Once managers have approved a suggestion, a team of volunteers is asked to work on developing a specific approach to implementing the suggestion. Members of the team receive any training they need to follow the project through to its completion.

Employee involvement (EI)

A formal approach to creating a spirit of teamwork that will lead to widespread process improvements.

Commitment 4: A Commitment to Data-Based Decision Making

Managers almost always make their decisions based on some kind of data. Often, however, they do not process the data correctly, they base their decisions on the wrong type of data, or they interpret the data incorrectly because of personal biases. Managers may also fail to understand the limitations of the available data and the ramifications of those limitations. In other words, they may jump to conclusions.

Statistical tools can help decision makers to process data correctly. While they should not overlook their intuition (that is a data point, too), whenever possible they should validate their intuition with appropriately generated statistical results. Quality experts universally agree that the effective use of statistical tools is critical to the improvement of processes, products, and customer satisfaction.

Shifting Paradigms of Management

A **paradigm** is a way of thinking, a pattern or model that serves as an example. Making the commitments required by TQM has forced organizations to radically change the way they view the world and conduct their business. In short, it has forced managerial thinking to shift from the traditional functional paradigm to the TQM paradigm. Table 4.2 summarizes several aspects of this change in thinking.

Paradigm

A way of thinking, a pattern or model that serves as an example.

Table 4.2

The Paradigm Shift to Total Quality Management

Traditional Approach	Total Quality Approach
Analytic Thinking	**Holistic Thinking**
• Functional management • Local performance measures	• Process management • Global performance measures
Focus on Acceptability	**Focus on Desirability**
• Meeting specifications • Performance plateaus	• Pursuit of perfection • Continuous improvement
Focus on Short-Term Financial Performance	**Focus on Long-Term Market Share**
• Financial control • Results oriented	• Managerial leadership • Process oriented
Reactive Response to Customers	**Proactive Solutions for Customers**
• Add on treatments for symptoms • Focus on product elegance	• Addressing the root cause • Focus on customer satisfaction
Competitive Sourcing	**Supply Chain Management**
• Large base of suppliers • Bidding for contracts • Buyer mandates • Short-term, contract-focused relationship	• Select set of suppliers • Single-supplier sourcing • Supplier input in design decisions • Long-term, improvement-oriented relationship
Class-Conscious Thinking	**Team Thinking**
• Hourly versus salaried • Labor versus management • Skilled versus unskilled • Functional classifications and competition	• Focus on teamwork • Focus on system improvement • Focus on satisfying internal customers • Functional excellence supportive of system improvement

ANALYTIC VERSUS HOLISTIC THINKING

In the analytic approach used in traditional management, complex problems are broken down into independent sub-problems that can be understood more easily. The idea is that if each part works correctly, the whole system will work correctly. Thus the analytic approach enhances a manager's understanding of subsystems, improves subsystems' efficiency, or better controls the portion of a problem that is under study. However, in using this divide-and-conquer strategy to solve problems, decision makers may fail to recognize that an understanding of each part does not necessarily confer an understanding of the whole. Because all parts of a system must interact to form a cohesive whole, the whole is much more than the sum of its parts. In the holistic approach to problem solving, subsystems are studied in the context of a clear understanding of the system as a whole.

Building a system out of the parts (the analytic approach) is substantially different from building the parts for a system (the holistic approach). To fully understand their processes, firms that implement TQM must take advantage of both approaches. For many companies, that means de-emphasizing functional management and local performance measures (such as departmental reject rates) in favor of process management and global performance measures (such as customer satisfaction).

ACCEPTABILITY VERSUS DESIRABILITY

The Ford Motor Company's experience in the late 1970s and early 1980s illustrates the practical implications of these two orientations. Based on an extensive analysis, Ford managers had concluded that the majority of the company's problems originated in parts manufacture. Despite the similarity of the two manufacturing plants involved, transmission-related warranty costs were roughly ten times greater for those made in Ohio than for those made in Japan.

Why was the performance of the Mazda transmissions significantly superior? Ford found that American employees defined a quality part as one that was built to specifications. A **specification**, or "spec," defines the boundary between that which is acceptable and that which is not. When asked where the specifications had come from, employees pointed to the process engineers. The process engineers, too, defined quality as conformance to specifications, but they maintained that those specifications came from the product engineers. The product engineers defined quality as the precision of specifications—but they believed that making a specification more precise would raise both manufacturing costs and quality. They wrote their specifications so as to achieve acceptable cost and quality levels.

When they studied a set of parts made in both plants, Ford's engineers noticed that the Mazda-built parts were roughly four times more likely to deviate from specifications than Ford's American-made parts. But, while they were outside the original specs more often than the American-made parts, the Mazda parts had much less variability than those made by Ford. Mazda workers also made improvements to the part's specs when applicable, whereas the Ford workers were asked only to meet specs. Mazda's engineers defined quality in terms of functionality and meeting the desired needs of internal customers. For example, they were more ready to heed the suggestion of a customer to shorten a part so that it would fit better with other parts or lengthen it so that it would attach more easily for the next person on the line. Seeking to continuously improve the desirability of a part's design rather than settling for the acceptability of meeting a given set of specs appeared to be the primary reason for the superiority of the Mazda transmissions.

SHORT-TERM PERFORMANCE VERSUS LONG-TERM MARKET SHARE

In the West, managers are frequently evaluated, rewarded, and promoted on the basis of short-term financial performance, partly because of the analytic orientation of Western culture and partly because of the tendency of stockholders to transfer their assets into companies whose shares are appreciating in value. The practice of rewarding short-term financial performance is widely seen as an obstacle to quality improvement efforts. Decisions that are made to generate short-term gains can send signals that overpower any or all of the four TQM commitments. For example, the desire to generate quarterly profits can lead to a decision to put off an improvement that everyone knows is necessary. Such a decision is inconsistent with both a commitment to the customer and a commitment to the process.

Specification

An instruction set that defines the boundary between that which is acceptable and that which is not.

Japanese firms tend to place greater emphasis on garnering long-term market share, and they frequently sacrifice short-term profits in pursuit of that goal. Their emphasis on long-term market share is consistent with the commitment to customer satisfaction, continuous process improvement, employee involvement, and data-based decision making. Indeed, if a company expects its market share to grow, long-term investments in these areas are justifiable.

Brian Joiner, a well-known quality consultant, and his co-author, Peter Scholtes, have pointed out the following negative outcomes of short-term managerial control:

1. Measurable short-term accomplishments get attention, even though organizational survival may depend on unmeasurable activities with long-term consequences.

2. Short-term control systems always intensify organizational conflict. For example, to make a sale in order to reach a monthly quota, marketing personnel might make a promise that production personnel cannot keep.

3. When measurable controls are not practical or feasible, workers and managers play games with performance numbers to make themselves look better.

4. Playing games closes down open communication and can lead to dishonesty, finger pointing, blame games, and excuse making.

5. Blame games may cause "covering your rear" to become more important than doing the job.

6. Employees are motivated by fear.

7. Management focuses inward rather than on the customer.

REACTIVE RESPONSE VERSUS PROACTIVE SOLUTIONS

If an organization has not made the four commitments of TQM, it is likely to pursue objectives that are stated explicitly in financial terms. By the time customer problems or unique requests get the attention of managers, the matter has usually become urgent. As a result, managers are often willing to pay dearly for a quick fix.

One way that proactive quality efforts pay off is in repeat business, that is, when satisfied customers return to purchase more. Repeat customers are less expensive to attract than first-time customers, they require less effort and expense to acquaint with existing service processes, they are inclined to spend more on additional items and services, and they spread the positive word of mouth that is the lifeblood of any organization. The following list1 provides several additional reasons for managers to proactively focus on long-term quality improvement:

- The average business only hears from 4% of its dissatisfied customers. Of the 96% who do not bother to complain, 25% have serious problems.

- The 4% who complain are more likely to stay with the supplier than the 96% who do not complain.

- About 60% of the complaining customers would stay as customers if their problems were resolved; 95% would stay if the problems were quickly resolved.

- A dissatisfied customer will tell from 10 to 20 other people about his or her problem, but a customer whose problem has been resolved will tell approximately five people.

These statistics suggest that it is very important to have a recovery plan for the times when a customer is dissatisfied. This is especially important in service environments where customer contact is high. The term **service recovery** refers to converting a customer who is dissatisfied with a service into one who is satisfied. Unlike warranty-based product replacements that could occur months after a purchase, service recovery often has to happen at the time the service is being provided. For example, a patient receiving treatment from a physician might not get the relief she expected, even though the office featured the best equipment and techniques. An organization without a service recovery plan might not even have a way to find out that the customer is dissatisfied, and if they do learn of the dissatisfaction might simply chalk up the dissatisfaction to a "you can't win them all" philosophy. An organization with a proactive approach to service recovery, however, will seek to find out if their customers are satisfied and will act quickly to rectify any problems.

Key elements of a service recovery program include

1. Recruiting, hiring, training, and promoting employees for excellence in service recovery

2. Actively seeking customer complaints through such tools as toll-free customer service phone numbers, follow-up phone or mail surveys, and questioning customers about the service during service delivery

3. Measuring the costs of dissatisfied customers and matching investments in quality improvement to the level of these costs

4. Giving authority to front-line employees to take corrective action immediately upon learning of a customer's dissatisfaction

5. Making managers easily available to customers

6. Rewarding employees for superior service recovery efforts

7. Including service recovery as part of the business strategy

8. Committing top managers to strive for both service perfection and effective recovery plans

When customer satisfaction is the key focus of the organization, managers will be proactive about customer service objectives in addition to financial goals. In such companies, customer concerns have management's attention continuously, not just when things get out of hand. Therefore, managers actively eliminate the root causes of potential problems in order to prevent problems from occurring or recurring. Instead of seeking quick fixes and expensive solutions, managers in these companies seek solutions that add value from the perspective of the customer.

COMPETITIVE SOURCING VERSUS SUPPLY CHAIN MANAGEMENT

Companies that frequently put their contracts up for bid in order to make their suppliers compete with one another generally find it difficult to get anything extra from their suppliers. This approach might be okay when a company is buying candy to give away at trade shows, but it will not work as well if a firm is purchasing jet engines or critical avionic instruments. Short-term suppliers have little incentive to get involved in design projects with their customers, invest significantly in information systems links to their customers' facilities, or make capacity and facility plans more favorable to their customers. Such cooperation and its benefits are available only to customers who foster long-term relationships with suppliers. Obviously, the benefits of cooperating with suppliers often outweigh the short-term material cost advantages that might come from awarding business solely on the basis of a competitive bidding system.

Service recovery

The process of converting a customer who is dissatisfied with a service into one who is satisfied.

In the pursuit of quality, many firms are choosing to move toward using a single supplier or a select group of suppliers for a given type of item. During the 1980s, for example, Xerox reduced the number of its suppliers from more than 5,000 to approximately 400. Such an approach may limit a buying organization's ability to bargain for the most competitive price, and it may also expose the buying firm to the risk of supply shortages. On the other hand, it gives the buying firm time to investigate the costs of producing the item and to justify the price requested. It also enables buyers to work with suppliers to modify product or component designs, processes, or buyer-supplier linkages. By concentrating on improving the supply chain rather than administering contracts, firms can reduce both waste and the total cost of sourcing. The improved relationship with the supplier allows the firm to generate improvements over the long term. This is also true in service businesses—for instance, McDonald's pursues long-term relationships with its suppliers.

The benefits of a cooperative supplier-purchaser relationship accrue not just to the buyer but to the supplier as well. Benefits to suppliers include long-term business commitments, more competitive customers, better information for use in planning and control, advance notice of new product designs and technologies, and assistance in making improvements.

CLASS THINKING VERSUS TEAM THINKING

Consider the view expressed by Kaoru Ishikawa:

> *Companies exist in a society for the purpose of satisfying people in that society. This is the reason for their existence and should be their primary goal. . . . If people do not feel happy and cannot be made happy, that company does not deserve to exist. . . . The first order of business is to let the employees have adequate income. Their humanity must be respected, and they must be given an opportunity to enjoy their work and lead a happy life. The term "employees" as used here includes employees of subcontractors and affiliated sales and service organizations. . . . Customers come next. They must feel satisfied and pleased when they buy and use goods and services. . . . The welfare of shareholders must also be taken into consideration. . . . Each company must make sufficient profit to provide stock dividends for shareholders. (Ishikawa 1985, 97–99)*

The quality paradigm emphasizes that employees are human and must be treated with respect because of their humanity. It emphasizes the importance of each individual's contribution and the need for a team-oriented work environment. A person's job classification—salaried or hourly, management or labor—simply signals that he or she is an internal customer whose requirements must be met. At the very least, every employee should receive the same amount of respect as the firm's customers. Every function must contribute its unique expertise, not just to improve the system, but to satisfy the person who is the firm's ultimate customer. The focus shifts from job classes to teamwork, from organizational position to process improvement, and from cross-functional competition to cross-functional cooperation.

Leaders of the Quality Movement in the United States

The movement toward total quality management in the United States can be attributed to the enduring work of three crusaders: W. Edwards Deming, Joseph M. Juran, and Philip Crosby.

W. EDWARDS DEMING

W. Edwards Deming (1900–1993) is best remembered for his ideas related to:

▶ The Deming Chain Reaction

▶ The PDCA Cycle, and

▶ His 14-point management philosophy.

Deming's major idea, the Deming chain reaction (see Figure 4.2a), was that quality improvement is not a costly business option but a strategic imperative that is essential to business survival. If quality improves, productivity will improve, because fewer defects imply less waste. Productivity improvement, in turn, confers the ability to lower prices. Coupled with higher quality, lower prices can lead to increased market share, which implies the ability not only to stay in business but also to provide more jobs. This message, while it sounds quite reasonable in retrospect, was once a revolutionary one to American managers, who have traditionally focused on cost containment for the sake of enhanced short-term financial performance.

The **P-D-C-A cycle** (also called the Shewhart cycle, or the Deming cycle) is a set of steps to be repeated in the pursuit of continuous improvement. These steps are Plan, Do, Check, and Act (see Figure 4.2b). Both Japanese and American managers now apply this cycle to specific processes, as well as in their general approach to running their

P-D-C-A cycle

A set of steps to be repeated in the pursuit of continuous improvement.

Figure 4.2

(a) The Deming chain reaction

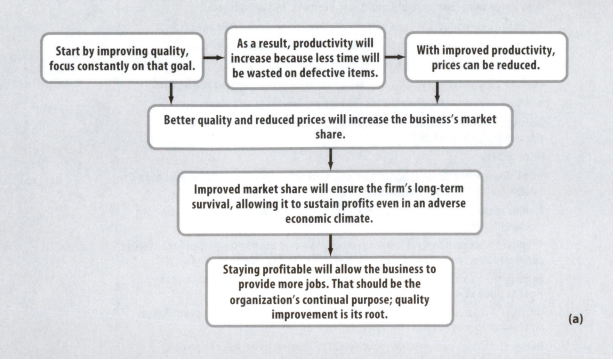

(a)

Figure 4.2

(b) The Deming P-D-C-A cycle (c) Deming's four-teen-point philosophy

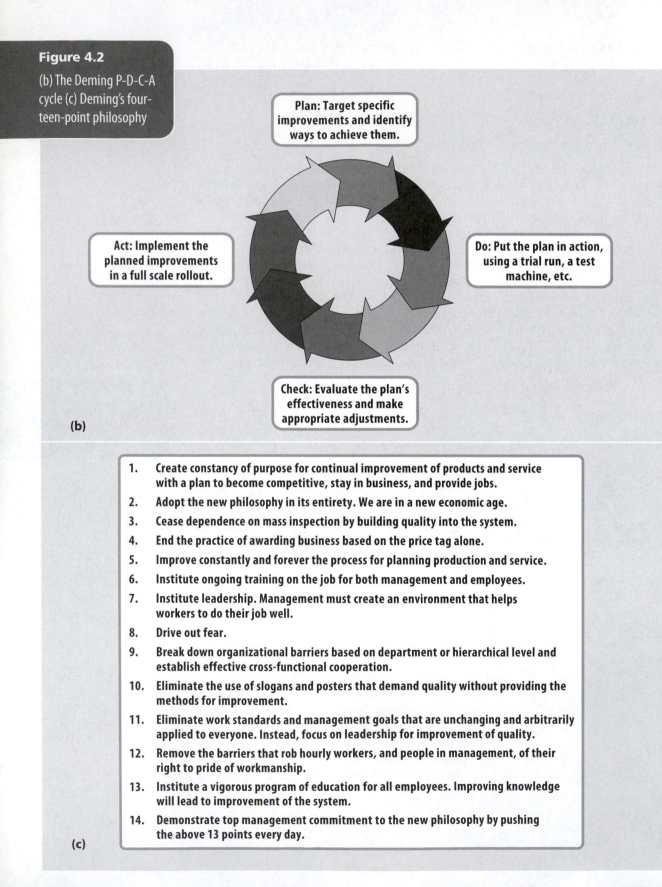

Plan: Target specific improvements and identify ways to achieve them.

Act: Implement the planned improvements in a full scale rollout.

Do: Put the plan in action, using a trial run, a test machine, etc.

Check: Evaluate the plan's effectiveness and make appropriate adjustments.

(b)

1. Create constancy of purpose for continual improvement of products and service with a plan to become competitive, stay in business, and provide jobs.

2. Adopt the new philosophy in its entirety. We are in a new economic age.

3. Cease dependence on mass inspection by building quality into the system.

4. End the practice of awarding business based on the price tag alone.

5. Improve constantly and forever the process for planning production and service.

6. Institute ongoing training on the job for both management and employees.

7. Institute leadership. Management must create an environment that helps workers to do their job well.

8. Drive out fear.

9. Break down organizational barriers based on department or hierarchical level and establish effective cross-functional cooperation.

10. Eliminate the use of slogans and posters that demand quality without providing the methods for improvement.

11. Eliminate work standards and management goals that are unchanging and arbitrarily applied to everyone. Instead, focus on leadership for improvement of quality.

12. Remove the barriers that rob hourly workers, and people in management, of their right to pride of workmanship.

13. Institute a vigorous program of education for all employees. Improving knowledge will lead to improvement of the system.

14. Demonstrate top management commitment to the new philosophy by pushing the above 13 points every day.

(c)

organizations. They do so by first planning an improvement, then doing what they have planned, perhaps on a test basis. They then check to see whether the results are consistent with their expectations. When they are convinced that a plan is working, they act to fully implement it. They then improve the newly implemented plan by putting it through another P-D-C-A cycle.

Deming's fourteen-point philosophy is summarized in Figure 4.2c. The fourteen points should not be seen as a menu from which managers may pick and choose. Rather, they represent a complete package in which each individual point is essential to the whole.

For further information on Deming, see http://www.deming.org.

JOSEPH M. JURAN

Joseph M. Juran (1904–), an industrial engineer by training, established a global consulting agency called the Juran Institute (see http://www.juran.com) and published numerous books on quality. His primary contributions included managerial methodologies and systems, such as a classification of quality costs and the breakthrough sequence, which can be used to generate significant improvement in quality.

Juran suggested that quality costs be divided into four categories: internal failure costs, external failure costs, appraisal costs, and prevention costs. **Internal failure costs** are expenditures associated with products, subassemblies, or components that are not fit for use and have not yet been transferred to the customer. The cost of dealing with scrap and rework (such as reinspection, downgrading, and failure analysis costs), and avoidable process losses (such as container overflow) are all internal failure costs. **External failure costs** are expenditures associated with items that are not fit for use but have nevertheless been transferred to the customer. Warranty charges and the costs of investigating customer complaints, returning and replacing materials, and making concessions to customers are all external failure costs. **Appraisal costs** are expenditures associated with the inspection and testing of materials and services at any point in a value-adding process. **Prevention costs** are expenses accrued in efforts to prevent failure and appraisal costs. Process control costs, as well as the cost of product design reviews, quality audits, supplier evaluations, training, and quality planning, are prevention costs.

In recent years, it has become clear that in many settings, companies can achieve 100% conformance to quality specifications through the use of modern technologies, fail-proofing devices, multiple sequential inspections of process output, vigorous inspection and maintenance of equipment, and the effective design of products and processes. (Conformance to a quality specification simply means meeting the specification. A company with 100% conformance over a given period has experienced no nonconforming (or defective) items during that time.) The long-term goal of most organizations is to achieve 100% conformance. For such organizations, Figure 4.3a illustrates the relationships among prevention, appraisal, and failure costs. Efforts to eliminate defects through prevention and appraisal become more costly as 100% conformance is approached, yet failure costs continue to decline. As a result, the total quality costs are at their lowest when the company attains 100% conformance.

In certain situations 100% conformance may not be feasible, especially in the short run. Figure 4.3b illustrates this second situation:

▶ If an organization is operating to the left of the minimum point on the total quality cost curve, managers will be motivated to spend more on appraisal and prevention because a small expense in these areas can lead to significant savings in failure costs, thus lowering the total quality costs.

▶ If an organization is operating to the right of the minimum point, managers are likely to cut back on inspection or product testing or find other ways to reduce

Internal failure costs

Expenditures associated with products, subassemblies, or components that are not fit for use and have not yet been transferred to the customer.

External failure costs

Expenditures associated with items that are not fit for use but have nevertheless been transferred to the customer.

Appraisal costs

Expenditures associated with the inspection and testing of materials and services at any point in a value-adding process.

Prevention costs

Expenses accrued in efforts to prevent failure and appraisal costs.

Figure 4.3

Juran's description of quality cost relationships: failure costs, appraisal costs, and prevention costs.

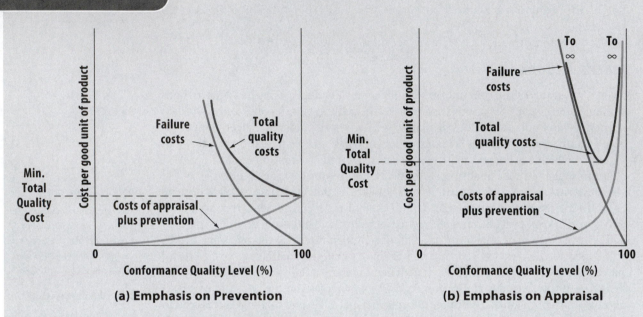

(a) Emphasis on Prevention

(b) Emphasis on Appraisal

Source: Juran, J. M. and Frank M. Gryna. *Quality Planning and Analysis, 3rd Edition,* New York: McGraw Hill, 1993, p. 25

appraisal and prevention costs. Realizing that failure costs are likely to increase with such an action, they will look for ways to scale back the appraisal and prevention costs that have the smallest impact on failure costs.

▶ Organizations that are operating close to the minimum point on the total quality cost curve will try to continue balancing appraisal and prevention costs with failure costs in the way that led them to this minimum point.

Once an organization has performed a cost-of-quality analysis, managers will begin to think of quality improvement in financial terms. In fact, they might realize that quality improvement projects offer a far superior return than stock buybacks, the purchase of equity in other firms, or new product development. Thinking about quality in financial terms also helps top managers to see the importance of their own participation in quality-related activities. Juran's breakthrough sequence, summarized in Table 4.3, is designed to enable companies to successfully identify and complete quality improvement projects with desirable financial returns.

PHILIP CROSBY

Unlike Juran and Deming, Philip Crosby (1926–) began his career in quality as an inspector and worked his way up through the ranks of quality professions. Along the way he was also a tester, an assistant foreman, a junior engineer, a reliability engineer, a group engineer, a section chief, a manager, and a director, and he ended his corporate

Table 4.3
Juran's Breakthrough
Sequence

Prove the need for breakthrough and management's willingness to support necessary changes. Management must recognize its responsibility for the system and the competitive importance of improvements that eliminate chronic waste. Quantum leaps in quality performance can come only from management-sponsored system changes. A quality council of the top executives of the company should be formed. The quality council should include representation of all key business functions. A diagnostic group composed of quality professionals and analysts should also be formed to aid the quality council.

Identify desirable projects and prioritize them. "Pareto analysis" should be used by the diagnostic group to help the quality council distinguish between the vital few projects and the useful many. Often, the vital few will be cross-functional in nature and require the quality council's sponsorship. The useful many projects frequently pertain to only one department. They do not require the direct attention of the quality council because they can be implemented within the improvement plans of the department affected.

Organize project teams. It is important to publish the projects and team members selected and to make the projects part of the business plan. This provides rights for the teams to call meetings, get help from experts, request sensitive information, and the like. Each team has its own organizational structure—a leader, members, rules for attendance, etc. A team should have a sponsor because it is not a part of the organizational hierarchy.

Verify the project need and mission. Each team should be supervised by a mission statement, which may be drafted by the diagnostic group, but must be approved by the quality council. Team members should begin by documenting the specifics of the situation for which their mission gives them responsibility.

Diagnose the causes. The team must begin with a "diagnostic journey" involving analysis of symptoms, developing theories as to the causes of the problems, testing the plausible theories, and finally establishing the root of the problem being addressed.

Provide a remedy and prove that it works effectively. The diagnostic journey is followed by a "remedial journey" that requires the development of alternative remedies for the problem, testing the various options to select the preferred solution, testing the selected solution in simulated conditions, testing the remedy in real world conditions, and establishing controls for the new situation.

Deal with resistance to change. Anticipate that the remedy will be met with natural resistance to change—and will be new to everyone outside of the team unless the team has worked hard to build bridges to the new methods that others can cross. It is important to treat people with dignity, provide for participation, provide ample time for consideration, work with recognized leaders, include no excess baggage, and clearly establish the need for the change. Resistance to change must be addressed directly. Negative attitudes that sabotage improvement efforts must be overcome.

Institute controls to hold gains. Process changes should be designed to be irreversible, and the new system should be sustainable under real operating conditions. New operating procedures must be developed and appropriate training provided to those who are affected by the change.

career as ITT's vice president of quality. According to Crosby, this tour of duty helped him to see quality management in terms of who does what specific job and to view these concepts in a people-oriented way. It comes as no surprise, then, that he felt one of the most important components of a quality improvement program was training. In 1979, he formed the Crosby Quality College (see http://www.philipcrosby.com/) to train managers in quality improvement. The practical suggestions included in Crosby's training programs have been used by hundreds of managers.

Baldrige Award
The United States' national quality award, believed to have played a significant role in promoting quality management practices. Named after Malcolm Baldrige, U.S. Secretary of Commerce from 1981 to 1987, whose managerial excellence is credited with long-term improvements in the efficiency and effectiveness of the U.S. government.

Quality System Effectiveness Measurement Processes

Today people do not talk about Deming, Juran, and Crosby or the TQM paradigm shift as much as they once did. The contributions of these innovators, however, remain evident in the practices of modern businesses. The TQM managerial approach can be seen still in the form of today's quality award programs, such as the U.S. National Quality Award program (called the Baldrige Award) or the Excellence Award bestowed by the European Foundation for Quality Management. The impact of the trio's work is also apparent in the work of the International Organization for Standardization, which maintains and administers the International Organization for Standardization (ISO) certification program.

Courtesy of the Baldrige National Quality Program at the National Institute of Standards and Technology

The Baldrige Award

The **Baldrige Award**, as mentioned above, is the United States' national quality award. Created by an act of Congress in 1987, it has played a significant role in promoting quality management practices. The purpose of the Malcolm Baldrige National Quality Award is to highlight the performance of firms that have attained excellence in quality management. Many firms, perhaps thousands, conduct internal assessments of their quality practices based on the Baldrige Award criteria. They then use the information they have obtained to identify opportunities for improvement. Figure 4.4 shows the Baldrige Award criteria framework and its interrelationships among the examination criteria. For more on the Baldrige Award, see http://www.quality.nist.gov.

ISO 9000 Certification

The International Organization for Standardization is a worldwide federation of national standards organizations (see http://www.iso.ch). The United States' representative is the National Institute for Standards and Technology (NIST). One division of NIST, the American National Standards Institute (ANSI), is responsible for developing any unique standards used by American industry. ANSI maintains the American version of the ISO 9000 standard in cooperation with the American Society for Quality Control (ASQC).

The Baldrige Award is America's top quality award. See their web site at http://www.quality.nist.gov/ for a list of winners.

Figure 4.4

The baldrige award criteria framework

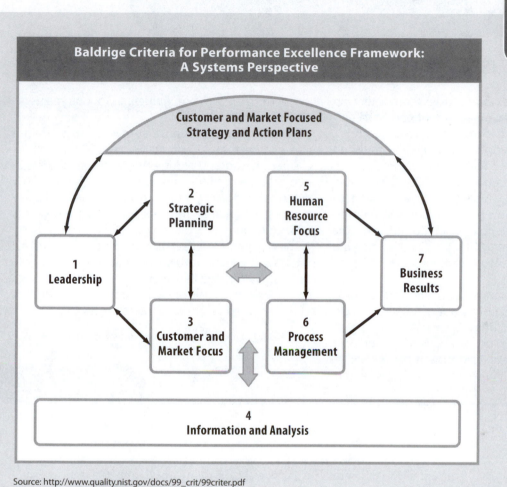

Source: http://www.quality.nist.gov/docs/99_crit/99criter.pdf

The International Organization for Standardization first established its uniform quality standards in 1987 and updated these in 2000. The **ISO 9000 standards** are actually a series of standards, the primary pair being:

▶ ISO 9001:2000—A standard under which an organization may be certified. Certification is the result of analysis of the company's management system by an accredited ISO auditor. ISO 9001:2000-certified companies can be expected to consistently meet their customer's needs and expectations as well as regulations applicable to their operations.

▶ ISO 9004:2000—A guideline for the development of quality management systems, a guidance standard. This standard helps managers understand how to use ISO 9001:2000 to develop and improve their quality management system. For example, it indicates how to do a self-assessment under the 9001 standard and provides a managerial perspective on a firm's quality management activities.

ISO 9000 standards

A series of uniform quality standards, covering requirements for design, development, production, installation, servicing, and manufacturing.

INTEGRATING OM:

Satisfying Customers at Intel Corporation

Intel Corporation is the world's largest computer chip maker and a leading manufacturer of personal computer, networking, and communications products. Like other influential companies, Intel has established performance awards for its suppliers: the Supplier Continuous Quality Improvement (SCQI) award and the Preferred Quality Supplier (PQS) award. These awards acknowledge outstanding quality and performance among Intel suppliers. In addition to the awards, Intel recognizes SCQI and PQS winners with an advertisement in the *Wall Street Journal*'s American and Asian editions.

To qualify for SCQI status, suppliers must attain a score of more than 625 points out of 1,000 on a self-assessment based on Baldrige Award criteria (scores in each of seven sections must be above 55%), and 95% performance against set improvement plans. In addi-

tion, performance to firm guidelines for one year is required to qualify.

To qualify for PQS status, suppliers must attain a score of more than 525 points out of 1,000 on a self-assessment based on Baldrige Award criteria (scores in each of seven sections must be above 50%), and 80% performance against set improvement plans. In addition, performance to firm guidelines for one year is required to qualify.

The SCQI and PQS awards are part of Intel's SCQI process, whose goal is to encourage Intel's key suppliers to strive for excellence and continuous improvement. A key supplier is one who provides a product or service deemed essential to Intel's success.

Source: Adapted from http://pentium.intel.com/pressroom/archive/releases/cn32698c.htm

▶ A significant benefit of ISO certification is the market access it provides. ISO certification was originally intended as a requirement for doing business in certain industries within the European Community (EC) and with the governments of EC countries. The idea was that a common standard would prevent a company from having to comply with separate standards in every country where it did business. Even outside the EC, obtaining such certification frequently allows firms to avoid meeting the requirements of various supplier certification programs promoted by their customers. In fact, many firms now require their suppliers to be ISO certified, and even more prefer ISO-certified suppliers over those that are not certified.

Quality Detection, Prevention, and Improvement Processes

Detection Processes

In business today, one often hears the saying "You can't inspect quality into the product." This is true particularly if quality is defined in terms of customer satisfaction and the inspection occurs after the product is complete. Yet inspection is a skill critical to any quality program, especially these days, when data-based decision making lies at the heart of quality management. Inspection provides the data used in any decision-making application. Without reliable data gathered under a well-reasoned plan for inspection, even the most sophisticated statistical techniques are useless.

Inspection generally refers to the process of comparing the characteristics of a product or service with the characteristics that define its acceptability. Historically, the term has been used to refer to the measurement of certain dimensional or physical characteristics that represent important properties of component products and service outcomes. Dimensional properties describe a product's size and weight, including measures such as length, diameter, ground clearance, or liquid volume. Physical characteristics can include the color, density, or porosity of an item; the legibility of printed matter; the fit of a joint; the cleanliness of a facility; the duration of a telephone service encounter; and the presence or absence of a handshake, eye contact, or a smile in a personal service encounter.

Physical and dimensional characteristics can be **attribute measures** (which are measured in categories), but they provide more information when they are **variable measures** (which are measured on a continuous scale). Obtaining a variable measurement usually costs more than an attribute measurement; hence, the choice of measurement must be based on the need for the data. For example, a child's height is measured as an attribute at amusement parks, where a quick comparison with a cutoff point marked on a measuring stick indicates whether a child is tall enough for a particular ride. In that setting, there is no reason to take the time to measure the exact height of each customer. On the other hand, to properly assess the child's growth, a pediatrician would measure a child's height as a variable, not an attribute.

Historically, inspection has been distinguished from **testing**, which refers to the measurement of the performance of complex assemblies and service systems. We speak of the test weight of fishing line, tests of the reliability of a computer system, or the "torture chamber" test used to try the durability of an automobile's paint job.

In an academic setting, professors typically use both testing and inspection to determine the grade that best reflects a student's performance. Taking attendance or giving a fixed number of points for participation in a particular exercise amounts to inspection. True/false and multiple-choice questions are arguably forms of inspection, in that they measure only whether or not the student knows (or can guess) the meaning of a term or acronym. On the other hand, complex homework problems, programming assignments, and integrative essay questions represent a testing of the student's performance. They can be used to evaluate the level of development of some combination of skill and understanding. Whether the information on a student's performance comes from inspection or testing, it is valuable only to the extent that it is relevant to the learning objectives set out in the course syllabus. That is why professors rely primarily on objective test questions in survey courses, which are designed to provide broad exposure to a particular topic, and on subjective questions in upper-level courses, which are designed to explore a subject in depth.

Today, the terms "testing" and "inspection" are often used interchangeably. Both are sources of the data used in quality management. In fact, without inspection, there could be no assessment of quality and no data-driven decision making. Each week many firms may manufacture thousands of items or experience thousands of service encounters, which implies that some clear plan for inspection is critical. Whatever the plan, it must be cost effective, and it must provide the data needed for the managerial purposes of detection of nonconformities, prevention of nonconformities, and process improvement.

Inspection

The process of comparing the characteristics of a product or service with the characteristics that define its acceptability.

Attribute measures

Measurements of physical and dimensional characteristics in categories.

Variable measures

Measurements of physical and dimensional characteristics on a continuous scale.

Testing

The measurement of the performance of complex assemblies and service systems.

INTEGRATING OM:

Satisfying Customers at Ritz-Carlton Hotels

Imagine a hotel where employees get more than 100 hours of customer service training annually, check-in is smooth and quick, guest rooms are renovated every 90 days, and every employee works as an individual customer service department interrupting his or her duties whenever necessary to help a guest. Systematic changes such as these have helped the Ritz-Carlton Hotel company revolutionize its service industry, for which it won the Malcolm Baldrige National Quality Award. The Atlanta-based firm was the first hotel company to win the award and has won it twice. In the meantime, consistent with the results experienced by other winners, it has increased productivity, market share, customer satisfaction, and employee satisfaction.

The daily Service Quality Indicator (SQI) is displayed throughout the hotel, enabling all departments to monitor key production and guest-service processes up to the minute to address challenges and areas of need immediately. The SQI of all hotels is displayed on flat-screen monitors in the corporate office, ensuring immediate communication of hotel issues and strategies to upper managment. All employees are empowered to make a difference. Using tools ranging from quality improvement teams to guest surveys, employees examine every process in the hotel to ensure that the most efficient and customer-service driven practice is in place. Examples include:

◗ A front-desk project team in Osaka reduced check-in time by 50%.

◗ In response to an increase in family travel, a cross-functional team from the two Atlanta hotels and the corporate office developed a guest room child safety program, POLO (Protect Our Little Ones).

◗ A guest-recognition database (CLASS—Customer Loyalty Anticipation Satisfaction System) is the company-wide tool used to meet and anticipate preferences and requirements of repeat customers.

◗ A team developed CARE (Clean and Repair Everything) by merging the deep-cleaning housekeeping processes with the engineering preventative maintenance schedule. CARE guarantees all guest rooms to be defect-free every 90 days.

◗ By staggering the lunch hours of the housekeeping supervisors, a cross-functional team of hourly employees in Barcelona tackled the problem of ensuring guest room readiness when a guest checks in.

◗ Based on the results of customer inputs, business and leisure travelers on The Club level are checked in according to the specific needs of each group. Business travelers are checked in quickly and efficiently, whereas leisure guests are given the option of having a more pampered check-in, receiving Champagne and a more thorough presentation of the hotel services and amenities.

◗ A team of catering managers created the first comprehensive wedding program in the hospitality industry designed to meet the bride's needs from initial telephone call to the first anniversary.

Source: Adapted from http://www.ritzcarlton.com

Acceptance sampling

A tool that uses information gained from a sample of finished items to determine whether or not to accept the entire batch from which the sample was taken.

ACCEPTANCE SAMPLING

Acceptance sampling uses information gained from a sample of finished items to determine whether or not to accept the entire batch from which the sample was taken. This type of sampling should be used only when the supply process is unstable and the cost of acceptance sampling is less than the cost of 0% or 100% inspection. (When the supply process is stable, 100% or 0% inspection will always be less expensive than sampling.)

Sampling Plans Using acceptance sampling, inspectors may reject a batch of thousands of items based on the presence of a small number of nonconforming items in a sample. In the sampling plan shown in Figure 4.5a, a production batch of 10,000 items is evaluated by taking a sample of 200 items. The letter *c* is usually used to represent the acceptance number or the cutoff point between acceptance and rejection of the entire batch. In this example, $c = 5$, meaning that if five or fewer of the 200 items are found to be nonconforming, the entire batch will be accepted, but if six or more of the items are found to be nonconforming, the entire batch will be rejected. Depending on the costs of inspection and of the items being inspected, a rejected batch would then be subjected to 100% inspection or it would be discarded.

For example, let's say that Fred buys electronic chips from a supplier in Southeast Asia. Waiting for a replacement for a rejected batch might disrupt his production schedule. In that case, Fred would probably pay local inspectors, either in his own company or in an outside firm, to go through the entire batch and sort out the problem chips. (If Fred's supply contract provided for such a circumstance, he might even be able to charge the supplier for the cost of inspecting the batch, as well as the cost of the rejected chips.) Nonconforming items found during the 100% inspection would be set apart for repair or disposal. Finally, because errors can occur even in a 100% inspection, the batch might have to be inspected once again using acceptance sampling.

The acceptance sampling plan shown in Figure 4.5a is called a "single sampling" plan because the decision to accept or reject the lot is based on just one sample. Figure 4.5b shows a "double sampling" plan that is comparable to the single sampling plan. In this double sampling plan, the sample size (*n*) is 125, and there are two cutoff points for the first sample, an upper limit of five and a lower limit of two nonconforming items. If the number of nonconforming items in the first sample is two or less, inspectors will accept the entire lot; if it is five or more, they will reject the entire lot. If the number of nonconforming items falls between two and five, the plan suggests that the inspector dig a little deeper and take a second sample of 125 items (making the

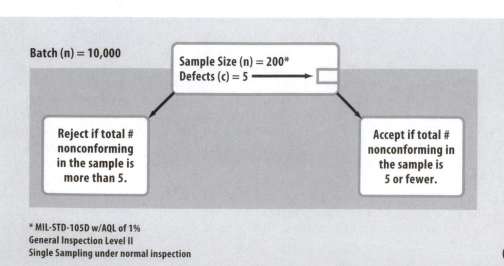

Figure 4.5

(a) Single acceptance sampling

Batch (n) = 10,000

Sample Size (n) = 200*
Defects (c) = 5

Reject if total # nonconforming in the sample is more than 5.

Accept if total # nonconforming in the sample is 5 or fewer.

* MIL-STD-105D w/AQL of 1%
General Inspection Level II
Single Sampling under normal inspection

(a)

Figure 4.5

(b) Double acceptance sampling

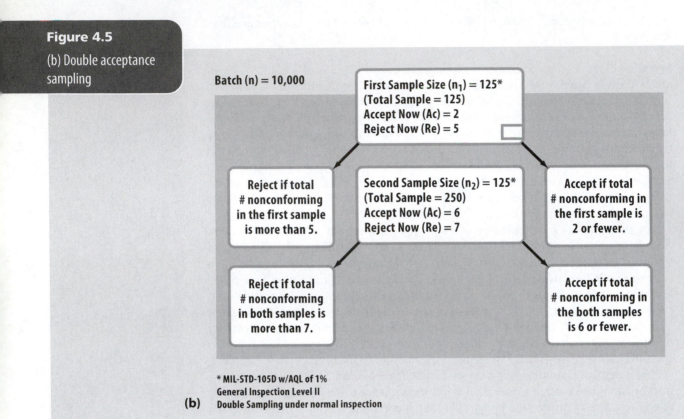

Batch (n) = 10,000

First Sample Size (n₁) = 125*
(Total Sample = 125)
Accept Now (Ac) = 2
Reject Now (Re) = 5

Reject if total # nonconforming in the first sample is more than 5.

Second Sample Size (n₂) = 125*
(Total Sample = 250)
Accept Now (Ac) = 6
Reject Now (Re) = 7

Accept if total # nonconforming in the first sample is 2 or fewer.

Reject if total # nonconforming in both samples is more than 7.

Accept if total # nonconforming in the both samples is 6 or fewer.

(b)   * MIL-STD-105D w/AQL of 1%
General Inspection Level II
Double Sampling under normal inspection

Sampling error

A situation where a sample is biased, or unrepresentative of the batch.

Inspection error

A mistake that occurs when the measurement applied to the sample is observed, recorded, or interpreted incorrectly.

Type I error

When a lot that should be accepted is rejected.

Producer's risk

The risk of making type I errors.

total sample size 250). Note that in the second sample, the cutoff points, six and seven, refer to the total number of nonconforming items in both samples.

When quality is typically either very good or very poor (that is, when it is bimodal), double sampling may be more cost-effective than single sampling because decisions will often be made based on the initial sample and the second sample will not be taken. But when the distribution of lot quality is *not* bimodal, double sampling can be more expensive than single sampling because, in order to make a conclusion regarding the quality of the batch, both samples will have to be taken. (Recall that the single sampling plan was based on a sample size of 200 rather than 250.) For example, Fred's chip supplier might have two different factories—one in Indonesia and another in Malaysia—but one central distribution center in Singapore. Let's say the chips from Malaysia typically meet Fred's acceptance criteria, but the chips from Indonesia typically do not. If Fred has no way of knowing the source of the chips he receives, he might be able to tell the difference based on a very small sample. Occasionally, he might need a second sample to make a final determination regarding the acceptability of a lot. Because he typically makes his decision based on the first sample, he will save money over time by using double sampling.

Another type of plan, "sequential sampling," extends the process of double sampling through several iterations. Figure 4.5c shows a sequential sampling plan. Note that the entire lot could be accepted or rejected on the basis of a first sample size of just 50 items.

Error, Risk, and Tolerance Levels Acceptance sampling is not a foolproof procedure. Based on the results of acceptance sampling, inspectors can reject lots that should be

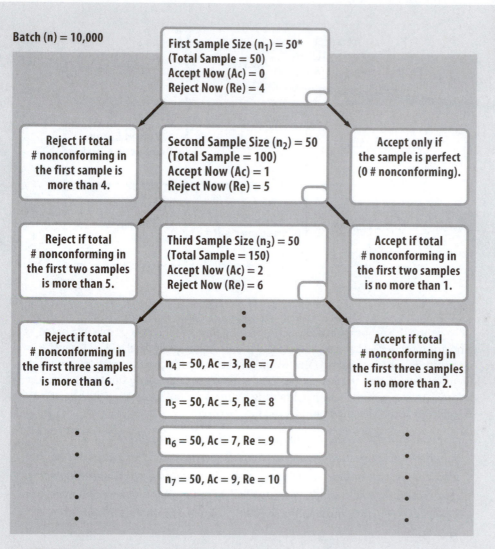

Figure 4.5

(c) Sequential acceptance sampling

Batch (n) = 10,000

First Sample Size (n_1) = 50*
(Total Sample = 50)
Accept Now (Ac) = 0
Reject Now (Re) = 4

Reject if total # nonconforming in the first sample is more than 4.

Second Sample Size (n_2) = 50
(Total Sample = 100)
Accept Now (Ac) = 1
Reject Now (Re) = 5

Accept only if the sample is perfect (0 # nonconforming).

Reject if total # nonconforming in the first two samples is more than 5.

Third Sample Size (n_3) = 50
(Total Sample = 150)
Accept Now (Ac) = 2
Reject Now (Re) = 6

Accept if total # nonconforming in the first two samples is no more than 1.

Reject if total # nonconforming in the first three samples is more than 6.

$n_4 = 50$, Ac = 3, Re = 7

Accept if total # nonconforming in the first three samples is no more than 2.

$n_5 = 50$, Ac = 5, Re = 8

$n_6 = 50$, Ac = 7, Re = 9

$n_7 = 50$, Ac = 9, Re = 10

* MIL-STD-105D w/AQL of 1%
General Inspection Level II
Sequential Sampling under normal inspection

(c)

accepted and accept lots that should be rejected. Such mistakes may result from errors in sampling or inspection or both. A **sampling error** occurs when a sample is biased or unrepresentative of the batch. An **inspection error** occurs when the measurement that is applied to the sample is observed, recorded, or interpreted incorrectly.

When a lot that should be accepted is rejected, a **type I error** has occurred. The risk of making type I errors, which is referred to as **producer's risk**, is represented by the Greek letter α (alpha). When a lot that should have been rejected is accepted, a **type II error** has occurred. The risk of making a type II error, which is called **consumer's risk**, is represented by the Greek letter β (beta). Figure 4.6 summarizes the potential errors and risks associated with acceptance sampling.

Type II error

When a lot that should be rejected is accepted.

Consumer's risk

The risk of making a type II error, represented by the Greek letter (beta).

Figure 4.6

Sampling errors

Batch Really Is: \ We Decide To:	Accept	Reject
Acceptable	Correct decision….	**Type I Error (Producer's Risk)**
Not acceptable	**Type II Error (Consumer's Risk)**	Correct decision….

Acceptable quality level (AQL)

The proportion of non-conforming items acceptable in a batch. This is the level of quality the customer would only expect to be rejected very infrequently (recognizing the limitations of a supplier's process, the limitations of acceptance sampling, and the cost of obtaining higher levels of quality).

Lot tolerance percent defective (LTPD)

The level of quality that the customer would expect the sampling plan to very infrequently accept (recognizing that such a failure rate could disrupt production schedules, damage other inventory, and otherwise harm the product's quality). This is sometimes called the rejectable quality level.

To define the proportion of nonconforming items that is acceptable in a batch, statisticians have devised a parameter called the **acceptable quality level (AQL)**. This is the level of quality at which the customer would expect a product to be rejected only infrequently (recognizing the limitations of a supplier's process, the limitations of acceptance sampling, and the cost of obtaining higher levels of quality). With regard to the AQL, Juran and colleague Frank Gryna have written:

> *It should be emphasized to both internal and external suppliers that* all *product submitted for inspection is expected to meet specifications. An acceptable quality level does not mean the submission of a certain amount of nonconforming product is approved. The AQL simply recognizes that, under sampling, some nonconforming product will pass through the sampling scheme. (Juran and Gryna, 1993, 466–467)*

As the following illustration points out, the use of the term *acceptable* in AQL is not entirely consistent with common use. In the early 1980s, IBM decided to try purchasing manufactured parts from a Japanese supplier. Engineers at IBM established specifications for the parts and set a limit, three parts out of 10,000, on the number of nonconforming parts that would be considered acceptable. With the first delivery, the Japanese supplier enclosed a letter stating, "We Japanese have a hard time understanding North American business practices. But the three defective units per 10,000 have been included and wrapped separately. Hope this pleases" (*Toronto Sun*, April 25, 1983, p. 6).

The **lot tolerance percent defective (LTPD)**, sometimes called the rejectable quality level, is the level of quality that the customer would expect the sampling plan to accept very infrequently (recognizing that such a failure rate could disrupt production schedules, damage other inventory, and otherwise harm the product's quality).

Figure 4.7 illustrates both the LTPD and the AQL as a percentage of nonconforming items in a lot. The higher the value on the horizontal axis, the poorer the quality of

Figure 4.7

OC curves

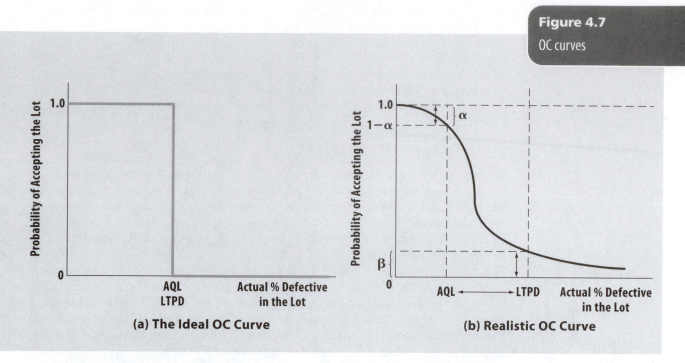

(a) The Ideal OC Curve

(b) Realistic OC Curve

the lot. The probability of acceptance of lots of various quality levels can be shown on an **operating characteristics (OC) curve**. OC curves can be used to describe the risk of type I and type II errors in an acceptance sampling plan. The ideal OC curve is shown in Figure 4.7a. (Again, notice that the higher the value on the horizontal axis, the poorer the quality of the lot.) This discontinuous curve represents a perfectly discriminating plan that allows no type I or type II errors. The probability that acceptable lots will be accepted is 1.0, and the probability that unacceptable lots will be accepted is 0. With such an acceptance plan, the AQL need not be distinguished from the LTPD; the only relevant issue is the quality threshold that marks the difference between what is acceptable and what is not.

Unfortunately, because of sampling error and inspection error, no acceptance sampling plan is perfectly discriminating. No real-world sampling plan has the OC curve shown in Figure 4.7a. Figure 4.7b presents a realistic OC curve, which is essentially defined by the two points (AQL, 1-α) and (LTPD, β). The probabilities α and β represent the producer and consumer risk, respectively—in other words, the risk of error in the sampling or inspection process. From zero to the AQL on the horizontal axis, lots are seldom rejected; beyond the LTPD level, lots are seldom accepted. Between the AQL and the LTPD, the chance that the lot will be accepted declines as the percentage of nonconforming items rises. If the curve in Figure 4.7b were steeper, both α and β would be smaller, as would the range of quality levels between the AQL and LTPD. Steeper OC curves represent more discriminating sampling plans; from that perspective, they are desirable. On the other hand, an OC curve may be made steeper only by increasing the size of the sample; thus, the more discriminating the plan, the more costly.

If the sample size is held constant, the steepness of the OC curve cannot be changed. But by changing the acceptance number (c), buyers can increase α and decrease β, or vice versa. Increasing the acceptance number makes it easier for inspectors to accept rejectable lots and more difficult for them to reject acceptable lots. Therefore, it increases the risk of type II error, β, and reduces the risk of type I error,

Operating characteristics (OC) curve

A representation of the probability of acceptance of lots of various quality levels.

α. Conversely, decreasing the acceptance number will increase the risk of type I error, α, and reduce the risk of type II error, β.

Ultimately, the consumer will pay for the sampling plan and for both types of error, because producers pass their costs on to consumers. It is therefore important that industrial buyers consider the risks and costs associated with various acceptance sampling plans when choosing an acceptance plan. Studying and comparing the OC curves and the costs associated with various plans will help buyers to select an appropriate plan.

STATISTICAL PROCESS CONTROL

In contrast to acceptance sampling, in which inspection is used to decide whether to accept or reject finished output, process control inspection helps managers to decide whether or not a production process is operating as expected. Rather than waiting until a production batch has been finished, inspectors use process control techniques to detect the symptoms of problems while a batch is being produced, and then make any necessary adjustments.

Process control may be accomplished through real-time inspection of 100% of the product passing through some control point, or it may be done using a mechanical device that automatically adjusts for process changes. For example, some firms in the paper industry use Measurex™ machines to continuously monitor the thickness of paper in process and automatically adjust process controls. One alternative to 100% inspection is to take samples at specified time intervals. In beer brewing, certain variables need only be monitored at specific intervals in the fermentation process. When processes are monitored and adjusted on the basis of sample data, **statistical process control (SPC)** is being used. SPC helps managers determine what type of variation is present in the process they are monitoring.

Types of Variation in a System   One type of variation, called **common cause variation** (also referred to as **random variation**), is the natural variation inherent in any system. It arises from a large number of unidentifiable and random causes. Deming and Juran have

Statistical process control (SPC)

When processes are monitored and adjusted on the basis of sample data.

Common cause variation (or random variation)

The natural variation inherent in any system.

Efforts to improve the quality of a firm's product service bundle or the way in which it is produced should be based upon data and facts when ever possible.

Flying Colours Ltd/Digital Vision/Getty Images Inc.

suggested that 85% of the variation in a production system is common cause variation inherent in the design of the system.

When common cause variation is the only type of variation present in a system or process, the system or process is said to be in **control**, meaning that management need not take any special action. For example, if some unidentifiable random event causes outstanding or poor performance, the outstanding performance should not be rewarded with a bonus, nor should poor performance be punished. Instead, managers should attempt to identify and reduce the root cause(s) of outstanding or poor performance. Juran's breakthrough sequence can be used to make radical system improvements by attacking the vital few causes on a project-by-project basis. In addition, worker teams can be empowered to make ongoing incremental improvements by attacking the useful many causes of variation.

Unlike common cause variation, the presence of **special cause variation** (also called **assignable variation**) usually reflects a significant change in the system. Typically, the root cause of such a change is identifiable; managers and workers should therefore seek to identify it.

If the unusual symptom is desirable—for example, fewer nonconformities than usual—managers should find a way to ensure that the symptom's root cause is preserved and incorporated in the system at all times. For instance, if the root cause is that a worker has consistently and effectively performed her job in a new way, her job description might be changed and she might be rewarded with a bonus. Or if the root cause is the use of particularly efficient equipment, it might be used in comparable parts of the process. For example, let's say that Tom Jackson's airline discovered that departures at one airport have been late much less often than usual. In searching for the cause of this desirable variation, managers found that the standard baggage-handling machine had been replaced at that airport with a newer model. If so, the airline should consider installing that type of baggage-handling machine at comparable airports the airline serves.

If the unusual symptom is undesirable—for example, more nonconformities than usual—managers should find a way to eliminate the root cause. A disgruntled worker who is unwilling to perform according to his job description or who is purposely undermining the system might be fired. Or if the root cause is inefficient equipment, that equipment might be removed. If, for example, Tom's airline found that departures at one airport have been late much more often than usual because a particular baggage-handling machine has been breaking down frequently, the appropriate response would probably be to replace that machine.

When managers respond to a common cause variation by taking some special action, they introduce more variation into the system. The cause of this type of variation, which is assignable to management, is referred to as **tampering**. Tampering amounts to playing games with the measurement system.

A fourth type of variation, **structural variation**, is caused by patterns in the system. For example, workforce performance may vary by shift; an individual worker's performance may vary by the time of day; and a machine's performance may vary with the maintenance interval or the plant's ambient temperature.

Sampling Distributions

How do managers distinguish among the different types of variation in a production system? One way is to examine the sampling distribution for the process. A **sampling distribution** identifies the probability that a particular sample statistic will take on a given value if common cause variation is the only type of variation present in the system. In other words, the sampling distribution answers the question: What are the

Control

A situation where common cause variation is the only type of variation present in a system or process. In this case, management need not take any special action.

Special cause variation (or assignable variation)

Unlike common cause variation, the presence usually reflects a significant change in the system.

Tampering

When managers respond to a common cause variation by taking some special action, which introduces more variation into the system.

Structural variation

Changes caused by patterns in the system.

Sampling distribution

The probability that a particular sample statistic will take on a given value if common cause variation is the only type of variation present in the system.

chances that this process is operating as expected? By taking a sample and calculating the statistics for which the sampling distribution is known, managers can make inferences about the likely nature of the system from which the sample was taken. If both the sample and the sampling distribution suggest that the behavior of the system is unusual, managers can conclude that special cause variation is present. That is, the process is not operating as expected; either the results are too good to be true, or there is some problem that must be dealt with.

Consider the distribution of height measurements among the students in your class. Unless you are attending a special class for basketball players, there is probably quite a lot of variation in height among your classmates. If you were to place your classmates into groups of two, three, four, and so forth, and average the heights of the members of those groups, the averages would vary much less than the individual heights, because the tall people and the short people would tend to cancel each other out. The same logic can be applied to the output of a production system.

The central limit theorem, which describes the sampling distribution of means illustrated in the last paragraph, states that if a population has a mean of μ ("mu") and a standard deviation of σ "sigma"), and if all possible samples of size n are taken and their means ($\bar{X}$s) calculated, the sampling distribution of those means will have a mean of μ and a standard deviation of $\sigma/\sqrt{n}$ and as n increases the distribution will approach normality. Figure 4.8a illustrates the central limit theorem. In Figure 4.8b,

Figure 4.8
Central Limit Theorem

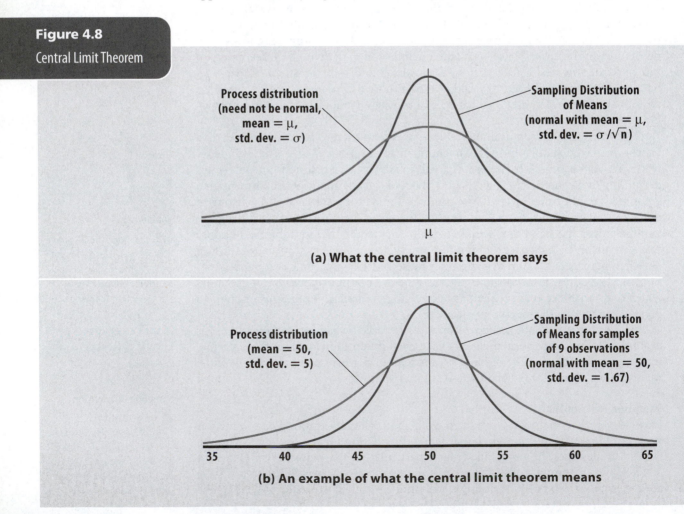

Process distribution (need not be normal, mean = μ, std. dev. = σ)

Sampling Distribution of Means (normal with mean = μ, std. dev. = $\sigma/\sqrt{n}$)

μ

(a) What the central limit theorem says

Process distribution (mean = 50, std. dev. = 5)

Sampling Distribution of Means for samples of 9 observations (normal with mean = 50, std. dev. = 1.67)

35   40   45   50   55   60   65

(b) An example of what the central limit theorem means

Figure 4.9

Type I & II errors with Shewhart limits

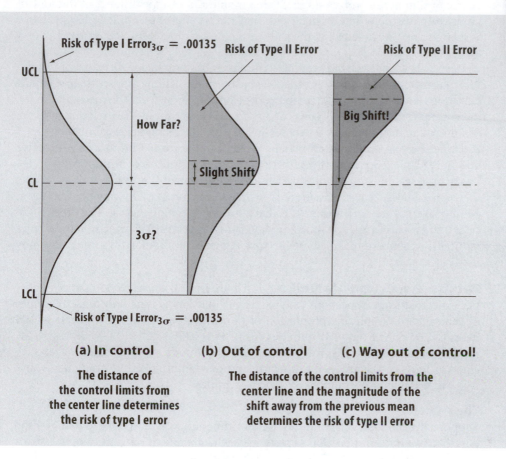

(a) In control

The distance of the control limits from the center line determines the risk of type I error

(b) Out of control   **(c) Way out of control!**

The distance of the control limits from the center line and the magnitude of the shift away from the previous mean determines the risk of type II error

we apply the theorem by setting the mean, μ equal to 50; sample size, n, equal to 9; and standard deviation, σ, equal to 5, which implies that the sampling distribution of means has a mean, $\mu_{\bar{x}}$, of 50 and a standard deviation ($\sigma_{\bar{X}}$) of $5/\sqrt{9} = 1.67$. Now, suppose we took a sample of nine observations from this theoretical system and obtained a sample mean higher than 55. With very low risk of a type I error, we could conclude that special variation exists in this system.

Control Charts and Rules of Run **Control charts** are statistical tools that allow decision makers to distinguish processes that are in control from those that are out of control. As Figure 4.9a shows, a control chart has a center line (CL), an upper control limit (UCL), and a lower control limit (LCL), all of which are calculated using information about the sampling distribution for the statistic plotted on the chart. (A **control limit** is a value used to distinguish between commonly expected and unusual values for a sample statistic.) Sample statistics are plotted against these limits; any point that falls outside the limits is considered an indicator of special cause variation in the system that generated the sample.

As Figure 4.9a shows, the distance of the upper and lower control limits from the center line determines the risk of both a type I error (concluding that the process is out of control when it is really in control) and a type II error (concluding that the process is in control when it is not). Figure 4.9a also shows that when a process is in control, the probability of a value falling outside either of the control limits is very small.

Control charts

Statistical tools that allow decision makers to distinguish processes that are in control from those that are out of control.

Control limit

A value used to distinguish between commonly expected and unusual values for a sample statistic.

Figures 4.9b and c show that the probability of a type II error is a function of both the degree of shift in the process statistic being monitored and the distance of the control limits from the center line. A small shift may not be of as much practical significance as a large shift. Fortunately, as the shift in the process increases, the probability of a type II error decreases.

Walter Shewhart, who has been called the father of statistical quality control, was the first to use such charts. Shewhart suggested using control limits that are three standard deviations (of the appropriate sampling distribution) away from the mean. In theory, there is no reason why three sigma (or 3σ) control limits should be preferred to limits of some other distance from the center line. Rather, the relative costs of making type I and type II errors should determine the distance of the control limits from the center line. In the United States, however, three sigma control limits are commonly used.

We have seen that any point that falls outside a control chart's limits may indicate that some special cause variation is affecting the process. In practice, however, additional rules are used to conclude that a process is out of control. The other rules, called the "rules of run," are based on patterns in the control chart. Using these rules reduces the chance of making type II errors. Figure 4.10 summarizes some commonly used rules of run.

Statistical Process Control by Attribute Attribute control charts rely on sample statistics generated from inspections yielding results that can assume only a fixed number of values. For example, the proportion of nonconforming items in a sample of 100 items can be one of only 101 numbers (0.00, 0.01, 0.02 . . . 0.99, 1.00). Similarly, the number of nonconformities must be an integer. Common attribute control charts include *p*-charts, which are used to study the proportion of nonconforming items, and *c*-charts, which plot the number of nonconformities.

The *p*-Chart

Suppose, like Tom Jackson, you work for an airline, and you have noticed that over the past three years, the proportion of passengers who are told to go to the wrong gate for departure has averaged 2%. The ability to direct passengers to the correct gate is, obviously, a critical process attribute. Airline employees will not hold a plane for a passenger who fails to reach the gate by departure time. At the same time, the airline's goal is to satisfy customers completely, and passengers are not satisfied until both they and their luggage have reached their destination on time.

If you found that in a sample of 500 passengers, 20 had been given faulty instructions, what would you think? Is this an unusual situation that needs to be investigated? Should the person at the information desk be reprimanded or trained better? Or, is this just a normal variation in the complex process of assigning planes to gates and communicating those assignments to passengers through computer monitors and airline personnel? What would you think if on each of the last four days, samples of 500 passengers yielded only one faulty instruction? Would you consider that result too good to be true? Or would you think there had been some real improvement in your airline's service—or that someone is covering up his errors?

Unless you know the distribution of the percentage of faulty instructions the airline has experienced in the past, you cannot answer these questions. Knowing that the average has been 2% (or 10 out of 500) is not sufficient information. What you must know is whether the deviation from the mean represented by a sample with 20 faulty instructions is a common deviation or an unusual one. The same statement applies to the samples with only one faulty instruction.

Fortunately, statistical theory can provide a picture of the distribution of the percentage of faulty instructions, called the sampling distribution of the proportion

Figure 4.10

Rules of runs

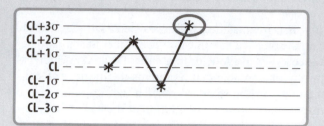

1 point more than 3σ above (or below) the center line.

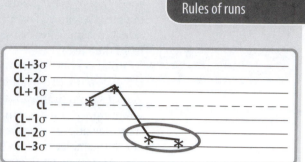

2 points in a row more than 2σ above (or below) the center line.

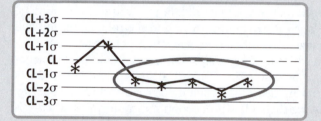

5 points in a row more than 1σ above (or below) the center line.

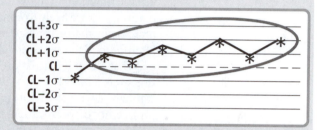

7 points in a row above (or below) the center line.

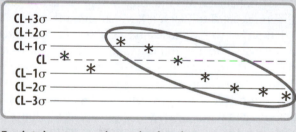

7 points in a row moving up (or down)

nonconforming, or the sampling distribution of p. The sampling distribution of p has a mean of $\bar{p}$ and a standard deviation of σ_p. The formulas for these variables are:

Sample size $= n$

proportion nonconforming in i^{th} sample $= p_i = \dfrac{\#\ nonconforming\ in\ sample\ i}{n}$

average proportion nonconforming $= \bar{p} = \dfrac{\displaystyle\sum_{i=1}^{m} p_i}{m}$

standard deviation of proportion nonconforming $= \sigma_p = \sqrt{\dfrac{\bar{p}(1-\bar{p})}{n}}$

In the case of the process for informing passengers of the correct departure gate, you were given $\bar{p}$ (it was 2%, or 0.02). You can now find σ_p. Using this formula, you discover that σ_p is 0.0062609. Because the proportion of nonconforming instructions in the sample with 20 faulty instructions was 20/500 = 0.04, and $\bar{p}$ is 0.02, the proportion nonconforming for that sample is $(.04 - .02)/0.0062609 = 3.194$ standard deviations from the mean.

What are the odds that no unusual circumstances will exist when a sample attribute is 3.194 standard deviations from the mean? The value for the number of standard deviations from the mean is the z-score, which allows us to use the standard normal distribution. (Z is the continuous random variable that represents the number of standard deviations away from the mean in the standard normal distribution.) If you check the table of values for the standard normal distribution at the back of this text (see Appendix 1), you will discover that the probability is approximately equal to $(1 - .99929) = 0.00071$. (To get the normal probability used above with a computer, use the function "(1-NORMSDIST(3.194)" in an Excel spreadsheet.) Given this information, you are likely to conclude that you need to find the root cause of the dramatic increase in the percentage of faulty instructions. If you find the root cause, you will attempt to institute system changes that will prevent a repetition of the problem.

What about the situation in which for four straight days, only 1 out of 500 instructions was faulty? Here $p = .002$; thus, z is $(.002 - .02)/0.0062609 = -2.875$, or 2.875 standard deviations below the mean. Using the standard normal distribution table, the probability of your sample having such a low proportion nonconforming when $\bar{p}$ is 0.02 is approximately 0.0021. The probability of the same result occurring four times in a row can be found using the rule of probability, $P(A \cap B) = P(A) \times P(B)$. Therefore, the probability of obtaining four consecutive samples with only one faulty instruction is equal to $(0.0021)^4$, which amounts to less than two chances in 100 billion. In this case, you would again conclude that something unusual must be going on. Since you like the results, you will want to discover the root cause of such excellent performance and institute controls to ensure that it continues.

Control charts, more specifically p-charts, help managers and workers to deal with the kinds of problem we have just discussed. Instead of going to the standard normal distribution table and looking up a z-score every time they take a sample, they use a control chart to decide whether or not a variation is unusual by comparing $\bar{p}$ for the sample to the limits of the p-chart. Charting the values over time also allows managers to see any patterns, or runs, in the data.

Because this chapter follows American practice, which is based on Shewhart's suggestion of 3σ limits, the formulas for the upper control limit (UCL), center line (CL), and lower control limit (LCL) on a p-chart are as follows:

$$UCL_p = \bar{p} + 3\sigma_p = \bar{p} + 3\sqrt{\frac{\bar{p}(1 - \bar{p})}{n}}$$

$$CL_p = \bar{p}$$

$$UCL_p = \bar{p} - 3\sigma_p = \bar{p} - 3\sqrt{\frac{\bar{p}(1 - \bar{p})}{n}}$$

To return to the airline example, suppose you took 10 samples of 500 departure instructions each and found the following numbers of incorrect instructions in each sample: 10, 12, 6, 14, 11, 9, 4, 14, 13, 10. You could construct a p-chart and plot these observations as follows. The chart's center line and limits are $CL = 0.02$, $UCL = 0.02 + 3(0.0062609) = 0.0387829$, and $LCL = 0.02 - 3(0.0062609) = 0.001217$. Figure 4.11 shows the finished p-chart.

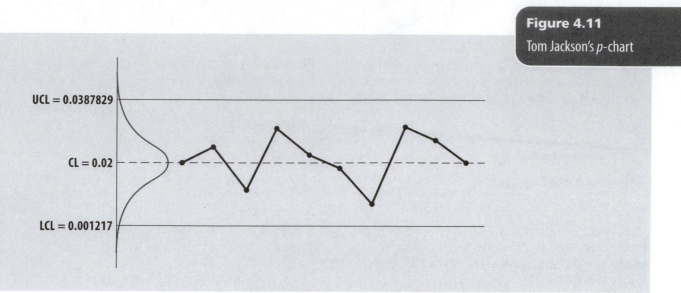

Figure 4.11

Tom Jackson's *p*-chart

The *np*-Chart

Often it is easier to maintain and interpret a *p*-chart by converting it from representation of the proportion nonconforming to the number nonconforming in a sample. This can be done very simply by multiplying the center-line, UCL, and LCL values for the *p*-chart by the sample size used to calculate *p*. Thus, any value pertinent to the *p*-chart can be converted to a value for an *np* chart as follows:

$$UCL_{np} = n\bar{p} + 3n\sigma_p = n\bar{p} + 3\sqrt{n\bar{p}(1-\bar{p})}$$

$$CL_{np} = n\bar{p}$$

$$UCL_{np} = n\bar{p} - 3n\sigma_p = n\bar{p} - 3\sqrt{n\bar{p}(1-\bar{p})}$$

(Note: We may refer to $n\sigma_p$ as σ_{np}, the standard deviation for the *np*-chart.)

In the case of the airline example above, the center-line of the corresponding *np*-chart is $500 \times 0.02 = 10$ and represents the average number of incorrect instructions per sample. The standard deviation, σ_{np}, is $500 \times (0.0062609) = 3.13045$. Thus, the UCL and LCL for the *np*-chart are $10 + 3 \times 3.13045 = 19.39135$ and $10 - 3 \times 3.13045 = 0.60865$ respectively. The actual number of incorrect instructions in each sample (10, 12, 6, 14, 11, 9, 4, 14, 13, 10) would be plotted on this *np*-chart.

The *c*-Chart

A *c*-chart is an attribute control chart that monitors the number of nonconformities. A *c*-chart may be used instead of a *p*-chart for at least two reasons. First, it monitors nonconformities themselves rather than the proportion of nonconforming items in a sample. Second, items that are not considered to be nonconforming may still contain nonconformities. For example, a fender with a mainly functional use could be slightly misshapen and have dents, paint drips, and scratches, yet not be considered nonconforming. Frequently, nonconformities have a significant influence on an item's appearance, but do not influence its function. Thus, though an item with just one nonconformity of function may be termed nonconforming, usually several appearance-related nonconformities are required for an item to be judged nonconforming.

Example 4.1

When Luis receives shipments of wood he selects 100 boards at random and determines whether each board is acceptable for use in his furniture factory. In the past 10 days, his samples have yielded the following results:

Day	1	2	3	4	5	6	7	8	9	10
# of Nonconforming Boards	10	6	14	3	17	6	12	9	13	10
Proportion Nonconforming (p)	.10	.06	.14	.03	.17	.06	.12	.09	.13	.10

Construct a p-chart that Luis could use to see if there was any special cause variation in the proportion of nonconforming boards he has received on a given day.

Step 1: Find the center line for the chart, which is the average proportion nonconforming ($\bar{p}$).

$$\bar{p} = \frac{\sum_{i=1}^{10} p_i}{10}$$

$$= \frac{(.10 + .06 + .14 + \cdots + .10)}{10}$$

$$= .10$$

Step 2: Find the standard deviation for the p-chart (σ_p).

$$\sigma_p = \sqrt{\frac{\bar{p}(1 - \bar{p})}{n}}$$

$$= \sqrt{\frac{0.1(0.9)}{100}} = 0.03$$

Step 3: Find the upper control limit (UCL_p).

$$UCL_p = \bar{p} + 3\sigma_p$$
$$= 0.10 + 3(0.03)$$
$$= 0.19$$

Step 4: Find the lower control limit (LCL_p).

$$LCL_p = \bar{p} - 3\sigma_p$$
$$= 0.10 + 3(0.03)$$
$$= 0.01$$

Step 5: Graph the chart.

$UCL_p = 0.19$

$CL = 0.10$

$LCL_p = 0.01$

Step 6: Interpret the chart.
At present, there appear to be no special causes of variation.

Example 4.2

Construct the control chart from the previous boxed example using a spreadsheet.

Step 1: Enter the data observed by Luis and calculate the proportion nonconforming using a spreadsheet cell reference formula for the first sample and copy the formula to compute the proportion for all other samples.

A	B	C	D	E	F	G
Day	number inspected	number nonconforming	proportion nonconforming			
1	100	10	0.1		=C2/B2	
2	100	6	0.06			
3	100	14	0.14			
4	100	3	0.03			
5	100	17	0.17			
6	100	6	0.06			
7	100	12	0.12			
8	100	9	0.09			
9	100	13	0.13			
10	100	10	0.1			

Step 2: Calculate the average proportion nonconforming, UCL, and LCL using spreadsheet cell reference formulas for the first sample and copy these values for all other samples.

A	B	C	D	E	F	G
Day	number inspected	number nonconforming	proportion nonconforming	p-bar	UCL	LCL
1	100	10	0.1	0.1	0.19	0.01
2	100	6	0.06	0.1	0.19	0.01
3	100	14	0.14	0.1	0.19	0.01
4	100	3	0.03	0.1	0.19	0.01
5	100	17	0.17	0.1	0.19	0.01
6	100	6	0.06	0.1	0.19	0.01
7	100	12	0.12	0.1	0.19	0.01
8	100	9	0.09	0.1	0.19	0.01
9	100	13	0.13	0.1	0.19	0.01
10	100	10	0.1	0.1	0.19	0.01

Step 3: Use the spreadsheet graphing wizard to create the chart.

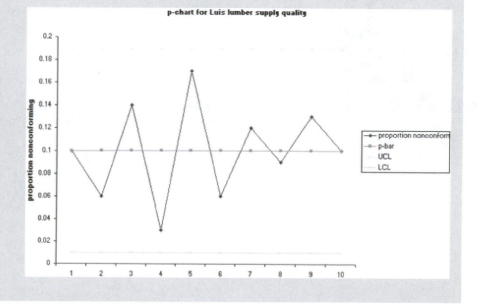

p-chart for Luis lumber supply quality

Formulas for the *c*-chart are:

$$UCL_c = \bar{c} + 3\sigma_c = \bar{c} + 3\sqrt{\bar{c}}$$
$$CL_c = \bar{c}$$
$$LCL_c = \bar{c} - 3\sigma_c = \bar{c} - 3\sqrt{\bar{c}}$$

Suppose Luis is evaluating a new supplier of fabric for his popular Southwestern-style furniture collection. He has requested fifteen separate production runs of the same pattern in order to evaluate the supplier's ability to produce the design with consistency. Critical nonconformities in a bolt of fabric would include a color that did not match the standard, a flaw in the weaving, a margin that is narrower than specified (making the fabric difficult to stretch in cutting), and loss of color when the fabric is subjected to dry cleaning. Let's assume that Luis is particularly concerned about flaws in the weaving. In inspecting the fifteen bolts the supplier has provided, he finds the following numbers of flaws on each bolt:

BOLT #	1	2	3	4	5	6	7	8	9	10	11	12	13	14	15
# of Nonconformities	25	32	51	63	44	42	39	45	47	32	58	43	44	28	40

Using these data, Luis would find $CL_c = \bar{c} = 42.2$, $UCL_c = 61.69$ and $LCL_c = 22.71$. The resulting *c*-chart is presented in Figure 4.12. It shows some indication of a lack of control: Bolt number four has sixty-three nonconformities, which is just above the upper control limit. Thus, Luis should investigate the value for bolt number four. Was the bolt inspected correctly? If so, where on the bolt were the nonconformities? Can the supplier identify the cause of the nonconformities on this bolt? If so, can the root cause of the nonconformities be eliminated, and when? Based on the answers to these questions, Luis may decide that bolt number four is not representative of the supplier's output when the process is in control. He could then eliminate that bolt from consideration and construct a new *c*-chart based on the fourteen remaining bolts, which appear to be representative of the supplier's process when it is in control.

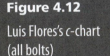

Figure 4.12

Luis Flores's *c*-chart (all bolts)

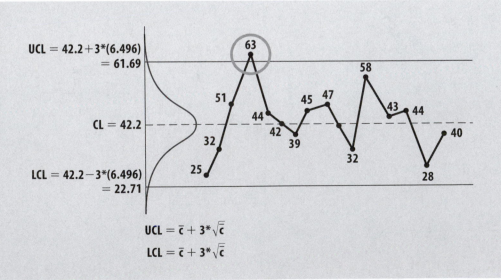

UCL = 42.2 + 3*(6.496) = 61.69

CL = 42.2

LCL = 42.2 − 3*(6.496) = 22.71

$$UCL = \bar{c} + 3*\sqrt{\bar{c}}$$
$$LCL = \bar{c} + 3*\sqrt{\bar{c}}$$

Example 4.3

When Luis receives shipments of upholstery fabric he selects ten square meters at random from each bolt to determine whether the fabric quality is consistent with that used in the past. Any nonconformity on the sample is counted. Common nonconfor-mities include knots in the weave, printing flaws, color irregularities, stains of any type, and holes or tears in the fabric. The past ten bolts of fabric have yielded the following results:

Bolt	1	2	3	4	5	6	7	8	9	10
# of nonconformities	110	130	100	130	95	160	120	105	140	120

Construct a *c*-chart that Luis could use to see if there was any special cause variation in the number of nonconformities on a given bolt of fabric.

Step 1: Find the center line for the chart, which is the average number of nonconformities.

$$\bar{c} = \frac{\sum (\# \, of \, nonconformities)}{\# \, of \, samples}$$

$$= \frac{1210}{10}$$

$$= 121$$

Step 2: Find the standard deviation for the *c*-chart (σ_c).

$$\sigma_c = \sqrt{\bar{c}}$$

$$= \sqrt{121}$$

$$= 11$$

Step 3: Find the upper control limit (UCL$_c$).

$$UCL_c = \bar{c} + 3\sigma_c$$

$$= 121 + 3(11)$$

$$= 154$$

Step 4: Find the lower control limit (LCL$_c$).

$$LCL_c = \bar{c} - 3\sigma_c$$

$$= 121 + 3(11)$$

$$= 88$$

Step 5: Graph the chart.

Step 6: Interpret the chart.
Sample 6, with 160 nonconformities, appears to have a quality level that is inconsistent with other samples. Luis should try to find the special cause for this variation and, if possible, prevent that cause from recurring.

Example 4.4

Construct the control chart from the previous boxed example using a spreadsheet.

Steps 1 and 2: Enter the data observed by Luis and calculate the center line, UCL, and LCL values. See the spreadsheet below.

Step 3: Use the spreadsheet graphing wizard to create the chart.

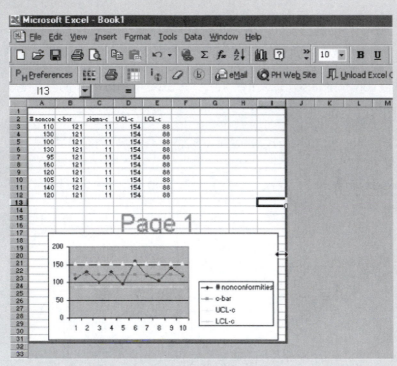

Luis's new c-chart would have the following values: $CL_c = \bar{c} = 40.71$, $UCL_c = 59.86$ and $LCL_c = 21.57$. Because the new chart has no indications of a lack of control, Luis may conclude that this supplier's fabric will have an average of 40.71 nonconformities per bolt. Unless there is some special cause of variation in the supplier's process, individual bolts will have between twenty-two and fifty-nine nonconformities. If this level of quality, along with the supplier's other capabilities, meets the needs of Luis's company, Luis should feel free to proceed with the contract negotiations.

Statistical Process Control by Variable As processes improve, they become less apt to produce nonconformities or nonconforming items. As a result, the tools that were used during the detection phase become obsolete. Using a tool that relies on nonconforming material is expensive when nonconformities are difficult to identify.

Suppose, for instance, that a machine that fills 1-gallon milk jugs is being monitored with a p-chart. Let's say a nonconforming jug is defined as one that has more than 1.02 gallons or less than .98 gallons. That means that 1.02 is the upper specification limit (USL) and 0.98 is the lower specification limit (LSL). (A **specification limit** defines the minimum level of conformance to a design target required for an item to be

Specification limit

The minimum level of conformance to a design target required for an item to be acceptable.

deemed conforming.) Inspecting just one milk jug may cost as much as $1, because in addition to the actual cost of the inspection, the inspected jugs cannot be sold. What would be the implications of an improvement in the proportion nonconforming, p, from 0.01 to 0.005?

If p is 0.01, the sample size would probably be at least 400, because when only one in a hundred items is nonconforming, inspectors usually need to look at several hundred items to get a good estimate of p. (The actual sample size required depends on the amount of variation in the sampling distribution of p; it could be much higher than 400.) With an inspection cost of $1 per item, then, obtaining just one point to plot on the p-chart would cost at least $400. If p were improved to 0.005, the required sample size to get a reasonable estimate of p would double, as would the cost of using the p-chart. This simple example clearly illustrates that as a process improves, attribute control techniques become more expensive. Indeed, for very good processes, the cost of using attribute control may be prohibitive.

One alternative to attribute control is variables control. In the case of the machine that fills 1-gallon milk jugs, the machine's performance can be monitored by tracking the volume of the milk that is placed in the jugs. A reasonable estimate of the average amount of milk being placed in the jugs could be obtained by inspecting only a fraction of the 400 jugs needed to plot one point on a p-chart when $p = 0.01$. In fact, inspectors might well need to examine only five jugs. Because obtaining a data point for the control chart would be far less expensive using this approach, inspectors might also take samples more frequently. Finally, if the common cause variation in the process is small enough, the information provided by these samples might even allow inspectors to recognize situations in which the machine is starting to drift away from its target of 1.000 gallons per jug long before any nonconforming jugs are created. Variables control, then, has the potential to prevent the creation of nonconforming products or services.

The most commonly used variables control charts plot sample means and ranges and are called $\overline{X}$ and R-charts. Two statistics, the sample mean and the sample range, are plotted for each sample. The three control limits for the $\overline{X}$ and the R-charts may be found using computational factors that are based on estimates of the relationship between the average range, $\overline{R}$, and the process standard deviation (see Table 4.4). As a rule, at least twenty samples are required to get a good estimate of $\overline{R}$ if the computational factors are used to estimate variability.

The equations for the $\overline{X}$ and the R-chart are:

$$UCL_{\overline{X}} = \overline{\overline{X}} + 3\sigma_{\overline{X}} \approx \overline{\overline{X}} + A_2\,\overline{R}$$

$$CL_{\overline{X}} = \overline{\overline{X}}$$

$$LCL_{\overline{X}} = \overline{\overline{X}} - 3\sigma_{\overline{X}} \approx \overline{\overline{X}} - A_2\,\overline{R}$$

$$UCL_R = \overline{R} + 3\sigma_R \approx D_4\,\overline{R}$$

$$CL_{\overline{R}} = \overline{R}$$

$$LCL_R = \overline{R} - 3\sigma_{\overline{R}} \approx D_2\,\overline{R}$$

It might have been better if the $\overline{X}$ and R-chart had been named the R and $\overline{X}$-charts, because the R-chart should always be interpreted before the $\overline{X}$-chart. The R-chart monitors a system's variability; thus an R-chart that is in control indicates that the system's precision has not changed. Because the control limits on the $\overline{X}$-chart are a function of the system's variability, they should be used only when that variability is known with some confidence—and that can be the case only when the R-chart shows no

Table 4.4

Computational Factors for the $\bar{X}$ and R-Chart

n	A_2	D_3	D_4	n	A_2	D_3	D_4
2	1.880	0.000	3.267	14	0.235	0.329	1.671
3	1.023	0.000	2.575	15	0.223	0.348	1.652
4	0.729	0.000	2.282	16	0.212	0.364	1.636
5	0.577	0.000	2.115	17	0.203	0.379	1.621
6	0.483	0.000	2.004	18	0.194	0.392	1.608
7	0.419	0.076	1.924	19	0.187	0.404	1.596
8	0.373	0.136	1.864	20	0.180	0.414	1.586
9	0.337	0.184	1.816	21	0.173	0.425	1.575
10	0.308	0.223	1.777	22	0.167	0.434	1.566
11	0.285	0.256	1.744	23	0.162	0.443	1.557
12	0.266	0.284	1.716	24	0.157	0.452	1.548
13	0.249	0.308	1.692	25	0.153	0.459	1.541

Source: Table B$_2$ of the *A.S.T.M. Manual on Quality Control of Materials*, p. 115. Used with permission.

indications of a lack of control. When the R-chart demonstrates a process variability that is in control, the $\bar{X}$-chart provides an indication of the system's accuracy.

The difference between precision and accuracy is subtle. Figure 4.13 illustrates the two concepts in terms of a bull's-eye target. Assume that the points on the targets represent the performance of machines that center watermarks on paper stationery. Figure 4.13a shows the precision and accuracy of a machine that is demonstrating only common cause variability. Both the $\bar{X}$ and the R-chart for this machine are in control. Figure 4.13b shows the performance of a machine whose R-chart is out of control, but whose $\bar{X}$-chart is in control. Though this machine's precision has been lost, its performance is still reasonably accurate.

Now, suppose inspectors identify and remove the special cause of the variation— say, a loose bolt—shown in Figure 4.13b. Suppose further that the operator learns that the customer would prefer to have the watermark appear in the upper right-hand quadrant of the paper. Figure 4.13c shows the results after the machine's precision has been brought under control and the process retargeted. Based on the *old* specifications, this process is precise but not very accurate. In Figure 4.13d, the process has moved out of control on the $\bar{X}$-chart, though the watermarks appear to be placed with greater precision than normal. If the precision remains this good, eventually a run will fall below the center line of the R-chart, leading to an investigation into the cause of

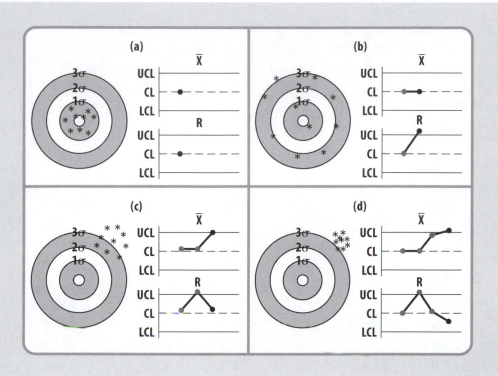

Figure 4.13

Accuracy vs. precision

the variation. New limits will be established for the two charts based on the new target and the reduction in variability.

Now return to the control chart in Example 4.5, which illustrates the performance of the machine that fills milk jugs. Notice that none of the rules of run illustrated in Figure 4.10 have been violated on the R-chart in Example 4.5. Consequently, we can go on to interpret the $\overline{X}$-chart for this machine. We see immediately that two points are out of control. These indicators of a shift in the mean should be investigated and corrected, as should all special cause variations.

Does being in control mean that a machine is not producing any nonconforming items? Certainly not. It means only that there is no special cause variation in the process. A process that is in control may or may not produce nonconforming items. As we shall see in the next section, the relationship between the variation in the process and the tolerance for variation represented by the product specifications determines whether or not a process that is in control is capable of nonconformity-free operation.

Prevention Processes

CAPABILITY INDEXES

The ability of a process to meet specifications, called **process capability**, is measured by comparing the variation in the process with the allowance for variation provided by the specifications. A capability index allows us to express process capability in numeric terms. Four commonly cited capability indices are the C_p index, the C_{pk} index, the CPU

Process capability

The ability of a process to meet specifications is measured by comparing the variation in the process with the allowance for variation provided by the specifications.

Example 4.5

Table 4.5 presents sample computations for an $\bar{X}$ and R-chart based on the example of the machine that fills milk jugs. The chart itself was computed using the factors in Table 4.4.

Table 4.5
Computations for an Example $\bar{X}$ and R-Chart

	Observation (Milk Jug)					Sample Mean($\bar{X}$)	Sample Range(R)
Sample	1	2	3	4	5		
1	1.005	1.008	1.000	.999	1.003	1.0030	0.0090
2	1.004	1.004	1.010	0.998	1.004	1.0040	0.0120
3	1.000	0.997	0.998	1.003	1.001	0.9998	0.0060
4	0.996	0.999	0.989	1.001	0.999	0.9968	0.0120
5	1.002	0.998	0.997	0.993	1.003	0.9986	0.0100
6	0.993	0.995	0.994	0.997	0.999	0.9956	0.0060
7	1.000	1.005	1.002	0.998	0.998	1.0006	0.0070
8	0.997	0.998	1.004	1.006	0.994	0.9998	0.0120
9	0.996	1.006	1.004	1.005	1.002	1.0026	0.0100
10	1.003	0.995	0.998	0.999	0.991	0.9972	0.0120
11	1.012	1.015	1.006	1.007	1.008	1.0096	0.0090
12	1.005	1.006	1.009	1.000	0.999	1.0038	0.0100
13	0.997	0.996	0.995	0.999	1.000	0.9974	0.0050
14	0.999	1.000	1.005	1.003	0.997	1.0008	0.0080
15	0.987	0.990	0.994	0.990	0.989	0.9900	0.0070
16	1.000	1.002	0.995	0.994	0.999	0.9980	0.0080
17	1.003	1.003	1.002	1.004	0.998	1.0020	0.0060
18	0.992	0.997	1.008	0.998	0.999	0.9988	0.0160
19	0.994	1.006	1.003	1.005	1.000	1.0016	0.0120
20	1.006	1.003	1.000	1.000	0.995	1.0008	0.0110
21	1.011	1.008	1.000	1.004	1.001	1.0048	0.0110
22	0.999	0.991	0.995	1.000	1.001	0.9972	0.0100
23	0.998	0.988	1.000	1.001	1.002	0.9978	0.0140
24	0.999	1.000	1.001	1.002	1.001	1.0006	0.0030
25	0.998	0.995	0.993	0.998	0.999	0.9966	0.0060
					Averages	$\bar{\bar{X}} = 0.9999$	$\bar{R} = 0.0093$

Factors from Table 4.4					
A2	D3	D4			
0.577	.000	2.115	UCL	1.0053	0.0196
			LCL	0.9946	0.0000

(continued)

Example 4.5

(*continued*)

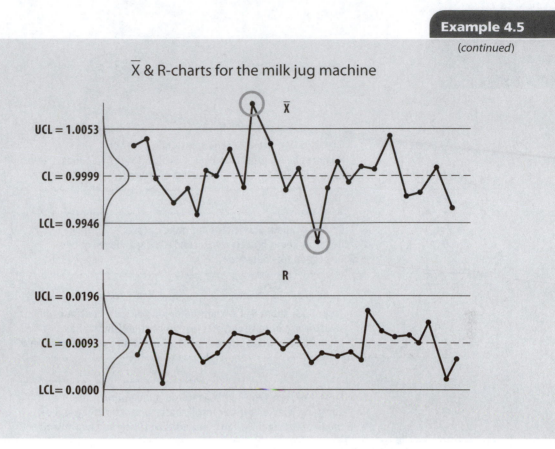

$\overline{\text{X}}$ & R-charts for the milk jug machine

index, and the CPL index. They are computed as follows:

$$C_p = \frac{(USL - LSL)}{6\sigma}$$

$$C_{pk} = min\left\{\frac{\overline{\overline{X}} - LSL}{3\sigma}, \frac{USL - \overline{\overline{X}}}{3\sigma}\right\}$$

$$CPU = \frac{USL - \overline{\overline{X}}}{3\sigma}$$

$$CPL = \frac{\overline{\overline{X}} - LSL}{3\sigma}$$

Each of the capability indexes yields different information. The C_p index indicates the process's *potential* capability, because it assumes that the distribution of process output is centered perfectly between the **specification limits**. Large values are desirable on the capability indexes. Thus, a C_p of 1.0 would mean that about 3 parts in 1,000 can be expected to be "out of spec"; a C_p of 1.33 would mean that about 64 parts per million (PPM) can be expected to be out of spec; and a C_p of 1.67 would indicate a nonconformity rate of about 1 PPM. In general, a process with $C_{pk} \leq 1.0$ is said to be "not capable"; a process with $C_{pk} \geq 1.0$ is said to be "capable." Figure 4.14 summarizes and illustrates this information. It shows that as process capability improves, the use of

Figure 4.14
Process capability
indexes

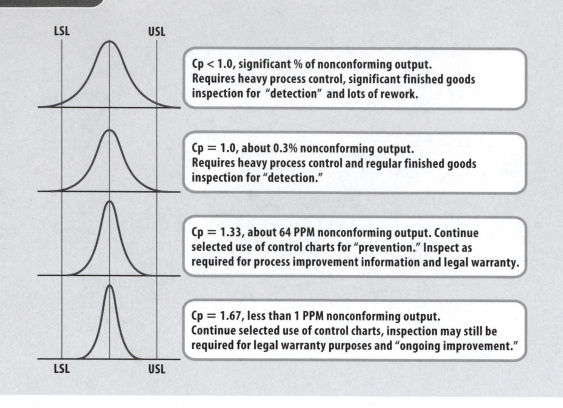

LSL   USL

Cp < 1.0, significant % of nonconforming output.
Requires heavy process control, significant finished goods
inspection for "detection" and lots of rework.

Cp = 1.0, about 0.3% nonconforming output.
Requires heavy process control and regular finished goods
inspection for "detection."

Cp = 1.33, about 64 PPM nonconforming output. Continue
selected use of control charts for "prevention." Inspect as
required for process improvement information and legal warranty.

Cp = 1.67, less than 1 PPM nonconforming output.
Continue selected use of control charts, inspection may still be
required for legal warranty purposes and "ongoing improvement."

LSL   USL

quality control tools such as final goods inspection, acceptance sampling, and statistical process control should decline.

When a process is centered exactly between the LSL and USL, the C_p index and the C_{pk} index will have the same value. The C_{pk} index indicates the *actual* capability of a process, whether or not its mean is perfectly centered between the USL and LSL. In reality, process output distributions frequently are *not* centered between the product specifications, so most large industrial companies use the C_{pk} index to describe their expectations of process capability in supply contracts. For example, many industrial firms require their suppliers to demonstrate process C_{pk}s above 1.33 or C_{pk}s of 1.67 in order to maintain their contracts.

The difference between the values of the C_p index and the C_{pk} index indicates how much the actual process capability could be improved by moving the mean to the center of the specification limits, without reducing variation in the process. This information is valuable, because changing the mean of a process is usually much easier than reducing process variation. For example, if a process has a C_p index of 1.33 and a C_{pk} index of 0.90, it is obvious that the process can be made capable by simple centering adjustments and without any reduction in process variability. As Figure 4.14 indicates, this scenario would call also for process control by variables to prevent production of nonconforming output. By detecting any shift of the process mean away from its target value, process control would ensure timely adjustments and maintenance of the process.

The CPU and the CPL are used less frequently than the C_{pk}. They are of particular interest only with one-sided specifications or when managers are concerned about either the LSL or the USL.

SIX-SIGMA PROGRAMS

You may have heard the term 6σ *quality* (or "six-sigma" quality), which means that specification limits are six standard deviations away from the process mean. Major companies such as Motorola and General Electric have made 6σ quality famous. This standard equates to a C_p index of 2.0. In a process with an output distribution centered between the specifications and $C_p = 2.0$, the proportion nonconforming would best be measured in parts per billion. When shifts in the process average are common, 6σ design is particularly useful. Even if the output distribution of a 6σ process were to move off center by $\pm 1.5\sigma$, only 3.4 PPM would be out of spec.

The 6σ quality concept is as applicable to service output as to manufacturing output. For example, the FAA defines "on time" as arrival within 15 minutes of schedule. This specification is important for air traffic control purposes, because having planes arrive early is as problematic as having them arrive late from a controller's point of view. If Tom Jackson's airline were to find a way to ensure that on average, flights arrived at the scheduled time, with a standard deviation equal to 2.5 minutes or less, it would achieve 6σ quality. Managers would be able to tell the FAA that the airline's planes are always "on time" and that continuously tracking the airline's performance is a waste of the FAA's resources.

Six-sigma programs are a management approach that involves employees in improvement project teams seeking to create essentially error-free processes. Each project follows a five-step process summarized by the letters D-M-A-I-C. The steps are:

▶ *Define* a project in terms of its specific, measurable, customer critical business objective.

▶ *Measure* the process, documenting its operation and effectiveness.

▶ *Analyze* the process to learn the sources of variation and why defects are created.

▶ *Improve* the process by finding ways to remove variability and prevent defects.

▶ *Control* the process by placing systems and tools in place to ensure that improvements are sustained.

▶ Six-sigma programs have become common in business and have expanded well beyond their roots in manufacturing processes to pervade improvement activities throughout many large corporations. These programs involve a wide spectrum of employees in all functional areas and at all managerial levels. Senior executives provide organizational commitment to the program through allocation of resources for training, personal involvement, and employee reward systems. Other managers become 6σ champions, identifying worthy projects and providing help to the teams whose projects they champion. Still other employees receive training and conduct improvement projects to become 6σ green belts, black belts, or master black belts.

▶ The investments companies make in 6σ training lead to corporate cultures that continuously improve their product-service bundles. The results of 6σ programs are also positive from a shareholder perspective, with companies such as Motorola, GE, Allied Signal, Ford Motor Company, and Citibank attributing significant cost savings to their programs. In 2001, for example,

Six-sigma programs

A management approach that involves employees in improvement project teams seeking to create essentially error-free processes.

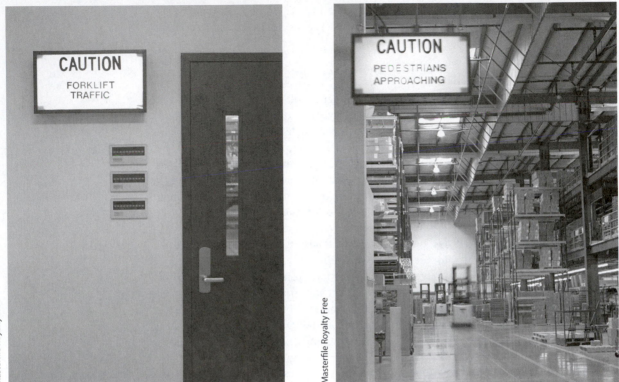

Proactive efforts to prevent mistakes and accidents can have a significant impact on quality and costs.

Ford attributed a \$300 million contribution to their bottom line and a two-percent increase in customer satisfaction to their 6σ program.[1] Between 1987 and 1994, Motorola used its 6σ program to reduce in-process defect levels by a factor of 200, reduce manufacturing costs by \$1.4 billion, and increase stockholder's share value fourfold (among other things). And GE, which started its program in 1995, estimated annual savings to be \$6.6 million by the year 2000.[2]

FAIL-PROOFING METHODS

In all the methods of statistical analysis discussed so far, nonconformities are prevented through a process of sampling and monitoring. At best, these techniques provide only partial assurance that the proportion nonconforming will be acceptable and that the special cause variation will be spotted. But the real goal of most companies is zero nonconformities. Obviously, to produce no nonconformities, a process must be unable to fail. Fail-proofing a process is therefore a much better form of nonconformity prevention and process control than is statistical process control.

The Japanese term for "fail proof" is **poka yoke.** A *poka yoke* device used at the Cummins Engine Company makes sure the correct transmission is placed in the company's midrange diesel engines. Electric "eyes" on the supply rack at the workstation check to "see" what type of transmission parts (automatic or manual) the assembly worker at the station picks up. The assembly line is also monitored by a computer

Poka yoke

The Japanese term for "failproof." For example, a device used at the Cummins Engine Company makes sure the correct transmission is placed in the company's midrange diesel engines.

program that keeps track of each engine during its assembly, based on the engine's bar-coded serial number. Before the computer allows the engine to advance to the next workstation, it checks the specifications for this particular engine. If the worker takes parts for an automatic transmission out of stock when the engine is supposed to have a manual transmission, the engine will not advance to the next point on the assembly line. In fact, it will not advance until the correct transmission parts have been removed from stock. Other examples of fail proofing in manufacturing environments include warning lights to indicate when tools are worn or out of tolerance, master templates to indicate when production samples are out of spec, and checklists to indicate that all steps required to complete a process have been performed.

Japanese operations expert Shigeo Shingo first introduced the concept of fail proofing a production process. Though Shingo devised the idea of *poka yoke* devices for use in manufacturing processes, the concept is applicable to service processes as well. In some states, driver's licenses show individuals under 21 years of age in profile rather than full face. The practice is intended to fail-safe the process of checking a person's age before alcohol or tobacco is sold to that person. This practice essentially eliminates the likelihood that a salesclerk who is checking the age of a minor will read a birth date incorrectly or calculate the individual's age incorrectly. Other examples of fail proofing in services include:

▶ Signs along customer waiting lines that list information and items the customer will need to receive service (for example, cash only)

▶ The McDonald's french fry scoop that measures a consistent quantity of fries

▶ ATM machines that require users to remove their card prior to completing a transaction

Improvement Processes

THE QUALITY IMPROVEMENT STORY

The **quality improvement (QI) story** is a structured process that allows the use of both numeric and subjective data to solve problems. It provides a way for group members to organize their interactions, collect and analyze data, and monitor their progress. This method was originally conceived as a technique for communicating the rationale a group used in arriving at a proposed solution. In reality, groups that use the QI story are able not only to communicate their solutions; but they are also better able to obtain input from non-team members and more productive in their problem solving. The QI story is composed of seven logical steps taken in sequence. The first step establishes the groundwork for the second, the second for the third, and so forth:

> **QI story**
>
> *A structured process that allows a group to use both numeric and subjective data to solve problems.*

Step 1. Establish the reason for improvement: Select a theme.

Step 2. Describe the current situation, including gaps between the existing state and the desired state.

Step 3. Analyze and identify possible root causes, and rank their impact on the project theme.

Step 4. Identify countermeasures, rank them, and establish a plan for testing them.

Step 5. Test the countermeasures with a prototype, trial period, or trial department. If the countermeasures fail, go back to step 4. If the plan works, move on to step 6.

Step 6. Standardize the solution and ensure that processes do not revert to the status quo.

Step 7. Continue the improvement cycle with another theme.

By this point in your college career, you should be familiar with, and may have used, many of the tools for data collection and analysis that are used by quality improvement teams. The tools themselves are shown in Figure 4.15, parts a–k. The following bullet list summarizes those tools in the context of the QI story. Figure 4.16 on page 167 places some of the tools shown in Figure 4.15 in the context of the QI story.

Figure 4.15

(a) Checklist

Setup Approval Checklist

Product to be made:_____   Name:_____   *IED Activities:*   *Time/Initial*

Customer:_____   Date:_____   Mach. maintenance:_____

Quantity to be made:_____   Begin time:_____   Tool removal:_____

Fixtures needed:_____   Location:_____   Tool installation:_____

Machine tool needed:_____   Machine ID:_____   Batch prototype:_____

Setup operator:_____   Prototype inspection:_____

OED Prep Activities :   *Time/Initial*   Approval request:_____

Die inspection:_____   Prodn. go ahead: _____

Die maintenance:_____   Signature: *OED Wrap-up Activities:*   *Time/Initial*

Fixture maintenance:_____   Die inspection:_____

Setup tool retrieval:_____   Die maintenance:_____

Fixture retrieval:_____   Fixture maintenance:_____

Begin checklist for setup: _____   Tool storage:_____

Prepare toolkit for setup:_____   Fixture storage:_____

Get material needed for prodn.:_____   File checklist for setup:_____

(a)

Figure 4.15

(b) Check sheet
(c) Cause-and-effect
(fishbone) chart
(d) Pareto chart

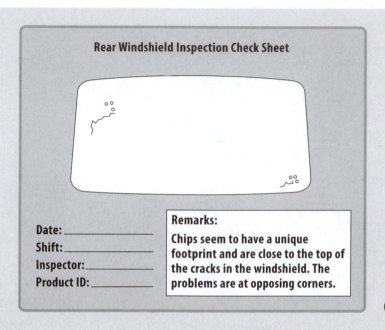

Rear Windshield Inspection Check Sheet

Date: _____
Shift: _____
Inspector: _____
Product ID: _____

Remarks:
Chips seem to have a unique footprint and are close to the top of the cracks in the windshield. The problems are at opposing corners.

(b)

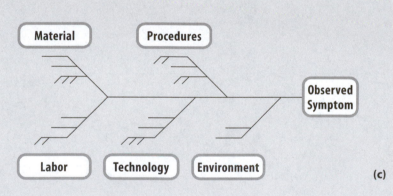

(c)

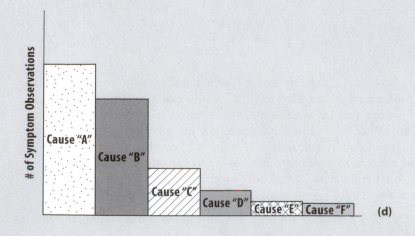

(d)

Figure 4.15

(e) Flowchart
(f) Control chart

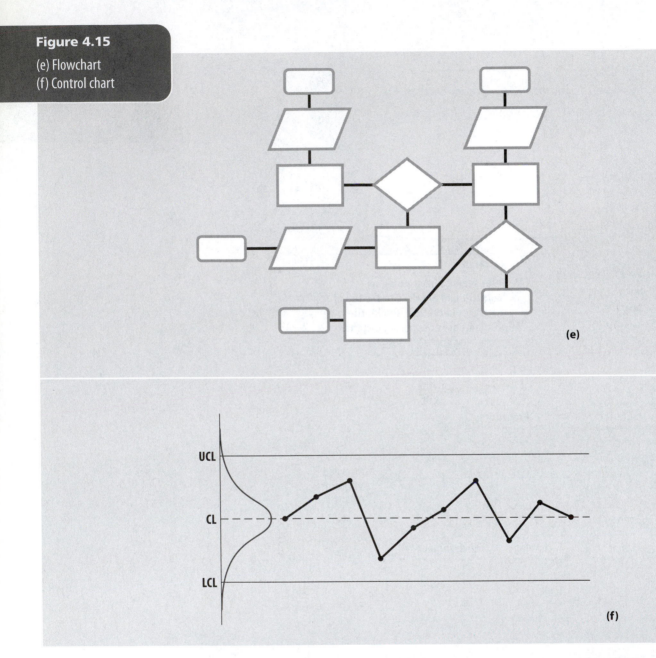

(e)

(f)

Checklists

A guide to accomplishing a task.

Check sheets

Much like a checklist, a checksheet is more oriented toward collecting data and less oriented toward guiding activity.

▶ **Checklists:** A checklist is a guide to accomplishing a task or set of tasks. It is particularly useful for standardizing the way that routine tasks are done and making note of any unusual occurrences in the process. In addition, when completed checklists are signed by workers and saved, they can provide an audit trail for the work that was done. For example, a "knock off" checklist at a restaurant could itemize the various cleaning tasks and machine shutdowns that have to be done before the staff can leave. The manager knows, by looking at the completed checklist, that it is okay to let employees "knock off."

▶ **Check sheets:** A check sheet is much like a checklist, but it is more oriented toward collecting data and less oriented toward guiding activity. A check sheet is a

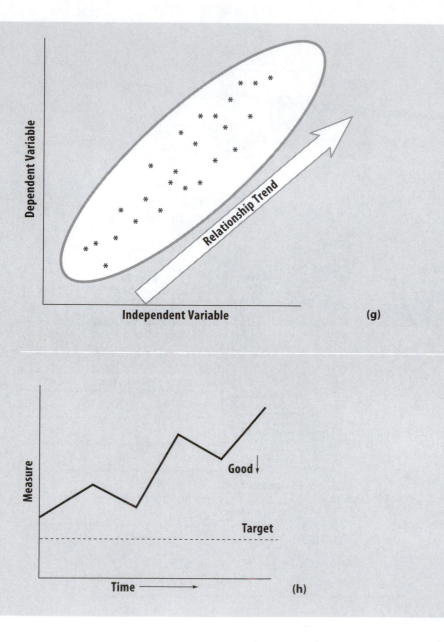

Figure 4.15

(g) Scatter diagram
(h) Run chart

template that provides the structure used to record data. For instance, a check sheet used to record nonconformities in windshields might include spaces for the inspector to record the batch inspected and the equipment used for inspection. It might also contain a picture of the windshield on which the inspector could mark the location of observed nonconformities.

▶ **Brainstorming:** Brainstorming is a well-known technique used to generate an extensive list of ideas pertinent to a particular problem, such as identifying root causes or suggesting possible solutions. During brainstorming, no judgment should be made of the value of any idea, because this tends to inhibit input. Brainstorming is a particularly effective way of gathering subjective data.

Brainstorming

A well-known technique used to generate an extensive list of ideas pertinent to a particular problem.

Figure 4.15

(i) Stratified pareto chart
(j) Countermeasures
matrix (k) Gantt chart/
action plan

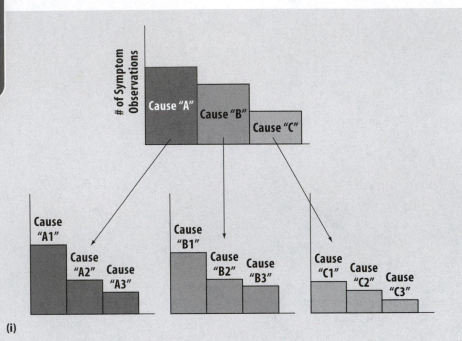

(i)

	Feasibility	Effectiveness	Cost
Solution #1	5	1	3
Solution #2	4	5	2
Solution #3	5	4	5
Solution #4	2	5	2
Solution #5	4	3	3

(j)

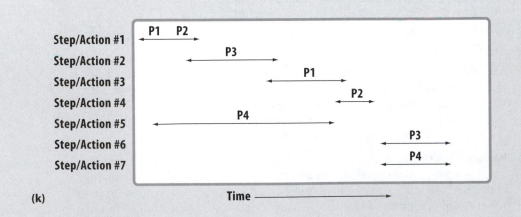

(k)

Figure 4.16

QI story

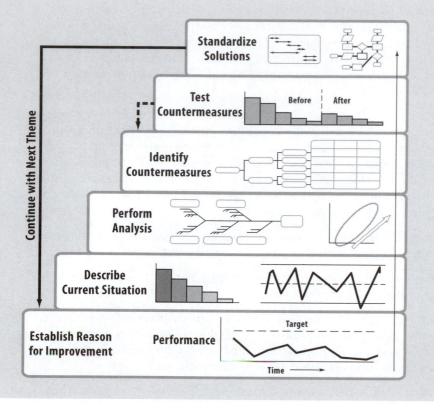

- **Cause-and-effect diagrams (fishbone charts):** Fishbone charts categorize the potential reasons for a situation that is observed. These diagrams, an example of which is shown in Figure 4.15c, may list causes of a problem that were identified in a brainstorming session, organizing them broadly into groups such as "material," "method," "man," and "machine." The main groups form the major vertebrae of the "fish," and these can also be subdivided.

- **5 Ws and an H:** The "5 Ws and an H" refer to the set of questions that identify the root of a situation: why, why, why, why, why, and how. This approach can also be used to determine whether a fishbone diagram is correctly constructed. When a problem arises, by asking a series of "why" questions we can move to the root cause on a fishbone. For example, if a FedEx delivery was late, we ask why. If the reason is that a sorting machine broke down at the Memphis distribution hub, we again ask why. If reason is because the machine overheated, we again ask why. If the wrong type of lubricant had been used, we again ask why. If the lubricant labels had been changed by the supplier to meet new environmental labeling requirements, we need not ask why again. Instead, we would ask how we can make sure the problem does not recur. Maybe we would ask the supplier to educate the maintenance department about the new labeling scheme.

- **Pareto charts:** Pareto charts are bar charts used to distinguish "the vital few from the trivial many." The design of these charts is based on the Pareto principle, also known as the "80/20 rule." In terms of quality, the 80/20 rule

Cause and effect diagrams (fishbone charts)

Charts which categorize the potential reasons for a situation that is observed.

5 Ws and H

A set of questions that can help identify the root cause of a problem.

Pareto charts

Bar charts used to distinguish "the vital few from the trivial many." They are based on the Pareto principle, also known as the "80/20 rule."

means that 80% of the problems come from 20% of the causes. Pareto charts typically deal with category data.

▶ **Histograms:** A histogram is a bar chart that presents a frequency distribution. Unlike the Pareto chart, which uses category data, a histogram can be used to characterize the relative frequency of process output along a scale that is divided into equal regions. A histogram can tell us whether product output is "skewed" in any particular direction, is "bimodal," or is balanced around the distributions mean.

▶ **Flowcharts:** Flowcharts are tools that are especially effective in describing a process by graphically depicting all of the steps in the process in sequence. In operations, we stress the importance of using flowcharts to understand both product flows and information flows. You can use flowcharts to highlight places where problems are most likely to occur (or opportunity for improvement is greatest) by comparing a flowchart of the process as it is with a flowchart of the process as it would be under ideal circumstances.

▶ **Control charts:** Control charts, which were discussed at length earlier in this chapter, are used to determine whether there is special cause variation in a process.

▶ **Scatter diagrams:** Scatter diagrams can be used to pictorially present the underlying relationships between two variables.

▶ **Run charts:** Run charts document the value of a particular variable over time. Like control charts, run charts allow us to track process changes over time. Unlike control charts, they usually are based on all output, not on samples, and they do not include limits based on past experience.

▶ **Stratification:** Stratification is a way of breaking data down by category. When data has been aggregated, it often loses its usefulness. For example, the percentage of the popular vote that a presidential candidate receives is not necessarily interesting in itself to political scientists. When this percentage is broken down by state, county, income level, gender, or profession, however, the data becomes much more useful.

▶ **Countermeasures matrix:** A countermeasures matrix provides a way of ranking a variety of possible solutions on a variety of criteria, such as effectiveness, feasibility, safety, environmental impact, and cost. By giving different weights to the various criteria, preference for one of many solutions can be established.

▶ **Gantt chart:** A Gantt chart is used to display planned (and actual) progress over time. Displaying planned timing of activities on a time line helps team members recognize which activities are critical and how well they are maintaining a project's schedule.

Although most managers are well prepared to use tools such as these, the typical hourly wage earner may lack the educational background or communication skills. Training should therefore be made available to workers, so that they will be able to use these tools. In addition to addressing the tools themselves, this training should cover skills such as interpersonal communication, effective writing, effective collaboration, and group decision making—skills that are often lacking in the general workforce. Just-in-time training should also be available, in case a team needs special training to deal with a particular problem or requires a refresher course. (Just-in-time training is

---

Histograms

A bar chart that presents a frequency distribution.

Flowcharts

Tools that are especially effective in describing a process by graphically depicting all of the steps in the process in sequence.

Scatter diagrams

Used to pictorially present the underlying relationships between variables.

Run charts

Graphs which document the value of a particular variable over time. Like a control chart, they allow a business to track process changes over time.

Stratification

A way of breaking data down by category. When data has been aggregated, it often loses its usefulness.

Countermeasures matrix

A tool that provides a way of ranking a variety of possible solutions on a variety of criteria such as effectiveness, feasibility, safety, environmental impact, and cost.

Gantt chart

Bar graphs that show a resource's scheduled area and available time. By displaying the planned timing of activities on a time line, team members recognize what activities are really critical and how well they are keeping up with their project's schedule.

not training about just-in-time production systems, but is training given at the time when a team needs to learn something to move their project forward.)

Most organizations make a facilitator available to quality improvement teams; often the facilitator is the person responsible for the employee involvement program. The facilitator can act as a sounding board for teams, monitor their progress, put them in touch with experts from other functions or divisions when necessary, and help them to work through interpersonal conflicts.

KAIZEN WORKSHOPS

Kaizen is a Japanese term that can be translated roughly as "continuous improvement." The Kaizen workshop was developed at Toyota in the 1950s to promote active ongoing improvement. The technique has gained recognition in the United States as a valuable approach to improving operations. For instance, DaimlerChrysler has promoted the technique aggressively with suppliers, both internally and externally.

A "Kaizen workshop" is an action-oriented, three-to-five-day, on-site event that focuses on improving a specific process. Participants in the workshop form a cross-functional team that includes both those who know the process well and those who can provide fresh perspectives. This team is given the mission and the authority to take immediate action to revise the process in order to achieve breakthroughs in quality, productivity, inventory reduction, manufacturing cycle time, and floor space utilization.

The workshop begins with a training session that is usually several hours long. The group then proceeds to study the process and determine what changes should be undertaken. Typically, the team will make small improvements immediately. Improvements that require only two or three days of concentrated effort will generally be made by the end of the workshop. Other improvements will be left with the "owner" of the process, to be completed by clearly specified dates. Table 4.6 outlines a typical schedule for a Kaizen workshop.

CROSS-FUNCTIONAL QUALITY IMPROVEMENT TEAMS

Earlier in this chapter, we stressed that all functions in a business make significant contributions to any quality management system, though the functional areas might use different kinds of quality improvement tools. Given that quality is everyone's responsibility, getting a variety of people together to solve a quality problem makes a lot of sense. People with different backgrounds and training will see the same problem from different perspectives and will think of different solutions.

Compared to the homogeneous workforce in many other countries (notably Japan), the American workforce is quite diverse—a strength that is partially responsible for the famous "Yankee ingenuity." Because of the cultural base that accommodates diverse strengths and weaknesses, a cross-functional team of American workers can be expected to come up with a creative solution to virtually any problem when empowered to do so. However, while diversity generates creativity, it also tends to slow the move to consensus. (When everyone thinks the same way, creativity may be limited but consensus is easy to achieve.) Therefore, learning how to communicate effectively and to work together in groups is important to the American workforce.

Because the goal of any improvement to business processes is ultimately to improve customer satisfaction, no function can be disinterested in continuous improvement projects. In fact, quality problems that have not been solved within a function usually require coordinated changes in several functions. This is another fundamental reason why cross-functional quality improvement teams are needed.

Kaizen

A Japanese term that can be translated roughly as "continuous improvement." The Kaizen workshop was developed at Toyota in the 1950s to promote active ongoing, continuous improvement. Recently, the technique has been gaining recognition in the United States as a valuable approach to improving operations.

Table 4.6

Generic Schedule for
a Kaizen Workshop

Time	Activities
Before the Workshop	• Select a project • Set project objectives • Select a team leader and team members • Take care of the logistical issues • Inform affected employees of the upcoming workshop
Day 1	• Deliver any training • Study the process as it is and gain an understanding of the workshop's key objectives
Day 2	• Analyze the process • Brainstorm for improvement ideas • Develop solutions
Day 3	• Implement solutions • Refine the solutions/improve the process further • Monitor the new process • Begin to prepare a presentation
Day 4	• Confirm results of the changes implemented • Complete a presentation • Make a presentation to management
After the Workshop	• Conduct a 30-day follow-up audit • Complete a follow-up report for management

SUMMARY

During the latter decades of the twentieth century, the concept and practice of total quality management (TQM) became popular with leading businesses. Championed by such visionaries as W. Edwards Deming, Joseph Juran, Armand Feigenbaum, and Philip Crosby, this approach spread to virtually all types of organizations. When it was introduced, many people believed that TQM was just another business fad. Today, some people say TQM is dead. Yet, for many companies, the practice of management is now completely different because of the positive impact of quality management and statistical process control.

For most American firms, adopting a quality management approach required significant changes in their way of doing business. Those changes required a paradigm shift in managers' understanding of the importance of customer satisfaction, process improvement, employee involvement, and data-based decision making. They also increased managers' appreciation for holistic thinking, single sourcing, a long-term focus on market share, the pursuit of perfection, the proactive treatment of quality issues, and respect for the humanity of workers.

Quality management has spread well beyond the manufacturing sector. Quality awards such as the Baldrige Award are offered to services, government entities, and health-care providers in addition to manufacturers. The growing importance of process standardization is reflected in the international recognition of the ISO 9000:2000 series of quality standards, which have become the globally accepted requirement for market entry.

Companies have integrated statistical process control (SPC) and other tools into their managerial systems. Acceptance sampling may serve as a starting point because it allows companies to determine the acceptability of a given shipment of material when the supplying process is not stable. To create a more stable supply process, attribute- or variables-based SPC may be used to determine when the process is subject to special cause variation that could require managerial intervention. *Poka-yoke* devices may be used to fail proof processes, and process capability indices may be used to monitor the ability of processes to operate without producing nonconformities.

Even the most capable processes can be improved by putting all employees to work in quality improvement teams using a whole variety of tools within the context of a six-sigma (6σ) program, QI story, or Kaizen workshop. This ongoing improvement requires a company to build a personnel system that provides workers with the needed training, motivation, and time to contribute to process improvement. The set of tools, managerial perspectives, and improvement steps we have described in this chapter now pervade the workplace of most modern organizations and are suited for application in virtually any operational setting.

KEY TERMS

5Ws and an H, 167
Acceptable quality level (AQL), 138
Acceptance sampling, 134
Appraisal costs, 127
Assignable variation, 141
Attribute measures, 133
Baldrige Award, 130
Brainstorming, 165
Cause-and-effect diagram (fishbone chart), 167
Checklist, 164
Check sheets, 164
Common cause (random) variation, 140
Consumer's risk, 137
Control, 141
Control charts, 143
Control limits, 143
Countermeasures matrix, 168
Employee involvement (EI), 119
External failure costs, 127

Flowchart, 168
Gantt chart, 168
Histogram, 168
Inspection, 133
Inspection error, 136
Internal failure costs, 127
ISO 9000 standards, 131
Kaizen, 169
Lot tolerance percent defective (LTPD), 138
Operating characteristics (OC) curve, 139
Paradigm, 119
Pareto chart, 167
P-D-C-A cycle, 125
Poka yoke, 160
Prevention costs, 127
Process capability, 155
Producer's risk, 136
QI story, 161
Random variation, 140

Run chart, 168
Sampling distribution, 141
Sampling error, 136
Scatter diagram, 168
Service recovery, 123
Six-sigma programs, 159
Special cause (assignable) variation, 141
Specification, 121
Specification limits, 152
Statistical process control (SPC), 140
Stratification, 168
Structural variation, 141
Tampering, 141
Testing, 133
Total quality management (TQM), 115
Type I error, 136
Type II error, 137
Variable measures, 133

SOLVED PROBLEMS

1. Luis has a process that can drill holes in furniture components for subsequent assembly. While it is used to drill holes to a variety of depths and diameters, it has a normal amount of depth variation where the standard deviation of each hole is equal to about ½ of a millimeter.

   a) What would be the standard deviation of the sample means if the sample size was equal to sixteen holes drilled?

   b) What would be the standard deviation of the sample means if the sample size was equal to twenty-five holes drilled?

Solution:

   a) Standard deviation of the sample means = .5 mm/($\sqrt{16}$) = .5 mm/4 = .125 mm

   b) Standard deviation of the sample means = .5 mm/($\sqrt{25}$) = .5 mm/5 = .100 mm

2. Using Luis's process from the last question, the average range of the samples of sixteen is .6 mm with a standard deviation of .1 mm. What would be the upper and lower limits on a R-chart for this process?

Solution:

   $UCL_R = .6$ mm $+ 3 \times .1$ mm $= .9$ mm

   $LCL_R = .6$ mm $- 3 \times .1$ mm $= .3$ mm

3. Tom's airline tracks the average turnaround time of its planes as they land, restock fuel and supplies, and board and unload passengers. In the past, the average time from landing till take off was 20 minutes. This did not count planes whose scheduled maintenance required longer down times. The standard deviation was approximately 5 minutes.

   a) What is the probability of a given flight randomly requiring 30 minutes for turn around? Do you feel there is reason to investigate?

   b) What is the probability of a given flight randomly requiring 4 minutes for turn around? Do you feel there is reason to investigate?

Solution:

   a) $Z = (30 - 20)/5 = 2$ (i.e., a 30 minute turnaround is two standard deviations above the mean). A value outside two standard deviations would likely happen about 5% of the time so it is likely a normal random occurrence.

   b) $Z = (4 - 20)/5 = -3.2$ (i.e., a 4 minute turnaround is 3.2 standard deviations below the mean). A value outside 3.2 standard deviations would likely happen about .14% of the time (or fourteen times in 10,000 flights) so it is likely due to some explainable reason. While it is faster, which seems to be good, you should still investigate to see why the apparent improvement has occurred.

4. An operator will sometimes find broken or defective spindles coming out of the lathe process in Luis's factory. Occasionally a knot or crack in the wood will cause the spindle to break while being turned. A series of samples over the last few months resulted in an average percent defective of 4%. The sample size is 400.

   a) What is the value of $\overline{np}$?

   b) What are the values of σ_p? and σ_{np}?

   c) If the most recent sample had thirty-two defectives in it, would you think this a normal random variation?

   d) If the two most recent samples had six and seven defectives in them, respectively, would you think this a normal random variation?

Solution:

   a) $\overline{np} = 4\% \times 400 = 16$

   b) $\sigma_p = \sqrt{[(.04 \times .96)/400]} = .00979$, $\sigma_{np} = .00979 \times 400 = 3.919$

   c) $Z = (32 - 16)/3.919 = 4.08$ or more than four standard deviations above the mean. That would happen randomly less than three times in 100,000 samples. (The probability is so small it is off the chart in Appendix 1. For the actual probability enter the formula

"1-NORMSDIST(4.08)" in an Excel spreadsheet.) We must conclude that the process is out of control.

d) $Z = (6 - 16)/3.919 = -2.55$ and $Z = (7 - 16)/3.919 = -2.29$. Because NORMSDIST($-2.55$) gives the result 0.0053861, a sample with six defective items would occur randomly only .54% of the time. Similarly, because NORMSDIST(-2.29) gives the result 0.0110107, a sample with six defective items would occur randomly only 1.1% of the time. The odds of these sample results occurring randomly in sequence would be .54% $\times$ 1.1% or less than six times out of 100,000 samples. Again, we must conclude the process is out of control. Even when things are looking better, it is still necessary to find out why and institute the special cause since it is a change that will make the process better.

5. Cheryl's hospital is interested in the time required to admit a patient for same-day surgery. Over the past month her staff has timed the admission process for a wide cross-section of patients at all times of day. They have timed patients in samples of ten and have collected three dozen samples. Computing the mean admission time for each sample of ten patients, the average of the sample means is 15 minutes. They also computed the range of admission times for each sample with the average sample range equal to 3.5 minutes. Using the "Computational Factors for the $\overline{X}$ and R-chart" in Table 4.4, construct the upper and lower control limits for both the $\overline{X}$ and the R-charts.

Solution:

You have a sample size of 10, A2 = .308, D3 = .223, and D4 = 1.777. Thus:

$UCL_{\overline{X}} = 15 + .308 \times 3.5 = 16.078$

$LCL_{\overline{X}} = 15 - .308 \times 3.5 = 13.922$

$UCL_R = 1.777 \times 3.5 = 6.2195$

$LCL_R = .223 \times 3.5 = .7805$

6. Luis's staining and varnishing area produces hardwood tables that occasionally require additional buffing to remove minor flaws in the tables' finish. The number has historically averaged about seven flaws per eight-hour shift. A *c*-chart is to be kept

on this process; determine the upper and lower control limits.

Solution:

C bar = 7 and $\sigma_c = \sqrt{7} = 2.645$ thus

$UCL_c = 7 + 3 \times 2.645 = 14.935$

$LCL_c = 7 - 3 \times 2.645 = -.935$ which would be truncated to 0

7. The Fred and Barney Cookie Co. has been baking chocolate chip cookies for many years, yet is just now looking to implement statistical process control. Managers are particularly concerned about the number of burned or broken cookies coming out of the baking process and heading into the packaging process. Traditionally, they have sampled the finished product, but obviously it is better not to package burned or broken cookies at all. To get SPC up and running, they have decided to track burned cookies. Four times per day over the last five days they have taken twenty samples of 1,000 cookies each as batches came out of the oven and counted the burned cookies in each sample. Use the chart below to answer the following questions:

a) Are the managers dealing with a variable or an attribute?

b) What are the upper and lower control limits of their *np*-chart?

c) Is the process in control now?

Sample	Number of Burned Cookies
1	11
2	9
3	8
4	12
5	4
6	7
7	12
8	11
9	12
10	14

Sample	Number of Burned Cookies
11	12
12	11
13	12
14	13
15	11
16	7
17	9
18	10
19	12
20	11

Solution:

a) attribute

b)

Sample Size (n)	1000
$\overline{np}$	10.4
$n\sigma_p$	$1000 \times \sqrt{[(0.0104 \times .9896)/1000]} = 3.20809$
LCL_p	$10.4 - 3 \times 3.20809 = 0.7747$
UCL_p	$10.4 + 3 \times 3.20809 = 20.0243$

c) The process is not in control because samples 7–15 are all above the mean, which violates one of the "rules of run."

8. Tom Jackson's airline is concerned about capacity utilization on the Las Vegas–San Francisco route. The airline flies this route five times a day, five days a week (Monday–Friday). Managers have decided to collect data on the number of seats filled on each flight (the same type of aircraft is used for all flights). The following table shows the average number of seats filled each day and the range between the fullest and the emptiest flights each day.

   a) Will statistical process control help in addressing the managers' concern? How?

   b) Draw the $\overline{X}$- and R-charts.

   c) Is capacity utilization on the route under control? If not, what reason can you deduce from the data and/or the charts?

Day	DAILY Mean	DAILY Range
M	78	13
T	82	11
W	77	11
TH	83	12
F	79	27
M	86	14
T	80	12
W	79	13
TH	77	14
F	78	39
M	79	14
T	80	14
W	82	13
TH	83	12
F	84	31
M	79	12
T	86	13
W	84	11
TH	79	12
F	75	35
M	84	11
T	86	13
W	79	14
TH	80	11
F	81	37

Solution:

a) Yes, it will help to show how accurately they are hitting target capacity, as well as how consistently

b)

	CL	UCL	LCL
$\overline{\overline{X}}$	80.8	90.47052	71.12948
R	16.76	38.24632	0
$A_2,5$	0.577		
$D_3,5$	0		
$D_4,5$	2.282		

c) Check the second Friday on the R-chart, which may indicate a big fluctuation on Fridays. Might it be caused, in part, by the fact that business and pleasure travel combine on certain Friday flights?

9. A local soda-bottling plant uses a p-chart to monitor the percentage of bottles that are not capped correctly after they have been filled. Managers found a sampling mean of 5% nonconforming based on a sample size of 480 bottles (twenty cases of twenty-four bottles each). Over the last several samples, they have observed the following sample means: 5%, 5.1%, 4.8%, 5.1%, 4.9%, 5.0%, 2.2%, 2.3%.

a) What is the σ_p?

b) Is the system under control? Why or why not?

c) What should the managers do?

Solution:

a) $\sigma_p = \sqrt{[(5\% \times 95\%)/480]}$ = Approx. 1%; thus UCL = 8%, LCL = 2%

b) No; the last two samples were close to LCL, ref: rules of run

c) Stop and investigate why the process has become "too good to be true," based on original conditions. An assumption would be that something has changed for the better.

10. While Cheryl would like all the services provided by her hospital's housekeeping department to be perfect, she realizes that the patient services desk will always receive a small number of complaints. Over the past twelve weeks she has noted the log information that follows.

a) Can you help Cheryl apply statistical process control to this problem? What type of chart would be applicable?

b) Is the housekeeping process in control? If not, why not?

c) What interpretation could you offer?

Week	1	2	3	4	5	6	7	8	9	10	11	12
# of Complaints	9	7	8	10	5	9	6	9	17	17	5	6

Solution:

a) Yes; a c-chart is applicable

b) CL = 9, this is found by averaging the number of complaints across all samples. The square root of this number is 3, thus the $UCL_c = 9 + 3 \times (3) = 18$, and the $LCL_c = 9 - 3 \times (3) = 0$. The process seems to be in control except for weeks 9 and 10, where two "near misses" would appear to put it out of control based on rules of runs.

c) What went wrong that made that two-week period so different from the rest? Was someone on vacation those two weeks?

11. A rip saw in Luis's factory cuts pine boards to a wide range of specifications with a standard deviation of .25 millimeters. The specs for most products at this stage of their processing have a tolerance of .5 millimeters in either direction. Luis and a process engineer are discussing the ability of the saw to meet their needs.

a) What is the C_p ratio for the saw based on the majority of the products it will be used on?

b) How many parts will not meet specifications even while the process is in control?

c) Considering what you know about the furniture business, do you feel the machine meets the company's needs?

Solution:

a) $C_p = (.5 + .5)/(6 \times .25) = 1/1.5 = .66$

b) The LSL is exactly two standard deviations below the target and the USL is exactly two standard deviations above the target. Because Excel returns the value 0.0227501 for the function NORMSDIST(-2.0), the percentage of nonconforming parts below the LSL would be 2.28%. By symmetry, the same percentage would be found above the USL. Thus, the total percentage nonconforming would be approximately 4.56%

c) Probably not when making high-quality furniture.

12. The "Older Than Dirt" potting soil company wants to monitor the time it takes to fill, seal, and load a 75-pound bag of garden dirt. The managers check and find that the process takes a normally

distributed average time of 60 seconds, with a standard deviation of 10 seconds. What would be the standard deviation of the sampling distribution of means if managers were to randomly sample:

a) Sixteen bags at a time?

b) Two hundred twenty-five bags at a time (a full truckload)?

c) Describe the process distribution and the two sampling distributions of means on the same scale. Estimate the center and the three-sigma boundaries on each distribution.

Solution:

a) $10/(\sqrt{16}) = 10/4 = 2.5$

b) $10/(\sqrt{225}) = 10/15 = .667$

c) All are centered at 60 seconds. Three standard deviations on either side of the mean of the process distribution ranges from 30 seconds to 90 seconds. With $n = 16$ the comparable sampling distribution range is from 52.5 seconds to 67.5 seconds; with $n = 225$ the comparable sampling distribution range is from 58 to 62.

DISCUSSION QUESTIONS

1. A duke is hunting in a forest with his men-at-arms and servants when he comes upon a tree. Archery targets are painted all over it, and smack in the middle of each is an arrow. "Who is this incredibly fine archer?" cries the duke. "I must find him."

   After continuing through the forest for a few miles, he comes across a small boy. The child is carrying a bow and arrow and admits that it was he who shot the arrows plumb in the center of all the targets.

   "You didn't just walk up to the targets and hammer the arrows into the middle, did you?" asks the duke worriedly.

   "No, my lord," replies the boy. "I shot them from 100 paces. I swear it by all that I hold holy."

   "That is truly astonishing," says the duke. "I hereby admit you into my service. But I must ask one favor in return. You must tell me how you came to be such an outstanding shot."

   "Well," said the boy, "first I fire the arrow at the tree, and then I paint the target around it."

   a) From a quality management perspective, what would be the moral of this story?

   b) Explain the concepts of accuracy and precision in terms of the theory of variation such that the Duke would know what type of variation he

   should expect to observe when selecting expert archers?

2. What is the difference between inspection as it is understood today and inspection under the old paradigm of quality management? How would you apply the new paradigm to the grading of your work in this operations management course class?

3. Using the context of an advertising agency, how would you explain the difference between "quality control" and the broader range of "quality assurance activities associated with TQM"?

4. Pick a product-service bundle you have purchased lately. Define customer satisfaction in that context. Define customer dissatisfaction in that context. How do they different? Which is easier to measure? Which is more important? Why?

5. The manager of a restaurant has just come to your table and asked, "Is everything okay?" What does she they want to hear? What will that answer not tell her? What should she hear?

6. Why is employee involvement (EI) important into TQM? Can you think of a situation in which it is not important?

7. Does putting more emphasis on statistics in your business mean that managers should go out and

hire a bunch of statistics professors to act as consultants? Why or why not?

8. How might meeting the "specifications" of a hamburger at a fast-food restaurant differ from satisfies the customer?

9. Describe a situation in which you had a problem with a product or service and complained to the business about it. What did you tell the business? What do you think they did with the information? What should they have done with the information?

10. A cookie maker buys its chocolate chips from two different suppliers that it plays against one another to keep the price of chips low. Is this a smart strategy? What are the trade-offs of the arrangement?

11. What does winning the Baldrige Award say about a company that ISO 9000 certification does not, and vice versa?

12. List the business functions in which you have taken introductory courses. What contributions does each function make toward the attainment of customer satisfaction through quality management? What tools does each function emphasize that are useful for the improvement of quality?

13. Compare and contrast detection, prevention, and ongoing continuous improvement. Now, think about your own effort to improve the quality of your schoolwork. In which of those three stages would you place your efforts? Why?

14. What does a diverse cross-functional team add to a process improvement project that is hard to get from a homogeneous team drawn from a single function?

15. What is the difference between precision and accuracy? Can accuracy be assessed independently of precision? How would you apply the two concepts to an archery competition? Who would win the competition?

16. As the manager of a small winery, you sample incoming grapes, as well as outgoing bottles of several varieties of wine prior to their shipment. How would you describe your type I and type II error costs? How would they different from

your customer's error costs (the wholesaler's or retailer's)? From the ultimate consumer's?

17. Which would be more likely to use acceptance sampling: the dairy that buys milk by the truckload directly from the dairy farm, or the auto manufacturer that buys brake parts from a component supplier? Why?

18. A hotel manager has received several complaints over the last few weeks concerning the time the front desk takes to check guests in and out. After analyzing the process, she realizes that several steps are included in each procedure (waiting in line, filling out a registration form, checking the availability of a room, and so on). What type of control chart would you suggest the manager use to begin to improve the front desk's service? What might be second step the manager should take?

19. Tom Jackson wants to verify his airline's ability to get a passenger's luggage where it is supposed to go. Can you suggest a plan for action? What variables should Tom measure? What type of chart should he use?

20. What type of chart should the manager of a group of computer programmers use to monitor the "bugs" in the code they create? Why?

21. The registrar's office at your college or university encourages students to graduate no more than five years after matriculating. What type of chart should the registrar use to monitor compliance with this goal?

22. You are a bank manager. What characteristics of the check-clearing process define quality? How would you apply statistical process control to this process?

23. If you were to classify the clothes in your closet by how often you wear them, and then construct a Pareto chart from the results, what might the chart tell you?

24. Your parents are concerned about your grades. You realize that your poor grades are merely the measured symptoms of some underlying problem. Use a fishbone chart and try to identify those problems. Would a Pareto chart add anything to your analysis? How? How would you use the "5Ws and an H" to set your parents at ease?

PROBLEMS

1. When a flight does not leave or arrive on time (the FAA defines this as outside a 15-minute window), Tom considers it a defect. If the long run average for late departure/arrivals on his flights is equal to 12%,

   a) What would be the appropriate control charts for this situation?

   b) What would be the upper and lower limits for these charts if Tom samples 100 flights per day?

2. Using Tom's situation in problem #1: Today the sample averaged 18%. Is this likely normal variation? Should we investigate the process?

3. Using Tom's situation in problem #1: Today the sample averaged 23%. Is this likely normal variation? Should we investigate the process? Why?

4. Using Tom's situation in problem #1: Today the sample averaged 18% after averaging 19% yesterday. Is this likely normal variation? Should we investigate the process? Why?

5. Using Tom's situation in problem #1: The last five days have all averaged between 12% and 16%? What if the next two are also above 12%?

6. When a customer buys a new home from a builder, the builder may be called back from time to time to make minor repairs and or adjustments. Though these repairs are usually covered under a new home warranty, a local builder of identical track homes considers each occurrence to be a defect and wants to monitor the situation. Some homes never need adjustment work while others require that the builder make several trips. Assume the average number of minor adjustments to be thirty-six a month (they finish building and sell about ten homes a month).

   a) What would be the appropriate control charts for this situation?

   b) What would be the upper and lower limits for these charts?

7. Hawkeye Apple Orchards has a new bagging process that is supposed to be filling 4-pound bags with apples for distribution through grocery stores.

The bagging process has generated samples of twenty bags every hour for the last few days. The average weight for those samples has been 4.28 pounds, with an average range of weights within each sample of .55 pounds.

   a) Using the "Computational Factors for the $\bar{X}$ and R-chart" in Table 4.4, construct the upper and lower control limits for both the $\bar{X}$ and the R-charts.

   b) How would you explain the fact that the sample mean exceeds the target of 4 pounds? How would you address this?

8. The staff of a weekly magazine wants to track the number of typographical errors in their editions once each issue reaches the newsstand. While the staff members feel they have an effective process for editing and catching errors before the magazine is printed, a few mistakes always slip through.

   a) What would be the appropriate control charts for this situation?

   b) What would be the upper and lower limits for these charts if the average number of typos per edition were four?

   c) What would be the upper and lower limits for these charts if the average number of typos per edition were sixteen?

9. A packaging machine that fills cereal boxes has a standard deviation of .5 ounce when set to fill 18-ounce boxes. The company takes a sample of thirty-six boxes every hour to check the filling accuracy. The average range from heaviest to lightest box is usually .5 ounces with a standard deviation of the range equal to .11 ounce.

   a) What should they expect the standard deviation of the sample means to be?

   b) What would be the upper and lower control limits of the $\bar{X}$ chart for the process?

   c) What would be the upper and lower control limits of the R-chart for the process?

10. Which type of chart would be most appropriate to measure each of the following situations?

a) The number of broken eggs in a crate of egg cartons.

b) The number of accidents each week in the local police report.

c) The output of a process packaging meat into 1-lb. packages.

d) The people who fail a driving test.

e) The people who vote in an election.

f) The calls to a consumer hotline.

g) The consistency of cookie diameter coming out of a process.

h) The number of broken cookies coming out of the process above.

11. Fred has a machine etch a pattern onto a circuit board to a location with a standard deviation of 1 micron from its targeted position. The specifications for the circuit boards call for the etching to be within 2 microns of the targeted position.

a) What is the C_p ratio for the etching process?

b) How many parts will not meet specifications even while the process is in control?

c) Considering what you know about the electronics business, do you feel the machine meets the company's needs?

12. Fred buys firewood from a local company who uses a chain saw to cut the wood from fallen timber. Most customers of the firm, like Fred, expect the wood to be between 12 and 24 inches in length to fit in a standard residential fireplace safely. Assume the local woodcutter "eyeballs" the length of a cut piece of wood when using his chain saw and can usually hit the target midway between the specifications, say 18 inches, with a 1-inch standard deviation.

a) What is the C_p ratio for the chain saw process of cutting firewood?

b) How many pieces of wood will not meet specifications even while the process is in control?

c) Considering what you know about the firewood business, do you feel the process meets the company's needs?

13. The percentage of faulty computer chips produced by a factory in the Pacific Rim is of concern to a customer. Rather than wait for the chips to be shipped to the assembly plant in Canada, the customer has sent a group of managers to the supplier's factory to start statistical process control there. As each batch of chips comes out of the process, the managers collect a sample of 200 for testing. The chart below shows the number of malfunctioning chips found in each of the last twenty-four samples.

a) What is the average percentage of malfunctioning chips?

b) What would be the upper and lower control limits on a p-chart?

c) Is the process under control?

Sample	# of "Bad" Chips
1	8
2	4
3	3
4	5
5	4
6	6
7	5
8	4
9	5
10	6
11	3
12	4
13	6
14	7
15	5
16	11
17	4
18	5
19	4
20	3
21	0
22	0
23	6
24	3

14. As a manager, you know that orders traditionally take about three days to go through your company's shipping department. Every so often you check a couple of shipments to make sure things are going smoothly. You guess there is a standard deviation of about one day.

    a) What is the chance that the next order will take more than three days to go through shipping?

    b) What is the chance that without any change in the system, the next seven samples you check will be shipped in less than three days? If that were to happen, would the system still be under control?

    c) Given the situation described in (b), should you take any action?

    d) Is the situation that is described in (b) different from that in which a sample of orders takes seven days to be shipped?

15. Right now, Fred's company uses two suppliers for its injection-molded pager cases: Casey's Cases and Krank Cases. Managers at his company want to consolidate all the business for that part with one of the two suppliers, but before doing so they need to certify which supplier will be more likely to deliver a steady flow of reliable parts. As Fred's boss put it, "Don't put all your eggs in one basket, that is, unless you know it's a darn good basket." The managers agree that the weight of the casing has a lot to do with how well it fits together: if a casing is too light, the mold must not have filled properly; if it is too heavy, the mold may have overflowed. As a comparison, purchasing agents from Fred's company weighed random samples of incoming cases and tracked them by supplier. Samples of five cases each were taken from twenty daily shipments sent by each supplier. The data the agents collected is provided below. The target spec is between .9 and 1.4 ounces per case.

    a) What would be the UCL and LCL for each supplier's $\bar{X}$ and R-charts?

    b) Do the charts from part (a) indicate any lack of control?

    c) Assess the accuracy and precision of Casey's Cases and Krank Cases.

    d) How comfortable would you feel consolidating the supply of this part with either Casey's or

Krank Cases? Which company would you choose? Why?

Casey's Cases

Sample	Case #1	Case #2	Case #3	Case #4	Case #5
1	1.1	1.2	1.1	1.2	1.1
2	1.1	1.2	1	1.1	1
3	1.2	1.1	1.1	1.1	1.1
4	1.2	1.3	1.2	1.1	1.1
5	1.1	1.3	1.1	1.2	1.2
6	1.2	1.1	1.1	1.3	1.2
7	1.2	1.1	1.1	1.2	1
8	1.1	1.1	1.3	1.2	1.3
9	1.2	1.2	1.2	1.3	1.3
10	1.3	1.1	1.1	1.2	1.1
11	1.2	1.1	1.2	1.1	1.2
12	1.1	1.2	1.2	1.1	1.2
13	1.2	1.1	1.1	1	1.2
14	1.2	1.1	1.2	1.1	1.3
15	1.2	1.1	1.1	1	1.2
16	1.2	1.1	1.1	1.2	1.2
17	1.1	1.2	1	1.2	1.2
18	1.2	1.1	1.3	1.2	1.2
19	1.2	1	1.2	1.2	1.2
20	1.1	1.2	1	1.2	1.1

Krank Cases

Sample	Case #1	Case #2	Case #3	Case #4	Case #5
1	1.1	1.2	1.4	1.4	0.9
2	1.1	1.4	1.4	0.9	1
3	1	1.1	1.1	1.1	1.1
4	1.2	1.3	1.2	1.1	1.1
5	1.1	1.2	0.9	1.2	1.2
6	0.9	0.9	0.9	1.3	1.3
7	1.3	1.4	1.4	1.2	0.9
8	0.9	1.1	1.4	1.2	1.5
9	1	1.3	1.2	0.8	1.5

Sample	Case #1	Case #2	Case #3	Case #4	Case #5
10	1.3	1.1	1.4	0.9	1.1
11	1.2	1.4	1.4	1	1.4
12	1.1	0.9	1.2	1.1	1.2
13	1.1	0.9	1	0.9	1.2
14	1.3	1.1	1.4	0.9	1.3
15	1.4	1.1	1.1	1	0.9
16	1.4	1.5	1	1.4	1.4
17	1.3	1.2	1	1.2	1.2
18	1.2	0.9	1.3	1.2	1.2
19	0.9	1	1.2	1.2	1.2
20	1.1	1.2	0.8	1.1	1.1

16. You have just graduated, started your first full-time job, and bought a new car on loan, with payments you can barely afford. After a week or two of driving the car, you notice that it needs a few minor repairs and adjustments (a loose mirror, a slight rattle when you put the car in park, a burned-out turn signal). These minor nonconformities, which are under warranty, annoy you, and you tell the service manager about them when you take the car in for adjustments. The manager assures you that the assembly plant is always seeking to improve its performance, but there are an infinite number of minor nonconformities on a new car, and the dealer always takes care of them. Curious to test your newly certified capability for critical thinking, you press further and find that on occasion, the service manager does decide that the number of nonconformities is getting out of hand and calls the factory to find out what the problem is. You suggest you can help, so he provides you with the following data, recorded over the last few months. Assume that the dealer sells the same number and mix of cars each week, and that all come from the same factory.

Week	1	2	3	4	5	6	7	8
# of Adjustments	34	22	18	27	44	15	6	34

a) Will statistical process control help to solve this problem? What type of chart should you use?

b) Is the system under control now?

c) What set of rules would you suggest the service manager use? Can you reconcile this answer with the material in this chapter?

17. One way in which a paper mill measures performance is the number of web breaks, a major disruption that occurs when the flow of paper (the "web") is broken, due either to a flaw in the fiber or to unusual tension. Web breaks are a fact of mill life, and most mill managers monitor their occurrence. A mill with four production lines has collected the following data over the last few weeks. Being a fairly capital-intensive operation, the mill runs all four lines seven days a week for three shifts per day.

Week	1	2	3	4	5	6	7	8
# of Web Breaks	11	7	10	6	9	9	9	12

a) Can statistical process control help to monitor web breaks? What type of chart should be used?

b) Is the system under control now?

c) What set of rules would you suggest the plant manager use? Can you reconcile your recommendation with the material in Chapter 4?

18. In canoe making, small blemishes in the finish are common; unless there are several on a single canoe, the consumer generally will not notice. Several canoes may be produced without any blemishes, while a single canoe may carry more than one. The Cando Canoe Co. thinks this state of affairs is fine. As a consultant, assess the following data:

Week	1	2	3	4	5	6	7	8	9	10	11	12
# of Blemishes per 20 Canoes	4	5	4	6	4	4	5	7	8	9	12	13

a) Can statistical process control help? What type of chart would you use?

b) Is the system under control now?

c) What set of rules would you suggest the plant manager use?

19. Fred has a flow soldering process that solders chips onto a board that goes into his cell phones. The target thickness of the solder is 4.0 microns. Every hour a sample of sixteen boards is taken to a quality assurance (QA) station in the plant where the soldering is measured. Over the past few days many samples have been taken and measured, both the sample mean and the range of solder thickness within each sample have been plotted. The average sample mean has been 4.001 microns, and the average range within each sample has equaled .5 microns.

    Using the "Computational Factors for the $\overline{X}$ and R-Chart" in Table 4.4, construct the upper and lower control limits for Fred's $\overline{X}$-chart.

20. Using the $\overline{X}$-chart for Fred's flow soldering process described above and assuming the following series of sample means were found over an 11-hour period:

4.012	4.002	3.999	4.001	3.801	4.019
4.008	3.999	4.000	4.002	3.806	

    Does the process appear to have been under control during the time these samples were taken? If not, why not?

21. Using the $\overline{X}$-chart for Fred's flow soldering process described above and assuming the following series of sample means were found over an 11-hour period:

4.028	4.011	4.001	3.999	3.995	3.825
4.009	4.008	3.999	4.000	4.002	

    Is the process under control? If not, why not?

22. Using the $\overline{X}$-chart for Fred's flow soldering process described above and assuming the following series of sample means were found over an 11-hour period:

4.103	4.100	4.086	4.091	4.095	4.091
4.083	4.072	4.010	3.994	3.991	

    Is the process under control? If not, why not?

23. Using the $\overline{X}$-chart for Fred's flow soldering process described above and assuming the following series of sample means were found over an 11-hour period:

4.010	4.105	4.106	4.066	3.921	4.009
4.008	3.999	4.000	4.002	3.806	

    Is the process under control? If not, why not?

24. Using the $\overline{X}$-chart for Fred's flow soldering process described above and assuming the following series of sample means were found over an 11-hour period:

4.010	4.022	3.999	3.995	3.921	4.009
4.028	3.999	4.000	4.042	3.806	

    Is the process under control? If not, why not?

25. Use the information from Fred's flow soldering process that solders chips onto a board that goes into his cell phones (see the earlier questions). The average range in thickness of the soldered surface from each sample of sixteen boards has been .5 microns.

    Using the "Computational Factors for the $\overline{X}$ and R-Chart" in Table 4.4, construct the upper and lower control limits for Fred's R-chart.

26. Using the R-chart for Fred's flow soldering process described above and assuming the following series of ranges were observed over an 11-hour period:

.212	.543	.443	.801	.814	.432
.545	.498	.506	.555	.467	

    Does the process appear to have been under control during the time these samples were taken? If not, why not?

27. Using the R-chart for Fred's flow soldering process described above and assuming the following series of ranges were observed over an 11-hour period:

.612	.543	.555	.576	.611	.632
.645	.698	.506	.555	.467	

    Is the process under control? If not, why not?

28. Using the *R*-chart for Fred's flow soldering process described above and assuming the following series of ranges were observed over an 11-hour period:

.342	.443	.443	.601	.355	.432
.245	.698	.506	.555	.467	

Is the process under control? If not, why not?

29. Using the *R*-chart for Fred's flow soldering process described above and assuming the following series of ranges were observed over an 11-hour period:

.267	.399	.543	.411	.301	.874
.643	.445	.389	.286	.511	

Is the process under control? If not, why not?

30. Using the *R*-chart for Fred's flow soldering process described above and assuming the following series of ranges were observed over an 11-hour period:

.501	.498	.476	.486	.399	.401
.495	.404	.432	.453	.503	

Is the process under control? If not, why not?

CHALLENGE PROBLEMS

1. The "Older Than Dirt" potting soil company uses a machine to fill 40-pound bags of enriched potting soil. The machine has a process standard deviation of about 6 ounces. For years managers have just assumed that if the bags averaged 40 pounds each, nobody would complain. Now, a new industry group wants to set limits on what can be called a "40-pound" bag of dirt: a bag must weigh at least 39 pounds, 8 ounces and no more than 40 pounds, 8 ounces, though heavy bags can still be counted as good. At least no one but Joe Dirt, Jr., the company president, complains when the bags are a little too full!

   a) Which is the appropriate type of ratio for this process as currently configured: C_{pk}, C_p, CPL, or CPU? Why?

   b) Given the answer to (a), what is the ratio for the machine when bagging 40-pound bags, on average?

   c) How many bags will not meet specifications even while the process is in control?

   d) Considering what you know about the dirt business, do you feel the machine meets the company's needs?

2. The "Older Than Dirt" potting soil company (see the previous problem) uses a machine that is not precise enough to consistently meet the specs for filling 40-pound bags of enriched potting soil. Joe Dirt, III, the company marketing director, has suggested that manufacturing set the filling machine to a target of 40 pounds, 10 ounces in order to reduce the number of light bags that his customers will reject. The machine still has a process standard deviation of about 6 ounces.

   a) Now, which is the appropriate type of ratio for this process as currently configured: C_{pk}, C_p, CPL, or CPU? Why?

   b) Given the answer to (a), what is the ratio for the machine when bagging 40-pound bags, on average?

   c) How many bags will not meet specifications even while the process is in control?

   d) Joe Dirt, Jr., company president, is concerned about the extra dirt that they are giving away by overfilling. Can you estimate the percentage? Why is it being given away?

3. The "Older Than Dirt" potting soil company (see the previous two problems) currently uses a machine that is not precise enough to consistently meet the specs for to filling forty-pound bags of enriched potting soil. Joe Dirt, II, the company engineer and nephew of the company founder, Joe

Dirt I, has suggested improving the precision of the filling process so that the standard deviation of the process would be only 2 ounces. This would mean that they could set the machine to target exactly 40 pounds again.

a) Now, which is the appropriate type of ratio for this process as currently configured: C_{pk}, C_p, CPL, or CPU? Why?

b) Given the answer to (a), what is the ratio for the machine when bagging 40-pound bags, on average?

c) How many bags will not meet specifications even while the process is in control?

d) How much should they be willing to spend to improve the precision given the circumstances described in these three problems?

4. The Fred and Barney Cookie Co. has collected the following data over the past few days: They have a process that bakes and packages a targeted 11-ounce package of cookies. They take a sample of fifteen packages every 2 hours and have collected both the average net weight from each sample as well as the range of individual package weights over the last seven shifts (twenty-eight observations). As flour is the predominant ingredient for this type of cookie, the supplier of the flour used when each sample was taken is also provided. The company uses two major suppliers, Acme All-Rise, the primary supplier, and Baker's Best, which is currently used as a backup. While both suppliers seem fairly reliable, the cookie company uses Baker's as leverage against Acme to keep Acme's price as low as possible.

Sample (Shift#/Sample#)	Avg. Weight of Sample	Range of Sample	Flour Supplier
1.1	11.3	0.8	Acme All-Rise
1.2	11.2	0.8	Acme All-Rise
1.3	10.9	1.1	Acme All-Rise
1.4	12.1	0.8	Acme All-Rise
2.1	11	0.7	Acme All-Rise
2.2	10.9	1.5	Acme All-Rise
2.3	10.9	0.6	Baker's Best
2.4	10.8	0.5	Baker's Best

Sample (Shift#/Sample#)	Avg. Weight of Sample	Range of Sample	Flour Supplier
3.1	10.9	0.6	Baker's Best
3.2	10.8	0.5	Baker's Best
3.3	10.9	0.5	Baker's Best
3.4	11.2	0.7	Acme All-Rise
4.1	11.1	1.4	Acme All-Rise
4.2	11.2	0.9	Acme All-Rise
4.3	10.8	0.6	Baker's Best
4.4	10.8	0.4	Baker's Best
5.1	11	0.8	Acme All-Rise
5.2	11.7	1.7	Acme All-Rise
5.3	10.8	0.7	Acme All-Rise
5.4	11.2	0.8	Acme All-Rise
6.1	10.8	0.4	Baker's Best
6.2	10.8	0.4	Baker's Best
6.3	11	0.8	Acme All-Rise
6.4	11.2	1.1	Acme All-Rise
7.1	10.8	0.8	Acme All-Rise
7.2	11.2	0.7	Acme All-Rise
7.3	10.9	0.7	Acme All-Rise
7.4	11.6	1.5	Acme All-Rise

a) Using the "Computational Factors for the $\overline{X}$ and R-Chart" in Table 4.4, construct the upper and lower control limits for both the X-bar and the R-charts.

b) Is the process under control?

c) What would the $\overline{X}$ and R-charts look like if you separated samples of the cookies baked with Baker's flour from samples of those baked with Acme's flour? (Hint: If you have typed the data into a spreadsheet, deleting entire rows containing data for one supplier may adjust formulas to represent the remaining supplier. Do not forget to save the combined data first!)

d) Consistent with concepts of supply chain management, how would you explain this? How would you address these findings?

Case 4: NASA's Problems with Mars Probes Linked to Communication Failure

Several years ago, the National Aeronautics and Space Administration (NASA) initiated a long-term systematic program of Mars exploration, the Mars Surveyor Program (MSP). The scientific objectives of this program were to

▶ Search for evidence of past or present life

▶ Understand the climate and volatile history of Mars

▶ Assess the nature and inventory of resources on Mars

The goal of the Mars Surveyor Program was to carry out low-cost missions, each of which would provide important, focused, scientific data, the sum of which constitutes a major element of the scientific exploration of Mars. A series of lander and orbiter spacecraft began being launched at favorable opportunities, which occur approximately every 26 months. The Mars Surveyor Program launched the Mars Global Surveyor (MGS) in 1997, the Mars Climate Orbiter (MCO) in 1998, and the Mars Polar Lander (MPL) in 1999.

The MCO's mission was to use atmospheric instruments and cameras to provide NASA teams with detailed information about the surface and climate of Mars. As it prepared to enter orbit around the planet, the spacecraft was too close to the surface and either burned up in the atmosphere or continued past the planet into space.

The MPL was to execute the first landing in a polar region of Mars, near the southern polar cap. The lander was equipped with cameras, a robotic arm, and instruments to measure the composition of Martian soil. Two small microprobes, which constituted the Deep Space 2 technology mission, hitched a ride to Mars on the lander, with the goal of penetrating the Martian subsurface to detect frozen water. However, communication was lost as the lander began its entry into the Martian atmosphere. Flight controllers spent several weeks searching for the spacecraft to no avail. The Deep Space 2 probes were also lost.

"People sometimes make errors," said Dr. Edward Weiler, NASA's Associate Administrator for Space Science. "The problem here was not the error, it was the failure of NASA's systems engineering, and the checks and balances in our processes to detect the error. That's why we lost the spacecraft."

Preliminary findings indicated that when building the part of MCO that was to place the spacecraft in the proper orbit, one team used English units of measurement (in other words, inches, feet, and pounds), while the other team used metric units. "Our inability to recognize and correct this simple error has had major implications," said Dr. Edward Stone, director of the Jet Propulsion Laboratory. "We have underway a thorough investigation to understand this issue." NASA recognizes that mistakes occur on spacecraft projects. However, sufficient processes are usually in place on projects to catch these mistakes before they become critical to mission success. Unfortunately for MCO, the processes in place did not catch the root cause of its problem.

Factors that led directly or indirectly to the loss of the MCO included inadequate consideration of the entire mission and its post-launch operation as a total system, inconsistent communications and training within the project, and lack of complete end-to-end verification of navigation software and related computer models. Similar issues were suggested as causing the MPL failure. More specifically, issues that are thought to have contributed to the failures include the following:

1. Errors went undetected within ground-based computer models of how small thruster firings were predicted and then carried out on the spacecraft during its interplanetary trip to Mars.

2. The operational navigation team was not informed in detail about the way the Mars Climate Orbiter was pointed in space, as

compared to craft in the earlier Mars Global Surveyor mission.

3. A final, optional engine firing to raise the spacecraft's path relative to Mars before its arrival was considered but not performed for several interdependent reasons.

4. The systems engineering function within the project that is supposed to track and double-check all interconnected aspects of the mission was not robust enough, exacerbated by the first-time hand over of a Mars-bound spacecraft from a group that constructed and launched it to a new, multi-mission operations team.

5. Some communications channels among project engineering groups were too informal.

6. The small mission navigation team was oversubscribed, and its work was not peer reviewed by independent experts.

7. Personnel were not trained sufficiently in areas such as the relationship between the operation of the mission and its detailed navigational characteristics, or the process of filing formal anomaly reports.

8. The process to verify and validate certain engineering requirements and technical interfaces between some project groups, and between the project and its prime mission contractor, was inadequate.

SOME QUESTIONS TO THINK ABOUT:

1. How should NASA define quality?

2. What is the significance of Dr. Weiler's statement? What was he blaming for the loss of MPL?

3. Given the specific issues identified in the investigation of the MCO, does it sound like NASA has functional silos to contend with? How do they affect the quality of NASA's programs?

Source: Adapted from http://www.jpl.nasa.gov/news/

REFERENCES

Bergman, B., and B. Klefsjö. *Quality*. New York: McGraw-Hill, 1994.

Bureau of Business Practice. *Profiles of ISO 9000*. Needham Heights, MA: Allyn & Bacon, 1992.

Costin, H. *Strategies for Quality Improvement*, 2nd ed. Fort Worth: Dryden Press, 1999.

Crosby, P. *Quality Is Free*. New York: McGraw-Hill Book Company, 1979.

Feigenbaum, A. V. "Total Quality Control." *Harvard Business Review* (November–December 1956): 93–101.

Gabor, A. *The Man Who Discovered Quality*. New York: Times Books, 1990.

Gilow, H. S., and S. J. Gitlow. *The Deming Guide to Quality and Competitive Position*. Englewood Cliffs, NJ: Prentice Hall, 1987.

Hanna, M. D., and W. R. Newman. "Operations and Environment: An Expanded Focus for TQM." *International Journal of Quality and Reliability Management* 12, no. 5 (1995): 38–53.

Hercules Corporation. "Quality Council Communique." Unpublished draft, January 15, 1990.

Ishikawa, K. *What Is Total Quality Control? The Japanese Way*. (Translated by David J. Lu.) Englewood Cliffs, NJ: Prentice Hall, 1985.

Joiner, B., and P. Scholtes. "The Quality Manager's New Job." *Quality Progress* (October, 1986): 52–56.

Juran, J. M., and F. M. Gryna. *Quality Planning and Analysis*, 3rd ed. New York: McGraw-Hill, Inc., 1993.

Killian, C. S. *The World of W. Edwards Deming*. Washington, DC: CEEPress Books, 1988.

Neave, H. R. *The Deming Dimension*. Knoxville, TN: SPC Press, Inc., 1990.

Stratton, B., "A Few Words about the Last Word." *Quality Progress* (October 1993): 63–65.

United States Department of Commerce. *Malcolm Baldrige National Quality Award: 1996 Award Criteria*. National Institute of Standards and Technology, 1995.

Yoshida, K. "Deming Management Philosophy: Does It Work in the U.S. as Well as in Japan?" Columbia *Journal of World Business* (Fall 1989): 10–17.

5

The Project Management Process

Chapter Outline

Introduction   190
Integrating Operations Management Across the Functions   191
Building the Project Management Organization   194

The Project Management Body of Knowledge   199

Managing through the Project Life Cycle   199
Project Planning, Scheduling, and Control   205

Detailed Scheduling Using Network Modeling   206

Analyzing PERT/CPM Networks   209

Time-Cost Trade-offs or Project Crashing   218

Summary   226
Key Terms   227
Solved Problems   227
Discussion Questions   233
Problems   235
Challenge Problems   241
Case 5: Project Scope: To See the Birth of the Universe (and More)   244
References   245

Learning Objectives

After studying this chapter you should be able to

▶ Discuss the linkages between project management and the various functional areas of business

▶ Describe the common organizational forms used in project management firms and explain why they make sense

▶ List and discuss the nine major tasks included in the project management body of knowledge (PMBOK)

▶ Explain what happens and what management tasks are critical at each phase of the project life cycle

▶ Analyze project progress and budgets utilizing standard project management accounting terminology

▶ Describe the process of planning and control in project management organizations

▶ Draw and interpret simple PERT/CPM network diagrams and use them to make detailed scheduling decisions

▶ Analyze PERT/CPM networks to find critical activities and completion probabilities

. . . Back at the Rec Center

Fred is preparing to leave the rec center early. He hadn't said much all morning, but as he is on his way to the locker room, Luis asks him why he is leaving. "I've got to get in early this morning," Fred answers. "I have to meet with my team on this software implementation stuff again." Fred had mentioned this project off and on—mostly off—for several months. His company was planning to bring a new software system on line that would help them coordinate their entire supply chain. He had called it "SAP," but that was the brand name; at other times he called it "ERP" or "enterprise resource planning" software. It was a big deal for his company, which had set up teams of consultants from the software vendor, internal MIS staff who had experience with software implementation, third-party vendors, and staff from the various departments who would work with the software. That's when Fred came into the picture. His team had met a few times to sketch out the basic requirements of the system and to stake out some implementation parameters—but not much had happened for a few months. Now, as his mood indicated, things were heating up quickly.

"That was all of a sudden!" Luis says with surprise. "I just asked you about the project last week."

"Yeah, you said there wasn't much going on with that anymore," notes Tom.

"There wasn't," answers Fred. "Now everything is in a rush. This whole project has been nothing but hurry up and wait."

"Sounds like military planning to me!" laughs Tom. "But I'll bet there's some bigger picture that you're seeing only one part of."

"You're probably right," Fred sighs, as he looks at his watch. "I just have a hard time understanding why things can be so slow one minute and then become a super important deadline the next. You gotta remember, this whole thing is still a year or so away from when it's supposed to go online."

"Maybe you're slack," laughs Luis, as he worked his legs.

"Say what?!" asks Fred as he looks up, surprised, at Luis.

"I think," says Cheryl, as she tuned into the conversation, "what he's saying is that when it comes to implementing a system like that, some things have to follow a tight schedule to get the whole thing done on time and others don't. It's the ones that are tight, well, they're critical. Those that don't, well, they have slack."

"It's like building a house," says Luis. He describes how his brother-in-law, a general contractor, builds a house. He uses the plumbing as an example: As soon as the basement is excavated, the plumber has to rough in all the main floor drains and sewer taps before the concrete walls can be poured. There's usually a tight window for that process, as nothing else can happen until it's completed. Then the plumbers aren't needed again until most of the frame is up, explains Luis. "All the plumbing, electrical, heating, and air-conditioning people are really pushed so the dry wall people can get in and finish the walls. They then have to wait until the house is almost finished to set the fixtures, toilets, and showers."

Fred could see what Luis meant. Some things need to happen before others can be done. "I guess it's up to the plumber to find something to do in between," says Fred.

"That's a good point," agrees Cheryl. "That means guys like that have to be flexible and juggle their time between jobs."

"These kinds of systems guys must have had five or six irons in the fire," Fred laughs. He described how the systems people from his company and the vendor's people on his team were also on teams together at other plants. They were always talking about different jobs they were juggling all concurrently and all at different stages of completion.

"I guess they're just different from the system guys I'm used to working with," says Fred. "I mean, I'm used to IT guys I see every day. The guys that keep us up and running, they think just like the rest of us in my plant. They see the world in the time it takes a phone to get through the line and on to the customer—you know, hours and days. These new guys are really different. They're looking months and years down the road."

"That's another good point," says Cheryl. "They need a way to be looking farther down the road than most of us do in our jobs."

"Oh, they have a system," says Fred. He described how they came in a few months earlier and spent some time looking around and asking a lot of questions. Then they were gone. He said they came back a few weeks later to do some preliminary training and to ask more questions and then left again. There wasn't much going on with the team over the last few weeks. Now they're back with some new people and a very tight schedule. "It just seems like they'd be better off doing one thing at a time and seeing it through. It's more like what I'm used to," Fred adds.

"I'll bet it's like the plumbers," says Luis. "They probably had some things done in the beginning and then got out of the way. Something else had to happen next, and now they're back and making more work for you." Tom and Cheryl nod their agreement.

"Yeah, I guess so," says Fred. "They did give some of the guys in my area a 'to do' list as they were leaving the first time. They needed some information. They wanted things reorganized a bit, nothing big. I guess we must have got it done on time."

"And then they came back?" asks Luis.

"Yeah, they did," answers Fred.

"I get it," interjects Tom. "All the time Fred thought nothing was going on, the consultants were waiting on Fred's people to do their part, or like the second time, waiting for the techies to get the software up and running."

"So what you're saying is that the next time I'm stuck in the middle of highway construction and it doesn't look like anybody's doing anything, I shouldn't start yelling about wasted tax dollars," Fred laughs. He had stayed longer than he'd expected to. He gets up and heads to the men's locker room. "I should remember, it's all part of some bigger plan."

Introduction

Project

A set of tasks that is completed only once to create a unique product-service bundle.

A **project** is a set of tasks that is completed only once to create a unique product-service bundle. For example, we all notice big civil engineering projects, and we probably associate project management with the skills required to accomplish them. But project management does not apply only to enormous building projects such as the Great Wall of China, the Eiffel Tower, the Suez Canal, or the International Space Station. Instead, projects, large and small, are a part of daily life, and project management skills are useful in a wide variety of situations. Many businesses add value by completing projects for their customers; examples of these businesses are social services agencies, consulting firms, accounting firms, engineering firms, construction firms, advertising agencies, law firms, framing shops, caterers, and artists. The work that such businesses complete is one of a kind, usually done to the specifications of the customer, and with a great deal of customer interaction along the way.

In project-oriented organizations such as the ones mentioned above, personnel from various functions must work together effectively to satisfy their customers because no single function exists in a vacuum. Companies that exist primarily to manage projects are significantly different from the kinds of companies we have discussed so far. Project managing companies must deal with greater uncertainty than other types of businesses, because they are generally working on jobs that

▶ Have never before been done

▶ Are often of critical importance to their customers, although those customers may have difficulty defining exactly what they need

▶ Present many challenges in regard to workforce management. Skilled workers and experts must work together to understand the scope of the entire project

Because project management organizations and their workforces are different from other organizations, the body of knowledge applied by project managers is somewhat different from that required in other organizations. They form a generally accepted domain of expertise called the project management body of knowledge (PMBOK).

The life cycle of a project—whether it is erecting a building, an accounting project, or implementation of an ERP system—can be divided into four stages:

1. The need for the project is established, alternatives are considered, and consensus is built around one specific alternative.

2. Plans for project implementation are developed.

3. The project itself is under way.

4. The project is completed, payments to the project provider are finalized, and the customer begins to use the value provided by the project.

Project managers can anticipate the different managerial challenges and activities associated with each stage.

A project activity may be critical to the timely completion of the project or have virtually no impact on the completion time. The critical nature of an activity changes as a project moves forward and sequences of activities move ahead of or behind schedule. Detailed project scheduling is, therefore, necessary to ensure timely completion within budgetary constraints. In many cases, this detailed scheduling makes use

REC CENTER DILEMMA

Cheryl's Dilemma—Part I

Cheryl has been thinking of the conversation at the rec center (see above). She has just been given the responsibility of leading a project team that is responsible for opening a new pulmonary care center. The job will be complete only when the center is in operation. One of her first steps is to organize the project team. Who do you think she should include on the team, and why? How will she be able to obtain the full participation of these individuals?

of computer modeling techniques that can identify which resources (workers and equipment) to use for a given task at a given point in the project's development.

Project managers must keep up with a large number of details. Because resources may be assigned simultaneously to multiple projects, detailed records must be kept on both a project-by-project basis and an aggregate basis. Thus, in planning and controlling their projects, managers must adapt to progress updates from their entire set of current engagements and reassign resources accordingly. Projects are often managed under severe pressure to meet deadlines, which makes the issue of resource assignment among multiple projects a particularly difficult and important task.

Integrating Operations Management Across the Functions

Just like product-service bundles, each project has consumers and providers. Project consumers, however, often provide at least part of the project specifications, which makes projects similar to many services and unlike most manufacturing operations. For example, the client of a law firm provides information and objectives for the project whose value they consume.

Bruno de Hogues/Getty Images Inc.

Getting all the right workers with the right material to the right place at the right time for the construction of an airliner can be complex process. It is a great place to employ project management techniques.

Occasionally, projects are completed and consumed by a single function within a business. Financial managers might restructure a firm's finances in light of new tax laws or corporate opportunities. Accountants might set up the books for a new division or prepare a tax return. Human resource managers might select and install a new employee database. Marketing people oversee advertising projects for their company, engineers consult on projects to expand capacity, and many MIS professionals are constantly occupied in building, installing, or updating computer systems.

As Table 5.1 indicates, project management is a critical activity for professionals in any function, and every function can be critical for project management. For example:

▶ *Finance.* Because cost control is a critical issue in project management, finance is a critical function in the management of projects. It plays a role in each stage of the project life cycle, as well as in project planning and control. For example, additional financial costs are typically associated with expediting a project.

Table 5.1

Integrating Operations Management with Other Functions

Integration Perspective / Functional Area	Finance	Accounting
Why Cross-Functional Integration Matters in Project Management	Major projects often require special financing and financial control. Also, many financial managers are involved in managing projects such as IPOs, LBOs, mergers, acquisitions, and the like.	Accountants are often responsible for establishing budgets and tracking the costs of projects. Also, accountants participate in projects such as audits, tax preparation, restructuring of businesses, etc.
Key Issues	How will project risks and insurance be managed? How will project operations be funded? How will project assets be acquired and valued?	What will be the project budget? How will project expenditures be tracked? How will the contract be managed and what controls will be established to prevent fraud and ensure timely payments of contract expenditures?

▶ *Accounting.* Most of the work done by accountants is project work. This is true in large public accounting firms, smaller accounting services, and corporate accounting departments.

▶ *Human resources.* People drive a project's success. Especially because project workers typically have unique skills, the human resources function is critical, particularly to the successful management of multiple projects.

▶ *Marketing.* The characteristics of project management organizations are familiar to marketing professionals, for this form of organization is common in advertising agencies and promotional firms. Also, projects must be marketed to ensure that they gain and retain the support of all interested parties, not just during the conceptual phase but throughout the project life cycle.

▶ *Engineering.* More than any other function, engineers add value to a firm's operations by managing projects. Whether designing the product-service bundle or the value-adding system, most engineering work takes the form of projects.

Human Resources	Marketing	Engineering	Management Information Systems
Projects provide a unique HR challenge in that they often use short-term laborers and subcontractors with highly specialized skills. Recruiting and integrating these people into the company is an HR challenge.	Firms that manage projects have a unique marketing challenge due to the high stakes involved for most of their customers. Many marketing professionals manage projects such as advertising and PR campaigns, media development, and market research.	Engineers of every type are heavily involved in projects ranging from designing new products and structures to building these items, to conducting major overhauls and maintenance, to demolition and waste removal.	Information systems provide key data and decision support to project managers. Additionally, MIS professionals will manage projects such as system development, software/hardware acquisition, and user training.
How will project labor be recruited, especially in specialized fields? Which labor laws apply to project personnel and how can we ensure compliance with these laws and other safety standards? How will project workerperformance be appraised?	How should the project managing firm market its technical capabilities and managerial skills? What are the customer's requirements and how do these translate into the project scope?	What technical requirements must be satisfied for project success? What additional input from technical experts will be required?	What project data must be captured and how? How will access to project management software be managed? How will the project data be maintained?

◗ *Management information systems.* MIS professionals, who normally support existing computer systems, must occasionally select and implement new software packages. They may also maintain the company's project management software application. Consequently, they must understand the project planning and scheduling process that is used by others in their organization.

Figure 5.1 illustrates the major decision processes and concepts presented in this chapter as they integrate with other functions and the supply chain in general. They include:

◗ "Building the project management organization," which includes discussion of organizational structures commonly found in project management firms and the project management body of knowledge.

◗ "Managing through the project life cycle," the portion of the chapter that describes the changing demands that arise as a project moves from conception to completion.

◗ "Project planning and control," which details the network modeling and analysis tools often used to keep projects on time and within budget.

Figure 5.1
The project management process

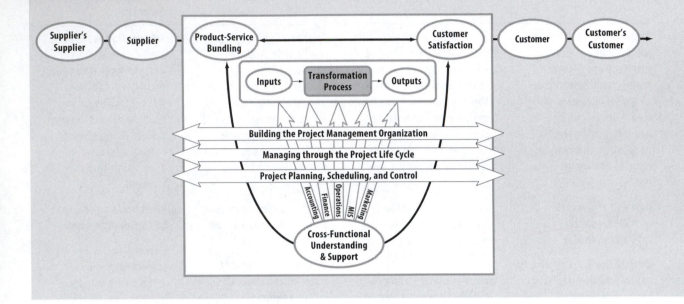

Building the Project Management Organization

Virtually every organization must manage some type of project from time to time, but, as mentioned before, some organizations are in the business of managing projects, such as engineering and construction firms, audit firms, consulting firms, law partnerships, research and development labs, insurance underwriters, and medical claims processors. This kind of company is unlike other businesses in many respects: Workers may move from project to project, often from one location to another. They might work with a different group of people on each project. And, while their expertise is of great value to clients, they often have difficulty communicating with clients without resorting to technical jargon.

From an organizational perspective, teams are common in project management companies. This type of structure makes a lot of sense, because while projects come and go, the employees remain. Workers need to retain some core organizational position, or identity, as they move from project to project. Figure 5.2 shows the traditional matrix organization that is often found in project management firms. With a **matrix structure**, employees may be assigned to one or more projects at a given time, but their home department does not change.

The matrix structure allows a company to develop and retain core capabilities and functional excellence. It also allows managers to classify and track personnel assigned to multiple projects. Each person has a department boss and a project boss. The project manager's job is to oversee and coordinate the work of personnel from various functions on the project. If a project manager has a problem with any function's performance on the project, he or she can take up the issue with the department

Matrix structure

The business theory that states employees may be assigned to one or more projects at a given time, but their home department will remain the same.

Figure 5.2

Hypothetical project management matrix

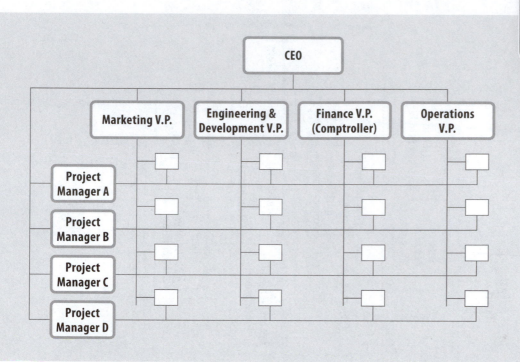

manager. It is the department boss's job to assign workers to specific projects and make sure their cumulative work loads are not excessive. The department boss also oversees contract pricing and scheduling to make sure the department's capacity is not exceeded.

Figure 5.3 shows two alternative team structures, a hierarchical structure and a customer-driven structure. With a **hierarchical team structure** (Figure 5.3a), projects come and go, but the team remains largely intact. Thus, project workers always report to the same project manager, who in turn reports to a senior manager (in Figure 5.3a, the regional director). The hierarchical structure is less flexible than the matrix structure. In a hierarchical structure, the team develops expertise with particular types of projects rather than individuals or departments developing functional capabilities. For example, a large law firm might create standing teams devoted to environmental practice, banking regulations, personal injury, labor law, incorporation, and so on. If the firm runs out of a particular type of work, however, and new cases are not well matched to a given team's expertise, a whole team of lawyers might well need to move on.

With a **customer-driven team structure** (Figure 5.3b), projects come and go, but the type of customer remains largely the same. As customers become familiar with the team they are working with, they can ask the team to take on a variety of projects. For example, an advertising agency might create a project team devoted exclusively to one client's account. The team might create a broadcast media campaign for one division in the client company, a web-promotion strategy for another, a print campaign for a third, and an overall marketing strategy for the corporation as a whole. Often, team leaders (the partners) in this type of structure represent the company's entire steering team, which is headed by a senior executive or partner in the firm. This steering team is responsible for

Hierarchical team structure

A business philosophy that states the team might remain largely the same as projects come and go. Project workers report to the same project manager, who would in turn report to a senior manager, probably the regional director.

Customer-driven team structure

A business philosophy that states projects come and go, but the type of customer remains largely the same.

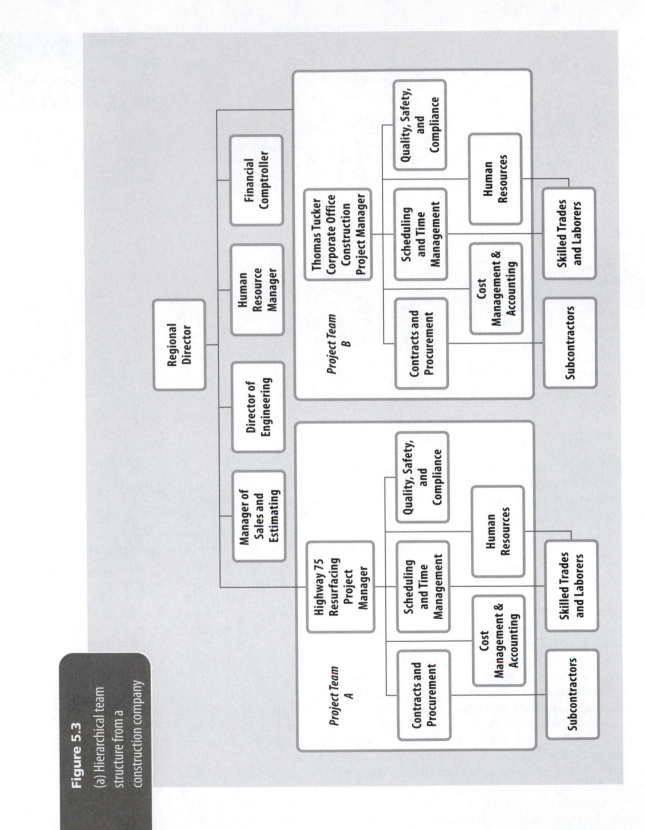

Figure 5.3
(a) Hierarchical team structure from a construction company

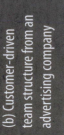

Figure 5.3

(b) Customer-driven team structure from an advertising company

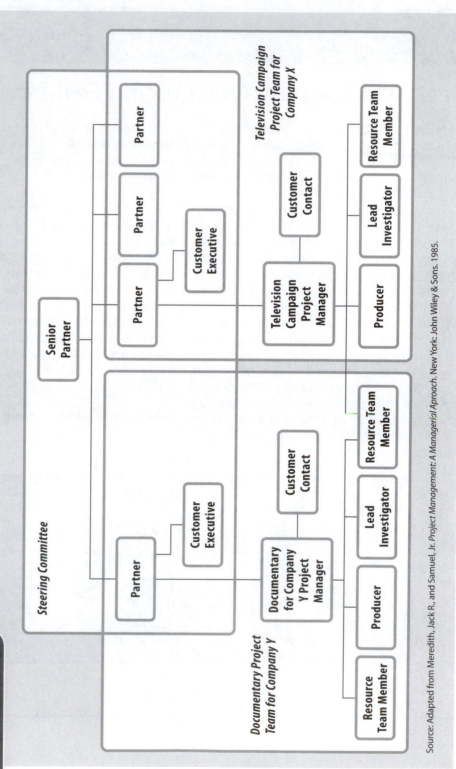

Steering Committee

Senior Partner

Partner   Partner   Partner

Customer Executive

Partner

Customer Executive

Television Campaign Project Team for Company X

Customer Contact

Television Campaign Project Manager

Producer   Lead Investigator   Resource Team Member

Documentary Project Team for Company Y

Customer Contact

Documentary for Company Y Project Manager

Resource Team Member   Lead Investigator   Producer   Resource Team Member

Source: Adapted from Meredith, Jack R., and Samuel, Jr. *Project Management: A Managerial Aproach.* New York: John Wiley & Sons. 1985.

INTEGRATING OM:

Project Management Outsourcing Gains in Popularity

A survey conducted by the Center for Business Practices (CBP), the research arm of project management consultancy PM Solutions, reveals an upward trend in the number of large international companies that are turning to project management as a cost-effective, long-term solution to product and process improvement efforts. In addition, the survey found that more of these companies are using project management consultants and augmented staffing to complete project implementations.

The survey, "Project Management: The State of the Industry," polled 1,000 project professionals and senior-level executives representing Global 2000 companies in industries including manufacturing, healthcare, and information technology.

According to survey respondents, 39% of the companies currently outsource project management functions or are considering it. More than half of the responding companies use consultants for project management, primarily for managing projects (66%) and augmented staffing (61%).

In addition, the study found that the most common functions currently outsourced are project delivery, project management training, and complete project management (at 40.7% each). . . .

[The results indicate] that most companies do not have a large enough in-house staff to successfully accomplish improvement project objectives . . . [and that such projects can cause managers to lose focus on their day-to-day activities and responsibilities. The results also suggest that increased levels of outsourcing project management functions, either entirely or through the use of consultants or augmented staffing companies, can help firms maintain their focus on the day-to-day operations. This can help them stay competitive and] achieve a higher project success rate at a lower cost.

Source: http://www.pmsolutions.com/press/, May 5, 2003

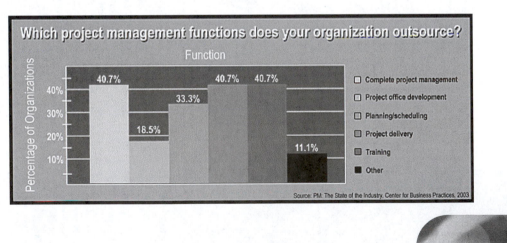

coordinating the efforts of the various customer-driven teams and creating opportunities for them to learn from each other. If any employees serve on more than one team, it is the steering team's job to ensure that they are not overburdened.

Regardless of the type of structure a project management organization has, all its projects share certain tasks and each progresses through a common life-cycle.

The Project Management Body of Knowledge

Table 5.2 summarizes the project management body of knowledge (PMBOK), which was developed by the Project Management Institute (PMI). PMI is the professional organization for project managers; it has almost 40,000 members worldwide and offers the project management professional (PMP) certification.

Notice that the PMBOK covers a wide area of expertise. It includes the detail-oriented aspects of project scheduling and budgeting, as well as the broad conceptual tasks of specifying a project's scope and integrating a project with existing systems. Not all projects will require the manager to apply every aspect of this body of knowledge, but the well-trained project manager should be prepared to cope with all these tasks.

Managing through the Project Life Cycle

As a project progresses through the four stages of its life cycle, the relative importance of the PMBOK areas changes, as illustrated in Figure 5.4.

In the first stage, the period of conceptual study, the primary required outcome is an organizational commitment to the project. This period can last for years and can raise numerous political and resource issues. The authors' university, for example, recently installed a $19 million fiber-optic data and video transmission network. Requests for such a network occurred for several years before the university committed to the project. Many issues had to be debated: Would the network cover all the buildings on campus, including dormitories and administrative buildings, or just academic buildings? Would the network be capable of carrying entertainment programming as well as educational channels? What bandwidth would be needed? Would the university operate the network or would an outside company operate it for profit? Finally, how would the school finance the network? These are only a few of the questions with which the university community had to come to terms when considering this project. Ultimately, the university president and board of trustees came to a consensus on the desired characteristics and capabilities of such a network and decided to install it. Their decision marked the end of the conceptual phase, which lasted roughly a decade.

Next, a team of technical experts and administrators began the second stage, the development phase, by writing a request for proposals (RFP). This request defined the scope of the project, indicating the university's needs and specifying the number of outlets, length of cable, and preferred standards and technologies for bidding purposes. It also specified an upper limit for bids on the project, a time limit for its completion, and the quality and performance measures that would be applied. Further development took place as development team conferred with prospective bidders, who began to consider how they would complete the project and what various alternatives would cost. The resulting proposals varied slightly, as did their price tags. Finally, the university accepted a bid and created a joint enterprise with NEC, which agreed to build the network for about 25% of its construction cost. In return, NEC would share in the revenues from the programming delivered over the network. This decision marked the end of the development phase of the project's life cycle, which lasted approximately one year.

During stage three, the implementation phase, which lasted about two years, an NEC project team worked with a university project manager to install the campus network. Various subcontractors were engaged to develop blueprints of the conduits and outlets; run underground cables; install cable buses, cable, and outlets; and test the installations. A lot of money was spent during implementation, so monitoring the cost, quality, and schedule established during the development phase was important.

Table 5.2
The Project Management
Body of Knowledge
(PMBOK)

PMBOK Area	Key Task(s)
Scope Management	Defining what must (and must not) be done in order to complete the project. Clients often have difficulty in defining this themselves—though they think they know what they want, it may be difficult for them to formally express that and cover all aspects of a project. Project managers with functional expertise and experience in previous projects can be very helpful in this regard.
Quality Management	Establishing metrics and standards to ensure that the client's expectations are met and making sure that the work is meeting those standards as it progresses. This area requires clear communication in subcontracting.
Cost Management	Establishing a project budget and making sure that the project stays within that budget. It is important to create checkpoints where project progress and expenses are evaluated relative to projections.
Contract Management/Procurement Management	Establishing and monitoring expectations of subcontractors. Purchasing or renting materials, equipment, training, and other resources as dictated by the project scope, quality standards, and cost structure.
Time Management	Scheduling work in order to complete the project in a timely manner. There may be penalties for late completion and rewards for early delivery. Project managers need to determine the value of time and find ways to use resources so that time is not lost and opportunities for improving the schedule are utilized.
Risk Management	Identifying potential project disruptions, their severity, ways to prevent their occurrence, and contingency plans should they arise. Risk management means more than buying an insurance policy; something this basic should not be overlooked.
Human Resources Management	Getting the right people assigned to the project at the right time. This area includes performance appraisal, discipline, compliance with labor law, and so on.
Communication Management	Keeping everyone on the same page with regard to the project. This area encompasses establishing regular team meeting times, creating formal communication channels such as e-mail, memos, newsletters, and websites, and establishing the needed informal channels of communication.
Project Integration Management	Fitting the project into existing organizations. For example, if the project is a new computer system, it has to be fit into the company where it will be used. That means that before, during, and after the project, or from the beginning to the end of the project's life cycle, the manager needs to be thinking about what will work in the environment where it will be deployed.

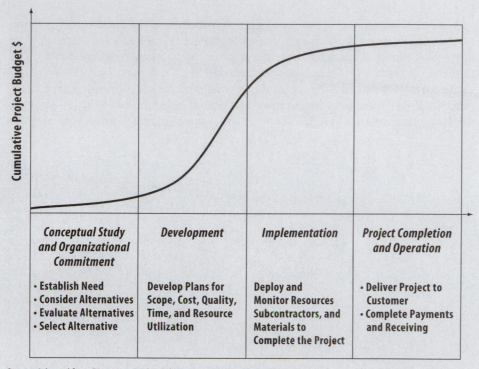

Figure 5.4

The project life cycle

Conceptual Study and Organizational Commitment

- Establish Need
- Consider Alternatives
- Evaluate Alternatives
- Select Alternative

Development

Develop Plans for Scope, Cost, Quality, Time, and Resource Utilization

Implementation

Deploy and Monitor Resources Subcontractors, and Materials to Complete the Project

Project Completion and Operation

- Deliver Project to Customer
- Complete Payments and Receiving

Source: Adapted from Dinsmore, Paul C., Editor. *The AMA Handbook of Project Management*. New York; Amacom, 1993.

When the network installation and testing were finished, the implementation phase of the project was complete, and the project team began to turn the network over to the personnel of the joint enterprise. The project team disbanded, but the network continues to operate, and NEC will receive shared revenue payments for years to come.

Figure 5.4 also lists some of the cost management, time management, quality management, and conceptual development tasks that are part of each phase of a project's life cycle. Notice that the early work in developing the project concept and obtaining cost estimates, schedules, and quality metrics provides the foundation for the entire project. Even though the cumulative financial outlays are most significant during the project's implementation phase, cost considerations are critical throughout the project. Similar statements could be made about time management and quality management. In fact, each area of the PMBOK is important in the early stages of the project. It logically follows any changes in a project's schedule, quality, cost, or scope should be made during the early stages because once the development phase is over, changing these particulars is both difficult and extremely costly. In particular, changes must be limited during the implementation phase.

Over the course of a project, estimates for cost, quality, and schedule become more and more certain. For that reason it is important to track these factors throughout a project. As for cost, project managers must look beyond their expenses and budget and carefully evaluate the progress of the project itself. Figure 5.5a shows the cumulative cost projections for a typical project. Notice that the project cost is only an estimate; the actual cost may be higher or lower than expected. Good managers will evaluate a project periodically and assess the risk of running over budget before the project can be completed. If the worst-case scenario is not tenable and the risk substantial, the project manager would be well advised to inquire whether the plan should be modified or even scrapped.

Figure 5.5b illustrates the many considerations in controlling project costs. It shows a common situation: The cumulative cost to date exceeds the budgeted cost to date. In other words, project managers have spent more money than they expected to. The monetary difference between the cumulative cost and the expected cost is referred to as the **current budget shortfall**. Note that even though the project is over budget, it is behind schedule: The value of the completed work, also called the **earned value**, is less than the budgeted expense. The difference between the budgeted cost to date and the

Current budget shortfall

The monetary difference between the cumulative cost and the expected cost.

Earned value

A situation where the value of the completed work is less than the budgeted expense.

Figure 5.5

Project cost projection

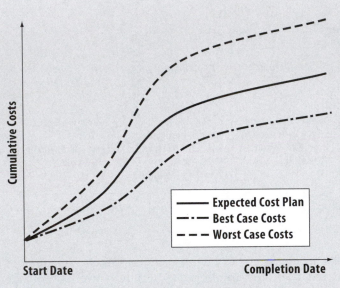

(a) Cost Projection at the End of the Development Phase

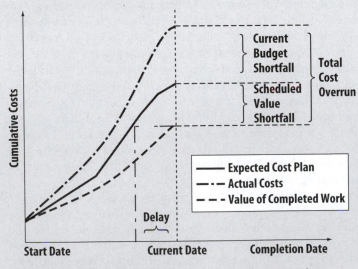

(b) Earned Value Analysis during Implementation

Figure 5.5

(continued)

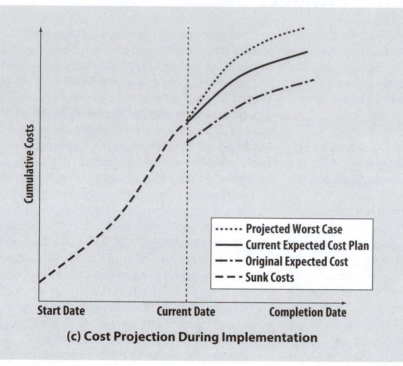

(c) Cost Projection During Implementation

Legend:
- Projected Worst Case
- Current Expected Cost Plan
- Original Expected Cost
- Sunk Costs

Axes: Cumulative Costs (vertical); Start Date, Current Date, Completion Date (horizontal)

earned value to date represents a variance from projected costs, which is called the **scheduled value shortfall**. The amount of time the project is running behind schedule is called the **project delay**. Managers must be concerned with both a current budget shortfall and a scheduled value shortfall, which together comprise the current **total cost overrun**. This analysis of project progress and expenditures relative to project targets is called **earned value analysis**.

Figure 5.5c shows how cost projections can be updated in the middle of the implementation phase. Notice that the projected (current expected) cost curve begins where the current cumulative expenses curve ends. The money that has been spent so far is called the **sunk cost**—that is, it represents an expenditure that cannot be recovered. Because information regarding actual costs is gained as the project progresses, the cost range from best case to worst case will continue to narrow as the project nears completion. Managers must continually evaluate and reevaluate a project's costs. If a cost overrun becomes large enough, they may need to downsize or modify the project. It may even be necessary, after millions or billions of dollars have been spent on a project, to abandon it. Sunk costs are not considered in these forward-looking decisions; they are irrelevant.

Large construction projects are not the only undertakings to be scrapped because of cost overruns. Many legal battles are dropped or settled out of court because of mounting costs. Research and development (R&D) projects can be high-risk ventures from the start, so many of them never make it past the "R" to the "D." Managers frequently back away from productivity improvement projects—from business process reengineering and total quality management (TQM) to computer system upgrades and equipment replacement. You may even have started some projects in your own home or back yard and never finished them because of a midstream reevaluation of the costs.

Scheduled value shortfall

The difference between the budgeted cost to date and the earned value to date. This represents a variance from projected costs, which is behind schedule.

Project delay

The amount of time the project is running behind schedule.

Total cost overrun

When a current budget shortfall and a scheduled value shortfall compromise together.

Earned value analysis

Analysis of project progress and expenditures relative to project targets.

Sunk cost

The money that has been spent on a project.

The Human Genome Project

The International Human Genome Sequencing Consortium, led in the United States by the National Human Genome Research Institute (NHGRI) and the Department of Energy (DOE), recently announced the successful completion of the Human Genome Project more than two years ahead of schedule. . . .

The international effort to sequence the 3 billion DNA letters in the human genome is considered by many to be one of the most ambitious scientific undertakings of all time, even compared to splitting the atom or going to the moon.

All of the project's goals have been completed successfully—well in advance of the original deadline and for a cost substantially less than the original estimates [shared with supporting agencies].

The flagship effort of the Human Genome Project has been producing the reference sequence of the human genome. A first draft of the human sequence was announced in June 2000. The working draft covered 90% of the gene-containing part of the sequence, 28% of which had reached finished form, and contained about 150,000 gaps. By 2003, researchers had converted the draft sequence into a finished sequence—one that is highly accurate and highly contiguous. The finished sequence produced by the Human Genome Project covers about 99% of the human genome's gene-containing regions, and it has been sequenced to an accuracy of 99.99%. The missing parts are essentially contained in less than 400 defined gaps. To help researchers better understand the meaning of the human genetic code, the project had numerous other goals, from sequencing the genomes of model organisms to developing new technologies to study whole genomes. As of April 14, 2003, all of the Human Genome Project's goals had been met or surpassed.

When the Human Genome Project was launched in 1990, many in the scientific community were deeply skeptical about whether the project's audacious goals could be achieved, particularly given its aggressive timeline and tight budgets. At the outset, the U.S. Congress was told the project would cost about $3 billion in FY 1991 dollars and would be completed by the end of 2005. It was finished two and a half years ahead of time. Costing $2.7 billion in FY 1991 dollars it was about $300 million under the original spending projections.

Effective coordination of scientific work was a major factor in the project's success. The consortium included hundreds of scientists at twenty sequencing centers in China, France, Germany, Great Britain, Japan, and the United States. The enormity of the Human Genome Project is unprecedented in biology. All of the sequence data generated by the Human Genome Project has been deposited into public databases and made freely available to scientists around the world, with no restrictions on its use or redistribution. The information is scanned daily by researchers in academia and industry, as well as by commercial database companies providing information services to biotechnologists.

Scientists have been quick to mine this new trove of genomic data, as well as to utilize the genomic tools and technologies developed by the Human Genome Project. For example, when the Human Genome Project began in 1990, scientists had discovered fewer than 100 human disease genes. Today, more than 1,400 disease genes have been identified.

With knowledge of all the components of the cells, we will be able to tackle biological problems at their most fundamental level. As we identify the similarities and the differences among the genes of mammals and other organisms, we will begin to gain valuable new insights into human health and disease. For example, researchers may now work toward:

◗ New tools to allow discovery of the hereditary contributions to common diseases, such as diabetes, heart disease, and mental illness.

◗ New methods for the early detection of disease.

◗ New technologies that can sequence the entire genome of any person for less than $1,000.

◗ Wider access to tools and technologies of "chemical genomics" to improve the understanding of biological pathways and accelerate drug discovery.

"The completion of the Human Genome Project should not be viewed as an end in itself. Rather, it marks the start of an exciting new era, the era of the genome in medicine and health," said NHGRI Director Dr. Francis S. Collins. "We firmly believe the best is yet to come, and we urge all scientists and people around the globe to join us in turning this vision into reality."

Source: http://www.genome.gov/11006929

Project Planning, Scheduling, and Control

Several supply chain management (SCM) issues confront project managers. Although every project is unique, SCM concepts remain relevant to the management of all projects. Many large projects are completed only after the creation of several levels of subprojects, each with its own subcontractors. For example, an advertising agency that is managing a large one-time media campaign might subcontract the print campaign. The subcontractor, in turn, would probably subcontract the artwork and writing. The advertising agency probably would also subcontract the printing of flyers, sportswear, and other documents to vendors who might then outsource some of the work. In other words, projects create supply chains of their own.

Because projects tend to be plagued by uncertainty, subcontractors and vendors need to be flexible in scheduling. Not only can they respond to changing demands, but they can benefit by structuring their contracts so that their flexibility is financially rewarded. The project's customer must likewise be flexible, providing schedule openings for the project when needed. For example, a software development and installation project might require the customer to provide windows of time for the project team to assess the system requirements, test software modules, conduct dry runs of the new system, run it parallel to the legacy system, and train workers in how to use it. The customer would also need to write formal statements of scope and accountability for the project manager and team.

Such scheduling issues are part of the time management aspect of the PMBOK. At the master scheduling level, managers must estimate the amount of work to be done on a weekly or monthly basis, while taking into consideration all the other projects the company has contracted to complete. The total workload is also an important consideration when bidding on and accepting new contracts. If there is a time conflict between two or more projects that require a single resource, managers must think about either turning down one project or finding ways to get both projects done.

One way to resolve such scheduling conflicts is to delay a project that is not critical in favor of one that is. **Critical activities** are those that cannot be delayed without delaying the entire project. Critical activities, in other words, have no **slack time**, which is the

Critical activities
Those activities on which the scheduled completion of the projects depends.

Slack time
The duration that an activity can be delayed without delaying the project's completion.

Though much less tangible in nature, a law firm's representation of a client through the duration of a trial (and potential appeals) is also very much a project. Many law firms use software like that described in this chapter to manage the process.

Michael Newman/PhotoEdit Inc.

Noncritical activities

A situation where the start of finish dates can be delayed without delaying the completion of the project.

Critical path

The longest path a project will take to complete its way through its network.

Crashing

Finding a way to complete an activity more quickly than expected.

Program evaluation and review technique (PERT)

A network modeling approach of time management that allows the expected duration of any activity to be expressed as a probability distribution.

duration that an activity can be delayed without delaying the project's completion. **Noncritical activities** do have slack time: Their start or finish dates can be delayed without delaying the completion of the project.

While this concept may sound simple, applying it can become quite complicated. Every project has a set of sequentially related critical activities, called the **critical path** that determines how long the project will take to complete. But as work on a project progresses, some activities may be delayed and others may proceed ahead of schedule. Therefore the critical path can change as the project moves forward. Activities that are critical can become noncritical, while activities that once had slack time can become critical.

If critical activities in separate projects are competing for resources, managers may try to "crash" one or more of the activities in order to deploy their resources more effectively. **Crashing** is finding a way to complete an activity more quickly than expected. It can be done by assigning more workers to an activity, using more or better equipment, approving more overtime, and so on. When a company has a number of projects on the master schedule, effectively deploying resources among them is a real challenge.

Project managers use two techniques to manage time and resources and break down a schedule into individual tasks. One is a network planning technique called **PERT**, which stands for **program evaluation and review technique**, and the other is **CPM**, or **critical path method**. Developed in the 1960s, both are network modeling approaches to time management. Originally, the only significant difference between the two was that PERT allowed the expected duration of any activity to be expressed as a probability distribution, while CPM did not. The two techniques are similar enough that many people use the terms interchangeably.

Currently available project management software, such as Microsoft's Project, is based on network modeling. Once the project network has been constructed, the software can be used to update the network and monitor progress, quality conformance, and costs. Because Project can track resources that are shared among multiple projects, it is extremely useful for making detailed capacity plans and allocating resources. Decisions about when subcontracted work and in-house activities should be completed and which activities should be crashed and which delayed are made much more easily with such programs. Recently, Eliyahu Goldratt, the developer of the theory of constraints, has developed a number of perspectives that are useful in managing projects. Given that projects contain multiple constraints, Goldratt's "Critical Chain Project Management" builds on the kind of network analysis and project management support provided by Project.

Peter Christopher/Masterfile

Next time you pass a construction site, remember that good project management is key to the project coming in "on time and under budget."

Detailed Scheduling Using Network Modeling

Detailed scheduling of projects begins with the identification of the specific activities that must be completed. A **work breakdown structure (WBS)**, which is a top-down view of the tasks included in a project, can be very useful in this process. Much like a bill of materials, the WBS breaks the project down into subprojects and then into sub-sub-projects, until it is reduced to the most basic work units that can be scheduled. These basic work units, which are referred to as **project activities**, are related in various ways to the other activities in the project. **Parallel (or independent) activities** are those that can be conducted simultaneously. **Dependent activities** are those that must be completed in a particular sequence—that is, one activity must be completed before another can begin. For example, in home construction, the land can be cleared while a request for a building permit is being processed. Those two tasks are independent activities. But the foundation cannot be poured until a building permit has been issued; those two tasks are dependent activities.

Figure 5.6 shows a simplified WBS for a political campaign. An actual WBS can be quite large, because it generally includes the subprojects to be handled by subcontractors in addition to all the individual activities in the project. While the activities in each subproject need not be listed, all the activities that will *not* be subcontracted should be. A complete enumeration of the project's activities is needed to estimate costs and create a **precedence table**, or a list of all the activities and their sequential relationships.

Figure 5.7 shows a precedence table for the political campaign outlined in Figure 5.6 (the table was created using Project). For the sake of simplicity, Figure 5.7 does not

Critical path method (CPM)

A network modeling approach to time management that doesn't allow the expected duration of any activity to be expressed as a probability expression.

Work breakdown structure (WBS)

A top-down view of the tasks included in a project.

Project activities

A basic work unit that's related in various ways to other activities in the project.

Parallel (independent) activities

Tasks that can be conducted spontaneously.

Figure 5.6

Work breakdown structure for a political campaign

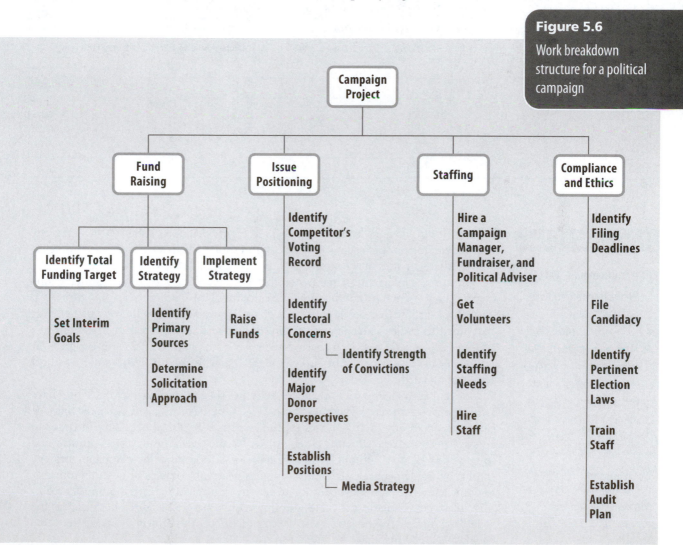

Figure 5.7

Precedence table for the political campaign

ID	Task Name	Duration	Start	Finish	Predecessors	Resource Names
1	Hire Manager	10d	Fri 10/9/06	Thu 10/22/06		Candidate
2	Hire Fundraiser	10d	Fri 10/23/06	Thu 11/5/06	1	Candidate,Manager
3	Hire Political Adviser	10d	Fri 10/23/06	Thu 11/5/06	1	Candidate,Manager
4	Hire Staff	30d	Fri 10/23/06	Thu 12/3/06	1	Manager
5	Get Volunteers	30d	Fri 12/4/06	Thu 1/14/07	4	Staff
6	Establish positions	60d	Fri 11/6/07	Thu 1/28/07	3	Candidate,Political Adviser
7	Compliance and ethics training	2d	Fri 1/15/07	Mon 1/18/07	2,3,5	Candidate,Political Adviser,Fundraiser,Staff,Volunteers
8	Begin fund raising	0d	Mon 1/18/07	Mon 1/18/07	7	
9	Raise funds	300d	Tue 1/19/07	Mon 3/13/08	8	Fundraiser
10	Implement Campaign Strategy	300d	Fri 1/29/08	Thu 3/23/08	7,6	Candidate,Manager,Staff,Volunteers
11	Vote	0d	Thu 3/23/08	Thu 3/23/08	10,9	Candidate,Manager,Political Adviser,Staff,Volunteers
12						
13						
14						
15						
16						
17						

REC CENTER DILEMMA

Cheryl's Dilemma—Part II

In reference to the project team she leads (see "Cheryl's Dilemma—Part I," page 190), Cheryl is now beginning to think of the tasks that will be involved in creating a pulmonary care center from scratch. What tasks will she need to include? What categories would you recommend she divide the work into? Which tasks have a parallel relationship and which ones have a dependent relationship?

include all the activities listed on the WBS in Figure 5.6. Notice the column that lists the predecessors for each activity—this column shows which tasks must be completed before other activities may begin.

Based on the information in the precedence table, the software can generate various graphical representations of the project. Notice the right-hand portion of Figure 5.7, a scrollable window that displays a Gantt chart. Figure 5.8 shows the complete Gantt chart for this project. The arrows on the chart indicate the precedence relationships among various activities. Such charts can display both planned and actual progress on a project's activities. They can also highlight the critical path by displaying critical activities in a dedicated color.

Notice that in Figures 5.7 and 5.8, the activities "begin fundraising" and "vote" have a duration of zero days. These less-than-brief activities are called **dummy activities** or **milestones**. Including such activities on the chart is sometimes necessary in order to keep the precedence of activities clear. In this case, the "begin fundraising" dummy had to be added because, although fundraising takes a long time, the campaign strategy cannot be implemented until fundraising has begun. In other words, though beginning the activity of fundraising is not an activity in itself, other activities must wait on this milestone. Similarly, the "vote" dummy activity had to be added because it is the milestone that marks the latest possible completion of the project. All activities must be completed by that date.

Figure 5.8
Gantt chart for the
political campaign

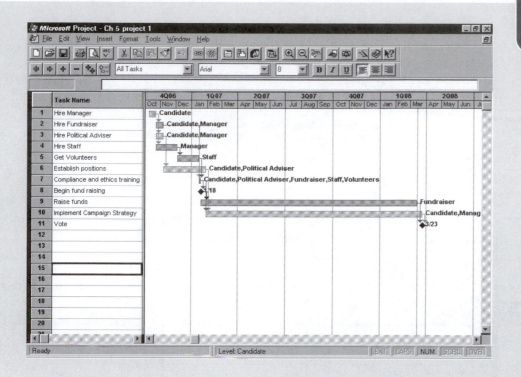

Figure 5.9 shows a PERT project network, which was also created using Project, for the political campaign. Each activity that is shown on the project's precedence table shows up as a *node* in this network. The *arcs*, or arrows, show the precedences between the activities. Project includes five fields on each node, which allow users to display information about activities directly on the diagram. In Figure 5.9 we have shown each activity's name, predecessors, duration, start, and finish. The critical activities and critical path are highlighted by the software with color and bold boxes; dummy activities are identified with a double box. As a project moves forward, the boxed activities change color to show that progress has been made.

In addition to its time management features, Project can be used to project, track, and control costs and resource requirements. For each resource, such as the campaign manager, fundraiser, or political adviser, data on capacity, cost, accrual rates, and work schedule can be entered into the project database. Once the resource requirements across all projects in the system have been compiled, the software can indicate when resources are overcommitted and when they are under committed. It can also generate resource-specific work calendars, such as the campaign manager's calendar for the fundraiser. Finally, as the actual activities of project personnel are recorded in the database, the software can be used to track the project's accrued costs.

Analyzing PERT/CPM Networks

A useful aid for understanding the relationships among the activities in a project is a network diagram. Two forms of such diagrams are in common use: **activity-on-node (AON)** and **activity-on-arrow (AOA)**. The AON network diagram is adequate for our

Dependent activities

Those activities that must be completed in a particular sequence.

Precedence table

A complete enumeration of the project's activities and their sequential relationships.

Dummy activities or milestones

Less than brief activities.

Activity-on-node

A useful aid for adequately understanding the relationships among activities to aide in illustrating ideas.

Activity-on-arrow

A useful aid for understanding the relationships among the activities in a project.

Figure 5.9

PERT network for the political campaign

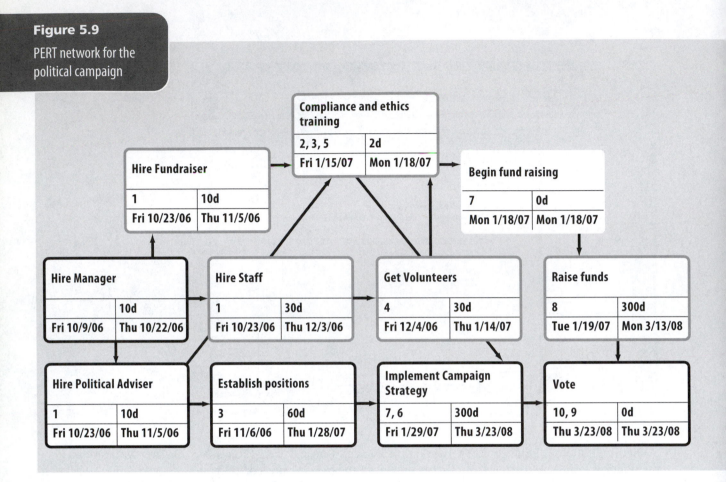

purposes and generally easier to construct than an AOA diagram, so we will focus on the AON approach to diagramming PERT/CPM network problems.

While a precedence diagram or AON network shows the structural relationships in the activity set, it is not sufficient for developing a project schedule. For scheduling purposes we need estimates of the time required to complete each activity in addition to the structural or precedence information.[1] By combining the individual activities' time information with the project's structural information, we can determine when each activity should start and may be expected to finish and how much flexibility we have in scheduling the activities.

Five times are associated with each activity in the project:

1. early start time
2. early finish time
3. late start time
4. late finish time
5. slack or float time

[1]If probability distributions of activity times are used rather than deterministic activity times, these will be the activities' *expected* completion times.

Use the immediate predecessors and activity time information given in Table 5.3 to determine the early start and finish times for a furniture factory expansion project. (Figure 5.10 is the AON network that arises from the precedence information in Table 5.3.)

Solution:

The list of activities, their immediate predecessors, and their times are repeated in Table 5.4, along with the early start and finish times as computed using the equations for ES_{act} and EF_{act}. The rationales for computation of the early start and finish times follow.

▶ Activity A has no predecessors, so it can start immediately ($ES_A = 0$), and taking 3 weeks, can finish as early as the end of week 3 ($EF_A = ES_A + t_A = 0 + 3 = 3$).

▶ Activity B has one predecessor, A, so B can start as soon as A is finished: $ES_B = EF_A = 3$. B takes 2 weeks, so B can finish as early as the end of week 5 ($EF_B = ES_B + t_B = 3 + 2 = 5$).

▶ Activity C has one predecessor, A, so C can start as soon as A is finished: $ES_C = EF_A = 3$. C takes 4 weeks, so C can finish as early as the end of week 7 ($EF_C = ES_C + t_C = 3 + 4 = 7$).

▶ Activity D has one predecessor, C, so D can start as soon as C is finished: $ES_D = EF_C = 7$. D takes 3 weeks, so D can finish as early as the end of week 10 ($EF_D = ES_D + t_D = 7 + 3 = 10$).

Table 5.3

Activities in Furniture Factory Expansion Project

Activity	Description	Immediate Predecessors	Time (weeks)
A	Develop initial plans	—	3
B	Secure financing	A	2
C	Develop final plans	A	4
D	Hire contractor	C	3
E	Secure permits	C	4
F	Construct addition	B, D, E	10
G	Order equipment	A	12
H	Install equipment	F, G	3

Figure 5.10

Activity on node network diagram for furniture factory expansion project

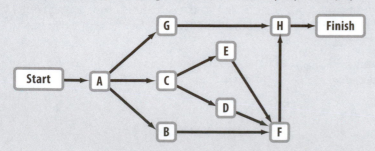

(continued)

Example 5.1

(*continued*)

Table 5.4
Early Start and Finish Times for Furniture Factory Expansion Project

Activity	Immediate Predecessors	Time (weeks)	Early Start	Early Finish
A	—	3	0	3
B	A	2	3	5
C	A	4	3	7
D	C	3	7	10
E	C	4	7	11
F	B, D, E	10	11	21
G	A	12	3	15
H	F, G	3	21	24

▶ Activity E has one predecessor, C, so E can start as soon as C is finished: $ES_E = EF_C = 7$. E takes 4 weeks, so E can finish as early as the end of week 11 ($EF_E = ES_E + t_E = 7 + 4 = 11$).

▶ Activity F has three predecessors—B, D, and E—so F can start as soon as all three are finished: $ES_F =$ maximum $\{EF_B, EF_D, EF_E\} =$ maximum $\{5, 10, 11\} = 11$. F takes 10 weeks, so F can finish as early as the end of week 21 ($EF_F = ES_F + t_F = 11 + 10 = 21$).

▶ Activity G has one predecessor, A, so G can start as soon as A is finished: $ES_G = EF_A = 3$. G takes 12 weeks, so G can finish as early as the end of week 15 ($EF_G = ES_G + t_G = 3 + 12 = 15$).

▶ Activity H has two predecessors—F and G—so H can start as soon as both are finished: $ES_H =$ maximum $\{EF_F, EF_G\} =$ maximum $\{21, 15\} = 21$. H takes 3 weeks, so H can finish as early as the end of week 24 ($EF_H = ES_H + t_H = 21 + 3 = 24$).

EARLY START AND FINISH TIMES

Early-start time (ES)

The earliest time at which something can begin if all activities preceding it start as early as possible and are completed in their estimated times.

Early-finish time (EF)

The time at which something will finish if it starts at its early start time and is completed in the estimated time.

Early start and finish times for an activity are based on the assumption that all activities will be done as soon as possible. An activity's **early start time (ES)** is the earliest time at which it can begin if all activities preceding it start as early as possible and are completed in their estimated times. An activity's **early finish time (EF)** is the time at which it will finish if it starts at its early start time and is completed in its estimated time. Because an activity cannot start until *all* of its immediate predecessors have been completed, its early start time must be at least as late as the early finish time of each of its predecessors. The early start and finish times of any activity ("act") may be computed from the following formulas:

$ES_{act} =$ maximum $\{EF_{pred1}, \ldots, EF_{predj}\}$, where "pred1", ..., "predj" are the immediate predecessors

of "act"

$EF_{act} = ES_{act} + t_{act}$, where t_{act} is the time required to complete "act"

Example 5.2

Use the immediate predecessors and activity time information given in Table 5.3 (see Example 5.1) to determine the late start and finish times for the furniture factory expansion project. Assume that the company wants to complete the project as soon as possible.

Solution:

The activities, their immediate predecessors, and their times are listed in Table 5.5, along with their late start and finish times computed using the equations for LF_{act} and LS_{act}. The computations were actually done in the reverse of the order shown in the table, beginning with the last activity or activities in the project and working back to the beginning.

▶ Activity H has no successors, so it must end at the desired completion time of the project. Assuming the company wants to complete the project as soon as possible, the desired completion time for the project is the same as the early finish time for H ($LF_H = EF_H = 24$). H takes 3 weeks, so it must

start no later than the end of week 21 ($LS_H = LF_H - t_H = 24 - 3 = 21$).

▶ Activity G has one successor, H, so G must end in time for H to start ($LF_G = LS_H = 21$). G takes 12 weeks, so G must start no later than the end of week 9 ($LS_G = LF_G - t_G = 21 - 12 = 9$).

▶ Activity F has one successor, H, so F must end in time for H to start ($LF_F = LS_H = 21$). F takes 10 weeks, so F must start no later than the end of week 11 ($LS_F = LF_F - t_F = 21 - 10 = 11$).

▶ Activity E has one successor, F, so E must end in time for F to start ($LF_E = LS_F = 11$). E takes 4 weeks, so E must start no later than the end of week 7 ($LS_E = LF_E - t_E = 11 - 4 = 7$).

▶ Activity D has one successor, F, so D must end in time for F to start ($LF_D = LS_F = 11$). D takes 3 weeks, so D must start no later than the end of week 8 ($LS_D = LF_D - t_D = 11 - 3 = 8$).

Table 5.5

Late Start and Finish Times for Furniture Factory Expansion Project

Activity	Immediate Predecessors	Time (weeks)	Late Start	Late Finish
A	—	3	0	3
B	A	2	9	11
C	A	4	3	7
D	C	3	8	11
E	C	4	7	11
F	B, D, E	10	11	21
G	A	12	9	21
H	F, G	3	21	24

(continued)

Example 5.2

(continued)

▶ Activity C has two successors—D and E—so C must end in time for both to start (LF_C = minimum $\{LS_D, LS_E\}$ = minimum $\{8, 7\}$ = 7). C takes 4 weeks, so C must start no later than the end of week 3 ($LS_C = LF_C - t_C = 7 - 4 = 3$).

▶ Activity B has one successor, F, so B must end in time for F to start ($LF_B = LS_F = 11$). B takes 2 weeks, so B must start no later

than the end of week 9 ($LS_B = L_B - t_B = 11 - 2 = 9$).

▶ Activity A has three successors—B, C, and G—so A must end in time for all three to start (LF_A = minimum $\{LS_B, LS_C, LS_G\}$ = minimum $\{9, 3, 9\}$ = 3). A takes 3 weeks, so A must start immediately ($LS_A = LF_A - t_A = 3 - 3 = 0$).

LATE START AND FINISH TIMES

Late-finish time (LF)

The latest time by which something must be completed if the end of the project is not to be delayed beyond its desired completion time.

Late-start time (LS)

The time by which something must start if it is to be completed in its expected time and is to be finished by its late finish time.

The late start and finish times for an activity are based on the assumption that all activities will be delayed as much as possible. An activity's **late finish time (LF)** is the latest time by which it must be completed if the end of the project is not to be delayed beyond its desired completion time. Its **late start time (LS)** is the time by which it must start if it is to be completed in its expected time and is to be finished by its late finish time. Because an activity must be finished in time for all of its successors to be completed by the desired ending time of the project, its late finish time must be no later than the late start time of each of its successors. The late finish and start times of any activity ("act") may be computed from the following formulas:

LF_{act} = minimum $\{LS_{suc1}, \ldots, LS_{sucj}\}$, where activity "suc1", . . . , "sucj" are the immediate successors

of activity "act"

$LS_{act} = LF_{act} - t_{act}$, where t_{act} is the time required to complete "act"

SLACK OR FLOAT

If you compare the early start (or finish) times in Table 5.4 with the late start (or finish) times in Table 5.5 (or Table 5.6), you will notice that for some activities they are the same and for others they are different. The difference between an activity's late and early start times (or between its late and early finish times), called its slack or float,[2] is the amount of time by which the activity's start or completion can be delayed without delaying the project's completion. Slack can be computed using the equation:

$TS_{act} = LS_{act} - ES_{act} = LF_{act} - EF_{act}$

Slack is a measure of how much flexibility there is in determining when an activity will start and end in the final project schedule. If an activity's total slack is 0, then there is no flexibility in scheduling it, as any delay in starting that activity will delay the completion of the project. If, on the other hand, an activity has positive slack, then its start can be delayed past its early start time—in fact, as late as its late start time—without delaying the completion of the project.

---

[2]This is sometimes called total slack or total float to distinguish it from other types of slack or float that have more restricted meanings. Since we will only discuss total slack or float, we will drop the "total."

Example 5.3

Use the early start and finish times given in Table 5.4 and the late start and finish times given in Table 5.5 to determine the slack for each of the activities in the furniture factory expansion project described in Example 5.1.

Solution:
The information in Tables 5.4 and 5.5 has been combined in Table 5.6. The slack times were computed using the equation for TS_{act}. For example:

$$TS_A = LS_A - ES_A = 0 - 0 = 0 \text{ or } = LF_A - EF_A = 3 - 3 = 0 \text{ and } TS_B = LS_B - ES_B = 9 - 3 = 6 \text{ or } = LF_B - EF_B = 11 - 5 = 6.$$

Table 5.6
Activity Timing for Furniture Factory Expansion Project

Activity	Immediate Predecessors	Time (weeks)	Early Start	Early Finish	Late Start	Late Finish	Slack
A	—	3	0	3	0	3	0
B	A	2	3	5	9	11	6
C	A	4	3	7	3	7	0
D	C	3	7	10	8	11	1
E	C	4	7	11	7	11	0
F	B, D, E	10	11	21	11	21	0
G	A	12	3	15	9	21	6
H	F, G	3	21	24	21	24	0

The problem with using slack as an indicator of scheduling flexibility is that it is shared by successive activities. While this is not an issue in the furniture factory expansion project, it is in the simple project summarized in Table 5.7 and Figure 5.11. While activities C and D each have 2 weeks of slack, it should be fairly obvious that they are the same 2 weeks. If the start of C is delayed at all, then the start of D will be delayed by the same amount of time, cutting into the time by which the start of D can be delayed beyond the amount by which its start is delayed due to the delay in C.

THE CRITICAL PATH

As noted above, the critical path for a project is the longest path through its network. Since it is possible, to carry out two or more activities simultaneously (subject to the precedence restrictions and the availability of required resources), the amount of time required to complete the project is not the sum of the activity times, but the length of the critical path. This assumes, of course, that all activities on the critical path are started and completed within the time limits established by their early and late start and finish times. Because the critical path is the longest path, it is the set of sequential activities with minimum total slack. If the late finish time for the final activity in the project is the same as its early finish time, then all the activities on the critical path will have zero total slack.

Table 5.7

Simple Network Example to Illustrate Slack

Activity	Immediate Predecessors	Time (weeks)	Early Start	Early Finish	Late Start	Late Finish	Slack
A	—	5	0	5	0	5	0
B	A	4	5	9	5	9	0
C	—	3	0	3	2	5	2
D	C	4	3	7	5	9	2

Figure 5.11

A simple project's network

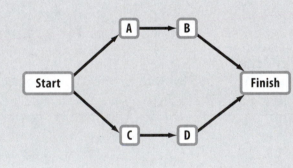

Example 5.4

Use Figure 5.10 and Table 5.7 to determine the critical path for the furniture factory expansion project described in Example 5.1.

Solution:

Looking at Figure 5.10, we see that there are four paths through the project network. Ignoring start and finish, which appear on all paths and are dummy activities taking 0 time, the paths and their lengths in weeks are:

Path	Length
A–B–F–H	3 + 2 + 10 + 3 = 18
A–C–D–F–H	3 + 4 + 3 + 10 + 3 = 23

Path	Length
A–C–E–F–H	3 + 4 + 4 + 10 + 3 = 24
A–G–H	3 + 12 + 3 = 18

The critical (longest) path is A–C–E–F–H with a length of 24 weeks, so the project will take 24 weeks. Looking at Table 5.6, we see that these are the activities for which slack equals 0.

Although we have referred to *the* critical path, it is important to note that there may be more than one path with the longest length. In this case there will be two or more critical paths, which may be completely distinct or may have some activities in common.

USING EXCEL TO MAKE THE COMPUTATIONS

There are many professional software packages for implementing PERT and CPM, including Project. However, it is also possible to use a standard spreadsheet application, such as Microsoft's Excel, to do the calculations. While there are a variety of ways of doing the calculations in a spreadsheet, we will use the simplest: implementing the equations given earlier in this supplement. This requires inserting formulas that compute the activities' early and late start and finish times and slack times into specific cells of the spreadsheet. An Excel spreadsheet for the furniture factory expansion project is developed in Example 5.5.

Example 5.5

Develop a spreadsheet model to determine the early and late start and finish times and slack times for the furniture factory expansion project, using the immediate predecessors and activity timing information given in Table 5.3 (see Example 5.1).

Solution:

The Excel spreadsheet for this project is shown in Exhibit 5.1. The activity, description, immediate predecessors, and activity time columns are taken directly from Table 5.3. The actual contents of the cells in rows 5 through 12 of the early start, early finish, late start, late finish, and slack columns (columns E through I of the spreadsheet) are formulas that implement the equations given in the text, leading to the numbers displayed in those cells. For example:

E10: = maximum (F6, F8, F9) to give the early start time for activity F

F10: = E10 + D10 to give the early finish time for activity F

H5: = minimum (G6, G7, G11) to give the late finish time for activity A

G5: = H5 − D5 to give the late start time for activity A

I5: = G5 − E5 to give the slack time for activity A

The only exceptions to the use of these formulas are the cells E5, which is set to equal 0, and H12, which contains = F12, so that the project will be completed as early as possible.

Microsoft Excel - Exhibit5-1

	A	B	C	D	E	F	G	H	I	J
1			Activity Timing for Furniture Factory Expansion Project							
2										
3			Immediate	Time	Early	Early	Late	Late		
4	Activity	Description	Predecessors	(Weeks)	Start	Finish	Start	Finish	Slack	
5	A	Develop initial plans	--	3	0	3	0	3	0	
6	B	Secure financing	A	2	3	5	9	11	6	
7	C	Develop final plans	A	4	3	7	3	7	0	
8	D	Hire contractor	C	3	7	10	8	11	1	
9	E	Secure permits	C	4	7	11	7	11	0	
10	F	Construct addition	B,D,E	10	11	21	11	21	0	
11	G	Order equipment	A	12	3	15	9	21	6	
12	H	Install equipment	F,G	3	21	24	21	24	0	
13										
14										

Sheet1 / Sheet2 / Sheet3 /

Ready

Time-Cost Trade-offs or Project Crashing

Suppose that a schedule has been developed for a project. For one reason or another, the project manager decides that it is going to take longer than would be desirable. For example:

▶ A platform is being erected for the use of the speakers at a political rally; if the platform is not ready by the time the speeches are scheduled, it will be of no use.

▶ The contract for constructing a new office building includes a penalty clause for completion after a specified due date or a bonus clause for completion before that date.

▶ The overhaul of a chemical plant requires that it be shut down while the maintenance is being performed. Because no product will be produced during that time, profits will be lost.

▶ A company is developing a new product; the longer the development process takes, the more likely that a competitor will bring a similar product to market first, thus reducing the company's profits from the new product.

Often, by using additional personnel or other resources to complete an activity, or by doing an activity in a different, more expensive way, one can reduce the time required for the project, thereby meeting a desired deadline or saving costs that are determined by the length of the project.

One of the original features of CPM was a procedure for determining how best to trade off increased activity costs for reduced project time. This **time-cost trade-off** process is also called project crashing. To conduct a project crashing analysis, we need, for each activity, three kinds of information:

1. The **normal time** for the activity and its associated **normal cost**. This will generally be the lowest cost way of doing the activity.

2. The minimum or **crash time** for the activity and its associated **crash cost**. This faster, higher cost way will require either additional resources or a different, more expensive way of doing the activity.

3. The functional relationship relating time and cost between these two extremes.

To illustrate the meaning of this last requirement, consider the four time/cost relationships shown in Figure 5.12. The usual assumption, and the one we will use here, is shown in Figure 5.12a, where the trade-off between reduced time and increased cost is linear. That is, any percentage of the time reduction can be obtained by paying the same percentage of the cost increase. The relationships shown in parts (b) and (c) of Figure 5.12 also allow for achieving any amount of the potential time reduction, but the relationship between time and cost is nonlinear. In Figure 5.12b, additional time reductions cost greater amounts of money. In Figure 5.12c, the relationship is reversed; additional time reductions cost lesser amounts of money. Finally, Figure 5.12d shows a discrete relationship, in which there are only two choices for time and cost. The activity may be done in either the long-time/low-cost way or in the short-time/high-cost way; there is no in between.

There are three different, but related, questions that one might ask about project crashing:

1. Which activities should be crashed and by how much in order to get to a specified project length at minimum cost?

Time-cost trade-off

A procedure for determining how best to trade off increased activity costs for reduced project time.

Normal time, Normal cost

Generally, the best ways of doing an activity.

Crash time, Crash cost

A higher, faster way will require either additional resources or a different, more expensive way of doing the activity.

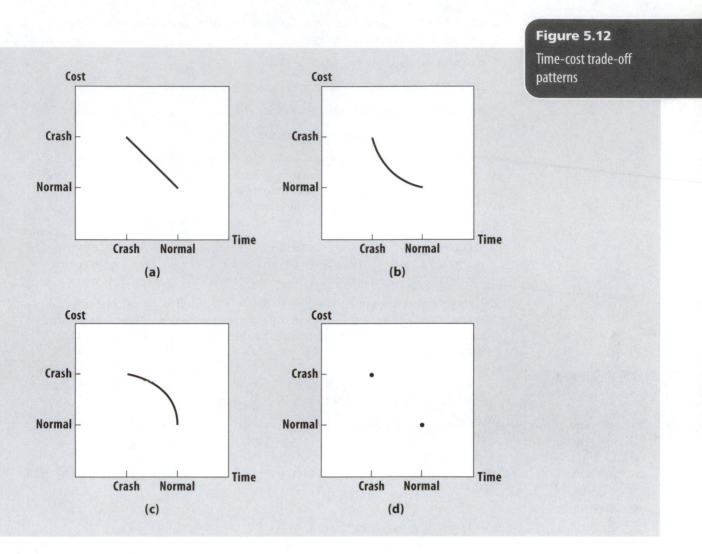

Figure 5.12

Time-cost trade-off patterns

2. What is the minimum length for the project, and which activities should be crashed and by how much in order to get to that length at minimum cost?

3. Considering both activity and project costs, what is the optimal project length, and which activities should be crashed and by how much in order to get to that length at minimum cost?

When working with small projects for which the linear time/cost trade-off assumption can be made, such as the ones we are considering here, the standard methods for answering all three sets of questions are based on the same approach, marginal analysis, conducted as follows:

1. For each activity, determine the marginal cost to crash it by dividing the difference between the crash and normal costs by the difference between the normal and crash times.

2. From among those activities that it makes sense to crash, identify that activity or set of activities that has the lowest marginal cost to crash.

3. Crash the chosen activity or set of activities by determining whichever of the following time factors is smaller:

   a) the maximum amount possible

   b) the amount required to reach the desired project length

   c) until another project path becomes a critical path

4. Repeat steps 2 and 3 as often as necessary.

Steps 2 and 3 of this process require a little more explanation. Which activities does it make sense to crash? To begin with, it only makes sense to consider activities that can be crashed, in other words, that are longer than their crash times. Beyond that, identifying activities that are candidates for crashing and limiting the amount by which the selected activity or activities should be crashed are based on the following two principles:

1. It makes sense to crash only activities that are on the critical path because the length of the project is determined by the length of the critical path. Reducing the length of any activity not on the critical path will not reduce the length of the project.

2. If there is more than one critical path, their lengths must all be reduced simultaneously or the length of the project will not change. This may be done by crashing one activity that is on all the critical paths or by crashing a set of activities that includes one from every critical path.

Example 5.6

The board of the hospital at which Cheryl is the administrator has decided that the hospital must upgrade its utility backup systems by adding a water storage tank and building an emergency utilities center with a generator and a pump connected to the water tank. Table 5.8 contains the information about the normal and crash times (in weeks) and normal and crash costs (in $1000s) developed by the

Table 5.8
Activity Information for Hospital Emergency Services Project

Activity	Description	Immediate Predecessors	Normal Time	Normal Cost	Crash Time	Crash Cost
A	Prepare site	—	3	30	2	45
B	Construct building	A	8	150	5	210
C	Install generator	B	3	40	2	50
D	Install water tank	A	5	60	3	70
E	Install pump	B	4	25	2	30
F	Connect generator	C	2	18	1	27
G	Connect pump	D, E	3	20	2	28
H	Test electric system	F	3	15	2	21
I	Test water system	G	2	20	2	20

Example 5.6

(continued)

Figure 5.13

AON network for hospital
emergency services project

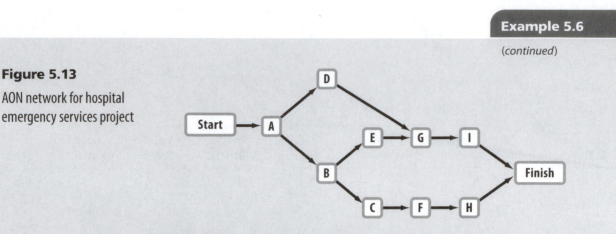

hospital's engineering office. The AON network for the project is shown in Figure 5.13.

1. Determine how long it will take and how much it will cost to construct and test the emergency systems if all activities are done in their normal time and at normal cost. Identify the critical path.

2. Determine which activities should be crashed and by how much if the hospital wants to have the emergency facility in operation within 16 weeks.

3. Determine the shortest amount of time in which the facility could be ready. Determine which activities should be crashed and by how much to be ready in this amount of time.

4. Because the current backup facilities are in such poor condition, the hospital board has decided it is prudent to rent temporary truck-mounted equipment until the new facility is ready. The cost of this temporary equipment will be $5,000 per week. Recognizing this, determine the amount of time that the hospital should take for this project and the activities that should be crashed, and by how much if the board wants to minimize the combined cost of completing the project and providing emergency backup facilities until the permanent facilities are ready.

Solution:

1. The early and late start and finish times and slack times if all activities are done in their normal times are shown in Table 5.9. The project will take 20 weeks. Adding up the normal costs, the project will cost 378, or $378,000. The critical path is A–B–E–G–I.

2. The first step in determining which activities to crash is to find the marginal crashing cost per week for each activity by dividing the difference between the crash and normal costs by the difference between the normal and crash times. The results are shown in Table 5.10.

First crashing: The activities on the critical path are A, B, E, G, and I. Of these activities, the one with the lowest marginal crashing cost is E, with a marginal cost of 2.5 or $2,500 per week. Crash E by one week, at which point there are two critical paths, the original one and A–B–C–F–H. The project time is now 19 weeks.

Second crashing: Because there are two critical paths, we can either crash one activity that is on both paths (the two possibilities are A and B) or crash a pair of activities, including one from each path (the possibilities are C, F, or H combined with E or G, because I cannot be crashed). The less expensive of the single activities to crash is A at a marginal cost of 15 per week. The least expensive pair of activities to crash is E and H at a combined cost of 2.5 + 6 = 8.5. Crash E and H by one week each, at which point both E and H have reached their limits. The project time is now 18 weeks and the same two paths are still both critical.

Third crashing: Because the same two paths are critical, we have the same choices as to what to crash except that neither E nor H can be crashed anymore, so the possible pairs are either C or F combined with G. The less expensive of the single activities is A at a marginal cost of 15 per week. The less expensive pair of activities to crash is F and G at a combined cost of 9 + 8 = 17. Crash A

Example 5.6

(*continued*)

Table 5.9
Activity Timing for Hospital Emergency Services Project

Activity	Immediate Predecessors	Time (weeks)	Early Start	Early Finish	Late Start	Late Finish	Slack
A	—	3	0	3	0	3	0
B	A	8	3	11	3	11	0
C	B	3	11	14	12	15	1
D	A	5	3	8	10	15	7
E	B	4	11	15	11	15	0
F	C	2	14	16	15	17	1
G	D, E	3	15	18	15	18	0
H	F	3	16	19	17	20	1
I	G	2	18	20	18	20	0

Table 5.10
Marginal Crashing Costs for Hospital Emergency Services Project

Activity	Normal Time	Normal Cost	Crash Time	Crash Cost	ΔC/ΔT
A	3	30	2	45	15
B	8	150	5	210	20
C	3	40	2	50	10
D	5	60	3	70	5
E	4	25	2	30	2.5
F	2	18	1	27	9
G	3	20	2	28	8
H	3	15	2	21	6
I	2	20	2	20	—

Fourth crashing: Because the same two paths are critical and A cannot be crashed any further, we can either crash B, at a marginal cost of 20 per week, or the lower cost pair, F and G, at a cost of 17 per week. Crash F and G each by one week, at which point the desired project time of 16 weeks has been reached. Also, G has now reached its minimum time and the same two paths are still critical.

Summarizing the results of these four crashes, the minimum cost way of completing the project in 16 weeks is to crash E by two weeks and A, F, G, and H each by one week. The added cost from crashing is 43, or $43,000, for a total project cost of 378 + 43 = 421, or $421,000.

Continue the process started in part b until the project's length cannot be reduced any further.

Fifth crashing: At this point there are still two critical paths, A–B–E–G–I and A–B–C–F–H. Because A, E, F, G, and H are all being done in their crash times, the only way of reducing the length of both paths simultaneously is to crash B at a marginal cost of 20 per week. B can be crashed by a maximum of three weeks, which

by one week, at which point A has reached its limit. The project time is now 17 weeks and the same two paths are still both critical.

Example 5.6

(continued)

reduces the length of the project to 13 weeks at an added cost of 60. At this point the only critical-path activity that can still be crashed is C, but doing so will only reduce the length of the path A–B–C–F–H, not the length of the project. Adding this information to the summary at the end of part (b), we find that the minimum project time is 13 weeks. The minimum cost way of reaching this length is to crash B by three weeks, E by two weeks, and A, F, G, and H each by one week. The added cost from crashing in this way is 103, for a total cost of 378 + 103 = 481, or $481,000. The entire series of crashes for parts (b) and (c) is summarized in Table 5.11.

Table 5.11
Summary of Crashing for Hospital Emergency Services Project

Project Length	Activity to Crash	Added Cost	Total Cost
20	—	0	378.0
19	E	2.5	380.5
18	E, H	8.5	389.0
17	A	15	404.0
16	F, G	17	421.0
15	B	20	441.0
14	B	20	461.0
13	B	20	481.0

3. Refer to Table 5.11. At a project length of 20 weeks (no crashing), the total cost, in $1000s, is 378 + 20(5) = 378 + 100 = 478, or $478,000. If the project is crashed to 19 weeks, the total cost is 380.5 + 19(5) = 475.5. If the project is crashed to 18 weeks, the total cost is 389 + 18(5) = 479. Crashing the project to 17 weeks or less will cost even more since the added crashing cost will be more than the amount saved by not having to rent the emergency backup equipment. Thus, the optimal length of the project, considering both the cost of completing the project and the cost of providing emergency backup facilities, is 19 weeks at a cost of 475.5, or $475,500.

4. Notice that activity D, install water tank, was not crashed at all, even though its marginal crashing cost is the second lowest of all the activities. Looking at the slack values in Table 5.9 shows us why: Activity D has so much slack that it never becomes part of a critical path, no matter how much other activities are crashed. This illustrates the first of the two principles stated for selecting activities to be crashed: It only makes sense to crash activities that are on the critical path since the length of the project is determined by the length of the critical path.

PROBABILITY IN PERT NETWORKS

So far, we have assumed that the time for an activity is deterministic—that is, we know exactly how long it will take to complete each activity. However, it is often impossible to say how long an activity will take, even with reasonable (if not exact) accuracy. To accommodate uncertainty about an activity's length, the original version of PERT used three time estimates for the length of each activity, rather than the single time estimate of CPM. These three estimates, which we will denote as o, m, and p, are, respectively, the optimistic, most likely, and pessimistic estimates of how long the activity will take.

Based on the characteristics of beta distributions, an activity's three time estimates are combined, using the following formulas, to estimate the mean and standard deviation of its duration:

$$\mu_i = \frac{o_i + 4m_i + p_i}{6} \qquad s_i = \frac{p_i - o_i}{6}$$

Assuming that the activities' durations are independent, their means and standard deviations may be combined, using the following formulas, to obtain a mean and variance for the length of the project:

$$\mu_p = \Sigma \mu_j \qquad \sigma_p^2 = \Sigma \sigma_j^2$$

where, for both μ_p, the mean time for the project, and σ_p^2, the variance of the project time, the summation is only for those activities on the critical path.

Once the project time's mean and variance have been determined from these formulas, the probability of completing the project within any specified amount of time can be computed by using the standard normal probability approach:

$$P(T_P \leq t_0) = p\left(Z \leq \frac{t_0 - \mu_P}{\sigma_P}\right)$$

Example 5.7

Table 5.12

Activity Information for New Product Development Project

Activity	Description	Immediate Predecessors	Activity Time Estimates		
			Optimistic	Most Likely	Pessimistic
A	Initial design	—	12	16	26
B	Survey market	A	6	9	18
C	Build prototype	A	8	10	18
D	Test prototype	C	2	3	4
E	Redesign product	B, D	3	4	11
F	Market testing	E	6	8	10
G	Set up production	F	6	8	10

The electronics company for which Fred works has been discussing developing a new personal communication device. The product development committee has put together the list of activities and time estimates (in weeks) shown in Table 5.12.

1. Find the mean and standard deviation of the time to complete each of the project's activities.

2. Using the activities' mean completion times, find the expected early and late start and finish times

for the activities. Determine the critical path and its expected length.

3. Find the probability that the project will be completed in no more than 50 weeks; in more than 60 weeks.

Solution:
1. The means and standard deviations of the times to complete the activities are shown in Table 5.13. For example, the mean and standard

Example 5.7

(*continued*)

Table 5.13

Means and Standard Deviations of Activity Completion Times for New Product Development Project

Activity	Activity Time Estimates			Mean Time	Standard Deviation
	Optimistic	Most Likely	Pessimistic		
A	12	16	26	17	2.3333
B	6	9	18	10	2.0000
C	8	10	18	11	1.6667
D	2	3	4	3	0.3333
E	3	4	11	5	1.3333
F	6	8	10	8	0.6667
G	6	8	10	8	0.6667

deviation of the time to complete activity A are computed as follows:

$$\mu_A = \frac{o_A + 4m_A + P_A}{6} = \frac{12 + 4(16) + 26}{6}$$

$$= \frac{102}{6} = 17.0$$

$$\sigma_A = \frac{P_A - o_A}{6} - \frac{26 - 12}{6} = \frac{14}{6} = 2.3333$$

The expected early and late start times and slacks for the activities are given in Table 5.14 (page 226). The critical path is A–C–D–E–F–G, with an expected length of 52 weeks.

The expected project completion time is the sum of the expected completion times of the activities on the critical path:

$$\mu_P = \mu_A + \mu_C + \mu_D + \mu_E + \mu_F + \mu_G$$
$$= 17 + 11 + 3 + 5 + 8 + 8$$
$$= 52 \text{ weeks}$$

The variance of the project completion time is the sum of the variances of the completion times of the activities on the critical path:

$$\sigma_P^2 = \sigma_A^2 = \sigma_C^2 = \sigma_D^2 = \sigma_E^2 = \sigma_F^2 = \sigma_G^2$$
$$= (2.3333)^2 + (1.6667)^2 + (0.3333)^2 + (1.3333)^2$$
$$+ (0.6667)^2 + (0.6667)^2$$
$$= 5.4444 + 2.7778 + 0.1111 + 1.7778$$
$$+ 0.4444 + 0.4444$$
$$= 10.9998 \text{ weeks}^2$$

The standard deviation of the project completion time is the square root of the variance:

$$\mu_P = \sqrt{10.9998} = 3.3166 \text{ weeks}$$

The probability that the project will be completed within 50 weeks is:

$$P(T_P \leq 50) = P\left(Z \leq \frac{50 - \mu_P}{\sigma_P} \right)$$

$$= P\left(Z \leq \frac{50 - 52}{3.3166} \right)$$

$$= P(Z \leq -0.60)$$

$$= .2743$$

Example 5.7

(*continued*)

Table 5.14
Activity Timing for New Product Development Project

Activity	Immediate Predecessors	Time (weeks)	Early Start	Early Finish	Late Start	Late Finish	Slack
A	—	17	0	17	0	17	0
B	A	10	17	27	21	31	4
C	A	11	17	28	17	28	0
D	C	3	28	31	28	31	0
E	B, D	5	31	36	31	36	0
F	E	8	36	44	36	44	0
G	F	8	44	52	44	52	0

The probability that the project will take more than 60 weeks is:

$$P(T_P > 60) = P\left(Z > \frac{60 - \mu_P}{\sigma_P}\right) = P\left(Z > \frac{60 - 52}{3.3166}\right) = P(Z > 2.41) = 1 - 0.9920 = .0080$$

Often there will be at least one additional path through the network with an expected length almost as long as the critical path. If such a path has a fairly high standard deviation, then there will be a reasonably high probability that when the project is actually done, this other path will turn out to be longer than the one identified as the critical path. Thus, the probability that the project will be completed by a specified time is not the probability that the "critical path" will be completed by that time, but the probability that *all* the paths through the network will be completed by that time. If these paths are completely independent of one another, then the project probability can be computed as the product of the path probabilities, each computed in the same way as the "critical path" probability. Unfortunately, however, the paths typically are not completely independent of one another because they have some activities in common. In this case, the only reasonable, although expensive, approach to estimating the project time probability distribution is simulation.

SUMMARY

In this chapter, we have covered a topic that is often taught as its own course, because project management is important to virtually every type of organization and in virtually every functional area of business. Some organizations, however, manage projects exclusively. For example, for construction companies that do only custom work, every job is a new project. Similarly, scientific organizations are in the business of advancing the frontiers of knowledge one research project at a time, even though they have some ongoing operations. Advertising agencies, consulting firms, law partnerships, and many other professional organizations are also primarily in a project management business. It is common to find matrix and team structures in companies that are simultaneously handling a large number of projects.

There is a recognized body of knowledge for project managers. This project management body of knowledge (PMBOK) includes scope management, quality management, cost management, time management, risk management, human resources management, communication management, and project integration management. This broad range of knowledge reflects the fact that a project manager has to manage all aspects of a unique value-adding system. In ongoing operations, unlike projects, these tasks might be divided among functional departments.

Projects typically have a life cycle comprised of four stages: conceptual study, development, implementation, and completion. Although all areas of the PMBOK are important at each stage, they are critical during the first and second stage of a project, because these stages set the foundation for the third stage. And, the decisions made during the earlier stages drive the costs incurred during the implementation phase, when most of a project's money is spent. Even projects that are canceled midstream because of fund shortages or other reasons must be terminated in some way, so in that sense, all projects go through all the stages of the project life cycle.

Although each project is unique and happens only once, supply chain management is relevant to all projects. Large projects require subcontractors, and those subcontractors may in turn employ subcontractors and vendors of their own. Project management teams also have customers. Generally speaking, flexibility in scheduling is needed most from project subcontractors, while access to information and resources is needed most from the project's customers.

Planning and control presents special challenges in project-oriented organizations. Managers need to keep up with several projects at once and coordinate the use of their human resources and equipment across all of them. Many managers use work breakdown structures to identify all the activities required to complete a project. After determining the precedence relationships among those activities, managers create a network model of the project and use it to conduct analyses that show where their attention is most needed. Software packages such as Microsoft Project provide computerized graphical displays of these planning aids, which help managers keep up with costs, resource allocations, schedules, and critical activities.

KEY TERMS

Activity-on-arrow (AOA) network diagram, 209
Activity-on-node (AON) network diagram, 209
Crash cost, 218
Crash time, 218
Crashing, 206
Critical activity, 205
Critical path, 206
Critical path method (CPM), 206
Current budget shortfall, 202
Customer-driven team structure, 195
Dependent activities, 207

Dummy activity, 208
Early finish time (EF), 212
Early start time (ES), 212
Earned value, 202
Earned value analysis, 203
Hierarchical team structure, 195
Late finish time (LF), 214
Late start time (LS), 214
Matrix structure, 194
Milestone, 208
Noncritical activity, 206
Normal cost, 218
Normal time, 218

Parallel (independent) activities, 207
Precedence table, 207
Program evaluation and review technique (PERT), 206
Project, 190
Project activity, 207
Project delay, 203
Scheduled value shortfall, 203
Slack time, 205
Sunk cost, 203
Time-cost trade-off, 218
Total cost overrun, 203
Work breakdown structure (WBS), 206

SOLVED PROBLEMS

1. The state highway department is going over the current state of the budget for its new 20-mile highway project. The 24 month $20 million project is just finishing its eighteenth month. The state has already spent $18 million of the budget while only 10 miles of the project have been built.

a) What is the estimated delay on the project?

b) What is the scheduled value shortfall?

c) What is the current budget shortfall?

d) What is the total cost overrun at this point in time?

Solution:

a) The estimated delay is 6 months. They should have completed 10 miles in 12 months rather than in 18.

b) The scheduled value shortfall is $5 million. By the eighteenth month, they should have completed three quarters of the $20 million project ($15 million) rather than just half ($10 million) thus $15 million − $10 million = $5 million.

c) The current budget short fall is $3 million. After 18 months, they would expect to have spent $15 million rather than $18 million, thus, $18 million − $15 million = $3 million.

d) The total cost overrun at this point is $8 million or the sum of the scheduled value shortfall and the current budget shortfall. In short, the first half of the project should have cost $10 million rather than $18 million.

2. Assume scheduling mishaps and poor weather for the project described above have contributed to the cost overruns and delays. Assume past overruns and spending to this point are sunk costs.

a) The best case for the project is that it can be finished based upon original budget expectations from this point on. What can we estimate for the project's best-case completion time and cost?

b) Poor weather is expected to continue with the project. If costs accumulate as they have, what would be the expected completion time and cost?

c) The worst-case is that costs rise as much as 10% from where they have already accumulated. What would you estimate the worst-case completion time and cost to be?

Solution:

a) Given we are only half way through and already 18 months and $18 million into the project, the best case would be completion after 30 months (18 + 12) and a total cost of $28 million ($18 million already spent + $10 more based upon the original budget).

b) Simply doubling where we are now and what we have spent, the expected completion time would be 36 months with a $36 million price tag.

c) Starting where we are and assuming the second half will cost an much and take as long as 10% more than the first half, the worst-case completion time would be 37.8 months (18 + 18 × 110%) and cost $37.8 million ($18 million + $18 million × 110%).

3. Pik-Fast, a chain of convenience stores, is planning to open a new store. The activities required, their immediate predecessors, and the optimistic, most likely, and pessimistic estimates of their times (in days) are given in Table 5.15.

a) Draw the project network.

b) Find the means and standard deviations of the activities' completion times.

c) Using the expected times from part (b), determine the expected early and late start and finish times and expected slack times for the activities. Identify the critical path.

d) Using the standard PERT approach, find the probability that the store will be opened within 80 working days; more than 84 working days.

Solution:

a) The activity-on-node (AON) network is shown below.

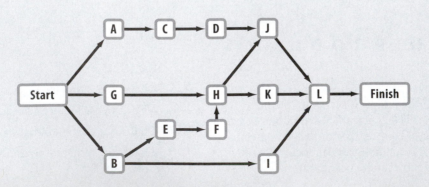

Table 5.15
Activity Information for Pik-Fast Store Opening Project

Activity	Description	Immediate Predecessors	Activity Time Estimates		
			Optimistic	Most Likely	Pessimistic
A	Select manager	—	10	12	20
B	Select site	—	8	15	22
C	Hire workers	A	17	21	31
D	Basic training	C	3	4	5
E	Secure permits	B	12	18	30
F	Construct building	E	26	30	40
G	Purchase equipment	—	30	45	60
H	Install equipment	F, G	4	6	8
I	Advertise opening	B	15	15	15
J	Final training	D, H	2	3	4
K	Stock store	H	4	6	8
L	Open store	I, J, K	1	1	1

Table 5.16
Means and Standard Deviations of Activity Completion Times for Pik-Fast Store Opening Project

Activity	Activity Time Estimates			Mean Time	Standard Deviation
	Optimistic	Most Likely	Pessimistic		
A	10	12	20	13	1.6667
B	8	15	22	15	2.3333
C	17	21	31	22	2.3333
D	3	4	5	4	0.3333
E	12	18	30	19	3.0000
F	26	30	40	31	2.3333
G	30	45	60	45	5.0000
H		6	8	6	0.6667
I	15	15	15	15	0
J	2	3	4	3	0.3333
K	4	6	8	6	0.6667
L	1	1	1	1	0

b) The means and standard deviations of the activity completion times are shown in Table 5.16. For example, the mean and standard deviation of the completion time for activity A are:

$$\mu_A = \frac{o_A + 4_A + P_A}{6} = \frac{10 + 4(12) + 20}{6} = \frac{78}{6} = 13.0$$

$$\sigma_A = \frac{P_A - o_A}{6} = \frac{20 - 10}{6} = \frac{10}{6} = 1.6667$$

c) The expected early and late start and finish times and expected slack times for the activities are shown in Table 5.17. The critical path is B–E–F–H–K–L.

The mean and variance of the project completion time are found by adding the means and variances of the times of the activities on the critical path:

$$\mu_P = \mu_B + \mu_E + \mu_F + \mu_H + \mu_K + \mu_L$$

$$= 15 + 19 + 31 + 6 + 6 + 1 = 78 \text{ days}$$

$$\sigma_P^2 = \sigma_B^2 + \sigma_E^2 + \sigma_F^2 + \sigma_H^2 + \sigma_K^2 + \sigma_L^2$$

$$= (2.3333)^2 + (3.0000)^2 + (2.3333)^2 + (0.6667)^2 + (0.6667)^2 + (0)^2$$

$$= 5.4444 + 9.0000 + 5.4444 + 0.4444 + 0.4444 + 0$$

$$= 20.7776 \text{ days}^2$$

d) The standard deviation of the project completion time is the square root of the variance:

$$\sigma_P = \sqrt{20.7776} = 4.5583 \text{ days}$$

The probability that the project will be completed within 80 weeks is:

$$P(T_P \leq 80) = P\left(Z \leq \frac{80 - \mu_P}{\sigma_P}\right)$$

$$= P\left(Z \leq \frac{80 - 78}{4.5583}\right)$$

$$= P(Z \leq 0.44) = .6700$$

The probability that the project will take more than 84 weeks is:

$$P(T_P > 84) = P\left(Z > \frac{84 - \mu_P}{\sigma_P}\right)$$

$$= P\left(Z > \frac{84 - 78}{4.5583}\right)$$

$$= P(Z > 1.32) = .0934$$

Table 5.17

Activity Timing for Pik-Fast Store Opening Project

Activity	Immediate Predecessors	Time (days)	Early Start	Early Finish	Late Start	Late Finish	Slack
A	—	13	0	13	35	48	35
B	—	15	0	15	0	15	0
C	A	22	13	35	48	70	35
D	C	4	35	39	70	74	35
E	B	19	15	34	15	34	0
F	E	31	34	65	34	65	0
G	—	45	0	45	20	65	20
H	F, G	6	65	71	65	71	0
I	B	15	15	30	62	77	47
J	D, H	3	71	74	74	77	3
K	H	6	71	77	71	77	0
L	I, J, K	1	77	78	77	78	0

Table 5.18

Activity Information for Solved Problem 4

Activity	Immediate Predecessors	Normal Time	Normal Cost	Crash Time	Crash Cost
A	—	5	30	3	36
B	—	7	35	4	41
C	A	4	16	3	20
D	B	4	20	2	25
E	B	3	6	2	7
F	C, D	5	20	3	23
G	E	8	32	4	38

4. Consider the project described in Table 5.18.

   a) Draw the network diagram for this project.

   b) Determine the early and late start and finish times and slack times for each of the activities, and find the critical path. What is the length of the project if all activities are completed in their normal times?

   c) Determine which activities to crash and by how much to achieve a project completion time of fourteen at minimum cost.

   d) Determine what the minimum project completion time is and which activities to crash and by how much to achieve that time at minimum cost.

   e) Suppose that there is a fixed cost of 4.0 per time period for the project. Determine the optimum project completion time and which activities to crash and by how much to achieve that time at minimum cost.

Solution:

   a) The AON network is shown in the figure below.

   b) The early and late start and finish times and slack times for the activities are shown in Table 5.19. The critical path is B–E–G with a length of 18 periods. The cost of the project is 159, found by adding the normal costs for all the activities.

   c) The first step in determining which activities to crash is to find the marginal crashing cost per week for each activity by dividing the difference between the crash and normal costs by the difference between the normal and crash times. The results are shown in Table 5.20.

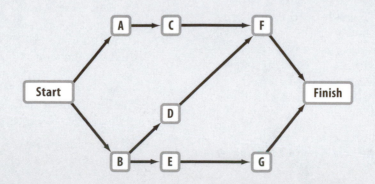

Table 5.19
Activity Timing for Solved Problem 4

Activity	Immediate Predecessors	Time (weeks)	Early Start	Early Finish	Late Start	Late Finish	Slack
A	—	5	0	5	4	9	4
B	—	7	0	7	0	7	0
C	A	4	5	9	9	13	4
D	B	4	7	11	9	13	2
E	B	3	7	10	7	10	0
F	C, D	5	11	16	13	18	2
G	E	8	10	18	10	18	0

Table 5.20
Marginal Crashing Costs for Solved Problem 4

Activity	Normal Time	Normal Cost	Crash Time	Crash Cost	$\Delta C/\Delta T$
A	5	30	3	36	3.0
B	7	35	4	41	2.0
C	4	16	3	20	4.0
D	4	20	2	25	2.5
E	3	6	2	7	1.0
F	5	20	3	23	1.5
G	8	32	4	38	1.5

First crashing: The activities on the critical path are B, E, and G. The least expensive of these to crash is E, with a marginal cost of 1.0 per period. Crash E by the maximum amount, one period. The project length is now seventeen periods.

Second crashing: The only activities on the critical path that can still be crashed are B and G. The less expensive alternative is G, with a marginal cost of 1.5 per period. Crash G by one period. The project length is now sixteen periods and there are two critical paths: B–E–G and B–D–F.

Third crashing: Because there are two critical paths, we can either crash one activity that is on

both paths (the only possibility is B) or a pair of activities that includes one from each path. The possibilities are G combined with either D or F. Crashing B will cost 2.0 per period. The less expensive pair of activities to crash is G and F at a combined cost of 1.5 + 1.5 = 3.0 per period. Crash B by two periods, to a time of five periods. The project length is now fourteen periods and there are now three critical paths: B–E–G, B–D–F, and A–C–F.

To summarize, the minimum cost way of reaching a project length of fourteen periods is to crash B by two periods, E by one period, and G by one period. The added crashing cost is 2(2.0) + 1.0 + 1.5 = 6.5, raising the total cost to 159 + 6.5 = 165.5.

d) Continue with the process started in part (c).

Fourth crashing: Because there are three critical paths, we can either crash one activity that is on all the paths (there is none) or a set of activities that includes one from each path. Because E has been crashed to its limit, the possible sets are A and B; A, D, and G; C and B; C, D, and G; F and B; and F and G. The least expensive of these combinations is F and G at a combined cost of 1.5 + 1.5 = 3.0 per period. Crash F and G each by two periods (the maximum allowable for F). The project length is now twelve periods. The same three paths are still critical.

Fifth crashing: Because F cannot be crashed any further, the possible sets for crashing are A and

B; A, D, and G; C and B; and C, D, and G. The least expensive of these combinations is A and B at a combined cost of 3.0 + 2.0 = 5.0 per period. Crash A and B each by one period (the maximum remaining for B). The project length is now eleven periods. The same paths are still critical.

Sixth crashing: Because B cannot be crashed any further, the possible sets for crashing are A, D, and G, and C, D, and G. The less expensive of these combinations is A, D, and G at a combined cost of 3.0 + 2.5 + 1.5 = 7.0 per period. Crash A, D, and G each by one period (the maximum remaining for both A and G). The project length is now ten periods. The same paths are still critical. There is now no combination of activities that can be crashed to reduce the length of the project since at least one activity out of every combination listed in the fourth crashing section above has reached its minimum time. Thus, the minimum length of the project is 10 periods.

To summarize, the minimum cost way of reaching this length (ten periods) is to crash A by two periods, B by three periods, D by one period, E by one period, F by two periods, and G by four periods. The total added crashing cost is 2(3.0) + 3(2.0) + 2.5 + 1.0 + 2(1.5) + 4(1.5) = 24.5, raising the total project cost to

159 + 24.5 = 183.5. The crashes discussed in parts (b) and (c) are summarized in Table 5.21.

e) Referring to Table 5.21, we see that each crashing down to a project length of twelve periods adds less than 4.0 to the cost. Each crashing below a length of twelve periods costs more than 4.0 per period. So, the optimal project length is twelve periods. The minimum cost way to reach that project length is: Crash B by two periods, E by one period, F by three periods, and G by three periods.

Table 5.21
Summary of Crashing for Solved Problem 4

Project Length	Activity to Crash	Added Cost	Total Cost
18	—	0	159.0
17	E	1.0	160.0
16	G	1.5	161.5
15	B	2.0	163.5
14	B	2.0	165.5
13	F, G	3.0	168.5
12	F, G	3.0	171.5
11	A, B	5.0	176.5
10	A, D, G	7.0	183.5

DISCUSSION QUESTIONS

1. A law office must juggle many cases at various stages of progression in order to both provide the best service it can to its clients and make a profit. What aspects of the project management body of knowledge would be most significant in such a context? How would they be managed?

2. An advertising agency specializing in television ad campaigns might share many of the same uncertainties as the law firm mentioned in the last question. They, too, need to balance the quality of many campaigns at different stages of development with the need to be efficient. What aspects of the project management body of knowledge would be most significant in such a context? How would they be managed?

3. Given what you know about the project management situations (construction companies, law firms, public relations firms, ship builders, etc.), what type of organizational style would you think most appropriate? Do you feel they would be more bureaucratic or entrepreneurial? What skill levels are expected of employees relative to production of more standardized product-service bundles?

4. Can you draw a PERT network describing the last time you researched, wrote, and turned in a term

paper? What was the critical path? How would you "crash" a critical activity? Did any noncritical activities ever become critical? Why? (Hint: procrastination?)

5. What aspects of the project management body of knowledge would be applicable to the administrator in your university's athletic department in charge of event staging? Can you draw a possible PERT diagram that shows the activities they might be responsible for?

6. Most student activity organizations at large universities have a concert board to book, coordinate, and stage concerts and other cultural events. What aspects of the project management body of knowledge would be applicable to that group? Can you draw a possible PERT diagram that shows the activities they might be responsible for?

7. Your job is to coordinate the implementation schedule of the software Fred was talking about in the conversation at the beginning of this chapter. Can you describe what each stage of the process life cycle might include in this context?

8. As consumers of services facilitated through project management (for example, kitchen remodeling, landscape design, or a professionally catered wedding reception), we understand how hard it is to know "exactly what we want" at the beginning of the process. How might this be the same as a business-to-business situation (for example, advertising campaigns, installing a new software solution, or designing a new football stadium)? How might they be different?

9. What is an activity, task, or job in a project? What is an immediate predecessor?

10. How is the critical path determined? Why is it important in project planning and control?

11. What is the classical PERT approach to determining the probability that a project will be completed by a specified time? What are the basic assumptions used in this approach?

12. What are the three possible objectives of a time-cost tradeoff analysis?

13. How do you determine which activities to crash when a time-cost trade-off analysis is done by hand?

14. One of the author's colleagues recently told us about the process of applying for disability benefits from the Social Security Administration. It is a Project (with a capital P)! When workers become disabled, they have to wait five months before they can apply for benefits. Next, the application process requires that you fill out forms, wait for Social Security to evaluate your request, wait for Social Security to assign a caseworker, and be interviewed by the caseworker. This application process generally takes at least a month. Once the application is complete, it must be processed. The administration subcontracts this processing task—and applicants do not know who the subcontractors are for their cases. Processing includes, among other tasks, fact checking the application to prevent fraud and ensure the applicant's eligibility. Applicants are told that processing will take at least 120 days and not to contact the Social Security office during that period because there will be no further information. After processing, a decision is made and communicated to the applicant. If the request for benefits is denied, the applicant can appeal up to four times. (A judge becomes involved on the third appeal.) Of course, applicants may secure the services of a lawyer at any point in the application process. Finally, when a request for benefits is accepted, the pay will be retroactive to the date when the applicant was first eligible for the benefits—but then a legal process might ensue to determine the appropriate interest. A recently approved payment included seven years of retroactive pay! Doesn't seven years seem like a long time for a disabled person to have to wait for disability benefits?

a) Draw a PERT diagram describing the application and evaluation process.

b) What aspects of the PMBOK are relevant to this type of project?

c) What would you do to improve the chances of a timely affirmative funding decision if you were applying for disability benefits from Social Security?

PROBLEMS

1. A local carpeting firm has a contract to carpet all 1,500 rooms of a new hotel project. They estimate their cost to be $2.5 million and have committed to a 75-day schedule.

   a) Assuming a steady rate of installation, how many rooms must they carpet per day?

   b) How much is the cost per room?

2. Using the same hotel carpeting project described above, assume we have gone 45 days into the project and have completed only 600 rooms, and that almost $1.3 million in costs have accumulated to this point.

   a) What is the estimated delay on the project?

   b) What is the scheduled value shortfall?

   c) What is the current budget shortfall?

   d) What is the total cost overrun at this point in time?

   e) How might this situation have occurred?

3. Big State University is in the midst of a new computer network project that entails installing almost 100 miles of fiber-optic cable in and among all campus buildings. The $50 million project was originally scheduled to be completed in 12 months; currently it is 8 months into the project, $40 million has been spent, and just over 75 miles of cable have been installed. Assume that the rest of the project should go as smoothly as everything up till now.

   a) What is the estimated delay on the project?

   b) What is the scheduled value shortfall?

   c) What is the current budget shortfall?

   d) What is the total cost overrun at this point in time?

4. Cheryl's hospital has been awarded a $10,000 government grant to do an experimental immunity screening in local schools. They are to check 500 children for immunity to an early childhood illness. Visiting local schools on Friday afternoons, the project was expected to take 10 weeks but they are now finishing the seventh Friday and have screened 400 children. They have accumulated costs to this point of $7500.

   a) What is the estimated delay on the project?

   b) What is the scheduled value shortfall?

   c) What is the current budget shortfall?

   d) What is the total cost overrun at this point in time?

5. Bob Heckman, manager of the MIS department at ASW Publishing, has received a request from Virginia Griner, the head of Human Resources, to develop an interactive icon- and menu-driven software package to be used by the benefits specialists in her department. Based on preliminary discussions with Virginia, Bob has identified two basically different types of functions that the package will have to serve, so he is planning on having it written in two modules. Based on this initial information, Bob has broken the project down into eight basic activities, listed in Table 5.22 along with their immediate predecessors and estimated times.

Table 5.22
Activity Information for Software Development Project

Activity	Description	Immediate Predecessors	Time (weeks)
A	Survey users for needs	—	2
B	Design graphic icons	A	3
C	Develop flowchart	A	1
D	Design input\output screens	B, C	3
E	Code module 1	C	4
F	Code module 2	C	5
G	Merge modules and graphics	D, E, F	1
H	Test program	G	2

a) Draw a project network.

b) Determine the early and late start and finish times and the slack times for the activities. Identify the critical path. How long will the project take if there are no problems or resource limitations?

6. Robinson Equipment Company has received a contract to build and deliver a new extrusion press for Continental Plastics to use in producing plastic components for Nippon Motors. Robinson's project manager has broken the project down into eight major activities, which are listed in Table 5.23 with their immediate predecessors and activity times.

a) Draw a project network.

b) Determine the early and late start and finish times and the slack times for the activities. Identify the critical path. How long will the project take if there are no problems or resource limitations?

7. Wordsworth Publishing has just received the complete first draft of a textbook from a prospective author. The activities that must be completed before this book could be available for adoption by schools and their times are given in Table 5.24.

Table 5.23

Activity Information for Robinson Equipment Company Project

Activity	Immediate Predecessors	Time (weeks)
A	—	3
B	A	4
C	A	3
D	A	8
E	B	4
F	C	6
G	D	5
H	E, F	3

Table 5.24

Activity Information for Wordsworth Publishing Project

Activity	Description	Immediate Predecessors	Time (weeks)
A	Appraisal by reviewers	—	8
B	Compare with competition	—	4
C	Assess marketability	A, B	2
D	Revisions by author	A	16
E	Sign contract	C	2
F	Edit final draft	D, E	8
G	Typeset text	F	6
H	Design artwork	F	4
I	Design and print cover	E	3
J	Proof and correct text and artwork	G, H	4
K	Print and bind book	I, J	6

a) Draw a project network.

b) Determine the early and late start and finish times and the slack times for the activities. Identify the critical path. How long will the project take if there are no problems or resource limitations?

8. Tom's airline is about to start offering flights into and out of a new (to them) airport. There are a number of activities that the airline must complete before starting this new service. The activities, their predecessors, and their times are summarized in Table 5.25.

a) Draw a project network.

b) Determine the early and late start and finish times and the slack times for the activities. Identify the critical path. How long will it be before the airline can start offering this new service if there are no problems or resource limitations?

Table 5.25
Activity Information for Airline Expansion Project

Activity	Description	Immediate Predecessors	Time (weeks)
A	Post notice for manager	—	3
B	Advertise for employees	—	4
C	Select manager	A	1
D	Train manager	C	2
E	Interview and hire employees	B, D	3
F	Renovate counter area	—	4
G	Purchase counter equipment	—	3
H	Install counter equipment	F, G	1
I	Purchase baggage carts	—	5
J	Train counter employees	E, H	2
K	Train ramp employees	E, I	1

Table 5.26
Activity Information for Problem 9

Activity	Immediate Predecessors	Normal Time	Normal Cost	Crash Time	Crash Cost
A	—	6	100	6	100
B	A	10	2000	4	2600
C	A	10	800	8	920
D	B	6	700	5	750
E	B	8	1000	6	1140
F	C, D	9	1400	7	1550
G	E	14	3000	10	3320
H	E, F	10	900	8	1020

9. Consider the project described in Table 5.26.

a) Draw a project diagram.

b) Using the normal activity times, determine the early and late start and finish times and slack times for the activities. Identify the critical path and the normal project time and cost.

c) Determine which activities to crash and by how much to achieve a project completion time of thirty-six at minimum cost.

d) Determine what the minimum project completion time is and which activities to crash and by how much to achieve that time at minimum cost.

e) Suppose there is a fixed cost of 125 per time period for the project. Determine the optimum project completion time and which activities to crash and by how much to achieve that time at minimum cost.

10. Consider the project described in Table 5.27.

a) Find the means and standard deviations of the activity times.

b) Draw a network for the project.

c) Using the mean activity times from part (a), determine the expected early and late start and finish times and the expected slack times for the activities. Identify the critical path. What is the expected length of the critical path?

d) Using the standard PERT approach, find the probability that the project will be completed within thirty time periods.

11. Consider the project described in Table 5.28.

Table 5.27
Activity Information for Problem 10

Activity	Immediate Predecessors	Activity Time Estimates		
		Optimistic	Most Likely	Pessimistic
A	—	1	2	3
B	A	1	2	4
C	A	3	5	9
D	B, C	4	7	10
E	D	2	3	6
F	C	6	11	14
G	E, F	3	4	7
H	E, F	4	5	6
I	G, H	2	5	9

Table 5.28
Activity Information for Problem 11

Activity	Immediate Predecessors	Activity Time Estimates		
		Optimistic	Most Likely	Pessimistic
A	—	1	6	11
B	—	3	7	11
C	A	2	6	10
D	B	4	6	8
E	C	3	9	15
F	D	5	9	13

Table 5.29
Activity Information for Problem 12

Activity	Immediate Predecessors	Normal Time	Normal Cost	Crash Time	Crash Cost
A	—	10	2000	7	2600
B	—	8	2400	6	2900
C	A	5	2000	4	2150
D	A, B	4	1600	2	2200
E	A, B	3	1500	2	1830
F	C, D, E	9	2400	7	2960
G	C, D, E	6	2000	6	2000
H	G	4	1200	3	1560

a) Find the means and standard deviations of the activity times.

b) Draw a network for the project.

c) Using the mean activity times from part (a), determine the expected early and late start and finish times and the expected slack times for the activities. Identify the critical path. What is the expected length of the critical path?

d) Using the standard PERT approach, find the probability that the project will take no more than twenty-four time periods; at least twenty-five time periods.

e) Find the probability that the noncritical path will take no more than twenty-four time periods; at least twenty-five time periods.

f) Using your results from parts d and e and assuming that the actual activity times are independent of one another, find the probability that the project will take no more than twenty-four time periods; at least twenty-five time periods. Compare your results with those from part (d). (Hint: Remember that $P[A \text{ and } B] = P[A] \times P[B]$ if A and B are independent events.)

12. Consider the project described in Table 5.29.

a) Draw a project diagram.

b) Using the normal activity times, determine the early and late start and finish times and slack times for the activities. Identify the critical path and the normal project time and cost.

c) Determine which activities to crash and by how much to achieve a project completion time of twenty-one at minimum cost.

d) Determine what the minimum project completion time is and which activities to crash and by how much to achieve that time at minimum cost.

e) Suppose that there is a fixed cost of 250 per time period for the project. Determine the optimum project completion time and which activities to crash and by how much to achieve that time at minimum cost.

13. Sociological Surveys, Inc. is a small social research consulting firm operated by two faculty members in the sociology department at a university. The firm has received an offer to submit a bid on a contract to conduct a study. In order to determine how long the project will take and how much it will cost, the firm's principals have identified the activities required and estimates of the amounts of time required to complete them, as shown in Table 5.30.

a) Draw a project network.

b) Determine the early and late start and finish times for the activities and their slack times.

Table 5.30

Activity Information for Social Research Project

Activity	Description	Immediate Predecessors	Time (weeks)
A	Design survey instrument	—	2
B	Design sampling procedure	—	1
C	Pilot test instrument	A	3
D	Redesign instrument	C	1
E	Recruit interviewers	B	3
F	Assign interviewers to districts	A, E	1
G	Train interviewers	A, E	2
H	Conduct interviews	D, F, G	6
I	Analyze results	H	4
J	Prepare report	I	2

Table 5.31

Activity Information for Little Lake Theatre Project

Activity	Description	Immediate Predecessors	Time (weeks)
A	Audition and hire actors	—	4
B	Design costumes	—	3
C	Make costumes	A, B	3
D	Design sets	—	3
E	Build sets	D	5
F	Design lighting	D	2
G	Create lighting	F	2
H	Rehearsals	A	3
I	Prepare advertising	A	1
J	Advertising campaign	I	3
K	Final rehearsals	C, E, G, H	1

c) Identify the critical path. How many weeks will it take to plan for and conduct the research project?

14. The Little Lake Theatre Company is planning a new production of *The Boyfriend*, scheduled to open during the second week of July. Will Disney, managing director of the company, has prepared a list of the activities (shown in Table 5.31) that must be completed before the play can open and has estimated the number of weeks for each.

   a) Draw a project network.

   b) Determine the early and late start and finish times for the activities and their slack times. Identify the critical path. How many weeks will it take before the play is ready to put on?

15. The marketing department at Bodnar Industries is developing a promotional campaign to introduce a new product. A listing of the various activities

required, their immediate predecessors, and estimates of their times (in days) is given in Table 5.32.

   a) Draw a diagram for the project.

   b) Find the means and standard deviations of the activity times.

   c) Using the expected activity times, find the expected early and late start and finish times and expected slack times of the activities. Identify the critical path. What is the expected length of the critical path?

   d) Using the standard PERT approach, find the probability that the project will be completed in less than 60 days; more than 65 days.

   e) How many days should the marketing manager allow for the project if he wants to be 99% sure that the project will be complete within the allowed time?

Table 5.32

Activity Information for Bodnar Industries Promotional Campaign Project

Activity	Description	Immediate Predecessors	Activity Time Estimates		
			Optimistic	Most Likely	Pessimistic
A	Rough brochure layout	—	2	3	5
B	Review brochure	A	6	8	10
C	Final brochure layout	B	4	6	8
D	Final brochure artwork	C	5	7	11
E	Design display	—	12	15	20
F	Rough display artwork	E	2	3	4
G	Review display	E	6	8	10
H	Revise display	G	2	3	4
I	Final display artwork	F, H	1	2	4
J	Make display plates	I	18	23	26
K	Make brochure plates	D, I	10	13	16
L	Make and ship displays	J	7	10	14
M	Print and ship brochures	K	6	8	10

CHALLENGE PROBLEMS

1. The city of West Hartford is going to build a new municipal pool in a corner of the main city park. Working with the city's director of Public Works, the contractor identified the various activities that will have to be completed and the normal and crash times (in days) and costs (in $1000s) for each. The activity information is given in Table 5.33.

   a) Draw a diagram for this project.

   b) Using the normal times, determine the early start and finish times and the slack times for all activities. Identify the critical path. How long will the project last if activities are done in their normal times? What will the project cost if activities are done in their normal times?

   c) Determine which activities to crash and by how much in order to achieve a project length of 63 days at minimum cost.

   d) Determine which activities to crash and by how much in order to complete the project in minimum time at minimum cost.

   e) Suppose that the contractor has a bonus clause that will pay an extra $5000 per day by which the pool is completed early. Determine the optimal project length and which activities should be crashed and by how much to achieve that length.

Table 5.33
Activity Information for Pool Construction Project

Activity	Description	Immediate Predecessors	Normal Time	Normal Cost	Crash Time	Crash Cost
A	Grade site	—	8	16	6	20
B	Excavate for pool	A	12	48	8	72
C	Excavate for pump house	A	3	12	2	17
D	Trench to connect pump house and water main	C	6	18	5	24
E	Trench to connect pool and pump house	B, C	3	9	2	15
F	Build pool frame	B	15	27	8	48
G	Pipe to connect pool and pump house	E, F	4	8	2	16
H	Pipe to connect pump house and water main	D	5	10	3	18
I	Build pump house and install pumps	G, H	20	30	16	52
J	Pour concrete for pool	G	8	40	6	54
K	Pour pool deck	J	6	24	4	33
L	Building for lockers and snack bar	K	10	12	6	28
M	Grade and pave parking lot	A	7	21	5	28
N	Landscape	I, L, M	6	6	4	9

2. Carlson Construction has a contract to build a small office building. The property is appropriately zoned for this type of use and all necessary permits have been obtained. Bill Carlson, head of the company, has prepared the following list of activities (shown in Table 5.34) that must be completed, along with estimates of the normal and crash times (in days) and costs (in $1000s) for each activity.

   a) Draw the project network.

   b) Using the normal activity times, determine the early and late start and finish times and slack times for the activities. Determine the critical path and the normal project time. Determine the normal cost for the project.

   c) Determine which activities to crash and by how much in order to reduce the length of the project to 45 days.

   d) Determine the minimum project length and which activities to crash and by how much in order to get to that length at minimum cost.

   e) Assume that Carlson Construction will receive a bonus of $2000 for every day by which it reduces the length of the project. Determine the optimal project length and which activities to crash and by how much to get there.

3. Presutti's Wood-Baked Pizzas operates a chain of restaurants specializing in pizza baked in wood-fired ovens. Bill Presutti, operations manager for the chain, is getting ready to open a new restaurant in an old warehouse in Richmond's Shockoe Slip district. The various activities required, along with their immediate predecessors and the optimistic, most likely, and pessimistic estimates of their times (in weeks), are given in Table 5.35.

   a) Compute the means and standard deviations of the activities' completion times.

   b) Draw the network diagram.

   c) Using the expected activity times, find the expected early and late start and finish times and expected slack times of the activities. Identify the critical path. What is the expected length of the critical path?

   d) Using the standard PERT approach, find the probability that the project will be completed within 19 weeks.

Table 5.34
Activity Information for Carlson Construction Project

Activity	Description	Immediate Predecessors	Normal Time	Normal Cost	Crash Time	Crash Cost
A	Excavate basement	—	6	6.0	4	9.0
B	Excavate for utility lines	—	3	3.3	2	5.0
C	Pour basement concrete	A	9	5.4	7	9.0
D	Connect utility lines	B, C	4	3.0	2	5.0
E	Erect building shell	B	25	25.0	20	31.0
F	Install rough plumbing	D, E	9	4.8	7	7.0
G	Install rough wiring	E	7	6.0	4	8.7
H	Finish exterior	E	9	18.0	6	22.2
I	Finish interior	F, G	12	25.0	8	31.4
J	Pave parking lot	H	5	15.0	4	18.0
K	Landscaping	J	6	4.5	3	6.9
L	Inspection	F, G	1	0	1	0

Table 5.35
Activity Information for Pizza Restaurant Project

Activity	Description	Immediate Predecessors	Activity Time Estimates		
			Optimistic	Most Likely	Pessimistic
A	Screen applicant for manager	—	2	4	6
B	Advertise for employees	—	2	3	5
C	Renovate building	—	8	12	16
D	Select manager	A	1	2	3
E	Interview employee applicants	B, D	4	5	8
F	Purchase equipment	—	6	8	12
G	Install equipment	C, F	2	3	4
H	Hire employees	E	3	4	6
I	Train employees	G, H	2	2	2

4. If the objective of project crashing is to determine how to achieve the minimum project time at minimum cost, there is an alternative approach: Set all activity times to the crash time. Solve the network and identify the critical path. Of those activities not on the critical path, identify the one with the highest value of $\Delta C / \Delta T$. Uncrash that activity back to its normal time or until its remaining total slack is used up. Repeat as often as possible. Apply this procedure to the project in Problem 9. Compare the result with that found in Problem 9d.

Case 5: Project Scope: To See the Birth of the Universe (and More)

Astronomers have begun a project that will include the design and construction of a generation of huge telescopes that will be able to see to the edge of the visible universe. The behemoth observatories planned by European and American astronomers will dwarf today's "big glass"—towering telescopes that sit on remote mountaintops in Hawaii and Chile—with huge mirrors that will be up to 100 meters across. The largest of the proposed projects is called OWL, or the Overwhelmingly Large Telescope. It is expected to gather more light and use more glass than all of the telescopes professional astronomers have built since Galileo first saw the moons of Jupiter.

Big enough to collect light from the time the first stars first began to form, the telescopes will also enable us to see things closer to earth. Steve Strom, associate director of the National Optical Astronomy Observatory in Tucson, Arizona, is coordinating design of the Giant Segmented Mirror Telescope—a 30-meter instrument whose primary mirror will be three times the diameter of today's largest telescope. He says these telescopes will be able to image and directly analyze earth like planets outside the solar system that now can only be detected indirectly by radio signals.

In the last decade, NASA's Hubble Space Telescope and ground-based observatories have worked together to study previously unseen black holes, planetary systems forming around other stars, and the birthplace of stars in glowing stellar clouds. Although the Hubble can "see" a distant object clearly from its place in orbit, only large ground-based telescopes can gather enough light to analyze the object's spectrum to discern what it is made of. With the launch of even more powerful space based telescopes in the next 10 years, astronomers will need even more powerful ground-based telescopes to keep pace with the observations from space—seeing light emitted billions of years ago to piece together details of the pre-galactic building blocks in a kind of archaeology of the cosmos.

It isn't yet clear where these telescopes will be built, when they will be completed, or who will pay for them. Likely locations are found in Chile, Hawaii or Mexico's Baja California. Still astronomers are moving ahead with the projects. Two former European competitors that had each been planning a 50-meter telescope—joined to work toward a single 100-meter instrument. To be built in the high desert region of Chile or the Canary Islands, the 15-year project could cost over $1 billion and challenges the bounds of technical and economic feasibility. To Europeans, its value is not merely an expansion of humanity's view of the universe because it would also dwarf a U.S. planned 30-meter telescope.

A 30-meter telescope poses major engineering challenges, let alone a 100-meter instrument. Some of these challenges are:

▶ Size and vibration: The world's largest telescopes currently are the 10-meter, twin-domed Keck Telescopes at Mauna Kea, Hawaii. These are eight stories tall and weigh 300 tons each. A 30-meter telescope would have to be shielded inside an 18-story steel dome because tiny vibrations induced by the wind could blur its images to uselessness. Electronic adjustments can correct the jitters, but the precision required exceeds anything in use today. Vibrations of only 1/400,000th of an inch could distort images beyond use. Construction of today's 10-meter telescopes was possible only because the primary mirrors, which were too large to be produced as a single piece, could be assembled as 36 hexagonal segments, each 1.8 meters in diameter. By comparison, a 100-meter telescope would have about 2000 highly polished segments.

▶ Manufacturing materials: Major breakthroughs in manufacturing are needed to build the mirrors of the new telescopes. The mirrors for the proposed 100-meter telescope would require more precision optics than have been produced throughout history.

▶ Financing: The twin Keck telescopes cost $140 million when they were built in the 1990s. Current estimates of a 30-meter telescope are around $700 million and experts admit that could be off by $100 million or more. That dwarfs the National Optical Astronomy Observatory's annual budget of $25 million. The National Science Foundation, the primary U.S. funding agency for big science, spent only $126 million this year on all of its major construction projects.

▶ Politics: "Projects of this size are going to require combined public and private money both to build and to operate," said Strom. "The science and politics of these telescopes are going to be an equal challenge."

Barring unforeseen technical problems, the Europeans think they can have their telescope in operation by 2015. The timetable for the Americans' 30-meter telescope calls for construction to be completed by 2012.

SOME QUESTIONS TO THINK ABOUT:

1. What is the scope of these projects and why would it be difficult to establish?

2. Describe the project management activities likely to be required in each phase of the project life cycle for these projects.

3. What role will the management of risk and uncertainty play with these projects?

4. What kinds of cooperation and or coordination may be required for all of these projects proceed ahead as planned?

5. Do you think the U.S. and European projects should be combined? Why or Why not?

Source: Adapted from the *Atlanta Journal Constitution*, http://www.ajc.com, May 20, 2003, reporter Mike Toner

REFERENCES

Barkley, B. T., and J. H. Saylor. *Customer Driven Project Management.* New York: McGraw-Hill, 1993.

Dinsmore, P. C., ed. *The AMA Handbook of Project Management.* New York: Amacom, 1993.

Duncan, W. R. *A Guide to the Project Management Body of Knowledge.* Upper Darby, PA: Project Management Institute, 1996.

Goldratt, E. M. *Critical Chain.* Great Barrington, MA: The North River Press, 1997.

Lewis, J. P. *Mastering Project Management.* New York: McGraw-Hill, 1998.

Meredith, J. R., and S. J. Mantel Jr. *Project Management: A Managerial Approach.* New York: John Wiley & Sons, 1985.

6

The Product-Service Bundle Design Process

Chapter Outline

Introduction   250

Integrating Operations Management Across the Functions   252

Product-Service Bundle Design Tasks   253

Designing Product-Service Bundles Using Cross-Functional Teams   257

Concurrent Engineering versus Sequential/Hierarchical Engineering   262

Group Technology, Modular Design, Product Simplification, and E-Commerce   264

Tools Used in Design Processes   266

The Kano Model   266

Quality Function Deployment   271

Computer-Aided Design   275

Service Blueprinting   276

Product Costing Methods   278

Summary   280
Key Terms   280
Solved Problems   280
Discussion Questions   282
Problems   285
Challenge Problems   287
Case 6: What's Bright Yellow, Takes a Beating Every Time It Comes Out, Yet Has Good Hair?   288
References   289

Learning Objectives

After studying this chapter you should be able to

▶ Demonstrate your understanding of the cross-functional linkages involved in designing product service bundles

▶ Describe the tasks involved in designing product service bundles

▶ Describe a cross-functional, team-based approach to designing product service bundles

▶ Compare and contrast a variety of tools that are useful in the design processes

▶ Use simple two-way break-even analysis to justify new products on the basis of volume

▶ Use a factor rating scheme to conduct competitor analysis as would be done to set design targets in the quality function deployment

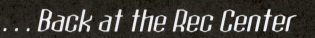

. . . Back at the Rec Center

Luis arrives late at the rec center this morning. Usually, when that happens, it's a sign that something has gone wrong at work over the weekend and that Luis has received a very-early morning call from the third-shift supervisor. (Many three-shift operations start the week on Sunday night or Monday morning.) But on this day, Luis was in a great mood.

"Hit it hard this morning, folks; Gatorade's on me!" he offers happily, as he bursts through the door doing his best "air guitar" routine. "They were rockin' on the third shift last night, and I just got the gold record!"

"Whoa, hold on there! What's the big celebration?" asks Fred, wondering what's going on. "Did you hit the lottery?"

"Nope, nothing like that," Luis assures the group, continuing to smile. "I got a call from the folks on the third shift just after they started using that new latex stain this morning." Luis was referring to a new stain being used on a best-selling line of bedroom furniture. He'd worked very hard with one of his company's better suppliers to develop the stain. The supplier had never produced anything like it, certainly not in the small quantities and wide array of colors Luis had asked for. He was very proud of the project, which had turned out well for the supplier, for Luis's company, and for Luis

himself. "They called to tell me it was working great. I was pretty sure everything was on track for the launch when I left on Friday, but they called just to tell me the first parts are out of the spray booths, and everything looks great!"

"Wait a minute. You're this excited about some new kind of paint?" Fred asks.

"It isn't just new paint," Luis replies, with some exasperation. "It's a stain that seals wood as well as anything we can get, but compared to the oil-based stuff, it's easier to use, easier to clean up, and it comes in more colors. The best part, though, was how we worked with the supplier to develop it. No quality problems at all."

Fred interrupts, saying, "Come on, you get word to your suppliers, tell them what you want; they each put a bid together, and the best price wins!" In Fred's mind, that's how it happens. The supplier's marketing representatives find out what the customer wants; the reps send the specifications to the engineers; the engineers use the specs to develop product designs; the designs are sent to the process engineers; the process engineers design the process and formulate a set of operating procedures for the folks who manufacture the product. After all that, marketing tries to deliver the new product to the customer on time. If the product isn't right, the customer sends it back to the factory and process starts over. You work out the kinks and move on. Eventually, everyone gets the specs straight and the customer is satisfied.

"That's how we used to do it," Luis replies. "Remember how I told you a while back that the EPA had been on our backs about solvent emissions? Remember the hassle we had with that other supplier, you know, when we were switching to latex-based paints because they didn't need the solvents to clean them up? Well, I made sure we didn't make the same mistake when we were looking for stains!"

To satisfy the EPA, managers at Luis's company decided to reduce the need for the solvents that were used to clean up oil-based paints during color changes in the spray booth. They asked their suppliers for latex-based paints that could be cleaned up with soap and water. They also wanted to schedule smaller and more frequent deliveries to keep paint inventory lower. A purchasing manager, the owner's nephew, had gone about obtaining a source for the paint much the way Fred had suggested it is done. The supplier's representative came in, listened to what the purchasing manager wanted, and told him she would be back in a couple of months with something Luis's company could use. After almost eight months, the representative came back without a workable solution. As it turned out, the representative could have been back much sooner if people at her company had been allowed to use their own expertise to calculate the right formula. Instead, bound by what they thought engineers and managers at Luis's company wanted, they struggled for months to come up with an acceptable solution. Not only did the supplier's delay throw off the introduction of

the company's new contemporary furniture collection; the colors didn't match the metal and plastic parts that held the furniture together. The whole process had to be repeated.

"I guess nobody was too happy with that the first time," Cheryl admits. "I remember you talking about all the damage control."

"I never did ask you what the problem was," Tom asks. "What took them so long to get the formula right? Why was the delivery schedule a problem?"

"We told them up front what we wanted the paint to look like, and what we wanted it to do," Luis explains. "But I guess a lot of what we wanted got lost in the translation. If we'd talked directly to their engineers from the start, it would have worked out a lot better. It was like a game of Telephone; the story changed each time it's retold. By the time the product design people formulated the stuff and the process people reengineered the production lines to make it, the consistency of the paint was way too heavy. The colors didn't match the samples. The new setup times killed them. Turns out they just didn't ask the right questions."

When the supplier tried to set up the production line, the change in formula and the heavier consistency complicated the setup and slowed production time whenever the color was changed. With a more expensive setup, the small quantities they were asking for would be unprofitable. The whole project ground to a halt while the marketing rep tried to negotiate a higher price to cover the higher cost. It turned out that the heavier consistency was caused by an additive that was no longer needed in the latex-based formula. Only after a lot of back and forth was the issue resolved. "The whole deal with longer setups became a nonissue" Luis laughs.

"Well, what you just described sounds typical for us," Fred offers. "What did you or your supplier do differently this time?"

"I've heard a lot about teams and concurrent engineering in my evening classes. After the paint problem, I convinced my boss to try a different approach with the stain. I wanted to get everybody talking up front," Luis replies. "One thing I did was to get together a team to meet with the supplier's people. We included representatives from purchasing, engineering, operations, even marketing. We met with a similar group from the supplier to talk the whole thing through. The combined groups talked about what we needed from them and what the supplier needed from us."

"Did you listen to each other? Did it work?" asks Cheryl. "I mean, I guess you must have, if this morning's news was so good."

"Yeah, we did. With everybody working off the same page, they got us a prototype sample much faster than before. We made everybody look like rocket scientists!" he says happily. "It sure would have saved a lot of headaches and delays if we'd used this process when we were getting the paint deal together! Now we know better. We even got some surprise benefits: Taking the additive out made it easier to get the color and tone of the samples right, solved a changeover problem our supplier had, and reduced the cost. There were lots of positive spin-offs like that."

"Well, I guess everything needs to happen faster these days," says Fred. What happened to 'Slow and steady wins the race'?"

"I think somebody saw you on the treadmill and rewrote the story!" chides Luis.

Introduction

Stop reading this chapter and take a moment to look around you. What products do you see? Over the past several days, what services have you used? Take a minute and list at least ten products and services you have used recently, and answer the following questions: What is unusual or unique about each item on your list? What are the standard features of each? If you purchased the items, why did you buy them rather than purchase competing products or services? If you begin to evaluate products and services in this way, before long you will be asking questions such as, "Why did they make or plan it that way?" "What could they have been thinking when they designed that?" or, "Hey—that's pretty cool; I wonder how they thought of that?"

Asking questions about products and services is not just something you should do when you are reading an OM book. As a consumer, you are always evaluating the design of the products and services you buy. For example, long before you finish a meal at a restaurant, you may form a number of opinions regarding the food and service you receive. Hours or even days after you finish your meal, your evaluation could change based on new information you gain from conversations with friends or from media reports.

Look back at your list of goods and services. There's a good chance that it includes some goods or services that did not exist 20 years ago. Does your list include an MP3 player, a DVD or CD player, a laptop computer, a cellular phone, a cash machine, a quick oil change, an electronic card catalog search, an overnight mail service, a facsimile machine, a diet soft drink sweetened with Splenda, an Internet movie rental service, or a soft drink in a can with no throwaway tab? These items, which we tend to take for granted today, were not available just 20 years ago.

Can you think of some goods and services that you are only beginning to anticipate, ones that might make a list of everyday items in the next 10 to 15 years? Will global positioning systems and interactive road maps be standard equipment on new cars? Will your telephone number be assigned to you and travel with you wherever you go, instead of being assigned to a specific location, as it most commonly is now? Will you still buy CDs, or will you buy network access to their content from an online library? Will you buy electricity the way that you currently buy long-distance telephone service? Will cars, appliances, and medical devices such as pacemakers have built-in maintenance monitors that are in constant contact with the producer and signal the need for a repair before a breakdown occurs? Will television programming be delivered to your cell phone/PDA on demand? No doubt, 10 years from now, you will be taking for granted countless goods and services that you cannot even imagine today. These are the issues faced by designers of product-service bundles, and this chapter describes how they do their job.

Designing product-service bundles is greatly facilitated if companies can manage cross-functionally. Marketing research might identify an idea for a product or service, but before they get a chance to sell it to a customer, many other departments will have affected the resulting product-service bundle. Research and development departments will have developed the product-service bundle and assessed its feasibility; process engineering departments will have created equipment and systems used to produce and deliver the package; purchasing and operations will have added the specified value; and finance will have created the budgets for capital acquisition and ongoing operations. In addition, customers and suppliers may be involved in the development of the product-service bundle.

Development of a product-service bundle requires the completion of a defined set of tasks:

◗ identifying a financially viable market opportunity

◗ physically designing the product-service bundle

◗ designing required value-adding processes

◗ developing systems for supply and operation of those processes

◗ establishing sales and service procedures

Traditionally, the design of product-service bundles has been seen as the job of marketing experts and product designers. But because the design of products and services often dictates the way in which they are made and delivered, design is also critical to operations management and other functions. All the functions involved in transforming an idea into a revenue-generating reality complete their part in the process independently and only in turn: Each stage of the work is passed from one department to the next until the design is complete. This traditional approach, allowing business functions to make independent decisions regarding design of the product-service bundle, will get the job done—but it may be too late or too far off targeted customer expectations and thus result in less-than-desirable commercial success.

The modern business environment presents many challenges to the traditional design approach. Today's global markets require designs that satisfy a large and diverse set of customer requirements. Global competition requires ever higher levels of quality, performance, and cost competitiveness. Technology and competitive strategies force businesses to respond quickly to changing customer requirements. Customers are more and more aware of alternatives and are less likely to accept partial satisfaction of their requirements. Finally, more and more customers are requiring "turnkey" solutions that effectively match manufactured products and services. Many customers want to tell the seller what they want with little if any interaction prior to delivery—and, most customers are not willing to develop new expertise to put the product or service into use. They simply want to "turn the key and drive off," as they would in a new car.

A team-based approach that concurrently includes the perspectives of all business functions as well as those of the customer is better suited to designing product-service bundles in the current business climate. This approach generally results in product-service bundle designs that are less expensive to make, are more in line with customer expectations, use more current technologies, and reach the market more quickly.

Many decision-making tools are used in the design process, including quality function deployment, computer-aided design, and various product-costing methods. Many statistical tools are also useful for making decisions in the presence of uncertainty.

Product-service bundle design is an ongoing activity in many organizations, but not every technological breakthrough or idea for a product improvement is a technical or financial success. Business history is littered with "white elephant" stories— many companies even keep these prototypes around to laugh about. Many of these products or services sounded great on paper and were technically elegant, but turned out to be hard to manufacture or deliver. Others, such as the peanut butter and jelly that came in the same jar, just never caught on. These and other failures actually benefit firms in the long run, however, because companies can learn important lessons about the design process, technology, and customer preferences with each new product-service bundle they design.

Integrating Operations Management Across the Functions

Table 6.1 highlights the main links between product-service bundle design and the functional areas of businesses, including operations management. Historically, the functions most involved in designing products and services were marketing and engineering: Marketing identified customer requirements and determined the extent to which various design proposals met those needs, then engineering developed the product-service bundle.

In contrast, modern design processes generally require cooperation across functions and, thus, draw upon cross-functional teams. Most companies recognize that separating design from other operational decisions can hinder efforts to satisfy customer requirements. Instead, product-service bundle design should play a significant role in the activities of each function and personnel from the various functional areas in a business should work together to evaluate design trade-offs and create design synergies. When this occurs, a firm can satisfy customers and gain competitive advantage. This approach is not a one-time event, however. Ongoing cross-functional management provides the necessary understanding and trust among the functions' employees that enables them to make design effective decisions on new product-service bundles. One consequence of this cross-functional activity is that businesses may more frequently redesign their products and services.

As Figure 6.1 indicates, product life cycles are getting shorter and shorter. While this fact allows companies to gain time-based competitive advantages from modern design processes, it also requires the various business functions to work together more effectively and more frequently. Each time a new or redesigned product is introduced, marketing needs to both promote the new product and sell the remainder of the old product. OM has to begin producing the new item to satisfy demand, while maintaining an adequate but not excessive supply of the old item. This transition requires that marketing and OM understand each other's processes, so that specific market requirements can be translated from marketing information into OM decisions.

The product-service bundle design process not only requires a cross-functional perspective but, as Figure 6.2 illustrates, it may require that the firm whose transformation process will produce the product-service bundle extend beyond its walls and into the supply chain. Luis's experience with the stain development (in the conversation at the beginning this chapter) is an example of supplier involvement in the design process. The coordination of material flows for existing products has been a major issue for SCM managers for several years. The same technology that enables coordination between functional areas inside the firm is beginning to be used to facilitate increased levels of collaboration between external supply chain entities when it comes to product-service bundle design.

Product-Service Bundle Design Tasks

The extent to which the design of product-service bundles is an everyday part of a firm's activity depends to some degree on the firm's strategy. The flexibility needed to continually introduce and maintain a wide variety of product-service bundles may be a major part of the strategy for businesses such as Luis's furniture factory or Cheryl's hospital. Or, the business strategy might be to maintain a narrower range of products and services in a cost-effective fashion, as in Fred's electronics business and Tom's airline. Figure 6.3 relates the rate of new product introduction to a firm's process type, level of dedication of its process technology, and order winners and qualifiers.

For firms on the right side of the scale in Figure 6.3 (batch processes and job shops), new product introduction is a more common aspect of daily operations. General-purpose technology can be used to produce a wide and changing array of low-volume products and services in a job or batch process. For example, the Parker-Hannifin Corporation plant in Brookville, Ohio, makes customized hydraulic tube fittings to match unique blueprints representing new product designs. Similarly, most fine restaurants introduce new entrees and customize existing ones to customers' tastes on an ongoing basis. Order winners, shown on the right side of the figure, include design quality, flexibility (the ease with which its output mix can be changed to match customer demand), and timeliness (the speed with which the firm can get new and customized products to the marketplace or rapid design and manufacturing capability). Cost, conformance, and delivery reliability need only meet levels necessary to qualify for the business. In such situations, the introduction of new products is generally integrated into most, if not all, systems, technologies, and other resources the firm employs.

For firms on the left side of Figure 6.3 (continuous flow and repetitive processes), however, the introduction of a totally new product or service design is a major

Table 6.1

Integrating Operations Management across the Functions

Integration Perspective / Functional Area	Finance	Accounting
Why Cross-Functional Integration Matters in Designing the Product-Service Bundle	The product-service bundle design has a huge impact on cash flows that are used to justify the business investments required to generate profits from the design. Financial managers must approve such investments and will want to know about the risk associated with them. Also, the design process itself requires financing.	Accounting systems are needed to track expenditures in the design project. Also, accountants must establish fiduciary systems to track the financial performance of the new product-service bundle.
Key Issues	What implications do design decisions have on the level of uncertainty associated with cash flows tied to the product-service bundle? Is the design project within budget? Are expenditures associated with the design project justified? How much can or should be invested in R&D?	How should the cost accounting system be set up for the new product-service bundle? What should be reported in SEC filings regarding potential impact of the design on financial balances and income?

undertaking because they use dedicated technology in a line or continuous process to mass-produce large quantities of standardized products and services. These companies win orders with low cost, conformance quality, and reliable delivery schedules. Flexibility, delivery speed, and design capability are usually defined by the market, and firms must meet these criteria in order to qualify for the business. Most car manufacturers, for example, must shut down for two weeks each summer just to retool their machinery to accommodate the relatively minor changes in product line from one model year to the next. Most auto companies feel they are doing a great job if they can introduce a totally new product in less than three years, from drawing board to showroom floor. In fact, many experts attribute much of DaimlerChrysler's resurgence during the late 1990s through the present to the company's ability to introduce a new product line about once a year, after about 30 months incubation time.

As Figure 6.3 illustrates, some firms engage heavily in product design and redesign to satisfy small market segments, while others redesign their offerings less frequently to satisfy large demand volumes. That does not mean that all companies on the right side of Figure 6.3 are small or that all companies on the left side are large. Microsoft

Human Resources	Marketing	Engineering	Management Information Systems
HR professionals are responsible for staffing the design team and working to ensure that the appropriate personnel systems and incentives are in place. Given the diverse set of professions involved in a design project over an extended project life cycle, this can be a significant challenge.	Marketing is responsible for translating customer requirements and market intelligence into design concepts, as well as for testing customer receptiveness to specific design alternatives. It will eventually have to distribute and sell the new product-service bundle.	Engineering creates the physical design of the product-service bundle, tests its performance characteristics, and develops the systems for its manufacture.	Design teams require an ability to share information and that information must be kept secure. For this they rely on the MIS function. Information Systems may also play a key supporting role by providing all or a part of the service value in the bundle.
What staffing is required in the design project and when? How will design professionals be recruited and compensated? What form of employee contracts will be used to ensure the security of proprietary design information?	What customer needs must the design meet? How will the bundle be packaged, distributed, promoted, and sold? How will customers respond to specific design alternatives?	What technical hurdles must be overcome during the design process? What type of equipment and process technology will be required to provide the new product-service bundle? How reliable will the design be? How safe? How will it perform? Etc.	Who on the design team needs access to what design information? What design software will be used, how will that be acquired and supported, and what hardware requirements must be satisfied? How will data be maintained and secured?

Corporation is continually adding to the mix of software and related product-service bundles it offers, while many small pizza places offer only a single product, pizza, in a limited number of sizes.

The magnitude of the tasks that must be accomplished in designing a new product-service bundle varies depending on a firm's operational strategy. In most cases, a common set of tasks must precede production. Typical tasks in designing product-service bundles and getting them to market may include:

▶ Doing market research to identify an opportunity

▶ Performing basic scientific research needed to develop the breakthroughs an opportunity depends on

▶ Choosing or developing a technology required to translate scientific breakthroughs into commercial concepts

▶ Developing specific applications, systems, and products and services

▶ Testing the performance of new applications, systems, and products and services

Figure 6.1

The product life cycle: past, present, and future

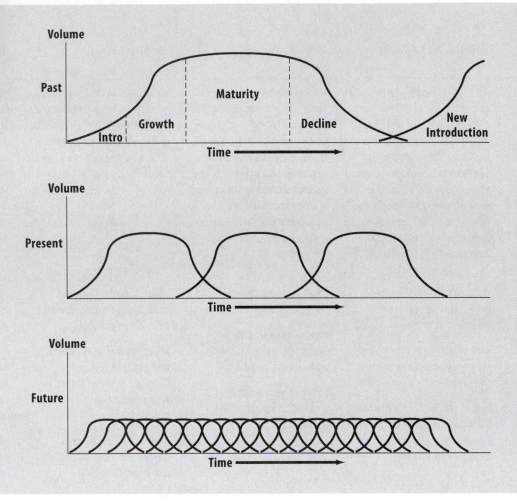

- ◗ Testing customer response to new applications and products and services

- ◗ Creating a value-adding system that is capable of delivering the new applications, systems, and products and services. This task includes the design and development of manufacturing processes to make specific product elements of the bundle; the development of service delivery systems to provide the service elements of the bundle; the development of systems to deliver maintenance and support services; the development of systems to deliver allied services and products (for example, toner for copiers); the development of supplier capabilities; and the development of an appropriate distribution system

- ◗ Ensuring the legal and regulatory compliance of new applications, systems, and products and services

- ◗ Obtaining patents, trademarks, and copyrights, as appropriate

- ◗ Developing a marketing plan and marketing the new applications, systems, and products and services. Such a plan must address the traditional marketing considerations of place, price, and promotion, as well as customer education

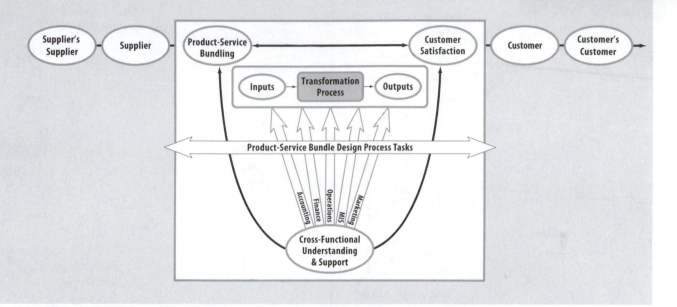

Figure 6.2
The product service bundle design process

Many of these tasks are sequentially related and may fit within the domain of a specific function. For example, the marketing department does the marketing research and planning, the legal department takes care of obtaining patents, and the product engineering department oversees product development. As a result, the design of product-service bundles has traditionally been accomplished one function at a time. The sequential relationship of the tasks, however, does not mean that the issues pertaining to the various tasks are best considered sequentially. Firms should be thinking about the availability of quality suppliers early in the development of a specific application, system, or product-service bundle. As a result, cross-functional product design teams that address several functional issues concurrently are becoming more common. The organizational approach used does not significantly change the set of core tasks required to design a new product-service bundle and bring it to market, however.

Designing Product-Service Bundles Using Cross-Functional Teams

As we have seen, the design of product-service bundles has traditionally included a set of sequentially related tasks, each represented by a different function. The sequential relationship of the tasks led to a design approach in which each function worked more or less in isolation from the others, as illustrated in Figure 6.4a. Once a function's work (functional output) has been completed and it "spins off" its contribution, its job is finished. This approach simply spans the gaps between functions; it does not "manage" or work across them. The customer is seen as being only the initiator of the

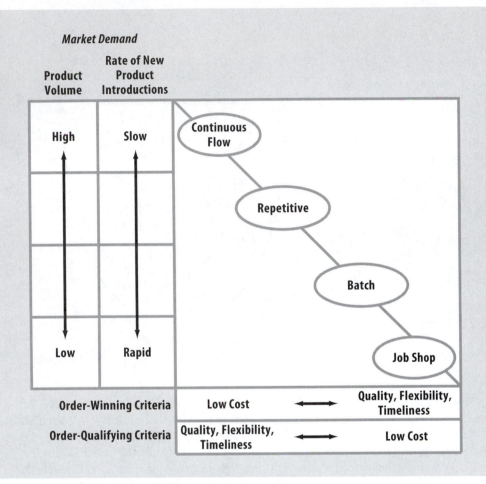

Figure 6.3

Rate of new product introduction vs. process choice, order winners

Concurrent engineering

An approach to product-service design in which the concerns of more than one function are considered simultaneously.

project and a potential user of the final product or service. At each stage of the design process, the emphasis is on only that one functional stakeholder's priorities.

As has been discussed, the modern approach to designing the product-service bundle emphasizes addressing the considerations of all functional area stakeholders throughout the design process. Figure 6.4b profiles this method, which is frequently referred to as **concurrent engineering**. In the concurrent engineering design process, all functions participate concurrently and a cross-functional team is established for the duration of the project to manage the entire process. Each function "spins in" its contribution, and the customer is seen as being a part of the design team. Because each function is represented on the design team, all functional concerns can be reflected in decisions that are normally influenced primarily by one function. Together, the functional "spin ins" and the customer-driven market opportunity move the design process forward. Though functional excellence remains an important goal, it is subordinated to customer satisfaction, the dominant concern of the entire team and the common goal that unifies its efforts. Because of the increased emphasis on consideration of all stakeholder concerns, and on the development of consensus solutions that will deliver customer satisfaction, no surprises should arise in the process of making and selling the new product-service bundle.

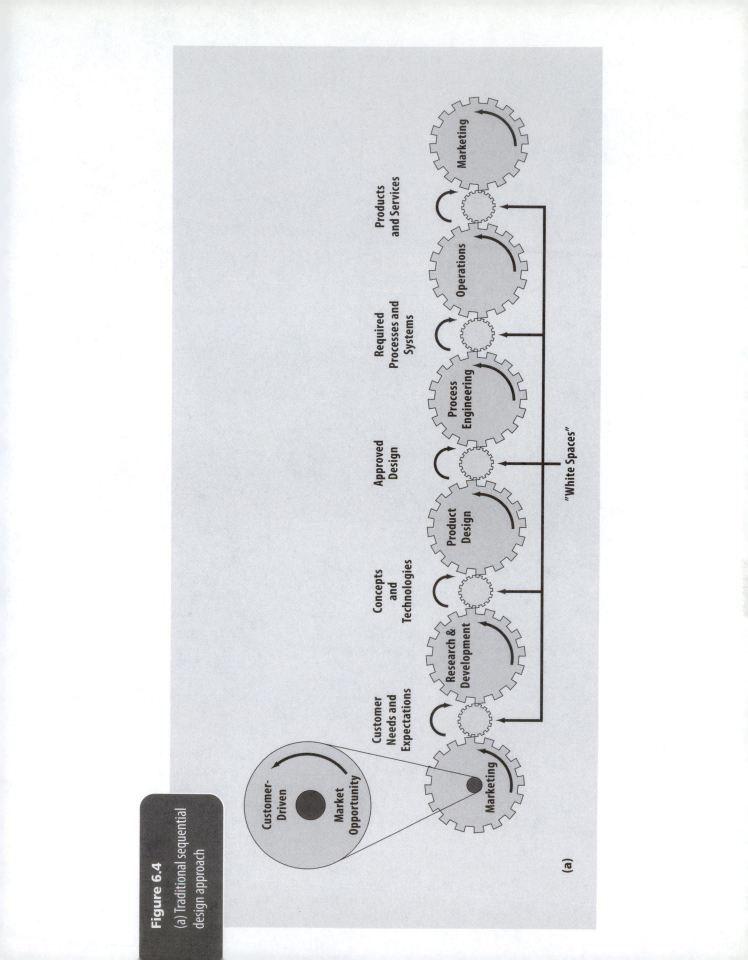

Figure 6.4

(a) Traditional sequential design approach

Customer-Driven

Market Opportunity

Marketing

Customer Needs and Expectations

Research & Development

Concepts and Technologies

Product Design

Approved Design

Process Engineering

Required Processes and Systems

Operations

Products and Services

Marketing

"White Spaces"

(a)

Figure 6.4

(b) Modern concurrent engineering design approach

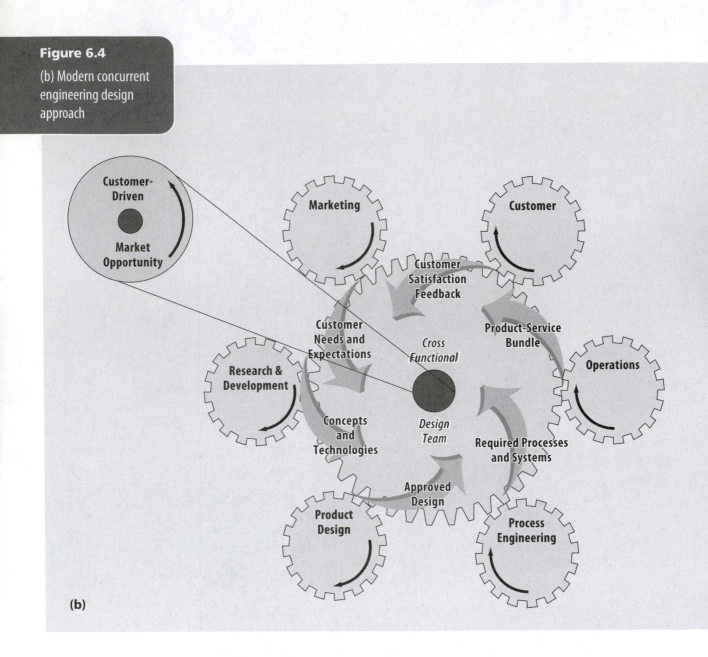

(b)

Figure 6.5 illustrates the timing of functional efforts in the traditional and modern approaches. Figure 6.5a shows that the sequential nature of the traditional approach creates significant variation in the allocation of effort for any given function over the life of a project. Figure 6.5b shows how the modern design approach allows for a steadier and concurrent allocation of effort for each functional area. Comparing parts (a) and (b) you will see that the design project is completed much more rapidly in the modern approach. Because allocation of staff to the project requires paying wages, the figure also illustrates the cost advantages of the modern approach.

Despite its seeming simplicity and apparent advantages, the concurrent team approach is not always easy to implement. Typically, teams go through a life cycle of their own. In the beginning, goals are not always clear and significant conflicts can

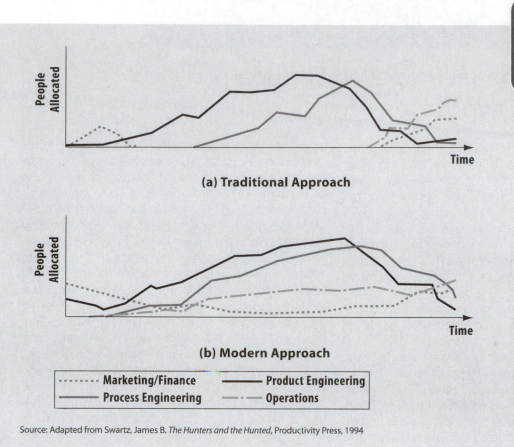

Figure 6.5

Functional involvement profile for product-service bundle design

(a) Traditional Approach

(b) Modern Approach

- - - - - Marketing/Finance   ——— Product Engineering
——— Process Engineering   —·—·— Operations

Source: Adapted from Swartz, James B. *The Hunters and the Hunted*, Productivity Press, 1994

arise. Individuals bring their own functional perspectives to the team and tend to be intolerant of the perspectives of others. Trust may be lacking, particularly in organizations with strong functional barriers where team members may fear that their allegiance to the team will hurt them in their own departments.

Putting such fears to rest can be difficult. As the team works through its initial conflicts, the project may seem to flounder. Team members must develop a common perspective on the project and a joint understanding of how it should proceed. Even when a team has effectively worked through its initial differences, honest differences based on functional biases may keep the group from coming to a clear consensus on key project decisions. At such times, it is vital that the team leadership be strong enough to move the project forward while maintaining mutual trust among team members.

One aspect of a successful design team is the ability of its members to make significant contributions to decision making at each stage of the design process. When a design team is working effectively, an operations manager or supplier can make relevant suggestions early in the design process. This requires, however, that the operations manager or supplier be able to interpret how early design choices will impact their functional areas later in the design process and to effectively communicate this to others. When teams have this kind of capability, they are able to concurrently consider multiple perspectives, which can result in the creation of superior designs that are completed faster.

INTEGRATING OM:

Designing the Jet Propelled Surfboard to Make Its Own Waves

West-coast inventor Bob Montgomery first learned to surf in Southern California in the 1960s. Like many other surfers, Montgomery imagined a dream machine—a one-man hydrokinetic rocket ship that would combine the freedom of surfing with a water ski's ease-of-use and maneuverability. "I wanted to ride a high-performance, motorized surfboard," recalls the 50-year-old ex-pro surfer. If you're like most people, you've probably shared his dream of "walking on the water" many times.

Now, with the help of space-age materials and CAD tools, he is seeing his dream come true. It has taken the form of the Igniter 360™ model Powerski™ Jetboard™, water craft that allows the rider to stand rather than sit, as is the case with most Jet Skis. The design of the Powerski Jetboard™ Ignitor 360™, which was a ten-year project, now enables high-speed planing and high-thrust G-force turns with simple shifts in the weight of a rear-mounted rider. The real key to this design breakthrough was packaging the jet drive system inside the hull under the rider's feet. (See http://www.powerski.com/.) The innovative new design, cleared numerous technical hurdles and won the *Popular Mechanics* Design and Engineering Award for the New Millennium.

As a pioneer in the industry, Montgomery saw changes in the personal watercraft (PWC) design. As a standup watercraft, he says, the typical Jet Ski was unstable—riders found it difficult to maintain a standing position because of the craft's forward center of gravity. Consequently, the Jet Ski became more like a boat than a surf board. That built up Montgomery's confidence in his plan for a standup watercraft. Where other designers chose sitdown, he would choose standup. Where they went heavy, he would go light.

Montgomery began in his garage during the late 1980s, working on prototypes. By 1990, to formally raise the funds necessary for taking the craft to the working prototype, pre-production stage, he had formed the HydroForce Group General Partnership. During the next few years that the Jetboard took shape, he operated a secret research and development campaign, strategically keeping the prototype hidden from the public (and competitors) as he slowly secured patents, trademarks, and other intellectual property rights protections. On one occasion he had to use his own fists to fight off would-be thieves intent on stealing his design. Once the Powerski Jetboard was fully protected, Montgomery revealed his prototype to the world, securing product placement stories in national magazines. In 1995, Montgomery co-founded PSI and moved to production facilities in Brea, CA, where he finished designing the Igniter.

The most significant challenge facing Montgomery in bringing his Jetboard idea into reality was the

---

Design for manufacturability (DFM)

A product development approach that explicitly considers the effectiveness with which an item can be made during the initial development of the product-service design. It is based on the belief that the cost of developing and running the value-adding system is as important as the functionality.

Concurrent Engineering versus Sequential/Hierarchical Engineering

In the concurrent engineering approach to product-service design, the concerns of more than one function are considered simultaneously. Examples include design for manufacturability, design for procurement, design for environment, and design for disassembly.

Design for manufacturability (DFM), a product development approach, explicitly considers the effectiveness with which an item can be made during the initial development of the product-service design. This approach is based on the belief that the cost of developing and running the value-adding system is as important as the functionality engine. After an extensive worldwide search failed to turn up a suitable prototype, he decided to build his own. The engine was designed using a computer assisted design system (CAD) where detailed 3-D drawings of the engine were used by the machinist for manufacturing. While the current production model is powered by a two-stroke aluminum engine, PSI also has prototyped a 320 cc version of the two-stroke that puts out 50–55 horsepower (hp). PSI is working on an environmentally friendly four-stroke engine, so that the Igniter 2000 can be as environmentally friendly as possible. Four-stroke engines emit 97% less pollution than conventional two-strokes, use half as much gas, and keep all oil inside instead of discharging it into the water and air.

To improve the engine's hp/weight ratio even further, PSI is considering manufacturing the production engines using a metal-matrix composite material, called Boralyn™, that is lighter than steel yet stronger. Used to make GM's EV-1 engine cradle, golf shafts for golf clubs, and satellites, boron-carbide is the third hardest material known to man. Even at high temperature, it's harder than diamond. Standing on and controlling a fast-moving, motorized surfboard through a "G-Force" turn requires a long handle. The design team developed a custom, ergonomic, ambidextrous handle unique to their PWC. The throttle switches on the handle at the end of the arm pole act as levers that let the rider regulate the supply of vaporized fuel that goes to the engine cylinders. "It's aggressive," notes Montgomery. "It doesn't take much pressure on the throttle switch to speed up this craft." To bring the craft's handle to reality, the PSI team again used a CAD system. "Coming into this process we had our designers do ergonomic studies so that the handle will fit the 85th percentile of people," says Montgomery.

The "rocket ship look" of the Igniter 360 comes from its streamlined, hydrodynamic, low-profile composite hull—8-ft-4-inches in length. Throughout the past 20 years, Montgomery has hand-built numerous operational prototypes. In designing and fabricating the Igniter hull, Montgomery and his team digitally scanned the hull of a hand-built model to create a digital "point cloud" on the computer. In the software, the PSI team improved Montgomery's hand-built design by lowering the profile by flattening the space in the hull where the craft's non-directional jet-drive system-engine, pump and propeller-is mounted. Another significant change: The engine is housed in a totally leak-proof, watertight compartment with an inflatable seal copied from technology used in jet-fighters and submarines. Riders can plunge underwater, float on the surface, or jump over wake without stalling due to a unique one-way valve on the exhaust and dual purge valves on the intake.

If you've ever thought about walking on water, or surfing without wind and waves, you might want to check out this new design (http://www.powerski.com) or one of its competitors (e.g., http://www.xboard.com).

Source: Adapted from "Engine Design and Packaging Are Key to Bringing Surfer Dream to Life," *Design News*, April 3, 2000, reporter John Lewis, Northeast Technical Editor; and press releases found on http://www.powerski.com and http://www.xboard.com Sept. 22, 2005

and aesthetics of the product-service bundle. DFM often relies on **Taguchi methods**— statistical studies that can be used to ensure that product design specifications are wide (or narrow) enough to accommodate likely levels of process variability. Obviously; a quick-lube shop would want to make sure that its garage door is wide and high enough to accommodate even the biggest vehicles. In the same way, when Motorola designs the various parts of its pagers, it needs to be certain that the parts can be easily assembled. Thus, manufacturability is considered concurrently with more traditional design criteria and becomes a key criterion in evaluating the designers' work.

Another concurrent engineering strategy, **design for procurement (DFP)**, explicitly considers component parts supply during the initial development of a product-service

Taguchi methods
Statistical studies that can be used to ensure that product design specifications are wide (or narrow) enough to accommodate likely levels of process variability.

Design for procurement
The explicit consideration of component parts supply during the initial development of a product-service design.

design. DFP involves designing to the capabilities and capacities of current and likely suppliers of parts and components used in the product or service. This involves:

▶ Determining the group of likely suppliers, called the supply base, for the required component parts

▶ Identifying the capacity of that supply base

▶ Estimating the cost, scheduling constraints, conformance quality, and other relevant performance levels likely to be achieved in procurement of parts and components for the product service bundle

▶ DFP extends the DFM concept beyond the internal operations of the firm to key participants in its supply chain.

Design for environment (DFE) is a product development approach that broadens the concept of design for manufacturability even further to include the environmental impact of a design, from the extraction of raw materials to the disposal of the physical product when the consumer is finished with it. This strategy is based on the concept of **sustainability**, which encourages companies to meet the needs of today's consumer without compromising the ability of future generations to meet their own needs. **Life-cycle analysis** is a tool used by designers to determine the environmental impact of a product from cradle to grave. In designing a new refrigerator, for example, manufacturers should be concerned with the availability of appropriate metals from new and recycled sources; the availability and effectiveness of chlorofluorocarbon (CFC)-free insulating materials; the availability and effectiveness of CFC-free cooling agents; the environmental impact of the processes that are used to manufacture, distribute, and service the refrigerator; the energy costs and other environmental impacts associated with the consumers' use of the refrigerator; the recyclability of the refrigerator and its components; and the ultimate disposal of those materials. Although the concepts of life-cycle analysis and sustainability are useful and appealing, universally accepted methodologies for life-cycle analysis do not exist. Furthermore, managerial incentives seldom take into account environmental risks; nor has society developed many economic incentives to encourage the practice of sustainability. From a practical perspective, designing for the environment is still a major challenge.

Another strategy, **design for disassembly (DFD)**, which explicitly builds parts and component recovery considerations into design decisions, has become increasingly important in the context of environmental regulation. Manufacturers are beginning to understand and accept the fact that they are responsible for the items they make, from start to finish. German law requires manufacturers to recover all the nonconsumable materials used in their products. Soft drink and beer makers have had little difficulty in meeting the requirement, but automobile manufacturers have found the process to be much more difficult. As a result of the legislation, BMW has designed the first completely recyclable car. In the United States, many manufacturers cannot shut down or sell their obsolescent manufacturing plants because of the site remediation costs and environmental liabilities associated with their disassembly. (Environmentally speaking, some things are best left alone.) Using a design-for-disassembly philosophy today can help to prevent such environmental liabilities in the future.

Group Technology, Modular Design, Product Simplification, and E-Commerce

Like design for disassembly, group technology, modular design, and product simplification have all been used primarily in a manufacturing context. Each method can be

Design for environment

A product development approach that broadens the concept of design for manufacturability even further to include the environmental impact of a design, from the extraction of raw materials to their disposal. This strategy is based on the concept of sustainability.

Sustainability

Encourages companies to meet the needs of today's consumer without compromising the ability of future generations to meet their needs.

Life-cycle analysis

A tool used by designers in an attempt to determine the environmental impact of a product from cradle to grave.

Design for disassembly (DFD)

A strategy that explicitly builds parts and component recovery considerations into design decisions.

Design for environment principles

- Use recycled and recyclable materials as raw materials.
- Reduce material variety.
- Avoid finishes and fillers that contaminate the material.
- Do not join dissimilar materials permanently or in ways that make separation difficult.
- Reduce the use of fasteners to keep the separation process simple.
- Mark all plastic components with ISO identification symbol.
- Minimize or eliminate the use of toxic materials or processes (e.g., PVC injection molding).
- Minimize the number of component parts, incorporate as many functions as possible into a single part.
- Design recoverable (or remanufacturable) components for reuse in new products.
- Design a modular product that allows for upgradeable components.
- Find multiple or second uses for the product.
- Ensure a product buy-back infrastructure is in place.
- Incorporate concurrent engineering philosophy to aid DFE effort.
- Reduce mass of components and products (i.e., downsize products).
- Reduce product packaging and/or utilize returnable packaging.
- Pursue waste reduction and reduce energy consumption during manufacture.

Source: Compiled by Thomas Gattiker, Ph.D., Networking, Operations, and Information Systems Department, Boise State University, Boise, Idaho

used in a team approach to concurrent engineering to speed the design process and create product-service bundles that involve simpler value-adding activities and are more easily managed.

Group technology is an engineering and manufacturing strategy based on the development and exploitation of commonalities among parts, equipment, or processes. For example, a company that makes metal parts might group its products according to shape and the type of metal or alloy each shape is made of. Doing so allows a designer who is choosing shapes and materials to see whether an off-the-shelf part would work as well as a newly designed part. The designer can also determine which shapes are compatible with which materials. By taking advantage of group technology, a design team can enhance the manufacturability of a design, speed up the design cycle, improve the company's profit margins, and save the customer money.

Modular design is an approach that allows designers to consider an item's components or subsystems independently. Because these modules can be installed and replaced individually, this concept is beneficial when requirements vary from one customer to the next and when customer needs may change over time. It is also useful in complex assemblies, because technological improvements to subsystems usually do not develop at the same rate. By using a modular design strategy, designers can update selected subsystems and components with newer modules. Thus, the firm can extend the usefulness of key technologies, while giving customers the benefit of the most recent technological developments. For example, Ford was able to use a transmission developed in the early 1990s in trucks and vans designed in the 1980s, because the transmission was designed as a replaceable module. Modular design makes sense for many service

Group technology (GT)

An engineering and manufacturing strategy for product and process design based on the development and exploitation of commonalities among parts, equipment, or processes.

Modular design

An approach that allows designers to consider an item's components or subsystems independently.

Product simplification

*A design (or redesign)
strategy that improves the
manufacturability,
serviceability, or reliability
of a product or service by
reducing the complexity of
its design.*

providers as well as manufacturers. Software development services, for example, rely particularly heavily on modular design. By putting together the right set of modules, or subroutines, an off-the-shelf information system can be tailored to fit many different unique customer applications.

Product simplification is a design (or redesign) strategy that improves the manufacturability, serviceability, or reliability of a product or service by reducing the complexity of its design. Often a product or part may be needlessly complex because of a designer or product engineer's bias toward technological sophistication or perhaps because of incremental design changes that have been made over a period of years. By reducing the number of parts or materials used, or changing the way in which parts are assembled, designers can realize significant benefits. For example, in a product simplification effort made during the design of the 1992 Seville, Cadillac cut the number of parts used by 20%. This resulted in cost savings, quality improvement, ergonomic gains, and shorter cycle times.

E-commerce can also play a big role in the design process. For example, several firms in the auto industry use the engineering services of the global firm MSX, which provides consistent solutions to the auto companies' engineering requirements. MSX uses computer-aided engineering tools so the auto companies can easily outsource design tasks that previously would have been kept in-house. Ford Motor Company, for example, uses MSX as a supplier of engineering drawings, and MSX keeps track of all of Ford's part designs. When Ford engineers want a part drawing, they get it from MSX and not internally. In a similar way, several auto companies use MSX to manufacture their design prototypes so that their existing assembly capacity can be devoted to the production of current models. MSX can easily undertake these jobs because they are equipped to receive and send the designs electronically.

We have just discussed a long list of strategies that can contribute to the work of design teams using the concurrent team approach. But what is the bottom line of all of these approaches? The customer. The concurrent design approach is successful only if it spins off a product-service bundle that delights the customer, both now and in the future.

Tools Used in Design Processes

Companies can use many tools to funnel customer-driven needs and expectations into the design of their products and services. These tools are used to understand customer needs and expectations, to evaluate design trade-offs, to enhance communication among members of the design team, to better communicate the rationale behind design decisions to outside parties, and to determine the financial feasibility of design alternatives. The tools described in the following paragraphs are a representative subset of the many available tools that can be useful in the process of designing product-service bundles.

The Kano Model

Figure 6.6 shows the Kano model, a diagram of the relationship between the extent to which a customer's needs (or requirements) are met by a hypothetical product characteristic and the level of satisfaction the customer derives from that characteristic. In this model, there are three types of product characteristics: must-do characteristics, expected characteristics, and excitement characteristics.

"Must-do characteristics" are those that meet a customer requirement but whose enhancement beyond a certain saturation point adds little value. Once the

Nissan Motor Corp/Getty Images Inc.

Concept cars show many of the upcoming exciting features in auto design. Some make it to production, others don't. Look at car magazines of the 1980's and compare what they thought would happen 20 years down the road to what is in the show room today.

customer's need has been met, customer satisfaction is not enhanced by these product characteristics. For example, the typical consumer would not value reductions in the emission levels of a new automobile that already satisfies all federal and state regulations. Similarly, improving the sound quality in the speaker at the Wendy's drive-up window, or increasing the insulation on a household extension cord will satisfy customers only to a given threshold; beyond that point the improvement will not enhance customer satisfaction. In fact, must-do characteristics are viewed as attributes of a product-service bundle rather than as features whose functionality and performance need to be assessed in the purchase decision. For example, did you "test" the seatbelts when you bought your last car?

On the other hand, enhancing an "expected characteristic" always increases customer satisfaction. Providing more of an expected feature always meets more of the customer's needs. Other things being equal, a car tire that lasts longer, a fishing line

Figure 6.6

Kano model

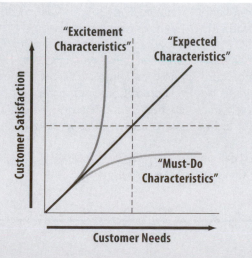

"I Don't Want No Satisfaction, I Want . . . LOYALTY!"

By Bill Fitzpatrick

July 18, 2002, 15:36 PST

Dear Mr. or Ms. Hampton Inn CEO:

You don't really know me, but back in 1996 when the Hampton Inn manager in Greenville, Mississippi, asked me if I would like coffee in the morning, and at what time would I like coffee in the morning, and that he was asking because some guests kind of liked their coffee delivered right to their room at no charge, wow, was I impressed. Though I know you have an important job running thousands of these Hampton Inn places and probably don't have time for too many of my personal details, I want to tell you anyway that I didn't have such a hot sales day that day. "Don't want to buy no fancy Point-of-Sale system," the Food & Beverage manager told me later that morning at the riverboat casino I had called on, and then he added, "Hell, over half the people who want to work here can't neither read nor write."

Now that depressing thought stuck in my throat like a wad of cold grits, so by the time I got to Memphis and checked into the Holiday Inn, I wanted something to clear my throat but the hotel bar was being renovated. I sat down in the dusty lobby where they had what they called a temporary bar, which, near as I can determine, since I've been in only one and that was it, is where they sell red Gallo for $4 in plastic cups that collect construction dust if you're not careful and the one waitress scowls like she is the one with the stuck wad of cold grits.

I know this is way out of order, but by the way, thank you for sending me my shiny Hilton Honors card last year. Confidentially, you didn't really have to do that because I was loyal without the card, which, in a backwards sort of way, brings me to the point of my letter and the enclosed check for $79.63.

Lots of the Information Systems executives I call on have been talking about something called CRM, or Customer Relationship Management. They're not exactly sure what it is, but I tell them heck, that's OK, nobody else does either, and that's one reason why NCR decided to fund the CRM Research Center at the Fuqua School of Business at Duke University to the tune of $1 million dollars per year. That sounds like a lot until you calculate, like the Gartner Group did, that worldwide CRM spending will reach $76.3 billion in 2005, up from $23 billion in 2000. Gartner analysts said that to be successful in business, a CRM strategy is essential and executives must understand and leverage technologies across all customer channels.

This whole idea of CRM (if you don't mind I'm just going to call it loyalty) is that since Americans aren't reproducing Americans like they use to, it's very important for businesses to not only get more money out of each shopper transaction, but to go all out to create a loyal customer; one that feels pulled to the offering, if you know what I mean. As smart as you are, I know that you aren't falling for that old 1980's trap where companies foolishly thought that by focusing on "customer satisfaction," customers would appreciate the good service so much they wouldn't shop anywhere else. Back then many well-meaning executives confused satisfaction and quality, with loyalty. Now I know that quality is all well and good, but I also know that many other companies make a quality cup of coffee but try telling that to one of those loyal Starbuck's fanatics. They might wallop you with a sack of black beans or worse, try to wipe the smirk off your face with a low-fat raspberry muffin. But let me finish that point on satisfaction versus loyalty by quoting a few facts, and then I promise I'll get to the point.

Forum Corporation reports that up to 40% of the customers in its study who claimed to be satisfied switched suppliers without hesitation.[1]

[1]David Stum and Alan Thiry, "Building Customer Loyalty," *Training and Development Journal*, April 1991, 34.

Harvard Business Review reports that between 65 and 85% of customers who chose a new supplier say they were satisfied or very satisfied with their former supplier.[2]

Dr. Peter ZanDan, whose company Intelliquest conducts market research studies for computer manufacturers worldwide, reports that in more than 30,000 interviews, his company has never found high levels of customer satisfaction to be a reliable predictor of repeat purchase.

Dr. Robert Peterson of the University of Texas found that in most surveys of customer satisfaction, 85% of an organization's customers claim to be "satisfied," but still show a willingness to wander away to other providers.[3]

That's some powerfully scary data, isn't it?

Well, the way I figure it, many companies attempt to separate themselves from the pack by offering free meals, free plane tickets, and free room-nights for frequent customers, and all of that is well and good, but now that I have ten cards in my wallet, I want to scream "what next?"

I say they better study the Kano Model.

The Kano Model, which is named for a Japanese quality expert, recognizes that customers experience value at three dimensions—the basic, the expected, and the unanticipated. Unanticipated value is delivered when companies provide well above and beyond what the customer expects. Only in operating in the unanticipated realm, so the Kano Model goes, can strong levels of customer loyalty be built.

And that's the whole point to my letter.

Be careful what you do with CRM, won't you? I know companies jump into CRM like it's a one-time project. Well, it's not. This whole idea takes a company effort to pull-off. Lawrence A. Crosby and Sheree L. Johnson, writing for the American Marketing Association, Marketing Management, put it as follows:

"CRM isn't just about collecting, processing, and deploying customer information. It is about serving customers in a fundamentally improved way. CRM needs to be about business strategy, supported by technology, not about reducing marketing costs or simply interacting more efficiently."

I suppose some day, by using my customer number and collecting my preferences, you will figure a way to turn on ESPN when my key hits the lock, my wake up call will be from Enya instead of a computer voice, my in-room coffee will be Seattle's Best, and instructions to the nearest Irish pub will be folded in the morning sports section. But we all know that it will be just a matter of time before your competition has all of that, too. I wish I had kept the name of that fellow who delivered that coffee to me in Greenville, Mississippi. I've never forgotten him.

I do have one last favor to ask, and it's kind of embarrassing. If you would, please see to it that the enclosed check for $79.63 gets credited to the Hampton Inn in Fort Smith, Arkansas. Just once, I decided to test the "and your satisfaction is always 100% guaranteed," line, even though I wasn't really peeved, and it worked. Every employee with your company says that line with such conviction, and at every opportunity they can, that I just had to put the policy to the test.

But when I started having sleepless nights, particularly when I was staying in Hampton Inns, I dashed to Confession. When Father Ralph told me that, "no, it wasn't enough to simply repent, you must send the money back," I thought it best to follow his advice. As soon as you cash this check I'm sure I'll start having blissful sleep and pleasant dreams.

That's about all I have to say. Sorry for being so long winded about this matter of loyalty, but I just felt like telling you how pleased I am with Hampton Inn.

[2]Frederick F. Recihheld, "Loyalty-Based Management," *Harvard Business Review,* March–April, 1993, 71.

[3]Robert A. Peterson and William R. Wilson, "Measuring Customer Satisfaction: Fact and Artifact," *Journal of the Academy of Marketing Sciences,* Winter 1992, 6.

Source: Bill Fitzpatrick is the Senior Vice President of Sales and Marketing for Spartan Computer Services, http://www.spartancomputer.com. This article first appeared in *Hospitality Upgrade,* Summer 2001, p. 124. Used with permission.

that holds more weight, and a hamburger patty that fills a larger bun all meet more of a customer's needs. With such product characteristics, one generally gets what one pays for. Expected characteristics are often tested by customers before a purchase decision is made. For example, energy and quality ratings play a large role in purchases of automobiles, electronics, and home appliances. Most of us would not buy a car without taking it for a test drive or sitting in the car to see how much leg room is available.

Have you ever been blown away by your first experience with a product? Customers may not always be able to articulate the characteristics of a product that, if available, would really turn them on. These hard-to-express characteristics, called "excitement characteristics" in the Kano model, add more than the usual amount of satisfaction to the customer's experience. As more of these features are added to the product-service bundle, they provide increasingly higher returns on the customer satisfaction scale.

Asked to identify the excitement features in a potential product or service, customers often can say only, "I'll know it when I see it." If designers are successful in identifying those characteristics that excite the customer, however, a large amount of customer satisfaction can often be generated through modest changes in the product-service bundle. Examples of recent successes include integrated digital cameras or PDAs on cell phones, Internet check-in for airlines, GPS systems for cars, and hospital web services that allow friends and families to receive patient updates.

Today's excitement characteristics can easily become tomorrow's expected characteristics and may eventually become must-do characteristics. For example, the automatic redial function on a touch-tone phone, an excitement characteristic of the 1970s, became an expected feature in the 1990s. Automobile safety features such as seat belts, 5 mph bumpers, antilock brakes, and air bags were once excitement characteristics for safety-conscious consumers. But as the technology became more widespread and public concern for safety increased, those features became must-do characteristics, in many cases because of legislation. Similarly, the mouse, the CD-ROM, high-resolution color screens, and dorm room connections to the campus intranet, which were originally excitement features, became expected or must-do features in succeeding generations of personal computers.

Quality Function Deployment is a process where a firm takes the needs, concerns, and ideas of the customer and converts them to the specifics of a product's design.

Noel Hendrickson/Masterfile

Quality Function Deployment

Quality function deployment (QFD) is a design methodology used to integrate customer expectations with decisions made throughout the product design process. Figure 6.7 shows a generic "house of quality" as it is used in QFD. The porch on the left side of the house lists the customer requirements, called "whats," in horizontal rows. These customer requirements are the must-do, expected, and excitement characteristics that are to be included in the product-service bundle. The porch on the right side of the house identifies the relative importance of each of these features, and presents a competitive assessment of the product-service bundle. Each column under the roof of the house represents a design characteristic that is required in order to meet one or more of the customer requirements. These design requirements are called "hows."

A triangular co-relationship matrix forms the roof of the house. The cells of this matrix provide information regarding the positive or negative tradeoffs between specific design characteristics. The main room of the house of quality is a matrix that is formed by the intersection of the customer requirements and the design requirements. This matrix provides critical insight into the importance of each design characteristic from the customer's perspective. The symbols in the cells of this matrix provide information regarding the importance of particular design characteristics to the satisfaction of the particular customer expectations the cells represent. Finally, the basement of the house provides information that is useful in technical assessment of the product-service bundle.

Once a product has been designed, its parts and subassemblies have to be designed. As a result, each column of the house of quality becomes a row in a new house that represents the design of a part or subassembly. In other words, the design requirements of the product-service bundle form internal requirements for the parts and

Quality function deployment (QFD)

A design methodology that is used to integrate customer expectations with decisions made throughout the product design process.

Figure 6.7
Generic house

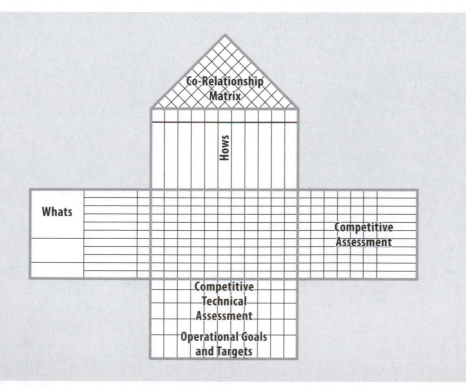

subassemblies. For example, the house of quality for a warehouse might have a row that identifies a storage capacity requirement and a column that specifies a rack system to meet that need. A design house for the rack system would show the requirements for the rack in the rows and the construction specs for the rack in the columns.

Once the product, its subassemblies, and its parts have been designed, the processes to make them must be designed. The rows of a process house can be derived from the columns of a part house. In this way, the design requirements of a part form the internal requirements for the process that is used to make the part. If the rack system for the warehouse was designed of steel, for example, then a particular type of process would be needed to build the racks. The process design characteristics would specify the required labor, equipment, method of transporting materials, and so on.

Similarly, once a process has been designed, operational procedures must be developed to run the process. The rows of the operations house are derived from the columns of the process house. The design requirements of the process house become the internal customer requirements for the operational systems that are used to run them. In the case of the process used to make warehouse racks, the operations house would determine how workers are scheduled, what training they receive, where they are located, how equipment is maintained, when materials are ordered and in what quantities, where materials are stored, and so forth.

The overlapping series of houses of quality produced in this process is illustrated in Figure 6.8. The central focus and overriding theme of all the decisions made in the QFD process is the development of products, parts, processes, and operational systems that are responsive to customer expectations and that will ultimately provide customer satisfaction. If at any point in the design or operation of a production system an individual is not sure why she is performing a particular task, she should be able to ask a series of "why" questions that establish a meaningful relationship between the task and a customer expectation.

QFD could be used in an over-the-wall design process, to help those who are performing each successive function to understand the reasoning behind earlier design

Figure 6.8

Cascading houses

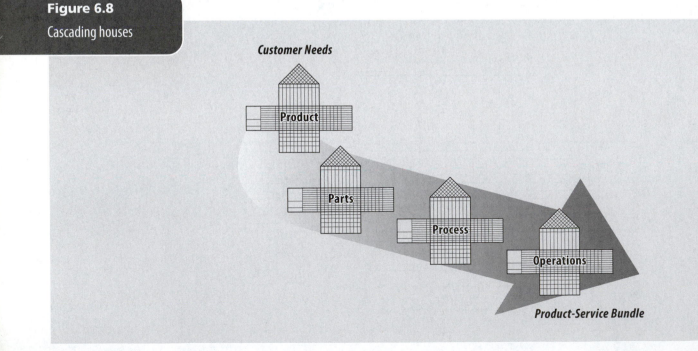

decisions. But QFD is particularly useful in concurrent design, because it gives structure to the design process. By working either forward or backward through the series of overlapping houses, teams can see the impact of early design decisions on other functions.

COMPETITIVE AND TECHNICAL ANALYSIS

Because QFD is geared toward the development of customer satisfaction, gathering information on customer satisfaction is a critical step in this method. Information may come from a competitor's customers as well as from the firm's present, past, and potential customers. Such information is used to develop a competitive analysis (the right porch of the house of quality) and a technical analysis (the basement of the house). Further input can come from analyzing a competitor's product-service bundle. By purchasing the competitor's outputs and disassembling them, employees can use *reverse engineering* to learn more about the product and the technological strategies used to produce it. They may also obtain useful information about reliability and performance capabilities and even gain clues about the competitor's plan for the future. The design team can then use this information to establish design targets that position the product-service bundle to best advantage from a competitive standpoint.

DESIGN TARGETS

In Figure 6.9, the use of a hypothetical product, the WriteSharp pencil, show how competitive and technical design targets might be set. As you can see, the competitive analysis compares the ability of the product-service bundle and benchmark competing products to satisfy customer needs. This analysis helps the design team to set its competitive targets. Similarly, the technical analysis compares the functional performance of the product-service bundle with that of benchmark competing products. It is used to set technical targets. In QFD, both the technical and the

Figure 6.9

(a) WriteSharp QFD

WHATs vs. HOWs Legend	Pencil Length (inches)	Time Between Sharpenings (written lines)	Lead Dust (particles per line)	Hexagonaility	Customer Importance Rating	WriteSharp (now)	Competitor X (now)	Competitor Y (now)	WriteSharp (target)
Strong Correlation △ 3									
Some Correlation ● 2									
Possible Correlation ■ 1									
Easy to Hold	●			●	3	4	3	3	4
Does not Smear		●	△		4	5	4	5	5
Point Lasts	■	△	●		5	4	5	3	5
Does Not Roll Away	■			△	2	3	3	3	4
WriteSharp (now)	5	56	10	70					
Competitor X (now)	5	84	12	80					
Competitor Y (now)	4	41	10	60					
WriteSharp (target)	6	100	6	80					

(a)

Source: Adapted from Business Week Jan. 15, 1991
Used with Permission

Figure 6.9

(b) Competitive analysis
(c) Competitive profile

"Whats" Importance Rating (5 = highest)	WriteSharp (now)	Competitor X (now)	Competitor Y (now)	WriteSharp (target)
3	3 × 4 = 12	3 × 3 = 9	3 × 3 = 9	3 × 4 = 12
4	4 × 5 = 20	4 × 4 = 16	4 × 5 = 20	4 × 5 = 20
5	5 × 4 = 20	5 × 5 = 25	5 × 3 = 15	5 × 5 = 25
2	2 × 3 = 6	2 × 3 = 6	2 × 3 = 6	2 × 4 = 8
Overall Rating	58	56	50	65
Market Price	$.15	$.18	$.14	$.16
Market Share	16%	12%	32%	20%
Profit (per unit)	$.02	$.03	$.02	$.04

(b)

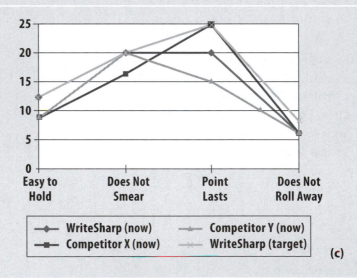

(c)

competitive targets are set by consensus of the design team. Though the targets need not always meet or exceed the competitive benchmarks on all criteria, they should add up to a composite target that is clearly superior to the competition. Performance profiles or arithmetic factor-rating can be used to assess the targets.

The competitive analysis performed in Figure 6.9b applies arithmetic factor-rating to the WriteSharp pencil example. The customer-determined importance rating is multiplied by the satisfaction rating the customers gave each pencil. Adding the score achieved for each "what" yields an overall rating. Note that while the current WriteSharp design has the highest overall rating, customer perception is that competitor X has the reputation for the highest quality, while competitor Y is the lowest-cost producer. Looking at the quantitative analysis in Figure 6.9b or the competitive performance profiles in Figure 6.9c, it is clear that WriteSharp is as good as or better than competitor X on all the "whats" except the most important: how long the point lasts. WriteSharp is also even with or ahead of competitor Y on all "whats," yet it makes the same profit per unit.

A similar factor-rating analysis could have been performed on the "hows." Using some estimate of the technical feasibility of the desired improvement for weight—analogous to the customer importance rating in Figure 6.9a—as well as the performance data in the basement of the house, an overall feasibility rating could be created for each "how." A technical performance profile could also be graphed from such data.

After looking at the relationships between the "whats" and the "hows" in Figure 6.9a, WriteSharp managers established a design team to investigate the most significant "how" related to the durability of the point, as measured by the time between sharpenings. The aim was to close the *performance gap* between the WriteSharp design and that of competitor X. A second team was set up to examine the pencil's shape, in an attempt to differentiate WriteSharp's design from that of the low-cost competitor, Y, and create a positive performance gap in the process.

The first team found that a better lead formulation was the key to increasing the time between sharpenings and eventually focused on the binder, or glue, used to form the lead. A new polymer was found that would wear down more slowly. This formulation also reduced the dust level by retaining more moisture, somewhat like a crayon. Thus, two customer concerns were addressed. Though the new binder was more expensive, it allowed for tighter production controls and actually cut production costs by $.01 per unit.

The second team examined the effect of switching from cedar to oak for the wood casing around the lead. When that idea did not work, the team decided to tighten production controls on the existing cedar design and improved the quality of the pencil's hexagonal shape, thereby reducing the likelihood of its rolling off the user's desk. Together, the two teams arrived at a design that met the target levels described in Figures 6.9a–c, and in the process increased the value to the customer enough to justify a $.01 price increase. Combined with the $.01 cost reduction, their work doubled the profitability of the product and was projected to increase market share.

Computer-Aided Design

Computer-aided design (CAD) uses computer software and hardware applications to generate digitized models representing a product's structural characteristics and physical dimensions. The models are displayed on a computer screen and can then be analyzed using special software, examined from a wide variety of perspectives, and printed out on a blueprint plotter or some other output device.

The Boeing 777 is one of the largest manufactured items ever designed using CAD. The technology allowed approximately 7,000 specialists to collaborate on one model. By using CAD software, Boeing significantly reduced rework and cut estimated total project costs by 20%. Atlanta's committee for the 1996 Olympic Games used CAD to design the Georgia Dome. Using the computer model to experiment with various seating configurations before the stadium was actually built allowed the committee to add thousands of extra seats (and sell thousands of extra tickets), to finalize security plans early, and even to identify the best places to locate television cameras.

When CAD is linked to a computer-aided manufacturing (CAM) system, designing for manufacturing considerations becomes even simpler. With a CAD/CAM system, a set of alternative CAD designs can be run through the CAM system to generate the

Computer-aided design (CAD)

An approach that uses computer software and hardware applications to generate digitized models representing a product's structural characteristics and physical dimensions.

programs that would be used to make the items with automated equipment. For instance, if a proposed part-manufacturing program is longer than another by a thousand lines of code, engineers can easily select the design that requires a shorter part-manufacturing program.

Going one step further, interfacing CAD with programs that simulate the value-adding system used to deliver the product-service bundle allows a design team to assess the technical feasibility, economic feasibility, and manufacturability of a design. Such simulation programs help designers to understand the impact of various design variables—such as dimensional specifications, materials, and product structure—on performance variables, including processing times, work-in-process inventory requirements, and process capacity requirements. Without simulations, these design variables have to be tested using actual prototypes and processes, which is far more costly.

For example, modern roller coaster designers rely heavily on CAD technology to build the world's most exciting, yet safe rides. In Minnesota, Valleyfair Amusement Park's "Wild Thing" takes riders up 200 feet before sending them hurtling across more than a mile of steel track at speeds up to 74 miles per hour. To design the $10 million ride, engineers created computer simulation models that show the effects of speed and force on riders, cars, and track. With this instant computer information, engineers were able to build a roller coaster with the sharpest possible curves and the steepest inclines to create the greatest illusion of imminent danger. With CAD tools now available, roller coaster designers are limited only by the degree of fright the average rider is able to endure.

Topham/The Image Works

The lines in front of the security checkpoints and ticketing desks at an airport are very much a part of the process. As the distinction between the product service bundle and the process providing it becomes blurred in service industries like air travel, techniques like service blueprinting help airlines improve their customers' overall experience.

Ultimately, although using CAD provides significant benefits on its own, CAD's potential is not fully realized until it is linked with other information technology-based systems. It is particularly useful in the context of group technology and modular design, because of the ease with which modules can be cut from one design and pasted onto another. In addition, design software is a critical building block of computer-integrated manufacturing systems that facilitate e-commerce. Finally, linking CAD with CAM and other information systems that assist with day-to-day operational decision making can provide significant synergies throughout a supply chain.

Service Blueprinting

The customer contact model developed by Prof. Richard Chase of University of Southern California is a valuable tool for designing the product-service bundle. High-customer-contact elements can be identified and enhanced to deliver personal satisfaction to the customer. Low-contact elements can be separated from high contact elements to drive down costs through standardizing, prioritizing, and automating.

The customer contact model's practical value comes from applying it to existing service environments to improve performance. The model essentially suggests that design improvements of existing services can be conducted using the following four steps:

1. Blueprint the service. A **service blueprint** is a visual diagram—usually a flowchart—that depicts all of the activities in the service delivery process.

2. These include activities involving information processing, customer interactions, and employee decisions. Figure 6.10 presents an example of a service blueprint. The flowchart is analyzed to identify the fail points in the delivery system. Fail points are steps in the service delivery process where meeting customer expectations is critical and perhaps more difficult to achieve. Resources, employee training, and management attention must be provided to these fail points to ensure that customer needs are met.

Identify customer contact points and reduce contact where appropriate. Customer contact activities are identified by a "line of visibility" that separates steps in the service delivery process where customers are present or actively participate. These contact activities should be examined to determine whether some elements may be removed from the customer's presence. For example, perhaps a bank teller conducts unnecessary data processing activity during each customer transaction. Such processing activities should be

Service blueprint

A visual diagram—usually a flowchart—that depicts all of the activities in the service delivery process.

Figure 6.10

Service blueprint for cashing checks in a bank

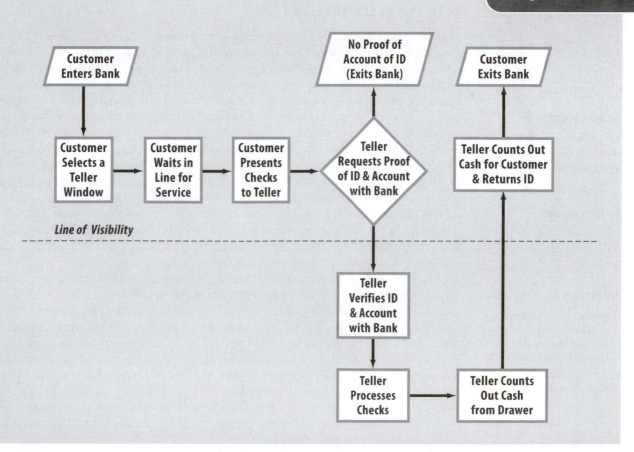

Luis gets an e-mail about his legs

Luis's company has an open-door policy whose purpose is to encour-age employees to make suggestions concerning processes that might add value or reduce costs. One such e-mail came from a lathe operator in a department Luis oversees. The operator explained that most of the spindles used in making tables and chairs have unique diameters, so she spends a lot of time changing her lathe settings and seems to be drowning in WIP inventory. To make her process more efficient, she suggested reducing the number of spindle diam-eters. , The operator thinks that using two or three standard dimen-sions would make her job a lot easier and that most customers would not notice the difference. Can you help Luis make an argument—one pro and one con—to take to senior managers on behalf of the lathe operator? How would customer preferences enter into the discussion?

reassigned to "backroom" areas where they do not interfere with customer service and where they can be more effi-ciently completed.

Improve the quality of contact. Where contact is criti-cal to the service, opportunities to enhance the cus-tomer's experience should be identified. Some examples include express lines in grocery stores, weekend and evening hours for dentists and car repair shops, and hir-ing and training people to deliver great customer service.

Improve efficiency in low-contact operations. In low-contact operations, costs can be reduced by standardiz-ing work procedures, prioritizing jobs, and adopting computerized and automated processing systems.

Product Costing Methods

The cost of providing a product-service bundle is crucial from the standpoint of both profitability and customer satisfaction, and as much as 85% of a product's lifetime costs are locked in before the first unit is ever produced. Ac-curate product costing, therefore, is a critical design issue. Whether one is designing a new product-service bundle or modifying an existing design, it is vital that one have some understanding of the cost implications of design decisions.

ACTIVITY-BASED COSTING (ABC)

A product-service bundle's cost is usually described as some combination of direct costs, which are related to the manufacture and delivery of the bundle, and indirect costs, which represent administrative overhead. Many of the product-costing tech-niques used today were developed at a time when product life cycles were longer, di-rect labor and materials were the primary cost drivers, and firms emphasized strate-gies designed to attain economies of scale. (An **economy of scale** is a reduction in variable cost per unit that can be used to justify higher fixed costs.) As a result, the overhead costs generated in the product design, administrative, and sales depart-ments were typically allocated to products based on their labor content. Many firms, however, now stress strategies based on economies of scope. An **economy of scope** is an economic advantage obtained through process flexibility. In today's highly auto-mated business world, with its greater emphasis on economies of scope, modular design, and group technology, the traditional product costing approach does not al-ways make sense. In certain industries, the cost of direct labor may be as small as 5%, while overhead may represent more than half a product's cost.

Today, financial software makes it easier to trace overhead costs to the products that required them. One alternative, **activity-based costing**, is an accounting method that allo-cates costs to the product-service bundle based on overhead activities performed. For example, using a dedicated machine to make a large volume of an old component may require very little direct labor. Using traditional cost-accounting practices, such an item would be allocated very little overhead cost. Yet that component might not fit with a new group technology. Trying to make the item work with a new design could require considerable engineering design time, additional assembly time, and so on. In contrast, a new component that requires more direct labor but works with group technology and can be made on more flexible equipment, would be allocated rather high overhead cost using traditional accounting methods. Yet the new approach might actually con-sume far less overhead and provide significant economies of scope to boot.

Economy of scale

The economic advantage that is often associated with the ability to operate at higher volumes.

Economy of scope

An economic advantage obtained through process flexibility.

Activity-based costing (ABC)

A managerial accounting method that allocates the costs to the product-service bundle based on overhead activities performed and aesthetics of the product-service bundle.

BREAK-EVEN ANALYSIS

Cost-volume break-even analysis is a financial tool that may be used to justify a new product-service bundle or a change to an existing one. This tool uses cost estimates of the type discussed above (whether derived through ABC or more traditional cost allocation approaches). Consider the following example:

A point-of-sale system manufacturer is proposing a change to its memory configuration. The manufacturer currently offers 128 megabytes of memory, delivered via an old memory board designed to accept two 64-megabyte chips. But increasing software memory requirements and the declining cost of memory may make a change in system architecture worthwhile. The company is considering switching to 128-megabyte memory slots. It has estimated that the up-front design cost of such a change in system architecture is approximately $5,000 per week, amortized over the system's three-year life. The average cost of memory is estimated at $45 per 128 megabytes if bought in 128-megabyte increments, or $55 per 128 megabytes if bought in 64-megabyte increments. The company assumes that no other costs will be influenced by the proposed design change.

Cost-volume break-even analysis can be used to compare these two alternatives and determine the weekly volume at which either alternative would be preferable. The relevant cost of the new alternative would be $5,000 per week plus $45 per unit. The relevant cost of continuing with the old design would simply be $55 per unit. By setting these two costs equal, we can find the *break-even volume* for the new design:

$$\$5000 + \$45X = \$55X$$
$$\$5000 = \$10X$$
$$500 = X$$

If the volume is expected to be greater than 500 units per week, changing the system design makes sense. Otherwise, the computer maker should stick with the old design.

Cost-volume break-even analysis

A capital investment justification tool that is well suited to modeling the costs associated with fixed automation. It may also be used to justify a new product-service bundle or a change to an existing one.

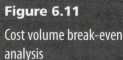

Figure 6.11
Cost volume break-even analysis

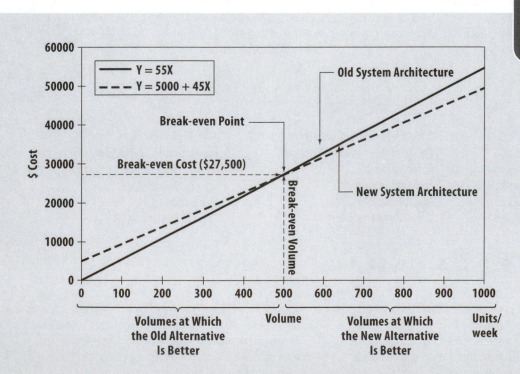

The break-even volume can also be found graphically, as shown in Figure 6.11. The cost of the new alternative can be graphed using the equation Y = \$5000 + \$45X; the cost of the existing approach would be Y = \$55X. Figure 6.11 illustrates the resulting graph. The *break-even point* is the point where weekly volume is 500 units and weekly cost is \$27,500—that is, (500, 27,500).

While break-even analysis is useful in estimating the viability of proposed design changes, it relies on inexact demand and cost estimates. Most organizations must therefore take further steps to justify design projects that require significant capital outlays. More detailed and complex techniques are covered in cost accounting and managerial finance classes; they are beyond the scope of this book.

SUMMARY

This chapter has covered several elements of product-service bundle design, including the specific tasks involved, the traditional approach, challenges generated by the traditional approach, the modern approach, and representative tools that are useful in the design process.

The tasks included in the process of designing the product-service bundle range from concept development to delivery of the first unit. In the traditional approach, these tasks are accomplished in functional silos, and work is passed over a series of walls until the design sequence has been completed. The traditional approach is not well adapted to the modern business climate, which is heavily influenced by time-based competition and frequently offers better returns through economies of scope than through economies of scale.

An approach that is better suited to the current competitive environment, concurrent engineering, relies on input from all functions throughout the design process. This modern approach stresses design for manufacture, design for procurement, and design for the environment. Other modern design concepts include group technology, modular design, product simplification, and design for disassembly.

Regardless of the approach that is taken to organize the design process, certain tools may be used to enhance its effectiveness and efficiency. They include computer-aided design/computer-aided manufacturing (CAD/CAM) systems, quality function deployment (QFD), and a variety of cost estimation and project justification techniques, such as cost-volume break-even analysis.

KEY TERMS

Activity-based costing (ABC), 278

Computer-aided design (CAD), 275

Concurrent engineering, 258

Cost-volume break-even analysis, 279

Design for disassembly (DFD), 264

Design for environment (DFE), 264

Design for manufacturability (DFM), 262

Design for procurement (DFP), 263

Economy of scale, 278

Economy of scope, 278

Group technology, 265

Life-cycle analysis, 264

Modular design, 265

Product simplification, 266

Quality function deployment (QFD), 271

Service blueprint, 277

Sustainability, 264

Taguchi methods, 263

SOLVED PROBLEMS

1. Luis could switch to a composite plastic veneer on his most popular table and cut the variable cost of production from \$25 to \$22. It would mean leasing a new machine to do the veneer however. The lease would add \$2600 per month to his overhead when staffing and other related fixed costs are totaled up. How much demand would he need to justify the change in his product's design?

Solution:

Given we do not know the current fixed costs, we will look at the incremental fixed costs and model the situation as follows:

$$\$25x = \$2600 + \$22x$$

$$\$3x = \$2600$$

x = 866.7 units per month to break even assuming all other costs remain the same.

2. Carrie's Custom Cabinets is a company that works with builders and homeowners to develop plans for cabinet layouts used in new or renovated kitchens and bathrooms. They then order and install the cabinets. The layouts are currently drawn to scale by hand. It can take several hours, however, to draft a reasonable likeness that the customer can use to evaluate their options. The draft may need to be redrawn more than once, increasing the time requirement. The variable cost per room with the current drafting process is approximately $120. There are currently no significant fixed costs. Drafting, redrafting, and ordering can add 2–3 weeks to the time required to deliver and install the cabinets. Total lead time from initial consultation to completion is 4–6 weeks.

   To reduce the time frame, Carrie is currently evaluating a CAD system that would use an electronic library of cabinet drawings. It could cut drafting time to under an hour per room and provide almost immediate revision capability. Carrie's staff, which is overworked to begin with, estimates that the CAD system would cut the variable cost to about $20 per room. Most rooms could be drafted, evaluated (redrafted if necessary), and ordered in one working day. The system and training would cost $25,750 up front, with a $2500 per year charge for software maintenance and support. Carrie's accountant suggests that the system be depreciated over 5 years. The accountant also suggests the gross margin on the average room is currently about $250.

   a) How many jobs per year must Carrie do using the new system to "break even" with it?

   b) How many jobs per year must Carrie do with the new system to get her annual costs lower than they would be drafting the plans by hand?

c) What other competitive issues come into play with the CAD system?

Solution:

   a) Using the straight line method and assuming no residual value, annual depreciation would be $25,750/5 or $5150. Adding the $2500 maintenance and support cost results in total annual fixed cost of $7650. With a $230 contribution margin per room, the break-even point is $7650/$230 or approximately 33.26 rooms (34 rooms) to be profitable.

   b) $7650 + $20/room × X = $120/room × X, X = 76.5 rooms. So if demand exceeds 76 rooms per year, order the CAD system. If not, then stay with the current manual system.

   c) The CAD system cuts the overall lead-time in half. Would the computerized image make it easier for the customer to "see" the options? Would it make them better able to meet the customer needs of the customer? Would there be fewer misunderstandings and negative surprises? Also, computerizing the design might improve the interface with the cabinet suppliers. Orders could be automatically generated and transmitted quicker with fewer mistakes on that end.

3. Ray-D-Os! has modified the design of its popular radio so that the component boards can be soldered without flux, a substance that requires the use of a toxic solvent in the cleanup process. The company is currently spending about $4 to manufacture each additional unit. The new design would save about $.75 per unit as the flux would no longer need to be purchased or cleaned off the radio's component board. It would, however, require an upgrade to the workstations, to allow for more precise soldering. That upgrade would add $25 per hour to the cost of running the plant. Without the solvents, the estimated cost of compliance with EPA regulations would be reduced by $1500 per month. Assume there are 20 production days per month, and the plant runs two eight-hour shifts per day.

   a) How many radios would the company need to build to make the design change worthwhile?

   b) What other important cost/revenue issues have not been quantified?

Solution:

a) $4/radio × X radios/month = $3.25/radio × X radios/month + $25/hour × 16 hours/day × 20 days/month − $1,500/month X radios/month = 8666.67

b) From a marketing point of view, what is the "green image" worth? While most people assume that being greener means being more expensive, the fact that the company can make the new design more cheaply than the old at volumes of more than 8667 units per month may make the change in design doubly advantageous. It is also a safe bet that a lot of overhead costs can be saved once the company is no longer handling the solvent, scheduling and managing the cleaning process, purchasing and inventorying it, dealing with the EPA, etc. Many of those costs might not have been accounted for in the decision as it has been formulated.

4. Consider the situation of the Ye Olde Motor Car Company described in discussion question 12 revised to:

a) Using the competitive analysis information in the QFD house of quality, how competitive is the current model X?

b) Using this analysis, where would you suggest improvement efforts be focused?

Solution:

a)

Customer "What"	Customer Importance Rating (out of 5)	Model X	Competitor Y	Competitor Z
Economy	3	3 × 3 = 9	3 × 1 = 3	3 × 5 = 15
Smooth Ride	4	4 × 3 = 12	4 × 1 = 4	4 × 3 =12
Safety	5	5 × 3 = 15	5 × 1 = 5	5 × 3 = 15
Performance	2	2 × 3 = 6	2 × 5 = 10	2 × 1 = 2
Fresh Styling	5	5 × 2 = 10	5 × 2 = 10	5 × 3 = 15
Sound System	3	3 × 2 = 6	3 × 4 =12	3 × 1 = 3
Totals		58	44	62

b) The Model X is rated just behind Competitor Z and well ahead of Competitor Y. Given the Model X is 10 years old and the largest competitive gap is in "Economy," they might look in that direction. However, the next largest gap (a close second as well), is in "Fresh Styling." Given the stronger weight and upside potential, a better opportunity may be in that direction.

DISCUSSION QUESTIONS

1. Make a list of five product-service bundles whose product life cycles you expect to be shorter than those of the product-service bundles they replaced. How does this decreased span impact the firm producing those products-service bundles?

2. What role do you believe the customer played in the design of the product-service bundles you listed response to Question #1?

3. How is the design for manufacturability concept inherent in the modern concurrent engineering approach to product-service design?

4. How is the concept of time to market related to the product life cycle?

5. Assume that in most of the term papers you have written to date, your writing process was analogous to the traditional approach to product design (define the topic, do the research, write the paper, get feedback, etc.). Would you compose papers in a different way if you were to take a modern, concurrent engineering approach to the writing process? How would you do it?

6. Assume that most computer software is written in a process that is analogous to the traditional approach to product design (define the system requirements, design the system, build the system, test the system, implement the system, etc.). Would your writing process differ if you were to adopt a modern approach to the project?

7. How is group technology (GT) related to the design of the product-service bundle? While GT is based on commonalities, it can also increase flexibility of design. How can those concepts be reconciled?

8. How does quality function deployment (QFD) improve the design of the product-service bundle? QFD might not be successful if used in the traditional approach to product-service bundle design. What might go wrong? Why?

9. What is meant by "design for environment"? Does the consumer always perceive this aspect of the product-service bundle? Can any kind of disposable product be consistent with this concept? Give some examples to support your position.

10. Create a service blueprint of a facility where you have worked, currently work, or have recently received service. Do you believe the line of sight is where it should be? What improvements would you make to the facility and how would the service blueprint change?

11. When visiting a service provider you usually face a customer service representative, but cannot see his computer screen. On some occasions, however, you are able to see the computer screen. Based on the concept of the line of sight in a service blueprint, should the service design provide a customer with a view of the computer screen? Why? Are there situations when customers should not be able to see the computer screen? Is so, provide examples of such situations.

12. Ye Olde Motorcar Company is doing a competitive analysis of its most popular platform, a small car identified as Model X. (Automobile manufacturers refer to each basic design as a platform.) Model X has historically been labeled a "tweener" by car experts. While it is significantly cheaper to buy than its sporty competitor, Model Y, many experts feel it does not offer the economy of Model Z. However, by many accounts, it does slightly outperform Model Z. A brief QFD analysis of Model X's current market position follows on page 284. In what direction should Ye Olde Motorcar Company move when updating the model's ten-year-old platform? What are some of specific parameters engineers should work on? Why? What is the next step in the design process?

13. The Ice Cream City (ICC) chain of ice cream parlors has been losing market share to its two major competitors, It's Vanilla and Mr. Neapolitan. ICC has long considered itself the Cadillac of the ice-cream parlor market, because it offers a larger variety of flavors, its ice cream has a richer texture than its competitors' product, and it introduces new flavors more frequently than its competitors. Customers perceive ICC's product to be high quality, so they do not consider the price of the ICC cone to be an issue, and they are willing to wait in long lines to buy the ice cream. Given the brief QFD analysis that is shown in the figure that follows on page 285, what changes to the overall product-service bundle would you recommend? Are those changes consistent with ICC's overall strategy? Why or why not?

For discussion question 12

HOWs vs. HOWs Legend
Positive Linkage   +
Negative Linkage   —

WHATs vs. HOWs Legend
Strong Correlation   △
Some Correlation   ●
Possible Correlation   ▪

	Wheel Base	Weight (00's lbs.)	Miles per Gallon	List Price ($000,s)	Watts (audio output)	Front Impact Test (passenger g's on impact at 35 mph)	Side Impact Test (passenger g's on impact at 35 mph)	0–60 mph Acceleration (seconds)	Unique Design Features per model year (3 year average)	60–0 mph Braking Distance (feet)	Driver Field of Vision (degrees obstructed)	Wind Noise (dbs)	Platform Age (yrs)	Customer Importance Rating (5 highest)	Current Design X	Competitor Y	Competitor Z
Economy	▪	▪	△	△				▪	●				●	3	3	1	5
Smooth Ride	△	△						●						4	3	1	3
Safety		△				△	△	▪		△	△			5	3	1	3
Performance	●	●						△		●				2	3	5	1
Fresh Styling						▪	▪		△		●		△	5	2	2	3
Sound System					△							●		3	2	4	1
Current Design X	94	22	30	15	12	7	8	11	3	150	50	10	10				
Competitor Y	98	24	16	28	100	6	7	6	4	175	75	15	6				
Competitor Z	96	23	32	13	10	7	8	12	2	145	60	12	8				

For discussion question 13

HOWs vs. HOWs Legend
Positive Linkage +
Negative Linkage —

WHATs vs. HOWs Legend
Strong Correlation △
Some Correlation ●
Possible Correlation ◼

	Number of Flavors	New Flavor Introductions (per month)	Selling Price (average of four – 2 dip cones)	Average Service Time (seconds in line till ice cream rec'd)	Average Number of Servers (for each 100 cones per hour)	Server Training (hours per month)	Texture (% fat content)	Customer Importance Rating	Ice Cream City	Vanilla R Us	Mr. Neopolitan
Economy/Low Price	◼	●	△		◼			2	2	5	4
Variety of Flavors	△	△						3	5	1	2
Speedy Service	●	●	◼	△	△	△		4	1	4	3
Homemade Taste							△	2	5	2	3
Cleanly Surroundings				●	●	●		4	2	3	4
Friendly Atmosphere				●	●	△		5	2	2	4
Ice Cream City	47	12	9	4	2	4	18				
Vanilla R Us	1	0	4	2	4	4	4				
Mr. Neopolitan	3	0	6	3	2	12	12				

PROBLEMS

1. Mama John's Pizza wants to switch from real pizza cheese to an artificial cheese-flavored material. Using the artificial material will cut the cost of an average pizza from $6 to $5.75. But, the company will have to buy the artificial cheese in very large quantities, so it will have to rent additional storage space for $100 a week. The company's current overhead costs are fixed at about $600 per week. They are open 4 nights a week and sell about 100–110 pizzas per night.

   a) What is Mama John's break-even point for investing in the storage space required for the artificial cheese?

   b) Should they go for it? Are there limitations on your recommendation?

2. Ice Cream City (ICC), a chain of ice cream parlors, has a central manufacturing facility in a Midwestern city. They are contemplating a change in the

equipment used to transport deliver the ice cream to their stores. While adding $125,000 per year in depreciation to the company's annual fixed costs, it will allow them to utilize cheaper and more environmentally friendly packaging material (making it easier to recycle), thus saving almost $.20 on each of the 5-gallon cartons that they use to ship product to their stores.

a) Should ICC invest in the new technology? If not, then what level of demand is required to support this initiative?

b) What assumptions are made as to the costs involved?

c) Are there intangibles that may sway your decision?

3. The Well-built Cart Company uses a five-piece design that bolts together the frame of their most popular wheeled golf cart. The fixed costs of this operation are $500 per week with a variable cost of $8 per cart. It has been suggested that the company use a new welding machine to produce a one-piece welded frame that is as good as or better than the original and that would reduce the variable costs per unit to only $6.50. The lease on the welding machine would increase fixed costs to $1400 per week. The company currently produces 800 units per week.

a) Should Well-built Cart invest in the new technology? If not, then what level of demand is required to support this initiative?

b) What assumptions are made as to the costs involved?

c) Are there intangibles that may sway your decision?

4. Responding to customer requests for faster service, a photo-developing lab is examining the economics of purchasing a larger and faster processing machine that does not require a manual changeover from one size of film to the next. Using the new machine, the company could process film on a first-come, first-served basis rather than holding film until a big enough batch of a given size has accumulated. In the past, the company processed about 4000 rolls a week and promised a turnaround time of three days. The new machine could turn film around in less than 1 hour, an improvement that the marketing department estimates could double demand for the service. The company currently earns a $1 profit margin on each roll. The new machine's capacity could handle the expected demand increase, plus 25 to 35% more if necessary, but would add $20,000 to the firm's total depreciation cost per week.

a) By how much would the company have to raise the price per roll in order to maintain its current level of profitability?

b) Do you think the company may be able to offer both 3-day service and 1-hour service?

c) What assumptions did you make to obtain your answers?

5. Bytes & Bits, a computer manufacturer, is contemplating redesigning its PCs to include a fax/modem as an integrated part of the motherboard. The company currently manufactures fax/modems on a separate card that is installed in the computers during final assembly. By integrating the fax/modem directly into the motherboard, the company can save $2.50 per unit in assembly and increase the system's reliability. The redesign would cost the company $50,000, an amount that would be depreciated over the next 2 years, after which the company will introduce a completely new system. Including the fax/modem feature in the new model, along with all the other improvements, would add only an additional $15,000 per year in depreciation.

a) What would you advise the company to do at this point?

b) What would you advise the company to do in 2 years?

6. Barney's Boston Bagel 'n' Bun Bakery is looking into a new type of bag tie that will better seal, and more important, better reseal the company's bagels after they have been taken home. According to a competitive analysis of Barney's bagels compared to those of the competition, the new bag ties would dramatically increase the shelf life of the bagels. Barney currently sells all the bagels the company can make, 5000 bags a week. The

new tie would cost $.02 more than the old one, but the longer shelf life would create incremental value to the customer.

a) Assume that the new tie would require a machine that would add $200 per week to the company's fixed costs. How much more would Barney have to charge per bag to maintain gross margin?

b) A faster machine, along with a second baker, would add $1500 per week to the company's fixed costs, but would triple the company's output. How much should the company add to the price of the bagels if it wants to increase gross margin by at least a $3000 per week?

7. The OM Ts clothing company is considering a change in its Major League Baseball genuine-replica jersey line. In responding to customer demand for more variety in size, the designer found that changing from a four-button to a five-button design would allow the company to add a larger, "oversized" style without going beyond a 6-inch gap between the buttons. (Too big a gap creates an unsightly fit; a smaller gap would not be an issue, even in children's sizes.) The new design will add approximately $.50 to the manufacturing costs of each shirt. It also will require a one-time up-front investment in tooling and reprogramming that will add $1000 per week to the firm's total depreciation cost. The company currently earns a gross margin of $2.00 per shirt on a weekly output of 1500 shirts. How much incremental demand must be satisfied to make the change to a five-button design worthwhile, relative to the company's current costs?

8. A local rock band is contemplating a new type of laser display to provide a backdrop to their performances. They currently use a large number of pyrotechnics that have a cost of more than $150 per performance. The band also has to maintain a license for the explosives, which costs $500 annually. If the band leases the laser device (they are sure that they cannot afford to purchase it out right) for $125 per month, they can get a safer but just as exciting effect, and the only additional cost would be the $25 per performance it would take to pay a "roadie" to operate the machine.

a) How many performances per year would the band need to average to make the laser machine pay for itself relative to the pyrotechnics?

b) What other intangible issues are involved?

CHALLENGE PROBLEMS

1. Consider the situation of the Ice Cream Company again (described in discussion question #13).

a) Using the competitive analysis information in the QFD House of Quality presented in that discussion question 12, how competitive is their current line of products and services?

b) Using this analysis, where would you suggest improvement efforts be focused?

2. A popular sports shoe manufacturer has been presented with a proposal to switch from cutting real leather to form the upper components of their shoes to buying a precut and formed synthetic version. The synthetic versions would cost an average of $3 per pair more than the current leather but by coming precut, they would eliminate the need for almost $1,500,000 in fixed costs associated with the labor and equipment required to cut and fabricate the leather. The source of the synthetic parts has indicated that their costs will go down as they accumulate experience in making the parts and as the demand for the parts increases. The shoe maker currently expects the demand to be 600,000 pairs per year for the next year or two but admits if the market accepts the new shoe, demand could increase dramatically.

a) How can break-even analysis fit here? If so, what is the break-even point?

b) How far would costs have to drop to make this break-even given current demand?

c) What can you suggest to them about this issue based upon current demand?

Case 6: What's Bright Yellow, Takes a Beating Every Time It Comes Out, Yet Has Good Hair?

The Wilson U.S. Open Tournament Select has been the official ball of the United States Open since 1979. Wilson is also used in the Australian Open, Davis Cup, and numerous other professional hard-court tennis tournaments. While tennis rackets have evolved from wood to metal to carbon fiber, Wilson's fuzzy yellow ball remains virtually unchanged. When it comes to tennis balls, constancy is essential. Not an easy task. It was one thing to design a ball to withstand the serve and volley of wooden rackets. Today's stronger breed of players with composite rackets serve the ball at 140 miles an hour or more. Since the ball is getting impacted much more severely than in the past Wilson's main focus has been to ensure that their product can take the punishment. In fact, the company's ongoing challenge is and has been to make the balls identical—and durable, yet lively. Given what seem to be contradicting needs, the answer is to walk a delicate balance.

For the U.S. Open in 2001, Wilson shipped more than 71,000 U.S. Open balls (12,000 pounds worth) to Flushing Meadows. While a player might occasionally want to blame the balls for a sub-par performance, every ball in play has to meet specifications of the International Tennis Federation (ITF) and the United States Tennis Association (USTA) for weight, size, hardness and rebound. In fact, the tennis balls now have to be more consistent than ever given what is at stake at the U.S. Open.

Wilson's engineers test the tennis balls for hardness using a machine (called the Stevens Machine) that places weight on the balls and measures the amount they get "smushed." The standard allowance for deformation, or change in shape, is from 0.220 to 0.290 inches. The U.S. Open has higher standards of uniformity: from 0.240 and 0.245 inches. According to Wilson testers, a pro playing with a 0.220 and then a 0.290 could feel the difference in hardness. Obviously, supplying balls that vary one to another wouldn't satisfy the players and organizers of million-dollar tournaments. Going further, players would ideally prepare by use the same brand for several months leading to a tournament.

The tennis ball's core is made of natural rubber and its covering is a heavy felt weave of New Zealand wool with a bit of nylon. (For match play, the felt on the men's ball is the slightest bit thicker than on the women's ball.) Of course, natural products have inherent variability. Tennis ball makers have to make sure the two natural products, rubber and wool, stay within certain governed parameters.

The balls' appearance is also important. The single biggest production challenge is getting two flat strips of wool and nylon (cut in shapes known as dog bones) to meet smoothly around the ball, joined by a white adhesive. "This part of the process will always be manual," according to Mr. Bill Bishop, principle engineer at Wilson's rackets technology labs in Elk Grove, Illinois. "You have to have a personal ball-coverer—that's what they do for a living—tweak it and make it look pretty." The ball-coverer's rule of thumb: the squarer the dog bones, the more the covering tends to wrinkle. Wrinkles and bad "hair" are also to be avoided in tennis balls. The more durable the felt, the more potential the ball has for getting "fluffy." The goal is to put enough "wig" on the ball that the racket face can grab it, but not enough to create aerodynamic drag, also balancing high durability with low fluff. When balls emerge from the heat and pressure of the manufacturing process, the felt is compressed, like the matted coat of a wet dog. It is then steam-fluffed in industrial driers that make the ball fuzzy so the balls won't fluff up dramatically during play.

Players know that fluff affects performance, and they will cull through balls looking for the kind of fuzz that will suit their game. "On the first serve, some players like to take the skinnier ball, where the fuzz is still down," said Tracey Austin, a two-time U.S. Open champion and USA Network analyst. "Those feel like they're going to go quicker through the air, come off the court quicker." Mr. Bishop added: "For the second serve they usually pick a scuffed-up ball." That allows them to hit the stuffing out of the first one, he said, "and put a little more English in the second serve to make sure it drops in."

When new, both the tennis ball and its packaging contain pressurized air. To make sure the balls have a consistent 12 pounds of pressure per square inch, a veterinarian's 20-gauge needle is attached to a test gauge and plunged into 10 percent of the balls. The cans should be at 13 pounds of pressure to guarantee the balls have a long shelf life. "Putting a metal lid onto a plastic container under pressure is an engineering feat in itself," according to Mr. Bishop. Wilson's canning machines come from the food industry, adjusted to insert pressure rather than create a vacuum. But the rubber ball itself is not a great insulator of air, Mr. Bishop said, nor is the

canister. "The plastic can leak; air permeates through the sidewall. And if you think of the necks of juice and soda bottles at the grocery store, the tennis ball canister opening is a very large one in the lid world."

SOME QUESTIONS TO THINK ABOUT:

1. From a QFD perspective, how would you define the "whats" that are important to a tennis pro at the U.S. Open? Is that different from a weekend player?

2. How has Wilson defined its "hows"?

3. How might QFD analysis have reached the actual manufacturing process in this situation?

4. Thinking about previous chapters, how does acceptance sampling come into play in this situation? C_p ratios?

Adapted from "Under Pressure to Withstand an Unforgivable Beating," the *New York Times*, Aug. 30, 2001, reporter Amy Goldwasser; and http://www.wilson.com/, Sept. 22, 2005

REFERENCES

Chase, R. B. "Where Does the Customer Fit in a Service Operation?" *Harvard Business Review* (November–December 1978): 137–142.

Costin, H. *Strategies for Quality Improvement, 2e.* Fort Worth, TX: Harcourt Brace and Company, 1999.

"Manufacturing Flexibility Nets Solid Savings." *DaimlerChrysler Times*, June 23, 2000.

Schlie, T. W., and J. D. Goldhar. "Product Variety and Time Based Manufacturing and Business Management: Achieving Competitive Advantage through CIM." *Manufacturing Review* 2, no. 1 (March 1989): 32–42.

Shostack, G. L. "Designing Services That Deliver." *Harvard Business Review* (January–February 1984): 133–139.

Shostack, G. L. "Service Positioning through Structural Change." *Journal of Marketing* 51 (January 1987): 36.

Stalk Jr., G. "Time—The Next Source of Competitive Advantage." *Harvard Business Review* (July–August 1988): 41–51.

Stephanou, S. E., and F. Spiegl. *The Manufacturing Challenge: From Concept to Production.* New York: Van Nostrand Reinhold, 1992.

Swartz, J. B. *The Hunters and the Hunted: A Non-Linear Solution for Reengineering the Workplace.* Portland, OR: Productivity Press, 1994.

7

Transformation Process Design Processes

Chapter Outline

Introduction   293
Integrating Operations Management Across the Functions   294
Matching Process Characteristics to Customer Requirements   295

Process Design Factors   297

Process Choice   316

Business Process Reengineering   320

A Reengineering Algorithm   322

Reengineering Principles   329

Summary   330
Key Terms   330
Solved Problems   330
Discussion Questions   333
Problems   334
Challenge Problems   335
Case 7: Hey, Where'd the Ticket Agent Go?   337
References   338

Learning Objectives

After studying this chapter you should be able to:

▶ Relate process design concepts to other business functions

▶ Describe the set of considerations involved in designing processes

▶ Describe fixed automation technologies and their impact on the competitive environment

▶ Solve cost-volume break-even analysis problems

▶ Describe flexible automation technologies and their impact on the competitive environment

▶ Solve cost-volume-flexibility break-even analysis problems

▶ Describe the impact of automation on the four basic process types

▶ Describe business process reengineering

...Back at the Rec Center

"It seems like I'm frustrated at work more than usual lately," says Luis, starting the group's dialogue on a recent Monday morning. "We just can't seem to meet our customer's expectations for variety and lead time without asking for a price that they choke on."

Luis's process is labor intensive, involving highly skilled people using general-purpose equipment to make just about anything anybody could want in the way of furniture. With all the different models the company makes, predicting capacity needs is difficult, and that means a lot of in-process inventory to keep everyone busy. Having a large inventory means having lots of jobs in process, therefore, each job takes longer to complete. The process that used to work doesn't anymore, and Luis isn't sure what to do about it. He knows the company will have to make some changes, and that they won't be easy or cheap, but somehow the firm has to compete.

"Have you looked into automation?" asks Cheryl. "I mean flexible high-tech stuff?"

"A few months ago we put some computer-controlled machines into a couple of departments," Luis responds. "The people who sold us the equipment said it would cut our labor costs and increase our speed and reliability, too." Luis sounds a little sarcastic. "The salespeople also told us we could switch back and forth

between models faster, and that meant we wouldn't have to batch our orders. That, we really liked!" Many times, to avoid unnecessary setups, Luis had waited until enough orders for a particular model accumulated before setting up a machine. But those batches of combined orders tended to flow through the shop together, increasing the amount of work-in-process inventory.

"And let me guess," says Tom, "the technology didn't deliver on the salespeople's promise? What you're talking about sounds a lot like the new airport systems. We've been through the same thing with technology like kiosk and on-line check-in, and before that with automated baggage handling systems. When we first put in a kiosk to let a customer check in at the airport without speaking to an agent, the only impact was to add another queue. Yeah, it gave the customer a choice, but it didn't change a thing for us beyond adding to the types of questions we had to answer. But then we started using it more and added the online check-in option. When it had taken hold—let's say achieved a critical mass—we could start thinking about the check-in process differently. For example, now we can start handling standby passengers at the gate a bit earlier, because lots of people who are pressed for time will check in before they leave their home. We don't have as many people showing up at the last minute to check in. If you think about it, the technology and automation we use for check-in is about the same as what we used when everyone had to line up and go to an agent at the counter. But by changing our check-in process to allow passengers to play a role, the technology has helped us improve in lots of ways."

"I guess that's right," says Fred. "Our choices about the technology we use have to fit with the way we put our value-adding systems together. I heard some management guru on TV talking about paving the cow paths. He said lots of companies spend lots of money on new technology to get better at what they're already doing, when they really ought to think about doing something different."

"I agree," Tom says. "It seems that modern technology is changing the way we all look at the systems we use to provide our products and services. Unless we want to end up with business processes designed for the past, we can't just focus on replacing the technology. Sometimes we have to work on the system, too!"

Introduction

In the past, little attention was given to the customer's role in designing the product-service bundle or the value-adding system. Nor was much thought given to the role of operations in the firm's overall strategy. Today, things are different, in two ways. First, the customer is at the center of decisions that have to do with process selection and the design of the service delivery system. Second, the design of processes and product-service bundles is addressed concurrently, in cross-functional teams that draw heavily on customer-driven definitions of quality.

This chapter describes the way in which companies commit their resources to value-adding systems that will deliver product-service bundles according to competitive priorities. A company's value proposition requires a system to back it up. That system, in turn, includes a significant role for employees in every functional area. As a consequence, it is easy to draw connections between value-adding system design considerations and every functional area of business.

Process design decisions need to be driven by the competitive position a company wants in the marketplace. The competitive considerations involved in designing the value-adding system can be assessed in four main areas: flexibility, technology choices, customer involvement, and supply chain configuration.

1. Flexibility: Processes designed to be efficient usually are capable of providing only a narrow range of product-service bundles. Flexible processes, which are capable of providing a wide range of product-service bundles, are usually less efficient. The degree of flexibility required is, therefore, a critical process design consideration.

REC CENTER DILEMMA

Fred's Dilemma

Fred's company has very automated processes and is quite efficient, but is not flexible. He has heard so much about Luis trying to adopt flexible automation technologies that he is starting to wonder if such technology could help his company, too. Luis is using it to increase efficiency without giving up flexibility. Fred wonders whether there might be a way to become more flexible without decreasing efficiency. It would allow him to be more responsive to demand generated by cell phone promotions. In addition, the company would save a lot by reducing the inventory of each model. And with the life cycle for cell phones getting shorter and shorter, it would help to have more flexible manufacturing equipment. Fred knows that the financial controllers are going to scrutinize any capital investment he comes up with very carefully to see how it impacts the manufacturing cost per unit. This will make it harder for him to provide the economic justification his company would require. How do you think he should approach this opportunity for improvement?

2. Technology: Technology is a critical component of any value-adding system. Used to make processes more efficient or to improve the conformance quality of process outputs, technology can even be used to make processes more flexible. Information technology has become a particularly pervasive aspect of value delivery in both manufacturing and services. In manufacturing, it can be used for process control and provides real-time information that allows managers to plan their operations and communicate their decisions more effectively. In services, it actually allows customers to add the value for themselves, in the ways they prefer, at the times they find most convenient. The potential impact of technology on system performance depends on the type of process—job shop, batch, repetitive, and continuous—being used.

3. Customer involvement: Many processes involve a participative role for the customer; this is particularly true of those where the primary aspect of the delivered value is service related. Other processes, especially those delivering very standardized manufactured goods, involve the customer in no way. Depending on the type of value delivered, process designers must provide for an appropriate amount of customer involvement.

4. Supply chain configuration: Firms with a variety of product-service bundles and those with a higher degree of vertical integration need to decide whether they will have a limited number of large multipurpose facilities or a larger number of smaller facilities that are more focused. Facility focus, another important process design factor, essentially addresses the question of where to set the boundaries of the firm's processes.

Many analytical tools are available to help managers choose between alternative technologies in designing value-adding systems. Perhaps the most commonly used is cost-volume break-even analysis (CVBA). This simple tool allows managers to determine the demand volumes at which various alternatives provide the greatest profit. An extension of CVBA is cost-volume-flexibility break-even analysis (CVFBA). This technique allows managers to determine demand volumes and levels of output variety for the alternatives that provide the greatest economic advantage. CVFBA is better suited for analyzing alternatives where one of the benefits under consideration is system flexibility.

Value-adding systems should not be designed and forgotten. Rather, they should be continuously improved by making incremental changes. Occasionally, despite efforts at ongoing improvement, some part of an existing value-adding system may need to be scrapped and completely redesigned. Business process reengineering is an approach well suited to such situations.

In many ways, then, process selection and the design of the service delivery system are pivotal components in operations management. After all, they focus on the development of the organization's value-adding system.

Integrating Operations Management Across the Functions

Table 7.1 highlights the cross-functional relevance of process design concerns. This topic is likely to be of particular interest to marketing and engineering majors. Marketing professionals play a large role in determining the best competitive position for a firm and explaining this to the rest of the organization. Thus, they are the conduit by which customer preferences become the driver of system design decisions. Engineers, on the other hand, must communicate the potential of alternative technologies to meet these competitive requirements. Changes in technology can open competitive opportunities, and a company's technical staff must be the conduit by which managers become aware of such opportunities.

System design factors have widespread applicability in other functional areas:

▶ Financial managers are crucial shareholders in the allocation of capital for system development and improvement. Ultimately, systems have to be financially viable, and tools for justification of system alternatives are discussed in this section.

▶ Human resources professionals focus on the skills, skill levels required, and appropriate staffing plans. HR strategies must be based on the mix of design factors selected.

▶ As we've already mentioned, the knowledge base of marketing and engineering personnel greatly facilitate the choices made in system design.

▶ Finally, information systems professionals will have to satisfy differing requirements depending on the choices made in system design.

Figure 7.1 illustrates the cross functional business processes described in this chapter. These processes involve (1) matching the transformation process's characteristics and capabilities to the customer requirements it will satisfy and (2) a technique used to make breakthrough improvements to existing business processes called business process reengineering.

Matching Process Characteristics to Customer Requirements

Because no business can be all things to all customers, businesses must set competitive priorities that rank the importance of factors such as low cost, flexibility, high-quality design, and speedy delivery. Establishing a clear set of competitive priorities is a critical part of strategic planning at the business level. It helps to define what the firm is and what it is not.

Along with clear competitive priorities, a clear definition of the product-service bundle is an important starting point in the design of any value-adding system. As Figure 7.2 shows, the definition of the product-service bundle sets in motion a series of related decisions, from the design of component parts and the process in which they are used to the system's day-to-day operation.

If you refer back to Chapter 6, Figure 6.4b on page 260 illustrates the cross-functional approach to system design, in which a cross-functional team uses concurrent engineering to select the value-adding system best suited to the product-service bundle. A certain amount of information on the design of the product-service bundle is necessary for work on the process design to begin, because the process must be capable of providing the bundle. But the product-service bundle need not be finalized for work on the process design to begin. As the product-service bundle moves from design concept to prototype through testing and toward final approval, the process requirements become clearer.

Using an iterative approach that allows designers to address process design issues in greater and greater detail as the product-service bundle's design becomes clearer

Table 7.1

Integrating Operations Management across the Functions

Functional Area Integration Perspective	Finance	Accounting
Why Cross-Functional Integration Matters to Process Design	Process resources, technologies, and equipment require financial justification.	Process investments must be valued and appropriately depreciated in the preparation of accounting statements.
Key Issues	How will investments in process resources and technologies be financially justified? What form of financing will be used for significant process investments? What financial controls will be established to monitor process investments?	How will process investments be valued on the balance sheet? What form of depreciation will be used to expense process investments on the income statement? How will intellectual property, in the form of proprietary process technologies, be valued?

makes sense. Such an approach allows product designers to modify the product-service bundle based on feedback from the process designers. They can evaluate various alternatives based on manufacturability, the implications for procurement (sometimes called "component sourceability"), and marketability. Designers can ask the question, From the customer's perspective, is the added value of this design characteristic worth the cost? Often a very small change to a product-service bundle's design can have a significant impact on the process design. Without such ongoing two-way communication, product designers might as well be working blindfolded; they cannot really know the implications of their decisions for the process and for customer satisfaction.

Finally, as we saw in Chapter 6, concurrent consideration of product design and system design issues significantly reduces the time to market for both new and modified items.

Human Resources	Marketing	Engineering	Management Information Systems
Staffing and HR development plans often depend on process design choices.	Process capabilities provide the backbone upon which marketers can build brand equity.	Engineers are generally responsible for the technical aspects of process design.	IS support is often key to effective utilization of automated process technologies. Selecting such technology would appropriately utilize input from MIS professionals.
What types of workers will be needed in the process?	Specifically, what must the process do in order to deliver the value customers expect from the company's brand?	What technologies will be used in the process?	How will information technologies be used in the process?
Will the process conform to OSHA and other regulations involving the use of human resources?		How will the technologies fit together to form a system?	What hardware and software will be used to support the process?
What job designs result from the process design?	Can unique process capabilities be leveraged for competitive advantages in the marketplace?	What will be the specific equipment selected, where will it be installed, how will it be maintained, what power supplies will be required, etc.?	How will system security and backup issues be handled?
What training will workers require?	What distribution requirements result from the process design?		What user training and support will be required?
What compensation and benefits package will be required to staff the process?	How should customer involvement in the process be structured, if at all?		

Process Design Factors

Designing the value-adding system requires decisions about the system's flexibility, customer involvement, supply chain configuration, and technology. These characteristics of the value-adding system are called system design factors. **Flexibility** refers to the system's ability to respond to uncertainty and variability in the business environment. **Customer involvement** pertains to the customer's role in creating or customizing a particular product-service bundle. **Supply chain configuration** defines the relationships between value-adding activities, both within and outside of the company. This includes *vertical integration decisions,* which focus on the determining extent of the value chain that a company's value-adding system will span. In backward vertical integration, the process includes upstream activities in the value chain (that is, activities that are close to the raw material source). In forward vertical integration, the process includes downstream activities (those that are closer to the ultimate consumer).

Flexibility

The system's ability to respond to uncertainty and variability in the business environment.

Customer involvement

The customer's role in creating or customizing a particular product-service bundle.

Supply-chain configuration

The relationships between value-adding activities, both within and outside of the company.

Figure 7.1

Transformation process design processes

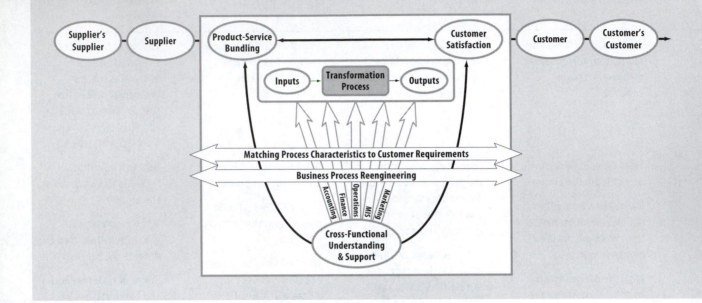

Technology selection

A variety of issues, including the degree and type of automation and the supplier of the equipment.

Finally, **technology selection** refers to a variety of issues, including the degree and type of automation and the supplier of the equipment. The choice of process type, or system type, includes alternatives such as the job shop, batch process, line flow, and continuous flow. As Figure 7.2 shows, this choice is determined largely by decisions about the design factors just discussed.

The four design factors cannot be considered independently; they are interrelated. For example, an inflexible system that is based on significant backward vertical integration and extensive automation could not deliver a high degree of customer involvement. Any customer who tried to influence such a system would quickly become frustrated. (Can you imagine a beauty shop where the stylists treat customers as if they were cars on an assembly line? Or imagine trying to get into one of GM's assembly plants so you can tell workers how to make the Corvette you just ordered. Do you think they would let you bring your own stereo and speakers, so the line workers could install them in the car?)

Obviously, the value-adding system needs to be designed in such a way that it will be capable of delivering customer satisfaction according to the firm's competitive priorities. Taken together, decisions on the four design factors must make sense. If they do, they can create a synergy that has the potential to satisfy the customer. If they do not, the system will not be able to satisfy the customer.

FLEXIBILITY

In the past, companies that wanted to build flexibility into their value-adding systems relied on general-purpose equipment and skilled workers. The per-unit variable cost of production was relatively high and fixed costs were low. Because companies were

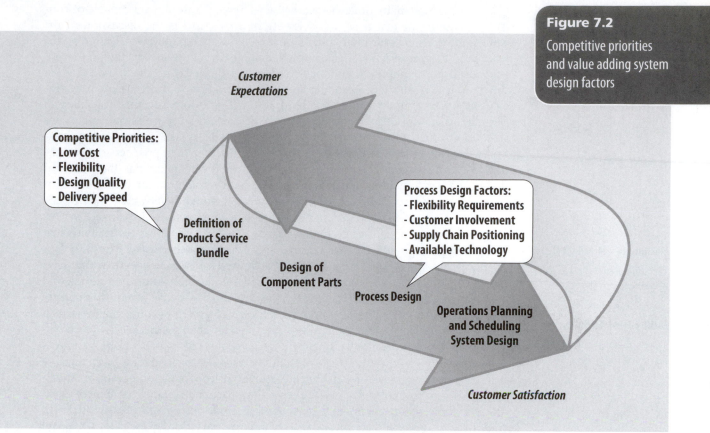

Competitive Priorities:
- Low Cost
- Flexibility
- Design Quality
- Delivery Speed

Customer Expectations

Definition of Product Service Bundle

Design of Component Parts

Process Design

Process Design Factors:
- Flexibility Requirements
- Customer Involvement
- Supply Chain Positioning
- Available Technology

Operations Planning and Scheduling System Design

Customer Satisfaction

using general-purpose equipment, they could provide a wide variety of items. Flexibility was further enhanced because equipment could readily be sold, traded, or acquired as needed; by definition, general-purpose equipment can be used to produce a wide array of outputs. In a typical day, firms with flexible processes might have made only a few units of a variety of items and justified the higher prices of those items as a legitimate reward for the firm's flexibility. Because prices were high and the product-service bundle could be provided with general-purpose equipment, barriers to entry were low in the market segments these firms served.

In the past, companies that chose *not* to build high levels of flexibility into their processes would have chosen to produce standardized goods and services in volumes large enough to justify the expensive special-purpose equipment required. To the extent that their volumes would support it, they would assume higher fixed costs to automate their processes. The automation of dedicated equipment, referred to as **hard automation**, adds very specialized capabilities to equipment. With hard automation, the fixed costs of production are high and the per-unit variable cost of production is low. Thus, hard automation typically provides economies of scale. This benefit, however, is obtained at the cost of reduced system flexibility.

In a typical day, such firms would produce a large quantity of only one item. Because the goods were standardized, customers would not pay a premium for them. Instead, firms would generate a profit as a reward for their ability to produce large volumes at a cost slightly below the low prices customers were willing to pay. Because of the low prices and high fixed costs, barriers to entry in such market segments were high.

Hard automation

The automation of dedicated equipment which adds very specialized capabilities to equipment.

Flexible automation

A variable process capable of controlling equipment that produces a variety of goods, making the discussion of the value-adding system's flexibility much more complex than it once was.

Today the availability of **flexible automation** technologies, which are capable of controlling equipment that produces a variety of goods, makes the discussion of the value-adding system's flexibility much more complex than it once was. Designing the flexibility of a process is no longer simply a matter of deciding between low-fixed-cost, general-purpose equipment, and high-fixed-cost, dedicated equipment. Indeed, given the trend toward shortened product lifecycles, production volumes are often insufficient to warrant processes that use hard automation. Moreover, the availability of flexible automation technologies allows firms with general-purpose equipment to consider trading higher fixed costs for lower per-unit variable costs without giving up flexibility. Thus, they can often provide considerable variety in their product-service bundles or even customize their bundles at unit costs not much higher than those of firms that use hard automation. Similarly, firms using hard automation can trade a small increase in per-unit variable cost for increased flexibility and thereby raise their prices.

Building a flexible system depends on more than equipment choices. In fact, variety of other structural and infrastructural decisions influence flexibility. The flexibility that arises from equipment is better referred to as **machine-level flexibility**. The flexibility of the system as a whole is referred to as **facility-level flexibility**. Besides machine-level flexibility, several factors contribute to facility-level flexibility, including design and engineering capabilities, adequate capacity in resources, effective inventory management policies, short lead times, short setup times, high quality of conformance (which reduces the need for rework), and the ability to readily change schedules.

Machine-level flexibility

Flexibility that originates from equipment.

Facility-level flexibility

The flexibility of a system that is referred to as a whole.

Workforce considerations also play a key role in facility-level flexibility. Cross-training workers so they can perform multiple tasks allows a company to change the product mix on an hourly basis, to quickly resolve bottlenecks and other capacity shortages, and to improve customer service. But there are barriers to the development of a flexible workforce. Fear of change or the loss of status, pride or the rivalries associated with trade or work group affiliations, and work standards that reward workers for speed and efficiency are all detrimental to the development of a flexible workforce. But the most formidable barrier is the restrictive collective bargaining agreements that are designed to provide job security for specific trades by giving them a monopoly of work in that trade.

In plants where such work rules have been included in a collective bargaining agreement, a simple one-hour maintenance task can take days. Suppose a small part of a cooling system pump needs to be replaced. First, the electrician has to be called to ensure that the power is off; that could take a day, depending on the worker's schedule. Next, a plumber has to be scheduled to disconnect the pipes and shut off all the fluid flows to the pump. Then maintenance technicians must be called in, trade by trade. If any special repairs are needed, workers from the appropriate trades must be scheduled. Finally, the plumber has to be called back to reconnect the piping and the electrician to reconnect the power.

Many times, the contribution that a single flexible resource makes toward facility-level flexibility can be rendered moot by a lack of flexibility in other resources. There are nine positions on a baseball team; if the best hitter can only play shortstop, it does not matter that several other players on the team are flexible enough to play shortstop in addition to their other positions. A lack of facility-level flexibility becomes obvious when the team needs better defensive skills at shortstop than the best hitter can offer—especially if the second-best hitter can only play shortstop as well.

CUSTOMER INVOLVEMENT

You may recall occasions when an instructor divided your class into small groups to perform an exercise or discuss a particular concept. Rather than deliver a lecture, to

Getting More Flexible but Not More Expensive at DaimlerChrysler

The introduction of new manufacturing techniques, called "flexible manufacturing," at DaimlerChrysler Corp. facilities has saved the company billions of dollars on product launches through 2004. A basis of flexible manufacturing is to design and create manufacturing facilities that can produce more than one type of vehicle simultaneously. This has allowed the company to increase product variety because of the ability to more quickly change production of vehicles to meet changes in consumer demand. "Flexibility enables us to produce a higher quality product, much sooner, for lower cost, less downtime and minimal production loss. This represents huge productivity and efficiency improvements," says Gary Henson, Executive Vice President–Manufacturing.

Much of the time and cost savings anticipated with flexible manufacturing comes from "rolling launches." Typically, a manufacturer loses several weeks' worth of production during the start of a new vehicle, or during model-year changeover, because production has to stop for new tooling and equipment to be installed, set up, and started. In a rolling launch, new preproduction vehicles are built, tested and launched on the same assembly line while current-model vehicles are still being manufactured. Production of the new vehicle is steadily increased (ramped up) so that production downtime and volume loss are minimized during the new product changeover.

Significant investments have been made in computer controlled technology with which it is easier to program for new models and even switch between models on the "fly." The use of computer-simulated manufacturing software also plays a role in the flexible manufacturing process. Using computer simulation programs, engineers can simulate and perfect the manufacturing process while the vehicle is still being designed and create an assembly process months ahead of the norm.

Flexible manufacturing concepts are part of a joint program that DaimlerChrysler has with the United Auto Workers (UAW) labor union. The involvement of assembly plant employees and the UAW is key to making the flexible manufacturing process work. A lot of ideas and the source of many improvements start with the experience of the worker on the line. Changing the mindset of workers, the union, and management to include employee involvement has been a long battle.

At the Toluca (Mexico) Assembly Plant, the company was able to start and increase production of the new Chrysler PT Cruiser while it was still building the Chrysler Sebring convertible. As a result, the company was able to shift assembly of the convertible to its Sterling Heights, Michigan, Assembly Plant and not lose any production. Sterling Heights has incorporated the flexible manufacturing concept and took on a third product line—the Sebring convertible—while it was launching the next-generation Dodge Stratus and Chrysler Sebring sedan. By adding production of the Sebring without expanding the plant, the company avoided $100 million in production launch-related costs.

Chrysler Group's Windsor (Ontario) Assembly Plant moved the company to the next level of flexible manufacturing by adding the 2004 Chrysler Pacifica sports tourer to the same production line as the 2003 Dodge Grand Caravan and Chrysler Town & Country minivans. The ability to produce these products under the same roof allowed the company to save millions of investment dollars, as well as bring a vehicle to market faster, with better quality and minimal downtime. With flexible manufacturing, the Chrysler Group saved nearly $100 million (U.S.) for the Pacifica launch while simultaneously reducing tooling and facilities capital expenditures by approximately 40%. An added benefit was the ability to produce pilot (or production prototype) vehicles. This reduced waste and improved initial model year quality by sensitizing workers and management to production issues related to the Pacifica, before large-scale production was launched.

Source: Adapted from "Manufacturing flexibility nets solid savings," *DaimlerChrysler TIMES*, June 23, 2000; and http://www.daimlerchrysler.com/dccom/, Sept. 27, 2005

which you would be only an observer, the instructor instead chose an educational process that would actively include you. Putting you into a small group made your participation critical to the learning process. It probably helped you to get more out of the class and may have allowed you to think about some topics that were important to you, but that otherwise would not have been on the instructor's agenda.

Similarly, in many business situations, the customer must be an integral part of the value-adding system. Including the customer in the process can improve the tailoring of the product-service bundle to the customer's expectations and reduce costs (see Table 7.2). For example, obtaining a patient history at the doctor's office helps the doctor to tailor her health care service to a specific patient. Working with a patient on an outpatient basis to build a healthier lifestyle may help to reduce the risk of costly hospital stays later on.

Situations in which the primary value is added to the product part of the product-service bundle are illustrated in the right-hand column of Table 7.2. Self-service at the gasoline pump is an example of the use of customer involvement to reduce the cost of a product-service bundle. Selling goods with "some assembly required" also reduces the cost of the product-service bundle. In addition, it increases the possibility for customization and reduces potential losses from quality problems during assembly. For example, computer desks that can be assembled at home can be shipped in flat, compact boxes that sustain little chance of damage during transit. This product-service bundle provides enough savings and requires a simple enough task (or so the assembly instructions suggest) that many customers opt not to buy preassembled desks.

Table 7.2

Examples of Customer Involvement

	Primary Source of Value Added	
Customer Involvement Results from Emphasis on	**Service Aspects of the Product-Service Bundle**	**Product Aspects of the Product-Service Bundle**
Low Cost	• Soda fountain at a fast-food restaurant • Automated Teller Machine • Laundromat • Co-op day care	• Self-service gasoline • "Pick your own" strawberries • Backyard swing set sold unassembled • TV dinners
High Level of Customization	• Personal fitness consultant • Psychotherapist • Full-service stock broker • Formal wear rental	• Personally designed greeting card kiosk • "Naked" furniture • "Tailor-made" clothing

When the primary value is added to the service portion of the product-service bundle, customer involvement is frequently required rather than optional. Making sure that the customer is consulted at the right times is therefore critical. For example, in medicine, a doctor cannot possibly diagnose a patient's needs without feedback from the patient, nor can the doctor effect a long-term cure without significant action on the patient's part. (Health-care providers, however, must sometimes prevent customer involvement at inappropriate times, for example, during surgery.) Similarly, lawyers, sports agents, advertising firms, and financial service institutions must rely on input from their clients in order to conduct their business effectively. The type of customer involvement is dictated partially by provider preferences, customer and provider expertise, technical requirements, and customer needs, but the timing and location of a service may well be dictated by the customer.

SUPPLY CHAIN CONFIGURATION

Numerous supply chain configuration issues arise in designing value-adding systems. Among these are the structure of information flows, the structure of material flows and distribution networks, and degree of vertical integration.

Information about demand and customer preferences must be made available to operational decision makers throughout the supply chain. This information flows from customers to suppliers in the opposite direction of material flows. Providing access to this information requires the design of interfaces that allow businesses to share information. Standards for the reporting and exchange of information—including security standards—must be established. Thus, information systems and communication technologies are a critical aspect of configuring a supply chain.

Just as important as designing the avenues of information exchange, material flows need to be thought out—especially in the case of manufacturing supply chains. This aspect of value-adding system design requires companies to think about where value will be added, how much capacity is needed at various stages in the creation of value, and how materials will be transferred between the stages of value creation.

Associated with the design of material flows is the design of the distribution networks that transfer materials between facilities that are sequentially related in the creation of value. Particularly with the advent of lean production systems, which do not provide for large quantities of excess inventory between stages of value creation, the reliability of the distribution network is crucial. The logistical system must be designed so that it is capable of consistently transferring material through the supply chain at the pace of material use in downstream operations. Without such logistical capabilities, inventory must be warehoused to protect against material shortages resulting from logistical disruptions.

Finally, supply chain configuration also involves vertical integration and outsourcing decisions. Companies must establish their core competencies and determine the extent to which they will own operations other than these. For example, an insurance company might outsource the claims processing part of their business in order to focus on the sale of policies. By outsourcing these operations, the companies limit their own financial risk and may reduce their costs by gaining access to greater economies of scale experienced by the supplying firms. By contrast, some companies will choose to buy, or internally develop, companies that are their suppliers or customers. Such vertical integration is likely to provide greater profit margins and may allow the company to more effectively control quality, material flows, and security.

TECHNOLOGY SELECTION

In the course of doing business, most companies will see opportunities to use new technology, either because of a need to improve their operations or because of promotional activity by vendors. The process of bringing new equipment and process technologies online falls into three stages, as summarized in Figure 7.3. In the first stage, managers define feasible technological alternatives and estimate their costs and benefits. This fact-finding exercise may include the use of a relatively simple break-even analysis, or it may require more complex analytical models or computer simulations. In the second stage, managers use their cost-benefit analysis to select the most desirable alternative. Their financial calculations will generally include a discounted future cash flow analysis, which can yield a net present value (NPV), or an internal rate of return (IRR). Worst-case estimates, likely estimates, and optimistic estimates should be presented for each alternative, along with information on the environmental

Figure 7.3

New technology adoption process

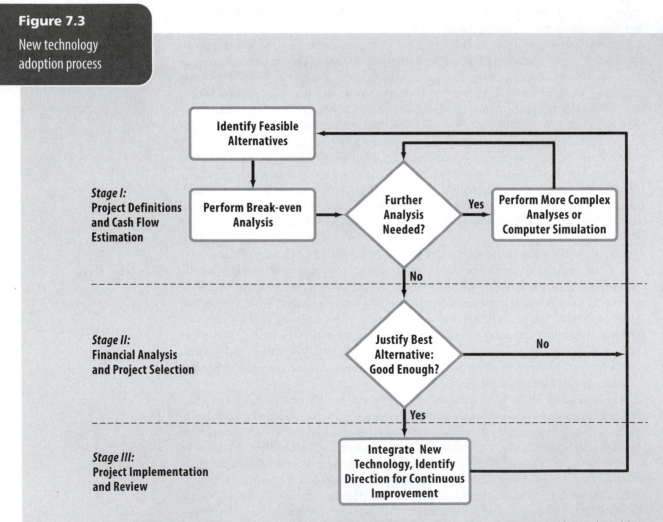

Source: Adapted from Hanna, Mark D., et al. "Adapting traditional breakeven analysis to modern production economics: Simultaneously modeling economies of scale and scope." *International Journal of Production Economics,* 29 (1993), p. 190 (Figure 1).

impact and other risks associated with each new technology. These figures are usually included in a formal proposal that is presented to managers who hold line responsibility for profit and loss.

After its approval by management, a new technology must be integrated into the existing system. This is the third stage of the new technology adoption process. As the technology is implemented, further opportunities for improvement may present themselves. For example, once a new bar code system has been adopted for storage and retrieval of inventory, managers may also want to use it to track units as they move through the plant, in order to generate information useful for scheduling and control purposes. Or a university that has adopted a single-card system for access to athletic events, recreational facilities, cafeterias, and ATM machines might find that with only slight modifications, the card could be used to allow access to students' dorm rooms as well. In many cases, these opportunities could not have been anticipated without an initial investment in the new technology. Before they are fully implemented, new uses for an installed technology must be analyzed thoroughly— meaning that managers must return to the first two stages of the new technology adoption process.

Many North Americans harbor strongly negative opinions of automation. They believe that automation threatens their job security and is therefore antilabor. Skilled workers fear that their craftsmanship and other creative skills that they have traditionally passed down the generations through various forms of apprenticeship may be lost forever because of automation. As their skills become rare, they become expensive, providing further incentive for companies to automate. Thus workers almost always oppose managerial attempts to improve a company's competitiveness by automation. Particularly in an era of corporate downsizing, when nobody's job is secure, managers should demonstrate their concern for the very real human costs that accompany a decision to automate.

Those who have a favorable opinion of automation believe that asking a worker to perform any task that can be done by a machine is disrespectful. In their thinking, respect for humanity means viewing workers as thinkers and problem solvers in a complex value-adding system. Whenever possible, those who favor automation feel, routine, dull, and dangerous tasks should be performed by machines. These people agree that job security is desirable, but they note that it is not guaranteed by the absence of automation. Technological progress is a force that will not be stopped by a manager's decision to preserve a worker's job. Job security is better guaranteed by making use of technology to keep a company competitive and providing training to enhance workers' problem-solving skills.

Over the long term, adjustments will be made in the labor markets, and society will benefit from automation. In the late 1700s, 95% of the U.S. population was engaged in some form of agricultural work; during the 1800s, railway and road work were highly labor intensive. Today, technology has rendered these economic sectors less labor intensive, freeing up the human capital that our society now relies on to staff other professions critical to our standard of living. Other long-term results of automation include a shorter workweek and a relatively high employment rate (about 94% at any given time). Your grandparents may well remember a time when the standard workweek was 48 hours. Less than a century ago, the standard workweek was 72 hours; today, many Europeans enjoy a standard workweek of just 32 hours. Over the same period, living standards have improved dramatically. Technological advances and automation are responsible in part for these positive changes, as well as for many positive improvements in worker health and safety.

Lots of automation and high enough production volume to spread out the increased fixed costs typically lead to low per-unit costs but may also mean little flexibility.

Cost-volume break-even analysis (CVBA)

A capital investment justification tool that is well suited to modeling the costs associated with fixed automation. It may also be used to justify a new product-service bundle or a change to an existing one.

Fixed Automation for Economies of Scale In Chapter 6, an economy of scale was defined as a reduction in variable cost per unit that can justify a significant fixed cost. Traditionally, automation has been possible only with dedicated equipment that produced large volumes of standardized product. In essence, any technology that replaced labor was adopted because of its potential to reduce variable costs.

Cost-Volume Break-Even Analysis Cost-volume break-even analysis (CVBA) is a capital investment justification tool that is well suited to modeling the costs associated with fixed automation. By graphing the total costs of various process options against the cumulative volume produced (or customers served), the analyst can determine the break-even volume for those options. The break-even volume is that volume at which the total costs of the two options are equal; it is found at the intersection between the two cost-volume lines. The break-even point may also be found algebraically, by setting the fixed costs (FC) plus variable costs (VC) for the two alternatives equal. For example:

$$FC_A + VC_A \times \text{Volume} = FC_B + VC_B \times \text{Volume}$$

Solving for the volume in this equation yields the following expression for the break-even volume:

$$\text{Break-even volume} = \frac{FC_A - FC_B}{VC_B - VC_A}$$

This formula for break-even volume assumes that all relevant costs can be categorized as fixed or variable, and that variable costs are a linear function of volume. This simple approach provides a good starting point for analysis of new equipment feasibility, but, as Figure 7.3 shows, further analysis may be required to justify equipment. Because graphs give analysts a feel for the sensitivity of a particular technology to changes in volume, drawing a break-even graph is usually a good idea, even if an algebraic solution has been used to find the break-even volume.

Consider the following example in which we assume that Gillette makes 1.8 billion razors a year, and the firm's board of directors recently approved a $10 million expenditure to test a laser welding system for manufacturing their state of the art razor blades. (Therefore, though there probably were other fixed costs, we assume the difference in fixed costs between the old and the new system is $FC_A - FC_B = \$10$ million.) If engineers had determined that Gillette could save, say, four-tenths of a cent ($VC_B - VC_A = \$0.004$) per razor blade by investing $10 million to modify the production process, then Gillette would have needed to sell 2.5 billion ($10 million/$0.004) razor blades to break even on the investment. Figure 7.4 shows the CVBA graph for this example.

Today, information technology is having a significant impact not just on the manufacturing sector, but on the service sector as well. Take, for example, the financial services sector. At one time in the banking industry, automation referred to the computerization of the machines that count money. But deregulation; the movement toward a cashless society; and electronic record-keeping, funds transfer, and trading in stocks, bonds, and commodities have had a significant effect on this industry. There is

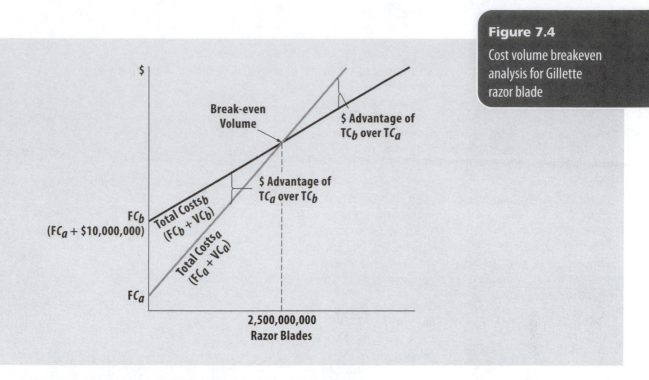

Figure 7.4

Cost volume breakeven analysis for Gillette razor blade

The use of flexible automation, like the robots shown in this picture, help reduce the loss of flexibility that comes from increasing the overall level of automation in a process.

Peter Yates/Corbis

Numerical control (NC)

A machine that can be programmed to operate automatically using coded instructions.

now no particular benefit to having a savings account in a "hometown" bank. If you live in Miami, you can access money that has been deposited in a Seattle bank just as easily as money deposited in a local bank. In either case, you would use the nearest ATM.

As a result, today no U.S. bank can consider its competitive arena to be the "local" market. Large banks have generated tremendous economies of scale by leveraging their investments in electronic technologies to serve a larger customer base. Similarly, discount brokers and financial services institutions have gained significant advantages over local stockbrokers by using technology to generate economies of scale.

In sum, making the right technological choices is critical to success in any business. Hugh McColl, former CEO of Bank of America, stated, "This thing (technology) is like a tidal wave. If you fail in the game, you're going to be dead." We agree. Attempting to use processes that go against the tide of technological change has led to the competitive failure of many businesses. On the other hand, riding the wave of technological change can lead to exceptional success.

Flexible Automation for Economies of Scope In recent years, computer-based technologies have made feasible the automation of processes that do not produce large volumes of standardized products. One basic foundation of such technologies is the concept of numerical control. A **numerical control (NC)** machine is one that can be programmed to operate automatically using coded instructions. The earliest forms of

Example 7.1

Engineers at Luis's factory have been exploring the possibilities of a computerized numerical control (CNC) lathe for use on a variety of spindle parts that go into chairs, tables, and other products they make. The current operation is very labor intensive. The three manually controlled lathes that may be replaced have a combined fixed cost of more than $1500 per week. A typical spindle costs $3 to produce in direct variable costs and the engineers estimate a demand of more than 12,500 spindles per week. The new CNC lathe would have fixed costs twice that but would be more automated and cut variables costs to slightly more than the cost of the material at $1.75 per spindle. The engineers have offered the following CVBA:

Step 1: Gathering the cost and demand information:

Current Lathes	CNC Lathe	Demand
Fixed Costs = $1500 per week	Fixed Costs = $4500 per week	2100 units per week
Variable Costs = $3 per unit	Variable Costs = $1.75 per unit	

Step 2: Computing the break-even value.

Break-even equation and calculation

$1500 + $3 × V = $4500 + $1.75 × V

$1.25 × V = $3000

V = 2400

Step 3: Graphing the alternatives.

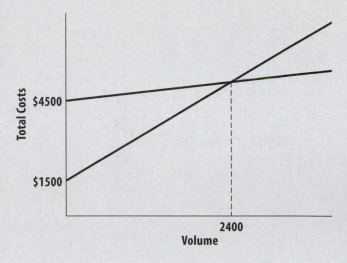

Step 4: Interpreting the analysis.

With demand of only 2100 units per week, the increased fixed costs do not seem to be offset by the reduction in labor and the associated variable costs. Perhaps there should be a more thorough investigation of all the costs involved?

---

numerical control used punch cards or circular paper tapes on which machining instructions had been encoded in the form of punched-out dots. One pass through the cards or one revolution of the tape on the numerical control machine would produce one unit of an item. (The unique set of machining instructions for making a particular item is called its part program.) Later, magnetic media such as cassette tapes and disks replaced punch cards and tapes. Numerically controlled general-purpose equipment can be used to produce low-volume items with higher levels of precision, consistency, and productivity than operator-controlled equipment.

Today, numerical control is often integrated into production equipment. A **computerized numerical control (CNC)** machine is a piece of equipment that has been

Computerized numerical control (CNC)

A piece of equipment that has been outfitted with a computer that can store part programs.

outfitted with a computer that can store part programs. If a part has been made on such a machine in the past, its part program is likely to be stored in the computer. The machine operator only has to instruct the machine to make that particular part; that person does not have to load a new part program into the machine each time a different part is made.

Distributed numerical control (DNC) (also called direct numerical control) refers to the use of a group of networked CNC machines run from a common server. The server is a computer that can download and store part programs from a centralized mainframe or server. It can also collect performance statistics and monitor the status of all of the machines in the network. With DNC, all part programs need not be stored on each CNC. Part programs for items that are made on only one machine can be stored on that machine's CNC. Programs for items that are made using several different machines can be stored on the local network server. Part programs for items that are manufactured in many different geographic locations can be stored on the mainframe computer. Figure 7.5 illustrates the concepts of numerical control, computerized numerical control, and distributed numerical control.

Besides material processing equipment, material handling and storage systems can be automated. An **automated storage and retrieval system (AS/RS)** is a resource that will place materials into a physical inventory location, maintain a record of their location, and return them when needed. AS/RS systems use bar code and/or radio frequency identification (RFID) technology to identify the materials arriving for or leaving inventory and a computer system to track them. When the materials are needed, the AS/RS again uses the computer system to identify the location of the needed inventory and the bar codes or RFID signals to ensure that the correct items have been retrieved. AS/RS systems not only provide accurate information about inventory on a real-time basis; they are programmed to "learn" patterns of material usage, so that commonly used

Distributed numerical control (DNC)

The use of a group of networked CNC machines that run from a common server.

Automated storage and retrieval system (AS/RS)

A resource that will place materials into a physical inventory location, maintain a record of their location, and return them when needed.

Figure 7.5

The evolution of numerical control

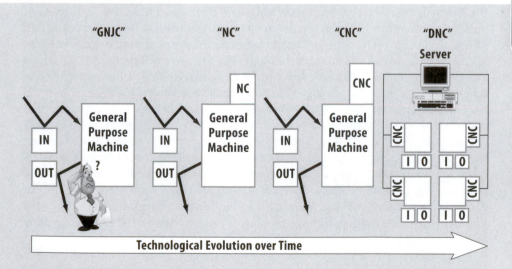

GNJC = Guy Named "Joe" Control
NC = Numerical Control
CNC = Computerized Numerical Control
DNC = Direct Numerical Control

Automated Guided Vehicle (AGV)

A tool used to transport materials without a human driver.

Group technology (GT)

An engineering and manufacturing strategy for product and process design based on the development and exploitation of commonalities among parts, equipment, or processes.

Flexible manufacturing system (FMS)

An automated manufacturing cell—a group of interconnected, numerically controlled machines with automated material-handling capabilities and a shared control system.

items can be retrieved quickly and easily, and less frequently used items stored in out-of-the-way locations.

An **Automated Guided Vehicle (AGV)** is a tool, much like a forklift, used to transport materials without a human driver. These vehicles can be programmed to avoid collisions and can be operated in environments considered unsafe for human material handlers. In many plants today, a grid of wires beneath the floor allows an AGV to "know" where it is and be instructed (by wireless transmission from a host computer) where to go next. In other settings, particularly where a standardized product is made in high volumes, AGVs follow a preprogrammed route along a visible line on the floor. **Group technology (GT)** is an approach to product and process design that is based on commonalities among parts. In this approach, similarities in the shape, size, material, or routing of parts are used to create product families. For example, in an existing product mix, a particular group of products may use the same resources. If it does not, a number of items may be redesigned in order to create a group that can use the same resources.

As for new products, they should not be designed from the ground up, because that approach might lead to new routings, new material sources, equipment needs, or the like. Designing each part from the ground up also produces a proliferation of designs, which can make the storage and retrieval of product designs difficult or expensive. Instead, whenever possible, new product designs should make use of existing components and design standards and should be made to fit into a specific product family. Because in group technology, each part within a group has the same routing and structural characteristics, companies that use GT can dedicate manufacturing cells to a particular product family. Dedicated cells offer great advantages in terms of product cost, quality of conformance, and delivery speed, in exchange for only a small loss in flexibility.

A **flexible manufacturing system (FMS)** is essentially an automated manufacturing cell—a group of interconnected, numerically controlled machines with automated material-handling capabilities and a shared control system. The automated material-handling system must be capable of loading and unloading materials on the NC machines, as well as transporting parts between them. An FMS, then, is capable of making a wide variety of parts, even in small quantities, without human intervention. Although flexible manufacturing systems are very expensive, they can frequently be justified in the context of group technology. Without group technology, an FMS is likely to be underutilized and eventually to be removed. Figure 7.6 illustrates the typical evolution of group technology cells and flexible manufacturing systems in a job shop or batch process. Part (a) shows a production setting in which similar equipment is placed together. For example, if work center A is a place where metal is cut, all metal-cutting equipment would be kept in that one work center. Note that there are four work centers in part (a): A, B, C, and D. Each work center has a number of general-purpose resources that could be either operator controlled or numerically controlled. Since the equipment in each work center is not specialized, the system is capable of producing just about anything. Although the picture shows the routing A–B–C–D, the number of possible routings through the shop is limitless, since a route could have any number of stops.

While this setup is flexible, it is not very efficient, nor is it well coordinated: Individual jobs are handled independently. If a firm found that much of a product mix could be produced using one common route, managers might use some of their general-purpose equipment to create a dedicated GT cell. Some companies might even redesign certain products to make them suitable for production in such a cell. Part (b) of Figure 7.6 shows such an arrangement. Note that the common route for the group of parts made in the GT cell is A–B–C–D. Finally, some firms might contemplate

**(a)
Typical Job Shop/Batch Process**

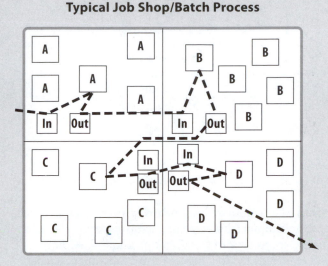

A large number of possible routings through the shop exists, many of which include the path A-B-C-D (or a subset of it).

**(b)
Typical Job Shop/Batch
Process w/Group Technology Cell**

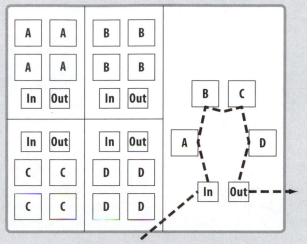

Based on sufficient volume over the path A-B-C-D, a group technology cell can be set up to include a machine from each of those departments. Parts sharing the common path A-B-C-D (or a subset of it) have that portion of their processing done in the cell area of the shop while all remaining work is done in the typical job shop/batch processing area.

**(c)
Typical Job Shop/
Batch Process w/
Flexible
Manufacturing
System**

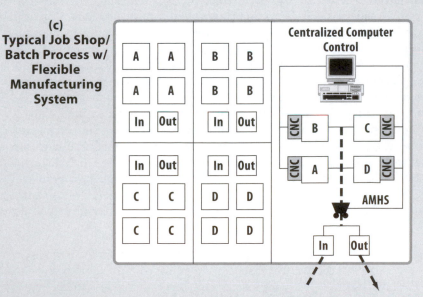

Based on the commonality of the group technology cell and the economic benefit of automation, a flexible manufacturing system (FMS) can be set up by adding hierarchical computer control and an automated material handling system (AMS). Like the group technology cell, parts sharing the common path A-B-C-D (or a subset of it) have that portion of their processing done in the cell while remaining work is done in the job shop/batch processing area.

Figure 7.7

Computer integrated manufacturing (CIM)

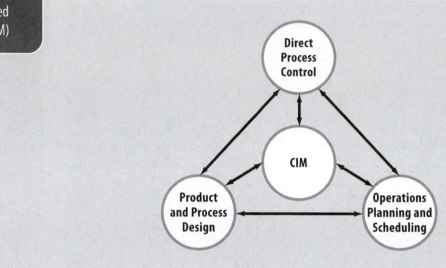

Computer-integrated manufacturing (CIM)

The process which combines automated process and material handling technologies with other computer-based manufacturing technologies, so that computers everywhere in the company can "talk" to one another.

Cost-volume-flexibility break-even analysis (CVFBA)

A tool that can be used to evaluate the economic tradeoffs in technology investments that may pay off through economies of scope.

establishing an FMS. Part (c) of Figure 7.6 shows an FMS that is an automated version of the GT cell in part (b).

Computer-integrated manufacturing (CIM) combines automated process and material handling technologies with other computer-based manufacturing technologies, so that computers everywhere in the company can "talk" to one another. (Computer-aided design [CAD] systems were introduced in Chapter 6, and subsequent chapters will discuss computerized planning and control systems.) A CIM system provides interfaces between these various systems. Figure 7.7 illustrates the role of CIM in linking product design, process design, and operations planning and control systems. As we saw in Chapter 6, there are significant benefits to such integration. Product design changes can quickly be tested for manufacturability, and accurate data on process performance can be made available for use in planning and control decisions. Moreover, the system architecture bridges functional boundaries, allowing managers in one function to gain a better understanding of the impact of their decisions on other functions.

Unlike fixed automation, the technologies used in flexible automation are not designed to generate economies of scale. Rather, they provide economies of scope or scale, depending on the competitive priorities they support. (Recall that on page 278 in Chapter 6, an economy of scope was described as an economic advantage that is obtained through process flexibility.) Cost-volume break-even analysis is therefore not well suited to describing the costs and benefits of flexible automation. **Cost-volume-flexibility break-even analysis (CVFBA)**, by contrast, is a tool that can be used to evaluate the economic trade-offs in technology investments that may pay off through economies of scope. In CVFBA, instead of finding a break-even volume, the analyst finds several break-even lines that represent combinations of volume and variety for which the process alternatives are equally attractive.

Cost-Volume-Flexibility Break-Even Analysis In the past, manufacturers focused almost exclusively on one of two competitive strategies: either low cost or flexibility and customization. A low-cost strategy usually meant using highly automated technology to mass produce a standardized product-service bundle. When a more customized fit was called for in order to differentiate a product-service bundle, a manufacturer would use a more labor-intensive technology to provide the necessary flexibility in the manufacturing process.

Today this type of either-or situation is becoming less and less common. Competing on the basis of a totally standardized product is becoming more and more difficult, no matter how competitive the price. Customers are beginning to expect a better match with their specific needs, whether in terms of timing, variety, or quantity. For example, if you want your hamburger served without a pickle at a fast-food restaurant, the manager cannot afford to treat you as if you come from outer space. Granted, in the past he might have suggested politely that "at our low prices, you can't ask for special favors." But today, the competing store next door will tell you that you can "have it your way" and make good on the statement quickly and at almost the same low price. To give another example, as recently as 1983, Anheuser-Busch, the world's largest brewer, produced only six varieties of beer in a handful of package options. Now, through product proliferation and licensing agreements with international companies, the firm produces several times that many products in about twice as many packaging options. The bottom line is that, except for a few rare markets (e.g., toothpick manufacturing, currency printing or coin minting, and oil refining), customers are demanding increased variety and customization in markets that have traditionally been highly cost competitive.

A similar situation is developing in markets in which companies have traditionally competed on the basis of flexibility. In these markets, companies are now being pressed to be more cost competitive. In the health care industry, express delivery services, and the machine tool industry, cost is no longer an afterthought—though the ability to provide a product-service bundle that precisely meets a specific customer's expectations is still the primary reason a company wins business.

Traditionally companies have used CVBA to evaluate a new process technology, followed sometimes by a more detailed analysis. In essence, a CVBA yields the point of intersection between the total cost curves of competing process alternatives, which shows the break-even volume, or the point at which the two alternatives are equally attractive. In most situations in the past, a CVBA model adequately captured the trade-off between the higher fixed costs of hard automation and the lower variable costs that resulted from labor savings. Because flexibility was not an issue, the model did not need to include some measure of the economic effect of variety in the product-service bundle on the choice of process. More often than not, when flexibility was an issue, cost was not. The need to justify technology from that perspective did not exist.

Today, business is not that simple. In most cases, a firm must consider the economic effect of variety in the product-service bundle when choosing a process. With today's flexible automation, the increased fixed costs of automation may be "buying" more than economies of scale, achieved through lower variable costs per unit. They may also be purchasing economies of scope, achieved through lower flexibility costs. In a significant number of cases, higher fixed costs cannot be justified based only on economies of scale. With today's flexible production technologies, the simplistic assumption that all costs can be categorized as fixed or variable can hinder effective decisions regarding new technologies. A third cost category, related to flexibility needs to be explicitly considered.

Fortunately, the CVBA model can be modified to include the economic impact of both volume (economies of scale) and flexibility (economies of scope). This modified model is CVFBA. By including both volume (variable costs) and flexibility (setup costs), we can define the total costs of two alternatives as:

Total Costs = Fixed Costs (FC) + Variable Costs (VC) + Setup Costs (SC)

Recall that modeling only two variables, fixed costs and variable costs, yields a total cost line for each alternative; the intersection of the total cost lines represents the volume at which the total costs of two alternatives are equal. Modeling *three* variables for each option (fixed costs, variable costs, and flexibility costs) yields a total cost *plane*. Just as the floor and wall of your classroom meet along a line, two total cost planes will intersect along a similar line. The points along that line represent the set of volume and flexibility combinations for which the combined total costs of two alternatives are equal. In this three-way break-even case, an entire line rather than a single point becomes the relevant equality. Combinations of volume and flexibility that fall to either side of the line are better served by one of the two alternatives.

For example, in a hospital, the fixed cost of a manually operated diagnostic testing machine might be $1000 per week. The cost to set up the machine for a different type of test might be $25. A second option might be a machine that incorporates a higher degree of flexible automation. The more automated machine might have a fixed cost of $2500 per week, but because a computer controls it, setup for a different type of test might be much more efficient, at an estimated cost of only $15. The more automated process might also be expected to reduce volume-related variable costs to only $3 per test, compared to $5 per test for the manually operated machine.

In making this decision, an analyst could model the total costs of each machine and set them equal to each other. Using traditional CVBA, one would see that a volume of 750 tests per week would be necessary to justify purchase of the automated machine based on volume alone ($1000 + $5 × 750 = $2500 + $3 × 750). On the other hand, if looking only at flexibility or at the reduced setup cost, one would find that at least 150 different setups per week would be necessary to justify the automated option ($1000 + $25 × 150 = $2500 + $15 × 150). But, what if the analyst considers both volume and flexibility, the results will be different? In the following equation, CFVBA is used to combine fixed costs with both volume and flexibility costs. The resulting relationship can be graphed as the line that separates those combinations for which one alternative is more economically advantageous than the other (see Figure 7.8).

$1000 + $5 × Volume + $25 × Setups = $2500 + $3 × Volume + $15 × Setups

or

$$\text{Volume} = 750 - 5 \times \text{Setups}$$

Graphing this relationship, we see that a volume of at least 750 tests per week, or at least 150 setups per week, or some combination of the two is needed to equate the usage costs of the two machines. Any point to the upper-right-hand side of the diagonal line would represent such a combination. Assuming that approximately 450 tests are done each week, a traditional break-even analysis based on volume alone would not justify purchase of the automated machine ($1000 + $5 × 450 < $2500 + 450 × $3). Assuming that the tests are done in batches of five similar tests each, the machine would be set up about 90 times a week. Again, an analysis based on economy of scope flexibility alone would not justify purchase of the more automated process ($1000 + $25 × 90 < $2500 + $15 × 90). But when the analysis is based on volume and flexibility combined, the variable cost savings on 450 tests plus the setup cost savings on 90 setups are more than enough to justify purchase of the automated machine.

The CVFBA approach can be helpful in making other types of choices. In a more traditional situation (one having to do with hard automation), lower variable costs might be obtained at the expense of higher fixed costs and flexibility costs. While in the past, low cost and high levels of flexibility rarely coexisted, that is not necessarily the case today. Consider the selection of an injection molding machine. One alternative might be a highly automated machine, with fixed costs of $150,000 per year, that can

Figure 7.8

CVFBA for diagnostic equipment

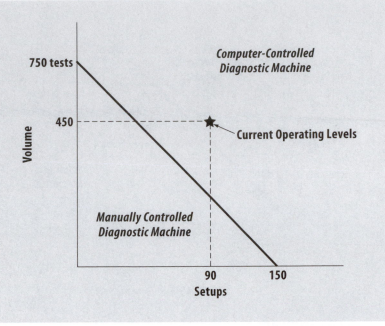

mold the outer shell of a pager out of hard plastic for about $.25 a unit. Retooling this machine to make a different model is estimated to cost about $15,000—very expensive. A smaller, less automated machine has a fixed cost of just $90,000 per year but a higher variable cost of $.45 per unit. Retooling this machine would be easier than the other and would cost only $6000. The firm currently produces 450,000 units per year of a single model. However, as product life cycles grow shorter, workers on the factory floor are switching to new models more and more often. Managers expect they will have to change models at least five times a year over the foreseeable future. What should they do?

Using traditional CVBA, only 300,000 units a year are needed to justify using the larger machine. However, that analysis ignores the cost of retooling to produce new models. Ten years ago, retooling costs might not have been an issue, but in today's competitive environment, flexibility costs cannot be ignored. Using the more comprehensive CVFBA model, managers could estimate the total costs of each injection-molding machine and set them equal to each other. The resulting relationship could then be graphed as the line that separates those combinations for which one alternative would be more economically advantageous than the other:

$$\$150,000 + \$.25 \times \text{Volume} + \$15,000 \times \text{Tooling} = \$90,000 + \$.45 \times \text{Volume} + \$6000 \times \text{Tooling}$$

or

$$\text{Volume} = 300,000 + 45,000 \times \text{Tooling}$$

If we graph this relationship (as in Figure 7.9), we can see a clear distinction between the two alternatives. If no additional retooling is required, any volume over 300,000 units per year would favor the larger machine. However, each new model raises the level of volume required to justify the larger machine by 45,000 units. Assuming that

Figure 7.9
CVFBA for injection molder

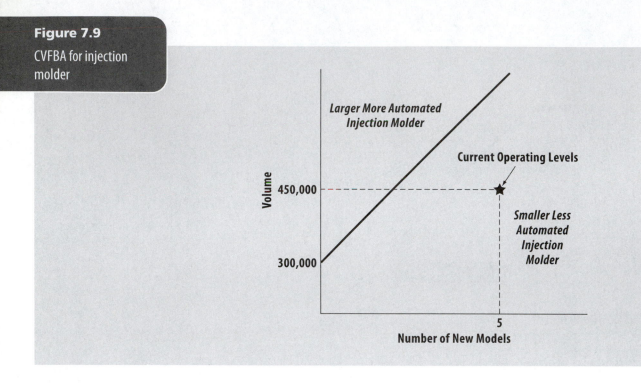

five new models are introduced in the coming year, a volume of 525,000 units would be required to justify use of the larger machine. Given that the plant's expected volume is only 450,000 and given the likelihood of an increasing need for flexibility over time, the firm is probably better off staying with the smaller machine.

Michael Rosenfeld/Getty Images Inc.

Grouping functionally similar machines and resources increases the flexibility in a process but may do so at the expense of efficiency.

Process Choice

The choice of a production process was first discussed in Chapter 2. Figure 7.10 summarizes the distinctions among the four major process types: the job shop, batch process, repetitive process, and continuous process. They include clear differences in the source of demand information, in the variety of inputs and outputs, and in the volume of the output. Managers of a job shop receive job specifications directly from their customers; they use general-purpose equipment to create a wide variety of outputs from a wide variety of inputs. Managers of a batch process limit the variety of specifications they will accept from a customer but do allow customers to specify volume and certain other characteristics of the output. Like the job shop, the batch process uses general-purpose equipment, but there is less variety of input and output and the volume of output is somewhat larger. In contrast, a repetitive process and continuous flow processes produce standardized outputs from standardized inputs using dedicated

Example 7.2

Engineers at Luis's factory are still investigating the possibility of the new CNC lathe for use on a variety of spindle parts that they make each week. Previous attempts to justify the new system on the volume of spindles and the associated reduction in variable costs fell short of the break-even point. Accountants have been looking at all aspects of the new technology and its impact on costs. Luis suggested to them that the machine might provide the flexibility necessary to make a wide variety of spindles, as it currently takes 30 minutes to change lathes when they switch from producing one part to another. The accountants estimate the cost of those 30-minute periods to be approximately $80 when labor costs and machine downtime are taken into account. The new machine can be retooled by simply loading a new program: a 2- to 3-minutes transition at an estimated cost of only $10. Luis estimates around 15 part changeovers per week, and he has worked with accounting and engineering to offer the following CVFBA:

Step 1: Gathering the cost and demand information.

Current Lathes	CNC Lathe	Demand
Fixed Costs = $1500 per week	Fixed Costs = $4500 per week	2100 units per week
Variable Costs = $3 per unit	Variable Costs = $1.75 per unit	15 part changeovers per week
Part Changeover Cost = $80	Part Changeover Cost = $10	

Step 2: Computing the break-even value.

Break-even

$$\$1500 + \$3 \times V + \$80 \times S = \$4500 + \$1.75 \times V + \$10 \times S$$

$$\$70 \times S = \$3000 - \$1.25 \times V$$

$$S = 42.857 - .017857 \times V$$

Step 3: Graphing the alternatives.

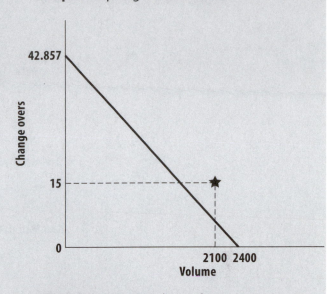

Step 4: Interpreting the analysis.

The break-even line defined in Step 2 and graphed in Step 3 above illustrates that more than 2400 units in total demand, more than forty-two part changeovers per week, or some combination of these that plots a point beyond the line would be needed to justify the new process. With demand of only 2100 per week or fifteen part changeovers per week, neither alone seems to meet the necessary minimums to justify the new machine. However, as you can easily see from the graph, when changeovers and demand are considered together, it becomes clear that the new machine is a better choice.

Figure 7.10

Process type choices

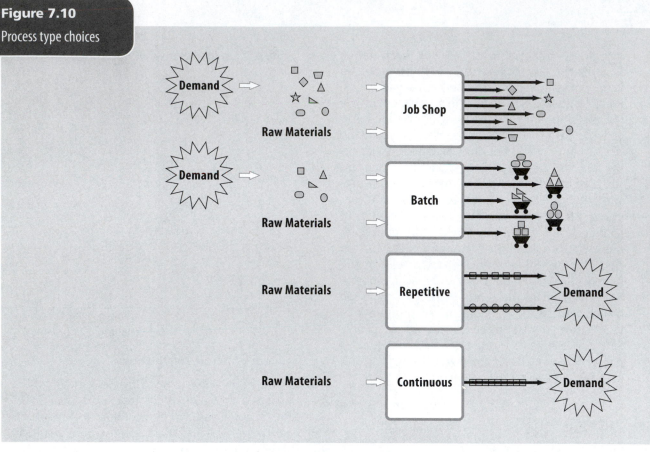

equipment. The only way that customers can "specify" what they wish to receive is by adjusting their rate of consumption.

Turn back for a moment to Figure 7.2 on page 297, which indicates that, taken together, decisions regarding the design of the value-adding system (flexibility, technology, vertical integration, and customer involvement) imply the choice of a particular type of process. That is, a particular set of decisions about the four major system design factors will lead to the choice of a job shop, another to the choice of a batch process, and others to the choice of a repetitive or continuous process. Figure 7.11 summarizes the relationship between the choice of process type and the design of the value-adding system. Generally speaking, job shops and batch processes are appropriate for systems in which orders are won on the basis of flexibility, design capacity, and delivery speed. Thus, the decision to use a job shop or batch process is associated with little vertical integration, considerable flexibility in product and process, and customer input in developing the product-service bundle. Conversely, a repetitive or continuous flow process would be preferred when the primary order winner is low cost. Those processes place more emphasis on vertical integration and dedicated process technologies (to reduce costs) and little emphasis on flexibility and customer involvement.

As Figure 7.11 shows, when competitive priorities have been neatly defined in terms of order-winning and order-qualifying criteria, system design factors have traditionally provided a clear set of either-or trade-offs, making the choice of a process type relatively

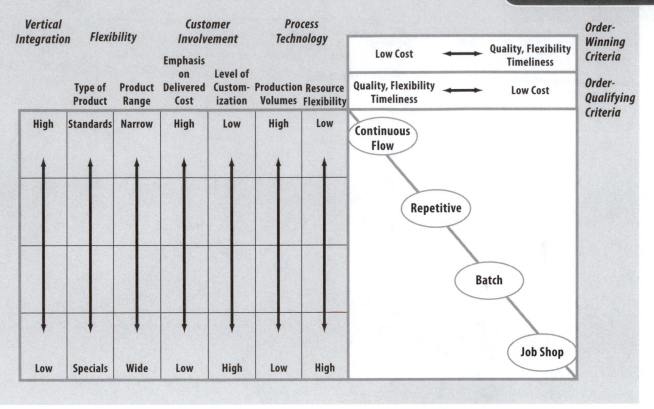

Figure 7.11

Process design factors
and the process type

simple. In some cases, however, the choice is not so simple. Some combination of process types, such as a group technology cell within a job shop, might be a beneficial hybrid. Multiple process types are combined in a hybrid process. For example, beverages are frequently prepared in a batch process and then canned in a continuous-flow process.

The advent of flexible automation technologies has further complicated the choice of process type (see Figure 7.12). Producing a single unit of twelve different items will probably never cost less than producing twelve units of a single item. Thus, the trade-off between flexibility and cost will probably always exist. Through CIM, however, job shops and batch processes, in which flexibility, design capacity, and delivery speed are the order winners, can now qualify for some orders on the basis of unit cost. Similarly, repetitive and continuous flow processes that normally win orders on the basis of cost, can now use CIM to qualify for some orders on the basis of flexibility, design capacity, and delivery speed.

REC CENTER DILEMMA

Cheryl's Dilemma

Cheryl has been thinking about how technology has and has not changed the way that doctors in her outpatient clinics keep patient records up to date. She knows that lots of doctors spend lots of time writing their charts at home, on nights and on weekends, but it seems that there are lots of times when the charts are not as complete as they should be. She proposed a voice recognition system, based on a PalmPilot-like device, that would automate the process and create electronic records. To her surprise, she received a lot of resistance to this change. Doctors said it was too costly and they did not want to have to learn the new technology. Nurses were afraid they would not get to "see" the charts. Clerical staff in the clinics thought it would be just more work for them, because doctors and nurses would "always be asking for printouts." Cheryl thinks it's important to move to this system, but wonders whether it is possible, given all of the resistance. What advice would you give her?

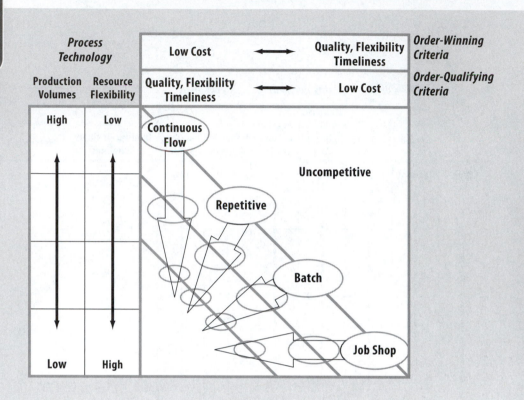

Figure 7.12

Flexible automation and the choice of process type

In short, the boundaries of the competitive playing field have become blurred. No longer can manufacturers that use flexible processes ignore the price differential between their product-service bundles and those of manufacturers using dedicated processes (or vice versa). Indeed, flexible producers may now be capable of providing product-service bundles at a low enough price to take some business away from low-cost producers. Likewise, the low-cost producers may be able to offer enough customization to take some business from even the most flexible producer.

Business Process Reengineering

The primary focus of this chapter has been the design of the process used to create a firm's product-service bundle. Conversion processes, for example, are the physical systems used by manufacturers and services to create their product-service bundle. For example, the system used at a cafeteria to prepare and deliver meals is a conversion process. So, too, are processes that make paper from wood chips, assemble cars from parts, and print tickets for a concert. Process reengineering (or process design) has been around for a long time in the context of conversion processes.

Managers tend to focus improvement efforts on these physical transformation aspect of the process. Perhaps this is because the physical process is visible or because managers associate it more closely with improvements to profitability than other processes. Or perhaps it is because management usually is not directly affected by changes to the physical process.

Unfortunately, customer dissatisfaction and the inability to improve customer satisfaction often stem more from a company's business processes than from its physical processes. Many business processes are truly cross-functional, but they are executed by employees who perceive themselves as working in functional silos. This perception creates a tendency for employees to maintain their resources, status, and power base within their functional silos, which makes it extremely difficult to change business processes. So, managerial practices that focus on improving only the physical aspects of a business' process do not address the additional or underlying issues generated by problematic business processes.

Two general approaches to business process improvement are making localized, incremental improvements or making radical improvements with widespread consequences (see Table 7.3). The first method, which uses the techniques of business process analysis, is typically referred to as **continuous improvement**. Continuous improvement is useful in both complex systems with many interrelated parts and simple systems with few interrelated parts. However, continuous improvement does not address the larger managerial issues mentioned above.

In contrast, **business process reengineering (BPR)** is a new and radical method that focuses primarily on managerial processes. BPR recognizes that all work is done in some process and that every employee, regardless of rank, has a customer and a supplier. In this context, many non-conversion business activities are reasonable targets for improvement. So, BPR uses process design tools to address administrative processes that accomplish such processes as hiring and scheduling employees, paying bills, identifying and paying suppliers, providing computer services, marketing products, raising capital, distributing finished goods, designing product-service bundles, and buying materials. For such processes BPR answers questions such as, Exactly what needs to be done? Who should do it? How? Where? When? For how long?

BPR has been called "starting over" or a "blow it up and start over from scratch" approach. More formally, it is defined as "the fundamental rethinking and redesign of business processes to achieve dramatic improvements in critical contemporary measures of performance such as cost, quality, service, and speed" (Hammer and Champy 1993). In contrast to the continuous improvement approaches of the total quality management system that make many small improvements, BPR seeks to accomplish the rapid and radical redesign of broad, cross-functional business processes. BPR is a higher-risk approach that "bets the farm" on a whole new way of doing things.

It does not make much sense to use BPR on a local (small) scale or with simple systems, because local subsystems and simple systems are constrained largely by outside factors. Thus, a complete redesign of a small subsystem can create many problems, yet has the potential to make only incremental improvements.

The advent of management information systems that use centralized databases has significantly changed the set of possible approaches organizations can use to make decisions. Today, managers and other decision makers frequently use data that they did not collect themselves. Data is available, frequently on a real-time basis, from many sites all over the world. Decisions that were once centralized because of the need of a hierarchy to collect and aggregate data can now be decentralized and made more quickly. As a result, BPR has often been called an MIS technique. We agree that MIS is frequently central to the success of BPR, and technology frequently does drive organizational change. MIS is an enabling technology for many positive process changes generally associated with e-commerce. Information systems, however, are only tools used to accomplish some objective. The sophistication of information systems is meaningless unless it improves organizational performance in some way. Thus, BPR is much more than an MIS technique.

Continuous improvement

The process of making localized, incremental improvements using the techniques of business process analysis.

Business process reengineering (BPR)

A "blow it up and start over from scratch" improvement technique frequently used to reinvent processes that are weak because they span functional boundaries in hierarchical organization charts but aren't coordinated across these boundaries.

Table 7.3

Reengineering Versus
Continuous Improvement

(a) Degree and Breadth of Change Desired

	Breadth of Areas Addressed	
Degree of Change	**Global and Broad in Scope**	**Local and Narrow in Scope**
Revolutionary	Process reengineering	May be suboptimal and doomed to die on the vine. Many times constrained by issues outside its scope. Might not fit with the rest of the business. Like working to put a 5-year supply of ink in a disposable pen that usually ends up lost, broken, stolen, or sat on within 3 to 4 weeks.
Incremental	Many times not worth the effort. Like getting an entire army lined up and in sync just to march a few yards.	Continuous improvement

(b) System Complexity and Breadth of Change Desired

	Breadth of Areas Addressed	
System Complexity	**Global and Broad in Scope**	**Local and Narrow in Scope**
Complex with Many Interrelated Parts	Process reengineering	Continuous improvement
Simple with Few Interrelated Parts	Should be obvious, should be done. "No-brainers" like moving from the telegraph to the telephone or from the typewriter to the word processor.	Continuous improvement

Source: Adapted from "Reengineering and Continuous Improvement," *Quality Digest*, July 1996: pp. 31–34, reporter J. Chris White

A Reengineering Algorithm

Each reengineering effort has unique goals, is shaped by a different team of individuals, and addresses a unique process, so every project proceeds differently. Thus, team members' creativity and ability to direct their project should not be compromised by

INTEGRATING OM:

Satisfying Customers at Toyota's Manufacturing Plants

The Toyota plant in Georgetown, Kentucky, builds more than 2000 cars a day. Though the process is very modern and efficient, Toyota employees are empowered to make it better every day. The company's *Kaizen* (or continuous improvement) teams generate ideas that improve the process. In 1997 they generated more than 3500 ideas that, when implemented, saved Toyota over $3 million. While allowing Toyota to make a better product less expensively, many of the process improvements were good for the environment as well, which is highlighted by the ISO 14001 certification the plant gained in 1998.

The painting operation in the plant generates about 40 tons of paint sludge each week. As cars are painted, the overspray is collected by a curtain of water and the collected water is distilled into a sludge. Each year since a *Kaizen* team came up with the idea in 1992, more than a thousand tons of the sludge have been dried and recycled into products such as a low-density asphalt and decorative landscaping blocks. Sludge used to be burned, but these disposal costs are no longer incurred and the air is cleaner.

Elimination of waste is even better than finding a use for it. One team looked at a different paint problem where too much paint was applied to the fuel tanks. Excess paint clumped up in places and chipped off. By adding a second robotic paint gun, the problem was solved cutting anti-chip touchup paint use by 41% and ozone-depleting volatile organic compounds (used to clean up the repair process) by more than 18 tons per year. Not only is waste eliminated, the paint job is of higher quality. In a similar innovation, paint is applied to the wheel-wells of vehicles with a roller rather than a spray nozzle. By saving paint, reducing emissions, eliminating the need for plastic masking, and holding down cleaning costs, this reduced waste in that part of the operation by 40%.

Local residents who were concerned, before the plant was built, about the wastewater it would put into their streams, are now pleasantly surprised. Toyota pretreats its waste water before it releases it to the local wastewater plant. As a result, tests show that Toyota's wastewater is cleaner than the water provided by local utilities. In fact, it is so clean that one team came up with the idea of mixing dog food with the treated water before sending it to the treatment plant so there would be enough "food" for the microorganisms used by the treatment plant to clean the water. Tests also show natural wildlife populations downstream from Toyota are now healthier than in the early 1980s before the plant was built.

As of the fall of 2005, the Georgetown plant had assembled over 6 million cars. Given that volume of operation, small improvements in efficiency make a big contribution to profitability and the environment. That's why the worker teams keep trying to improve, even though the plant can boast that their vehicles are 85% recyclable, 99% of scrap steel is recycled, over 90% of North American parts are received in returnable packaging, over 45,000 light bulbs are recycled annually and total recycling at the plant exceeds 100,000 tons per year.

Source: Adapted from "Toyota Workers to be Eco-Friendly," *Cincinnati Enquirer,* Aug. 16, 1998, and http://www.toyotageorgetown.com/, Sept. 27, 2005

requiring teams to follow predefined steps. Nevertheless, looking at a cross-section of reengineering projects reveals common procedural patterns, which we present below in the form of an algorithm, or set of sequentially related steps.

STEP 1: PRIORITIZE PROCESSES FOR REENGINEERING

A company's leaders are responsible for determining which processes to reengineer and when. Processes that are performing poorly and have significant impact on customer satisfaction and competitiveness are obvious candidates. It is common for a small percentage of business processes to account for a majority of the problems experienced by customers. Pareto analysis can be used to determine which processes are most important to address. When a firm uses BPR for the first time, it is wise to pick a relatively simple project with which to gain experience with the approach. This allows leaders to demonstrate early successes and helps to build support for other reengineering efforts.

STEP 2: ORGANIZE AND EDUCATE

Reengineering is done by people. The people who are chosen for a reengineering team are a major factor in determining the team's impact. Team members must be creative risk takers who can communicate well. Certainly, the team should include those who are involved in the process being changed. Because most business processes cut across several functions, most reengineering teams are cross-functional. It is important that team members be representative of, or at least respected in and accessible to, their home function. If people from a critical function are left out of the improvement effort, important insights may be missed and the project may be strongly opposed by that function. In some cases, reengineering will result in the elimination of certain work areas. When this occurs, the team members from that area may have the responsibility of selling that decision to their colleagues. Experts suggest that reengineering team members be exempted from most, if not all, of their normal duties and assigned full time to the reengineering effort.

Top-level managers whose power and authority can be leveraged to support the requests of the team also need to be assigned to the reengineering effort. The idea of letting workers make their own decisions about their own work area is useful in the context of continuous improvement, but top management sponsorship is essential in the context of BPR. Top management also needs to lead the implementation of BPR plans. Some respected consultants and authors recommend devoting at least 20% of the chief executive's time to the project during the design phase of a BPR project and 50% during the implementation phase. Allocating an additional 50% of another senior executive's time during the implementation phase is also recommended. BPR must be driven by customer priorities and strategically important—it is the "big time." And, to be successful, it must provide visible senior management leadership.

Put the right people on the reengineering team is only the start, however. In addition, team members need a budget and other resources with which to operate. For a BPR project to be successful, they team members must

- Have a place to meet
- Be paid, even if they are not assigned to a particular function
- Be able to travel, if necessary, to consult with other firms
- Have support staff, such as MIS professionals, to help them carry the project forward
- Be provided with an implementation budget

Choosing the best set of people for a reengineering team also means determining whether individuals are ready for the task at hand. A team member's former work experience may not have exposed him to every part of the broader process the team is preparing to change. Also, team members need to be familiar with the company's goals for the project so that their decisions will be consistent with those goals and with the firm's strategies, and so they will know when they have completed their task.

STEP 3: DOCUMENT THE CURRENT PROCESS

Reengineering teams have to start with the existing process and they must understand the process as a system. Later, they must be able to communicate and defend their suggested changes to others. As a result, it is important to document the process at the beginning of a reengineering effort. There are at least two major ways in which a process can be documented: (1) Flowcharts indicate what happens to information and material as it moves through a process, and (2) performance measures indicate the effectiveness of the process. This documentation, if well done, can be used as a baseline from which to measure the impact of a reengineering team.

The Supply Chain Operating Reference (SCOR) model is a tool for depicting and analyzing supply chains which was introduced in Chapter 3 (pages 65–110). You may recall that the process of developing a SCOR model was hierarchical, starting with a high-level overview of the supply chain (the Level 1 model) and working toward more and more detailed representations (the Level 2, Level 3, and Level 4 models).

In the context of process reengineering, process mapping is analogous to the SCOR model in the context of supply chain management. A **process map** may take the form of a system overview, which identifies suppliers, outputs, key deliverables, key material flows, key information flows, and feedback loops. Figure 7.13 is an example of a system map for a convalescent care facility. Developing such a system map is the natural

Process map

A system overview, which identifies suppliers, outputs, key deliverables, key material flows, key information flows, and feedback loops.

Figure 7.13

System map for a convalescent care facility

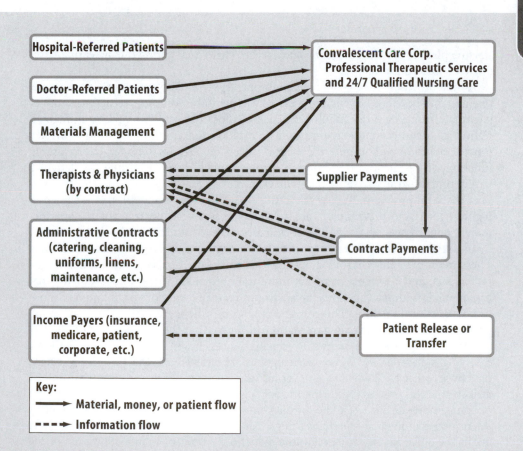

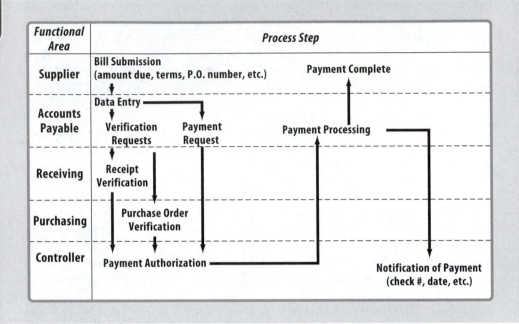

starting place for process mapping and can help with goal setting during early phases of a reengineering effort.

A macro-process map generally details one aspect of a system map. For example, the map may have one box for a process such as payroll accounting, receiving, supplier payment, hiring, or order fulfillment. Each of those is a business process in its own right. Each requires input and output from multiple functions. In addition to the key functional inputs and outputs, the macro-process map shows the interactions among functional areas. It does not, however, provide much detail regarding the activities within functional areas. Figure 7.14 is an example of a macro-process map for the supplier payment process in the convalescent care facility whose system map is shown in Figure 7.13. Macro-process maps are used to identify sources of large potential performance gains by synchronizing activities across all of the functional divides.

In contrast, micro-process maps detail the activities within a given functional area. These maps use a flowchart to show how that functional area converts inputs to outputs. Thus, micro-process maps are more useful for identifying improvements that can be made within a functional area without requiring support from and coordination with other functions. These improvements may be incremental from an overall process perspective, but may have significant impact on the functional area. For example, a micro-process map of the receiving process might show that paperwork for receiving is placed in an "in-box" when goods are received and that data entry is handled by an office clerk when receipt verification is requested from accounts payable. It is likely that this process results in time being wasted in a search for the paperwork. An obvious improvement would be for data entry to take place at the time of receipt by the receiving individual—perhaps using a new networked computer in the work area. While the dollar savings and cycle-time reductions from this change might not be big in terms of the macro-process shown in Figure 7.14, the reduction in frustration might make a big difference to those who work in the receiving area and have to hunt down the paperwork.

It may not be necessary to construct detailed process maps for every micro-process. Rather, companies can set priorities and goals for improvement on the basis of what they understand from their macro-process maps and system map. These maps can help companies identify opportunities of improvement that will yield measurable and immediate results (or "low-hanging fruit" in business jargon), as well as opportunities for significant improvement that may be more difficult to accomplish. The need to map micro-processes varies from one reengineering project to another and depends on the mix of identified opportunities for improvement.

Anecdotal evidence suggests that the four most common types of improvement opportunity identified through process mapping are non-value-adding steps, excessive inspection or control, ineffective or excessive handoffs, and excessive task specialization. Consequently, when managers examine a process map they need to challenge each step and verify that it is really adding value. They also need to determine whether the lack of confidence in their process, which leads to inspection and control points, is justified. A handoff occurs every time work is passed from one worker, or one part of the organization, to another. By expanding the work of individuals, and relying less on job specialization, handoffs are reduced, complexity is reduced, fewer non-value-adding steps may be required, and there is less potential for delay and miscommunication.

Process mapping identifies a process' current state as well as its potential future states. Therefore, it is an extremely useful tool for identifying and building consensus around both the need for change and the best change to make. Mapping enables managers to pinpoint inefficiencies in a process design. It also provides an opportunity for those impacted by the proposed change to verbalize their concerns and questions.

STEP 4: DEVELOP A VISION FOR THE FUTURE PROCESS

A reengineering team needs goals. These goals provide a shared vision for the team; without such a vision, there is little hope for success. In fact, a team's success should be measured against their goals as well as against the baseline of past performance. For example, a team reengineering a payroll system might begin with a process that employs 100 people, processes paychecks and tax payments with 99% accuracy, and accommodates voluntary deductions to as many as four different accounts. A team that reduces head count by 50%, eliminates 50% of the paycheck and tax payment errors, and increases the capability to handle voluntary deductions by 50% is successful when compared to prior performance. In reality, this same reengineering effort might have failed: If the team's goal was a 90% improvement in these areas, a 50% improvement is a failure.

How do reengineering teams set appropriate goals? Clearly, benchmarking other processes is one important aspect of the goal-setting process. By benchmarking other processes, a team may be able to challenge arguments that its goals are impossible. In fact, the existence of benchmark performances demonstrates not only what is possible, but what has been achieved. Having this information available helps the team members to come together in support of more ambitious goals.

Once benchmarks have been established, the team needs to consider the differences between their process and the benchmark, the theoretical extent of improvement possible, and the extent of improvement that customers and competitive factors would require. All of these issues play a role in the final determination of the group's goals.

STEP 5: STARTING WITH THE CURRENT PROCESS, DESIGN THE FUTURE PROCESS

Once a group has set goals for the process it is reengineering, it can begin to think about what process changes need to take place in order for the goals to be met. The team members probably will have identified some changes from benchmarking other processes and attempting to set project goals, as well as from their own frustration with existing processes and from the suggestions of others. These ideas must be studied objectively so that the best can be chosen for implementation. Teams make this determination by using a wide variety of analytical and conceptual tools, including service blueprints, value-added analysis, process simulation, flowcharts, and others discussed in Chapter 5.

STEP 6: DEVELOP AN IMPLEMENTATION PLAN

In most cases, process redesign results in losses of jobs, losses of employee status, or major changes in a company's social environment. Therefore, managers and redesign teams must determine the impact of their proposed changes on current employees before implementing those changes. It is natural for people to resist change—in fact, it is healthy for employees to question the value of change. To deal with this resistance successfully, managers need to communicate the rationale for the changes and the benefits that will accrue to the employees who are most affected by the plan.

In other words, the team must create an implementation plan that spells out a time line for process changes and defines the roles of individuals. For instance, it is important that senior managers devote significant time to the project, and the implementation plan should make this clear, so that managers commit to the project schedule and include it in their performance objectives. In addition, a good implementation plan should

- Include a period for measuring and testing results, potentially in a pilot study, prior to widespread application of the redesign
- Include plans for training on a wide-scale basis.
- Anticipate the financial costs of the proposed changes and establish an adequate budget
- Consider how progress will be communicated
- Provide for regular progress reports to both senior managers and to employees affected by the change
- Establish mechanisms for control in the new process. If the process is meeting objectives, those who take over its management on an ongoing basis need to maintain the gains that have been achieved and not allow any aspect of the process to revert to prior norms.

STEP 7: IMPLEMENT THE PLAN

Once a plan is in place, it can be implemented. During this phase of the reengineering project, the demands on managerial time and the rate at which money is spent are very high. (It has been suggested that as much as 50% of a senior manager's time, in addition to 20% to 50% of the chief executive's time, can be consumed during the implementation phase.) So, it is critical that managers and reengineering teams are prepared to devote significant time and energy to implementation and to take a hands-on approach. If the team members do not oversee the details of implementation, critical elements of the process change may be overlooked. Worse yet, employees may feel that management is not committed to the change. Inertia can easily overtake a reengineering project and lead to dismal results.

STEP 8: MEASURE, EVALUATE, AND REPORT RESULTS

For process changes to last, they must be demonstrably beneficial. Just as a person on a diet needs to have scales and use them regularly, process redesign efforts require a comprehensive measurement system that reports changes in quality, cost, flexibility, cycle time, and other variables of interest. Without an effective performance measurement system, it is difficult to determine whether the changes are leading to the desired improvements or whether aspects of the new process are not working as expected.

Reengineering Principles

Michael Hammer, one of the leading proponents of business process reengineering, has suggested principles of reengineering that should be used by process redesign teams as they move through the process outlined above. These principles are as follows:

1. *Organize around outcomes, not tasks.* People need to think of themselves more in terms of what their process is accomplishing than of their department or of the task they perform.

2. *Have those who use the output of the process perform the process.* For example, companies can use computer technology to allow customers to input the information regarding their purchase. Or departments can use available data in purchasing their own materials rather than having a purchasing department buy materials for them.

3. *Subsume information-processing work into the real work that produces the information.* For example, rather than having a salesperson prepare monthly sales reports, sales reports can be generated by information systems that schedule the operations resulting from sales.

4. *Treat geographically dispersed resources as though they were centralized.* For example, a company with fifty plants could have a central purchasing department that generates economies of scale by combining the orders required for each of the plants.

5. *Link parallel activities instead of integrating their results.* For example, when college students register for classes, they have to decide what classes to take and must clear their fees. At many universities, these parallel activities are handled separately, despite the fact that registration is not complete until fees are cleared on the basis of courses scheduled. At other universities, the fee calculation and scheduling activities are integrated into one process.

6. *Put the decision point where the work is performed, and build control into the process.* In other words, let employees have responsibility for their own work decisions, instead of giving that responsibility to a boss who's across the building, hidden behind a door and a desk. The old, departmentalized, hierarchical approach to management made more sense when employees had less education and training, but it is no longer as applicable and does not fit the process orientation suggested in step 1.

S U M M A R Y

This chapter has introduced many factors that must be considered in the design of value-adding systems. It is important to remember the contrast, first mentioned in Chapter 6, between sequential, over-the-functional-wall design processes and concurrent, team design processes. Managers need information about the product-service bundle in order to design an appropriate value-adding system, because this knowledge can significantly improve the competitiveness of the product-service bundle. For this reason, the system design issues covered in this chapter should be approached from the perspective of a cross-functional design team that also has influence over product-service bundle designs.

Those who design a value-adding system must make choices regarding the system's flexibility, customer involvement, degree of vertical integration, and technological options based on a firm's competitive priorities. Those choices ultimately determine the type of process—job shop, batch, repetitive, or continuous

flow—the value-adding system will use to deliver the product-service bundle. To remain competitive, a firm must regularly review the priorities behind each of the decisions made regarding its value-adding system. Managers must verify that the decisions are mutually supportive and serve a common set of objectives.

Competitive conditions and value-adding systems change. Companies that recognize the importance of their value-adding systems create processes for continuous improvement of the system. At some point, however, revolutionary improvements to an existing value-adding system may be needed. Continuous improvement generally is not the best approach to generate such radical improvements. Under these conditions, business process reengineering can be an effective way of maintaining the competitiveness of a firm's value-adding system by redesigning it "from the ground up." BPR can prove valuable to both corporations and public institutions.

K E Y   T E R M S

Automated Storage and Retrieval System (AS/RS), 309
Automated Guided Vehicle (AGV), 310
Business process reengineering (BPR), 321
Computer-integrated manufacturing (CIM), 312
Computerized numerical control (CNC), 308
Continuous improvement, 321

Cost-volume break-even analysis (CVBA), 306
Cost-volume-flexibility break-even analysis (CVFBA), 312
Customer involvement, 297
Distributed numerical control (DNC), 309
Facility-level flexibility, 300
Flexibility, 297
Flexible automation, 300

Flexible manufacturing system (FMS), 310
Group technology (GT), 310
Hard (fixed) automation, 299
Machine-level flexibility, 300
Numerical control (NC), 307
Process map, 325
Supply chain configuration, 297
Technology selection, 298

S O L V E D   P R O B L E M S

1. You are going into business with some college friends who want to build children's picnic tables. One option is to rent a garage from one of your friend's parents and make the tables with hand tools. This arrangement would keep your options open and has a fixed cost of just $150 per week. Yet it is labor intensive, with a variable cost of $8 per table. A second option is to rent the same garage and lease three air-powered nail guns. That option would cut labor and reduce your variable cost to $6 per table, but the lease would increase your fixed cost to $250 per week. A third option is to rent a larger garage, lease the nail guns, and buy an automated saw station that would reduce variable cost to only $3 per table (material cost would be $2.50 per table), but with increased rent on the larger garage and

depreciation on the saw, the fixed cost would climb to $500 per week. Regardless of which option you choose, the business plan you show the bank must include a cost analysis over potential levels of volume.

a) What should you show the bank?

b) If demand were estimated at 80 units per week, what would be your decision?

Solution:

a) $150 + $8 × volume = $250 + $6 × volume

   $2 × volume = $100

   volume = 50

   $250 + $6 × volume = $500 + $3 × volume

   $3 × volume = $250

   volume = 83.3

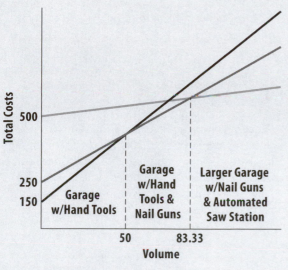

b) At 80 tables per week, you would be close to the break-even point between the garage with hand tools and nail guns and using a large garage with a saw. Assuming the costs are only estimates, a good manager would look for more information to differentiate. The points determined on the graph are only as good as the precision of the total cost curves in estimating the entire economic realty of the situation.

2. Operations managers from another division of Fred's electronics firm—one that considers flexibility to be a higher competitive priority than

does Fred's division—are attempting to make a case for upgrading an injection molding machine. They are under pressure in the marketplace to offer a wider variety of colors in their cellular flip-phones. The problem is that shutting down the current process to change to a different color is very difficult. To meet a demand of around 30,000 units per year, offer a wider variety of colors, and keep inventory at a reasonable level, the plant would need to change colors nearly 130 times a year. Managers estimate that the current cost to change from one color to another (in terms of labor and lost time on the machine) is about $500. A proposal involving a high level of flexible automation has been put forward. The new machine would increase the annual fixed cost of operating the process from $40,000 to $100,000, yet because it is computer controlled, the changeovers would require much less time and effort. Managers estimate the cost to change colors would fall to around $100 each time. Because the new machine is more automated, labor would be reduced, and material usage would be more tightly controlled. The variable costs per case are expected to fall from $2 per unit to around $.50. Typically, managers perform a cost-volume break-even analysis for a proposed equipment upgrade.

a) Will that type of analysis justify this investment?

b) How would you make the case for the new equipment? Can you model the trade-offs?

Solution:

CVBA:

a) $100,000 + $.5 × v = $40,000 + $2 × v

   v = 40,000 and since demand is only 30,000, the new equipment would not be a good choice based on volume considerations alone.

CVFBA:

b) $100,000 + $.5 × v + $100 × s = $40,000 + $2 × v + $500 × s

   v = 40,000 − 266.667 × s

Requiring 150 or more setups per year would justify the machine without even considering its volume related benefits. Similarly, annual volume of 40,000 units would justify the new machine without even considering its setup related benefits. Combinations of setups and benefits that fall above the line in the graph below, would also justify the new machine. The new machine, therefore, appears to be a justifiable investment with annual demand of 30,000 units and 130 setups per year. Other factors should always be considered, such as anticipated changes in demand, availability of capital, alternative uses of capital, and flexibility needs. Any of those might sway the decision.

TC(alt – new,130,30,000) = $130,000

TC(alt – current,130,30,000) = $175,000

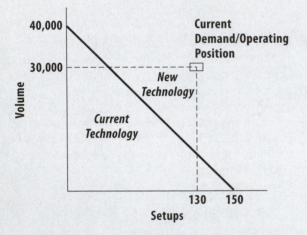

3. Bob's Bed Frames makes its popular bunk-bed frame in three new colors each year that are popular with young children. Bob wants to invest in a painting booth. Bob's fixed costs for this operation would go from $30,000 per year with the smaller of the two booths to $93,000 per year with the larger painting booth. The reduced and more efficient use of labor with the bigger booth cut the variable cost of painting a bunk bed frame from $12 to $5 per unit. Bob currently sells 8000 beds per year but has marketing's assurance that they could sell 12,000 per year if they could offer six additional new colors each year to bring the total to nine. The paint booths require a new painting head for each color they produce each season. The heads are only $1000 for the smaller of the two but cost $8000 per head for the large booth.

a) Can CVBA justify the bigger of the two booths?

b) What can CFVBA tell us about the use of more colors to increase demand to 12,000 units per week?

Solution:

CVBA:

a) $30,000 + \$12 \times v = \$93,000 + \$5 \times v$

$\$7 \times v = \$63,000$

$v = 9,000$ so demand of 12,000 per year would seem to justify the bigger booth when only volume related costs are being included in the analysis.

CFVBA:

b) (We will use the variable "c" to represent colors.)

$\$30,000 + \$12 \times v + \$1,000 \times c = \$93,000 + \$5 \times v + \$8,000 \times c$

$\$7 \times v = \$63,000 + \$7,000 \times c$

$v = 9000 + 1000 \times c$

Because volume related cost function has a positive slope the demand of 12,000 beds is not be enough to justify the new equipment when the additional cost of paint heads is included. In fact, it would take 18,000 units to break even with the larger paint booth. (See graph).

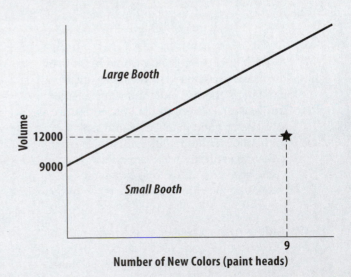

DISCUSSION QUESTIONS

1. If airlines fly the same routes quite often, what are their needs in terms of flexibility? How can modern technology help?

2. If group technology can be likened to "factoring out the constant," what might be some common examples of group-technology-like processes in a grocery store? A health club? A university? A bookstore? A bank?

3. How would you characterize the difference between continuous improvement and process reengineering? When a quarterback improves the way he reads a defense when calling the next play, is he engaging in continuous improvement or reengineering? When the coach brings in a completely new playbook?

4. Currently, Ford Motor Company fabricates a larger percentage of its own parts than DaimlerChrysler. Which company is more vertically integrated? What are the pros and cons of that approach?

5. What are some aspects of the process in Luis's furniture factory that might be well suited to group technology? What about the process in Cheryl's hospital?

6. A friend from high school calls and leaves a message on your answering machine that she wants to start a Tex-Mex restaurant. She says she has the menu done, and she wants you to acquire the process technology to operate the restaurant. Assuming you know something about Tex-Mex cooking, what else do you need to ask your friend about the project? Assuming you know nothing about what customers might want to see on the menu, why should your friend have talked to you before putting the menu together?

7. How does adding computer control to hard automation increase the flexibility of a process? Does it reduce the cost effectiveness of a process? Why or why not? What about computerizing a saw in a lumber mill? A sewing machine in a garment factory?

8. How does adding computer control to a piece of general-purpose equipment increase its precision and cost effectiveness? Does it reduce the flexibility of the equipment? Why or why not? What about computerizing a cash register? A soft drink dispenser at a McDonald's restaurant?

9. How might the process technology employed by the bakery that supplies packaged bread to a local supermarket differ from that of an in-store bakery that makes fresh-baked loaves? From that of a home kitchen?

10. A friend from high school calls and leaves a message on your answering machine that he wants to start a mail-order coffee business. He says he has already compiled the catalog and wants you to acquire the process technology to roast, grind, package, and ship the beans. Assuming you know something about grinding coffee, what else do you need to ask your friend about the project? Assuming you know nothing about customer needs, why should your friend have talked to you before putting the catalog together?

11. What aspects of the process in Luis's furniture factory might be well suited to flexible automation? Of the process in Cheryl's hospital?

12. Describe three manufacturing examples each of a job shop, a batch process, a repetitive process, and a continuous flow process. Can you do the same for processes that provide a service?

13. From the perspective of customer involvement, what are the trade-offs between a prepared salad and a salad bar? Between soft drinks served over the counter or at self-serve stations in a fast-food restaurants? Between an automatic car wash and a self-serve car wash? How do the competitive priorities differ in these cases?

14 In a co-op day care center, each parent assists the teacher three days a month; there are always two parents at the school on any day. Is this arrangement an example of customer involvement? Why or why not? What might be the reasons for making a day care center a co-op? A laundromat or buffet-style restaurant?

15. What services of the college or university you attend are outsourced to a supplier? Why? Do all

universities outsource the same services? Why or why not?

16. Compare and contrast flexible automation to hard automation. What is the best use for each?

17. Will we see more or fewer fully integrated companies in the future? Why or why not?

18. What are the basic components of computer integrated manufacturing? Must they all be implemented together?

19. Assuming that most restaurants are run as a job shop or batch process, is there any way to apply group technology to the industry? If so, what would be some examples? What impact would group technology have on the menus? Could

group technology be applied in Luis's furniture manufacturing facility? How would it affect the company's furniture catalogs? What about applying group technology in Cheryl's hospital? How would it affect patient treatment?

20. Besides sorting baggage, in what other ways would flexible automation be of use to Tom's airline? What value would it add to the service the airline provides?

21. Fred's company produces a somewhat standard product, low cost cell phones. How might flexible automation add to or detract from the company's competitive priorities? What about the competitive priorities at Ford, DaimlerChrysler, and other auto makers?

PROBLEMS

1. A laundry service needs to choose between leasing several smaller top-loading machines that cost $50 per week and process laundry at $.25 per pound, and leasing one larger machine that costs $125 per week but only $.20 per pound to clean clothes.

   a) What is the break-even volume between these two options?

   b) If demand were close to the break-even point, what other issues might you consider?

2. A regional brewery currently uses ten forklifts to load pallets of product onto trucks for distribution. The forklifts are owned by the brewery and add about $1000 a month to its deprecation, maintenance, and associated overhead budgets. The main cost of the loading operation is the $25 hourly rate paid to the drivers. A proposal is being floated to buy sixteen automated guided vehicles (AGVs) that, the company believes will have the same loading capacity as the forklifts. The AGVs have no real variable costs but would be leased for $8000 per month each. The downside to the AGVs is that they must be leased for a 3-year term while forklift drivers can be reassigned or laid off if demand falls.

   a) How many hours per month must the trucks be loading in order to justify the cost of leasing the AGVs?

   b) How reasonable is it for the brewery to bear this cost?

3. A new copier in your office can make copies faster and at only $.012 per copy as compared to the current $.015 per copy (assuming a standard 8.5" x 11" one-sided copy with average toner use). The kicker is the lease cost would rise from $175 per month to $265 per month.

   a) How many copies per month must be made to justify the additional cost?

   b) What is the value of "faster"? When would that be an issue?

4. Your summer grass cutting business is growing (ughhh). A push mower costs $250 and its cost can be spread over the 2 years it will likely last under heavy use. The riding mower you have been looking at will last for 5 years and has a $6500 price tag. You can bring in $30 per hour in revenue using the rider versus $20 using a push mower for the same jobs.

   a) How many hours must you mow in a season to make it worth investing in the bigger mower?

   b) What are the intangibles?

5. You are in charge of booking ground transportation for your school's marching band when it travels to competitions. The band's trips are usually scheduled to last an entire week; some destinations are close and others far away. If you rent a bus big enough to take everybody, the cost for the week will be $2800 plus $.50 per mile driven. If you take seven-seat minivans instead, you will need eight vans to accommodate the entire band. The rental on a minivan is $150 per week plus $.15 per mile driven. If you use cars from the school's motor pool, there will be no rental cost, but the mileage will be $.24 per mile, and the cars hold only four passengers comfortably; thus you will need fourteen cars.

   a) Assuming that all other costs for the week-long trip are about equal, which choice is best for short trips? Long trips? In-between trips?

6. You are asked to choose a new lens-grinding machine for an optician who promises one-hour service. A small tabletop machine has an annual depreciation cost of only $2500, yet the variable cost of producing a lens with that machine is $7 per lens. A version of the same machine that requires special plumbing for a special lubricant used in the process has an annual depreciation of $7000, but can produce a lens at a variable cost of only $5. A larger, more automated machine would increase depreciation to $10,000, but would cut variable costs to just $3.

   a) Depending on what your marketing people forecast for demand, what would you decide?

   b) Would you ever choose the small machine with special lubricant/plumbing?

7. A regional soft drink maker wants to expand into a neighboring country and wants to bottle the product in that country to avoid political issues and to enhance the product's local image. The company has identified three options for the expansion. The first is to build a single large plant in the capital city. Economies of scale would allow the firm to produce a can of soda for $.04 and distribute product across the country from a central location for $.07 per can. This facility would have $1,000,000 per year in fixed costs. The second option is to build two smaller plants, one in the capital and the other in the second largest city. Production costs would increase to $.05 per can, but as the market would be "cut in half," distribution costs would fall to $.02 per can. The fixed cost of each plant would be $650,000 per plant. The third option is to outsource production and distribution to a domestic company who would charge $.17 per can to both produce and distribute the product.

   a) Can you model the range of volume that would make each alternative attractive?

   b) What are some issues not modeled by your break-even model?

CHALLENGE PROBLEMS

1. Personnel at a stamping plant that supplies the automotive industry are trying to decide which type of machine they should buy to cut rolls of sheet metal into "blanks" that are later formed into bumpers, fenders, hoods, and other auto body parts. One alternative has fixed costs of $180,000 a year and variable costs of $12 per blank. The second alternative has fixed costs of only $75,000 per year but variable costs of $15 per blank. In either case, demand for the parts made by this machine would be about 15,000 parts per year. The first machine is computer controlled and can be changed over to the next part type with little or no direct cost. Like new fonts on a laser printer, new parts for this machine can be programmed automatically, with little retraining of the work force or retooling costs. The total cost of overhead and programming to introduce a new part on this machine is estimated at around $1000 per part. The second machine is traditional and, like an old typewriter, would require new tooling, fixtures, and setup training whenever a new part is introduced. This alternative is estimated to require a total of $15,000 of work to introduce a new part.

number of lines, and if this helps while helping the airlines, we're all for it. But there is always the problem of the technology not working as well as the airlines hoped."

Company Perspectives

Delta says ticket counter wait times at Cincinnati Northern Kentucky Airport, where the new system was first installed, had averaged 30 minutes at peak times. It was expected that waiting time would drop to 2 minutes with the new approach and double Delta's ability to handle customers at peak hours.

Delta officials credit the system with improving customer service, reducing staffing requirements, and significantly lowering costs. By Fall 2005, the company had placed over 800 kiosks in 90 cities. While the new technology and training costs totaled about $30 million, the company says the

reengineering of the check in process was a central part of their effort to reduce operating costs by $2.5 billion a year between 2003 and 2005.

SOME QUESTIONS TO THINK ABOUT:

1. How did Delta's check-in kiosks reduce waiting lines?

2. A reference was made comparing this technology to the banking industry. What was meant by that comparison? Is it a good one?

3. Which of the reengineering principles described in this chapter were utilized in the redesign of the check-in process?

4. How have the jobs of the agents who remain been changed?

Source: Adapted from "Delta plans more check-in speed with fewer people," *Cincinnati Enquirer*, Feb. 6, 2003, reporter James Pilcher; and http://www.delta.com/traveling_checkin/index.jsp, Sept. 27, 2005

REFERENCES

Hall, G., J. Rosenthal, and J. Wade. "How to Make Reengineering Really Work." *Harvard Business Review* (November–December, 1993): 119–131.

Hammer, M. "Reengineering Work: Don't Automate, Obliterate." *Harvard Business Review* (July–August, 1990): 104–112.

Hammer, M. and J. Champy. *Reengineering the Corporation: A Manifesto for Business Revolution*. New York: Harper Business, 1993.

Hanna, M. D., W. R. Newman, and S. V. Sridharan. "Adapting Traditional Break-Even Analysis to Modern Production Economics: Simultaneously Modeling Economies of Scale and Scope." *International Journal of Production Economics*, 29 (1993): 187–201.

Hill, T. *Manufacturing Strategy*, 2nd ed. Homewood, IL: Irwin, 1994.

Imai, M. *Kaizen: The Key to Japan's Competitive Success*. New York: Random House Business Division, 1986.

McMahon, C., and J. Brown. *CAD/CAM: From Principles to Practice*. Boston: Addison-Wesley, 1993.

Swamidass, P. M. *Manufacturing Flexibility*. Operations Management Association, Monograph #2 (January, 1988).

White, J. C. "Reengineering and Continuous Improvement." *Quality Digest* (July 1996): 31–34.

8

Building the Global Supply Chain: Capacity and Location Decision-Making Processes

Chapter Outline

Introduction   342

Integrating Operations Management Across the Functions   342

Capacity Decision-Making Issues   343

    Capacity Strategy   345

    Capacity Utilization   348

    Long-Term Forecasting   350

    Learning Curves and Capacity Requirements   352

    The Economics of Capacity Decisions   353

Location Decisions   363

    The Location Decision Hierarchy   363

    Locating Near Suppliers or Customers   367

    Supply Chain Management and Collocation   371

    Decision-Making Tools for Locating Facilities   371

Summary   386

Key Terms   386

Solved Problems   387

Discussion Questions   392

Problems   394

Challenge Problems   397

Case 8: Capacity and Location Issues in a Yacht Building and Repair Business?   398

Reference   399

Learning Objectives

After studying this chapter you should be able to

▶ Demonstrate your understanding of the linkages between the various business functions that are involved in making facility capacity and location decisions within an operational and supply chain context

▶ Describe the operational and supply chain issues that are involved in long-term capacity decisions

▶ Construct a learning curve for a given learning rate and relate this to capacity decisions

▶ Use quantitative tools to conduct economic analysis of capacity alternatives

▶ Describe the issues that are involved in facility location decisions at each level of the geographic hierarchy

▶ Use quantitative tools to evaluate location alternatives and make location decisions

▶ Set up a transportation tableau and obtain an initial solution to the transportation problem

...Back at the Rec Center

"That Great American ballpark in Cincinnati looks great," says Luis, as he skims the sports section one morning while riding the air bike.

"I heard the whole thing started when both the Reds and the Bengals threatened to leave if they didn't get new facilities," says Tom, as he works out on a stepper. "The fans lose when a team leaves, but so does the league. It leaves a big hole in the market."

"You're right," responds Luis. "Just look at what happened to Cleveland! How could the NFL not be in Cleveland those four years?"

"Not every city is going to get a major league sports franchise," counters Fred.

"Everybody has fast food, a dry cleaner, and even one of those quick-oil-change places, but not everybody has an NFL franchise! And when people do have one, the exact location of the stadium isn't such a big deal. Fans will always find the place, and besides, all the games are on TV. I always know where my TV is!"

"When you say location is no big deal, are you just talking football or are you talking fast food and everything else you mentioned?" asks Tom.

"Everything, all of it!" Fred replies. "The whole location thing is overblown. Provide a good product, with good promotion, price, and delivery—that'll bring the customers in. That's all you need. This side of the highway or that side, this neighborhood or that one—it all seems too petty for a baseball park. What difference does it make, as long as the team's in Cincinnati?"

"No, I think you're wrong, Fred," says Cheryl. "Location can be a big deal for Major League Baseball or for fast-food restaurants! Their perspectives may vary, but the issues are the same."

While Luis loves to give Fred a hard time, he had brought the issue up in the first place and he could see Fred's point. "What difference would a couple of blocks make?" he asks. "It's still the same city."

"That's part of it," Cheryl replies. "I'd even say that in some cases, location is part of what they're selling. You know, 'Let's root, root, root for the home team.' But you'd be surprised, especially in these cases. What would happen if they crossed the Ohio River into Kentucky? Would you still call them the Cincinnati Reds? Look how upset New Yorkers got over the Jets and the Giants playing in New Jersey!"

"It sure seemed like a big deal in Charlotte," agrees Tom. "I heard both North and South Carolina wanted the Panthers. I'll bet calling them the Carolina Panthers was a political compromise."

"I'm sure the NFL has to look at the big picture when it comes to locating an expansion team or deciding whether existing teams can move," says Luis. "I agree that market size and potential customer base is a big issue—but the detailed stuff?"

"Well, fast food is different from major league sports," Cheryl argues. "The economics are different. It makes sense to have hundreds or even thousands of small stores spread around the country, as opposed to just 30 franchises spread over major markets. Just look at Starbucks—they like to saturate a local market with stores, sometimes putting them less than a block apart." The economic benefit and prestige of having a major league franchise close by was obvious. Cheryl continues: "But deciding which 30 markets is just the first step. Which cities to choose might be the next step. Then someone has to decide the exact spot for each stadium or ballpark."

"That last part, the specific site, now that's just like fast food, right?" asks Luis.

"At that point they look at the same stuff," replies Cheryl, "but the scale of operation is so different that some of their specific concerns will differ. The idea of what makes a specific location good or bad, traffic flow, access, property cost, that kind of stuff is just as important for a retail franchise as it is for a big stadium."

"She's right," adds Tom. "There was a lot of talk in the paper about exactly where the stadium would go when the league decided to put the team in North Carolina. I heard it came down to Charlotte, North Carolina, or York County, in South Carolina. York County would have been a lot more expensive, even though the two sites are practically right next to each other."

"Why was that? What difference would it have made?" asks Fred, glancing skeptically at Tom.

"For one thing, York County didn't have the little things—the paper called them 'infrastructure'—to support the stadium," replies Tom. "The roads and highways in and out of the possible sites were more congested. Parking, mass transit—all that stuff would have had to be upgraded. For big bucks, too. And getting up to the speed necessary to handle the extra traffic flow would have taken a lot longer."

"I heard it would have taken two years," Cheryl says.

"Couldn't they have played somewhere else in the meantime?" asks Fred.

"They did that, anyway," exclaims Tom. "They played at Clemson for a year, as it was!"

"Didn't the paper also mention an NFL rule that says a stadium has to be cleared within 30 minutes after a game is over?" Cheryl asks. "Seems as if that would have been easier in North Carolina. You know, the access roads and whatnot."

"Okay, I see your point about location," Fred concedes. "But you have to admit that retailers and sports teams deal more with the consumer and marketing issues when picking locations. We, and other manufacturers, just look for the best place to put a facility, to find the skilled labor and materials we need, and the shipping. Most of our location decisions are made by looking at costs."

Introduction

REC CENTER DILEMMA

Cheryl's market expansion Dilemma

Cheryl has been involved in making a number of site selection decisions for outpatient care facilities in markets that are served by her corporation. The higher-ups have noticed, and they recently invited her to lead a team to advise the Board of Directors about expansion into new markets. She knows this is a great opportunity to demonstrate her potential for top corporate management positions, and suspects she might have been appointed to the committee as a test. She also knows that different issues will drive the decision about market expansion than have driven the site-selection decision. Can you help her identify what issues should drive her team's expansion study?

In designing any value-adding system, companies must address the important issue of required long-term capacity. One of the first considerations of an executive planning a new hospital wing or manufacturing plant would be the size of the facility. For a hospital, size can be stated in terms of number of beds, number of nursing stations, number of patients served per day, or square footage. For a manufacturing plant, size could be stated in terms of the number of units produced in a month, the dollar volume of sales per month, or the volume of raw materials used per month. The demand for the product-service bundle is the obvious starting point for any such discussion. The "size," or capacity, that decision makers settle on may in turn help to determine the best location relative to exiting supply chain considerations.

This chapter begins by addressing the strategic issues in capacity decisions. Which is better: a small number of large facilities, each of which serves a fairly large region (for example the twelve Federal Reserve banks)? Or a large number of smaller facilities, each of which serves a local area (such as the local branches of a big-city library system)? This fundamental question has a bearing on both capacity and location decisions. Industry factors play a role, too. Obviously, deciding where to put a large auto assembly plant presumes a different set of concerns than deciding where to put a fast-food store.

To analyze the economics of capacity decisions, this chapter describes tools used to evaluate capacity alternatives and discuss the economic trade-offs that come into play when choosing between large-scale facilities and smaller alternatives. We then present concepts relevant to making location decisions: a decision hierarchy, ranging from choice of country right down to selection of a specific site, along with the factors that most influence location decisions at each level of the hierarchy.

A number of other tools help decision makers decide where they should locate facilities. These include information systems (IS) tools, quantitative methods, market analysis techniques such as trade area studies, and so on. Decision makers rarely rely on just one of these tools to determine the location of a facility. Instead, using a combination of these tools, managers from a variety of business functions work together to ensure that the entire range of relevant considerations is included in the location decision.

Integrating Operations Management Across the Functions

Table 8.1 (shown on pages 344 and 345) highlights some of the reasons why cross-functional integration is important to facility capacity and location decisions from each functional perspective.

▶ For financial managers, the investment in added capacity or a new location requires justification on the basis of projected increases in revenue or reductions in cost. The decision to shut down capacity or close locations requires similar financial cost/benefit analysis.

▶ For accountants, capacity and location decisions change the company's assets and liabilities in ways that must be measured. Additionally, the cost structure of the company is changed when location and capacity changes are made and cost accountants will have to adjust their cost estimates so that decisions made in other functional areas utilize the appropriate data.

▶ Because any change in a company's location and capacity mix involves changing jobs and employee status, human resources professionals address labor relations issues. Labor supply and demographics, or labor regulation, can drive a company away from a particular region and toward another.

▶ Marketing concerns can drive location choices—especially for service and retail organizations. To a lesser extent, this can also be true for manufacturing firms. A location on Park Avenue may be a critical success factor for an advertising agency in New York City. Owners of a clothing boutique would prefer a location in the right shopping mall. Jack Daniels Distillery promotes their manufacturing location in the heart of Tennessee as a competitive asset (because of the marketable characteristics of the water in their local aquifer). At the very least, market demographics and projections have an impact on the financial justifiability of every location and capacity change proposal.

▶ Engineers and information systems professionals provide the expertise and support that makes any capacity expansion, or new location, operationally effective. Engineers design or specify the equipment that will be used to expand capacity or equip a new location and have an interest in ensuring that any operational location has the needed technical infrastructure in place. IS professionals not only provide decision support tools for those who make capacity and location choices, but once a new location is selected, they are responsible for extending the organization's information system to that location and supporting new users.

In total, location and capacity decisions are long-term business decisions that can be made only on a cross-functional basis. As such, they are generally approved only at higher levels in a corporate hierarchy, where a functional perspective does not limit decision makers. Also, because of the cross-functional and possibly supply chain related nature of these decisions, organizations commonly utilize cross-functional teams and even input from external sources such as consultants with specialized expertise, major customers, or key suppliers when considering location and capacity alternatives. Figure 8.1 illustrates the cross-functional reach of the capacity and location decisions covered in this chapter.

Capacity Decision-Making Issues

How many seats should a new major league baseball or football stadium have? A new church? What size moving van should a transfer and storage company buy? How many checkout registers should a grocery store have? How many copies per hour should a copy machine produce? How many cars per shift should an assembly line turn out? And what bandwidth will a new communications network require? All these questions address long-term capacity decisions.

Table 8.1

Integrating Operations Management across the Functions

Integration Perspective / Functional Area	Finance	Accounting
Why Cross-Functional Integration Matters to Facility Capacity and Location Decisions	Location and capacity decisions involve significant long-term commitments of capital. Corporate financial strategies have a large impact on the lease vs. buy decision.	Taxation, both from an income and property standpoint, is strongly affected by location and capacity decisions. Valuation of real estate is a key task in construction of balance sheets.
Key Issues	Should new capacity and locations be leased or bought?	How should new capacity and locations be valued on financial statements? How will old capacity be valued or depreciated?
	How should investments in new capacity and locations be financially justified?	How will real estate transactions be reported to investors?
	What capital requirements arise from location and capacity decisions, and how will that capital be raised?	How does new capacity impact operational costs?
	What insurance is needed to accompany new capacity?	What changes in property tax must be accommodated due to capacity and location changes?

Capacity

The maximum rate of output from a process.

From an operational perspective, **capacity** is defined as the maximum rate of output from a process. It can be easy to state from a theoretical perspective, but difficult to realistically estimate. For example, the theoretical capacity of an 8-ounce beverage glass is obvious—8 ounces. But you cannot expect a table server in a busy restaurant to deliver 8 ounces to the customer's table in a reasonably short period of time in an 8-ounce glass. Thus, the effective capacity is less than 8 ounces and difficult to estimate. The effective capacity of an 8-ounce glass depends on how busy the restaurant is, how experienced the server is, what type of beverage is involved, how far the server must walk, and other factors. Just like the restaurant glass, it can be easy to state the theoretical capacity of a service or manufacturing process, but a host of real-world considerations can make it hard to know the effective capacity of a process.

Long-term capacity choices are difficult to make because they must be arrived at in the face of great uncertainty about future demand, future costs, technological change, and competitors' capacity plans. What is more, a poor decision by one company can often cause significant long-term losses for an entire industry. For example, if an airline were to acquire more planes than it could fill, managers might try to cover fixed costs by discounting passenger fares, provoking a price war that would hurt the entire industry. Conversely, wise decisions about capacity can produce significant

Human Resources	Marketing	Engineering	Management Information Systems
Location and capacity decisions impact the demographics of the available labor pool and the staffing required, thus, they have a large impact on the HR plans of the firm.	Access to markets is often impacted by location choices. Target markets can drive the location choice. Capacity requirements are impacted by market size and share trends.	Engineering expertise is required to estimate the capacity of new or expanded facilities. The engineering function must make decisions regarding support capacity and its location.	IS provides tools that help analyze location and capacity decisions. The IS function must make decisions about required processing and support capacity.
What labor skills are required to staff new capacity and/or locations? Are these skills available and how will they be recruited, trained, rewarded, etc.? How will labor relations, particularly with unions, be impacted by capacity and location choices? When reducing capacity or abandoning locations, how will severance issues be handled?	How does location influence market potential, revenue potential, and brand awareness? Does market access depend on local content laws and public sentiment regarding locally produced items? How will market growth impact the economics of the location decision? What capacity will be required to satisfy the market? What is the market impact of a capacity shortage?	What capacity requirements must the production process satisfy? What technical infrastructure is required to maintain new capacity or new locations? Should new equipment be used to expand capacity or should existing equipment be enhanced? How do equipment and technology plans fit long-term capacity and location plans?	What locational and market data are used in location decisions, and how will they be accessed? What software will be used for location and capacity analysis, and how will it be supported? What hardware and software is required to support new locations and operating capacity? How will new locations be integrated into the company's ERP systems?

profitability and sustained competitive advantage over long periods. Because capacity choices have a significant impact on financial performance, almost any well-done financial analysis of a company's performance will include an assessment of long-term capacity.

Capacity Strategy

Capacity decisions encompass more than expansion; they can also include the closing or downsizing of facilities, the transfer of existing facilities, and the creation of brand-new facilities or prototype systems. Generally speaking, changing levels of demand or a need to become more competitive motivates all these decisions.

Compared to the relatively smooth pattern of demand changes, capacity changes typically come in large increments. Even though consumers buy airline tickets, cars, dishwashers, and gasoline in small quantities, the airports, factories, and oil tankers that provide these product-service bundles are all large-scale facilities. Even small, labor-intensive facilities expand and shrink their capacity in much larger increments than those in which they sell. Over time, therefore, imbalances between capacity and demand are bound to develop.

Figure 8.1

Building and improving the global supply chain: Capacity and location decision-making processes

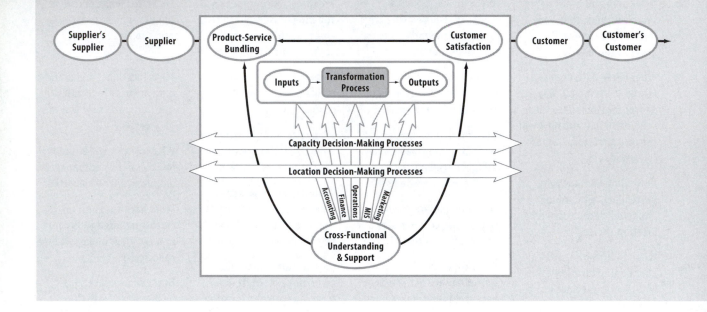

Capacity strategy

The set of long-term decisions a firm makes about the size of its plants and equipment.

Deciding how much to increase or decrease capacity, and when, is a strategic choice. The set of long-term decisions a firm makes about the size of its plants and equipment is its **capacity strategy**. Figure 8.2 illustrates a number of possible decision-making patterns. Based on industry factors and competitive strategy, a company will lean toward one of the three strategies shown in the figure.

Figure 8.2a illustrates a capacity cushion strategy that is used in many service operations to ensure that demand can be met from existing resources. Firms that cannot create an inventory or a demand backlog must have excess capacity in order to deal with the extremes of demand. For example, the fire department in a small town may possess several fire trucks that are seldom, if ever, on call all at once. Similarly, an electrical utility needs enough capacity to meet peak demand, which usually occurs early in the evening during the hottest part of the summer. A bank needs enough teller windows to handle traffic on the busiest days, like the Friday before the Fourth of July (which is a payday for many employers and retirement systems, a dividend payment time for many publicly owned companies, and the start of many workers' vacations). Finally, an Internet service provider, such as America Online, needs to have an adequate number of connections, so that customers will not cancel their accounts because of an inability to access the network.

A capacity cushion strategy is also useful in the growth stage of the product life cycle. Firms that seek to obtain first-mover advantages—as well as those that seek to gain the competitive advantages associated with flexibility, speed, and superior service—frequently adopt this strategy. A capacity cushion also works well with limited reliance

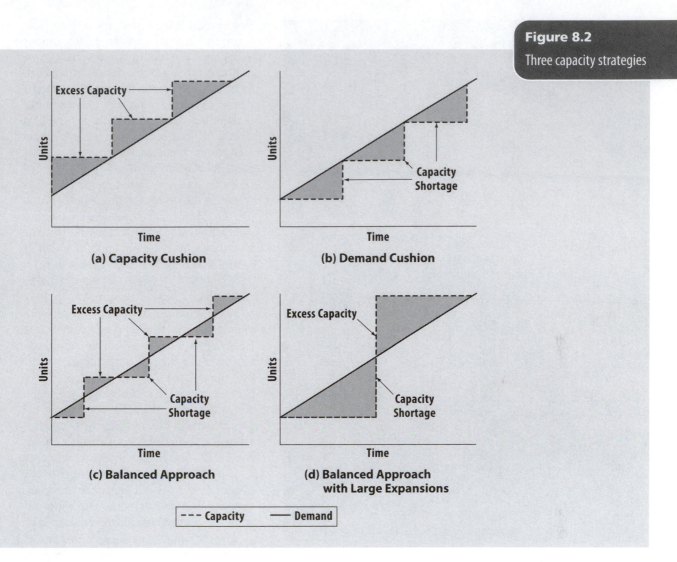

Figure 8.2
Three capacity strategies

(a) Capacity Cushion

Excess Capacity

Units

Time

(b) Demand Cushion

Capacity Shortage

Units

Time

(c) Balanced Approach

Excess Capacity

Capacity Shortage

Units

Time

(d) Balanced Approach with Large Expansions

Excess Capacity

Capacity Shortage

Units

Time

- - - Capacity —— Demand

on finished goods inventory, aggressive sales and marketing efforts, the use of customer incentives, and a great deal of product variety. Clearly, capacity decisions cannot be made in isolation by operations managers alone. Rather, they must fit the firm's business strategy as well as decision making in other functions, such as finance and marketing.

Financially, adding new capacity in anticipation of market growth can be risky. If the demand does not materialize, or if it is slower to materialize than expected, the fixed costs of the new capacity are not likely to be covered. The fact is, demand does not always grow. The same capacity cushion that provides a first-mover advantage in a growing market can provide a last-mover disadvantage in a declining market. And the firm that seeks to create a capacity cushion is likely to have higher fixed costs, which will limit its ability to harvest profits in the later stages of the product life cycle.

Figure 8.2b illustrates a demand cushion strategy, in which fixed costs are more easily covered. Firms that use demand cushions tend to maintain high inventory levels or large demand backlogs. They often compete on the basis of price and are likely to outsource certain noncritical tasks. These firms are less likely than others to try to be

While it is easy to identify the number of seats on an airplane, determining capacity requirements for an airline is not that simple. Realistic estimates of capacity must also consider air-safety regulations, baggage compartment size, ground facilities, and scheduling constraints.

BananaStock/Jupitor Images

first to market with new products and features, and they generally invest less money in aggressive marketing campaigns.

Though having excess demand may seem to be a luxury, problems can arise when a demand cushion is too large. For example, if there is a demand cushion for the OM course at your school and no additional sections are made available, some of those students who are unable to register for the class might find a way to take the class elsewhere. In the worst case, the capacity shortage could prevent some students from graduating on time. Situations like this one would eventually become public, and your school would find recruiting more difficult and costly. With fewer students and a higher recruitment expense, the school might have to increase tuition. As a consequence, firms should take care to add new capacity before their demand cushions become too large.

Figure 8.2c shows a third capacity strategy, the balanced capacity strategy. Firms that compete in cyclical industries and firms that are in the maturity stage of the product life cycle are likely to adopt this strategy. Such firms endeavor to match their capacity as closely as possible to near-term demand. Depending on the economic climate, they carry either excess capacity or excess demand. During recessions they will tend to have excess capacity; during economic expansions they may develop shortages. To such firms, effectively anticipating changes in the economic cycle is very important, as is flexibility in capacity. They may prefer to lease rather than own, rely on temporary employees rather than hire a permanent staff, or find alternative uses for their capacity by developing complementary businesses.

In addition to strategy, as Figure 8.2d illustrates, a key factor in capacity decisions is the size of capacity expansions. Because of capital requirements, technical factors, and desires for economies of scale in all facilities, many firms will make less frequent (but larger) capacity changes.

Capacity Utilization

Capacity utilization

The ratio of capacity used during a fixed period of time to the available capacity during that same time period.

Capacity utilization is the ratio of capacity used during a fixed period of time to the available capacity during that same time period. Figure 8.3a shows the aggregate capacity utilization rate for American industry in recent years. Published by the Federal Reserve, the industrial and manufacturing capacity utilization rates are watched closely by economists, because utilization is a useful indicator for forecasting long-term interest rates. Utilization is calculated as the ratio of actual output to potential full-capacity

Figure 8.3

(a) U.S. industrial
capacity utilization
(b) U.S. high-technology
industrial capacity
utilization

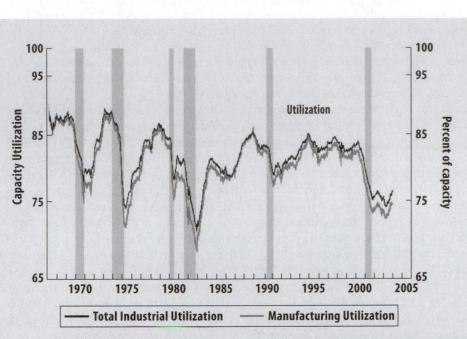

Notes: The shaded areas are periods of business recession as defined by the National Bureau of Economic Research (NBER).
See note on cover page.

Source: Adapted from http://www.federalreserve.gov/releases/g17/current/g17.pdf

(a)

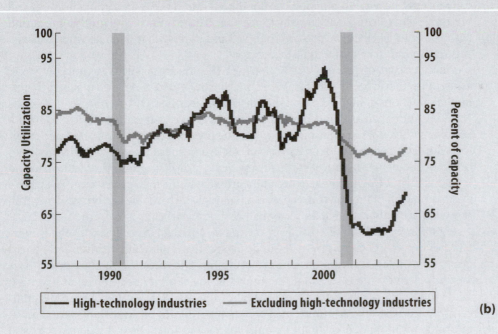

(b)

output. The industrial utilization graph includes manufacturing, mining, and utilities.
Obviously, the manufacturing utilization graph omits the mining and utilities sectors.

The higher the capacity utilization rate rises above some benchmark level—say,
85%—the tighter the plant capacity and the more difficulty factories will have meeting
their orders. Under such conditions, labor shortages and equipment breakdowns tend
to lead to supply shortages and higher production costs. The cost increases, in turn,

trigger a rise in the level of inflation, higher long-term interest rates, and lower levels of capital investment. Pressure mounts for manufacturers to expand their capacity—which is why aggregate capacity utilization rarely rises above 90%.

The capacity utilization rate falls during recessionary periods, such as the shaded ones in Figure 8.3. If it drops too low, manufacturers have difficulty covering their fixed costs and operating profitably. Pressure mounts to close down plants and lay off workers. As a result, the utilization rate rarely falls below 70%.

As you might imagine, the quality of long-term capacity decisions depends in large part on the quality of the economic forecasts on which they are based. Long-term forecasting is therefore one of the primary challenges for managers who make capacity decisions.

Occasionally, capacity decisions and utilization in one sector of the economy are substantially different from the norm—to the extent that they have an impact on the entire economy. Figure 8.3b shows one such instance. Prior to 2000, the high-tech industry was booming. As Figure 8.3b shows, utilization in the high-tech sector of U.S. industry exceeded 90%. What did that mean in terms or real life? Many firms, concerned about the Y2K software problem advanced their purchases of computer hardware and software and aggressively pursued software revision projects. E-commerce was also a big new trend with the World Wide Web relatively new and its business potential beginning to be exploited. ERP systems implementations were booming. The NASDAQ stock index—heavily weighted to the high-tech sector was approaching 5000. Managers were doing all they could, utilizing the collateral of their lofty stock values to finance capacity expansions and keep up with what they perceived to be a tidal wave of demand driven by the superiority of new technologies to traditional business systems. College students and professionals with any expertise in information systems were heavily sought after commodities—lured by heavy signing bonuses and big-time salaries from one company to the next. The economic situation of the period has now been labeled the "dot-com bubble" and that is what it is like when capacity gets really tight in an entire industrial sector.

It became clear on January 1, 2000, that the Y2K software problem was not going to be as disruptive as had been predicted. And soon, as virtual enterprises failed to generate profits, the valuations of high-tech firms began to be questioned. (By the middle of 2002 the NASDAQ index had lost more than 75% of its peak value, bottoming out close to 1000.). Speculative investors were losing money as company stock values plummeted, and creditors who had extended funds on the basis of stock values began to question their ability to collect on the loans to high-tech startup firms. Venture capital became very difficult to find high-tech firms. Unemployment became a problem in the high-tech sector. The wheels were coming off of the dot-com expansion. The high-tech bubble had burst. Figure 8.3b shows capacity utilization in the sector had dropped well below 65% by the end of 2001.

Figure 8.3b, and the discussion in the last two paragraphs, illustrates the importance of capacity decisions from a real life perspective. Following the thundering herd is not a formula for success in capacity planning. The recession of 2001 might have seemed relatively minor without the impact of the capacity decisions that had been made in the high-tech sector. The bursting of the dot-com bubble, however, significantly exacerbated the economic pain of the recession. To promote long-term corporate and employee well being, firms must follow a rational, data-driven strategy and remain cautious not to be overly reactive in their capacity decisions.

Long-Term Forecasting

No one knows for certain what the future holds; the further into the future one looks, the less certain one can be. But in a manufacturing or service facility, the equipment, processes, and technologies that are installed today must be useful over a time frame that is measured in decades. Because the decision to build, expand, or shut down facilities has long-term implications, it must be based on a long-term forecast.

In forecasting, the future is predicted on the basis of past occurrences. (Predictions that are not based on past experience—for instance, those that are based on the way a Coke bottle is pointed when it stops spinning—cannot be called forecasts.) If you were on a weekly class schedule, you would probably forecast where you will be at 10:00 a.m. tomorrow by looking at where you were at that time six days ago. Forecasting what you will be doing in 5 years is far more difficult. Many factors will have some bearing on that forecast, such as your health, your attitude toward risk, and your goals, technological changes, the economic climate, your employer's financial strength, and your coworkers' plans. Similarly, long-term forecasters try to assess the impact of a broad range of factors on a firm's capacity needs. They do not rely solely on the projections made by quantitative models. Instead, they examine qualitative and subjective information obtained from experts in various disciplines who understand past relationships among the many factors that could influence capacity.

Perhaps the best-known approach to generating forecasts from expert opinion is the **Delphi method**, in which the forecaster uses a series of surveys to develop a consensus of expert opinion on a subject. For example, a paper company might need to project paper usage in the years 2010 to 2030 in order to decide whether to build a new manufacturing plant. In the Delphi method, the forecaster would first develop a panel of experts, including leaders in the industry; leaders of supplying industries, such as forestry; leaders in customer groups, such as printers and publishers; representatives of competing technologies, such as the computer industry; and other relevant experts, such as economists, demographers, and futurists. This panel would be asked to respond to a series of questions relevant to the level of paper demand during the period of interest, usually in a mail survey. If the experts agree, their views can be used as a consensus forecast.

Chances are, however, that experts from such diverse fields will hold different viewpoints and will not agree on all questions. In that case, the forecaster would summarize the experts' views according to their fields of expertise, and then provide the information to the entire panel. Along with the feedback, the forecaster would provide another survey for the experts to complete. As the process is repeated, some degree of consensus among the experts might develop. Once a consensus has been reached, or if after several successive surveys it becomes clear that a consensus will never be attainable, the Delphi method should be stopped.

In another forecasting method, **scenario planning**, long-term planners deal with uncertainty by preparing for a variety of possible situations. By testing the performance of several alternative long-term plans under a wide range of potential scenarios, managers can gain a feel for the risks associated with each plan. They can then select the plan that represents the smallest exposure to negative consequences, or the greatest likelihood of good results, or the best results under certain circumstances. Their decision will reflect their willingness to take risks, as well as their beliefs about the likelihood of various scenarios.

Figure 8.4 illustrates the impact of uncertainty on two capacity strategies. Notice in Figure 8.4a that a strategy that is intended to provide a demand cushion, given forecasted demand, could result in a capacity cushion, given lower-than-expected demand. Similarly, in Figure 8.4b, a capacity cushion strategy could yield a demand cushion if actual demand were to be higher than forecasted demand. As a result, long-term forecasters (and managers who make decisions that have long-term implications) are usually more interested in the range of possibilities than in consensus, or middle-of-the-road, projections.

Delphi method

An approach to generating forecasts from expert opinion in which the forecaster uses a series of surveys to develop a consensus on a subject.

Scenario planning

A forecasting method where long-term planners deal with uncertainty by preparing for a variety of possible situations.

Figure 8.4

Forecasted demand uncertainty and capacity strategy

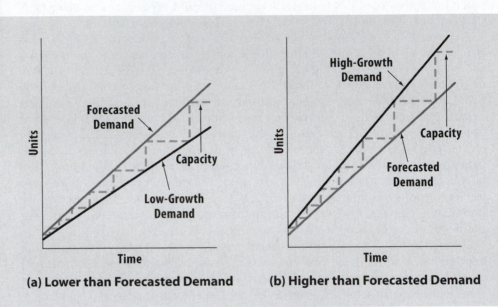

(a) Lower than Forecasted Demand   **(b) Higher than Forecasted Demand**

Learning Curves and Capacity Requirements

Learning curves

A graph of the time required to produce a unit of an item over time.

Learning rate

The percentage reduction in the time required to produce one unit each time production doubles.

It is obvious that a facility's production rate can increase as experience is gained with the production of a particular item. This learning results in changes in capacity that are especially important to recognize during the start of production. The ability to estimate long-term capacity is based on the ability to model organizational learning. This is done with **learning curves**. A learning curve is simply a graph of the time required to produce a unit of an item over time. Learning curves are usually negative exponential curves, which level out as production experience is gained. An example is shown in Figure 8.5.

Learning curves use a **learning rate** to describe the percentage reduction in the time required to produce one unit each time production doubles. The learning rate in Figure 8.5 was 70%. Thus, if the first unit took 100 hours to produce, the table below reflects the production time for cumulative units each time production experience doubles.

A 70% Learning Rate

Cumulative Production	Time per Unit (hours)
1	100
2	70
4	49
8	34.3
16	24.01
32	16.807
64	11.7649
128	8.23543

Learning curves are very easy to model using spreadsheets. To generate Figure 8.5, we used the Microsoft Excel graphing wizard to graph the above table, which was

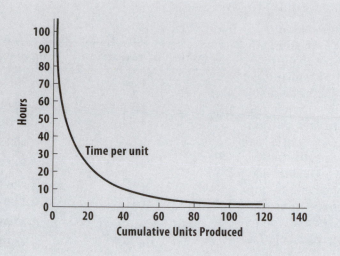

Figure 8.5

A 70% learning curve

developed in an Excel worksheet. As you can see, entering a formula that made each successive row assume a value twice that of the previous row generated the first column of the table. Entering a formula that made the value of each successive row 70% of the value of the former row generated the second column.

The boxed examples on pages 354 and 355 illustrate the computation of learning curves and the calculation of capacity requirements based on these curves.

The Economics of Capacity Decisions

Once a capacity strategy has been established, managers must address the economics of the capacity decision. What are the capacities of various facilities, and what are the costs and benefits associated with each? Seven different types of cost enter into a capacity decision:

1. Fixed costs

2. Variable costs

3. Total cost

4. Average fixed cost

5. Average variable cost

6. Average unit cost

7. Marginal cost

Fixed costs are the costs of inputs to the product-service bundle that cannot be changed over the short run. For example, a steel company has a quantifiable capital investment in each of its manufacturing plants, one that cannot be changed over the short run. Similarly, a doctor's office has to pay utility bills and salaries for employees at the front desk, regardless of the number of patients cared for in a given month. The total fixed cost for a facility is the sum of all its fixed costs over a particular period. Over the long

Fixed costs

The costs of inputs to the product-service bundle that cannot be changed over the short run.

Example 8.1

A specialty speedboat manufacturer wants to determine how long it will take to assemble components in a newly designed boat that uses a new type of fiber-composite shell. The manufacturer will use this information to establish adequate capacity to have a capacity cushion. Demand is expected to total 100 units during the first year and level out at roughly 200 units per year during the second through fifth years. In the past, the facility used to make this shell has shown a 92% learning rate. The first prototype required one crew (in one production center) 85 hours to assemble. Construct a learning curve to illustrate the expected time to produce a unit during the first 5 years of this product's life.

Step 1: Create a table of the learning curve values covering demand during planning period.

The cumulative demand during the first five years is expected to reach 900 units. Thus the table (shown at the right) will need to address production through the nine-hundredth unit. Note that the initial unit had a production time of 85 hours, and that each time the cumulative production doubles, the unit production time is reduced by 92%.

Step 2: Use the values in the table to graph the learning curve.

A 92% Learning Rate

Cumulative Production	Time per Unit (hours)
1	85
2	78.2
4	71.944
8	66.18848
16	60.8934016
32	56.02192947
64	51.54017511
128	47.41696111
256	43.62360422
512	40.13371588
1024	36.92301861

A 92% learning curve

Variable costs

The costs of inputs to the product-service bundle that vary with the number of units (or volume) produced or served.

Total cost

The sum of all the fixed and variable costs for a facility over a given period.

run, facilities can be shut down, downsized, or expanded, so the concept of fixed costs is not applicable to long-run cost functions.

Variable costs are the costs of inputs to the product-service bundle that vary with the number of units (or volume) produced or served. Over the short run, these costs may vary because of quantity discounts for large purchases, the relative size of production runs or shipments, the particular costs prescribed in collective bargaining agreements, and so on. For example, the cost of raw materials will vary according to the volume of output produced by a steel mill, and the cost of disposable products will vary according to the number of patients seen in a doctor's office. The total variable cost for a facility is the sum of all of its variable costs for the given period's volume. The sum of all the fixed and variable costs for a facility over a given period is the **total cost**.

Example 8.2

Consider the specialty speedboat manufacturer described in the last example. Assume the same 92% learning curve. Assuming they are still using a capacity cushion strategy, how many hours of capacity will be required of the company to meet production goals over the next 5 years?

Step 1: Determine the cumulative expected capacity required. (This is accomplished in the table below.)

Cumulative Production	Time per Unit (hours)	Cumulative Time Required
1	85	85
2	78.2	170
4	71.944	326.4
8	66.18848	614.176
16	60.8934016	1143.68384
32	56.02192947	2117.978266
64	51.54017511	3910.680009
128	47.41696111	7209.251216
256	43.62360422	13278.62224
512	40.13371588	24446.26492
1024	36.92301861	44994.72745

Notice that during the first year of production (in other words, the first 100 units) the time per unit will decrease from 85 hours to less than 51.55 hours. The cumulative time required column is computed as follows:

$$Ct_n = Ct_{n-1} + (Cp_n - Cp_{n-1}) \times T_{n-1}$$

Where:

Ct_n = Cumulative time required in row n,
Cp_n = Cumulative production in row n, and
T_n = Time per unit in row n

Because the firm seeks a capacity cushion, it is reasonable to estimate the cumulative capacity required over a production interval in the table above using the higher value of production time from the table. Thus, the formula uses Tn-1 as the multiplier for computation of production time during any production interval represented by the movement down one row of the table.

Step 2: Graph the cumulative time required against the cumulative production with demarcations for yearly production (see below).

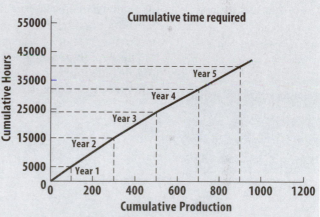

Step 3: Use the graph to determine yearly capacity required.

Note that roughly 5000 hours will be required during the first year, 10,000 during the second, 9000 during the third, and 8000 in years thereafter.

Fixed and variable costs may be used to calculate the average unit costs for the period. The **average fixed cost** is the fixed cost per unit of the product-service bundle. It is calculated by dividing the total fixed cost per period by the number of units created in the facility over the same period. The **average variable cost** is the variable cost per unit. It is computed by dividing the total variable cost for the volume in a period by the number of units created in the facility during the period. The sum of the average fixed cost and the average variable cost is the **average unit cost**.

Average fixed cost
The fixed cost per unit of the product-service bundle.

Average variable cost
The variable cost per unit.

Average unit cost
The sum of the average fixed cost and the average variable cost.

Marginal cost

The cost of providing one additional unit of the product-service bundle.

Finally, the **marginal cost** is the cost of providing one additional unit of the product-service bundle. For example, if your university has an open space in a summer class, the marginal cost of serving one additional student in that course would be very small. But if all the seats have been allocated to enrolled students and a larger classroom is not an option, the marginal cost of enrolling one more student would be much greater. At some point, the university might even have to schedule an additional section to enroll one more student.

Once the costs of various facilities have been identified, managers can use them to analyze the costs and benefits of each alternative. Simple break-even analysis is one way to estimate the volumes at which various facilities provide the most economical returns. An estimate of fixed costs and variable costs must be made for each facility. Once those estimates have been obtained, they can be plotted on a graph that shows which alternatives are better at various volumes. (This technique is described in detail in Chapters 6 and 7.)

A second method of determining the best capacity is based on an analysis of returns to scale. Because the fixed costs of operating a facility cannot be changed in the short-run, businesses need to operate at a sufficient volume to cover those costs. When a firm is operating at low volumes, it may experience **increasing returns to scale**, meaning that the average unit cost of producing $(n + 1)$ units is lower than the average unit cost of producing (n) units, as illustrated in Figure 8.6. Put another way, increasing returns to scale exist when a facility's average unit cost curve is downward sloping. For example, the average cost per patient in a 300-bed hospital is much lower when all 300 beds are full than when only 200 are full. Similarly, on an assembly line that has been designed to produce one car every 2 minutes, the production cost per vehicle will be lower at a production rate of 240 cars per 8-hour shift than at a rate of only 200 per shift.

The **law of diminishing returns** suggests that a facility cannot produce increasing returns to scale indefinitely. As volume rises, coverage of costs that are fixed over the short run may no longer dominate in the computation of average unit cost. Instead, variable

Increasing returns to scale

When operating at low volumes, the average unit cost of producing $(n + 1)$ units is lower than the average unit cost of producing (n) units, increasing returns to scale.

Law of diminishing returns

A facility cannot produce increasing returns to scale indefinitely.

Figure 8.6

Increasing and decreasing returns to scale

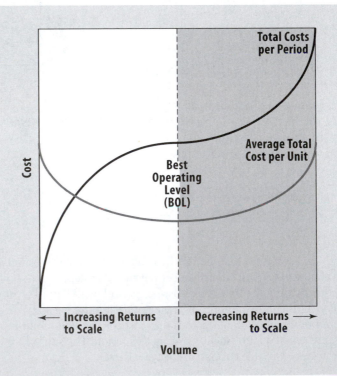

costs may begin to rise, due to problems associated with higher volumes. Thus, **decreasing returns to scale** set in: The average unit cost of producing $(n + 1)$ units rises above the average unit cost of producing (n) units, and the average unit cost curve begins to slope upward, as shown in Figure 8.6. For example, maintaining a steady level of 400 patients in a 300-bed hospital would probably require significant overtime expenditures, along with equipment rental costs and other unusual expenses. So, too, producing 400 cars per 8-hour shift on an assembly line designed to make just one car every 2 minutes would take an economic toll.

The volume, or scale of operations, at which average total cost per unit is minimized is called the facility's **best operating level (BOL)**, as shown in Figure 8.6. Suppose Tom's airline offers a daily flight from Ontario Airport in southern California to a small airport near some ski resorts in British Columbia. Service on the route is maintained year round, even though monthly ticket sales range from a low of about 500 in the summer months to a high of approximately 5500 in December and January. Table 8.2 provides information on the monthly costs associated with the airline's facilities in British Columbia. Tickets sell for $190 (column 2), and monthly fixed costs total $200,000 (column 3). The fixed costs include such items as lease payments on the aircraft that are locked in by contract, gate rentals, the fuel cost required to fly an empty plane over the route, and staffing for gates and flights at the minimal level required to offer the service. At a marginal cost of $60 per ticket (column 6), average variable cost is estimated at $60 per ticket (column 8) up to a volume of 3000 passengers (column 1). Variable cost covers such items as the additional fuel required per passenger, per passenger airport use fees, commissions paid to travel agents, and food and supplies consumed by passengers. What is this facility's best operating level? Its profit-maximizing level?

Notice that at volumes of 3000 passengers or fewer, per unit profit (column 11) increases. Thus, the airline enjoys increasing returns to scale at volumes of 3000 passengers or fewer. Beyond 3000 passengers a month, the airline may need to add some additional crew members or it may have to pay overtime to ground support personnel. As a result, marginal cost (column 6) grows to $180 per passenger for volumes between 3000 and 4500 passengers. In other words, at passenger volumes above 3000, decreasing returns to scale set in. The increase in volume reduces per unit profit (column 11) when volume rises above 3000 passengers a month. For the route to British Columbia, then, this facility's best operating level is 3000 passengers.

Figure 8.7 shows the short-run cost curves obtained from the data in Table 8.2. Notice that average total cost continues to decline as long as it is greater than the per unit marginal cost. Thus, the minimum point on the average total cost curve is the point where marginal cost and average total cost are equal.

Table 8.2 also shows that profit is not necessarily maximized at the best operating level. Indeed, up to the point where marginal cost exceeds marginal revenue, or price per unit (column 2), the airline will make more money by carrying more passengers. Beyond 3000 passengers the airline does not make as much money on each additional passenger, but it still makes a profit as long as it carries no more than 4500 passengers. With more than 4500 passengers a month, marginal cost reaches $360 per ticket, which exceeds the marginal revenue per ticket. Because marginal cost exceeds price per unit, total profit begins to decline. The profit-maximizing level is therefore 4500 passengers.

You may be wondering why an airline would consider booking beyond the profit-maximizing level. Over the short term, booking beyond the best operating level, or even the profit-maximizing level, is not uncommon. The airline sacrifices short-run profits to build customer satisfaction and ensure long-run profitability. A business may incur costly overtime or weekend labor costs if it gets an order out for a big or important customer. In fact, Tom's airline overbooks on purpose, offering a seat to everyone possible during the peak season, in order to build a loyal customer base

Decreasing returns to scale

A situation where variable costs may begin to rise due to problems associated with higher volumes.

Best operating level (BOL)

The volume, or scale of operations, at which the average total cost per unit is minimized.

Figure 8.7

Short-run costs for an airline route (from Table 8.2)

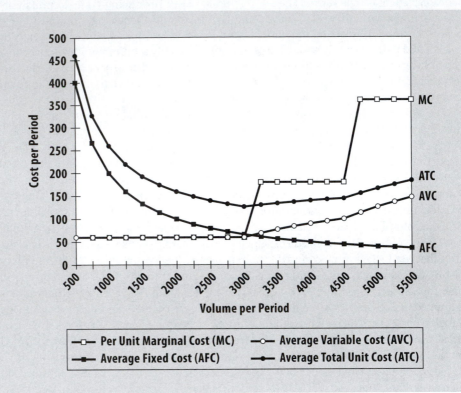

during the off-season. Sometimes the airline has to offer travel vouchers or hotel rooms to compensate passengers who have been bumped from an overbooked flight—a practice that obviously raises its costs.

Clearly, the scale on which a business operates has an economic effect on the business's returns. An **economy of scale** is the economic advantage that is often associated with the ability to operate at higher volumes. High levels of demand or required capacity, purchase discounts for large volumes, the practice of carrying large inventories, and the use of dedicated equipment to produce standardized product-service bundles can all provide economies of scale. The reverse of an economy of scale, a **diseconomy of scale**, is an economic disadvantage associated with operating at higher volumes. Low levels of demand, high costs for finished goods transportation, an inability to carry large inventories due to a limited shelf life, and the costs of paperwork and bureaucracy can produce diseconomies of scale.

Over the long run, based on expected demand, businesses will adjust their capacity to avoid diseconomies of scale and obtain economies of scale. Tom's airline could shut down, downsize, expand, or maintain the size of its current facilities in British Columbia. Such long-term capacity choices represent a variety of possible short-run cost curves. Tom's airline is considering upgrading its facility in British Columbia. At the airline's current terminal in British Columbia, Facility A, passengers must disembark via an outdoor stairway and walk to the terminal. The costs associated with this facility were summarized in Table 8.2. At the proposed Facility B, passengers could disembark via a covered walkway that connects directly to the terminal. Facility B would have relatively high monthly fixed costs of about $500,000 (see Figure 8.8a) but would lower variable costs to $40 per ticketed passenger, up to a monthly total of 9000 passengers. Beyond that point,

Economy of scale

The economic advantage that is often associated with the ability to operate at higher volumes.

Diseconomy of scale

An economic disadvantage associated with operating at higher volumes.

Table 8.2

Monthly Costs and Profits
for B. C. Airline Route

Vol. (1)	Price per Unit (2)	Fixed Cost (3)	Variable Cost (4)	Total Cost (5)	Per Unit Marginal Cost (6)	Average Fixed Cost (7)	Average Variable Cost (8)	Average Total Cost (9)	Total Profit (10)	Profit per Unit (11)
500	$190	$200,000	$30,000.00	$230,000.00	$60.00	$400.00	$60.00	$460.00	−135000	($270.00)
750	$190	$200,000	$45,000.00	$245,000.00	$60.00	$266.67	$60.00	$326.67	−102500	($136.67)
1000	$190	$200,000	$60,000.00	$260,000.00	$60.00	$200.00	$60.00	$260.00	−70000	($70.00)
1250	$190	$200,000	$75,000.00	$275,000.00	$60.00	$160.00	$60.00	$220.00	−37500	($30.00)
1500	$190	$200,000	$90,000.00	$290,000.00	$60.00	$133.33	$60.00	$193.33	−5000	($3.33)
1750	$190	$200,000	$105,000.00	$305,000.00	$60.00	$114.29	$60.00	$174.29	27500	$15.71
2000	$190	$200,000	$120,000.00	$320,000.00	$60.00	$100.00	$60.00	$160.00	60000	$30.00
2250	$190	$200,000	$135,000.00	$335,000.00	$60.00	$88.89	$60.00	$148.89	92500	$41.11
2500	$190	$200,000	$150,000.00	$350,000.00	$60.00	$80.00	$60.00	$140.00	125000	$50.00
2750	$190	$200,000	$165,000.00	$365,000.00	$60.00	$72.73	$60.00	$132.73	157500	$57.27
3000	$190	$200,000	$180,000.00	$380,000.00	$60.00	$66.67	$60.00	$126.67	190000	$63.33
3250	$190	$200,000	$225,000.00	$425,000.00	$180.00	$61.54	$69.23	$130.77	192500	$59.23
3500	$190	$200,000	$270,000.00	$470,000.00	$180.00	$57.14	$77.14	$134.29	195000	$55.71
3750	$190	$200,000	$315,000.00	$515,000.00	$180.00	$53.33	$84.00	$137.33	197500	$52.67
4000	$190	$200,000	$360,000.00	$560,000.00	$180.00	$50.00	$90.00	$140.00	200000	$50.00
4250	$190	$200,000	$405,000.00	$605,000.00	$180.00	$47.06	$95.29	$142.35	202500	$47.65
4500	$190	$200,000	$450,000.00	$650,000.00	$180.00	$44.44	$100.00	$144.44	205000	$45.56
4750	$190	$200,000	$540,000.00	$740,000.00	$360.00	$42.11	$113.68	$155.79	162500	$34.21
5000	$190	$200,000	$630,000.00	$830,000.00	$360.00	$40.00	$126.00	$166.00	120000	$24.00
5250	$190	$200,000	$720,000.00	$920,000.00	$360.00	$38.10	$137.14	$175.24	77500	$14.76
5500	$190	$200,000	$810,000.00	$1,010,000.00	$360.00	$36.36	$147.27	$183.64	35000	$6.36

Figure 8.8

Short-run costs for two airline gate arrangements

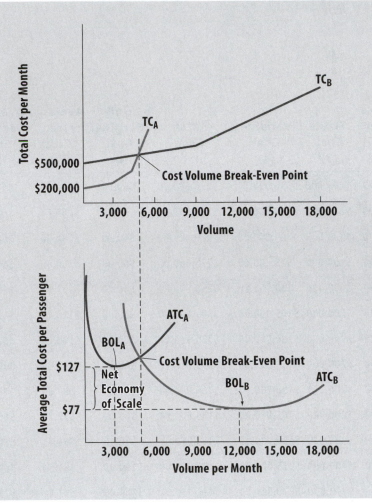

they would rise to $80 per passenger up to a maximum capacity of 18,000 passengers per month. What is the best operating level for each facility? The break-even volume?

Figure 8.8b shows that the best operating level for Facility A, BOL$_A$, is 3000 passengers at the minimum average total cost of $127 (also seen in Table 8.2). This passenger volume is much lower than the best operating level for Facility B, BOL$_B$, which turns out to be 12,000 passengers at the minimum average total cost of $77. The break-even volume—where the two average total cost curves, ATC$_A$ and ATC$_B$, intersect—is about 4600 passengers.

Thus, if the airline's long-term forecasts suggest a growth in demand on the route to British Columbia, managers might consider expanding the terminal's capacity. The net economy of scale associated with the move would be the difference between their best operating levels, about $50 per ticketed passenger. However, managers probably would not make the change unless they expected monthly demand to be higher than the break-even volume. If the demand for tickets to this destination grows beyond the break-even point during the off-season, managers should look into the larger facility.

Figure 8.9 shows a set of short-run average cost (SRAC) curves, which yield a long-run average cost (LRAC) curve. On this long-run curve, economies of scale are gained

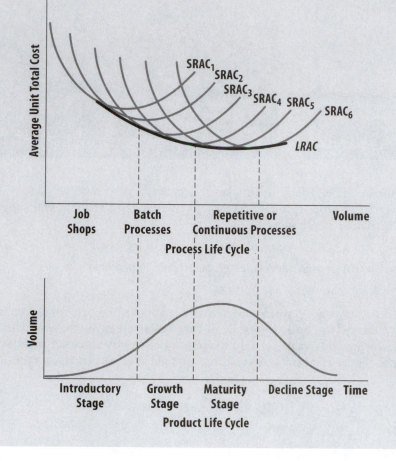

Figure 8.9

Long-run average cost across the product and process life cycles

up to a certain point by changing processes, which means moving from one short-run average cost curve to another. After a certain point, diseconomies of scale would cause long-run average costs to increase. Ideally, managers would avoid operating at a volume that is large enough to incur diseconomies of scale. Because of the relationship between the product life cycle (PLC) and long-run capacity decisions, the pattern of the long-run average cost curve is rather predictable up to the maturity stage. During the introductory stage of the product life cycle, demand is small, technological standards are less than certain, and customer preferences are still unclear. As a result, job shop and batch production facilities, which have low fixed costs and high variable costs, are best suited to this stage. During the growth stage of the cycle, firms begin to move to larger facilities with higher fixed costs and lower variable costs. This trend continues into the maturity stage, until product volume begins to decline, at which point large facilities with high fixed cost and low variable cost become less efficient. As the market continues to decline and volumes drop, the large facilities may be replaced with smaller facilities that have higher variable costs but lower fixed costs (such as batch processes and job shops). This cycle of process changes, which results from product life cycles, is referred to as the **process life cycle (PSLC)**.

Like the process life cycle, a firm's facility strategy will have a major impact on its long-run average cost curve. A facility strategy determines whether a firm will have a

Process life cycle (PSLC)

As the market continues to decline and volumes drop, the large facilities may be replaced with smaller facilities that have higher variable costs but lower fixed costs (such as batch processes and job shops).

The Image Works

AP Photo/Joerg Sarbach

Smaller bottling and packaging operations, such as the process at the microbrewery pictured at left rely much more heavily on labor than the automated but less flexible lines of large beverage companies as shown in the right-hand photo.

small number of large facilities or a larger number of small facilities, as well as what combination of product variety and geographic range its facilities will supply. For instance, facilities might supply:

◗ A wide range of products on a global, regional, or local basis

◗ A narrow range of products on a global, regional, or local basis

◗ Some combination of these options

Figure 8.10 shows how process and industry factors help to determine a company's facility strategy. The horizontal scale in this figure represents the extent to which manufacturing adds value to the product-service bundle. Product manufacturers appear at the far left; pure services at the far right. The vertical scale represents the

Figure 8.10

Common multi-plant strategies

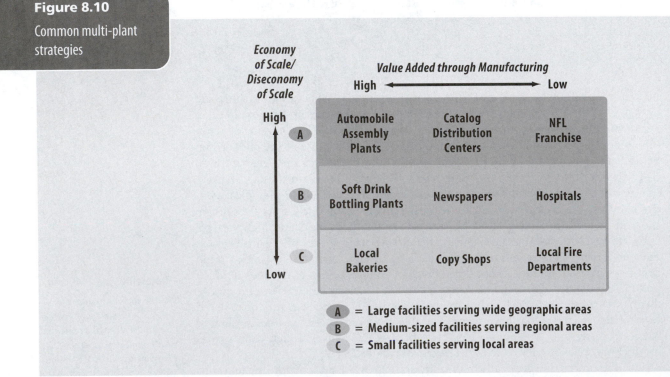

extent to which industry factors do or do not provide economies of scale. Where markets are large, product-service bundles are standardized, production volumes are high, and extensive personal interaction with the customer is not required, bigger facilities are usually better. In these cases, the economic benefits of a large-scale operation usually outweigh the economic drawbacks. This rule applies to services as well as to products. For example, National Football League (NFL) franchises, catalog distribution centers, and automobile assembly plants all benefit from economies of scale and all employ large facilities (see Figure 8.10). Similarly, bakeries, copy shops, and fire departments all experience diseconomies of scale. They are likely to be small and local in nature. As this discussion suggests, a facility's capacity is closely related to its location.

Location Decisions

If you have an address of your own, chances are you have made a *location decision*. Your complete address indicates your country, region (the first three digits of your zip code), state, city, street, and the exact location of your residence. Notice that the order of your address represents a clear hierarchy. When you chose your location, you probably did not have to decide on all levels of the hierarchy. You probably took the country where you would live for granted, and you may have had a clear preference for a particular region or state, based on your family and personal relationships. If you had already chosen a college or a particular job, even the city of your residence may have been predetermined. Thus, not all location decisions require explicit consideration of each level of the hierarchy. As individuals, we get into the decision-making loop at a particular level, then move to more and more specific levels.

Businesses, too, get into location decisions at varying levels of the location hierarchy. Bakeries, copy shops, and fire departments tend to be small-scale facilities that serve local areas. As such, their location decisions are dominated by local and site-specific concerns. Soft drink bottlers, newspapers, and hospitals are medium-sized facilities and must therefore consider regional issues as well as local and site-specific concerns. Large-scale service and manufacturing facilities, such as automotive assembly plants, catalog distribution centers, and NFL teams, must consider national and international issues as well as regional, local, and site-specific concerns.

The problem of locating a major league sports franchise or stadium is a good example of the hierarchical considerations in location decisions. Although the NFL may someday consider locating a franchise outside the United States, to date it has been unwilling to do so. To maintain a strong following throughout the United States, however, the NFL tries hard to be even-handed in locating new franchises. In deciding where to start new franchises or where to allow existing franchises to relocate, the NFL has considered regional demographics, business demographics (indicative of the market for luxury boxes among corporate clients), and the distribution of existing franchises. Local factors, such as a city council's willingness to fund the construction of a new stadium, are also important. Finally, before awarding a franchise to a city, the NFL must be certain that it has a suitable site for a stadium. Thus, the franchise location decision is an effort to obtain the best mix of regional, local, and site-specific factors.

The Location Decision Hierarchy

Table 8.3 lists the major issues in location decisions, categorized by their level in the location hierarchy. We will begin with the highest level global-international concerns.

Table 8.3

Considerations in the
Location Decision by Levels
in the Location Hierarchy

Level in the Location Hierarchy	Considerations That Are Usually Important to the Decision Maker
Global/International	• International trade issues (currency exchange risk, balance of trade, quotas, tariffs, etc.) • Market access issues (free trade agreements such as NAFTA, consumer sentiment toward imported goods, etc. • Labor issues (availability, wages, skills and training, regulations) • Supply issues (availability of raw material, local content laws, etc.) • Political concerns (stability of current regime, risk of asset nationalization, local ownership laws, etc.) • Cultural issues (compatibility of business practices and products with local culture) • Legal issues (environmental regulations, accounting and reporting requirements, etc.) • Quality of life issues (desirability as a place to live)
Regional	• Supply issues (availability of material inputs) • Market and demographic factors • Economic conditions • Costs of key inputs and advertising media • Labor climate • Quality-of-life issues
Community	• Transportation options and costs (by river, sea, rail, truck, pipeline, and air) • Utility options and costs • Civil services • Financial incentives • Legal climate and community receptiveness • Environmental concerns
Site Specific	• Fixed costs (land, construction, taxes, etc.) • Operating costs (maintenance, transportation, utilities, labor, etc.) • Access concerns (for customers, suppliers, utilities, etc.) • Work environment (crime statistics, nearby eating establishments, etc.) • Key questions, what mix has worked well for the firm in the past?

Decision makers who are considering expanding into a new country or geographic region must consider macroeconomic, demographic, and political issues of long-term significance. They must consider international trade issues, such as currency exchange risks, import-export quotas, and balance of trade. Access to a country's or trading block's market may also be important. The availability of skilled labor, materials, and support services; political, cultural, and legal concerns; and quality-of-life issues—all these global-international issues must be considered prior to a significant investment in a new country.

Once the decision has been made to locate a facility in a particular country or trading block, decision makers must choose a region based on regional issues like geographic, demographic, or cultural differences. For example, the geography, culture, and demographic trends of the southeastern United States are quite different from the geography, culture, and demographic trends of the Midwest, Southwest, Pacific Northwest, and New England.

Companies that want to locate close to their customer base commonly compare regions based on market characteristics, such as customer quality, customer quantity, and customer value. **Customer quality** refers to the portion of the market that matches the customer profile for which a product-service bundle is designed. It indicates how hard a company will have to work to get customers. **Customer quantity** is an indicator of market size, stated in terms of the total number of buyers—for example, number of households, number of individuals in a particular demographic category, or number of companies that use a product-service bundle. **Customer value** describes the spending potential of a spending unit. Average household expenditure, average disposable income, and average production volume (for industrial customers) are measures of customer value.

Once a firm has identified the right region for a new facility, it must find one or more specific communities in which to locate the facility. In evaluating various communities, decision makers will look at specific community issues, such as the cost of inputs and transportation, the quality of the infrastructure, environmental regulations and other legal issues, and so on. Frequently, communities will offer significant tax abatements and infrastructural improvements to a particular site, in the hope of attracting a new facility. When BMW chose to build an automotive assembly plant in Spartanburg, South Carolina, it received economic incentives worth more than $150 million from the state, county, and city and from local businesses, including millions of dollars worth of infrastructural improvements, from the purchase and removal of nearby residential buildings to the construction of new roads and utility pipelines. (To date, the economic benefits of these incentives to residents of the state of South Carolina, in the form of increased tax revenues and economic activity, have far exceeded their cost.)

Occasionally, rather than selecting a locality where support services are already in place, a company will look for an undeveloped area where it can start from scratch. Such facilities are called greenfields. The idea is to build exactly what the firm needs, rather than to live with the results of past decisions. The Saturn plant in Springhill, Tennessee, is a greenfield facility.

Companies tend to learn from their experiences in site selection. Often, two or three sites that seem to have identical location profiles yield vastly different operational results. After looking at many existing sites, managers begin to see what makes a location good for their specific purposes. They find that a good site for a McDonald's franchise is not necessarily a good site for a Wendy's. The best approach to site selection is to analyze the demographic and performance characteristics of the firm's existing sites and select new sites based on those factors most closely associated with superior operational results.

Virtually no detail is irrelevant to a site selection. You may not think that the side of the road makes much difference, but if the breakfast business is really important to your fastfood service, you will have a strong preference for locations on the right-hand side of the road for commuters on major arteries (in the U.S.). Or perhaps you think that the previous ownership and use of land does not matter. But in fact, under current law, property owners are liable for environmental remediation costs, even if an environmental problem was created by a past owner. Thus, the financial strength of previous owners, as well as the previous uses of the land, are of critical importance. These

Customer quality

The portion of the market that matches the customer profile for which a product-service bundle is designed. It indicates how hard a company will have to work to get customers.

Customer quantity

An indicator of market size, stated in terms of the total number of buyers—for example, number of households, number of individuals in a particular demographic category, or number of companies that use a product-service bundle.

Customer value

The spending potential of a spending unit such as average household expenditure, average disposable income, and average production volume (for industrial customers).

INTEGRATING OM:

Boeing Looks to the Windy City and Beyond

Boeing has a very large presence in the northwest state of Washington. Currently headquartered in Seattle, Boeing is one the state's largest single employer. However, with a rapidly changing industry, they have found coordinating their eastwardly growing enterprise of plants and suppliers from the west coast increasingly difficult and costly. Recently, Boeing selected Chicago for the location of their new world headquarters following an intense three-way sweepstakes that leaves the bulk of Boeing's Seattle work force behind. Passing over runners-up Dallas-Fort Worth and Denver, the aerospace giant ended months of suspense and made final its decision to move its corporate office from the city where it was founded 85 years ago. Boeing executives informed the cities of the verdict after their corporate jet took off from Seattle for a secret destination that turned out to be Midway Airport in Chicago.

The three cities had been competing since March, when Boeing announced plans to leave Seattle to save money and be more central to its operations in 26 states. Each city offered millions of dollars in tax breaks and other incentives. But Chicago offered the sweetest deal—state income tax breaks and other aid estimated at $25 million to $30 million—and its central location and air links are unmatched. "We looked at three very exciting metropolitan areas in which to base our company," Boeing chairman Phil Condit said in a news release issued while the jet was in flight. "It was a very difficult decision." However, Illinois state and local officials were jubilant. The Illinois House burst into applause at the announcement.

Boeing brings fewer than 500 executives to Chicago but immediately becomes Illinois' biggest company. Its $51.3 billion in 2000 revenues will rank it ahead of Sears, Motorola, McDonald's, and United Airlines. Boeing plans to move Sept. 4 to its new headquarters—a 36-story office tower on the west bank of the Chicago River, just north of the city's two main train stations. The building formerly was the headquarters of Morton International.

From a manufacturing standpoint, the company will keep its massive aircraft factories and design and development facilities in the Seattle area, where 79,000 of its 199,000 employees work. In fact, Everett, Washington, is the front runner in the location sweepstakes for winning the contract to build the new Boeing 7E7. The availability of an existing plant and a trained work force are the main factors in favor of Everett as well as a high quality of work life and a mild climate. Congested transportation, high cost of labor, and tough environmental laws work against Everett and have Boeing looking at other cities as well.

Other favorites under consideration include several cities in Texas where a business friendly government, lower labor costs, bigger congressional delegation, and large aerospace base work in their favor. Distance from ocean ports (except for Houston) and summer heat work against them.

Another front-runner state is Alabama, with potential sites near Decatur, Mobile, and Huntsville. Positives include an excellent recruitment track record, generous governmental incentives, lower labor costs, and existing Boeing operations. However, a lack of suitable existing plant capacity, sites that depend on river barge transportation, and other sites that are environmentally risky will be a negative for Alabama.

As the possibilities are considered, other contenders include Savannah, GA, Charleston, SC, Gulfport-Biloxi, MS, and several cities in Arkansas. The issues they will consider, as with the favorites, include labor cost, government incentives, and transportation between this plant and a network of existing plants across 26 states. What's the prize at the end of the sweepstakes? A $500 million plant and 1,200 jobs. What governor doesn't want that on their resume?

Source: Adapted from "Boeing lands on Chicago as its new headquarters," Associated Press, May 11, 2001, reporter Ted S. Warren; and "Boeing stakes favorite places for plant," *Tacoma News Tribune*, June 10, 2003

and other site-specific issues—such as land and building costs, utility costs, safety, and property taxes—are of great importance in selecting a location for a facility.

Locating Near Suppliers or Customers

We have seen that proximity to supplies and markets frequently dominates facility location decisions. But because the major markets for a company's products are rarely located in the same area as its raw materials, decision makers must often decide whether to locate close to their suppliers, close to customers, or somewhere in between.

The location of hungry customers is used to determine the location of the next fast food restaurant rather than where the buns, meat, and french-fries suppliers are located. That makes them a "weight added" businesses.

During the early 1980s when General Motors (GM) was planning the Saturn Corporation, location issues were obviously very important for them to consider. Both the need for economies of scale in automobile manufacturing and the unique Saturn concept made location important. For political reasons, the plant had to be located in the United States. For logistical reasons, potential supplier locations and geographic proximity to the U.S. market were critical. Therefore, GM narrowed the location to the Midwest. Governors from no less than nine states made pitches with economic incentives to attract the new company. By the time GM announced the choice of Spring Hill, Tennessee, in July 1985, it had looked at possibilities in all nine states, a number of cities, and numerous sites. Availability of skilled labor, economic incentives, and, most importantly, good logistical access for inbound supplies and outbound cars were all keys to the final choice.

Shipping weight, an indicator of transportation time and cost, is a critical factor in facility location decisions in manufacturing facilities. Depending on the product-service bundle, some facilities add weight to a product, while others reduce it. **Weight-added operations** tend to use converging material flows to produce items that are much more costly to transport than the supplies from which they are made. For example, assembling an airplane, large ship, or other construction project is a weight-added operation. For that reason most ships are assembled close to water, most airplanes are made close to a runway, and most construction projects are built entirely on site. Naturally, the facilities that are used to build a bridge must be located at the bridge. By contrast, mining, agriculture, and refining are **weight-reduced operations**, which use diverging material flows to stratify objects according to their market value. Transporting the dirt that clings to iron ore or copper over great distances makes little sense. Similarly, lumber is usually cut to standard dimensions and dried prior to shipment over long distances. Thus, it is advantageous to locate mining and lumber facilities near suppliers. Figure 8.11 illustrates the spectrum of weight-added and weight-reduced operations in manufacturing.

A quick look at some maps will demonstrate the significance of the weight-added, weight-reduced spectrum in facility location decisions. Figure 8.12 shows the location concentration of facilities in the wood and forest products industries. (Note that these maps are based on aggregate economic data and may not reflect the concentration of facilities for any one firm.) Figure 8.12a shows that the greatest concentration of logging activity is in the southeastern and western states. Sawmills, planing mills, hardwood dimension mills, and flooring mills all house weight-reducing activities—the

Weight-added operations

The use of converging material flows to produce items that are much more costly to transport than the supplies from which they are made.

Weight-reduced operations

The use of diverging material flows to stratify objects according to their market value.

Figure 8.11

The weight/access spectrum of operations

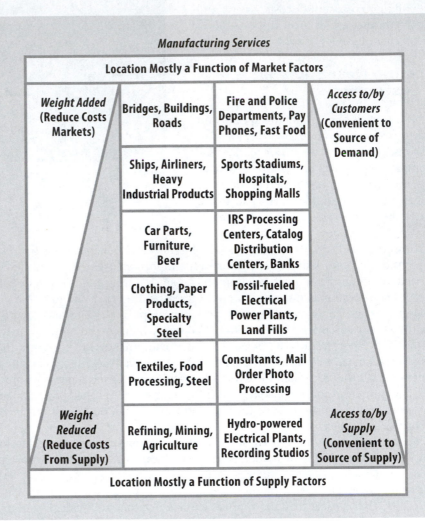

Manufacturing Services

Location Mostly a Function of Market Factors

Weight Added (Reduce Costs Markets)	Bridges, Buildings, Roads	Fire and Police Departments, Pay Phones, Fast Food	Access to/by Customers (Convenient to Source of Demand)
	Ships, Airliners, Heavy Industrial Products	Sports Stadiums, Hospitals, Shopping Malls	
	Car Parts, Furniture, Beer	IRS Processing Centers, Catalog Distribution Centers, Banks	
	Clothing, Paper Products, Specialty Steel	Fossil-fueled Electrical Power Plants, Land Fills	
	Textiles, Food Processing, Steel	Consultants, Mail Order Photo Processing	
Weight Reduced (Reduce Costs From Supply)	Refining, Mining, Agriculture	Hydro-powered Electrical Plants, Recording Studios	Access to/by Supply (Convenient to Source of Supply)

Location Mostly a Function of Supply Factors

conversion of raw timber of varying shapes, lengths, and water content into dried lumber cut to standard dimensions. Most of these plants are concentrated close to the timber sources in the Southeast. Wood products—for example, cabinets—that are made from the output of these lumber mills are manufactured closer to customers, in the Midwest and West, because they are heavy and bulky to ship (weight added).

Figure 8.12b shows the distribution of facilities that make and use paper products. This logging activity is also concentrated in the Southeast and West. Paper mills, however, are concentrated in the Midwest and Northeast—a distribution very different from that of the sawmills. The wood chips and dried pulp used in papermaking (whether they are the product of logging, a byproduct of lumber milling, or recycled material) can be transported easily, with no concern for damage. Paper, on the other hand, must be protected from the elements, because it can easily be damaged in storage and transit. Consequently, paper-making facilities are concentrated close to the areas where paper is used to print books and newspapers.

In the location of service facilities, managers must consider the logistics of access rather than material logistics issues. Convenient access to the demand source, customers, or the source of supply becomes more critical than the cost of moving

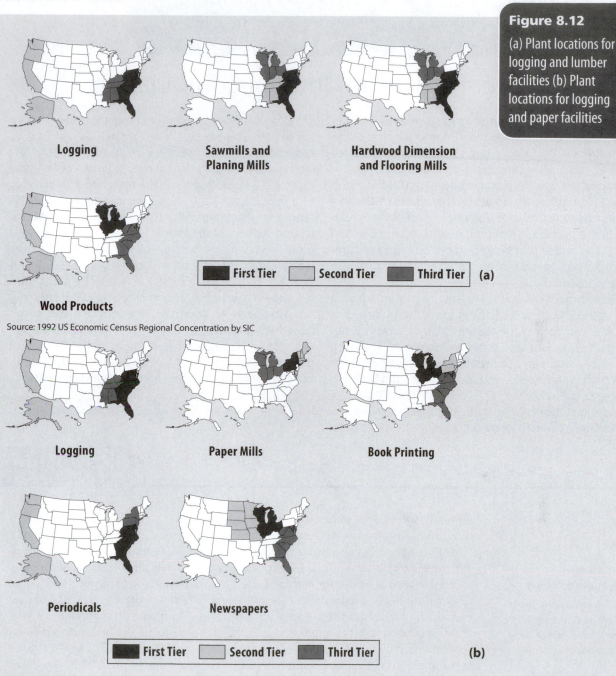

Figure 8.12

(a) Plant locations for logging and lumber facilities (b) Plant locations for logging and paper facilities

Logging

Sawmills and Planing Mills

Hardwood Dimension and Flooring Mills

Wood Products

First Tier   Second Tier   Third Tier   (a)

Source: 1992 US Economic Census Regional Concentration by SIC

Logging

Paper Mills

Book Printing

Periodicals

Newspapers

First Tier   Second Tier   Third Tier   (b)

Source: 1992 US Economic Census Regional Concentration by SIC

things. For example, Figure 8.11 also suggests that locating a fire department near the customer base is much more important than locating it near a training facility or to the homes of staff members. In these cases, a small force of professionals serves a large number of customers, most of whom would not want to pay taxes for a facility located an hour from their homes. In contrast, a large number of professionals at a research hospital may serve a relatively small group of patients. Traveling a day or two to such a facility is worthwhile if a patient benefits from the expertise of so many specialists.

INTEGRATING OM:

Fire and Water Provide an Unusual Combination

When the alarm sounds inside Fire Station 95 in Dublin, Ohio, a suburb of Columbus, some of the firefighters ride down a two-story tube slide rather than a pole. The twisting slide, built because of an abnormally tall vehicle storage bay, isn't the building's most unusual feature, however. That would be the two million gallons of water above the firefighters' quarters in the building. The combination water tower/fire station is an idea that's catching on nationally as communities struggle to locate services amid sprawling development.

Government officials favor the unusual structure, a fire station built within the support structure of a water tower, for several reasons. Within growing municipalities, vacant land is becoming scarce. The need for a fire station and fire protection sometimes overlaps with water needs, and the combination building saves tax dollars.

Administrators of the township where this fire station/water tower is located consider the project an example of governments working together to save tax dollars. The tower, owned by the City of Dublin, provides a multiple use at far less cost than purchasing land and constructing a new station. Washington township is leasing space in the tower from the city for $1 a year. Because the water tower already had an exterior shell, the required construction work for the fire station was primarily interior work. The idea gained momentum after township officials toured a similar water tower fire station in Downers Grove, Ill., and heard of another such facility in Texas. The fire station has drawn a lot of attention since its 1998 opening.

Living beneath two million gallons of water hasn't posed any problem for Dublin firefighters, and the 2 1/2 story tube slide, while it might delight kids at a playground, isn't for everyone. According to the Dublin fire chief, some firefighters prefer to take the stairs.

Source: Adapted from *Cincinnati Enquirer*, Dec. 5, 2002, A1, reporter Karen Vance; and http://www.cpmra.muohio.edu/washingtontownship/page5.htm, Sept. 29, 2005

Competitive clustering

An approach used by motels and automobile dealerships to locate themselves close to competitors.

Saturation marketing

An approach (used by Au Bon Pain, a croissant sandwich restaurant chain and others) that segments high-density urban areas into small, focused markets such as shopping malls and office buildings.

Similarly, since films can be easily distributed once they have been created, movie studios usually locate close to the sources of acting and editing talent (i.e., Hollywood).

Service operations also feature unique approaches to location decisions. For example, motels and automobile dealerships are purposefully located near competitors—a strategy known as **competitive clustering**. Motels cluster around major airports and tourist destinations because that is where the customers are. Auto dealerships are located near each other to take advantage of consumer behavior—comparison shopping.

The **saturation marketing** approach segments high-density urban areas into small, focused markets such as shopping malls and office buildings. Starbucks Coffee restaurants, for example, may be located within very short distances of one another. While some sales cannibalization among restaurants can occur with this strategy, extremely close proximity to customers (shoppers and office workers) is viewed as the key to increased sales.

Today, with e-commerce utilizing the World Wide Web to create clicks and mortar enterprises that compete with bricks and mortar systems, business need to consider virtual access through technology as well as physical access. Substituting virtual access through technology for physical proximity is a strategy used by many organizations such as libraries, call centers, health-care providers and retailers. In the case of health care, clinics are able to utilize technology to deliver services to remote or hard to reach areas (including prisons) that would otherwise not receive service. High-resolution cameras and real-time communications equipment permit physicians to diagnose problems and prescribe remedies without being physically present. Automatic payroll deposits and deductions, and banking by computer and telephone reduce the need for bank customers to travel to bank offices. University distance learning programs provide education access to people for whom traveling to campus is inconvenient. In these cases, technology enables organizations to increase their customer base and geographic reach without substantially increasing costs.

Supply Chain Management and Collocation

Clearly, the way in which suppliers and customers interact is an important consideration in facility location decisions. Businesses have been moving toward more cooperative supply chain management, in the interest of providing greater value to the customer. Rather than locate an operation near the customer, they may choose to locate inside a customer's facility. In fact, a Volkswagen facility in Brazil took this idea to an extreme. At this plant, suppliers are completely responsible for assembling that portion of the vehicle in which their material is used.

While locating one's assembly workers under a customer's roof is becoming a more common practice, stationing personnel with other responsibilities at a customer's facility is a well established practice. Suppliers' design personnel are often located at the customer's facility, where they are full-fledged members of the product design team. Much of the task of designing new products and services is in effect outsourced, without any proprietary information leaving the facility. Likewise, quality personnel routinely work at suppliers' and customers' plants, in order to perform inspections and resolve problems quickly. Rather than stationing transportation and logistical personnel in a facility of their own, they are better located in the facilities where shipments originate or where shipments are sent.

Finally, collocated suppliers frequently do not receive purchase orders telling them what to ship and when. Instead, their inventory planning and control personnel make those decisions at the customer's facilities. These people know the customer's material requirements and are responsible for making sure they are satisfied. Given the ability to electronically share sales information gathered by point-of-sale systems in retail establishments, many suppliers now "own" their part of an assembled product until that product has been sold to the consumer.

All these forms of collocation help firms to manage across functions and improve customer service. By breaking down communication barriers, they facilitate joint problem solving and process improvement.

Decision-Making Tools for Locating Facilities

Given the impact of location decisions, managers will use every tool at their disposal to make the best possible choices. In studying and using these decision-making tools, it is important to remember the old maxim, "Garbage in, garbage out." Managers must have accurate and current information in order to make good decisions. In fact, the quality of the information that is used may have a much more significant impact on the quality of the decision than the choice of decision-making technique.

Typically, managers will tap at least three sources of data in making a facility location decision. One source, **syndicated data**, is found in existing databases and provides demographic information about the lifestyles, needs, and expectations of potential customers. Syndicated data generally does not provide all the information managers need, and it may not be current or accurate. In that case, managers must be willing to incur the expense of gathering and maintaining the additional data they need. In conducting **primary research**, managers gather the specific information they need about past

Syndicated data

Information found in existing databases which provides demographic information about the lifestyles, needs, and expectations of potential customers.

Primary research

A process which involves managers in gathering the specific information they need about past and potential customers.

Point of sale (POS) data

Information that is captured when the customer actually makes a purchase. It is even more valuable than primary research because it indicates what customers do, not just what they say they do.

Spatial data warehouse

A database including geographic information that can be accessed by users of a client-server computer system.

Global positioning system (GPS)

A highly-effective mechanism for location identification.

Geographic information system (GIS)

A software tool that is used to improve spatially oriented decisions.

Geographic boundaries

The lines of demarcation that allow spatial data to be categorized.

and potential customers. Although this type of data is more expensive than syndicated data, it may be more meaningful, because the manager can choose the individuals to include in the study and the exact questions to be asked. Finally, **point-of-sale (POS) data**, captured when the customer actually makes a purchase, is even more valuable than primary research because it indicates what customers do, not just what they say they do. Rather than suggesting what the firm's customer base could be, POS data shows what the customer base really is.

GEOGRAPHIC INFORMATION SYSTEMS (GIS)

An estimated 80% or more of business data has some spatial context—a street address, plant name, or ZIP code. Until recently, however, many business databases did not include information about location. But the development of systems for storing and sharing large amounts of data, tagging data by location, and displaying it visually has put a wealth of information at decision-makers' fingertips.

A **spatial data warehouse** is a database that includes geographic information that can be accessed by users of a client-server computer system. Such databases may receive input from and transmit data to remote locations, either stationary or mobile, via communication links such as phone lines and digital satellite transmission. Thus, instead of building and maintaining a number of separate databases, companies can build one large database and use this to perform more extensive analysis of their business activities and market demographics.

The **global positioning system (GPS)** is a tool that provides precise location identification values for inclusion in spatial data warehouses. (Developed by the military to guide missiles, the satellite-based GPS can identify a location's latitude, longitude, and altitude to within a few millimeters.) GPS data enables decision makers to pinpoint business activity on maps. The applications are almost endless. Using a GPS receiver, a farmer can gather data on crop yields during harvest, in order to identify fields with low and high yields. Such information is useful in preparing fields and planting them the following year. Similarly, businesses can use the GPS to identify the location of rental cars, trucks, and service and maintenance vans, or the location of billboards carrying a particular advertisement. This type of information allows managers to make real-time decisions about staffing, routing, and the effectiveness of an advertising campaign. Over time, it can become the foundation for long-term decisions on facility location and capacity.

Information that is gathered through a global positioning system is often used in a **geographic information system (GIS)**, a software tool that is used to improve spatially oriented decisions. A GIS can display the relationship between business variables, like sales, and location variables, like customer residence. For example, a GIS can be used to display sales data on a map, a format that is much easier to understand than the usual spreadsheet approach of columns-and-rows. Cost factors, transportation times, and service quality issues can also be linked to specific locations. For example, Tom Jackson's airline could use a GIS to identify those airports where ground services are performed most cost effectively, and then use that information in routing, scheduling, and purchasing decisions. Figure 8.13 suggests some of the elements that might be part of such a system.

In order to interpret spatially oriented data, managers rely on **geographic boundaries**, lines of demarcation that allow spatial data to be organized into categories. In the United States, several approaches are used to define geographic boundaries, including:

▶ Physical geography: the natural boundaries established by surface and subterrestrial features, such as mountains, watersheds, forests, underground aquifers, soil,

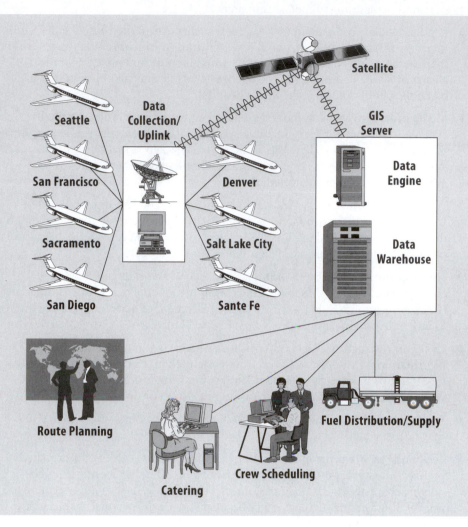

Figure 8.13
Basic GIS system for an airline

and so on. This form of geographic data has been found particularly useful in land management and was showcased in the fire-fighting operations surrounding several catastrophic fires in Southern California in 2003. Physical geography also has significant impact on site selection decisions.

▶ Census geography: block group, census tract, city, county, metropolitan statistical area, state, and township. Federal and state program managers rely on this data for allocation of government resources and placement of government service facilities.

▶ TIGER streets: short for the Census Bureau's "topologically integrated geographic encoding and reference" file, a set of computerized maps that provide the locational context for every street, highway, bridge, and tunnel in the United States. Vehicle routing and business location decisions depend heavily on this data.

▶ Congressional districts: information on a multitude of demographic variables can be found in many different databases. This is of obvious interest to politicians, but is also useful for the placement of business and industrial facilities and the planning of media campaigns.

▶ Landmarks: airports (about 600 commercial airports in the United States), universities (several thousand), population centroids for incorporated places (more than 20,000), and so forth. Thus, a GIS could identify and plot the location of all airports serving more than 100,000 travelers per year, all universities with business schools and all cities with a hospital.

▶ Media geography: geographic areas defined on the basis of broadcast media coverage—radio and television, cable systems, distribution of periodicals and directories such as the Yellow Pages, and so on. This allows marketing professionals and politicians to use a GIS to graphically identify the characteristics of the population reached by their media buys.

▶ Postal geography: the regions defined by the three- and five-digit ZIP codes. Using this information, businesses can identify the geographic characteristics of their customers, or mailing lists. For example, they could determine the impact of a direct advertisement campaign mailing on actual sales.

▶ Highway infrastructure: major interstates, federal and state highways, and county roads. Using a GIS to plotting this information along with customer and business locations could be critical to the placement of additional service outlets as well as billboard campaigns.

▶ Utility infrastructure: electrical lines, water mains, gas pipelines, and so on. This information is not only beneficial from a maintenance perspective for the utilities. It allows businesses to estimate the cost of infrastructure development when contemplating capacity expansion in existing or new facilities.

▶ Street intersections: tens of thousands of geographic points with which data may be associated.

▶ Telephone service geography: telephone exchanges, area codes, and designated prefixes. Much like postal codes, businesses can use this data identify the geographic characteristics of their customers. For example, they could determine the impact of direct phone solicitation on actual sales or the regional characteristics of users who access a service desk by phone.

Many of the different uses of GIS technology can be categorized by business function, as shown in Table 8.4.

CENTER OF GRAVITY METHOD

Suppose you own a laundry service based at several storefront locations. You decide to build a new central facility that will service all those locations. How would you go about selecting that location? One way would be to find the center of gravity of those storefront locations by pasting a map on a board and drilling holes where each of the storefronts is located. If you thread a string through each of the holes and attach a weight representing the volume of work handled at each location, then tie all the strings together and let go, the knot that joins all the strings together will land at the center of gravity. The center of gravity of a physical object is the point on which its entire weight could theoretically be balanced. With regard to facility location, the center of gravity is that place that best balances the transportation demands associated with operating a facility. The **center of gravity method**, then, is a mathematical technique that gives decision makers a rough idea of the most suitable location for a new facility.

Center of gravity method

A mathematical technique that gives decision makers a rough idea of the most suitable location for a new facility.

Table 8.4

GIS Applications Categorized by Business Function

Functional Area	GIS Applications
Finance and Accounting	• Accounting for environmental liabilities and the risks of weather and crime related losses. • Disaster planning • Loss management • Underwriting • Analyzing the flow of financial resources • Asset and inventory management • Locating financial service outlets, such as ATM's and branches.
Marketing	• Sales territory design • Sales forecasting • Sales district performance analysis • Marketing research • Direct marketing • Product Development • Media planning • Emerging market analysis
Operations Management	• Facility location (site selection, land economics, real estate demographics) • Facility layout • Facility network analysis and planning • Emergency management • Distribution system planning • Mobile asset management • Routing analysis
Human Resources	• Compensation planning • Social issues • Interorganizational networking and information flow • Demographic issues
Management Information Systems	• Systems development • Database design • Network planning • Data warehousing • Electronic data interchange • Privacy and security

The center of gravity can also be found mathematically. If you place a coordinate plane over the map and identify the coordinates of each of the storefronts, you can compute the coordinates of the center of gravity using Equations 8.1 and 8.2. Assuming n storefronts, each located at some point identified by the coordinates (x_i, y_i) and

Figure 8.14

Center of gravity method

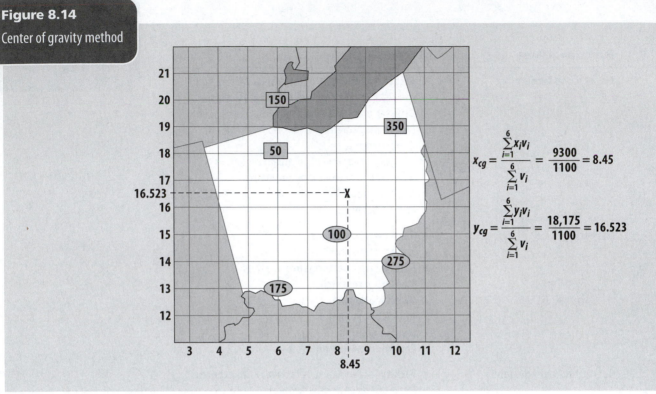

$$x_{cg} = \frac{\sum\limits_{i=1}^{6} x_i v_i}{\sum\limits_{i=1}^{6} v_i} = \frac{9300}{1100} = 8.45$$

$$y_{cg} = \frac{\sum\limits_{i=1}^{6} y_i v_i}{\sum\limits_{i=1}^{6} v_i} = \frac{18{,}175}{1100} = 16.523$$

doing a weekly volume of business equal to v_i, the center of gravity would be the point (x_{cg}, y_{cg}).

$$x_{cg} = \frac{\sum\limits_{i=1}^{n} x_i v_i}{\sum\limits_{i=1}^{n} v_i} \qquad \textit{Equation 8.1}$$

$$y_{cg} = \frac{\sum\limits_{i=1}^{n} y_i v_i}{\sum\limits_{i=1}^{n} v_i} \qquad \textit{Equation 8.2}$$

Suppose an employment agency has obtained a contract to place 550 summer employees with a large company that has service facilities in Detroit, Toledo, and Cleveland. Of the employees, 350 will be assigned to Cleveland, 150 to Detroit, and 50 to Toledo. After reviewing a large number of applications, the firm's managers have decided to conduct a two-day screening of 175 students from Miami University (Ohio), 100 from Ohio State University, and 275 from Ohio University. On the first day, screenings will be conducted off campus; on the second day, at one of the three facilities where the new employees will work. Each student will be reimbursed for mileage, and all must be present at one location for the first day of screening. Use the center of gravity method to determine the most cost-effective location for the first day's screening.

Figure 8.14 shows the solution to this problem graphically. The data are summarized in Table 8.5. The computations are also shown in the figure. Based on this method of analysis, managers should look for a site near the point marked X on the map in Figure 8.14.

Table 8.5

Market and Source Data for the Center of Gravity Method

Raw Material Source/ Market Concentration	Volume (V_i)	x_i	y_i
Miami University	175	6	13
Ohio State University	100	8	15
Ohio University	275	10	14
Cleveland Market	350	10	19
Detroit Market	150	6	20
Toledo Market	50	6	18

While the center of gravity method is used most often to find a specific site, it can also be used on higher levels of the location hierarchy. For example, if a company intends to serve several regions with a new facility or to receive materials from several regions, the center of gravity method could be used to identify the most suitable region.

One caveat: The ideal location may not be a feasible location. Murphy's Law suggests that the center of gravity location will probably fall right in the middle of the local forest preserve or in a neighborhood with a residential zoning. Even when the center of gravity location is feasible, it should be seen only as the starting point in the search for a location. Managers should consider a variety of alternatives before selecting any one location.

TRADE AREA ANALYSIS

Trade area analysis

Determines the impact of one facility on the business of others. It is especially important for service.

Trade area analysis, which determines the impact of one facility on the business of others, is especially important for service franchises because it can be used to ensure that a new facility will not take significant business from existing facilities. Managers can then target the new facility at customers located within an area that is underserved. Table 8.6 presents some information that could be used for a trade area analysis.

One way to perform such an analysis is to graph the percentage of customers the business could serve as a function of their distance from the site. Such information can also be displayed on a map of the trade area (see Figure 8.15). Managers can examine the map to see where customer concentrations are heaviest.

Figure 8.16 shows a "distance decay curve" obtained from this data. Clearly, significant business could be lost if a new facility is built within 5 miles of the existing facility. The accompanying map shows that most of the customers from outside the 70% ring do not reside in the northeastern quadrant, even though household incomes in that quadrant seem similar to those inside the 70% ring. If other demographic factors do not contradict this information, the distance decay curve and map suggest that locating a new facility in the northeastern quadrant could significantly expand sales without a major reduction in sales at the existing facility.

MULTIPLE-FACTOR RATING SYSTEMS

We have seen that a variety of factors are important to decision makers at each level of the location decision hierarchy. What is their relative importance, and which factor is most important? The answers to these questions vary from one decision to the next,

Table 8.6

Data for Distance Decay
Report in Trade Area
Analysis

Distance from Site (Miles)	Cumulative Number of Customers	% Customers
0.9	57	5
1.5	200	15
1.9	377	25
2.6	499	35
3.1	566	40
3.4	637	45
3.7	681	50
4.0	752	55
4.4	851	60
4.8	890	65
5.6	956	70
6.7	1023	75
8.0	1095	80
9.9	1162	85
12.3	1232	90
16.9	1302	95
45.8	1370	100

Source: Adapted from *Business Geographics*, Feb. 1997, pp. 20–23, reporter Jim Laiderman; and
http://www.geoplace.com/bg

Multiple-factor rating systems

A comparison of the attractiveness of several locations on the basis of more than one criteria.

but rating the factors according to their general importance can help decision makers to avoid placing too much emphasis on the wrong factors. **Multiple-factor rating systems** can be used to compare the attractiveness of several locations on the basis of more than one criterion.

The relative attractiveness of a given location can be estimated mathematically using equation 8.3. In this equation, the rating of location i on factor j is referred to as r_{ij}, and the weight assigned to factor j is referred to as w_j. The number of different factors is assumed to be m.

$$\text{Location attractiveness for location} \quad i = \sum_{j=1}^{m} r_{ij}\, w_j \qquad \textit{Equation 8.3}$$

Let's say a young entrepreneur wants to open a medical and legal transcription service and is considering three different locations. One is in the town square, which offers many amenities for workers and is close to the law practices but suffers from

Figure 8.15

Trade area analysis

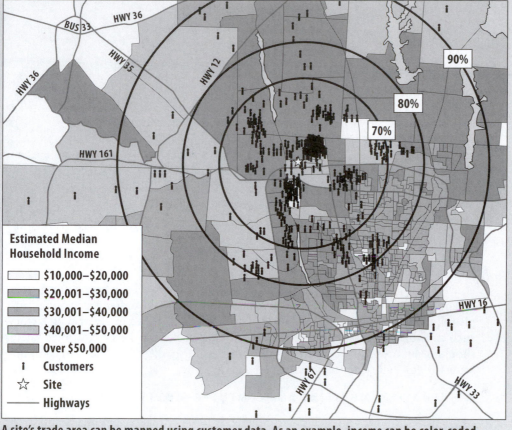

Estimated Median Household Income

- $10,000–$20,000
- $20,001–$30,000
- $30,001–$40,000
- $40,001–$50,000
- Over $50,000
- Customers
- ☆ Site
- Highways

A site's trade area can be mapped using customer data. As an example, income can be color-coded, and the cumulative concentration of customers can be shown using the concentric circles above. The same information can be shown in either tabular or graphical form.

Source: Adapted from *Business Geographics*, Feb. 1997, Vol. 5, No. 2, pages 20–23, http://www.geoplace.com/bg, reporter Jim Laiderman

inadequate parking and poses considerable safety concerns for the employees which generally work mostly in the late evening and middle of the night. Another location is next to a lake, on the outskirts of town. The lakeside location has plenty of parking and is the safest place for late-night workers, but it has few amenities and is out of the way for customers. A third location is in a small new shopping center close to several medical practices on the main highway that links the town to the larger metropolitan area. Its primary drawback is the lack of amenities for workers. Use multiple-factor rating to help select the best location.

Table 8.7 shows the factor ratings and weights for the three locations. Notice that the third location got the highest location attractiveness score, even though it got only medium ratings on most factors. Decision makers are sometimes surprised by the results of weighted-factor ratings, especially if they are not fully aware of their own biases. For example, a decision maker who subconsciously values high visibility among the legal services clientele would have located the business in the town square.

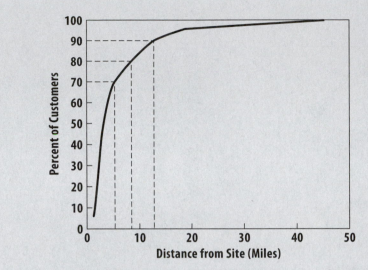

Figure 8.16

Trade area analysis (distance decay curve)

Source: Adapted from *Business Geographics*, Feb. 1997, page 20–23, http://www.geoplace.com/bg, reporter Jim Laiderman

Obviously, factor-rating systems can be used only when certain overriding factors will not eliminate some locations from consideration. The entrepreneur in our example might have eliminated several locations at the outset, based on overriding factors such as projected cost or the availability of a retail permit. Perhaps worker safety should be an overriding concern for this business. If so, there is no need to compute attractiveness ratings for the town center location.

MATHEMATICAL MODELING AND COMPUTER SIMULATIONS

Mathematical models are quantitative methods to determine an optimal solution to real-world problems. For example, decision makers might use a mathematical technique to identify a location that maximizes service potential or minimizes costs. Before computers became widely available, these decision-support models were limited in scope by the time required to find their solutions. Based on a limited number of variables and a small number of equations, of necessity they aggregated many variables into one. By today's standards these mathematical modeling tools were crude.

Over time, as computing power increased and became less expensive, decision-making models became more sophisticated. Today, computers can solve models with thousands of equations and variables. While the mathematical models provide an optimal solution for a business decision, the value of that solution is only as good as the match between the formulated model and reality. Though they are better than the less sophisticated models of the past, today's mathematical models retain certain shortcomings. For example, the weekly volume of shipments between two facilities is often treated as a constant, rather than a variable. What is more, decision-making

REC CENTER DILEMMA

Luis's Patio Line Dilemma

Luis's company has decided to produce a new line of outdoor patio furniture. Existing facilities are operating close enough to capacity and producing products that are dissimilar to the new line, so the company realizes it needs a new facility. They have narrowed the choice down to three sites: (1) an industrial park in Phoenix, where a facility could be built close to their existing facilities; (2) a warehouse that is for sale at a Metamoros, Mexico, maquiladora factory; and (3) an existing injection molding factory that is for sale in Los Angeles (one of their major markets), because the owner is ready to retire. What factors do you believe Luis should include as he evaluates the three options?

Table 8.7

Factor Ratings for the Three Location Alternatives for the transcription business

Factor	Factor Weight (On a scale of 1 to 10 how important is this factor? 1 is bad, 10 is good.)	Location Rating (Converted from any previous measurement to a scale of 1 to 10, where 1 is bad and 10 is good.)		
		Town Square	Beside the Lake	On the Highway
Safety	10	2	10	8
Convenience for Customers	5	4	1	6
Cost of Operation	7	1	7	6
Convenience for Workers	3	8	2	2
Availability of Workers	5	8	4	5
Forecasted Sales Volume	7	10	2	4
Impact of Sales Taxes on Margin	4	1	10	10
Location Attractiveness Score (sum of the ratings multiplied by each corresponding factor weight)		185	234	251

models usually quantify variables that are inherently qualitative. For example, the quality of the water supply for a soda bottler might be translated into a financial cost.

Seldom is the answer to a complex problem so simple as one optimal solution. Decision makers need to know how much a model's assumptions could change without changing the optimal solution. This kind of information is provided by **sensitivity analysis**. For example, sensitivity analysis would allow a decision maker to determine how much the weekly volume of shipments between two facilities can increase before the selected location becomes less than optimal.

Unlike mathematical models, computer simulation models generally do not provide optimal solutions. They do, however, allow decision makers to model extremely complex systems and to incorporate probabilistic and qualitative variables, as well as quantitative variables. Given the computing speed that is available to virtually all businesses today, the user-friendliness of simulation software, the availability of vast amounts of relevant information in spatial data warehouses, and the benefits of GIS, managers are increasingly dependent on computerized decision support systems for location decisions.

Sensitivity analysis

A special type of linear programming model for finding each source destination. Decision makers need to know how much a model's assumptions could change without changing the optimal solution.

Example 8.3

The campus postal service, currently operating from an off campus facility, seeks to identify an ideal on-campus location for distribution of pouches to mail carriers. The campus has been mapped on a Cartesian plane to identify building coordinates. The mail is distributed and collected twice daily by three carriers to ten separate buildings, as indicated in the table below. What is the center of gravity for the postal operations? (Assume that no extra pouches are carried with each delivery, so no extra trips are made to provide empty pouches.) Calculate your solution based on the information in the table below.

Building	Coordinates	Average Daily Volume of Mail Delivered (pouches)	Average Daily Volume of Mail Picked Up (pouches)
Science & Math	(64, 15)	4.3	1.4
Business	(10, 40)	3.4	3.2
Graphic Arts	(50, 20)	6.1	8.2
Music & Theater	(40, 15)	3.0	2.5
Athletics	(85, 70)	2.1	5.2
English	(30, 30)	2.0	2.0
Social Sciences & History	(21, 19)	3.1	3.2
Engineering	(85, 30)	5.2	4.3
Administration	(48, 53)	3.5	5.4
Health	(65, 70)	2.3	2.1

Solution:

Step 1: Determine the product of the x-coordinate and total daily volume for each building. These values are as follows:

Building	x-coordinate	Average Daily Volume (total)	Product of x-coordinate and Average Daily Volume
Science & Math	64	7.7	492.8
Business	10	6.6	66
Graphic Arts	50	14.3	715
Music & Theater	40	5.5	220
Athletics	85	7.3	620.5
English	30	4	120
Social Sciences & History	21	6.3	132.3
Engineering	85	9.5	807.5
Administration	48	8.9	427.2
Health	65	4.4	286

Example 8.3

(*continued*)

Step 2: Determine the sum of the products computed in Step 1.

This sum is 3887.3. ($492.8 + 66 + \cdots + 286 = 3887.3$)

Step 3: Determine the sum of the average daily volumes for all buildings.

This sum is 74.5. ($7.7 + 6.6 + \cdots + 4.4 = 74.5$)

Step 4: Compute the x-coordinate for the center of gravity.

This coordinate is the ratio of the resulting values from steps 2 and 3.

$$x_{cg} = \frac{3887.3}{74.5} = 52.1785$$

Step 5: Determine the product of the y-coordinate and total daily volume for each building. These values are as follows:

Building	y-coordinate	Average Daily Volume (total)	Product of y-coordinate and Average Daily Volume
Science & Math	15	7.7	115.5
Business	40	6.6	264
Graphic Arts	20	14.3	286
Music & Theater	15	5.5	82.5
Athletics	70	7.3	511
English	30	4	120
Social Sciences & History	19	6.3	119.7
Engineering	30	9.5	285
Administration	53	8.9	471.7
Health	70	4.4	308

Step 6: Determine the sum of the products computed in step 5.

This sum is 2563.4. ($115.5 + 264 + \cdots + 308 = 2563.4$)

Step 7: Compute the y-coordinate for the center of gravity.

This coordinate is the ratio of the resulting values from steps 6 and 3.

$$y_{cg} = \frac{2563.4}{74.5} = 34.4081$$

The center of gravity of (52.1785, 34.4081) is close to the Graphic Arts, English, and Administration buildings. These would be obvious candidates for the location of the central mail distribution facility. Among these three, the largest volume of mail goes to and from the Graphic Arts building, thus, this might be a good place to start. Of course, to finalize their decision, the postal service could calculate what their projected distribution costs would be with each of these three buildings as their central distribution point.

Transportation model

A special type of linear programming model.

Transportation tableau (transportation matrix)

A special format used to summarize the information for a transportation model.

The Transportation Model Many companies produce the same product at several factories and distribute it through a number of different warehouses. In such systems, a basic question is how much to produce in each location and how much to ship to each warehouse. The transportation model is a special type of linear programming model that can be useful in solving this type of problem. In this section we explain how to construct a table, called the **transportation tableau** or **transportation matrix**, that illustrates the transportation problem. Supplement B: Mathematical Optimization illustrates the use of such a table to find an optimal solution to the transportation problem. Note that, when considering several potential new locations, finding the optimal solution to the transportation problem for each potential location allows decision makers to determine which location is financially preferable from an operating perspective and by how much.

The basic structure of a transportation model is as follows: A given product is available in specific limited quantities at each of a number of sources (for example, factories) and is required in specified amounts at each of a number of destinations (for example, warehouses). The cost of shipping a unit from each source to each destination is known and is the same for every unit shipped on that route. The problem is to determine how much material to ship from each source to each destination so as to minimize the total shipping cost.

A transportation tableau summarizes the information relevant to the transportation model. The tableau has a row for each source and a column for each destination. Written in the corner of each cell of the matrix is the cost of shipping a unit from the row's source to the destination's column. Written to the right of each row is the availability at that row's source, and at the bottom of each column is the requirement at that column's destination.

Example 8.4

Suppose that Fred's company produces cell phones at three plants in Phoenix, Chicago, and Atlanta. The Phoenix plant has a capacity of 100,000 units per month, while each of the other two plants has a capacity of 150,000 units per month. The products are distributed nationally through warehouses in San Diego, Dallas, Detroit, Charlotte, and Philadelphia. The monthly demand from each warehouse is as follows: San Diego (70,000), Dallas (40,000), Detroit (50,000), Charlotte (70,000), and Philadelphia (90,000). The cost (in $100s) to transport 1000 units from each plant to each warehouse is given in the table below.

	Warehouse				
Plant	**San Diego**	**Dallas**	**Detroit**	**Charlotte**	**Philadelphia**
Phoenix	10	8	13	16	18
Chicago	12	7	6	9	9
Atlanta	17	12	10	5	9

Formulate a transportation tableau to summarize the information about production and distribution of cell phones in Fred's company and provide a possible solution to the transportation problem.

Solution:

Step 1: Determine the number of rows and columns needed.

Example 8.4

(continued)

Because there are three sources and five destinations we need a three-by-five matrix, as shown below.

Plant	San Diego	Dallas	Detroit	Charlotte	Philadelphia	Available
Phoenix	10 / 70	8 / 30	13	16	18	100
Chicago	12	7 / 10	6 / 50	9 / 70	9 / 20	150
Atlanta	17	12	10	5	9 / 70	150
	70	40	50	70	90	400 / 320

Step 2: Add the plants' capacities, in thousands of units, along the far-right column edge of the above matrix.

Step 3: Add the warehouses' requirements, also in thousands of units, along the bottom row of the above matrix.

Step 4: Add the transportation costs for the appropriate plant-warehouse pair in the upper-right-hand corner of each cell (see above).

Step 5: Find an initial solution to the problem.

The italicized numbers in each cell shows an initial solution. This solution was obtained by starting in the "northwest corner" cell and placing the maximum allowable shipment in the cell (based on unused warehouse demand or plant capacity for that row and column). Because the Phoenix factory can produce 100,000 units, but the San Diego warehouse can take only 70,000, we place a "70" in this cell to indicate that 70,000 units will be shipped from Phoenix to San Diego per month.

Next, we move to the new northwest corner and repeat the allocation procedure. Because the San Diego column is now full, the new northwest corner is the Phoenix-Dallas cell. We can allocate 30,000 units to ship along that route because the Dallas warehouse can receive 40,000 units each month, but the Phoenix factory has only 30,000 left to ship.

The new northwest corner is now the Chicago-Dallas cell. We can allocate 10,000 units to that route because the Dallas warehouse can receive only 10,000 more units.

Continuing the iterative process described above we ultimately come to the initial solution depicted in the transportation tableau above.

An alternative, cost sensitive, method to finding an initial solution is presented in Solved Problem 2 on page 387. There the cells are filled with shipment volumes starting with the least expensive cell, completing rows and columns until the initial solution is complete.

SUMMARY

This chapter describes the processes of making location and capacity decisions, which have long-term implications for the operating structure and profitability of every organization. Deciding how large a facility should be or where it should be located requires the attention of personnel in all of the functional areas of business, for such decisions have significant implications for every function in the business. Mistakes can damage the firm's profitability for decades, while good decisions can ensure a sustained competitive advantage. The uncertainty surrounding long-term forecasts complicates the decision-making task considerably. To safeguard against faulty decisions, some firms adopt a demand-cushioning or capacity-cushioning strategy. Others use scenario planning to identify capacity and location options that will prove workable in a variety of situations.

In selecting a place to do business, companies must consider global, regional, community, and site-specific issues. This range of issues is referred to as the location decision hierarchy. Firms whose operations add weight to their product-service bundle, often choose to locate close to their customers. Firms whose operations reduce the weight of the product-service bundle often locate close to their suppliers. A variety of supply chain management issues enters into such decisions.

Capacity decisions are very closely related to location decisions. For instance, a company that has chosen to build a large plant in order to generate economies of scale is not likely to maintain a large number of locations. Firms that seek economies of scope rather than economies of scale might choose to maintain a large number of plants. The scale of an organization's facilities also helps to determine what elements of the location decision hierarchy are relevant to the decision.

Recently, geographic information systems have become available to managers who must choose facility locations. These tools allow managers to visualize the impact of their decisions through maps. They provide a much more effective method of analysis and communication of spatial data than the models available to decision makers in the past and are likely to be widely used. Other tools that are useful in making location decisions are the center of gravity method, trade area analysis, factor rating, mathematical modeling (including the transportation method), and computerized simulation.

KEY TERMS

Average fixed cost, 355
Average unit cost, 355
Average variable cost, 355
Best operating level (BOL), 357
Capacity, 344
Capacity strategy, 346
Capacity utilization, 348
Center of gravity method, 374
Competitive clustering, 370
Customer quality, 365
Customer quantity, 365
Customer value, 365
Decreasing returns to scale, 357
Delphi method, 351
Diseconomy of scale, 358

Economy of scale, 358
Fixed costs, 353
Geographic boundaries, 372
Geographical information system (GIS), 372
Global positioning system (GPS), 372
Increasing returns to scale, 356
Law of diminishing returns, 356
Learning curve, 352
Learning rate, 352
Marginal cost, 356
Multiple-factor rating system, 378
Point-of-sale (POS) data, 372
Primary research, 371
Process life cycle (PSLC), 361

Saturation marketing, 370
Scenario planning, 351
Sensitivity analysis, 381
Spatial data warehouse, 372
Syndicated data, 371
Total cost, 354
Trade area analysis, 377
Transportation model, 384
Transportation tableau, 384
Transportation matrix, 384
Variable costs, 354
Weight-added operations, 367
Weight-reduced operations, 367

SOLVED PROBLEMS

1. Cheryl's hospital lab is looking at a new diagnostic device with which it will initially take a technician approximately 1 hour to run a common battery of tests frequently requested by the medical staff. The manufacturer has suggested that a learning curve of 90% may be appropriate for the technician operating the device. The test is requested about 10 times per week.

   a) How long should it take to run the test once they have had the new diagnostic device up and running for 6 months or so?

   b) At the current rate of demand, how long will it take to get the time required for the test to be around 20 minutes?

   c) How would an increase in the demand for the test affect the required capacity for the test?

Solution:

   a) Assuming a 90% leaning curve, the following table would represent the time per test battery as the accumulated experience with the diagnostic device builds. With a demand of about ten tests per week, they should accumulate close to 256 tests over the next six months and the testing time should be down to under 26 minutes by then.

Accumulated Experience	1	2	4	8	16	32	64	128	256	512	1024	2048	4096
Completion Time per Test (minutes)	60	54	48.6	43.7	39.4	35.4	31.9	28.7	25.8	23.2	20.9	18.9	16.9

   b) A 90% leaning curve projects the time per test will be at 20.1 minutes after 1024 tests have been performed. That is about 2 years at the current rate of demand.

   c) The bad news is that an increase in demand would mean more capacity is needed in the lab, possibly requiring a second machine. The good news is that as experience accumulates, the time per test will decrease as the leaning curve projects thus reducing the incremental need for additional capacity.

2. An IT consulting firm has three offices in a metropolitan area with a fifteen full-time consultants assigned to each one. They currently have six projects pending in various nearby cities to which consultants need be assigned. Based upon where they are driving from each week assignments should be made to keep transportation costs to a minimum. The table below details the number of consultant required for each project and the cost of commuting each week from each office.

Project	Demand for Consultants	Miles from Downtown Office	Miles from the Northern Branch	Miles from the Southern Branch
Gattiker Inc.	8	2	5	8
Snavely Concrete	7	6	6	2
Rocky's Pizza	6	3	8	5
Porcano Motors	9	2	8	7
Redhawk Brewery	4	7	1	5
Schwarz's Woodworking	11	6	2	5

a) Assuming commuting costs are proportional to distance and all other issues are equal, set this problem up using the transportation model.

b) What might be a good first cut at a solution?

Solution:

See below.

a) See the Transportation Tableau below. Demand for consultants and capacity at facilities are shown in the tableau as given by the problem statement. The costs shown in the tableau match the commuting distances for the consultants.

b) We determined this initial solution using a cost sensitive approach. To begin allocating branch consultants to specific jobs we found the cell with the smallest cost (Northern Branch-Redhawk Brewery) and allocated as many consultants as possible to that cell. Four consultants from the Northern Branch were allocated to Redhawk Brewery because that project required a total of four consultants. Next, we found the lowest cost cell remaining in the Northern Branch column and allocated as many consultants as possible to that cell. Thus we allocated eleven consultants from the Northern Branch to Schwarz's Woodworking.

This completely used the remaining capacity at Northern Branch and completely satisfied the demand for consultants at Schwarz's Woodworking. Using the same algorithm, we completed the initial solution with the following allocations (in order):

▶ Nine consultants from the Downtown office to Porcano Motors. (Because several cells were tied for lowest cost at "2," for our next allocation we chose the one where we could allocate the most consultants.)

▶ Six consultants from the Downtown office to Gattiker, Inc.

▶ Two consultants from the Southern Branch to Gattiker, Inc.

▶ Seven consultants from the Southern Branch to Snavely Concrete

▶ Six consultants from the Southern Branch to Rocky's Pizza

3. A local printer who specializes in silk-screening T-shirts and sweatshirts for various affiliates of your university has a capacity problem. She is currently in her second year of business, and has seen solid growth over the last few months. The business began conservatively, with student helpers

Project	Downtown Office		Northern Branch		Southern Branch		Demand for Consultants
Gattiker, Inc.		2		5		8	
	6				2		8
Snavely Concrete		6		6		2	
					7		7
Rocky's Pizza		3		8		5	
					6		6
Porcano Motors		2		8		7	
	9						9
Redhawk Brewery		7		1		5	
			4				4
Shwarz's Woodworking		6		2		5	
			11				11
Branch Capacity	15		15		15		Total = 45

who are paid by the hour, a small spinning printing rack, and a single oven to cure the ink after printing. The rack-printing process, which allows a single worker to print designs of up to six colors, is very labor intensive. The oven employs a conveyor to move the garments through, much as in some of the new pizza places. The owner, whose shop prints just over 5000 shirts per week, expects her operation will soon grow out of its low-tech process. Current fixed costs (for rent, depreciation on the printing rack and oven, and utilities) are $1600 per week. Because one worker must apply as many as six colors to a single shirt, variable costs are estimated at an average of $2 per shirt.

One alternative would be to replace the current single-station rack with a multi-station, semi-automated rack that accommodates up to nine workers and eight ink colors simultaneously. With one worker assigned to apply each of the eight colors, the owner can realize significant labor savings on each shirt. Though fixed costs would increase to $2500 per week, the more efficient and specialized use of labor would decrease variable costs to an average of $1.80 per shirt.

Another option, suggested by one of the student workers would be to keep the old rack and buy the new one as well. The old one could be used for one- and two-color jobs (a significant proportion of the shop's work), and the new rack for jobs requiring three or more colors. By using resources even more efficiently, this approach would push variable costs down even further, to $1.75 per shirt. Without the trade-in on the old machine, however, fixed costs would rise to $2800 per week.

Which alternative should the owner select? On what assumptions do you base your recommendation? How sensitive is your recommendation to those assumptions?

Solution:

Cost volume break-even analysis:

$$\$1{,}600 + \$2 \times v = \$2{,}500 + \$1.80 \times v$$

$$v = 4{,}500$$

$$\$2{,}500 + \$.1.80 \times v = \$2800 + \$1.75 \times v$$

$$v = 6{,}000$$

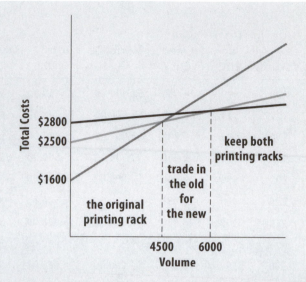

With demand growing beyond 5000, the new rack seems a good investment. Depending on how solid the future growth projections seem, keeping the old rack might also be a good idea.

4. Tom Jackson's airline offers five flights a day between Phoenix and Los Angeles. The ten legs of this schedule, less than an hour each, are scheduled from 6 a.m. to 10 p.m. All are handled by the same aircraft at the same gate. Fixed costs are estimated at $30,000 per day, with a variable cost per ticketed passenger of $20 up to 600 passengers. When more than 600 passengers are booked each day, variable cost increases to $60 per passenger. The aircraft holds 92 passengers, so the maximum capacity for five round-trip flights is 920 passengers per day. The airline charges $99 per passenger each way.

Use a spreadsheet to put together a worksheet that looks like Table 8.2 (on page 358). What is the best operating level on this route? How many passengers does the airline need to book to make a profit? What should the airline charge to break even on a half-full plane?

Solution:

The BOL (about 600) and break-even levels (about 275) are shaded. You would have to charge about $64 a ticket to break even between 450 and 475 passengers per day (approximately 50% seat utilization).

Volume	Price per Unit	Fixed Cost	Variable Cost	Total Cost	Per Unit Marginal Cost	Average Fixed Cost	Average Variable Cost	Average Total Cost	Total Profit	Profit per Unit
100	$99	$20,000	$2,000.00	$22,000.00	$20.00	$200.00	$20.00	$220.00	−12100	($121.00)
125	$99	$20,000	$2,500.00	$22,500.00	$20.00	$160.00	$20.00	$180.00	−10125	($81.00)
150	$99	$20,000	$3,000.00	$23,000.00	$20.00	$133.33	$20.00	$153.33	−8150	($54.33)
175	$99	$20,000	$3,500.00	$23,500.00	$20.00	$114.29	$20.00	$134.29	−6175	($35.29)
200	$99	$20,000	$4,000.00	$24,000.00	$20.00	$100.00	$20.00	$120.00	−4200	($21.00)
225	$99	$20,000	$4,500.00	$24,500.00	$20.00	$88.89	$20.00	$108.89	−2225	($9.89)
250	$99	$20,000	$5,000.00	$25,000.00	$20.00	$80.00	$20.00	$100.00	−250	($1.00)
275	$99	$20,000	$5,500.00	$25,500.00	$20.00	$72.73	$20.00	$92.73	1725	$6.27
300	$99	$20,000	$6,000.00	$26,000.00	$20.00	$66.67	$20.00	$86.67	3700	$12.33
325	$99	$20,000	$6,500.00	$26,500.00	$20.00	$61.54	$20.00	$81.54	5675	$17.46
350	$99	$20,000	$7,000.00	$27,000.00	$20.00	$57.14	$20.00	$77.14	7650	$21.86
375	$99	$20,000	$7,500.00	$27,500.00	$20.00	$53.33	$20.00	$73.33	9625	$25.67
400	$99	$20,000	$8,000.00	$28,000.00	$20.00	$50.00	$20.00	$70.00	11600	$29.00
425	$99	$20,000	$8,500.00	$28,500.00	$20.00	$47.06	$20.00	$67.06	13575	$31.94
450	$99	$20,000	$9,000.00	$29,000.00	$20.00	$44.44	$20.00	$64.44	15550	$34.56
475	$99	$20,000	$9,500.00	$29,500.00	$20.00	$42.11	$20.00	$62.11	17525	$36.89
500	$99	$20,000	$10,000.00	$30,000.00	$20.00	$40.00	$20.00	$60.00	19500	$39.00
525	$99	$20,000	$10,500.00	$30,500.00	$20.00	$38.10	$20.00	$58.10	21475	$40.90
550	$99	$20,000	$11,000.00	$31,000.00	$20.00	$36.36	$20.00	$56.36	23450	$42.64
575	$99	$20,000	$11,500.00	$31,500.00	$20.00	$34.78	$20.00	$54.78	25425	$44.22
600	$99	$20,000	$12,000.00	$32,000.00	$20.00	$33.33	$20.00	$53.33	27400	$45.67
625	$99	$20,000	$13,500.00	$33,500.00	$60.00	$32.00	$21.60	$53.60	28375	$45.40
650	$99	$20,000	$15,000.00	$35,000.00	$60.00	$30.77	$23.08	$53.85	29350	$45.15
675	$99	$20,000	$16,500.00	$36,500.00	$60.00	$29.63	$24.44	$54.07	30325	$44.93
700	$99	$20,000	$18,000.00	$38,000.00	$60.00	$28.57	$25.71	$54.29	31300	$44.71
725	$99	$20,000	$19,500.00	$39,500.00	$60.00	$27.59	$26.90	$54.48	32275	$44.52
750	$99	$20,000	$21,000.00	$41,000.00	$60.00	$26.67	$28.00	$54.67	33250	$44.33
775	$99	$20,000	$22,500.00	$42,500.00	$60.00	$25.81	$29.03	$54.84	34225	$44.16
800	$99	$20,000	$24,000.00	$44,000.00	$60.00	$25.00	$30.00	$55.00	35200	$44.00
825	$99	$20,000	$25,500.00	$45,500.00	$60.00	$24.24	$30.91	$55.15	36175	$43.85
850	$99	$20,000	$27,000.00	$47,000.00	$60.00	$23.53	$31.76	$55.29	37150	$43.71
875	$99	$20,000	$28,500.00	$48,500.00	$60.00	$22.86	$32.57	$55.43	38125	$43.57
900	$99	$20,000	$30,000.00	$50,000.00	$60.00	$22.22	$33.33	$55.56	39100	$43.44

5. A supplier of auto parts is looking for a suitable location for its new stamping plant, which has been planned in response to increased domestic demand from foreign automakers with plants in the United States. The new plant will receive sheets of rolled steel from a steel processor located in Middletown, Ohio. It will supply four auto plants situated along the Interstate 75 (I-75) corridor between Michigan and Kentucky. Because I-75 runs north/south through the region where both the auto plants and the steel source are located, managers have decided to use their location relative to I-75 as a basis for their analysis. They have represented the volume of both stamped parts and steel sheets in terms of truckloads, as that is the primary method in which they will be transported in and out of the proposed plant.

The following table shows how far south of the northernmost customer, and how far east or west of I-75, each potential location is, along with the monthly volume of each. Based on the center of gravity method, where would you suggest the company plan to locate the new plant?

Location	Distance South	Distance East (-West) of I75	Volume
C-Maz1	0	−15	1500
C-Chry	45	5	2000
C-Maz2	145	−65	1000
C-Toy	275	10	2500
S-Steel	195	−5	7200

Solution:

Note that the sum of the "Volume" column is 14,200. Using a weighted average of the locations and their volumes, you get the following:

Distance South × Volume	Distance East (−West) × Volume
0	−22500
90000	10000
145000	−65000
687500	25000
1404000	−36000
------------	---------
2326500	−88500

Miles South of Northern Most Cust/Sup Plant	Miles East (−West) of I-75
163.84	(6.23)

So, a good place to start looking would be in the vicinity of 160–170 miles south of the existing northernmost plant and about 5–10 miles west of I-75. That might mean looking for a site somewhere in west central Ohio convenient to the interstate. In fact, if all of the freight will travel on I-75, the east-west center of gravity is irrelevant and the site should be as close to the interstate as possible. (And, it doesn't matter whether that is east or west of the interstate.)

6. A large beer maker has narrowed the search for its next brewery to four locations. Managers will consider 4 major criteria in making the final choice: water quality, labor pool, local attitude, and property costs. (All other criteria are deemed equal.) Water quality has received the highest weight (.4); the availability of a pool of high-quality labor, the second-highest weight (.3). Local attitude (.2) and property costs (.1) are the least important of the four factors. The ratings for the three locations, made by an independent consultant on a scale of 1–10, follow. Where should the firm build the brewery?

Location	Water	Labor	Attitude	Property Costs
Barleyville, OR	4	8	2	8
Hopsburg, MN	8	9	2	8
Ricetown, SC	6	2	7	2
Yeastings, VT	3	7	7	2

Solution:

Location	Water	Labor	Attitude	Property Costs	Weighted Average
Barleyville, OR	4	8	2	8	5.2
Hopsburg, MN	8	9	2	8	7.1
Ricetown, SC	6	2	7	2	4.6
Yeastings, VT	3	7	7	2	4.9
Weights	0.4	0.3	0.2	0.1	

The better labor pool of Hopsburg gives it the edge over the rest.

DISCUSSION QUESTIONS

1. Airlines fly the same routes quite often. Where do they begin in the location decision-making hierarchy? How do they use modern technology in these decisions? How would an airline's location decision process differ from McDonald's?

2. What economies of scale exist for an airport? What diseconomies of scale? Would you consider an airport a weight-added or a weight-reduced operation? Why?

3. Explain the current trend toward smaller major league baseball parks and larger National Football League stadiums (as evidenced in the declining number of multipurpose stadiums)?

4. Skipper's, a great new sandwich place across from the health club, has a steadily growing lunchtime clientele. However, sometimes the owner, Andy, has difficulty dealing with fluctuations in demand.

   a) As a customer of Skipper's, what strategy would you suggest to Andy: a demand cushion, a capacity cushion, or a combination of the two strategies? Why?

   b) Just 2 days ago, Skipper's started opening early for breakfast. Business was slow the first day, but on the second day a waiting line extended out the door. On the third day, Andy tells you that he is thinking about getting a small business loan in order to double his seating and serving capacity. What advice can you give him? What is the role of forecasting in this situation?

   c) How would the advice you gave Andy in parts (a) and (b) differ if he were running a manufacturing operation?

5. Why is Fred unlikely ever to see 100% capacity utilization in his factory? What about Luis and Cheryl? Why might Tom have mixed feelings about a full plane?

6. Which strategy would you suggest Tom adopt: a demand cushion or a capacity cushion? Why? What strategy would work best in Cheryl's hospital? In Luis's furniture factory? In Fred's electronics factory?

7. You have just been charged with finding the location for the next low-grade nuclear waste storage and disposal facility, to be operated by the federal government. How do you start, and what are the issues you must deal with? How is

your task similar to General Motors's task in finding a site for the first Saturn factory? How is it different?

8. In the area where you live, every city and town buys its own fire trucks, which spend more time being shown off in parades than putting out fires. Why not just have one central fire department at the state capital? Frame your answer in terms of weight-reduced and weight-added operations.

9. The enrollment in the campus daycare center at your university varies over time. How could the center's manager apply the Delphi method to forecast long-run staffing needs? Who, both inside and outside the center, might be included in the staffing decision?

10. a) Tom Jackson's airline is trying to decide what size airplane to use on a given route. Describe some of the costs that would be considered in this decision, including: fixed costs, variable costs, total cost, average fixed cost per unit, average variable cost per unit, average total cost, and marginal cost per unit. In terms of capacity, would the goal be to maximize total profit or average unit profit? Can you think of a situation in which the optimal volume for maximizing total profit might not be the same as the optimal volume for maximizing average unit profit? Why or why not?

b) Figure 8.8 illustrates the economic trade-offs associated with a terminal expansion. Could you use that figure to explain the trade-offs discussed in part a? How?

11. What variables would be relevant to the decision to locate the following facilities in a particular community?

a) A new regional state university

b) A new steel mill

c) A maximum-security prison

d) A dairy processing plant

e) A fast-food restaurant

f) A multiplex movie theater

g) A new auto plant

h) A bicycle manufacturing plant

i) A bicycle assembly and service shop

12. If you worked for General Motors, what interest would you have in the company that sells steel to GM's ball bearings supplier? What could that interaction do for you? What could you offer them?

13. a) Describe the situation in which an airline seeks to increase the number of ticketed passengers on a flight in terms of fixed costs, variable costs, marginal costs, and profits. Under what conditions would the airline realize increasing returns to scale? Might it ever experience decreasing returns to scale? When?

b) Apply the question in part (a) to bed utilization in Cheryl's hospital.

14. A salesperson for Luis's furniture factory refers to her list of customer names and addresses as a geographic information system (GIS). Is she correct? Explain the difference between the two, and state the advantages of a GIS to a furniture business.

15. Cheryl is considering establishing a GIS of patient data for her hospital. How would such a system help Cheryl? What types of decisions does such a system support?

16. Several international auto manufacturers have built plants in the United States, including Honda, Toyota, BMW, and Mercedes. What issues are relevant to such a decision?

17. Of what use would the center of gravity method be (or not be) to a car company? To a banking and finance firm?

18. The executives of Miller Brewing have asked you to find the best location for their next brewery. (Your basement is not one of the options.) The facility will brew several million barrels a year to distribute to the eastern states. The choice has been narrowed to three sites.

a) What criteria should be included in the multiple-factor rating system that will be used to select a site?

b) How might those criteria differ from the criteria for a small brewery two recent graduates are trying to start in your hometown? (Their choice has been narrowed to three sites as well.)

19. What type of information would you need and what tools would you use if you had to pick the best place to sell or distribute the following items on your college campus?

a) T-shirts commemorating the basketball team's conference championship

b) Jewelry made by students in the art program

c) New carpeting for students moving into the dorms

d) Flyers for a candidate for student body president

e) A computer program for connecting students' personal computers to your school's computer network

20. Each spring the National Collegiate Athletic Association (NCAA) invites sixty-five men's basketball teams and sixty-four women's basketball teams to take part in a single elimination tournament to decide the year's national champion. The first round of the men's tournament is played in four different regions—West, East, Southeast, and Midwest, each of which hosts two groups of eight teams each. In the first round, eight men's teams play at each of eight different locations. The first round of the women's tournament is conducted at sixteen different sites—each with four teams. In both tournaments, the thirty-two winners of the first round play a second round in the same location as the first round. Sixteen teams (the sweet sixteen) qualify to participate in the regional championships that yield the Final Four. The regional championships of each championship are held at four different sites, which are usually different from the first- and second-round sites. The four women's regionals and four men's regional comprise eight individual sites. Finally, the four winners of the regional championships of each tournament meet in the finals, which are usually held at yet another site—with the men's and women's tournaments at different locations.

The NCAA wants to optimize its ticket revenues from the tournaments. How should it determine the best mix of sites for the first-round, second-round, regional, semifinal, and championship games? Are there different considerations for the women's tournament than the men's tournament? Should there be?

PROBLEMS

1. Federated Express delivers small document packages to a large number of clients in a west coast city. Currently located on the outskirts of town, the company pays $15,000 rent per month. If its sorting and distribution center was located closer to the center of the city, then the company could deliver faster and cheaper with variable costs per delivery averaging $2. The current location requires a longer drive into the city and results in a variable cost for each delivery of $2.20. What monthly volume must they have to justify moving into the city?

2. Fred is setting up a new production line that is more labor intensive than most of the others in his plant. He expects the cycle time to be 3 minutes the first week. His engineers estimate an 80% learning curve.

a) What do you project the cycle time to be in the second week?

b) After a month?

c) Two years?

d) Will it eventually get to zero?

3. George Jefferson is expanding his dry cleaning business. He has already expanded to six stores, all of which are located southeast of his original store and all are located in the same metropolitan area. He is now looking for a centralized location in which to build a new processing plant. The table below shows the amount of dry cleaning (pounds) that each store will have processed at the new plant. It also shows the number of miles south and east of his first store where each later store is

located. Using the center of gravity method, where would you suggest he start looking?

	# Miles East	# Miles South	Pounds of Dry Cleaning
First Store	0	0	1000
Store #2	2	5	1500
Store #3	2	7	1200
Store #4	8	1	2200
Store #5	9	4	1750
Store #6	9	5	2500

Project	Daily Milk Production (gallons)	Miles from the Main Plant	Miles from Plant #2	Miles from Plant #3
Jones' Farm	45,000	2	8	14
Jersey Dairy	30,000	6	5	2
Dave's Dairy	65,000	9	2	7
Smith Dairy	75,000	2	8	5
Dan's Dairy	95,000	12	1	4
Garland's Dairy	25,000	1	12	6
Mabry Farms	10,000	7	3	11
Rupel Dairy	25,000	3	7	7
Total	370,000			

4. A recent college graduate works in downtown Boston for a "Big Four" accounting firm. She can rent an apartment literally across the street from the office with only a 6-minute commute (going down the elevator, across the street and up another elevator). However, the rent would be $2500 per month for the one-bedroom apartment. She could live in a small town in New Hampshire and rent a comparable apartment for $600 per month, but would have 45-minute commute to the office by train and subway. Assume that she values her time at $40 per hour and the cost of the train would be $5 daily.

a) How many trips a month must she make in to work to make living in the city worth the added cost?

b) Assuming that as she moves up the corporate ladder, her time becomes more valuable. If she makes twenty-five trips a month to the office, how much would her time need be worth in order to justify the city apartment?

5. A regional dairy company has three processing plants that collect milk each morning from eight large dairy farms for pasteurization and packaging. The main plant can process 150,000 gallons daily while Plant #2 and Plant #3 can each process 170,000. The distance between each farm and the three plants is listed below as well as the daily output of each farm.

a) Assuming hauling costs are proportional to distance and all other issues are equal, set this problem up using the transportation model.

b) What might be a good first cut at a solution?

6. A frozen food packing company currently operates two processing plants in small towns located near rail yards. Each began as a separate company more than 75 years ago, but about 10 years ago one bought out the other. Currently, the combined fixed costs are approximately $15,000 per day; at optimal capacity, each can produce a box of frozen vegetables for about $.50 in variable costs. Demand, which is projected to grow over the future, is estimated at 148,000 boxes of frozen vegetables per day for the next year. Managers feel that volume may be more than the two plants can handle efficiently, given their current configuration.

Managers are presently considering a proposal to consolidate the two plants, at a site more convenient to the interstate highway system. The new plant would eliminate redundant overhead and more than double the firm's capacity, but the cost of additional automaton would push fixed costs to $20,000 per day. Decreased direct labor costs and more cost-effective shipping would reduce variable costs to $.47 per box.

Should managers go ahead with the new plant? On what assumptions do you base your conclusion? How sensitive is your conclusion to those assumptions?

7. The owner-operators of a single facility dry cleaning business are thinking of moving closer to their customers in order to offer free delivery by 4 p.m. of any clothes brought in by 10 a.m. They are currently processing 2700 garments per week at a converted convenience store beneath their second-story apartment. They pay $400 per week in rent, plus some other fixed costs. The new location they are considering would cost them $1800 per week, including their daily commute to work. However, the owners estimate that being closer to their customers would reduce their average variable cost from the current $1.75 per garment to an estimated $1.25 per garment, due to a reduction in delivery fees, which are charged on a per mile and per stop basis, as well as in the fees for occasional temporary help. The shorter delivery time would give them more time in which to meet their "in by 10, delivered by 4" promise.

Should the owners move to the new location? On what assumptions do you base your conclusion? How sensitive is your conclusion to those assumptions?

8. An oil company is looking for a location in which to build a new distribution center, to service all the retail gasoline stations in a large city on the eastern seaboard. Existing stations are listed in the table below, in terms of their daily volume (in gallons) and the number of miles east (-west) and north (-south) of the city's center.

Using the center of gravity method, determine approximately where in relation to the city center the oil company should try to locate its new distribution center.

Location	East (-West) from City Center	North (-South) from City Center	Volume
Station 1	5	−15	2500
Station 2	−15	5	12,000
Station 4	12	12	3700
Station 7	−7	−11	4800
Station 3	6	−5	2900
Station 12	1	15	11,300
Station 14	12	10	2900
Station 9	15	−5	7200

9. A newly hired Vice President of Operations for a large West Coast lumber business is trying to find a location in which to buy a house. She has narrowed her choices down to two suburbs of Portland, Oregon, where her company is headquartered: Green Hills and Burlingame. The two places are equal in all respects except for five: quality of the local schools, commuting time to her job, her husband's commuting time to his new job, the availability of recreational activities, and property taxes. She and her husband have weighted the quality of the schools their highest priority, at .5; the other factors they have weighted equally at .125.

The following ratings (on a scale of 1–10) were obtained from the local chamber of commerce, the real estate company, and coworkers at the executive's new company. In which community should the executive begin to look for a house? How would your recommendation change if the quality of the schools in Green Hills were to be reduced by 50%?

For Problem 9

Location	Schools	Her Commute	His Commute	Recreation	Property Taxes
Green Hills	7	4	6	2	7
Burlingame	5	6	4	9	3

10. A producer of television commercials has reduced the potential locations for a new studio to three options: an upper Midwestern city, a large city in the Southwest, and a small town on the East Coast. The criteria on which they will base the decision include proximity to a major airport, political climate, average number of days of sunshine per year, and the availability of catering service.

The following figures are based on a scale of 1–100. Where should the new studio be located? How likely is the answer to this question to change?

Location	Airport	Sunshine	Politics	Catering
Midwest	25	40	80	90
Southwest	40	80	32	25
East coast	15	30	45	90
Weights	0.2	0.5	0.2	0.1

11. A large electronics manufacturer has several manufacturing sites located all over the country. Each year the firm hires interns, who are trained first at corporate headquarters, to work at its plants. The vast majority of the interns are hired from three schools in Michigan, Arizona, and Ohio. Managers would like to find a centrally located site where the interns can meet twice a year for a week of orientation. They plan to pick an airport, rent a block of hotel and meeting rooms, and fly all the interns in for a 2-day meeting at the beginning and end of their internships.

Managers would like to minimize travel time for all concerned. Using the center of gravity method and the table below, which lists the potential locations

and their distances east-west and north-south of corporate headquarters; the number of students needed at each plant; and the number historically hired from each school, suggest where managers should begin looking.

Location	East (-West) from Corp. Headquarters	North (-South) from Corp. Headquarters	Volume
Plant 1	5	−15	8
Plant 2	−350	118	7
Plant 12	−900	375	3
Plant 3	450	−1100	9
Plant 8	−1800	−1200	11
Plant 4	180	−11	2
Plant 5	1	1	12
School 1	100	65	20
School 2	175	−250	20
School 3	−1500	−1100	12

CHALLENGE PROBLEMS

1. Officials at Fairbanks International Airport (FIA) in Alaska are planning the expansion of their parking facilities. They have two options on the table at the moment. Building a parking garage close to the terminals for long-term parking will have the highest construction costs ($22 million dollars for 2000 spaces) as the land is more valuable and construction will be very disruptive. Yet this option provides the best access—customers can walk to the terminals—so operating cost are minimal. Assuming staffing, maintenance, and convenience are considered in estimating variable costs, airport managers assume variable operating costs of $3 per car, per stay utilizing the facility.

Another option is to locate the facility across the interstate highway from the airport. Land is cheaper, construction would not disrupt any current operations and there is ample room for expansion (the airport managers expect 2000–3000 more spaces will be needed by 2010). However, it would require a shuttle that would add to the cost of each car utilizing the facility. Construction cost would only be $6 million for 4000 spaces as most parking could

be on the ground level. Operating costs, including the extra cost of the shuttle and an allowance for customer convenience would be estimated at $6 per car, per stay. Assume construction costs can be amortized over 10 years without interest (because of to a state development loan program) and that average revenue is about $12 per car, per stay.

a) What is the break-even number of customer cars for each parking facility?

b) How many times must a space turn over in a year to break even for the close in facility? The remote facility? How would you determine the facilities' annual capacity? Which is more feasible?

c) How would the intangibles factor into this decision?

d) Under what conditions is each option financially profitable? Would it ever make sense to build a garage that is unlikely to break even?

2. A new school district has been formed by consolidating existing schools from three nearby small

towns. One town's students exceeded capacity of its local school while another's was significantly below capacity. The newly elected School Board must now draw the boundaries for which kids go to which school based upon current demand, balancing school utilization, all while minimizing the cost of busing. The enrollment demand for each if the three towns, the capacity of each school and the daily cost of busing a student from one town to the other's school is listed below.

Town	Enrollment Demand	Existing School Capacity	Cost of Busing from (within) Marshalltown	Cost of Busing from (within) Laineville	Cost of Busing from (within) Bethsburg
Marshalltown	800	550	$1.50	$4.00	$5.00
Laineville	400	600	$4.00	$1.00	$1.75
Bethsburg	500	650	$5.25	$2.00	$1.25

a) Assuming that transportation costs are the main issue, can this be set up with the transportation model?

b) What would be a good solution?

c) What other issue might come into play in addition to transportation costs?

3. A local assembly operation for a consumer appliance manufacturer has fixed costs of $5000 a day. Variable costs are about $1 per unit for materials and $3.50 per unit for labor on the first production shift. Given the shift differential (due to increased pay on the second and third shifts), increased costs of supervision, and other variable overhead costs, managers estimate the marginal cost per unit (excluding materials) to be $5.00 on the second shift and $7.25 on the third shift. The plant can produce up to 2000 units per shift.

Use a spreadsheet to put together a worksheet like the one in Table 8.2 (on page 358). What is the plant's best operating level? How many units must be assembled before the operation makes a profit? At what volume is the plant's total profit maximized?

4. Tom is looking at a new type of fueling truck use at the airport his airline uses most. The company has been testing one for almost a week, and it has the potential to significantly cut the time required to refuel a plane while at the gate. The first time the equipment was used, the crew was not very familiar with it and they needed 60 minutes to refuel a plane that took 30 minutes with the old equipment. By the time the thirty-second plane had been fueled with the new equipment the time was down to 35.42 minutes. Assume a truck and crew are scheduled to refuel six planes per day for the immediate future.

a) Can you estimate the learning curve?

b) How long till they get it down to less than the time required for the old system?

c) What should the time be in 6 months?

d) What impact will that have capacity of the trucks and the way they are scheduled?

e) Will it have any impact on the capacity and scheduling of planes?

Case 8: Capacity and Location Issues in a Yacht Building and Repair Business?

Savannah-based yacht builder Intermarine, was tied up for months as embattled WorldCom Inc. sorted out its assets in U.S. Bankruptcy Court. Recently it was released for sale to Palmer Johnson, a Wisconsin-based yacht maker with a boat yard in nearby Thunderbolt, Georgia. (Palmer Johnson Inc. in Sturgeon Bay, Wisconsin, builds a wide range of custom and semi-custom luxury motor yachts, sport fishing and sailing yachts ranging from 80 feet to more than 200 feet. The company is one of the world's leading builders of custom yachts as well as a leading provider of yacht refit/repair services.) The 21-acre Intermarine manufacturing facility joins Palmer Johnson's more than 30-acre Thunderbolt facility and an interior design facility convenient to the nearby Savannah Hilton-Head International Airport. The Thunderbolt location is one of the largest paint, service, and refit yards on the East Coast, while the 65,000-square-foot operation close to the airport serves as an interior fabrication facility for yachts and executive jets. Combining both operations makes Palmer Johnson's Savannah-area operation one of the world's largest such facilities.

The consolidation of the two yacht makers was at first assumed to be a boost for both. The hope was that by no longer competing against each other, the merged operations would be more efficient. For example, when one yard is slow and another busier personnel can be shifted and capacity more fully utilized.

With the more visible merged Savannah facility also came the possibility that some capacity could be dedicated to production of new yachts. This would allow city officials to further develop plans to build a mega yacht marina, attracting more yacht traffic to Savannah as owners either visit or use the city as a home port.

Clearly the Palmer Johnson expansion, by acquisition of Intermarine, held the promise of expanded business and new jobs for Savannah residents. However, not long after the sale of Intermarine was announced, rumors of layoffs and shut downs in Wisconsin surfaced for Palmer Johnson. In fact, the Sturgeon Bay company soon filed for bankruptcy and layoffs of workers began. The financial woes and threats of eviction at Palmer Johnson Inc.'s facility in Sturgeon Bay, Wis., were claimed to have no bearing on the health of the yacht builder's newly expanded facility in Savannah because Palmer Johnson, Inc. was a separate and distinct corporation from Palmer Johnson Savannah. Issues of what money and work was moved between the two facilities (including a 131-foot custom yacht—an $18.9 million dollar project) became the focus of legal wrangling by creditors and subsequent court actions.

By June of 2003, while Palmer Johnson officials continued to deny the linkage of the two corporate entities, Thunderbolt yard employees were being laid off and concerns arose that Palmer Johnson Savannah would have to close its Thunderbolt shipyard due to entanglements with the Wisconsin bankruptcy. Management conceded the luxury yacht builder had moved its headquarters to the company's Savannah River yard, former site of Intermarine Savannah while continuing to deny plans to close the Thunderbolt yard.

SOME QUESTIONS TO THINK ABOUT:

1. In what ways is the Savannah location better than the Sturgeon Bay site for Palmer Johnson? Would this hold for every company building luxury yachts?

2. What does the case say about economies of scale in this industry? How about the scope of the product-service bundles provided?

3. How would government officials in both locations see the developments? Why?

4. What are the ethical factors in what may have been PJ's long-run strategy all along?

Source: Adapted from "Intermarine Sold to Palmer Johnson," *Savannah Morning News*, Feb. 6, 2003, reporter Mary Carr Mayle

"Palmer Johnson Buys Intermarine Assets," *Savannah Morning News*, Feb. 7, 2003, reporters Mary Carr Mayle and Ben Werner

"Smooth Sailing," *Savannah Morning News*, Feb. 9, 2003, reporter Mary Carr Mayle

"Despite problems in Sturgeon Bay, Palmer Johnson Savannah healthy, officials say," *Savannah Morning News*, March 4, 2003, reporter Mary Carr Mayle

"Tale of two companies," *Savannah Morning News*, March 12, 2003, reporter Mary Carr Mayle

"Bankruptcy filing further muddles Palmer Johnson picture," *Savannah Morning News*, June 11, 2003, reporter Mary Carr Mayle

"Palmer Johnson changing its Savannah focus," *Savannah Morning News*, June 26, 2003, reporter Mary Carr Mayle

REFERENCE

Gray, A. E. *Process Fundamentals.* Harvard Business School Teaching Note, 1995. Harvard University, Cambridge, MA

9 Facility Layout Design Processes

Chapter Outline

Introduction   404
Integrating Operations Management across the Functions   405
General Layout Types   406

Fixed-Position Layouts   406

Product Layouts   408

Process Layouts   410

Cellular Layouts   410

Hybrid Layouts   411

Layout Decisions and Competitiveness   412

Considerations That Drive Layout Decisions   416

Tools to Help with Process-Oriented Layout Decisions   417

Summary   443
Key Terms   444
Solved Problems   444
Discussion Questions   447
Problems   448
Challenge Problems   450
Case 9.1: Intel's "Seedy" Plant Cloning Process   453
References   454

Learning Objectives

After studying this chapter you should be able to

- Demonstrate your understanding of the linkages between the operational issues involved in making facility layout decisions and the concerns arising from other functional areas of business

- Identify and describe the generic types of facility layouts

- Describe the relationship between facility layout and competitiveness

- Summarize the considerations that drive layout decisions

- Utilize tools that are helpful in making process oriented layout decisions

- Balance assignment of work to optimize product oriented layouts

. . . Back at the Rec Center

Luis arrived with everybody else this morning, but he seems more interested in socializing than in exercising. Now, about 10 minutes earlier than usual, he's getting ready to head for the lockers.

"What's the rush? You hardly worked out this morning," notes Tom. "You have a big day coming up at work, or what?"

"No, not really," Luis replies. "I'm just a little drained this morning. I went to one of those really big health clubs last night. A guy at work has been talking about this new circuit training he's doing there, and I wanted to check it out."

"Oh, I get it. You don't like us anymore! You're going to leave us high and dry," Fred chimes in, with as maudlin a look as he could muster. He was just giving Luis some good-natured ribbing, with his visit to the larger club serving as the excuse.

"No, no, no," Luis interrupts defensively. "That's not it at all. My friend keeps talking about how he gets such a great workout in such a small amount of time. It sounded interesting. He kept asking me to join him, so finally I said okay. I'll try anything once."

"Well, what did you think? Was it what you expected?" asks Cheryl.

"Yes and no," replies Luis. "Most of the equipment is grouped by type, like it is here. All the bikes were in one place, the steppers in

another—even the weight stations were clustered. It was set up the same way we group our machines at work, by department—you know, by what they do."

Equipment at the two health clubs was laid out much the same way as the machines in Luis's factory. Luis had heard his factory referred to as a functionally organized job shop, so he assumed that the layout of the health clubs could be called the same. It seemed that the clubs' layouts made getting a workout as inefficient and time consuming as his factory's layout made building a batch of tables. Though Luis realized he came to the rec center's club for more than just an efficient workout, he'd thought he might as well check out the other club's setup to see whether he might learn something about getting a good workout and running a factory at the same time.

"But how is that different from what we have here?" asks Fred, interrupting Luis. "I've seen the place you're talking about from the street. It looks huge! They must have twenty of everything. We're lucky to have four of anything! Besides size, what's the big deal?"

"Yes, it's very big!" confirms Luis. "The different areas, or sections, all had a staffer who specialized in one activity. It was pretty cool. They really knew their stuff." He told the group about how aerobics were held in a separate room that was closed during classes. You could talk even when there was a class in session; music from a boom box didn't drown out conversation. He told them the other club even had a couple of rooms just for day care. "But all that's not really why I went," he says. "I went to try an area where they had a sequence of stations set up for circuit training."

Luis realized that there might be some advantages to the size of the club (the specialization and all), but he was sure it took a lot of memberships to pay for such a huge operation. As big as the club was, Luis had noticed that some sections were particularly crowded, with a lot of people waiting to get on the machines. Those parts didn't seem to move any faster than they did at rec center's club. In fact, in the smaller club, you could look across the room to see whether the upcoming stations or machines were busy and adjust the order of your workout accordingly. In the larger club, Luis had noticed that some of the machines he liked to use were at opposite ends of the building. While he didn't mind the walk, by the time he got there and discovered that a machine was busy, it was a pain to go look for something else to do. Besides, when he got out of line to check another area, he lost his spot in the place where he had been working out. That part of the new club didn't seem any more efficient than the smaller one— maybe even less so. But that wasn't why Luis had gone there. "What I really went there for was the circuit training," he repeated.

"I've heard something about that kind of stuff, but not much," Cheryl says, curious. "What was it like?"

"Pretty nice," Luis answers. "They had a series of stations set up in a fixed sequence. You went from one to the next in two-minute intervals. What you did at each one took about a

minute to a minute and a half. You got a few seconds to recover and then went right on to the next one. First it was some easy stretching stuff, then a strider, a bike, some weights for the legs, bench press—a lot of stuff. By the time we were done, we had really pretty much hit all the bases. Right down the line. Real quick and to the point! I was really feeling the burn in about 30 minutes."

"What if you wanted to skip something or go in a different order?" asks Tom.

"Yeah, that sounds like trying to get a McDonald's hamburger without a pickle!" adds Fred.

"It sounds like the same tradeoff you might make in a fast-food restaurant, a factory, or even a hospital," interjects Cheryl. She knew from experience that flexibility and efficiency don't often go hand in hand. "You get through the circuit predictably as long as you want to do the same basic stuff—you know, use it the same way as everybody else. Try to get some variety—take a slower pace than the rest of the crowd or go back to get something you forgot—well, I bet that's different!"

"You're right, you can't do that on the circuit—not without a hassle, anyway," says Luis. I guess if you want variety or something unique, you need to use those specialized sections I mentioned earlier."

"I see what you mean," says Tom. "The circuit is a great idea if there are enough people who want the same type of workout at the same pace. Kind of like having enough people who are willing to buy the same type of car, hamburger, or even a seat to Dallas six times a day! You set up an assembly line," he adds.

"Sounds like our cell phone assembly," says Fred. "You can have them any way you want them, as long as it's the one way we make them!"

"But like Tom said," notes Cheryl, explaining her point further, "that's not a problem if there's enough demand for that particular cell phone. You can keep the costs down when you do it that way, right?"

"Costs down?" asks Luis. "That place of Fred's costs bazillions! How can that be cheap?"

"Volume, volume, volume!" replies Fred. "Just like Tom's airline, we spread costs out over volume. Everything we do, we do to get the numbers up! That helps keep the cost down. But we wouldn't invest unless we knew the numbers were there. This new club must figure a lot of people want that type of circuit training."

"Maybe somebody should open up a club just for circuit training?" asks Tom.

"Well, for now, this may be a good compromise—you know, until they see the interest is going to last," Cheryl replies. She recognized that management could always move the circuit machines back to the areas they came from. From the description, it sounded as if the club had not spent much money on things that couldn't easily be undone.

"Yeah, but when it's all said and done, this deal reminds me of what I like about my factory and this club," summarizes Luis. "It's flexible enough to give me what I need, even if I do have to wait for Tom to quit hogging the treadmill once in a while!"

"Right, and it's small enough to be comfortable!" adds Cheryl. The others agreed. Tom grins at Luis as he adds 5 more minutes to the treadmill timer.

Introduction

In this chapter we introduce a variety of general layout types, describe the impact of layout decisions on competitiveness, summarize the considerations that drive layout decisions, and present a number of quantitative tools that can help managers who make layout decisions.

The choice of a layout for a factory or service operation is a significant one. Such decisions are particularly crucial in big cities, where office rents are extremely expensive. Total occupancy costs per year based on prime headline rents (the achievable rental value for a unit of 10,000 square feet in a prime location) in London's West End, Midtown Manhattan, Tokyo, and Paris, were $149.16, $118.40, $114.51, and $88.76[1] per square foot, respectively. In most cases, rents have actually declined from higher levels of the 1990s. Consider what the occupancy cost for prime office space could cost in these cities. Surely, Lloyd's of London could easily charge ten times the average rent in London to insurers wishing to rent an office or cubicle in its headquarters.

Think about the practical implications of these costs for layout planners. Using valuable floor space for a

REC CENTER DILEMMA

Luis wants to use circuit training to make tables:

Luis liked the efficiency of the new club's circuit training area. He is thinking about how he might apply the concept to his work. As he drives in that morning, he is thinking about moving the equipment needed for a family of tables and chairs together to make a "circuit." Help him make an argument to his boss. Can you anticipate his boss' objections?

[1] As of the first quarter of 2003. Source: Insignia Richard Ellis, 2003.

wastebasket costs an additional $100 per month. A large desktop with space for horizontally stored files costs a great deal more than an upright filing cabinet. All in all, layout decisions can have a significant impact on the cost of operating a facility, the effectiveness of employees from all functional areas, and the ability of the facility to meet the firm's operational goals.

Moreover, though moving furnishings within a facility is easier than relocating the entire facility, layout decisions are usually seen as long-term decisions. Once a facility has been set up in a particular way, it tends to stay that way for some time, because changing the layout disrupts a firm's operations.

Integrating Operations Management Across the Functions

As illustrated in Table 9.1, layout issues are important within every functional area, as every part of every organization needs its workspace to support its functional excellence. Although it may be less obvious, the layout of facilities is also a business decision with cross-functional importance. Figure 9.1 depicts the layout design process as not only as cross-functional in nature but also as a function of the competitive requirements of the firm as it creates value for the customer.

Rearranging resources within a facility must be financially justified. Layout decisions can determine cash flow and profit potential. Efficiency, also driven by layout, is often a consideration in the financial analysis that compares a company's performance to industry averages and benchmarks.

Because layout determines the approach to cost accounting, managerial accountants are particularly interested in layout decisions. Allocation of costs to cost centers, budgeting, and financial control can all be impacted by layout decisions.

Layout decisions also are important from a human resource perspective. Job descriptions and requisite skills vary greatly depending on layout type. Additionally, schemes for motivation and reward must be tailored to the particular environment, and Occupational Safety and Health Administration (OSHA) regulations must be satisfied.

Particularly in services with greater degrees of customer involvement, layout can be a critical market factor. Consider how important it is for nonsmoking areas in restaurants to actually be smoke free. Or think about how little variety you will find in the layouts of franchised businesses such as fast-food restaurants or retail chains such as Wal-Mart. In these service examples the layout itself is a part of the brand image. In addition to services with extensive customer involvement, layout is a key determinant of the capability of the value-adding system. The need to sell this capability drives marketing strategies.

The engineering and management information systems (MIS) functions provide key support to those making layout decisions. Industrial engineers are often involved in technical analysis of layout alternatives. IS professionals provide computer-aided design (CAD) and other drafting tools, as well as the decision support systems used in location decisions.

Layout decisions are best described as business decisions that have a bearing on every function and must be synchronized with other all other aspects of the value-adding system through the involvement and consideration of all functional areas.

Table 9.1

Integrating Operations Management across the Functions

Integration Perspective / Functional Area	Finance	Accounting
Why Cross-Functional Integration Matters to Facility Layout Decisions	**Layout decisions impact both earning potential and efficiency. Office layout is important within the finance function.**	**Cost accounting systems will vary by layout type. Office layout is important within the accounting function.**
Key Issues	**How will the layout impact a firm's earning potential and thereby, its valuation?**	**How will layout choices impact allocation of costs to cost centers?**

General Layout Types

Regardless of a firm's competitive priorities, the layout of its facilities impacts the way those facilities are run and therefore, the firm's competitiveness over the long run. Different layouts present different managerial challenges and opportunities to satisfy unmet customer needs. As a result, a strategic perspective, geared toward customer satisfaction, is required to make the right layout choices. In the following sections, we will examine the advantages and disadvantages of five basic layouts:

1. Fixed-position layouts
2. Product layouts
3. Process layouts
4. Cellular layouts
5. Hybrid layouts

Fixed-position layout

A layout in which value-adding resources travel to the customer, but materials do not travel through a value-adding system.

Fixed-Position Layouts

In a **fixed-position layout**, value-adding resources travel to the customer or need, but materials do not travel through a value-adding system as they may in other layouts. A fixed-position layout may be used, for example, to film a movie on location, to repair or manufacture a boat in dry dock, to build a house, or to assemble a swing set. In

Human Resources	Marketing	Engineering	Management Information Systems
Layout decisions impact worker morale and job designs. Office layout is important within the HR function.	Layout decisions influence the capability of the value adding system. Layout impacts customer perception in retail and other service operations. Office layout is important within the function.	Engineers may be called upon to aid other functional areas with layout decisions. Office layout is important within the function.	IS tools are helpful in drafting and layout analyses. Office layout is important within the IS function.
How will layout choices impact job designs, incentive systems, worker safety, and worker morale?	How will layout choices impact marketing strategies?	How can a facility layout be optimized and what structural changes will be required?	What layout and drafting software will be supported by the IS function and what system requirements follow this decision?

This luxury ocean liner is being assembled to in a ship yard using a fixed position layout. All the means of transformation come here to the shipyard and the dry dock where the ship is being built rather than building it somewhere inland and trucking it to the ocean.

Reuters/Corbis

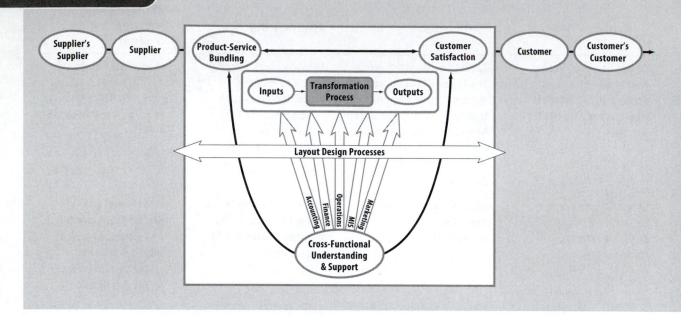

Figure 9.1
Layout design processes

addition, manufacturers of large industrial equipment frequently use a fixed-position layout for final assembly, either immediately prior to shipment or at the customer's manufacturing facility.

The benefit of a fixed-position layout is that highly specialized experts, materials, and resources can be brought together to work on the product-service bundle. When you build a new house on site, you can bring in any subcontractor you choose to customize it to your taste. But when you build a house using prefabricated parts shipped from a factory, your choice of materials, resources, and expertise is much more limited. The disadvantages of the fixed-position layout include a lack of efficiency, difficulty in scheduling and communicating with widely dispersed resources, and a potential for significant cost overruns and quality problems.

Product Layouts

Product layout

A layout in which the value-adding resources are arranged in the order in which materials or customers must flow to complete the product-service bundle.

In a **product layout**, the value-adding resources are arranged in the order in which materials or customers must flow to complete the product-service bundle. The resources in the product layout are dedicated solely to the creation of one product-service bundle and cannot be used for other purposes. This layout is typically used in mass-production assembly operations that might manufacture cell phones and other electronics. If you have ever had the feeling of being herded through a crowded airport, you may have been reacting to its product-oriented layout. Ultimately, the primary value the airport terminal adds is to assemble planeloads of passengers and move them through check-in, seat assignment, and boarding, while the ground crews service the aircraft. Figure 9.2a shows a rough sketch of Redhook Ale's product layout. Though the diagram does not include layout elements such as the square footage allocated to each step in the process or the location of inventory and offices, it illustrates a basic product layout.

Figure 9.2

(a) Product layout—
Redhook Brewery
(b) Process layout—
Thompson-Shore
publisher

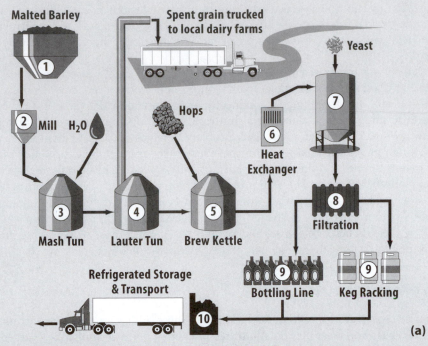

Source: Redhook Brewery's website at http://www.redhook.com/

(a)

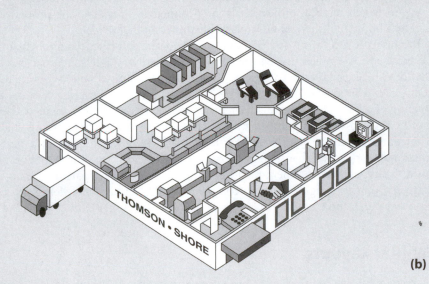

(b)

Source: Thomson-Shore's website at http://www.tshore.com/DesktopDefault.aspx?tabid=27

Using product layouts allows production and material-handling tasks to be automated, thus reducing the need for skilled labor. If demand is large enough, a product layout will enable the production of large quantities of the same item at very low cost. This advantage is particularly important when customers are willing to accept a standardized product-service bundle but demand low prices and high quality. From a financial perspective, the outcome of such high-volume operations can be large profits.

The disadvantage of a product layout is its lack of flexibility. An automobile assembly operation is a good example. To introduce a new model, a car company must make a significant investment in new tooling, the installation of which disrupts the production line and potentially involves a shut-down of production for weeks. Moving to a new product presents an even bigger problem in terms of cost and disruption. When customer preferences change or substitute product-service bundles become available, demand declines and the company has difficulty spreading its high fixed costs over a large number of units. The dual problem of high per-unit costs and unattractive offerings reduces the company's profits—in extreme cases driving it into bankruptcy. From a human perspective, the result is usually reduced income or widespread layoffs for workers. (These wage losses and layoffs usually affect those workers who are least equipped to handle them—namely, those with low-skill jobs.)

Process Layouts

Process (or functional) layout

A layout in which value-adding resources are arranged in groups based on what they do.

In a **process layout**, also called a **functional layout**, value-adding resources are arranged in groups based on what they do. All the resources that perform similar tasks are located together, so that materials can be routed through the resources in any order. The rec center health club where Cheryl, Fred, Luis, and Tom meet has a process layout, as does Luis's furniture factory. Cheryl's hospital, like many others, is supported by a process layout in which medical professionals are grouped by specialty. The process layout used by a book publisher, for example, is illustrated in Figure 9.2b.

Because process layout is flexible, it can be used to provide highly customized product-service bundles. It also fosters an environment in which functional excellence can flourish. Skilled workers are likely to learn from each other and take pride in their technical capabilities. However, this flexibility and functional excellence come at the expense of efficiency and quick response time and bring with them a complex managerial environment. Coordinating a set of diverse jobs is a tremendous challenge in an environment in which workers tend to think of themselves as a part of a functional work area rather than as a part of a broader value-adding system. Employees in this type of environment might be more loyal to their department than to the company, or they might be more concerned with technical excellence than with customer satisfaction.

Cellular Layouts

Cellular layout

Layout in which a facility is made up of value-adding cells.

As discussed earlier in this chapter, fitness equipment in most health clubs is organized into a process layout. An exercise circuit created alongside that process layout is a value-adding cell—a place in which general-purpose resources are dedicated to a particular group of products, parts, subassemblies, or services. A facility made up entirely of such cells would be said to have a **cellular layout**. Each cell in such a layout is, in effect, a pseudo product layout. Figure 9.3 shows the cellular layout used at a Harley-Davidson plant.

Figure 9.3

Sample cellular layout

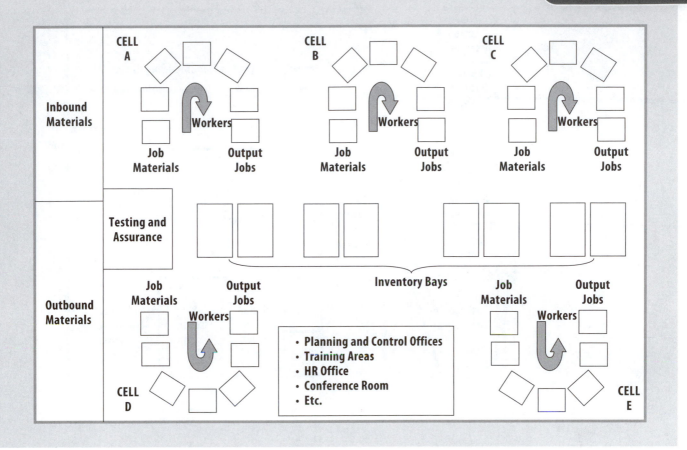

Cellular layouts are designed to obtain much of the efficiency of a product layout without sacrificing flexibility. Using many cells, a facility with such a layout can make a variety of items. More flexible than product layouts and more efficient than process layouts, cellular layouts can deliver a mixture of the advantages and disadvantages of process and product layouts.

Hybrid Layouts

Many facilities have multiple purposes. For instance, the Honda of America plant in Marysville, Ohio, both makes parts and assembles cars. Such facilities are said to have **hybrid layouts**, which combine product, process, and cellular layouts. Figure 9.4 shows the layout of a manufacturing plant owned by Mazak, a machine tool manufacturer in northern Kentucky. Mazak fabricates its parts in one of six cells, assembles the major parts for large machines in fixed assembly stations, and does the final assembly at the customer's site. Note that the part of the plant where the assembly takes place has a fixed-position layout. Mazak indicates that the fabricating cells provide 95% of the firm's part-making value added. This figure suggests that the company has used the cellular layout within its hybrid layout effectively.

Hybrid layouts

Layout in which one facility has multiple purposes.

Figure 9.4

Hybrid layout—mazak
machine tools

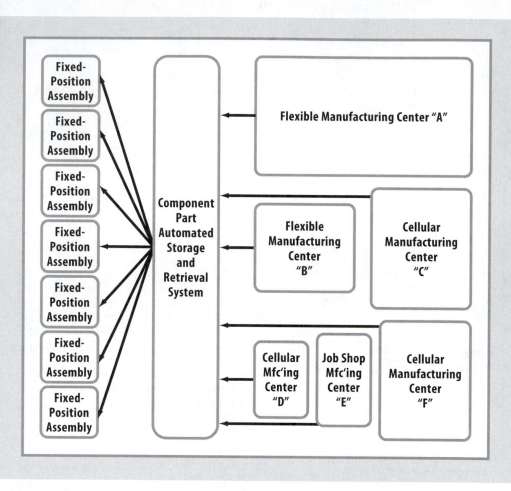

Layout Decisions and Competitiveness

You have probably come to the conclusion that process layouts are well suited to job shops and batch processes, while product layouts lend themselves to continuous flow and repetitive processes. If so, you are exactly right. The reason for this relationship is simple: The firm's competitive priorities should be reflected in all its operational decisions, including those that have to do with the layout of its facilities. If the firm's product-service bundles require customization, then process flexibility, design capability, and delivery speed are of paramount importance. A process-oriented layout will help the firm to attain those strategic advantages. Conversely, a product-oriented layout will provide highly standardized, low-cost product-service bundles on a fixed schedule. Figure 9.5 revisits the discussion of process choice in Chapter 7 (see page 316–319) from the perspective of layout type rather than process choice. Notice that though the correlation between process type and layout is strong, more than one type of layout can be used in any type of process.

Facility layout decisions do have a significant impact on competitiveness. One of the authors of this book once worked for a printing firm called Dependa Graphics. Figure 9.6a shows the initial layout at one of the company's facilities. As you can see, there

Figure 9.5

Process design factors, layout type, and process type (revisited)

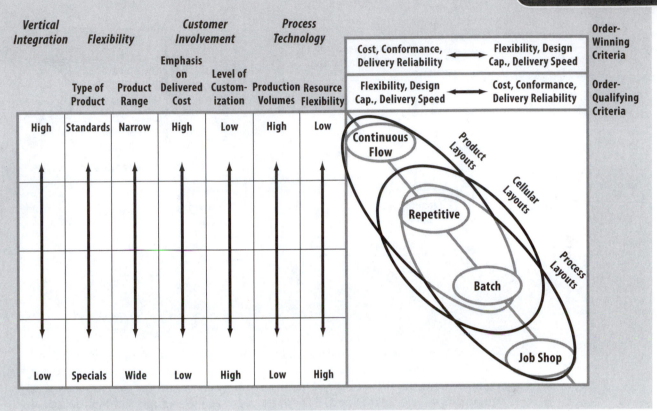

was very little room for inventory in that process layout. Basically, unused materials were kept in boxes in the hall. If materials were ordered too long before they were to be printed or were not picked up immediately after printing, the facility faced a significant space shortage. During busy periods, the business could not meet the needs of all its customers, and jobs over a certain size simply were not feasible. Because the business could not grow, its profitability was severely limited. When the layout of the Dependa Graphics facility was modified as shown in Figure 9.6b, the firm experienced a large increase in both the volume of its business and its profitability. One year after the change, the owner sold the business at a substantial profit—a result he could not have achieved without the positive financial performance enabled by the change in layout.

This example illustrates two things. First, layout decisions cannot always be made starting from scratch. Often, the ideal layout cannot be accomplished because of existing structural realities. For example, the company's building might be too small, a load-bearing wall might be in the wrong place, or the required investment might be too large. Even so, a company should not overlook opportunities to make incremental improvements to a layout. Second, a company should not automatically write off a new business opportunity just because it does not fit the existing layout. Dependa Graphics was able to significantly expand the range of job sizes it could handle by making a small change in layout.

Figure 9.6

Dependa graphics' facility layout

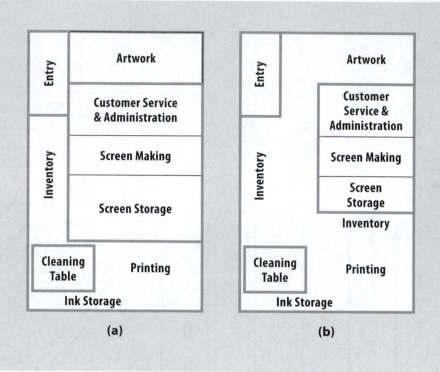

(a)   (b)

Ford Motor Company's auto assembly operations, which use a product-oriented layout, had to make some changes in order to accommodate customer demand for T-tops in the early 1980s. Ford's Mustang assembly line could not accommodate that product option. Until the line could be revamped, managers set up an off-line functional work area in which fully roofed car bodies could be converted to T-tops. For a short period, Ford's layout was less than ideal, but the company nonetheless took advantage of a significant new market opportunity and satisfied an unexpected customer requirement.

In addition to competitiveness, facility layout can have a large impact on service rates and customer satisfaction. For example, in the 1990s, the layout of carry-on luggage security stations at the Minneapolis/St. Paul (MSP) airport was causing significant delays for passengers who transferred to connecting flights. The security stations were located at the entry to each concourse. This ensured that any person on a concourse had been through the security checkpoint. Those who were not on a concourse were not forced to undergo needless inspection. Unfortunately, this layout also caused unnecessary delays for passengers who deplaned on one concourse and needed to board a plane on another concourse. Because these passengers had already passed through a security checkpoint at their airport of origin, it was redundant to check them again for connecting flights. When it was determined that about 40% of the people passing through the checkpoints were doing so to make flight connections, the security stations were moved so that connecting passengers no longer had to pass through security checkpoints. The layout change virtually eliminated the security checkpoint bottleneck and improved the satisfaction of both the travelers whose flights originated at MSP and those who were making connecting flights with no reduction in the effectiveness of the security precautions.

Chrysler Group's Windsor Assembly Plant Launches Next Phase of Flexible Manufacturing

Chrysler Group's assembly plant in Windsor, Ontario, became an example of the next level of flexible manufacturing when it added the 2004 Chrysler Pacifica sport tourer to the same production line as its best-selling 2003 Dodge Grand Caravan and Chrysler Town & Country minivans. The ability to produce several products under the same roof allowed the Chrysler Group to save millions of investment dollars, as well as bring a vehicle to market faster, with better quality and less downtime. With flexible manufacturing, the Chrysler Group estimates it saved nearly $100 million for the Pacifica launch alone while simultaneously reducing tooling and facilities capital expenditures by approximately 40%.

The company's flexible efforts support the addition of five new products to the current long-range product plan. "For the first time ever, a Chrysler Group manufacturing facility is able to produce two entirely different products on the same production line as a result of flexible manufacturing initiatives," said Tom LaSorda, Executive Vice President Manufacturing, Chrysler Group. "Flexibility lends to better use of our capacity, which will ultimately increase our ability to meet market demand more quickly, with less cost, while enhancing our competitive position within the industry."

KEYS TO FLEXIBILITY

The key to Chrysler Group's flexible manufacturing is the order in which the body is assembled, using a standardized underbody palette system in the body shop. The same flexible palette system has also been used at the company's Sterling Heights Assembly Plant in Michigan, which makes Chrysler Sebring and Dodge Stratus sedans, and the Toledo North Assembly Plant in Ohio, home of the Jeep(r) Liberty and Wrangler. This means that the same production system may be used to build sedans, convertibles, minivans, sport-utility vehicles, and now, sport tourers in virtually any order or sequence.

While the Pacifica is now built in the same plant as Chrysler and Dodge minivans, the vehicle is not built on any one of the company's short or long-wheelbase minivan platforms. Chrysler Pacifica is built on its own unique platform, but will use existing corporate components, including the same 3.5-Liter V6 engine that powers the Chrysler 300M.

The vehicles also share several production resources. For example, Windsor's flexible body shop uses common processes of underbody framing and panel lines, paint systems, and final assembly between the Chrysler Pacifica and Chrysler and Dodge minivans. A few unique body sub-assembly systems (engine box, underbody sub-assembly, and body sides) for the Chrysler Pacifica are in satellite areas within the Windsor Assembly Plant.

With the production of both Chrysler Pacifica and Dodge and Chrysler minivans, the Windsor Assembly Plant employs approximately 5,900 employees, and maintains a line-speed of 1,325 units per day, or more than 330,000 combined units annually on a three-shift operation.

PILOT VEHICLES

The ability to build multiple products on the same line enables the company to effectively build pilot vehicles, or test prototypes, in the assembly plant much earlier in the launch phase. Building pilot vehicles on the same line as production vehicles allows the company to train employees as well as detect and address any remaining issues to meet stringent quality levels. This uninterrupted and continuous approach to production will allow the company to increase Pacifica production as the market dictates.

Source: Adapted from http://www.daimlerchrysler.com/index_e.htm

Considerations That Drive Layout Decisions

What considerations are important in making a layout decision? Obviously, the answer will not be the same in all situations. As a rule, the needs of customers and employees will play a significant role in any decision. Some of those needs are included in the partial list that follows:

▶ To reduce unnecessary activities, including non-value-adding activities, such as material handling, packaging, and removal of packaging

▶ To prevent damage to inventory through material handling, packaging, and removal of packaging

▶ To enhance communication among individuals, groups, or departments. For example, the Chrysler Technology Center in Auburn Hills, Michigan, is designed to enhance teamwork among functions. Each function has its own wing in the building, and each platform team its own floor. The building has several hubs where the wings come together, each with a public area containing displays of mutual interest to the various functional groups in the adjoining wings. A ring of meeting rooms surrounds each hub. Thus, the whole layout of the Chrysler Technology Center reflects Chrysler's matrix organizational structure and its emphasis on teamwork.

▶ To prevent rework. Frequently rework results from poor communication about requirements. Getting the job done right the first time has a great deal to do with effective communication of expectations between and among functional groups—which is enhanced by an appropriate layout.

▶ To discourage communication between particular individuals, groups, or departments. A single facility might house the value-adding systems for several different product-service bundles. If competitive priorities and customer expectations differ significantly from one bundle to the next, companies with multiproduct facilities might use an arrangement like the *plant within a plant* to keep employees focused on the relevant customer expectations. Some common examples include the pharmacy at the grocery store, the snack bar at the discount store, and the cosmetics counter in a large department store.

▶ Similarly, when incompatible processes or materials are housed under the same roof, they need to be separated. For example, finishing wooden or metal items usually requires some kind of dust-producing operation followed by a color coating. If the two processes were not physically separated, the dust from the first operation would spoil the second. Thus, great care is always taken to seal off the paint booth from other operations. And you probably recall that your high school band room wasn't located next door to the library.

▶ To provide privacy. Because privacy discourages unwanted communication, separating certain departments, such as payroll or human resources, from others makes sense. Furthermore, in certain service environments, privacy is a luxury that can be used to generate significant additional revenues. The luxury box at the ballpark, the private hospital room with attached toilet and shower, and the separate banquet hall all command a premium price.

▶ To provide for safety of employees, customers, and neighbors. The pharmaceutical company that makes both aspirin and morphine obviously needs to keep the two processes and packaging operations separate.

▶ To provide for security of resources. For example, a movie theater that stays open later than the neighboring retail stores will be located on the perimeter of the mall and have separate access. Similarly, an ATM that is accessible after hours must be carefully placed.

▶ To enhance labor skills and functional excellence through specialization. For example, professors in the accounting department will be located in the same area, so that they can interact and keep up-to-date in their field.

▶ To enhance the quality of work life. Cummins Engine Company's Mid-Range Engine Plant, which is located close to Columbus, Indiana, provides an interesting example of this need. The parking lot of this manufacturing facility is on the roof, and most of the exterior is covered with windows. Thus, the interior is filled with natural light, and workers gaze out on flora and fauna rather than on parking lots. Though employees must still perform repetitive tasks, they have less reason to dread going to work in the morning.

▶ To provide for customer involvement in the value-adding process. Particularly in service operations, individual customers often need to be included in the value-adding process. For this reason, the psychologist has a counseling office, not a counseling classroom. Similarly, at better restaurants customers are served at their tables rather than on a cafeteria line or at a take-out window.

Simplified systematic layout planning (SSLP)

A tool used to develop process-oriented layouts in service organizations and other settings where the need for proximity between departments is influenced by a number of qualitative factors.

Tools to Help with Process-Oriented Layout Decisions

Planners often think of layout decisions in horizontal terms, which is fine if a facility has only one floor. Many facilities, however, are housed in buildings with more than one floor or level. These may include retail establishments, office buildings, factories, restaurants, aircraft, ships, and trains. In such cases, thinking of alternative layouts one floor at a time is a temptation, because the spaces and distances are easier to visualize that way—similar to taking the roof off a dollhouse or architect's model in order to view the interior.

Conceiving of multiple-story facilities in terms of three-dimensional space is very helpful, but, until recently, it has been difficult to do. Today's computer modeling tools help planners to visualize three-dimensional spaces from a variety of angles and perspectives. Doing so helps to eliminate problem layouts and tends to produce better layouts than those that are planned one level at a time. Particularly when the creation of the product-service bundle requires a high degree of customer interaction, computer modeling can help to optimize the design of a facility from the customer's perspective. It allows layout planners to ask themselves, How will this layout look and feel to the customer?

Michael Rosenfeld/Getty Images Inc.

Designing the layout of this restaurant kitchen has obvious criteria, some of which are easily measured objectively (i.e. volume), while others are more subjectively measured (i.e. the head chef's desire to be involved in some key steps of the process). Simplified Systematic Layout Planning can be used in such situations.

SIMPLIFIED SYSTEMATIC LAYOUT PLANNING

Simplified systematic layout planning (SSLP) is a tool used to develop process-oriented layouts in service organizations and other settings where the need for proximity between departments is influenced by a number of qualitative factors. The first step in this

INTEGRATING OM:

Fantastic Food Facts from the "Fun Ship" Fleet

Taking a cruise is about warm climates, exotic destinations, relaxation, entertainment, and food. Lots of food!

If you have ever taken a cruise, you know that the food prepared onboard runs the gamut from buffet style on the upper decks to elegant gourmet fare in the formal dining rooms. The Carnival Cruise Line is no exception. The ability to prepare to order several meals a day for each of the thousands of passengers cruising on their 17 ships requires a challenging combination of mass production and customization. The layout of the ship's galley is therefore a critical factor in cruising success. (See figure below.)

Catering on this grand scale requires a great deal of planning, and preparation. It requires lots of hours in a well designed galley. Fleet-wide weekly food and beverage consumption on the "Fun Ships" reflect Carnival's tradition of keeping its pampered guests happy by serving them eight meals and snacks on every day of their vacations at sea.

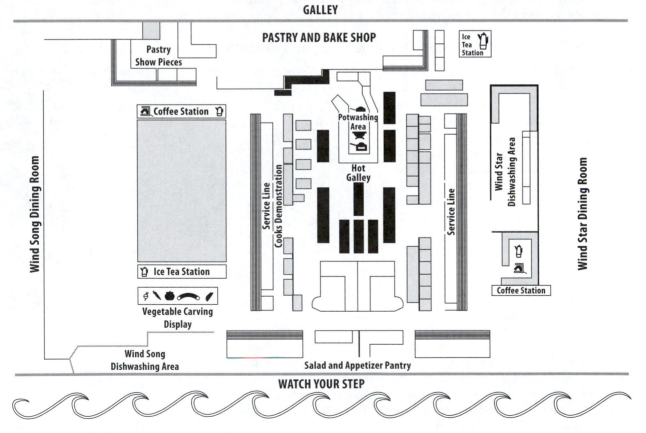

Source: Galley tour of MS Ecstasy; used with permission of Carnival.

The Carnival fleet—in just a week—will serve its guests:

- 39,900   pounds of tenderloin
- 83,700   pounds of chicken
- 13,240   Cornish game hens
- 8,020   whole ducks
- 386,000   shrimp
- 13,100   pounds of veal
- 68,200   hot dogs
- 91,900   hamburgers
- 10,700   pounds of ham
- 8,000   pounds of salmon
- 4,390   pounds of nova (smoked salmon)
- 16,500   pounds of lobster

And for breakfast lovers:

- 568,340   eggs
- 14,070   gallons of fruit juices
- 587,700   bacon slices
- 8,250   pounds of link sausages
- 18,370   pounds of coffee
- 13,230   gallons of homogenized milk
- 20,850   bagels
- 20,970   pounds of butter
- 1,540   pounds of grits
- 74,270   individual boxes of breakfast cereal

What about fruits and vegetables:

- 138,680   tomatoes
- 224,100   potatoes
- 82,480   heads of iceberg lettuce
- 29,990   bell peppers
- 17,465   cucumbers
- 94,420   bananas
- 49,675   apples
- 24,620   melons
- 21,750   fresh pineapples

Pastries are all made aboard "from scratch," using in part:

- 25,570   pounds of cake mixes
- 84,410   pounds of flour
- 22,810   pounds of shortening

Thirsty "Fun Ship" guests drink their way through:

- 351,860   cans of soft drinks
- 6,530   gallons of soda from the bar fountain
- 456,130   domestic and imported beers
- 30,840   quarts of fruit juice for exotic drinks
- 25,000   bottles of champagne and sparkling wines
- 63,108   bottles of wine
- 13,355   liters of Scotch
- 12,330   liters of rye and Canadian whiskey
- 11,825   liters of vodka
- 7,750   liters of gin
- 10,830   liters of rum
- 9,300   liters of tequila and vermouth
- 2,660   liters of cordials and liqueurs
- 1,260   fifths of brandy and cognac

Designing a galley capable of satisfying the expectations of thousands of passengers daily requires careful planning in terms of storage, production flow and menu selection. Appetizers, salads, entrees, drinks, and desserts are prepared in advance in a central galley then placed along a service line to be collected by servers as they flow through the galley and back to one of two dining rooms. Support stations for drinks, salads, appetizers, and desserts are strategically placed to maximize the flow as well. All in all the galley of a typical carnival cruise ship will serve over 1.5 million meals per year!

approach is to classify the need for each department to be adjacent to other departments. Planners generally use an A-E-I-O-U-X taxonomy, as follows:

A—adjacency is absolutely necessary

E—adjacency is especially important

I—adjacency is important

O—ordinary closeness is okay

U—proximity is unimportant

X—proximity is undesirable

Obviously, these classifications should not come out of the blue. Rather, the eventual users of the facility, including the department heads who will operate and maintain it, should be consulted regarding the real need for proximity and distance between various departments.

Once department pairs have been rated using the A-E-I-O-U-X taxonomy, planners must attempt to develop a layout that is consistent with those ratings. The second step in the SSLP is to build department clusters based on the "A," or absolutely necessary, requirements. In the third step, planners add to these "A" clusters based on the "E" (especially important) requirements, and so on, until all the requirements have been included. The result is a set of clusters that indicates the preferred location of departments relative to each other.

Once the relative location of departments has been determined, the actual layout can be planned. Planners take into account variations in the amount of space required from one department to the next and attempt to develop several alternative layouts, all based on the relative locations they have developed. Based on the symmetries present, there may be several different ways to arrange departments without changing their relative locations. In the sixth and last step, planners select one of those alternatives and finalize the layout. The Miami University (Ohio) Recreational Sports Center was planned using SSLP. Table 9.2 shows the adjacency requirements for the various departments in the facility. This table, called a REL chart, shows the relationships among departments (REL is short for "relationship"). Table 9.3 shows only the requirements from Table 9.2, with the rows and columns sorted to clarify the clustering that results from a consideration of the A requirements. Figure 9.7 shows

Figure 9.7

Step 2—form "A" clusters (designated by triple lines)

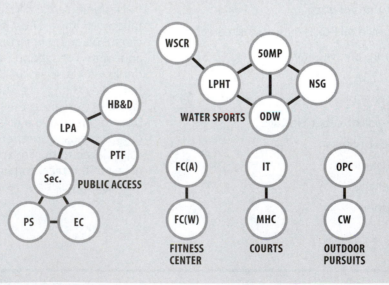

Table 9.2
Adjacency Requirements (REL Chart)

	Recreational Sports Office	Pro shop	Men's Locker Room and Toilets	Women's locker room and toilets	Family locker room and toilets	50 Meter Pool	Olympic diving well	Natatorium Spectator Gallery	Leisure pool and hot tub	Multipurpose hardwood courts	Indoor track	Racquet courts	Exercise Performance Rooms	Watersports classroom	Fitness Center (Aerobic)	Fitness Center (Weight lifting)	Equipment checkout	Security	Lounge and public areas	Public toilet facilities	Outdoor Pursuit Center	Climbing Wall
Recreational Sports Office																						
Pro shop	E																					
Men's locker room and toilets	X	X																				
Women's locker room and toilets	X	X	E																			
Family locker room and toilets	X	X	E	E																		
50 Meter Pool	X	O	I	I																		
Olympic diving well	X	O	I	I	A																	
Natatorium Spectator Gallery	X	U	I	I	A	A																
Leisure pool and hot tub	X	O	I	I	A	E	U															
Multipurpose hardwood courts	X	O	I	I	X	X	X	X														
Indoor track	U	O	I	I	X	X	X	X	A													
Racquet courts	U	O	I	I	U	X	X	U	A	U												
Exercise Performance Rooms	O	O	I	I	U	X	X	U	U	U	U											
Watersports classroom	O	O	I	I	E	E	U	A	X	U	U	U										
Fitness Center (Aerobic)	X	O	I	I	X	X	X	X	I	U	U	U	U	A								
Fitness Center (Weight lifting)	X	O	I	I	X	X	X	X	I	U	U	U	U	A	A							
Equipment checkout	E	A	I	I	U	X	U	U	U	U	U	U	U	U	U	U						
Security	E	A	I	I	U	U	E	U	U	U	U	U	U	U	U	U	A					
Lounge and public areas	I	E	O	O	U	E	U	U	U	U	U	U	U	U	U	U	U	A				
Public toilet facilities	I	O	I	I	U	E	U	A	U	U	U	U	U	U	U	U	U	U	A			
Outdoor Pursuit Center	I	U	U	U	U	U	U	U	U	U	U	U	U	U	U	U	U	U	U	U		
Climbing Wall	U	U	U	U	U	U	I	U	U	U	U	U	U	U	U	U	U	U	I	A	A	
Health Bar & Deli	I	O	U	U	U	E	U	U	U	U	U	U	U	U	U	U	U	U	U	A	U	U

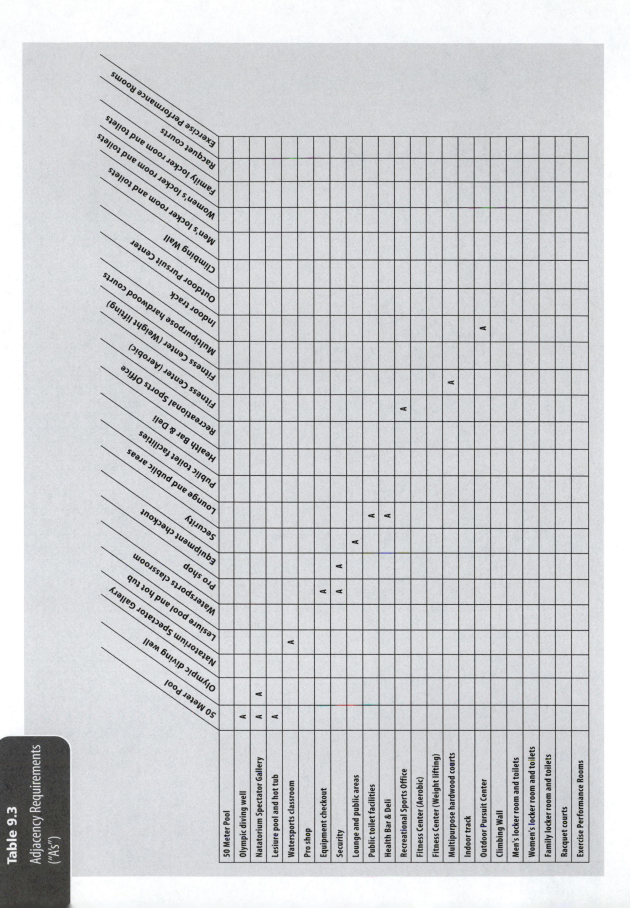

Table 9.3

Adjacency Requirements ("A's")

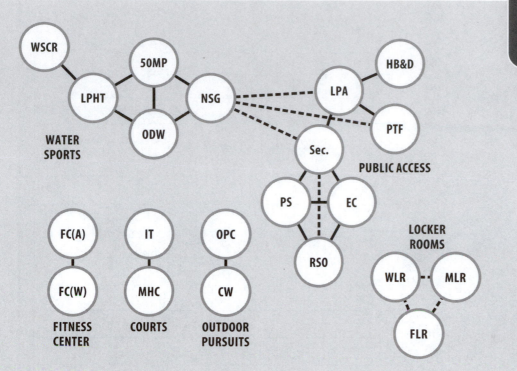

Figure 9.8

Step 3—add "E" clusters (designated by double lines)

the clusters obtained in this second step of the SSLP. Note that there are five separate clusters and that a number of departments are not included in any of them. For convenience, we will call these five initial clusters "water sports," "public access," "fitness center," "courts," and "outdoor pursuits."

Table 9.4 adds the E requirements to the "A" requirements in Table 9.3. The clusters obtained in this third step of the SSLP are shown in Figure 9.8. (To distinguish among the various requirements, heavy solid line connect the "A" requirements, heavy dashed the "E" requirements, and light solid line the "I" requirements.) Notice that another cluster, which we call the locker rooms, has been added. The public access and water sports clusters have been joined at the natatorium spectator gallery (NSG), and a recreational sports office has been added to the public access cluster.

Table 9.5 (page 426) adds the "I" requirements to the "A" and "E" requirements in Table 9.4. Figure 9.9 (page 425) shows the clusters after this fourth step in the SSLP. The picture has been simplified so that only one line represents all the "I" requirements between any two clusters; otherwise, the lines would have made this figure begin to look like a plate of spaghetti. At this point, all areas have been attached, and it has become clear that the locker rooms should be centrally located. Because all areas have been included in Figure 9.9, it is not necessary to draw another figure showing the clustering after consideration of the "O" requirements.[2]

---

[2] Often, layout planners will use four, three, two, and one lines to represent the "A," "E," "I," and "O" requirements, respectively. Because we chose not to show the "O" requirements, we began with three lines. In addition, some planners use colors or different line weights or styles to distinguish among the types of requirement.

Table 9.4
Adjacency Requirements
("A"s & "E"s)

	50 Meter Pool	Olympic diving well	Natatorium Spectator Gallery	Lesiure pool and hot tub	Watersports classroom	Pro shop	Equipment checkout	Security	Lounge and public areas	Public toilet facilities	Health Bar & Deli	Recreational Sports Office	Fitness Center (Aerobic)	Fitness Center (Weight lifting)	Multipurpose hardwood courts	Indoor track	Outdoor Pursuit Center	Climbing Wall	Men's locker room and toilets	Women's locker room and toilets	Family locker room and toilets	Racquet courts	Exercise Performance Rooms
50 Meter Pool																							
Olympic diving well	A																						
Natatorium Spectator Gallery	A	A																					
Lesiure pool and hot tub	A	E																					
Watersports classroom	E	E		A																			
Pro shop					E																		
Equipment checkout					A	A																	
Security					A	A	E																
Lounge and public areas							A	E															
Public toilet facilities								A															
Health Bar & Deli								E															
Recreational Sports Office																							
Fitness Center (Aerobic)																							
Fitness Center (Weight lifting)													A										
Multipurpose hardwood courts																							
Indoor track															A								
Outdoor Pursuit Center																							
Climbing Wall																	A						
Men's locker room and toilets																							
Women's locker room and toilets																			E				
Family locker room and toilets																			E	E			
Racquet courts																							
Exercise Performance Rooms																							

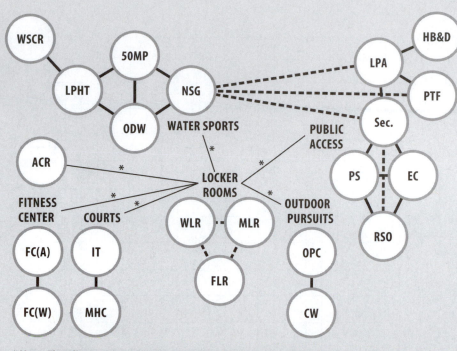

Figure 9.9

Step 4—add "I" clusters (designated by single lines)

* Note: These lines represent the many "I" relationships between each part of one cluster and the corresponding parts of the other cluster.

Based on the information developed in the first four steps of the SSLP, planners considered a number of possible layouts (step 5) before selecting a final layout. Figure 9.10 (page 429) shows the final layout for this facility. The Miami University Recreational Sports Center was one of six winners of *Athletic Business* magazine's Facility of Merit award in 1995 and has hosted several regional and national swimming meets.

DISTANCE- AND LOAD-BASED DECISION-MAKING TOOLS

In developing process-oriented layouts, the costs of material and customer movement should be considered. Using mathematical modeling techniques based on assumptions about future demand for various product-service bundles, it is possible to minimize the distance customers must travel or the pound-feet of materials that must be moved. However, process-oriented layouts must usually be developed in the face of significant uncertainty about future demand. Therefore, decision makers commonly use a "cut-and-try" approach to develop a layout that will accommodate a variety of possible demand patterns.

For example, assume that a manufacturer of specialty papers has recently had some problems with overtime and timely delivery of materials. Managers have decided to evaluate the plant's existing layout, to see if alterations might improve performance. Figure 9.11 (page 432) shows the plant's current layout. The only physical walls inside the facility are located around the roll-paper storage and papermaking areas; the lines

Table 9.5

Adjacency Requirements ("A's," "E's," & "I's")

	50 Meter Pool	Olympic diving well	Natatorium Spectator Gallery	Lesiure pool and hot tub	Watersports classroom	Pro shop	Equipment checkout	Security	Lounge and public areas	Public toilet facilities	Health Bar & Deli	Recreational Sports Office	Fitness Center (Aerobic)	Fitness Center (Weight lifting)	Multipurpose hardwood courts	Indoor track	Outdoor Pursuit Center	Climbing Wall	Men's locker room and toilets	Women's locker room and toilets	Family locker room and toilets	Racquet courts	Exercise Performance Rooms
50 Meter Pool		A																					
Olympic diving well	A		A	A																			
Natatorium Spectator Gallery	A	A		E	E																		
Lesiure pool and hot tub	A	E	E		A																		
Watersports classroom	E	E		A																			
Pro shop							E	E	E										–	–			
Equipment checkout						A		A	A		E								–	–			
Security						A	A		E	A	E								–	–			
Lounge and public areas						E	A	E		A	I							–	–	–			
Public toilet facilities								A			–								–	–		–	
Health Bar & Deli								A				–							–	–		–	
Recreational Sports Office											A		A										
Fitness Center (Aerobic)											–			–					E	–		–	
Fitness Center (Weight lifting)													A	–					–	E		–	
Multipurpose hardwood courts														A						–		–	
Indoor track											–				A					–			
Outdoor Pursuit Center																		A		–			
Climbing Wall																A			–	–		–	
Men's locker room and toilets																				–			
Women's locker room and toilets																		E	E				
Family locker room and toilets																		E	E	–		–	
Racquet courts																		–	–				
Exercise Performance RoomsN																		–	–				

Example 9.1

Assume the following table of adjacency requirements was provided by a doctor's office that is seeking your help with the layout of their new facility.

Use the SSLP clustering procedure, assume a simple rectangular building, and determine a suitable arrangement of the six areas within the facility.

	Restrooms	Office	Exam Rooms	Break Rooms	Waiting Room	Storage
Restrooms	******	E	I	U	A	U
Office		*****	A	E	E	I
Exam Room			*****	U	A	I
Break Room				*****	U	U
Waiting Room					*****	X
Storage						*****

Doctor's Office Adjacency Requirements

Step 1: Identify the adjacency requirements. This has been accomplished in the table provided.

Step 2: Identify clusters based on "A" adjacencies. Connect resources in the cluster with heavy solid lines. (See figure below.)

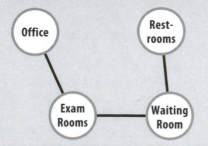

Step 3: Add the "E" adjacency requirements to the clusters and form new clusters as required. Use a heavy dashed line to represent the "E" adjacency requirements.

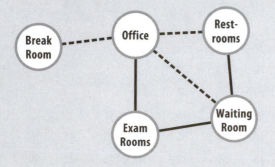

Step 4: Add the "I" adjacency requirements to the clusters and form new clusters as required. Use a light solid line to represent the "I" adjacency requirements. A two-directional arrow may be added to show "X" adjacencies.

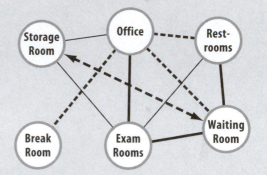

Step 5: Establish a general layout pattern based on the clustering algorithm. (See figure below for the result.)

Here is how we arrived at that result. (Note that this layout may not be the only suitable alternative based on the adjacencies given and the clustering algorithm.) We started with the three-line cluster ("A" adjacencies), placing the restrooms and waiting room together for the sake of patient convenience, the office and exam rooms together for doctor convenience, and the exam rooms and waiting room together to facilitate patient flow. Because the "E" requirements for the waiting room and restrooms

(continued)

Example 9.1

(continued)

were well accommodated this way, we simply placed the break room as close as possible to the office when considering the "E" requirements. To accom- modate the "X" adjacency, we swapped the original placement of the break room when adding the stor- age room and accommodating the "I" requirements.

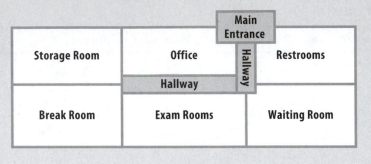

Table 9.6

The Paper Co. Distance Matrix (Current)

	Receiving	Paper Making	Roll Paper Storage	Recyclable Paper & Pulp Storage	Laminating	Embossing	Cutting	Packaging	Shipping
Receiving									
Paper Making	60								
Roll Paper Storage	60	50							
Recyclable Paper & Pulp Storage	50	70	20						
Laminating	75	30	20	55					
Embossing	85	50	30	50	20				
Cutting	105	40	60	80	20	25			
Packaging	125	100	60	100	30	20	40		
Shipping	100	130	40	40	60	30	115	45	
Assembly	140	110	85	120	50	30	25	25	90

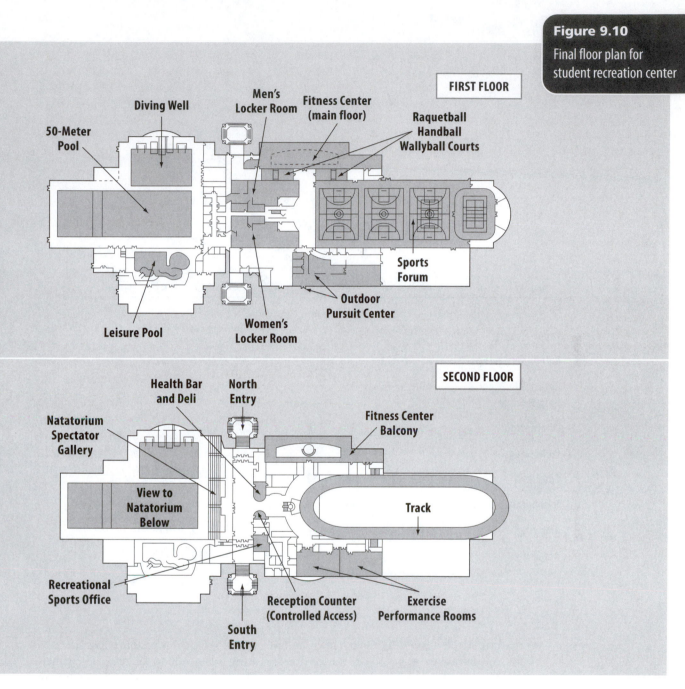

Figure 9.10

Final floor plan for student recreation center

FIRST FLOOR

Diving Well

Men's Locker Room

Fitness Center (main floor)

Raquetball Handball Wallyball Courts

50-Meter Pool

Sports Forum

Leisure Pool

Women's Locker Room

Outdoor Pursuit Center

SECOND FLOOR

Health Bar and Deli

North Entry

Fitness Center Balcony

Natatorium Spectator Gallery

View to Natatorium Below

Track

Recreational Sports Office

Reception Counter (Controlled Access)

Exercise Performance Rooms

South Entry

between other functional areas represent aisles that are used for transporting materials. Paper pulp and paper rolls are received via rail and truck. The pulp goes to the roll paper machine, where it is made into rolls of a variety of colors and weights. These rolls are then sent to roll paper storage, where they are kept along with rolls from outside vendors. Defective rolls go into recyclable paper storage.

When a customer such as a greeting card company, a publisher of annual reports, or some other specialty printer orders paper for a production run, the stock is pulled from roll storage and converted as necessary in the laminating, embossing, and cutting centers. (Laminating or embossing must be done before cutting.) Depending on

Table 9.7

The Paper Co. Volume Matrix

	Receiving	Paper Making	Roll Paper Storage	Recyclable Paper & Pulp Storage	Laminating	Embossing	Cutting	Packaging	Shipping
Receiving									
Paper Making	15								
Roll Paper Storage	75	75							
Recyclable Paper & Pulp Storage	0	25	5						
Laminating	0	0	10	0					
Embossing	0	0	30	2	0				
Cutting	6	0	105	12	10	30			
Packaging	0	0	0	0	0	0	0		
Shipping	0	0	0	7	0	0	0	150	
Assembly	0	0	0	0	0	0	150	150	0

their size, leftover rolls are sent to either roll paper storage or recyclable paper storage. Non-laminated paper that is wasted due to cutting is also sent to the recyclable paper storage area, for eventual use in making new rolls. Customer orders are put together in the assembly area prior to packing and shipping. All outbound shipments are placed on a railcar, which is dispatched daily to the distribution center across town.

Table 9.6 (page 428) shows the distance (in meters) between each pair of work centers, as they are currently arranged. Table 9.7 indicates the average weekly volume shipped between each pair of work centers over the past six months. Multiplying the distance by the volume for each pair of work centers provides the distance-volume figures shown in Table 9.8. Notice that although the layout shown in Figure 9.11 makes sense from the perspective of materials flow, the volume of paper being embossed or laminated is small relative to the amount being cut. The weekly shipment from roll

Table 9.8

The Paper Co. Distance *
Volume Matrix (Current)

	Receiving	Paper Making	Roll Paper Storage	Recyclable Paper & Pulp Storage	Laminating	Embossing	Cutting	Packaging	Shipping	Totals
Receiving										
Paper Making	900									900
Roll Paper Storage	4500	3750								8250
Recyclable Paper & Pulp Storage	0	1750	100							1850
Laminating	0	0	200	0						200
Embossing	0	0	900	100	0					1000
Cutting	630	0	6300	960	200	750				8840
Packaging	0	0	0	0	0	0	0			0
Shipping	0	0	0	280	0	0	0	6750		7030
Assembly	0	0	0	0	0	0	3750	3750	0	7500
										35570

storage to cutting of 6300 ton-meters is significantly greater than other shipments to and from roll storage. This imbalance indicates a potential source of improvement in materials handling.

Figure 9.12 (page 433) shows an alternative layout for this plant. Notice that only the cutting, embossing, and laminating areas have been moved. The new distance matrix is shown in Table 9.9, and the new distance-volume matrix in Table 9.10 (page 434). Notice that the number of ton-meters traveled between roll storage and the embossing and laminating centers has risen. In fact, jobs that are embossed or laminated are now traveling much farther than they did before. This increase is more than offset, however, by the reduction in travel distance for jobs that require only cutting. Note that the total weekly material handling (in ton-meters) has fallen almost 10%.

Table 9.9
The Paper Co. Distance Matrix (Alternative)

	Receiving	Paper Making	Roll Paper Storage	Recyclable Paper & Pulp Storage	Laminating	Embossing	Cutting	Packaging	Shipping
Receiving									
Paper Making	60								
Roll Paper Storage	60	50							
Recyclable Paper & Pulp Storage	50	70	20						
Laminating	100	35	60	75					
Embossing	110	55	70	90	20				
Cutting	80	40	20	40	20	25			
Packaging	125	100	60	100	30	20	40		
Shipping	100	130	40	40	60	30	115	45	
Assembly	140	110	85	120	50	30	25	25	90

Figure 9.11

The paper company's existing layout

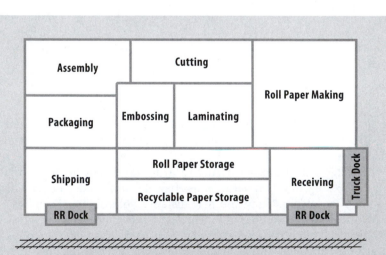

*Note: All outbound shipments go by rail to the company's distribution center across town. Pulp and roll paper are received by rail and truck, therefore, shipping and receiving can't be moved. The roll paper making area also can't be moved because doing so would require changing the plumbing.

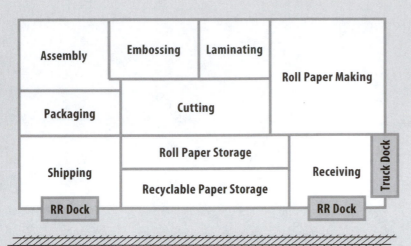

Figure 9.12

The paper company's alternative layout

*Note: All outbound shipments go by rail to the company's distribution center across town. Pulp and roll paper are received by rail and truck, therefore, shipping and receiving can't be moved. The roll paper making area also can't be moved because doing so would require changing the plumbing.

LINE BALANCING FOR PRODUCT-ORIENTED LAYOUTS

In contrast to the process-oriented layouts, product-oriented layouts are designed to be especially efficient in the creation of a standardized product-service bundle. In product-oriented layouts, including assembly lines, all value-adding resources are arranged in a suitable sequence; tasks are performed repetitively, with little variation in processing time; and virtually no inventory is kept between workstations. Thus, stations cannot operate independently, and the pace of the slowest workstation determines the pace of the entire system. (You have heard the old saying, "A chain is only as strong as its weakest link"; similarly, an assembly line is only as fast as its slowest workstation.) The difference between the pace of the slowest workstation and the pace of other stations represents wasted time.

On an assembly line, the time allowed for each workstation to complete its portion of the work on one unit of output is called the **cycle time**. Typically, the cycle time is determined either by the rate at which the product-service bundle is consumed in the marketplace or by the time the slowest workstation requires to complete its assigned tasks. The market rate of consumption may be considered **maximum cycle time**. The total time a unit spends on the line, which can be found by multiplying the line's cycle time by the number of workstations on the line, is called the **production lead time**. The ratio of the time a workstation requires to complete its assigned tasks to the cycle time is called the **workstation utilization**. The average utilization of workstations on the line, which is the ratio of the total time to complete all tasks on the line to the production lead time, is called the **utilization of the line**.

To illustrate these key terms, let's look at a very simple example of an assembly line. Suppose you and two friends decide to help a local mayoral candidate by stuffing, sealing, and labeling envelopes. You have been given the folded letters,

Cycle time

On an assembly line, the time allowed for each workstation to complete its portion of the work on one unit of output.

Maximum cycle time

The market rate of consumption.

Production lead time

The total time a unit spends on the line.

Workstation utilization

The ratio of the time a workstation requires to complete its assigned tasks to the cycle time.

Utilization of the line

The average utilization of workstations on the line.

Table 9.10

The Paper Co. Distance *
Volume Matrix
(Alternative)

	Receiving	Paper Making	Roll Paper Storage	Recyclable Paper & Pulp Storage	Laminating	Embossing	Cutting	Packaging	Shipping	Totals
Receiving										
Paper Making	900									900
Roll Paper Storage	4500	3750								8250
Recyclable Paper & Pulp Storage	0	1750	100							1850
Laminating	0	0	600	0						600
Embossing	0	0	2100	180	0					2280
Cutting	480	0	2100	480	200	750				4010
Packaging	0	0	0	0	0	0	0			0
Shipping	0	0	0	280	0	0	0	6750		7030
Assembly	0	0	0	0	0	0	3750	3750	0	7500
										32420

preprinted labels, and envelopes preprinted with a return address and postal permit number. To minimize the amount of time spent on the task, you decide to use an assembly line. One of you stuffs an envelope, then passes it to the next person, who seals it and passes it on to the third person, who labels it. The process is illustrated in Figure 9.13. Stuffing, sealing, and labeling take 5.1, 6.0, and 3.8 seconds, respectively. Obviously, one envelope can be completed every 6.0 seconds. If you chose to work at that pace, your cycle time would be 6.0 seconds. Assuming that it is, the production

Figure 9.13

Envelope stuffing line

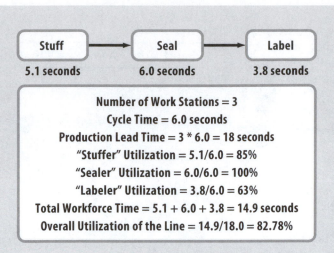

lead time for one envelope will be 18 seconds (6.0 seconds times three workstations). The utilization of the three workstations will be:

$$\frac{5.1}{6.0} = .85,$$

$$\frac{6.0}{6.0} = 1.00, \text{ and}$$

$$\frac{3.8}{6.0} = .63, \text{ respectively.}$$

The total time required to complete all tasks is:

$$5.1 + 6.0 + 3.8 = 14.9 \text{ seconds.}$$

Therefore, utilization of the line is:

$$\frac{14.9}{18} = .8278.$$

Is there any way to improve on these measures? In the very simple assembly line just described, where we are limited to three employees, probably not. But in more complex operations, tasks might be divided among workstations so as to minimize the line's cycle time. **Line balancing** is a procedure that can be used to optimize the assignment of tasks to work centers. In real-world assembly operations, line-balancing problems are very complex. They generally encompass many thousands of **elemental tasks**—operations that cannot be divided, because of technical reasons or managerial preference—each with variable processing times. As a result, line-balancing heuristics do not guarantee optimal task assignment. The largest elemental task's duration is called the **minimum cycle time**. Because of their complexity, tasks are typically built into computer programs, and only simple assembly operations are balanced with paper

Line balancing

A procedure that can be used to optimize the assignment of tasks to work centers.

Elemental tasks

Operations that cannot be divided, because of technical reasons or managerial preference.

Minimum cycle time

The largest elemental task's duration.

Example 9.2

Provided below are the current layout and the load and distance matrices for Luis's furniture factory. The load information was recently collected because Luis felt that the production mix had changed significantly, with recent furniture product introductions requiring a superior finish and additional sanding compared to the more "rustic" items that had fallen out of style. Values in the distance matrix can be thought of as the number of doors between the pair of work centers. Values in the volume matrix reflect the average number of transfer requests per week from a 6-week study of material handling activity.

Use the load and distance calculations to propose a modification to Luis's current layout and determine the expected savings associated with the change.

Sanding	Ripsaw
Turning	Router
Assembly	Rought Plane
Paint	Drilling

Volume

	Sand	Turn	Asm	Pnt	Rip	Rout	RfP	Drl
Sand		100	325	250	2	300	200	75
Turn			10	15	0	0	0	5
Asm				275	25	100	0	175
Pnt					150	100	0	100
Rip						200	350	100
Rout							100	0
RfP								0
Drl								

Distance

	Sand	Turn	Asm	Pnt	Rip	Rout	RfP	Drl
Sand		1	2	3	1	2	3	4
Turn			1	2	2	1	2	3
Asm				1	3	2	1	2
Pnt					4	3	2	1
Rip						1	2	3
Rout							1	2
RfP								1
Drl								

Step 1: Compute the distance * load matrix for Luis's factory by multiplying the values of cells in the distance matrix by the corresponding values of cells in the load matrix (see below)

Volume * Distance

	Sand	Turn	Asm	Pnt	Rip	Rout	RfP	Drl
Sand		100	650	750	2	600	600	300
Turn			10	30	0	0	0	15
Asm				275	75	200	0	350
Pnt					600	300	0	100
Rip						200	700	300
Rout							100	0
RfP								0
Drl								
Total = 6257								

Step 2: Identify department pairs that are unnecessarily close or distant using the load * distance matrix.

It appears that little is being gained by having the "Turning" work center adjacent to the router or assembly. In fact, there is little work for this work center and it could become less centrally located. By contrast, the "Sanding" work center interacts heavily with the "Assembly," "Paint," "Router," and "Rough Plane" work centers and should be more

Example 9.2

(*continued*)

centrally located. Thus the proposed revised layout, volume, and revised distance matrices below would probably be a good choice.

Turning	Ripsaw
Sanding	Router
Assembly	Rought Plane
Paint	Drilling

Revised Distance

	Sand	Turn	Asm	Pnt	Rip	Rout	RfP	Drl
Sand		1	1	2	2	1	2	3
Turn			2	3	1	2	3	4
Asm				1	3	2	1	2
Pnt					4	3	2	1
Rip						1	2	3
Rout							1	2
RfP								1
Drl								

Step 3: Compute the new volume * distance matrix using the revised matrices from Step 2 (see below).

Revised Volume * Distance

	Sand	Turn	Asm	Pnt	Rip	Rout	RfP	Drl
Sand		100	325	500	4	300	400	225
Turn			20	45	0	0	0	20
Asm				275	75	200	0	350
Pnt					600	300	0	100
Rip						200	700	300
Rout							100	0
RfP								0
Drl								

Total = 5139

Step 4: Compute the savings.

Swapping the "Turning" and "Sanding" work centers reduced the weekly material handling "cost" from 6257 to 5139. This represents an improvement of almost 22%. (Note that the 6257 and 5139 are not actual dollar values, but would be related to the actual dollar values in a linear fashion. Thus the percentage savings above is meaningful. For example, if Luis's weekly material handling costs were 10,000 dollars before the change, he could expect to save almost $2,200 per week with the revised layout.)

Step 5: Evaluate the revised layout and consider further changes.

We have not necessarily found the optimal layout with the one swap and may want to look at further changes using the procedure outlined above. (For example, we might want to see if any savings could be gained by moving the "Ripsaw" and "Rough Plane" work centers closer together.)

Additionally, we would need to consider whether the disruption to operations would be worth the savings gained and whether there were any technical constraints preventing the proposed change. It may be that the "Sanding" work center has intentionally been placed at the corner of the building because of dust generated in that work center, ventilation requirements, potential safety issues, and so forth. Thus, while a proposed change may provide financial savings, it could present other problems and hidden financial costs.

and pencil. To help in visualizing the line, planners often draw or print out a **precedence diagram**—a schematic drawing that shows the order and duration of the required tasks.

An **assignment rule** is a procedure that forms the basis for choosing an elemental task for assignment to a workstation. Because there is no guarantee that a given assignment rule will maximize utilization of the line, managers tend to assign tasks based on rules that they believe will work well. A common assignment rule is the Longest Task Time rule, which states that once the tasks that take a long time have been assigned to workstations, adding tasks of shorter duration should be easy. Conversely, assigning the shortest tasks first may make the assignment of longer tasks difficult without creating additional workstations. This approach is similar to packing the biggest things in a suitcase first, then filling in with smaller items.

Unfortunately, the process of line balancing does not always work out as well as it did in Example 9.3, where we were able to divide the work evenly enough to achieve the theoretical minimum number of stations. Often, task times do not fit together so neatly, and additional workstations are needed to achieve the required cycle time.

You may also have noticed that the time required to complete a work assignment varied from one workstation to the next. Workers at stations I, II, and III had to complete 3.00 minutes of work, while those at stations IV and V had to do only 2.50 and 2.00 minutes of work, respectively. What do you think would happen if you hired five college students for a week, paid them the same wage, and made three of them work substantially harder than the others? Unless they were unusual people, assigning jobs in this way would produce a great deal of dissension. Job dissatisfaction and low levels of motivation could be the result. Clearly, there is a great deal more to job design than assigning tasks to workstations. (Job design is discussed more thoroughly in Chapter 10.) Once tasks have been assigned to workstations, facility layout decisions can be made. Obviously, if managers know the tasks that must be performed, determining what equipment and materials will be required at each workstation is a reasonably straightforward matter.

Caution should be exercised in using and interpreting the results of line-balancing heuristics. Planners should question the assumptions made during the process:

▶ How did they come up with the time required to do the elemental tasks? Was it a guess? Was it determined experimentally? Was it determined in a real work environment? Did it take into account learning effects?

▶ What if demand were to change so that the cycle time becomes too long, or utilization of the workstations becomes too low? Will it be possible to readily adapt the line to changing conditions based on the planned allocation of tasks to work centers?

▶ What if the product needs to be modified in some way: Would the facility need a completely new line?

Moreover, one must remember that though the estimates of demand and task times used in line-balancing heuristics are constants, they represent variables with probabilistic distributions. Practically speaking, a real-world assembly line is not going to operate like clockwork, no matter how well it has been balanced.

Example 9.3

Suppose the manager of a department store has decided to employ college students on winter break to assemble Radio Flyer wagons for sale during the holiday season. The assembly tasks are listed in Table 9.11; a drawing of the parts to be assembled is shown in Figure 9.14 (page 440). The manager expects to sell 800 assembled wagons over the holiday season but would like to employ the students for only one 40-hour week at the beginning of their winter break. She wants to set up an assembly line that will be capable of assembling 800 wagons in 40 hours, using the smallest possible number of workers. The line-balancing process for this operation may be summarized as follows:

Step 1: Draw the precedence diagram.

Figure 9.15 (page 440) shows the precedence diagram for the wagon assembly line. All the information required to draw the diagram is found in Table 9.11.

Step 2: Find the required cycle time.

To assemble 800 wagons in 40 hours, workers will need to put them together at an average pace of 1 per 3.00 minutes.

$$\frac{[40 \text{ hrs} \times 60 \text{ min/hr}]}{800 \text{ units}} = 3 \text{ min/unit.}$$

Step 3: Find the theoretical minimum number of workstations.

The total time required to assemble each wagon is 13.5 minutes. Because the work must be accomplished within the cycle time of 3 minutes, at least five stations will be required (13.5 min./ 3 min./station = 4.5 stations, or 5, rounded up to the next highest integer). Thus, if the work can be divided more or less evenly, the manager will be able to accomplish her goal of assembling 800 wagons in one week using only five workers. But

Table 9.11
Tasks, Duration, and Precedence for the Toy Wagon

Task	Description	Duration	Immediate Predecessor(s)
1	Unpack box and distribute parts	2.00	None
2	Inspect wheels	1.00	1
3	Place tires on wheels	2.00	2
4	Attach first wheel to axles	0.50	3
5	Attach second wheel to axles	0.50	8,9
6	Attach hubcaps	1.00	5
7	Inspect tray	0.50	1
8	Attach front axle to tray	0.50	4
9	Attach rear axle to tray	0.50	4
10	Inspect handle	0.50	1
11	Attach handle to tray	0.50	7,10
12	Lubricate axles	0.50	8,9
13	Lubricate handle	0.25	11
14	Attach decals	0.50	7
15	Inspect and test wagon	0.75	13,8,9
16	Remove assemble wagon to storage	2.00	15
		13.50	

(continued)

Example 9.3

(continued)

Figure 9.14

Wagon parts & subassembly diagram

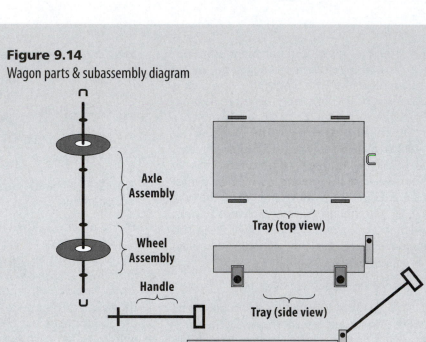

Figure 9.15

Wagon assembly precedence diagram

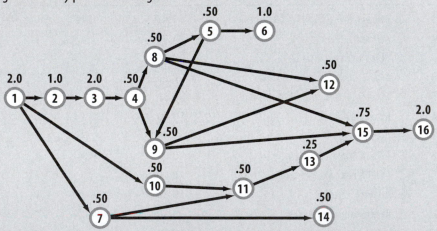

if the work is not evenly divisible, more than five workers or one week might be required to get the job done. One indivisible task may take a long time. Or, a set of tasks, where each task has a duration just long enough to prevent its combination with other tasks, may complicate the process.

Step 4: Assign the tasks to work centers.

Tasks are assigned to workstations using a priority rule. Most planners start with the first tasks in the sequence; they place them in the first workstation, as many as can be added without exceeding the required cycle time. In this example, when more than one task is adjacent to tasks already assigned to a work center, we will use the Longest

Example 9.3

(continued)

Task Time priority rule—adding the task of longest duration to the work center first. When two or more such tasks are of the same duration, we will add the task that is followed by the greatest number of activities.

Table 9.12 shows this assignment algorithm at work. When we begin, no tasks have been assigned to any station, and the only task with no unassigned predecessors is task 1. Thus, the only assignable task for workstation I is task 1. Once task 1 has been assigned to workstation I, tasks 2, 7, and 10 become assignable. Each has a duration less than or equal to the remaining 1.00 minute at workstation I, and none has an unassigned

predecessor. We select task 2 because it takes the longest time. At that point, no more time remains to be assigned at workstation 1.

We can now begin to assign tasks to workstation II. We continue assigning tasks to stations until all the tasks have been assigned. Notice that by the end of Table 9.12, we have managed to assign all tasks to only five workstations, the theoretical minimum number of stations. Figure 9.16 shows the precedence diagram for this operation. We now know that the manager can accomplish her goal of assembling 800 wagons in one week using just five workers.

Table 9.12

Workstation Task Assignments

Work station	Task(s) assigned	Assigned Time	Remaining assignable time	Assignable tasks
I	None	0.00	3.00	1
	1	2.00	1.00	2, 7, 10
	1, 2	3.00	0.00	None
*****				
II	None	0.00	3.00	3, 7, 10
	3	2.00	1.00	4, 7, 10
	3, 4	2.50	0.50	7, 8, 9, 10
	3, 4, 7	3.00	0.00	None
*****				
III	None	0.00	3.00	8, 9, 10, 14
	8	0.50	2.50	9, 10, 14
	8, 9	1.00	2.00	5, 10, 12, 14
	8, 9, 5	1.50	1.50	6, 10, 12, 14
	8, 9, 5, 6	2.50	0.50	10, 12, 14
	8, 9, 5, 6, 10	3.00	0.00	None
*****				
IV	None	0.00	3.00	11, 12, 14
	11	0.50	2.50	12, 13, 14
	11, 12	1.00	2.00	13, 14
	11, 12, 14	1.50	1.50	13
	11, 12, 14, 13	1.75	1.25	15
	11, 12, 14, 13, 15	2.50	0.50	None
*****				

Example 9.3

(continued)

Table 9.12
Workstation Task Assignments (continued)

Work station	Task(s) assigned	Assigned Time	Remaining assignable time	Assignable tasks
V	None	0.00	3.00	16
	16	2.00	1.00	None

Figure 9.16
Task Assignments to Workstations

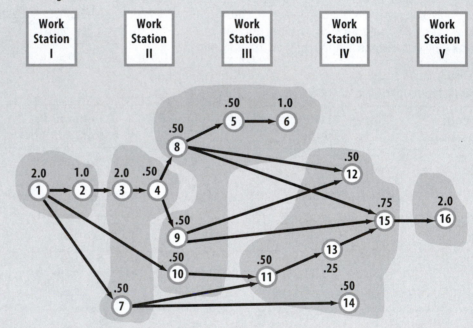

Fred Wonders why balancing his line is so difficult

Fred went to lunch with one of his process engineers to discuss re-balancing one of the cell phone lines. They determine the line has about 100 separate operations that cannot be divided any further. A few, less than half, must be sequenced in a particular order. The time required for each task ranges from 3 to 20 seconds. Fred really needs a 10-second cycle time (six phones per minute) to meet demand. He does not see what would be so hard about finding the best possible solution through trial and error. Can you frame the complexity of the problem for him? Can you suggest options for how can he get a 10-second cycle time?

For example, if the elemental task times in the preceding example were average times, then the total of 3.00 minutes required to perform the tasks assigned to workstation I was also an average time. That means that half the time, the worker at station I will not be able to complete the work in the given cycle time. Thus, unless there is enough inventory between each workstation to accommodate fluctuations in task times, the worker has only two options: (1) delay the line, causing delays in delivery to customers, or (2) cut corners, sacrificing quality and pride of workmanship. Neither option is acceptable. (W. Edwards Deming, one of the leaders in the U.S. quality movement, advised managers to "remove barriers that rob employees of their pride of workmanship." See Chapter 4, page 125.) To remedy this problem, what if the time estimates for elemental tasks were set at the average time plus three standard deviations? Doing so might build too much idle time into the line. Obviously, managerial judgment is required to use a quantitative technique such as line balancing effectively. There is much more to managing an assembly line than assigning tasks to workers and expecting them to execute those tasks repetitively, for hours on end.

Gary Cralle/Getty Images Inc.

The typical auto assembly line must complete a car or truck about once every 60-70 seconds. That means the 20 plus hours normally required to assemble a vehicle must be broken down into jobs that fit inside that cycle time. Balancing the assignments of tasks in such a way as to maximize efficiency yet consider the of the worker's environment can be a complex problem.

SUMMARY

This chapter presented five facility layout types: fixed-position layout, product layout, process layout, cellular layout, and hybrid layout.

The fixed-position layout requires that resources move to the location where the product-service bundle is needed. It is often used to make large capital goods, such as bridges and buildings.

The product layout is arranged in the order in which materials or customers are needed to complete the product-service bundle. It is used primarily in assembly operations that produce large volumes of a standard product-service bundle.

In the process layout, resources are grouped by function in order to produce customized product-service bundles. This arrangement provides flexibility and promotes functional excellence.

In the cellular layout, resources are grouped by cell and dedicated to a particular group of products, parts, or subassemblies. Each cell can be used to perform a commonly required series of value-adding steps.

The hybrid layout is constructed of some combination of the first four layout types.

A firm's layout should reflect its competitive priorities, as misalignment of the layout will undermine its operations. In fact, improvements to a facility's layout often expand a firm's market opportunities. Other important facility layout considerations include the need to reduce non-value-adding activity, such as materials movement; the need to improve communication and enhance teamwork; and the need to ensure safety on the job.

Helpful computer-modeling and quantitative tools include simplified systematic layout planning (SSLP) and load-weight-based decision tools are useful in designing process-oriented layouts. Line balancing is used extensively in designing product-oriented layouts. But such tools merely provide a starting point for layout planners, who must ultimately allocate space for all the resources to be housed in a facility.

KEY TERMS

Assignment rule, 438
Cellular layout, 410
Cycle time, 433
Elemental task, 435
Fixed-position layout, 406
Functional layout, 410

Hybrid layout, 411
Line balancing, 435
Maximum cycle time, 433
Minimum cycle time, 435
Precedence diagram, 438
Process (or functional) layout, 410

Product layout, 408
Production lead time, 433
Simplified systematic layout
    planning (SSLP), 417
Utilization of the line, 433
Workstation utilization, 433

SOLVED PROBLEMS

1. If your company needed a line capable of producing 100 "flexible fliers" per hour, with each unit requiring a total assembly time of 5 minutes, then:

   a) What would be the maximum cycle time possible?

   b) What would be the theoretical minimum number of workstations?

   c) If you could have a maximum of only six workstations, what would be the line's hourly potential output (assuming it is perfectly balanced)?

Solution:

   a) $\dfrac{(60 \text{ seconds/minute} \times 60 \text{ minutes/hour})}{(100 \text{ units/hour})}$

   = 36 seconds/unit, thus, the maximum cycle time should be no more than 36 seconds.

   b) $\dfrac{(5 \text{ minutes/unit} \times 60 \text{ seconds/minute})}{(36 \text{ seconds/unit})}$

   = 8.333 or nine workstations

   c) $\dfrac{(5 \text{ minutes/unit} \times 60 \text{ seconds/minute})}{6}$

   = 50 seconds/unit or 72 units/hour

2. Suppose you are the manager of the department store whose line-balancing problem was illustrated in Example 9.3 (page 439). Suppose further that your demand is 850 wagons per week rather than 800. (All other information remains the same.)

   a) What is the new required cycle time?

   b) What is the theoretical minimum number of workstations?

   c) Using the Longest Task Time heuristic to balance the line, what workstation assignments would you make?

   d) Why does the answer to part (c) require a different number of workstations from that suggested in part (b)?

Solution:

   a) $\dfrac{(40 \text{ hours per week} \times 60 \text{ minutes per hour})}{850 \text{ units per week}}$

   = 2.8235 minutes per unit at a maximum.

   b) $\dfrac{13.5 \text{ minutes total work per unit}}{2.8235 \text{ minutes per unit maximum}}$

   = 4.78, or 5 workstations minimum.

   c) They would be allocated as follows: ws#1 (1, 7), ws#2 (2, 10, 11, 14, 13), ws#3 (3, 4), ws#4 (8, 9, 15, 5, 12), ws#5 (16), and ws#6 (6).

   d) The task times are not uniform or infinitely divisible, thus, they do not fit evenly into five workstations.

3. A local grocery store has built a new building and is renovating the interior of its old building for an Internet shopping service that delivers customer orders to homes. In the past, the store was organized like most grocery stores—to sell as much merchandise as possible, not to minimize customer travel. (For example, milk and bread were located in the rear of the store, not the front.) The following table represents the proximity requirements of the six departments considered responsible for the bulk of the store's business. The store is currently utilizing three perimeter areas and three central

areas on its floor plan. Each is defined by the permanent electrical and plumbing infrastructure, and can support any department. If you could locate any department in any area, where would you put each department? Why? Use the SSLP approach.

Proximity Requirements

	Meat	Dairy	Frozen Foods	Canned Foods	Dry Foods	Bakery
Meat	—	A	I	O	O	E
Dairy		—	I	O	O	E
Frozen Foods			—	O	O	O
Canned Foods				—	O	E
Dry Foods					—	O
Bakery						—

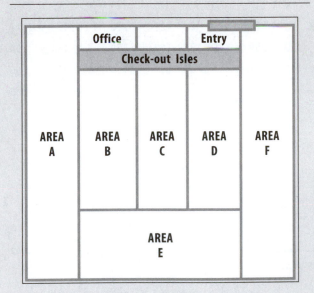

Solution:

The cluster diagram and one potential layout are shown in the following figure. We constructed the cluster diagram, as described in the chapter, by working from A relationships on the REL chart, to E relationships, to the I relationships, and finally to the O relationships. Taking our cue from the cluster diagram, we started the actual layout by placing the Dairy and Meat departments in the center of

the facility. Next we added the Bakery as close to the Dairy and Meat Departments as possible and Canned Foods as close to the Bakery as possible. Then we placed Frozen Foods as close to Dairy and Meats as possible. Finally, we added Dry Foods in the remaining space.

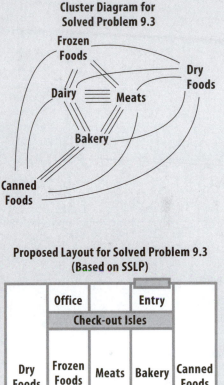

Cluster Diagram for Solved Problem 9.3

Proposed Layout for Solved Problem 9.3 (Based on SSLP)

The managers of the grocery store described in Problem 4 want to evaluate the same problem using a distance-load approach. The following summary indicates how many times a week an item from one department is included in an order from another department (indicating that a customer walked from one department to the other). The table shows the distance from the center of one area to the center of the others. Examine the data. Do you still want to locate the departments in the areas you chose in answer to problem 3?

Number of Times (in Thousands) an Item from One Department Was in the Same Order as Something from Another Department

	Meat	Dairy	Frozen Foods	Canned Foods	Dry Foods	Bakery
Meat	—	35	7	4	11	34
Dairy		—	8	2	2	17
Frozen Foods			—	5	2	3
Canned Foods				—	9	5
Dry Foods					—	2
Bakery						—

Distance between Areas

(Feet)	Area A	Area B	Area C	Area D	Area E	Area F
Area A	—	100	175	250	125	350
Area B		—	75	150	125	250
Area C			—	75	100	175
Area D				—	125	100
Area E					—	125
Area F						—

Solution:

Use the distance * volume totals for the layout suggested in #2:

	Meat	Dairy	Frozen Foods	Canned Foods	Dry Foods	Bakery
Meat	—	35 × 100 = 3500	7 × 75 = 525	4 × 175 = 700	11 × 175 = 1925	34 × 75 = 2550
Dairy		—	8 × 125 = 1000	2 × 125 = 250	2 × 125 = 250	17 × 125 = 2125
Frozen Foods			—	5 × 250 = 1250	2 × 100 = 200	3 × 150 = 450
Canned Foods				—	9 × 350 = 3150	5 × 100 = 500
Dry Foods					—	2 × 250 = 500
Bakery						—

Total = 18,875 units

The biggest totals are meat-dairy(3500), canned foods-dry foods (3150), and bakery-meat (2550), so switch canned foods with frozen foods. We left the other two areas alone because the pairs are already adjacent.

	Meat	Dairy	Frozen Foods	Canned Foods	Dry Foods	Bakery
Meat	—	35 × 100 = 3500	7 × 175 = 1225	4 × 75 = 300	11 × 175 = 1925	34 × 75 = 2550
Dairy		—	8 × 125 = 1000	2 × 125 = 250	2 × 125 = 250	17 × 125 = 2125
Frozen Foods			—	5 × 250 = 1250	2 × 350 = 700	3 × 100 = 300
Canned Foods				—	9 × 100 = 900	5 × 150 = 750
Dry Foods					—	2 × 250 = 500
Bakery						—

New totals: 17,525 units (It is possible that the assignment of A, E, I, O, U, and X may not have been consistent with the data collected by the POS terminals, especially with regard to the canned foods-frozen foods pair.)

DISCUSSION QUESTIONS

1. Imagine you are the dean of a small business school that includes six departments (accountancy, economics, finance, marketing, management, and management information systems). The school employs forty full-time faculty members. Some faculty members primarily teach specialized courses in their major, others primarily teach core classes required of all undergraduate business students. The new building in which the school is to be housed will have two floors. Each floor will include several classrooms and two office suites. What impact could the layout of the offices and assignment of faculty to offices have on the development and delivery of the school's curriculum? What factors are likely to play a role in the actual layout decision? What layout choices would you recommend? Why?

2. What criteria would be important to Luis in planning to improve the layout of his facility? To Cheryl, Fred, and Tom? (In Tom's case, consider service both before and after passengers get on and off a plane.)

3. What approach would you suggest Luis use in evaluating the layout of his factory? What would you suggest the others use?

4. In balancing a line, what aspects of the result are important to the worker? To the manager? Can these two perspectives be reconciled? Would your answer differ with respect to the short-term and the long-term?

5. What type of layout was used in the place where you worked last summer? Was the facility laid out well? Why or why not?

6. What are the tradeoffs between the SSLP approach to planning a process-oriented layout and the distance-load-based models?

7. Most of the time a fixed-position layout implies that the means of production must go to the site where the product will be built (that is, to the construction site). Can you think of any situation in which a product is built in a "factory" using a fixed-position layout and then transported to the customer?

8. What is a heuristic? How do planners use heuristics to solve layout problems?

9. In balancing an assembly line, planners compute the theoretical minimum number of workstations, always rounding it to the next highest integer. Why? Can a line always be balanced with the theoretical minimum number of workstations? Why or why not?

10. How would you categorize the layout of your college or university? What criteria are important to consider?

11. What is an elemental task? Why do planners bother to break the production process down into such detail?

12. Trying to squeeze all the requirements for an undergraduate degree into just eight semesters, or twelve quarters, in order to graduate in four years is difficult. It is something like trying to squeeze all the elemental tasks of a production process into the theoretical minimum number of workstations. What other similarities can you see between the two undertakings? What assignment rule will you use to pick your classes next semester?

13. Luis thinks that a cellular layout might make sense in fabricating some of the common parts for a family of kitchen and office chairs and swivel stools. How would you suggest he go about investigating the idea? Might Cheryl find similar uses for this layout in her hospital? What might be some places to look for commonalities in a service operation like a hospital?

14. You have been assigned the job of balancing a small, labor-intensive assembly line. You find that the largest single elemental task takes longer than the cycle time needed to meet the desired demand. Is that a problem? Why or why not? How might you deal with this situation?

15. How would you classify the layout of a typical amusement park—Disney World, Six Flags, or Cedar Point? If you were building an amusement park from scratch and the layout was up to you, what basic principles would you use to lay it out? What more pragmatic issues might become critical?

16. You are employed as an urban planner. Can you see any parallels between the process of laying out a new city (including the development of zoning regulations) and the process of laying out a job shop?

PROBLEMS

1. Assume that there are 480 minutes of production time available per day. Demand for your product is sixty units per day. There are thirteen elemental tasks involved with the product's production, each taking 2 minutes. Assuming that the tasks can be placed in any order:

   a) What is the maximum allowed cycle time?

   b) Theoretically, how many workstations will be necessary?

2. A small assembly line producing simple radios in one of Fred's other divisions requires 20 elemental tasks each of which takes 30 seconds to complete.

   a) If demand is 80 units per hour, what is the maximum cycle time that can still meet demand?

   b) Theoretically, how many workstations will be necessary?

   c) Is this possible?

   d) How many will it take? Why?

3. A set of tasks required to assemble bag lunches for distribution on Tom's airline requires the following task times (all in seconds): 8, 12, 6, 20, 14, 8, 14, 10, 12, 4, and 14.

   a) If demand is 120 units per hour, what is the required cycle time?

   b) What is the theoretical minimum number of workstations?

   c) If demand needs to be maximized, what is the fastest cycle time possible?

4. The layout of the Dean's office staff at your university is being reconsidered. Currently, there are four offices that open to a shared hallway. Each office has a door and it is 5 meters between the doors of adjoining offices. Given a matrix showing the number of trips made between offices each week and a description of the current layout of offices:

Trips per Week

	Dean's Office	Associate Dean's Office	Assistant Dean's Office	Administrative Assistant to the Dean's
Dean's Office	***	30	10	40
Associate Dean's Office		***	60	50
Assistant Dean's Office			***	10
Administrative Assistant to the Deans				***

Current layout:

Hallway

Dean's Office	Associate Dean's Office	Assistant Dean's Office	Administrative Assistant to the Deans

a) Evaluate the current layout in terms of how efficiently time is spent walking between offices.

b) A consultant was asked to suggest a new layout. It is shown below. How would you compare it to the current layout?

Layout proposed by the consultant:

Hallway

Dean's Office	Administrative assistant to the Deans	Associate Dean's Office	Assistant Dean's Office

5. The typical automobile requires 18 hours of actual task time for assembly. If demand equals 400 vehicles per 8-hour shift of continuous operation, and the line is balanced to 80% efficiency, then:

   a) What is the implied cycle time for the workstations?

   b) How many workstations will be needed?

   c) How many workstations would be needed if demand increased by 25% and efficiency stayed the same?

6. Using the information from the previous problem, assume that consultants from local universities helped the company rebalance the line such that efficiencies increased to 95%.

   a) With demand of 400 cars per shift, how many workstations are required?

   b) With the 25% increase in demand, how many workstations are required?

7. Using the data from the previous problem, assume that two of the elemental tasks have been lengthened to 5 minutes in duration (now there are eleven @ 2 minutes per task and two @ 5 minutes per task):

   a) How many workstations would it require to achieve production goals now?

   b) Assuming there was demand for your product, what is the fastest cycle time possible?

   c) How many workstations would be required to achieve the fastest cycle time?

8. Ida Cook, layout analyst for Mass-Bake Cookies, Inc., is designing a product layout for a new cookie. She plans to use this production line 8 full hours a day in order to meet projected demand of 480 units per day. Accordingly, she has prepared the following table describing the tasks necessary to produce this product:

Task	Predecessor	Time (Seconds)
U	—	30
V	U	52
W	U	6
X	W, V	24
Y	X	54
Z	Y	30

   a) If Ida desires that output rate equals demand, what is the desired cycle time (in seconds)?

   b) If Ida desires that output rate equals demand, what is the theoretical minimum number of workstations needed?

   c) If Ida uses the "longest task time" heuristic to balance the line, then what would be the tasks assigned to each workstation?

   d) What is the efficiency of Ida's line if she "balanced" it as follows (note, this balance is *not* necessarily the answer to anything above nor is it necessarily a good one):

   u, w, v, x, y, z

9. Assume you are given the task of determining this plant's layout. The plant currently makes imitation apples, oranges, and bananas. It is currently made up of three departments that must be laid out in the three rooms shown as follows. Rooms 1 and 2 are 100 feet apart, rooms 2 and 3 are 100 feet apart, and rooms 1 and 3 are 200 feet apart. Every month you must make ten batches of apples, fifteen batches of oranges, and thirty batches of bananas. A batch of apples costs $8.00 per foot to move, a batch of oranges costs $6.00 per foot to move, and a batch of bananas costs $2.00 per foot to move. Apples have a processing route from Dept. A-> Dept. B-> Dept. C. Oranges go from Dept. B-> Dept. A-> Dept. C. Bananas go from Dept. B-> Dept. C-> Dept. A.

Room 1	Room 2	Room 3

a) What is the optimal layout?

b) What would be your material handling costs?

c) How would your answer change if the bananas were outsourced to another plant leaving only apples and oranges?

10. Fred's other division produces televisions on an assembly line. They currently producing 1600 televisions during each 8-hour shift.

   a) What is the implied cycle time for the line assuming 100% efficiency?

   b) How many workstations would be needed assuming the line is operating at 100% efficiency?

   c) What would be the cycle time if the line were operating at 80% efficiency?

   d) How many workstations would be needed assuming the line is operating at 80% efficiency?

11. The manager of a product layout used for assembling the toy cars that come in the kid's meal sold at fast-food restaurants has been asked to rebalance the line to accommodate a new model. The eight elemental tasks, which can be done in any order, have the following task times, in seconds: 5, 5, 5, 3, 3, 3, 4, and 4.

   a) If demand requires that 4800 units be assembled in an 8-hour day, what is the maximum cycle time allowable?

b) What is the theoretical number of workstations needed?

c) What is the actual number of workstations needed to meet the demand? Why?

d) What is the production lead time?

e) What would be the efficiency of the workstations? The line?

12. You have been asked to consult on the layout of a new department store. The floor plan is shown below as a three by two set of "zones" within the store. Each Department must be assigned to a zone based upon SSLP. The following matrix contains relationships gleaned form a survey of customers from other similar stores. (Only the A's, E's, I's, and X's are shown. Consider the rest to be O's and U's.) How would you lay out the store?

Zone #A	Zone # B	Zone #C
Zone # D	Zone #E	Zone #F

Department	1	2	3	4		6
1	***		A	X		A
2		***		A		
3			***		I	
4				***	I	
5					***	I
6						***

CHALLENGE PROBLEMS

1. Managers of the factory where Luis works have once again decided to rearrange the eight rooms in the facility. Long-term demand seems to have changed and the new estimates of flow between departments is shown in the matrix below. As in Example 9.2, each room is capable of housing any of the factory's eight department sand the distances between rooms is assumed proportional to how many rooms are between them.

   a) Starting with the improved layout from Example 9.2, what would be a good first attempt at reorganizing the departments in these eight rooms? Given your swap, what would be the total number of "load-rooms" traveled?

   b) Can this first layout be improved? If so, how, and how many "load-rooms" would be saved each week?

# of Trips/Week between Department Pairs in Luis's Factory

	Sanding	Turning	Assembly	Paint	Ripsaw	Router	Rough Plane	Drilling
Sanding	—	100	325	100	20	300	200	15
Turning		—	10	15	0	0	0	250
Assembly			—	25	25	100	0	175
Paint				—	150	100	0	100
Ripsaw					—	200	100	350
Router						—	100	0
Rough Plane							—	0
Drilling								—

2. The athletic ticket office at your university has asked that you help them set up a small assembly line for processing season ticket renewals. The various tasks, task times, and necessary preceding tasks are listed below:

Open Returned Envelope	Task #	Task Time (secs)	Immediate Predecessor
Remove Renewal Forms/Check/Money Order	1	10	N/A
Scan Forms/Checks/Money Order For Completeness	2	10	1
Update Ticket History on Computer	3	25	2
Put Check/Money Order into Drawer	4	5	1
Pull and Staple the Tickets Off Printer as History Is Updated	5	20	3
Pull Return Envelope from Bin	6	5	N/A
Peel Return Mailing Label Printed as History Is Updated	7	25	3
Put Return Label on Return Envelope	8	5	6, 7
Insert Tickets and Order Form into Return Envelope	9	5	5
Pull New Schedule	10	5	N/A
Insert New Schedule	11	5	10
Seal Return Envelope	12	10	4, 9,11
Meter the Return Envelope	13	15	8,12

a) If demand indicates eighty units are needed in an hour, what is the maximum cycle time allowable?

b) What is the theoretical number of workstations needed?

c) Draw the precedence diagram.

d) Using the Longest Task Time heuristic to assign tasks to workstations (use the greatest number of followers as a tiebreaker), what is the actual number of workstation needed to meet demand requirements? What tasks would be assigned to them?

e) What is the production lead time?

f) What would be the efficiency of each workstation? The line as a whole?

3. A fire recently forced an entire floor of a freshman dormitory at a large state university to be vacated while repairs were made. Now after 6 weeks in temporary housing, the residents are to be moved

back into room on their old floor. As dorm director, you thought it might make sense to improve on the arbitrary selection of roommates made at the beginning of the year. You had students fill out a confidential rating sheet describing who they most wanted to live with or close to. You yourself noted that students 1 and 5 both dated the same person last semester and thought it best to keep them at opposite ends of the hall! Using SSLP, the following matrix contains the results. (Only the A's, E's, I's, and X's are shown. Consider the rest to be O's and U's.)

Student	1	2	3	4	5	6	7		9	10	11	12	13	14	15	16
1	***	I			X		A								E	A
2		***		A			I								I	I
3			***		I	A	E									
4				***	I	I	E						A		E	
5					***									A		
6						***			A		I	I				
7							***			A	E	E	E			
8								***								
9									***		A			A		
10										***						
11											***		A			
12												***				
13													***			
14														***		
15															***	A
16																***

Given the eight rooms on the floor are configured like the following and that two students are assigned to each room, who should be assigned to each room?

Room 1	Room 3	Room 5	Room 7
→ Entry		HALL	
Room 2	Room 4	Room 6	Room 8

4. Assume you are planning the layout of your school's dining hall on days when submarine sandwiches are served as part of a standard lunch complete with a bag of chips and a piece of fruit. All meals are to be standardized for this day and your job is to suggest a set of workstations that will balance assignment of work, be capable of assembling 200 lunches per hour. You are also to advise the manager as to:

a) The maximum cycle time

b) The minimum cycle time

c) The theoretical minimum number of workstations

d) The utilization of the line

You have been provided with the following information:

Task #	Elemental Task	Estimated Task Time	Immediate Predecessor
1	Place plastic sheet on tray	6 seconds	n/a
2	Slice bun in half and place on plastic	11 seconds	1
3	Place roast beef slices on bun	5 seconds	2
4	Place turkey slices on bun	5 seconds	2
5	Place cheese slices on bun	6 seconds	2
6	Place lettuce slices on bun	6 seconds	2
7	Spread mustard on sandwich	8 seconds	3, 4, 5, 6
8	Place banana peppers on sandwich	5 seconds	7
9	Place tomato slices on sandwich	5 seconds	7
10	Put top bread slice on sandwich	5 seconds	9
11	Cut sandwich in half	10 seconds	10
12	Wrap sandwich	10 seconds	11
13	Place bag of chips on tray	5 seconds	2
14	Place milk on tray	5 seconds	2
15	Place fruit on tray	5 seconds	2
16	Place napkin on tray between milk and fruit	3 seconds	15
Total		100 seconds	

Case 9.1: Intel's "Seedy" Plant Cloning Process

Intel Corp. has more than 2,000 Ph.D.s on staff to generate and develop new ideas. But innovation also depends on people like Trish Roughgarden, an Air Force veteran whose job is to copy carefully. Ms. Roughgarden is known inside Intel as a "seed," an unofficial title for technicians who transfer manufacturing know-how from one Intel chip factory to another. Her current job is to help ensure that Intel's latest plant, works just like an identical plant in Hillsboro, Oregon. Several hundred other seeds will copy the same techniques to a third plant in Ireland.

It is all part of a major Intel strategy known as "Copy Exactly," which discourages experimentation at individual factories. Instead, engineers and technicians painstakingly clone proven Intel manufacturing techniques from one plant to the next-down to the color of workers' gloves, wall paint or other features that would seem to have no bearing on efficiency. The strategy emerged when variations between factories in the early 1980s hurt productivity and product quality. Japanese competitors nearly drove Intel out of business. Today, Copy Exactly is helping accelerate the relentless pace of technology improvements at Intel.

Copy Exactly contradicts most current thinking about employee motivation, involvement, and empowerment. Most experts suggest pushing decision making as far down into the organization as possible. They would seek to tap into potential insights for product and process improvement that come from the experience of the work force. Many experts would suggest a process whereby: a culture of empowerment is developed; information—in the form of clear goals and boundaries for decision making—is shared; competency—in the form of training and experience—is developed and leveraged; resources to be effective in their jobs, are provided; and the encouragement of risk taking—is provided. Every employer uses these concepts to some extent, though it is often thought of as delegation. But most of Copy Exactly seems to fly in the face of them.

Intel's resolve is reflected in 200,000 square feet of new factory space where Ms. Roughgarden is working. Linked to an existing 300,000-square-foot facility this creates what Intel believes is the world's largest semiconductor "clean room." One corridor stretches 900 feet, an avenue of white, ventilated flooring intersecting side streets called bays and chases. The price: more than $2 billion, roughly the same as the Oregon and Ireland additions.

Copy Exactly doesn't just help start new manufacturing lines. Seeds in Intel's plants help minimize the potential sources of unexplained variation. For example, when identical tools in two factories kept producing different defect rates, Intel learned that one worker group was cleaning the tool by wiping a towel in a circular motion; the other wiped back and forth. One motion went against the grain of the metal, spreading dirt particles rather than removing them. The strategy also helped solve a mystery that emerged after Intel transferred a production process to a plant in Hudson, Massachusetts, purchased from Digital Equipment Corp. It turned out that an East Coast vender delivered oxygen with a slightly fewer impurities than the gas Intel bought for other plants. Who would have suspected a problem with oxygen that is too pure!

Some of Intel's practices are now commonplace. AMD, for instance, has "Copy Intelligently." Though few computer chip making companies besides Intel sell enough of a single product to require multiple production lines, Copy Exactly allows Intel to more easily shift products and workers from plant to plant as needed, and have engineers in multiple locations simultaneously tackle problems that pop up.

While it prohibits willy-nilly changes, the Copy Exactly methodology encourages Intel workers to come up with ideas to boost productivity or make chip features smaller. But the ideas must pass a committee called the "Process Change Control Board," which requires workers to come up with tests to prove the value of their suggestions. There may be fewer structural changes to the Intel manufacturing processes than you'll find in other corporations of similar size, but because of Intel's "seedy" Copy Exactly strategy, each change can be expected to be implemented more quickly and have a more significant impact.

Finally, though it seems counter-intuitive, Copy Exactly has increased the flexibility of Intel's factory network. Because each factory is nearly identical work partially completed in one can easily be completed in another.

SOME QUESTIONS TO THINK ABOUT:

1. Describe the layout of Intel chip making facilities. (In addition to a geometric description, use the most appropriate terms you learned in this chapter.)

2. Among Fred, Luis, Cheryl, and Tom, whose situation would benefit most from programs like "Copy Exactly"?

3. Does a program like work for or against "Moore's Law"? How?

4. The opening paragraph of the case indicates that innovation at Intel depends on copy exactly. How so?

5. What other industries might benefit from this approach? Which ones would likely not?

Source: Adapted from Don Clark, the *Wall Street Journal,* Oct. 28, 2003, p. B1, http://cache-www.intel.com/cd/00/00/10/28/ 102853_pp023306_sum.pdf (accessed on May 1, 2006); and www.intel.com/pressroom/kits/manufacturing/copy_exactly_bkgrnd.htm (accessed on May 1, 2006)

REFERENCES

Muther, R., and J. D. Wheeler. *Simplified Systematic Layout Planning.* Kansas City, MO: Management and Industrial Research Publications, 1961.

Koretz, G. "Less of a Gulf in Office Rents: America's Costs Are Up; Asia's Down." *Business Week* (June 16, 1997): 28.

10

Job Design Processes

Chapter Outline

Introduction   458

Integrating Operations Management Across the Functions   459

Job Design with a Focus on Work Standards   461

Standard Times   462

Standard Procedure   464

Task Familiarity in Job Design   464

Job Specialization and Skill Set Stratification   465

Designing Jobs with a Focus on Their Motivating Potential   465

The Motivating Potential Score   468

Improving a Job's Motivating Potential   469

Designing Jobs Including Socio-Technical Systems Perspectives   469

Designing Jobs for Employee Involvement and the High-Performance Workplace   472

Encouraging Teamwork   472

Rewarding Employee Involvement   474

The Service Profit Chain   475

Job Design and Competitive Priorities   477

Summary   479

Key Terms   480

Discussion Questions   480

Case 10: Southwest Airlines Feels the Pain of Growing Older   481

References   483

Learning Objectives

After studying this chapter you should be able to

▶ Demonstrate your understanding of the linkages between job design decisions and the other functional areas of business

▶ Describe work standards approaches to job design

▶ Demonstrate your understanding of the job characteristics model and its implications for job design

▶ Describe the socio-technical systems approach to job design

▶ Explain the impact of employee involvement practices on job design and worker performance

▶ Use the service profit chain model to contrast employee roles in the cycles of success and failure

▶ Describe the impact of competitive priorities on the design of jobs

. . . Back at the Rec Center

"I just don't understand people," mutters Luis, mostly to himself, as he pumps away at one of the weight stations. The others had noticed his disposition and had been giving him more space than usual. After a few more minutes of working out his frustrations, Luis looks around and notices the impact his mood was having on the group's normally friendly dynamics. "Okay, I'm sorry," he says, a little sheepishly. "It's just that I've got a mess on my desk to face when I get in, and I'm not really looking forward to it. But hey, I'm okay now. I won't bite!"

"Well, I wasn't sure for a while," laughs Tom.

"So, what's the mess you have to clean up? Yours or somebody else's?" Cheryl asks from the treadmill across the room.

"Actually, it's both. I've been trying to get my people to think for themselves a little—you know, give them some room to do what they need to do," Luis replies. He said some of them took to it "like ducks to water," but others didn't want anything to do with the idea. Luis, who's resting now, having worked up a good sweat, goes on to describe his efforts to share decision making with the people who work on the shop floor. He calls the idea "empowerment," something he'd heard about in the organizational behavior class he was taking in a part-time MBA program. "Some of them just don't want to make any decisions," he complains. "They just want to be told what to do!"

"So?" asks Fred. "I've got a lot of people like that, it works out just right." Fred is sitting on an air strider next to Luis. "I don't want the guy who's putting the board in the cell phone to just up and change something some morning. That could mess up my whole line!"

"It's not the same," answers Luis. "I run a job shop. We make decisions about work order changes on the floor all the time. Sometimes we change the quantity; sometimes we bump a job to let another go ahead. Sometimes we rethink how we're going to make something, who's going to do what when, or what the thing's going to look like."

"Okay, okay, I'll give you that," Fred replies. "We think it all through, set up the process, and then train the line workers. We get it together up front and then practice until everyone knows the drill. There aren't a lot of decisions to make on the fly."

"Well, we have a different situation. We have to make decisions," says Luis. "And we need to figure out who decides what. I don't want to have to make all the decisions, especially not when the workers are closer to the problem than I am."

"We've been down this road, too," notes Cheryl. "What happened?"

"Well, we had a problem in the staining booth yesterday," explains Luis. An operator had stained a batch of 1500 spindles a very dark color. Earlier in the day, the same operator had stained 300 seats for the kitchen stools he knew those spindles were meant for—only he'd stained them a much lighter shade. When Luis questioned him about it, he admitted he'd been aware of the difference in color and had thought it was odd. But as Luis explains, "He said he didn't think much about it, but when he did, well, he figured the best thing to do was to follow the work order. Why didn't he use some common sense? Why didn't he stop and check it out? Now I'm sitting on a large batch of seats that don't match the spindles and spindles in a shade I may not need for months, if ever. All of this makes us likely to be late in delivering the order of kitchen stools, which are for a good customer. I just can't believe the guy didn't check it out!" Luis exclaims, exasperated.

"Well, what do you pay him to do?" asks Tom.

"Well, umm, I—I mean, we pay him to run a painting and staining booth," says Luis. He was somewhat taken aback by the question, which seemed to have such an obvious answer. "Why, what are you getting at?"

"I mean, it seems to me that you pay him for painting and staining a wide variety of things," suggests Tom. "I'll bet he never heard his job was to second-guess the system!"

"Well, he knows we don't make only vanilla either!" says Luis.

"I think I see where Tom is going with this," says Cheryl, as she stops her treadmill. "Let me ask you a question, Luis. Have you ever fired someone for doing what the work order said to do?"

"No," Luis answers.

"Have you ever fired someone for *not* doing what the work order said to do?" she asks.

"Probably," Luis answers. "I don't know about just once, but maybe if it's a chronic problem. It's definitely not going to get anybody a raise, though!"

"Well, maybe it should," Cheryl replies.

"I suppose I should give raises, too—you know, to people who don't do what we assign them to do!" Fred says, his voice loaded with sarcasm.

"No, not at all," says Cheryl. "I'm just saying that if you want to empower people to do something, make it part of the job. Reward them for it. In Luis's job shop, an immediate improvement in either the product or the process design is more likely to be noticed on the floor than in the manager's office. In a job shop, responsibility and authority can be built into a job to reward workers for facilitating improvements. If you want someone to look beyond the blinders of the work order, make it part of his job," concludes Cheryl.

"Exactly," adds Tom. "You need to design jobs so that you get what you want from the workers."

Everyone agreed that on Fred's assembly line, making an immediate change in either the process or product design might not work. There the physical composition and layout of the process was a reflection of the product. You couldn't change the product design without serious implications for what was usually a big capital investment. Rarely could an individual line worker see enough from the vantage point of his workstation to appreciate all the implications of a change he might suggest. The individual worker's part in the process was just a small slice of the pie. But a line worker might well see the potential for streamlining the process and quite possibly the interface with stations up and down the line.

"In your case, Fred," adds Tom, "you might want the line workers' job description to include focusing on the process—keeping their eyes open and making suggestions to improve the process. Just make sure *somebody* is looking at the big picture. In Luis's case, maybe the workers' job description should include focusing on both the process and the product. You might even think about getting people into groups or teams with different perspectives."

"Seems to me," says Cheryl, "that the important thing is to structure the job descriptions and the reward system to encourage what you want from workers and still give them what they need. Empowerment is an important issue, but there's a lot more to it than making people feel good by talking about it. Some people need it more than others. Some situations call for it more than others. Bringing those variables into

line with each other is a tough assignment. You guys ought to see how tough it gets in the hospital. We've got to empower and reward our people in a way that allows them to balance what the patients think they should be getting with what we think they should be getting. I can't imagine you have it any easier, Tom."

"No, you're right," Tom answers. "The presence of a customer makes the game tougher to play. I mean, should a flight attendant recheck the head count so the plane can take off on time, or help a passenger to find someone to swap seats with? We can't anticipate every conflict and tell the attendants what they should do in every case. They have to make the call."

"Well, I'm beginning to see what you're getting at," says Fred, sliding under the bench press station, which seemed a bit overloaded for him. "With all this talk about job design, empowerment, and who does what, do you think I can empower this?" He attempts, without much success, to move the bar.

"Well, between plain old inertia and plain old gravity," laughs Cheryl, "you've got your job cut out for you, big guy!"

Introduction

In modern history, Adam Smith's experiment with the manufacture of pins may have been the starting point for the purposeful design of work. Smith, an English economist and philosopher, popularized the concept of the division of labor, or job specialization, in England in the late 1700s. Working alone, a worker could produce twenty pins a day. Smith demonstrated that a small group of workers, each of whom repeatedly performed a limited portion of the work of making a pin, could produce 48,000 pins a day.

More recent developments in job design are detailed (more or less chronologically) in this chapter. These have included the use of time and motion studies to develop work standards for repetitive jobs—guidelines for what must be done, the technique to be used, and the time allotted for completion. Time and motion studies are very mechanistic, focusing primarily on the physical aspects of jobs. Researchers using other, more behavioral approaches have sought to enhance the motivational characteristics of work. Often, a worker's rate of output is determined less by the physical ability to complete a task correctly in a given period than by the desire and willingness to do so.

Socio-technical systems theory was developed to match the mechanical with the human elements of the work environment. This theory emphasizes the impact of the production process on workers' social structure. Employees have many objectives besides the creation of a product-service bundle; thus, it is important to consider their social needs when designing a job. Likewise, employee involvement programs seek to unleash workers' creativity. Such programs allow workers to shape their own work environment, solve persistent problems, and respond to opportunities for improvement that others seldom notice.

Integrating Operations Management Across the Functions

Table 10.1 highlights some of the primary interactions of this chapter's content across the various functions of business. The design of jobs is a critical factor in the effectiveness of any organization and any function within that organization. Jobs that are poorly designed can drain employee motivation; create conflict between workers and management; create conflict between departments or functions; lead to worker illness, injury, or death; increase cost and reduce efficiency; and so on. In sum, poorly designed jobs rob employees of the opportunity to satisfy customers and contribute to worker dissatisfaction, turnover, morale problems, and low motivation. On the other hand, job designs that empower, motivate, and stimulate the worker can raise levels of job satisfaction and productivity at the same time. These job design implications hold true regardless of the function where the work will be done. To be effective in the long run, the job design process not only must consider various functional perspectives but must also be consistent with the competitive priorities and physical realities of the business. Figure 10.1 emphasizes the cross-functional nature of the job design process.

Financial managers are concerned with job designs across the organization from at least two perspectives. First, when jobs are redesigned or when new motivational and incentive schemes are adopted, there may be significant up-front costs that require financial justification. Second, from a risk management perspective, financial managers should be aware of the potential hazards associated with the work of employees so that appropriate insurance can be acquired and legal records maintained.

The accounting managers have to synchronize payroll accounting and cost tracking systems with any changes in job design.

Human resources (HR) professionals play a critical role in job design decisions. Jobs must comply with labor law, and labor relations considerations (including collective bargaining agreements) must be brought to bear in every job redesign. Additionally, HR is concerned with the workforce development and training that should accompany any changes to the way workers accomplish their tasks and responsibilities. Finally, HR professionals play a significant role in the design of incentive packages and motivational schemes, adapting the social structure of work to its technical requirements, and through a wide variety of recruitment, selection, promotion, retention, and compensation decisions.

Because job design decisions can have a huge impact on a company's competitive position, marketing managers also should take an active role in the job change process,

Table 10.1

Integrating Operations Management across the Functions

Functional Area / Integration Perspective	Finance	Accounting
Why Cross-Functional Integration Matters in Job Design	The effectiveness of financial operations depends on the design of jobs in that area. Additionally, modifications in motivation schemes often have significant financial implications that require justification.	The effectiveness of accounting operations depends on the design of jobs in that area. Also, payroll systems must take into account job designs.
Key Issues	What will be the justification of investing in improved job design? How will we minimize risk and obtain the necessary insurance related to potential work injuries and other labor liabilities? How will we ensure compliance of financial operations with labor laws? How will we improve the design of jobs within the finance function?	What will be the payroll accounting implications of job design and motivation schemes? How will we ensure compliance of accounting operations with labor laws? How will we improve the design of jobs within the accounting function?

especially in service-intensive businesses. Later in this chapter, we will discuss the service profit chain, a model that describes the role employees play in developing cycles of success and failure for their employers. This model ties together job design considerations, financial issues, and marketing concerns, such as customer loyalty. It explains why the design of jobs provides either the foundation for ongoing success or the basis for intractable problems.

Technology and information systems are ubiquitous in today's workplace, but they sometimes fail to deliver all of the expected benefits because of conflicts with the existing job design or social structure. Engineers and management information systems (MIS) professionals, who develop and install new technologies and systems, benefit by first understanding the social context in which their machines and computerized systems will be used. These considerations highlight the relevance of job design to the functional areas of engineering and MIS.

Human Resources	Marketing	Engineering	Management Information Systems
Job design is a primary HR activity and input to the design of value-adding systems.	The effectiveness of marketing operations and that function's interaction with other areas depends on their job designs.	Industrial Engineers are often called upon to provide critical analysis in the support of job design and assist in ensuring the safety of workers jobs.	The effectiveness of the IS function depends on the design of jobs in that area. Also, the interaction of technical systems with human and social systems is a critical aspect of job design.
How will we ensure compliance of job designs across the organization with labor law?	What will be the impact of job design decisions on competitive position?	What will be the ergonomic design of jobs?	What will be the impact of automation when considering socio-technical systems factors?
How will we optimize worker motivation and safety through design of jobs and incentive packages?	How will we ensure compliance of marketing operations with labor laws?	How do will we appropriately accommodate handicapped workers?	How will we ensure compliance of IS operations with labor laws?
What will be the job training and workforce development needs?	How will we improve the design of jobs within the marketing function?	How will we optimize job design (possibly utilizing time and motion study)?	How will we improve the design of jobs within the IS function?
		What will be the impact of automation when considering socio-technical systems factors?	
		How will we ensure compliance of engineering operations with labor laws?	
		How will we improve the design of jobs within the engineering function?	

Job Design with a Focus on Work Standards

If you have ever held a job, you probably remember a time when another worker said something like, "Slow down or you're going to make us all look bad." Often, this comment is made during your first few days on the job and continues to be made until you adapt your pace to that of the leading bully in your work area. This social pressure to perform your work in a particular way is called **worker soldiering**. Through such social mechanisms, workers determine the rate at which work is done. When they do, they take over part of management's traditional role in job design.

While Frederick Taylor, the father of scientific management, was taking night classes in mechanical engineering, he worked the day shift in a steel mill. There Taylor observed that worker soldiering played a major role in determining the rate at which work

Worker soldiering

The social pressure to perform your work in a particular way.

Figure 10.1

Job design process

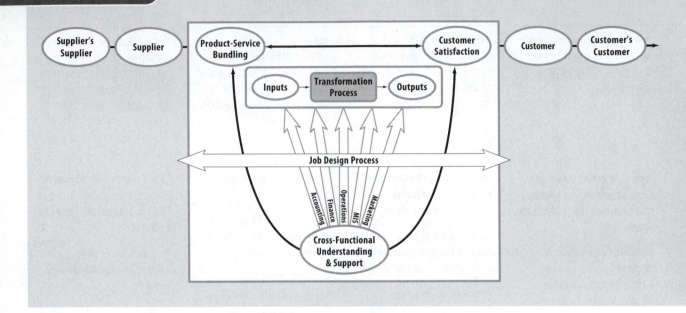

was done. He felt strongly that instead of allowing workers to determine production rates, managers should use quantitative and motivational techniques to determine and control the pace of work. Later, Taylor and his fellow researchers, Frank and Lillian Gilbreth, suggested the use of time and motion studies in setting job standards.

Standard Times

Time and motion studies

Job standards are determined by breaking a task down into its basic movements and measuring the time required to complete those movements.

Work standard

A defined procedure for the completion of a task including a clearly stated task duration.

Work sampling

Research gathered through the process of timing workers with a stopwatch as they performed the various tasks that made up their jobs.

In **time and motion studies**, job standards are determined by breaking a task down into its basic movements and measuring the time required to complete those movements. The Gilbreths identified fourteen such motions, which they called "Therbligs" (the plural of "Gilbreth" spelled backward). Therbligs included activities such as grasping with a hand, searching visually or with a hand, selecting one part from among several, moving an item by hand, moving an empty hand, mental planning, and resting to overcome fatigue. The Gilbreths theorized that by eliminating unnecessary motions and training workers to perform only required motions, they could standardize any job for all capable workers. The time required to complete the job could then be computed by adding the times allowed for each of the Therbligs in the job. Thus, a **work standard** is a defined procedure for completion of a task and includes clearly stated task duration. In another approach to setting work standards researchers timed workers with a stopwatch as they performed the various tasks that made up their jobs. They then used the distribution of times observed to determine an acceptable work standard.

Work sampling is a technique used to establish work standards for less structured jobs such as those held by librarians, policemen, or sales managers. In work sampling employees record their allocation of time to their various responsibilities and this information is used to determine future staff requirements and compensation. Obviously,

Athletes often cover a fixed distance faster during a timed workout than during a game. Similarly, work-studies in industry often underestimate the time required to complete a job because the conditions of the study were not the same as typical work conditions.

a work standard is useful only if workers can be made to conform to the standard. Determining an appropriate standard is far easier than imposing it on workers, however. Thus, companies that use work standards must find a way to get workers to accept them. The most common approach has been to select those workers who are best suited to the task, train them to complete the task in the manner required to achieve the standard, and motivate them to achieve the standard using some piece rate system. Taylor, who suggested the approach, favored a piece rate pay system for those who accomplished the standard and a bonus for those who exceeded it.

One advantage of work standards is that they allow managers to separate the planning and doing of work. If managers can effectively estimate the rate at which work will be done, they can also plan schedules, estimate the labor requirements for a given period, tell customers how long a job will take, estimate the labor cost attributable to a particular product-service bundle, and so on. This advantage was particularly important in the past, when managers dealt with a large pool of workers with limited reading, writing, and analytical skills. On the other hand, managerial systems that separate planners from doers tend to reinforce "we versus they" attitudes. Workers often complained about managers who pushed them to achieve a standard while "sitting up in their air-conditioned office without lifting a finger to help." Indeed, managers were often so concerned with the standards, they seemed uninterested in the workers' feelings. They saw the imposition of a work standard much as the process of setting a knob on a machine. But while a work standard is fixed, human strength and concentration vary over time and environmental conditions. From the worker's perspective, work standards were not a very caring approach. Not surprisingly, scientific management techniques provoked a strong worker backlash in the early decades of the twentieth century. Indeed, many scholars attribute the growth of unions in the first half of the century to the failure of scientific management.

Standard Procedure

Eventually, the field of industrial engineering grew out of scientific management. Together, these two approaches to the management of work contributed many of the advances in operational efficiency that support our current consumptive lifestyle. Even today, industrial engineers conduct time and motion or work sampling studies. Because most workers today can read, write, and perform many of the analytic tasks once reserved for managers, separation of the planning and doing of work is now not so essential. Instead, members of a work group in a repetitive manufacturing environment might ask an industrial engineer to help them design the jobs in their work area. In fact, in many workplaces, autonomous groups of workers bear full responsibility for staffing, scheduling, and improving their work processes. Even unionized blue-collar workers in heavy industry have accepted this approach.

A work standard tells how much work a worker should be expected to do in a given period. Originally, when jobs tended to be quite repetitive, that focus was considered relevant. If a worker was expected to complete sixty defect-free pieces in an hour, he or she could be reprimanded for completing only fifty-five or rewarded for completing sixty-five. Quality was inspected after the fact, and consistency was ensured through the worker's familiarity with the work.

But today, most repetitive jobs have been automated. Not many jobs require a worker to repeat a one-minute task for eight hours. Instead, workers have been cross-trained to perform a variety of tasks in any given day; they are multiskilled. As a result, work standards now focus on the question of *how* a task should be completed. Job standardization provides uniformity of procedure, even though most procedures are conducted by a variety of employees. If a job is done incorrectly, a mistake is made, or production rates become excessively slow, the managers ask, have we been following the standard procedure? Producing sixty units an hour rather than fifty-five is less important than following standard procedure.

ISO 9000 certification requirements (described on pages 130–131 in Chapter 4), which have become essential in many manufacturing firms, reinforce this emphasis on the standardization of work procedures. To become and remain ISO 9000 certified, workers must know and follow the standards for the jobs they perform. They must also be able to look up the documentation for the standards if they have questions.

Task Familiarity In Job Design

To illustrate the importance of task familiarity in developing job standards for routine work, the Gilbreths developed some experiments that focused on the activities of individual workers. Though their experiments have not been widely used in the West, they have been used extensively by Japanese managers since the 1930s. The Japanese call these experiments "table top experiments," because they can be done at a desk.

For example, one experiment shows that workers' familiarity with a task makes a big difference in the rate at which they can perform it. The experiment requires the worker to write the words "industrial engineering" ten times. An observer provides the subjects with blank cards and times them. Naturally, some improvement occurs, but because the task is familiar and simple, the improvement is not significant. The workers are then told that their work is being "cut in half": They must write "industrial engineering" ten times, leaving out every other letter. (The result should be "idsra egneig.") Again, an observer provides blank cards and times the subjects, this time exhorting them not to slack off or create defects.

As you might imagine, subjects take much longer to do "half of the work," making more errors in the process. They also reveal an interesting pattern of learning. They typically complete the first card faster than the second and third, yet take significantly less time to complete the last card. Experimenters theorize that subjects take longer to complete the second and third cards because they feel a need to go back and check what they have written.

In other experiments, workers were asked to write the words backward, as they would appear in a mirror. These and other experiments illustrated the significance of a worker's familiarity with the task standard, the order of tasks, and the way in which tasks are learned. Scholars now believe that some of these experiments, along with lessons learned from Henry Ford and other key U.S. industrial figures, became the foundation for the Japanese management system in the latter half of the twentieth century.

Job Specialization and Skill Set Stratification

If a job requires more than one skill, a manager may want to take advantage of **job specialization**, which divides work according to the type of skill or knowledge required for its completion. Designing jobs so as to optimize worker skills makes sense, particularly in the delivery of services that require a highly skilled worker to be supported by less-skilled workers. Examples can be found at doctors' offices, restaurants, repair services, and beauty salons. You may have noticed that at certain beauty salons, some stylists only cut and style hair, while other employees make appointments or shampoo, dry, and sweep up hair. Designing jobs by skill set optimizes the salon's income. You may prefer to go to a barber or beautician who does it all—shampoos, cuts, styles, dries, and sweeps. If so, the price you pay will be higher than elsewhere, or the business will be making less money than other salons, because you will be paying a skilled stylist to do tasks that don't require much skill.

Job specialization

The process of dividing work according to the type of skill or knowledge required for its completion.

Designing Jobs with a Focus on Their Motivating Potential

The primary shortcoming of the scientific management approach to job design is clearly its mechanistic treatment of workers. Workers have feelings; no matter how well they are selected, trained, and paid, if they are treated like machines they will resent it. Workers' feelings about their work and their motivation to perform it are stressed in the Job Characteristics Model of work proposed by Hackman and Oldham (1976); see Figure 10.2. This model summarizes a long stream of behavioral research into the relationship among job design, worker motivation, and job performance.

According to the job characteristics model, the job design variables important to worker motivation include:

▶ **Skill variety**—the extent to which a job includes different activities requiring different skills and talents.

▶ **Task identity**—the extent to which a job requires the completion of a recognizable product-service bundle. In other words, can workers tell a customer that they are responsible for the product-service bundle just purchased?

▶ **Task significance**—the extent to which a job affects other people, including fellow employees, customers, community members, and so on.

▶ **Autonomy**—the extent to which a worker is free to do a job in her or his own way. The ability to schedule a job, determine the techniques and procedures to be used, and judge the quality of the finished work all add autonomy to a job.

Skill variety

The extent to which a job includes different activities requiring different skills and talents.

Task identity

The extent to which a job requires the completion of a recognizable product-service bundle.

Task significance

The extent to which a job impacts other people.

Autonomy

The extent to which a worker is free to do a job on her or his own.

INTEGRATING OM:

Things Get Dicey When the Job Description Includes the "Look"

Abercrombie & Fitch store managers are known to approach physically attractive customers and offer them jobs. The managers are just following company policy. They're instructed to approach good looking young people with the idea that if they have the best-looking college kids working in their store, everyone will want to shop there.

Abercrombie's aggressive approach to building an attractive sales force may be a growing trend in American retailing. Businesses including Abercrombie, L'Oréal, the Gap, and others are openly seeking workers who are sexy, sleek, or simply good-looking.

Hiring for looks is old news in some industries. But many companies have taken that approach to sophisticated new heights in recent years, hiring workers to project an image. In doing so, some have been accused of violating antidiscrimination laws and had to face private and government lawsuits. While hiring attractive people is not necessarily illegal, discriminating on the basis of age, sex, or ethnicity is. That is where things can get confusing. Hiring by looks can potentially result in unintended discrimination on the basis of race, national origin, gender, age, or even disability. While it might make sense for a retailer of athletic goods to insist on hiring only athletic-looking people, this could be viewed as discriminating against a person in a wheelchair. Employers who insist on a height requirement might be discriminating against racial groups that tend to be shorter. In fact the Equal Employment Opportunity Commission (EEOC) has accused several companies of practicing race and age discrimination by favoring youthful and attractive whites in their hiring.

Some chains, most notably the Gap and Benetton, pride themselves on hiring attractive people from many backgrounds and races. However, some feel that Abercrombie's "classic American" look, pervasive in its stores and catalogs and on its Web site, is blond, blue-eyed, and preppy. Abercrombie finds such workers and models by concentrating its hiring on certain colleges, fraternities, and sororities, approaching certain customers, and discretely rating walk-in applicants. While the company denies that it discriminates, lawsuits have been filed by Hispanic, Asian, and black job applicants who feel otherwise. In many cases, plaintiffs feel the company ignored past retail work experience or lack thereof. Several plaintiffs said in interviews that when they applied for jobs, store managers steered them to the stockroom, not to the sales floor.

Abercrombie's communications have acknowledged that the company seeks to hire sales assistants, known as brand representatives, who "will represent the Abercrombie & Fitch brand with natural classic American style, look great while exhibiting individuality, project the brand and themselves with energy and enthusiasm, and make the store a warm, inviting place that provides a social experience for the customer."

While the company has denied job bias, in late 2004 it agreed to pay $50 million to settle lawsuits claiming it discriminates against minorities and women. The settlement required the company to implement new policies and programs to promote diversity and prevent discrimination in its workforce. Abercrombie has also created an office of diversity and hired a vice president for diversity.

Retailers defend that approach to hiring as necessary and smart, and industry experts see their point. Yet the federal government has accused some businesses of going too far. The hotel entrepreneur Ian Schrager agreed to a $1.08 million settlement three years ago after the EEOC accused his Mondrian Hotel in West Hollywood, California, of racial discrimination for firing nine valets and bellhops, eight of them non-white. Documents filed in court showed that Schrager had written memos saying that he wanted a trendier group of workers and that the fired employees were "too ethnic."

Stephen J. Roppolo, a New Orleans lawyer who represents many hotels and restaurants, said: "Hiring someone who is attractive isn't illegal per se. But people's views on what's attractive may be influenced by their race, their religion, their age. If I think Caucasian people are more attractive than African-American people, then I may inadvertently discriminate in an impermissible way. I tell employers that their main focus needs to be hiring somebody who can get the job done. When they want to hire to project a certain image, that's where things can get screwy."

Source: Adapted from "Going for the Look, but Risking Discrimination," *New York Times*, July 13, 2003, reporter Steven Greenhouse, and http://www.npr.org/templates/story/story.php?storyId=4174147, October 7, 2005

▶ **Feedback**—the extent to which a worker is informed about her or his effectiveness on a routine basis.

The job characteristics model suggests that job design, in and of itself, can motivate workers by altering their psychological state. Some job designs are more apt than others to provide experiences through which workers attribute meaningfulness to their work, assume responsibility for their work, and gain feedback on the results of their work. Jobs that provide these psychological benefits are more likely than others to produce positive personal and work outcomes, including higher levels of motivation,

Feedback

The extent to which a worker is informed about her or his fellow employees, customers, community members, and so on.

Figure 10.2
The job characteristics model

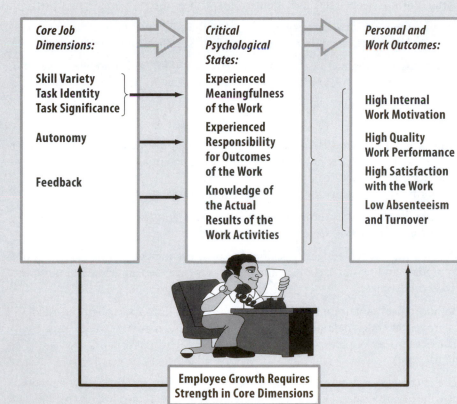

Source: Hackman, J. R. and G. R. Oldham. "Motivation through the design of work: Test of a theory." *Organization Behaviour and Human Performance, 16* (1976), pp. 250–279.

higher performance levels, higher satisfaction with work, and lower rates of absenteeism and turnover. Furthermore, research suggests that for most of these outcomes, the impact of improved job design will be more significant if individual workers possess a strong need or desire for personal growth.

The Motivating Potential Score

The motivational potential of a particular job, called its motivating potential score (MPS), may be calculated using this equation.

Motivating Potential Score (*MPS*) =
(skill variety + task identity + task significance) × autonomy × feedback

Because the MPS is a multiplicative combination of job dimensions, a job design will not motivate workers if feedback, autonomy, or a combination of skill variety, task identity, and task significance is missing. That means workers will have to be motivated by other means, such as a combination of rewards, punishment, and their own internal desire to do the work. Conversely, the more of the five core job dimensions a job design includes, the greater the job's motivating potential.

Consider the work of a short-order cook at a fast-food breakfast chain's restaurant:

▶ The establishment offers a limited menu of similar items, all prepared in the same manner; thus, skill variety is low.

▶ The cook does not buy materials and in many cases does not even mix up the batter, but just heats it up. Task identity is low then, too.

▶ Though the cook's work is very important to the customer, his recipes are not going to be printed in culinary magazines. Task significance is therefore low.

▶ Autonomy is nonexistent in the short-order cook's job: He is told when to come to work, when to leave, and is given no choice in what to prepare and when.

▶ Finally, no formal feedback loop requires customers to compliment the cook's efforts.

Little wonder that the classifieds are filled with help-wanted ads for short-order cooks! Turnover is high because the job's motivating potential score is close to zero—and its extrinsic rewards are not significant, either.

In contrast, let's consider the job of head chef at a five-star restaurant:

▶ Because the chef must prepare a variety of desserts, entrees, appetizers, seasonal dishes, and drinks, skill variety is high.

▶ Task identity is high, too, because the chef buys the ingredients, determines how to prepare and season each dish, and even takes care to arrange the items attractively on the plate.

▶ Because a five-star restaurant has a reputation, the chef's recipes will be regarded as proprietary information until they are published and may even win awards. The rich and famous are likely to patronize the chef. Thus, task significance is high.

▶ The chef is also autonomous, preparing the foods he or she chooses when and how he or she wishes. Diners are expected to relay their compliments to the chef via the garçon or maitre d'.

For all these reasons, the MPS of the head chef's job is high. Turnover and absenteeism are low; a chef might remain at one restaurant for decades.

Improving a Job's Motivating Potential

Ideally, every job should include some combination of the five core job characteristics. Fortunately these job design variables can be manipulated in a number of ways. Common strategies for improving a job's motivating potential score include the following:

▶ **Job enlargement** adds skill variety through the addition of new tasks.

▶ **Job rotation** adds skill variety by moving workers through a series of different jobs over a prescribed period.

▶ **Job enrichment** adds task significance and enhances autonomy by combining some planning and controlling with the doing of work. For example, a job can be enriched by allowing workers to decide what methods to use, train new hires, schedule their own work, solve their own operational problems, and control part of their budget. The establishment of responsibility for internal and external customer relationships provides task significance, task identity, and feedback.

▶ **Job-contained feedback channels** provide private, timely, and accurate data on job performance. For example, if client relationships and quality evaluation requirements are built into a job, workers will get feedback straight from the customer's mouth. This type of feedback is generally superior to any feedback a supervisor could provide. Moreover, when feedback comes from a supervisor, the employee will seek to satisfy the supervisor; but when feedback comes from the customer, the employee is more likely to satisfy the customer.

Job enlargement

Adds skill variety through the addition of new tasks.

Job rotation

Adds skill variety by moving workers through a series of different paths.

Job enrichment

Adds task significance and enhances autonomy by combining various jobs.

Job-contained feedback channels

Private, timely, and accurate data provided on job performance.

Designing Jobs Including Socio-Technical Systems Perspectives

According to socio-technical systems theory, there are two systems in any workplace: a social system and a technical system. The technical system has only one purpose: to create a product-service bundle that will satisfy customers. The social system, on the other hand, may have numerous objectives, only one of which is creating the product-service bundle. Other objectives may include providing for the material needs of workers' families, uplifting the community's quality of life, keeping the environment clean, and making life at work more enjoyable. Often, to the people who make up the social system, these other objectives are much more important than the technical systems.

Figure 10.3 illustrates a common situation. The technical system is designed to be highly effective at meeting a product's design specifications. The social system, on the other hand, has evolved over time to meet the interests and needs of the employees. Because the social system's objectives do not match the technical system's objectives, the socio-technical system is not particularly well suited to providing the product-service bundle the customer desires. The idea behind socio-technical systems theory is that in any organization, there is a best match between the technical system and the social system. That match, which is best suited to satisfying customer requirements, is a critical aspect of job design.

While automation is usually seen as a change in the technical system, in reality, any change in the technical system will change the social system as well. The decision to automate a worker's job creates a new type of job to support the new technology. Changing the makeup of the workforce also creates fear of job loss, mistrust, and insecurity in the workforce. Often, managers will automate a process to achieve higher levels of productivity, trusting that their goal can be met solely through a change in the technical

The Cost of Addiction

Addiction costs corporate America billions of dollars a year in lost productivity, absenteeism, and higher health care expenses. Based on a National Institute on Drug Abuse and Arizona State University study, employers can estimate a lower bound on what drug abuse costs them by figuring that at least 10% of the workforce is involved, that these workers experience at least a 25% reduction in productivity, and that 20% of healthcare costs are attributable to the problem.

In addition to costing companies, drug abuse is costly to users—it derails many once-promising careers. Because of this, more companies are willing to help, especially their higher-level or high potential employees. Workers are, understandably, still reluctant to take advantage of company help, for fear of jeopardizing their positions.

High-level professionals have many delicate issues to navigate. How, for example, can they avoid being stigmatized by colleagues? And how can they explain gaps on a résumé after a long treatment period? Many employees who receive treatment—whether for alcoholism or for drug, gambling, or food addictions—will undoubtedly have some difficulties in the beginning, experts say, but as they recover, so too will their careers.

Abuse of some drugs has been climbing in the workplace. According to Quest Diagnostics, which provides workplace drug tests, the number of workers and job applicants who tested positive for amphetamine use rose 17% in 2002 from the previous year. At the Waismann Institute, in Beverly Hills, Calif., 60% of the patients, mostly high-powered business people, are addicted to painkillers like OxyContin and Vicodin, up from about 10% four years ago as today's workers seek ways to curb their anxieties and depression.

One of the biggest difficulties is seeking help in the first place. Underlings who are more than willing to help cover up the problem may surround managers. A recent survey by the Caron Foundation of its patients found that 75% of executives in recovery said they had secretaries or assistants who went to great lengths to cover for them. Ninety percent said their peers had to work extra hours to compensate for their addiction.

Another issue is confidentiality. Many workers, particularly executives, hesitate to seek help through their company's employee assistance programs or human resources departments, out of fear of looking weak or even harming the company's reputation. To help make executives feel more comfortable about seeking help, some companies are offering programs that promise heightened confidentiality, including one with a substance-abuse counseling program that can be completed entirely by telephone.

Law experts argue that employers are generally under no obligation to keep workers with untreated substance-abuse problems on the payroll and that the Americans With Disabilities Act does not protect these employees. But employers are much more likely to support those who request help rather than those whose problems were discovered through drug testing or other means.

After seeking help, patients should avoid trying to keep up workloads during treatment. In fact, job designs that place excessive responsibility or too much work on an individual are often seen as a contributor to the development of addictions in the first place. For assembly line workers this point has been forcefully illustrated by Ben Hamper's book, *Rivethead*. Hamper worked in auto assembly operations for many years and came from a family and community of autoworkers. He colorfully chronicles psychological impact of being required to perform mundane operations repeatedly for hours per shift over the course of a career and the potential of that environment to drive workers toward substance abuse.

Career experts suggest the many who return to work during treatment for substance abuse are so fearful of losing their jobs, especially in an economic downturn, that they step up the pace of their work and don't take vacations, or even lunch breaks. They suggest easing back into the workload, perhaps even working part time for a few weeks if possible. Once the person is back to a full-time schedule, he should set boundaries on the job, by taking time out for lunch each day, for example.

The cost of addiction can be high but the cost of replacing valuable employees can be higher. And, getting to one possible root of the problem, the human impact of a job design should be considered in such a way as to reduce the likelihood that it will contribute to development of substance abuse and addiction problems.

Don't let drugs derail your career. For facts visit the National Institute of Drug Abuse website (http://www.nida.nih.gov/). If you're already dealing with an addiction problem, seek help. One place to start: http://www.addiction-help-line.com/.

Source: Adapted from "Dealing With Addiction, and What Comes After," *New York Times*, July 20, 2003, reporter Melinda Ligos; http://www.addictionalternatives.com/products/costto1_2.html, October 7, 2005; http://www.nida.nih.gov/; and http://www.addiction-help-line.com/

system. Later, when they cannot use the new technology effectively because it does not fit the existing social system, they realize they have made a costly blunder.

Just as the changes in the technical system can force changes in the social system, changes in the social system can drive technical considerations. Two examples are the increasing concern for ergonomics and worker safety. Automating jobs that are dangerous or highly repetitive makes a great deal of sense. Indeed, workers might tend to avoid dangerous, monotonous, or difficult jobs through tardiness, absenteeism, and other social mechanisms. Where these problems exist or where operational equipment is not designed with the user in mind, managers should use technology to remedy the social problem.

Figure 10.4 illustrates the constant pressure for change in job design. While all managers hope that the existing job design and work organization are consistent with company strategy, structure (building and equipment), and infrastructure (decision making, training, procedures, and systems), those relationships cannot be set in concrete. Technological change, change in customer preferences, and social change will eventually create mismatches that require jobs to be redesigned.

Figure 10.3

Matching technical and social objectives to satisfy customer expectations

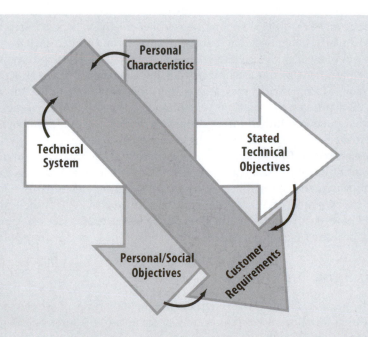

Figure 10.4

The ongoing need to redesign jobs

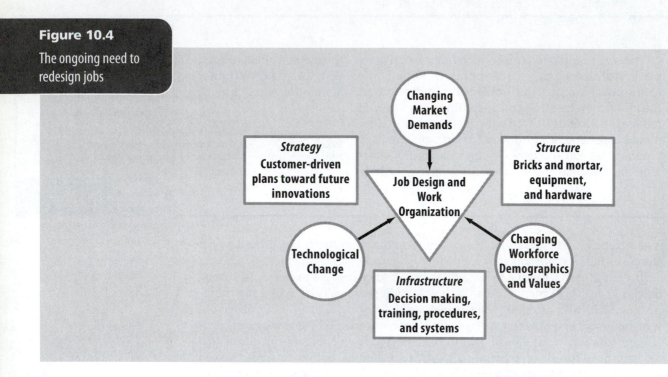

Designing Jobs for Employee Involvement and the High-Performance Workplace

Today, most employers realize that to remain competitive, they need to capitalize on the brain power and creativity of their workforce. Job designs that include only physical tasks and treat workers like machines are on the way out. If the physical tasks in a job are so repetitive that they do not require worker creativity, the job is frequently automated. Similarly, the notion that management plans and controls what workers do has fallen out of favor in many companies. As a value-adding system resource, workers are notably different from machines in that they can adapt, learn, interact with others, and grow. Machines can't make suggestions that will improve customer service, worker safety, product reliability, or environmental performance. Workers, on the other hand, can make hundreds of suggestions each year, and they can cooperate with others to make the improvements they have suggested a reality.

Employee involvement (EI) is a management approach that allows workers to participate regularly in the operating decisions that affect them, including planning, job design, process improvement, goal setting, performance measurement, and problem solving. Designed to give employees more pride, responsibility, and reward for their companies' success, EI has been an extremely effective approach, because it places the power to address both problems and opportunities in the hands of those workers best able to do so.

Encouraging Teamwork

One of the most common ways to harness the mental power of workers is to form worker teams. Teams are used in just about every area of business and at just about every organization. They are the engine behind any successful effort to implement the

Employee involvement (EI)

A formal approach to creating a spirit of teamwork that will lead to widespread process improvements.

Total Quality philosophy and rely heavily on quality tools, such as the Quality Improvement story (see pages 161–169 in Chapter 4).

Regardless of the context of teamwork, the assignment of workers to teams has a significant impact on the design of their jobs. Communication, analytical skills, functional knowledge in multiple areas, goal-oriented behavior, and consensus-based decision making all become critical to job performance. Teamwork also means that job performance cannot be fully described, measured, or rewarded solely in terms of hourly output. In a team environment, therefore, managers must act as leaders who value employee input and participative decision making. They cannot simply oversee administrative procedures and guard the status quo.

Teams are a way of life at many organizations today. The job design tools and techniques described in this chapter are often used by teams themselves to design their own jobs. As a result, the benefits of teamwork are now widely recognized. As a former president of Ford Motor Company has said, "No matter what you're trying to do, teams are the most effective way to get the job done."[1] Some of the specific benefits teams have generated for their companies include:

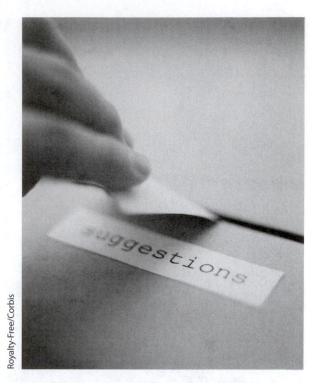

Many of the suggestions for improved work place design come from employees themselves.

▶ Cost reductions in materials, overhead, and labor

▶ Improvements in product reliability and usefulness

▶ Process improvements, including reduced setup and operating time, improved flexibility and quality of conformance, a reduction in unexpected downtime, and improved reliability of delivery

▶ The reduction or elimination of waste, including transportation, rework, shrinkage, packaging, storage cost, and paperwork

▶ Improvements in worker safety, health, knowledge, engagement, skill, and morale

▶ Improved environmental performance

▶ Improved supplier, customer, and community relations

Companies that are serious about EI design the system so as to facilitate and reward worker participation. Typically, in each facility, managers called **facilitators** support the teams' efforts and respond to workers' suggestions for improvement. The facilitator's job is to provide any necessary training, which often includes coaching in problem solving and communication. Facilitators can also put teams in touch with functional experts, customers, or outside vendors who have the knowledge and information they need. Having enough facilitators to support the level of team activity present in a facility is critical. Frequently, facilitators will report to a director of EI, who reports in turn to a corporate vice president for quality.

Facilitators

Managers that support the teams' efforts and respond to workers' suggestions for improvement.

One of the keys to successful teamwork is the knowledge and skill of team members. Consequently, most successful EI programs provide significant training to employees. Performing effectively as a team member will be difficult if an employee's reading, writing, speaking, listening, or basic data analysis skills are limited.

---

[1] This comment was made in a presentation by Thomas Page (former Executive Vice President of Ford Motor Company) at the dedication of Miami University's Page Center for Entrepreneurship, September 26, 1994.

Understanding group dynamics—how to conduct meetings, develop a consensus, and include less-outgoing members—is also important. Team members must understand the proper roles of leaders, facilitators, and others in the group, as well as the importance of preparing for a meeting. All these general skills must be developed in the workforce; one cannot assume that a new hire has them.

In addition to general skills, team members may require training specific to a project. For example, a team that is trying to reduce setup time on a specific machine might need training in the Single-Minute Exchange of Dies (SMED) system for reducing setup time. Similarly, a team that is trying to prevent equipment breakdowns might need training by the manufacturer of the equipment or training in total productive maintenance. Or a team might need help in comprehending the production process as a whole. Process-oriented experiments (similar to table top experiments, except that they are applied to a whole process) can help team members to understand the dynamics of a complex production process, including the impact on productivity of bottlenecks, inventory buffers, quality problems, and process disruptions. Experimentation of this nature is particularly useful for teams that design their own jobs and work as an autonomous group. It not only helps members to better understand and design their jobs, but it improves the effectiveness of the group as a whole.

Awards and other work place recognitions can provide high levels of motivation.

Fisher/Thatcher/Getty Images Inc.

Rewarding Employee Involvement

As for rewards, most companies compensate workers generously for their participation. At Honda of America Manufacturing (HAM), for example, workers who make suggestions for improvement and then serve on teams to implement their suggestions receive small cash bonuses. Every bona fide suggestion is compensated with a $3, $6, $20, $50, or $100 bonus in the next paycheck. Simple, run-of-the-mill suggestions are evaluated by supervisors and facilitators and rewarded at the lower levels. Suggestions that have a significant impact beyond the local work area are forwarded to higher levels of management. The higher a suggestion goes, the greater the monetary reward.

In addition to small bonuses, employees can earn between ten and fifty points for each suggestion, and fifty points for completing a team project, such as investigating, planning, and implementing a suggestion. As workers accumulate points, they begin to receive prizes. Workers who reach the 300-point milestone receive a plaque from the plant manager. At 1000 points, they receive an $800 cash bonus. At the 2500-point milestone, the participating employee can choose a new Honda Civic or pay the difference and get an Accord. At 5000 points, the grand prize includes a new Accord, a paid 2-week trip for two anywhere in the world, and a cash bonus worth 4 weeks' pay. Honda also pays monthly bonuses for perfect attendance and on-time arrival, as well as an annual profit-sharing bonus based partly on the company's profitability and partly on the employee's performance. Because of this voluntary program, a large percentage of Honda's workforce is highly motivated to improve the company's operating system. Though the work may be monotonous and all workers have the same title and receive the same wage, without regard to seniority, Honda of America turns away thousands of job applicants each year.

To recognize groups of employees, most large companies hold team competitions. Honda, for example, has one competition for supplier teams and another for internal teams. Teams present their projects and showcase the problem-solving processes they used, allowing all employees to learn from their experiences. The winners at each facility go on to a national competition; the national winners compete internationally. Organizations such as the Association for Quality and Participation (AQP) and state manufacturers' organizations also sponsor team competitions. The travel and recognition that are associated with these competitions are a significant reward for the workers who participate.

Given the key elements of a well-designed EI program—excellent facilitators, readily available training, a well-designed reward system—one can see that teamwork requires a significant investment in the workforce. Does it pay? Many companies are convinced that it does. Honda of America executives believe they get back more than five dollars for every dollar they spend on the EI program. In many cases, the financial return is ongoing, because while the improvements are paid for only once, their benefits last for many years. Large organizations may generate more than a million worker suggestions a year; many estimate the combined return on their suggestion and EI programs to be roughly 100 to 1. For every penny they spend, they are getting back roughly a dollar.

In the United States, some legal objections have been raised to certain manufacturers' EI programs. Union leaders may suspect that manufacturers might be using EI programs to thwart or even replace the unions' role in meeting workers' needs. Thus, companies must be careful to ensure that teams in their EI programs do not violate national labor law. Generally speaking, team activities may be illegal if they (1) address labor issues that affect employees who do not belong to the team; (2) address matters such as wages, grievances, hours, or working conditions; (3) include deals with management on certain issues; or (4) represent employees being "led through the hoops" by managers, rather than operating autonomously.

The Service Profit Chain

Heskett, Sasser, and Schlesinger (1987) developed the concept of the service profit chain. Illustrated in Figure 10.5, the model suggests that employees drive service value, which drives customer satisfaction and loyalty, which drives revenue and profit growth. In short, the service profit chain recommends that primary attention be paid to the role of employees as a key driver of profits. This concept, despite its name, is not limited to service environments. Whether an organization primarily manufactures a product or delivers services involving high customer contact, its employees are critical to quality and financial performance.

In Figure 10.5, the box labeled "Operating Strategy and Service Delivery System" encompasses the elements of employee performance. "Capability" refers to recruiting, hiring, and training employees who can do the work and find fulfillment in the work. "Satisfaction" comes from a work environment that provides both extrinsic financial rewards and intrinsic rewards.

Employees who are equipped to accomplish excellence and are satisfied with the rewards that come from high performance will become loyal to the employer. They will be less likely to quit or look for work elsewhere. This is because employers who devote proportionately more resources to employee hiring, training, and motivating than competing area employers quickly become known in the community as "employers of choice." Word spreads fast among potential job applicants when an employer offers higher-than-average wages, health and dental benefits, and such perks as on-site daycare facilities. Employers of choice enjoy a larger pool of better-qualified job applicants because they are the most desirable employer in the community. Employee turnover rates at employers of choice can be as low as 1% to 2% annually.

Figure 10.5

The service profit chain

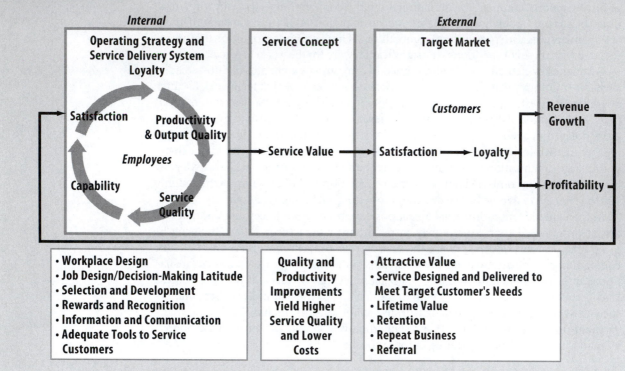

Source: *The Service Profit Chain*, Heskett, Sasser, and Schlesinger, Free Press, 1987, p.19

Loyal employees become more productive employees over time. They learn more skills, they become experts in the organization's product-service bundle, they help train new employees, and they often develop important relationships with customers and suppliers. The result is high service quality delivered by employees. The circle of arrows in the "Employees" box in Figure 10.5 indicates the synergy that is created through the interaction of the different elements of employee performance.

The middle box labeled "Service Concept" in Figure 10.5 is the combination of low costs and high service quality that result from an effective employee strategy. The customer, as depicted in the "Customers" box on the right ultimately determines service value. High service value means that customers will be satisfied with their purchases, will become loyal, and will spread positive word of mouth in the community. Repeat customers are cheaper to serve and tend to purchase more per transaction. New customers, by contrast, are more expensive to attract and serve, and tend to spend less per transaction.

The output of the service profit chain model is revenue growth and profitability. It represents a "breakthrough" strategy for organizations that are frustrated by industry convention. The fast-food industry provides a good context for applying the service profit chain model. Fast-food restaurants are plagued with low pay, low morale, boring work tasks, and high employee turnover. Fast-food employers claim they cannot pay more because they must keep their costs in line with competitors. The result is that no employer is an employer of choice. To job applicants, one employer is the same as another and no reason for loyalty exists. Customer service is frequently slowed because of worker shortages, poor worker attitudes, or inadequate levels of worker training. Poor customer service, in turn, leads to lower service value, lower customer satisfaction, lower loyalty, and less revenue growth and profitability. With less revenue and profitability, it becomes more difficult to improve worker wages and training. This self-perpetuating mess is called the "cycle of failure."

Several years ago, the croissant sandwich restaurant chain Au Bon Pain tried to turn the cycle of failure into the cycle of success. Their new approach slashed the number of part-time employees and created full-time positions that promised a 50-hour weekly work schedule, with 10 hours paid as overtime. This arrangement provided the financial incentive for the new full-time employees to be loyal to their Au Bon Pain jobs. The overtime provided an incentive to avoid missing work, because a missed day meant a loss of the 10 hours of overtime pay. The full-time employees became more knowledgeable, faster, and more accurate in filling customer orders. Customer "regulars" became acquainted with employees who worked the same shifts every day. The result was a high level of comfort and familiarity for the customers. This led to repeat business, positive word of mouth, increased store sales, and greater profits. Through the service profit chain, Au Bon Pain did, in fact, turn the cycle of failure into the cycle of success.[2]

> **REC CENTER DILEMMA**
>
> **Tom needs to explain his airlines' success with people:**
>
> *Tom feels that the service profit chain is an appropriate way to describe a great deal of his airline's success, and the company has been moving in a positive direction for several years now. However, there is pressure to cut costs. Some of the cuts would come from key aspects of the employee involvement programs. Tom feels that these programs are central to the airline's success. Can you help him articulate an argument to keep funding the programs? Help him use the service profit chain in reverse to demonstrate how this might negatively affect the airline.*

Job Design and Competitive Priorities

The modern worker and work environment are quite different from the workers and factories of the past. Today, even the least educated workers are better educated than workers were forty or fifty years ago: Most are high school graduates. Furthermore, today's workers enjoy a great deal of job mobility; the idea of spending one's entire life doing just one job is a thing of the past. Temporary workers ("temps") are used much more widely today than in the past. Finally, the present focus on satisfying a firm's internal and external customers makes the current workplace very different from the workplace of times past.

As a result of these changes, job design has changed. While specialization and scientific management, which stressed the separate planning and execution of work, did improve productivity significantly in the early twentieth century, managers today recognize that jobs can become too specialized. Improving a single worker's productivity, for example, may harm the production flow and overall system performance. With too much specialization, a company might lose sight of customer satisfaction. Given the dynamics of today's workforce, cooperation and teamwork may be more important than individual performance. In working together as a team, individuals may need to sacrifice their own productivity to improve the overall productivity of the system. The team approach also helps to overcome some of the problems associated with a transient workforce. That is not to suggest that the tools once used in job design are irrelevant today, but those tools must be used selectively by workers themselves.

Figure 10.6 shows that not all job design considerations are of equal importance in all operational settings. The figure suggests that competitive priorities and process

[2] This information on the service profit chain is adapted from: James L. Heskett, Thomas O. Jones, Gary W. Loveman, W. Earl Sasser, Jr., and Leonard A. Schlesinger, "Putting the Service Profit Chain to Work," *Harvard Business Review* (March–April, 1994): 166; and W. Earl Sasser Jr. and Lucy Lytle, "Au Bon Pain: The Partner/Manager Program," Case No. 9-687-063, Boston: Harvard Business School Publishing Division, 1993.

Figure 10.6

Job design factors by layout and process type (revisited)

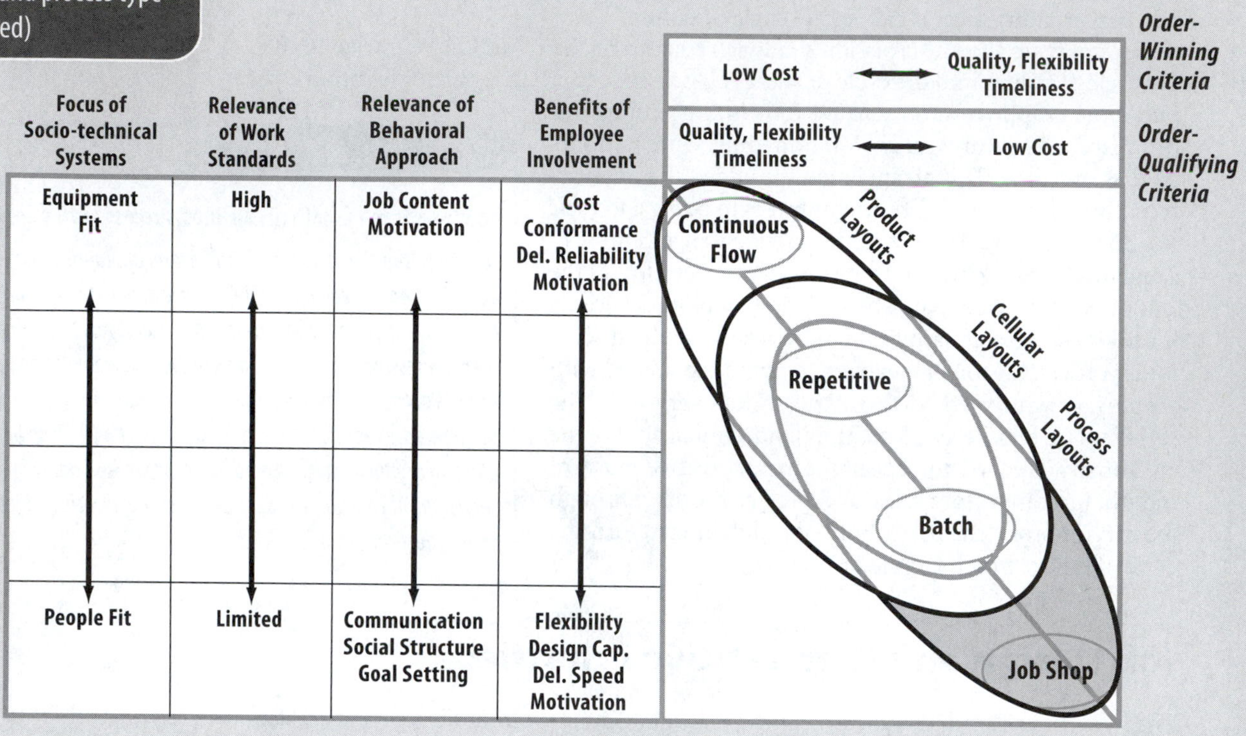

Focus of Socio-technical Systems	Relevance of Work Standards	Relevance of Behavioral Approach	Benefits of Employee Involvement
Equipment Fit	High	Job Content Motivation	Cost Conformance Del. Reliability Motivation
↕	↕	↕	↕
People Fit	Limited	Communication Social Structure Goal Setting	Flexibility Design Cap. Del. Speed Motivation

Order-Winning Criteria: Low Cost ⟷ Quality, Flexibility Timeliness

Order-Qualifying Criteria: Quality, Flexibility Timeliness ⟷ Low Cost

Continuous Flow — Product Layouts

Repetitive — Cellular Layouts

Batch — Process Layouts

Job Shop

type are a large factor in the design of jobs. Specifically:

▶ In product layouts, where equipment requirements tend to be more rigid and special purpose equipment is used by less skilled workers, socio-technical systems approaches focus more on fitting work to the equipment. By contrast, where worker skill is a more critical factor, socio-technical systems place a greater emphasis on adapting equipment and organization to the skills and needs of the workforce.

▶ Work standards, which first became popular in the age of mass production, are still highly relevant in companies that win orders on the basis of cost, conformance, and reliable delivery. But with the growing importance of customization and the increasing flexibility of operational systems, such standards are becoming far from universal in their application. Work standards are not as valuable to firms that compete on the basis of flexibility, where there is greater task variety and limited opportunity to design jobs that are repetitive in nature.

▶ In continuous flow or repetitive manufacturing environments, the behavioral approach to job design recognizes the low motivating potential of job designs that assign repetitive tasks on short cycle times. These approaches focus on improving job content in order to enhance worker motivation. In batch processes and job shops, however, the behavioral approach to job design focuses more on communication, social structure, and goal setting. The EI approach seems applicable to any production environment and should result in improved worker motivation wherever applied. The focus of employee teams, however, will depend on the firm's competitive priorities. For each type of production process, managers will seek to generate EI program benefits that are consistent with their order-winning criteria. Teams are more likely to seek cost reductions, improvements in conformance quality, and improvements in delivery reliability in continuous flow and repetitive environments. In job shops, improvements in flexibility, product design quality, and delivery speed.

SUMMARY

Employees' jobs are part of the value-adding system, so customer satisfaction depends to some degree on the design of those jobs. Throughout this book, we emphasize that the value-adding system should fit a company's competitive priorities. The jobs that employees are asked to do should support the company's operations strategy. Where the competitive priority is cost, jobs will be designed to provide efficiency. Where the competitive priority is flexibility, jobs will be designed to enhance creativity, innovation, and communication.

The work standards approach to job design makes sense in operations in which workers do not have the analytical skills to make decisions about their own work, or in which the production of a highly standardized product-service bundle cannot be automated. Traditionally, work standards have focused on *how much* work should be done in a given period. Workers were motivated with extrinsic rewards. Today, work standards are used to standardize tasks and procedures that are performed by many different workers. This approach, which facilitates job rotation, requires a more broadly skilled workforce but adds interest to workers' lives.

The job characteristics model, which represents a behavioral approach to job design, focuses on the need to motivate workers. The motivating potential score measures a job's motivational ability—the extent to which the job provides skill variety, task identity, task significance, autonomy, and feedback. Because low-MPS jobs are associated with turnover, absenteeism, and even quality problems, employers should try to eliminate those positions whenever possible.

Socio-technical systems theory emphasizes the need to effectively match the mechanical and human elements in the work environment. Too frequently, jobs must be made to fit the technical constraints of machines designed by engineers who are more concerned with technological sophistication than with user-friendliness. When workers must adjust to a machine's shortcomings, they lose their motivation and pride of workmanship. This theory, then, suggests that the design of both machines and jobs should focus on satisfying customer requirements.

Today, employees are expected to assist in the improvement and ongoing operation of the systems in which they work. This expectation has altered both the jobs workers do and the way in which they are managed. Employee Involvement is an approach that emphasizes the use of teams to leverage workers' brainpower. As workers become decision makers, management's role evolves from direct supervision to facilitation of teamwork.

The service profit chain is one model that effectively links job design to the ongoing performance of firms. When jobs are well designed, one should expect higher levels of productivity, output quality, service quality, performance capability, employee satisfaction, and loyalty. Thus customers receive greater value, are more satisfied, and become more loyal. Consequently revenue can more easily be grown and profitability can be enhanced. These business results allow managers to further enhance the workplace and satisfaction of employees, which continues the cycle. An ongoing and sustainable cycle of success, therefore, can begin with the effective design of jobs. By contrast, poor design of jobs can lead to a cycle of failure that is very difficult to escape.

The options available to a firm in regards to job design are constrained by the competitive choices that they have made to position their product-service bundle in the marketplace. As mentioned in Chapter 2, the value-adding system and the product-service bundle must fit the competitive priorities of the firm. Because job design is a part of the value-adding system's design, job design choices must fit a firm's competitive priorities. Companies that are trying to compete on the basis of cost are more likely to pursue cost efficiency, quality of conformance, and delivery reliability while designing jobs. By contrast, companies that compete on the basis of flexibility are more likely to pay attention to issues such as communication, social structure, and skill development.

KEY TERMS

Autonomy, 465

Employee involvement (EI), 472

Facilitators, 473

Feedback, 467

Job-contained feedback channels, 469

Job enlargement, 469

Job enrichment, 469

Job rotation, 469

Job specialization, 465

Skill variety, 465

Task identity, 465

Task significance, 465

Time and motion studies, 462

Work sampling, 462

Worker soldiering, 461

Work standard, 462

DISCUSSION QUESTIONS

1. We have always assumed that Luis's furniture factory was fairly labor intensive. What would a typical job description for that factory sound like? A typical work standard? How would the job descriptions and work standards for Fred's cell phone factory differ?

2. Given your answer to question 1, how should Luis go about expanding the jobs in his factory? What approach might work for him but not for Fred? Also, what approach might work for Fred but not for Luis?

3. Can you think of a work standard you have experienced that focused on *how* the job was done? On *how much* was done?

4. You are trying to come up with a proper compensation package for a new sales manager. In addition to time spent on commission sales, this person will spend a significant amount of time managing a group of representatives who sell only on commission. How do you determine their base salary so as to arrive at a fair combination of salary and commission?

5. How should the school you attend reward your professor? What approach would help to measure the amount of time he or she spends on teaching, scholarship, and institutional service?

6. How are job specialization and skill set stratification related? What examples of each would you expect to see in Luis's furniture factory? At Tom's airline? In Cheryl's hospital? At Fred's cell phone factory? At a restaurant? Your last summer job?

7. Where in a hospital might you find a time and motion study being done? At an airline? Would the emphasis in each place be on *how* or *how much*?

8. How would an employee involvement (EI) program have worked at your last summer job? In your OM class? (Assume that you and your classmates are the employees and your professor is the supervisor.)

9. How do TQM tools fit into an employee involvement program?

10. Fifty years ago, some employees were paid to think and others to do. What line currently separates management from labor?

11. How is working on a team different from a traditional work assignment? Draw on your experiences in study groups to explain the difference.

12. Why would identifying with a group or team tend to make you feel better about your job? Have you had experiences that would support the positive effect of teamwork?

13. Under what conditions would you rather have work assigned to a group rather than to you individually? Why? Under what conditions would you want it assigned individually? Have you had an experience in which either arrangement worked well or poorly? Explain.

14. In Luis's or Tom's companies, where would you draw the boundaries between autonomous work groups? For example, would you group pilots, flight attendants, and ticket agents separately?

15. How would you characterize the motivating potential score (MPS) for a truck driver's job? A surgeon's? A lifeguard's? A college professor's? A bank teller's? A bank robber's? A computer programmer's?

16. When you button your shirt or blouse, do you button it from the top down or the bottom up? Try the procedure the other way; does it take longer? Try reversing it for a week; does the time required to complete the procedure shorten as the week wears on? What do the results of your experiment suggest about job design?

17. Studies have shown that the placement of keys on the standard computer keyboard, which is based on the standard keyboard for typewriters, is far from efficient and can cause occupational problems for typists. Think about the tabletop experiments. Why not change the keyboard layout?

Case 10: Southwest Airlines Feels the Pain of Growing Older

Family, love, and Golden Rule behavior. No one would be surprised to hear these words at a marriage workshop or during a church service. But Southwest Airlines President Colleen Barrett turned heads—about 400 of them—during a recent address to the Texas Society of Association Executives' annual conference when she used the warm, fuzzy words to explain the airline's success.

Southwest, recently the only profitable airline among the nine U.S. majors, owes much of its success to an extraordinary culture that binds and motivates workers. By offering a generous profit sharing and stock-option plan, and creating a "we're all family" culture with office parties and advancement opportunities, Southwest has spurred its employees to continually boost productivity and profits. (In the mid-1970s, Southwest became the first airline to start a profit-sharing plan, and added a stock-purchase plan in 1984 and a stock-option plan for employees in 1991. The stock, which has risen more than a thousand-fold since 1972, has produced millionaires throughout company ranks, down to mechanics and flight attendants. Even with recent stock declines, a $10,000 investment in early July of 1984 would be worth just over $200,000 today.) Southwest Airlines has had a history of hiring and promoting honest people. Hiring for values has also contributed to its competitive advantage as well as combining fun with values. Along the way, the company's workforce has gained the reputation of being fiercely loyal and competitive.

But now that culture is showing signs of strain, just as Southwest flies toward crucial new challenges—from adapting to a new CEO to maintaining its growth during the worst downturn in aviation history. Southwest's labor unions have become more vocal and aggressive. Workers who scrimp and sweat to boost earnings are seeing less return from profit sharing and pummeled stock. And some employees say that after pushing themselves to increase productivity for years, they just can't give any more. In response Southwest has started "culture" programs in all 58 cities it serves, appointing ambassadors to disseminate corporate news and hold parties and picnics to foster team spirit. A "second wind" team helped establish seminars to address employee burnout.

With so much of employees' personal holdings and compensation tied to the company's performance, peer pressure to keep costs down grew intense. Workers still routinely challenge each other on questionable sick calls, overuse of office supplies, and requests for overtime pay for "stupid things." Employees recycle everything possible, saving paper clips and making scribble pads out of old mail. In 1994, a flight attendant suggested using plain trash bags on airplanes, instead of printing ones with the airline's logo. The switch saved $300,000 a year.

Flight attendants pitch in to hurriedly clean planes to get them back in the air within 25 minutes; some even help when they're traveling off-duty. Pilots have helped ramp agents load bags to keep flights on time, and they log more flight hours per day on average than their peers at other airlines.

In 2002, Southwest's unit labor costs—which track the cost to fly one seat one mile—were 22% below those at Continental Airlines, even though the two airlines' average salaries were about the same, around $60,000. Southwest's costs were 41% below those at AMR Corp.'s American Airlines, but American's average salary was nearly $80,000.

Such results have helped Southwest post 30 consecutive years of profits and turn it into the fourth-biggest airline in terms of U.S. domestic service. Many carriers, new and old, are trying to emulate Southwest's low-cost, no-frills formula. Yet that formula is under mounting pressure. Southwest, which led the industry in on-time performance for most of the 1990s, slipped to second in 1999 and has bounced in and out of the lead ever since. In 2002, it ranked sixth among the nine major carriers. Executives cite increased security measures as one reason for the change. They also note that Southwest hasn't reduced its flight schedule during the industry slump, as most other airlines have.

Lately, unions have increasingly sought "big airline" pay to match the airline's growing success, as opposed to the old days, when they'd settle for other incentives to help their underdog airline fly higher. In 1994, for example, in exchange for a stock-option awarded in their contract, pilots agreed to a five-year wage freeze that would help the company keep costs in check.

But now, many of the company's top motivational techniques aren't working as well as they used to. Consider stock options and profit-sharing, which have lost a lot of their allure during the airline slump. Southwest's net income fell 53% to $241 million last year from $511 million a year earlier. Its stock (NYSE: LUV) fell to a low of $10.90 last year. Shares have inched back up to around $18, well below the five-year, split-adjusted high of nearly $24. Unions are showing more frustration during negotiations, unlike the old days, when deals would generally be made more quickly and amicably but union officials say they have no lingering hard feelings toward management.

The slump has hit morale in other ways. Southwest's growth—as measured in the seating capacity of its fleet—has slowed to 4% to 5% annually from its traditional 8% to 10%. The airline typically launches service in at least two cities a year. It hasn't done so in 21 months. That restricts advancement opportunities for pilots, station managers and many others, and employees lose the excitement of conquering new territory.

At the same time, Southwest has found it tougher to maintain its underdog fighting spirit. Southwest, which now has more planes than Continental, often finds itself playing the incumbent under attack from new upstarts, such as JetBlue Airways.

Growth has also made upper management more remote from the rank and file. In the early days of the company, corporate people could send hand-written notes of compliment or condolence to many of the company's 517 employees. They still write notes, but to a fraction of the company's more than 35,000 workers, who are spread from Manchester, N.H., to San Diego.

Some employees say that newer hires just don't get how special the culture is. "Southwest treats its employees so well, and really takes care of them if they stay," says Susan Goodman, who joined Southwest in 1975 as a flight attendant and now coordinates legislative efforts among employees, such as organizing petition drives. "I think some of the younger ones don't understand."

Southwest executives say recent complaints from employees don't necessarily indicate waning loyalty. An overwhelming number of employees remain devoted to the company's success and are proud of their high productivity, executives say. They are also doing their part to keep the culture alive. While some used to disapprove of the company's annual daylong Halloween celebration; dressing up in costumes and doing comedy sketches didn't seem productive. But after coming to see that the party preparations were a model of teamwork and employee bonding, last year the CEO paraded through the headquarters in a judge's robe and wig, evaluating the workers' sketches with a smile.

All work and no play makes life dull. At least that is what President Barrett told those executives in Texas. "There is nothing wrong with enjoying what you do every day. Much of the advice for avoiding overload has placed emphasis on having fun: Workers are taught to value "kid spirit" by taking "joy breaks," such as staging yo-yo contests or hopscotch games in the office. They are also taught to look at every weekend as a "mini-vacation," so that they'd have something to plan and look forward to each week.

SOME QUESTIONS TO THINK ABOUT:

1. What was it about the Southwest culture that motivated workers in the early years?

2. How did the stock options and profit sharing plans fit into the culture and motivation of Southwest's employees?

3. Do you believe there is actually a business benefit (such as improved customer service or profitability) to making "fun and games" a part of the job design at Southwest? Why or why not?

4. Would the "fun and games" approach work elsewhere? Explain why or why not.

Sources: Adapted from

"New Atmosphere Inside Southwest Airlines, Storied Culture Feels Strains," *Wall Street Journal*, July 11, 2003, p. A1, reporter Melanie Trottman

Cohan, Peter S. *Value Leadership*. San Francisco: Jossey-Bass, 2003

Colleen Barrett, Southwest President, "Family, Love, and Golden Rule Behavior" Speech to Texas Society of Association Executives, September 21, 2004

REFERENCES

Frei, F., M. Hugentobler, S. Schurman, W. Duell, and A. Alioth. *Work Design for the Competent Organization*. Westport, CT: Quorum Books, 1993.

Hackman, J. R., and G. R. Oldham. "Motivation through the Design of Work: Test of a Theory." *Organizational Behavior and Human Performance,* 16 (1976): 250–279.

Hackman, J. R., and J. L. Suttle, eds. *Improving Life at Work*. Glenview, IL: Scott Foresman, 1977.

Hillkirk, J. "New Award Cites Teams with Dreams." *USA Today* (April 10, 1992).

Miner, J. B., T. M. Singleton, and V. P. Luchsinger. *The Practice of Management: Text Readings and Cases*. Columbus, OH: C. E. Merrill Publishing Co., 1985.

Robinson, A. G., and M. M. Robinson. "On Table Top Improvement Experiments of Japan." *Production and Operations Management*, 3, no. 3 (1994): 201–216.

Susman, G. I. *Autonomy at Work: A Sociotechnical Analysis of Participative Management*. New York: Praeger Publishers, 1976.

11

The Demand Forecasting Process

Chapter Outline

Introduction 488

Integrating Operations Management Across the Functions 488

Using Forecasts for Planning and Control 489

Choosing a Forecasting Method 494

Forecasting Model Types 494

Time-Series Components 495

Short-Term Forecasting 498

Measuring Forecast Accuracy 503

Estimating Trend 506

Estimating and Using Seasonal Indexes 509

Summary 515
Key Terms 515
Solved Problems 516
Discussion Questions 519
Problems 520
Challenge Problems 523
Case 11: Data: How Much Is Enough? 525

Learning Objectives

After studying this chapter, you should be able to

▶ Demonstrate an understanding of the linkages between forecasting and decisions made in various functional areas of business

▶ Explain the role of forecasts in operational decision making

▶ Describe various types of forecasting models

▶ Identify time series components

▶ Prepare short-term forecasts using moving averages and simple exponential smoothing

▶ Compute and interpret measures of forecast accuracy

▶ Estimate trend in a time series

▶ Estimate and use seasonal indices

...Back at the Rec Center

Luis notices how empty the rec center seems this morning. Fred, Cheryl, and he had made it in, but Tom was still unaccounted for. It's the Monday after Thanksgiving, a day that usually is very busy, with long lines at every station or machine. However, a surprise early winter snowstorm had snarled up the flights into and out of the airport last night. Luis guesses that driving on snow-choked roads or getting much-needed sleep after enduring travel delays are good enough reasons to push workout plans to another day. But, in anticipation of a big crowd, the rec center had scheduled a lot of extra staff—staff that now had little to do.

"Wow, even Tom's sleeping in after last night," suggests Luis. "He must have had a tough night dealing with the storm!" he says, looking at the other two. "Bet he worked really late; he's usually pretty anxious to get in here after a holiday!"

"Yeah, I heard every airport west of the Mississippi was tied up with flights trying to avoid the storm. And this of all weekends!" replies Cheryl, sliding the last plate over on the bar. Just the week before Tom had described how his planners forecast the day before and the weekend after Thanksgiving as one of the biggest demand periods of the year. Forecasts called for a record number of passengers to fly

that weekend, and when the snowstorm hit, it undoubtedly made a mess of his schedule and operations. "He probably could use a little stress relief right now," she smiles knowingly.

"Probably has workers sitting around in some places and going crazy in others!" Fred says, in between the deep breaths and hissing sounds that usually accompany his repetitions on the bench press. "Eeevvennn the best fore-casters," he says, struggling a bit with the final rep, "don't see it coming every time!"

"Tom's not the only one who missed the target judging by all the extra help around here this morning," Cheryl observes as she switches places with Fred on the bench press. Luis and Fred nod as they glance around. "It's hard to anticipate what you'll need," says Cheryl. "Just when you anticipate a big day like this and get everybody and everything together, something happens. Weather or whatever throws a mon-key wrench in the works and everybody's stand-ing around with nothing much to do. We see it all the time at the hospital."

"Guess so," replies Fred. "You live by your forecasts and hope that they're close to being on target. We have to make it and have it ready when the customer calls. We're lucky though, only a couple models to worry about!"

"I envy you on that," adds Cheryl. "Demand forecasts are behind almost every decision we make, long or short run. And we're no better than the weather guys on TV!"

Luis, the final one to use the bench, begins lifting. As Cheryl and Fred step back from the bar, they see Tom coming into the weight room. "Hey, you made it!" they say, all three smiling.

"Yeah, long night, didn't get home till after 3 a.m.!" sighs Tom. "I'm just going to ride a bike to blow off some stress, shower, and head back to the airport." Tom describes the impact the storm had on his airline's schedule, how it delayed some flights and cancelled others. Fred had been right, the storm did idle a lot of his people while it created a lot of extra work for others—all with a serious impact on customer satisfaction.

Tom picks up the conversation as he gets off the bike he's been riding. "We do a lot of forecasting," he says. He describes how his company forecasts long-term demand in order to know how many planes to operate and used this information for lease and maintenance agreements. He goes on to suggest that the company forecast overall monthly demand by city in order to budget payroll and cash flow, as well as to give catering and fuel suppliers an overall idea of what the airline will need in the upcoming months. "Our marketing people get with me weekly as well," he says. Because most of his flights are fixed months ahead, he needs to look at short-term forecasts in order to make adjustments to the schedule, offer last-minute discounts for cities that haven't sold well, order fuel and food, and assign personnel. "All kinds of business decisions are forward looking," he summarizes, "and based upon demand forecasts."

"Our marketing and operations people spend a lot of time working from demand forecasts, too," Luis says.

"True, you do," Cheryl says, smiling as she cuts him short, "but . . . !" She explains how in comparison, Luis and Fred have it easier than the other two because they can use inventory and backorders to buffer themselves when their forecasts were off. "You can't do that in a hospital or with an airline," she laughs. She suggests that Luis has it easier because his business was mostly "make to order," so that he can wait till the order is placed to start most jobs.

Luis steps over to start taking the weight off the bar. He acknowledges her point. "You're right, but we still need to look at projections out over the coming months to keep our head count on target," he says. "On top of that, we have to forecast overall demand levels for each line on a weekly basis so we can order materials. We do a lot of forecasting," he adds. "But I'll admit it is easier for use because we simply keep inventory and use it later if the forecasts were off. I guess that would be hard to do in a service situation."

Luis reminds Tom that he'd forecasted a big holiday travel day. "Big, yeah, just not in the way we expected it to be big!" Tom laughs. He describes how past experience, recent demand data, and seasonal patterns had all been taken into account to forecast peak demand for the holiday weekend. While the weather doesn't normally have that large an impact on their demand, this storm wasn't expected, and its surprise appearance had a huge impact on their operations and their ability to meet the demands of a big weekend.

"We can't sell yesterday's capacity!" laughs Tom. "We're always looking back over our past numbers trying to anticipate trends, patterns, cycles, whatever we can see. There's still random variation to deal with. You do the best you can to understand your demand, and then deal with the random variations."

Introduction

Forecasting is important to business decisions in virtually every business area. Operations managers depend primarily on demand forecast. It is important for them to have an estimate of future demand in the short term, intermediate range, and long term. Short-term forecasts are used to make detailed resource scheduling decisions. Intermediate-range forecasts help determine what demand will be satisfied over that time frame and are a critical element of production planning. Long-range forecasts are used for capacity planning and other structural decisions.

This chapter covers the basics of time-series forecasting methods, which estimate a future value of a variable on the basis of past patterns in the value of that variable. Time-series techniques are relatively easy to understand, and they illustrate well the factors in forecasting demand that have a major impact on operational planning. Any forecast can be "wrong," however. In fact, it is unusual for any forecast to exactly match the actual value it predicts. It is important to measure, understand, and plan for forecast error, because, by studying forecast error, managers can improve their forecasts and make better decisions.

REC CENTER DILEMMA

Luis may want to pay more attention to forecasts

Luis took note of Cheryl's comment. His company does make most of its product to order, and it seems as if they still have a lot of raw material and component-part inventory around. He thinks that having raw material in inventory when someone places an order allows them to quote a shorter delivery time. But that assumes he has some capacity available to do the work. Without time on the machine or the people, inventory or not, it still takes a long time. How would better forecasts improve this? Can you help him think through the relationship between forecast accuracy and inventory, capacity, and delivery lead time? What if he forecasts demand for aggregated product families rather than individual products?

Integrating Operations Management Across the Functions

Forecasts affect every business function within an organization, as illustrated in Table 11.1. All business decisions tend to be forward looking; therefore, managers who understand forecasts, forecasting methodologies, and forecast errors are well suited to succeed within their functional areas. In a broader sense, every functional area within a business must actively participate in the forecasting process for a firm to operate effectively. Figure 11.1 suggests the cross-functional aspect of the demand forecasting process must also integrate with the supply chain.

Forecasts are at the heart of financial planning and investment decisions. While this chapter focuses primarily on demand forecasting for intermediate- and short-term operational planning, these forecast techniques correlate directly to financial performance forecasts over the same time frame.

Accountants regularly create "pro forma" (i.e., forward-looking) statements and are generally responsible for establishing budgets. For public corporations, required financial reporting often includes forward-looking expectations and the risks associated with these expectations.

Human resources professionals, responsible for establishing plans for staffing and skill development, must either forecast staffing and training needs themselves or be familiar with forecasting techniques so that they can interpret and use the forecasts created by others.

Product development plans, sales targets, promotion planning, distribution planning, pricing, and many other marketing decisions are based on forecasts. Indeed, the ability to anticipate trends and changes in customer preference from demographic data

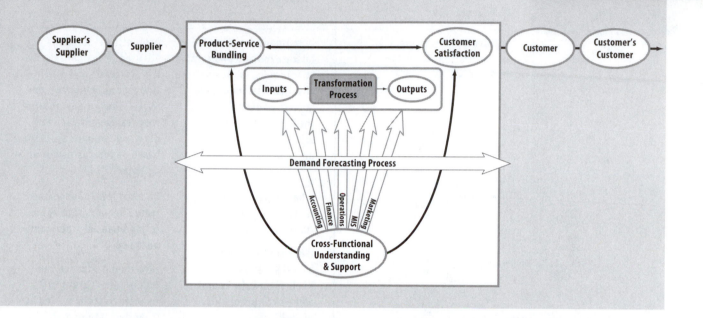

Figure 11.1

Transformation process design processes

and from market intelligence is one of the key ways that the marketing function helps an organization to satisfy (or even delight) customers and gain competitive advantage. Because the systems and technologies used by companies can change rapidly, and superior systems are always under development, engineers and MIS professionals base many of their decisions on long-term technology forecasts. Once companies decide to implement new technology or systems, engineers and MIS professionals plan the deployment and utilization of new technologies and systems using intermediate and short-term forecasts.

In sum, businesses must plan for the future to operate effectively within their supply chain and every function must be involved in such planning. As a result, familiarity with forecasting techniques is important in all functional areas of business.

Using Forecasts for Planning and Control

It has been said, "Nothing happens until a sale is made." While this statement points out the vital importance of sales and marketing to any organization, imagine how a business would have to operate if that were the whole truth. The wait for items of necessity would be horrendous. It would be impossible to fully satisfy customer expectations. And every function in the company would anxiously wait to respond to demand, not knowing whether they had enough capacity, materials, workers, and other resources to meet the demand. Planning has to start before the phone rings or a sale is made. In fact, operational planning must be an ongoing activity, and a great deal has to happen in order for marketing to be in a position to make a sale.

Table 11.1

Integrating Operations
Management across the
Functions

Integration Perspective \ Functional Area	Finance	Accounting
Why Cross-Functional Integration Matters to Forecasting	Investment decisions are forward looking and rely on forecasts. Additionally, financial managers need to understand the business risk that arises from forecasts' uncertainty.	Accounting statements are used to compare results with forecasts and may include forward looking comments. Thus, risk associated with forecasts must be understood. Budgets are also based on forecast levels of activity.
Key Issues	What degree of uncertainty (i.e., risk) is associated with the forecast? What are the worst case, best case, and most likely future states and what is the probability of each? On the basis of the stated forecast risk and outcome probabilities, what discount rates should be applied to forecast earnings when making investment decisions?	On what level of expected future demand should pro forma financial statements be based? How should advance bookings or other future business contracts be valued in financial statements? How will operational resources be allocated during the budgeting process?

Operational plans regarding the future are made on the basis of information. The greater the degree of certainty about this information, the more reliable the plans are likely to be. Some information may provide a great deal of certainty regarding future demand, such as a delivery contract. In contrast, an estimate of demand for a new product with no sales history, no competing or substitute products, and no delivery contracts would be associated with a great deal of uncertainty. Business planners, like everyone else, prefer to have less uncertainty in their estimates regarding future demand. Greater uncertainty requires greater flexibility of plans, which consequently drives up the cost of doing business.

Companies have tried a number of alternatives to reduce the uncertainty they face with regard to future demand. One of the recent initiatives has been collaborative planning, forecasting, and replenishment (CPFR). An example of this technique is

Human Resources	Marketing	Engineering	Management Information Systems
Staffing and human resource development plans are forward looking and rely on demand forecasts.	Marketing plans, product development decisions, and even pricing strategies are all forward looking and rely on forecasts.	Engineering decisions rely on the forecasted direction of technology. Engineers also must rely on forecasts demand as well as those of equipment effectiveness and efficiency to justify process change investments.	MIS professionals rely on forecasts of industry and hardware trends in system development. System and hardware justification and support plans are based on usage forecasts.
What is the appropriate level of staffing in each area of the organization? (From which will follow hiring and layoff policies.)

What training and development activity needs must be accommodated?

What budget requests are justified in the human resources functional area? | What sales targets should be set?

What promotions will be required in order to achieve sales objectives?

How will prices be set?

What characteristics are critical to new or updated product-service bundles?

What budget requests are justified in the marketing functional area? | What technology should be selected when making process and product design decisions?

How long will equipment last?

When should maintenance be scheduled?

What output rate can be expected from a given process?

What budget requests are justified in the engineering functional area? | What functionality will users require and what software and hardware should be selected?

When should software and hardware be upgraded?

What training and support will users require?

What budget requests are justified in the IS area? |

described in the boxed example on TrueValue, the hardware store cooperative. Under CPFR, customers and their suppliers plan and forecast together so that the operational plans of each can be based on better information with less uncertainty. Effective forecasting is important to every business and plays a major role in reducing uncertainty about future demand.

Forecasts are used to support every form of operational planning at every level of an organization. Forecasts may apply to the business as a whole, product groups, or individual items. And forecasts support long-term, intermediate range, and short-term operational decisions. Figure 11.2 provides an overview of the planning and control activities covered in this section of the book. The center column describes the forecasting activities that support materials planning and capacity planning decisions.

True Value Hardware Improves Forecasting with CPFR

True Value, the hardware store cooperative owned by Tru-Serve, based many of its logistical decisions for its 7,600 independently owned retail units, 1,700 stocking vendors, and 14 distribution centers on short-term demand forecasts. This approach resulted in cash flow pressures, dissatisfied customers and franchise owners, and millions of dollars in excess inventory, and the cooperative believed that these all that stemmed from forecasting and logistical problems. As a first step in addressing these issues, the $2.2 billion hardware retailer initiated the development of a collaborative forecasting program with Delta Faucet, a key supplier in their supply chain.

To address these problems, TrueValue established a new collaborative planning, forecasting, and replenishment (CPFR) system. This system has enabled TrueValue to collaborate with suppliers like as Delta Faucet to establish a single, shared demand forecast. By electronically sharing demand information with suppliers such as Delta Faucet, the suppliers can better anticipate demand and support a higher level of customer service with less inventory. The retailer and its partners have been working together to develop a single source of promotional and inventory information. The resulting forecasts and subsequent logistical decisions are improving inventory availability and optimizing replenishment timing with some joint inventory ownership.

Starting in late 1998, the collaborative forecasting relationship was initiated having recognized the need to streamline supply chain processes. TrueValue completed an internal audit of existing systems and determined that a collaborative approach was a win-win situation. The company submitted RFPs to various software vendors. By the middle of 1999, after reviewing several presentations, TrueValue selected E3's E3TRIM software suite. TrueValue and E3 conducted meetings to define the goals of the partnership on a step-by-step basis, as well as the proper implementation methodology necessary to satisfy the demands of all involved partners. Then, the company established connectivity to its resident E3 system via the Internet, allowing TrueValue and its suppliers (such as adhesive manufacturer Manco, Black and Decker, L.R. Nelson, and HyKo Products) access to the same supply chain data in real-time.

In early 2001 TrueValue approached Delta Faucet concerning participation in the CPFR initiative. Following discussions, the two companies met with E3 and established a front-end agreement. With measures, goals, and procedures established and agreed upon, Delta staff training began. This included defining best practices, functional training, certification, and a review of TrueValue policies. Live execution of the system followed. Following live execution, a series of scorecard reviews and additional category planning integration occurred.

During this initial implementation of CPFR with Delta, TrueValue learned that to effectively alter established supply chain processes, changes in behaviors and attitudes were needed. Issues of trust, cooperation, sharing and security need to be looked at under a new paradigm. This required support of management and a new project leader. The hardware cooperative also learned that technology can only function as a facilitator for this changing paradigm of how supply chains interact, specifically in this case with respect to demand forecasts. Technology alone should not be used as the sole basis to make strategic implementation decisions.

CPFR has enabled TrueValue to improve inventory service levels—meaning it experiences fewer stockouts. The cooperative is better able to understand the market impact of its sales promotions; its forecasts are more accurate; and it has reduced inventory across the distribution network. As a result, gross sales have increased by 10 to 20% above previous levels for vendors that are participating in the program. As a consequence, TrueValue will continue to increase its CPFR partners and expand the capabilities of its CPFR system.

Recognizing the need to organize a supply chain that included numerous independently owned retail units and multiple suppliers, TrueValue invested in time and resources to embrace CPFR in a scalable (or expandable) fashion. The retailer can now quickly and easily add trading partners to the CPFR process, thus further increasing the value of its investment.

Source: Adapted from http://logistics.about.com/library/weekly/uc021802.htm, "TrueValue Initiates CPFR with Delta Faucet," reporter Gregory Belkin; and "Surviving a Sticky Situation," *Supply Chain Technology News*, reporter Daniel Jacobs, June 2003

Figure 11.2

Forecasts and planning decisions

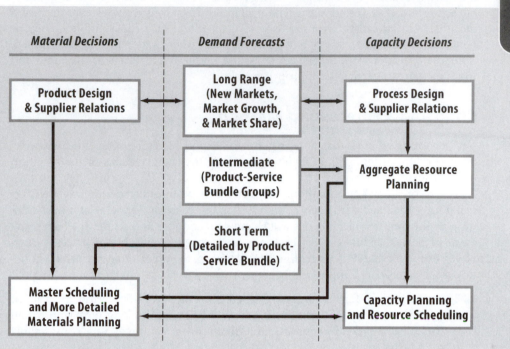

Three types of forecasting activity are listed:

1. Long range

2. Intermediate

3. Short term

Long-range forecasts are prepared and updated, perhaps on an annual basis, by a corporate staff or committee. These forecasts are used by senior decision makers to make strategic planning decisions about product designs, process design, facility location, facility capacity, and other factors as described in the "Effective Alignment of Operational Decisions" section of Chapter 2, beginning on page 44. Often, these forecasts analyze the business as a whole, rather than analyzing only the creation of products. The decisions made by senior management on the basis of long-range forecasts not only have a long-term impact on a firm's operating structure and competitiveness but they also establish constraints for the ongoing operations of the firm.

Intermediate-range forecasts, which might be prepared on a monthly basis, are often used by middle managers to make decisions about staffing, build-ups of inventory, and budgets. These forecasts can help suppliers determine the general level of expected business in general product categories, and they can help customers recognize potential supply constraints. The decisions made based on intermediate-range forecasts provide the resources that allow a firm to operate at a given level. Just as intermediate-range forecasts are constrained by long-term capacity decisions, they, in turn, constrain short-term decisions.

Short-term forecasts, perhaps prepared on a weekly basis, are used at the lower levels of the corporate hierarchy to make the detailed materials management and capacity allocation (i.e., resource scheduling) decisions that are required to generate the master schedule. For example, these forecasts are used to determine what quantity of each product-service bundle will be available during any given week over the next 6 months. This information can be used to determine which subassemblies, components, and other supplies to buy or make, and when. Once that is determined, purchase orders or work orders can be issued, and resources (such as machines and workers) can be assigned the appropriate tasks.

Choosing a Forecasting Method

No forecasting system is best, or even good, for all possible situations. Choosing an appropriate forecasting method involves matching the characteristics of the situation with those of the method.

When considering the situational characteristics, we must first ask ourselves what is being forecasted and why. Are we interested in the value of a variable at a particular time; in the time at which a series will change direction; or in the time at which some event of particular interest (for example, the next generation of some technology) might occur? Besides this overriding consideration, the other situational characteristics usually considered important include:

1. The time horizon for the forecast, divided generally into short-term (up to about 3 months), intermediate-term (from 3 months to 2 years), or long-term (more than 2 years). These time divisions are somewhat arbitrary and may vary considerably from industry to industry.

2. The level of detail, or how much aggregation there will be. For example, are we talking about a product, a product line, a company's division, or the entire company?

3. The number of items. If we are developing forecasts for thousands of items on a monthly basis, we probably want to use a simpler technique than if we are forecasting the demand for only one or two items once or twice a year.

4. The stability of the situation. If we can assume basic patterns that held in the past will continue to hold in the future, we can use a different approach than if we are attempting to deal with a great deal of change.

Forecasting Model Types

Quantitative forecasting

A method of using one or more equations to turn a set of numerical or categorical inputs into a forecast of a value or set of values for one or more variables.

Qualitative forecasting

A planning method based on the subjective assessments of individuals, working separately or in groups, rather than on formal equations.

We can categorize forecasting models in two general ways:

▶ Quantitative versus qualitative

▶ Time series versus causal

Quantitative forecasting models use one or more equations to turn a set of numerical or categorical inputs into a forecast of a value or set of values for one or more variables.

Qualitative forecasting models are subjective. They are based on the subjective assessments of individuals, working separately or in groups, rather than on formal equations. Probably the best-known of the qualitative methods is the Delphi method, which is discussed in Chapter 8 on page 351. Given the amount of time and the cost required to use the Delphi method, it is most often used for long-range decisions with significant implications for capital expenditures or the organization's future direction. At the other extreme, a qualitative method sometimes used for annual demand forecasting is the grass-roots method, in which individual salespeople estimate next year's sales for their territories and the results are added up (with or without adjustment for perceived bias) to get sales for the district, the region, and the company.

Time-series models are based on extrapolating the historical pattern for the variable of interest and projecting it into the future. The model's inputs may include all or selected past values of the variable and, possibly, the forecast errors for all or selected past periods. As time-series models are most often used for short time frames, they will be our primary focus.

Causal models estimate the value of the variable of interest, called the dependent variable, on the basis of a second set of variables, called the independent variables, which are believed to determine the value of the dependent variable. For example, a school system can do a very good (but not perfect) job of forecasting its kindergarten enrollment by looking at the number of births 5 years earlier. Two popular techniques for building causal models are regression analysis and simulation.

Time-Series Components

A time series is simply a time-ordered set of the values of a specific variable. Examples include the monthly, quarterly, or yearly sales of a product or the daily number of passengers for an airline or daily number of cases seen at a hospital emergency room. The variable's value in any specific time period is a function of four factors:

1. Trend
2. Cyclic effects
3. Seasonality
4. Randomness

TREND

Trend refers to a general pattern of change over time, and some of the many possible basic trend patterns are shown in Figure 11.3. The most basic pattern is level or horizontal, Figure 11.3a, which pattern implies that there is no basic change expected over time. Figures 11.3b and 11.3c show increasing and decreasing linear trends. A linear trend implies a constant *amount* of change from one period to the next. Figures 11.3d and 11.3e depict exponential growth and decay patterns, which imply a constant *percentage* change from one period to the next. Figure 11.3f is an S-shaped growth curve, which is typical of the cumulative demand for a product over its lifetime. S-shaped growth curves show a pattern of slow growth, followed by a period of rapid growth, and, finally, slow growth again as the product nears the end of its life cycle.

CYCLIC EFFECTS

Cyclic effects arise from changes in the economy as it moves through the phases of growth and decline in the business cycle, a process that generally takes several years. For any particular item, cyclic effects may be very important or not important at all, depending on whether the item is or is not influenced by the phases of the business cycle. Figure 11.4 shows a wave-like cyclic effect superimposed on an increasing linear trend.

Incorporating cyclic effects into a forecasting model is extremely difficult because it requires the ability to forecast the timing of the turns in the business cycle and the rates of growth and decline between those turns. Experience has shown that doing so is

Time series

Models based on extrapolating the historical pattern for the variable of interest into the future.

Causal models

Causal Models that estimate the value of the dependent variable on the basis of the independent variables.

Trends

Refers to a general pattern of change over time.

Cyclic effects

Changes in the economy as it moves through the phases of growth and decline in the business cycle, a process that takes several years.

Figure 11.3
Examples of trend patterns

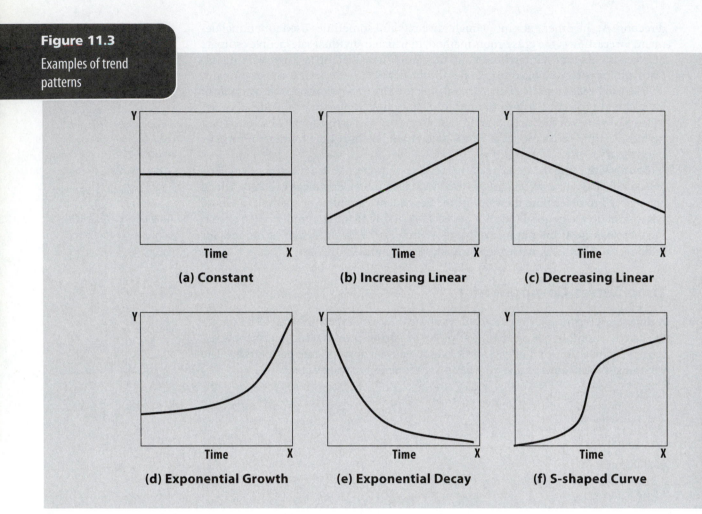

(a) Constant   (b) Increasing Linear   (c) Decreasing Linear

(d) Exponential Growth   (e) Exponential Decay   (f) S-shaped Curve

Figure 11.4
Linear trend and cyclical effects

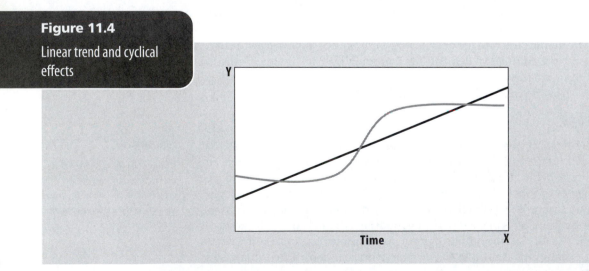

Stephen Chernin/Getty Images Inc.

The demand for many products will follow a very strong and well defined seasonal pattern. Hallmark and other greeting card companies build this into their planning. Chances are that, in a couple weeks, this card rack will be full of St. Patrick's day and Easter greeting cards.

extremely difficult, if not impossible, in spite of the enormous amounts of money that have been spent on the development of macroeconomic forecasting models. For this reason, cyclic effects are often ignored, at least in those models that forecast only a few months or quarters ahead.

SEASONALITY

Seasonality refers to any regular pattern recurring within a time period of no more than 1 year, and seasonality effects are often related to the seasons of the year (hence the name). Increased demand for snow tires in the winter, for air conditioners in the summer, and air travel around major holidays are examples of seasonality. However, such effects may occur in a time frame of less than a year and may be based on causes that have nothing to do with the yearly seasons or holidays. For example, banks experience regularly recurring patterns in the level of deposits, based on the monthly, semimonthly, biweekly, and weekly pay schedules of their corporate customers. Hospital emergency rooms and police departments experience weekly demand patterns based on the typically increased level of accidents on weekend nights. And 911 operators experience a fluctuating pattern of calls over the course of a day.

Regardless of the nature or cause of the pattern, its recognition can make a forecasting model considerably more accurate. In Figure 11.5, an annual seasonal pattern has been added to the trend and cyclic effects of Figure 11.4.

RANDOMNESS

Randomness refers to all other factors that cause the actual observed value of a variable to differ from that predicted by the trend, cyclic, and seasonal effects. Randomness essentially refers to the many—real, yet unpredictable—causes of variation. It is the portion of a variable's behavior that cannot be systematically explained.

Seasonality

Any regular pattern recurring within a time period no more than a year.

Randomness

A situation where all other factors that cause the actual observed value of a variable differ from that predicted by the trend, cyclic, and seasonal effects.

Demand for the amusement park and food stands in this photo may have looked much different on a sunny day. Random demand fluctuations can be tied to the weather in a variety of situations.

Dennis MacDonald/PhotoEdit

Simple moving average (SMA)

Forecasts the value for the next period simply by estimating the height or level of the horizontal line around which the actual values are randomly scattered.

Simple exponential smoothing (SES)

A popular item series model for averaging when there is no seasonality by forecasting the value for next period simply by estimating the height of the horizontal line around which the actual values are randomly scattered.

Short-Term Forecasting

When there is no trend in a time series, a naive (but sometimes useful) short-term forecasting approach is to assume that the value of the variable will be the same next period as it is this period. Of course, this approach ignores the effect of seasonality, if it is relevant, but it also causes the forecasts to jump around from period to period in response to the randomness.

One way to compensate for this jumpiness in the forecasts is to use averaging. Two popular time series models for averaging when there is no seasonality[1] are the **simple moving average (SMA)** and **simple exponential smoothing (SES)**. Both forecast the value for next period simply by estimating the height or level of the horizontal line (see Figure 11.3a on page 496) around which the actual values are randomly scattered.

Figure 11.5

Linear trend, cyclical effects, and seasonality

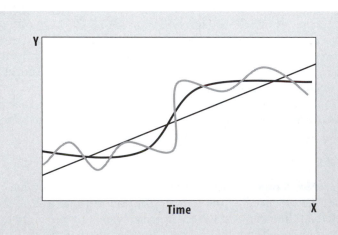

---

[1] As we shall see later, both methods can be adapted to work with seasonal data.

Example 11.1

The demand for a particular type of chairs at Luis's furniture company has been fairly stable. The actual numbers of chairs ordered for the past 18 months are given in Table 11.2 and graphed in Exhibit 11.1

Table 11.2

Monthly Demand for Chairs

Month	Demand	Month	Demand	Month	Demand
1	122	7	105	13	99
2	90	8	105	14	107
3	131	9	118	15	114
4	87	10	135	16	139
5	123	11	108	17	80
6	127	12	91	18	119

Exhibit 11.1

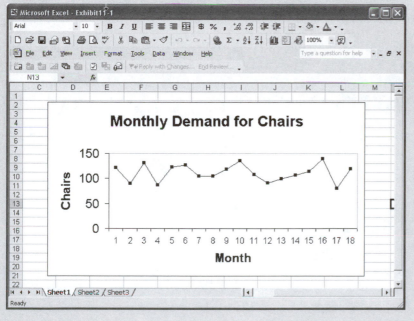

Find the 6-month simple moving average forecasts for months 7 and 8.

Solution:

The 6-month SMA forecast for month 7 is:

$$F_7 = \frac{Y_6 + Y_5 + Y_4 + Y_3 + Y_2 + Y_1}{6}$$

$$= \frac{127 + 123 + 87 + 131 + 90 + 122}{6}$$

$$= \frac{680}{6} = 113.333$$

The 6-month SMA forecast for month 8 is:

$$F_8 = \frac{Y_7 + Y_6 + Y_5 + Y_4 + Y_3 + Y_2}{6}$$

(continued)

Example 11.1

(continued)

$$= \frac{105 + 127 + 123 + 87 + 131 + 90}{6}$$

$$= \frac{663}{6} = 110.5$$

A comparison of the two equations in this example shows why this model is called a simple *moving* average. As the period to be forecasted moves up by one, the periods for which the actual values are averaged also move up by one; the oldest data value is dropped and replaced by the new one.

This simple model is easy to automate with a spreadsheet, either by building the equation into the sheet directly or by using the spreadsheet's built-in procedure. Exhibit 11.2 shows the results of applying the moving average procedure from data analysis in Excel to the data in Table 11.2. Notice that there are no forecasts for the first 6 months, because we cannot get an average until we have 6 months of data. Also notice that, because of the averaging, the line for the forecast does not bounce around as much as the line for the actual data. If we used more periods in the average, the forecast line would fluctuate even less.

Exhibit 11.2

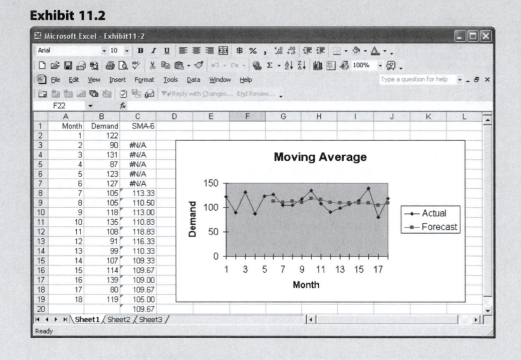

SIMPLE MOVING AVERAGE

If we could assume that the height of the line around which the actual values are randomly scattered has always been the same, then the simplest way to estimate it and forecast the value for the next period would be to average all past values of the variable. Because we cannot always make this assumption, a reasonable compromise is to use the average of the last few periods. This approach is called the simple moving average model. Letting F_t be the forecast for period t and Y_t be the actual value, the n-period

SMA forecast for period t+1 is:

$$F_{t+1} = \frac{Y_t + Y_{t-1} + \cdots Y_{t-n+1}}{n}$$

SIMPLE EXPONENTIAL SMOOTHING

While the simple moving average forecast is easy to compute and the concept is easy to understand, it has two possible drawbacks: (1) it treats all values used equally, regardless of their age, and (2) it requires a fair amount of storage (although this drawback has become less of a problem as computer storage became cheaper). An alternative to the SMA model is simple exponential smoothing (SES), which differs from SMA in three important respects:

1. The model implicitly uses the entire past history of the time series, not just the most recent periods.

2. The weights assigned to the values decrease[2] with the age of the data, rather than being 1/n for each.

3. Less storage is required: Only the value of the smoothing constant (α in the equations to follow) and the most recent forecast are needed.

There are two alternative, but equivalent, forms of the SES model. The first,

$$F_{t+1} = \alpha Y_t + (1-\alpha)F_t$$

states that the new forecast is simply a weighted average of the most recent actual value, Y_t, and the old forecast, F_t. The **smoothing constant**, α, is a number between 0 and 1. A value close to 0 produces a lot of smoothing (similar to a large value for n in an SMA model), while a value close to 1 yields a forecast that responds quickly to changes in the data pattern.

By doing a little algebra on the equation above, we get the second form of the equation:

$$F_{t+1} = F_t + \alpha(Y_t - F_t).$$

This equation shows that the new forecast is simply the old forecast corrected by a percentage of the amount by which that forecast was in error ($Y_t - F_t$).

Just as the n-period SMA model could not produce a forecast before period n+1, so the SES model cannot give a forecast for period 1 unless, for some reason, there are values for F_0 and Y_0. Common practice, then, is to let $F_1 = Y_1$ and start the forecasts with t = 2.

FORECASTING MORE THAN ONE PERIOD AHEAD

Because the basic data pattern assumed for the SMA and SES models is random scatter around a horizontal line, the forecast is simply the estimated height of that line. Although the equations given above for these models assume that we are forecasting only one period ahead (F_{t+1}), we can just as easily use them to forecast two, three, or as many periods ahead as desired by using the same value. Of course, as with any model, the further into the future we attempt to forecast, the larger our forecast error is likely to be.

Smoothing constant

A number between 0 and 1.

---

[2] While we will not go through a derivation, the reason this model is called simple exponential smoothing is that each period's weight is a constant percentage of the weight for the next (later) period's weight. That is, the weights decline exponentially with the age of the data values.

Example 11.2

Refer to Example 11.1. Find the SES forecasts for months 2 and 3. Use $\alpha = 0.3$.

Solution:

Letting $F_1 = Y_1 = 122$ (from Table 11.2), the SES forecast for chairs in period 2 with $\alpha = .3$ is:

$$F_2 = \alpha Y_1 + (1-\alpha)F_1 = (.3)(122) + (.7)(122) = 122$$

The forecast for period 3 is:

$$F_3 = \alpha Y_2 + (1-\alpha)F_2 = (.3)(90) + (.7)(122) = 112.4$$

As with the SMA model, the simple form of the SES model is easy to automate with a spreadsheet, either by building the equation into the sheet directly or by using the spreadsheet's built-in procedure. Exhibit 11.3 shows the results of applying the exponential smoothing procedure from data analysis in Excel to the data in Table 11.2.[3] As with the graph for the SMA model, note that the SES forecasts are much less variable than the actual data. With a smaller value for α, there would be even less variability.

Exhibit 11.3

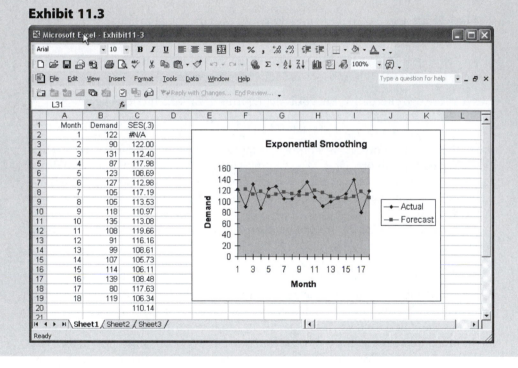

OTHER SHORT-TERM FORECASTING MODELS

The two short-term forecasting models discussed are both designed for situations where the basic data pattern is random scatter around a horizontal line. Of course, in many cases we will have either trend or seasonality (or both). How to incorporate seasonality into these models will be discussed later, after we have shown how seasonal factors can be estimated. There are also moving average and exponential smoothing models that build the estimation and use of trend effects directly into short-term forecasts. These models are beyond the scope of this book, but the models are available in many software packages.

---

[3] Excel's Exponential Smoothing dialog box asks for the value of the damping factor, which is 1-α, rather than the smoothing constant, α.

Measuring Forecast Accuracy

An important consideration in the selection and use of a forecasting model is how well it will perform, i.e., how close the forecasts come to the actual values of the variable of interest. Four popular measures of **forecast accuracy** are the **mean forecast error (MFE)**; the **mean squared error (MSE)**, which is analogous to a sample variance in basic statistics; the **mean absolute deviation (MAD)**; and the **mean absolute percentage error (MAPE)**. All four start with the same basic forecasting error measurement:

$$e_t = Y_t - F_t$$

The MSE, MAPE, and MAD actually tell us about the average magnitude of error terms. Any of these three accuracy measures can be used as the basis for comparing forecasting models or as the basis for selecting parameter values for a given model type. Either the MSE or MAD, with appropriate adjustments, can be used for finding forecast intervals (similar to confidence intervals in basic statistics).

The average error term, that is the mean forecast error (MFE), does not tell us how accurate our forecast is. The MFE can, however, tell us whether our forecast consistently over- or underestimates demand. For this reason the MFE is also called the forecast **bias**. Forecast bias is considered large when its magnitude is a significant percentage of the MAD. Large negative values for the MFE indicate that our forecasts are consistently higher than demand, while large positive values suggest that our forecasts are consistently low.

The presence of bias is an indicator of at least three possibilities. First, a large bias indicates that the forecasting technique can be improved; any consistent pattern in the forecast error terms can be analyzed and exploited to improve the forecast. Second, if a forecasting technique becomes biased over time but was not biased to start with, the underlying demand pattern must have changed. (For example, there could have been a turning point in a product life cycle, or a new seasonal effect could have developed, etc.) Third, bias may result from deliberate attempts to manipulate forecasts. For example, marketing personnel or valued customers might attempt to inflate demand forecasts to guarantee the availability of supply. In reality, such attempts are counterproductive because they foster uncertainty, undermine trust, and hinder integrated cross-functional decision making. Decision makers in all functions rely on forecasts to make their decisions. They should all be using the best information available. Rather than manipulating forecasts to influence decisions, managers should get the best forecast possible, then consider their range of options to make the most effective decision. There is ample opportunity for cross-functional influence on decisions once an unbiased forecast has been developed.

MEAN SQUARED ERROR (MSE)

Similar to the procedure for measuring variation in a sample in basic statistics, the mean squared error compensates for the problem of positive/negative error cancellation by squaring the forecast errors, summing them, and then taking their average.

$$MSE = \frac{\sum_{t=1}^{n} e_t^2}{n} = \frac{\sum_{t=1}^{n} (Y_t - F_t)^2}{n}$$

Just as we take the square root of a sample variance to get the standard deviation, which is used in finding a confidence interval in statistics, we can take the square root

---

Forecast accuracy

A measurement of the selection and use of a forecast model.

Mean forecast error (MFE)

A measure of forecast accuracy that gives the average error term.

Mean squared error (MSE)

A measure of forecast accuracy which is analogous to a sample variance in basic statistics.

Mean absolute deviation (MAD)

A measure of forecast accuracy that tells about the average magnitude of error terms.

Mean absolute percentage error (MAPE)

A measure of forecast accuracy.

Example 11.3

Use Excel to compute the mean squared error and root mean squared error for the simple exponential smoothing forecasts with $\alpha = .3$ for the chair demand data found in Example 11.2. Use the results to find an approximate 95% forecast interval for chair demand in month 19.

Solution:

The Excel spreadsheet in Exhibit 11.4 shows the computed MSE and RMSE for the chair demand data in Table 11.2. (The forecast values from using SES with $\alpha = .3$ come from Exhibit 11.3). We see that the MSE is

$6915.58/17 = 406.80$ and the RMSE is 20.17. Using this value for the RMSE and, from the spreadsheet, the forecast value of 110.1 for $t = 19$, we can get an approximate 95% forecast interval of:

$$F_{19} \pm 2(\text{RMSE}) = 110.1 \pm 2(20.17)$$

$$= 110.1 \pm 40.34$$

$$= (69.76, 150.44)$$

We could say that we are roughly 95% sure that the demand for chairs in month 19 will be between 70 and 150.

Exhibit 11.4

	A	B	C	D	E	F	G
1	Month	Demand	SES(.3)	error	error^2	|error|	|error/Demand|
2	1	122	#N/A				
3	2	90	122.00	-32.00	1024.00	32.00	35.56
4	3	131	112.40	18.60	345.96	18.60	14.20
5	4	87	117.98	-30.98	959.76	30.98	35.61
6	5	123	108.69	14.31	204.89	14.31	11.64
7	6	127	112.98	14.02	196.55	14.02	11.04
8	7	105	117.19	-12.19	148.50	12.19	11.61
9	8	105	113.53	-8.53	72.77	8.53	8.12
10	9	118	110.97	7.03	49.40	7.03	5.96
11	10	135	113.08	21.92	480.49	21.92	16.24
12	11	108	119.66	-11.66	135.86	11.66	10.79
13	12	91	116.16	-25.16	632.98	25.16	27.65
14	13	99	108.61	-9.61	92.38	9.61	9.71
15	14	107	105.73	1.27	1.62	1.27	1.19
16	15	114	106.11	7.89	62.26	7.89	6.92
17	16	139	108.48	30.52	931.67	30.52	21.96
18	17	80	117.63	-37.63	1416.29	37.63	47.04
19	18	119	106.34	12.66	160.18	12.66	10.64
20	19		110.14				
21							
22			Sum =	-39.53	6915.58	295.98	285.86
23			Average =	-2.33	406.80	17.41	16.82
24			RMSE =	20.17			

Root mean squared error (RMSE)

A basis for a forecast interval.

of the MSE, called the **root mean squared error (RMSE)**, and use it as the basis for a forecast interval:

$$\text{RMSE} = \sqrt{\text{MSE}}$$

Following the basic approach for finding a confidence interval in statistics, a forecast interval for any particular level of confidence can be found as:

$$\text{Forecast} \pm Z \text{ (standard error of forecast)}$$

MEAN ABSOLUTE DEVIATION (MAD)

An alternative approach to compensating for the positive/negative error compensation problem is to take the absolute values of the errors and average them to obtain the mean absolute deviation:

$$\text{MAD} = \frac{\sum_{t=1}^{n} |e_t|}{n} = \frac{\sum_{t=1}^{n} |Y_t - F_t|}{n}$$

As we can see by comparing the values of MAD and RMSE in Exhibit 11.4, the mean absolute deviation is generally smaller than the root mean square error. However, it has been found that, for a normal probability distribution, MAD tends to be about 80% of the standard deviation, so we can get a good estimate of the standard deviation of forecast errors by using 1.25MAD.

MEAN ABSOLUTE PERCENTAGE ERROR (MAPE)

A large forecast error is less of a problem when the value being forecasted is large than when it is small. An alternative to using the actual error is to use the relative or percentage error, which is found by dividing the error by the value being forecasted and, if desired, multiplying the ratio by 100. The absolute percentage errors can then be averaged to get the mean absolute percentage error or MAPE:

$$\text{MAPE} = \frac{\sum_{t=1}^{n} 100 \times \left|\frac{e_t}{Y_t}\right|}{n} = \frac{\sum_{t=1}^{n} 100 \times \left|\frac{Y_t - F_t}{Y_t}\right|}{n}$$

REC CENTER DILEMMA

Luis looks for a trend in his forecasts

Luis has been using a simple 4-week moving average to forecast the aggregated demand for a new family of tables his company introduced last season. The tables have not really taken off yet, and most of the demand for them is to make stock. Luis tried a new approach and generated a demand forecast for the total number of tables in all three finishes and both sizes combined. This worked well for 6 months, but the last four monthly forecasts have fallen way short of actual demand. What is Luis missing?

Example 11.4

Use Excel to compute the mean absolute deviation for simple exponential smoothing forecasts with $\alpha = .3$ for the chair demand data found in Example 11.2. Use the results to find an approximate 95% forecast interval for chair demand in month 19.

Solution:

Exhibit 11.4 also shows the computation of the value of the MAD for the chair demand data in Table 11.2, using SES with $\alpha = .3$. From the spreadsheet, we see that the sum of the absolute values of the forecast errors = 295.98 and MAD = 295.98/17 = 17.41.

Using this value for MAD and, from the spreadsheet, the forecast value of 110.1 for t = 19, we can get an approximate 95% forecast interval of:

$$F_{19} \pm 2(1.25\text{MAD}) = 110.1 \pm 2.5(17.41)$$
$$= 110.1 \pm 43.525$$
$$= (66.575, 153.625)$$

We could say that we are roughly 95% sure that the demand for chairs in month 19 will be between 67 and 154. This interval is, of course, not exactly the same as the one found above using RMSE, but that is to be expected since neither RMSE nor 1.25MAD is exactly equal to the true standard deviation of forecast errors.

Example 11.5

Use Excel to compute the mean absolute percentage error for simple exponential smoothing forecasts with $\alpha = .3$ for the chair demand data found in Example 11.2.

Solution:

Exhibit 11.4 also shows the computation of the value of the MAPE for the chair demand data in Table 11.2,

using SES with $\alpha = .3$. From the spreadsheet, we see that the sum of the absolute percentage forecast errors is 285.86 and *MAPE = 285.86/17 = 16.82*. That is, the forecast is, on average, in error by 16.82% of the demand value.

While useful as a way of comparing alternative forecasting methods or comparing different parameter values for a particular forecasting method, MAPE does not lend itself to serving as the basis for constructing forecast intervals.

MEAN FORECAST ERROR (MFE)

The mean forecast error, or *bias*, is simply the average of the error terms as indicated in the equation below.

$$MSE = \frac{\sum\limits_{t=1}^{n} e_t}{n} = \frac{\sum\limits_{t=1}^{n} (Y_t - F_t)}{n}$$

Because summing positive and negative error terms is involved in computing the MFE, the statistic cannot be used as an indicator of error magnitude. On the other hand, if the MFE is not close to zero, or very small relative to the MAD, we know that our forecasts are prone to overestimating or underestimating demand.

Estimating Trend

While some time series can be expected to stay at a relatively constant level, at least for the near future, others will show a consistent pattern of growth or decline. Many different patterns are possible. Computer programs for forecasting have built into them a variety of trend equations, including the ones in Figure 11.3.

Example 11.6

Use Excel to compute the mean forecast error for simple exponential smoothing forecasts with $\alpha = .3$ for the chair demand data found in Example 11.2.

Solution:

Exhibit 11.4 also shows the computation of the value of the MFE for the chair demand data in

Table 11.2, using SES with $\alpha = .3$. From the spreadsheet, we see that the sum of the forecast errors is -39.53 and the MFE = $-39.53/17 = -2.33$. That is, the forecast is, on average, in error by 2.33 units higher than actual demand.

Given an aging baby boomer population, the impact of those demographic trends should be considered in the demand for many products.

The simplest form of trend equation is linear, for which the data is randomly scattered around a straight line, given by the equation

$$T_t = b_0 + b_1 t.$$

In this equation, t is the period number; T_t is the forecasted value that has been adjusted for trend for period t (we will call it the "trend value" or "trend" for short); b_0 is the intercept, corresponding to the trend value in period 0; and b_1, the slope of the line, gives the change in the trend value from period to period.

Estimating and Using Seasonal Indexes

Seasonal indexes are used for two purposes:

1. To deseasonalize raw data, in order to compare values from different seasons or to use them in a basic forecasting model
2. To incorporate seasonality into a forecast made by a basic model that does not include seasonal effects

Seasonal indexes may be either "additive" or "multiplicative." When seasonality is additive, the magnitude of seasonal effects does not vary with changes in the underlying demand pattern. Thus, whether demand grows or declines, the seasonal effect remains the same. When seasonality is multiplicative, the magnitude of seasonal effects is proportional to the underlying demand. Thus, when demand grows the seasonal effect also grows, and if demand declines the seasonal effect also declines.

An **additive seasonal index** is the expected difference between the value of a time series (in the period for which the index applies) and the value, as called for by any trend and cyclic components. For example, if the additive seasonal index in a period is 0, the value of the time series in that period is expected to be exactly what the trend and cyclic components call for. If the additive seasonal index is 100, the time series value is expected to be 100 units larger than what trend and cycle call for. If the seasonal index is –50, the time series value is expected to be 50 units less than what the trend and cycle

Additive seasonal index

The expected difference between the value of a time series and the value, as called for by any trend and cyclic components.

Example 11.7

A year ago, as part of its community wellness program, Cheryl's hospital started a Saturday morning aerobics program. Since then, the average number of registrants per week has been growing steadily, as can be seen in Exhibit 11.5.

Use regression analysis from data analysis in Excel to estimate the trend equation for these data and interpret the results. Use the equation $T_t = b_0 + b_1t$ to forecast average weekly attendance for the next 6 months.

Solution:

The regression results are shown in Exhibit 11.6. From that output we see that the estimated trend equation is:

$$T_t = 20.114 + 3.069t$$

With $R^2 = .97$, the line fits the data very closely, as shown by the straight line in the graph in Exhibit 11.5. The slope coefficient is $b_1 = 3.069$, which means that, on average, the hospital can expect the average weekly number of registrants to increase by a little over three per month.

Exhibit 11.5

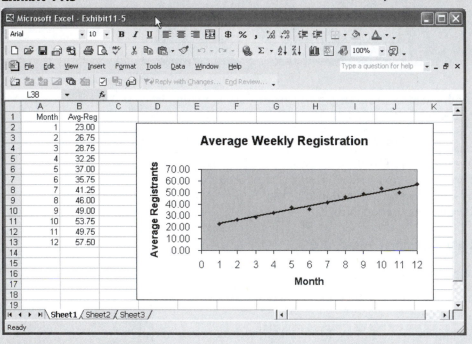

Assuming that the trend will remain the same (a big assumption), the hospital can use the same equation to forecast the average number of registrants per week for the next 6 months, as follows:

Month	Trend
13	$20.114 + 3.069(13) = 60.01$
14	$20.114 + 3.069(14) = 63.08$
15	$20.114 + 3.069(15) = 66.15$
16	$20.114 + 3.069(16) = 69.22$
17	$20.114 + 3.069(17) = 72.29$
18	$20.114 + 3.069(18) = 75.36$

Example 11.7

(continued)

Exhibit 11.6

	A	B	C	D	E	F
1	SUMMARY OUTPUT					
2						
3	*Regression Statistics*					
4	Multiple R	0.98540005				
5	R Square	0.97101325				
6	Adjusted R Square	0.96811458				
7	Standard Error	2.00521065				
8	Observations	12				
9						
10	ANOVA					
11		*df*	*SS*	*MS*	*F*	*Significance F*
12	Regression	1	1346.931927	1346.932	334.9852	5.09813E-09
13	Residual	10	40.20869755	4.02087		
14	Total	11	1387.140625			
15						
16		*Coefficients*	*Standard Error*	*t Stat*	*P-value*	
17	Intercept	20.1136364	1.234121844	16.29793	1.57E-08	
18	Month	3.06905594	0.167684139	18.3026	5.1E-09	

call for. Because additive seasonal indexes show how to adjust the values of individual periods up or down from "normal," they must average 0.0 across a full set of seasons.

A **multiplicative seasonal index** is the expected ratio of the value of a time series in the period for which the index applies to the value, as called for by any trend and cyclic components. For example, if the seasonal index in a period is 1.0, the value of the time series in that period is expected to be exactly what the trend and cyclic components call for. If the seasonal index is 1.25, the value is expected to be 25% larger than what trend and cycle call for. If the seasonal index is .90, the value is expected to be only 90% of (10% lower than) what the trend and cycle call for. Since multiplicative seasonal indexes show how to adjust the values of individual periods up or down from "normal," they must average 1.0 across a full set of seasons.

Multiplicative seasonal index

The expected ratio of the value of a time series in the period for which the index applies to the value as called for by any trend and cyclic components.

ESTIMATING MULTIPLICATIVE SEASONAL INDEXES

The basic multiplicative time series model says that the value of the variable (Y) is the product of its four component parts: trend (T), cycle (C), seasonality (S), and randomness (R). That is:

$$Y = T \times C \times S \times R$$

This leads to a four-step process for estimating multiplicative seasonal indexes:

1. Estimate the value of $T \times C$ in each period.
2. Divide the value of Y by the estimate of $T \times C$ in each period, giving an estimate of $S \times R$ for that period.
3. Average the $S \times R$ values for all periods of the same type or season to get raw seasonal indexes.
4. Average the raw seasonal indexes. If the average is not 1.0, divide the raw indexes by the actual average to get adjusted seasonal indexes.

There are a number of ways to implement this process. They differ in the way in which the $T \times C$ estimates are obtained (step 1). We will consider two approaches, one for basically horizontal data patterns and one for trend. Both approaches assume that cyclic effects are negligible and can be ignored.

HORIZONTAL DATA PATTERNS

If the basic data pattern is horizontal, its level can be estimated simply by averaging the values for all time periods (step 1 of the process described above). To make this estimate as valid as possible, the same number of each type of season should be included in the average. For quarterly indexes, the average should be based on 4, 8, 12, etc. periods. For monthly indexes, the average should be based on 12, 24, 36, etc. periods.

TREND DATA PATTERNS

If the basic data pattern exhibits a trend, the basic trend value for a period can be estimated from the appropriate trend equation (step 1 of the process described above). The seasonality ratio for each period is then found by dividing Y_t, the actual value for that period, by T_t, the trend estimate (step 2 of the process).

USING SEASONAL INDEXES

Deseasonalizing Raw Data
Since the multiplicative model incorporates the seasonal effect by multiplying by the seasonal index, seasonality is removed by the reverse process, dividing. That is, you can

Example 11.8

Exhibit 11.7 shows a department store's quarterly sales of lightweight men's pajamas over a period of 3 years. The graph shows that the basic pattern is horizontal, but with a pronounced up and down quarterly pattern.

Use Excel to estimate the quarterly multiplicative seasonal indexes.

Solution:

Exhibit 11.8 shows an Excel spreadsheet for calculating the seasonal indexes. The actual sales values in column C are divided by their average (in C15) to obtain the quarterly ratios in column D. These ratios are grouped by year in columns G–I; the quarterly averages are shown in column J. Notice that these raw indexes average 1.0 as expected for a complete set of multiplicative seasonal indices. This indicates that the seasonal effect has been effectively estimated and the indices can be used.

Example 11.8

(continued)

Exhibit 11.7

Microsoft Excel - Exhibit11-7

	A	B	C
1	Year	Quarter	Sales (Y)
2	1	1	88
3		2	129
4		3	88
5		4	72
6	2	1	105
7		2	136
8		3	116
9		4	66
10	3	1	105
11		2	108
12		3	108
13		4	68

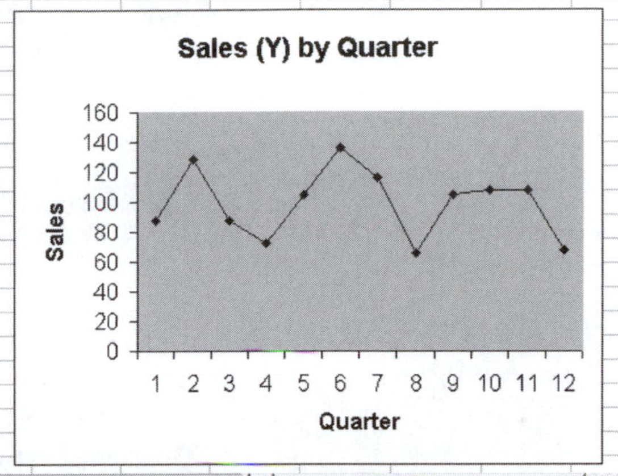

Sales (Y) by Quarter

Exhibit 11.8

Microsoft Excel - Exhibit11-8

	A	B	C	D	E	F	G	H	I	J
1	Year	Quarter	Sales (Y)	Ratio		Quarter	Ratio1	Ratio2	Ratio3	Average
2	1	1	88	0.888		1	0.888	1.060	1.060	1.003
3		2	129	1.302		2	1.302	1.373	1.090	1.255
4		3	88	0.888		3	0.888	1.171	1.090	1.050
5		4	72	0.727		4	0.727	0.666	0.686	0.693
6	2	1	105	1.060						
7		2	136	1.373					Average =	1.000
8		3	116	1.171						
9		4	66	0.666						
10	3	1	105	1.060						
11		2	108	1.090						
12		3	108	1.090						
13		4	68	0.686						
14										
15		Average =	99.08333							

Deseasonalize

The process of removing seasonality by dividing the actual value by the appropriate seasonal index.

deseasonalize a data value by dividing the actual value by the appropriate multiplicative seasonal index.

Incorporating Seasonality

To use multiplicative seasonal indexes to incorporate seasonality into a forecast made with an unseasonalized model, multiply the basic value by the appropriate multiplicative seasonal index.

Example 11.9

Exhibit 11.9 shows the quarterly demand for in-house continuing education at Fred's company over the past 2 years. The basic data pattern exhibits both upward trend and quarterly seasonality. Estimate the linear trend equation and quarterly multiplicative seasonal indexes.

Exhibit 11.9

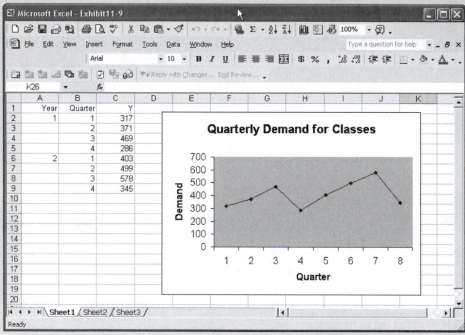

Solution:

The results from Excel's regression analysis procedure (found in the "Data Analysis" tool pack within the "Tools" menu) are shown in Exhibit 11.10, along with the computed trend values for each period (column C) and the ratios of actual to trend values (column D). The seasonal indexes are computed as follows:

Quarter	Quarterly Seasonal Index
1	$S_1 = (0.909 + 0.966)/2 = 0.938$
2	$S_2 = (1.014 + 1.149)/2 = 1.082$
3	$S_3 = (1.225 + 1.281)/2 = 1.253$
4	$S_4 = (0.715 + 0.737)/2 = 0.726$

Because these raw indexes average 1.0 (to three decimal places), we can assume that the multiplicative seasonal indices are suited to use.

(continued)

Example 11.9

(continued)

Exhibit 11.10

	A	B	C	D	E
1	Regression Model				
2		Coefficients	Standard Error	t Stat	P-value
3	Intercept	331.464	76.026	4.360	0.0048
4	t	17.119	15.055	1.137	0.2989
5					
6					
7					
8	Period (t)	Y	Trend	Ratio	
9	1	317	348.583	0.909	
10	2	371	365.702	1.014	
11	3	469	382.821	1.225	
12	4	286	399.940	0.715	
13	5	403	417.060	0.966	
14	6	499	434.179	1.149	
15	7	578	451.298	1.281	
16	8	345	468.417	0.737	

Example 11.10

Refer to Example 11.8. Suppose the sales of light-weight men's pajamas during the four quarters of the next (fourth) year are:

Quarter	Sales
1	95
2	116
3	89
4	73

Use simple exponential smoothing with $\alpha = .2$ to find the base level forecast for the first quarter of year 5. Assume the base level forecast for the first quarter of year 4 was 99.1.

Solution:

First use the seasonal indexes found in Example 11.8 to deseasonalize the raw data for year 4. Then use these deseasonalized values in an SES model with $\alpha = .2$ to obtain a base-level forecast for quarter 1 of year 5. These operations have been carried out in the spreadsheet in Exhibit 11.11, which shows that the base level forecast is 96.75 units. Note that, since the exponential smoothing procedure in Excel assumes that $F_1 = Y_1$, we had to trick it into using a different value for F_1. This was done by inserting a period 0, with $Y_0 = 99.1$, the value we want to use for F_1.

(continued)

Example 11.10

(continued)

Exhibit 11.11

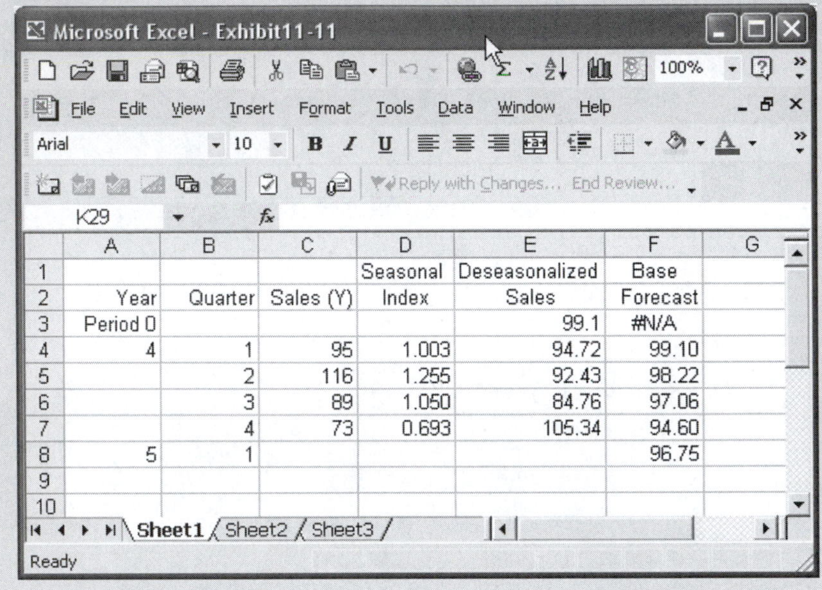

	A	B	C	D	E	F	G
1				Seasonal	Deseasonalized	Base	
2	Year	Quarter	Sales (Y)	Index	Sales	Forecast	
3	Period 0				99.1	#N/A	
4	4	1	95	1.003	94.72	99.10	
5		2	116	1.255	92.43	98.22	
6		3	89	1.050	84.76	97.06	
7		4	73	0.693	105.34	94.60	
8	5	1				96.75	
9							
10							

Example 11.11

Refer to Example 11.9. Forecast the demand for in-house continuing education classes at Fred's company for the four quarters of next year. for each of the four quarters. Then multiply the trend values by the seasonal indexes found in Example 11.9, to get the forecasts, as follows:

Solution:

Use the trend equation found in Example 11.9, $T_t = 331.464 + 17.119t$, to determine the trend value

Quarter	t	Trend	x Index =	Forecast
1	9	$331.464 + 17.119(9) = 485.535$	0.938	455.4
2	10	$331.464 + 17.119(10) = 502.654$	1.082	543.9
3	11	$331.464 + 17.119(11) = 519.773$	1.253	651.3
4	12	$331.464 + 17.119(12) = 536.892$	0.726	389.8

SUMMARY

Two basic ways of categorizing forecasting models are quantitative versus qualitative and time-series versus causal. Quantitative models use equations to estimate the value of the variable of interest, while qualitative forecasts are based on the subjective judgment of knowledgeable people. Time series models identify a pattern in the past values of the variable and project it into the future, while causal models estimate the value a variable on the basis of the values of other variables that are assumed to affect it.

The basic components of a time series are:

1. Trend, a general pattern of growth or decline

2. Cyclic effects due to the general economic cycle

3. Seasonality, a pattern that repeats itself within a time period of no more than a year

4. Randomness

Two approaches to short-term forecasting—when there is no trend or seasonality—are simple moving averages and simple exponential smoothing. A simple moving average uses the average of the last few periods' values as the forecast for the next period. In simple exponential smoothing, the forecast is updated from period to period by adding a percentage of the amount by which the last forecast was in error.

When the trend to be estimated is linear, simple linear regression is an appropriate technique to use in forecasting demand.

There are a number of ways of estimating multiplicative seasonal indexes. They are all based on averaging, for a set of comparable periods, seasonality ratios found by dividing the actual time series value by a base-level estimate determined by the trend and cyclic components of the model. Multiplicative seasonal indexes are used to incorporate seasonality into a forecast by multiplying the base value by the index, and to deseasonalize data by dividing the actual value by the index.

Four popular measures of forecast accuracy are:

▶ The mean forecast error, found by averaging the error terms for a number of periods

▶ The mean squared error, found by averaging the squared forecast errors for a number of periods

▶ The mean absolute deviation, found by averaging the absolute values of the forecast errors for a number of periods

▶ The mean absolute percentage error, found by averaging the absolute values of the forecast error divided by the actual value

A standard deviation to be used as the basis for a forecast interval can be estimated by using either the square root of the mean squared error, called the root mean squared error, or by using 1.25 times the mean absolute deviation.

KEY TERMS

Additive seasonal index, 507
Bias, 503
Causal model, 495
Cyclic effects, 495
Deseasonalize, 512
Forecast accuracy, 503
Mean absolute deviation (MAD), 503

Mean absolute percentage error (MAPE), 503
Mean forecast error (MFE), 503
Mean squared error (MSE), 503
Multiplicative seasonal index, 509
Qualitative forecasting models, 494
Quantitative forecasting models, 494
Randomness, 497

Root mean squared error (RMSE), 504
Seasonality, 497
Simple exponential smoothing (SES), 498
Simple moving average (SMA), 498
Smoothing constant, 501
Time series model, 495
Trend, 495

SOLVED PROBLEMS

1. Demand for a basic pager model produced by Fred's company has been fairly stable over the past year. Weekly demand (in hundreds) for the past 16 weeks is:

Week	Demand	Week	Demand
1	56	9	58
2	52	10	50
3	52	11	51
4	44	12	61
5	50	13	47
6	50	14	52
7	51	15	44
8	47	16	52

a) Compute 4-week and 8-week simple moving average forecasts for as many periods as possible. Compare them with respect to mean squared error, mean absolute deviation, and mean absolute percentage error.

b) Compute simple exponential smoothing forecasts for as many weeks as possible using α of .25 and .75. Compare them with respect to mean squared error, mean absolute deviation, and mean absolute percentage error.

Solution:

a) The first week for which a forecast can be developed when using a 4-week simple moving average is week 5. The 4-week SMA forecast for week 5 is:

$$F_5 = \frac{Y_4 + Y_3 + Y_2 + Y_1}{4}$$

$$= \frac{44 + 52 + 52 + 56}{4} = \frac{204}{4} = 51$$

Similarly, the first week for which a forecast can be developed when using an 8-week SMA is week 9.

The 8-week SMA forecast for week 9 is:

$$F_9 = \frac{Y_8 + Y_7 + \dots + Y_2 + Y_1}{8}$$

$$= \frac{47 + 51 + 50 + 50 + 44 + 52 + 52 + 56}{8}$$

$$= \frac{402}{8} = 50.25$$

The remaining computations for both SMA forecasts are shown in Exhibit 11.12.

Exhibit 11.12

	A	B	C	D	E	F	G	H	I	J	K	L	M
1	Week	Y	MA-4	error	error^2	|error|	|%error|	MA-8	error	error^2	|error|	|%error|	
2	1	56											
3	2	52	#N/A					#N/A					
4	3	52	#N/A					#N/A					
5	4	44	#N/A					#N/A					
6	5	50	51.00	-1.00	1.0000	1.00	2.00	#N/A					
7	6	50	49.50	0.50	0.2500	0.50	1.00	#N/A					
8	7	51	49.00	2.00	4.0000	2.00	3.92	#N/A					
9	8	47	48.75	-1.75	3.0625	1.75	3.72	#N/A					
10	9	58	49.50	8.50	72.2500	8.50	14.66	50.250	-7.750	60.0625	7.750	13.36	
11	10	50	51.50	-1.50	2.2500	1.50	3.00	50.500	0.500	0.2500	0.500	1.00	
12	11	51	51.50	-0.50	0.2500	0.50	0.98	50.250	-0.750	0.5625	0.750	1.47	
13	12	61	51.50	9.50	90.2500	9.50	15.57	50.125	-10.875	118.2656	10.875	17.83	
14	13	47	55.00	-8.00	64.0000	8.00	17.02	52.250	5.250	27.5625	5.250	11.17	
15	14	52	52.25	-0.25	0.0625	0.25	0.48	51.875	-0.125	0.0156	0.125	0.24	
16	15	44	52.75	-8.75	76.5625	8.75	19.89	52.125	8.125	66.0156	8.125	18.47	
17	16	52	51.00	1.00	1.0000	1.00	1.92	51.250	-0.750	0.5625	0.750	1.44	
18			48.75					51.875					
19													
20	Sum =				314.94	43.25	84.17			273.30	34.13	64.98	
21	Average =				26.24	3.60	7.01			34.16	4.27	8.12	
22													

From the spreadsheet we find that MSE = 26.24, MAD = 3.60, and MAPE = 7.01% for the 4-week SMA, and that MSE = 34.16, MAD = 4.27, and MAPE = 8.12% for the 8-week SMA. All three measures are lower for the 4-week SMA than for the 8-week MSA. The shorter moving average would appear to give more accurate forecasts.

b) Without having a value given for F_0, the first week for which a forecast can be developed using SES with any value for α is week 2. Following the usual practice, let $F_1 = Y_1 = 56$. Then the SMA forecasts for weeks 2 and 3 using $\alpha = .25$ are:

$$F_2 = \alpha Y_1 + (1-\alpha)F_1 = (.25)(56) + (.75)(56)$$
$$= 56.0$$

$$F_3 = \alpha Y_2 + (1-\alpha)F_2 = (.25)(52) + (.75)(56)$$
$$= 55.0$$

For $\alpha = .75$ they are:

$$F_2 = \alpha Y_1 + (1-\alpha)F_1 = (.75)(56) + (.25)(56)$$
$$= 56.0$$

$$F_3 = \alpha Y_2 + (1-\alpha)F_2 = (.75)(52) + (.25)(56)$$
$$= 53.0$$

The remaining computations for both SES forecasts are shown in Exhibit 11.13.

From the spreadsheet we find the MSE = 28.42, MAD = 4.08, and MAPE = 8.16% for the SES with $\alpha = .25$, and that MSE = 57.57, MAD = 6.64, and MAPE = 12.83% for the SES with $\alpha = .75$. With SES, the model with more smoothing ($\alpha = .25$) gave lower values for all three error measures than did the model with less smoothing.

Exhibit 11.13

Week	Y	SES(.25)	error	error^2	|error|	|%error|	SES(.75)	error	error^2	|error|	|%error|
1	56	#N/A					#N/A				
2	52	56.00	-4.00	16.0000	4.00	7.69	56.00	4.000	16.0000	4.000	7.69
3	52	55.00	-3.00	9.0000	3.00	5.77	53.00	1.000	1.0000	1.000	1.92
4	44	54.25	-10.25	105.0625	10.25	23.30	52.25	8.250	68.0625	8.250	18.75
5	50	51.69	-1.69	2.8477	1.69	3.38	46.06	-3.938	15.5039	3.938	7.88
6	50	51.27	-1.27	1.6018	1.27	2.53	49.02	-0.984	0.9690	0.984	1.97
7	51	50.95	0.05	0.0026	0.05	0.10	49.75	-1.246	1.5527	1.246	2.44
8	47	50.96	-3.96	15.6968	3.96	8.43	50.69	3.688	13.6049	3.688	7.85
9	58	49.97	8.03	64.4578	8.03	13.84	47.92	-10.078	101.5637	10.078	17.38
10	50	51.98	-1.98	3.9148	1.98	3.96	55.48	5.481	30.0362	5.481	10.96
11	51	51.48	-0.48	0.2342	0.48	0.95	51.37	0.370	0.1370	0.370	0.73
12	61	51.36	9.64	92.8727	9.64	15.80	51.09	-9.907	98.1579	9.907	16.24
13	47	53.77	-6.77	45.8629	6.77	14.41	58.52	11.523	132.7826	11.523	24.52
14	52	52.08	-0.08	0.0063	0.08	0.15	49.88	-2.119	4.4911	2.119	4.08
15	44	52.06	-8.06	64.9534	8.06	18.32	51.47	7.470	55.8038	7.470	16.98
16	52	50.04	1.96	3.8239	1.96	3.76	45.87	-6.132	37.6070	6.132	11.79
		50.53					50.47				
Sum =				426.34	61.21	122.38			460.58	53.08	102.67
Average =				28.42	4.08	8.16			57.57	6.64	12.83

2. Three years of quarterly sales data for cases of de-caffeinated diet cola at a local bottling plant are:

Quarter

Year	1	2	3	4
1	6,080	8,234	12,209	10,413
2	7,115	9,411	13,959	11,140
3	7,634	9,791	14,514	12,002

a) Determine a linear trend equation and multiplicative seasonal indexes for this data.

b) Use your results from part (a) to forecast quarterly demand for year 4.

Solution:

a) Exhibit 11.14 shows the results of using Excel's regression analysis procedure in data analysis to fit the regression line. The linear trend equation is $T_t = 7766.14 + 375.75t$. The predicted (trend) values computed by Excel are shown in column C in Exhibit 11.15, with the ratios of Y/T in column D. In columns G−I, the ratios for the 3 years have been grouped by quarter and averaged, giving seasonal indexes of 0.723, 0.919, 1.312, and 1.045.

b) To obtain forecasts for the four quarters of year 4 (quarters 13, 14, 15, and 16), first estimate the trend values by using the trend equation, $T_t = 7766.14 + 375.75t$, and then multiply each

quarter's trend value by the appropriate seasonal index to get the seasonally adjusted forecasts. The results are:

Quarter	Trend	Seasonal Index	Forecast
13	12650.86	0.723	9146.6
14	13026.61	0.919	11971.5
15	13402.36	1.312	17583.9
16	13778.11	1.045	14398.1

Exhibit 11.14

	A	B	C	D	E	F	G
1	SUMMARY OUTPUT						
2							
3	*Regression Statistics*						
4	Multiple R	0.50655257					
5	R Square	0.25659551					
6	Adjusted R Square	0.18225506					
7	Standard Error	2418.53877					
8	Observations	12					
9							
10	ANOVA						
11		*df*	*SS*	*MS*	*F*	*Significance F*	
12	Regression	1	20189705.06	20189705	3.451627	0.092841173	
13	Residual	10	58493297.94	5849330			
14	Total	11	78683003				
15							
16		*Coefficients*	*Standard Error*	*t Stat*	*P-value*		
17	Intercept	7766.13636	1488.507717	5.217397	0.000391		
18	t	375.748252	202.2483724	1.857856	0.092841		
19							

Exhibit 11.15

	A	B	C	D	E	F	G	H	I	J
1	Quarter	Sales	Predicted Sales	Ratio		Quarter	Ratio1	Ratio2	Ratio3	Average
2	1	6080	8141.884615	0.747		1	0.747	0.738	0.685	0.723
3	2	8,234	8517.632867	0.967		2	0.967	0.939	0.850	0.919
4	3	12,209	8893.381119	1.373		3	1.373	1.343	1.220	1.312
5	4	10,413	9269.129371	1.123		4	1.123	1.034	0.978	1.045
6	5	7,115	9644.877622	0.738						
7	6	9,411	10020.62587	0.939				Average =		1.000
8	7	13,959	10396.37413	1.343						
9	8	11,140	10772.12238	1.034						
10	9	7,634	11147.87063	0.685						
11	10	9,791	11523.61888	0.850						
12	11	14,514	11899.36713	1.220						
13	12	12,002	12275.11538	0.978						

DISCUSSION QUESTIONS

1. Identify the basic approaches to forecasting and describe how they differ.

2. Identify the basic components of a time series and explain how they differ from one another.

3. How are simple exponential smoothing and simple moving average forecasting models alike? Different?

4. What would be the effect on the forecasts of increasing the number of periods in an SMA forecasting model?

5. What would be the effect on the forecasts of increasing the value of the smoothing constant in an SES forecasting model?

6. Explain how multiplicative seasonal indexes work and what they can be used for.

7. Identify the basic components of a linear regression trend model and explain what each is.

8. Explain the difference between dependent and independent variables in causal forecasting models.

9. Explain how MSE and MAD are alike and how they differ as measures of forecast accuracy. Explain how both MSE and MAD differ from MAPE as measures of forecast accuracy.

10. Explain how MFE differs from MSE, MAD, and MAPE.

11. If you could pick only two error terms, which would you select? Why?

PROBLEMS

1. Quarterly demand for cordless phones at a discount electronics store for the past 4 years has been:

Year	Quarter			
	1	2	3	4
1	500	370	406	444
2	374	304	458	378
3	402	438	330	480
4	376	344	438	372

a) Develop four-quarter SMA forecasts for as many periods as possible.

b) Develop eight-quarter SMA forecasts for as many periods as possible.

c) Compare the two sets of forecasts with one another and with the actual time series.

2. Using the data from Problem 1:

a) Develop SES forecasts for as many periods as possible with $\alpha = .2$.

b) Develop SES forecasts for as many periods as possible with $\alpha = .4$.

c) Compare the two sets of forecasts with one another and with the actual time series.

3. Using the results from Problems 1 and 2:

a) Find the MSE for each of the forecast series. Identify which forecasting model appears to be the best based on this measure of accuracy.

b) Find the MAD for each of the forecast series. Identify which forecasting model appears to be the best based on this measure of accuracy.

c) Find the MAPE for each of the forecast series. Identify which forecasting model appears to be the best based on this measure of accuracy.

d) Use the RMSE from the SES model with $\alpha = .2$ to find an approximate 95% forecast interval for demand in the first quarter of year 5. Repeat using MAD. Compare the two forecast intervals.

4. The laboratory supervisor at Cheryl's hospital is interested in developing a forecasting model for the number of tests to be performed each week. She has collected the following data from the laboratory's records:

Week	Tests	Week	Tests	Week	Tests
1	611	6	641	11	626
2	640	7	614	12	597
3	628	8	608	13	622
4	616	9	607	14	645
5	604	10	572	15	619

a) Compute forecasts for all possible periods using SMAs with 3 and 6 weeks and SES with $\alpha = .3$ and $\alpha = .5$.

b) Compute the MSE, MAD, and MAPE for each model in part (a). Which model would you recommend on the basis of MSE? On the basis of MAD? On the basis of MAPE?

c) Use simple exponential smoothing with $\alpha = .3$ to find the forecasted number of tests for week 16. Find an approximate 95% forecast interval based on the RMSE; based on MAD. Compare the two intervals.

5. The monthly demands for a new music video magazine at a record store last year were:

Month	Demand	Month	Demand
Jan	145	Jul	328
Feb	182	Aug	375
Mar	202	Sep	404
Apr	236	Oct	452
May	286	Nov	413
Jun	273	Dec	489

a) Use simple linear regression to fit a linear trend line to the data. Interpret the model results.

b) Use the model developed in part (a) to forecast the demand for the magazine in January, June, and December of the current year.

6. As the demand for digital cellular phones increases due to reductions in cost, improvements in quality, and increased advertising, the demand for analog cellular phones has been decreasing. The demand for analog cellular phones at one local service center for the past 10 months has been:

Month	1	2	3	4	5	6	7	8	9	10
Demand	455	385	384	361	324	329	320	320	251	261

a) Use simple linear regression to fit a linear trend line to the data. Interpret the model results.

b) Use the model developed in part (a) to forecast the demand for analog cellular phones for the each of next 6 months.

7. The MBA program at Downtown University operates on a quarter system. While the number of students enrolled is fairly stable, there are quarterly seasonal effects, with enrollment lower in the summer due to vacations. Quarterly enrollment for the past 3 years has been:

Year	Quarter			
	1	2	3	4
1	319	289	295	190
2	321	285	303	196
3	322	291	302	193

a) Estimate the quarterly multiplicative seasonal indexes.

b) Use the indexes found in part (a) to deseasonalize the data.

c) Use SES with $\alpha = .2$ on the deseasonalized data to give a base level forecast for the first quarter of year 4.

d) Forecast enrollments for the four quarters of year 4.

8. Being located in a rapidly growing area, Campbell's Nursery, a gardening supply center, has experienced fairly steady demand growth for most of its product lines over the past few years. However, since gardening is definitely a seasonal activity, there has also been pretty strong quarterly seasonality in sales. Quarterly demand for fertilizer for the past 4 years has been:

Year	Quarter			
	1	2	3	4
1	239	988	669	421
2	299	951	742	431
3	323	1,002	825	420
4	331	1,010	705	476

a) Use simple linear regression to estimate linear trend.

b) Estimate quarterly multiplicative seasonal indexes.

c) Forecast fertilizer demand for the four quarters of year 5.

9. Bagel City is open seven days a week. Other than fairly regular fluctuations on a day-of-the-week basis, demand for bagels has remained basically steady. Daily demand over the past 4 weeks has been:

Week	Day						
	Mon	Tue	Wed	Thu	Fri	Sat	Sun
1	782	920	755	856	868	1,012	1,036
2	921	847	800	804	1,013	1,026	999
3	885	748	669	871	761	1,000	1,048
4	814	657	821	729	826	1,087	1,028

a) Estimate daily multiplicative seasonal indexes for bagel demand at Bagel City.

b) Use the seasonal indexes found in part (a) to deseasonalize the data.

c) Use SES with $\alpha = .25$ on the deseasonalized data (starting with the first period) to develop a base forecast for Monday of week 5.

d) Forecast the daily demands for bagels for week 5.

10. Monthly gasoline sales at a station located at an interstate highway exit show a fairly steady increase over time. In addition, the station experiences higher than normal sales during the summer months (June, July, and August) due to vacation travel and in months with a major travel holiday (May, July, September, November, and December). Monthly sales (in thousands of gallons) for the past 2 years are:

Month	Year 1 Sales	Year 2 Sales	Month	Year 1 Sales	Year 2 Sales
Jan	63.7	68.9	Jul	69.3	70.0
Feb	65.0	67.2	Aug	67.3	70.1
Mar	67.2	68.9	Sep	68.5	70.0
Apr	66.6	69.2	Oct	66.2	68.8
May	67.4	69.3	Nov	67.8	71.2
Jun	68.9	69.7	Dec	67.6	70.1

a) Use simple linear regression to estimate linear trend.

b) Estimate monthly multiplicative seasonal indexes.

c) Forecast monthly gasoline sales for the first 6 months of year 3.

11. The use of ATMs (automated teller machines) has been growing at Third Bank and Trust. As at most banks, the use is heaviest over the weekend when the bank offices are not open as long, so the work processing transactions is heaviest on Mondays. Data collected on the hundreds of transactions to be processed each day for the past 3 weeks are:

Week	Mon	Tue	Wed	Thu	Fri
1	149.0	47.3	35.4	44.3	91.7
2	162.9	53.5	39.5	49.5	93.4
3	168.0	67.4	55.2	40.4	100.7

a) Use simple linear regression to estimate linear trend.

b) Estimate daily multiplicative seasonal indexes.

c) Forecast the daily transaction processing workload for week 4.

12. The demand for mountain bikes at Lewis's Bike Shop has grown each year over the 3 years that the shop has been open. In addition, due to the popularity of bicycles as Christmas presents and their greater use during the summer, there has been a definite seasonal pattern to sales. Quarterly sales of these bikes over the last 3 years have been:

Year	Quarter			
	1	2	3	4
1	117	179	251	214
2	146	183	285	301
3	153	242	306	340

a) Use simple linear regression to estimate linear trend.

b) Estimate quarterly multiplicative seasonal indexes.

c) Forecast the quarterly demand for mountain bikes for the next year.

13. Tom's airline has experienced fairly stable demand for tickets on its Phoenix to San Diego route over the past 2 years. Actual demand (in thousands) over this period has been:

Month	Year 1	Year 2
Jan	18.5	18.9
Feb	15.5	20.1
Mar	18.8	16.0
Apr	17.8	19.2
May	14.7	23.5
Jun	21.3	16.5
Jul	19.6	18.3
Aug	15.3	10.8
Sep	19.1	22.1
Oct	12.2	12.8
Nov	23.9	21.5
Dec	18.0	21.1

a) Estimate multiplicative monthly seasonal indexes to three decimal places.

b) Use the seasonal indexes found in part (a) to deseasonalize the data.

c) Use SES with $\alpha = .3$ on the deseasonalized data to develop a base forecast for January of the next year.

d) Forecast demand for the next 3 months.

14. All-Points Moving and Storage has been experiencing fairly steady growth in demand with, as is usual in the moving industry, strong seasonal effects. Data on monthly contracts to move families out of town over the past 2 years are:

Month	Year 1	Year 2	Month	Year 1	Year 2
Jan	35	38	Jul	82	115
Feb	22	40	Aug	107	140
Mar	32	39	Sep	63	83
Apr	35	48	Oct	53	60
May	38	54	Nov	39	53
Jun	100	130	Dec	41	54

a) Use simple linear regression to estimate linear trend.

b) Estimate quarterly multiplicative seasonal indexes.

c) Forecast the monthly out-of-town trip demand for the next year.

15. In an effort to improve the scheduling of its buses and drivers, the Metropolitan Transit Authority is reviewing the records on the numbers of riders by the day of the week. Daily riders (in thousands) for the past 4 weeks are:

Day	Week 1	Week 2	Week 3	Week 4
M	232	201	156	220
T	200	179	206	212
W	219	186	212	216
T	187	212	190	193
F	227	228	224	222
S	140	164	162	158
S	42	52	45	51

a) Estimate daily multiplicative seasonal indexes.

b) After the daily multiplicative seasonal indexes were calculated, one of the transit authority managers pointed out to the analyst that Monday of week 3 was a federal holiday and that government offices, banks, and a variety of other offices (although not all) were closed. How does recognition of this fact affect the daily seasonal indexes?

c) Using SES with $\alpha = .2$, develop forecasts for the numbers of daily riders for the next week.

CHALLENGE PROBLEMS

1. The local bakery has developed a new confection that they are selling at the rec center deli. Called RedHawk feathers, it is being marketed as a light, low-cal energy and electrolyte replenishment snack. Sales since the introduction 4 weeks ago

have been as follows:

Week	Day	Sales
	Monday	30
	Tuesday	33
	Wednesday	35
1	Thursday	39
	Friday	44
	Saturday	58
	Sunday	40
	Monday	51
	Tuesday	53
	Wednesday	55
2	Thursday	60
	Friday	63
	Saturday	79
	Sunday	61
	Monday	69
	Tuesday	71
	Wednesday	76
3	Thursday	80
	Friday	81
	Saturday	99
	Sunday	79
	Monday	91
	Tuesday	93
	Wednesday	96
4	Thursday	98
	Friday	104
	Saturday	120
	Sunday	97

a) Graph the demand pattern.

b) Use SES with $\alpha = .7$ and the original Forecast $(F_1) = 30$ to forecast demand for the fifth week.

c) Find the MAD, MFE, MAPE, and MSE for the forecast developed in part (a).

d) Describe the seasonality in the demand pattern. (Is it additive or multiplicative? How many seasons are there? What are the seasons?)

e) Incorporate seasonality into your forecasting method and forecast demand for the fifth week.

f) Find the MAD, MFE, MAPE, and MSE for the forecast developed in part (d).

g) How did the change in forecasting method impact the MAD, MFE, MAPE, and MSE?

h) Describe the trend in the demand pattern.

i) Incorporate trend into the forecasting method used in part (d) and forecast demand for the fifth week.

j) Find the MAD, MFE, MAPE, and MSE for the forecast developed in part (h).

k) How did the change in forecasting method impact the MAD, MFE, MAPE, and MSE? Could this have been foreseen?

l) Graph the demand pattern and forecast developed in part (h) together. Does this graph give you a degree of confidence regarding your forecasts for the next week? Why or why not?

2. The rec center sells cookies from the local bakery. Sales during the most recent 4 weeks have been as follows:

Week	Day	Sales
	Monday	223
	Tuesday	221
	Wednesday	218
1	Thursday	215
	Friday	215
	Saturday	111
	Sunday	105
	Monday	208
	Tuesday	204
	Wednesday	203
2	Thursday	199
	Friday	197
	Saturday	97
	Sunday	98

Week	Day	Sales
	Monday	189
	Tuesday	187
	Wednesday	183
3	Thursday	179
	Friday	177
	Saturday	79
	Sunday	79
	Monday	171
	Tuesday	168
	Wednesday	166
4	Thursday	163
	Friday	163
	Saturday	60
	Sunday	55

a) Use the additive approach to deseasonalize the data. (Use two seasons. One season is weekday the other is weekend.)

b) Determine the forecast (seasonalized) for week 5 using SES with $\alpha = 0.7$.

c) Compute the MAD and MFE for the forecast developed in part (b). Based on the values of MAD and MFE, do you believe the forecast can be improved? Why?

d) Determine the forecast (seasonalized) for week 5 using linear trend and the deseasonalized data from part (a).

e) Compute the MAD and MFE for the forecast developed in part (d).

f) Which of the two forecasts is better? Why?

Case 11: Data: How Much Is Enough?

The *New York Times* recently ran a story describing the "Always On" executive. The story described an individual, Charles Lax, as a man whose "brain is on speed." You know the profile: a go-getter who is in a meeting and at the same time has an ear-pod getting a news broadcast, responding to text messages on a cell phone, and surfing the Net on a laptop. (Let's hope that's not you in your OM class—but it is a problem professors have experienced with classrooms that provide Internet links or wireless web access.) Many of us in the twenty-first century are addicted to information and feel lost without our mobile devices and laptops. Without these, we are bored, restless, agitated, and sometimes depressed. Strange as it may seem, we might feel that we can have a better conversations while we are "Always On," than when we are isolated from such input. As the subject of the *New York Times* article stated, "It's hard to concentrate on one thing. I think I have a condition."

Many with the condition described above legitimately fear they will fall behind if they disconnect, but they also acknowledge feeling compulsively drawn to the constant stimulation provided by incoming data. Psychologists are calling it O.C.D. — online compulsive disorder.

Two professors from Harvard, Edward M Hallowell and John Ratey, among others, are assessing how technology affects attention span, creativity, and focus. Their term for this condition, pseudo-attention deficit disorder, refers to the way individuals subjected to the pace of modern life have developed shorter attention spans, have difficulty with long-term projects, and physically crave the bursts of stimulation from checking e-mail or voice mail or answering the phone. Hallowell and Ratey claim the addiction is real and that some cannot cope with down time or quiet moments.

Though many experience information overload today, things haven't always been that way. According to the *Wall Street Journal*, the challenge facing forecasters in the 1920s (before computers, econometric models, and time-series analysis) was quite different. There wasn't a standard definition of many economic terms such as Gross

Domestic Product (GDP). Measures for unemployment and many other economic variables were compiled from scattered sources, which were often just city or statewide estimates derived using varying methodologies. In total there was a lot of data, but the data was incomplete, inconsistent, and not suited for large analytic models. In fact, even after the stock market crash of 1929, the country's leading economists couldn't predict the Great Depression using all available data and many produced rosy economic forecasts! Without the kinds of economic measures and statistical analysis rigorously developed over the past 70 years or so, the forecasters of the 1920s were severely limited. In fact, researchers have concluded that with the data available to forecasters at the time, "the Depression was not forecastable."

SOME QUESTIONS TO THINK ABOUT:

1. How are the problems of Mr. Lax and the economists of the 1920s the same? How are they different?

2. Can there be such a thing as too much data, when it comes to forecasting?

3. How does establishing a formal forecasting methodology help solve the problems experienced by both Mr. Lax and economists of the 1920s?

Source: Adapted from "The Lure of Data: Is It Addictive?," *New York Times*, July 6, 2003 (online edition), reporter Matt Richtel; and "Before the Depression, Economic Indicators Forecast Rosy Future," *Wall Street Journal*, August 6, 2003, p. B1, reporter Cynthia Crossen

12

Aggregate Sales and Operations Planning Processes

Chapter Outline

Introduction   530

Integrating Operations Management Across the Functions   531

Planning for the Intermediate Term   533

Aggregate Planning Variables   538

    Special Aggregate Planning Considerations in Service Environments   540

General Aggregate Planning Strategies   542

    The Level Production Strategy   542

    The Chase Demand Strategy   545

    The Peak Demand Strategy   546

    Mixed Strategies   548

Aggregate Planning Methods   551

    Optimizing Methods   551

    Methods that Model Manager Decisions   554

    The Cut-and-Try Method   554

E-Commerce, Supply Chain Management, and Aggregate Planning   555

Summary   555

Key Terms   556

Solved Problems   556

Discussion Questions   560

Problems   561

Challenge Problems   563

Case 12: Resizing the Workforce in the Netherlands and the U.S.   567

Learning Objectives

After studying this chapter you should be able to

▶ Demonstrate your understanding of the linkages between the various functional areas of business that are important in the process of aggregate planning

▶ Describe the importance of planning for the intermediate term

▶ Identify the variables used in aggregate planning

▶ Describe special considerations relevant to aggregate planning in services

▶ Describe aggregate planning strategies

▶ Describe quantitative methods useful in aggregate planning and apply the cut-and-try method

▶ State the implications of current trends in e-commerce and Supply Chain Management on the practice of aggregate planning

...Back at the Rec Center

"Know what I like about our factory?" asks Fred, as he and the others finish stretching one morning. He's referring to the factory that supplies his division with mass-produced, standardized cell phones. "We crank 'em out at whatever pace the annual plan calls for, pile 'em up at the end of the line, and ship 'em when we sell 'em. If we run out for a week or two, we back order," he says, with obvious satisfaction. "Planning is easy. Get the monthly numbers from the marketing people, adjust the line, get some lunch, and call it a day. What a life!"

"I don't think it's quite that easy, even in *your* business," Luis doubts aloud.

"Yeah," suggests Tom, "even though a lot of the decisions are hardwired into the production line, it can't be easy to rebalance the jobs all the way down the line every time marketing wants to change the pace."

"It isn't, and that's why we don't do it very often," says Fred. "It's cheaper to let inventory build up. Nobody likes back orders, either, but we do it when we have to."

"That's okay for a mass-marketed cell phone, but you can't use inventory to set a broken leg or get someone home for the holidays!" laughs Luis, as he gets on a stepper. "You can't inventory services!"

"Right, Luis, but you know, you're a lot more like us than you are like Fred," says Cheryl. "You guys do most of your work to order. You don't inventory much finished furniture either."

"You're telling me!" Luis responds. "And have you seen how many different pieces of furniture we make? With all the labor we use, we could never keep our line as smooth as Fred's. We still plan ahead, though: hiring, layoffs, raw materials, overtime, temps—all that stuff. We put it all together with our forecasts and make everything line up for the next few months. We can't just change everything over breakfast and have it on the floor by lunch! Just the time it takes to hire a machine operator—all said and done, we're looking 8 to 10 weeks down the road."

"We make only a couple of different cell phones, so plugging in the right numbers based on a new forecast is pretty straightforward," Fred responds, as he looks around the room. "How do you know what your orders will be if you do as much custom work as you say you do?" he asks Luis.

"It's hard," says Luis. "We don't know what our orders will be until we get them. We do forecasts, though. We just add up the labor hours we'll need to get the stuff out the door. For us, labor is the hardest thing to plan. If we can estimate our total needs—you know, a monthly head count over the next year or so—we can figure out what we need each day when the time comes."

"It's funny, we do sort of the same thing," replies Tom, who's moved over to the biceps curl station. "It's a little different, though. We're planning for personnel and equipment. We forecast all the demand on each flight over the next year or two—booked flights and forecasts together. Then we boil them down into one big number per month, as far ahead as we can see. We talk about total passengers and passenger miles. We can't sweat the specifics at that point—too much can happen. We don't assign equipment, personnel, or gates until much later."

"We try to match total available equipment, personnel, and airport resources to the demand forecast for each month," Tom laughs. "It'd be hard for us to pile up inventory the way Fred does. We can't just go out and buy a plane or hire a pilot the same morning, either. Just like at Cheryl's hospital, some of our months are heavier than others. We need to look way down the road to adjust our capacity. We hire temps, lease equipment, manage our vacation times, and move scheduled maintenance around so that most of the time the totals match up. It's not so bad when we can see a crunch coming— when people book tickets well in advance and future ticket orders are predictable. Then we can usually handle it. The two things we can't control are the weather and who actually shows up for the ride. But again, we build in some room to maneuver, so that with planning it all tends to work out. We usually manage to get people where they want to go."

A minute or two later, Tom's look of confidence vanishes, as he remembers the unpleasant task he has to deal with that day.

"You know what we were just talking about? How well we plan and schedule our flights? Well, it doesn't always work out that well," Tom says. "I have to call Boeing this morning and try to work out some problems with them." Tom's airline owns more than 200 jets, all of them Boeing 737s. "We ordered a few new 737s awhile back," he continues. "Nothing special, just what we always order. But now everything is delayed. They have a real logjam up there, I guess. Everything is 6 months behind schedule."

"I think I read something about that in the *Wall Street Journal*," says Cheryl. "It sounded as if they just missed the boat on their planning."

"*Plane*, they missed the *plane!*" interrupts Luis.

"Good one," laughs Tom. "That's exactly what they did." He explains that Boeing's forecasting people had predicted a period of slow demand. Thinking it would be a good time to make some changes, top management had decided to downsize and restructure some business processes. The people at the top also thought it would be a good time to install some new technology and implement a production quality system that had been in the works for some time. "The only problem was, after a good part of the workforce had been laid off in preparation for the changes, the orders for new planes just took off!" says Tom.

"Booo, that was bad," laugh Cheryl and Luis.

"Well, in any case, they've got a huge backlog in the factory, and they think it'll be a year or more before they can catch up," Tom says. "And it's not just affecting their customers. Besides downsizing their own employees, Boeing's managers had cut back on multiple suppliers of certain parts or components. Now the firm had fewer suppliers to turn to and was leaning very hard on the ones that were left. It's not good for anybody," Tom concludes, as he heads for the locker room. "It's going to be an interesting few months."

"Makes you wonder about those forecasts, doesn't it?" asks Luis, as he starts his second set.

Introduction

We have looked closely at the operational decisions that determine the structure within which a company operates. Such decisions are generally related to long-term demand forecasts, which are updated at least once a year based on projections many years into the future. These decisions have long-term implications; they typically take years to implement; they affect the entire range of a company's product-service bundles, and they cannot easily be reversed.

You have probably noticed that many classrooms at your college or university have forty or fewer seats. Class size is considered to be a factor in the quality provided by an educational institution: the smaller, the better. If the biggest classroom at a school has only forty chairs, professors must satisfy the demand for a popular course through several small sections rather than one large lecture class. Thus, a bricks-and-mortar structural decision that was made years ago has a direct impact on today's scheduling decisions.

Or consider a hotel at a large resort. When it was built, demographic projections and other long-term forecasts suggested that with expected growth in convention and tourist business, 3000 rooms could eventually be filled during peak periods. Now the housekeeping and administrative staff must be able to meet the needs of such a large capacity, particularly on days when all the rooms are occupied. Thus, structural operating constraints establish the boundaries for intermediate-range operational plans. The hotel knows how many housekeepers to hire, and the college or university knows how many sections to schedule, because of structural characteristics that are relatively permanent.

Beginning with this chapter, we will focus on the operation of existing systems. First, we will concentrate on intermediate-range issues in the operation of value-adding systems and decision-making tools that set the stage for more detailed planning in every functional area. For example, cash flow projections in finance, sales projections in marketing, and hiring plans in human resources must all take into account the overall capacity plans of the firm.

Intermediate term operational plans strive to ensure that resources are in place to meet overall demand 6 to 18 months in the future. In a university, this kind of work is usually done by department chairs, who must determine how many sections will be taught by their department and develop suitable staffing plans. In this planning process, all sections taught by the department are treated as equal—no

REC CENTER DILEMMA

Tom's dilemma:

Though he knows it will be more than 6 months from now, Tom is calling Boeing to get a better feel for when his planes will be ready. How specific a delivery date does he need to ask for? How will he be able to use the information? How would your answers to the previous two questions change if the delivery date were within the next month?

specific classes are distinguished from others. (Because demand has been aggregated across multiple products, this approach is called aggregate planning.) The actual scheduling, which matches individual instructors to specific class sections, can be done later.

Aggregate planners have a very limited set of variables to use. They can change workforce size through hiring and layoff decisions. They can make plans to extend the hours contributed by each worker through such mechanisms as overtime. In some situations they can shift capacity to a later month by building inventory or shift demand to a later month by extending a back order. In some cases, subcontracting can be used to expand capacity. In service environments, the options are often even more limited than in manufacturing. It is often not possible to inventory, subcontract, or backlog a service, but there are other strategies to employ in service environments.

Aggregate planners may pursue a variety of different strategies in their attempt to match resource availability to expected demand, including:

▶ Keeping capacity stable at an average demand level

▶ Matching capacity to expected changes in demand

▶ Ensuring adequate capacity for peak demand periods

▶ Combining the other three strategies in some way

The strategy selected by an aggregate planner is generally a function of their business, process type, and competitive strategy.

Numerous quantitative methods have been suggested and used by aggregate planners, including methods that model manager decisions, optimizing methods, and the spreadsheet-based "cut-and-try" approach. While it would seem that managers should use techniques that provide an optimal solution, this is often not possible because of the uncertainty surrounding demand projections.

E-commerce and supply chain management (SCM) practices have had a positive influence on the effectiveness of aggregate planning. In particular, SCM and e-commerce have created closer links and greater trust between organizations and their customers, which can result in plans that are both more effective and more stable.

Integrating Operations Management Across the Functions

Table 12.1 highlights some of the critical linkages between the operational issues involved in aggregate planning decisions and other functional areas. Intermediate-range plans, by their very nature, have to take into account the considerations of all functions, because the more detailed plans in each area have to fit within this plan:

The cash flow projections and working capital plans prepared by financial managers must be consistent with the aggregate plan for operations.

Accountants have to prepare pro forma statements, allocate costs, and value operating assets, such as inventories, in a way that is consistent with the intermediate-range plans of the firm.

Human resource (HR) professionals must make necessary adjustments to workforce size and contracts based on the aggregate plan. Workforce size adjustments and other personnel contract issues arise from the aggregate planning process and require

Table 12.1

Integrating Operations Management across the Functions

Functional Area Integration Perspective	Finance	Accounting
Why Cross-Functional Integration Matters in Aggregate Planning	**Cash flow projections and working capital requirements must be consistent with the level of activity indicated on the aggregate plan.**	**Pro forma accounting statements and operating budgets must be consistent with the aggregate plan and operating assets, such as inventories need to be valued appropriately. Cost estimates used in aggregate planning may be prepared by accounting.**
Key Issues	**How much working capital will be needed to support intermediate-range operational plans?** **Are economic forecasts consistent with demand projections?** **How will the aggregate plan impact intermediate-range financial results?**	**What will be the appropriate costs (of carrying inventory, hiring, laying off workers, and subcontracting) to use in aggregate planning?** **What operational budgets can be anticipated on the basis of the aggregate plan?** **If pro forma accounting is used, does it reflect the operational plans?**

follow-through on the part of HR. This may be particularly true in certain services where inventories cannot be used to prepare for demand increases and the only way to adjust capacity is through personnel changes.

Marketing programs, including advertising and promotional budgets, are generally critical to accomplishing the aggregate plan and must be consistent with it.

Engineering changes applied to products and processes must be timed correctly and play a role in intermediate-range performance expectations.

Finally, management information systems need to be capable of providing the same information to managers in all functional areas. When managers are all working with the same data and operational plans, their decisions are more likely to be consistent and they are more likely to accomplish the results they desire.

Figure 12.1, illustrates the importance of cross-functional understanding if the aggregate sales and production planning process is to effectively support a firm's transformation process, integrate decisions with those of supply chain partners, and satisfy customers.

Human Resources	Marketing	Engineering	Management Information Systems
Staffing requirements will be directly impacted by the aggregate plan and worker contracts must be consistent with the aggregate plan.	Advertising and promotional budgets may be critical to achieving the demand levels against which the aggregate plan is prepared and must be consistent with the aggregate plan.	Engineering changes and design work will be required of engineering in levels correlated to operational volumes in the aggregate plan, especially in the make to order environment.	By supporting the firm's internal information systems and/or extranet, MIS makes it possible to have consistent intermediate-range plans across all functions and facilitates coordination with supply chain partners.
What hiring and/or severance activities will be called for by the aggregate plan? What HR budgets should be anticipated based on the aggregate plan? Does the aggregate plan fit within the context of existing labor contracts and/or employee relations programs?	Is the aggregate plan consistent with intermediate-range sales targets? What marketing budgets should be anticipated based on the aggregate plan? Does the aggregate plan fit within the context of promotional plans?	What engineering budgets will be required to support the aggregate plan? What engineering staffing will be required to support the aggregate plan?	Is the firm's IS infrastructure providing consistent data to intermediate-range planners in the various functional areas? Can the firm and its supply chain partners share and receive (or electronically access) data that are useful for intermediate range planning?

Planning for the Intermediate Term

Intermediate-range planners typically look 6 to 18 months forward; they plan in monthly increments and generally revise their plans each month based on intermediate-range forecasts. Some firms look further forward than others, depending on their time frame for decision making. For example, Boeing relies on a skilled workforce and therefore cannot rapidly change its production plans. Its intermediate-range plans cover a relatively long period. A copy shop or restaurant, on the other hand, need not look so far forward.

In the intermediate range, separate plans are made for groups of product-service bundles with similar value-delivery characteristics or marketing requirements. Resources are then allocated to product groups according to those plans. For example, a carpet manufacturer could aggregate its demand according to major carpet types, such as Berber, plush, pile, and indoor-outdoor. The intermediate-range forecast

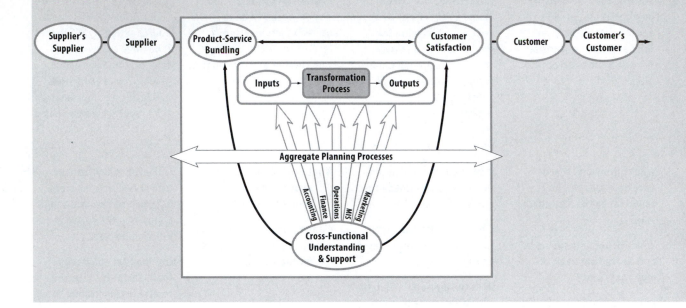

would indicate how many million square yards of carpet would be needed in each category, but the aggregate plan would not specify specific colors or patterns. Similarly, a large accounting and consulting firm would aggregate its personnel or billable hours by group or division, such as auditing, tax accounting, and process consulting.

An **aggregate plan** indicates the ways in which existing resources will be used to meet expected levels of demand for product groups over the intermediate range. It sets target levels for the size of the workforce, the extent of subcontracting, the monthly production rate, and the level of inventory. These decisions must typically be made several months in advance.

In contrast, short-term plans address day-to-day decisions with relatively short lead times. In this type of operations planning, time is divided into weekly or daily increments, and plans must continually be revised. The short-term plan includes a **master schedule**, or detailed description of delivery commitments for the product-service bundles over the near term. It also indicates how workers and equipment will be used, how the in-house creation of various parts of the product-service bundle will be coordinated, and how outsourced materials and services will be procured. Figure 12.2 summarizes the differences between short- and intermediate-range planning.

The firm's competitive priorities determine what is included in its intermediate- and short-range plans. Companies that emphasize customization of their product-service bundles, like job shops, must cope with a great deal of complexity and uncertainty in their planning. Every job is different; each goes through a different set of work centers, and no one knows how long its passage through the factory will take. For companies that emphasize low-cost delivery of a standardized product-service bundle,

Aggregate plan

The ways in which existing resources will be used to meet expected levels of demand for product groups over the immediate range.

Master schedule

A detailed description of the product-service bundles scheduled to be completed over the near term.

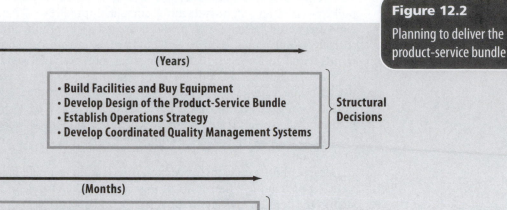

Figure 12.2

Planning to deliver the product-service bundle

planning and control of operations is much simpler. Because the product is standardized, so is the process; therefore, the main task is to schedule operations at a flow rate that matches the level of demand.

Short-term plans must be closely monitored to ensure their feasibility. Managers may be tempted to make unrealistic commitments in order to please customers, but in most organizations, there is usually very little flexibility in short-term capacity. As a result, companies need to be effective in their short-term scheduling and very careful about the promises they make to customers regarding delivery dates.

Regardless of the time frame, operations planning is based on a **rolling planning horizon**, which is a planning period whose beginning- and endpoints slide forward with the passage of time. At least once a year, the long-range plan will be updated, across both the product and process life cycle. Of course, the definition of *long range* varies from one industry to the next; the product life cycle for a new computer chip is much shorter than the life cycle for potato chips. While a 5- to 10-year plan might seem very long range to a microprocessor manufacturer such as Intel, forest products companies such as Georgia Pacific and Weyerhauser need forecasts that look at least 30 years forward.

Intermediate-range plans are updated more frequently than the long-range plan, often on a monthly basis, and they pay particularly close attention to staffing needs. If more skilled workers are needed and the labor market is particularly tight, the time horizon for the intermediate-range plan may need to be longer than a year. If labor is readily available, the intermediate-range plan might not extend so far forward.

Rolling planning horizon

A planning period whose beginning and endpoints slide forward with the passage of time.

Production lead times also affect the length of the intermediate-range plan. A ship builder or large aircraft manufacturer can reliably predict workforce requirements several years ahead, because such products are always in production for several years. A specialty clothing manufacturer will not have the same luxury, however. Once fashion trends have become clear, the manufacturer must respond rapidly to staffing needs.

Short-range plans are updated on an ongoing basis, daily or weekly. If the cumulative lead time required to provide the product-service bundle is 6 weeks, schedules will need to be revised at least once a week, looking at least 6 weeks forward. In that case, planners will usually create a tentative schedule that looks forward more than 6 weeks (say, 10 to 20 weeks), so that the company will be prepared for an unusually busy or slow period.

Because short-range, intermediate-range, and long-range plans all pertain to the same set of resources, they must fit together. A small change in the long-range plan, such as the decision to delay an expansion, could produce very different scenarios over the short and intermediate ranges. Similarly, a decision by intermediate-range planners to limit the use of overtime could cause significant capacity shortages and reduce flexibility over the short run. Finally, short-range decisions can affect the intermediate- and long-range plans. For instance, week-to-week scheduling that produces a continually growing backlog may lead to heavier use of subcontracting over the intermediate range or even to a decision to expand capacity.

Different types of manufacturing processes produce vastly different levels of complexity in short-term scheduling. From a planning standpoint, job shops and batch processes that produce customized product-service bundles are a highly complex environment. At the most detailed level, that of a job shop, planners must deal with a varying number of jobs, each of which is unlike any other that has been done in the past. Because each job follows its own unique route through the facility, the planner can only estimate processing times in the various work centers. Because each work center may have a number of jobs queued up for processing, the waiting time at each work center is usually unpredictable. Despite the inherent uncertainty, job shops must give customers some indication of when their jobs will be completed. In contrast, planning and control for a continuous or repetitive process such as an assembly line is quite simple. All the inputs and outputs are standardized, so the only real question planners must answer is, How fast should we run the process?

For high-volume assembly lines that create standardized product-service bundles, "deterministic approaches" to planning and control are most useful. In these environments, the schedule is "hardwired" into the process, so that it represents a firm commitment to a rate of production. The planner's task is simply to specify the rate of production for each product-service bundle. Then, on the basis of the resulting schedule, suppliers will provide parts, supervisors will prepare work and overtime schedules, and the sales force will sell product-service bundles. A Saturn dealer, for example, can tell customers the exact day on which the car they have ordered will be delivered. So, too, Saturn's suppliers do not have to be told which parts to ship on any given day; they can determine that information from Saturn's production schedule. An automatic car wash is another example. Because the time a car takes to go through the car wash is predetermined, a customer's waiting time can be determined easily based solely on the number of cars queued up for service. This type of production environment is easy to model and schedule.

Whenever a group of jobs must compete for limited resources, however, the planning environment becomes complicated. Highly complex environments like the job shop, where many different product-service bundles are produced and value is added in a variety of ways, cannot be modeled in a deterministic way. In these environments, "probabilistic approaches" to planning are more useful. Planners first estimate processing times, waiting times, transfer times, and the probability of breakdowns. They

INTEGRATING OM:

Planning Milk Production the New Zealand Way

Fonterra Co-operative Group Ltd is a leading multi-national dairy company, owned by 11,600 New Zealand dairy farmers. They are the world's largest exporter of dairy products, exporting 95% of production. The co-op's global supply chain encompasses everything from shareholders' farms and twenty-nine manufacturing sites in New Zealand through to customers and consumers in 140 countries. Collecting about three and a half billion gallons of milk a year, the co-op's members manufacture and market about 1.8 million metric tons of dairy products annually, making them the world's leader in large-scale milk procurement, processing and management.

In recent years Fonterra has moved to switch from pushing products to meeting market demand using a project they called JEDI. The co-op's 2003–2004 annual report states:

> The JEDI programme has defined and introduced a single set of processes to work across all geographies, all functions and all customers. Our operations are now more aligned to customer demand than in the past. After balance date, a significant step forward was taken with the implementation in mid-June of "Empower," our SAP-based order management and logistics system. This system incorporates a new set of business processes and redevelopment of our inventory and warehouse management system.

The SAP has helped the company reverse the logic in its business processes by scheduling manufacturing operations to meet forecast sales orders, rather than asking sales teams overseas to market predicted output. In the process, Fonterra scrapped an inventory and production planning system, which used to fulfill the key role of allocating production from its various manufacturing plants to orders received by marketing offices overseas. The global rollout of the SAP software was a multi-year project that began in corporate offices in New Zealand in 2004.

SAP's Advanced Planning and Optimization (APO) software module is designed to match demand and supply in an industry such as Fonterra's that include a huge number of supply sources, manufacturing facilities, inventory items, end products, distribution patterns, planning and scheduling decision makers, and customers. APO combines sales forecasts from business development staff overseas with information on the amount and characteristics of milk coming to Fonterra, manufacturing plants to create proposed production schedules and transport options. This is used to build a schedule that is, at least in theory, the most efficient plan as to how much of each item to manufacture, where, when, and how to get product to market.

The technology relies in part on accurate sales forecasts. One of the biggest changes is to move from a "push" value chain to a "pull" system based upon real demand. In the past, the company tended to produce ingredients and then look for customers. Now the model places increased expectations on customers to accurately predict their own demand, but the idea behind a system such as APO is that it can learn from past experience and do some of that forecasting for customers. With APO, each month's plan should be better than the last. For it to work, a high level of compliance to the plan is needed—therefore increasing the importance of customer relationships based on trustworthy information. Requiring accuracy above 80%, the methodology is a cultural change for Fonterra. Less accuracy than that and too many exceptions must be made. If a plan keeps changing, it's not a plan, it's just reacting.

APO produces an initial production plan based on inputs from all supply chain partners. This initial plan is then adapted in light of "exceptions" such as product with no buyers or customers with unfulfilled demand. For future planning iterations, the algorithm at the heart of APO can be tweaked to learn from such real-world mistakes so that the initial solution it provides is closer to the final schedule.

Source: Adapted from "Turn of the Jedi," *Dominion Post*, July 28, 2003, p. 12; http://www.dompost.co.nz; and http://www.fonterra.com (accessed on May 4, 2006)

Make-to-stock

A policy where a company wants to allow for immediate product availability by building inventories of finished product based on forecasted customer demand. The entire schedule is based on forecasted demand figures.

Companies who are seeking short term labor availability in order to avoid the fixed costs and investments associated with hiring permanent workers often turn to temporary agencies. This resource alternative is becoming a growing part of our economy and our culture.

then make planning and control decisions based on expected processing times and lot sizes. But while managers can indicate when they expect a job to be completed, delays can occur for many reasons. When the value-adding steps are executed, they may take more or less time than expected. The schedule is therefore more a guideline than a binding commitment, and time buffers are built into most job completion estimates.

To better appreciate why a complex business environment cannot be modeled deterministically, think about an amusement park. Imagine one person trying to plan out a day at Six Flags, Disneyland, or some other park—what rides to take, in what order, and at what time. Now imagine trying to do the same for all the visitors on a given day. Consider the timing of employees' breaks, unexpected absences, the length of waiting lines, and the possibility of equipment breakdowns. Such an environment can be modeled effectively only in a probabilistic way.

Figure 12.3 illustrates the relationships between intermediate- and short-range planning and control in various environments that we have just discussed and illustrates how subsequent chapters relate to this chapter. Chapter 13 covers the supply chain-related issues of inventory management and master scheduling for all environments. Chapters 14–16 deal with detailed planning and scheduling issues one environment at a time, starting with simple environments and moving to greater and greater levels of complexity.

Aggregate Planning Variables

To understand aggregate planning, one must first have at least a basic understanding of the forecasting process. To begin with, because demand follows patterns, future demand is predictable, or "forecastable." However, the precision with which future demand can be predicted decreases the farther into the future one attempts to look. Depending on the planning system a business uses, this characteristic of forecasting may be more or less significant.

Some companies use make-to-order planning and control systems; others, make-to-stock or assemble-to-order systems. In a **make-to-stock** system, the entire schedule is based on forecasted demand figures. For example, a paper pulp manufacturer is likely to forecast demand for its standardized product, make that product in the volume the forecast calls for, and supply its customers from the inventories it has created. In contrast, in **make-to-order** systems, managers have purchase orders in hand when they are planning, so they know the demand for products and services at least as far forward as their processing lead times. Looking several months forward, however, their forecasts may be based primarily on predicted orders. For example, a manufacturer of customized machine tools and dies can only know what to make when orders have been received, but can estimate the number and type of orders that its likely to get. **Assemble-to-order** systems are a combination of the make-to-stock and make-to-order approaches: Production

Figure 12.3

The management of operational systems

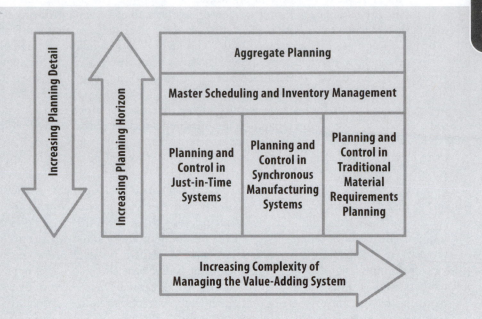

Increasing Planning Detail

Increasing Planning Horizon

Aggregate Planning

Master Scheduling and Inventory Management

Planning and Control in Just-in-Time Systems

Planning and Control in Synchronous Manufacturing Systems

Planning and Control in Traditional Material Requirements Planning

Increasing Complexity of Managing the Value-Adding System

of customer orders are scheduled using components and subassemblies that have been made to stock. For example, a computer assembly firm might keep a stock of processors, circuit boards, disk drives, and other components to be used for assembly once a customer orders the machine. Dell is one firm known to use such a system.

Fortunately, the precision of a forecast can be estimated. Thus, an aggregate plan can be based on expected demand, best-case scenarios, and worst-case scenarios. As more information becomes available, forecasts are (or should be) updated. The aggregate plan is effectively based on a moving target.

Typically, in the intermediate time frame, no new facilities can be built, no old facilities can be shut down, and no productivity improvement programs can have their full effect. These kinds of structural changes simply take too long to plan and implement. Though the firm's structure is fixed in the intermediate term, the demand for each family of product-service bundles is likely to vary from month to month. Aggregate planners must therefore determine how to vary monthly volumes in order to meet demand in the most effective way.

The set of planning variables available to the aggregate planner is quite limited: It includes only the inventory account, the monthly production rate, the size of the workforce, and the extent of subcontracting. Of course, not all these variables are equally available to all businesses. Like many other service businesses, a hospital cannot inventory services; the freedom to hire and fire staff may also be limited in many skill categories. In capital-intensive processes such as steel making, production rates and workforce requirements are largely fixed.

The inventory account, if there is one, may be positive or negative. A positive inventory account indicates that the plan is to have materials on hand. A negative inventory account indicates a planned production **backlog**, or a deliberate amount of unmet demand. The planned level of the inventory account can be changed by producing more or less in any given month than the forecasted level of demand. This goal may be

Make-to-order

A policy where managers have purchase orders in hand when they are planning, so they know the demand for products and services at least as far forward as their processing lead times. They do not actually start the production process until the customer places an order.

Assemble-to-order

A combination of the make-to-stock and make-to-order approaches. The production of customer orders are scheduled using components and subassemblies that have been made to stock.

Backlog

An amount of unmet demand.

accomplished in several ways. The planned monthly production rate can be changed by varying the number of overtime hours worked in a month. The planned size of the workforce can be changed by hiring or laying off workers. To meet demand during a holiday rush, retailers often hire temps to staff their stores and catalog operations. Finally, subcontracting plans can be changed, within certain limitations and for a limited time.

To the aggregate planner, each of these variables has a cost. No checks are actually written to cover the cost estimates associated with an aggregate plan; rather, the figures are used to model the cost of meeting demand through various approaches. The cost of carrying inventory, for instance, is much higher than the investment income lost on money tied up in warehoused goods. It includes items such as the rental fee for warehouse space, the administrative expense associated with monitoring and tracking the extra inventory, potential loss from damage to goods in storage or transit, tax and insurance costs, and the risk that the warehoused materials will become obsolete while they are in storage. By comparison, the cost of a planned backlog includes sales lost due to delays in customer service, the administrative expense associated with keeping track of unfilled orders, and the cost of maintaining the systems that respond to customer inquiries about orders. Changing the production rate by adding extra overtime typically inflates the hourly cost of labor at least 50%. Hiring or laying off workers obviously requires a significant amount of administrative time and record keeping. New workers must be trained and oriented; laid-off workers usually receive some severance pay or outplacement services or both. Finally, subcontracting requires extra administrative effort and may erode profit margins or the quality of customer service.

Ultimately, the aggregate planner's goal is to meet customer requirements, based on some forecasted demand pattern, through whatever mix of inventory, overtime, workforce size, and subcontracting minimizes the firm's costs. An alternative goal, particularly when the service component of the product-service bundle is significant, might be to ensure sufficient capacity to meet the expected peak level of demand. For example, the aggregate plan for a hospital emergency room should ensure that enough doctors are scheduled to handle the highest expected level of monthly demand. In a small college town, that would probably mean scheduling more doctor-hours during the academic year than during summer vacation. In operations in which service is not a significant part of the product-service bundle—such as a factory that makes a standardized, mass-produced product—maintaining a level workforce might be important. In those cases, inventory might be varied in order to level production.

Special Aggregate Planning Considerations in Service Environments

Aggregate planning in service environments is especially challenging because services typically cannot be inventoried in anticipation of future demand. Planning sufficient service capacity is the main approach to satisfying customer demand. The benefits of satisfied customers, however, must be weighed against the risks and costs of excess capacity.

STRATEGIES FOR MANAGING SERVICE DEMAND

1. *Segmenting customers.* An orthodontist group that serves both adults and children might benefit by segmenting customers. The group schedules short checkups (15 minutes or less) for children in the early morning before school starts and in the late afternoon after school is out. Adult patients may come in for short checkups anytime. However, both children and adults must schedule long appointments for mid- to late morning and early afternoon. Because orthodontia patients have many more short appointments than long ones, this scheduling policy minimizes

the frequency of children missing school to attend an appointment. It also maintains high flexibility in short appointments to accommodate adult schedules, while keeping capacity utilization consistently high by forcing long appointments into the middle of the day.

2. *Differential pricing.* Most of us are familiar with the strategy of using price discounts to encourage customers to purchase services at nonpeak times. Utilities offer special rates for off-peak electricity and phone usage. Restaurants promote "early bird specials" to fill tables before peak dining hours. Movie theaters sell discount tickets for matinee shows. Resorts reduce their rates for periods when business is slow. Some organizations have highly sophisticated pricing strategies, where different service "packages" can be priced at different rates. For example, Chicago's Shedd Aquarium divides its facilities into (1) regular exhibits of species from around the world, (2) the dolphin and beluga tanks, and (3) special shows such as a traveling exhibit of sea horses; various ticket packages provide different amounts of access to the aquarium's facilities. Pricing can be an effective tool to maintain high capacity utilization and maximize total revenue.

3. *Counterseasonal products and services.* Many services suffer from demand seasonality. Summer resorts, universities, bicycle shops, and other specialty retailers all suffer from excess capacity when the peak sales season passes. Adding counterseasonal services is one way to combat this problem. In recent years, scores of summer resorts in Minnesota have insulated their cabins and now offer winter accommodations to snowmobile and cross-country skiing enthusiasts. Universities offer group retreats and sports camps during the summer months. In northern states, specialty bicycle shops sell ice skates and skis during the fall and winter months, while motorcycle dealers sell snowmobiles.

4. *Complementary products and services.* A common strategy for Las Vegas hotels is to offer a complete package of services to keep guests (and their money) in the hotel's complex and away from competing facilities. A full-service Las Vegas hotel offers reasonably priced rooms, multiple restaurant and bar options, extravagant Broadway shows, and of course, extensive gambling opportunities.

5. *Reservation systems.* Airlines, hotels, restaurants, hair salons, and numerous other services use reservations to match future service capacity with future demand. Customers who request reservations that are already filled often can adjust to other options, thereby smoothing demand across a broader range of service capacity. Reservations are convenient to both customers and service providers. Problems with this strategy include customers who do not show up for their appointment and providers who overbook their services and cannot serve everyone with a reservation. One way of dealing with customer "no-shows" is to collect the service payment in advance and not issue refunds to no-shows, such as nonrefundable tickets sold by airlines. Another approach is to charge a minimum fee if the customer does not cancel a reservation or appointment within 24 hours. Overbooking costs the service provider money in compensation paid to inconvenienced customers and the loss of future business when customers are alienated.

STRATEGIES FOR MANAGING SERVICE SUPPLY

1. *Schedule employees to match demand patterns.* No customer at a fast-food restaurant will deny that it makes sense to schedule a sufficient number of employees to meet demand peaks that occur at breakfast, lunch, dinner, and perhaps a late-night "bar rush." However, it is critical for controlling labor costs that some workers finish their shifts at the end of these demand peaks.

2. *Customer participation.* Customers provide their own service when they bag their own groceries, check themselves out of the library, complete loan applications prior to meeting with a loan officer, cut their own Christmas trees, and fill their cars with gasoline. Problems can occur with this approach when customers lack sufficient training in procedures or equipment operation. Customers may also cause problems if they try to cheat the system (for instance, drive away without paying for gas) or by causing quality problems (for example, contaminating bulk foods in the grocery store).

3. *Contingent employees.* Part-time and temporary full-time workers are called "contingent" employees. They benefit the company by quickly filling supply gaps that occur when demand picks up. Contingent workers are used in both service and manufacturing environments. Retail stores hire contingent workers during the busy holiday sales seasons, and universities hire fixed-term professors to fill in for professors who are on leave.

4. *Adjustable capacity.* A favorite saying with fast-food managers is, "If you've got time to lean, you've got time to clean." During slack periods between meal rushes, employees spend their time conducting supportive tasks such as cleaning, staging food supplies, and replenishing napkin and condiment dispensers. When the peak periods begin, the workers can be reassigned to focus on essential tasks in serving customers. University classrooms are sometimes separated by floor-to-ceiling partitions, which can be removed to create large lecture rooms, then easily repositioned for smaller classes. Sports stadiums may be designed to accommodate multiple sporting and entertainment events in a variety of configurations.

5. *Shared capacity.* Airlines that overbook often can move "extra" passengers to flights on competing airlines. Hotels have similar arrangements with one another to handle overbooking problems. Accounting firms often outsource work during the busy tax season. During periods of excess capacity, an airline may lease its aircraft to other airlines or freight shipping businesses. Universities and colleges may lease classroom space to other institutions that conduct special workshops, programs, and classes.

Charles E. Rotkin/Corbis

Starting up and shutting down a steel mill can be very expensive. They must find an efficient level of operation and level their production for long periods of time using inventory and back orders to absorb demand fluctuations.

Level production strategy

A process where demand is met by altering only the inventory account.

Chase demand strategy

The process where demand is met by matching planned monthly production with forecasted demand, while the inventory account is held constant.

Peak demand strategy

A situation where capacity is varied to meet the highest level of demand at particular times.

General Aggregate Planning Strategies

Aggregate planners may employ several strategies to meet expected customer demand, as summarized in Table 12.2. In a **level production strategy**, demand is met by altering only the inventory account. In a **chase demand strategy**, demand is met by matching planned monthly production with forecasted demand, while the inventory account is held constant. In a **peak demand strategy**, particularly useful in service settings, capacity is varied to meet the highest level of demand at particular times. Planners can also combine aspects of these approaches. The strategy that planners select should depend on the company's competitive priorities and the ways in which its product-service bundles add value for customers.

Table 12.2

Aggregate Planning
Strategies

Strategy	Variables Used	Compatible Competitive Priorities	Environments Where Most Common
Peak Demand Strategy	Undertime (Excess capacity) Subcontracting	Delivery Speed Conformance Quality Flexibility	Emergency Services Easily Obtainable Substitutes Cost of Back Orders High
Level Production Strategy	Inventory/Backlog	Low Cost Design Quality Delivery Speed	Repetitive Manufacturing Continuous Processes Highly Skilled Professionals Cost of Capacity Changes High
Chase Demand Strategy	Workforce Size Overtime/Undertime Subcontracting	Flexibility Design Quality Delivery Speed	Pure Service Job Shops Batch Manufacturing Cost of Inventory High

The Level Production Strategy

In the level production strategy, changes in the inventory account are used to balance mismatches between monthly demand and output. Workforce size, production rates, and subcontracting are held constant. This strategy boosts worker morale, because it eliminates the disruptions in employment associated with changing production rates. From the employer's viewpoint, it also eliminates the cost and paperwork associated with the hiring and laying off of workers, while providing a low-cost, high-quality production system. But other benefits are lost in a level production strategy, including flexibility, the ability to provide a high level of customization, and the ability to always satisfy all a customer's requirements.

The level production strategy is especially desirable in businesses that can afford to hold inventory or carry backlogs. Capital-intensive businesses, such as steel manufacturers and other basic materials producers, are often forced by the nature of their processes to use this strategy. The strategy is also compatible with make-to-stock planning and control systems. For example, you might find a toy manufacturer working at a steady pace year round even though most of their demand occurs in the November–December holiday shopping season. However, many service businesses cannot employ a level production strategy, because most of the value they add cannot be held in inventory or back ordered.

Table 12.3
Fred's Cell Phones Level Production Strategy

Safety Stock Desired	12000
Units/Worker Hour	20
RT Hours/Month	160
RT Wage/Hour	$12
OT Wage/Hour	$18
Subcontract Cost/Unit	$2.50
Hiring Cost/Worker	$500.00
Layoff Cost/Worker	$1,500.00
Inventory Cost/Unit/Month	$0.05
Back-Ordering Cost/Unit/Month	$0.50

Total Cost = $378,525.00

Month	(1) Beginning Inventory	(2) Expected Demand	(3) Production Required	(4) Worker Hires (Layoffs)	(5) Workforce Size	(6) Reg. Time Hours	(7) Overtime Hours	(8) In-House Production	(9) Subcontracted Production	(10) Cumulative Production	(11) Cumulative Demand	(12) Ending Inventory	(13) Hiring Cost	(14) Layoff Cost	(15) Inventory Cost	(16) Backlog Cost	(17) Subcontracting Cost	(18) Reg. Time Cost	(19) Overtime Cost
May	12000	12500	12500	0	10	1600	0	32000	0	44000	12500	31500	$0.00	$0.00	$1,575.00	0	$0.00	$19,200	$0
June	31500	13000	−6500	0	10	1600	0	32000	0	76000	25500	50500	$0.00	$0.00	$2,525.00	0	$0.00	$19,200	$0
July	50500	16000	−22500	0	10	1600	0	32000	0	108000	41500	66500	$0.00	$0.00	$3,325.00	0	$0.00	$19,200	$0
August	66500	35000	−19500	0	10	1600	0	32000	0	140000	76500	63500	$0.00	$0.00	$3,175.00	0	$0.00	$19,200	$0
September	63500	45000	−6500	0	10	1600	0	32000	0	172000	121500	50500	$0.00	$0.00	$2,525.00	0	$0.00	$19,200	$0
October	50500	47500	9000	0	10	1600	0	32000	0	204000	169000	35000	$0.00	$0.00	$1,750.00	0	$0.00	$19,200	$0
November	35000	48000	25000	0	10	1600	0	32000	0	236000	217000	19000	$0.00	$0.00	$950.00	0	$0.00	$19,200	$0
December	19000	52000	45000	0	10	1600	0	32000	0	268000	269000	−1000	$0.00	$0.00	$0.00	500	$0.00	$19,200	$0
January	−1000	13000	26000	0	10	1600	0	32000	0	300000	282000	18000	$0.00	$0.00	$900.00	0	$0.00	$19,200	$0
February	18000	17000	11000	0	10	1600	0	32000	0	332000	299000	33000	$0.00	$0.00	$1,650.00	0	$0.00	$19,200	$0
March	33000	17000	−4000	0	10	1600	0	32000	0	364000	316000	48000	$0.00	$0.00	$2,400.00	0	$0.00	$19,200	$0
April	48000	28000	−8000	0	10	1600	0	32000	0	396000	344000	52000	$0.00	$0.00	$2,600.00	0	$0.00	$19,200	$0
May	52000	30000	−10000	0	10	1600	0	32000	0	428000	374000	54000	$0.00	$0.00	$2,700.00	0	$0.00	$19,200	$0
June	54000	35000	−7000	0	10	1600	0	32000	0	460000	409000	51000	$0.00	$0.00	$2,550.00	0	$0.00	$19,200	$0
July	51000	45000	6000	0	10	1600	0	32000	0	492000	454000	38000	$0.00	$0.00	$1,900.00	0	$0.00	$19,200	$0
August	38000	45000	19000	0	10	1600	0	32000	0	524000	499000	25000	$0.00	$0.00	$1,250.00	0	$0.00	$19,200	$0
September	25000	45000	32000	0	10	1600	0	32000	0	556000	544000	12000	$0.00	$0.00	$600.00	0	$0.00	$19,200	$0
October	12000	43000	43000	0	10	1600	0	32000	0	588000	587000	1000	$0.00	$0.00	$50.00	0	$0.00	$19,200	$0
													$0.00	$0.00	$32,425.00	$500.00	$0.00	$345,600.00	$0.00

Table 12.3 shows an aggregate plan for Fred's cell phone factory. The upper-left-hand corner of the spreadsheet displays a group of fixed production parameters, including the desired safety stock, the production rate in units per worker hour, the number of regular time (RT) hours in a month, the normal wage per hour, and other costs. The main portion of the spreadsheet shows the level production plan and the costs associated with it. At the beginning of May, Fred expects to have 12,000 units in inventory (column 1). Beginning inventory in other months will depend on production and usage after this starting point. The expected demand column (column 2) shows the demand forecasts for cell phones.

Fred's factory has ten workers at the beginning of May (column 5); the size of the workforce in any given month will depend on the amount of firing and hiring that occurs after this point. The number of regular time hours in the month (column 6) is a function of the workforce size. The assumption is that each worker works and is paid for all the regular time hours in the month. Overtime and subcontracted hours (columns 7 and 9) are numeric values plugged in by the aggregate planner.

Monthly in-house production is simply a function of the production rate (units per worker hour) and the number of regular time and overtime labor hours in the month. Ending inventory (column 12) is equal to cumulative production minus cumulative demand (column 11). Notice that monthly production stays the same, while the inventory account (whether beginning or ending) changes from month to month. Costs are a direct function of the aggregate plan. Thus, the last seven columns in Table 12.3 relate directly to the cost parameters in the upper-left-hand corner.

The two graphs presented in Figure 12.4 better explain the level production strategy. Figure 12.4a (graphs monthly demand and monthly production from Fred's cell phone company's aggregate plan that was developed using the level production strategy (in Table 12.3). Notice that demand is quite variable. Because cell phones would not seem to have a seasonal demand pattern, most likely the demand variability arises from promotional strategies of the company. The timing of these promotional strategies could also be related to financial concerns. For example, the promotions might be intended to move demand forward into a fiscal year. Despite the variability in demand, you will notice that the monthly production rate is constant. The graph gives clear meaning to the term "level strategy."

Differences between demand and production in a given month of the level strategy developed in Table 12.3 and illustrated in Figure 12.4a result in changes in the amount of inventory on hand. According to Table 12.3, Fred's company wanted to keep 12,000 units of inventory on hand as safety stock. A level production strategy, starting with ten workers did not achieve this goal. In fact, Table 12.3 shows a production backlog (a negative inventory) of 1,000 units at the beginning of January. While this cannot be seen in Figure 12.4a, it is evident in Figure 12.4b, which plots cumulative production and cumulative demand. In fact, one of the primary benefits of plotting cumulative production and cumulative demand is that comparing the two patterns indicates patterns in inventory growth and depletion. This information can be helpful if the aggregate planner wishes to modify the strategy to achieve target inventory levels, reduce costs, or improve their plan in some other way.

The Chase Demand Strategy

In the chase demand strategy, changes in the use of overtime and the size of the workforce are used to adjust monthly output to match changes in forecasted demand. Inventory levels are held constant. This strategy is suitable for both manufacturing and service operations in which holding inventory or keeping a backlog is costly or

Figure 12.4

Fred's cell phones—level production strategy

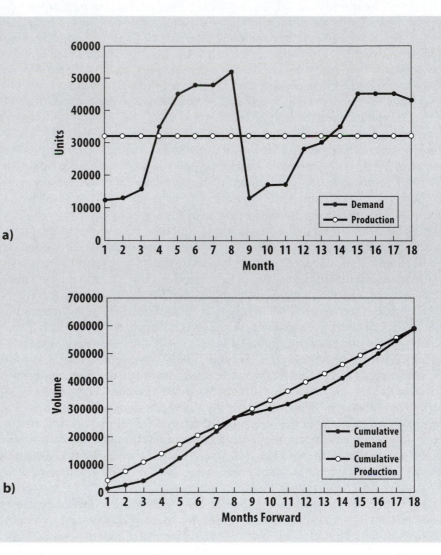

a)

b)

impossible. It is particularly appropriate in operations that produce highly customized product-service bundles, as well as in make-to-order environments in general.

Table 12.4 shows an aggregate plan for Luis's furniture factory. This spreadsheet was generated using the same set of formulas as that used in Table 12.3; however, in this plan, the goal was to match monthly production with monthly demand. Notice that the inventory account does not change from month to month, but the size of the workforce and the amount of overtime vary, depending on forecasted demand. Figure 12.5a shows the close relationship between cumulative production and cumulative demand in a chase demand strategy. Note that the two lines are on top of each other. Also note, in Figure 12.5b, that the lines are parallel. Thus, the inventory level does not change.

The Peak Demand Strategy

In the peak demand strategy, changes in overtime and in the size of the workforce are used to match monthly capacity to the anticipated maximum monthly demand. This

Table 12.4

Luis's Metal Sofa Frames
Chase Demand Strategy

Safety Stock Desired	28
Units/Worker Hour	0.1
RT Hours/Month	160
RT Wage/Hour	$18
OT Wage/Hour	$27
Subcontract Cost/Hour	$30.00
Hiring Cost/Worker	$500.00
Layoff Cost/Worker	$1,500.00
Inventory Cost/Unit/Month	$20.00
Back-Ordering Cost/Unit/Month	$4.00
Maximum Overtime/Month	100 hours

Total Cost = $193,620.00

	(1)	(2)	(3)	(4)	(5)	(6)	(7)	(8)	(9)	(10)	(11)	(12)	(13)	(14)	(15)	(16)	(17)	(18)
Month	Beginning Inventory	Expected Demand	Worker Hires (Layoffs)	Workforce Size	Reg. Time Hours	Overtime Hours	Subcontracted Hours	Total Production	Cumulative Production	Cumulative Demand	Ending Inventory	Hiring Cost	Layoff Cost	Inventory Cost	Backlog Cost	Subcontracting Cost	Reg. Time Cost	Overtime Cost
May	28	75	0	4	640	100	10	75	103	44	28	$0.00	$0.00	$560.00	0	$300.00	$11,520	$2,700
June	28	56	(1)	3	480	80	0	56	159	100	28	$0.00	$1,500.00	$560.00	0	$0.00	$8,640	$2,160
July	28	48	0	3	480	0	0	48	207	148	28	$0.00	$0.00	$560.00	0	$0.00	$8,640	$0
August	28	40	(1)	2	320	80	0	40	247	188	28	$0.00	$1,500.00	$560.00	0	$0.00	$5,760	$2,160
September	28	40	0	2	320	80	0	40	287	228	28	$0.00	$0.00	$560.00	0	$0.00	$5,760	$2,160
October	28	35	0	2	320	30	0	35	322	263	28	$0.00	$0.00	$560.00	0	$0.00	$5,760	$810
November	28	45	0	2	320	100	30	45	367	308	28	$0.00	$0.00	$560.00	0	$900.00	$5,760	$2,700
December	28	100	4	6	960	40	0	100	467	408	28	$2,000.00	$0.00	$560.00	0	$0.00	$17,280	$1,080
January	28	80	(1)	5	800	0	0	80	547	488	28	$0.00	$1,500.00	$560.00	0	$0.00	$14,400	$0
February	28	40	(3)	2	320	80	0	40	587	528	28	$0.00	$4,500.00	$560.00	0	$0.00	$5,760	$2,160
March	28	30	(1)	1	160	100	40	30	617	558	28	$0.00	$1,500.00	$560.00	0	$1,200.00	$2,880	$2,700
April	28	40	1	2	320	80	0	40	657	598	28	$500.00	$0.00	$560.00	0	$0.00	$5,760	$2,160
May	28	35	0	2	320	30	0	35	692	633	28	$0.00	$0.00	$560.00	0	$0.00	$5,760	$810
June	28	40	0	2	320	80	0	40	732	673	28	$0.00	$0.00	$560.00	0	$0.00	$5,760	$2,160
July	28	50	1	3	480	20	0	50	782	723	28	$500.00	$0.00	$560.00	0	$0.00	$8,640	$540
August	28	40	(1)	2	320	80	0	40	822	763	28	$0.00	$1,500.00	$560.00	0	$0.00	$5,760	$2,160
September	28	40	0	2	320	80	0	40	862	803	28	$0.00	$0.00	$560.00	0	$0.00	$5,760	$2,160
October	28	40	0	2	320	80	0	40	902	843	28	$0.00	$0.00	$560.00	0	$0.00	$5,760	$2,160
												$3,000.00	$12,000.00	$10,080.00	$0.00	$2,400.00	$135,360.00	$30,780.00

Service industries can't build inventory for use in a busy period. They must build capacity to meet the peak levels of demand that they feel can be justified over time. If the demand for the Teacups in this photo gets too long, people will not pay to come to the park.

Pascal Le Segretain/Getty Images Inc.

strategy is generally used in service operations in which the immediate availability of customized service is critical. The lonely Maytag repairman just might be needed someday, so he waits patiently for the customer's phone call. So do firefighters, pizza makers, and physicians in an emergency room. In fact, many services are useless unless they are available on demand. Because these types of service cannot be inventoried, the peak demand strategy may be thought of as a special case of the chase demand strategy. (If there is no inventory, then obviously there can be no variation in inventory.) The peak demand strategy is particularly appropriate in operations in which the product-service bundle is highly customized.

Table 12.5 shows an aggregate plan for Cheryl's emergency room; along with Figure 12.6, it illustrates the chase demand strategy. Notice that there is no inventory at any time. (How could emergency health services be inventoried?) Apart from the absence of inventory, however, the arithmetic in this spreadsheet is identical to that in Tables 12.3 and 12.4. While the inventory account does not change, the size of the workforce and the amount of overtime vary from month to month, depending on forecasted demand. In months in which the size of the workforce is more than adequate to meet demand, the emergency room simply carries extra capacity—just in case it is needed. Thus, the extent to which the cumulative curve for patients covered and expected load diverges indicates the cumulative unused capacity. Figure 12.6b illustrates the efficiency of the aggregate plan.

Mixed Strategies

In mixed strategies, changes in subcontracting, the production rate, and the size of both inventory and the workforce are used to adjust monthly output. By manipulating all these variables, planners can often significantly reduce costs, minimize the disruption of operations, enhance customer service, or otherwise improve on an aggregate plan based on a pure strategy. For example, the hiring costs associated with a chase demand strategy might be significantly reduced by holding a small quantity of inventory for a month or two. Or the well-timed use of temporary personnel could offset a significant amount of the inventory holding cost or back-ordering cost associated with a level production plan, with no reduction in quality or customer service. Mixed

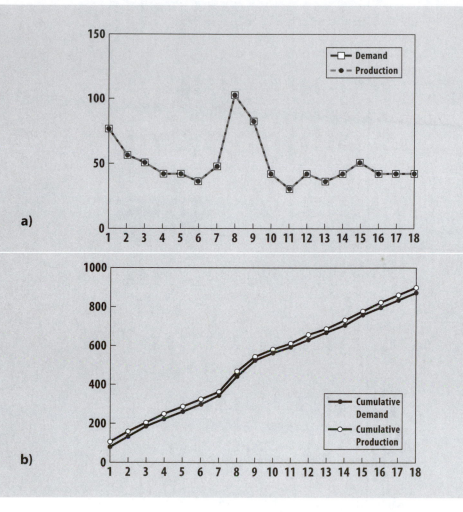

Figure 12.5
(a) Luis's sofa frames—chase demand strategy (b) Luis's metal sofa frames—chase demand strategy

strategies may be used in both manufacturing and service operations in which some form of inventory (perhaps only partially complete) can be held.

Table 12.6 shows a revised aggregate plan for Fred's pager factory. Note that the level production strategy shown in Table 12.3 has been adapted by allowing some variation in hiring, layoffs, and overtime. This plan is not based on a chase demand strategy, because the inventory levels vary. A similar mixed strategy could be used in Luis's furniture factory, if inventory could be built up in periods preceding an anticipated surge in demand. (Even though Luis's company does not make furniture in high volumes, partially completed furniture could be inventoried for later finishing. For example, a sofa frame could be used to make a variety of different sofas.) In periods following a surge in demand, the backlog could be worked off.

As was mentioned earlier, a graph of cumulative demand versus cumulative production can be helpful in determining how to improve an aggregate plan; that is certainly the case with a mixed strategy (see Figure 12.7). The distance between the two curves shows the size of the inventory or production backlog. If the graph for a level production plan shows that the inventory (or backlog) is growing rapidly, then clearly layoffs (or hiring) are likely. Similarly, a rapid change in the slope of the

Table 12.5

Cheryl's Emergency Room Peak Demand Strategy

Total Cost = $4,947,280.00

Patients/Doctor Hour	3
Hours/Month for Staff Doctors	168
Doctor-on-Duty Wage/Hour	$200
Doctor Call Fee per Patient (OT Pay)	$100
Hiring Cost/Doctor	$2,500.00
Layoff Cost/Doctor	$2,500.00
Current Staffing Level (Doctors)	10

Month	(1) Expected Patient Load	(2) Doctor Hires (Layoffs)	(3) Staff Size	(4) Staffed Hours	(5) Staff-Covered Patients	(6) On-Call Patient Load	(7) Monthly Patients Covered	(8) Cumulative Patients Covered	(9) Cumulative Expected Load	(10) Hiring Cost	(11) Layoff Cost	(12) On-Call Cost	(13) Reg. Time Cost
May	5000	0	10	1680	5040	0	5040	5040	5000	$0.00	$0.00	$0.00	$282,240
June	5200	0	10	1680	5040	160	5200	10240	10200	$0.00	$0.00	$16,000.00	$282,240
July	6000	1	11	1848	5544	456	6000	16240	16200	$2,500.00	$0.00	$45,600.00	$310,464
August	5500	0	11	1848	5544	0	5544	21784	21700	$0.00	$0.00	$0.00	$310,464
September	5000	0	11	1848	5544	0	5544	27328	26700	$0.00	$0.00	$0.00	$310,464
October	4000	(3)	8	1344	4032	0	4032	31360	30700	$0.00	$7,500.00	$0.00	$225,792
November	3500	(1)	7	1176	3528	0	3528	34888	34200	$0.00	$2,500.00	$0.00	$197,568
December	5000	3	10	1680	5040	0	5040	39928	39200	$7,500.00	$0.00	$0.00	$282,240
January	5000	0	10	1680	5040	0	5040	44968	44200	$0.00	$0.00	$0.00	$282,240
February	3000	(4)	6	1008	3024	0	3024	47992	47200	$0.00	$10,000.00	$0.00	$169,344
March	3000	0	6	1008	3024	0	3024	51016	50200	$0.00	$0.00	$0.00	$169,344
April	4000	2	8	1344	4032	0	4032	55048	54200	$5,000.00	$0.00	$0.00	$225,792
May	5000	2	10	1680	5040	0	5040	60088	59200	$5,000.00	$0.00	$0.00	$282,240
June	5200	0	10	1680	5040	160	5200	65288	64400	$0.00	$0.00	$16,000.00	$282,240
July	6500	3	13	2184	6552	0	6552	71840	70900	$7,500.00	$0.00	$0.00	$366,912
August	5600	(2)	11	1848	5544	56	5600	77440	76500	$0.00	$5,000.00	$5,600.00	$310,464
September	5100	(1)	10	1680	5040	60	5100	82540	81600	$0.00	$2,500.00	$6,000.00	$282,240
October	4000	(2)	8	1344	4032	0	4032	86572	85600	$0.00	$5,000.00	$0.00	$225,792
										$27,500.00	$32,500.00	$89,200.00	$4,798,080.00

Figure 12.6
Cheryl's ER—peak
demand strategy

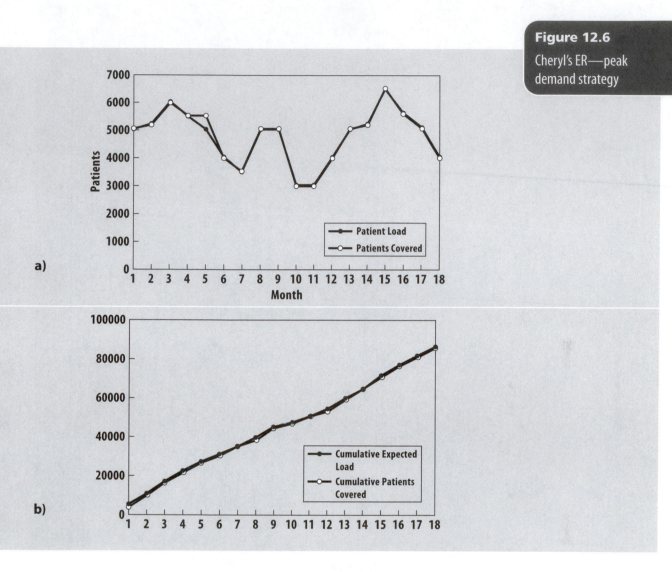

curve for a chase demand plan indicates a period in which inventory might be used to significantly reduce costs. Inventory is selectively used to level out significant changes in the slope of the cumulative production line. You will notice that by using a mixed strategy, Fred can meet his safety stock requirement (of keeping 12,000 units on hand) while keeping production almost level and costs slightly higher.

Aggregate Planning Methods

Optimizing Methods

Optimizing methods, used to minimize the cost of an aggregate plan, include:

▶ Linear decision rule (LDR) models, in which the costs of the aggregate plan are represented in the form of quadratic equations, and differential calculus is used to find the lowest-cost plan

Table 12.6
Fred's Pagers Mixed Strategy

Safety Stock Desired	12000
Units/Worker Hour	20
RT Hours/Month	160
RT Wage/Hour	$12
OT Wage/Hour	$18
Subcontract Cost/Unit	$2.50
Hiring Cost/Worker	$500.00
Layoff Cost/Worker	$1,500.00
Inventory Cost/Unit/Month	$0.05
Back-Ordering Cost/Unit/Month	$0.50
Beginning Workforce Size	10

Total Cost = $400,295.00

Month	(1) Beginning Inventory	(2) Expected Demand	(3) Production Required	(4) Worker Hires (Layoffs)	(5) Workforce Size	(6) Reg. Time Hours	(7) Overtime Hours	(8) In-House Production	(9) Subcontracted Production	(10) Cumulative Production	(11) Cumulative Demand	(12) Ending Inventory	(13) Hiring Cost	(14) Layoff Cost	(15) Inventory Cost	(16) Backlog Cost	(17) Subcontracting Cost	(18) Reg. Time Cost	(19) Overtime Cost
May	12000	12500	12500	1	11	1760	0	35200	0	47200	12500	34700	$500.00	$0.00	$1,735.00	0	$0.00	$21,120	$0
June	34700	13000	−9700	0	11	1760	0	35200	0	82400	25500	56900	$0.00	$0.00	$2,845.00	0	$0.00	$21,120	$0
July	56900	16000	−28900	−1	10	1600	0	32000	0	114400	41500	72900	$0.00	$1,500.00	$3,645.00	0	$0.00	$19,200	$0
August	72900	35000	−25900	0	10	1600	0	32000	0	146400	76500	69900	$0.00	$0.00	$3,495.00	0	$0.00	$19,200	$0
September	69900	45000	−12900	0	10	1600	0	32000	0	178400	121500	56900	$0.00	$0.00	$2,845.00	0	$0.00	$19,200	$0
October	56900	47500	2600	0	10	1600	0	32000	0	210400	169000	41400	$0.00	$0.00	$2,070.00	0	$0.00	$19,200	$0
November	41400	48000	18600	1	11	1760	0	35200	0	245600	217000	28600	$500.00	$0.00	$1,430.00	0	$0.00	$21,120	$0
December	28600	52000	35400	0	11	1760	10	35400	0	281000	269000	12000	$0.00	$0.00	$600.00	0	$0.00	$21,120	$180
January	12000	13000	13000	−1	10	1600	0	32000	0	313000	282000	31000	$0.00	$1,500.00	$1,550.00	0	$0.00	$19,200	$0
February	31000	17000	−2000	0	10	1600	0	32000	0	345000	299000	46000	$0.00	$0.00	$2,300.00	0	$0.00	$19,200	$0
March	46000	17000	−17000	0	10	1600	0	32000	0	377000	316000	61000	$0.00	$0.00	$3,050.00	0	$0.00	$19,200	$0
April	61000	28000	−21000	0	10	1600	0	32000	0	409000	344000	65000	$0.00	$0.00	$3,250.00	0	$0.00	$19,200	$0
May	65000	30000	−23000	−1	9	1440	30	29400	0	438400	374000	64400	$0.00	$1,500.00	$3,220.00	0	$0.00	$17,280	$540
June	64400	35000	−17400	0	9	1440	60	30000	0	468400	409000	59400	$0.00	$0.00	$2,970.00	0	$0.00	$17,280	$1,080
July	59400	45000	−2400	0	9	1440	60	30000	0	498400	454000	44400	$0.00	$0.00	$2,220.00	0	$0.00	$17,280	$1,080
August	44400	45000	12600	0	9	1440	0	28800	0	527200	499000	28200	$0.00	$0.00	$1,410.00	0	$0.00	$17,280	$0
September	28200	45000	28800	2	11	1760	60	36400	0	563600	544000	19600	$1,000.00	$0.00	$980.00	0	$0.00	$21,120	$1,080
October	19600	43000	35400	0	11	1760	10	35400	0	599000	587000	12000	$0.00	$0.00	$600.00	0	$0.00	$21,120	$180
													$2,000.00	$4,500.00	$40,215.00	$0.00	$0.00	$349,440.00	$4,140.00

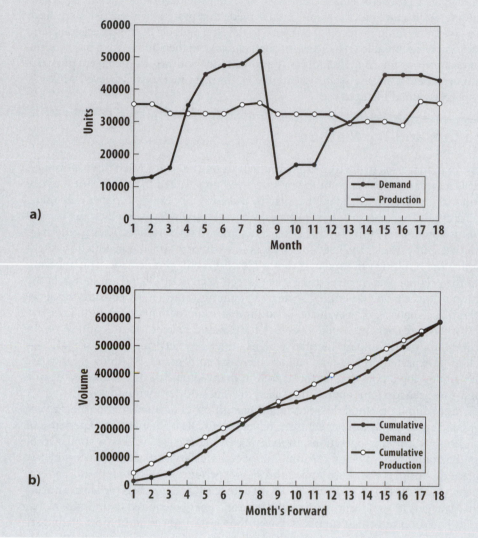

Figure 12.7
Fred's cell phones—
mixed strategy

- Search decision rule (SDR) models, which use a mathematical search process to find the best plan among thousands of possible alternatives

- Linear programming (LP) models, which use algebra to build and optimize mathematical models of the aggregate planning problem

While they may sound impressive, these optimizing methods are optimizing only to the extent that they fit the real situation. Because the aggregate plan is based on relatively imprecise forecasts and is updated regularly, many managers question the practical value of so-called optimal plans.

Methods that Model Manager Decisions

The management coefficients method (MCM) is another technique used in aggregate planning. In this method, the assumption is made that past managerial decisions have been good, and multiple regression is used to develop a model of those decisions. The regression weights (called management coefficients) can then be used as a basis for future decisions or for an evaluation of the consistency with which managers pursue a given aggregate planning strategy. Like the optimizing methods, however, MCM is complicated and difficult to use.

The Cut-and-Try Method

How do managers actually come up with their aggregate plans? Most often, seasoned managers rely on experience, or the pure strategy most suited to their business to develop a trial plan and then adapt that plan by tinkering. For example, paper pulp manufacturers and toy manufacturers may prefer a level strategy based on their use of continuous flow and repetitive processes to make standardized products. They would start with that, but consider the need for changes in workforce size and production rate if they felt the resulting variation in inventory levels became problematic. The tinkering with the original plan involves using spreadsheets such as those that are shown in the section of this chapter describing aggregate planning strategies. By considering alternative plans, managers can evaluate the cost implications of their decisions to hire, lay-off workers, use overtime, build inventory for demand in later months, and so on. In addition, they can compare alternative plans under a variety of demand scenarios—such as unexpected declines and sudden increases in demand. By doing so, they are likely to develop a plan that performs well in many situations and is acceptable in a worst-case scenario. This approach is called the "cut-and-try method."

The cut and try method does not sound scientific, but for many reasons it is a very workable approach. It can benefit from reliance on years of managerial experience in planning and running operations. In many cases, managers have seen a similar forecasted demand pattern before. No amount of technical sophistication can completely replace the insights they have gained through experience with that demand pattern. Furthermore, the aggregate plan is based on a forecast, and forecasts are always uncertain. Managers are not likely to invest the time and energy required to optimize a plan that is based on uncertain numbers. Given the level of uncertainty most businesses face as they look forward 6 to 18 months, a plan that performs well in many situations and has an acceptable worst-case outcome may be better than a plan that minimizes costs based on the assumption that demand forecasts are correct.

What is more, the aggregate plan is typically updated on a monthly basis. Forecasts will change as more information becomes available; inventory levels will change based on actual events; personnel decisions will change the composition of the workforce. Because of the dynamic nature of the value-adding system, managers recognize the necessity of taking an adaptive approach to aggregate planning. They are not overly concerned with developing an optimal plan based on the data available at a given time. Finally, an "optimal" solution often has a narrow focus that renders it problematic. For example, most optimizing methods attempt to minimize the costs associated with an aggregate plan. Sometimes that requires a lot of hiring and firing—clearly not an ideal plan from the standpoint of worker morale. Minimizing the costs of an aggregate plan may also reduce the company's ability to respond effectively to customer expectations based on competitive priorities such as quality and flexibility.

E-Commerce, Supply Chain Management, and Aggregate Planning

Supply chain management and e-commerce systems may have a significant bearing on aggregate planning practices. In particular, rather than sending individual purchase orders each time material is required, managers commonly work with suppliers on the basis of long-term contracts. Many firms now establish bulk capacity agreements with their suppliers. Rather than establishing capacity levels on the basis of expected demand, the available capacity levels can be established on the basis of the customer's contractually stated requirements for capacity. Suppliers then use this capacity as demand occurs, often without any purchase orders, by simply producing what is called for by the customer's electronically accessible production schedules. Suppliers are responsible for handling the scheduling details and ensuring that there's adequate capacity to provide the needed materials when required by their customers. Customers, likewise, are responsible if there's a lack of balance between the amount of capacity they reserved and the amount they have used. These arrangements provide aggregate planners with much better knowledge of the intermediate-range demand to which their aggregate plan must respond, resulting in more effective and stable plans.

E-commerce requires a lot more than electronic connections between a customer and supplier. It takes a high degree of trust for a supplier to establish capacity levels (for example, by hiring workers) and commit its capacity to a customer, without any formal orders. It also takes trust for a customer to enter bulk capacity agreements and give up the detailed scheduling of component delivery. The relationship between companies becomes broader than one based on business transactions alone—thus relationship marketing takes on a significant role for the supplier, and vendor development becomes important to the customer. The value provided by the supplier is much greater than that of the physical product: It includes the service of synchronizing deliveries and fitting in with the customer's system. For this value to be fully developed and the connection between the two value-adding systems to become seamless, some level of integration between the vendor's and customer's information systems is generally required.

SUMMARY

The aggregate plan is an intermediate-range plan that indicates the available capacity for a family of product-service bundles. This kind of planning is an important function of senior managers, such as plant managers, group vice-presidents, and product managers. If it is done well, there should be sufficient money in budgets, adequate arrangements for subcontracting, and a large enough workforce to meet customer expectations, even at busy times. If the aggregate plan does not provide a way to meet a rise in demand, operations managers will be limited in their ability to respond. As a result, customers may experience unusual delays in service, or cost and quality may become problematic. Similarly, if the aggregate plan does not provide a way to adjust for periods of unusually low demand, excess capacity, and significant economic loss could be the result. The operations management tasks described in the following chapters cannot be effectively carried out without some sort of aggregate planning.

To create an aggregate plan, companies must rely on forecasts. The aggregate plan determines how capacity will be adjusted in response to forecasted variations in demand. Adjusting capacity in the intermediate term may mean changing the size of the workforce, planning for overtime, subcontracting some tasks, or varying the level of inventories or backlogs. Typically, senior managers will revise the aggregate plan once a month based on their experience and a trial-and-error technique referred to as the cut and try method.

Managers generally prefer different aggregate planning strategies for different business environments. For instance, in service businesses that cannot hold inventory or in businesses in which inventory is expensive to hold, does not keep well, or becomes obsolete quickly, planners are likely to prefer a chase demand strategy. In each period they will try to provide sufficient capacity to meet demand. In other environments, perhaps those in which skilled labor is difficult to obtain and labor agreements limit overtime, managers will prefer a level production strategy, in which changes in inventory or backlog levels are used to even out differences between capacity and demand. In still other cases, economic criteria, competitive priorities, or customer service objectives will require some combination of the chase demand and level production strategies. These combination strategies are called mixed strategies.

Recent developments, including movement toward supply chain management and e-commerce have had an impact on aggregate planning practices. Because of these trends, information used by aggregate planners is likely to be superior to forecasted demand values that are generated within the company. Thus, the aggregate plans more effectively match supply to demand and need less revision.

KEY TERMS

Aggregate plan, 534
Assemble-to-order, 539
Backlog, 539
Chase demand strategy, 542

Level production strategy, 542
Make-to-order, 539
Make-to-stock, 538
Master schedule, 534

Peak demand strategy, 542
Rolling planning horizon, 535

SOLVED PROBLEMS

1. A local plumbing and heating company estimates the cost of hiring and training a new plumber to be $4200. They also feel that to lay someone off would cost an estimated $2200. They pay workers $20 per hour and schedule them to work 160 hours per month. Given they see an increase in demand expected over the next few months, at a minimum, how many months should they plan on keeping a new hire rather than simply working overtime with the current staff?

Solution:

The combined "one time" costs of hiring and then firing a plumber would be $4200 + $2200 = $6400.

Overtime would be $1.5 \times \$20/\text{hour} = \$30$ per hour or $10/hour greater than the regular rate of $20/hour.

Therefore, one more plumber would save 160 hours/month $\times$ $10/hour = $1600 per month.

If the one-time costs of saving $1600/month are $6400, then $6400 / $1600 = 4 months at a minimum. If they can expect to keep the new hire busily employed for more than 4 months, then it would be better to hire him or her. If not, working overtime with existing staff would be advantageous.

2. A law office has five associates supervised by a senior partner with a combined capacity of up to 800 billable hours a month. The associates are paid a monthly salary of $6400. When their billable hours exceed 160 hours per month, they receive a bonus of $60 per hour for the extra hours. To avoid "burnout," associates are expected not to exceed 300 billable hours in any one month, nor to work more than 200 billable hours per month in 2 successive months. The senior partner can hire a new attorney for what she believes to be a one-time cost of $25,000. She estimates the cost of a

downsizing to be $35,000 in severance pay, as well as long-term damage to the firm's reputation. Members of the firm have an ad hoc relationship with several professors at a local law school; the professors will consult with the firm on a case-by-case basis at an hourly rate of $250 per billable hour. Given current cases and an estimate of work expected in the future, the demand for billable hours for the associates over the next 9 months can be estimated as follows:

Month	1	2	3	4	5	6	7	8	9
Billable Hours	815	680	690	1100	1400	500	680	800	800

a) What should the firm's capacity plan for the next few months look like?

b) What would be the cost of maintaining the current staff of five and "making do" with bonuses and ad hoc consultation with the law professors?

c) Would maintaining the staff at its present level be a good idea? Why or why not?

d) Are there issues in this problem that are not captured by the cost information?

e) What complications would the firm encounter in "disaggregating" this plan?

Solution:

a) The aggregate capacity plan might look like the following:

Month	Monthly Reqts. (Billable Hours)	Associates	Reg. Billable Hours	Bonus Hours	Subcontracting "Consultants"
1	815	5	800	15	0
2	680	5	800	0	0
3	690	5	800	0	0
4	1100	5	800	200	100
5	1400	5	800	600	0
6	500	5	800	0	0
7	680	5	800	0	0
8	800	5	800	0	0
9	800	5	800	0	0

b) The cost would include significant bonuses in the fourth and fifth month. Consultants should be hired in the fourth month so as not to exceed 200 hours of billable hours per associate (160 hours of regular hours plus 40 bonus hours) for 2 straight months. The high cost of consultants relative to bonus hours and the limit on consecutive months makes it cheaper to use 100 consultant hours in month 4 and save the higher limit on bonus hours for month 5 when there is greater demand to satisfy. The costs would be $288,000 in regular salary, $48,900 in bonus hours, and $25,000 in consultant's fees for a total of $361,900.

c) Yes, unless there was a sustained increase in demand, the cost of hiring a new associate and then possibly downsizing when demand returns to normal is very high compared to paying bonus hours or hiring the occasional consultant.

d) Yes. For one thing, the level of productivity is assumed to be the same for regular, bonus, and consultant billable hours. It also assumes that all associates are interchangeable and that the forecasts are accurate. The further these assumptions are from the truth, the further this plan will be from reality.

e) Will the actual mix of cases and the load they place on the resources of the firm match the specific resource capacities of the firm when the work is actually assigned to associates? The extent to which they don't will be a problem. For example, suppose most of the cases in the fifth month were litigation cases and very few involved probate or tax situations. The "mix" might not line up with the availability of lawyers by specialty.

3. Review the situation of the law office described in problem 2. Assume for the sake of simplicity that the estimated demand for clerical staff hours is the same as the demand for associate's billable hours. However, no more than 40 hours of overtime is allowed in a month. There are currently five clerical staff on the payroll and assume that the hiring

costs are estimated to be $500 and firing costs for the clerical staff are estimated at $1000. Overtime is 150% of the base rate of $16 per hour, while the cost of hiring temporary workers from a local agency is 175%of the base rate.

a) What should the firm's capacity plan for clerical work over the next few months look like?

b) What would be the cost of the plan described in (a)? (Assume the clerical workers will be paid for a minimum of 160 hours per month.)

c) Would maintaining the clerical staff at its current level be a good idea? Why or why not?

d) What complications would the firm encounter in "disaggregating" this plan?

Solution:

a)

Month	Monthly Reqts. (Clerical Hours)	Clerical Staff	Regular-Time Hours	Overtime Hours	Temporary Worker Hours
1	815	5	800	15	0
2	680	4	640	40	0
3	690	4	640	50	0
4	1100	7	1100	0	0
5	1400	7	1120	280	0
6	500	3	480	20	0
7	680	4	640	40	0
8	800	5	800	0	0
9	800	5	800	0	0

b) $112,640 for regular salary (with 7 workers in month 7 the clerical force must be compensated for 7×160=1120 hours), $10,680 in overtime, $2500 to hire new staff, and $5000 to lay people off.

c) The relatively low cost of hiring and firing the clerical staff makes it appear more economical to hire and fire as needed to avoid overtime, unneeded workers, or hiring temporary workers from and agency. The combined $1500 hiring and firing costs makes layoffs of only a month worthwhile in order to avoid paying the $2560 monthly wage (160 hours × $16 per hour) to someone who's labor is not needed. Hiring an additional person to avoid overtime saves

$1280 per month (160 hours × $8 per hour overtime premium) therefore the combined hiring and firing costs are more than offset when someone is needed for 2 or more months.

d) Just as with the professional staff, the level of productivity is assumed to be the same for regular, overtime, and temporary worker hours. It also assumes that all staff members are cross-trained and interchangeable. Some may be better or worse at any given activity, which may make it hard to assign tasks within the aggregate totals planned. The further these assumptions are from the truth, the further this plan will be from reality.

4. Assume the following about a furniture factory much like Luis's:

▶ Aggregate planning is usually done in terms of direct labor hours.

▶ Each of the firm's workers can provide 200 hours of regular-time direct labor per month for a salary of $2000 per month.

▶ Overtime is limited to 50 hours per worker per month, at a cost of $15 per hour.

▶ The factory currently employs two workers, and can hire additional workers for an esti-mated $1000 hiring expense per worker. Layoffs are estimated to cost $500 per worker.

▶ Inventory is considered to cost $5 per hour's worth of material carried over per month, while back orders are assumed to cost $25 per hour's worth of demand not met each month. (Both inventory and back order charges are based on the ending balance for each month.)

▶ Subcontracting is unlimited at a cost of $20 per hour.

Expected demand over the next 6 months, in terms of total hours required each month, is as follows:

Month	1	2	3	4	5	6	7	8	9	10
Demand	200	600	200	1000	1000	200	200	800	800	1000

a) Given a constant workforce (no overtime or subcontracting) and the production rate required by the situation just described, how many workers would be needed each month to just satisfy demand over the next 6 months (i.e., ending inventory in month 10 = 0)? What would be the cost of this plan?

b) What would be the total cost over the next 10 months of hiring and firing as needed in order to use only regular time and avoid overtime, sub-contracting, and inventory or back-order costs?

c) What would be the lowest total costs for the next 10 months if the factory could not hire or fire any workers, and no back orders were allowed? (Carrying inventory is permissible.)

Solution:

a) The average demand is for 600 hours per month, therefore three workers could use regular time and satisfy demand. The costs would be $60,000 for regular time wages and $21,000 in inventory carrying costs.

Month	1	2	3	4	5	6	7	8	9	10
Demand	200	600	200	1000	1000	200	200	800	800	1000
RTProduction	600	600	600	600	600	600	600	600	600	600
Inventory	400	400	800	400	0	400	800	600	400	0
Inv. Cost	$2000	$2000	$4000	$2000	0	$2000	$4000	$3000	$2000	0

Total = $81,000

b) The costs would be $60,000 for regular time wages and $13,500 in hiring and firing costs.

Month	1	2	3	4	5	6	7	8	9	10
Demand	200	600	200	1000	1000	200	200	800	800	1000
RT Production	200	600	200	1000	1000	200	200	800	800	1000
Workforce	1	3	1	5	5	1	1	4	4	5
Hiring/Firing Cost	$500	$2000	$1000	$4000	0	$2000	0	$3000	0	$1000

Total = $73,500

c) The costs would be $40,000 for regular time
    wages, $5000 in inventory carrying costs, $6000

in overtime costs, and $32,000 in subcontract-
ing costs.

Month	1	2	3	4	5	6	7	8	9	10
Demand	200	600	200	1000	1000	200	200	800	800	1000
RT Production	400	400	400	400	400	400	400	400	400	400
Workforce	2	2	2	2	2	2	2	2	2	2
Inventory	200	0	200	0	0	200	400	0	0	0
Inv. Cost	$1000	0	$1000	0	0	$1000	$2000	0	0	0
Overtime	0	0	0	100	100	0	0	0	100	100
OT Cost	0	0	0	$1500	$1500	0	0	0	$1500	$1500
Subcontract	0	0	0	300	500	0	0	0	300	500
SC Cost	0	0	0	$6000	$10000	0	0	0	$6000	$10000

Total = $83,000

DISCUSSION QUESTIONS

1. What aggregate planning strategies would be appropriate for a police department? For an automotive assembly plant? A steel mill? A law office? For J. C. Penney during the Christmas rush? For McDonald's?

2. How does the level of labor skill required by a process relate to its capital intensity? What do those factors have to do with the way in which managers develop an aggregate plan for the process?

3. In Luis's furniture factory, there is a cost to hiring or laying off an employee. Can you explain what that cost represents? How might an accountant estimate the cost?

4. When is holding inventory an option and when is it not an option? Could Luis use inventory as a variable in his aggregate planning? Could Cheryl? Why or why not?

5. What are the "pure" strategies for aggregate planning? When would you be willing to use them?

6. What are some of the shortcomings of the more heavily quantitative approaches to aggregate planning? What are the advantages?

7. Refer to the planning hierarchy illustrated in Figure 12.3. How far into the future should McDonald's attempt to look on each of the three levels of planning? What about General Motors? The college or university you attend? Major League baseball?

8. What would be the common planning unit in the following businesses: a dry cleaner, a photo processor, a restaurant, a furniture factory, a dentist's office, and a university? How about a lumber mill? A quarry? A farm?

9. Why aren't the mathematical models discussed in the chapter used much in the real world? What can be said about an "optimal" answer to one of those models?

10. How does aggregate planning for Tom's airline affect the marketing and finance functions? Would the issues be the same in Fred's pager factory?

11. What is the difference between an optimal solution to an aggregate planning problem and a spreadsheet or seat-of-the-pants solution?

12. Assume you are the director of nursing in a hospital like Cheryl's. Describe your aggregate planning

process. How would it differ from that of the manager of a rental car agency? Of a lawn-care service?

13. Managers in the steel industry try harder than managers in other industries to achieve level output; why? Why do managers of utilities tend to focus on peak demand?

14. How does a supplier benefit by becoming part of a customer's aggregate planning process? Can you explain the benefits in terms of the relationship between Tom's airline and the companies that supply jet fuel? What about Luis's furniture factory and the companies that supply the factory with lumber? Would the relationship between the factory and the paint and stain suppliers be different? If so, how?

PROBLEMS

1. The pizza store down the road from your school has very seasonal demand. Hiring and training a pizza maker can cost as much as $1000 while letting them go is estimated to cost the store $800 in severance costs. They pay the pizza makers a weekly salary of $400 per week. Overtime comes into the picture after 40 hours and is $15 per hour with a limit of 20 hours per week. They are currently using four pizza makers and can either require each of the four to work 10 hours of overtime each week or hire a fifth pizza maker. How long they need to employ the fifth pizza maker to justify hiring and firing costs?

2. Using the information in question 1, assume the demand for pizza makers over the next 12 months is shown below in terms of labor hours required:

   a) On average, how many pizza makers are required?

   b) Would maintaining the exact average number of pizza makers through out the year be a feasible idea? If so, would it be a good idea?

   c) What would be the cost of maintaining the exact average number of pizza makers through

out the year (assume 4 weeks are in every month)?

3. Again using the data from problems 1 and 2:

   a) What would be the cost of hiring and firing pizza makers such that the capacity and demand were matched each month?

   b) What are the benefits of such a plan? The draw backs?

   c) Would you support deviating from this plan in October and March? How?

4. A local cable TV office schedules repair calls and new installations for its field crews. A typical repair call takes 1 hour of labor, while an installation takes 2 hours in new construction and 4 hours in existing buildings. Being in a college town, a large part of the repair and existing building installation business is seasonal. Assume a field worker logs 120 hours per month (significant time is spent in transit between sites). The number of calls over the next 12 months is projected as follows:

For Problem 2

Month	Aug	Sept	Oct	Nov	Dec	Jan	Feb	Mar	Apr	May	Jun	Jul
Hours	480	960	1440	1280	1280	480	960	800	960	320	320	320

Call Type/ Month	Nov	Dec	Jan	Feb	Mar	Apr	May	Jun	Jul	Aug	Sep	Oct
Service	200	100	300	80	80	80	400	100	100	300	110	110
New Construction Installation	25	15	5	10	10	10	20	30	30	50	60	80
Existing Building Installation	50	50	500	125	125	125	200	500	100	550	400	100

a) Assume the number of crews was flexible, how many field crew workers would be required each month?

b) If the number was not flexible, how many would need be hired to meet peak demand. Is this economically feasible? Why or why not?

c) What suggestions would you offer the service manager?

5. A small carpet manufacturer makes three styles of carpeting in a variety of colors. The rate at which the mill can produce the carpeting is based upon the cut and pile density of the style. A standard cut can be produced at 2000 square yards per hour. A heavy industrial cut can be produced at a rate of 800 yards per hour while thicker plush cut for residential use slows the mill to 600 yards per hour. Marketing has forecast the overall demand for the next 9 months by style:

	Month								
Style	1	2	3	4	5	6	7	8	9
Heavy Industrial	150,000	200,000	200,000	250,000	250,000	225,000	173,000	150,000	150,000
Standard	200,000	250,000	250,000	300,000	252,000	250,000	225,000	225,000	200,000
Plush	75,000	75,000	85,000	120,000	110,000	75,000	75,000	75,000	75,000

Assume the mills run three shifts per day in order to spread out fixed costs. Also assume a monthly inventory carrying cost estimate of $200 per month for each hour's equivalent output placed into inventory or on a back order list.

a) What would be the aggregated demand for monthly production hours over the next 9 months?

b) What will be the inventory position and carrying costs associated with a schedule that includes 20 production days each month?

c) How many production days will be required to just meet demand over the planning horizon? What would be the inventory carrying costs of this plan?

d) If operating the plant beyond 20 days per month means a $50,000 per day overtime premium above the normal daily operating costs, would you still schedule overtime to meet demand in this case?

6. The local appliance superstore offers free delivery and installation within a 30-mile radius of the store. Managers have asked you to set up a process for planning the capacity of the store's delivery and installation resources over the next few months. Currently, two truck crews work out of the store. Considering the cost of labor and fuel and lease payments on the trucks, managers estimate the cost of each two-person crew to be $1600 per week. The crews typically work a 40-hour week, but when needed can work an extra 20 hours a week at

an hourly overtime rate of $60 per hour. Assume for planning purpose that there are 4 weeks in every month. Managers can lease a new truck and hire an additional crew for an up-front cost of $1500; the cost of ending the lease early and laying off the crew is estimated at $2000. Alternatively, managers can hire a trucking company to do the overflow deliveries and installations. In this case, capacity is unlimited, but the cost is a flat $100 per hour, including all labor and equipment costs.

Because all deliveries and installations must be completed on demand, back orders are not an option. Deliveries usually average an hour; the time for installations varies, depending on the item to be installed. Stoves and refrigerators take an additional half-hour beyond the hour to deliver them, while satellite dishes require 2 additional hours, and dishwashers, 3 additional hours.

Expected demand over the next few months is as follows:

| | Month | | | | | | | | | | | |
Appliance	1	2	3	4	5	6	7	8	9	10	11	12
Refrigerators	125	140	140	90	80	80	110	170	220	500	100	70
Stoves	30	30	30	20	20	30	40	40	120	20	20	30
Satellite Dish	12	10	10	30	30	40	40	50	50	60	60	100
Dishwasher	45	45	40	40	40	40	40	40	40	30	30	30

a) What would be the cost of sticking with just two crews and "making do" with overtime and ad hoc use of subcontractors?

b) Would maintaining the workforce at the current level be a good idea? Why or why not? Should managers hire a new crew? Support your answer with cost information.

c) What should a more reasonable plan for the store's capacity over the next few months look like? How long must they keep a crew on the payroll to justify avoiding overtime? Subcontracting?

d) What would the plan look like if they insisted all work be done with regular crews on regular time (no overtime or subcontracting)?

CHALLENGE PROBLEMS

1. A local hospital attempts to plan nursing staff levels for the coming year according to the forecasted level of bed occupancy. The following parameters are assumed to be true:

▶ A patient in intensive care utilizes an average of 8 hours of nursing capacity per 24-hour day. (Another way of putting this is to say that a nurse in the intensive care unit can support up to three patients at the same time.)

▶ A patient in pediatrics utilizes an average of 6 hours of nursing capacity during a 24-hour day.

▶ A patient (with child) in maternity requires an average of 8 hours of nursing capacity during a 24-hour day.

▶ A patient in neo-natal intensive care utilizes an average of 12 hours of nursing capacity during a 24-hour day.

▶ A patient in the general ward utilizes an average of 6 hours of nursing capacity during a 24-hour day.

▶ A full-time nurse is scheduled for a maximum of 160 hours per month, with a salary of $3200 per month. (The base rate becomes $20 per hour when the nurse is scheduled to monthly capacity.) Overtime of up to 50 hours per month can be required, at one-and-a-half times the base rate. Nurses who are not scheduled for a full 160 hours are still paid the entire monthly salary.

▶ Nursing "temps" may be hired on a month-to-month basis at a rate of $50 per hour.

▶ The hospital estimates the cost of hiring a new nurse (a one-time expense) to be $3500. When nurses are laid off, the hospital sustains a one-time cost of approximately $3500 for severance pay and increases in unemployment insurance.

▶ They currently have 90 nurses on staff.

▶ Over the next 12 months, the hospital anticipates the following bed occupancy levels, in bed/days (e.g., twenty beds, each occupied for 15 days, would total 300 bed/days):

Level	Month											
	1	2	3	4	5	6	7	8	9	10	11	12
General Ward	1250	1400	1400	1000	800	800	1400	1700	2200	500	500	800
Pediatrics	300	300	300	250	250	350	400	400	600	300	300	300
ICU	125	100	100	110	120	120	130	130	100	100	100	100
Neonatal ICU	45	45	40	40	40	40	40	40	40	30	30	30
Maternity	150	250	350	500	280	250	200	200	150	150	110	250

Use a spreadsheet to aggregate the demand for nursing services.

a) What would be the cost of maintaining a level workforce over the next 12 months, without using subcontracting (a form of peak demand strategy)? Could the cost be reduced with subcontracting? What intangibles would be included in this plan?

b) What would be the cost of chasing demand, using no overtime or subcontracting? What intangibles would be assumed in such a plan?

c) How would your answers to questions a–c change if the cost of hiring temporary nurses went down to $30 per hour? To $25 per hour? How would your answers change if the cost of hiring and firing rose to $5500 and $4500, respectively?

2. Assume that the following statements describe the activity at the RedHawk Soda Company's bottling plant:

▶ Aggregate planning is usually done in terms of product gallons.

▶ Each of the plant's bottling lines is normally available for approximately 320 hours per month (in two shifts, for 5 days per week). Each line fills 1200 gallons of product per hour. The cost of labor and variable overhead is approximately $300 per hour per line.

▶ Each month, the plant must commit to either shutting down or operating with a one- or two-shift operation. The first- or second-shift crew can be laid off or called back at an estimated one-time cost of $10,000. The cost of temporarily "mothballing" a single line (when no production is scheduled for the month) is estimated to be $25,000. The cost of taking a whole line out of "mothballs" is the same.

- Overtime is limited to 80 hours per line per month, at a cost of $450 per hour (direct labor plus variable overhead).

- The factory is currently operating four lines. Managers can subcontract with a local brewery on a month-by-month basis when demand exceeds current capacity. The charge is $600 per hour on a line with the same capacity as the factory's soft drink lines.

- Inventory is considered to cost $15 per thousand gallons per month for material that is carried over from one month to the next. Back orders are assumed to cost $150 per thousand gallons of demand. Backorders from the plant cause retailers' inventory to fall to uncomfortably low levels and may cause stockouts. Both inventory and back order charges are based on the month's ending balance.

- Subcontracting is limited to 120 line hours per month.

- Demand over the next 6 months, in terms of total number of UNITS required each month for the three flavors and three package sizes, is as follows:

	Month					
Product	1	2	3	4	5	6
Red Hawk Soda (12 oz. Can)	500,000	1,000,000	1,000,000	500,000	450,000	400,000
Red Hawk Soda (16 oz. Bottle)	1,000,000	1,500,000	1,600,000	1,000,000	800,000	700,000
Red Hawk Soda (64 oz. Bottle)	300,000	350,000	350,000	300,000	300,000	250,000
Hawk-sa-Cola (12 oz. Can)	700,000	750,000	850,000	700,000	700,000	600,000
Hawk-sa-Cola (16 oz. Bottle)	1,000,000	1,000,000	2,000,000	1,000,000	800,000	780,000
Hawk-sa-Cola (64 oz. Bottle)	400,000	500,000	650,000	500,000	400,000	350,000
Hawk-sa-Lite (12 oz. Can)	300,000	300,000	350,000	300,000	300,000	250,000
Hawk-sa-Lite (16 oz. Bottle)	750,000	750,000	750,000	750,000	450,000	350,000
Hawk-sa-Lite (64 oz. Bottle)	125,000	125,000	125,000	125,000	85,000	65,000

Use a spreadsheet to aggregate the demand for soda.

a) What would be the cost of maintaining level production over the next 6 months, without using subcontracting?

b) What would be the cost of chasing demand, with no inventory or back orders allowed?

c) What would be the advantage of seeing a forecast that extends beyond month 6?

d) What intangibles are not captured in this assessment of the Redhawk Soda Company?

3. Assume you are assigned to help do aggregate planning for a small plant in another division of Fred's Company. You are to use direct labor hours as a unit of aggregate demand/capacity. For now, they hand assemble two products with the following parameters:

Labor Cost	$60/hour
Regular Time	160 hours/month
Overtime	40 hours/month
Hiring Cost:	$2,000
Firing Cost	$8,000
Subcontract Cost	$110.00/hour (400 hours/month limit)
Inventory Cost	Demand not met but back ordered: $45/hour/month Product made but not sold: $25/hour/month
Two Products	Product A requires 6 hours direct labor/unit Product B requires 4 hours direct labor/unit
Current Inventory	Product A: 10 units Product B: 20 units
Current Workforce	15

The marketing department came up with the following demand forecast covering the next 12 months:

Period	Product A	Product B
1	200	180
2	220	180
3	500	180
4	600	180
5	500	180
6	130	40
7	120	40
8	560	40
9	580	200
10	600	200
11	300	200
12	150	365
Totals	4460	1985

a) Use a spreadsheet to build a tool for aggregating the demand forecast above into direct labor hours.

b) One strategy would be to choose a level workforce and produce only on regular time, the least expensive hourly rate, throughout the year. Further develop this tool for computing the itemized and total monthly costs of this level workforce plan. The tool should be generalized enough as to be capable of evaluating other potentially feasible plans for meeting the aggregated demand forecast.

c) Using the spreadsheet developed in part (a), construct a graph that compares monthly output with demand.

d) Using the spreadsheet developed in part (a), construct a graph that compares cumulative output to cumulative demand over the length of the plan.

e) Using the spreadsheet developed in part (a), evaluate an alternative strategy where overall production chases demand each month without the use of inventory or backordering in any month. Do the graphs help put light on the issues?

f) Using the spreadsheet developed in part (a), evaluate an alternative strategy where workforce levels (including overtime and subcontracting limitations) are matched to peak demand rates. Do the graphs help put light on the issues?

Case 12: Resizing the Workforce in the Netherlands and the U.S.

When PinkRoccade wanted to lay off 700 workers last year to cut costs, the information technology (IT) services company had to get creative. A Dutch agreement between management and labor adopted in the 1980s—and hailed as part of worker rights that bolstered a Dutch "economic miracle"—required companies to consult frequently with unions and justify layoffs by negotiating with a worker's council. As a way to get around the requirement, PinkRoccade started laying off employees in groups of 19. To get around another labor rule that didn't allow layoffs of more than 19 in any region of the country, they moved affected workers around the country. If the number of desired layoffs exceeded the limit for one region, the company reclassified workers based on where they lived rather than where they worked. And to avoid laying off too many talented young programmers as part of a "last in, first out" policy, PinkRoccade reassigned some of them to divisions where the layoff quota had already been met.

Facing the first economic contraction in more than 20 years, the Netherlands's dependence on exports has always made it especially vulnerable to the global downturn. However, economists now say the country's labor relations may also be a major factor in the slump. Throughout the 1990s, the Netherlands was lauded for low unemployment and high growth. The labor agreement negotiated in the early 1980s set the foundation for three underpinnings:

1. Labor unions would restrain wage demands.

2. The government promised to keep corporate taxes down.

3. Employers promised to hire more workers and consult labor unions on key staffing positions.

The first two elements helped companies keep production costs down, making exports—ranging from consumer electronics to beer—more competitive. And the approach worked during good times. There was near-zero unemployment and a national growth rate of more than 3% in the late 1990s, while the rest of Europe grew at about 2.5%. Relatively low corporate taxes and a location in the heart of Western Europe also helped lure foreign investment. But now, experts point out that as the Dutch system is characterized by consensus and cooperation between workers and employers, it makes it difficult for companies to adapt quickly when the economy turns. Companies, swollen with workers and committed to a collaborative approach to hiring and firing, waited too long to streamline their businesses. And when they finally did, they faced labor laws that allowed unions to impose limits on some company staffing decisions. For example, in 2002, when ABN Amro Bank decided to outsource a chunk of its IT services to Electronic Data Systems and reassign 2,000 ABN Amro employees, it was forced to spend more than 3 months in talks with unions.

Some Dutch employers resort to putting able-bodied workers on disability to get rid of unwanted full-time employees, government officials say. According to the Dutch Economics Ministry, about 13.5% of the labor force, roughly 950,000 workers, is classified as "sick" or "disabled"—among the highest rate in Europe. That number is projected to rise to 15% by 2006. In response, the government is making plans to investigate suspicious disability claims for bad backs—on of the most frequent ailments cited.

The flexibility of the Dutch system does offer advantages. The unions allow for more part-time work. In one case, consumer electronics giant Phillips Electronics employs a larger number of factory workers on a part-time basis. The arrangement, introduced in 2002, allows workers to juggle family, school, and other commitments and saves the company money as the part-time employees receive fewer benefits.

Still, companies such as PinkRoccade are frustrated. Faced with a decline in demand for its IT services, the company was not able to cut 700 employees from its workforce of 8,000 in less than a year. Even with all its juggling to get around government restrictions, it was forced to layoff some of its more talented programmers and leave some regions overstaffed while cutting workers in other areas. And, while PinkRoccade's 19-at-a-time layoff strategy saved the company hundreds of thousands of dollars by allowing it to avoid union negotiations during its first round of layoffs, it also strained labor relations. As a result, the company eventually opted to abandon the 19-at-a-time strategy and negotiate with unions for the last 450 of the 700 layoffs.

American companies that have a long history of labor relations challenges have developed adapting mechanisms that may seem as strange as the 19-at-a-time layoff strategy. One example is provided by Delphi, a one time General Motors (GM) subsidiary that was spun-off to create a separate company in 1999. Why did GM spin off Delphi? One answer is that GM's UAW contract included Delphi workers, whereas many competing parts suppliers had non-unionized workers. Because of the wage differences, GM's Dephi manufactured parts were more costly than the parts many of its competitors were using. The wage differential didn't just make GM products less competitive on a cost basis, because of work rules, layoff restrictions and retirement coverage in the union contract Delphi's staffing options were more limited than those of other parts suppliers. In sum, some would argue that by spinning off Delphi, GM was trying to find a way to lay off a large number of Delphi's 145,000 employees. And the prime targets could be found among the parts maker's 33,000 U.S. unionized workers.

Even though GM had tried to sell the restructuring as a way for Delphi to get more business and make their jobs more secure, the unionized employees at Delphi were opposed to the GM restructuring in which their company was spun-off. The negative impact of GM's divestiture on Delphi workers became even clearer in 2005. On October 10, 2005, Delphi filed for Chapter 11 bankruptcy protection and spelled out plans for a major downsizing of its North American manufacturing capacity. At that point it appeared that many of the company's off-shore, non-unionized workers would be kept, while many of the North American unionized workers would be laid off. Fortunately for the unionized Delphi workers, GM agreed to guarantee some of their pensions and benefits when the company was spun-off. But for this concession, GM might have actually accomplished a 33,000-worker-at-a-time firing through corporate restructuring and bankruptcy protection.

SOME QUESTIONS TO THINK ABOUT:

1. This case points out that time requirements for making adjustments to workforce levels varies by country. What impact might that have on the length of the aggregate planning timeline? What does that say about forecasting accuracy?

2. If layoffs are restricted, what would be the logical reaction of Dutch companies to fluctuating demand requirements? Would the answer be the same for U.S. companies with union legacies such as GMs? What problems does this situation create for current workers?

3. In the short run, can these labor issues explain large amounts of overtime but high unemployment at the same time? In the long run, what would it say about the Netherlands ability to attract new business and new jobs?

4. Would a company with multinational operations have an advantage over a local Dutch company when in comes to making output adjustments in the intermediate range? Why did Delphi's multinational operations not work in favor of its unionized U.S. workforce?

Source: Adapted from "The Dutch Way of Firing: Even with Flexible Labor Laws, the Netherlands Feels the Global Chill," *Wall Street Journal*, July 8, 2003. p A14, reporter Dan Dilefsky; and "Delphi CEO Sees Major Downsizing in Bankruptcy," *Wall Street Journal*, October 10, 2005, reporters Jeffrey McCracken and John D. Stoll

13

Supply Chain Coordination: Master Scheduling and Inventory Management Processes

Chapter Outline

Introduction   572

Integrating Operations Management Across the Functions   572

Master Scheduling: Supply Chain Coordination Decisions   573

Building the Master Schedule   577

The Supply Chain Perspective: Fitting the Master Schedule to Competitive Priorities   580

Rough-Cut Capacity Planning   581

Independent Demand Inventory: Competitive Considerations   582

Negative Aspects of Inventory   582

Positive Aspects of Inventory   583

Finding the Right Inventory Level   586

Independent Demand Inventory Models   587

ABC Inventory Analysis   587

The Basic Fixed Order Quantity Model   589

Fixed Order Quantity with Price Discounts   592

Fixed Order Quantity with Variable Demand and Lead Times   595

Fixed Order Quantity with Non-Instantaneous Replenishment   602

Fixed Interval or Periodic Review Models   603

Periodic Review Systems When Demand Is Probabilistic   605

Supply Chain Management—Based Improvements to Master Scheduling and Inventory Management   606

Enterprise Resources Planning Systems   606

Improving on "Optimal" Order Quantities   609

Summary   611
Key Terms   612
Solved Problems   612
Discussion Questions   616
Problems   617
Challenge Problems   620
Case 13: Inventory Tracking with RFID Chips   621
Reference   622

Learning Objectives

After studying this chapter you should be able to

▌ **Demonstrate your understanding of the linkages between the functional areas of business and the operations management activity of master scheduling**

▌ **Describe the master scheduling process and the impact of master scheduling on competitiveness**

▌ **Describe the linkage between master scheduling and capacity leveling decisions**

▌ **Demonstrate your understanding of the competitive factors influencing independent demand inventory decisions**

▌ **Use a variety of basic independent demand inventory models to make inventory and scheduling decisions.**

▌ **Describe the current trends in inventory management.**

...Back at the Rec Center

It's a Monday morning late in the year. The group has been working out regularly for several months now and their relationship is no longer limited to the early-morning workouts at the health club. In fact, Luis and his wife hosted the group at their house for a dinner the previous Friday. It was the first time the foursome's significant others had finally met the people they'd heard so much about, and the evening had gone well. During this morning's workout, talk turns to the wine served with dinner.

"Neither of us is a wine connoisseur," Luis says, "but it's been really easy for us to learn. We found this great little shop just a few doors down here in the strip mall, and we've been picking the owner's brain for suggestions. Some have been better than others, but everything she's suggested has been really good. Being here by the club, it's easy to stop on the way home from work. We'll pick up a bottle to have with dinner, sometimes a couple extra, you know, if people are coming over, maybe stock up a bit if something we like is on sale. Actually, we bought the wine we served last night a few weeks ago. We tried it and liked it enough to buy a case. That was one less thing we had to worry about in getting the dinner together!"

"Well, it worked out great!" says Cheryl. "I just wish I could stock up on nursing hours like you do the Merlot!" she adds as she finishes her bicep curls and exhales deeply. "I could use a case or two of nursing hours this week!"

"Did you have to mention work?" asks Fred with a pained look.

"I'm sorry," says Cheryl. "I'm thinking shop again!

"It's just that coming up with a schedule this week is going to be tough," she laments.

"I'm short staff on all three shifts from scheduled vacation and to top it off, I had two more first-shift nurses called in on jury duty! I'm short staffed in the labs as well. Even when you know it's coming, planning to make do with overtime, temps, and juggling people between departments can be tough. Then, boom! Jury duty!"

Tom nods in agreement, but Fred and Luis are a little slow to see the issue. "That's what makes your job so easy," Cheryl says, now turning the table to give Fred a hard time. "You and Luis, you two can see this sort of stuff coming and work ahead. You know, build your inventory. A couple of squirrels, putting away nuts for the winter!" The other three laugh. "You just can't store up your extra nurses and lab techs when things are slow, then pull them out in the winter!"

Tom stops to listen to Cheryl. "Yeah, we have the same problem with empty seats. It'd sure be nice if we could bank a few to use on those Friday and Sunday flights when we're way overbooked!" he says.

"Hey, wait a minute, we're trying to apply some just-in-time thinking, getting rid of inventory, shorter quality feedback loop, and all that. Don't forget that, you know," replies Luis.

"Yeah, but even in the best cases, you still use inventory to some extent," says Cheryl.

"Maybe it's a popular chair you keep so you have it when a customer calls. Maybe it's raw material you bought in bulk to get a great deal, WIP just in case something happens. There are lots of times when you can try to be as JIT as the best of 'em but you still have the option of inventory when it makes sense. Tom and I don't have that option. You can't inventory a service too easily! It's sort of like the wine you served at dinner," she adds, almost as an afterthought.

"Okay, let's see where you're going with this one," Luis says with a grin.

"Well, you said a minute ago you sometimes buy a couple of extra bottles when there is an occasion or something, right?" Cheryl asks.

"Yeah, so?" replies Luis.

"Simple, if you were really into JIT at home as you say you're trying to be at work, you'd always buy one bottle at a time just when you need it. You'd never buy a case or any extra for later," Cheryl says.

"I guess you're right," Luis responds. "I just never looked at what we buy at home the same way as what we deal with at work. I have to admit we stock up at home on a lot of things because neither of us really likes to shop. Maybe we just dislike shopping more than the hassle of finding a place to put everything! But let's go back to Cheryl's point. I think she's right. My wife and I both enjoy stopping at the wine shop. We like talking wine with the owner and, like I said, it's convenient for either of us."

"So?" asks Fred.

"It's easy," says Tom. "Luis is saying that the hassle of shopping for this particular item is pretty much zero—in fact, it sounds like he actually enjoys it. That means he only buys what he needs that day or for that occasion. There's no need to stock up! You make zillions of one pager because of the hassle of switching your lines between models. You stock up because you don't like changeovers; but Luis doesn't stock up because he likes shopping for different varieties."

"But Luis, you said you sometimes buy a case?" asks Fred.

"Yes, we've done that when we've had a big occasion like last Friday," Luis answers. "We've also bought a case when the owner of the shop wasn't sure she could get more of a vintage we particularly like. Actually, that was what happened last time, with that case of Merlot we had last Friday. But the owner also gave us a 10% discount on buying by the case. I'm just not sure if that is worth it."

"Well, if you set aside the fact that you like going to the store and just look at the savings of buying in quantity, it might be a good idea," answers Cheryl. "That is to say, if you'd be drinking wine at dinner regularly, like say a bottle a week. You'd drink it long before it would ever go bad. Then it's just a little money and space that you'd have tied up in the wine until you finish it off."

"Okay, so even if I'm not planning something big where we'll use it all, or something bigger like building a wine cellar of my own, you're saying buying by the case is a good 'inventory' policy!" laughs Luis. "Does that mean we need to start buying those big 10-pound packs of ground beef, as well? You know, the ones where you save 10 cents a pound by buying in bulk?"

"I suppose you could," says Tom, "but as fast as the two of you are likely to go through it, the green you'd be saving after a week or so might be growing in your refrigerator and not your bank account!"

Introduction

A master schedule indicates the planned delivery time for the product-service bundles a company sells.

Master scheduling decisions are constrained by the capacity decisions made during the aggregate planning process described in the last chapter. Obviously, master schedulers should not commit to accomplishing work for which they do not have sufficient capacity. Part of master scheduling involves attempts to keep capacity requirements as level as possible from week to week. Heavy use of capacity can lead to problems with worker morale, equipment failure, quality, and customer service. It can also reduce efficiency. Low use of capacity leads to low levels of productivity and can influence worker morale, customer service, and quality.

In manufacturing firms like Fred and Luis's, there is a strong link between master scheduling and inventory, because an increase or decrease to scheduled production changes the inventory balance. Therefore, no discussion of master scheduling is complete without some focus on inventory decisions. In this chapter, we will address competitive considerations in inventory management, several common inventory models, recent trends, and quantitative models for inventory management.

REC CENTER DILEMMA

Tom's Dilemma:

Tom's airline has recently added a Chicago-Newark-Myrtle Beach-Orlando-Miami round-trip route to their master schedule. For more than a year the plan has been to run that route twice daily with crews from Chicago and Miami returning home each day. Now, just 1 month before the first flight, it appears that demand is not as high as expected, and one of the planes will be used on a more profitable Indianapolis-St. Louis-New Orleans-Orlando-Nassau route. There has been some talk of starting that route, but it has never actually been on the schedule. Even though none of these flights has started, Tom is frustrated by the change because he has been gearing up for one schedule and is now going to have to plan differently. How justified is his frustration? How much advance notice should be given for such changes and why?

Integrating Operations Management Across the Functions

Master scheduling is the focal point for many interactions between operations and the marketing and finance functions. In make-to-order (MTO) companies, salespeople need access to the master schedule in order to tell customers when their purchases will be available. In make-to-stock (MTS) companies, marketing people want to ensure that the timing and quantities of planned output effectively meets forecast demand. Finance people are concerned with the master schedule because it affects their ability to project earnings for investors and make appropriate preparations for the cash flows associated with the plans. When agreeing to a particular master schedule, the purchasing and operations functions are essentially saying they can get the job done. In other words, the master schedule is the game plan and thus, a critical linking point for all functions.

Capacity requirements may be estimated in greater detail based on a master schedule than is possible with an aggregate plan. In fact, capacity implications need to be considered before a master schedule is finalized. Ideally, the capacity used from week to week should be relatively stable over the short term—thus limiting the strain on workers that comes with particularly busy weeks and reducing the productivity losses that can result from slow weeks. Work scheduling implications often arise from capacity issues in the master scheduling process, necessitating the involvement of human resources professionals. For several reasons, inventory decisions directly influence company competitiveness.

First, inventory is reflected on a company's balance sheet as an asset, with a value established and monitored by the accounting function. As an asset, the inventory represents one of many possible investments for a company's capital. Recent changes in cost accounting practices have led to changes in the ways inventory is managed.

Second, from a financial analyst's perspective, changes in the levels of inventory must be reflected on the balance sheet of the firm and need to have a rational explanation. For example, growth in inventory could result from reduction in sales and indicate problems in the company's competitiveness—yet the inventory would be reported as an asset on the balance sheet. Alternatively, growth in inventory could result from increasing sales and the need for materials to satisfy the increased demand.

Third, the level of inventory that is maintained can influence a company's responsiveness, flexibility, performance in regard to customer satisfaction, and numerous other competitive variables.

Fourth, computer systems have become a key facilitator to inventory and scheduling decisions, so MIS professionals provide real time information regarding inventory levels and usage throughout the supply chain to decision makers at each stage of value creation. Finally, inventory decisions need to reflect the competitive priorities with which the company goes to market. For all of these reasons, as illustrated in Table 13.1, it is important to view inventory decisions from a cross-functional perspective. Figure 13.1 further emphasizes the fact that supply chain coordination processes, including master scheduling and inventory decision making, are an important support to the transformation process and are cross-functional in nature. Through their support of the transformation process, these business processes are critical to customer satisfaction and supplier relations.

Master Scheduling: Supply Chain Coordination Decisions

From the supply chain management perspective, the master schedule is an important link between a company and its customers and suppliers. The activities or items on the master schedule will ultimately be needed to satisfy some customer's requirements (and perhaps the requirements of a customer's customer). Similarly, many of the parts, components, and services that are needed to satisfy the demand on the master schedule will come from suppliers and suppliers of suppliers. The scheduling decisions of one company can have huge consequences on customer satisfaction throughout an entire chain of value-adding customers and suppliers. Ultimately, the long-term competitiveness of each company depends on the effectiveness of the entire supply chain as much as on its internal operations. For this reason, many companies practice supply chain management, or the coordination of decisions across a series of suppliers and customers in order to more effectively satisfy the needs of end-users of the product-service bundle. Because master scheduling is one of the strongest points of linkage between companies, as well as between the various functions of a single company, it is a critical activity in virtually every organization.

Refer back to Figure 12.3 on page 539, which compares various planning and control systems. Notice that master scheduling decisions have a shorter planning horizon than aggregate planning. The aggregate plan is typically revised monthly

Table 13.1

Integrating Operations
Management across the
Functions

Integration Perspective \ Functional Area	Finance	Accounting
Why Cross-Functional Integration Matters to Supply Chain Coordination	Cash flows and income projections are closely related to the master schedule. Inventory decisions are investment decisions that may be improved if undertaken from a financial perspective.	Accounting for inventory is an important task for the functional area. Additionally, preparation of pro forma statements is enhanced by the availability of stable operational plans—represented in this chapter by the master schedule.
Key Issues	What will be the impact of the planned schedule on profitability? Is the current set of income projections in line with the master schedule? Are current inventory policies appropriate from a capital allocation standpoint? What is the return on these investments?	How often and when should inventory cycle counting occur? Are inventory values accurately reflected on the balance sheet? Are pro forma financial statements in line with the master schedule? From a fiduciary perspective, are inventory control policies adequate?

Freeze window

A fixed period of time at the beginning of the schedule for which the master schedule is final and not subject to revision.

based on a 6- to 18-month planning horizon. Master schedules are typically revised at least once a week, and though they may look forward 6 months or more, the emphasis is on agreement about satisfaction of near-term customer requirements. Typically, a **freeze window** is established on the master schedule. This is a fixed period of time at the beginning of the schedule for which the master schedule is final and not subject to revision.

Figure 13.2 illustrates the contextual fit of this chapter within our coverage of planning and control in OM. Because master scheduling decisions require a higher level of detail than the aggregate planning decisions discussed in Chapter 12, as Figure 12.3 suggests, master scheduling requires disaggregation of the aggregate plan. Aggregate plans set the stage for the execution of a master schedule by making funds available for overtime, subcontracting, changes in workforce size, and the accumulation of inventory to meet periodic surges in demand. Thus, the level of demand accommodated in the master schedule needs to match the level of demand anticipated in the aggregate plan. For example, Luis's aggregate plan might have called for 100 hours of overtime in a particular month; the master schedule would then specify the product-service bundles to be made with that capacity. The plan may be disaggregated further during

Human Resources	Marketing	Engineering	Management Information Systems
While the aggregate plan establishes required staffing levels, the master schedule will help HR determine staffing needs by work area and skill.	The master schedule tells marketing what will be available to sell (or promise to customers) and when. Marketing wants the needs of customers (reflecting all market demand which needs to be satisfied) to appear on the master schedule.	Especially in the make-to-order environment, and to a lesser extent in others, engineering and design work, as well as engineering support of processes (e.g., maintenance), will be required in accordance with the master plan.	Information systems allow customers, marketing, operations and other areas to exchange demand and supply information in the master scheduling process.
What specific staffing changes are required (skill type and timing) in order to simultaneously accomplish the master schedule and not carry excess capacity?	What delivery promises can be made to customers? Are product promotion plans and sales force incentives accurately reflected in the master schedule? Are market and competitive strategies appropriately reflected in the master schedule? Will the master schedule satisfy demand?	What maintenance and replacement inventories are needed and what inventory policies will apply to these items? In make to order environments, is there adequate engineering staffing to accomplish the schedule?	How will the functional areas and supply chain partners share and receive (or electronically access) demand, inventory, and schedule information? Can IS provide tools and methods to enhance the scheduling process and/or optimize schedules?

planning for the timely availability of parts for the product-service bundle (see Chapters 14, 15, and 16). In the end, if aggregate planning has been done well, a company is likely to be able to meet the demand for its products and services effectively.

Figure 13.3 provides a view of the relationships between material decisions, demand forecasts, and capacity decisions. Demand forecasts provide guidance at each stage of the planning process. Long-range forecasts, whether qualitative or quantitative, play a significant role in the design of product-service bundles (a material decision) and the other structural decisions of the firm (such as process design). Infrastructural decisions are made within the context established by these structural decisions and rely on intermediate- and short-range forecasts.

Aggregate planning, for example, relies on intermediate-range forecasts of demand for groups of products. Likewise, master scheduling, a material decision, relies on detailed product-service bundle demand forecasts. Across the board, material planning decisions and capacity planning decisions have to be synchronized with each other and with demand projections. Operations cannot be scheduled without available capacity of the required resources. Therefore, master scheduling relies on capacity planning decisions, ranging from aggregate resource planning to detailed capacity plans.

Figure 13.1

Master scheduling and inventory planning processes

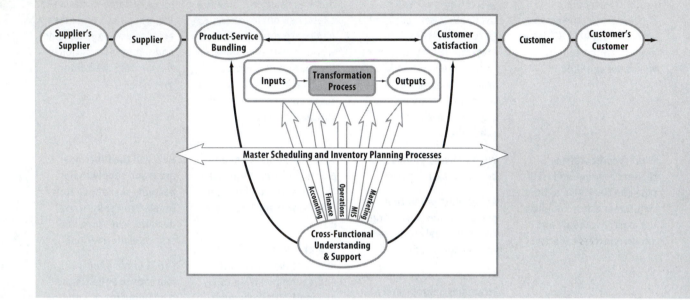

Not all companies are able to make scheduling decisions, project the most detailed capacity implications of these decisions, and then make adjustments to schedules based on capacity utilization issues. So, not all of the links depicted in Figure 13.3 will be present in all operational planning systems. Regardless, the goal in master scheduling is to create a material plan that is feasible in light of capacity considerations, which are

Figure 13.2

The management of operational systems

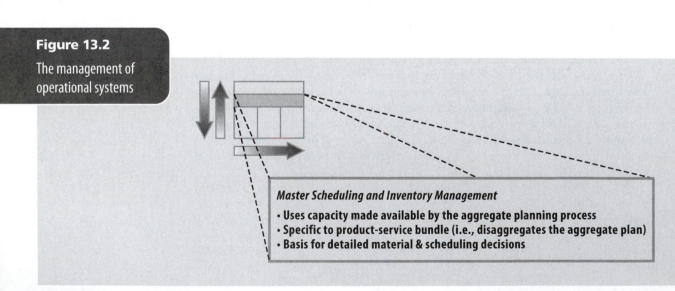

Master Scheduling and Inventory Management

• **Uses capacity made available by the aggregate planning process**
• **Specific to product-service bundle (i.e., disaggregates the aggregate plan)**
• **Basis for detailed material & scheduling decisions**

Figure 13.3

The management of operational systems

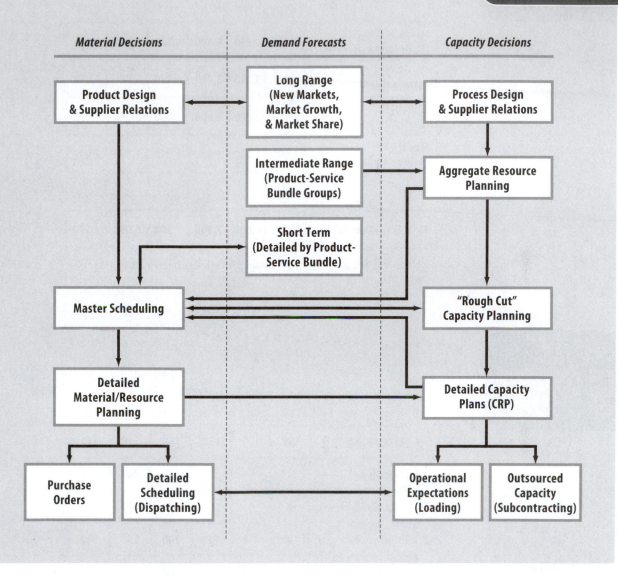

dependant upon material requirements. (In subsequent chapters, we will demonstrate ways that material decisions result in actual capacity allocations through **loading decisions** that assign work to resources and **dispatching decisions** that determine the sequence in which that work will be completed.)

Building the Master Schedule

Figures 13.4, 13.5, and 13.6 present sample master schedules for a variety of environments. For the cosmetic surgery department at Cheryl's hospital (Figure 13.6), the

Loading decisions

Choices made to help assign work to resources.

Dispatching decisions

The choices which determine the sequence in which that work will be completed.

Figure 13.4

Master schedule for the pager line in Fred's factory

| | Week of: | | | | | |
	1/6	1/13	1/20	1/27	2/3	2/10
Model 37b (Basic Numeric)	2,000	2,000	4,000	4,000	6,000	6,000	· · · · ·
Model 37c (Deluxe Numeric)	3,000	3,000	3,000	3,000	1,000	1,000	· · · · ·
Model 47b (Basic Alpha-Numeric)	2,000	2,000	3,000	3,000	2,000	3,000	· · · · ·
Model 47c (Deluxe Alpha-Numeric)	1,000	1,000	1,000	1,000	1,000	2,000	· · · · ·
	⋮	⋮	⋮	⋮	⋮	⋮	
Total Line Minutes*:	6,000	6,000	7,500	7,500	6,000	7,500	· · · · ·

* Line cycle is approximately 1 minute for deluxe model and 30 seconds for basic models.

Figure 13.5

Master schedule for tables in Luis's furniture factory

| | Week of: | | | | | |
	10/1	10/8	10/15	10/22	10/29	11/5
Tbl-h36r-oak	150	150	150	150	150	150	· · · · ·
Tbl-h48r-oak	0	0	0	300	200	200	· · · · ·
Tbl-h48x66-ov-oak	0	0	0	200	200	200	· · · · ·
Tbl-k36r-chy	400	450	400	200	150	100	· · · · ·
Tbl-k48r-chy	500	500	500	100	100	100	· · · · ·
Tbl-k48x66-ov-chy	100	100	100	300	300	300	· · · · ·
Tbl-k48x72-ov-chy	200	200	200	200	200	200	· · · · ·
	⋮	⋮	⋮	⋮	⋮	⋮	
Total Tables:	1,350	1,400	1,350	1,450	1,300	1,350	· · · · ·

Week of:

	12/1	12/8	12/15	12/22	12/29	1/5	
Liposuction	10	12	12	18	20	12	·····
Nose Reconstruction	15	15	15	15	15	15	·····
Face Lifts	10	10	10	15	30	12	·····
"Tummy Tucks"	5	5	5	8	8	5	·····
Skin Grafts	12	12	12	12	12	12	·····
	⋮	⋮	⋮	⋮	⋮	⋮	
Total Nursing Hours:	???	???	???	???	???	???	·····

schedule indicates the number of times each type of procedure is to be conducted in a given week. Figure 13.4 indicates the planned production of each of the pagers that is produced in Fred's factory, and Figure 13.5 shows the planned production of furniture in Luis's factory.

In these master scheduling examples, the time increment is weekly and the information refers to specific product-service bundles. The focus has narrowed from the aggregate plan, which dealt with entire product lines and monthly capacity requirements. Nevertheless, there must be a correlation between the aggregate plan and the master schedule: The total monthly demand for the items shown on a master schedule should be close to the demand anticipated in the corresponding aggregate plan. In master scheduling, however, the actual demand might not be distributed evenly from week to week. (Having 160 hours of capacity a month does not necessarily mean you can schedule 80 hours for 2 weeks and take 2 weeks off.) As a result, it is necessary to assess the feasibility of the master schedule more directly.

The weekly requirements included on the master schedule are derived from a detailed forecast. For make-to-order companies, this forecast is based largely on customer orders expected over the near term. Looking further into the future, however, orders will be less specific and the master schedule will be based more on forecasted demand for the product-service bundle. Figures 13.5 and 13.6 fit the MTO category, as do the master schedules of many service organizations. For example, at the rec center, customized training programs; group activities, such as the ropes course at the Outdoor Pursuit Center; and group reservations of facilities are all made to order. In an MTO setting, the freeze window should include the entire production lead time (the duration between placing and receiving an order). That way, there will be no chance of canceling or changing an order once processing has begun.

In make-to-stock organizations, the demand shown on the master schedule is based on forecasted rates of demand for the various product-service bundles. Figure 13.4 illustrates an MTS environment. So, too, the pagers Fred's factory makes may or may not be sold, but they are available for shipment to customers. In MTS environments the freeze window on the master schedule should be at least as long as the time suppliers need to respond to purchase orders. A staffing schedule in a service facility is similar. For example, the rec center is staffed and remains open based on projected usage; thus the open schedule for walk-in customers is the MTS-like part of the center's master schedule. Whether the center is empty or full—that is, whether the facilities are used or not—it is available to patrons during regular hours.

The Supply Chain Perspective: Fitting the Master Schedule to Competitive Priorities

Because master scheduling is clearly linked to a company's competitiveness, decisions made in the master scheduling process should fit a firm's competitive priorities and promote customer satisfaction in a way that is consistent with the company's other operational decisions. In building a master schedule that will satisfy customers, it is critical to consider the number and frequency of orders or product-service bundles that can be accommodated; the level of uncertainty in demand forecasts; and the impact of scheduling decisions on the firm's competitive priorities.

In some cases, firms may need to reconsider their inventory approach. On one hand, MTO systems are appropriate in settings where flexibility is important and general purpose equipment is available. Such systems can handle frequent orders and are better able to deal with demand uncertainty. Thus, the size of the production run and service delivery options can be based on customer requirements. On the other hand, the MTO approach can have negative consequences on cost, quality of conformance, and delivery reliability, because of lower capacity utilization, schedule changes, and the coordination costs associated with high variety.

If the demand forecast is reasonably certain, an MTS approach is a good fit for companies that emphasize low cost and high quality of conformance and provide mass-produced, standardized product-service bundles. In these companies, the finished goods inventory provides a "buffer" or "decoupling point" between the producer and the customer. Therefore, the system can operate independently of individual customers' demand patterns. This independence from the customer allows the company to choose efficient scheduling alternatives, to order inputs and produce outputs with less frequency, and to level the firm's output rates over time. It also allows the use of dedicated, specialized equipment that is capable of meeting high quality specifications. The obvious downside that accompanies the MTS approach is a lack of operational flexibility and limited ability to rapidly respond to changes in customer preferences.

Consider the Supply Chain Operating Reference (SCOR) Model that we first introduced in Chapter 3. Figure 3.5 on page 88 illustrated the use of standardized process categories to configure a company's approach to scheduling such that it would be internally consistent and fit with the processes used by customers and suppliers. Once it's supply chain has been configured using the SCOR model to meet a specific set of competitive priorities, a company can use the Supply Chain Council's repository of benchmarking performance data to determine how well their actual schedules and operational performance measure up to that of comparable supply chains. This, in turn, helps them to establish realistic goals for improvement.

Rough-Cut Capacity Planning

The right column of Figure 13.3 shows three different types of capacity decisions that may be a factor in master scheduling, in order of increasing detail: aggregate planning, rough-cut capacity planning, and detailed capacity planning. The aggregate plan provides for adequate monthly capacity to meet demand, but that does not mean that a master schedule based on the same level of monthly output is feasible. (In the same way, 16 credit-hours might seem feasible to you until all your professors schedule major assignments to be completed on the same day.) As a consequence, the feasibility of master schedules must be verified, a process that is called **rough-cut capacity planning**.

Rough-cut capacity planning typically relies on overall estimates of capacity requirements. For example, a large accounting firm might estimate the data entry, legal, auditing, and tax accounting hours required for a standard audit of a firm with revenues between $500 million and $1 billion. Then, in developing a master schedule, managers would determine the projected weekly totals of data entry, legal, auditing, and tax accounting hours needed. If the results indicate that the schedule is feasible, does their rough estimate mean that all the firm's audits will be completed on schedule and under cost? Of course not; clearly, each audit is unique, and rough-cut capacity planning gives only a general sense of the schedule's feasibility.

Ultimately, a master schedule that looks feasible based on rough-cut capacity planning might not be feasible because of the processing requirements associated with various components and subassemblies. For example, making the body parts for one type of Indy car might take just 1 week, while manufacturing the body parts for another type might take 2 weeks. Therefore, leveling the schedule for assembly of the cars, so that 10 cars are assembled each week, might throw off the schedule for parts fabrication. Once a detailed materials plan has been done and a procurement plan for the components and subassemblies completed, however, a detailed capacity check can be constructed. At this point, businesses with highly sophisticated planning and control systems can engage in **closed loop planning**, a process in which information from detailed capacity planning is used to level (and ensure the feasibility of) the master schedule.

A simple example from your own experience may illustrate these three levels of capacity planning. As a freshman you no doubt looked over your selected academic program to get an idea of how many hours you could and would take per semester. At that point you were not thinking much about the specific courses you would take in particular semesters; you were just trying to get an idea of how you would spread your required and elective courses over a certain number of semesters. This first look at your schedule was analogous to aggregate planning.

At some point you registered for the current semester and decided exactly what courses you needed to take. This second step was analogous to master scheduling. As you scheduled your courses, however, you probably looked at a weekly calendar and tried to divide your coursework between Tuesday/Thursday (TR) and Monday/Wednesday/Friday (MWF) time slots. If your TR schedule looked too crowded with required courses, you probably tried to find electives given on MWF. Even though you probably had not seen the syllabus for any of these classes, you were nevertheless making decisions about the feasibility of your schedule. Based on those decisions, you made adjustments to even out your schedule and finally settled on a plan that seemed satisfactory. This course-scheduling activity is analogous to rough-cut capacity planning.

At the beginning of the semester you received a syllabus for each of your classes. At that point you began to look at the specific assignments required in each class, and you

Rough-cut capacity planning

A planning method where the feasibility of master schedules must be verified.

Closed loop planning

A process in which information from your detailed capacity planning is used to level (and insure the feasibility of) the master schedule.

dedicated specific blocks of time throughout the semester to those activities. This last step is analogous to detailed capacity planning. Looking at your daily planner for the coming week, you can probably identify specific blocks of time that you set aside to complete specific assignments. Although you may have tried to level your schedule for the entire semester, you may have some weeks in which the workload on specific days is well beyond feasible. In those cases, you might ask for extensions on particular projects or you might request your assignments ahead of time, so you can get an early start on your work. In a worst-case scenario, you might actually have to drop a course or take an "incomplete." The fact is, very few students can figure out all the implications of a schedule early enough in the semester to both drop and add courses. Those who can are able to close the loop between their detailed capacity planning and their course scheduling. In other words, they can consider detailed information about their courses (the timing and requirements of assignments, the timing of tests, and so forth) in setting up their semester schedules.

In MTO companies, the master schedule is built by incrementally adding orders to an existing schedule. Planners cannot just add new orders indiscriminately; rather, they must first check to see if there is adequate capacity for the order. Usually this check is based on an overall estimate of the time required to process the order in each work center. When customers are particularly time sensitive, the master scheduler usually attempts to add the order as early as possible, in the hope that it can be completed within a satisfactory period. This practice is referred to as **forward scheduling**.

In MTS companies, planners typically use **backward scheduling** to develop the master schedule. They determine from the forecast when a stock of outputs will be needed, then place orders on the master schedule so as to ensure the availability of outputs by that time. When all of the anticipated demand has been scheduled, the rough-cut capacity planning can be done. Just as in an MTO company, this rough-cut check is based on an overall estimate of the time required to process the orders in each work center. If the initial schedule is not feasible, adjustments can be made by splitting orders so as to defer the production of some items; or the schedule can be leveled in other ways.

Independent Demand Inventory: Competitive Considerations

The inventory that is addressed by the master schedule is referred to as **independent demand inventory**, because it is material that the firm produces for sale. Typically, some or all of this type of demand must be forecast. **Dependent demand inventory**, by contrast, is the material that goes into the product-service bundle. This demand can be calculated once the master schedule has been agreed upon.

Negative Aspects of Inventory

Earlier chapters of this text emphasize many of the negative consequences of an over-reliance on independent demand inventory. Those adverse consequences include:

❱ Overdepending on inventory can prohibit meaningful feedback on the quality of the product-service bundle. With large inventories, there is usually a long delay between the creation of an item and its use. When problems are discovered, it is usually too late to investigate and remedy the causes.

Forward scheduling

When customers are particularly time sensitive, the master scheduler will usually attempt to add the order as early as possible in the hope that it can be completed within a satisfactory period.

Backward scheduling

A process where companies determine when a stock of outputs will be needed, then place orders on the master schedule so as to ensure the availability of outputs by that time. In MTS companies, planners typically use this to develop the master schedule.

Independent demand inventory

Inventory that is addressed by the master schedule is preferred because it is material that the firm produces for sale.

Dependent demand inventory

The material that goes into the things the firm sells.

▶ Large inventories hide operational problems that might be solved if they were discovered. When a worker finds a nonconforming item and inventory provides an immediate replacement, the worker has very little incentive to communicate the fact that a defective item was created. Indeed, the cost to the worker of reporting the defective item might exceed the cost of replacing it with conforming inventory.

▶ The financial cost of carrying excess inventory represents the lost opportunity to invest that money elsewhere, as well as the rental cost for the space used to house the inventory (including utilities, security, and insurance on the structure and the inventory itself).

Accountants put inventory on the asset side of the balance sheet. However, if it sits in a warehouse too long, it becomes money sitting idle, taking up space, slowing down the process flow, and in many cases, making it hard to see underlying problems in the value adding process.

▶ The risk of damage to goods held in inventory. The larger the inventory, the more likely items are to be handled before shipment. Often, warehouse workers have to move and replace large quantities of inventory just to find a specific item. Each time an item is handled, there is a chance that it will be damaged.

▶ The cost of tracking and accounting for inventory. Inventory records are often quite inaccurate; thus, accountants and auditors frequently spend days locating and counting specific items. Much productivity is lost because of time wasted searching for inventory that has been moved without updating warehouse records. Though the bar-coding systems that have become commonplace in most businesses help track inventory, the technology is not without cost. Systems currently under development will allow an entire warehouse to be scanned at one time, alleviating the necessity of having to run each item across a bar-code reader. But while these new systems should significantly improve the capability of firms to track their inventory, they will be even more costly than bar code–based tracking systems.

▶ Large inventories are associated with a risk of product obsolescence and losses due to depreciation.

▶ Large inventories can have a significant impact on the flexibility of the value-adding system. When a firm has invested in particular technologies and inventories, it must use them until the inventories are depleted. Technological advances and product innovations cannot be adopted while preexisting inventories appear on the balance sheet.

Positive Aspects of Inventory

Clearly, carrying more inventory than is needed is not advisable. On the other hand, inventory listed on the balance sheet as an asset does have a positive impact on operations when used in moderation. Sometimes managers find it hard to draw the line between inventory that adds value (or facilitates the adding of value) and inventory that is needed only to cover some solvable problem in the value-adding system. Some of the potential benefits of inventory that managers might consider include:

▶ Inventory can allow managers to decouple operations. That is, placing inventory between two work centers, or between a customer and a supplier, allowing them to operate independently. Therefore, the two separate value-adding processes can each operate in the most efficient manner, based on local considerations. Decoupling operations also allows producers to set aside material for later use by customers, and customers to receive immediate delivery of in-stock items. In this sense, inventory is particularly useful in complex systems. Conversely, using inventory to decouple operations might discourage managers from creating mechanisms to reduce the need for inventory or from otherwise solving operational problems.

▶ Inventory protects one part of an operating system from disruptions in other parts of the system. When a worker at one work center calls in sick or a machine requires maintenance, others can continue to work if inventory is available. At the same time, the presence of inventory might encourage managers to accept preventable disruptions rather than eliminate them.

▶ Inventory can be used to reduce the number of times orders are placed or the number of setups required to meet demand. Time and money spent in preparation to meet demand can be reduced. However, the willingness to carry inventory might keep managers from looking for ways to handle setups and logistics more efficiently.

▶ Inventory can provide a hedge against inflation. On the other hand, inventory held for this reason will prevent managers from looking for superior substitutes.

▶ Some inventory, such as pipeline inventory, is an integral part of the system. The Alaskan oil pipeline, for example, is 800 miles long and 4 feet in diameter, and its "bazillion" barrels of oil inventory are just part of the system! (If you remember your high school geometry, you may determine the pipeline can actually hold about 9.778 million barrels. Assuming the pipeline is full and the spot price for crude oil is $25 per barrel, that oil is worth more than $244 million. If the money could have been invested elsewhere with a 10% rate of return, the opportunity cost of holding that oil is about $24 million a year.) The same output rate could be achieved with a pipe diameter half the size, at a flow rate twice as fast. The system cost of the additional oil inventory contained in the 4-foot pipe must be lower than the operational costs associated with higher flow rates in a smaller pipe. In a similar way, inventory may reduce a firm's need for additional capacity or manufacturing flexibility. Using inventory in this way is justified by the accompanying savings in capital requirements and/or operational costs.

▶ Inventory allows firms to take advantage of quantity discounts from suppliers. If used for this purpose, however, the availability of inventory might reduce the supplier's incentive to provide small shipments more efficiently.

▶ Inventory allows firms to meet unexpected demand. On the other hand, this safety net allows firms to be less proactive in their attempts to understand customers' needs and to use supply chain management to coordinate their relations with downstream customers.

Finding the Right Inventory Level

Within companies, people from different functions often debate the question, How much inventory is enough? Financial managers and controllers commonly question the use of inventory, because they are concerned about tying up funds in this way and unsure of the benefits. But operations managers know that inventory, if strategically used, can simplify operations, and they see it as an asset. Salespeople, too, like to be able to satisfy customers immediately.

The right inventory level clearly depends on the level of uncertainty surrounding demand, the potential for system disruptions, and the characteristics of the operating

INTEGRATING OM:

Improving Video and DVD Rental Inventory Management

Many companies that rent videos, DVDs and computer games struggle to track their inventory. Two specific problems they face are: (1) Movies are often picked up by customers and put back in the wrong place. And (2), thieves find ways to lift the movies they want most—which are usually those with the greatest revenue potential.

Now, companies in the RFID chip market have created systems that use RFID tags to track rental inventory and may solve both problems. These systems put RFID tags on the items to be tracked and RFID readers situated on the store shelves, above the return bins and at the exits. The unique serial number on the tag is linked to the rental title by the systems' software.

Stores are using these RFID based systems to keep track of each title's position on the shelf. If someone picks up the item and continues shopping, its status is changed to "roaming." When the person checks out, the system is updated so that when the customer passes the exit reader, no alarm sounds. When the title is tossed into the return bin, a reader scans the tag, and the item is automatically checked back into inventory so it can be rented again immediately.

Because the system is designed specifically for the video rental industry it is easy to install and use. The tags initially cost about 50 cents each, and the smart shelf technology, which is added to a company's existing shelves, costs about $30 or $40 for each three-foot section. Prices will come down as volumes go up.

Such systems are cost justifiable in large video stores because rental companies save the labor costs associated with taking inventory, reduce losses due to theft. But the biggest benefit may be increased revenue. Rental companies derive 70 percent of their revenue from new releases rented on Friday and Saturday night, so knowing where all the copies of hot movies are in real time increases inventory turns. Having the hot movies available when customers want them is important to repeat business in this industry. Inventory management, therefore, provides a competitive advantage. Knowing what they have available and what customers want to rent and don't want to rent could make or break stores operating on thin margins.

Source: Adapted from "RFID Tracks Video and DVD Rentals," *RFID Journal*, August 2003, http://216.121.131.129/article/articleprint/540/-1/1/; http://www.symbol.com/products/rfid/rfid.html, October 19, 2005; and http://www.rapidrental.com/, October 19, 2005

system. The greater the degree of uncertainty surrounding demand and the greater the potential for system disruptions, the more inventory is required to effectively satisfy customer requirements.

Fortunately, as far as the short term is concerned, the uncertainty surrounding demand can be estimated. One way to do so is to use the error statistics from demand forecasts, such as the mean absolute deviation (MAD), mean forecast error (MFE), or mean squared error (MSE), as discussed in Chapter 11. A similar approach is to simply compute the standard deviation of periodic demand. The potential for system disruptions can also be estimated using measures such as the variability of the time required to complete orders or the variability of the time required for suppliers to fill orders.

In MTS environments, firms will hold inventories of raw materials, work-in-process, or finished goods. In MTO environments, firms are likely to stock only commonly used raw materials, as the more flexible operating systems typically require less

Figure 13.7

Handling uncertainty with buffers

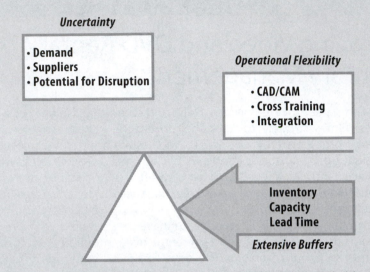

Source: Adapted from Newman, W. Rocky, et al. "Dealing with the Uncertainties of Manufacturing: Flexibility, Buffers and Integration," *International Journal of Operations and Production Management*, Vol. 13, No. 1, 1993, p.25.

inventory. Figure 13.7 illustrates the relationship between uncertainty of demand, operational flexibility, and buffers such as inventory. Where the operating system is not very flexible and demand is uncertain, or the potential for system disruption is significant, companies tend to use buffers of inventory, capacity, or lead time. For example, a fast-food restaurant such as Wendy's might ask customers to place their orders while waiting in line. This practice moves the waiting line along more quickly, by eliminating some of the uncertainty about what customers want and thereby reducing the time they spend at the cash register. Rather than increasing lead time, Wendy's could choose to improve the flow in the system by carrying excess capacity—for example, by opening another cash register. Or Wendy's could use inventory to take up the slack, by preparing burgers of every variety in advance. McDonald's, which does not encourage customers to customize their orders as Wendy's does, uses the latter strategy. Buffering the operating system with inventory allows a firm to satisfy customer requirements without investing in system flexibility; thus, a company can avoid the cost of product redesign, automation, or cross training of workers. However, carrying inventory to compensate for uncertainty or inflexibility can actually lead to greater uncertainty and a greater need for capacity, lead time, or inventory buffers. For example, if Wendy's was working to build an inventory of cooked beef patties between 11:30 a.m. and noon, this would reduce their ability to respond to a school bus of students who wanted to order chicken nugget meals (or any other form of unanticipated demand). The result might be a decision to have more capacity, or an

REC CENTER DILEMMA

Fred's Dilemma:

Fred's company uses an MTS schedule. While demand is usually very stable, a newly released music video prominently featured one of their products, which resulted in some regional product shortages and even a brief nationwide stock-out. In light of this event, the company is thinking of several policy changes, including carrying a safety stock and reducing the freeze window on their master schedule. Fred thinks all of the ideas are crazy because, as he says, "Who cares if customers had to wait a day or two for the phone this one time? We've never had a problem like this before." How would you advise the company to approach this problem? What direction would your advice lean?

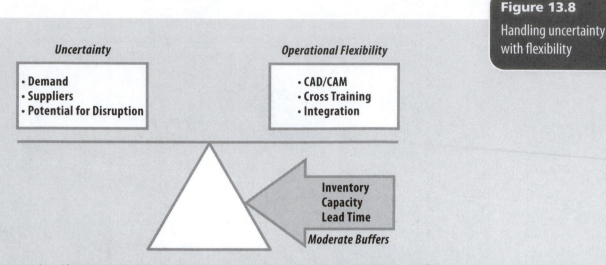

Source: Adapted from Newman, W. Rocky, et al. "Dealing with the Uncertainties of Manufacturing: Flexibility, Buffers and Integration." *International Journal of Operations and Production Management*, Vol. 13, No. 1, 1993, p.25.

Figure 13.8
Handling uncertainty with flexibility

inventory of chicken nuggets, or simply a longer wait. The same holds with inventories in manufacturing firms.

When operational flexibility is sufficient to accommodate the levels of uncertainty a firm faces, there is less need for standby inventory, capacity, and lead time (see Figure 13.8). As we noted in Chapter 7, there is a cost associated with creating and maintaining a highly flexible value-adding system. In industries where rapid change and time-based competition are a part of life, that cost might be a necessity for long-term profitability. In such situations, managers might rely on temporary buffers of inventory, capacity, and lead time while working on system improvements. The long-term goal of such operations should be to reduce uncertainty and buffers and increase flexibility, as dictated by the firm's competitive priorities.

Independent Demand Inventory Models

Inventory modeling is a well-established part of operations management and assists in setting inventory policies on the basis of competitive considerations such as cost and customer service. The most common inventory models include:

ABC analysis

several variations of the fixed order quantity model

fixed order interval models

ABC Inventory Analysis

ABC inventory analysis is a form of Pareto analysis, which is based on the rule that 20% of the items in inventory will account for 80% of the value of inventory. In the context of inventory management, Pareto (ABC) analysis is used to distinguish between highly

ABC inventory analysis

A form of Pareto analysis, which is based on the rule that 20% of the items in inventory will account for 80% of the value of inventory.

Figure 13.9

Inventory items at Lainey's lectronics

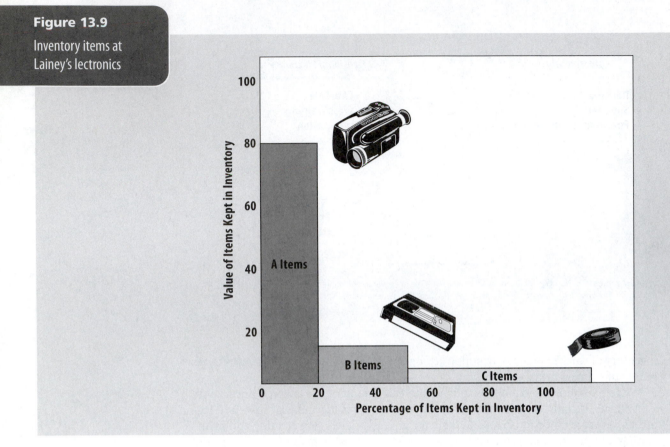

Cycle counting

A periodic audit of inventory quantities to ensure accuracy.

important inventory items and those that are less important. "A" inventory items require tight control policies and close managerial scrutiny, including frequent policy review and **cycle counting**, a periodic audit of inventory quantities to ensure accuracy. Typically *A* items are so designated either because they are critical items or because they represent an unusually high dollar value (see Figure 13.9). *B* inventory items, which are of moderate importance, receive less frequent managerial attention than *A* items. The *C* classification is reserved for items that are inexpensive, infrequently used, or do not otherwise significantly impact customer satisfaction.

Figure 13.10 presents a simple example of ABC analysis at Lainey's Lectronics, a small electronic products retailer. The top table (a) lists twenty inventory items, and the lower table (b) ranks those items by annual dollar volume. The far-right-hand column of table (b) divides the inventory items into four A items, six B items, and ten C items. At Lainey's store, the A items are displayed, but the customer must get them from a secured stockpoint. These items are restocked immediately, unless the manufacturer is planning to introduce new models in the near future. The B items are displayed in cases and on shelves within clear view of the cash register; their inventory is replenished each week. The C items are dispersed throughout the store on shelves; replenishment orders are placed monthly.

The ABC classification Lainey's uses is not an irreversible decision. Rather, because demand patterns change over time, certain A or C items could become B items, and vice versa. No doubt outdoor antennas were once a popular item, but with the advent of cable television, Lainey's does not seem to be selling many of them.

Figure 13.10

ABC analysis at Lainey's lectronics

Item	Monthly Volume	Item Value($)
VCR's	125	$150.00
TV's	75	$375.00
TV Cable (50')	150	$28.00
T160 VCR Tapes	400	$2.00
T120 VCR Tapes	2500	$2.00
Stereos	75	$300.00
Speaker Wire (100')	300	$6.00
Patch Cables	75	$3.00
Indoor TV Attenna	75	$30.00
Deluxe T120 VCR Tapes	1000	$4.00
D Cell Batteries	50	$0.80
Camcorders	100	$600.00
Camcorder Batteries	250	$30.00
Cable Splitters	25	$2.00
C Cell Batteries	100	$0.80
Audio Tape (90 minute)	2000	$1.10
Audio Tape (60 minute)	2500	$0.50
AC/DC Converters	150	$20.00
AAA Cell Batteries	2000	$1.00
AA Cell Batteries	100	$0.50

(a)

Item	Monthly Volume	Item Value($)	Volume ($)		
Camcorders	100	$600.00	$60,000.00		
TV's	75	$375.00	$28,125.00		
Stereos	75	$300.00	$22,500.00	"A" Items	
VCR's	125	$150.00	$18,750.00	$129,375.00	78.79%
Camcorder Batteries	250	$30.00	$7,500.00		
T120 VCR Tapes	2500	$2.00	$5,000.00		
TV Cable (50')	150	$28.00	$4,200.00		
Deluxe T120 VCR Tapes	1000	$4.00	$4,000.00		
AC/DC Converters	150	$20.00	$3,000.00	"B" Items	
Indoor TV Attenna	75	$35.00	$2,625.00	$26,325.00	16.03%
Audio Tape (90 minute)	2000	$1.10	$2,200.00		
AAA Cell Batteries	2000	$1.00	$2,000.00		
Speaker Wire (100')	300	$6.00	$1,800.00		
Audio Tape (60 minute)	2500	$0.50	$1,250.00		
T160 VCR Tapes	400	$2.00	$800.00		
Patch Cables	75	$3.00	$225.00		
C Cell Batteries	100	$0.80	$80.00		
Cable Splitters	25	$2.00	$50.00		
AA Cell Batteries	100	$0.50	$50.00	"C" Items	
D Cell Batteries	50	$0.80	$40.00	$8,495.00	5.17%

(b)

The Basic Fixed Order Quantity Model

Ultimately, the required level of independent demand inventory comes down to customer demand for those items and the timing of their production, as planned in the master schedule. Figure 13.11 presents a basic model for determining the timing and quantity of orders for independent demand inventory items. The graph illustrates a fixed-quantity ordering system with constant demand and lead time. In this situation, the time to place an order is when inventory has been reduced to the point at which it is sufficient to cover only the demand during lead time. This level of inventory, referred to as the **reorder point**, is simply the product of the demand per day and the lead time in days. The time between orders, called the order interval, is identical to the time between receipts of successive shipments.

Clearly, to use a reorder point based inventory model, a manager must have a perpetual record of on-hand inventory, such that he or she is aware when the reorder point has been reached. Not all inventory items are vital enough to warrant such close scrutiny, making use of this model most applicable to A inventory items.

We will consider two cases: one in which the lead time is shorter than the length of an order interval, and another in which the lead time is longer than the length of an order interval.

Reorder point

The product of the demand per day and the lead-time in days. An order should be placed when the amount of inventory available for use during lead time exactly equals the amount that will be required during the lead time.

Figure 13.11

Fixed order quantity model—constant demand and lead time

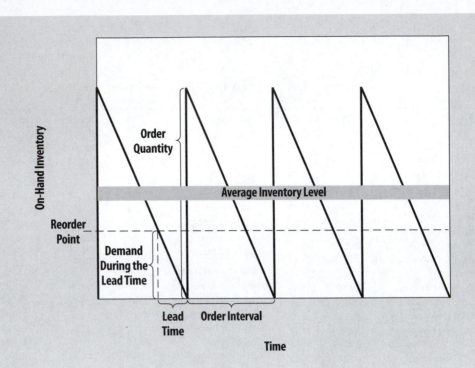

SHORT LEAD TIME

If the lead time is shorter than the length of an order interval, then an order should be placed when the amount of inventory on hand will exactly cover the demand during the lead time, as shown in Figure 13.12a. That is:

R = Ld, where
R = the reorder point, L = the lead time in days, and d = the daily usage rate.

LONG LEAD TIME

If the lead time is longer than the length of an order interval, then an order should be placed when the amount of inventory on hand or on order (called the book inventory or inventory position) will exactly cover the demand during the lead time. Because the on-hand inventory will never be enough to cover all the demand during the lead time, we must order during one cycle for delivery during a later cycle, as shown in Figure 13.12b. The reorder point is still given by short lead time equation if we base it on the book inventory or the inventory position. But if we want to base it on on-hand inventory, then:

R = Ld − n* Q* where
Q* is the order quantity, and n* is the maximum integer value less than or equal to Ld/Q*.

That is, subtract from Ld as many full-order quantities as possible (to recognize the orders placed during earlier order intervals that have not yet been received), and the remainder is R, the reorder point in terms of on-hand inventory.

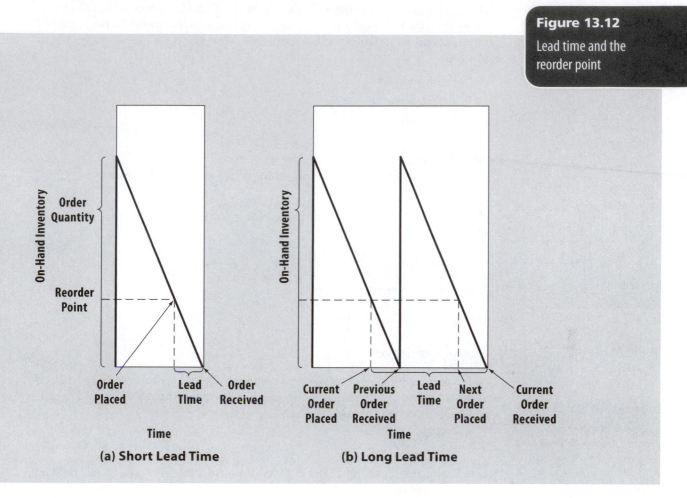

Figure 13.12

Lead time and the reorder point

(a) Short Lead Time

(b) Long Lead Time

Example 13.1

Cheryl's hospital uses approximately 1000 boxes of non-sterile disposable examining gloves per year. Usage is fairly regular from day to day. The hospital pays $5 per box for the gloves. The accounting department has estimated the cost of placing and receiving an order for this item to be $40 and uses a 20% annual carrying rate for nonperishable inventory (which means the annual holding cost is 20% of the price). The company that supplies examining gloves to the hospital quotes a delivery time of 2 weeks (14 days), and Cheryl orders enough to last more than 100 days each time she places an order. Determine the reorder point for gloves.

Solution:

The lead time, L, is 14 days. Daily demand, d, is 1000 ÷ 365 = 2.74. Because the lead time (14 days) is shorter than the length of the order interval (more than 100 days), the reorder point is:

$$R = Ld = 14(2.74) = 38.36 \text{ or } 39 \text{ boxes}$$

The previous discussion has addressed the issue of when an order should be placed. We now describe how policies are set regarding how much to order. To begin we will define a number of variables relevant to the inventory model shown in Figure 13.11 as follows:

Q = order quantity

D = annual demand

d = daily demand

L = lead time

H = the cost to hold one unit for 1 year

S = the cost to place an order (including order preparation, shipping, handling, and receiving costs

Applying these variables and simple geometry to the model in Figure 13.11, it is easily determined that:

$$\text{Average inventory} = \frac{Q}{2}$$

$$\text{Number of orders per year} = \frac{D}{Q}$$

$$\text{Annual holding cost} = \frac{Q}{2}H$$

$$\text{Annual ordering cost} = \frac{D}{Q}S$$

If the purchase cost per unit is not a function of the order size, the relevant annual total cost function to minimize in an order sizing decision is simply the sum of the annual holding and annual ordering costs:

$$TC = \frac{Q}{2}H + \frac{D}{Q}S$$

Figure 13.13a graphically illustrates the relationship among order size, annual holding cost, and annual ordering cost, and annual total cost. In this simple inventory model, demand rate and lead time are treated as a constants. (The **demand rate** refers to the amount of inventory used in a given time period. **Lead time** is the duration between placing and receiving an order.) Using differential calculus, it can be shown that the cost-minimizing order quantity is the amount that perfectly balances annual ordering costs and annual holding costs. This amount, referred to as Q^* in Figure 13.13, is frequently referred to as the **economic order quantity**, or **EOQ**. The formula for the EOQ is given below:

$$EOQ = \sqrt{\frac{2DS}{H}}$$

Figure 13.13b shows the calculation of the EOQ and total cost in a simple scenario where annual demand 40,000 units, the cost to place an order is $100, and the cost to hold a unit of inventory for a year is $0.50. The resulting EOQ is 4000 units at an annual total cost of $2000.

Fixed Order Quantity with Price Discounts

Referring back to the information in Example 13.1 and Figure 13.13, let's suppose that the supplier is willing to offer discounts that reduce the per item price from $1.00 to $0.99 for orders of 5000 or more, and to $0.98 for orders of 6000 or more. Would it make sense to order the EOQ of

---

Demand rate

The amount of inventory used in a given time period.

Lead time

The duration between placing and receiving an order.

Economic order quantity

The cost-minimizing order quantity, which is the amount that perfectly balances annual ordering costs and annual holding costs.

When you are thirsty, you may buy more soda than you want at the moment and keep the rest for later. Why would you buy a case of 24 when you only want a few cans today? Why would the company price a case of 24 cans less than what 2 cartons of 12 would cost?

Michael Newman/PhotoEdit

Figure 13.13

Economic order quantity for scrub kits

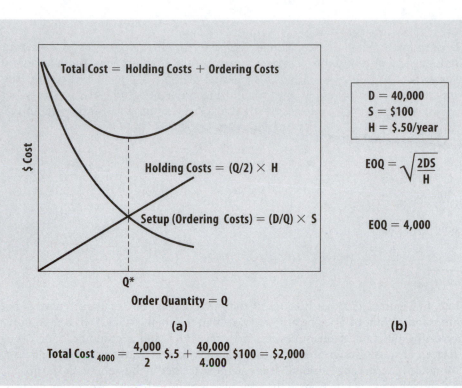

(a)

$$\text{Total Cost}_{4000} = \frac{4,000}{2}\ \$.5 + \frac{40,000}{4.000}\ \$100 = \$2,000$$

D = 40,000
S = $100
H = $.50/year

$$EOQ = \sqrt{\frac{2DS}{H}}$$

EOQ = 4,000

(b)

4000 units, or should the purchasing agent buy 5000 or 6000 at a time? Figure 13.14 illustrates this situation. Because cost is now a function of the quantity ordered, we need to consider purchase costs in our order sizing decisions. Letting C represent price, we know that the annual purchase cost of the item is CD (price times annual demand). The appropriate annual total cost function to minimize is, therefore:

$$TC = \frac{Q}{2}H + \frac{D}{Q}S + CD$$

Example 13.2

Fred orders plastic pellets to use in the injection molding equipment that makes the cell phone cases. He uses about 200 boxes (each weighing 50 lbs.) of these pellets each year. It costs $80 to place an order and costs about $10 to carry a pound of pellets in inventory for a year. How many pounds of the pellets should Fred order at a time?

Fred needs to find the EOQ.

Annual Demand (D) = 200 × 50 = 10,000 pounds.
Holding cost (H) = $10 per pound per year.
Ordering Cost (S) = $80 per order.

$$EOQ = \sqrt{\frac{2DS}{H}}$$

$$= \sqrt{\frac{2(10,000)(80)}{10}}$$

$$= 400$$

Fred will order 400 pounds of pellets at a time, or eight boxes.

Example 13.3

Based on Example 13.2, determine what Fred would spend each year holding and ordering the plastic pellets for cell phone cases.

$$\text{Annual Holding Cost} = \frac{Q}{2}H$$

$$= \frac{400}{2}10 = \$2000 \text{ per year}$$

$$\text{Annual Ordering Cost} = \frac{D}{Q}S$$

$$= \frac{10,000}{400}80$$

$$= \$2000 \text{ per year}$$

Notice, consistent with Figure 13.13 and our expectations, annual holding and annual ordering costs are equal at the EOQ. As stated earlier, "the cost minimizing order quantity is the amount that perfectly balances annual ordering and annual holding costs."

Note, in Figure 13.14 that because of the price breaks, the total cost curve is not continuous. Without price breaks, we know that the total cost curve is a monotonic decreasing function at quantities less than the EOQ, and a monotonic increasing function at quantities greater than the EOQ. (Who said you'd never use calculus?) "Monotonic decreasing" means that as you move farther to the right on the horizontal axis, the value of the function on the vertical axis only decreases. "Monotonic increasing" means that as you move farther to the right on the horizontal axis, the value of the function on the vertical axis only increases. Consequently, we need only consider ordering the EOQ versus ordering the minimum quantities required to receive the price breaks at quantities greater than the EOQ. In our example, that means comparing the total cost of ordering 4000 units at a price of $1 each to the cost of ordering

Figure 13.14

Quantity discount model for scrub kits

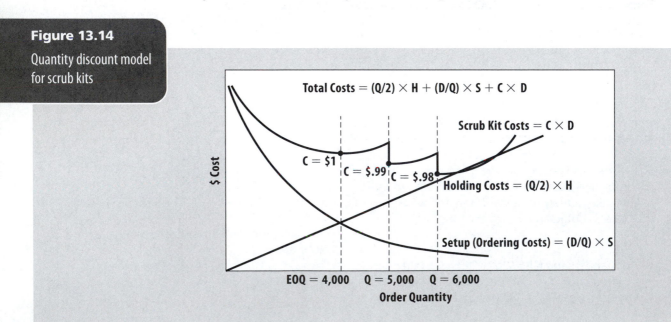

5000 units at a price of $0.99 each or 6000 units at a price of $0.98 each. Using the formula given in Figure 13.14, the total costs may be computed as follows:

$$TC = \frac{Q}{2}H + \frac{D}{Q}S + CD$$

$TC_{4000} = (4{,}000/2) \times 0.50 + (40{,}000/4{,}000) \times 100 + 1.00 \times 40{,}000 = \$42{,}000.00$
$TC_{5000} = (5{,}000/2) \times 0.50 + (40{,}000/5{,}000) \times 100 + 0.99 \times 40{,}000 = \$41{,}650.00$
$TC_{6000} = (6{,}000/2) \times 0.50 + (40{,}000/6{,}000) \times 100 + 0.98 \times 40{,}000 = \$41{,}366.67$

Based on these computations, it is clear that the savings from the price discount and a reduction in the frequency of ordering more than offset the increase in holding costs associated with the 6000 unit order quantity. As a result, the optimal order quantity would be 6000 units, and the order interval would increase to 6000/109.589, or 54.75 days.

Fixed Order Quantity with Variable Demand and Lead Times

The fixed order quantity model shown in Figure 13.13 assumed that demand and lead time were constant. In reality, the demand for independent demand items is rarely constant. Lead times might be known, but they frequently vary. As a consequence, managers usually do not set the reorder point at the expected usage during lead time. Instead, they set it a bit higher to maintain a certain margin of safety. To give a common example of this approach, most people refill their gas tank well before they are about to run out of gas. In the same way, managers are more comfortable with an inventory model that includes some safety stock, such as the one presented in Figure 13.15. Notice that the lead time in this figure varies from one order to the next. So, too, does the usage rate. The order quantity remains constant.

To accommodate the uncertainty of demand and lead times in Figure 13.15, managers have added safety stock to the on-hand inventory, which makes the reorder point the sum of the safety stock and the expected demand during lead time. Without safety

Example 13.4

Using the information from Examples 13.2 and 13.3, determine the best order quantity if Fred's supplier normally charges $1.00 per pound of plastic pellets but offers a 2% discount for orders of at least 1000 pounds (i.e., orders of twenty boxes or more). We determined in Example 13.2 that the EOQ was 400 pounds, thus we need only compare total costs at order sizes of 400 and 1000 pounds to determine the best alternative.

$$TC_{400} = \frac{Q}{2}H + \frac{D}{Q}S + DC$$

$$= \frac{400}{2}10 + \frac{10{,}000}{400}80 + 10{,}000 \times (1.00)$$

$$= \$14{,}000$$

$$TC_{1000} = \frac{Q}{2}H + \frac{D}{Q}S + DC$$

$$= \frac{1000}{2}10 + \frac{10{,}000}{1000}80 +$$

$$10{,}000 \times (1.00 \times .98)$$

$$= \$15{,}600$$

Clearly, the better choice for Fred is to forego the discount and continue ordering 400 pounds at a time. The savings associated with lower priced bulk orders are more than offset by the increase in annual holding costs.

INTEGRATING OM:

Satisfying Customers Requiring Financial Advice

In a May 17, 1993, "Money Angles" column in *Time* magazine, financial guru Andrew Tobias suggested that the rate of return on price discounts warrants bulk purchases of commodities for everyday use. A letter to the editor concerning an apparent oversight in the article and Tobias's response to the letter were published in a subsequent issue (June 14, 1993).

Tobias's original column claimed that a consumer could save money by buying in bulk, noting that if you bought a case of wine every 12 weeks at a 10% discount, you would save more than 40% a year. A letter writer questioned this position and claimed that the yearly savings would still total only 10% (just off a bigger total), not more than 40%.

Tobias responded by correcting himself as follows: "Oops. I should have said you'd earn 40%, not save it. Say the wine was $5 a bottle. That's $60 for 12 bought one a week, or $54 if they were all purchased up front, by the case, with a 10% discount. If you were going to buy the wine anyway, that's a $6 tax-free return on tying up $54 for 12 weeks, or 11%. At an annual rate of return, that is well in excess of 40%."

Perhaps Tobias wasn't thinking of the investment in terms of the fixed quantity inventory model, but that's really what's going on here. If he had been thinking in terms of Figure 13.11, he would have realized that you aren't tying up $54 for 12 weeks—the investment

declines each week. When comparing the $54 investment up front with the option of spending $5 each week, the initial investment was only $49. A week later, the incremental investment would only have been $44, and so on.

Figure 13.11 fits this situation perfectly—demand is constant and there's no appreciable lead time. Using Figure 13.11 you could estimate that the average inventory is ½ of the initial inventory, and the average amount of money tied up is ½ of the $54 value of that inventory. Over the course of the year, you would save $6 four times or $24. So the average investment of roughly $27 gives an annual savings of $24. The quarterly rate of return is $6/$27 = 22%. When compounded annually, the return on that investment exceeds 88%.

A lot of people think Tobias is silly to recommend buying household items such as toothpaste and soap in bulk just to save 5% or 10%. Granted, you have to store the stuff and keep track of it; but from the financial point of view it makes plenty of sense. Tobias might have gotten some of the numbers wrong, but he's right about the investment value of such price discounts.

By the way, while you do have the negligible cost of storing the wine, you also save yourself 11 of the 12 trips to the store. (Or do you like to shop?)

Stock-out

A zero inventory balance.

stock there is about a 50% chance of running out of inventory before a new order comes in (based on reasonable assumptions regarding the distribution of demand during lead time). When the safety stock is added to the reorder point, the average inventory level increases by the amount of the safety stock, and the chance of a **stock-out**, which is a zero inventory balance, decreases. In short, the safety stock protects against shortages that could occur due to higher demand rates or unusually long lead times.

The amount of safety stock to carry can be statistically determined, such that stock-outs will occur in only a certain percentage of order cycles. Alternatively, the level of safety stock can be set such that a certain percentage of demand is satisfied from stock. Detailed information regarding the calculation of safety stock quantities is addressed in the next section of this chapter.

Figure 13.15

Fixed order quantity model—variable lead time and demand

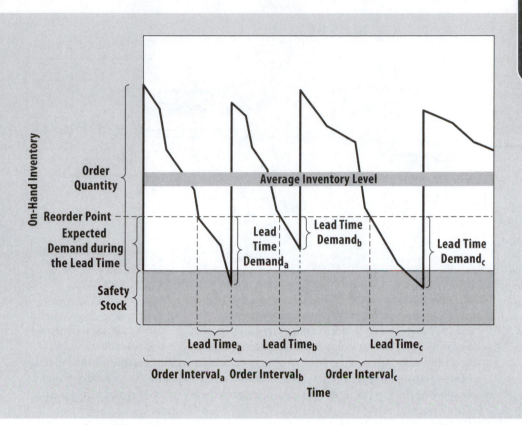

The variability of demand and lead time requires constant monitoring of the level of available inventory. If demand rates were constant, predicting the time when the next order should be placed would be easy. But because demand is variable, the only way to know when to place an order is to keep a perpetual count of inventory. Doing so makes sense for very expensive or important A inventory items, but, for other items, the cost or effort required to keep track of on-hand quantities is prohibitive.

Simple alternatives, such as inventory reserves and two-bin systems, have been developed to keep track of less-important inventory items. A departmental secretary who keeps a stock of overhead transparencies in a locked desk drawer is using a reserve system. When a faculty member complains that the department has run out of transparencies, the secretary simply places the reserve transparencies in the supply closet. The reserves should be adequate to cover the department's needs during the lead time for reordering the transparencies. The reserves provide built-in notification that the time to reorder transparencies has arrived. (As a side benefit, the secretary gets to look like a lifesaver.) A two-bin system like the one illustrated in Figure 13.16 works in a similar way. In this scenario, it takes no more than 2 days to receive an order of copier paper and the usage rate is about one ream per day, but never more than two reams per day. The office manager unpacks the box of paper when it arrives and places a re-order notice in the stack above on the two bottom reams. (Signified in this figure by the blue layers marked with an "x.") When users of the copy machine get to the re-order notice, they simply give it to the office manager and the order is placed.

Figure 13.16

Two-bin system for ordering copier paper

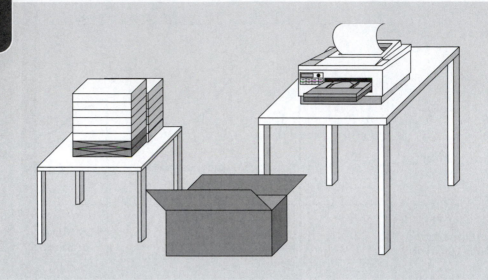

You may have seen a two-bin system in use at local retail outlets, particularly hardware stores. An open box holds items available for purchase; underneath sits a full, unopened box of the same item. When the top box is emptied, the second is opened, and the label from the empty box is used to order a replacement. The reorder point is reached when the top box is empty. Again, there is no need for daily counts or a usage tracking system.

When the demand during the lead time is a random variable, it will sometimes be less than expected, so some inventory is still left when the next order is received. At other times it will be more than expected, so that a stock-out will occur.

As is suggested in Figure 13.15, one way of coping with this uncertainty is **safety stock**, which is extra inventory that is held to reduce the chance of a stock-out. Then:

Safety stock

Extra inventory that is held to reduce the chance of a stockout.

$$R = \mu_{DDLT} + SS$$

where R is the reorder point, μ_{DDLT} is the expected demand during lead time, and SS is the safety stock.

There are a number of ways to determine the amount of safety stock to carry. We shall consider two: a policy-based approach and a cost-based approach. First, we need to consider the idea of a *desired service level*.

DESIRED SERVICE LEVEL

Service level

The measure of how well an inventory system meets demand.

The **service level** of an inventory system is a measure of how well it meets demand. One of two approaches, which are somewhat related, is typically used:

1. The probability that a stock-out will not occur during an order interval, i.e., the probability that all demand during an order interval will be filled from stock.

2. The probability that a unit of demand will be filled from stock.

The first measure relates directly to the graph of inventory level in Figure 13.15. In the second order interval shown, the demand during lead time was low, less than the reorder point, so there would not have been a stock-out even if there were no safety stock. During the first and third order intervals in Figure 13.15, the demand during lead time was higher than expected; a stock-out would occur if the safety stock had not been fairly high. With half as much safety stock, there would have been no stock-out during the first cycle, but a stock-out would occur during the third cycle when the demand during lead time was higher. Within the three cycles shown in Figure 13.15, one of three possible outcomes might have resulted, depending on the level of safety stock:

▶ With no safety stock, a stock-out would occur during two of the three cycles.

▶ With a moderate level of safety stock a stock-out would occur during one of the three cycles.

▶ With a high level of safety stock (the actual case), no stock-outs would occur.

The second measure of the service level indicates the amount of demand facing a stock-out rather than whether or not a stock-out happens. This is a fairly common measure of service level in practice; many inventory control departments track their **fill rate**, which is the percentage of demand filled from stock.

Fill rate

The percentage of demand filled from stock.

These two measures of service level are obviously related: A stock-out occurs (measure 1) whether one unit of demand or many cannot be filled from stock (measure 2). The second measure is more complicated, because it not only recognizes the existence of a stock-out, but also indicates how much demand goes unmet during the stock-out.

While either stock-out measure can be used to set the safety stock level, the second measure requires more complicated analysis than we will deal with here. We will focus on the first measure: the probability that a stock-out will not occur during an order interval.

A POLICY-BASED APPROACH TO SETTING SAFETY STOCK

A policy-based approach to setting safety stock specifies the maximum allowable probability that there will be a stock-out during an order interval. To do this, we must have a probability distribution of **demand during lead time (DDLT)**. There are a variety of ways to develop such a probability distribution. One approach would be to develop a relative frequency distribution based on past history. A second approach would be to use a forecasting system such as simple exponential smoothing to estimate the mean demand during lead time and base the standard deviation on the forecast error measure (see Chapter 11).

Demand during lead time (DDLT)

A variety of ways to develop a probability distribution.

If we can assume that the lead time is a constant, with the only variability in demand during the lead time coming from the variability in day-to-day (or week-to-week, etc.) demand, and further assume that demand is independent from day to day, then determining the mean and standard deviation of demand during lead time is simpler. From basic probability theory, we get:

$$\mu_{DDLT} = L\mu_d$$

$$\sigma_{DDLT} = \sigma_d\sqrt{L}$$

where μ_d and σ_d are the mean and standard deviation of daily demand.

Regardless of how the probability distribution of demand during lead time is estimated, we can then determine the reorder point (and safety stock) that would give the desired maximum allowable probability of stock-out, as shown in Figure 13.17. If we can assume that demand during lead time has a normal distribution, then the reorder point is given by:

$$R = \mu_{DDLT} + Z_\alpha\sigma_{DDLT}$$

where R is the reorder point, μ_{DDLT} is the expected demand during lead time, σ_{DDLT} is the standard deviation of demand during lead time, and Z_α is the value of Z, the standard normal variable that gives α, the allowable probability of a stock-out.

Figure 13.17

Probability of stock-out
with reorder point R

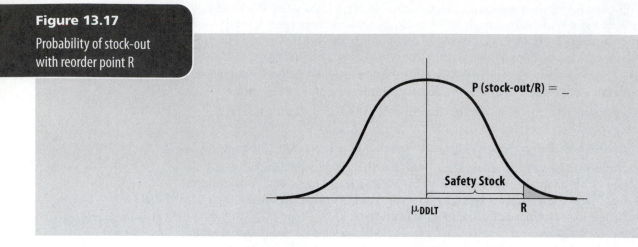

$P\,(\text{stock-out}/R) = \_$

Safety Stock

μ_{DDLT} R

A COST-BASED APPROACH TO SETTING SAFETY STOCK

If it is possible to determine the cost of incurring a stock-out, then it is possible to determine what the probability of a stock-out should be in order to balance the cost of carrying extra inventory (more safety stock) against the expected cost of stock-outs without that extra inventory. The simplest approach to determining what the reorder point and safety stock should be in order to balance these costs is to determine the expected economic payoff of a slightly larger reorder point and the expected economic loss from a slightly reduced reorder point. This would be called a marginal analysis on the reorder point level.

A table describing the economic payoffs for marginal analysis on the reorder point level (called a payoff table) is shown in Figure 13.18. Suppose that the reorder point is

Example 13.5

While the company that supplies examining gloves to Cheryl's hospital (Example 13.1) does average 14 days for delivery, as quoted, historical records indicate that demand during lead time has a standard deviation of 5.3 boxes. Assume demand during lead time has a normal distribution.

 a) What should the reorder point be if the hospital is willing to accept a stock-out in one cycle out of 20, on average?

 b) What will the safety stock be with this reorder point?

Solution:

 a) Averaging one stock-out out of 20 cycles means that P(stock-out) = .05 for any given cycle. The value of Z that gives this probability 1.645. Mathematically we could write Z(1.645)

=> P(stock-out) $\leq$ 0.05. From Example 13.1, the expected demand during a lead time averaging 14 days is 38.36 boxes. Using the "reorder point" equation, we can determine the reorder point:

$R = \mu_{DDLT} + Z_{\alpha}\sigma_{DDLT} = 38.36 + 1.645(5.3)$

$\quad = 38.36 + 8.72$

$\quad = 47.08$ boxes

 b) This result can be rounded down to 47 boxes, which will raise the probability of a stock-out to a little more than .05, or be rounded up to 48 boxes to guarantee the desired service level.

If R = 47, the safety stock is 47 − 38.36

$\quad = 8.64$ boxes.

Figure 13.18

Payoff table for decision about whether or not to increase reorder point and safety stock

	I-P (Stock-out/R) (Last Unit Not Needed)	P (Stock-out/R) (Last Unit is Needed)
Did Not Increase Reorder Point to R + 1 Units	0	V
Did Increase Reorder Point to R + 1 Units	H(Q/D)	H(Q/D)

R. The question is, Should it be increased to R + 1? The two decision alternatives are: (1) do not increase, and (2) increase. There are also two states of nature: (1) Unit R + 1 is not needed, and (2) unit R + 1 is needed. The probability that unit R + 1 is needed is P(stock-out|R), i.e., the probability that there will be a stock-out if the reorder point is kept at R. The probability that unit R+1 is not needed is simply $1 - $ P(stock-out|R).

The costs for the four cells in Figure 13.18 may be explained as follows:

▶ If unit R + 1 is not stocked and not needed, then there is no cost.

▶ If unit R + 1 is not stocked but is needed, then there will be a stock-out, which will cost V.

▶ If unit R + 1 is stocked but is not needed, then unit R + 1 will have been carried in inventory for the entire length of the order interval. Carrying this unnecessary unit of inventory will cost a fraction of H (the annual holding cost per unit of inventory). This fraction of H would be the length of an order interval relative to the length of a year. The demand during an order interval averages Q units, relative to the demand during a year averaging D units, so the relevant fraction is Q/D.

▶ If unit R + 1 is stocked and is needed, then unit R + 1 will have been carried in inventory for *almost* the entire length of the order interval, because we are considering the last unit stocked. Rather than trying to determine the small amount by which the holding cost could be reduced, we will simply use the same carrying cost shown in the lower left corner of the table.

Using Figure 13.18, we can see that the reorder point should be increased if the expected cost of an increase is less than or equal to the expected cost of no increase. That is, if:

$$H(Q/D) \leq V \times P(\text{stock-out}|R) = V \times P(DDLT > R)$$

Doing a little algebra on this inequality, we get the following result: Set the reorder point at the highest value R for which:

$$P(\text{stockout}) = (P(DDLT) > R) \leq \frac{H(Q/D)}{V} = \frac{HQ}{VD}$$

Example 13.6

Refer to Example 13.5. Cheryl's hospital has worked out an arrangement with neighboring hospitals to back each other up in the event that any of them runs out of commonly used supplies. If a hospital stocks out of examining gloves, the materials management department director will send a van to one of the neighboring hospitals to pick some up. When the new order comes in, the borrowed boxes will be replaced. The cost of the emergency restocking procedure is estimated to be $50. Given this information, what should the reorder point and safety stock be?

Solution:

From the information presented here, V = $50. From Example 13.1, we find that H = $1 per box per year, D = 1,000 boxes per year, and Q = 283 boxes per order.

The desired probability of a stock-out is:

$$P(\text{stockout}) = \frac{HQ}{VD} = \frac{(1)(283)}{(1,000)(50)}$$

$$= \frac{283}{50,000} = .0057$$

From a normal distribution table, Z = 2.53 provides P(stockout) $\leq$ .0057. Using the reorder point equation:

$$R = \mu_{\text{DDLT}} + Z_{(1-.0057)}\sigma_{\text{DDLT}} = 38.36 + 2.53(5.3)$$

$$= 38.46 + 13.41 = 51.77$$

The reorder point should be 52 boxes, and the safety stock will be 52 – 38.46 = 13.64 boxes.

Fixed Order Quantity with Non-Instantaneous Replenishment

When goods are purchased from an outside vendor, it is reasonable to expect the entire order to be delivered at once. The fixed order quantity model in Figure 13.11 assumed instantaneous replenishment. But internal orders for parts might not be received all at once; rather, the materials are likely to become available as they are produced. In this situation, each order cycle will be composed of two distinct periods: a period during which both production and usage occur, and a period during which only usage occurs. Figure 13.19 illustrates this situation. It is similar to the situation that develops when you bake four dozen cookies but have only three dozen left when you are done, because some of them got eaten in the process.

Because material is used while it is being produced, the average inventory level is lower when replenishment is non-instantaneous and the optimal production order quantity is slightly larger than the EOQ. In fact, as Figure 13.19 shows:

$$\text{Avg inventory w/noninst replenishment} = \frac{\left[Q\left(1-\frac{d}{p}\right)\right]}{2}$$

where p is the periodic production rate (for example, the number of units produced per day).

The cost-minimizing production order quantity is frequently referred to as the **economic production quantity (EPQ)**.

Economic production quantity (EPQ)

The cost-minimizing production order quantity.

$$\text{EPQ} = \sqrt{\frac{2DS}{H(1-\frac{d}{p})}}$$

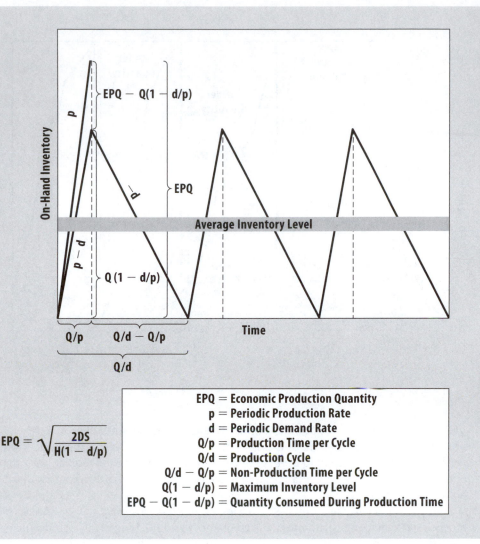

Figure 13.19

Fixed order quantity model—non-instantaneous replenishment

The instantaneous and non-instantaneous replenishment models are really not different. In fact, the term "instantaneous" simply means that an order is received before any more stock can be used. In other words, the production rate, p, is really fast relative to the usage rate, d. That makes the ratio d/p close to zero, in which case the formulas for the EOQ and the EPQ are identical.

Fixed Interval or Periodic Review Models

With a steady rate of inventory usage, the EOQ may be considered the amount of on-hand inventory required for a fixed period. Consequently, we can talk about an optimal order interval. For example, Cheryl might know that at her hospital, the optimal order quantity for latex gloves will last about 2 weeks. In that case, it is probably easier to establish a standing order for delivery every 2 weeks rather than to place a special

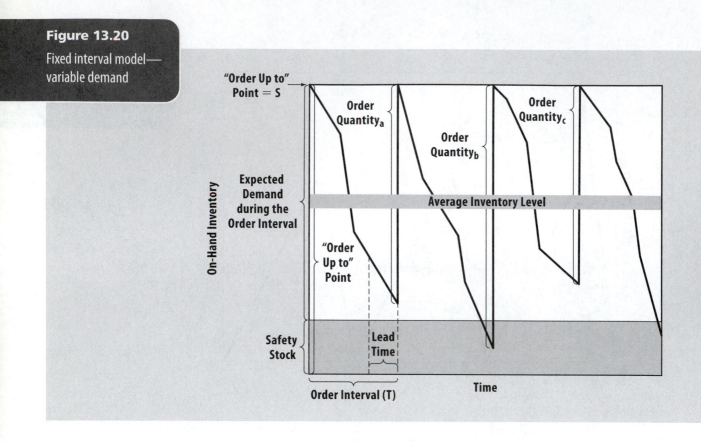

Figure 13.20

Fixed interval model—variable demand

order whenever the reorder point is reached. If Cheryl does so, she will probably carry a bit of safety stock to cover the surges in demand that might occur during any 2-week period. Figure 13.20 presents a number of equations, starting with the formula for the optimal order quantity, which can be used to convert the optimal order quantity to the optimal order interval.

Many salespersons are aware that ordering items regularly every 1, 2, or 3 weeks is much easier than planning to order a fixed quantity and tracking the use of inventory until the next order point. They know the economics behind their customers' purchase quantities and visit their customers at fixed intervals that are convenient for reordering. This approach gives customers confidence in the salesperson's ability to meet their needs. It also provides some assurance that their orders will be placed at stock levels reasonably close to the reorder point.

Many companies receive their shipments from suppliers on a fixed interval schedule. Each shipment replaces only those items that have been used since the last shipment. This situation is particularly common in retailing, especially among chain stores and franchises that receive most or all of their independent demand inventory from a central warehousing facility. The local fast food establishment knows when the next truck will be arriving and places its order in time to ensure that items used since the last shipment will be replaced. Figure 13.20 illustrates the fixed interval model.

If demand varies and the order interval is fixed, the quantity that is ordered will vary, depending on the inventory that is on hand at the time the order is placed. The amount that is ordered will be the amount needed to replace the stock used since the last order. Typically, the amount of inventory on hand immediately after an order is received should be sufficient to last through an entire order interval, including lead time, plus safety stock and minus on-hand inventory. As a result, the order quantity would be:

q = average daily demand × (order interval + lead time) +
 safety stock − on-hand inventory

Fixed interval models are not often used with *A* inventory items. Inventory management policies based on these models do not require a perpetual inventory record or close managerial scrutiny; they simply require an inventory check prior to placement of an order. Items that are reordered on a fixed interval model are therefore subject to stock-out at any time during the order interval or lead time. This risk of a stock-out necessitates higher levels of safety stock than would be required with a fixed quantity inventory model. The combination of a higher risk of stock-out and higher required levels of safety stock is not appropriate for vital or expensive *A* items. Only if the savings that can be realized by ordering several items together outweigh the cost of additional safety stock would a fixed interval model be appropriate for use with *A* items.

Periodic Review Systems When Demand Is Probabilistic

While it is possible to determine the optimal length of the review period, T is usually based on the frequency with which a supplier's representative makes deliveries. The issue we deal with here is how to determine the desired **stocking level**, S, when the demand rate is variable.

    The basic idea in determining the desired stocking level, S, in a periodic review system is similar to that in determining the reorder point, R, in a continuous review system: The amount of stock available should be sufficient to cover expected demand until the next order arrives, plus an allowance to cover uncertainty. The main difference between the two models is in the safety stock. As shown in Figure 13.15, in a fixed quantity system, the safety stock needs to supply stock-out protection for the relatively short time between placing and receiving the order, which is the lead time, L. In a periodic review system, however, the time between placing orders is fixed, not variable. The safety stock must supply stock-out protection for the relatively long time between placing an order and receipt of the following order, because that is the next time it will be possible to satisfy any unusually heavy demands. That is, the safety stock must cover the uncertainty of demand over the time interval T + L, not just L. As a result, the safety stock will be larger than in a periodic review system, even if the average time between orders, the lead time, and the variability in daily demand are the same.

Stocking level

The amount of stock available

DETERMINING THE DESIRED STOCKING LEVEL, S

As just stated, the basic concept in determining the desired stocking level is: The amount of stock available should be sufficient to cover expected demand until the next order arrives, plus an allowance to cover uncertainty. Because the time until the next order arrives is T + L—the time until the next order will be placed, T, plus the time until that order is delivered, L—the desired stocking quantity is:

$$S = \mu_d(T + L) + SS$$

where μ_d is the expected daily demand, T is the length of the review period in days, L is the lead time in days, and SS is the safety stock.

Because some inventory is likely to exist at the time the order is placed, the actual order quantity will be given by:

$$Q = S - I$$

where Q is the order quantity and I is the existing inventory.

DETERMINING THE SAFETY STOCK

The process of determining the amount of safety stock to carry in a periodic review system is the same as in a reorder point system, however the length of time for which the safety stock must provide stock-out protection is different. The desired safety stock can be determined with a policy-based approach or a cost-based approach; the procedures are identical to those used previously except for the probability distribution used. As stated, the safety stock must provide stock-out protection for the period T + L, so the probability distribution used must be for that amount of time rather than L.

In particular, if we can assume that L, the length of the lead time, is a constant, as is the length of the review period, T, and the only variability in demand during the period T + L comes from the variability in day-to-day demand; and if we can further assume that demands from day to day are independent, then as basic probability theory tells us, the mean and standard deviation of demand during the time period T + L are given by:

$$\mu_{T+L} = (T + L)\mu_d$$

$$\sigma_{T+L} = \sigma_d \sqrt{T+L}$$

where μ_d and σ_d are the mean and standard deviation of daily demand. Then, for a desired stock-out probability α, the stocking level S is given by:

$$S = (T + L)\mu_d + Z_\alpha \sigma_{T+L}$$

Supply Chain Management—Based Improvements to Master Scheduling and Inventory Management

Business practices that span many functional areas are at the heart of many of the recent changes in inventory management. Advances in information systems and communication technologies provide the opportunity for greater coordination of decisions among marketing, operations, purchasing, and accounting within one company and across company boundaries within a supply chain. Enterprise resources planning (ERP) systems facilitate this coordinated decision making. Similarly, improving processes that cut across functional boundaries often results in significant reductions in ordering or setup costs and stock-out risks. This allows firms to reduce their order quantities and reorder points and results in leaner inventory policies.

Enterprise Resources Planning Systems

Today most corporate information systems are based on client server technology, whereby many personal computer users can share the same information. This means that the computers in the marketing department share information back and forth

Example 13.7

Oxygen and other gases are delivered to Cheryl's hospital every Thursday. The quantity delivered is based on an order called in by the hospital on Monday, 3 days before. The average daily usage of oxygen is six tanks, with a standard deviation of 1.2 tanks.

a) Determine the desired stocking level if the hospital wishes to take no more than a 2% chance of running out of oxygen between orders.

b) If there are 10 tanks on hand on a given Monday, what should the order be?

Solution

a) We are given that $T = 7$ days (review every Monday) and $L = 3$ days (the Monday order is delivered on Thursday). The mean daily usage is $\mu_d = 6$ tanks and the standard deviation of daily usage is $\sigma_d = 1.2$ tanks. The allowable stock-out probability is given as 0.02, which, from a normal distribution table, gives a Z value of $Z_{0.98} = 2.05$. The desired stocking level is:

$$S = (T + L)\mu_d + Z_\alpha \sigma_d \sqrt{T + L}$$
$$= (7 + 3)(6) + 2.05(1.2) \sqrt{7 + 3}$$
$$= 60 + 7.78 = 67.78$$

which we round up to 68.

b) On the Monday when there are ten tanks on hand, the order should be for $68 - 10 = 58$ tanks.

with those in finance, OM, purchasing, accounting, logistics, and so on. Up-to-date information regarding sales is readily available to decision makers who forecast earnings, schedule operations, purchase materials, and track costs. Similarly, information regarding operations schedules is available to those who sell, purchase, forecast earnings, and track costs. Really, it is hard to imagine a functional decision that does not benefit from current business information coming from other functional areas. From an inventory management perspective, this information allows firms to more effectively plan the location, quantity, and timing of material availability to more effectively satisfy their customers with lower total inventory costs.

ERP systems do not only span functional areas; they also span geographic distances and potentially multiple businesses in a supply chain. This means that business decision makers can factor the plans and activities of their customers and suppliers—from any location in the world—into their current decisions. It means that they can more easily see inventory throughout their supply chain and compare the efficiency of facilities. As a result, many companies have been able to improve the coordination of their supply chain and dramatically reduce redundant or excessive inventories, planning lead times, working capital requirements, while increasing bargaining power with suppliers, and improving customer service. At the same time, the middle managers whose job it was to accumulate data and pass it through the hierarchy have seen their jobs become obsolete. By re-engineering their scheduling and inventory management systems to take advantage of ERP system capabilities, therefore, companies not only become more efficient, they also become less bureaucratic and more responsive to customer needs. Numerous large companies have credited ERP systems with annual savings in excess of $100 million a year.

The market for ERP software is itself a multibillion dollar market. To date it has been dominated by the German firm SAP. Other mainstream ERP system providers

Scott Olson/Getty Images Inc.

Innovations like Radio Frequency Identification devices (RFID) will completely transform the way data collection can be automated. Such technology will lead to many diverse and profound changes in the way we use IT to support the operation and management of business.

Figure 13.21

Coordinating business decisions with ERP systems

Warehousing and Logistics
• Allocates available inventory to customer orders and handles shipping arrangements
• Updates order status as shipping information becomes available

Operations Management
• Tracks demand to schedule production as additional finished goods are needed
• Monitors and updates order progress
• Monitors and inputs employee hours and performance
• Monitors and inputs product quality information

International Field Sales Personnel
• Use notebook computers during sales call to check prices, availability, customer's credit history, business terms, etc.
• Enter the order

Accounting/Corporate Finance
• Issues invoices in the appropriate language
• Tracks receivables and payables
• Issues payroll checks
• Issues supplier checks per contract and delivery details
• Maintains customer credit histories and authorizes customer credit on orders

Data Warehouse Available to Users via the Internet

Human Resources
• Establishes staffing plans and takes care of hiring or layoffs as dictated by corporate policy and production schedules
• Tracks employee hours and performance statistics for payroll and benefit purposes

Purchasing
• Establishes supply contracts and based on the production schedule establishes delivery dates for materials.
• Inputs contract payment terms

Order Tracking
• Customers can get order status online at any time by logging on to the company's website
• Company employees from any function can get any information needed to enhance their decisions—up to date—via online queries of the database

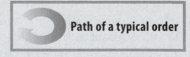 Path of a typical order

Source: Adapted from *Business Week*, Nov. 3, 1997, pp. 164–165

include Oracle, J. D. Edwards, PeopleSoft, and Baan. Figure 13.21 provides a simple overview of the way that SAP's R/3 software could be used to coordinate an order fulfillment process for a hypothetical sneaker company spanning several functions, facilities, and time zones.

Despite the potential benefits of ERP systems, they are no magic bullet. It is clearly possible for companies to spend millions of dollars on new computer systems— without making any change in their underlying operational and decision-making processes. The result is an expensive system that becomes the scapegoat for ongoing business problems.

Improving on "Optimal" Order Quantities

In the past, the attitude that analytically determined order quantities were optimal led many companies to accept large lot sizes. Recently, managers have come to realize that inventory management policies are closely linked to improvement efforts. As a consequence, they have begun to focus on changing the cost structure that lies behind the EOQ calculations. The EOQ is the optimal lot size only for a given set of costs.

Recently, many firms have made a concerted effort to reduce the transaction costs associated with placing purchase orders or the setup costs associated with in-house orders. When a system has bottlenecks, setup times and costs should not be a deterrent to small lot sizes. Activity-based costing (ABC) might be used to estimate the actual cost of the setup, which is probably close to zero if the firm has extra capacity. Furthermore, a better understanding of the drawbacks associated with holding large inventories has highlighted hidden costs that are not accounted for in the classical EOQ model. As a result, "optimal" order quantities are being reduced, and firms are experiencing fewer of the negative consequences associated with large orders and high inventory levels.

When inventory items are managed using a fixed order quantity model, electronic technologies can be used to reduce the cost of tracking inventory. In fact, it has become much easier to maintain a perpetual inventory record with today's information systems and stock tracking systems that identify individual items of inventory with an inexpensive bar code or electronic chip. As such, the cost of constantly monitoring inventory levels is decreasing. Other improvement programs that can also be used to reduce inventory and improve customer service include electronic data interchange (EDI); improved logistics capabilities and less-than-truckload (LTL) transfer arrangements available from freight carriers; and improvements in supplier processes, such as supplier setup-reduction programs.

As Figure 13.22 shows, ordering costs can also be reduced in fixed interval systems, as can the setup costs for internal orders. Thus, the "optimal" order quantity determined using an inventory model should be viewed as optimal only over the short run. Firms need to take a long-term focus on improving customer service by reducing their reliance on inventory. They can do so by reducing the potential for disruption in their value-adding systems, by reducing the uncertainty that they face, and by improving their ordering and setup capabilities.

Recently, suppliers have questioned the efficiency of the classical EOQ model. The bike shop example in Figure 13.23 illustrates the type of problem that can arise when one member of a supply chain adheres rigidly to a particular inventory model. Marshall's bike shop assumes a constant demand for bicycles, its independent demand inventory item. Yet its ordering policy can create very lumpy demand patterns for its parts suppliers.

Thus the "optimal" ordering policy, when applied by one company, can produce boom-and-bust cycles (no pun intended) for suppliers. To deal with the resulting variations in demand, a supplier must carry excess capacity (which is rather inefficient), offer a high level of flexibility (which is costly to develop and maintain), or provide a low level of customer satisfaction. Recognizing that the customer will ultimately pay the supplier's costs, none of these alternatives is very appealing. Our

Figure 13.22

Inventory management—focus on improvement

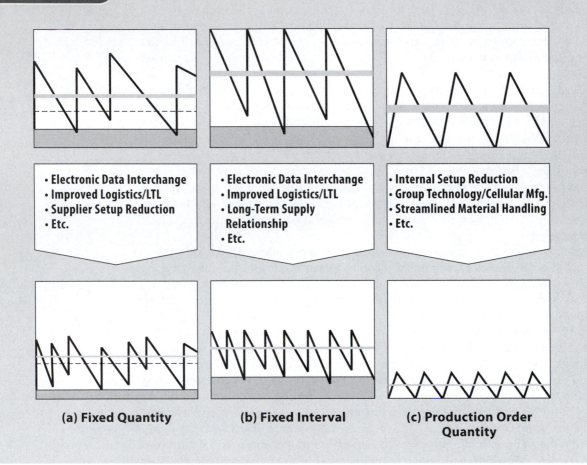

- Electronic Data Interchange
- Improved Logistics/LTL
- Supplier Setup Reduction
- Etc.

- Electronic Data Interchange
- Improved Logistics/LTL
- Long-Term Supply Relationship
- Etc.

- Internal Setup Reduction
- Group Technology/Cellular Mfg.
- Streamlined Material Handling
- Etc.

(a) Fixed Quantity   **(b) Fixed Interval**   **(c) Production Order Quantity**

discussion of supply chain management in Chapter 3 also details recent trends in decision making that recognize the joint interests of all value-adding firms in a supply chain.

In the final analysis, recent trends support the view that the more managers know about the value-adding system and the role of inventory within it, the more likely that their inventory decisions will be consistent with other decisions and will support the firm's competitive priorities. Extending this logic, the more managers know about the supply chain upstream and downstream, the better they will be able to make inventory and scheduling decisions that enhance customer satisfaction. Consequently, the recent surge in use of e-commerce applications has the potential to result in improved master scheduling and inventory management decisions.

Figure 13.23
Impact of inventory management on suppliers

Market Demand for Bikes at Marshall's Bike Shop

Week	1	2	3	4	5	6	7	8	9	10	11	12	13	14
Demand	12	12	12	12	12	12	12	12	12	12	12	12	12	12

Marshall's On-Hand Inventory (Order Quantity = 48)

48

24

0

Time

Demand on Marshall's Bike Supplier (Order Quantity for Wheels = 192, Seats = 300)

Week	1	2	3	4	5	6	7	8	9	10	11	12	13	14
Demand	0	0	0	48	0	0	0	48	0	0	0	48	0	0

Demand on Bike Maker's Wheel Supplier

Week	1	2	3	4	5	6	7	8	9	10	11	12	13	14
Demand	0	0	192	0	0	0	0	0	0	0	192	0	0	0

Demand on Bike Maker's Seat Supplier

Week	1	2	3	4	5	6	7	8	9	10	11	12	13	14
Demand	0	0	300	0	0	0	0	0	0	0	0	0	0	0

S U M M A R Y

Master scheduling and inventory management decisions are all about how existing capacity (established by long-term value-adding system design and the aggregate plan) will be used to satisfy customers. Master scheduling determines the planned timing of completion for the firm's product-service bundles—what is to be done and when. This activity is central to the satisfaction of customers and as a result becomes a critical linking point among marketing, operations, finance, and purchasing. If master scheduling is done right, scheduling decisions will be consistent with those of all other functions and operations. This achievement allows a firm to set itself apart in the customer's eyes. Being able to give customers what they want when they want it leads to competitive advantage.

Inventory decisions are closely related to scheduling decisions, because inventory is often needed to conduct scheduled activities and, at least in manufacturing operations, is created by scheduled activities. We have discussed a number of inventory models in this chapter, including ABC analysis, fixed quantity models, and fixed interval models. Recently, some of the negative consequences of excessive reliance on inventory have become clear. As a result, firms are looking for ways to do without large stocks of material. They are using technologies to enhance their flexibility and reduce the uncertainty they face. They are also beginning to coordinate their systems across entire supply chains. This strategy allows firms to remove many of the uncertainties that necessitate inventory in the first place.

KEY TERMS

ABC inventory analysis, 587
Backward scheduling, 582
Closed loop planning, 581
Cycle counting, 588
Demand during lead time (DDLT), 599
Demand rate, 592
Dependent demand inventory, 582
Dispatching decisions, 577

Economic order quantity (EOQ), 592
Economic production quantity (EPQ), 602
Fill rate, 599
Forward scheduling, 582
Freeze window, 574
Independent demand inventory, 582
Lead time, 592
Loading decisions, 577

Reorder point, 589
Rough-cut capacity planning, 581
Safety stock, 598
Service level, 598
Stocking level, 605
Stock-out, 596

SOLVED PROBLEMS

1. It takes 4 days to order more popcorn at Tuffy's Snack Shop in the student union. Demand is 10 pounds a day and the manager has suggested 5 pounds of safety stock.

   a) What should the reorder point be in their popcorn inventory system?

   b) What would be the likely chance of a stock-out if they did not use safety stock?

Solution:

   a) Use the reorder point formula on page 598.
   R = 4 × 10 + 5 = *45 pounds.*

   b) If no safety stock is being carried, the re-order point is the expected (or mean) usage during lead time. Thus the risk of stock-out is *50%.*

2. Ms. I. Kanby, Materials Management Specialist for Custom Classic China, periodically needs to place orders for graphite, one of the raw materials used in producing dishware. Ms. Kanby knows that manufacturing uses graphite at a rate of 50 kilograms each day (they produce 250 days per year), and that it costs $10.00 per year to carry a kilogram of graphite in inventory. She also knows that the clerical costs for placing an order for graphite are $100 per order, and that the lead time between placing and receiving the entire order is 4 days. Orders are received in one shipment.

   a) At what point should Ms. Kanby reorder ?

   b) If Ms. Kanby were to order 2500 kilograms of graphite at a time, what would be the length of an order interval (time between orders)?

   c) If Ms. Kanby were to order 1000 kilograms of graphite at a time, what would be average annual total costs, *excluding* the cost of the graphite?

   d) What is Ms. Kanby's economic order quantity for graphite?

   e) What is the total cost of managing the inventory when the EOQ is used?

Solution:

a) $R = L \times d = 4 \times 50 = 200$ KG

b) Order Interval $= Q \div d = 2500 \div 50 = 50$ days

c) $TC = \dfrac{Q}{2}H + \dfrac{D}{Q}S + CD$

$= \dfrac{1000}{2}(\$10) + \dfrac{12500}{1000}(\$100)$

$= \$6250$

d) $EOQ = \sqrt{\dfrac{2DS}{H}} = \sqrt{\dfrac{2 \times 12500 \times 100}{10}} = 500$

e) $\dfrac{500}{2}(\$10) + \dfrac{12500}{500}(\$100) = \$5000$

3. Suppose Luis's upholstery department uses 40,000 yards of material per year. The supplier quotes you a price of $8.50 per yard for an order size of 999 yards or less and a price of $8.40 per yard for an order of 1000 or more yards. You assign an annual holding cost of $12.00 per yard to this inventory. Assume ordering cost is $80/order.

   a) What is the EOQ without considering the price of the material?

   b) What order quantity would you use if the objective is to minimize total annual costs of holding, ordering, and the price of the material? (Show the total costs and the savings you expect relative to the other choice.)

Solution:

a) $EOQ = \sqrt{\dfrac{2DS}{H}} = \sqrt{\dfrac{2 \times 40000 \times 12}{80}}$

$= 730$ yards per order

b) $TC_{1000} = \dfrac{1000}{2}(\$12) + \dfrac{40,000}{1000}(\$80)$

$+ 40000(\$8.40) = \$345,200$

$TC_{730} = \dfrac{730}{2}(\$12) + \dfrac{40,000}{730}(\$80)$

$+ 40,000(\$8.50) = \$348,763.56$

Therefore, the policy should be to request 1000 yards per order.

4. Fred's company buys three pager components from the same supplier. The company has been using a fixed interval system for the three components, but each has a unique order interval (i.e., one is weekly, another is every 10 days, etc.). Fred would like to consolidate shipping and receiving as much a possible, and coordinate the three intervals in order to reduce shipping costs. Consider the following information about the three parts:

Part	76hf-1	76hj-1	76hk-1
Cost of checking stock and placing the order (S)	$93.75	$104.17	$375
Annual cost of holding the item in inventory (H)	$.50	$2.50	$.50
Annual Demand	150,000	300,000	150,000

Assume 300 production days per year.

   a) What would be the desired fixed intervals based upon the EOQ equation?

   b) What would you suggest in order to consolidate the shipments?

Solution:

a) The EOQ for 76hf-1 is 7500 units, or about 15 days' worth; thus, the interval is likely to be every 15 days. The EOQ for 76hj-1 is 5000 units, or about 5 days' worth; thus, the interval is likely to be every 5 days. The EOQ for 76hk-1 is 15,000 units, or about 30 days' worth; thus, the interval is likely to be every 30 days.

   b) The company should schedule a truck every 5 days and order 76hj-1 every time, 76hf-1 every third truck and 76hk-1 every sixth truck.

5. Luis's company stocks frequently demanded replacement parts for furniture that is ordered frequently. They range from simple chair spindles to complete "hideaway" bed mechanisms for sleeper sofas. In the table on the top of next page is a selected list of the items kept in the warehouse.

   a) Can you suggest which items might be *A* items? *B*s? *C*s?

   b) What implications would your analysis have on how the warehouse is managed?

Item	Monthly Volume	Item Value($)
u-343-12-xw	500	$4.00
u-343-12-xt	675	$6.00
u-343-12-t	500	$15.00
u-256-27-l	50	$20.00
u-234-23-l	700	$6.00
48t-ch	15	$20.00
44l-23-p	100	$20.00
38-23-ch	500	$8.00
36t-ok	245	$250.00
34-t-ok-l	100	$350.00
34-p-ok-l	150	$30.00
344-36t-ok	100	$4.00
343-36t-ok	7	$100.00
32x48ct-ok	150	$9.00
122-34-t-ok	75	$175.00

For Problem 5

Solution:

a) Three *A* items account for 78% of the dollar volume, five *B* items account for 17%, and seven *C* items account for approx. 5% of the dollar volume.

b) Spend more effort on *A*s, less on *B*s, and even less on *C*s.

6. Hegele Electronics has decided to bring production of a stamped metal component previously purchased from an outside vendor in house and produce it on an existing press. The press is shared with other items they stamp for their products, so determining an economic production quantity is important. The company will need fifty units per hour while they can stamp out 200 per hour. They produce 8 hours a day and are running 250 days per year. The accounting and human resource departments have looked at the labor and time needed to change over the tooling

	Item	Monthly Volume	Item Value($)	Volume ($)		
1	36t-ok	245	$250.00	$61,250.00		
2	34-t-ok-l	100	$350.00	$35,000.00	*A* ITEMS	
3	122-34-t-ok	75	$175.00	$13,125.00	$109,375.00	78%
4	u-343-12-t	500	$15.00	$7,500.00		
5	34-p-ok-l	150	$30.00	$4,500.00		
6	u-234-23-l	700	$6.00	$4,200.00		
7	u-343-12-xt	675	$6.00	$4,050.00	*B* ITEMS	
8	38-23-ch	500	$8.00	$4,000.00	$24,250.00	17%
9	44l-23-p	100	$20.00	$2,000.00		
10	u-343-12-xw	500	$4.00	$2,000.00		
11	32x48ct-ok	150	$9.00	$1,350.00		
12	u-256-27-l	50	$20.00	$1,000.00		
13	343-36t-ok	7	$100.00	$700.00		
14	344-36t-ok	100	$4.00	$400.00	*C* ITEMS	
15	48t-ch	15	$20.00	$300.00	$7,750.00	5%
				$141,375.00		

on the press. They estimate the cost of changing the tooling to be about the same as processing a purchase order, which is $500. The annual cost of carrying inventory is estimated to be 80% of the item's value. This particular stamping is valued at $20.

a) If they were still purchasing the part, what EOQ would you suggest? How long would the average interval between orders be?

b) Now that they are making the part in house, what would be the EPQ? How long would the production run last? How often would they set up to stamp the part?

c) Why is the EPQ larger than the EOQ?

Solution:

a) If they were still buying the part and they arrived all at once then the EOQ = $\sqrt{\dfrac{2DS}{H}}$

$$= \sqrt{\frac{2 \times (50 \times 8 \times 250) \times 500)}{(.8 \times 20)}} = 2500$$

parts per order. At a demand of 50 parts/hour, each order would last $2500 \div 50 = 50$ hours or a little more than 6 days.

b) Making the part in house would result in EPQ

$$= \sqrt{\frac{2DS}{H(1-\frac{d}{p})}} = \sqrt{\frac{2(50 \times 8 \times 250) \times 500}{(.8 \times 20)(1 - \frac{50}{200})}} =$$

2887 parts per production run. At a production rate of 200 parts per hour, each run would take $2887 \div 200 = 14.43$ hours to complete. Again, with a demand of 50 parts/hour, each run would last $2886 \div 50 = 57.7$ hours or a little over 7 days.

c) The EPQ is bigger because, by making the parts in house, a significant amount can be used as they are produced. Thus average inventory will be lower and inventory costs will be lower. Balancing holding and setup costs, therefore requires a larger order quantity.

7. Fly-at-Night Express uses 10,000 #3 envelopes per month. It costs $50 to order and receive a shipment of these envelopes. The envelopes cost $.40 each,

and Fly-at-Night uses an inventory carrying cost rate of 30% per year.

a) Determine the economic order quantity, the average inventory level, and the time between orders if Fly-at-Night operates 307 days per year.

b) What should the reorder point be if the envelope supplier takes ten working days to deliver?

c) If the usage rate given is an average and the standard deviation of daily usage of envelopes is 75, what should the reorder point and safety stock be if Fly-at-Night wants to take no more than a 5% chance of running out of stock of envelopes during any given order cycle?

Solution:

a) We are given that D = 10,000 per month or 120,000 per year, S = $50 per order, and H = .30 × $.40 = $.12 per envelope per year. From the formula for the EOQ, we get:

$$Q^* = \sqrt{\frac{2(50)(120,000)}{.12}} = 10,000$$

The average inventory level is $Q^*/2 = 5,000$. The time between orders is $Q^*/D = 10,000/120,000 = .08333$ years, or $0.08333 \times 307 = 25.6$ days.

b) Daily usage is $120,000/307 = 390.9$ envelopes per day, so the reorder point should be $R = Ld = 10 \times (390.9) = 3909$ envelopes.

With L = 10 days, $\mu_D = 390.9$, and $\sigma_D = 75$, the mean and standard deviation of demand during lead time are:

$$\mu_{ddlt} = L\mu_d = (10)(390.9) = 3909$$

$$\sigma_{DDLT} = \sigma_d \sqrt{L} = (75)\sqrt{10} = 237.17$$

c) For a maximum stock-out probability of $\alpha = .05$, $Z_\alpha = 1.645$ from a normal distribution table. Thus the reorder is:

$$R = \mu_{DDLT} + Z_\alpha \sigma_{DDLT} = 3909 + 1.645(237.17) = 3909 + 390.15 = 4299.15$$

which we can round off to 4299 or round up to 4300. With R = 4299, the safety stock is 390 envelopes.

DISCUSSION QUESTIONS

1. How does the concept of the master schedule differ from that of the aggregate plan described in Chapter 11?

2. Fred was a marketing manager before he took his current job. He once mentioned that the master schedule always seemed to be a compromise between himself and the operations manager (when he said "compromise," his tone and body language seemed to mean "battle"). Can you explain what he meant? Assuming that Fred is talking about producing "plain vanilla," how would his "compromise" differ from the one Luis faces?

3. How far into the future should the master schedule extend? When would you expect notes penciled into the schedule to be based on firm orders? When would you expect to see forecasts? Can you have both?

4. Assume the furniture in Luis's factory takes as many as 8 weeks to make its way from raw materials to finished goods. However, some customers want delivery in 4 weeks. How can Luis do this? How will his decision be reflected on the master schedule?

5. Describe the master schedules for an auto repair shop, advertising agency, and law office. How far into the future should they go? Should they use forward or backward scheduling? Both?

6. A cell phone takes only a few hours to make its way down the line in Fred's factory. How far ahead does Fred need to project his master schedule? Why? Should he fill it up with forecasts or firm orders? Why?

7. Does your dentist have a master schedule? How about your hair stylist? What do they use them for?

8. What are the purposes of inventory? Is it necessary? How does it facilitate operations in a Wal-Mart store? What function does it perform in an auto assembly plant? In a pizza place? In the Alaskan oil pipeline? What about the last remaining soda in your refrigerator, left over from the 12-pack you bought last week?

9. What is ABC analysis? How would you use it to classify the inventory in Luis's furniture plant? How would you classify the fuel Tom uses to run his planes? How would the same fuel be classified if it were used to run the forklifts in Luis's furniture factory? If there is a difference, why?

10. How would you use ABC analysis to classify the clothes in your closet? Would your classification be accurate? How about your CD collection? The food in your refrigerator? How would thinking about your things in this manner help you manage your time and your "stuff"? Could these be the same issues a business manager deals with in managing inventory?

11. Think back to the last time you bought some soda to take back to your dorm or apartment. How many cans did you buy? A 12-pack or a 24-pack? Explain your decision using the concept of the EOQ. Could you use that same line of thinking when you buy milk? What is the difference between the two products? Would the manager of a hardware store think any differently in determining the best quantity in which to buy hammers or drill bits? How about the manager of a music store buying the newest CD release?

12. Explain the EOQ model in words. What are some critical assumptions of the model? How should you deal with them when they are not true?

13. How do the fixed order interval and the economic quantity model differ? More important, how are they alike? When you get cash from an ATM, which model do you use? Do other people use the other model? What issue is the determining factor?

14. What is assumed in the EPQ model that is different from the EOQ model? Where would you expect to see each used?

15. Assume your job is to determine the best batch size for making chocolate chip cookies. How could the baker's appetite determine whether you should use the formula for the EOQ or the EPQ?

16. Explain the impact of quantity discounts on the EOQ model. When would you take a quantity

discount? When would you not take it? Why would a supplier give you a quantity discount in the first place?

17. Why would Fred's company be willing to give a price break to a customer who would buy the same number of phones each year but in bigger order quantities? How would you reconcile such an arrangement with the concepts of just-in-time and supply chain management?

18. Is a "frequent flier" program the same as a quantity discount? How would it be different from a discount based on the size of the traveling party (or an offer of a free tour to groups of at least sixteen travelers)?

19. When you are managing the inventory of gas in your car, what is the reorder point? What is the safety stock? What are the costs of determining the reorder point?

20. Considering ABC analysis, how would the way in which you think about safety stock change from A to B to C items? In terms of your own personal finances, describe what you consider to be the reorder point and safety stock for cash withdrawals from your checking account. How about the blank checks that come with your checking account?

21. What is cycle counting? How does the IRS use a version of it? How would a retail store manager use it?

PROBLEMS

1. If the demand for milk in gallon at the local supermarket is 72,000 gallons per year (assume that they are open 365 days per year) and the cost of placing an order with the dairy is estimated to be $50 for the delivery truck. The holding cost of a gallon is estimated at $.05 per day (it spoils quickly).

   a) What is the best order quantity?

   b) If the dairy wanted to fix the order interval based upon the answer to (a), what would it be?

2. It takes 3 days for the local hardware store to order from its warehouse. The demand for a popular brand of light bulb is twenty-five bulbs per day. If the manager wishes to maintain fifteen bulbs as safety stock, then what should the reorder point for the bulbs be in their inventory system?

3. As a computer retailer, you buy a certain type of computer for resale. It costs $2000, and the annual holding cost is 30% of the cost. Annual demand is 450, and the cost of placing an order is $100.

   a) What is the approximate economic order quantity from your point of view?

   b) If a salesperson from the supplier said that they need to charge a 1% surcharge on orders of less than twenty-five units (something to do with the shipping cost), what do you suggest?

4. Assume we now make the computers mentioned in the problem above "in house." We can make five per day. Also assume 225 production days per year.

   a) In that case, what should be the approximate production order quantity?

   b) How long would the order cycle be?

5. Average demand for an inventory item is 200 units per day, lead time is 2 days, safety stock is 100 units, and the desired order quantity is 2800 units.

   a) What should the reorder point be?

   b) How long is the order cycle?

   c) If we should decide to switch over to a fixed interval based upon the desired order quantity, what would the "order up to" point be?

6. As you discuss the time value of money in your finance class, you think back to a debate you and your roommate had about paying the cable TV bill. As poor students, you only have basic cable costing $10 per month. Your roommate argues it is better only to pay 1 month at a time and keep the money in the bank earning 5% interest per year. You argue that even if the cost of the stamp were the only "setup cost" associated with mailing in the bill on a monthly basis that you considered, it would still be better to pay several months at a time.

a) How can the EOQ be used here?

b) How many months should you pay at a time?

c) Are there other costs you might consider?

7. Bonnie's Bikes manufactures bikes to customers' orders for all ages and budgets. When a customer calls in an order or sends it via the Internet, Bonnie's Bikes will try to build a bike to order and ship it the next day. There follows a listing of the major component categories and the number of unique variations offered in each category. The average cost of a component and the average volume for each variation in a category are also listed.

a) Using ABC analysis, can you help Bonnie's Bikes sort out which items to pay more attention to?

Item Category	# Unique Variations	Average Unit Cost	Avg. Monthly Vol./Part Type
Tires (26")	6	$11.00	170
Tires (24")	6	$4.00	100
Tires (20")	6	$3.00	80
Tire Valves	2	$0.08	1000
Tire Tubes	3	$2.00	1000
Spokes	3	$0.14	22000
Rims (26")	3	$2.12	170
Rims (24")	3	$2.00	200
Rims ("20")	2	$1.75	200
Reflectors	27	$0.05	100
Pumps	3	$11.00	170
Lights	6	$3.00	90
Frames (Women's)	9	$60.00	30
Frames (Men's)	12	$55.00	500
Frames (Children's)	3	$45.00	100
Forks	24	$40.00	55
Fenders	6	$10.00	35
Derailer	5	$20.00	1000
Chains	2	$1.00	500
Bells	2	$3.00	100

8. Bob's Box Top Stuffers is a company that processes all the special offers you see on the back of a cereal box. You have seen them; they are the offers for free watches with the cereal logo on it or a CD with your favorite cartoon character singing on it. Bob's company operates a number of post office boxes, which they constantly monitor and when the pile gets big enough, they set up and process a batch of orders. They provide this service 7 days a week to major cereal companies in hundreds of different situations processing a variety of order types. Bob estimates that a typical offer results in 300 arrivals per day. Even though the fine print for these offers always reads. "allow 4–6 weeks for delivery," Bob also knows that the time an unprocessed offer sits in the post office box costs the cereal company and, ultimately, his company money. He estimates it to be $.25 per week on average. Bob knows he spends about $195 to get a crew set up and running but Bob doesn't know how many to do at a time. In other words, how big should he let the pile in the post office box get before processing the orders?

a) What should be the batch size for processing orders?

b) If it were easier to set up a rotation with a fixed interval between batches, how big would the typical one be?

c) How long with the average order sit in a box prior to being processed?

d) As a customer, what do you think of this situation?

9. Luis's furniture factory makes a common table leg on a machine (a lathe) that is also used to make several other parts. The legs can be turned out at a rate of more than 800 per day yet are used at a rate of 200 per day. It takes five people an hour to set up the machine each time it is switched over to a new part. Machine time is valued at $300 per hour. Luis estimates his labor costs to be $20 per hour, while the cost of carrying a table leg in inventory is estimated at $5 per year. His factory works 250 days per year.

a) How many table legs should he run before switching to something else?

b) How long will that take?

c) How often will he make this part?

d) Should he fix the run length or the interval between runs?

e) His boss wants all current production intervals or quantities cut in half, what should Luis tell his boss? What should he do?

10. A pet supplies store sells 800 cases per year of Arfo dog food. The cost to place and receive an order with the supplier is $50 and it costs the store $1.60 to keep a case in inventory for a year. Determine:

a) The economic order quantity to the nearest case

b) The average inventory level

c) The average number of orders per year

d) The optimal time between orders

11. Mitre Industries uses 10,000 of a special type of insulator per year, paying $5 per unit. It costs $50 to place and receive an order for this insulator. Mitre uses an inventory carrying cost of 20% per year. Determine:

a) The economic order quantity to the nearest integer

b) The average inventory level

c) The average number of orders per year

d) The optimal time between orders

12. Another way of looking at Mitre Industries' usage of this type of insulator (see previous problem) is in terms of the dollar amount used. Express annual usage in dollars and redo all parts of the previous problem. Verify that the answers are the same.

13. Wilshire Farms uses 6000 pounds per year of a special feed supplement that costs $5 per pound. The supplement's supplier offers a two percent discount (to $4.90 per pound) if it is ordered in quantities of 3000 pounds or more at a time. It costs $100 to place and receive an order. Wilshire uses an inventory carrying charge of 40 percent of value per year. Determine the economic ordering quantity.

14. United Transformers produces its Model 417 transformer at a constant rate of 6000 per year, working 240 days per year. One of the components of this transformer, a coil, is produced on a separate production line, which is capable of turning out 30,000 coils per year if it produces nothing else. It costs $180 to set the coil assembly line up to produce and $2.40 to hold a coil in inventory for a year. Determine:

a) The optimal production quantity for coils

b) The average length of a production run

c) The average time between the starts of production runs

d) The average level of coil inventory

15. Peterson's Paint Supply sells paint roller covers. The expected demand for roller covers during the lead time to deliver from the supplier is fifty covers, with a standard deviation of ten covers. If Mr. Peterson wishes to have a stock-out probability of no more than 10% of the order cycles, what reorder point should be used? What is the safety stock? (Assume that the demand during the lead time is normally distributed.)

16. Southeast Community Hospital uses gauze pads at an average rate of ten packages per week with a standard deviation of two packages. It takes 3 weeks for delivery of a gauze pad order. It costs $40 to place and receive a pad order and $1.50 to hold a package of pads in inventory for a year. If a stock-out occurs, Southeast can arrange for an emergency shipment of pads at an added cost of $6 per package. Determine the optimal order quantity and reorder point. (Assume that the demand during the lead time is normally distributed.)

17. Computer Sales, Inc. sells an average of twenty-five boxes of diskettes per week with a standard deviation of 5 boxes. It costs $40 to place and receive a diskette order and $2.40 to keep a box in inventory for a year. The lead time for delivery is 2 weeks. Computer Sales' sales manager estimates that the lost profit and goodwill associated with a stock-out is $7 per box. Determine the optimal order quantity and reorder point. (Assume that the demand during the lead time is normally distributed.)

18. Morton's Cafeteria orders lettuce once a week, on Wednesday, with delivery 2 days later, on Friday.

Lettuce is used seven days a week, with an average daily use of twenty-five heads and a standard deviation of four heads. Determine what the stocking level and safety stock should be if the cafeteria manager wishes to have no more than a one percent chance of a stock-out during each review period. (Assume that the demand during the lead time and review period is normally distributed.)

19. Millicent's Yard Goods orders fabric from a distributor every 4 weeks. The distributor takes 1 week to deliver. For one particular type of denim, the average usage is 30 yards per week with a standard deviation of 5 yards. Determine the stocking level and safety stock required to limit the stock-outs to an average of one every other year. (Assume that the demand during the lead time and review period is normally distributed.)

CHALLENGE PROBLEMS

1. Watson's Office Supply stocks a special type of bond paper. The average rate of demand for the paper is twenty packages per week with a standard deviation of ten packages. It costs $30 to place and receive an order for this type of paper and $.45 to carry a package of paper in inventory for a year.

   a) What is the EOQ for this type of paper?

   b) If the lead time for paper is constant at 2 weeks, and Mr. Watson uses a reorder point of fifty packages, what is the probability of a stock-out? (Assume that the demand during the lead time is normally distributed.)

   c) What reorder point should Mr. Watson use if he wishes the stock-out probability to be no more than 2%?

   d) Suppose that Watson's Office Supply decides to switch to a fixed interval period review policy for this bond paper, ordering every 16 weeks. Determine what stocking level and safety stock will give a 2% stock-out probability. (Assume that the demand during the lead time and review period is normally distributed.)

   e) Given the EOQ calculated earlier, what advice would you give Watson about his order period?

2. Steve's Beta House, a popular sandwich place on campus, has decided to bake its own buns. While demand for the basic bun is 180 dozen per day (the shop is open from noon to midnight, 300 days per year, and closed on Sundays), the company is currently buying buns every Monday and Thursday from a bakery about 2 hours away. The driver checks the stock of buns and leaves whatever it takes to get stock levels to 565 dozen. Steve has checked the invoices recently and found the average delivery to be about 540 dozen. Steve worked out the schedule based upon the bakery's estimated delivery cost ($300 per trip) and Steve's estimate for keeping buns in stock. Assume Steve can lease an oven that could bake 36 dozen buns per hour and have a setup cost of $36 per order. The oven could only be operated while the shop is open but its capacity during that time could be shared by other products used at Steve's.

   a) What is the safety stock level currently implied by the ordering policy?

   b) What is the cost of holding inventory implied by the current ordering policy? Given the short shelf life of baked goods, does this seem reasonable?

   c) How many buns should Steve bake before switching to something else in the oven (EPQ)?

   d) What would be the time required to bake that quantity?

   e) How long would that batch of buns last before Steve would need to set up and bake another batch?

   f) What would be the maximum inventory level under this policy? Can you explain this given the EPQ is greater than the current average order size?

   g) What impact would this change in maximum inventory level have on bun freshness if any?

Case 13: Inventory Tracking with RFID Chips

Many people in the auto identification business (which deals with inventory tracking—not car tags) used to say that RFID will never replace bar codes, that bar codes will always be used for applications where even a five-cent RFID tag is too expensive. We now know that may not be so. In late 2002 researchers at Infineon, the large German chipmaker, successfully integrated plastics electronic circuits on commercially available packaging. The breakthrough makes it possible that ordinary bags of potato chips and boxes of cereal will have RFID microchips and antennas printed on them during the commercial printing process—much the way bar codes are printed on most products today. That means an infrastructure built to track pallets and cases with silicon-based RFID tags could be extended to track everything companies make, move, and sell.

Researchers discovered back in 1977 that certain polymers could act as semiconductors. Cheaper than silicon, the hope has always been that they could be turned into very inexpensive microchips. But researchers developing plastic chips have never been able to come close to matching the performance of silicon. Nor have they found suitable application for plastic chips they could produce until now.

Dr. Guenter Schmid, is head of Infineon's polymer activities. Schmid and his team found a way to increase the performance of plastic, thin-film chips. With this new technique and new materials, the Infineon team created an integrated circuit on ordinary aluminized foil used to keep potato chips and other products fresh. "In principal, [our technique] should work on almost anything," Schmid says. Food packaging paper may need to be coated first. Packaging with metal in it can be used directly or a layer of metal can be laminated to it.

What will the chips cost? "We hope we can do it for a cent or two," says Schmid. "When they are being mass-produced, then it will drop even a little more." Most of the research around thin-film organic semiconductors has focused on using inexpensive polymers. However, they must be purified using chlorinated solvents, which are highly toxic (chlorinated solvents are banned in Germany and other countries). Instead Schmid's team has focused on organic semiconductors, which perform better than polymers and are feasible from both a cost and environmental perspective. He believes it is now possible to print low-cost RFID chips right on cheap packaging materials. "RFID tags don't require high performance," Schmid says. "Our main focus is to get the functionality, to prove that RFID or other circuits are possible in polymer electronics. The second step is to move it to a cheap manufacturing process."

Retailers that dream of one day being able to track every single item in the store, including bars of soap and packs of gum, now have reason to be optimistic. Infineon feels commercialization of the technology could occur by 2008. Before chips can actually be printed onto commercial packaging, the printing industry will need to refine its machinery. Up to now, printers have had no need to improve resolutions because any improvement would be undetectable by the human eye. But electronics could drive new innovations in printing technologies.

SOME QUESTIONS TO THINK ABOUT:

1. How would the availability of disposable RFID chips, costing a penny or less, along with reliable inventory tracking hardware devices and software influence the usefulness of ABC inventory analysis?

2. How will the eventual low price of the chip change the way retail stores can monitor inventory and make replenishment decisions? Hint: A good way to answer this question is to create a table with two columns and two rows. One column will be for retailers without RFID based inventory control and one for retailers with inventory control. One row of the table would depict what the retailers can do, the other what they cannot.

3. How will the availability of RFID inventory control impact the need for safety stock? Considering the costs of carrying inventory, do you believe it's likely that a one-cent RFID chip would be financially justifiable on a $1.50 bag of snack food? What about a $0.60 candy bar sold in a vending machine?

4. What are the concerns that consumers would have about RFID technology? Do you believe these concerns are justified?

Source: Adapted from "Breakthrough on 1-Cent RFID Tag," http://www. rfidjournal. com/article/view/273; and http://www.rfidjournal.com/faq, October 19, 2005

REFERENCE

Newman, W. R., M. Hanna, and M. J. Maffei. "Dealing with the Uncertainties of Manufacturing: Flexibility, Buffers and Integration." *International Journal of Operations and Production Management,* 13, no. 1 (1993): 19–34.

Detailed Scheduling and Control Processes with Lean Thinking and the JIT System

Chapter Outline

Introduction   626
Integrating Operations Management Across the Functions   627
Overview of JIT Systems   630

JIT, Toyota Production System, and Lean Systems   632

The Enormous Impact of JIT and Lean Systems   632

The Applicability of Lean Thinking and JIT   633

Scheduling and Capacity Management in JIT Systems   635

Level Scheduling   636

JIT Perspectives on Inventory   637

Supply Chain and E-Commerce Considerations in JIT   644

Material Planning   648

Lot Sizes and Setup Time   648

Outside Suppliers and Logistical Issues   651

Kanban Systems   654

Controlling Inventory Levels with Kanbans   656

Lean Systems in Services   660
Summary   662
Key Terms   662
Solved Problems   663
Discussion Questions   665
Problems   666
Challenge Problems   668
Case 14: J.C. Penney "Tailors" Its Inventory Management to the Twenty-first Century   669

Learning Objectives

After studying this chapter you should be able to

▶ Demonstrate your understanding of the linkages between operational planning and control decisions and the concerns of other functional areas in firms that use JIT systems

▶ Provide an overview of JIT systems and lean thinking

▶ Create a level schedule and describe its capacity implications

▶ Demonstrate your understanding of material planning in JIT systems

▶ Describe the kanban scheduling system and calculate the number of kanbans required in a particular workstation

...Back at the Rec Center

"What a weekend!" says Luis, as he enters the fitness center just after the rest of the group had arrived one spring Monday morning. "I think I worked harder this weekend than I do in a month at my real job! We had a pancake breakfast fundraiser for the little league team I coach. Remember I was pushing tickets last week?" Luis laughs. "I haven't work so hard in years! It was a regular production line!"

"Oh! That's right! I bought the ticket but forgot to go! How was it?" asks Fred.

"I went, and I thought it was great," Tom says. "The lines moved quickly, and you even had three kinds of pancakes to choose from. Look out, IHOP! I flipped my share of pancakes when my kids were in that league. It's a lot of fun once you get things up and running. It's like a small factory, everybody running around and making things, everybody sort of falls into a system or routine."

"You flipped flapjacks, too?" asks Cheryl, who was sitting down to do leg extensions.

"Oh, yeah!" Tom answers. "Pancake Day craziness has been going on for some time. No organization, too much batter here, not enough there, cold sausage and coffee, long lines of people waiting to get in, and volunteers standing around up to their elbows in stuff, but not the right stuff. And waiting, a lot of waiting."

"Well, I'd heard some horror stories from people who'd done it before," says Luis. "But as the new guy, I didn't know what to expect. The more I heard about it in the planning committee meetings, the more I thought it would be fun to try and run it like a factory."

Luis took a pen hanging from a clipboard on the wall and started to draw on the back of a signup sheet for an upcoming racquetball tournament. "Here, let me show you how we laid it out. It was really pretty simple," he says with pride. "I'm not sure how it was done before, but I heard they tried to wait till people came in to do anything, like made-to-order or something. When that didn't work and lines were too long, people tried to guess what they would need and made up big batches of sausage and batter. Everybody had different ideas about how much was enough, how long was too long. Things got confused. We simplified it a lot," he says as he finishes drawing and leans over to show the group his "floor plan" (see Luis's Floor Plan Figure).

"We bought the batter in 5-gallon pails from a supplier but still had to stir it with a mixer before it could be used at a griddle," he continues. "In the past, they kept a big pail at each griddle and dipped in pitchers with which they poured the batter onto the griddle. This year, we kept a pail or two at the mixer. We would fill up a pitcher at the mixer station and run it up to the griddle, where

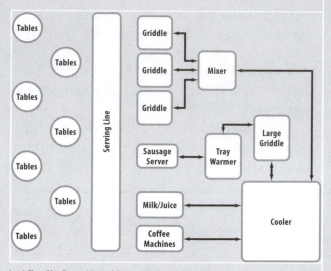

Luis's Floor Plan Figure: Material Flows at the Pancake Fundraiser

we made the pancakes as people came in. It was slow at first, but we started to keep the griddles full as things got more crowded. In the past, people waited as the pancakes cooked on the griddle. This year we put trays near the griddle, the same trays we use to serve the sausage, to hold a few pancakes made up in advance when things were slow. The trays kept the pancakes warm, and having pancakes ready and waiting helped keep the lines moving when the place got busy. When we filled a tray, we stopped cooking; that way, the pancakes stayed warm and fresh," he explains.

"As the pitchers used at the griddles were emptied," he went on, "Little Leaguers would bring the empty ones back to the mixer, where they were refilled from the central location and taken back to the parents and coaches who were running the griddles. We decided to stir some blueberries or chocolate chips directly into the pitchers with a big spoon, right there at the griddle. It was just an afterthought, but it worked out well."

"Didn't that mean a pitcher of each type batter at each griddle?" asks Fred.

"Yes," says Luis, "but that's a lot easier to handle than a 5-gallon pail at each griddle, let

alone three pails. The best part was that when it got really busy, we got a few more pitchers out. As it slowed down, we would take a few away."

"What happened when the mixer was out of stuff?" asks Tom.

"We had lots of kids to do the running back and forth," answers Luis. "When the mixer emptied a pail, we'd send kids back to the cooler with the empty one, and they would bring a full one back. We generally had one pail at the mixer already stirred up and another on the mixer being stirred. As things got busy, we put third and fourth pails into the system. That way, one could be used to refill the pitchers, a second was on the mixer being stirred, a third pail was open and ready to go on the mixer, and the fourth pail was 'in transit' back to the cooler. Near the end, things slowed down and we could scale it back to where we had one pail refilling the pitchers. When it was empty, what was in the pitchers could hold us till the empty pail could be taken to the cooler and the replacement brought back to the mixer and stirred up."

"Did you do drinks the same way as we used to?" asks Tom.

"Yes, milk and juice were all donated in gallon jugs. We kept them in the cooler till they were needed," Luis answers. He said we used the empty jugs as a signal here as well. "We put the recycling container near the cooler," he says. "That way, when we took the empties back to throw them away, we brought up the same number of full ones. When things slowed down, though, we didn't keep as many jugs up front."

"It all sounds like you had a good handle on it—better, in fact, than we probably did," says Tom. "But what about the coffee? That was always a pain. When that big 80-cup percolator was empty, it seemed to take forever to brew another pot. The lines got real long and everybody got sick of waiting."

"It's funny you should ask," Luis responds. "That big ol' monster was dead on arrival this year. It wouldn't turn on. The committee wanted to replace it with another one just like it, but one parent suggested two to three smaller coffee makers would be better—that way somebody could be changing the coffee grounds of one while the other percolates and a third is being used."

"Well your whole system sounds like a 'just-in-time' system to me," says Fred, "Sounds a lot like making cell phones."

"Yeah, but you don't smell like maple syrup till the Fourth of July when you make phones all day!" laughs Luis.

Introduction

This chapter covers detailed planning and control in just-in-time (JIT) operational systems. We are particularly concerned with how a JIT company can translate the plans in its master schedule into a detailed operational plan, so that every employee knows exactly what to do with which resources at any time. As operations managers, we are concerned with the planning through which commitments to customers are converted into detailed plans for action.

The system a company uses to make detailed planning and control decisions, be it JIT or another method, has implications for the conduct of work in every functional area of the firm. Because many companies have recently adopted JIT systems, it is easy to describe the systems' implications for other functional areas—and spanning the gaps between functional areas—in terms of the changes that occurred when JIT was adopted.

JIT systems rely on a level scheduling approach, which ensures that inventory levels remain stable, value is added close to the time that customers purchase value, and the level of managerial effort required to coordinate system activities is quite low. This makes material planning in a JIT system quite simple. If the schedule is the same for any hour of the week (or month), then the materials required to execute the schedule are also the same for any hour or the week or month. Essentially, then, the level master schedule creates a rate at which components and other material supplies are consumed. Material planning simply requires that supplies of these items are replenished at the rate at which they are consumed.

One way JIT systems tell workers what to do in order to replenish consumed materials is through the use of kanban systems. By placing cards or other visual cues in work centers to signal the need for replenishment of materials, it takes very little effort for managers to control inventories and regularly provide detailed work assignments to employees.

REC CENTER DILEMMA

Luis's Dilemma:

Luis had been reading about lean production systems before the pancake breakfast and wanted to share what he learned with the others, but he had not had a chance. Thinking back to this morning's conversation (above), he was thinking he might have actually done that, although without using any of the terminology. He wonders which aspects of lean systems were present in the pancake system and which were missing from it. He is making a two-column list on a sheet of paper. What do you think he should put in the "Lean elements included" column and what should he put in the "Lean elements absent" column? Was the pancake system a lean production system?

JIT systems were developed in a manufacturing environment, have been most commonly implemented by manufacturers, and have had a huge impact in manufacturing operations. However, JIT and elements of the JIT philosophy are also beneficial in service-intensive businesses.

Integrating Operations Management Across the Functions

As large numbers of companies have adopted JIT, the way business is conducted has changed significantly, not just in operations and purchasing, but in all functions. For example, in the discussion in Chapter 8 of capacity planning (pages 343–362) we suggested that the widespread adoption of JIT practices may have had a dampening effect on the cycle of recession and growth experienced in the U.S. economy. Since many firms adopted JIT in the 1980s, reduced reliance on inventories from that point forward could help explain the pattern of milder recessions with slower recoveries which seem to have started with the recession of 1990–91. Because companies using JIT are better able to match their production to current demand, they do not have to shrink output as much to clear inventories early in the recession and they do not have to rapidly expand output to rebuild inventories at the beginning of a recovery.

Marketing practices changed, too, as a result of JIT. A regional manager of The Pillsbury Company indicated that prior to the company's adoption of JIT practices, she had worked with the sales force to get "good" demand forecasts for products several weeks into the future. The information was generally gathered from managers or buyers at the grocery stores. If the forecast was a little high, warehouse space was adequate to store the extra items produced. Clearly that was better than experiencing shortages. Consequently, managers and salespeople had an incentive to pad their forecasts. When the company adopted JIT, the sales force toured the production facility to gain confidence in the new approach to planning and control, which was said to be capable of responding to customers' requirements within a day. The company's refrigerated warehouse would no longer be needed under the new system. Because store managers no longer needed to estimate demand weeks into the future, sales representatives stopped padding their forecasts. Instead, just two days prior to delivery they submitted their actual orders.

Store managers later began to wonder why the special pricing deals and store displays they had once used to attract customers had disappeared. Pillsbury's sales manager had to explain that periodically lowering the price also lowered the margin on the product and therefore was not good business practice. Furthermore, the whole reason for the price "blow-outs" had been the need to liquidate warehouse inventories accumulated as the result of incorrect forecasts or large lot production. Clearly, for Pillsbury and many other companies, the movement to a JIT planning and control system had a significant impact on marketing and customer relations.

The movement to JIT has had significant impact on the finance and accounting functions as well. During the 1980s, warehouse space requirements were significantly reduced by the adoption of JIT. Prior to that time, mortgages backed by warehouse space had been a major component of virtually every private bond fund. Indeed, fund managers associated that sector of the mortgage market with high performance and low risk. With the advent of JIT, the mortgages on those warehouses suddenly became high-risk investments. Today, the declining use of inventory and the ever-present possibility of further reductions in inventory discouraged many financial managers from investing in warehouse space.

Table 14.1

Integrating Operations Management across the Functions

Functional Area / Integration Perspective	Finance	Accounting
Why Cross-Functional Integration Matters to JIT and Lean Systems	Financial justification for operational equipment and inventory storage capacity requires some knowledge of its potential utilization—and this depends on an understanding of the planning and control system in use.	For companies using JIT/Lean Production, effective managerial accounting requires an understanding of the system. Also, with lean operations and close supplier relationships, parts and supplies inventory ownership and accounting may take on unique dimensions.
Key Issues	How will equipment be utilized and capital expenditures justified in the JIT system? What risks to projected earnings arise from the operational plans of the business? From an investment perspective, what is the impact of lean production operations on an equity's attractiveness or a facility's mortgage risk?	How will costs be allocated within the lean production system? Who owns inventory at what point? How will it be accounted for? When and how will suppliers be paid? When and how will customers be billed?

For accounting managers, the process of making payments for purchases and receiving payment for the delivery of product-service bundles has changed. Even the question of who owns the inventory has become debatable. For example, many suppliers own and maintain stocks of materials in their customers' plants. In some cases, materials are purchased when the company that assembles the product-service bundle uses the material. In other cases, the supplier owns the material until the product-service bundle is actually sold. As a result, paperwork is minimized; the supplier is paid based only on the products that have been sold.

For example, a company that assembles hospital beds knows that if it has sold 100 beds, it has used 100 mattresses. If inventory is low and demand is strong, why not pay suppliers on the basis of deliveries to customers? Suppliers who might be tempted to push overproduced stock onto the customer will not be paid until that stock is actually sold. If inventory is kept too lean and stock-outs occur, then the supplier's revenues suffer also. These changes in supplier-customer relationships have interesting implications for accountants. If the inventory is under some other company's roof, and formal purchase orders and other contractual paperwork are de-emphasized, when

Human Resources	Marketing	Engineering	Management Information Systems
Lean systems depend on employee commitment and involvement because it is vulnerable in the context of labor disturbances. HR's role in labor relations is critical to the effectiveness of JIT planning and control systems.	Marketers must understand their own planning and control system, along with those of customers and other supply chain partners, in order for a company to satisfy their customers—particularly from a distribution perspective.	Maintenance and reliability of processes are key to the effectiveness of the JIT/lean system. Additionally, engineering activities support lean systems via reduction of complexity in design of products, machine tools, and fixtures.	JIT systems rely on current information about all aspects of materials management. Information sharing with part suppliers, logistics providers, and internal users is essential to the effectiveness of the system.
How will employee commitment to the system be developed and maintained? How will employee involvement be rewarded? How will the employee involvement system be managed? Is the labor contract appropriate to the lean production system?	With the emphasis on reduction in complexity in operations, how (and to what extent) will needs for customization be handled? What product distribution system will best fit the lean operating system?	What equipment should be used? And how, when, and by whom will it be maintained, to ensure the JIT system does not face unwarranted disruptions? Can technical changes to product or process designs reduce the process and equipment complexity and/or reduce changeover times?	How will suppliers and logistics providers deliver advance notice of shipments and/or delivery delays to both upstream and downstream supply chain partners? How will real-time information about the status of operations be displayed within a facility?

and how should audits be performed? What are the tax, security, and insurance implications of such arrangements? How often should inventory counts be taken?

Consistent with Table 14.1 and the discussion above, Figure 14.1 illustrates the importance of cross-functional understanding in the implementation of JIT planning and control processes.

Finally, the human resources function is handled very differently in JIT companies. In unionized environments, employees can take concerted actions, such as strikes, slowdowns, and protests, which disrupt the value-adding system. Even in nonunionized environments, without inventory buffers and extra capacity, disgruntled individuals and small groups of employees can create serious problems. Teamwork, improvement, coordination, and cooperation all require a participative workforce. Consequently, distinctions between white-collar and blue-collar jobs, excessive reliance on job classification schemes, and traditional piece rate incentives are out of place in a JIT company.

Table 14.1 highlights some of the major links between JIT and the other functional areas of business. For companies using JIT, effective financial management, managerial accounting, HR management, marketing, engineering, and management of the IS function all depend greatly on understanding the operational system.

630

Chapter 14

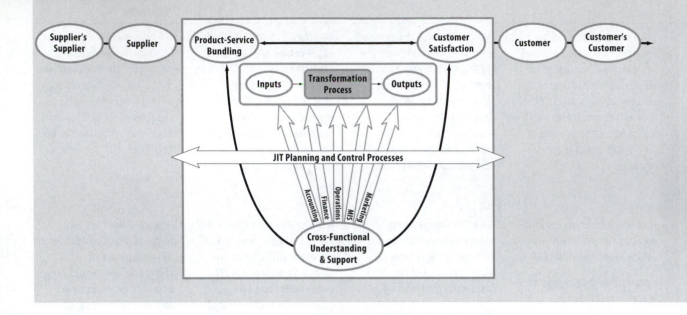

Figure 14.1 JIT planning and control processes

Overview of JIT Systems

It has been said that as a young man, Eiji Toyoda (heir to the Toyoda industrial establishment) was sent to learn the management practices of Henry Ford. Yet one of his most inspiring lessons came from a grocery store. Toyoda was amazed that despite the large variety of items the store carried, the shelves were always completely restocked when he returned the following day. He realized that the store handled more parts than are required to build an automobile and wondered why his family's production facilities always suffered from parts shortages and excesses. His observation, along with the effectiveness with which Ford had synchronized the manufacture of parts and the assembly of cars, provided the seed bank from which the just-in-time system would one day be developed.

Following World War II, executives at the Toyota Motor Company became particularly interested in narrowing the gap between their firm's capabilities and those of the Western automotive industry. They did not have a cash hoard to invest and their facilities weren't fancy or new, so they focused on reducing costs, eliminating waste, and improving productivity. Over many years of trial and error, under the direction of Taiichi Ohno, Shigeo Shingo, and other visionary leaders, Toyota tested a number of unique approaches which together came to be known as the Toyota Production System. After the oil crisis of 1973, which sparked a crisis of survival in many Japanese firms, the Toyota Production System spread to other industries. In the 1980s, during similar crises resulting from international competition, companies all over the world began to use the system, now called the just-in-time (JIT) system. In short, the JIT

INTEGRATING OM:

Satisfying Customers at General Motors

Is the new "lean" approach to manufacturing embraced by many modern automakers in the United States an advantage or a disadvantage when it comes to labor issues and, in the most critical situations, labor stoppages? Have today's tight inventory systems, associated with JIT systems, played into the hands of organized labor by giving selected "surgical" strikes an even bigger impact? Events at General Motors (GM) may give you some ideas upon which to base your own conclusions.

In 1996, 2700 union workers at the Dayton, Ohio, GM brake plant went on strike over work rules and outsourcing disagreements. The strike by workers that supply more than 90% of GM's brake parts effectively ended shipments of brake parts to nearly all twenty-nine North American assembly plants. With its JIT approach to inventory and logistics throughout its value-adding system, the company had limited inventory of brake parts at the assembly plants and production had to shut down within three days. Within a week, twenty-one of GM's twenty-nine North American assembly plants had shut down, idling 87,000 hourly workers. As the assembly plants shut down, the demand for parts made at other part plants also dried up. This forced the layoff of thousands at part factories around the world. Before the 17-day strike ended, virtually all North American production by GM (estimated at over 178,000 workers) was brought to a standstill. The after-tax cost of the strike was estimated to be more than $900 million (Associated Press, June 10, 1998).

In 1998, history repeated itself. Workers in a Flint, Michigan, plant that stamps body parts from sheet metal went on strike over what the company called "outdated" work rules that it claimed stifled both productivity and flexibility. Union leaders feared GM wanted to close the plant and consolidate stamping operations elsewhere. The company claimed it had no choice but to force union concessions on issues that were critical for the productivity and flexibility gains it needs to survive, even if it meant surviving as a smaller, more streamlined corporation. Again, the JIT approach to inventory and logistics throughout GM's value-adding system forced the impact of the relatively small strike (3400 workers) to grow quite rapidly. Within a week, some 35,000 workers had been idled and the entire North American workforce—296,000 laborers—was threatened. Some economists suggested the strike could throw a monkey wrench into the whole country's economy.

Ironically, despite the similar events just two years earlier, the price of GM's stock shares barely slipped when news of the strike and its potential began to hit the wires (AP June 10, 1998). Many business analysts felt GM had no choice but to push for the very necessary concessions (*Wall Street Journal*, June 12, 1998) as a matter of survival. Some even saw the strike as a sign of progress by the automaker.

But what about the speed at which these strikes spread and the rate at which their costs escalated? Some would argue that JIT's lean manufacturing practices helped by quickening the awareness of internal problems. Others counter that JIT gives unions too much leverage at times when significant changes need to be hammered out on both sides. Who is right? Is this an example of what is right or what is wrong about JIT? Is this an overblown response to what could be viewed as a small thorn in the giant's side at a small and relatively insignificant plant? Or, does it quickly point out the significance of a problem that could be systemic to the entire corporation? Would a larger stash of inventory at each level within the value-adding system have bought the company more time to solve its problems? Or would it have allowed the company to ignore an issue longer and just intensify the impact of the inevitable breakdown that would be coming? Whatever the answer is to these questions, GM's experience highlights the extreme importance of worker relations to any JIT system.

system allows managers to plan operations that reduce variability of demand, enhance responsiveness of operational resources, and attempt to conduct value-adding operations as close as possible to the time that value is consumed.

JIT, Toyota Production System, and Lean Systems

As we indicated in the last paragraph, the "Toyota Production System" and "the JIT system" are terms that have been used interchangeably for some time. These terms are both associated with: (1) movement toward small batches delivered as needed, (2) the idea of continuous improvement of internal processes, and (3) the context of repetitive manufacturing operations. The use of JIT techniques has now expanded to the point that aspects of the JIT system can be found in many different environments—and the term **lean manufacturing** is commonly used as a synonym for JIT.

Lean manufacturing

A commonly used synonym for JIT.

Some consider lean manufacturing different from JIT in the following ways:

1. Lean is externally focused on customer value. JIT is internally focused on continuous improvement.

2. Lean approaches waste elimination by determining first what customers value and improves processes by targeting those activities not contributing to the customer value. JIT is more likely to focus on predefined waste types such as overproduction, poor quality, capacity imbalances, and the like.

3. Whereas lean thinking is applicable in virtually any service or manufacturing environment, some aspects of a JIT system are best suited to repetitive manufacturing environments.

On the basis of these distinctions, it would be fair to say that all JIT systems are lean production systems, but not all lean systems are JIT systems. Some people have even use the term "little JIT" for JIT systems and "big JIT" for lean systems. Though the terms "JIT" and "lean manufacturing" are frequently used interchangeably in practice, because of these perceived differences highlighted in this paragraph, "JIT systems" is the term that you will see most frequently in the rest of this chapter.

The Enormous Impact of JIT and Lean Systems

The improvements that resulted from the change to JIT were impressive. Harley-Davidson, which called its JIT system "material-as-needed" (MAN), claimed that over the first few years of its use, the system reduced inventory by 70%, scrap by 50%, warranty claims by 70%, and rework by 90%. As a result, productivity increased by 40%, and the company regained 15% of the American motorcycle market and survived the most significant crisis in its 80-year history. This level of improvement is typical of companies that adopt JIT. In fact, companies that adopt JIT can expect:

Visual and straight forward performance measures are a key to JIT operation.

Courtesy of Magnatag

▶ Manufacturing cycle time reductions

▶ Inventory reductions of raw materials, work-in-process, and finished goods

▶ Labor cost reductions in both the direct and indirect labor categories

▶ Space requirement reductions

▶ Quality cost reductions

▶ Material costs reductions

In addition to improvements in these areas, lean thinking is often credited with substantial improvements in customer responsiveness.

Additionally, we have learned that adopters of JIT begin to think more broadly about managing their supply chains effectively. In the eighties, early JIT users with economic clout over their suppliers were accused of simply using the system as no more than a ploy to transfer raw materials inventory from their accounts into their supplier's warehouses. Most firms, however, learned very quickly that their long-term supplier relationships were critical to their business success and that dictating terms of purchase contracts via strong-arm tactics was often counter-productive. As a result attempts to work with suppliers in improvement efforts and to understand supplier processes became the method by which companies sought reduce supply uncertainty, and thereby reduce the need for raw materials inventory. It could well be said that one of the most significant impacts of JIT was its role as a catalyst for adoption of supply chain management practices.

The Applicability of Lean Thinking and JIT

Obviously, detailed plans that specify what workers must do must also provide for the necessary materials and equipment capacity to get the job done. Figure 14.2 illustrates

Figure 14.2

Short-term planning and control in a JIT system

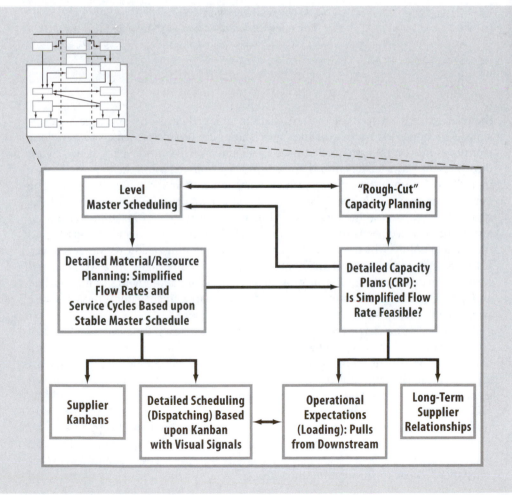

Figure 14.3

System characteristics of
JIT planning and control

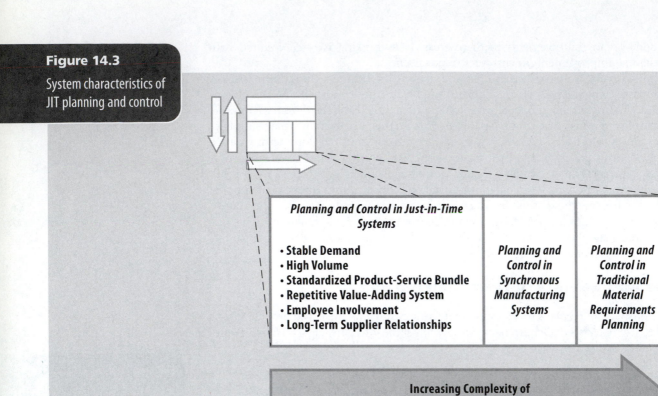

the relationships between the master schedule, material decisions, and capacity decisions. The upper-left portion of the figure shows the broader scheme of operations planning and control systems discussed in Chapter 13. The lower part of this figure illustrates the short-term planning and control tasks and describes their characteristics in a JIT environment—involving primarily dependent demand inventory issues. The decisions are not based directly on forecasts, which are probabilistic estimates of demand. Rather, because the master schedule has been set, decisions are based on an agreed-upon schedule. As the figure indicates, JIT systems rely on a level approach to master scheduling, which makes the more detailed planning decisions much simpler. If the master schedule is level, material and capacity requirements are also stable and easily calculated. Furthermore, the most detailed decisions about who should do what, and when, can be made without a great deal of management supervision because people will be doing standardized work in a repetitive way.

Figure 14.3 summarizes the system characteristics where a JIT planning and control system fits best. If these characteristics are not present, some different planning and control system (discussed in a later chapter) might be a more logical choice. Though aspects of lean thinking could be applied in any setting (i.e., Little JIT), JIT systems are a good fit when demand is reasonably stable and high-volume repetitive value-adding systems can be used to make standardized product-service bundles. Effective use of JIT also requires the cooperation and coordination of employees and suppliers.

The JIT system is most effective in settings such as Toyota's, where a repetitive value-adding system is in use and product variety is limited. These qualities allow for a balanced capacity throughout the value-adding system. If capacity is balanced throughout the system and product variety is limited, there is little need for day-to-day and moment-to-moment adjustments to the system. The planning and control decision boils down to how many units the system will create in a given period, not how many units of what. Simply removing the "of what" makes the planning and control task more like turning a knob to control the rate of flow from a garden hose.

Interestingly, very complex product-service bundles are frequently created using JIT systems. Most of us would consider an automobile a complex assembly. Touring an automobile assembly plant, we would probably say that the value-adding system was complex as well. Yet, we have just described JIT as a system that works well in simple, not complex, environments. To understand this apparent paradox, we must distinguish between complexity in the product-service bundle; complexity in the value-adding system; and complexity in planning, scheduling, and controlling the operation of the value-adding system. When making only one model of a vehicle, with a very limited set of options, the system should be very good at making that model. In turn, many of the operational decisions, such as how many of what to make, with what equipment, and when, can be built into the repetitive system. Consequently, the planning and control environment becomes simple.

Complex planning and control environments are those in which there is significant uncertainty regarding demand and in which a great deal of product variety is accommodated with general-purpose equipment. JIT is not well suited to such environments. The presence of a lot of customers, a lot of suppliers, a lot of differently designed (or heterogeneous) products, or a lot of options or varying features can greatly complicate the operation of the value-adding system. Many of the decisions that are hardwired into simpler systems must be addressed on a case-by-case basis. As the complexity of planning, scheduling, and controlling the system increases, making those decisions deterministically becomes more difficult, and managers may need to take a more probabilistic approach. (Subsequent chapters cover those types of systems.) Figure 14.4 illustrates the differences between operating a simple and a complex value-adding system.

Continuous improvement and employee involvement are core aspects of the JIT system: Every worker is responsible for making sure that things are working right and finding ways to make things work better.

Suppliers of JIT companies are often required to provide shipments on 1-, 2- or 3-hour cycles with materials loaded so that they come off the truck in the order in which they will be used. As a result, it is very helpful if the supplier can operate its processes in sync with those of customers. **Takt time** is the rate at which material is used by the customer's value-adding system. Suppliers will have much greater success in satisfying a JIT customer if their systems also operate at that rate. Because manufacturing cells can be made to operate in takt time, a cellular manufacturing arrangement is an ideal characteristic of JIT suppliers.

Takt time

The rate at which material is used by the customer's value-adding system.

Scheduling and Capacity Management in JIT Systems

Managers must address several parameters in the JIT approach to master scheduling, capacity decisions, inventory decisions, and business relationships with suppliers and customers. In particular, JIT planning and control relies on (1) a level master schedule, (2) prefers excess capacity to excess inventory, and (3) works with suppliers and customers to reduce complexity and uncertainty, while (4) simultaneously improving the system's responsiveness to customer requirements.

Figure 14.4
Simple vs. complex
value-adding systems

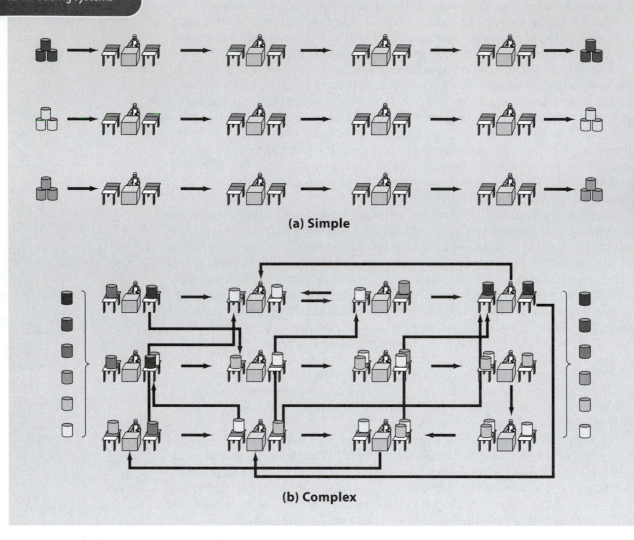

(a) Simple

(b) Complex

Level Scheduling

Level master schedule

A schedule in which the same mix of product-service bundles is created repeatedly over the period for which the master schedule has been frozen.

JIT planning and control relies on a **level master schedule**, or one in which the same mix of product-service bundles is created repeatedly over the period for which the master schedule has been frozen. For example, assume that the United States Mint had only one printing press and in a given week had to print 25 million one-dollar bills, 10 million five-dollar bills, 5 million ten-dollar bills, and 1 million twenty-dollar bills, for a total of 41 million bills. The most level schedule they could envision, to spread them out evenly and proportionally, would be to print twenty-five out of every forty-one bills in the one-dollar denomination, ten out of forty-one in the five-dollar denomination, five out of forty-one in the ten-dollar denomination, and every forty-first bill

Example 14.1

A small engine maker similar to Briggs and Stratton operates an assembly line two shifts per day and five days per week. A shift is 8 hours, but production stops for two 15-minute breaks and a half-hour lunch. Demand for all of the small engines assembled on this line is about 4000 units per week. What is their takt time?

Step 1: Find the total time (seconds) in the demand period

Total time = 5 days/week $\times$ 2 shifts/day
$\times$ 7 hours/shift $\times$ 60 minutes/hour
$\times$ 60 seconds/minute
= 252,000 seconds

Step 2: Determine takt time

Takt time = # seconds per time period
/ demand per time period
= (252,000 seconds per week) /
(4000 engines per week)
= 63 seconds per engine

would be a twenty! For example, the following sequence of bills would be printed a million times each week:

1-1-5-1-1-5-1-10-1-1-5-1-1-5-1-10-1-1-5-1-1-5-1-10-20-1-1-5-1-1-5-1-10-1-1-5-1-1-5-1-10

If this were the sequence in which the money was printed—even if a customer needed a bill that was not in stock—the bill would be printed within one millionth of a week. That places the creation of value and its consumption very close to one another. You could even say that the money is printed just in time. (Now, of course the mint does not print bills this way, but the idea is interesting; see Discussion Question 1 at the end of this chapter.)

Independent demand inventory models (as presented in the last chapter) base the determination of order quantities on the idea that overall costs are minimized when ordering and holding costs are balanced. The economics (also presented in Chapter 13) are just as valid for JIT systems as for any other type of system. Note that the schedule for the mint would mean frequently changing over from printing one-dollar bills to five-dollar bills and so forth. In fact, that approach to scheduling would require 31 million setups each week. At the other extreme, if the whole week's demand for each demarcation (printed piece of currency) were printed before moving on to another demarcation, only four setups per week would be required. However, a holding cost would be incurred Because at least a week's supply would need to be on hand whenever the printing of a given demarcation had been completed. (The Federal Reserve Bank would not want to run out of one-dollar bills because of supply problems at the United States Mint.)

JIT Perspectives on Inventory

Figure 14.5 presents the JIT view of inventory. Problems in a value-adding system are illustrated as rocks at the bottom of the lake. Inventory is the water. If we have enough inventory, we can sail through just about any system—despite all the problems that might exist just below the surface. In fact, the inventory will not only keep us from

Example 14.2

Assume, the small engine manufacturing company whose takt time was determined in Example 14.1, assembles several different types of engines on its line. Engines come in two-, three-, or five-horsepower sizes. They may be for marine or land-based applications. And they may be two- or four-cycle. That means twelve different configurations are offered (three sizes × two applications × two cycle types). The last three digits of the engine serial number are used to identify the engine configuration. For example, the digits 5M2 would refer to a five-horsepower, marine, two-cycle engine and a 2L4 would be a two-hp, land-based, four-cycle engine. Given the weekly demand for the next 12 weeks (in Table 14.2), determine a level production schedule for the company.

Table 14.2

						Week						
Item	1	2	3	4	5	6	7	8	9	10	11	12
2M2	50	80	30	40	50	60	60	40	50	40	50	50
2M3	300	350	200	300	300	350	200	300	300	350	350	300
2M5	200	150	200	240	220	220	160	200	210	160	220	220
2L2	430	440	500	430	410	520	440	450	410	500	410	460
2L3	40	50	50	40	40	50	40	50	50	60	50	80
2L5	290	290	240	340	290	290	340	290	290	290	330	320
4M2	150	240	90	120	150	180	180	120	150	120	150	150
4M3	650	775	500	600	600	675	500	675	675	700	700	750
4M5	300	225	300	360	330	330	240	300	315	240	330	330
4L2	1,260	1,310	1,500	1,250	1,200	1,470	1,290	1,250	1,200	1,400	1,210	1,260
4L3	200	320	120	160	200	240	240	160	200	160	200	200
4L5	70	50	70	40	50	60	40	50	60	40	30	40
Total	3,940	4,280	3,800	3,920	3,840	4,445	3,730	3,885	3,910	4,060	4,030	4,160

Step 1: Determine the demand totals by item and the ratio of total demand represented by each item.

Item	Item Total Demand (12 weeks)	Percentage
2M2	600	1.25
2M3	3600	7.5
2M5	2400	5.0
2L2	5400	11.25
2L3	600	1.25
2L5	3600	7.5

Item	Item Total Demand (12 weeks)	Percentage
4M2	1800	3.75
4M3	7800	16.25
4M5	3600	7.5
4L2	15,600	32.5
4L3	2400	5
4L5	600	1.25
Overall Demand Total (12 weeks)	48,000	100

Example 14.2

(continued)

Item	Units per Shortest Possible Sequence	Production Frequency*
2L2	9	8.888889
2M3	6	13.33333
2L5	6	13.33333
4M5	6	13.33333
2M5	4	20
4L3	4	20
4M2	3	26.66667
2M2	1	80
2L3	1	80
4L5	1	80
Total	**80**	

*Production frequency values are interpreted as follows: One out of every x items, where x is the value in the cell. So, the production frequency of 3.077 for the 4L2 indicates that one in every 3.077 engines needs to be a 4L2.

Step 2: Determine the shortest possible sequence of production slots that could be used to schedule production. (That sequence would be a repeatable production pattern, or rotation, in which we would make at least one engine of each type—spreading out the demand for each item as evenly as possible over the course of the sequence, the day, the week, and the 12-week planning horizon.)

Shortest possible sequence = (Overall demand total)/(smallest item total demand)

= 48000 engines /600 engines

= 80 production slots.

Therefore, a production sequence can be created that, when repeated 600 times (48,000/80) over the course of the next 12 weeks, will result in supply of the exact total of demand for each item.

Step 3: Determine the duration of the shortest possible sequence.

Duration of shortest possible sequence
= shortest possible sequence × takt time

= 80 × 63 seconds

= 5,040 seconds

= 84 minutes

Step 4: Determine the frequency with which each item will appear on the production schedule. This frequency is ratio of the shortest possible sequence and the product of the demand percentage shown in Step 1 and the shortest possible sequence. For example, demand for 4L2 is 32.5% of the overall demand total. Consequently, 32.5% of the eighty slots, or twenty-six slots, in the shortest sequence will be devoted to producing 4L2. Dividing 80 by 26 gives us 3.0769, hence, in the most level schedule roughly every third engine would be a 4L2. We show this calculation for all twelve items in the table below. Notice that we have sorted the table's rows such that we start with the item whose demand is greatest and end with those whose demand is lowest.

Step 5: Create the level schedule by spreading the production of each item evenly across the shortest possible sequence using the frequencies provided by the calculations in Step 4.

Many possible sequences could be created. One simple way is to start with the item with highest demand and allocate production slots to that item, then move to the next highest and fill in its production until the schedule sequence is complete. Using this approach, our first step would be to assign the twenty-six slots contained in the set {1, 4, 7, . . . , 76} to production of the 4L2 engine. We would then assign the thirteen slots contained in the set {2, 8, 14, . . . , 74} to production of the 4M3. The partially completed schedule after assigning these two items to production slots is illustrated in the table below.

Item	Units per Shortest Possible Sequence	Production Frequency*
4L2	26	3.076923
4M3	13	6.153846

Production Slot	Item
1	4L2
2	4M3
3	
4	4L2
5	

Example 14.2

(continued)

Production Slot	Item
6	
7	4L2
8	4M3
9	
10	
11	
12	
13	
14	4M3
...	...
74	4M3
75	
76	4L2
77	
78	
79	
80	

Next we would place nine units of 2L2 on the schedule spacing them in the same way and continue the process until all engine types had been placed on the schedule. As we continue to assign the engines to slots, we would occasionally find that we would like to use a slot that had already been assigned. When that occurred, we would simply find a nearby slot to use. When all eighty slots are assigned, the result would be a schedule such as the one shown in Table 14.3.

Repeating the eighty-slot sequence shown in the above table 600 times over the next 12 weeks (once every 84 production minutes) would result in level production of the projected demand. If a customer needed an engine that was not in stock, he or she could be shown the production schedule and could choose the engine to be produced in a given slot. This sequence would benefit suppliers by allowing them to produce at a level rate. By contrast, if we did not use a level schedule and made all of the 4L2s in one batch, the supplier of the engine casting for that item would have two choices: (1) Devote twenty-six eightieths of the month to production of the 4L2 and find a different set of customers to work with for the remainder of the month. Or (2), produce the castings to stock all month long with a level schedule and satisfy our engine assembly company from inventory.

From a supply chain management perspective, this engine company would share the finalized schedule (perhaps electronically) with their suppliers, thereby making suppliers responsible for ensuring that their production was scheduled and parts were available as needed to complete the assembly schedule. In many cases, when the schedule is fixed and level, it is up to the supplier to manage all parts inventories until they are used in production. This practice is called vendor managed inventory (VMI).

Table 14.3

Production Slot	Engine	Production Slot	Engine	Production Slot	Engine	Production Slot	Engine
1	4L2	21	2L2	41	4L3	61	4L2
2	4M3	22	4L2	42	2M3	62	4M3
3	2L2	23	2L5	43	4L2	63	2L5
4	4L2	24	4M5	44	4M3	64	4L2
5	2M3	25	4L2	45	4M2	65	4M5
6	2L5	26	4M3	46	4L2	66	2L2

Example 14.2

(continued)

Production Slot	Engine	Production Slot	Engine	Production Slot	Engine	Production Slot	Engine
7	4L2	27	2M2	47	2L2	67	4L2
8	4M3	28	4L2	48	2L5	68	4M3
9	4M5	29	2L2	49	4L2	69	2M3
10	4L2	30	2M3	50	4M3	70	4L2
11	2L2	31	4L2	51	4M5	71	4L5
12	2M5	32	4M3	52	4L2	72	2M5
13	4L2	33	2M5	53	2M5	73	4L2
14	4M3	34	4L2	54	2M3	74	4M3
15	4M2	35	2L5	55	4L2	75	2L2
16	4L2	36	2L2	56	4M3	76	4L2
17	4L3	37	4L2	57	2L2	77	2L5
18	2M3	38	4M3	58	4L2	78	4M5
19	4L2	39	4M5	59	2L3	79	4M2
20	4M3	40	4L2	60	4L3	80	4L3

If deliveries of supplies to the line are relatively infrequent compared to the duration of the shortest possible sequence, it may not be necessary to completely balance the schedule. For example, our sequence duration was 84 minutes. If supplies are delivered to the assembly line only once per day, it might make sense to produce the engines in small batches. (At two 7-hour shifts, the production day is 840 minutes. Thus, the sequence given above could be done ten times each day or once per day with each production slot representing a batch of ten identical engines.) However, because supplies may come from many different sources, with differing lead times and delivery frequencies, JIT producers will generally try to keep the schedule as level as possible.

noticing the problems, it will keep us from solving the problems. Just-in-case inventory can save the day, if:

⬤ A schedule doesn't synchronize production with customer demand

⬤ We receive a shipment of bad parts

⬤ A machine breaks down

⬤ A worker is absent

⬤ A supplier fails to come through

⬤ A truck gets delayed in transit

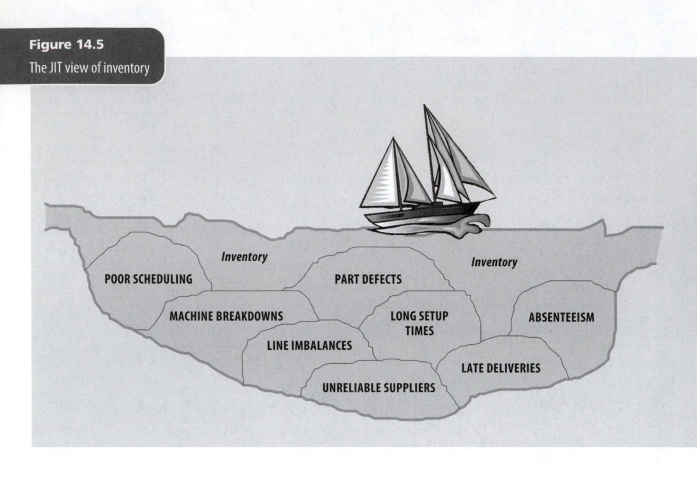

Figure 14.5

The JIT view of inventory

> ▶ A process is idle for a long time

> ▶ A capacity imbalance develops

If we do not have just-in-case inventory, we expose the problems in our value-adding system and create a strong incentive to eliminate them. The "rocky" problems listed in Figure 14.5 are common examples of faults that can affect any firm's system. Without inventory to cover over these problems, firms may suffer immediate breakdowns, but they also have an opportunity to gain an understanding of their system's weaknesses. When a firm hits a "rock," wise managers learn from the experience—the key is to avoid hitting any given rock twice. Thus, JIT is a philosophy that not only helps managers to find problems but motivates them to find remedies.

Figure 14.6 ties problem covering, or just-in-case inventories, to a model introduced in the previous chapter (see Figure 13.15 on page 598). There we saw that safety stock is often used to provide a margin of safety against disruptions in the supply of independent demand inventory items. A variety of reasons make this margin of safety needed in any environment, including:

> ▶ *Supply uncertainty.* Keeping some inventory in case a shipment from a supplier is late or full of bad parts. To reduce the need for this aspect of the margin of safety, a company needs to be sure that their suppliers have adequate capacity, processes capable of delivering the required quality, input into planning decisions (whether monthly, weekly, or daily), availability from their suppliers, positive employee relations, and so on.

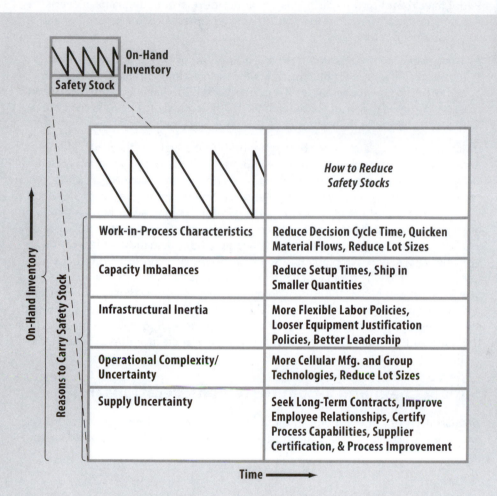

Figure 14.6

The need for a margin of safety

- *Operational complexity/uncertainty.* This is inventory in the system due to long setup or production lead times. In order to reduce the need for this part of the safety margin, companies should seek ways to simplify product and process designs through the use of group technology; reduce lot sizes; and gain a better understanding of their customers' demand patterns.

- *Infrastructural inertia.* This portion of the safety margin results from policies such as piece rate pay systems, layoff policies, idle labor policies, equipment justification issues, volume purchase discounts, communication policies, and incentive systems that emphasize full utilization of resources. It is hard to overcome the "We do it that way because we've always done it that way" mindset. Nevertheless, companies should recognize the impact that such policies have on their inventory levels. It takes real courage and leadership for a manager to change existing policies and overcome inertia.

- *Capacity imbalances.* Full truckload shipment preferences and mismatches between the capacity of suppliers and customers can lead to artificially inflated production lot sizes and transfer lot sizes. For example, most carpet stores do not have room for full truckloads, let alone entire production runs of every color they sell. This can lead to redistribution costs, warehousing, and extra handling and rehandling.

▶ *Work-in-process (WIP) characteristics.* The amount of WIP in the system reflects a number of factors, including the cycle time for decisions and paperwork, labor and material flow reporting, lot sizes, quality levels, packaging requirements, and so on. As noted earlier in the chapter, the JIT system enabled firms in the 1980s to shave 70–90% of WIP inventory.

Inventories such as safety stock buffers are built in throughout the value-adding systems of many industries. As soon as inventory is added at one point in the system, an element of supply uncertainty or operational complexity is created, to which other parts of the value-adding system respond by adding inventory. For example, when a manufacturer keeps a safety stock of parts, its supplier may never know whether an order represents a need to satisfy demand, to rebuild a safety stock inventory, or both. As a result, the supplier has to be ready to supply both demand and just-in-case inventories and may choose to keep a stock of inventory to protect from the demand uncertainty created by the manufacturer's safety stock. The JIT system emphasizes improving and simplifying the value-adding system so that inventory can begin to be removed from the system and the rest of the supply chain. When inventory is removed, eliminating an element of supply uncertainty or operational complexity, other parts of the value-adding system can respond by eliminating their inventory, as illustrated in Figure 14.7.

Supply Chain and E-Commerce Considerations in JIT

Because decisions at one point in the value-adding system influence decisions elsewhere, it is worth considering the impact on customers and suppliers of a company's

Figure 14.7

The effects of operational improvement on inventory

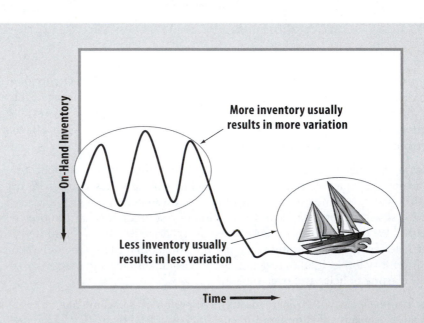

use of JIT planning and control. This impact is summarized in Figure 14.8. Companies that choose to use JIT systems will attempt to work with their suppliers to effect both structural and infrastructural improvements.

On the structural side, suppliers are encouraged to improve their responsiveness and efficiency via group technology and cellular manufacturing. Reduced inventory at suppliers should result in lower space requirements and, therefore, lower fixed costs. On the infrastructural side, JIT emphasizes maintaining a relationship that is beneficial to both parties. Communication lines need to remain open at all times: Information regarding costs, quality, and process capability must be shared without reservation. Along with relationship management, the suppliers of JIT companies need to be capable of providing product-service bundles in small quantities with frequent deliveries, which allows for smoother master schedules and shorter lead times. When improvements are made, all parties in the supply chain, including the customer, should share the benefit of these improvements through higher profit margins and lower costs.

Relationship management is also a critical aspect for customers of JIT users. From an infrastructural perspective, customers will be expected to place frequent small orders, eliminate their just-in-case inventories, and work with their downstream customers to establish smoother demand patterns. From a structural standpoint, they will be encouraged to design their product-service bundles for manufacturability and procurement, establish electronic data interchange (EDI) systems to remove demand uncertainty, and reduce their inventories of purchased materials.

INTEGRATING OM:

Coke Cuts Inventory through Better Planning

When Coca-Cola was packaged only in little green bottles and was the soft-drink maker's single brand, replenishing stores was a simple matter. Drivers loaded their trucks with product and dropped whatever was needed at the businesses on their route. It's not so simple today for Coca-Cola Bottling Co. Consolidated in Charlotte, N.C., CCBCC is Coca-Cola's second-largest bottler in the U.S. With five production centers, seventy sales and distributions centers and 6000+ employees, it bottles, packages and distributes a wide range of soft-drinks, juices, and other beverages whose brands are owned by the Coca-Cola company. Its business provides thousands of different SKUs to about 200,000 customers in 11 Southeastern U.S. states, and moves more than 125 million cases of product each year. (Murphy, 2002)

CCBCC's considers its end-user population to be greater than 18 million consumers. Nearly all of its retail customers engage in frequent promotions and aggressive discounting to garner sales from these end-users—often providing little or no notice to the bottler—that can result in dramatic swings in volume for particular products. It's critical for the company to know what to produce and how much to ship to which locations.

Although CCBCC claims to be very efficient at producing product, it simply cannot react quickly enough to market demands. The company is in a very retail-driven sales environment, and on any given day one of its major retail chains might alter what they are promoting. For example, a grocery store chain might decide to feature a two-liter bottle of Classic Coke instead of a 12-pack. That can change the whole dynamic of what CCBCC needs to produce and ship. By the time managers realized they were not producing the right product, CCBCC already had a lot of the wrong inventory sitting on the floor. The result was that the company suffered sporadic stock-outs while holding too much inventory overall. As the company continued to grow and as Coca-Cola introduced more new products, CCBCC was facing the expense of adding 10 to 15 new warehouses to its then already large network of 73. Because warehouses average $5 million each, this represented a huge capital investment.

When the company began looking for solutions, it had three goals in mind. First, it wanted to cut finished-goods inventory in half, from 12–14 days to six—four days at the plant and two days at the distribution center, or in the store for the small number of instances where CCBCC ships direct. This achievement also would result in fresher product on the shelf. Second, it wanted to improve customer service levels and reduce stock-outs by having the right product in the right place. And, finally, it wanted to reduce large-scale capital investments in warehousing.

To accomplish these goals, the company knew it needed to have better visibility to actual demand and more flexibility in production. CCBCC decided to partner with Manugistics whose software products aim at improving their production planning through collaboration with customers (Collaborative Planning And Forecast Replenishment—or CPFR). The project drove a fundamental change in the way CCBCC managed its business. Previously, forecasting and production had been completely decentralized. Each manufacturing plant created its own forecasts and scheduled production and delivery to its associated distribution centers (DCs) based on that. Forecasts typically looked out four weeks and were updated weekly by each plant's sales and marketing personnel. Once these forecasts were consolidated, there was no visibility between plants or distribution centers, so an inventory surplus in one location could not easily be shifted to make up for a shortage elsewhere.

Under the new system, forecasting, production and replenishment are managed by a centralized planning group. With centralized management, the company has visibility throughout all its facilities. And because the entire forecast and production plan can be rerun in less than an hour they are able to be far more proactive than before. The current process begins with the marketing and customer-development group feeding in price plans from the company's largest customers — ones that in a given week can run CCBCC out of

stock if they run a big advertisement. The group also inputs estimated demand from other customers, along with known promotions and price points, and information about new product introductions or other system wide events. Every Thursday the forecast is updated and sent to the area sales managers, who are aligned with specific distribution centers. They review the forecast, making notes and modifications that are based on new or changing promotions among their customer base and on specific local knowledge, such as a fair coming to town or foul weather that may prompt people to stock up on bottled water.

This input is not a blank check. If changes alter the initial forecast more than a set amount, the system triggers an automatic alert to the demand analyst, who can communicate with that sales manager. This feature helps catch errors caused by somebody keying in a wrong number or a sales manager turning in an overly optimistic sales forecast. The demand plan drives production and scheduling, which is locked in three days out. Distribution is planned every day, with shipments going out in the evening for next-day delivery.

Since its inception, this project has exceeded CCBCC's initial goals. Overall inventory has been reduced by about half. Forecast accuracy has improved and now is more than 90% accurate. Finally, the company has achieved significant reductions in capital expenditure. Not only did CCBCC refrain from spending approximately $50 million on new warehouses, it actually closed more than a dozen existing facilities—a process that continues.

CCBCC anticipates doing more collaboration with its suppliers by feeding suppliers information on a regular basis, because, when CCBCC plans change, suppliers' plans also have to change. CCBCC already shares information on a weekly basis with a number of its largest suppliers and plans to allow them access to CCBCC's internal system on an ad hoc basis, so that suppliers can retrieve information in the format they prefer. Eventually CCBCC managers would like to migrate towards vendor-managed inventory, where suppliers manage their own inventory within the CCBCC production system.

Source: Adapted from "Forecasting Tool Lowers Coke Bottler's Inventory," *Global Logistics & Supply Chain Strategies*, Nov. 2002, reporter Jean V. Murphy, at http://supplychainbrain.com/archives/11.02.coke.htm; and www.cokeconsolidated.com/, Oct. 20, 2005

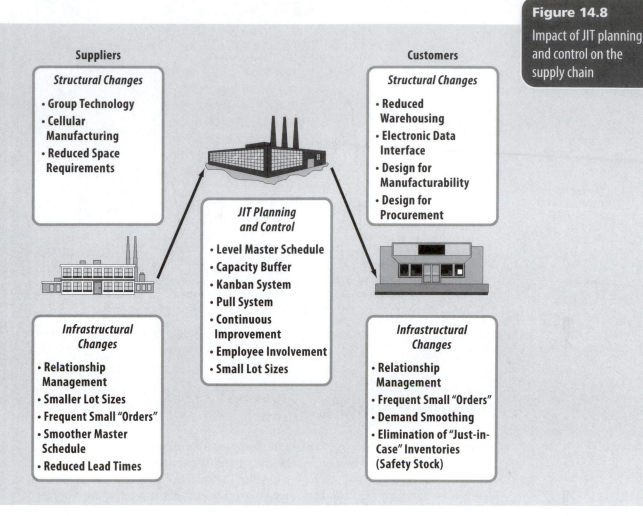

Figure 14.8

Impact of JIT planning and control on the supply chain

In reality, it is quite difficult to use JIT at only one stage in the creation of value. Variability and complexity travel through a supply chain much like waves in a Slinky® hanging vertically from your hand. Let it hang there until it stops bouncing, then wiggle your hand just a little. What happens? The effect ripples through the entire length. In the same way, if only one company in a supply chain introduces variability or complexity, even just a bit, the slight change creates a big bounce at the bottom of the supply chain. Fortunately, just the opposite can happen, too. That is, smoothing the schedule for independent demand product-service bundles can lead to significantly smoother schedules in the work centers or supplier companies that provide materials for that bundle. This Slinky analogy, first introduced in Chapter 2, is known as the bullwhip effect and is illustrated in Figure 14.9. As demand becomes more variable, as is the case for companies at the top of the supply chain (see Figure 14.7), more and more capacity is needed to maintain a particular service level. This increase in capacity has a significant cost in efficiency, which in turn leads companies to produce larger (more efficient) quantities. The change in strategy introduces uncertainty elsewhere in the supply chain, sending the wave back through the Slinky in the other direction.

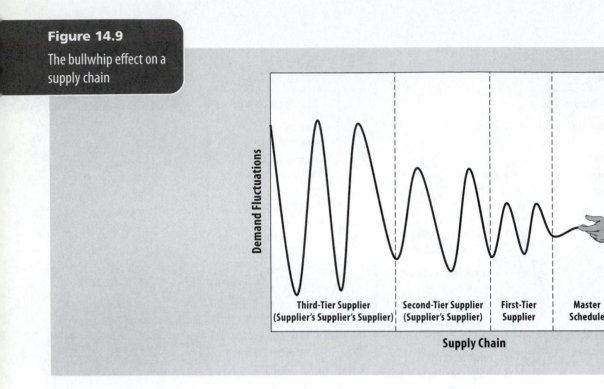

Figure 14.9
The bullwhip effect on a supply chain

Material Planning

To the largest extent possible, JIT planning and control systems rely on a level master schedule, which means daily (or even hourly) material requirements may be identical throughout the week. In such scenarios, detailed material planning means establishing a daily (or hourly) *flow rate* for dependent demand aspects of the product-service bundle. For example, you might find suppliers delivering identical shipments on a 2-hour cycle. With frequent shipments, lot sizes need not be large and setups must not take long.

Naturally, service aspects of the value-adding system, such as the transportation of parts, also have to operate on that same cycle. If the capacity of the value-adding system is adequate to sustain the material flow rate and service cycle times established by the leveled master schedule, then facilities can be loaded and scheduled using a system of built-in signals, such as empty storage bins, to "pull" replenishments of materials from one work center to another. (This approach is much like Luis's "pancake breakfast" system of using empty pitchers to signal that more batter is needed at the griddle. We will discuss pull scheduling in detail in the next section, Kanban Systems.) By relying on long-term supplier contracts and trustful relationships, managers can guarantee adequate capacity and replenishment of materials from outside as well as inside suppliers and vendors.

Lot Sizes and Setup Time

Based on a level master schedule, JIT requires workers to prepare various aspects of the product-service bundle as needed. For suppliers—in-house or external—this requirement implies the need to provide materials in very small quantities on a regular basis.

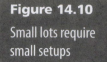

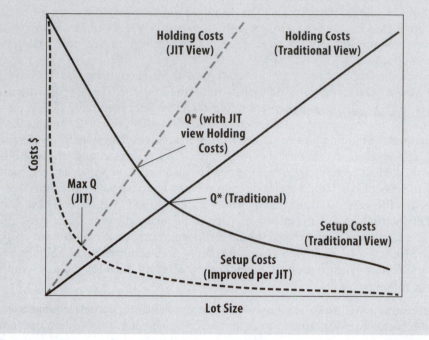

That is impossible if setup costs (or ordering costs) are too high. In the preceding chapter we noted that the optimal lot size is one that balances ordering and holding costs. To accommodate small orders, setup costs have to be drastically reduced. Figure 14.10 summarizes the economics of this approach. In the general situation described in Chapter 13, the optimal order quantity was that quantity which balanced holding and setup costs. In a JIT setting, with its bias against holding inventory, holding costs are probably higher than estimated because of the negative repercussions associated with inventory. That alone makes the "optimal" lot size smaller, but some method of reducing setup costs is still be needed to get to small-lot production.

The story of a team of workers at a Cadillac plant illustrates the reduction in setup times that can be achieved with JIT. A team of workers was formed at a stamping operation where metal is cut or folded into various shapes using a hydraulic press that can be fitted with various dies. In setting up the press, workers must remove one die and install another that matches the shape to be stamped. To improve the quality of the operation, Cadillac's stamping team decided to reduce its setup time, which averaged 8 hours and 11 minutes. (Long setup times can lead to large production runs and large inventories, which tend to inhibit feedback on quality.)

The team received from training in setup reduction techniques and set a goal: to achieve a certified setup time of less than 5:00 minutes. Within 2 years they had demonstrated a consistent time of 4:59 minutes. But having had some training in statistics, team members realized that they had not achieved their goal. Statistically speaking, 4:59 minutes is not significantly different from 5:00 minutes. They went back to work and within two additional years had established a standard setup time of 3:37 minutes.

You may be wondering why Cadillac would ever have taken 8 hours to accomplish something that could be done in less than 5 minutes. The reason is that managers did not think it could be done in less than 5 minutes—setups had always taken a long time.

Typically, when a large production run was finished, workers were tired and wanted to take a break. They usually had not thought about what the next task would be. When they finally got started on the next setup, they realized they had to find the appropriate die for the next job. (The die might not have been put away correctly following its last use, because workers or managers may have been anxious to demonstrate some productivity. And it might not have received the necessary maintenance after its last use.)

Once the workers found the correct die and ascertained that it was fit to use, they "tore down" the last setup and began to build the new one. The new die might have come from a different supplier and might therefore have required different fixtures. (Because dies are expensive—as much as $300,000—they are usually bought through a competitive bidding process. Different suppliers might follow slightly different design conventions, so that their dies might attach to the press in different ways.) Once the old die had been removed and the new die attached, the appropriate raw material had to be located. Finally, a preproduction run of a few parts would be completed, and the parts inspected to ensure that they met specifications. Depending on how busy the quality control lab was, the inspection itself could take some time.

The idea that a setup can and should be done in a matter of minutes was proposed in the 1960s by Shigeo Shingo, a Japanese management consultant. The Shingo system for quick setups, called the **single minute exchange of die system (SMED)**, reduces setup time in the following ways:

Single minute exchange of die system (SMED)

Shingo system for quick setups.

Inside exchange of die (IED)

Activities that can be done only while a machine is stopped.

Outside exchange of die (OED)

Activities in which the next die is ready for use prior to the start of a setup.

▶ A distinction is made between **inside exchange of die (IED)** and **outside exchange of die (OED)** activities. IED activities are those which can be done only while a machine is stopped. For example, a die cannot be removed from a machine until a production run has been completed, and a new die must be placed on the machine before a new production can begin. In the SMED system, die maintenance is considered an OED activity, and the next die should be ready and waiting for use prior to the start of a setup.

▶ Whenever possible, IED activities are converted to OED activities. A simple example of this tactic can be seen in a doctor's office. With only one examining room, one patient must be moved out and the next moved in before a new examination can begin. Vital signs must be taken, and a screening interview may have to be conducted. With two examining rooms, however, the exchange of patients, collection of vital statistics, and screening can be done while the doctor is attending another patient. Adding a room allows the doctor's staff to convert IED activities to OED activities.

▶ IED activities are streamlined or eliminated. Figure 14.11 shows several ways to standardize dies and fixtures. Doing so usually means that setup can be done correctly the first time, thus eliminating the need for a preproduction quality assurance check. Using a setup kit with tools prepared and lined up in the order in which they are needed is another way to streamline IED activities. Setup teams often videotape their setups to discover sources of wasted time.

▶ OED activities are streamlined or eliminated. When the IED portion of the setup time is shortened, it might fall below the OED portion, limiting the impact of further reductions in setup time. If a doctor's exam takes less time than screening and setting up new patients, the doctor will experience costly downtime. Likewise, if a die can be changed in 3:37 minutes, and the whole production run takes only 20 minutes, it is important that the OED portion of the setup not take more than 23:37 minutes.

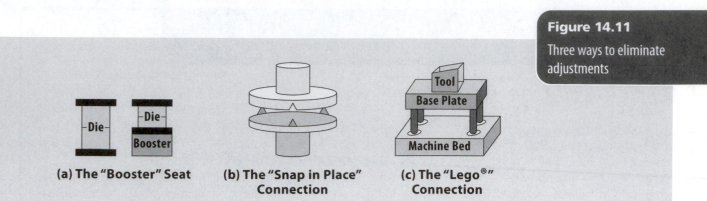

Figure 14.11
Three ways to eliminate adjustments

(a) The "Booster" Seat   (b) The "Snap in Place" Connection   (c) The "Lego®" Connection

Reducing setup time can be just as important in service operations as it is in manufacturing. Airline managers realize that planes do not make money while they are on the ground. Customers, too, find that delays in boarding mean they are not able to get their business done in one day. That means the airlines have got to come up with ways to make quick turnarounds. According to the *Wall Street Journal* (August 4, 1994), US-Airways recently improved its turnaround time on one hundred 737-200s to the point where those planes could fly seven trips a day rather than six. In doing so, the airline was able to sell an additional 12,000 seats per day.

Some other techniques the airlines have used to speed turnaround times include:

▶ The "10-minute rule," which requires passengers to board 10 minutes or more before departure time. In SMED terminology, boarding the aircraft is an IED activity, so this rule is part of an effort to streamline IED.

▶ The carryon luggage "sizer box," which is used to determine whether a passenger's carryon bags are too large before boarding actually begins. This technique converts an IED to an OED activity, reducing the time spent handling unusual carryon items and thus streamlining the boarding process.

▶ Reliance on a single type of aircraft, which, like die standardization, allows an airline to know exactly what equipment and personnel will be needed for changeovers.

▶ Cleaning of cabins on an as-needed-only basis. This technique eliminates an IED activity.

▶ In-flight inventorying and reporting of drink and snack stocks by flight attendants. Thus, caterers know exactly what supplies will be needed before a plane lands. This tactic converts an IED to an OED activity.

Outside Suppliers and Logistical Issues

JIT planning and control requires trustworthy suppliers, so in the JIT environment, letting supply contracts out for bids has serious drawbacks. By allowing for multiple sources of material inputs, it introduces variability and

INTEGRATING OM:

Quick-Change Artists

Mike Grammel, plant manager at Chardon Rubber Co., knew it regularly took up to 45 minutes to changeover dies between customer batches. That meant lengthy downtime for Chardon Rubber's machines. And when its machines aren't running, Chardon Rubber isn't making money. Grammel didn't know how to make the plan more efficient without a substantial cash infusion. He invited the Work In Northeast Ohio Council (WINOC) to use his plant as a host site for a hands-on manufacturing process-improvement seminar. Using SMED, WINOC's class saw several ways to fine-tune the workflow:

Improving the availability of materials. Large, stackable containers of the raw rubber strips were brought closer to the production line making them more accessible. Before this, boxes were stored in a separate room, sometimes behind other boxes and high up on shelves.

They increased activity while machines are operating. Tool carts were brought to the production line while the machine was operating. Previously, production-line employees waited until the machine was shut down before retrieving new tools and dies and often retrieved them one tool at a time from across the room.

They purchased an additional die. One task that slowed the production line was that workers had to clean the single tool and die before replacing it on the machine and running the next product batch. For $500, Chardon Rubber bought a duplicate die. Now workers replace the die, start the machine, then clean the one that was removed. That move alone shaved 14 minutes off the changeover time.

They created a task checklist. Two lists of jobs were determined: external and internal. The external list handles tasks that must be completed before the machine can be shut down. The internal checklist provides an ordered list of jobs to follow to get the machine up and running.

They began to chart their progress. The pilot program has resulted in a 60 percent reduction in changeover time—down to an average time of 18 minutes. They've also posted a chart at the end of the production line. After each changeover, the total time is recorded, along with any notes. Looking for any patterns and other ways to cut time, the goal is a single changeover in less than 10 minutes.

According to WINOC's Fletcher Birmingham, "a good observation, followed by improvements, can usually cut your changeover time in half without spending a significant amount of money." For Chardon Rubber, it's resulted in a shorter lead time for customers and less materials waste because smaller batch sizes can be produced. Without adding manpower or machines to the plant, Chardon Rubber now fills its customers' orders faster and supplies rubber products to more customers at a lower cost.

Source: Adapted from *Cleveland's Small Business News*, October 1998, reporter Dustin S. Klein; and www.winoc.org/newsletter188161.html

reduces the customer's ability to interact with the sup-plier. It also eliminates any possibility of cooperation between manufacturer and supplier in the creation of the synergies and distinctive competencies that lead to a competitive advantage. For these reasons, long-term relationships with trustworthy suppliers are best suited to the JIT system.

This aspect of the JIT system may be easier to implement in countries like Japan, which, geographically is quite small relative to the United States. Japanese culture places a heavy emphasis on cooperation, trust, and long-term relationships, and many Japanese corporations belong to a **Kieretsu**, or a group of companies that cooperate with one another. For example, Mitsubishi's Kieretsu includes a merchant banker, a shipping company, a steel manufacturer, several electronics companies, an automobile maker, and several other companies. A large portion of the stock of each company is held by other companies in the Kieretsu, and the directors of the companies meet regularly. In addition, small companies that do not belong to the Kieretsu often align themselves with the group. In Toyota City, for instance, there are a large number of small businesses whose primary reason for existence is to provide supplies for Toyota.

Although U.S. business culture emphasizes independence, and legal barriers forbid anticompetitive practices, working closely with suppliers is still important. Indeed, the geographic distances between manufacturers and suppliers may require it. For example, getting regular 2-hour shipments to a facility in Detroit from a supplier in Mexico City is a great challenge. To meet such challenges, U.S. companies have developed two significant innovations: the in-plant supplier and sole source logistics providers.

The Bose Corporation of Framingham, Mass., pioneered the concept of the **in-plant supplier**. In planning Bose's new facilities, managers added extra office space for the company's suppliers, so that those employees could work on site. Bose would provide the office space and the necessary support; the supplier would provide the employee's compensation. Today, the in-plant supplier may work full time at the Bose facility or may be there only a certain number of days each week. Suppliers' personnel often mix with Bose personnel in meetings and during cafeteria breaks. The constant interaction between the two improves coordination with suppliers. The result is greater certainty about the supply of materials and greater efficiency throughout the supply chain.

Product design also benefits from the presence of in-plant suppliers. Even if an engineer from a supplier spends just one or two days a week at the Bose facility, at the very least that person will meet Bose design engineers during cafeteria breaks. When Bose designs a new stereo system, the design engineers will already know what off-the-shelf technologies are available from the supplier. Often, they will be able to avoid designing a new component from scratch, because something that was used in another application is available. Time, money, and energy would have to be expended in developing such components without the in-plant supplier's presence.

One of Bose's in-plant suppliers, Yellow Freight, is also Bose's **sole source logistics provider**, meaning that it handles all inbound and outbound freight. Because Yellow Freight attends schedule meetings and has complete knowledge of Bose's schedule, there is no need for Bose employees to arrange for the shipment of purchased materials and finished goods—Yellow Freight takes care of it automatically. In fact, Yellow Freight can anticipate Bose's needs and ensure more efficient shipment of supplies. For example, if the Yellow Freight representative knows that a shipment of raw materials will be available at a Bose supplier in California in 2 hours, the rep can delay an eastbound truck long enough to carry those materials and reroute the truck to ensure that the pickup and delivery take place. The result is greater efficiency in transportation services. Yellow Freight runs more smoothly, Bose gets better service, and a lot less paperwork is required.

Since the advent of JIT, the sole sourcing of logistical services has become common. Most major freight lines now offer turnkey solutions for manufacturers, meaning that they use their logistical expertise, their knowledge of cost factors, and their sophisticated computer models to benefit the manufacturer. Thus, they can provide much

Kieretsu

A group of companies that cooperate with one another.

In-plant supplier

Suppliers who are provided office space and support on-site at a facility they service.

Sole source logistics provider

A supplier that handles all aspects of a company's particular need.

Figure 14.12

Size of the transfer batch vs. the time through the process

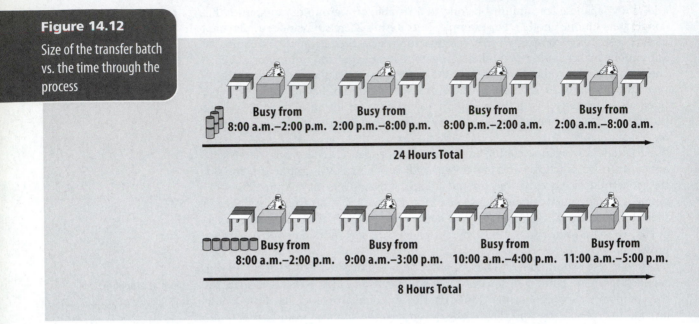

more economical service than would be available if manufacturers were to determine shipping quantities, schedules, and routes themselves. Work is reduced for both suppliers and their customers, and service improves throughout the supply chain. Note that in this sense, JIT manufacturing relies on a service operation for much of its success.

Figure 14.12 illustrates one of many potential benefits that could arise from improved logistical services. Often, to keep things simple, managers make transfer batches the same size as production batches. In other words, all the work on a particular order will be completed before any of it is transferred from one work area to another. This rule frequently holds true whether the work is being transferred from suppliers to customers or from one work area to another. The top half of the figure shows an order for six units being transferred and processed all at once. If the processing time at each of eight work stations is 1 hour per unit and the processed goods will not be transferred until all are finished, 24 hours will pass before any finished goods become available. But if the items can be transferred one at a time (bottom half), some finished goods will become available in just 8 hours. (Remember that on-hand inventory is proportional to the time a product takes to go through the process.) The producer who uses the latter system can afford to be more responsive and adaptive to customer requirements.

Kanban system

A signal that something needs to be done.

Pull scheduling

A system in which work is pulled through the value-adding system by signals from end users.

Kanban Systems

Sooner or later, in any operation, one must determine who should do what with which resources on a moment-to-moment basis. In JIT systems, detailed scheduling is often done using a **kanban system**. "Kanban" is the Japanese word for "card"; in the context of detailed scheduling, a kanban is simply a signal that something needs to be done. The kanban system is a **pull scheduling** system, meaning that work is pulled through the

In high school, possessing a hall pass meant you had permission to be out of class and on your way somewhere the same way a Kan Ban card signals permission to produce something. The card stays with the product until it is used by the next step in the process. The number of students in the hall could be controlled by adjusting how easy it is to get a pass or how many are in circulation. The amount of inventory in the system can be similarly controlled by the number of Kan Bans issued to the system.

value-adding system by signals from end users. Unless a downstream customer uses a material, its production and replenishment will never be authorized.

Figure 14.13 illustrates a simple two-stage kanban system. Department 24K receives material that is described on the card labeled "A" and converts it into something labeled "B." Department 97X converts the material called "B" into something called "C." When a customer uses up a bin full of part C, a chain reaction pulls more of that material through the system. When the customer needs the part, he or she takes the material and leaves the kanban behind. Workers in Department 97X see the "free kanban" and replace the used material according to the instructions shown on the card.

Figure 14.13

A simple, two-stage kanban system

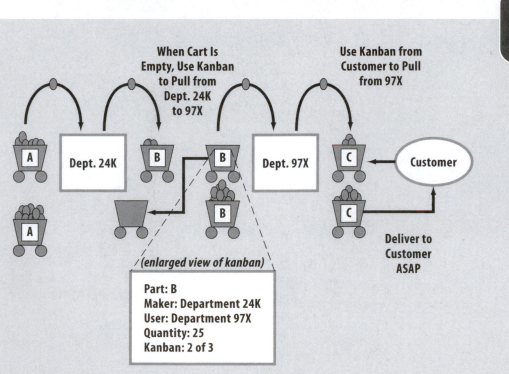

In doing so, they will use up a bin of part B, leaving the B kanban free. Workers in Department 24K will then use a bin of part A to make a bin of part B, freeing the A kanban and drawing more of that material into the system. Thus, the kanbans authorize workers to perform specific tasks, translating customer needs into work orders without management intervention.

Though cards are typically used in modern kanban systems, there are many other ways to signal workers. For example, as Figure 14.14 shows, an empty space can serve as a kanban. At the pancake breakfast described at the beginning of this chapter, empty pitchers were used as kanbans to signal the need for more pancake batter. In other situations, kanbans can be transmitted electronically to employees' workstations.

Controlling Inventory Levels with Kanbans

Management can control the amount of inventory in a value-adding system by adding or removing kanbans. Notice that in Figure 14.13, there were two A kanbans, two C kanbans, and three B kanbans. As a rule, only enough kanbans are needed to ensure

Figure 14.14

An empty space as a kanban ("work only if there is a space to put the completed job")

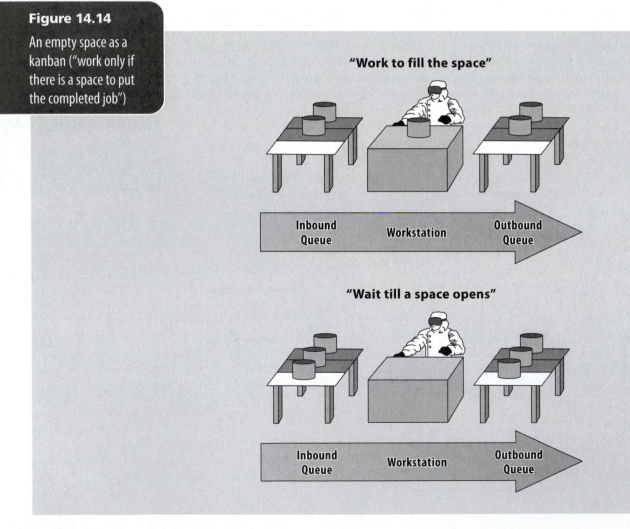

that users of a particular material do not suffer stock-outs. The following formula is useful in establishing the number of kanbans needed:

$$\# \, Kanbans = \frac{d(l + \alpha)}{c}$$

where:

   d = the leveled pull rate experienced at the workstation
   L = the expected lead time (time from use of the material to its replenishment)
   $\propto$ = the safety stock factor, to cover foreseeable variability in L
   c = the container or bin size
   (i.e., the number of units authorized by each kanban)

As Figure 14.15 illustrates, the kanban system works extremely well in simple environments in which the master schedule has been effectively smoothed and workstation capacities essentially balanced. The beauty of the system is that it can provide all the necessary information about work priorities to each workstation in the system

Example 14.3

Assume the company in Examples 14.1 and 14.2 is using a kanban system to procure engine castings from an outside supplier for their 4L2 model engine. Empty trailers, specially outfitted to transport, load and unload the castings will be used as kanbans. These trailers are unloaded at a dock situated at the beginning of the assembly line, so that no inventory staging occurs within the facility. Rather, the castings are in the trailer until use. Each trailer holds 30 engine castings. The supplier's location is normally an 80-minute drive each way, but traffic and weather conditions could make the drive as long as 120 minutes. The time required to load a truck is estimated at 15 minutes, but would not exceed 20 minutes. The company expects a safety factor of 60 minutes will provide a reasonable level of protection against loading and traffic disruptions. How many kanbans should the company use for the ongoing procurement of this part?

Step 1: Estimate the demand rate (d), lead time (L), and safety factor (α) in consistent units.

Based on the level schedule created in Example 14.2, the 4L2 will be produced at a rate of twenty-six engines per 84 minutes. That translates to 18.5714 *per hour*.

The lead time is the expected value of the time required for an empty truck to make a round trip, returning full. That would be 80 minutes in transit each way plus 15 minutes for loading, a total of 175 minutes (or 2.9167 *hours*).

The safety factor of 60 minutes translates to 1.00 *hours*. (Note: we chose to use *hours* as the consistent time unit. We could have used minutes, seconds, etc.)

Step 2: Calculate the number of required kanbans.

$$K = [d(L + \alpha)] / c$$
$$= [18.5714(2.9167 + 1.00)] / 30$$
$$= 2.4246$$

We can determine that three kanbans will be required. Any result greater than 2.0000 would require three kanbans. By rounding up, the actual margin of safety (or α) becomes larger than required. In fact, you could figure out that with three kanbans the actual margin of safety is 1.94 hours. (Find this by working backward—setting K equal to 3 and solving for α.) Because the actual margin of safety is greater than that specified, the company has the option of reducing the number of engines per kanban (trailer). Because 2.42 shipments of thirty engines is roughly the same volume as three shipments of twenty-three, the number of engines per kanban could be reduced to twenty-three while still maintaining the level of safety specified.

Figure 14.15

Kanban pull from the preceding workstation in simple environments

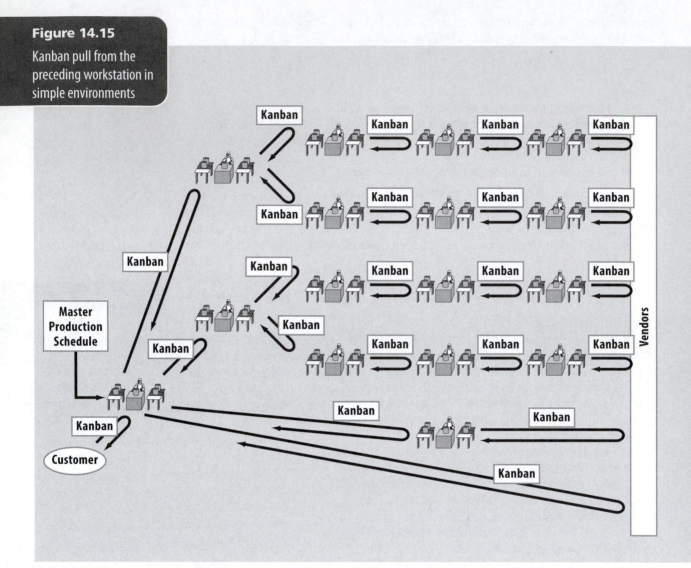

without managerial intervention. It does so based on the pull rate of internal and external customers, so that no workstation will get ahead of others and no unnecessary inventory will accumulate. If a workstation has no free kanbans, workers will not create more inventory—indeed, they cannot. But that doesn't mean that their time has to be wasted. For example, downtime caused by a lack of free kanbans can be used to help other workers—particularly if the reason for not having a free kanban is that some other work center has experienced a disruption. Alternatively, free time can be used to perform productive maintenance or to pursue ideas for improvement. Too much or too frequent idle time, however, could be a sign of an imbalanced schedule (i.e., a rock from figure 14.5). A worker who creates inventory simply to look busy is putting water back into the pond and potentially submerging the rock hiding the problem.

The kanban system breaks down when the demand pull comes from multiple sources, when workstation capacities are not balanced, or when demand is not level, as illustrated in Figure 14.16. Adding the complexity of multiple customers and suppliers

Figure 14.16

Kanban breaks down when the pull comes from multiple sources

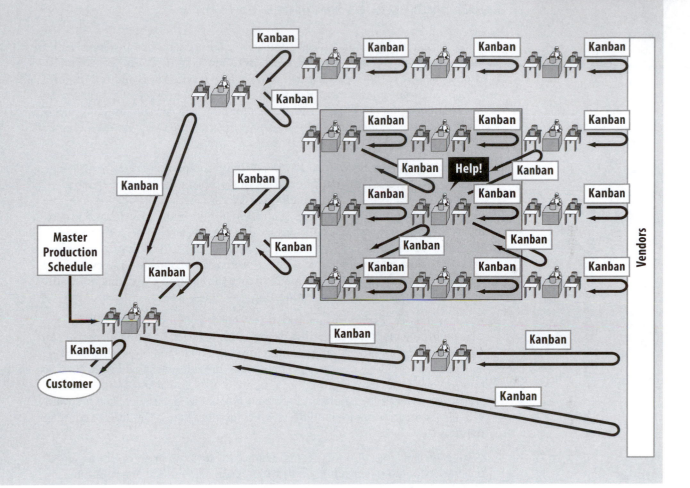

to just one workstation introduces the question of which kanban will receive top priority and why. This weak point will eventually cause the whole system to unravel.

Finally, on an assembly line in which workers perform the same task over and over again using the same materials, there is no need to put routine instructions on kanbans. That doesn't mean that workers don't need information regarding their progress, but simply that they need less detailed information less often. In this type of operation, andon boards are often used. An **andon board** is a large electronic sign that provides real-time operational performance and system status information. Typically andon boards communicate the daily production goal, current progress toward that goal, whether the assembly line is ahead of or behind target, and the amount of time that has been lost to work stoppages. When work has been stopped, the andon board also tells where the disruption occurred. Workers are allowed, even encouraged, to stop the assembly

Andon board

A large electronic sign that provides real-time operational performance and system status information.

line when they find a quality problem or experience some other disruption. When they do, other workers can identify the location of the disruption and aid in an effort to eliminate the problem.

Lean Systems in Services

As noted earlier in the chapter, service-intensive environments can benefit from lean thinking. For example, developing value driven relationships with suppliers of materials used by service businesses can enhance inventory service levels and reduce inventory costs. But lean systems involve more than timing the delivery of tangible goods. Below we identify ten ways that services can adopt the lean cornerstones of customer focus, waste elimination, continuous improvement, employee involvement, and reduced uncertainty.

1. *Organize continuous improvement teams.* A utility company, Florida Power and Light (FP&L), creates teams to address specific problems and customer complaints. (The teams use QI story method and tools described in Chapter 4 on page 159.) Most importantly, when improvements are made, policies and procedures are permanently changed to ensure that the new level of performance is sustained. For example, an FP&L team determined that cars hitting utility poles—especially those on the outside of curves—was a major contributor to customer outages. The team helped the company change the location of existing poles and revised the company's method for locating new poles.

2. *Reduce employee absenteeism and turnover.* A major source of uncertainty in service environments is employee absenteeism and turnover. Creating incentives and compensation programs to improve employee reliability and loyalty helps to keep experienced employees on the job. Fairfield Inn provides extra paid vacation days for employees who have no absences. Employees may also arrange with other employees to cover their shifts and not have it count as an absence. The program provides some freedom for employees while providing the reliability the company requires.

3. *Cross train employees.* Productivity is enhanced when employees can be assigned to a variety of tasks, depending on the immediate needs of the organization. Cross-trained employees can handle a greater variety of customer requests, fill in for absent coworkers, and improve their compensation and job satisfaction. For example, employees at a call center help desk who are experts at more than one software package may be more valuable to their employer, enable their firm to provide better service, and be more highly compensated than employees whose expertise is limited to one package.

4. *Blueprint the service process.* Blueprinting plays a key role in identifying and removing waste in the system. For example, waiting is a common problem for students who visit their university's walk-in health clinic. The reasons for long delays in the clinic's process can be pinpointed by identifying and timing the steps involved, including check-in, chart retrieval, triage, treatment by a care provider, and supplemental services, such as X-rays and lab work. Blueprint analysis helps identify service bottlenecks and sources of unnecessary delays.

5. *Update equipment and process technology.* Technology can improve service responsiveness while containing costs. Target stores place telephone call boxes throughout the store so customers can call for assistance. Call boxes help maintain customer service while keeping labor costs down. Target also uses intercom headsets so store employees can communicate with one another without blaring announcements that could annoy customers over a public-address system.

6. *Level demand.* Demand is a major source of uncertainty for any business environment. Leveling demand allows companies to reduce inventories or improve response time. One-hour photo labs usually have higher prices for the 1-hour service and lower prices for next-day and 2-day service. Pricing helps segment demand and spread it more evenly throughout the day. The shops can therefore schedule labor and developing machines with more certainty. Costs are kept low and customer expectations are met consistently.

7. *Have a service recovery plan.* Because uncertainty cannot be completely eliminated in most businesses, companies should have a service recovery plan to minimize the impact on customers when things go wrong. One of the authors of this book was shopping at Target on a busy Saturday when all computerized cash registers went down. The store manager immediately announced the temporary outage over the public-address system and requested the customers to be patient. Announcing the incident to all shoppers immediately lowered their expectations regarding the checkout service. It prevented customers from being surprised and disappointed when they arrived at the registers. Several store managers stationed in the register area handed out $3 vouchers to every customer while apologizing for the delay. The managers also assigned all store personnel to the registers (note the use of cross-trained employees) so customers could be served as quickly as possible once the registers were back on-line. After 15 minutes the registers began operating and the customer backlog was quickly processed. In this case, what could have been a customer service nightmare turned out to be a minor incident.

8. *Eliminate unnecessary activities.* Understanding customer priorities is the key to eliminating activities that the customer does not care about. Bagging your own groceries became popular in many stores when managers recognized that customers associated self-service bagging with lower prices. It also saved the stores in resources. Some stores allow customers to price-scan their own groceries—a move that allows customers an alternative to checkout lines.

9. *Change the facility layout.* Customers can often be better served and costs saved by simply changing the layout of the service facility. For example, various congregations have removed bolted-down church pews in favor of movable seating solutions that allow their facility to be used for multiple functions and banks that use a single line for waiting customers provide better service than those that use multiple waiting lines because demand is distributed evenly among the tellers.

10. *Use demand-pull scheduling.* Service technicians, retail store personnel, real estate agents, and funeral home employees are among the numerous service sector employees who provide on-call services. For example, Lanier's copier service and repair orders can be entered on the web by a customer. When a repair order is entered, the computer automatically notifies all service personnel who could respond to that need by pager, e-mail, and/or cell-phone of the need for their

services. Based on the incentive scheme by which these employees are compensated, it is a sure bet that the nearest available individual will notify the system that he or she is taking that service opportunity. The service technicians are graded for their services effectiveness as well as the speed of response—and customer service ratings are very high.

SUMMARY

In this chapter we have described short-range planning and control for dependent demand items in repetitive value-adding systems. The JIT system has become one of the most common approaches to handling material and capacity decisions in such environments. JIT was developed by Toyota Motor Company in the 1950s and 1960s, and took root in the rest of the world by the late 1980s. Its use has influenced the practice of business in virtually every function and is often simply referred to as lean manufacturing.

The simpler the value-adding system, the better the JIT system works. JIT is not well suited to complex value-adding systems, such as batch processes or job shops. JIT emphasizes the reduction of wasteful inventories through the improvement of processes and the elimination of uncertainty. Lower levels of inventory are often achieved through smaller lot sizes that are made possible by extremely low setup costs. Low setup costs are often achieved through a setup-time reduction technique referred to as SMED.

The JIT approach to planning and control relies on a leveled master schedule for independent demand inventory items. A level schedule can be seen as a completion sequence for all of the items that are on the master schedule for a specific planning period. The sequence is repeated until all of the requirements on the master schedule have been met. The more rapidly the sequence can be completed, the more level the schedule. With a more level schedule, inventory levels can also be kept lower, because value can be added at a rate that is consistent with its consumption.

Day-to-day and moment-to-moment scheduling of the JIT environment is accomplished with visual signals such as kanbans and andon boards. The kanban system is designed to allow workers to respond to the demand pull of downstream customers. Thus, workers do not need managers to tell them what to do next. In fact, much of the power and efficiency of the JIT system comes from simplifying the system to the extent that it can run itself. This approach eliminates the need for an army of middle managers to handle production planning and control, and renders the operational system flexible, efficient, and responsive to customer requirements.

The JIT philosophy that stresses employee involvement, uncertainty reduction, and continuous improvement has many applications in service-intensive businesses. Services may try to reduce uncertainty through such mechanisms as demand-pull scheduling; employee cross training; and incentive systems based on employee skills, length of service, and attendance record. Continuous improvement in services often comes from employee teams, applications of technology, service blueprinting, changes in facility layout, and elimination of unnecessary activities.

KEY TERMS

Andon boards, 659
In-plant supplier, 653
Inside exchange of die (IED), 650
Kanban system, 654
Kieretsu, 653

Lean manufacturing, 632
Level master schedule, 636
Outside exchange of die (OED), 650
Pull scheduling, 654

Single minute exchange of
 die (SMED), 650
Sole source logistics provider, 653
Takt time, 635

SOLVED PROBLEMS

1. A bicycle factory assembles various frame sizes of its most popular 12-speed mountain bike through a series of work stations. The line operates one shift a day and with breaks and lunches considered, is running 400 minutes per shift. They work a five-shift week.

   Weekly demand for the bikes is as follows:

Frame Size	19"	20"	21"	22"	23"	24"
Weekly Demand	150	200	250	300	250	200

   What is the necessary Takt time?

Solution:

   Total weekly demand = (150 + 200 + 250 + 300 + 250 + 200) = 1350 frames

   Total weekly work time = (400 minutes per shift × 5 shifts per week × 60 seconds per minute) = 120,000 seconds

   Takt time = 120,000 seconds ÷ 1350 frames = 88.88 seconds per frame

2. A printing company has multiple work centers over three primary stages of production that print, cut, and assemble business forms. Currently a kanban system is used to pull work from each work center to its downstream "customer" operation. The steps required for most jobs are very similar and almost never change, thus material flows are also somewhat stable but fluctuate from time to time. All material is transferred by forklifts that move single pallet jobs from one work center to the next downstream work center. The forklift drivers simply scan the work areas for free kanban cards, then retrieve full pallets from the upstream operations that provide the part or material described on the kanban. As an assembly area supervisor, you realize that for any given part, it usually takes the forklift driver about 90 minutes to return with a full pallet from the supplying workstation. If the upstream machines are having problems, forklifts have been known to take as much as 150 minutes to return with parts. Your assembly operations use one pallet of parts or material in about 40 minutes under normal conditions.

   a) How many kanban cards would be needed to keep your assembly work station supplied with that one part under normal conditions (assuming average stock retrieval time)? What does rounding up to the next higher integer number of kanban imply for a default value for $\propto$? If rounding does take place yet you wish ($\propto = 0$, what does that imply about the number of parts per pallet?

   b) If you wanted to protect your assembly areas from running out of material due to upstream issues, how many kanbans would you need? What does rounding up to the next higher integer number of kanban imply for a new default $\propto$? Is this of value?

   c) Who is the most critical person to material flow in the current system? Why?

   d) How might this process be improved?

   e) What might cause the complexity of the situation to increase, and how might that affect the response of upstream operations to the downstream operations? Would the answer to (c) have any impact on downstream operations?

Solution:

   a) Given: # kanbans = $[d(L + \propto)]/c$, assuming no safety stock (or that ($\propto = 0$), an average replenishment of L = 1.5 hours, demand = 1.5 pallets per hour, and c = 1 (as demand is expressed in pallets), then the number of kanbans required should not exceed 2.25 or rounded to 3. Rounding to 3 kanbans and solving for $\propto$ means a default of 30 minutes protection (.75 extra kanban/1.5 kanbans required per hour). It would also be possible to use three kanbans with the number of parts or material per kanban reduced to 75% of the current pallet capacity. You can determine this by setting K = 3, d = 1.5, L = 1.5, $\propto = 0$, and solving for c.

   b) Assuming the worst case is 150 minutes (2.5 hours) for delivery turnaround, then 3.75 rounded to 4 kanbans would be needed. In this case $\propto$ = 1.16 hours or 70 minutes (1.75 extra kanbans/1.5 kanbans required per hour). If the delivery never requires more than an extra

60 minutes (as the problem implies), then it would be better to reduce the quantity per pallet as the additional safety stock inventory in the system is of no value.

c) In the current system, the forklift driver is the most critical person in the system as they have to notice a kanban card is available and deliver it to the upstream workstation responsible for replenishing it and deliver it back within the normal 2-hour maximum time window. In order to maintain a high utilization of the forklift drivers, much like servers in a restaurant, they may be juggling kanbans and delivery of several items at a time.

d) Communication between the fork lift driver, the user of the part, and the maker of the part controlled by the kanban is critical. If the time between the user determining a need for the part and notification of part's maker and the forklift driver can be reduced, the replenishment time and thus the number of kanbans in the system can be reduced. This may take the form of a computerized system notifying all parties instantly or possibly an electronic voice communication system. The simplest improvement might be anything that makes the need and availability of parts more visual. Such as the series of lights used in a restaurant to signal that an order is "up."

e) Complexity might increase if the number of possible user workstations a forklift driver has to check increases, or if the customer/supplier workstation pairings become less stable, then the turn-around time would increase. An increase in the number of downstream workstations that send a kanban back to a given workstation would also increase turn around time (i.e., complexity). In either case, the number of kanbans required would increase in proportion to the turn around time. This will increase

amount of inventory in the system and reduce the responsiveness of the overall process and make it harder to find the "rocks" (i.e., identify problems when they occur). This effect could be due to an increase in the number of products or variety of product routes through the system.

3. A local firm assembles four different models (named after a variety of fruit) of a home computer for wholesale distribution. Assembled from similar purchased parts, the models vary only in hard-disk capacity and chip speed. The shop is in operation over a single 400-minute shift each day, 5 days a week. The following represents their schedule over the next 6 weeks:

Model/Week	1	2	3	4	5	6
Pear	180	180	100	100	120	120
Orange	150	150	200	250	170	200
Cherry	50	50	50	30	70	70
Lime	20	20	50	20	30	20
Total	400	400	400	400	390	410

a) Given the schedule above, what would be the necessary takt time for the shop over the next 6 weeks?

b) In order to both spread out and level production for the four models, how many units would comprise the shortest possible production sequence that includes at least one unit of all four models?

c) How would you spread the models over that sequence such that demand is met in a level fashion?

Solution:

a) Weekly and overall demand totals for the facility are as follows:

Model/Week	1	2	3	4	5	6	Total
Pear	180	180	100	100	120	120	800
Orange	150	150	200	250	170	200	1120
Cherry	50	50	50	30	70	70	320
Lime	20	20	50	20	30	20	160
Total	400	400	400	400	390	410	2400

Therefore:

Takt = production time / aggregate demand

= (60 seconds per minute × 400 minutes per day × 5 days per week × 6 weeks) ÷ 2400 units

= 720,000 seconds ÷ 2400 units

= 300 seconds per unit

b) With the overall demand total of 2400 and the smallest item demand of 160 (for the item named Lime):

Required length of Shortest Possible Sequence = 2400 production slots ÷ 160 Units of Lime = 15 Production Slots per Unit of Lime.

The proportion of each model is as follows:

Model	Proportion of Total Demand	Proportional Number of Slots Out of 15	Production Frequency of Each Model in the Sequence
Pear	0.333333	5	3
Orange	0.466667	7	2.14
Cherry	0.133333	2	7.5
Lime	0.066667	1	15

c) Thus, a production sequence approximating the suggested production frequency of each model would be as follows:

Production Sequence Slots	Model in Each Production Slot
1	Pear
2	Orange
3	Pear
4	Orange
5	Cherry
6	Orange
7	Pear
8	Orange
9	Pear
10	Orange
11	Lime
12	Orange
13	Pear
14	Orange
15	Cherry

DISCUSSION QUESTIONS

1. How much do you think the United States Mint actually relies on JIT planning and control? Identify some of the costs the mint faces because of demand variability and large printing lots.

2. How is JIT related to TQM? Can you illustrate the relationship in terms of Tom's airline? Luis's factory?

3. What was the role of the "hall pass" (usually some big piece of wood or other conspicuous object) your fourth-grade teacher gave you when you asked to get a drink of water? How was that role different from that of a kanban?

4. Give some everyday examples of setup time and how it can be reduced. What does reduced setup time have to do with inventory?

5. How would JIT apply to the stocking of inventory in the pro shop at Miami University's recreation center? (That's the small shop in the lobby that sells a limited variety of athletic wear and equipment.) How would it apply to the snack counter?

6. Explain the idea of buffers. How do they fit into the "lake and rocks" analogy of Figure 14.5?

7. Assume your job requires you to respond rapidly in a standard way (i.e., providing a standard

product-service bundle) to the unpredictable timing of kanbans from a downstream operation. (This situation is similar to that of the butler who responds when the head of the house rings a bell.) How hard would your job be if you had no other responsibilities? How would your job change if the number of downstream operations that could send you kanbans increased? What if the variety of kanban types increased? What if both complications ensued at once—in what ways would you be forced to change the way you plan and execute your day?

8. How is the analogy of reducing the water (inventory) in a pond (the process) until you hit a rock (a problem) similar to the way a doctor in Cheryl's hospital would prescribe an antibiotic to cure a simple throat infection? Would inventory be analogous to taking an aspirin for the sore throat?

9. Recent strikes by single facilities in the auto industry have idled thousands of workers in just a few days. The fact that the impact of the strikes spread so quickly over such large numbers of workers and facilities is attributed to JIT practices. Is this phenomenon an example of what is good about JIT, or is it an example of what is bad about JIT?

10. What would make the kanban system difficult to implement in Luis's furniture factory?

11. Tom would argue that the time an airplane spends on the ground is comparable to the time spent on a machine setup. In terms of reducing setup time, what are some internal and external activities that Tom might focus on improving? Do you have any suggestions on how to do it?

12. In many household devices (digital radio tuners, digital thermostats, belts with prepunched holes), setup adjustments have been eliminated. Can you identify anything in your classroom that was designed with the same purpose?

13. How complex would the scheduling of Luis's furniture factory be compared to that of Fred's pager factory? How would Tom's airline compare to Cheryl's hospital? (Hint: The route map on the back of the airline's on-board magazine may be misleading.) Which ones could use a kanban system more easily than the others?

14. Think back to your last summer job. Could you suggest ways to streamline, simplify, or integrate the value-adding system? Do not let organizational inertia limit your answer.

PROBLEMS

1. Assume a major dining hall at your university serves 1200 students with three lines during the 2-hour lunch period. An analysis revealed that there are five basic work stations that the typical student progresses through as they "assemble" their meal:

   a) What is the implied takt time that would be necessary in order to get all the students through the line in the 2-hour period? Assume they arrive evenly through out the lunch period.

   b) If the line is not moving smoothly and the main entree station is an apparent issue, what would you suggest?

2. Fred's cell-phone factory uses a kanban system to "pull" printed circuit boards from the fabrication area (at one end of the plant) to the assembly area (at the other end of the plant). The empty cart serves as the kanban. Each cart holds 120 printed circuit boards that are used to supply assembly lines with a 15-second cycle time. Basically, when material handlers notice an empty cart, they take it

For Problem 1

Station	1	2	3	4	5
Description	Silverware, Tray, and Napkins	Main Entree	Salad	Drinks	Condiments

back to the fabrication area for reloading. When workers in the fabrication area fill a cart, they take it to the assembly area.

a) If it takes exactly 2 hours from the time a cart is emptied to the time it is filled and taken back to the assembly area, how many carts (or kanbans) are needed to assure smooth production in a given assembly area?

b) Assume delays are possible and while almost all carts return in less than 3 hours it has taken as long as 4 hours to get full carts back. How many carts would be needed to protect against an extra hour's delay? All delays given history to date?

c) What are some of the "rocks" (or problem areas) that you might uncover if the number of carts were reduced?

d) How might the system described here be improved?

e) Who is the critical person in this system?

3. A major auto manufacturer's assembly plant receives stamped body parts from a supplier about 3 hours away. While anything can happen, over the last 6 years, no truck has taken more than 5 hours to deliver parts. (A couple of traffic accidents have delayed shipment for more than 5 hours, but accidents happen so sporadically that they are not considered here.) After a brief check-in, trucks are moved to a receiving dock near the spot on the line where the parts are used, and are unloaded and stored very near the line, with no incoming inspection. Then the empty trucks are moved away from the receiving dock to make room for the next full truck. Empty trucks are immediately driven back to the supplier, who uses their arrival as a signal to send another full truck. The assembly line makes equal numbers of three different models, but the parts supplied by truck are used in only two models. The line has a 60-second cycle time, and a truck can hold parts for 160 cars.

a) How many trucks are needed in the loop between the supplier and the assembly plant?

b) What are some of the "rocks" (or problem areas) that you might uncover if the number of trucks in the system were reduced?

c) How does the number of car models that use these parts affect the situation?

d) How would the scheduled mix of the cars made on the line affect this situation?

4. Cheryl's grandparents used to tell her about the dairy truck that once delivered milk to their door in glass quart bottles. When the bottles were empty, they would put them on their doorstep the night before a scheduled delivery. The next morning they would find full bottles in their place.

a) The dairy that delivered to Cheryl's grandparents had a daily demand for retail home delivery of about 1000 gallons of milk, though it could increase to as much as 1200 on any given day. If the dairy took 4 days to get an empty bottle cleaned, refilled, and back on the delivery truck, how many bottles were needed to assure that everyone had milk to pour over corn flakes each morning given normal demand?

b) How many bottles would they need to keep their customer happy if demand peaked?

5. A modern grocery chain now has its own dairy plant that supplies thirty stores. The chain uses a similar system (to that of the previous problem) for "pulling" dairy products to the stores' dairy cases. Milk products are packaged in a variety of containers, each of which comes in a special color-coded plastic crate. The delivery people collect the empty crates at the store and return them to the dairy, where the milk is packaged according to the mix of empty crates returned on the delivery truck each day. From the time a crate is emptied, it takes a maximum of 5 days to fill it and get it back to the store.

a) If the demand for gallon jugs of skim milk across all thirty stores ranges from 4000 to 6000 gallons per day, and a crate holds four 1-gallon jugs, how may crates of skim milk would be needed to ensure that everybody has skim milk for their granola each morning?

b) What are some of the "rocks" (or problem areas) that you might uncover if the number of milk crates were reduced?

c) How might the system be improved if the potential problems you listed in part b) actually occurred?

d) How would the system begin to break down as the variety of product and container combinations proliferated?

6. A local bistro "assembles" boxed lunches for their catering business. The sandwiches are made, the vegetables cut and wrapped, etc. over a handful of work stations. They need to schedule workers during a 2-hour window of time each morning over the upcoming week. The aggregate demand for lunches over that period is as follows:

a) What is the necessary takt time each day?

b) Given an average of 3 minutes work involved with assembling each lunch, what can you say about the number of workers needed each day?

Monday	Tuesday	Wednesday	Thursday	Friday	Saturday	Sunday
150	150	240	240	180	90	60

CHALLENGE PROBLEMS

1. For the next 5 weeks, Fred will be evenly spreading the production of 3 basic phone models over one production line. Each week they will need to make 3000 of Model 16A, 18,000 of the more popular Model 16b, and 12,000 of the new Model 18A. The production line is in operation 420 minutes per day and 5 days per week.

   a) What is the takt time?

   b) What is the smallest number of phones in a production sequence that includes at least one of all three models and meets demand over the next 5 weeks?

   c) How long will it take to produce each sequence?

   d) How many times will it be repeated each week?

   e) What would be the sequence?

2. Wally's Weed Whackers, Inc. (they used to go by the acronym WWW until they found out that it was being used elsewhere) assembles three different models of their popular gas-powered weed whackers. They make the original Wally Whacker 1, the bigger Wally Whacker 2, and the newest model, the streamlined Wally Whacker 3. Assume one shift that operates (taking out time for lunch and breaks) 410 minutes per day over a 5-day week.

The following demand is forecast for the upcoming 8 weeks:

   a) What is the takt time needed to meet demand over the next 8 weeks?

   b) What is the smallest number of whackers in a production sequence that includes at least one of all three models and meets demand over the next 8 weeks?

   c) How long will it take to produce each sequence?

   d) How many times will it be repeated each week?

   e) What would be the sequence?

For Problem 2

Model									
WWW1	650	600	500	500	500	500	600	600	550
WWW2	1700	1800	1800	1900	1600	1600	1500	1500	1600
WWW3	300	200	400	200	200	400	400	200	200

Case 14: J. C. Penney "Tailors" Its Inventory Management to the Twenty-first Century

When a customer walks into a J. C. Penney store in the U.S. and buys a dress shirt, they set in motion a global replenishment supply chain. In fact, on the following morning in Hong Kong, a procurement professional will receive a computer record of the sale (and others like it) and within two more days a factory Taiwan will ship an identical replacement shirt back to replenish the inventory at the J. C. Penney store.

This expedited replenishment process has given J. C. Penney a competitive edge in an industry where the goal is rapid inventory turnover Penney stores now hold almost no extra inventory of house-brand dress shirts. Less than a decade ago, Penney would have had thousands of them warehoused across the U.S., tying up capital and slowly going out of style.

Surprisingly, the process is not even managed by Penney's. The entire program is designed and operated by TAL Apparel Ltd., a closely held Hong Kong shirt maker. TAL, is a generally unknown but very large company. It is the maker of one in eight dress shirts sold in the U.S., employs 18,000 workers worldwide, and by processing over 40 million pieces had sales of $580 million in its 1999–2000 fiscal year.

Though you might not have heard of TAL before, you've probably worn apparel that the company manufactured. That's because TAL also supplies labels such as J. Crew, Calvin Klein, Banana Republic, Tommy Hilfiger, Liz Claiborne, and Ralph Lauren, Nike, Levi, and Talbots.

TAL collects point-of-sale data for Penney's shirts directly from stores in North America. It then runs the numbers through a computer model it designed. Next the Hong Kong company decides how many shirts to make, and in what styles, colors, and sizes. The manufacturer sends the shirts directly to each Penney store, bypassing the retailer's warehouses—and most of the corporate decision makers. For Lands' End, TAL stitches made-to-measure pants in Malaysia and flies them straight to U.S. customers, with a shipping invoice that carries the Lands' End logo.

As retailers strive to cut costs and keep pace with consumer tastes, they are becoming more dependent on flexibility and quick response from suppliers. This opens value-added service opportunities for manufacturers. TAL has capitalized on such opportunities by starting to take over such critical areas as sales forecasting and inventory management. Instead of asking Penney what it would like to buy, "I tell them how many shirts they just bought," says Dr. Harry Lee, TAL's managing director.

Retailers have been willing to cede some functions once seen as central because TAL can do them better and more cheaply. Rodney Birkins Jr., vice president for sourcing of J. C. Penney Private Brands Inc., describes as "phenomenal" the added efficiency Penney has been able to achieve with TAL. Before it started working with TAL a decade ago, Penney would routinely hold up to six months of inventory in its warehouses and three months' worth at stores. Now, for the shirt lines that TAL handles, "it's zero," Mr. Birkins says.

While TAL has no plans to vertically integrate into retailing, Dr. Lee points out that his approach is a natural for clothing retailers. It made a lot of sense for dress shirts, which are basic replenishment items, but also makes sense for fashion items. His view on fashion is that because retailers can never be sure what a customer will buy, the smart ones will reduce their risk by test marketing the fashion and then following up with very quick replenishment.

With decisions made at the factory, TAL can respond instantly to changes in consumer demand: stepping up production if there is a spike in sales or dialing it down if there's a slump. The system "directly links the manufacturer to the customer," says Mr. Birkins. "That is the future."

The degree of power Penney turned over to TAL is radical. "You are giving away a pretty important function when you outsource your inventory management," says Wai-Chan Chan, a principal with McKinsey & Co. in Hong Kong. "That's something that not a lot of retailers want to part with."

Penney, too, was reluctant, and took the step only after building up trust over years of working with TAL. But Penney now has let TAL take the arrangement a step further: designing new shirt styles and handling their market testing.

TAL's design teams in New York and Dallas come up with a new style, and within a month its factories churn out 100,000 new shirts. For a test, these are offered for sale at 50 Penney stores. Not nearly all will sell, but offering a wide array of colors and sizes helps to provide a true test of consumer sentiment. After analyzing sales data for a month, TAL—not Penney—decides how many of the new shirts to make and in what colors.

Because TAL manages the entire process, from design to ordering yarn, it can bring a new style from the testing stage to full retail rollout in four months, much faster than Penney could on its own.

The system in effect lets consumers, not marketing managers, pick the styles. "When you can put something on the floor that the customer has already voted on is when we make a lot of money," says Penney's Mr. Birkins.

TAL learned the supply chain business the hard way. In 1988, a U.S. wholesaler that handled its shirts, Damon Holdings Inc., failed. TAL, fearing a loss of sales and figuring they understood the wholesaling business, bought Damon. The result was "a big shock." A manager TAL had put in charge of Damon went on a buying spree, and soon its warehouses were crammed with two years' worth of shirt inventory that was going out of style. Shirts that cost $10 to make had to be sold for $3. By the time TAL closed Damon in 1991, it had lost $50 million.

Around the same time, TAL had begun supplying Penney with house-brand shirts. Mr. Lee saw that Penney was holding up to nine months of inventory, twice what most competitors kept. He floated a radical solution: Why not have TAL supply shirts directly to Penney stores instead of sending bulk orders to a Penney warehouse? Mr. Birkins was skeptical. But he saw that savings could be huge. It cost Penney 29 cents a shirt to have its warehouse workers sort out orders in the U.S. TAL could do it for 14 cents.

And such a system would let Penney respond more quickly to consumer demand. This had been a problem for the retailer, which often needed months to restock hot-selling styles. Stores ended up missing sales of these styles while holding less-popular models that they had to move at a discount.

There was one clear downside to the new system: If a store sold out of a style of shirts, it couldn't quickly get some more from a regional warehouse. So TAL agreed to sometimes send shirts to stores by air freight—a costly step but one TAL would take to keep the customer happy.

Soon TAL saw another opportunity. Penney's sales forecasts often missed, sometimes overestimating shirt needs by as much as two months' worth. Sales forecasting is one of the most difficult tasks for retailers, yet one that's increasingly important to get right as inventories get tighter. Using data straight from the stores, TAL began to forecast how many shirts Penney's stores would need each week, ordering more fabric and increasing production where needed.

Because TAL's computer model was better than the system Penney used, stores now keep half as much in stock as before. However, one time when TAL underestimated Penney's needs significantly, TAL's factory had to expedite Penney's order and send some shirts by air freight, which cost ten times as much as ocean shipping.

It's worth noting that TAL is part of a trend toward e-commerce systems in global supply enterprises. Financial institutions, government import/export regulators, suppliers, and buyers are all moving in a similar direction. For example, it has been estimated that the value of products sources through traditional methods between 1998 and 2001 fell from US$120 billion to US$89 billion per year. During the same period, use of electronic speed sourcing (last-minute ordering) and continuous replenishment systems increased by roughly 100% to US$97 billion per year.

While e-commerce has already provided faster response time, reduced inventory, enhanced supply chain performance, a marketing niche, and a new value-added service to customers, TAL is thinking of ways to push the idea to the next level. One possibility is to form a joint venture with Penney that would allow TAL to manage the supply chain for some other manufacturers that supply the retailer.

SOME QUESTIONS TO THINK ABOUT:

1. What is the product and what is the service in TAL's product-service bundle?

2. Use the "lake and rocks" analogy from this chapter to explain the new system utilized by TAL and J. C. Penney. How do the companies remove the rocks that are exposed by their dramatic reduction in inventory?

3. How does the reduced amount of inventory between the two companies help facilitate the designing of new styles and fashion conscious merchandising?

4. What role does technology play in this new system?

5. Compare and contrast the TAL replenishment system described in this case, with the JIT system for operations planning and control?

Sources: Adapted from "Made to Measure: Invisible Supplier Has Penney's Shirts All Buttoned Up," *WSJ.Com*, Sept. 11, 2003, Pg. 1, reporter Gabriel Kahn; and information on company and trade-related websites, including http://www.tapgroup.com/, http://www.tradecard.com/, http://www.lawson.com/, http://www.tdctrade.com/, and http://www.info.gov.hk/

15

Detailed Scheduling and Control Processes in Synchronous Environments with TOC

Chapter Outline

Introduction   676

Integrating Operations Management Across the Functions   677

Optimizing Revenues in a Simple Synchronous Value-Adding System   681

Applicability of Synchronous Planning and Control   690

Overview of TOC   694

Performance Measures and Capacity Issues   695

Cost Accounting   697

The Management Process   698

Supply Chain Impact of Synchronous Planning and Control   700

Detailed Scheduling: The Drum-Buffer-Rope System   702

Summary   710

Key Terms   710

Solved Problems   711

Discussion Questions   713

Problems   715

Challenge Problems   719

Case 15: The Advanced Regional Traffic Interactive Management and Information System—ARTIMIS   721

References   722

Learning Objectives

After studying this chapter you should be able to

▶ Explain what a bottleneck is and how it impacts the value-adding system

▶ Explain how the various functional areas of a business can work together to effectively identify and manage bottlenecks in the value-adding system

▶ Identify the bottleneck in a value-adding system and determine how to synchronize the system in order to maximize its profitability

▶ List the environmental characteristics of those systems that are best suited to synchronous planning and control

▶ Explain how performance should be measured and costs accounted for in synchronous value-adding systems

▶ Describe the impact of synchronous planning and control systems on a firm's suppliers and customers

▶ Schedule resources using a drum-buffer-rope scheduling system

...Back at the Rec Center

"Hey, Fred, did you get a chance to use the new bike machines with the road race simulators?" asks Luis, arriving in the work out room.

It was barely past 6:00 a.m., and there were only a few people in the rec center. The center had recently purchased three bike machines with computerized simulations of several types of road races that users could choose from as they worked out. Using these, riders could race another computer-generated rider over realistically simulated race courses. Riders could even select their opponent's level of strength to make the "race" competitive.

The new machines were very popular and in heavy demand. In fact, people who wanted to use the bikes had to sign up for 20-minute time slots. The center even had to schedule an additional supervisor to keep the schedule and monitor the use of the machines. The lines had been getting really long, and sometimes people selected a longer course, which only made the situation worse.

"They're really cool," Luis says to Fred. "You kind of forget you're working out and get caught up in the race on the screen. What a great way to work out!"

"No, I haven't had a chance to try one yet," says Fred, with some disappointment. "I couldn't get a time slot that fits my schedule until next week. I went over to look at them, and even though there was only one person waiting, the student supervisor told me I had to sign up for a time slot." He looks up and sees Cheryl and Tom coming in. Tom is looking toward the new bikes as he walks in. "Don't even think about it unless you have an appointment," says Fred.

"So those are the new ones I've been hearing about!" Cheryl says, admiringly. "I guess it makes sense to set up a schedule on them while they're the hot ticket. That'll give more people a chance to try them out and will keep anybody from hogging them. Remember when they opened the new racquetball courts?"

"Yes, I do," Tom says, with an annoyed tone. He's just sitting down to start stretching. "What a mess that was. It was 'first come, first served,' and then it became a challenge court, with the winner staying and taking on all comers. A lot of people got discouraged and never even tried to get on."

"That's right," says Cheryl. "I remember how word got around about the wait, which scared people off, and the courts actually sat empty during the late morning and afternoons. A sign-up sheet does make sense, at least until something else becomes the hot ticket. By that time, people who want to use the new item can get a feel for the typical wait at the times they want to come in, and they can plan accordingly."

She uses Tom's routine as an example: "Tom likes to come in and do six stations in his workout. Most of the time there's a small wait for a spot on a machine or stepper to open up before he can get on. He plans on about 15 minutes total for each station. So, with a few minutes spent talking with his friends in the group and a quick shower, he probably needs between an hour and a half and two hours each morning. If he has to be at work by 8, he needs to be at the rec center by 6 a.m."

"I come in earlier if I want to do something extra," says Fred. "That's why I got here early today. I wanted to try those bikes."

"Well, the bikes are a bottleneck right now, and the sign-up system makes the most sense until that changes," says Cheryl. "It keeps the bikes busy and the lines short."

"But what happens when somebody signs up for a time slot and then doesn't show?" Fred asks. "I don't even think the next person showed up this morning."

"Well, that's not right," says Tom. "Never let the hot ticket sit idle! That's why we overbook a flight when it gets full. Somebody invariably doesn't show, and we make good money only when all the seats are full."

"But you lose when more people than you expect show up. Don't the costs and problems from bumping customers add up?" asks Fred.

"Sure they do," says Tom, "so we have to be careful and try and balance the amount we overbook with the cost of giving out vouchers and flying empty seats on a heavily demanded flight. We don't mind having a few people wanting to fly standby, too."

"Wouldn't you really rather just have the people who book the flight just show up or cancel in time for you to sell the seats to somebody else?" asks Cheryl.

"That would be nice," says Tom. "We're linked by computer to travel agents, ticket agents, Internet sales sites, other airlines—the whole ball of wax. That gives us a better idea of what we need than we used to get in the old days. Someday, maybe we'll get it all figured, but for now that's still too complicated. We just play the percentages and hope for the best."

"Well, nobody likes getting bumped at the airport, and nobody wants to find they're double-booked on a bike at 6 a.m.!" laughs Cheryl. "There are other ways to keep the bottleneck moving."

"Yeah," says Luis, "maybe they could do what the restaurant my wife and I visited last night does." He told them how the restaurant inside a local shopping mall had a waiting line estimated to be 30 to 45 minutes long. The staff gave everyone who was waiting a small pager that worked only within a couple of hundred yards of the restaurant. That way, people who were waiting were free to shop around the mall and could come back to the restaurant when their table was ready. "It was great," laughs Luis. "We didn't have to sit around waiting, and the other stores in the mall must like the system, too. We spent more money in the other stores 'waiting' than we did for dinner!"

"This bottleneck issue happens here, too," Tom replies. "Sometimes you can't plan it; you just go with the flow. Every once in a while, there'll be a long line at one of the machines I want to go to next on my circuit. I just try to work around it. If the line at the next station looks long, I'll try a different one. Sometimes I've even cut it short on one machine to get over to the busiest-looking machine when I can sneak in between other users. I can always go back to the less-busy machines."

"Well, whether it's scheduled ahead of time or fit in between other users," laughs Fred,

"I want a crack at those new bikes. And I could sure set them up with free pagers if that would help!"

Introduction

Synchronous value-adding systems

Systems whose effective management, because of the presence of a bottleneck, requires that the timing of value-adding activities be coordinated (or synchronized) throughout the system.

Bottleneck

Any resource that has insufficient capacity to satisfy requirements.

REC CENTER DILEMMA

Cheryl's Dilemma:

Cheryl has noticed that there has been a strong spike in the number of complaints she gets from family physicians and their patients about the length of time it takes to get an appointment with the doctors in her hospital's orthopedic surgery practice. She remembers how good she felt a few months ago, when they hired an orthopedic surgeon who specialized in the reconstruction of damaged vertebrae. The new surgeon replaced a doctor who had been with the practice for many years and got a lot of referrals, but Cheryl discovered that the new surgeon was not perceived by the family practitioners as being a general orthopedic, as well as spinal, surgeon, so she was not getting nearly as many referrals as her predecessor had. To remedy the situation, Cheryl ran a marketing campaign introducing her to the local medical community, and the campaign had gone very well. After the campaign, the new doctor's load for general orthopedic procedures was more consistent with that of the remaining doctors in the practice. Now, Cheryl is wondering what has caused the increased time to get orthopedic surgery and what to do about it. What's your advice?

This chapter covers planning and control issues in **synchronous value-adding systems**—systems whose effective management, because of the presence of a bottleneck, requires that the timing of value-adding activities be coordinated (or synchronized) throughout the system. From an operational point of view, a **bottleneck** is any resource that has insufficient capacity to satisfy requirements. It is usually easy to find a bottleneck: it exists where a large number of customers or jobs are waiting for service. For example, in cities where a bridge is the primary way out of the city, many commuters avoid the bridge route at rush hour because they have come to expect traffic to be backed up there. (The bridge is the bottleneck, and the commuters are customers waiting for service.) When a value-adding system has a bottleneck and other activities are not coordinated with that resource, the bottleneck's capacity might be wasted, unnecessary inventories might be created, and customer service may suffer.

Not all systems are plagued by bottlenecks. If you went to a public elementary school, you were probably never closed out of a course. That is because everyone moved together through a standardized curriculum. The value-adding system was the same for each pupil, and if capacity had to be increased in a particular grade, the need would be clear from the number of students in the next lower grade. Typically, there were no enrollment problems, because potential bottlenecks could be anticipated and eliminated by appropriate staffing decisions. Essentially, the students flowed through the system together, with no special arrangements made for any particular group of students. Planning and control for this type of system was covered in Chapter 14.

In college, however, you may have experienced difficulty getting into a class you wanted to take. Because college-level students may take electives and can change their program of study at will, the level of certainty regarding the demand for particular course offerings is much lower than at an elementary school. Though student-demand patterns are continually changing, the faculty of academic departments does not change quickly. As a result, enrollment bottlenecks crop up in various course sequences, and department chairs must manage them by shifting teaching assignments or limiting enrollments. The dean of a business school with excess demand for a senior level advertising class might attempt to solve the problem by canceling a section of the introductory marketing prerequisite and shifting the professor's assignment to the senior level course. If you have ever been closed out of a course you needed in order to graduate on time, you know how important it is for academic administrators to synchronize course offerings.

You will better understand the concept of a synchronous value-adding system if you briefly consider its opposite, **asynchronous value-adding systems**, which are systems that allow separate value-adding activities to be scheduled independently. A local community college with a high continuing education enrollment and many part-time students who take courses only occasionally cannot synchronize the course offerings in non-degree programs. Administrators do not even try to accomplish this. Instead, they compile a list of offerings and hope for adequate enrollments. Each course faces a go/no-go decision based on current demand. Chapter 16 deals with planning and control issues in asynchronous value-adding systems.

This chapter begins with an explanation of the relevance of bottlenecks to employees in all functions in a synchronous value-adding system. To effectively manage such a system, the functions must be well coordinated across the entire synchronous value-adding system.

Asynchronous value-adding systems

Systems that allow separate value-adding activities to be scheduled independently.

Integrating Operations Management Across the Functions

Table 15.1 describes the cross-functional relevance of synchronous value-adding systems and other functional areas of business. Any functional area of any business can include a bottleneck or create one:

▶ Marketing policies that reward a sales force with commissions based on the dollar volume of sales generated, for example, can lead to large sales of low-margin items that are time consuming to produce.

▶ Financial management policies that require detailed expense reporting can tie up employee time; to the extent that such policies keep employees from value-adding activities, the paperwork itself may become a bottleneck. Investment policies that require a particular localized rate of return can prevent a company from expanding its capacity at a bottleneck, even though the expansion would improve the firm's profitability. Budgetary policies that limit cash flow can make the financing process a bottleneck in and of itself.

▶ Information systems often limit a firm's capability. For example, many retail companies use bar code readers to determine customer bills at cash registers and point-of-sale (POS) terminals, but their information processing capacity is insufficient to use the data for reordering. That is why, even though the checkout register "knows" what has been sold, you may still see clerks going through the aisles of some grocery stores with handheld scanners.

▶ The operations function itself often contains one or more bottlenecks. The problem might be inadequate parking space for a service facility, too few examination rooms in a doctor's office, a machine with temporarily insufficient capacity in some part of the value-adding system, a limitation in the availability of some highly demanded material, a shortage of skilled or unskilled labor, or insufficient space for inventory storage.

Table 15.1

Integrating Operations
Management across the
Functions

Integration Perspective / Functional Area	Finance	Accounting
Why Cross-Functional Integration Matters to Planning and Controlling Synchronous Value-Adding Systems	Financial justification for operational equipment and inventory storage capacity requires some knowledge of its potential utilization—and this depends on an understanding of the planning and control system in use.	Effective managerial accounting requires an understanding of the operational system. The Theory of Constraints (TOC) has much to say with regard to managerial accounting in the context of cost and productivity measurement.
Key Issues	How will equipment be utilized and capital expenditures justified in the Theory of Constraints (TOC) system? What risks to projected earnings arise from the operational plans of the business? From an investment perspective, what is the impact of synchronous operations on an equity's attractiveness or a facility's mortgage risk?	How will costs be allocated within the TOC system? How will inventory be valued? How will operating expense and throughput be measured? When and how will suppliers be paid? When and how will customers be billed?

When a company has unused capacity because of low levels of demand, the market itself is the system bottleneck.

Regardless of where a bottleneck is located, decision makers in other functions can harm their company if they are not aware of the bottleneck and its implications. An operations manager who does not know about a market bottleneck might make too much of the wrong product-service bundles and not enough of the right ones. A salesperson or marketing manager might promote low-profit items, which are difficult and time consuming to make at a bottleneck work center, because they are easy to sell and generate high commissions. Financial managers who are unaware of a bottleneck in another part of the firm are likely to overestimate the revenue potential from investment opportunities that depend on the bottleneck. In fact, one can imagine a host of scenarios in which decision makers' lack of awareness of bottlenecks in other functions results in regrettable choices, from the perspective of the firm or its

Human Resources	Marketing	Engineering	Management Information Systems
HR systems for employee selection, retention, motivation, and reward need to be consistent with the needs of the operating system.	Marketers must understand their own planning and control system, along with those of customers and other supply chain partners, for a company to satisfy their customers. In the TOC system, marketing priorities may arise from operational constraints.	Maintenance and reliability of bottlenecks are key to the effectiveness of the TOC system. Additionally, engineering activities support these systems by determining ways to enhance and exploit bottleneck capacity.	TOC systems rely on current information about workstation schedules to identify bottlenecks and optimize the system's throughput. Communicating bottleneck throughput and buffer capacities effectively is essential to these systems.
How will employee commitment to the system be developed and maintained? Is the labor contract appropriate to the TOC operating system? How will a system perspective be developed in all employees?	How will marketing plans and promotions adapt to operational changes resulting from tactics to exploit system bottlenecks? What product distribution system will best fit the TOC operating system?	What equipment should be used? And, how, when, and by whom will it be maintained, to ensure the JIT system does not face unwarranted bottleneck disruptions? Can technical changes to product or process designs reduce elevate bottleneck capacity?	How will bottleneck performance and buffer capacity be communicated across the system? How will workstation demand, capacity, and performance be monitored across the system?

customers. Clearly, effective management of a synchronous value-adding system presupposes effective management across the white spaces of the organizational chart.

The key to effective management of such systems is to recognize and exploit a system bottleneck wherever it exists.

General guidelines for the various functions might be stated as follows:

- Operations managers should make whatever is most profitable for the firm, not what generates the best local performance results or piece rate bonuses.

- Financial managers should support efforts to improve performance at the bottleneck. When traditional capital justification techniques are used, the system return on improvements to bottleneck performance is usually understated, because those techniques look at resources in isolation. On the other hand, one must be careful about expecting a return on an investment in a non-bottleneck work center; there is no financial benefit to improving performance at an underutilized resource. Finally, financial managers who are responsible for creating operational budgets need to recognize that in many firms, cash flow problems create operational bottlenecks.

▶ Accountants must approach cost and performance measurement in nontraditional ways. Activity-based costing, the balanced scorecard (page 698), and other recently developed performance measurement methods that focus on systemwide rather than local performance are necessary if cost information is to adequately support managerial decision making in a synchronous value-adding system.

▶ Human Resources personnel need to reward systems consistent with the needs of the operating system. It is particularly important that local incentives not be allowed to over-ride system requirements that are generated by managing to increase bottleneck throughput.

▶ Marketing professionals should be promoting and selling what is most profitable, not necessarily what carries the highest commission. This could mean refusing an order if a bottleneck will limit the firm's ability to profitably deliver the product-service bundle to the customer's satisfaction.

▶ Engineering, operational, financial, and marketing professionals who serve on design teams need to design (or redesign) product-service bundles for manufacturability. That means they need to be aware of existing and potential bottlenecks and create designs that can bypass these system constraints.

▶ Management information systems personnel need to clearly understand the information requirements of managers. Particularly in complex value-adding systems, synchronizing operational, marketing, purchasing, and financial decisions frequently requires the use of decision support systems.

Figure 15.1

Synchronous planning and control processes

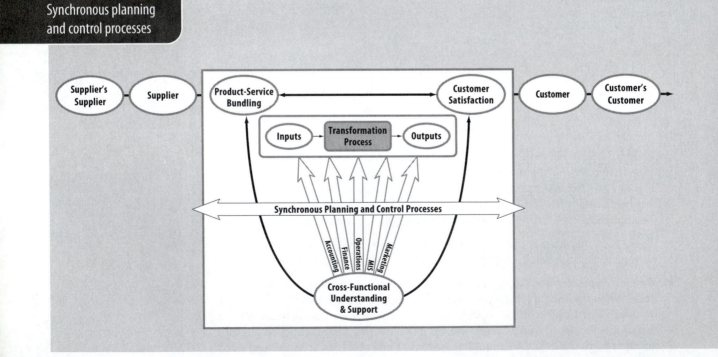

Figure 15.1 illustrates the important role that cross-functional understanding plays in planning and control of synchronous processes. Cross-functional understanding improves the support of the transformation process, and hence also the ability of the value-adding system to work with suppliers and to satisfy customers.

Optimizing Revenues in a Simple Synchronous Value-Adding System

Figure 15.2 illustrates a fairly simple screen-printing operation. The printing process requires that a screen be prepared for each color of a print. Screen preparation and setup takes 30 minutes per screen (5 of those minutes are devoted to setup). The screen is then set up on one of two presses, the garments printed, and the ink cured in the firm's single oven. (A conveyor belt runs through the oven, so curing the ink is not as much work as it would be if you were to do it in your kitchen oven.) The time required to accomplish each of these operations is indicated in Figure 15.2, along with the available capacity at each of the resources.

    Two employees are required to run this operation: an artist-screen maker, who makes the screens and does setups, and a printer, who uses the presses to print the garments. Both these employees are expected to be available for 2400 minutes each week. During any given week, the company cannot change the available capacity of any of its resources, human or capital, in the short term—they are fixed. The mix of jobs in the facility, however, will vary from one week to the next, depending on customer needs.

Figure 15.2

A simple screen—printing value-adding system

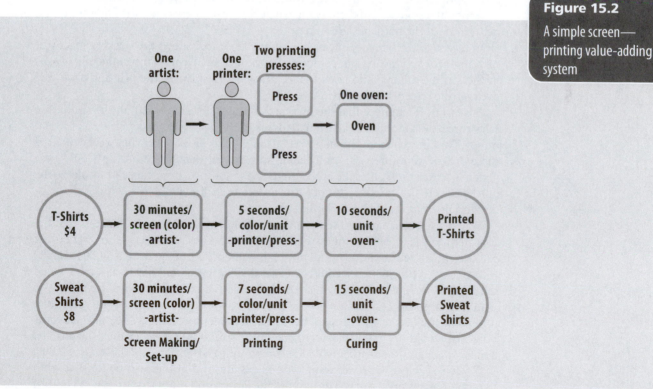

The company buys its sweatshirts for $8 and its T-shirts for $4. It sells the sweat-shirts for $16 with one-color prints, and $17, $18, and $19 for two-, three-, and four-color prints, respectively. T-shirts sell for $10, $11, $12, and $13 for one-, two-, three-, and four-color prints, respectively.

Consider the following questions pertaining to the screen-printing operation just described:

▶ Suppose the sales commission is 10% to 7% of the dollar value of sales (declining as the order size increased) plus an additional 10% for orders from new cus-tomers. If you were a salesperson, what kind of jobs would you shoot for? The answer: Based on these incentives, you would look for a lot of new customers and you would try to sell them a lot of expensive items. You would push the four-color items and, because of the declining percentage, you would not push too hard for larger jobs. Result: many small four-color jobs.

▶ What effect would your decision have on the printing operation? The answer: Recall that each screen takes 30 minutes to make. Because a four-color job requires four screens, the printing operation can handle only twenty of these each week (and it can do that only if there are no other jobs). As a result, the commission structure would motivate the sales force to sell work that cannot be completed. The firm's revenues would be far lower than they might be otherwise, and friction would develop between marketing and operations.

Obviously, the situation we have just described is not a desirable one. What if the sales commission was 10% of sales for on-time jobs, paid only upon delivery and verifica-tion of customer satisfaction? In that case, the sales force would be motivated to sell whatever product would generate the greatest revenue from the printing operation. It would not do the salesperson any good to sell something that could get held up in production. Result: The sales force would be continually trying to assess the status of operational resources and then selling whatever product generates the highest margin per minute at the bottleneck resource.

In regard to the screen-printing operation, Table 15.2 shows the weekly capacity of each resource and the margin per minute or per screen. Depending on the mix of jobs in the facility, the operational bottleneck may be the printer, the printing press, the oven, or the screen-making operation.

For example, suppose that the market potential (perhaps based on the size of the sales force) was around 10,000 units a week, and the typical order size was for 300 units. (That means there will be about $10,000/300 = 33.33$ orders per week.) If all of these orders were three- and four-color jobs, screen making and setup would be a system bottleneck. If all of the orders were one-color jobs, oven capacity would be the bottleneck. If the mix was twenty-five orders each for 400 shirts with three-color designs, printing would be the bottleneck.

When screen making and setup is not the bottleneck, Table 15.2 suggests that the best item to sell would be the two-color T-shirt, because at a margin of $42.00 per minute, the margin at the oven and printer is highest. This suggests that 42.00×2400 min/week $= $100,800$/week could be generated by the system if the sales force could sell 14,400 two-color shirts in forty or fewer designs. Thus, the average order size would need to be $14,400/40 = 360$ shirts. (If, as we suggested above, the market is limited to 10,000 shirts because of the size of the sales force, the weekly gross income potential would be only $70,000 [10,000 units $\times$ $7.00 margin per unit].) Thus, the ability to expand the market would be worth up to $100,800 - $70,000 = $30,800$.

Of course, customers will want various designs and not all will be satisfied with two-color prints on T-shirts. The point of the illustration is not to say it is good to turn away customers because they do not want 360 two-color T-shirts. It is not the job of

Table 15.2

Cost Breakdown on T-Shirts and Sweatshirts

	Sweatshirts				T-Shirts			
Price/Shirt	$16	$17	$18	$19	$10	$11	$12	$13
Cost/Shirt	$8	$8	$8	$8	$4	$4	$4	$4
Margin/Shirt	$8	$9	$10	$11	$6	$7	$8	$9
Screen Making and Setup	80	40	26.66	20	80	40	26.66	20
Capacity (orders per week)								
Printing Capacity (shirts per week)	20,571	10,285	6,857	5,142	28,800	14,400	9,600	7,200
Oven Capacity (shirts per week)	9,600	9,600	9,600	9,600	14,400	14,400	14,400	14,400
Margin/Screen*	$2,400	$1,350	$1,000	$825	$1,800	$1,050	$800	$675
Margin/Printer Minute	$68.57**	$38.57**	$28.57	$23.57	$72**	$42	$32	$27
Margin/ Oven Minute	$32	$36	$40**	$44**	$36	$42	$48**	$54**

*Assumes an average order size of 300 units

**These margins for the oven and the printer are not currently attainable, because the printer will not be able to keep up with the oven with three- and four-color images, and the oven will not be able to keep up with the printer with one- and two-color sweatshirts and one-color T-shirts.

the sales force to make customers conform to the needs of the value-adding system. The example is designed to illustrate that marketing targets for number of colors and job size can be developed from an understanding of operational issues.

Managers would attempt to optimize the revenues generated from the system by aligning sales force incentives and marketing promotions in light of the characteristics of the value-adding system. In doing so, they would make the most of their bottleneck resources. In situations where the market is not limited, some work has to be turned away. Using the logic contained in this example, managers can determine which orders are most desirable. This decision would not occur once and for all time. Rather, based upon the current mix of orders already promised for a given week on the master schedule, management (or the sales force) can prioritize the new order possibilities.

Table 15.3 illustrates a situation where the master schedule for a given week already includes five orders for two-color T-shirts totaling 4000 shirts and ten orders for one-color sweatshirts also totaling 4000 shirts. As you can see, this schedule has the oven most heavily utilized and the screen-making artist has very little work to do. Thus, because the margin per oven minute (shown in Table 15.2) is highest for four-color Ts, it would make sense to promote these shirts for this particular week of the master schedule. Because oven time is getting scarce, not many more shirts can be sold;

Table 15.3

With the Oven as the Bottleneck: Promote Multicolor Shirts

	Current # of Order	Number of Colors	Total Number of Shirts	Screen Making/Setup (Minutes)	Printing Press (Minutes)	Oven (Minutes)	Printer (Minutes)
T-Shirts	5	2-color	4000 shirts	300	716	666	666
Sweatshirts	10	1-color	4000 shirts	300	516	1000	466
Total Minutes Required				600	1232	1666	1133
Total Weekly Capacity				2400	4800	2400	2400
Utilization %				25%	25.7%	69%	47.16%

but there is still plenty of screen making and printing capacity to sell. Thus, orders for multicolored shirts, which are heavy users of such capacity, are desirable in this week.

Table 15.4 illustrates the master schedule of another week. Ten orders for a total of 12,000 two-color shirts are already scheduled, and four orders for a total of 800 four-color sweatshirts. The printer is the most highly utilized resource. With utilization at 98.9%, the weekly capacity is, for all practical purposes, fully committed. Table 15.2 shows that two-color T-shirts provide the highest margin per printer minute. It makes sense, therefore, to give printing priority to the two-color Ts in this situation. If there is any lost time during the week and the full capacity cannot be used, at least the time that has been used will have been dedicated to items with the highest margin per minute.

When the screen-making artist is the bottleneck, Table 15.2 suggests it is best to sell one-color jobs because this provides the highest margin per screen. This suggestion makes sense. Who would not sell jobs that make the best use of your scarce resource? Table 15.5 gives another, more specific, example of this situation. It considers a product mix consisting of ten orders for three-color T-shirts averaging 400 units in size and eleven orders for four-color sweatshirts averaging 200 units in size. If this were the existing demand for a given week, it is clear that the screen-making artist is the most heavily utilized resource. At 92.5% screen-making utilization, you are about to run out of capacity for new work, even though the oven and printing presses are barely being used half of the time. This calls for the sales force to promote large orders for one-color shirts, so that scarce resource can be best leveraged to create additional system revenues by providing work for the underutilized resources.

Finance and accounting majors reading this chapter might be wondering why the company is carrying two printing presses. After all, there is only one printer, and in every example so far, the utilization of the two printing presses has been less than 100%. Having a second press allows the screen-making artist to set up for a printing

Table 15.4

With the Printer as the Bottleneck: Give Priority to Two-Color Ts

	Current # of Order	Number of Colors	Total Number of Shirts	Screen Making/Setup (Minutes)	Printing Press (Minutes)	Oven (Minutes)	Printer (Minutes)
T-Shirts	10	2-color	12,000 shirts	600	2100	2000	2000
Sweatshirts	4	4-color	800 shirts	480	453	200	373
Total Minutes Required				1080	2553	2200	2373
Total Weekly Capacity				2400	4800	2400	2400
Utilization %				45%	53.2%	91.6%	98.9%

Table 15.5

With the Artist as the Bottleneck: Promote Large Orders for Single-Color Shirts

	Current # of Order	Number of Colors	Total Number of Shirts	Screen Making/Setup (Minutes)	Printing Press (Minutes)	Oven (Minutes)	Printer (Minutes)
T-Shirts	10	3-color	4000 shirts	900	1165	666	1000
Sweatshirts	11	4-color	2200 shirts	1320	1246	550	1026
Total Minutes Required				2220	2411	1216	2026
Total Weekly Capacity				2400	4800	2400	2400
Utilization %				92.5%	50.2%	50.7%	84.4%

job while the printer is still working on the prior job. This converts all internal exchange of die (IED) setup tasks to outside exchange of die (OED) setup tasks, which was a primary suggestion of the single minute exchange of dies (SMED) system described in Chapter 14. However, having a second press ties up capital, requires floor space, and eats up maintenance dollars, so the financially minded are right to require justification of such an arrangement.

If typical capital justification procedures were used, the second press would have to justify itself on the basis of the revenues it could generate on its own. A common mistake is to look at the utilization of the resource in isolation from the rest of the system to see if it is worth keeping (or buying). So, for example, if the average utilization of each printing press is 52.4%, analysts would say that the second press brings in incremental revenues of only 4.8% (52.4% $\times$ 2 = 104.8%, or 4.8% more than one press used continuously). Because Table 15.2 shows that the margin per minute for the printer is at best $42, that means that for 4.8% of 2400 minutes per week, the second printer brings in incremental revenues of just $42 per minute, or a total of $4838.40 per week ($42 $\times$ .048 $\times$ 2400 = $4838.40).

Table 15.6 illustrates a hypothetical situation in which there is only one press, and it is utilized at the rate of 107%. (Actually, the press cannot be utilized at more than 100%—this really means that demand exceeds press capacity by 7%.) If a second press were added, the utilization would be 53.5%. (Note that this situation is similar to the one just described, in which the second press, considered in isolation, appears to provide only an additional $4838.40 per week in revenues.) Because there is only one printer and only one press, however, the number of minutes available for actually printing shirts is reduced by the number of minutes required for setups. Because the setup time per color is 5 minutes, 100 minutes will be required to set up ten two-color jobs, and 200 minutes to set up ten four-color jobs. Consequently, though the printer is idle only 6% of the time, the press is unavailable due to setup 300/2400 = 12.5% of the time. That means that 6.5% (12.5% − 6%) of the week, the printer is idle because of downtime due to setup on the press.

Table 15.6

Making the Case for the Second Printing Press

	Current # of Orders	Number of Colors	Total Number of Shirts	Screen Making/Setup (Minutes)	Printing Press (Minutes)	Oven (Minutes)	Printer (Minutes)
T-Shirts	10	2-color	8000 shirts	600	1433	1133	1333
Sweatshirts	10	4-color	2000 shirts	1200	1133	500	933
Total Minutes Required				1800	2566	1833	2266
Total Weekly Capacity				2400	2400	2400	2400
Utilization %				75%	107%	76%	94%

Here is the crux of the matter: Adding a second press would turn that 6.5% of the week into productive time for the printer. Considering the system as a whole, the improvement in the utilization rate resulting from the additional press is not 4.8%, but 6.5% + 4.8% = 11.3%. The incremental revenue resulting from the additional press is 11.3% × 2400 × $42.00 = $11,390.40 per week. Thus, in synchronous value-adding systems, financial analyses of the need for capital equipment must consider the *systemwide* impact of the resource.

Compared to virtually any real-world business, this example is quite simple; there are only two types of shirts, only four steps to the process (screen making, setup, printing, and curing), and operation times have been kept simple. Still, this example illustrates the challenges facing managers of such systems. In more complex operational situations, applying the concepts illustrated in this chapter requires the use of sophisticated decision support systems, which have the computing power to handle the required mathematical calculations.

Peter Christopher/Masterfile

Air traffic controllers deal with a variety of resources and variables that may create bottlenecks in many different ways on any given day. Weather, mechanical failures, labor availability, and last second changes in demand can force them to change schedules or priorities on a moment's notice.

Example 15.1

There are four work centers, (labeled A, B, C, and D) in the production system depicted below. These are used to process three raw materials (RM1, RM2, and RM3) and a purchased part. There are two products (P and Q). The diagram should be interpreted as follows: Work center D assembles product P using a purchased part, output from work center C that contains RM1 and has been pre-processed by work center A, and output from work center C that contains RM2 and has been pre-processed by work center B.

Similarly, work center D assembles product Q using output from work center B that contains RM3 and has been pre-processed by work center A, and output from work center C that contains RM2 and has been pre-processed by work center B. The times listed in the boxes refer to the number of minutes required per unit of output. Operating expenses reflect the fixed costs of the operation. The only variable costs are those for parts and materials.

(Continued)

Example 15.1

(Continued)

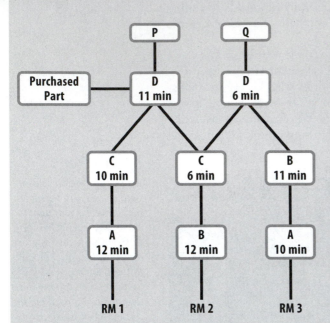

Applicable demand, cost, and supply information is as follows:

	P	Q
Demand Per Week	120	65
Selling Price	110	90
Raw Material Costs		
RM1	25	
RM2	25	25
RM3		30
Purchased Part	6	

Time available at each work center = 2400 min.
Purchased part, RM1, and RM3 have unlimited supply.
Only 180 units of RM2 are available each week.
Operating expense per week = $6500.

Find the bottleneck in the system.

Step 1: Determine the amount of each resource required to meet weekly demand. These computations are shown in the table below.

		P	Q		
Demand (Weekly)		120	65	**Available**	**Total Requirement**
Weekly Resource Requirements if All Demand Is Satisfied	RM1	120	0	unlimited	120
	RM2	120	65	180	185
	RM3	0	65	unlimited	65
	Purchased Part	120	0	unlimited	120
	Work Center A	120(12) = 1,440 min	65(10) = 650 min	2400 min	2090 min
	Work Center B	120(12) = 1,440 min	65(12 + 11) = 1,495 min	2400 min	2935 min
	Work Center C	120(10 + 6) = 1,920 min	65(6) = 390 min	2400 min	2310 min
	Work Center D	120(11) = 1,320 min	65(6) = 390 min	2400 min	1710 min

Step 2: Compare the requirements calculated in Step 1 with the available capacity to find the bottleneck(s).

Comparing required resources with available resources we see that we do not have sufficient supply of RM2 to meet all demand for both products. We only have 97.3% of what is needed (180/185 = 0.9730). We also lack sufficient capacity at work center B to meet weekly demand for both products. We only have 81.77% of the capacity we need (2400/2935 = 0.8177). Because the shortfall of capacity at work center B is much more severe than the shortage of RM2, this is the bottleneck. (Due to the capacity constraint at work center B, we will not be able to use even 180 units of RM2.)

Example 15.2

For the production system described in Example 15.1, determine the optimal production mix. (That is, the weekly output of P and Q that will maximize profit.)

Step 1: Find the margin per minute at the bottleneck work center. This is done in the first two rows of the table below. The margin per minute for P is $4.50 and for Q it is $1.52.

Step 2: Assign production priorities to products based on the margin per minute at the bottleneck

work center. This is done in the third column of the table below. The first priority is product P and product Q is the second priority.

Step 3: Allocate capacity at the bottleneck work center based on the production priorities. This is done in the last four rows of the table below. Note that our resulting production mix is 120 units of P and 41.7391 units of Q.

	P	Q
Demand (Weekly)	**120 units**	**65 units**
Profit Margin per Unit	$110 − $56 = $54	$90 − $55 = $35
Profit Margin per Minute at the Bottleneck Resource	$54/12 = $4.50	$35/23 = $1.52
Production Priority	1	2
Weekly Production of Priority 1 Item	120 units	
Capacity Used at Bottleneck Resource per Week by Production of Priority 1 Item	120(12) = 1440 min	
Capacity Remaining After Production of Priority 1 Item	2400 − 1440 = 960 min	
Weekly Production of Priority 2 Item If All Remaining Capacity Is Used		960/(12 + 11) = 41.7391 units
Total Weekly Production	120 units	41.7391 units

Example 15.3

Determine the total profit at the optimal production mix.

Step 1: Determine the margin generated by total weekly production. This is calculated by multiplying weekly production of each item by the margin for that item and summing across all items.

$$\text{Weekly margin} = 120(54) + 41.7391(35)$$
$$= \$6480 + \$1460.87$$
$$= \$7940.87$$

Step 2: Find the total profit by subtracting operating expenses from the weekly margin. If

the margin generated by the total weekly production is not sufficient to cover the fixed operating expenses, a loss will result. This situation would not be sustainable and if it were recurring, the company would seek ways to shut down production rather than producing the predetermined product mix. In essence, the optimal mix would be zero units of each item. Because weekly operating expenses total $6500.00, the total profit is positive and the product mix determined in Step 1 (above) is sustainable. The weekly total profit from that product mix is $1440.87. (That is $7940.87 − $6500.00.)

Applicability of Synchronous Planning and Control

In general, it makes sense to synchronize system planning and control when operations and demand patterns are too complex for a kanban system to work, and system bottlenecks can be found quickly. In Chapter 14, we noted a number of conditions that limit the effectiveness of the just-in-time (JIT) approach to planning and control. Specifically, kanban systems will not work when the demand pull comes from multiple sources and has not effectively been leveled through master scheduling. As Figure 15.3 suggests, when scheduling complexity is introduced in one part of an otherwise simple kanban system, a bottleneck is likely to develop. When that happens, system planning and control calls for an option better suited to the job than JIT.

The **theory of constraints (TOC)** is a general approach that can be used to synchronize value-adding systems containing bottlenecks. You have probably applied this theory without thinking about it at some point in your life. For example, if you have wanted to keep a group of drivers together on the interstate, you have probably put the slowest vehicle (i.e., the team bus) in the front and required the others to follow. The soonest

Theory of constraints

A general approach that can be used to synchronize such value-adding systems containing bottlenecks.

Figure 15.3

The Kanban system does not work with a bottleneck in the system

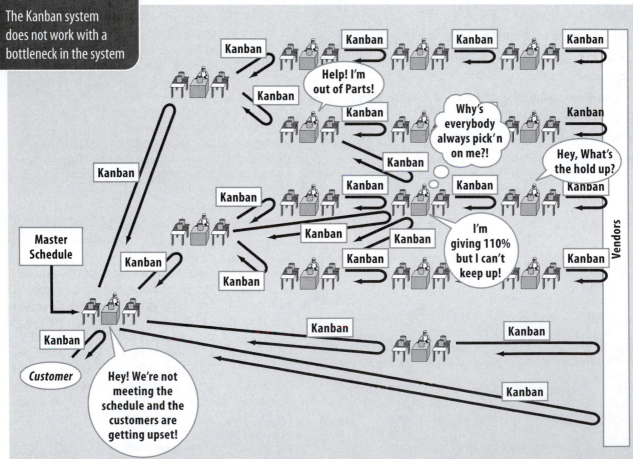

The World's Highest Bottleneck—The Hillary Step

The summit of Mt. Everest, which is the world's highest peak at an elevation of 29,028 feet above sea level, was first reached by Sir Edmund Hillary and Sherpa Tensing Norgay. (*Sherpa* is a Nepalese term that refers to the high-altitude porters used by climbing expeditions.) The final significant obstacle that they encountered was a 40-foot rock cliff on the eastern ridge of the mountain a few hundred feet below the summit. Ultimately, Hillary's mountaineering skills were sufficient to negotiate the inescapable obstacle, and the summit was reached on May 29, 1953. Since that initial attempt to achieve the summit, hundreds of climbers have scaled Everest, and the vast majority of these have used the route established by Hillary and Norgay. The 40-foot obstacle near the summit is still called The Hillary Step (see photograph).

In recent years, an interesting product-service bundle has been offered to affluent mountain climbers: a guided expedition. For $40,000 to $70,000, you can buy a spot on a guided expedition to Everest. (The price depends on how deep your pockets are and the prior success of the guide in getting clients to the summit.) The expedition provides clients with materials, logistical support, expedition management, health care, food, water, and personal guidance. In turn, clients must have a minimum level of mountaineering experience, be in shape, and be willing to follow directions.

There is only a short window of time when it is safe to attempt the summit—in the spring, between the cold of winter and the storms of the monsoon. During this brief window of time, the mountain's summit must be reached early in the day, because even in this relatively calm period, afternoon storms are an almost daily occurrence. Finally, real success lies in climbing Everest *and* getting back down—so every climber has to traverse the Hillary Step twice. It is a lot easier to climb Everest than to climb Everest and get back down *alive*. These factors combine to make the Hillary Step the world's highest bottleneck.

In May of 1996, Everest was an unusually busy place: Guided expeditions from South Africa, United States, and New Zealand were on the mountain at the same time. In addition, the IMAX Everest project was being filmed. All of these climbers were seeking the summit using the route established by Sir Edmund Hillary and Tensing Norgay. In his book *Into Thin Air: A Personal Account of the Mount Everest Disaster*, Jon Krakauer, who was a guide for one of the climbing expeditions, describes some of the bottleneck-management approaches that were used on the mountain in 1996.

First, it was decided that each expedition should attempt the summit on separate days. Unfortunately, each team wanted to climb the last stretch on the best day—so, unknown to each other, all three expeditions planned a summit attempt on that one day. Second, it was suggested that a Sherpa for one of the expeditions should reach the Hillary Step ahead of time and secure ropes that the climbers could follow on their arrival. This did not happen, either, and hours were lost while a group of climbers gathered at the foot of the step. Finally, Krakauer and a climber from another expedition climbed the step and secured rope for the remaining climbers. By then, 2 hours of precious time had been lost at the bottleneck. Six climbers were caught in the afternoon storm and died from exposure before they could make it back to camp. Krakauer suggests that this tragedy can be primarily attributed to the time lost at the Hillary Step bottleneck.

Clearly, the Everest expeditions would qualify as product-service bundles delivered with the world's highest value-adding systems. And the Hillary Step is, without question, the world's highest bottleneck.

that all of the vehicles can arrive at the destination is determined by the schedule of the bus (bottleneck). When you identified this bottleneck, you subordinated the schedule of all other vehicles to it. You might have even attempted to increase the capacity of the bottleneck by towing a trailer of band instruments with another vehicle or taking two smaller buses.

The same principles are in use when an airline allows elderly or disabled passengers to board first. The time needed to board passengers is not changed much by this practice, but it does make the boarding process more pleasant for most passengers, because they can wait in the lounge, where they are more comfortable, rather than standing in line in the Jetway or on the plane, waiting to find their seats. The theory of constraints also applies when a student group decides on a meeting time based on the schedule of the busiest team member or when a small-town university with a large stadium crowd allocates special parking spaces for RVs, cars, and buses at weekend football games.

Figure 15.4 summarizes the characteristics of synchronous planning and control systems. This approach is very useful when demand varies from week to week, the number of product-service bundles is manageable and does not require extensive individual customization, and operational volume is moderate. These characteristics are generally descriptive of batch processes. Also, there are usually some dominant material flows, which carry the lion's share of the system's load, and system complexity is somewhat lessened through limits in product variety. This approach is likely to be useful wherever customers or materials are batched in order to simplify the scheduling of operations.

Some situations are too complex for full implementation of the theory of constraints; we have reserved discussion of such systems for Chapter 16. Maybe the complexity of the product-service bundle is too great because of the high level of customization that is offered. Maybe the value-adding system is so flexible, because of the need for customization, that capacity requirements have become difficult to predict.

Figure 15.4

System characteristics of synchronous planning and control

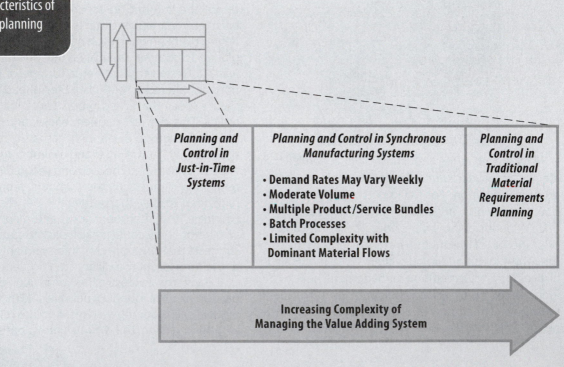

Maybe by the time managers find the bottleneck and get a plan in place to deal with it, demand patterns have changed and the bottleneck has moved.

Today, improvements in computing power and information systems have made it easier to find bottleneck(s), interact with customers and suppliers, understand the system capacity requirements for customized work, and synchronize the value-adding system at the same time. The line between systems that can be synchronized (this chapter) and those that cannot (Chapter 16) is moving. It is likely that systems that cannot be synchronized today may be synchronized sometime in the future. Companies that can make that kind of improvement will gain a competitive advantage in the marketplace. Figure 15.5 summarizes short-term planning and control in a synchronous value-adding system. At the master scheduling level, product mix decisions are made. These decisions are about what orders to accept or reject and are based on the orders' profit potential at the system bottleneck. Material plans will then be made to ensure that parts and components are available to support the schedule at the bottleneck. Detailed capacity plans focus on the bottleneck and optimizing throughput at this resource. All operations are synchronized using a **drum-buffer-rope (DBR) system**. DBR is a method for scheduling resources that seeks to ensure that the system is never starved for work. The bottleneck's pace is the primary factor in the scheduling of

Drum-buffer-rope (DBR) system

The most detailed level of scheduling, in which managers must decide who should do what and with which resource.

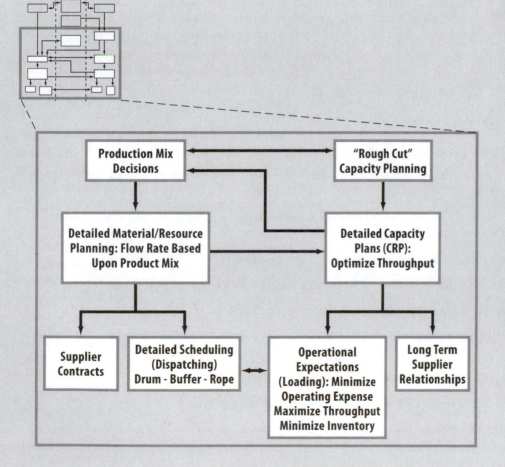

Figure 15.5

Short-term planning and control in a synchronous system

non-bottleneck resources. The goal is to maximize throughput while minimizing inventory and operating expense for the given product mix.

While the schedules for various resources can be computed deterministically in a JIT system, in which the master schedule is leveled, that is not possible in a system with enough complexity to require synchronization. According to the theory of constraints, the bottleneck schedule can be arrived at deterministically, but other resources must be scheduled based on probabilistic assumptions (using the "DBR" approach described later in this chapter). The bottleneck is generally scheduled using what is called a **forward finite scheduling** approach. Managers start with current jobs waiting at the bottleneck and assign time to them—from the present onward—based on the jobs' relative priorities. They do not schedule more work than the bottleneck can process over a given period. Other resources will have excess capacity, and these resources are scheduled with a **backward infinite scheduling** approach—starting with the time the work must arrive at the bottleneck and working backward in time. In other words, the schedule of non-bottleneck resources is determined so as to ensure that work gets to the bottleneck when it is needed. Because these resources have excess capacity, managers aren't concerned about scheduling more work than they can process in a given period.

Overview of TOC

In the 1980s, Eliyahu Goldratt published a book called *The Goal*, which popularized the principles underlying a software package he had developed called Optimized Production Technology (OPT). (The principles are detailed in Table 15.7.) The book

Forward finite scheduling approach

A process where managers start with the current jobs waiting at the bottleneck and assign time to them—from the present onward—based on their priorities.

Backward infinite scheduling approach

A process where managers start with the time they must arrive at the bottleneck and work backward in time.

Table 15.7
The OPT Principles

1. Balance the flow of materials through the system, not the capacity of resources.
2. Utilization levels for non-bottleneck resources are not determined based on their own capacity, but by the capacity of the system bottleneck.
3. Utilization and activation of a resource are not the same thing. You can create useless WIP by activating a resource. Only useful WIP counts toward utilization.
4. Any time lost at the bottleneck is lost to the system and cannot be recovered.
5. Any time saved at a non-bottleneck is irrelevant because it already has time to spare.
6. The bottleneck is the key to improving throughput or lowering system inventory.
7. You do not have to complete an order at one work center before you transfer WIP forward allowing the next work center to begin.
8. Batch sizes are not set in stone; their size can affect rates of throughput and inventory levels.
9. Schedules for each resource should simultaneously consider all system constraints.
10. Because the system and its constraints can change over time, schedules change over time and lead times will also vary.

dealt primarily with the importance of bottlenecks in a value-adding system. The lead character in the book, Alex Rogo, learns that an hour lost at a bottleneck is an hour lost for the entire system, while an hour lost at a non-bottleneck is inconsequential. He also learns that it helps not to begin work on jobs that cannot be accommodated at a bottleneck. For example, if a customer's order must wait, it is better for it to wait as an unstarted job, with no investment in materials, than as a partially completed order representing a partial investment in materials and processing time. Not only is money tied up when an order waits as work in process but scheduling flexibility is lost.

Performance Measures and Capacity Issues

One issue that comes up in attempting to synchronize the schedule of resources across an entire facility is the question of how performance will be measured. The traditional approach to operational performance measurement relies on local performance measures, in which worker performance and resource utilization are measured against a work standard and resource capacity. In other words:

1. Workers are considered to be performing to expectations if they are doing their jobs as fast as we believe they can.

2. Resources are considered to be well managed if the operation is producing the volume of output it is capable of generating.

3. Output is measured in units completed at the individual resource.

4. Work-in-process inventory is accounted for as an asset whose value increases with each additional operation it passes through.

5. Capacity and, therefore, operating expenses are essentially fixed at the output level individual resources are able to provide.

In synchronous systems, relying too heavily on local performance measures can lead to a frustrating phenomenon called the "hockey stick syndrome," in which daily output resembles the pattern shown in Figure 15.6. Note the high levels of output at the end of reporting periods, followed by low levels of output for the majority of the reporting period; thus the name hockey stick syndrome. You have probably had some experience with this syndrome. For example, you may tend to complete term papers and major projects the weekend or night before they are due. That is probably because

Figure 15.6

The "Hockey-Stick" Syndrome

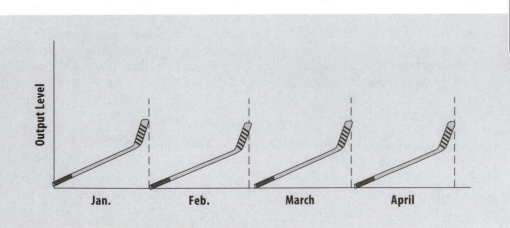

for weeks you have been too busy learning about the topic to write it up (at least, that is the explanation your professors get). When the goal changes from learning to showing what you have learned, your rate of output changes dramatically.

Why do companies experience the hockey stick syndrome? When accountants compute local performance measures, they generate information that managers use to make decisions about worker performance, resource utilization, and asset allocation. These decisions ultimately influence workers' pay and the quality of their jobs. As a result, workers and managers are motivated to look good on local performance. But their goal-directed behavior creates problems for anyone who is trying to synchronize operations across an entire system. When decisions are made based on local performance, operations are not synchronized and customers' orders get bottled up in the value-adding system. At the end of the month, when financial performance has to be reported to key stakeholders, managers become very interested in performance measures such as net profit, return on assets (ROA), and cash flow. Unlike the local performance measures that influence employees' behavior for most of the month, these financial measures are global performance measures: They indicate the effectiveness of the entire value-adding system, not just one resource. So toward the end of the month, decisions are made with system performance in mind, and the system generates rapid output.

To synchronize operations, local operational performance measures must be replaced with global measures. These broader operational measures should help decision makers and workers to coordinate their activities for the customer's benefit every day of the month, not just when financial results must be reported. Goldratt has suggested that the following operational performance measures replace traditional local measures:

1. **Throughput:** the rate at which the system generates money through sales. It is desirable to increase throughput.

2. **Inventory:** all the money invested in purchasing items the system intends to sell. It is generally desirable to reduce inventory.

3. **Operating expense:** the money the system spends in converting inventory to throughput. It is generally desirable to reduce operating expense.

These global operational measures differ from local measures in several critically important ways. By definition, they focus on performance of the whole system, not that of individual resources. For example, getting lots of passengers' baggage checked in at Tom's airline creates no throughput. Throughput is only created when satisfied customers collect their baggage and leave the terminal in the city of their destination. Similarly, cutting lots of table legs at Luis's factory would require a large amount of work at one particular work center and would look great on the traditional measures of worker output and resource utilization. On Goldratt's measures, however, it would create no throughput, but instead increase inventory and operating expense. It might even hold back other jobs and thereby reduce throughput, while further increasing inventory and operating expense.

Goldratt's measures are better linked to the global financial measures that become important at the end of the month, because their unit of measurement is money, not output units. Increasing throughput, decreasing operating expense, and decreasing inventory will each lead to an increase in net profit, ROA, and cash flow. Because Goldratt's operational measures are well aligned with the financial measures, companies that utilize these measures throughout the month are less likely to adjust their behavior at the end of financial reporting periods and therefore less likely to suffer

Throughput

The rate at which the system generates money through sales.

Inventory

All the money invested in purchasing items the system intends to sell. It is generally desirable to reduce inventory.

Operating expense

The money the system spends in converting inventory to throughput. It is generally desirable to reduce operating expense.

from the hockey stick syndrome. A consistent rate of throughput provides a more stable operating environment and improves quality-of-work-life for employees by eliminating the stressful activity that would otherwise occur just prior to reporting deadlines. It can also improve customer satisfaction by reducing lead times and making them more predictable.

Ultimately, to use global measures of performance effectively, managers must change their view of resource capacity needs. When performance is measured locally, any activity is presumed to be productive; thus, "resource activation" is confused with "resource utilization." If Tom's meal catering facility is capable of preparing twice as many meals as needed for his flights, it does no good for that resource to be active 100% of the time as only half that activity would have practical utility. But if the value-adding system is synchronized, the catering facility cannot create throughput any faster than the system as a whole. The more appropriate view of the capacity of the catering facility is the rate at which the system can create satisfied customers.

REC CENTER DILEMMA

Cheryl's Dilemma:

Cheryl has been evaluating the overhead costs in her outpatient operating room. She is particularly interested in this area, because she has noticed that doctors' practices are charged a fixed amount per hour to use that facility, but procedures vary in regard to staffing, prep and recovery time, and liability. She is thinking that because she charges by the hour, her price structure favors doctors who provide low-margin procedures over those who provide higher-margin procedures. Do you agree? Why? What could Cheryl do to correct the problem?

Cost Accounting

Like performance measures, cost-accounting practices need to fit the value-adding system to which they are applied. An ongoing problem for accountants and decision makers has been the question of how to estimate the indirect and overhead costs affiliated with particular product-service bundles. Historically, when less computing power was available, cost accountants would apply overhead costs to product-service bundles based on the estimated percentage of overall indirect costs required to support the particular bundle. For example, suppose one of Cheryl's lab technicians tests a variety of different types of samples from four different parts of the hospital. (Let's say they are throat cultures from an outpatient clinic, blood samples from the wellness center, tissue samples from the oncology center, and samples of collagen purchased for use in the plastic surgery practice.) Cost accountants would need to determine how the cost of the lab technician's salary and benefits would be allocated to these four product-service bundles.

Accurate allocation of these costs is essential to good decision making. Suppose the lab technician's time is dominated by time-consuming tissue testing for the oncology clinic, but because the accountants are not lab technicians and do not know for sure what product-service bundles dominate the technician's schedule, the overhead cost is distributed evenly over the four areas. Cheryl will consider the oncology clinic's services to be more profitable than they really are. Similarly, the other areas will look less profitable than they really are. As a result, when it looks as if the lab is too busy, she will be likely to send wellness, plastic surgery, and outpatient clients to competing hospitals so that lab technicians can concentrate on the oncology. At the end of the accounting period, she will find that the hospital's earnings are lower than expected, and she may not understand why. Cheryl may be particularly confused when she sees the improved performance of her competitors, who will benefit from the work she has sent their way.

With the advent of synchronous value-adding systems, cost accountants have had to develop new approaches that provide more useful information for decision makers. Two of the better-known approaches currently in use are activity-based costing and

Activity-based costing (ABC)

A managerial accounting method that allocates the costs to the product-service bundle based on overhead activities performed and aesthetics of the product-service bundle.

the balanced scorecard. **Activity-based costing (ABC)** is a managerial accounting approach that rests on the principle that activities cost money and operations consume activities. Cheryl's lab technicians, for example, cost money, and their services are consumed in the creation of the various product-service bundles the hospital offers.

ABC seeks to provide greater accuracy in allocating overhead costs to the direct value-adding activities than is possible using the historical percentage allocation method. In this approach, the accountant first enumerates all the overhead activities and their costs. Next, the accountant determines the product-service bundles whose creation consumes these overhead activities. The overhead cost for each product-service bundle is the sum of the costs of the activities consumed in its creation. Though this approach is not conceptually difficult, the level of detail required was prohibitive prior to the advent of modern information systems.

If ABC leads to more accurate estimates of the indirect costs that go along with the creation of each product-service bundle, then it is particularly useful to managers of value-adding systems that contain a bottleneck. These managers have to decide how to ration bottleneck capacity among various product-service bundles. If their indirect cost estimates are not accurate, they might well think they are allocating bottleneck capacity to the most profitable product-service bundles, when they are actually wasting critical capacity on unprofitable items.

Balanced scorecard

Information about performance in key categories.

Robert Kaplan of the Harvard Business School suggested another managerial accounting approach, the **balanced scorecard**, which includes information about performance in key categories which may also include nonfinancial measures. Part of the idea behind the balanced scorecard is that often the very decisions that optimize short-term financial performance ultimately lead to disappointments in long-term performance. Kaplan's approach suggests that a company should consider its strategic goals in establishing its cost measurement system. Luis's company, which emphasizes flexibility and quality, for example, would use a different scorecard from Fred's, which focuses on low-cost standardized product-service bundles.

The balanced scorecard might include measures representing the customer perspective, the internal business process, and innovation and learning. For example, the customer perspective might be measured by customer retention ratios, on-time deliveries, and customer satisfaction surveys. The internal business process perspective might be represented by cycle time, throughput, yield, and quality defect rates. Innovation and learning could be measured by product development lead time, new product introduction rates, number of employees cross trained, and percentage of sales from new products. By measuring performance from each of these perspectives, in addition to the financial perspective, managers can work to balance various stakeholder concerns.

The Management Process

The theory of constraints suggests that managers use a five-step process to manage their value-adding system. The five steps are:

1. Identify the system constraints.
2. Determine how to exploit the system constraints.
3. Subordinate every other decision to the decision made in Step 2.
4. Elevate the system constraint.
5. If the constraint has changed with the passage of time or the process of moving through steps 1 through 4, go back to Step 1.

INTEGRATING OM:

Enhancing the Capacity of a Bottleneck to Global Trade

On the surface, you might not immediately think of the watershed of a tropical rainforest as a bottleneck with global geopolitical and business ramifications. The watershed has great ecologic significance, providing habitat for roughly 70 amphibian, 112 reptilian, and more than a hundred thousand tree species. At the same time, it provides drinking water for almost all of a nation, and is home to numerous indigenous cultures. Yet, the Panama Canal watershed is a bottleneck with global trade consequences, affecting operational volumes and the local economy in port cities—especially those on the eastern coast of the United States that handle large volumes of Asian imports.

Building the Panama Canal exacted a huge cost in both financial and human terms. An estimated 80,000 persons took part in the canal's construction and more than 30,000 lives were lost during approximately 34 years of construction. Together the French and American expenditures totaled $639 million.

It's obvious why the canal is so important to international trade. Its 50-mile traverse of the isthmus of Panama saves cargo ships 7,872 miles of potentially rough sailing. Consequently, the canal services more than 140 different transportation routes involving virtually every significant commercial port in the world. There are about 14,000 transits through the canal per year, involving more than 170 million long tons of cargo, which amounts to about 5% of world trade. Annual tolls generate in excess of $419 million. With approximately 9 thousand employees and the Canal operates 24 hours a day, 365 days a year.

The Canal uses a system of locks to raise ships from sea level (the Pacific or the Atlantic) to Gatun Lake (26 meters above sea level); ships then sail the channel through the Continental Divide and traverse another set of locks to return to sea. The water used to raise and lower vessels in each set of locks comes from Gatun Lake. And that's where the bottleneck arises. (Until the building of the Hoover Dam formed Lake Mead, Gatun Lake was the largest artificial body of water in the world.) The water comes into the lake from the Panama Canal Watershed and flows through the locks by a gravity-fed system. It is the fresh-water from the watershed that is used to raise (and lower) the ships—and not saltwater from either the Pacific or Atlantic oceans. Once the water has been used for this purpose, it empties from the locks into the oceans—it is not pumped back up to Gatun lake. Thus, a significant disruption to the ecosystem of the watershed, such as might lead to an extended drought or major soil erosion (which would make Gatun Lake more shallow) would have disastrous consequences on the global economy. Not to mention the impact on the human population and bio-diversity of the watershed.

Recognizing the importance of enhancing the capacity of this vital bottleneck, the Panama Canal Authority recently began a dredging project to deepen the navigation channel in Gatun Lake and the Gaillard Cut navigation channel. This project will remove about 7.1 million cubic meters of soil. It will raise the lake's active water storage volume by nearly 45 percent, from 770 million cubic meters to 1,420 million cubic meters. This will provide enough water for an additional six transits per day, and may delay the time when someone has to decide to limit canal traffic due to the ecological or human needs of the watershed's residents.

The project is being applauded by ports of call, especially on the East Coast of the U.S., that depend on the canal for the operational volumes. The dredging project has a price tag of over $200 million and is a part of a $1 billion canal modernization effort. By understanding and applying some of the bottleneck management concepts presented in this chapter, you may quickly come to the conclusion that the cost to "enhance the capacity of the bottleneck" is well justified in this case.

Source: Adapted from "Panama Canal Dredging Likely to Increase Shipping Calls Here," *Savannah Business Report and Journal*, September 22–28, 2003, pp. 1 and 15, reporter Jason Harvey; "Panama Canal at Crossroads," *Wall Street Journal*, p. B1, Jan. 7, 2004, reporter Neil King, Jr.; http://www.pancanal.com/eng/general/asi-es-el-canal.html; http://www.pancanal.com/eng/cuenca/la-cuenca.html; and http://www.ared.com/kora/java/pcc/javaani.html

To see how straightforward this five-step process is, consider the screen-printing example presented on pages 681–687:

- ▶ **Step 1:** We can use Tables 15.2 to 15.6 to identify the constraints, or bottlenecks, by comparing the capacity required at each resource with the capacity available.

- ▶ **Step 2:** By finding the margin per unit of the scarce resource (see Table 15.2), we can determine how to exploit that constraint.

- ▶ **Step 3:** In synchronizing the unconstrained activities with the constraint, we will subordinate every other decision to the decision made in Step 2.

- ▶ **Step 4:** If the constraint is a long-standing problem, we can seek ways to elevate it. For example, we might consider buying a second printing press as a way of eliminating a long-standing bottleneck.

- ▶ **Step 5:** Finally, if the action we took in Step 4 alleviates the problem, we should go back to Step 1 and identify the new system constraint.

Bottlenecks anywhere in the supply chain can have a big impact on the rest of the supply chain. When Hurricane Katrina struck the Gulf Coast in late summer 2005, refineries forced off line caused an immediate spike in gasoline prices.

Dave Einsel/Getty Images Inc.

Supply Chain Impact of Synchronous Planning and Control

Figure 15.7 indicates some of the ways that synchronous planning and control systems impact the firms that are a company's customers and suppliers in the supply chain.

From the supplier's perspective, several options might be used to improve relations with a customer who uses a synchronous system. Some of the value the supplier provides could be duplicated in the customer's non-bottleneck operations. At little incremental cost, capacity requirements could be shifted from the supplier to the customer through a temporary outsourcing agreement. Conversely, suppliers can occasionally reduce the customer's bottleneck capacity requirements by providing enhanced product-service bundles. (That is what happens when you have pizza delivered rather than going out to eat during final exam week.) Suppliers whose revenue potential is limited by customer bottlenecks should consider seeking additional customers for their output. When possible, they should also consider supplying technological alternatives to their customers, so as to reduce the severity of the bottleneck.

From an infrastructural perspective, the most important concern for suppliers of customers with synchronous systems is to guarantee the supply of critical bottleneck materials. Additional features and options, better material quality, and price discounts are of little interest to a customer whose bottleneck has been idled by a supply shortage. Guaranteeing the supply of critical materials means that the supplier's scheduling decisions must be synchronized, to some extent, with the bottleneck schedule. Occasionally, the supply of materials is itself the bottleneck in a value-adding system. In

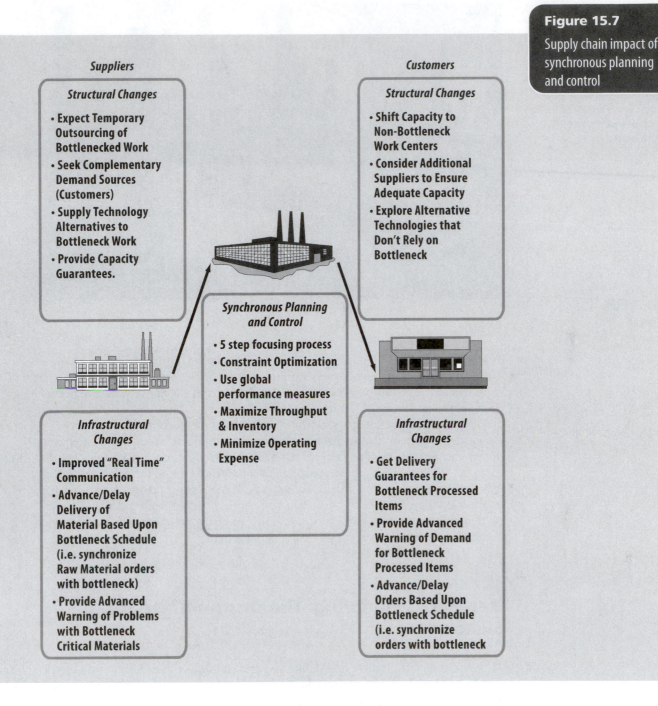

Figure 15.7

Supply chain impact of synchronous planning and control

Suppliers

Structural Changes

- Expect Temporary Outsourcing of Bottlenecked Work
- Seek Complementary Demand Sources (Customers)
- Supply Technology Alternatives to Bottleneck Work
- Provide Capacity Guarantees.

Customers

Structural Changes

- Shift Capacity to Non-Bottleneck Work Centers
- Consider Additional Suppliers to Ensure Adequate Capacity
- Explore Alternative Technologies that Don't Rely on Bottleneck

Synchronous Planning and Control

- 5 step focusing process
- Constraint Optimization
- Use global performance measures
- Maximize Throughput & Inventory
- Minimize Operating Expense

Infrastructural Changes

- Improved "Real Time" Communication
- Advance/Delay Delivery of Material Based Upon Bottleneck Schedule (i.e. synchronize Raw Material orders with bottleneck)
- Provide Advanced Warning of Problems with Bottleneck Critical Materials

Infrastructural Changes

- Get Delivery Guarantees for Bottleneck Processed Items
- Provide Advanced Warning of Demand for Bottleneck Processed Items
- Advance/Delay Orders Based Upon Bottleneck Schedule (i.e. synchronize orders with bottleneck

such cases, the supplier needs to work with customers, using the five-step process to make the best use of the limited supply of materials.

From the customer's perspective, several potential structural and infrastructural options need to be considered to reduce the level of dependence on a supplier bottleneck. From a structural perspective, the customer can often shift work from a bottleneck center by changing the make-or-buy decision, and making instead

Greeters at a restaurant may ask customers to wait even though there are obviously empty tables available. This is to balance the use of resources based upon server area, size of party, or reservations being held, in order to avoid bottlenecks.

Michael Newman/Photo Edit

of buying a portion of an item that had been purchased. Other structural changes that can reduce dependence on a supplier bottleneck include seeking additional suppliers and developing alternative technologies that do not require the bottleneck resource.

From an infrastructural perspective, it is important for customers to reserve capacity for their orders in advance. Doing so allows the supplier to assess resource requirements and provide reliable delivery dates. It also provides an opportunity for the customer to interact with the supplier and make decisions about the timing of orders. If as a group, customers are willing to cooperate, it is possible to reduce lead times and improve customer service by advancing or delaying orders based on demand for the bottleneck capacity. Customer cooperation allows the entire supply chain to be synchronized, not just the company's value-adding system.

Detailed Scheduling: The Drum-Buffer-Rope System

At the most detailed level of scheduling, in which managers must decide who should do what and with which resource, the drum-buffer-rope system (DBR) is often used. This detailed scheduling approach is most useful in value-adding systems that contain a bottleneck. The term "drum" refers to the bottleneck; like a marching band, its rate of throughput sets the pace for all other work centers. The "buffer" is time that is maintained in front of the bottleneck or other strategic points in the system, to make certain the bottleneck never sits idle for lack of work. (This extra time results in an inventory of materials that will accumulate in front of the bottleneck.) Finally, the "rope" refers to communication links between the buffers and the gateway work centers.

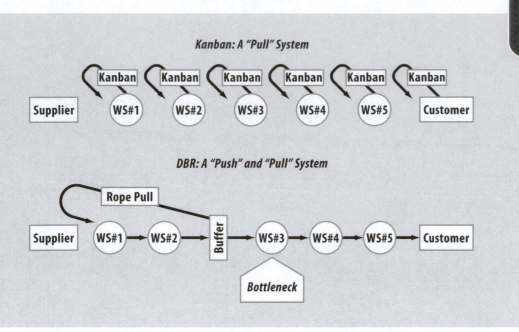

Figure 15.8

Kanban vs. drum-buffer-rope scheduling systems

These communication links keep workers from starting jobs for which there is no room in the buffer. The purpose of the drum-buffer-rope system is to ensure that bottleneck resources are fully utilized and that all other resources work at the pace of the bottleneck.

Figure 15.8 compares the kanban scheduling system described in Chapter 14 with the drum-buffer-rope system. The kanban system is a "pull" scheduling system; nothing moves from one work center to the next and nothing new is made unless a customer has used an item and it needs to be replaced. In a kanban system, it is essential that capacity be reasonably balanced throughout the operational system. The master schedule, which establishes the pull rate, must be leveled. The drum-buffer-rope system is a "pull and push" scheduling system: Work is pulled into the value-adding system based on the schedule at the bottleneck and the expected time needed for it to move from the gateway work center to the bottleneck buffer. Once it is in the system, however, orders are pushed through their prescribed routing. Rather than waiting for a free kanban to know what to do, workers wait for incoming orders and the work-in-process that accompanies them. When employees complete their work on a particular order, they simply send it on to the next station.

Of course, operations rarely are that simple. Figure 15.9 illustrates the drum-buffer-rope scheduling system in a more realistic environment that includes multiple product flows. Notice that the master schedule directly determines the schedule of the bottleneck in addition to the timing of customer shipments. The **bottleneck buffer** is extra lead time in the supply of material to the bottleneck, which results in work that is waiting to be processed at the bottleneck and protects the bottleneck from any idle time that might result from upstream operating disruptions. When there is space in the buffer (units of time) for additional work, the

Bottleneck buffer

Work that is waiting to be processed at the bottleneck.

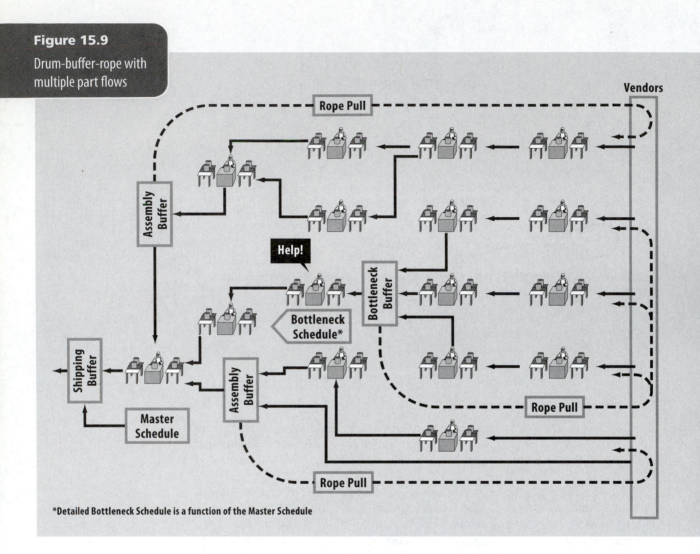

Figure 15.9

Drum-buffer-rope with multiple part flows

*Detailed Bottleneck Schedule is a function of the Master Schedule

communication link symbolized by the rope releases more work into the facility. Because the rate of work at the bottleneck determines the rate at which work enters the facility, no resource supplying the bottleneck will work at a rate greater than that of the bottleneck. Thus, the bottleneck determines the rate at which all other resources in its material flow must operate—whether upstream or downstream from the bottleneck.

Figure 15.9 includes three types of buffers: bottleneck buffers (discussed above), assembly buffers, and shipping buffers. An **assembly buffer** is extra time resulting in a collection of work wherever material flows that do not include the bottleneck join work that has been through the bottleneck. These buffers ensure that work does not get held up on its way to the customer for want of components or subassemblies that come from another material flow. Ropes from these buffers to the gateway work centers ensure that these resources, which aren't in the bottleneck material flow, nevertheless operate at the pace of the bottleneck.

Many customers would prefer not to receive their shipments early, while many suppliers would like to build in a margin of safety against late delivery of their

Assembly buffer

A collection of work placed wherever material flows that doesn't include the bottleneck join work that has been through the bottleneck.

product-service bundles. The **shipping buffer** is an amount of time (which usually results in an inventory of finished work) used to enhance the probability of correctly timed shipments. It is useful if outbound logistics include a bottleneck, or if the market itself is the bottleneck, or simply to decouple the production system from the outbound logistical system. In all such cases, the rope from the shipping buffer to the gateway work center prevents overproduction, ensuring that more only product-service bundles than can be shipped or consumed in the marketplace are produced.

Managing buffers is a critical aspect of improving the synchronous system. You will remember from Chapter 14 that inventory is like water in a river: It helps the system work smoothly, but it hides problems. Because a time buffer is reflected by the inventory required to keep a bottleneck busy for a specified period of time, it helps to ensure that the bottleneck stays busy and the system runs smoothly. Managers who don't want the bottleneck to stop running because of material shortages will want to have a large bottleneck buffer in place "just to be safe." On the other hand, the larger the buffer, the longer the quality feedback loop will be. Suppose you have a 2-day buffer at the bottleneck and discover a problem with material while processing it in the bottleneck. Whoever created that material will not hear about the problem for at least 2 days. Furthermore, the quality of all of the work done during these 2 days is suspect. The larger the buffer, the longer the required planning horizon must be. If you reduce your buffer size by 2 days, the system lead time required to complete the product-service bundle and the planning horizon will also be shortened. This suggests there is a benefit to keeping buffers as small as possible.

The buffer is basically safety stock. New work is ordered (i.e., brought into the process) based on the expected lead time between the gateway operation and the bottleneck. The inventory between the gateway operation and the bottleneck includes the work in upstream work centers and the buffer. Essentially, then, the reorder point (i.e., the time to start working on another order) is expected upstream process inventory plus safety stock. In Chapter 13, we suggested that safety stock levels and reorder points could be set based on the lead-time demand distribution and the level of safety desired. In the DBR system, buffer sizes can also be set based on these considerations. The lead-time supply distribution will indicate the mean and variance of the lead time required for material to travel from the gateway work center to the bottleneck. Based on the relative costs of bottleneck stock-outs and the cost of carrying inventory in the buffer, managers can establish a buffer service level, which is simply a probability that the buffer will stock-out. With this information, the approach to finding safety stock levels discussed in Chapter 13 can be used to determine the appropriate size of a buffer.

Suppose, for example, that it takes an average of 3 days (with a standard deviation of half a day) from the instant work begins on a job until it shows up at the bottleneck buffer. As illustrated in the top curve of Figure 15.10, if no buffer was present and work orders were released exactly 3 days before their processing was to begin at the bottleneck, the chance of idling the bottleneck would be 50% for each order (a normal distribution of the lead time is assumed). On the other hand, as the bottom portion of Figure 15.10 illustrates, if the planned buffer was 1 day (i.e., two standard deviations of the lead-time demand distribution), work orders would be released exactly 4 days before their processing was to begin. Based on the cumulative normal distribution, which contains about 97.5% of its area to the left of $z = 2.00$, this would reduce the probability of idling the bottleneck to about 2.5% for each order.

You might wonder how anyone would know the variability (or standard deviation) of the time needed for work to travel from the gateway work center to the buffer,

Shipping buffer

An inventory of finished work used to enhance the probability of correctly-timed shipments.

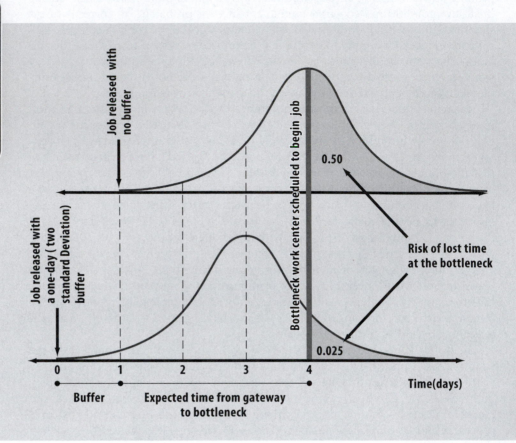

Figure 15.10

Buffers and the risk of lost time at the bottleneck (Average time from gateway to bottleneck is 3 days with a standard deviation of 0.5 days)

especially if the system might bottleneck at a different place each week. Because we are dealing with a fairly simple situation, most managers are likely to know the variability of their key processes—at least to some extent. We can quickly gauge the system's total upstream variability by adding the variances at all the work centers. The standard deviation of total upstream processing time (i.e., the standard deviation of the lead-time supply distribution) is simply the square root of this sum of variances. This value, in turn, can be used to determine the appropriate size of the buffer.

Figure 15.11 illustrates the effect of inventory levels on the material flow that feeds the bottleneck just described. A similar graph might be drawn for assembly and shipping buffers. The plan is for 1 day's worth of inventory to be in the buffer and 3 days' worth in process upstream of the bottleneck, for a total of 4 days' inventory in the upstream portion of the system. But the bottleneck will process one order at a time, and the work will enter the facility one order at a time; thus inventory levels will decrease and increase by the size of the orders, rather than one item at a time. Consequently, at any given moment the upstream inventory level may be somewhat different from the intended level. Situation A illustrates the intended level of upstream inventories.

In situation B, the buffer has grown larger than intended, while the upstream process inventory is as intended. This situation can only occur if work in the bottleneck

Figure 15.11

Buffer management situations

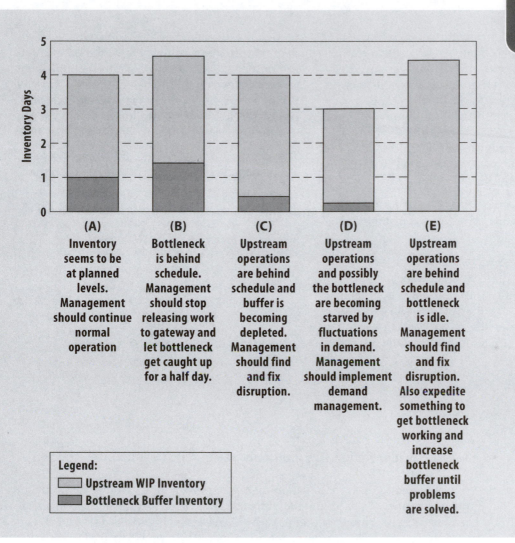

has been disrupted and fallen behind schedule. A manager who observes this situation would stop releasing jobs to the gateway workstation until work in the bottleneck caught up. Effort would also be expended to fix the problem that slowed the bottleneck and thereby improve throughput.

Situation C shows more than 3 days' worth of inventory in upstream processes and a smaller than intended buffer. Managers would realize that there was some upstream process disruption if they observed this inventory situation. They would try to fix the problem with the upstream resource and might increase the planned buffer to more than 1 day's worth until they were sure work was back to normal.

In situation D, the upstream work centers have been starved for work because of demand shortages. If there is no order from a customer, no work can be released to upstream work centers. We have included this situation primarily to

Example 15.4

Assume in Figure 15.8 that the average time to process an order is 10 hours at WS1 with a standard deviation of 0.8 hours. At WS2 the average time to process an order is 6 hours with a standard deviation of 0.6 hours. Assuming no time is required to transfer materials, what is the average length of time between release of materials to WS1 and their arrival at the bottleneck? What is the standard deviation of the time required for material to travel from the gateway to the bottleneck?

Step 1: Find the average time on the routing by summing the means of processing times at individual work stations.

Because averages are additive, the average length of time between release of materials and their arrival at the bottleneck is just the sum of the average times for the work stations on the routing between the gateway and the bottleneck. In our case, that is the 10 hours at WS1 plus the 6 hours at WS2, a total of 16 hours.

Step 2: Find the standard deviation of the time required for material to travel from the gateway to the bottleneck. Begin by squaring the individual standard deviations on the routing to find the variances on the routing. (We are doing this because, unlike averages, standard deviations are not additive. However, variances are additive.)

The variance, σ^2, for WS1 is $(.8 \text{ min})^2 = .64 \text{ min}^2$. The variance, σ^2, for WS2 is $(.6 \text{ min})^2 = .36 \text{ min}^2$.

Next, determine the variance of expected time on the routing by summing the individual variances on the routing.

$$\text{Routing variance} = 0.64 \text{ min}^2 + 0.36 \text{ min}^2$$
$$= 1.00 \text{ min}^2$$

Finally, determine the standard deviation of the expected time on the routing by taking the square root of the routing variance.

$$\text{Routing standard deviation} = \sqrt{1.00}$$
$$= 1.00$$

emphasize that operations is not the only function that can influence the bottleneck schedule.

Finally, situation E is the situation managers most want to avoid. The upstream problem has not been fixed, and the entire buffer has been used up at the bottleneck. The system's most critical resource has been idled because of process disruptions at an upstream resource. Like an army of ants, workers will be trying to fix the problem that disrupted the upstream resource's schedule. Upstream jobs that can be quickly completed will also be expedited, so that work at the bottleneck can resume. After such an event, the buffer might be increased until managers are confident of the reliability of upstream resources.

Order sizes are likely to vary depending on customer requirements, so Figure 15.11 does not present a fixed order size model. All things being equal, however, the risk of a stock-out is greater with big orders and the system is more difficult to manage. The issue we are alluding to, which is highlighted by OPT principles 7 and 8 in Table 15.7 (see page 694), is batch sizing in the drum-buffer-rope scheduling system. A **production batch size** is the number of items a resource is asked to process with one setup. A **transfer batch size** is the number of items that are moved from one resource to the next on a material routing. If production and/or transfer batch sizes are small, jobs spend less time at each resource. Consequently, the time required for a job to move from a gateway operation to a bottleneck

Production batch size

The number of items a resource is asked to process with one setup.

Transfer batch size

The number of items that are moved from one resource to the next on a material routing.

Example 15.5

How large would the bottleneck buffer and total lead time from the gateway to the bottleneck (in Figure 15.8) need to be in order to have a 99% level of confidence that disruptions at WS1 and WS2 would not result in a stoppage of work at the bottleneck?

Step 1: Determine the z-score that would provide a 99% level of confidence.

This z-score can be found in the cumulative standard normal distribution table—see the appendix at the end of this book. The value for z, which corresponds to a cumulative probability of 0.9901, is 2.33. Alternatively, a calculator or spreadsheet function will return a more exact value. Typing the Excel function = NORMINV(0.99,0,1) in a cell, will result in the exact value of z-score we are looking for (because we are looking for a cumulative probability of 0.99 and the mean and standard deviation of the standard normal distribution are 0 and 1 respectively). The exact value of the z-score is 2.326342.

Step 2: Calculate the buffer's duration. (Use the standard deviation of the expected time of 1 hour found in Example 15.4.)

The buffer's duration can be calculated as follows:

$$\text{Buffer duration}_{(sl)} = z_{sl} \times (\sigma_L)$$

where sl = the level of confidence we seek, and σ_L = the standard deviation of the expected time.

In our case:

$$
\begin{aligned}
\text{Buffer duration}_{(0.99)} &= z_{0.99} \times (\sigma_L) \\
&= 2.33 \times (1.00 \text{ hours}) \\
&= 2.33 \text{ hours}
\end{aligned}
$$

Step 3: Determine the total time that should be allowed between the gateway and the bottleneck including the buffer. (Use the expected time of 16 hours found in Example 15.3 and the standard deviation of the expected time of 1 hour found in Example 15.4)

$$
\begin{aligned}
\text{Total lead time from gateway to bottleneck} &= \text{expected time} + \text{buffer} \\
&= 16 \text{ hours} + 2.33 \text{ hours} \\
&= 18.33 \text{ hours}
\end{aligned}
$$

Note: Because the distribution of expected time has a mean of 16 and standard deviation of 1, if we were using an Excel spreadsheet we could get this value directly by using the following function:

" = NORMINV(0.99,16,1)."

buffer is short and relatively predictable. There is also less inventory in upstream processes.

Typically, for the sake of simplicity, transfer batch sizes and production batch sizes are kept the same, and production batch sizes are determined based on the tradeoff between holding costs and ordering costs at some level of completion. In a DBR system, smaller batches are preferred, because they reduce both inventory levels and the risk of material shortages at the bottleneck. Specifically, it is common to base production order sizes on customer requirements, shown on the master schedule, but to allow transfer batch sizes to be smaller than production batch sizes. Doing so allows an upstream operation to feed a bottleneck, even when all the materials needed to complete a production batch have not been processed. In general, small batch sizes (whether production batches, transfer batches, or both) reduce lead times and planning horizons, making processes become simpler to manage.

SUMMARY

To effectively run a synchronous planning and control system, every business function must become concerned with maximizing bottleneck resources. Accountants need to verify that their traditional costing methods are appropriate and revise their approach where necessary. Financial managers have to understand the value-adding system to the extent that they will know the system value of capacity at both bottleneck and non-bottleneck resources. Marketing professionals need to work with customers to make the most of resources with limited capacity. Engineers and others on design teams need to consider the capacity implications of their decisions. Senior managers have to ensure that incentives and performance measurement systems for employees in all of the various functional areas are set up to encourage cooperation and synchronized operations. Synchronous planning and control systems will only work for certain value-adding systems. They are not a good choice where there is so much complexity that it is difficult to identify the bottleneck quickly enough to synchronize other resources accordingly. On the other hand, where there is no bottleneck because demand has been leveled and resource capacities have been balanced, JIT is a better choice for system planning and control.

The most well-known approach to synchronizing value-adding systems is the theory of constraints developed by Eliyahu Goldratt. The system management principles and five-step focusing process that are based on the theory of constraints were made famous by a book called *The Goal*. Recognition of many of these principles has also begun to impact on cost accounting. At least in part, recently developed approaches to accounting such as activity-based costing and the balanced scorecard owe their acceptance to the awareness of operational issues created by the work of Goldratt and others who have tried to explain synchronous planning and control systems.

In a synchronous planning and control system, detailed decisions about who does what with what resource and when are made with the drum-buffer-rope scheduling approach. The fundamental idea of DBR is that the bottleneck's pace should be the average pace for all resources. Because non-bottleneck resources have excess capacity, it is okay for them to run faster and slower than the bottleneck for short periods of time. Communication ensures that no more work enters the value-adding system than can be handled at the system bottleneck. This guarantees that the average output of non-bottleneck resources cannot continually exceed that of the bottleneck. A buffer is used to keep the bottleneck from running out of work, thus preventing wasted time at the system's most critical resource. Buffers are also used to make certain that work that has been processed at the bottleneck is delayed as it proceeds onward to the customer. The entire approach is geared toward maximizing system throughput while minimizing inventory and operating expense.

KEY TERMS

Activity-based costing (ABC), 698
Assembly buffer, 704
Asynchronous value-adding system, 677
Backward infinite scheduling, 694
Balanced scorecard, 698
Bottleneck, 676

Bottleneck buffer, 703
Drum-buffer-rope (DBR) system, 693
Forward finite scheduling, 694
Inventory, 696
Operating expense, 696
Production batch size, 708

Shipping buffers, 705
Synchronous value-adding systems, 676
Theory of constraints (TOC), 690
Throughput, 696
Transfer batch size, 708

SOLVED PROBLEMS

1. The "case goods" section of Luis's furniture factory is the area that makes wood furniture without any upholstery. The departments that make up that end of the business are listed in the table below. Also included in the table is the average amount of time needed by the four basic product lines as they flow through those departments. Also listed below are the demand for the coming week (from the master schedule) and the gross margin on each product line.

   a) Where is the bottleneck? Assuming each department is available 4800 minutes per week (two shifts of 8 hours for 5 days), can the schedule be met?

   b) What advice would you give the scheduling manager in order to maximize the profitability of the shop next week?

   c) What advice would you give the sales people for adding additional orders to the shop next week?

   d) A new salesperson came in excited about a special favor he had agreed to for a big customer. It effectively doubled the demand for bookcases next week. How does that change your answer to part (b)?

   e) Assume additional orders doubled the demand for chairs. Orders for all but 25 bookcases were canceled and all the desk orders for next week were canceled. How does that change what you said for part (c)?

Department/ Product Lines	Chairs (minutes/unit)	Tables (minutes/unit)	Desks (minutes/unit)	Bookcases (minutes/unit)
Rip Saws	2	4	6	6
Cross-Cut Saws	2	4	6	6
Planing	1	4	10	12
Lathes	3	3	0	0
Finish	2	3	8	8
Assembly	2	2	8	6

Product	Demand	Margin
Chairs	200	$15
Tables	150	$45
Desks	200	$50
Bookcases	200	$40

Department	Load for the Week (Minutes)
Rip Saws	3400
Cross-Cut Saws	3400
Planing	5200
Lathes	1050
Finish	4050
Assembly	3500

Solution:

a) Listed below is the load for the week for each department. The planing department is clearly the bottleneck department. Because its capacity is only 4800 minutes per week, it cannot meet the schedule.

b) Given the margin per bottleneck minute (see the following table), They should be prioritized: chairs, tables, desks, and then bookcases.

Product	Margin per Minute in Planing
Chairs	15
Tables	11.25
Desks	5
Bookcases	3.333333

Product	Margin per Minute in Planing
Chairs	5
Tables	15
Desks	Unlimited*
Bookcases	Unlimited*

c) Do not promise anything else for next week, as everything will use planing to some degree. If orders must be taken, prioritize them is the same fashion as the answer to part (b).

d) It effectively makes everything tighter except the lathe department, In fact, now finishing is also over utilized. That just further emphasizes the need to do items with higher priority.

Department	Load for the Week (Minutes)
Rip Saws	4600
Cross-Cut Saws	4600
Planing	7500
Lathes	1050
Finish	5650
Assembly	4700

e) With 400 chairs, 150 tables, and only 25 bookcases ordered, the load by department is as follows:

Department	Load for the Week (Minutes)
Rip Saws	1550
Cross-Cut Saws	1550
Planing	1300
Lathes	1650
Finish	1450
Assembly	1250

The bottleneck would now be the lathe department. And the margin per bottleneck minute would be:

* With no lathe time required for desk or book cases, marketing should push orders for those over chairs or tables until another department becomes the bottleneck in place of the lather department.

2. A five-step process has a bottleneck in the fourth step this week. The average upstream flow time from the gateway to the fourth step is about 3 days with a 6-hour standard deviation. Assume the process is in operation 8 hours per day.

a) How many hours' worth of inventory should usually be upstream from the bottleneck not counting any buffer in front of the bottleneck?

b) If the bottleneck was to be protected from any shutdowns due to blockages or delays in upstream operations with a 97.7% confidence level, how big should the buffer in front of the fourth step be? 99.86%?

c) What might cause the buffer to exceed the levels suggested in part (b)?

d) What would you suggest if the buffer drops below the level determined in part (b)?

Solution:

a) 24 hours (3 days × 8 hours/day), which is the mean upstream flow time.

b) 12 hours (two standard deviations above the mean will result in approx. 97.7% confidence level). Get this in one of two ways: (1) Using Excel enter the formula = norminv(.977,24,6). This gives the result 35.97. Because 24 of the 35.97 hours is expected time, the remaining 11.97 hours are buffer time. (2) Using the cumulative normal distribution table at the back of the book, find the value closest to .9770 in the body of the table. The Z value corresponding to this is 2.0. Thus two standard deviations or 12 hours of buffer time are required. Similarly, norminv(.9986,24,6) results in the value 41.93. With 24 of these hours being expected time 17.93 hours are buffer time. From the cumulative normal table you will find that 2.99 standard deviations above the mean will result in approx. 99.86% confidence level, thus, $2.99 \times 6 = 17.95$ hours of buffer time are needed.

c) Some small fluctuations would be normal but if the upstream operations allow product into the gateways faster than the bottleneck's capacity, significant excesses of inventory will build up at the bottleneck buffer. If after placing a drum-buffer-rope system in place and the bottleneck is somehow interrupted for a significant amount of time, then the buffer might back up. At that point a lack of pulls on the "rope" should keep any more work from entering the gateway operations and other workstations would slow down or stop when they don't hear the "drum." At that point, the buildup of the buffer should stop.

d) You would want to look for whatever is delaying the flow to the bottleneck starting with the gateway operations and following the flow to the bottleneck.

3. Further study of the process described in Problem 2 found the following flow times and standard deviations by process. Assume the bottleneck is still in the fourth step and the process is in operation 8 hours per day.

Step	1	2	3	4	5
Average Flow Time	6	14	6	18	6
Standard Deviation (Hours)	2	5	4	2	2

a) How many hours worth of inventory should usually be upstream from the bottleneck not counting any buffer in front of the bottleneck?

b) If the bottleneck was to be protected from any shutdowns due to blockages or delays in up-stream operations with a 97.7% confidence level, how big should the buffer in front of the fourth step be? 99.86%?

Solution:

a) 26 hours (or 3 1/3 days), which is the mean upstream flow time.

b) The accumulated variances would be the accumulation of the standard deviations squared or ($2^2 + 5^2 + 4^2 = 45$). The square root of the accumulated variances would be the standard deviation of the combined steps ($\sqrt{45} = 6.7$), thus (using z values from the previous solved problem of 2.0 and 2.99) a 97.7% confidence level would be 6.7×2 or 13.4 hours in the buffer and a 99.86% confidence would be 6.7×2.99 or 20.1 hours.

DISCUSSION QUESTIONS

1. As a manager of a popular fast-food restaurant, you notice that during peak lunch hours, things get congested at the register where customers order. Customers are not always sure how to order what they want, which slows things down. What could you do to better utilize the bottleneck at the register?

2. What is the difference between a production batch and a transfer batch? Why would Luis want them to be the same in most cases? Where would he be willing to consider them separately?

3. How can the bottleneck be starved if it supposed to be the resource with the largest load? How would this happen with the bikes mentioned in the conversation at the beginning of the chapter? How could it happen at Luis's furniture factory? How could it happen in the most heavily demanded course at your school? How could it happen at an amusement park? (Hint: When entering a busy amusement park like Disney's Epcot Center as the gates open in the morning, most veteran park-goers will tell you to go directly to the rear of the park and work your way forward.)

4. Consider yourself a cog in your own personal supply chain. How might understanding the bottlenecks of your employer (your customer) affect

how your job changes from week to week? How might understanding the bottlenecks of businesses where you spend your money (your suppliers) affect your day-to-day activities? (Hint: If you are not busy, do you need to pay for your pizza to be delivered?)

5. The drum-buffer-rope system can be a very effective scheduling system. Can you think of circumstances where it might break down and not be effective?

6. How could understanding the bottleneck affect pricing on Tom's airline?

7. Assume Tom can identify the bottleneck in his airline's operation this week. For example, is it the equipment? Pilots? Baggage handlers? What things might he do in scheduling other flights and services with respect to the bottleneck that might allow him to better run his airline?

8. How could understanding the bottleneck affect job scheduling in Luis's furniture factory? When would someone split a production batch? When would an extra setup on a lathe be significant? When would it be trivial?

9. Does the hockey-stick syndrome apply to the way you keep up with your studies? How about the reading for this class? Explain why or why not.

10. How might the hockey stick syndrome apply to the local auto repair shop? How about the local copy shop where your course packets are reproduced?

11. Think of the most popular night spot in your college town. Does a line of patrons form when it gets busy? If so, what is the bottleneck? What is the drum? The buffer? The rope?

12. Why do we need an assembly buffer if nothing in it went through the bottleneck? For most pizza shops, the market is the bottleneck. What would be the assembly buffer and why would you have it? What might be the tradeoffs in terms of local versus global performance measures?

13. When going to the Magic Kingdom Park at Florida's Disney World, the ticket gates can become a bottleneck in the morning. How does the use of the monorail train and the ferryboat across the man-made lake between the gates and the main

parking lot help the process? How does it shift the buffer? Is that good or bad?

14. What would be the shipping buffer in Luis's furniture shop? Why would it be important? What might be the tradeoffs in terms of local versus global performance measures?

15. Luis wants to cut inventory from his bottleneck and shipping buffers. How might that affect throughput or operating expense? What might be the tradeoffs in terms of local versus global performance measures?

16. Luis wants to cut operating expense, so he limits overtime in all departments (which, obviously, includes any bottlenecks for the week). How will that affect inventory? Throughput? What might be the trade-offs in terms of local versus global performance measures?

17. A small pallet manufacturer (pallets are the wooden "crates" that material is stacked on so a forklift can move it easily) pays laborers who saw the wood by the hour but pay the people who nail them together by the completed unit, because it is easy to measure. Depending upon the type of wood used and the particular type of pallet being produced, processing times will vary at both workstations. Given what you know about local versus global performance measures, what do you think of the arrangement?

18. Again thinking about the pallet manufacturer described above, if the person sawing the wood works a full day despite an obvious bottleneck in the nailing area, how would you describe the level of utilization? Activation? Given the current bottleneck, would you want any buffer of sawed wood in front of the nailer?

19. The sawyer described above usually cuts batches of 200 to 300 boards before a forklift operator transports them to the nailing area. They usually have a fairly set schedule of board sizes and wood varieties to cut for the day. Under what conditions should they change their schedule? When would they ship less than a complete batch?

20. Let's say you went to a large amusement park with 35 fraternity or sorority friends and some in the group insisted that you all stay together as you go

from ride to ride. How does that affect the number of rides you might all ride in a day? What would happen if you split up into smaller groups? Keep in mind that one ride you all want to go on, the world's fastest and tallest roller coaster, is very popular and tends to have very long lines during the peak hours of the park's operation.

21. A local dairy has a lot of uncertainty in day-to-day operation. The milk will come in from local dairy farms in varying quantities whenever the farmer can finish milking and get it to the dairy. Depending on the mix of products to be produced that day (i.e., whole milk in gallons, skim milk in quarts, 2% in half gallons, etc.), a bottleneck can move between the raw milk storage area, the pasteurizer, the homogenizer, the packaging line, and even the truck staging area (typically, packaged milk is moved to a cooler adjacent to the dock where the returning trucks will be loaded for their next delivery). Can you discuss a possible drum-buffer-rope system for this dairy? Would you need an assembly buffer? A shipping buffer?

22. A recording company will sign artists to contracts for new albums, record various tracks, edit the tracks together, create artwork, produce the CDs, and promote and sell the finished products. As the mix of artists under contract changes—especially with new unproved groups being signed for the first time versus currently popular groups—bottlenecks can develop from time to time. As the manager of this recording label, how might you manage this business using TOC principles?

23. Other common environments where bottlenecks may be found include a doctor's office, restaurants with table service (think of Applebee's), computer networks, and bakeries (think of your local donut shop). What are the common bottlenecks in such businesses and what aspects of the TOC system have you seen them employ?

PROBLEMS

1. Tom Jackson's airline has four popular flights that include five connecting "legs" between major airports. As the airline looks ahead and forecasts demand for the flights, they can estimate the varying demand for seats or load on each of the five popular connecting "legs" and use that information to revise pricing and reservation policies. The loading is as follows:

Flight/Leg	A (Seats)	B (Seats)	C (Seats)	D (Seats)	E (Seats)
#12	2500	2500	0	2500	0
#34	3000	3000	3000	0	0
#56	1500	0	1500	1500	1500
#78	0	4500	0	0	4500
Leg Capacity	9000	10500	6000	6000	8000

Tentative pricing is as follows:

Flight	Initial Price Estimate
#12	$250
#34	$285
#56	$400
#78	$200

a) Where is the bottleneck?

b) What recommendations would you make to the airline concerning advance reservation time frames for flights that include the bottleneck leg? Flights not including the bottleneck leg?

c) What recommendations would you make to the airline concerning pricing for flights that include the bottleneck leg? Flights not including the bottleneck leg?

For Problem 2

Workstation	Sanding	Taping/Masking	Paint Shop	Drying/Buffing
Average Job Flow Time (Hours)	8	2	6	10
Standard Deviation (Hours)	3	1	2	3

d) What recommendations would you make to the airline concerning scheduling and prioritizing for flights that include the bottleneck leg? Flights not including the bottleneck leg?

2. The flow of work through an auto painting business typically follows a set sequence from sanding to taping/masking, to painting, and finally to drying/buffing. The bottleneck can fluctuate depending on the jobs to be completed each week. Listed below are the four departments and the average time required to get a job through each department (along with fluctuations in those times).

a) If the drying/buffing becomes the bottleneck this week, then how many hours' worth of inventory should usually be upstream from the bottleneck not counting any buffer in front of the bottleneck?

b) If the drying/buffing department bottleneck was to be protected from any shutdowns due to blockages or delays in upstream operations with a 97.7% confidence level, how big should the buffer in front of the bottleneck be? 99.86%?

c) What might cause the buffer to exceed the levels suggested in part (b)?

d) What would you suggest if the buffer drops below the level determined in part (b)?

3. In the auto painting business described in the last problem, the estimated job time for each of the four types of paint jobs they offer is listed as well as the demand for them over the next 4 weeks:

Paint Job Type	Sanding Time (Minutes)	Taping/Masking Time (Minutes)	Painting Time (Minutes)	Drying/Buffing Time (Minutes)
Basic	160	30	120	260
Two-Tone	150	35	190	280
Clear Coat	150	30	120	330
Metallic Enamel	150	30	170	360
Department Capacity (Minutes)	6000	2000	6000	12,000

Week 36	Week 37	Week 38	Week 39
15	8	8	10
6	16	6	6
6	6	6	6
8	8	18	10

a) What department is the bottleneck each week?

b) Given the low utilization of the taping/masking department (assume they have one worker available for 400 minutes per day over a 5-day week), what would you suggest to ease the effects of the bottleneck?

4. Using the product and process data from the previous two problems, now assume the following margins per product:

Paint Job Type	Margin
Basic	$200
Two-Tone	$270
Clear Coat	$250
Metallic Enamel	$300

Given the bottleneck each week, how would you prioritize your production schedule?

5. In golf, assume the expected number of shots required to play a hole is somewhat correlated to the length of the hole and the number of hazards surrounding it. The "par" for the hole usually reflects this and also correlates with the time required playing the hole. If you were designing a nine hole course where the green from one hole should be close to the tee for the next to encourage sequential play (okay, that is normal isn't it?), and you typically include two par 3s, two par 5s, and four par 4s, then:

a) As a way of keeping the course from getting to full, what type of hole should be first?

b) What else, in terms of course design, could you do to ensure that the course does not become too full?

c) How would you schedule the course differently from the "off season" to "peak season"?

6. The upholstered furniture section of Luis's factory is the area that makes furniture with upholstered sections. The departments that make up that end of the business are listed in the table below. The average amount of time needed by the four basic product lines as they flow through those departments is included in that table. Also listed below is the demand for the coming week along side the gross margin on each product line.

a) Where is the bottleneck? Assuming each department is available 4800 minutes per week (two shifts of 8 hours for 5 days), can the schedule be met?

b) What advice would you give the scheduling manager in order to maximize the profitability of the shop next week?

c) What advice would you give the sales people for adding additional orders to the shop next week?

d) Assume additional orders for couches went to 175 and orders for all but 100 footstools were canceled and all the reclining chair orders for next week were canceled. Love seats stayed at 150. How does that change what you said for part (c)?

Department/ Product Lines	Reclining Chairs (Minutes/unit)	Couches (Minutes/unit)	Footstools (Minutes/unit)	Love Seats (Minutes/unit)
Fabric Die Cut	6	8	1	6
Sewing	4	14	2	12
Framing	14	4	2	4
Inspection	8	6	2	6
Foam Cut and Prep	4	12	2	8
Assembly	8	8	2	6

Product	Demand	Margin
Reclining Chairs	275	$35
Couches	50	$50
Footstools	200	$15
Love Seats	150	$30

7. A lumber milling operation has six basic steps: Rough rip cut, kiln drying, final rip cut, cross cut, stamping, and banding. The average and standard deviation upstream flow time through each step is shown below. The bottleneck will vary depending on the mix of finished products required each week. For example, when more 8-foot 2x4s and fewer 16-foot 2x4s are in the mix then the cross cut operation is more heavily loaded as it is this week. Assume the process is in operation 8 hours per day.

Step	Rough Rip Cut	Kiln Drying	Final Rip Cut	Cross Cut	Stamping	Banding
Average Flow Time (Hours)	6	16	8	16	2	2
Standard Deviation (Hours)	2	3	4	4	1	1

a) How many hours' worth of inventory should usually be upstream from the cross cut operation not counting any buffer in front of the bottleneck?

b) If the bottleneck was to be protected from any shutdowns due to blockages or delays in upstream operations with a 97.7% confidence level, how big should the buffer in front of the cross cut step be? How about for a 99.86% confidence?

c) What would happen if there were no buffers?

d) What might cause the buffer to exceed the levels suggested in part (b)?

e) What would you suggest if the buffer drops below the level determined in part (b)?

8. A police lab that tests evidence collected at crime scenes will face a varying mix of demands each week. The following table shows the cases on schedule for next week and the time they will require of the various lab resources. All cases are equally important and should be completed as soon as possible.

Case/Resource	A (hours)	B (hours)	C (hours)	D (hours)	E (hours)
#124	2	0	3	5	1
#245	0	3	13	3	13
#356	4	2	5	1	12
#467	3	3	13	0	0
#578	12	12	12	2	2
#689	9	11	10	13	9

a) How should you prioritize the cases?

b) Once you start a lab procedure, it usually must be completed in a defined amount of time. How could you keep the lab from being congested?

c) Does your suggestion in part (b) conflict with maximizing total throughput over the week?

CHALLENGE PROBLEMS

1. A printing company specializing in business forms has a five-step process for most of its products. Depending on the mix of orders each week, the bottleneck can shift around from one workstation to the next. Information concerning the five basic steps in the process, the five primary product lines, average demand, next week's demand, and the times required (minutes per 1000 forms) in each workstation are listed below:

Product/ Workstation	Slitting (Minutes)	Coating (Minutes)	Printing (Minutes)	Cutting (Minutes)	Assembly (Minutes)
#234I (Invoices)	2	1	3	5	2
#987CC (Credit Card Slips)	2	4	4	2	2
#12KB (Kanban)	2	2	1	1	2
#2340F (Order Forms)	3	1	3	3	2
#154RC (Rain Checks)	3	2	1	1	2

Product	Average Demand/ Week (1000s)	Demand for Upcoming Week (1000s)
#234I (Invoices)	200	300
#987CC (Credit Card Slips)	300	150
#12KB (Kanban)	200	50
#2340F (Order Forms)	100	150
#154RC (Rain Checks)	200	200

With a significant amount of accumulated experience, the following information can be estimated with respect to delays at the various workstations:

Workstation	Slitting (Minutes)	Coating (Minutes)	Printing (Minutes)	Cutting (Minutes)	Assembly (Minutes)
Typical Delay (Minutes)	30	45	45	30	15
Worst Case Delay (Minutes)	90	180	120	60	60

A "typical" delay in one workstation (while independent of delays in other stations) has a 20% chance of happening at a workstation some time during an average day. A "worst case" delay may occur once every 20 days or so.

a) Based upon average demand, does there appear to be a long-term bottleneck? What should they do at this point?

b) Based upon the upcoming week's demand, where is the bottleneck?

c) Given the upcoming week's demand, where would you place a buffer?

d) Given the upcoming week's demand, how big would the buffer need to be if you want to protect against any shut down in the bottleneck? What is the probability that any of the worst case delays would occur on a given day? What is the probability that they all would on the same day? What do you think the buffer should the buffer be?

e) Given this week's demand and a 45-minute buffer at the bottleneck, what is the likelihood that you might still starve the bottleneck due to upstream delays?

2. Tom's Tubs—a hot tub and spa manufacturer—has a process for assembling and packaging its various tubs. The bottleneck seems to shift from week to week. Assume all tubs follow the same flow through the workstations of the plant as described below:

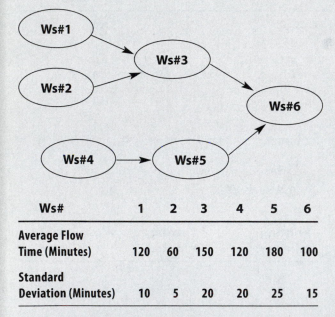

Ws#	1	2	3	4	5	6
Average Flow Time (Minutes)	120	60	150	120	180	100
Standard Deviation (Minutes)	10	5	20	20	25	15

a) Assume that Ws#6 is this week's bottleneck. How many minutes of inventory should usually be upstream from the bottleneck not counting any buffer in front of the bottleneck?

b) Again assuming that Ws#6 is this week's bottleneck and that it is to be protected from any shutdowns due to blockages or delays in

upstream operations with a 97.7% confidence level, how big should the buffer in front of the Ws#6 be? What if a 99.86% confidence level is desired?

c) Assume that Ws#3 is this week's bottleneck. How many minutes' worth of inventory should usually be upstream from the bottleneck not counting any buffer in front of the bottleneck?

d) Again assuming that Ws#3 is this week's bottleneck and that it is to be protected from any shutdowns due to blockages or delays in upstream operations with a 97.7% confidence level, how big should the buffer in front of the ws#6 be? What if a 99.86% confidence level is desired?

3. A local florist shop has six basic arrangements that they ship all over the metropolitan area. The arrangements follow a variety of paths through the shop but impose the following work time requirements on each of shop's six workstations. Also listed are the workstations' weekly capacity in terms of minutes and staff (assume a 400 minute day, 5 days a week).

The work requirements by arrangement and workstation (minutes) are:

Arrangement Type	WS1	WS2	WS3	WS4	WS5	WS6
A	10	10	15	10	10	60
B	15	10	50	10	15	10
C	10	10	15	10	5	60
D	15	5	50	10	10	10
E	10	5	5	10	15	10
F	15	5	5	10	15	10

	Ws1	Ws2	Ws3	WS4	Ws5	Ws6
Capacity (Staff)	4	4	8	4	8	12
Capacity (Minutes)	8000	8000	16000	8000	8000	24000

While demand fluctuates each week, the basic mix is fairly seasonal. The seasonal demand and gross margin earned on each product are listed below.

Arrangement Type	$ Margin/Unit	Weekly Demand *Winter* (Units)	Weekly Demand *Summer* (Units)
A	$30	100	250
B	$30	150	50
C	$20	100	150
D	$20	150	50
E	$15	50	100
F	$15	50	100

a) Can you estimate the bottleneck for the winter season?

b) Can you estimate the bottleneck for the summer season?

c) How would you prioritize the arrangement types during each respective season?

d) If the fixed weekly operating expenses are $13,500, will they be able to earn a profit in the winter? The summer?

e) What suggestions might you have to help balance the flow of work in each of the seasons?

Case 15: The Advanced Regional Traffic Interactive Management and Information System—ARTIMIS

ARTIMIS is a project to manage bottlenecks, the worst kind of bottlenecks, traffic jams! Whether due to temporary lack of capacity, accidents, disabled vehicles, etc., ARTIMIS provides real-time information in a way that helps keep traffic moving on 88 miles of freeway in the Cincinnati–Northern Kentucky area. Similar systems exist in other large metropolitan areas.

As our nation's freeways become more congested, transportation officials are looking at new technologies that can help ease the burden on highways and lessen the frustrations of motorists. Emerging from this search are new methods of traffic technology, collectively known as Intelligent Transportation Systems (ITS).

This is the first project of this type in Ohio and Kentucky. The estimated benefits to date of ARTIMIS include:

▶ Reducing interstate highway accidents by at least 10%

▶ Cutting 45 tons of hydrocarbon and nitric oxide emissions annually

▶ Saving 1 million gallons of fuel each year

▶ Total financial savings arising from reduced traffic delays, fuel consumption, and accidents is estimated to be $15.9 million per year

ARTIMIS is also helping bring the Greater Cincinnati–Northern Kentucky area into compliance with federal ozone standards.

The ARTIMIS system includes 80+ cameras, 57 center-lane miles of fiber optic cable, approximately 1,100 detectors of various types, 40 fixed changeable message signs, 3 portable changeable message signs, 2 highway advisory radio frequencies, 5 freeway service patrol vans, and a control center in downtown Cincinnati. ARTIMIS officially began limited operations in June of 1995 with the launch of its traveler advisory telephone service. In March of 1997, operations from the control center began. On January 8, 1998, the first 23 of the 40 changeable message signs were placed into operation and the system was immediately put to the test when a tractor-trailer carrying hazardous material overturned and ruptured on I-75. The result was a total closure of the interstate for approximately 3 hours. Motorists followed the alternate routes that were posted and later analysis of the incident indicated that ARTIMIS conservatively saved approximately $100,000 in motorist use costs.

Other services provided by the system besides the changeable message signs include:

▶ An automated telephone system in which travelers can use cell phones to check traffic conditions. The system is updated approximately 1150 times per day.

▶ A website where users can check conditions before they leave home or the office. The site includes links to real time video showing the area's potential hot spots (major interstate junctions, stadiums, arenas, amusements parks, etc.). The site is updated approximately 480 times each day. Apple users can even install a dashboard widget with a link to ARTIMIS for a regular "heads-up" check each morning as they head out the door. Links to portable PDA type devices are not far off.

The system also provides links that average 30 calls per day to local law enforcement and emergency dispatchers for faster response to incidents and congestion. Using a common radio frequency, the system has improved communication between many police and fire agencies including a freeway service patrol sponsored by local business to provide free roadside assistance in non-emergency situations.

Information collected by the system is distributed and or shared with local TV (25 traffic reports daily), 10 radio stations (e-mailed every 10 minutes), and 10–20 dispatches to local public mass transit agencies. Dispatches also go to major media outlets on an ad hoc basis when major incidents occur and even local school districts when those incidents affect bus routes.

SOME QUESTIONS TO THINK ABOUT:

1. How easy is it to match the capacity with demand for an interstate highway around and through a major city?

2. When problems do occur, how does ARTIMIS help deal with them?

3. Can you relate checking the system before you begin your commute to a sales rep checking the factory before committing an order to a customer?

4. Can you relate the ARTIMIS system to one designed to help update a customer on an order already in the process?

Source: Adapted from http://www.artimis.org/about.php and http://www.apple.com/downloads/dashboard/transportation/artimisforcincinnati.html

REFERENCES

Umble, M. M., and M. L. Srikanth. *Synchronous Manufacturing: Principles for World Class Excellence.* Cincinnati: Southwestern Publishing Company, 1990.

Goldratt, E. *The Goal.* Croton-on-Hudson, NY: North River Press, 1986.

Kaplan, R. S., and D. P. Norton. *The Balanced Scorecard: Translating Strategy into Action.* Boston: Harvard Business School Press, 1996.

Kaplan, R. S., and R. Cooper. *Cost and Effect: Using Integrated Cost Systems to Drive Profitability and Performance.* Boston: Harvard Business School Press, 1998.

16

Detailed Scheduling and Control Processes in Complex Environments with MRP

Chapter Outline

Introduction 726
Integrating Operations Management Across the Functions 727
Where to Use MRP Planning and Control 731
Overview of a Material Requirements Planning System 733
MRP System Logic 735
An MRP Application 737

The Product Structure 737

From Master Schedule to Material Plan 739

Reducing Lumpiness and Lead Time 742

Managing MRP Systems 743

Choosing a System 748

Expediting Orders 748

Combining MRP with JIT and TOC 748

Applying MRP in Service Operations 749

Yield Management Systems 750

Supply Chain Impact of an MRP System 752
Detailed Scheduling in an MRP Environment 753

Local Priority Rules 754

Local Priority Rules: An Application 756

Gantt Charts 759

Summary 763
Key Terms 764
Solved Problems 764
Discussion Questions 772
Problems 773
Challenge Problems 777
Case 16: To Varian Semiconductor, Speed Is the Key to Success 780
References 781

Learning Objectives

After studying this chapter you should be able to

▶ Explain how the various functional areas of business can work together to effectively manage complex value-adding systems using manufacturing resources planning (MRP II) systems

▶ Describe the environmental characteristics best suited to the use of material requirements planning (MRP) systems

▶ Explain how master scheduling, material requirements planning, capacity requirements planning, and detailed scheduling decisions fit together in a manufacturing resources planning system

▶ Compute material requirements from master schedules

▶ Describe the managerial challenges presented by MRP systems

▶ Schedule value-adding systems using local priority rules and Gantt charts

...Back at the Rec Center

"This rec center is well run," Tom blurts out one morning while taking a short break. The group was nearing the middle of its workout, having been there for about half an hour. "I mean, we get here really early, when you would expect things to be slow, but I've come back a few times later in the day or on a weekend with lots of people around, and everything still flows smoothly, no glitches." The rest of the group agrees. They seldom had to wait long for machines; there were plenty of towels; and more than enough staff was on hand to help out with a problem, keep things neat, restock whatever was needed, spot somebody on the free weights, offer encouragement, or just make training suggestions. In general, the staff did what needed to be done. The center even seemed to be open longer hours when the demand called for it. Tom was amazed at what a good handle the center's managers had on planning operation.

"Other clubs I've been in haven't been run as well," Tom continues. "There never seems to be enough staff, and you have to wait a long time for help. Other times, there are plenty of people around looking busy, but they're not doing what you need them to be doing."

"Yeah, I've seen those places too," says Luis, as he starts a set of sit-ups on the incline board.

"Lots of people, lots of equipment, but you still end up waiting for the stuff you want."

"I have enough of those kinds of headaches at work. Sure glad we don't have it here. Maybe I should take lessons," Tom adds, in exasperation.

"Sounds like you're not looking forward to working this morning," says Cheryl, wiping away the sweat of a 15-minute stint on the treadmill. "Problems?"

"New problems no, just a chronic pain," Tom answers. "We always do it, and we do it as well as anybody, but it's always a pain to get people to the right places at the right time." He adds that he's always scrambling at the last minute to get a crew somewhere or find enough agents for the gates. "I wish we could run things at work like this club is run! Sometimes I almost think it was easier in the old days, you know, before deregulation."

"Hearing this ought to make Fred happy with the plant he's in now," Luis says. "He may have complained about 'plain vanilla' before, but he's got it pretty smooth now—just put people in a job, start the line, and everything goes. No changes, no surprises, real plain, real smooth."

"That's what I mean about deregulation," says Tom. "It used to be a lot simpler to fly the same few routes over and over. Now, we couldn't make it more complicated if we wanted to."

Fred has been listening from a stepper with a smug look. "Sounds like you guys want my job!" he laughs.

"Not really, just a little bit of the 'down the line and out the door' simplicity of scheduling it now and then," Luis says.

"It's the complexity of planning, scheduling, and then running a process that gives us headaches," adds Cheryl. Luis and Tom nod in agreement, but she sees a puzzled look on Fred's face, so she explains: "Even building a simple product with basic technology, like wooden furniture, can be complicated if there are enough orders for enough other products competing for the same resources, changing colors, quantity, design, that kind of stuff."

"And all at the last minute!" Luis adds.

"Yeah, Fred, you have us on this one," says Cheryl. "Things are just more complex for Luis and me, even more so than what Tom's talking about. You might have it easy now, but remember what it was like in your old job." Fred had been head of marketing for a division that manufactured all of the newer products and prototypes, a wide variety of things in very small quantities. The group remembers him talking about the same kind of problems when he was at that job, many worse than what Cheryl and the others had to contend with now.

"Yeah, I remember those weekly resource planning meetings. We'd get all the orders together, we'd have 'em all lined up nice and neat," Fred reminisces. "That lasted until the operations people got there. They'd always want to talk about capacity, materials, priorities, and time fences, all kinds of reasons to tell us why they couldn't tell us exactly when we could have what we wanted. Is that what you mean?"

"That's the whole point," Cheryl says. "When you only have a couple of products to produce,

even if they are complicated products, it's easy to figure out what it will take to make them. Then you get the resources in place and go to it."

"Okay, I can see what you're talking about when I think of my old job and compare it to this one," says Fred, "but I wonder about something else. Stuff does happen and customers do change their minds. How do you coordinate it all? How do you ever meet your master schedule?"

"Information," says Cheryl.

"That sounds simple," says Fred.

"Believe me, it's not," Cheryl responds. "But think about what you need to know in order to schedule your shop. If you know what the customer wants, how to make it, and can match resources to it, then you have a schedule. In simple value-adding systems, those decisions could be hardwired into the system. It gets tougher as things become more complicated."

"Well, how do you handle it then, Luis?" asks Fred.

"We use something called MRP, or material requirements planning," says Luis. "It's more of an information system." He describes how the system generates schedules for his work centers by using information about customer orders, the list of components that go into each product, and each component's routing through the plant. He says it's a great planning tool and helps the employees in the work centers be more proactive, to plan ahead. "It's not perfect and it depends on a lot of data from the shop," he explains, "but it gives us a plan." The data includes some guesswork on the part of management, such as determining how long a component usually takes to get through a department, but the more accurate the data fed into the MRP system, the better it helps them run the shop. "It's like my drive home on the beltway," says Luis. "When the radio traffic report says an exit is closed or that a wreck has

caused a lane closure, the best route home still requires some guesswork, but you can make a better guess."

Introduction

Material requirements planning (MRP)

A system needed to identify the quantity and timing of materials required for individual orders and to track the progress of those offers through each part of the value-adding system.

Yield management system

A service-orientated system that performs a function similar to materials requirement planning.

If you have read Chapters 14 and 15, you are accustomed to the general flow of our chapters on detailed planning and control. Like those chapters, this one looks at short-term operations planning and control. This chapter, however, focuses on very complex value-adding systems, such as job shops, airlines, rental businesses, and hotels. These are environments where each customer's order may be unique and the resources required to satisfy the customer must be—at least in part—probabilistically estimated. Planning and control approaches such as just-in-time (JIT) and theory of constraints (TOC) are not flexible enough to deal with the managerial tasks required by such complex value-adding systems. These situations call for a system that can identify the quantity and timing of materials required for individual orders and track the progress of those orders through each part of the value-adding system. Systems of this nature used in manufacturing are typically referred to as **material requirements planning (MRP)** systems. Service-oriented systems that perform a similar function track the availability of capacity relative to demand and are commonly called **yield management systems**.

MRP systems are used to convert customer demand information into operational plans that are useful for the procurement of the parts, components, and subassemblies that go into the product-service bundles on the master schedule. A material requirement is simply something that is needed in order to carry out an order. For example, if your friend were running for student council president, she might ask you to fold, stuff into envelopes, label, stamp, and mail the letters she is sending to off-campus voters. You would probably think she was crazy if she asked you to do that job without providing the letters, envelopes, labels, or stamps you needed. Those are the material requirements associated with the order she gave. The situation is the same in business. Employees would think their boss was crazy if they got work orders without the materials necessary to complete the order.

Services that cannot store their capacity in the form of inventory may use yield management systems to perform the same planning function. The process would begin with planning departments determining what services are for sale at what price. For example, an airline might decide on the set of flight schedules and fares to offer in a given period or a hotel may decide the number and types of conferences and events to accommodate. This is much the same as master scheduling in manufacturing environments. Next, however, yield management systems determine how much of each service-price combination to make available, realizing that each uses a different set of

REC CENTER DILEMMA

Luis's Dilemma:

In the last paragraph of the conversation, Luis outlines the way that his company plans production schedules. He has noticed that the more complex a product is, and the more steps it requires for production, the greater the chance that it will end up getting to the customer late. What do you think Luis should do to enhance the odds that orders for such products will be completed on time and in the right quantity?

resources. Customers are required to buy and cancel their services through a computer system. Thus, the mix of available service-price combinations and unused capacity is always known. Management can adjust the availability of service-price combinations, in real time, to manage their capacity and maximize their revenues.

Integrating Operations Management Across the Functions

Compared to just-in-time (JIT) and synchronous systems, MRP systems allow for a higher degree of variety in the product-service bundle and far greater variety in the scheduling of each resource from one week to the next. Planners, therefore, must determine exactly what should be done when and at what resource on the basis of specific orders on the master schedule. The JIT approach, in which a group of resources (such as an assembly line) are scheduled together, and the synchronous approach, in which all resources are scheduled based on the system bottleneck, are much simpler. The greater complexity of the MRP environment means that there are more decisions to be made, creating a tremendous need for effective communication across functional areas—even though the various functions may not coordinate their internal decisions as closely as in other systems. Table 16.1 highlights some of the cross-functional linkages between this chapter's content and other business functions.

Because an MRP system handles many different product-service bundles, operations personnel must interact frequently with financial managers, accounting personnel, and marketing people in order to establish guidelines for new products. Management must address issues such as new product costing, pricing, and promotion; delivery lead times; and priorities in material and resource usage.

From a financial perspective, the operational complexity of a system that accommodates variable volumes of multiple product-service bundles creates some interesting challenges as well. Cash flows, both in and out, will vary, depending on the mix of orders and the resulting mix of lead times and profitability. That means managers' budgets and investors' financial forecasts need to be just as flexible. The complexity of the bundle also implies a data-rich financial environment: lots of things to keep up with mean lots of data to enter and maintain. The limited accuracy of such data, along with the complexity of the system, can complicate the auditing task.

Accounting personnel are consulted to establish costing parameters for new products. Management must address issues such as new product costing. This is not ongoing interaction regarding an individual product or product family, but intermittent contact regarding new or redesigned offerings. The flexibility of the operational system and the diversity of product-service bundles accommodated lead to frequent contact between the various business functions.

Where customized items are being made with general purpose equipment you will find skilled workers. Often, these skill workers are organized into unions. This can create scheduling difficulties from an operational perspective, and it certainly requires the human resources (HR) area to have personnel who are adept in their relations with the unions. Even if the unions are not a factor, skilled labor is often scarce and especially so during busy times for business. The ability of the HR function to attract and retain skilled workers is critical to the prosperity of the firm.

From a marketing perspective, salespersons need to be able to follow up on customer orders. If operational problems delay time-sensitive orders, operations

Table 16.1

Integrating Operations
Management across the
Functions

Integration Perspective / Functional Area	Finance	Accounting
Why Cross-Functional Integration Matters to Planning and Control in Material Requirements Planning Systems	**Financial justification for operational equipment and inventory storage capacity requires some knowledge of its potential utilization—and this depends on an understanding of the planning and control system in use.**	**Effective managerial accounting requires an understanding of the operational system. Managerial accounting in the context of complex operating systems is quite different from that seen in simple or synchronous systems.**
Key Issues	**How will equipment be utilized and capital expenditures justified in this operating system?** **What risks to projected earnings arise from the operational plans of the business?** **From an investment perspective, what is the impact of MRP based operations on an equity's attractiveness or a facility's mortgage risk?**	**How will costs be allocated within the system?** **How will WIP inventory be valued and accounted for?** **When and how will suppliers be paid?** **When and how will customers be billed?** **Will an order tracking system be used for pricing and audits?**

managers need to be sensitive to customer needs and communicate with marketing personnel. Often, operations managers get wrapped up in their own work and fail to alert sales and service personnel to problems with specific orders, making the marketing people's job difficult. Conversely, given the flexibility inherent in this type of value-adding system, marketing personnel too often assume that operations can perform extremely difficult or time-consuming feats (because they once did something similar). They may make promises to customers that create problems or raise costs in operations. As a consequence, there is often a great deal of conflict and lack of understanding between OM and marketing personnel in this type of system. While marketing

Human Resources	Marketing	Engineering	Management Information Systems
HR systems for employee selection, retention, motivation, and reward need to be consistent with the needs of the operating system.	Marketers must understand their own planning and control system, along with those of customers and other supply chain partners, in order for a company to satisfy their customers. In complex systems, marketing knowledge of the operating system plays an important role in customer satisfaction by establishing reasonable delivery expectations.	Engineering will be heavily involved in product modification and design to support complex operations. Knowledge of the planning and control system will allow engineering to set appropriate job priorities and optimize designs.	ERP systems with information about product designs, workstation priorities, inventory status, and so forth have become essential to planning and control in most complex environments.
How will employee skills be developed and maintained? How will skilled employees be rewarded and retained? Is the labor contract appropriate to the MRP based operating system?	With the emphasis on flexibility in operations, how (and to what extent) will needs for customization be identified and promoted? What product distribution system will best fit the MRP based operating system?	Can customer supplied product designs be manufactured? At what cost? With what routing? In what time frame? Etc. Can technical changes to customers' designs improve manufacturability? How will flexible equipment be maintained?	What MRP software will best meet the company's needs? How will MRP users be trained? How will data integrity be assured in the MRP system? How will operational and inventory data be collected and updated in the system? When will MRP updates be run?

personnel need not know how to manage the operational system, the more they know about operations, the more reasonable their customer promises are likely to be.

The engineering function is heavily involved in the design of the product-service bundle. In situations where customization is offered, engineers are involved in figuring out exactly what operational specifications are to be used and what process steps will be required to provide the bundle. The choices they make have a big influence on the quality, cost, and lead time the customer gets. That means they must be familiar with the implications of their choices on the firm's operations and intimately familiar with the managerial issues and planning and control system of the business.

Manufacturing Resources Planning (MRP II)

A broad information system for manufacturing environments.

Not surprisingly, information systems are at the heart of any MRP system. From the dawn of business information systems, computers have been used to crunch numbers for material planners. At first, the acronym MRP stood for material requirements planning, which is sometimes referred to today as *little MRP*, or simply *mrp*. Later, a broader information system for manufacturing environments, called **manufacturing resources planning**, became known as *big MRP*, or **MRP II**. These commercially available software programs are complete decision support systems. In addition to the MRP module, most contain modules for forecasting, master scheduling, quality control, cost accounting, scheduling, and capacity planning.

In today's client-server information systems environment, in which employees from every function make decisions based on a common database, operations managers rely heavily on information systems (IS) personnel to maintain accurate data and facilitate access to data. IS personnel must meet these expectations while guaranteeing the security and reliability of the information system. The term "MRP II" is not prevalent in business today because of the advent of enterprise resources planning (ERP) systems, which more effectively link all functional areas and may be capable of linking customers and suppliers electronically. Thus, IS personnel must meet the information needs of a large and diverse group of users. To do so, they must manage not only across the functional areas within their own firms but across corporate boundaries as well.

Reflecting the above discussion, Figure 16.1 illustrates the importance of cross-functional understanding to the effectiveness of MRP-based operations planning and control systems.

Figure 16.1

Material requirements planning and control processes

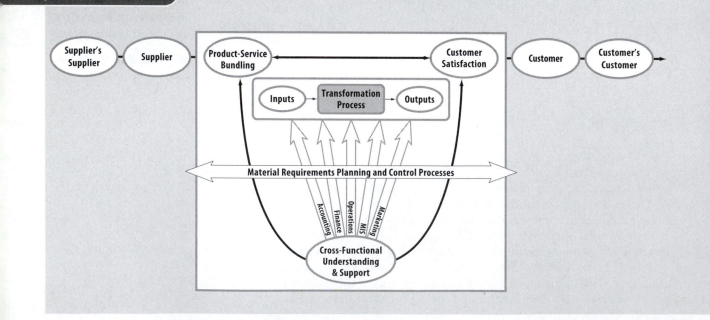

Where to Use MRP Planning and Control

Figure 16.2 illustrates the manufacturing process and common product flows in Luis's furniture factory. Like this illustration, many functionally organized environments have common (or dominant) product flows, but each specific job has its own route through the process. Furthermore, each week the mix of jobs changes. Some of the large jobs require little time at each work area per unit. Others may look simple because the parts inventory is small, but may nevertheless turn out to be very time consuming. Typically, by the time managers discover one bottleneck, another has developed somewhere else in the facility. Determining how all the jobs will flow through the shop in any week is difficult, then, because a bottleneck can develop at any

Figure 16.2

Example of a complex system

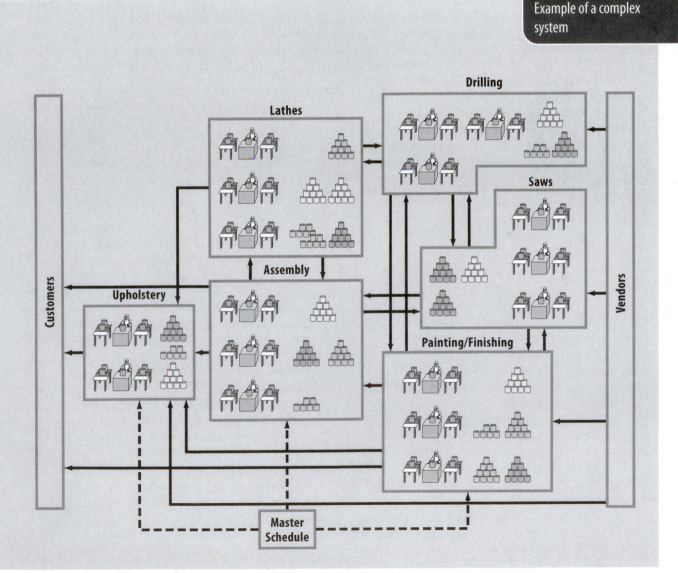

work center at any time. The complexity of such an environment makes systematic use of TOC or JIT impractical. As a rule, managers spend little effort trying to coordinate schedules across the entire facility. Rather, each work area schedules the work that has been assigned to that area, for which materials are in stock.

In a make-to-order environment, in which customers can specify the options and delivery schedule of their choice, scheduling and material planning are quite complex. Demand rates are highly variable and small orders are commonplace, so the value delivery system must be flexible enough to deal with a wide variety of product-service bundles. The typical process type required in such settings is a job shop or at least a facility with a functional layout. As Figure 16.3 illustrates, MRP systems are best suited for use in such complex environments. The computer system takes information regarding delivery commitments, current inventory levels, and the design of the product-service bundle and converts it into planned orders that can be released for scheduling.

When managerial decision-making tasks become very complex, managers use probabilistic approaches. Think for a moment about how long it takes to complete a typical homework assignment for this class: probably no more than a few hours. But the instructor probably gives you several days to get the job done. The instructor delays the due date sufficiently to allow you time for everything else in your life, without causing you undue hardship. The busier you get, the harder it is for professors to

Figure 16.3

Characteristics of materials requirements planning system

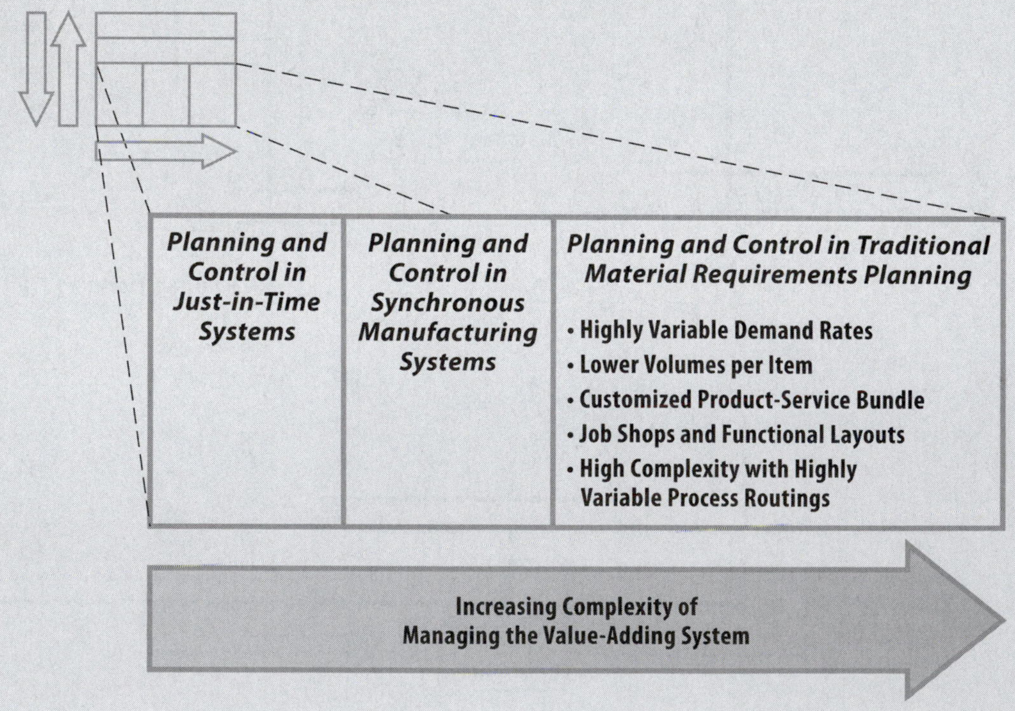

Planning and Control in Just-in-Time Systems	Planning and Control in Synchronous Manufacturing Systems	Planning and Control in Traditional Material Requirements Planning
		• Highly Variable Demand Rates • Lower Volumes per Item • Customized Product-Service Bundle • Job Shops and Functional Layouts • High Complexity with Highly Variable Process Routings

Increasing Complexity of Managing the Value-Adding System

predict how much time you will need to complete the assignment, so they give you a week for a 3-hour assignment. That is probably enough time for most students.

The dry cleaner in whose window hangs a sign that reads, "In by 10:00 a.m., Ready by 3:00 p.m.—Guaranteed" is taking the same approach. How can the store manager make that promise without knowing how much laundry you have? (Maybe there are not many signs like that close to campus dormitories, for good reason.) Basically, the manager has made an assumption about the range of demand for dry cleaning and has estimated the time that would be required under reasonable circumstances to provide same-day service. An unusually large order would create problems.

In all complex value-adding systems, planning and control decisions are much like the case of the professor who is creating a course schedule or the dry cleaner who is stating a guaranteed service cycle time. Generally, managers estimate the time required to complete a job probabilistically and then create a master schedule based on that estimate. Then they calculate the timing of the steps in the value-adding process deterministically.

Overview of a Material Requirements Planning System

Figure 16.4 summarizes the short-term planning and control activities seen in most MRP systems. In complex environments, the master schedule typically represents those commitments that have been, or are expected to be, made to customers. The near-term portion of this schedule consists almost entirely of order commitments from customers, whereas the more distant portion includes only a few commitments and many expected (or forecasted) orders.

In addition to these independent demand product-service bundles, the master schedule may include certain dependent demand items. For example, if replacement parts are sold to customers, the demand for those parts will be included on the master schedule. In environments where lead times are so long that satisfying customer delivery dates usually is not possible, or in which group technology has enabled the manufacture of numerous end items from many of the same parts, managers may adopt an assemble-to-order strategy. In these situations, companies may include some of the common parts or modules on the master production schedule. This practice means that common subassemblies are ready for use whenever they are needed, providing customers with more rapid service.

MRP programs convert such master scheduling information into plans for all dependent demand items. In other words, by analyzing information on what customers need and when, the programs generate information about when parts, components, and subassemblies will need to be ordered. This output information can then be used by MRP planners to allocate purchase orders and internal shop orders to specific operational resources, a process called **loading**. The MRP output can also be used for **capacity requirements planning (CRP)**, which alerts managers to capacity shortages resulting from schedules based on the orders planned by MRP systems. If CRP reveals vendor capacity problems, it can be used to help planners determine which vendors should get what orders and when.

If there are so many material requirements in a given week that it is not possible to load all the work on existing resources and vendors, some companies will adjust their master schedules. Companies that can do so based on their CRP output are referred to as **closed-loop MRP users** and are said to have "what-if capability." This capability allows

Loading

Information that can be used by MRP planners to allocate both purchase orders and internal shop orders to specific operational resources.

Capacity requirements planning (CRP)

Alerts managers to capacity shortages resulting from schedules based on the orders planned by MRP systems.

Closed loop MRP users

Companies that adjust their master schedules because there are so many material requirements in a given week that it is not possible to load all the work on existing resources and vendors, said to have a what-if? capability.

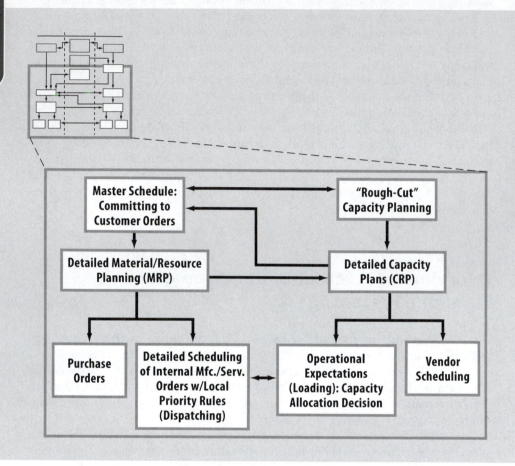

Figure 16.4

Short-term planning and control in a materials requirements planning system

schedulers to determine the impact of a change in the master schedule on an overutilized work center and it allows a salesperson to determine whether to accept a special rush order. For example, if one of Luis's most important customers were to ask for expedited delivery of a truckload of sofas, the salesperson could determine the feasibility of guaranteeing the desired delivery.

Once the planner actually releases the orders to specific work centers, work teams or area supervisors determine their priority. If material planning has been done correctly, materials will be available to complete the order; they will have been pushed forward from the upstream work center. (That is why you see so much inventory piled up at each work center in Figure 16.2.) Usually, local priority rules are used to schedule, or "dispatch," the jobs in any work center. The hope is that each order will eventually obtain the highest priority in the work center, will be processed, and will move to the next work center on its route. Jobs that get hung up at some point on their route will eventually become critical, at least from the customer's perspective. When that happens, they will usually be expedited. **Expediting** is a process of walking a job through a facility, overriding local scheduling decisions at each point on the route in order to give it top priority. Often, a job that has seen no action in weeks can be completed in hours with an expediter's attention.

Expediting

A process of walking a job through a facility overriding local scheduling decisions at each point on the route in order to give it top priority.

Bill of materials

A list indicating what parts and subassemblies go into independent demand items.

Inventory status file (ISF)

A record which indicates particulars such as inventory on hand, required lead-time, lot size, vendor, and so forth.

The quantity of a component produced in a single batch, or lot, can impact how long that batch takes to get through the process (i.e. lead time) and then by default, how far ahead production schedules are planned.

Getting all the ingredients of a product to arrive at the right place at the right time in the right quantity can be complicated. MRP systems are used to help plan the purchase of raw materials and also schedule the flow of materials through the process.

MRP System Logic

Figure 16.5 describes the basic inputs and outputs of the MRP program. Three primary inputs are shown: the master schedule, the bill of materials, and the inventory status file. As you already know, the master schedule indicates which end items need to be delivered to customers and when. The **bill of materials (BOM)** indicates which parts and subassemblies go into these independent demand items. For each end item, part, and subassembly, the **inventory status file (ISF)** indicates particulars such as inventory on hand, required lead time, lot size, vendor, and so forth. Using this information, the MRP program generates three types of documents:

▶ planned purchase orders, for release to vendors

▶ planned internal orders, for release to workstations within the facility

▶ exception reports, which indicate a problem that requires a planner's attention—a material shortage or late delivery that threatens the timely completion of some order, for instance. In such cases, the planner must determine how to resolve the problem and take corrective action. If the problem cannot be resolved, the customer must be notified of the expected delay.

Figure 16.6 shows a planning template which embodies the logic used in MRP computations. Though the numbers in the data rows vary, the structure of the template

Figure 16.5

Inputs and outputs in a material requirements planning system

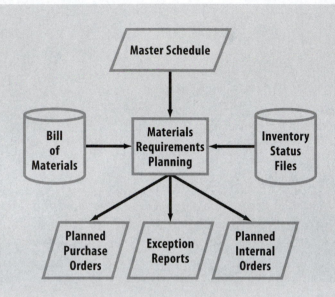

remains the same. "Gross requirements" are materials required during a particular week. Their value is calculated from the planned orders for the items of which they are a part. For example, an order for 125 tables would generate a gross requirement for 500 table legs.

"Scheduled receipts" are deliveries scheduled to be received at the beginning of the week. Figure 16.6 shows a scheduled receipt for 1000 table legs in the first week; therefore, an order must have been released at some point. "Planned on hand" is inventory that is expected to be available at the beginning of the week. These parts can be used to satisfy some of the gross requirements. In this case, 132 units of inventory are on hand, and the plan appears to be to keep a stock of at least that many on hand at all times.

Figure 16.6

A material requirements planning template

Week		1	2	3	4	5	6	7	8	9	10
Gross Requirements		500	0	500	0	500	0	500	0	500	0
Scheduled Receipts		1000									
Planned On Hand	132	132	632	632	132	132	632	632	132	132	632
Net Requirements		0	0	0	0	368	0	0	0	368	0
Planned Order Receipts		0	0	0	0	1000	0	0	0	1000	0
Planned Order Releases		0	0	0	1000	0	0	0	1000	0	0

"Net requirements" are calculated from these three amounts, as well as any safety stock the material plan may call for. When the quantity Gross Requirements − Scheduled Receipts − Planned On Hand + Desired Safety Stock is positive, that amount is the net requirement for the week. For example, the gross requirement for table legs in week 5 is 500; there are no scheduled receipts; and 132 table legs are planned on hand. Therefore, net requirements in week 5 are 368 table legs. When the result of the "gross to net" calculation is less than or equal to zero, there is no net requirement (a result that is expressed as a zero on the planning template).

"Planned order receipts" are determined based on net requirements and a lot-sizing rule. There are many different lot-sizing rules. For example, if a lot-for-lot (L4L) sizing rule is being used and the net requirement for table legs is 368, the planned order receipt would be for 368 table legs. If a fixed lot size of 100 table legs is used, the planned order receipt for any net requirement between zero and 100 would be 100 units; for any net requirement between 101 and 200, it would be 200 units. Sometimes a minimum lot size is specified. For example, with a minimum lot size of 1000, the planned order receipt would be large enough to cover the net requirement or 1000 units, whichever is greater. That is the lot-sizing rule used in Figure 16.6.

Often, the lot-sizing decision in MRP comes down to whether to order this period's net requirement or combine this period's order with the order for an upcoming period (or periods). Combining orders can reduce ordering (or setup) costs, but a carrying cost is incurred in the process. The carrying cost is directly proportional to the number of "part-periods" of inventory resulting from the combined order. Because the lot sizing decision is based on an attempt to minimize the total cost of ordering and holding inventory in the system, a "part-period balancing" approach to lot-sizing would combine current demand with the demand of future periods in the way that most closely matches ordering cost with the holding cost resulting from the order.

Finally, "planned order releases" are directly correlated with planned order receipts: They simply indicate when an order must be released to be received at the planned time. Thus, if the lead time required to receive an order is one week and the planned order receipt is for 1000 table legs in week 5, 1000 table legs would need to be ordered in week 4. (When the planned order release is actually executed by an MRP planner, the planned order receipt becomes a scheduled receipt.)

An MRP Application

The Product Structure

Figure 16.7a presents a set of end items, subassemblies, and components sold by Bonnie's Candle Shop. Bonnie's assembles wall- and table-mounted electric candle fixtures in a variety of configurations. Only twelve of the more popular end items are shown in the figure. End items are referred to as level (0) items. Notice that level (1) items are used to assemble level (0) items, level (2) items to assemble level (1) items, and so on. In other words, planned order releases for level (0) items would generate gross requirements for level (1) items.

Figure 16.7b shows pictorial bills of materials for two of the end items Bonnie's sells. These are "low-level-coded" BOMs, which means that each item always appears at the same level of the BOM, regardless of which end item it is being used in. For

Example 16.1

Suppose the net requirements for an item in weeks 5, 8, and 9 are 200 units, 250 units, and 100 units, respectively; the net requirements for all other weeks are zero. Also assume the ordering cost is $200, and the carrying cost per unit per week is $0.25. Determine the weekly planned order receipts with:

1. lot-for-lot sizing,

2. a fixed order quantity of 100 units, and

3. part-period balancing.

1. With lot-for-lot we would plan to receive exactly what is needed when it is needed, thus the planned order receipts would be zero units for all periods except weeks 5, 8, and 9. The planned order receipts would be 200 units in week 5, 250 units in week 8, and 100 units in week 9.

2. With a fixed order quantity of 100, we would plan to receive at least enough of the item to meet our net requirements in each period. Thus, we would have planned order receipts of zero in all periods except weeks 5, 8, and 9. In weeks 5, 8, and 9, the planned order receipts would be 200 units, 300 units, and 100 units, respectively. (Because the fixed lot size exceeded demand by fifty units in week 8, there would be fifty extra units available in week 9. And because the planned receipt for week 9 covers that week's demand, these

fifty units would also be available moving into week 10.)

3. With part-period balancing we would need to decide whether to order 200 units, 450 units, or 550 units in week 5. In any case the cost of the order would be $200. If we order 200 units, the holding cost would be $0.00 because we are ordering only the current period's net requirements. If we order 450 units, we will also incur 750 part-periods of inventory (for holding the 250 units for the three weeks from week 5 until week 8). At $0.25 per unit per week, the 750 part-periods would cost:

$$750 \times \$0.25 = \$187.5$$

If we order 550 units, we will incur 1150 part periods of inventory (by holding 250 units for three periods and 100 units for four periods). This would result in a holding cost of:

$$1150 \times \$0.25 = \$287.50$$

Because the cost of ordering and holding inventory resulting from the order are best balanced with the order of 450 units, the planned order receipts would be 450 units in week 5, 100 units in week 9, and zero units for all other periods. (Of course, if we could see the net requirements further into the future we would consider combining that demand with the planned order receipts for week 9.

Summary of planned order receipts:

Lot-Sizing Rule	1	2	3	4	5	6	7	8	9
Lot-for-Lot	0	0	0	0	200	0	0	250	100
Fixed Quantity of 100	0	0	0	0	200	0	0	300	100
Part-Period Balancing	0	0	0	0	450	0	0	0	100

Weekly Planned Order Receipts

example, notice that the candle fixture base appears at level (2) on the wall-mounted fixture's BOM, even though it could have been placed at level (1). Because level (2) is the highest level on which the candle fixture base could appear on the BOM for the table-mounted fixture, that part can appear no higher in any other BOM. An alternative way to represent this type of BOM uses indented text. The "indented BOMs" that correspond to the low-level-coded BOMs in Figure 16.7b are shown in Table 16.2.

From Master Schedule to Material Plan

Figure 16.8 shows the linkage between the master schedule for the end item "Triple-C-Table" (ct333) and the material plan for that item. The master schedule in this figure shows five orders for the ct333, which represent delivery commitments to customers. These product-service bundles must be provided in L4L fashion. Notice that all the commitments are for some multiple of seventy-five items, a common situation that results from the size of shipping containers. (The packaging used to ship the ct333 is a box designed to hold seventy-five fixtures.)

The orders on the master schedule are translated into gross requirements for the item in the bottom portion of Figure 16.8. This part of the material plan details how

Figure 16.7

(a) Bonnie's candle shop products and components

(a) *Traditional* **Table Family**   **(b)** *Traditional* **Wall Mount Family**

Level (0)

(c) *Contemporary* **Table Family**   **(d)** *Contemporary* **Wall Mount Family**

Level (1)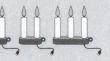

Level (2)

Level (3)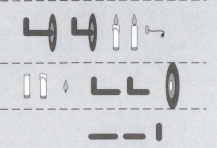

Figure 16.7

(b) Pictorial bills of materials for two types of candle fixtures

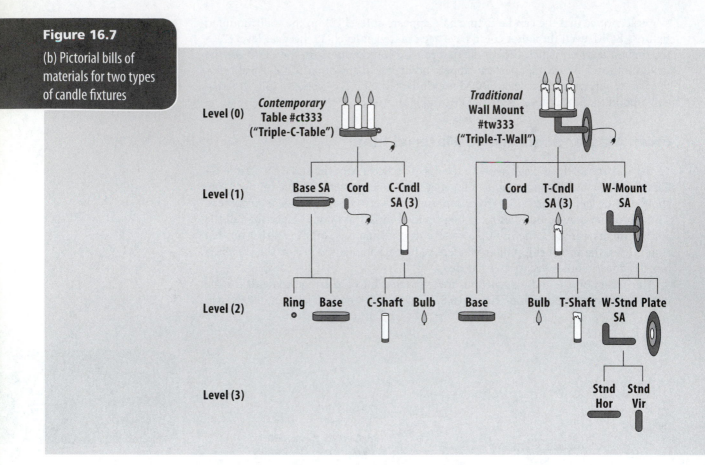

Bonnie's Candle Shop intends to fulfill its delivery promises. Inventory policies for the ct333 have been captured on the left side of the planning template. The item is assembled in the final assembly workstation in lots of seventy-five units; the estimated lead time required to fill an order is 1 week; current on-hand inventory is 130 units; and the company intends to keep a safety stock of 75 units on hand. Because of the company's lot-sizing policy, whenever the net requirement is positive, enough lots will be ordered to satisfy that demand, and planned order receipts will always be for some multiple of seventy-five.

You might wonder how Bonnie's could end up with 130 units of ct333 planned on hand for week 1. After all, the lot size is seventy-five, and with a safety stock level of seventy-five, you might expect all the numbers in this table to be multiples of seventy-five. If a box holds seventy-five fixtures, how could Bonnie's end up with a partial box of fifty-five (130 − 75) fixtures? This situation is not uncommon and can happen in different ways. Fixtures may have been lost because of quality problems that were discovered during final assembly. Fixtures may have been withdrawn for use as marketing samples, without being noted in the computer system. Or a customer may have returned the unused portion of an order because of quality problems. Even though demand for dependent demand inventory items can be calculated from the requirements for independent demand items, surprises are commonplace. Physical inventory counts often do not match computer records exactly.

Table 16.2

Indented Bills of Materials for Two Types of Candle Fixtures

Triple-C-Table (#ct333)

    Base Subassembly (Base SA)
        Ring
        Base

    Cord

    Contemporary Candle Subassembly (C-candle SA)
        Contemporary Shaft (C-shaft)
        Bulb

Triple-T-Wall (#tw333)

    Base

    Cord

    Traditional Candle Subassembly (T-candle SA)
        Traditional Shaft (T-shaft)
        Bulb

    Wall Mount Subassembly (WSA) Plate
        Arm
                Vertical Rod (V-rod)
                Horizontal Rod (H-rod)

Figure 16.9 shows the rest of the material plan for the ct333. The MRP links the planned order releases for the level (0) ct333 to gross requirements for all the level (1) materials used to make it. Thus, the planned order releases from Figure 16.8 (which are shown in the top rows of Figure 16.9) establish the gross requirements for the base SA, the cord, and the candle SA. Based on these gross requirements, planned order releases for level (1) items can be determined using the basic MRP formula described earlier. Planned order releases for level (1) items can then establish the gross requirements for level (2) items. For example, the planned order releases for the base SA are used to determine the gross requirements for ring and base components. So, too, planned order releases for the candle SA determine the gross requirements for shafts and bulbs.

Within each planning template, the MRP logic is essentially the same; only the inventory policies and the resulting numbers differ. For example, while the ct333 has a lot size of seventy-five, the base is ordered in lots of 400 units minimum; the ring is ordered lot-for-lot; and all the other parts have fixed lot sizes ranging from 50 to 4000 units. Because the cord is a common item in all the light fixtures, not just the ct333, its lot size is fairly large. This simple example shows the planning for a single end item. By the time the demand for all other end items is considered, the material plan for the cord will include many more large orders. Similarly, the large lot size for bulbs is warranted because bulbs are common to many items. If the rest of the items on the master schedule had been built into this example, the plan would call for many more bulbs to be ordered.

Figure 16.8

Master schedule and material requirements plan for the Triple-C-Table fixture final assembly

								Master Schedule									
							Week	1	2	3	4	5	6	7	8	9	10
							#ct333	500		325		300		250		750	

Work Center	Lot Size	Lead Time	On Hand	Safety Stock	Lower Level Code	Item ID	Week	1	2	3	4	5	6	7	8	9	10
							Gross Requirements	500	0	325	0	300	0	250	0	750	0
							Scheduled Receipts	450									
Final Assembly	75	1	130	75	0	#ct333	Planned On Hand 130	130	80	80	130	130	130	130	105	105	105
							Net Requirements	0	0	320	0	245	0	195	0	720	0
							Planned Order Receipts	0	0	375	0	300	0	225	0	750	0
							Planned Order Releases	0	375	0	300	0	225	0	750	0	0

Reducing Lumpiness and Lead Time

Notice in Figure 16.9 (on page 744) that the gross requirement of 750 units of end item ct333 in week 9 ultimately leads to all of the following planned order releases:

Week	Units
4	2400 C-shafts
	500 bases
	750 rings
6	1800 C-cndl SAs
	1200 cords
	750 base SAs
8	750 ct333s

Thus, work on the order actually begins 5 weeks before its delivery to the customer. If the company is working in a make-to-order mode, it might make sense to tell customers that their orders cannot be changed within 5 weeks of the due date. But that kind of policy can be hard for customers to understand. A typical order for fixtures might represent only 20 hours' worth of work in a value-adding system that employs many people, each working full-time. Indeed, with expediting, such an order might be completed in a day. Why, then, should a customer be satisfied with a 5-week lead time?

An alternative to this approach would be to adopt an assemble-to-order strategy. Two weeks could be cut off the lead time by keeping a stock of the candle SA and the base SA on hand for use in assembling end items. Demand for these subassemblies could be handled using the reorder point system described in Chapter 13.

In Figure 16.9 the weekly variation in the gross requirements of the level (0) item (final assembly) was much smaller than the corresponding variation in requirements for level (3) inventory items. Even though the material plan for the ct333 showed an order every other week, ranging in size from 250 to 750 items, only one order for the bulb was planned during the 10-week period and that was for 4000 units. Much like the bullwhip effect described in discussions of supply chain management earlier in this book, demand tends to become lumpier as you move to lower levels of the BOM.

Alamy Images

When a dry cleaner claims "Same Day Service," they base that claim on the normal daily demand for their services, not an ability to take infinite capacity.

Leveling the master schedule, as has been done in Figure 16.10, can help to reduce the lumpiness but will not eliminate the problem. By adding lot-for-lot ordering policies to a perfectly leveled master schedule, managers can remove the lumpiness at lower levels of the BOM. While that approach may make sense in theory, it is of little use in practice, because the whole idea behind MRP is to accommodate a variety of demand patterns and product-service bundles. The complexity of the value-adding systems where MRP is used can also make it costly to have a level master schedule which requires a large number of very small orders.

Managing MRP Systems

While MRP logic is quite simple, MRP systems are actually difficult to manage. Inventory levels for items at all levels of the BOM are continually changing: Any worker can remove items from inventory, process and change them, and replace items

Figure 16.9

Material requirements plan for the Triple-C-Table fixture

Work Center	Lot Size	Lead Time	On Hand	Safety Stock	Lower Level Code	Item ID	Week		1	2	3	4	5	6	7	8	9	10
Final Assembly	75	1	130	75	0	#ct333	Gross Requirements		500	0	325	0	300	0	250	0	750	0
							Scheduled Receipts		450									
							Planned On Hand	130	130	80	80	130	130	130	130	105	105	105
							Net Requirements		0	0	320	0	245	0	195	0	720	0
							Planned Order Receipts		0	0	375	0	300	0	225	0	750	0
							Planned Order Releases		0	375	0	300	0	225	0	750	0	0
							Week		1	2	3	4	5	6	7	8	9	10
Welding	50	2	410	20	1	Base SA	Gross Requirements		0	375	0	300	0	225	0	750	0	0
							Scheduled Receipts		0									
							Planned On Hand	410	410	410	35	35	35	35	60	60	60	60
							Net Requirements		0	0	0	285	0	210	0	710	0	0
							Planned Order Receipts		0	0	0	300	0	250	0	750	0	0
							Planned Order Releases		0	300	0	250	0	750	0	0	0	0
							Week		1	2	3	4	5	6	7	8	9	10
Purchasing	1200	2	465	80	1	Cord	Gross Requirements		0	375	0	300	0	225	0	750	0	0
							Scheduled Receipts		0									
							Planned On Hand	465	465	465	90	90	990	990	765	765	1215	1215
							Net Requirements		0	0	0	290	0	0	0	65	0	0
							Planned Order Receipts		0	0	0	1200	0	0	0	1200	0	0
							Planned Order Releases		0	1200	0	0	0	1200	0	0	0	0
							Week		1	2	3	4	5	6	7	8	9	10
Sub Assembly	1,800	2	240	120	2	C-cndl SA	Gross Requirements		0	1125	0	900	0	675	0	2250	0	0
							Scheduled Receipts		0	1800								
							Planned On Hand	240	240	240	915	915	1815	1815	1140	1140	690	690
							Net Requirements		0	0	0	105	0	0	0	1230	0	0
							Planned Order Receipts		0	0	0	1800	0	0	0	1800	0	0
							Planned Order Releases		0	1800	0	0	0	1800	0	0	0	0

Ring — Purchasing | L4L | 2 | 105 | 100 | 3

Week	1	2	3	4	5	6	7	8	9	10
Gross Requirements	0	300	0	250	0	750	0	0	0	0
Scheduled Receipts	0	375								
Planned On Hand 105	105	105	180	180	100	100	100	100	100	100
Net Requirements	0	0	0	170	0	750	0	0	0	0
Planned Order Receipts	0	0	0	170	0	750	0	0	0	0
Planned Order Releases	0	170	0	750	0	0	0	0	0	0

Base — Purchasing | 400 | 2 | 75 | 75 | 3

Week	1	2	3	4	5	6	7	8	9	10
Gross Requirements	0	300	0	250	0	750	0	0	0	0
Scheduled Receipts	0	400								
Planned On Hand 75	75	75	175	175	325	325	75	75	75	75
Net Requirements	0	0	0	150	0	500	0	0	0	0
Planned Order Receipts	0	0	0	400	0	500	0	0	0	0
Planned Order Releases	0	400	0	500	0	0	0	0	0	0

C-shaft — Purchasing | 2400 | 2 | 375 | 150 | 3

Week	1	2	3	4	5	6	7	8	9	10
Gross Requirements	0	1800	0	0	0	1800	0	0	0	0
Scheduled Receipts	0	2400								
Planned On Hand 375	375	375	975	975	975	975	1575	1575	1575	1575
Net Requirements	0	0	0	0	0	975	0	0	0	0
Planned Order Receipts	0	0	0	0	0	2400	0	0	0	0
Planned Order Releases	0	0	0	2400	0	0	0	0	0	0

Bulb — Purchasing | 4000 | 1 | 200 | 150 | 3

Week	1	2	3	4	5	6	7	8	9	10
Gross Requirements	0	1800	0	0	0	1800	0	0	0	0
Scheduled Receipts	0									
Planned On Hand 200	200	200	2400	2400	2400	2400	600	600	600	600
Net Requirements	0	1750	0	0	0	0	0	0	0	0
Planned Order Receipts	0	4000	0	0	0	0	0	0	0	0
Planned Order Releases	4000	0	0	0	0	0	0	0	0	0

Figure 16.10

Leveled master schedule and material requirements plan for the Triple-C-Table fixture final assembly

								Master Schedule									
							Week	1	2	3	4	5	6	7	8	9	10
							#ct333	213	213	213	213	213	213	213	213	213	213

Work Center	Lot Size	Lead Time	On Hand	Safety Stock	Lower Level Code	Item ID	Week	1	2	3	4	5	6	7	8	9	10
Final Assembly	75	1	130	75	0	#ct333	Gross Requirements	213	213	213	213	213	213	213	213	213	213
							Scheduled Receipts	225									
							Planned On Hand 130	130	142	79	91	103	115	127	139	76	88
							Net Requirements	0	146	209	197	185	173	161	149	212	200
							Planned Order Receipts	0	150	225	225	225	225	225	150	225	225
							Planned Order Releases	150	225	225	225	225	225	150	225	225	0

Example 16.2

The low-level-coded BOM for end item A is as follows:

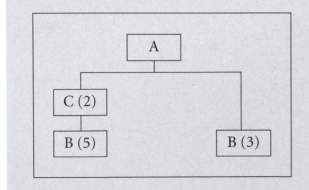

End item A has a lot-for-lot ordering policy, a lead time of 1 week, and gross requirements of 100 units in week 5 and 250 units in week 7. Currently, 20 units of item A are on hand. Component B has a 3-week lead time and a fixed-quantity lot size of 100 units. 200 units of B are currently on hand. Subassembly C has a lead time of 1 week, lot-for-lot ordering policy, and 300 units on hand.

Determine the Planned order releases for A, B, and C using standard MRP logic.

Note that the BOM is low level coded. This tells us we will prepare our plan for A first, then for C and finally for B. The resulting plan is as follows:

(continued)

Example 16.2

(*continued*)

Inventory Policies	Item A	Week 1	2	3	4	5	6	7
	Gross Requirements	0	0	0	0	100	0	250
	Scheduled Receipts							
LT=1 Week, Beginning On-Hand=20, Lot-for-Lot	Planned On Hand	20	20	20	20	20	0	0
	Net Requirements	0	0	0	0	80	0	250
	Planned Order Receipts	0	0	0	0	80	0	250
	Planned Order Releases	0	0	0	80	0	250	

Inventory Policies	Item C	Week 1	2	3	4	5	6	7
	Gross Requirements	0	0	0	160	0	500	0
	Scheduled Receipts							
LT=1 Week, Beginning On Hand=300, Lot-for-Lot	Planned On Hand	300	300	300	300	140	140	0
	Net Requirements	0	0	0	0	0	360	0
	Planned Order Receipts	0	0	0	0	0	360	0
	Planned Order Releases	0	0	0	0	360	0	

Inventory Policies	Item B	Week 1	2	3	4	5	6	7
	Gross Requirements	0	0	0	240	1800	750	0
	Scheduled Receipts							
LT=3 Weeks, Beginning On Hand=200, Lot-size=100	Planned On Hand	200	200	200	200	60	60	10
	Net Requirements	0	0	0	40	1740	690	0
	Planned Order Receipts	0	0	0	100	1800	700	0
	Planned Order Releases	100	1800	700	0			

in inventory. At times, however, even the most conscientious employees may forget to note their actions on the company computer. Occasionally, workers will purposely understate or overstate their output in order to manipulate their pay or work schedules. As for the bill of materials, when parts are temporarily unavailable, permanent changes may be made to the product without being noted in the computer file. Finally, the master schedule is generally made up of both forecasted demand and customer orders, either of which can change. As a result, the value of an MRP system is quite limited if a company cannot establish order and discipline in its operations and information gathering. One of the primary benefits of an MRP system, in fact, may be that it imposes discipline on complex environments, making them more understandable and manageable.

Choosing a System

Generally, there are two types of MRP systems, regenerative and net change. Regenerative MRP systems typically update the material plan once a week, usually over the weekend. Thus, orders that have come in during the week, changes in inventory levels that resulted from operations during the week, changes in orders, and shortages resulting from quality problems are not reflected in the material plan until the Monday morning following the change. On Monday morning, the MRP planner receives a clean set of planned orders that reflects all the prior week's activities. The regenerative approach to MRP is justified by the complexity of many manufacturing environments, whose thousands of parts, subassemblies, and end items require a great deal of computer processing time. Usually the plan is relatively close to actual figures throughout the week, and MRP planners can keep track of critical changes in inventory until a fresh computer run has been completed.

In "net change MRP systems," material plans are updated as new data becomes available. If a material shortage is noted in a shipment from a supplier, the net change system will note it immediately and adjust the material plans for all the items in which it is used. The major benefit of a net change system is this ability to make real-time adjustments. Yet real-time adjustments can also produce **system nervousness**, or problem-causing fluctuation in the material plan. When material plans are not stable and orders change frequently, workers and material planners tend not to trust the information they have been given. They might try to speed up production before an order gets canceled, or delay work on a difficult but important job in the hope it will be canceled or reduced. Alternatively, workers might hide some inventory in order to be prepared for order changes. Such behavior only worsens system nervousness. As a result, the regenerative approach is used more often.

Expediting Orders

Many companies that use MRP systems employ expeditors to walk a job through the facility and ensure on-time delivery. If asked, "Do you do any expediting here?" many managers respond with pride, "Oh yes! Every day. Customer satisfaction is very important to us!" Expediting, however, is a sign that an operation's planning and control system is not working as well as it should. If possible, expediting should be avoided, and the system should be adjusted so that it is not needed. When expeditors are given the authority to override scheduling decisions in any work area and place a customer's job at the head of the line, they throw a monkey wrench into a company's scheduling system. Expeditors introduce variability into a system that is already difficult enough to manage.

Combining MRP with JIT and TOC

Unlike JIT and theory of constraints (TOC), MRP systems do not have a built-in mechanism for reducing inventory over time in order to streamline operations. Think back to the analogy of the rocks and the river in Chapter 14 (see Figure 14.5 on page 642): MRP does not place any emphasis on lowering the water level to improve

System nervousness

A problem-causing fluctuation in the material plan.

the system. That does not mean that quality and improvement are irrelevant. Certainly, one of the most important considerations in an MRP system is whether computers are automating and facilitating unnecessary complexity. If, based on customer preferences, firms find that complexity is not warranted, they should eliminate it and move toward a TOC or JIT system through techniques such as group technology.

Many companies use some combination of MRP, JIT, and TOC in their operations planning and control. For example, highly effective closed loop MRP users can use such a system to guarantee JIT delivery to both internal and external customers. At the Kawasaki plant in Lincoln, Nebraska, JIT is used to schedule the production of roughly a dozen end items, including motorcycles, snowmobiles, and jet skis. MRP is used to do the material planning for these items, as it is in most TOC implementations so that both internal and external suppliers receive advance notice of material requirements on a weekly basis. Product deliveries are scheduled using a JIT pull system. Similarly, a Jergens factory in Cincinnati makes dozens of different soaps and lotions using MRP to schedule weekly material requirements as much as months in advance. Managers can still call a supplier the night before a delivery to adjust the required quantity upward or downward. The actual materials are pulled into the mixing operation using bins that serve as kanbans.

Applying MRP in Service Operations

While MRP is used primarily to support manufacturing operations, it is applicable to services as well. Many service operations require kits of tools or parts needed to complete a specific task. MRP can be quite useful in that context.

An article in the *Journal of Operations Management* (Steinberg, Khumawala, and Scamell 1982) described how the Park Plaza Hospital in Houston, Texas, used MRP to guarantee adequate supplies for its surgical suite. The data inputs required in this service application closely paralleled the inputs required in a manufacturing environment. Physicians who used the surgical suite were required to schedule their activity well in advance of the time of surgery; cancellations could not occur within a given period of the scheduled operation. This type of schedule was clearly analogous to the master schedule found in any operational context. The particular procedure being performed by a given physician was defined as the level (0) item. The schedule for these level (0) items was obtained by the advance notice that physicians were required to give.

The parallel to the bill of materials in this application was the preference sheet each physician filled out, indicating the instruments preferred for use in each of the procedures being performed. As each surgeon completed this form, the information needed to purchase the lower-level items became available. Because surgical operations cannot be stored, and many surgical instruments are sterilized and reused, inventory considerations were somewhat more complex than in a standard manufacturing operation. To calculate net requirements, managers had to subtract on-hand inventory, scheduled receipts, and sterilized items receipts from the gross requirements for an instrument. Using MRP provided several advantages to the Park Plaza Hospital:

▶ Assurance that materials would be available when needed

▶ Protection against over-investment in an inventory of facilitating goods

▶ Guidance in formulating and adjusting inventory reordering policies

▶ A way to analyze and control spending on supplies

Yield Management Systems

Many services are now employing yield management systems in order to more fully utilize their service capacity and maximize their revenue. These information systems require planners to generate a set of paired service-price offerings. They then gather data regarding customer transactions (sales and cancellations) as they occur. Managers are able to modify availability of the service-price offerings on the basis of current information, in order to maximize the revenue they obtain from their use of capacity.

American Airlines pioneered the use of yield management with their SABRE reservation system. At the outset, the airline required that all reservations be made through SABRE. This allowed the company to monitor the sale of seats at particular prices for its own flights and, to some extent, those of competitors. It could then alter the availability of the fares and seats on the basis of real-time demand information. If it looked as if there was insufficient demand for the expensive seats, more discounts could be offered. If it seemed that there was strong demand for expensive seats, the number of available discounted seats could be reduced. The system also allows the airline to modify its mix of flights on the basis of weather conditions and other factors that might lead to delays (or other lost revenue events) in particular airports.

The environments to which yield management systems apply are just as complex as those where MRP is used. One factor that adds complexity for airlines is that of connecting flights. Because passengers can get from point A to point B with many different flight combinations, the airline has to take into account the volume of traffic on each leg of the trip whenever a discount fare is offered. Additional complexity comes from the fact that many services have perishable inventory. (Services like hotels and airlines consider the seats on upcoming flights or the rooms for upcoming nights their inventory. Revenue from an unsold seat or hotel room is lost forever if the flight takes off or the reservation date passes.)

The success of yield management at American Airlines has led many other services to adopt the practice. It is most beneficial to service firms with:

▶ Relatively fixed capacity

▶ Perishable inventory

▶ Ability to sell their service in advance of consumption

▶ Ability to segment markets

▶ Fluctuating demand

▶ Low marginal sales costs

▶ High marginal costs to change capacity

Yield management is now widely used in the hotel industry, rental businesses, and travel industries—and with the advent of deregulation has even gained a foothold in electrical utilities.[1]

The growing use of yield management strategies has created new business opportunities and spawned companies that bargain for customers. There are now many clubs and newsletters that advise customers who seek to minimize the price they pay for services that are managed with yield management strategies. Priceline.com, for example, is a web-based business that allows customers to make an offer for a flight,

---

[1] Sheryl E. Kimes, "Yield Management: A Tool for Capacity-Constrained Service Firms," *Journal of Operations Management* 8, no. 4 (Oct. 1989): 348–363.

Satisfying Customers at United Airlines

An IBM RS6000/SP2 supercomputer, nicknamed "Deep Blue" by its developers, beat world chess champion Gary Kasparov in 1997. Now it's helping United Airlines determine how to price the seat you fly on your next trip. It is also helping United (and others like it are helping many airlines) find ways to better schedule their flights in order to maximize safety and economy. The parallel architecture of several data processors working together to form this new supercomputer vastly outperforms the older system where 12 processors worked in serial fashion and frequently became bogged down with an ever-increasing need for crunching data. The new system allows United to process more data concerning passenger demand, weather, mechanical problems, and schedule variation. More precise and timely information about these issues allows the airline to make better pricing and scheduling decisions, both of which are directly related to the bottom line.

The next time you fly, don't ask your fellow passengers what they paid for their ticket. The answers would probably upset you and could start a riot. The variance can be staggering. Many people feel booking ahead will get the best price. While airlines will offer discounts to people who book in advance, they also save seats for travelers to get where they need to go with little, if any, advance notice. Advance booking helps the airlines plan efficient use of equipment and helps cash flow. By contrast, these last-minute travelers (mostly business travelers) will pay very high fares, which means a lot of profit for the airline. The airlines also offer very deep discounts to fill remaining seats with another type of last-minute traveler, those looking for a cheap "getaway" who are very flexible about where they go. Deep Blue will help United use past demand for flights and moment-to-moment changes in advance bookings to help the airline decide how many seats to book in advance and how many to save for last-minute business travelers. Finally, it will also help them decide when to release those seats and free them for impulse buyers.

Not all that unlike the complexities of a manufacturing environment where MRP might be applicable, issues that make the airline situation complex include the 3,000 different flights, passengers with different destinations or origins sharing a leg of a connecting flight, volume between various destinations and points of origin, and the sometimes unpredictable way in which passengers book their flights. The old system could only look at the flight as a whole and aggregated a lot of the details based upon average profiles for that flight. The new system, able to process more data and faster, can produce more precise information by including all 350,000 different paths that passengers will take each day. Decisions are now made faster and based upon much more certainty than before. Using yield management to more completely fill each plane, improves revenues, and it can be argued that better utilization of seats will help everyone in the long run.

When it comes to scheduling the airline, decisions are made at operations control center that also depend upon fast availability of reliable information. Mechanical problems, the weather, and last-minute bottlenecks at an airport can make life very difficult for those making the schedule and executing it. Art Pappas, American Airlines managing director of operations control, said, "We want to minimize customer inconvenience and maximize profit." As an example, when weather causes a problem at an airport that limits the window on flights in and out, then a lot of information is needed quickly. The goal is to make sound decisions that keep the impact on passengers to a minimum. That information would include weather forecasts estimating the duration or the severity of the weather's impact, flights due in during the affected time, and the flights due out during that time. Of the flights due in, a distinction is also made between those that are already in the air and those still on the ground. Of those due out, another issue to note is where passengers are making connections. Mechanical problems that take a plane out of service can create similar problems. Just like the issue of pricing, faster computers that can provide more precise information based upon more specific data makes the scheduling process more timely and more exact, thus more effective.

Source: Adapted from "IBM's Deep Blue Takes to the Skies," *Chicago Tribune*, Business Technology section, Nov. 17, 1997, reporter John Schmetlzer; and "The Inexact Science of Keeping an Airline on Schedule," *Wall Street Journal*, Sept. 11, 1996, reporter Scott McCartney

REC CENTER DILEMMA

Cheryl's Dilemma:

Cheryl has often wondered whether there is anything she can do about customers who arrive late or do not show up for an appointment because these customer behaviors result in long delays for other patients and lost revenue for the medical practices. She has been intrigued by the idea that yield management might be part of a solution in practices where appointments (and not emergencies) are the primary schedule drive. At the same time, she has been reluctant to try it because she is afraid of the impact it could have on waiting times and/or customer satisfaction. Do you think yield management would be a good idea for her doctors' offices that are appointment scheduled? Why? Or, why not?

hotel room, or other service within particular timing parameters. Service providers then have the opportunity to accept or reject the customer's bid within a fixed period of time.

Yield management allows companies to tailor the use of their capacity to specific customer preference. In Chapter 2, we suggested that companies cannot be all things to all customers and therefore needed to focus their value-adding systems on a specific set of competitive priorities. In the context of yield management, however, an airline can provide different value propositions within the context of one service. For example, airlines can offer cheap fares for customers who just want to get away but do not care so much about when and where they travel. At the same time, they can command top dollar from customers, potentially with identical iteneraries, who have to reach a specific destination and must travel within a specific window of time. The yield management system allows airlines to meet the requirements of both types of customers using their single value-adding system.

Supply Chain Impact of an MRP System

Figure 16.11 describes some of the supply chain impacts of MRP planning and control systems. As a rule, MRP users interact with customers and suppliers on an order-by-order basis. Because MRP users make planning and control decisions order by order, they must track orders and monitor quality on the same basis. This approach generates a lot of information to monitor, and keeping that information current and accurate is difficult. Because of the weekly regeneration system most companies use and the decentralized approach to scheduling that is inherent in MRP, total lead times on customer orders tend to be long.

Careful product design can improve lead times in an MRP system. The flatter the BOM, the fewer the steps required to create the product-service bundle. Total lead times are shorter and the system is easier to manage with a flat, wide BOM than with a deep, narrow BOM.

Suppliers of MRP users need to track quality by order, maintain accurate inventory records (so that their shipments do not come up short), and promptly communicate foreseeable shortages or delays. From a structural perspective, suppliers can greatly facilitate their interactions with MRP firms by using information systems that allow them to receive or anticipate orders electronically via some form of electronic data interchange (EDI). Such systems allow customers to obtain updates on an order's progress when needed. Updates to item lead times, perhaps based on material shortages or capacity considerations, can also be taken into account, and changes in the BOM, inventory status, or schedule can be passed on easily. For all the same reasons that MRP users find a flat BOM beneficial, suppliers do as well.

Like suppliers, customers of MRP users must interact with them one order at a time. They, too, must assess incoming quality order by order, implement compatible information systems, and flatten their BOMs. Unlike suppliers, however, customers

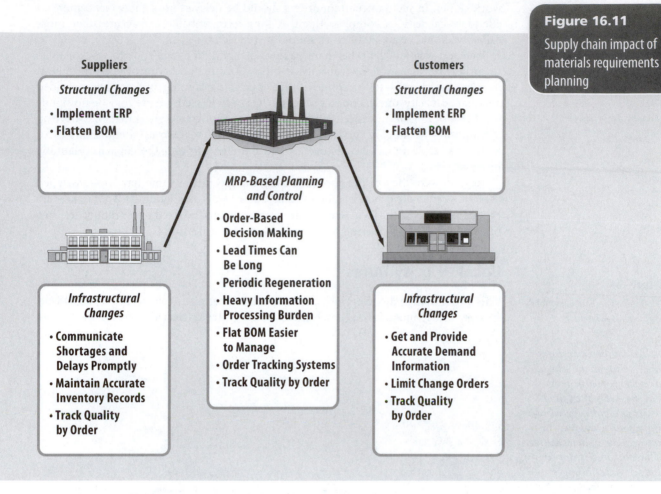

Figure 16.11

Supply chain impact of
materials requirements
planning

drive the MRP system's material planning decisions. Timely and accurate demand information and restraint in changing orders is essential in an MRP customer.

Detailed Scheduling in an MRP Environment

Once the material requirements have been calculated by the MRP system, orders may be released to specific work centers by the MRP planners. This assignment of work to specific resources is referred to as *loading*. Two approaches to loading exist: finite loading and infinite loading.

Finite loading limits the amount of work that is released to a given work center on the basis of capacity considerations. One simple way to do this is with **input/output control**, a system that monitors the work assigned to a resource (input) and the work completed by a resource (output). Input/output control can also be applied to a group of resources or a whole facility. It is based on the premise that over time, the inputs and outputs at any work center should balance out. If, over an extended period of time, the input rate is greater than the output rate, a large backlog of work accumulates in the

Finite loading

The process which limits the amount of work that is released to a given work center on the basis of capacity considerations.

Input/output control

A system that monitors the work assigned to a resource (input) and the work completed by a resource (output).

work center. In such a situation, orders should be delayed until the work center has adequate capacity to complete them. A long-term imbalance indicates that more capacity should be added or work should be turned away.

Infinite loading, on the other hand, allows planners to assign jobs to work centers regardless of their available capacity. If other planning and control tasks have been handled effectively—for example, if the aggregate planning process has provided adequate capacity and the master schedule has been leveled—there may be no significant risk of long-term capacity imbalances. Even though a work center may develop a temporary backlog, in the long term it will be able to keep up. Requirements for additional capacity can be discovered and handled through the capacity planning process.

Regardless of the loading approach used, the specific jobs that have been assigned to a work center are generally scheduled based on local considerations. That is, jobs are ranked in terms of the local work center's priorities and worked on in that order. Two basic methods of prioritizing work are local priority rules and Gantt charts.

Local Priority Rules

This process of sequencing jobs through a work center is referred to as **dispatching**. In complex manufacturing environments, a job's characteristics are often used to

Infinite loading

A process which allows planners to assign jobs to work centers regardless of their available capacity.

Dispatching

The process of sequencing jobs through a work center.

When complexity creates uncertainty in the schedule, a backlog of work or an "in" basket is often used to act as a buffer between the resource and the uncertainty of the schedule. The more uncertainty in the schedule, the bigger the backlog needed to ensure that the resource stays busy.

Royalty-Free/Corbis

determine its relative priority. The rules used to assign priorities to jobs based on their characteristics are called **priority rules**, **dispatching rules**, or **sequencing rules**. Let's consider several commonly used dispatching rules and their benefits and drawbacks.

Priority rules dispatching rules, sequencing rules

Rules used to assign priorities to jobs.

FIRST COME, FIRST SERVED

The first-come, first-served (FCFS) rule is particularly useful in service settings, where the customer considers "cutting in line" unfair. If you are waiting in line at a local restaurant that does not take reservations, you would be upset if the town mayor, who arrived after you, was seated before you. Under FCFS, it does not matter how hungry you may be, the time you need to leave the restaurant, how important the mayor is, or who eats more quickly. In other words, FCFS does not take into account the urgency of a job based on due date criteria, the importance of a job, efficiency in sequencing jobs, or any other relevant criteria.

EARLIEST DUE DATE

This earliest due date (EDD) dispatching rule gives highest priority to the job with the nearest due date, and ranks job priority on that basis alone. Thus, the job that is due tomorrow has a higher priority than the job that is due next week or next month. When customers are particularly sensitive to late deliveries, this rule serves them well, presuming that all jobs have relatively uniform processing times. The weakness of this rule is that it does not consider efficiency in sequencing and ignores the time required to complete a job. For example, it gives a higher priority to a job due 2 days from now that requires 1 day's work than to a job due 3 days from now that requires 5 days' work.

MINIMUM SLACK

Slack is the difference between the time until a job is due and the processing time required to complete it. Obviously, jobs with negative slack are behind schedule; those jobs might require expediting to get caught up. Under the minimum slack (MS) rule, jobs are sequenced based on their slack: Those with the most slack receive the lowest priority and those with the least slack receive the highest priority. Though this sequencing rule was devised to overcome one of the stated weaknesses of EDD, like EDD it ignores efficiency issues.

CRITICAL RATIO

The critical ratio (CR) is the time until a job is due divided by the processing time required to complete it. A 4-day job that's due in 5 days would have a CR = 5/4, or 1.25. In the critical ratio rule, jobs are sequenced from lowest CR to highest CR. Those with a CR less than one are considered behind schedule. Like MS, this sequencing rule is meant to overcome one of the stated weaknesses of EDD, but it too ignores efficiency.

SHORTEST PROCESSING TIME

The shortest processing time (SPT) dispatching rule gives highest priority to the job with the shortest processing time, allowing a work center to process a large number of jobs very quickly. This rule generally increases efficiency and can have a positive effect on an operation's cash flow. In fact, it can be proven mathematically that SPT minimizes average flow time, or the average amount of time that a job spends in a work center, including waiting and processing times. Flow time is highly correlated with inventory levels. For this reason, it can serve as a proxy for efficiency. This rule is especially helpful when a work center is close to the beginning of a job routing, because it allows work to move forward quickly to other work centers. Though minimizing flow time has a positive effect on due date performance, SPT does not explicitly consider due dates in the sequencing of jobs. Thus, if processing times vary, long jobs will receive a low priority and short jobs will continually take precedence over them.

LONGEST PROCESSING TIME

The longest processing time (LPT) sequencing rule is often used by those who want to attack the toughest job first and get it out of the way. Because it is diametrically opposed to SPT, this rule could not be recommended for either efficiency or due date performance. Using LPT in work centers that are early in a job's routing is a bad idea, because the other work centers might become starved for work. For example, in a copy shop with a typesetter and a printer, the time required to print a job is generally independent of the time required to do the typesetting. So if the typesetter picked a really tough job to work on first and took a lot of time to complete it, the printer might quickly run out of work. Indeed, apart from the psychological benefit some workers derive from getting a tough job over with, there is little justification for using LPT.

Local Priority Rules: An Application

Figure 16.12 shows the tasks waiting to be scheduled at the paint booth in Luis's factory. Six batches of furniture need to be painted; they vary in size, due date, expected time to

Figure 16.12

Jobs waiting to be processed at Luis's painting/finishing booth

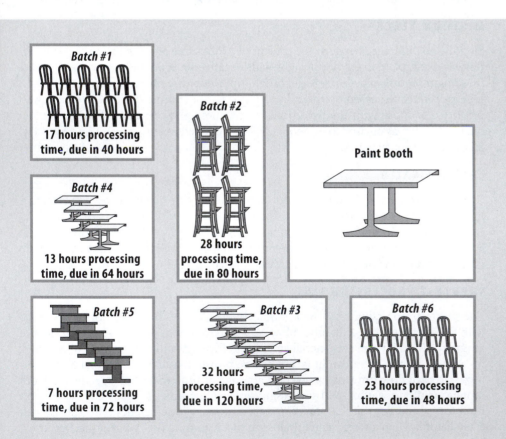

Batch #1
17 hours processing time, due in 40 hours

Batch #2
28 hours processing time, due in 80 hours

Batch #4
13 hours processing time, due in 64 hours

Paint Booth

Batch #5
7 hours processing time, due in 72 hours

Batch #3
32 hours processing time, due in 120 hours

Batch #6
23 hours processing time, due in 48 hours

completion, and even their location in the work center. Workers might have to move one job aside to get access to another job. This picture illustrates why jobs in complex, functionally organized manufacturing environments typically spend 90% or more of their lead time waiting in line, and less than 10% of their lead time actually being worked on. As more jobs arrive at the booth, the competition for this resource intensifies.

Figure 16.13a–f shows the schedules that result from using six different dispatching rules to order the jobs waiting at the paint booth. Notice that the total processing time for all the jobs that have been loaded on the work area, called the **make span**, is 120 hours. Regardless of the sequence in which the six batches are processed, 120 hours worth of work will be required. By contrast, **flow time** (the time a job will spend in the work area including both waiting time and processing time) is a function of the sequencing of jobs. If the crew at the paint booth can complete several jobs quickly, fewer jobs will have a lengthy wait and the flow time will be relatively short. Dividing total flow time by the make span yields the average number of jobs in the system.

In the discussion of sequencing rules starting on page 754, we saw that SPT minimizes average flow time. That result can be seen in Figure 16.13: SPT yields the lowest total flow time and the lowest average flow time. Study Figure 16.13 and you are likely to recognize the following:

▶ If Luis wants to schedule the paint booth on the basis of efficiency, he will use SPT.

▶ If Luis is more concerned about due date performance, he will notice that EDD provides the lowest average lateness with this mix of jobs. While EDD, MS, and SPT provide comparable results, they are far better than the other choices. Both EDD and MS are slightly better than SPT in regard to average lateness with this set of jobs. Interestingly, in this case, SPT provides better due date performance than CR. One downside to using SPT in this setting might arise if the booth must frequently process jobs requiring less than seven hours. Because batch 3 requires 7 hours of processing time, it would never move from the back of the line under SPT. Sooner or later, the customer for that job would complain, and batch 3 would have to be expedited.

Make span

The total processing time for all the jobs that have been loaded on the work area.

Flow time

The time a job will require to complete the sequence of activities needed.

Figure 16.13

(a) Results of six different local priority rules

(a) First Come, First Served (FCFS)

	Processing Time (hours)	Due (hours from now)	Flow Time (hours)	Late (hours)
Batch 1	17	40	17	0
Batch 2	28	80	45	0
Batch 3	32	120	77	0
Batch 4	13	64	90	26
Batch 5	7	72	97	25
Batch 6	23	48	120	72
			Average Flow Time (hours)	**Average Lateness (hours)**
			74.33	20.50

Figure 16.13

(b–d) Results of six different local priority rules

(b) Shortest Processing Time (SPT)

	Processing Time (hours)	Due (hours from now)	Flow Time (hours)	Late (hours)
Batch 5	7	72	7	0
Batch 4	13	64	20	0
Batch 1	17	40	37	0
Batch 6	23	48	60	12
Batch 2	28	80	88	8
Batch 3	32	120	120	0
			Average Flow Time (hours)	**Average Lateness (hours)**
			55.33	3.33

(c) Longest Processing Time (LPT)

	Processing Time (hours)	Due (hours from now)	Flow Time (hours)	Late (hours)
Batch 3	32	120	32	0
Batch 2	28	80	60	0
Batch 6	23	48	83	35
Batch 1	17	40	100	60
Batch 4	13	64	113	49
Batch 5	7	72	120	48
			Average Flow Time (hours)	**Average Lateness (hours)**
			84.67	32.00

(d) Earliest Due Date (EDD)

	Processing Time (hours)	Due (hours from now)	Flow Time (hours)	Late (hours)
Batch 1	17	40	17	0
Batch 6	23	48	40	0
Batch 4	13	64	53	0
Batch 5	7	72	60	0
Batch 2	28	80	88	8
Batch 3	32	120	120	0
			Average Flow Time (hours)	**Average Lateness (hours)**
			63.00	1.33

Figure 16.13

(e–f) Results of six
different local
priority rules

(e) MIN Slack (MS)

	Processing Time (hours)	Due (hours from now)	Slack (hours)	Flow Time (hours)	Late (hours)
Batch 1	17	40	23	17	0
Batch 6	23	48	25	40	0
Batch 4	13	64	51	53	0
Batch 2	28	80	52	81	1
Batch 5	7	72	65	88	16
Batch 3	32	120	88	120	0
				Average Flow Time (hours)	Average Lateness (hours)
				66.50	2.83

(f) Critical Ratio (CR)

	Processing Time (hours)	Due (hours from now)	Critical Ratio	Flow Time (hours)	Late (hours)
Batch 6	23	48	2.09	23	0
Batch 1	17	40	2.35	40	0
Batch 2	28	80	2.86	68	0
Batch 3	32	120	3.75	100	0
Batch 4	13	64	4.92	113	49
Batch 5	7	72	10.29	120	48
				Average Flow Time (hours)	Average Lateness (hours)
				77.33	16.17

Gantt Charts

Schedules can be displayed graphically using **Gantt charts**, or bar graphs that show a resource's scheduled work and available time. Figure 16.14 shows the Gantt chart for Luis's paint booth based on the FCFS rule. This simple figure shows the planned schedule at only one resource. Other versions of Gantt charts include both the planned schedule and time spent at the resource to date, allowing operators to see whether they are behind schedule or ahead.

Multiple resource Gantt charts can also be created to track the progress of a job through its routing. In fact, some companies use a Gantt chart as the weekly plan for their operation, using it to predict and track a job's progress through the factory.

Gantt chart

Bar graphs that show a resource's scheduled area and available time. By displaying the planned timing of activities on a time line, team members recognize what activities are really critical and how well they are keeping up with their project's schedule.

Example 16.3

Corporate Event Management, a company that processes group ticket orders for a variety of concerts and sporting events has the following set of jobs to process.

Customer/Job Sequence Number	Date Order Received	Hours Till Packet Due	Processing Time in Hours
A/200310001	10/05/03	5	2
A/200310002	10/05/03	13	4
B/200310004	10/06/03	13	5
C/200310003	10/06/03	4	2
D/200310005	10/05/03	10	8

Determine the average lateness, number of late jobs, and average flow time for a

1. The job sequence that minimizes average flow time

2. The job sequence resulting from the EDD priority rule

3. The job sequence resulting from the minimum slack priority rule

Wherever a tiebreaker is needed to assign priority between jobs use FCFS as the tiebreaker.

Solution:

1. The sequence that minimizes average flow time is SPT. The sequence and flow time and lateness calculations are as follows:

Customer/Job Sequence Number	Date Order Received	Processing Time in Hours	Hours Till Packet Due	Flow Time	Lateness
A/200310001	10/05/03	2	5	2	0
C/200310003	10/06/03	2	4	4	0
A/200310002	10/05/03	4	13	8	0
B/200310004	10/06/03	5	13	13	0
D/200310005	10/05/03	8	10	21	11

The average flow time is 9.6 hours. (This is simply the average of the five numbers in the column labeled "Flow Time.") The average lateness is 2.2 hours. (This is the average of the five numbers in the column labeled "Lateness.") One of the five jobs was late.

2. The EDD sequence and its flow time and lateness calculations are:

Customer/Job Sequence Number	Date Order Received	Processing Time in Hours	Hours Till Packet Due	Flow Time	Lateness
C/200310003	10/06/03	2	4	2	0
A/200310001	10/05/03	2	5	4	0
D/200310005	10/05/03	8	10	12	2
A/200310002	10/05/03	4	13	16	3
B/200310004	10/06/03	5	13	21	8

Example 16.3

(continued)

The average flow time is 11 hours, the average lateness is 2.6 hours, and three of the five jobs were late.

3. The minimum slack sequence and its flow time and lateness calculations are:

Customer/Job Sequence Number	Date Order Received	Processing Time in Hours	Hours Till Packet Due	Slack	Flow Time	Lateness
C/200310003	10/06/03	2	4	2	2	0
D/200310005	10/05/03	8	10	2	10	0
A/200310001	10/05/03	2	5	3	12	7
B/200310004	10/06/03	5	13	8	17	4
A/200310002	10/05/03	4	13	9	21	8

The average flow time is 12.4 hours, the average lateness is 3.8 hours, and three of the five jobs were late.

Summary: Notice, in this case, that SPT not only has the lowest average flow time, it also performs better than the supposedly due date sensitive rules in terms of average lateness, and number of late jobs.

Figure 16.14

Gantt chart for Luis's paint/finishing booth (first come, first served)

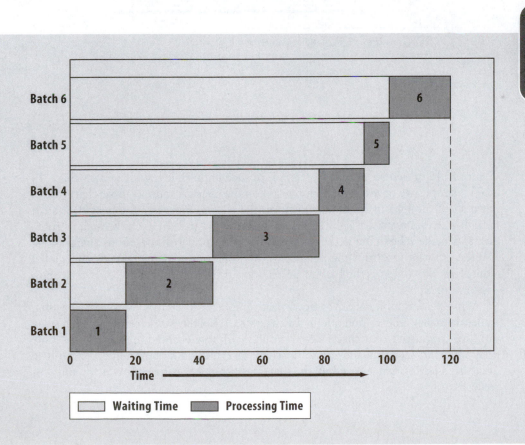

Batch 6 — 6
Batch 5 — 5
Batch 4 — 4
Batch 3 — 3
Batch 2 — 2
Batch 1 — 1

Time

☐ Waiting Time   ▨ Processing Time

Figure 16.15

Gantt chart showing progress of "Batch #1"

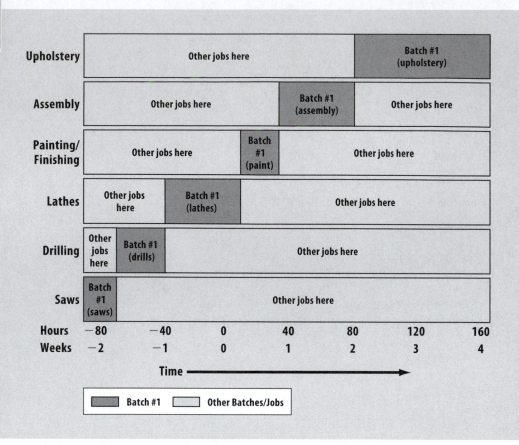

Figure 16.15

Gantt chart showing progress of "Batch #1"

Figure 16.15 presents a simplified example of such a multiple resource Gantt chart. To keep it simple, we have only shown one job on the chart. A more realistic chart would have all of the jobs in the shop shown on the chart. Obviously, the benefit of such a multiple resource chart is the ability to track the progress of a job through its routing and make scheduling decisions based on both local considerations (what is the highest priority job from the perspective of work center performance) and global considerations (what is the highest priority job from the perspective of overall shop performance).

A recent development in computerized graphical interfaces for Gantt charting, called **leitstands**, allows operations managers to schedule work centers and display multiple resource Gantt charts electronically. With the leitstand, managers can easily play "what-if?" scenarios and adjust the schedules at individual work centers to improve a facility's performance based on due date performance, average flow time, and cost criteria.

Leitstands

A recent development in computerized graphical interfaces which allows operations managers to schedule work centers and display multiple resource charts electronically.

SUMMARY

Material requirements planning (MRP) is a computerized planning and control system that determines the need for dependent demand items and the timing of their orders directly from the master schedule. It is best suited for use in complex value-adding systems such as job shops, where the process is functionally organized and customer expectations are quite diverse.

In complex value-adding systems with a lot of variety in its product-service bundles, communication between operations and other functions is essential. For marketing, making a single sale might entail multiple conversations with finance and operating personnel to price and schedule a customer's desired order. For operations to successfully complete an order, they might need to verify a number of different customer preferences with marketing. Accounting personnel will be challenged to keep up with the multitude of different items that could be inventoried on an ongoing basis. The complexity of the environment makes communication on customer preferences critically important on each order processed.

The planning and control system that generally is used in MRP systems is an order-based system. For each order from a customer that is placed on the master schedule, it determines when to order the parts, components, and subassemblies that are required. Based on the timing of these orders, the system can use capacity requirements planning (CRP) to verify that adequate capacity exists to accomplish the master schedule. Ultimately, all of the orders for end items and the dependent demand items associated with each end item must be released to work centers through a facility loading process. These orders must then be scheduled in each work center.

The MRP logic is simple. Gross requirements for independent demand items are found on the master schedule. For other items, gross requirements are a function of planned orders for the items of which they are a part. MRP programs convert gross requirements to net requirements by accounting for planned on-hand inventory and scheduled receipts. When the net requirements are positive, planned receipts will be scheduled by placing an order according to a defined lot-sizing rule. Finally, planned orders have to occur a specified period of time in advance of planned receipts. This period of time—between when orders are placed and when they are received—is called the lead time.

If the MRP logic is simple, managing in the MRP environment is not. MRP output is only as good as the input data. There is always some uncertainty surrounding the master schedule, inventory records are very difficult to keep up-to-date and accurate, and even bill of materials files can contain faulty information. As a consequence, a major responsibility for management in firms using MRP is to enforce a disciplined approach to decision making and record keeping. In fact, many experts agree that one of the major benefits of MRP is that it forces such discipline on its users.

The primary supply chain impact of a firm's use of MRP is that interaction with customers and suppliers is generally order driven. Companies need effective order tracking systems in order to field questions of suppliers and customers regarding their business. Quality must be assessed on an order-by-order basis. Payments and terms are also generally handled on an order-by-order basis. Enterprise resources planning systems can help to improve the performance of the supply chain. These systems that allow electronic interaction between companies help by giving decision makers access to more data than they would otherwise see and in a more timely way. Design initiatives that flatten a product-service bundle's bill of materials (BOM) are also helpful to customers of a supply chain, because they shorten delivery lead times.

Detailed scheduling in environments where MRP is used generally happens one work center at a time. Little coordination of schedules across a facility is seen. Instead, jobs are sequenced through individual work centers and the materials are pushed on to the next point in their routing, where they will eventually meet up with an order. The sequence in which orders are processed is often determined using a local dispatching rule, which is chosen on the basis of the type of performance measurement that is stressed in the work center. For example, if efficiency and cash flow are the primary performance measures, the shortest processing time (SPT) sequencing rule is a logical choice. When due date performance is the primary measure, some other rule such as earliest due date, minimum slack, or critical ratio might be used. Frequently, Gantt charts are also used to display the planned schedule as well as progress against that schedule.

KEY TERMS

Bill of materials (BOM), 735
Capacity requirements planning
   (CRP), 733
Closed loop MRP users, 733
Dispatching, 754
Dispatching rules, 755
Expediting, 734
Finite loading, 753

Flow time, 757
Gantt chart, 759
Infinite loading, 754
Input/output control, 753
Inventory status file (ISF), 735
Leitstands, 762
Loading, 733
Make span, 757

Manufacturing resources planning
   (MRP II), 730
Material requirements planning
   (MRP), 726
Priority rules, 755
Sequencing rules, 755
System nervousness, 748
Yield management systems, 726

SOLVED PROBLEMS

1. Luis is currently using a lot-for-lot approach to schedule assembly for a popular table. However, he is considering an override of the system based upon a "part-period balancing" approach. He is afraid that given the frequency with which the table is scheduled over the coming few weeks, he will spend too much in setup costs as opposed to the inventory cost of that result from combining multiple orders. Assume the assembly department has a $350 setup cost. Luis estimates it will cost $2 per week to carry an assembled table in inventory. There is a 1-week lead time for the assembly department. Given the following MRP inventory record for the table:

Table #48 (oak round traditional)

Week	1	2	3	4	5	6	7	8	9	10
Gross Requirements	150	250	150	100	50	50	150	50	50	100
Scheduled Receipts	150									
Planned On Hand 0	0	0	0	0	0	0	0	0	0	0
Net Requirements	0	250	150	100	50	50	150	50	50	100
Planned Order Receipts	0	250	150	100	50	50	150	50	50	100
Planned Order Releases	250	150	100	50	50	150	50	50	100	0

a) What would be the setup cost associated with using lot-for-lot over the course of this schedule?

b) What would be the inventory cost associated with using a "part-period balancing" approach to schedule the tables?

c) What would be the cost of setups and carrying inventory estimated for that schedule? What would you suggest to Luis?

Solution:

a) There would be $3150 in setup costs for nine orders over that period.

b) Ordering only 250 in Week 1 will mean no additional inventory.
Ordering 400 in Week 1 will mean $300 in inventory (150 × $2 × 1 week).
Ordering 500 in Week 1 will mean $700 in inventory (150 × $2 × 1 week + 100 × $2 × 2 weeks).

Result: As adding Week 3's demand to the order costs more in incremental carrying costs ($400) than the cost of an additional setup ($350), order only 400 in Week 1.

Ordering 100 in Week 3 will mean no additional inventory.

Ordering 150 in Week 3 will mean $100 in inventory (50 × $2 × 1 week).

Ordering 200 in Week 3 will mean $300 in inventory (50 × $2 × 1 week + 50 × $2 × 2 weeks).

Ordering 350 in Week 3 will mean $1200 in inventory (50 × $2 × 1 week + 50 × $2 × 2 weeks + 150 × $2 × 3 weeks).

Result: As adding Week 6's demand to the order costs more in incremental carrying costs ($900) than the cost of an additional setup ($350), order only 200 in Week 3.

Ordering 150 in Week 6 will mean no additional inventory.

Ordering 200 in Week 6 will mean $100 in inventory (50 × $2 × 1 week)

Ordering 250 in Week 6 will mean $300 in inventory (50 × $2 × 1 week + 50 × $2 × 2 weeks).

Ordering 350 in Week 6 will mean $900 in inventory (50 × $2 × 1 week + 50 × $2 × 2 weeks + 100 × $2 × 3 weeks).

Result: As adding Week 9's demand to the order costs more in incremental carrying costs ($600) than the cost of an additional setup ($350), order only 250 in Week 6.

Ordering 100 in week 9 will mean no additional inventory.

Result: Order 100 in Week 9.

c) The resulting schedule would be:

Week	Week 1	Week 2	Week 3	Week 4	Week 5	Week 6	Week 7	Week 8	Week 9	Week 10
Gross Requirements	150	250	150	100	50	50	150	50	50	100
Scheduled Receipts	150									
Planned On Hand 0	0	0	150	0	100	50	0	100	50	0
Net Requirements		250	0	100			150			100
Planned Order Receipts	0	400	0	200	0	0	250	0	0	100
Planned Order Releases	400	0	200	0	0	250	0	0	100	0

The resulting costs would be:

Four setups × $350 + $900 in inventory carrying costs = $2300. Thus, you should suggest the part-period balancing approach, as it saves $300 over the period of the schedule.

2. The Peter's Pliers Producers Co. makes the deluxe pliers (#101) pictured below and described by the pictorial bill of material.

   a) What would the indented bill of material look like for this model?

   b) How many of each part would be required to make 100 pairs of pliers?

Pictorial BOM:

Solution:

It appears that Peter's Pliers buys both top and bottom parts that are stamped out of steel. They drill holes in both the top and bottom part then assemble each of the drilled parts to on of two identical plastic sleeves. The drilled and sleeved parts are then assembled into the finished pliers with a purchased rivet.

a) Indented BOM:

Pliers (101)

  (1) Drilled sleeved upper (UDS101)

    (1) Drilled upper (UD101)

      (1) Blank (UB101)

    (1) Sleeve (S100)

  (1) Drilled sleeved bottom (BDS101)

    (1) Drilled bottom (BD101)

      (1) Blank (UB101)

    (1) Sleeve (S100)

  (1) Rivet (R100)

b) Pliers (101)—100

Drilled sleeved upper (UDS101)—100

Drilled upper (UD101)—100

Rivet (R100)

Drilled sleeved bottom (BDS101)—100

Drilled bottom (BD101)—100

Blank (UB101)—200

Sleeve (S100)—200

3. Consider the following indented bill of material for a high-backed chair made in Luis's factory:

Chair (#244h)

Chair back (#200bh)

    (1) Back frame (#200bhf)

    (75) Caning slats (#4)

(1) Chair seat

    (1) Seat frame (#200sf)

    (50) Caning slats (#4)

(4) Chair legs (#200lc)

    (4) Leg castors (#24)

    (4) Leg base (#200l)

(4) Bolts (#18)

(4) Nuts (#12)

a) What would the material list look like if an order of 150 chairs was placed?

b) What is the lower level code for each item?

c) If I already had a batch of seventy-five seats in WIP, how would that change the answer to (a)?

Solution:

a) 150 Chairs (#244h)
    150 Chair backs (#200bh)
    150 Chair seats
    600 Chair legs (#200lc)
    600 Bolts (#18)
    600 Nuts (#12)
    150 Back frames (#200bhf)
    150 Seat frames (#200sf)
    18750 Caning slats (#4)
    600 Leg castors (#24)
    600 Leg base (#200l)

b) 0 Chairs (#244h)
    1 Chair backs (#200bh)
    1 Chair seats
    1 Chair legs (#200lc)

1 Bolts (#18)
1 Nuts (#12)
2 Back frames (#200bhf)
2 Seat frames (#200sf)
2 Caning slats (#4)
2 Leg castors (#24)
2 Leg base (#200l)

c) 150 Chairs (#244h)
    150 Chair backs (#200bh)
    75 Chair seats
    600 Chair legs (#200l)
    600 Bolts (#18)
    600 Nuts (#12)
    150 Back frames (#200bhf)
    75 Seat frames (#200sf)
    15000 Caning slats (#4)
    600 Leg castors (#24)
    600 Leg base (#200l)

4. The master schedule and inventory information for the chair described in #2 above is as follows:

Week	1	2	3	4	5	6	7	8	9	10
Chair #24h	150	0	150	0	150	0	150	0	150	0

Work Center	Lot Size	Lead Time	On Hand	Safety Stock	Lowe-Level Code	Scheduled Receipts
Final Assembly	350	1	82	25	0	350 in Week 1

What would the MRP inventory record for the chair #24h look like?

Solution:

Chair # 24h

Week		1	2	3	4	5	6	7	8	9	10
Gross Requirements		150	0	150	0	150	0	150	0	150	0
Scheduled Receipts		350									
Planned On Hand	82	82	282	282	132	132	332	332	182	182	32
Net Requirements		0	0	0	0	43	0	0	0	0	0
Planned Order Receipts		0	0	0	0	350	0	0	0	0	0
Planned Order Releases		0	0	0	350	0	0	0	0	0	0

5. Luis's factory manufactures a round 48" table with a removable center section that when in place extends the dimensions to 48" by 60". The indented bill of material for levels 0–2 is shown below along with the inventory records and the master schedule for the coming weeks. Use the information below to draw a set of MRP records for the table.

Table (#t200)

(2) Table Top Half (#t248/2)
    (1) Table Top Half (unsanded) (#t248UF)
(1) Track Sub Assembly (#t248trsa)
(4) Table Legs (#t200l/4)
(1) Table Insert (#t248I)

Work Center	Lot Size	Lead Time	On Hand	Safety Stock	Lower-Level Code	Scheduled Receipt	Item ID
Final Assembly	L4L	1	27	25	0	82 in week 1	Table (#t200)
Planing	80*	2	27	20	1	160 in week 2	Table Top Half (#t248/2)
Purchasing	200	2	172	50	1	none	Track Sub Assembly (#t248trsa)
Subassembly	480	2	240	120	1	480 in week 1	Table Legs (#t200l/4)
Purchasing	200*	2	110	25	3	none	Insert (#t248I)
Saws	280	2	105	50	2	280 in week 1	Table Top Half (#t248UF)

*Package size—order in multiples

Master Schedule

Week	1	2	3	4	5	6	7	8	9	10
Table (#t200)	77	0	83	45	88	0	67	76	0	98

Solution:

Table (#t200)

Week		1	2	3	4	5	6	7	8	9	10
Gross Requirements		77	0	83	45	88	0	67	76	0	98
Scheduled Receipts		82									
Planned On Hand	27	27	32	32	25	25	25	25	25	25	25
Net Requirements		0	0	76	45	88	0	67	76	0	98
Planned Order Receipts		0	0	76	45	88	0	67	76	0	98
Planned Order Releases		0	76	45	88	0	67	76	0	98	0

Table Top Half (#t248/2)

Week		1	2	3	4	5	6	7	8	9	10
Gross Requirements		0	152	90	176	0	134	152	0	196	0
Scheduled Receipts		0	160								
Planned On Hand	27	27	27	35	25	89	89	35	43	43	87
Net Requirements		0	0	75	171	0	65	137	0	173	0
Receipts		0	0	80	240	0	80	160	0	240	0
Planned Order Releases		80	240	0	80	160	0	240	0	0	0

Track Subassembly (#t248trsa)

Week		1	2	3	4	5	6	7	8	9	10
Gross Requirements		0	76	45	88	0	67	76	0	98	0
Scheduled Receipts		0									
Planned On Hand	172	172	172	96	51	163	163	96	220	220	122
Net Requirements		0	0	0	87	0	0	30	0	0	0
Planned Order Receipts		0	0	0	200	0	0	200	0	0	0
Planned Order Releases		0	200	0	0	200	0	0	0	0	0

Table Legs (#t200l/4)

Week		1	2	3	4	5	6	7	8	9	10
Gross Requirements		0	304	180	352	0	268	304	0	392	0
Scheduled Receipts		480	0								
Planned On Hand	240	240	720	416	236	364	364	576	272	272	360
Net Requirements		0	0	0	236	0	24	0	0	240	0
Planned Order Receipts		0	0	0	480	0	480	0	0	480	0
Planned Order Releases		0	480	0	480	0	0	480	0	0	0

Insert (#t248I)

Week		1	2	3	4	5	6	7	8	9	10
Gross Requirements		0	76	45	88	0	67	76	0	98	0
Scheduled Receipts		0	0								
Planned On Hand	110	110	110	34	189	101	101	34	158	158	60
Net Requirements		0	0	36	0	0	0	67	0	0	0
Planned Order Receipts		0	0	200	0	0	0	200	0	0	0
Planned Order Releases		200	0	0	0	200	0	0	0	0	0

Table Top Half (#t248UF)

Week		1	2	3	4	5	6	7	8	9	10
Gross Requirements		80	240	0	80	160	0	240	0	0	0
Scheduled Receipts		280	0								
Planned On Hand	105	105	305	65	65	50	50	50	50	50	50
Net Requirements		0	0	0	65	160	0	240	0	0	0
Planned Order Receipts		0	0	0	65	160	0	240	0	0	0
Planned Order Releases		0	65	160	0	240	0	0	0	0	0

6. You have just finished the first day of class, and when you check the syllabi for your classes, you see you have the following assignments due at some point over the semester. Each one has an estimated time to complete (under normal working conditions) and a due date.

	Work Time (days)	Due Date (days)
Accounting Project	5	15
Finance Term Paper	1	4
Investment Portfolio Analysis	4	14
Market Research Project	2	5
OM Spreadsheet Project	6	12

a) What would be the average flow time if we did them in the order in which they were assigned (the original order listed)? Average lateness?

Solution:

	Work Time (days)	Due Date (days)	Flow Time	Late (days)
Accounting Project	5	15	5	0
Finance Term Paper	1	4	6	2
Investment Portfolio Analysis	4	14	10	0
Market Research Project	2	5	12	7
OM Spreadsheet Project	6	12	18	6
Total			51	15
Average			10.2	3

b) What would be the average flow time if we did them in the order of their due dates? Average lateness?

Solution:

	Work Time (days)	Due Date (days)	Flow Time	Late (days)
Finance Term Paper	1	4	1	0
Market Research Project	2	5	3	0
OM Spreadsheet Project	6	12	9	0
Investment Portfolio Analysis	4	14	13	0
Accounting Project	5	15	18	3
Total			44	3
Average			8.8	0.6

c) What would be the average flow time if we did them in the order of shortest to longest? (That way, we can turn a bunch in early and get PR points.) Average lateness?

Solution:

	Work Time (days)	Due Date (days)	Flow Time	Late (days)
Finance Term Paper	1	4	1	0
Market Research Project	2	5	3	0
Investment Portfolio Analysis	4	14	7	0
Accounting Project	5	15	12	0
OM Spreadsheet Project	6	12	18	6
		Total	41	6
		Average	8.2	1.2

d) What would be the average flow time if we did them in the order of longest to shortest? (We just want to knock off some of the big ones and get them out of the way.) Average lateness?

Solution:

	Work Time (days)	Due Date (days)	Flow Time	Late (days)
OM Spreadsheet Project	6	12	6	0
Accounting Project	5	15	11	0
Investment Portfolio Analysis	4	14	15	1
Market Research Project	2	5	17	12
Finance Term Paper	1	4	18	14
		Total	67	27
		Average	13.4	5.4

e) What would be the average flow time if we did them in the order of their critical ratio? Average lateness?

Solution:

	Time	Due Date (days)	Critical Ratio	Flow time (days)	Late (days)
OM Spreadsheet Project	6	12	2	6	0
Market Research Project	2	5	2.5	8	3
Accounting Project	5	15	3	13	0
Investment Portfolio Analysis	4	14	3.5	17	3
Finance Term Paper	1	4	4	18	14
			Total	62	20
			Average	12.4	4

DISCUSSION QUESTIONS

1. Using a hospital bed manufacturer as an example, what are the major inputs to an MRP system?

2. What would the bill of material look like for a Value Meal at McDonald's? What level on the bill of material would you schedule on the master schedule?

3. Assume a local restaurant does use something like an MRP system to schedule the flow of food through the kitchen to the customers at their tables. Can you think of any reasons why 100% inventory accuracy would be difficult? Can you think of any reasons why the bill of material might not be 100% accurate? As a manager, how might you encourage better records?

4. Can you imagine a value-adding system where the product-service bundle emphasizes the service aspect that might use MRP? Would it be of use in Cheryl's hospital? A dentist's office?

5. Would MRP make sense in an oil refinery? A pizza shop? A furniture factory? A jet airplane remanufacturing shop? Why? Why not?

6. Using Luis's furniture shop as an example, what would be the difference between a planned order receipt and a scheduled receipt?

7. Do the lead times used in an MRP system directly reflect the actual production time? Why is the lead time typically independent of order size? Does your answer make sense in terms of Luis's shop?

8. How might MRP apply to the scheduling of classes at your university? What is the master schedule? The bill of material? What is the inventory?

9. Again applying MRP to scheduling classes at your university, what are the lot-sizing issues? How would you describe the logic used at your school?

10. What aspects of MRP would you consider probabilistic? What do you gain by accepting that aspect of the system?

11. Compared to the last question, what aspects of MRP would you think need to be considered deterministic?

12. Is the logic of MRP a recent advance? Why do you think it did not become popular until the late 1960s?

13. Can you describe the bill of material for a PC? What are the first-level components? Second-level?

14. What is the bill of material for a hamburger? Do you see MRP-like logic in the back of a fast-food restaurant?

15. Could the people scheduling production in Fred's plant use MRP? If so, should they? Why or why not?

16. If you work as an MRP planner and notice a "negative" on-hand value for a key part scheduled in the upcoming week, in general what does that mean? Looking deeper, you find the schedule shows the part to be negative to the next 2 weeks, yet the part has a 4-week lead time. Can you deduce what happened? If no changes are made to the plan from this point, what can you expect? What can you do at this point to improve the outlook? MRP and kanban have been known by the terms "push" and "pull" for some time. Can you explain what is meant by the terms? Which of the two systems would make sense for Luis? For Fred? Why?

17. When would you choose to use "lot-for-lot" as a lot-sizing rule over some fixed lot size? When would you choose to fix the interval between order releases? Given what we know about Luis's shop, can you think of a case where each may be appropriate?

18. What does "closing the loop" mean? What is meant by the what-if? capability of an MRP system? How is this concept expanded when we consider ERP?

19. How would you describe the difference between MRP and MRP II? ERP? Could Fred's plant use ERP? If so, should they? Why or why not?

20. Some people have argued that MRP can be too accepting of uncertainty and complexity within a business. What do they mean? Do you agree?

21. MRP has been called an operational planning and control system. Is its true strength in planning or control? How would you compare that to kanban? To the drum-buffer-rope system within TOC?

22. In the 1970s, some viewed MRP as a panacea. Later kanban and TOC were viewed the same way. Can you explain that? Can you argue for the viability of each system? When? Where? How do you see the when and where changing over the coming years?

23. Can a component part, say a car's steering wheel, ever have independent demand? Why? Why not?

PROBLEMS

1. Sequence (schedule) the following four jobs using the critical ratio rule:

Job	Remaining Production Time	Days Until Job Is Due
A	5 days	25
M	8 days	30
S	2 days	12
X	10 days	16

2. Sequence (schedule) the following four jobs using the MIN slack rule:

Job	Remaining Production Time	Days Until Job Is Due
A	5 days	25
M	8 days	30
S	2 days	12
X	10 days	16

3. Sequence (schedule) the following five jobs:

Job	Remaining Production Time	Days Until Job Is Due
A	8 days	8
B	4 days	18
C	2 days	12
D	6 days	6
E	1 day	16

a) Using the first-come, first-served rule (assume they arrive alphabetically)

b) Using the shortest processing time rule.

c) Using the earliest due date rule.

d) What do you think of the results?

4. Today is day 85 on the production control calendar, and a company has six new jobs waiting to be produced on a single machine:

Job	Due Date	Production Time Remaining
U	106	3
V	92	6
W	105	10
X	96	4
Y	90	2
Z	87	8

   a) Sequence (schedule) the six jobs using the critical ratio rule and calculate the average lateness and average flow time.

   b) Sequence (schedule) the six jobs using the earliest due date rule and calculate the average lateness and average flow time.

   c) Sequence (schedule) the six jobs using the shortest processing time rule and calculate the average lateness and average flow time.

   d) Sequence (schedule) the six jobs using the min slack rule and calculate the average lateness and average flow time.

   e) Assume the jobs arrived alphabetically, sequence (schedule) the six jobs using the first-come, first-served rule and calculate the average lateness and average flow time.

   f) How would you compare the results of each rule?

5. Bill's Bells from Bellevue, Ohio, manufactures the "Big Bill Bell" listed bellow. Can you suggest what the pictorial as well as indented bills of material should look like? This bell is assembled from a purchased steel bell, a three-piece clapper (welded from a steel rod, a steel ball, and a steel ring that bolts it to the bell and the handle), a plastic handle injection molded from 4 ounces of purchased plastic, and a bolt and nut to fasten the bell to the handle and the clapper.

6. Marshall's Toy Wagon Manufacturing assembles the basic wagon shown below. (Those of you with a good eye for toy wagons will remember we balanced the assembly line for the wagon in Chapter 9.) The toy's design is illustrated below:

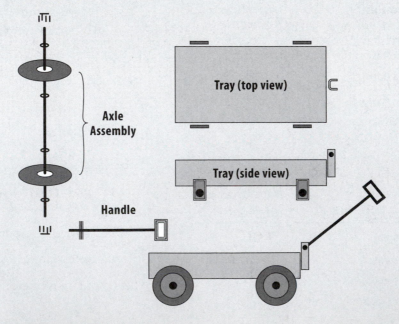

a) What would the pictorial bill of material look like?

b) What would the indented bill of material look like?

7. The master schedule at Marshall's Wagon Company (see problem #2) is being finalized for the coming 10 weeks. Given the following master schedule and inventory information concerning model #MTN:

Week	1	2	3	4	5	6	7	8	9	10
#Wagon MTN	75	75	275	25	150	50	250	10	150	70

Work Center	Lot Size	Lead Time	On Hand	Safety Stock	Lower-Level Code	Scheduled Receipts
Final Assembly	150*	1	46	10	0	150 in Week 1

* Minimum

a) What would the MRP inventory record for the #MTN Wagon look like?

b) Why is the safety stock there if you never plan on using it?

c) What would happen if you could somehow streamline (smooth out) the obviously "lumpy" master schedule? What would the table look like?

d) What would it look like if you could reduce the minimum lot size to 115?

8. There are four lab tests (listed below) that need to be run in the lab at Cheryl's hospital. The technician who does the testing can do only one test at a time, but each test has a duration and due date. In all four cases, the test results are coordinated with the results of other tests done in separate labs, so missing the deadline can delay a diagnosis. The tests are numbered as they come in to the lab but not all tests go through this department.

	Test Time (hours)	Due Date (hours from now)
Test #104	3	9
Test #108	2	7
Test #112	5	7
Test #132	6	14

a) What would be the average flow time and lateness of the tests if they were done in the order in which they arrived (FCFS)? Why would someone choose this rule?

b) What would be the average flow time and lateness of the test if they were done from shortest processing time (SPT) to longest? When would this rule make sense?

c) What would be the average flow time and lateness of the test if they were done based upon the critical ratio? Is this better than SPT?

d) What would be the average flow time and lateness of the test if they were done in order of their due date (DD)? When would this rule make sense?

9. The Oxford Copy Shop and Typing Pool is a local copy shop that produces course packets. Professors take copies of handouts and other course related materials and the "Copy Shop" duplicates them and sells them to students as they come in. The number of pages and the number of students in a course determine the run time of a job, and the first day of a given class determines the due date. J. C. Rupel, the owner, is asking your help in suggesting a prioritizing rule for scheduling jobs. As a sample, the following five jobs have been

brought in over the last few days and represent the current backlog:

	Time (days)	Due Date (days)
MGT 302	2	8
MKT 291	1	3
MIS 235	4	8
MGT 305	5	16
ACC 321	3	13

a) In trying to get the professors to bring the originals to the shop in a timely fashion, he has thought about always doing the jobs in order of their arrival (FCFS). What would be the average flow time and lateness of the packets if they were done in that order? What do you think of this rule?

b) What would be the average flow time and lateness of the packets if they were done from shortest (SPT) to longest? When would this rule make sense?

c) What would be the average flow time and lateness of the packets if they were done based upon the critical ratio? Is this better than SPT or FCFS?

d) What would be the average flow time and lateness of the packets if they were done in order of their due date (DD)? When would this rule make sense?

10. Your university food service department has a menu planned for the upcoming academic calendar that "feeds" into an MRP-like system. Cheddar cheese is used in several dishes as well as at the salad bar. As the food service uses such large quantities, it can get a deeply discounted price by having the supplier ship directly to the food service warehouse on campus. However, there is a $200 shipping fee per order. The inventory holding cost associated for the cheese is estimated to be $.10 per pound per week. Given the following demand schedule for the next 12 weeks, use a part-period balancing approach to determine the order schedule from the cheese supplier. Assume a week's notice is needed for delivery.

Week	1	2	3	4	5	6	7	8	9	10	11	12
Demand (pounds)	300	500	700	700	1000	1400	2200	1800	700	600	400	200

11. The team shop office for the arena where your favorite NBA team plays is planning the delivery of logo merchandise. The setup cost for ordering logo basketballs is $500. The cost of carrying ball in the shop's inventory is about $.50 per ball per week. The demand will fluctuate greatly depending on the number of home games during a particular week. Assume a 2-week delivery time on the balls. They currently have 700 balls in inventory. Given the estimated demand over the next 15 weeks, use part-period balancing to determine an ordering schedule.

Week	1	2	3	4	5	6	7	8	9	10	11	12	13	14	15
Demand	500	0	1000	750	1500	0	0	500	0	0	1500	750	500	0	1000

CHALLENGE PROBLEMS

1. Joe Jackson's Dental Kit and Supply Company sterilize and pack dental equipment into kits for office use. They package disposable parts along with reusable instruments that have been sterilized into a variety of kit configurations that are custom tailored to the needs of individual dental offices. Joe's will purchase disposable components and sterilize reusable components collected from dental offices by their distribution staff. They then deliver complete kits back to the dental offices based upon their projected demand. (Assume that enough of the reusable components are already in circulation and customers are willing to return used ones for sterilization. Therefore, no new item will need to be ordered to supplement receipts back from current customers.) Joe's company offers hundreds of configurations; the most popular is described below in an indented bill of material:

Basic Cleaning Kit #12

    Basic Instrument SA

        Mirror—RU

        Explorer/Probe—RU

        (2) Cotton Pliers—DisP

        Air/Water Tip—DisP

    Prophy Angle—DisP

    Clng-hand Instmnt SA

        Anterior Scaler

        Ball 5/6 Scaler

        7/8 Curette

The Basic Instrument Subassembly is common to most kits they package, while the Prophy Angle and the Hand instrument subassembly are specific to a cleaning kit and a given customer preference. Joe's uses an MRP system to schedule the batches of work flowing through their shop.

Inventory Records

Work Center	Lot Size	Lead Time	On-Hand	Safety Stock	Lower-Level Code	Schedule Receipts	Item ID
Final Assembly	150	1	105	50	0	none	Basic Cleaning Kit #12
Subassembly—Main	500	1	235	75	1	none	Basic Instrument SA
Sterilizing	00	1	86	75	2	none	Mirror—RU
Sterilizing	500	1	240	120	2	none	Explorer/Probe—RU
Purchasing	1200	2	181	120	2	2000 Wk 2	Cotton Pliers—DisP
Purchasing	800	2	121	75	2	800 Wk 1	Air/Water Tip—DisP
Purchasing	375	2	232	50	1	none	Prophy Angle—DisP
Subassembly—Main	400	1	203	40	1	none	Clng-hand Instmnt SA
Sterilizing	750	1	197	150	2	none	Anterior Scaler
Sterilizing	500	1	112	100	2	none	Ball 5/6 Scaler
Sterilizing	750	1	165	150	2	750 Wk 2	7/8 Curette

Master Schedule

Week	1	2	3	4	5	6	7	8	9	10
Basic Cleaning Kit #12	46	72	58	34	113	105	45	87	58	101

a) What would the entire set of MRP inventory records look like given the indented bill of material, master schedule, and component inventory information above?

b) How would it change if the seventy-two kits in Week 2 was increased to 122? What problems develop?

c) What would you suggest to help the issue in part (b)?

d) How would your approach to this problem change if returns of used implements for sterilization were not adequate to completely satisfy upcoming demand for kits and some new implements had to be ordered to keep up with demand?

2. Sylvia's Silverware Warehouse contracts with a local metal stamping plant to produce their everyday line of table service. A typical design will be created and an entire set of table service stamped out in a common pattern. Blanks are punched form standard metal stock and the blanks are heated and drop forged (or stamped) from the heated blanks. Utensils are stamped from stainless steel or sterling. Some stainless utensils go on for silver plating. A given quantity of each type of utensil will then be packaged and shipped. Various accessory sets are also stamped and assembled to compliment the basic service set. A typical service would include teaspoons, salad forks, dinner forks, soup spoons, and case knives in services for six, eight, and twelve. A typical accessory pack might include a serving ladle, serving spoon, and cake server, all in a pattern common to the basic table service. The indented bill of material list below is for the "Classic" pattern for eight in stainless steel. Also shown is the master schedule for shipping the "Classic-8" to Sylvia's over the next few weeks:

Classic-8

    (8) soup—classic

        (1) mid—blank

            (.18m) stainless bar stock

    (8) teaspoon—classic

        (1) sml—blank

            (.16m) stainless bar stock

    (8) sldfrk—classic

        (1) sml—blank

            (.16m) stainless bar stock

    (8) dnrfrk—classic

        (1) mid—blank

            (.18m) stainless bar stock

    (8) csnv—classic

        (1) lgblank

            (.22m) stainless bar stock

Master Schedule

Week	1	2	3	4	5	6	7	8	9	10
Classic-8	200	100	100	300	100	200	200	200	200	200

Work Center	Lot Size	Lead Time	On Hand	Safety Stock	Lower-Level Code	Schedule Receipts	Item ID
Final Assembly	300	2	327	50	0	500 in Wk 2	Classic-8
Stamping	6000	2	430	300	1	0	soup—classic
Stamping	12,000	2	6200	1000	1	0	teaspoon—classic
Stamping	8800	2	862	600	1	0	sldfrk—classic
Stamping	8000	2	240	400	1	8000 in Wk 1	dnrfrk—classic
Stamping	6000	2	420	300	3	0	csnv—classic

(*continued*)

Work Center	Lot Size	Lead Time	On Hand	Safety Stock	Lower-Level Code	Schedule Receipts	Item ID
Punch-press	20,000	2	105	50	2	20,000 Wk 1	sml—blank
Punch-press	13,000	2	7200	600	3	0	mid—blank
Punch-press	8000	1	200	150	3	8000 inwWk 1	lg—blank
Purchasing	10,000	1	200	150	3	0	stainless bar stock

a) What would the entire set of MRP inventory records look like given the indented bill of material, master schedule, and component inventory information above?

b) What other sources would contribute to the gross requirements of the "mid—blank"? Is this something you would want to encourage or discourage?

c) Can you move the deliveries scheduled in Week 4 of the master schedule into Week 3? Why? Why not?

d) What would be the total set of demand placed on the schedule for stainless bar stock?

3. Luis has another popular table (similar to the "Table #48 oak rnd trad" table whose schedule was examined in the Solved Problems for this chapter) that is produced on a fairly regular basis. Assume the assembly department has a $650 set up cost for this table Luis estimates it will cost $3 per week to carry an assembled table in inventory. There is a 1-week lead time for the assembly department. Also, assume the following MRP inventory record representing the gross requirements for the next 10 weeks:

Table #60 oak oval trad.

Week	1	2	3	4	5	6	7	8	9	10
Gross Requirements	50	100	150	100	50	50	150	50	150	100
Scheduled Receipts	150									
Planned On Hand	0 0	0	0	0	0	0	0	0	0	0
Net Requirements	0									
Planned Order Receipts	0									
Planned Order Releases										

a) How would Luis finish the MRP Inventory Record using a "part-period balancing" approach to lot sizing of this table?

b) What would be the setup and inventory carrying cost associated with using part-period balancing?

c) How would Luis finish the MRP inventory record using a lot-for-lot approach to lot sizing of this table?

d) What would be the setup and inventory carrying cost associated with using lot-for-lot over the course of this schedule?

e) If the assembly area asked to fixed the lot size at 250 tables, how would Luis finish the MRP inventory record using such a fixed lot size for this table?

f) What would be the setup and inventory carrying cost associated with a fixed lot size of 250 tables over the course of this schedule?

Case 16: To Varian Semiconductor, Speed Is the Key to Success

Gloucester, Mass.-based Varian Semiconductor (http://www.vsea.com) is a leading producer of ion implantation equipment, which is used very early in the semiconductor manufacturing process, essentially to impregnate silicon wafers with energy particles. The machines are large. They weigh 20 tons and are as big as a small room or a two-car garage. To make semiconductors, they use 11,000 pound electromagnets to accelerate a beam of ions toward a single wafer that can easily be held in your hands. The machines are customized, with commonly available options and special features specified by each customer.

Supplier lead times are very important to Varian for several reasons:

1. Customers are looking for *exact* on-time delivery. They don't care if a late order is late because of a problem at Varian or a problem at a supplier. They just want the parts or machines on time.

2. Lead times play a role in reducing their cash-to-cash cycle—from receipt of order to "first silicon" processed by the customer.

3. There is a very competitive aftermarket for consumable parts, which comprise a large percentage of the goods sourced by Varian. Quick delivery by suppliers can help them earn a significant profit in a very competitive market for those consumable replacement parts. Varian can't afford calls from customers saying that their machine is down and that they're losing a million dollars an hour because they are waiting for a $25 spare part!

4. Varian Semiconductor needs to maintain an exceptionally high gross margin goal of 50% to pay for their cutting edge R&D. Reducing their cash-to-cash cycle time and that of their suppliers has a direct effect on ROI. Maintaining exceptional delivery performance from suppliers helps Varian Semiconductor to turn inventories rapidly, a big part of the company's strategy for achieving its high gross margin goal.

For all of the above reasons and more, while many companies look to e-business to reduce costs, Varian has pursued e-procurement to increase supply speed. In that effort they built an electronic sourcing system—a supplier portal—with the goal of effective, increasingly rapid, supply chain performance.

The idea for a supplier portal sprang from Varian Semiconductor's customer-facing e-commerce system, a tool they used so their customers could come in, view and order parts, check availability, check delivery status, etc. The thought was to turn the tool around and use it with their inbound materials. Instead of customers using it to place demand on the company, Varian could use it to place demand on suppliers.

In its phase-one incarnation, Varian Semiconductor's supplier portal was essentially a communications tool for orders that had already been placed. "The deals are done, pricing and lead times are set," says Jim White, director of SCM for Varian. Varian Semiconductor's MRP reports are generated internally by exploding their own master schedule against the bill of materials for a product and their own inventory records. Along with generating the necessary work orders internal to Varian, procurement requirements flow directly from the MRP system into the portal. Each day, Varian's buyers or commodity specialists log into the portal to review MRP reports and determine if adjustments—either in or out—need to be made to suppliers' delivery dates. If changes are needed, Varian's buyers first verify the changes with the MRP system, then transmit demand signals to their suppliers.

Suppliers, meantime, designate agents to access their own secure areas of the Varian web site. "They can sort by what is due for delivery, what's being pulled in, pushed out, or canceled," White says. If there's a change, suppliers can accept the new delivery date, counter it, or refuse the change while providing a narrative explaining their refusal.

The biggest advantage of the portal is its provision for two-way communications. If a supplier feels they can't meet a new delivery demand, they can explain why or suggest what needs to happen to allow them to meet the demand. A supplier might say, 'I would love to deliver this power supply, but I'm missing a particular diode stack.' Varian can possibly counter by saying they have access to the part or know of another source.

Varian Semiconductor's supplier portal also serves as an automated conduit for a supplier's on time and quality performance metrics and as a way to manage supplier corrective action requests coming out of its quality management (QM) process.

To aid suppliers in planning their production more effectively, Varian Semiconductor broadcasts six-month demand forecasts for its products, which can be exploded directly through the MRP system, to estimate forecast demand from their suppliers. Not firm commitments, the broadcasts are simply a window into Varian's future plans, which should give suppliers a head start on their own production planning. Varian's MRP system combines original equipment demand with consumable spare part demand to give suppliers a look at their aggregated demand from Varian over a six-month window.

Varian Semiconductor runs various metrics to gauge the success of its portal at delivering shorter supplier lead times. Varian Semiconductor is also running reports to see if on-time delivery-to-commit dates are improving. Based on these reports, Varian Semiconductor is convinced that the portal has helped suppliers achieve substantial on-time delivery improvements.

SOME QUESTIONS TO THINK ABOUT:

1. How would you characterize the importance of Varian's internal MRP system to the supplier portal and vice versa?

2. How would Varian have found out a supplier could not meet a delivery date in the past? What is the potential for integrating the portal with the MRP system to improve that?

3. How does the potential for improved supplier performance relate to Varian's ROI goals?

4. How does improved supplier performance help reduce Varian's internal build times and thus ROI goals?

Source: Adapted from "Velocity Is Prime Mover in Equipment Maker's Portal," *Purchasing Magazine Online*, Jan. 16, 2003, reporter Anne Millen Porter; "Varian Develops Portal for Suppliers," *Purchasing Magazine Online*, March 3, 2003, Staff; "Varian Semiconductor Launches Website; Portal Promotes Real-Time Information Exchange Reducing Lead Times," *Business Wire*, Oct. 1, 2002; "Chips and Flexibility," *The Manufacturer*, March 2004; and http://www.vsea.com/, Oct. 24, 2005

REFERENCES

Kanet, J. J., and V. Sridharan. "The Electronic Leitstand: A New Tool for Shop Scheduling," *Manufacturing Review 3*, no. 3: 161–170.

Steinberg, E., B. Khumawala, and R. Scamell. "Requirements Planning Systems in the Health Care Environment," *Journal of Operations Management 2*, no. 4 (Aug. 1982).

Appendix

The Cumulative Standardized Normal Distribution

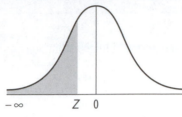

Entry Represents Area Under the Cumulative Standardized Normal Distribution from —∞ to Z

Z	.00	.01	.02	.03	.04	.05	.06	.07	.08	.09
−3.9	.00005	.00005	.00004	.00004	.00004	.00004	.00004	.00004	.00003	.00003
−3.8	.00007	.00007	.00007	.00006	.00006	.00006	.00006	.00005	.00005	.00005
−3.7	.00011	.00010	.00010	.00010	.00009	.00009	.00008	.00008	.00008	.00008
−3.6	.00016	.00015	.00015	.00014	.00014	.00013	.00013	.00012	.00012	.00011
−3.5	.00023	.00022	.00022	.00021	.00020	.00019	.00019	.00018	.00017	.00017
−3.4	.00034	.00032	.00031	.00030	.00029	.00028	.00027	.00026	.00025	.00024
−3.3	.00048	.00047	.00045	.00043	.00042	.00040	.00039	.00038	.00036	.00035
−3.2	.00069	.00066	.00064	.00062	.00060	.00058	.00056	.00054	.00052	.00050
−3.1	.00097	.00094	.00090	.00087	.00084	.00082	.00079	.00076	.00074	.00071
−3.0	.00135	.00131	.00126	.00122	.00118	.00114	.00111	.00107	.00103	.00100
−2.9	.0019	.0018	.0018	.0017	.0016	.0016	.0015	.0015	.0014	.0014
−2.8	.0026	.0025	.0024	.0023	.0023	.0022	.0021	.0021	.0020	.0019
−2.7	.0035	.0034	.0033	.0032	.0031	.0030	.0029	.0028	.0027	.0026
−2.6	.0047	.0045	.0044	.0043	.0041	.0040	.0039	.0038	.0037	.0036
−2.5	.0062	.0060	.0059	.0057	.0055	.0054	.0052	.0051	.0049	.0048
−2.4	.0082	.0080	.0078	.0075	.0073	.0071	.0069	.0068	.0066	.0064
−2.3	.0107	.0104	.0102	.0099	.0096	.0094	.0091	.0089	.0087	.0084
−2.2	.0139	.0136	.0132	.0129	.0125	.0122	.0119	.0116	.0113	.0110
−2.1	.0179	.0174	.0170	.0166	.0162	.0158	.0154	.0150	.0146	.0143
−2.0	.0228	.0222	.0217	.0212	.0207	.0202	.0197	.0192	.0188	.0183
−1.9	.0287	.0281	.0274	.0268	.0262	.0256	.0250	.0244	.0239	.0233
−1.8	.0359	.0351	.0344	.0336	.0329	.0322	.0314	.0307	.0301	.0294
−1.7	.0446	.0436	.0427	.0418	.0409	.0401	.0392	.0384	.0375	.0367
−1.6	.0548	.0537	.0526	.0516	.0505	.0495	.0485	.0475	.0465	.0455
−1.5	.0668	.0655	.0643	.0630	.0618	.0606	.0594	.0582	.0571	.0559
−1.4	.0808	.0793	.0778	.0764	.0749	.0735	.0721	.0708	.0694	.0681
−1.3	.0968	.0951	.0934	.0918	.0901	.0885	.0869	.0853	.0838	.0823
−1.2	.1151	.1131	.1112	.1093	.1075	.1056	.1038	.1020	.1003	.0985
−1.1	.1357	.1335	.1314	.1292	.1271	.1251	.1230	.1210	.1190	.1170
−1.0	.1587	.1562	.1539	.1515	.1492	.1469	.1446	.1423	.1401	.1379
−0.9	.1841	.1814	.1788	.1762	.1736	.1711	.1685	.1660	.1635	.1611
−0.8	.2119	.2090	.2061	.2033	.2005	.1977	.1949	.1922	.1894	.1867
−0.7	.2420	.2388	.2358	.2327	.2296	.2266	.2236	.2006	.2177	.2148
−0.6	.2743	.2709	.2676	.2643	.2611	.2578	.2546	.2514	.2482	.2451
−0.5	.3085	.3050	.3015	.2981	.2946	.2912	.2877	.2843	.2810	.2776
−0.4	.3446	.3409	.3372	.3336	.3300	.3264	.3228	.3192	.3156	.3121
−0.3	.3821	.3783	.3745	.3707	.3669	.3632	.3594	.3557	.3520	.3483
−0.2	.4207	.4168	.4129	.4090	.4052	.4013	.3974	.3936	.3897	.3859
−0.1	.4602	.4562	.4522	.4483	.4443	.4404	.4364	.4325	.4286	.4247
−0.0	.5000	.4960	.4920	.4880	.4840	.4801	.4761	.4721	.4681	.4641

(continued)

The Cumulative Standardized Normal Distribution (*continued*)

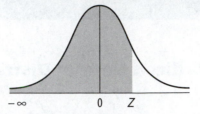

Entry Represents Area Under the Cumulative Standardized Normal Distribution from $-\infty$ to Z

Z	.00	.01	.02	.03	.04	.05	.06	.07	.08	.09
0.0	.5000	.5040	.5080	.5120	.5160	.5199	.5239	.5279	.5319	.5359
0.1	.5398	.5438	.5478	.5517	.5557	.5596	.5636	.5675	.5714	.5753
0.2	.5793	.5832	.5871	.5910	.5948	.5987	.6026	.6064	.6103	.6141
0.3	.6179	.6217	.6255	.6293	.6331	.6368	.6406	.6443	.6480	.6517
0.4	.6554	.6591	.6628	.6664	.6700	.6736	.6772	.6808	.6844	.6879
0.5	.6915	.6950	.6985	.7019	.7054	.7088	.7123	.7157	.7190	.7224
0.6	.7257	.7291	.7324	.7357	.7389	.7422	.7454	.7486	.7518	.7549
0.7	.7580	.7612	.7642	.7673	.7704	.7734	.7764	.7794	.7823	.7852
0.8	.7881	.7910	.7939	.7967	.7995	.8023	.8051	.8078	.8106	.8133
0.9	.8159	.8186	.8212	.8238	.8264	.8289	.8315	.8340	.8365	.8389
1.0	.8413	.8438	.8461	.8485	.8508	.8531	.8554	.8577	.8599	.8621
1.1	.8643	.8665	.8686	.8708	.8729	.8749	.8770	.8790	.8810	.8830
1.2	.8849	.8869	.8888	.8907	.8925	.8944	.8962	.8980	.8997	.9015
1.3	.9032	.9089	.9066	.9082	.9099	.9115	.9131	.9147	.9162	.9177
1.4	.9192	.9207	.9222	.9236	.9251	.9265	.9279	.9292	.9306	.9319
1.5	.9332	.9345	.9357	.9370	.9382	.9394	.9406	.9418	.9429	.9441
1.6	.9452	.9463	.9474	.9484	.9495	.9505	.9515	.9525	.9535	.9545
1.7	.9554	.9564	.9573	.9582	.9591	.9599	.9608	.9616	.9625	.9633
1.8	.9641	.9649	.9656	.9664	.9671	.9678	.9686	.9693	.9699	.9706
1.9	.9713	.9719	.9726	.9732	.9738	.9744	.9750	.9756	.9761	.9767
2.0	.9772	.9778	.9783	.9788	.9793	.9798	.9803	.9808	.9812	.9817
2.1	.9821	.9826	.9830	.9834	.9838	.9842	.9846	.9850	.9854	.9857
2.2	.9861	.9864	.9868	.9871	.9875	.9878	.9881	.9884	.9887	.9890
2.3	.9893	.9896	.9898	.9901	.9904	.9906	.9909	.9911	.9913	.9916
2.4	.9918	.9920	.9922	.9925	.9927	.9929	.9931	.9932	.9934	.9936
2.5	.9938	.9940	.9941	.9943	.9945	.9946	.9948	.9949	.9951	.9952
2.6	.9953	.9955	.9956	.9957	.9959	.9960	.9961	.9962	.9963	.9964
2.7	.9965	.9966	.9967	.9968	.9969	.9970	.9971	.9972	.9973	.9974
2.8	.9974	.9975	.9976	.9977	.9977	.9978	.9979	.9979	.9980	.9981
2.9	.9981	.9982	.9982	.9983	.9984	.9984	.9985	.9985	.9986	.9986
3.0	.99865	.99869	.99874	.99878	.99882	.99886	.99889	.99893	.99897	.99900
3.1	.99903	.99906	.99910	.99913	.99916	.99918	.99921	.99924	.99926	.99929
3.2	.99931	.99934	.99936	.99938	.99940	.99942	.99944	.99946	.99948	.99950
3.3	.99952	.99953	.99955	.99957	.99958	.99960	.99961	.99962	.99964	.99965
3.4	.99966	.99968	.99969	.99970	.99971	.99972	.99973	.99974	.99975	.99976
3.5	.99977	.99978	.99978	.99979	.99980	.99981	.99981	.99982	.99983	.99983
3.6	.99984	.99985	.99985	.99986	.99986	.99987	.99987	.99988	.99988	.99989
3.7	.99989	.99990	.99990	.99990	.99991	.99991	.99992	.99992	.99992	.99992
3.8	.99993	.99993	.99993	.99994	.99994	.99994	.99994	.99995	.99995	.99995
3.9	.99995	.99995	.99996	.99996	.99996	.99996	.99996	.99996	.99997	.99997

A

Supplement A: Decision Analysis

Supplement Outline

Supplement A: Decision Analysis   786

    The Components of a Decision Problem   786

    Types of Decision Problems   787

    Decision Making Under Uncertainty   787

    Decision Making Under Risk   790

    Decision Trees: An Alternative to Payoff Tables   792

    Utility: An Alternative to Dollar Value   797

Summary   799

Key Terms   799

Solved Problems   799

Discussion Questions   803

Problems   803

Supplement A: Decision Analysis

The Components of a Decision Problem

The three basic components of a decision problem are the decision alternatives; the possible environments, conditions, or states of nature within which a decision is to be implemented; and the outcomes or payoff functions that will result from each possible combination of alternatives and states of nature.

The **decision alternatives** are those actions from among which the decision maker must choose. That is, they are the aspects of the decision situation over which the decision maker has direct control.

The **states of nature** are those aspects of the decision situation over which the decision maker does not have direct control. They certainly include things over which he or she has no control, such as the weather, the general state of the economy, or actions taken by the national government. They may also include things which he or she might influence to some extent, but cannot determine completely. The market response to a new product (which is partly determined by the price charged and advertising) or a competitor's actions (which may be at least partly determined by choices made by the decision maker) are conditions the decision maker cannot determine completely. Making a decision and implementing it within a state of nature will result in some outcome, which may be either a gain or a loss. The **payoff function** specifies what that outcome is for every possible decision/state-of-nature combination. The payoff function may be given either as an equation or, when the possible decision alternatives and states of nature are relatively limited, as a payoff table or matrix. For example, Table A.1 shows a payoff table for a proposed cardiac catheterization service at Cheryl Sanders's hospital.

Decision alternatives

The set of definable alternatives from which the decision maker must choose

States of nature

Aspects of the decision situation over which the decision maker does not have direct control.

Payoff function

A tool which specifies what that outcome is for every possible alternative/state-of-nature combination.

Example A.1

Cheryl Sanders has been approached by the head of the hospital's cardiac care unit about the possibility of starting a cardiac catheterization service at the hospital. Doing so would require either the conversion of existing space in the hospital (which would allow for the development of only a small unit) or the construction of an addition (which would make it possible to build a larger unit). Additional equipment would also have to be purchased.

Before taking this idea to the capital expenditure review committee for the chain that owns the hospital, Cheryl gets information on the costs of the two possibilities from the hospital architect and asks the hospital's marketing department for a preliminary assessment of the possible levels of demand for this type of service. Putting this information together, Cheryl creates the payoff table in

Table A.1. The hospital chain uses a five-year planning horizon for major capital expenditures. The 5-year returns shown in the table are stated in millions of dollars of net present value over that time horizon.

Table A.1

Payoff Table for Cardiac Catheterization Service

Alternative	Demand Level		
	Low	Medium	High
Build addition	−3	1	7
Convert space	−1	2	5
Do nothing	0	0	0

Types of Decision Problems

There are three basic types of decision problem, each with its own mode of analysis:

1. **Decision making under certainty**: In this type of problem, the state of nature is known, so the payoff table has only one column. In principle, the analysis is simple: Choose the alternative with the best payoff. In practice, it is not always that easy, because an "alternative" may actually represent the values for many decision variables. However, solution procedures have been developed for many problems of this type. For example, the supplement to Chapter 8 presents an introduction to linear programming, a popular technique for decision making under certainty.

2. **Decision making under uncertainty**: In this type of problem, decision makers have the payoff table, but no information on the relative likelihood of the states of nature. A number of approaches to this type of problem are possible, several of which will be discussed in this supplement.

3. **Decision making under risk**: In this type of problem, in addition to the payoff table, decision makers have the probabilities for the different states of nature. The standard approach is expected value analysis, which will be discussed in this supplement.

Decision Making Under Uncertainty

As noted above, in decision making under uncertainty we have a payoff table but no information about the relative likelihood of the different states of nature. A number of procedures have been developed for choosing an alternative under these

Decision making under certainty

A basic type of decision problem where decision makers have the payoff table, but no information on the relative likelihood of the states of nature.

Decision making under uncertainty

A basic type of decision problem where decision makers have the payoff table, but no information on the relative likelihood of the states of nature.

Decision making under risk

A basic type of decision problem where the state of nature is known, so the payoff table has only one column.

Example A.2

Find the maximum solution to Cheryl Sanders's cardiac catheterization service problem described in Example A.1.

Solution:

From Exhibit A.1, the maximum payoffs for the decision alternatives are:

Build addition:	7
Convert space:	5
Do nothing:	0

The largest maximum payoff is 7, so the "maximax" decision is to *build an addition.*

Exhibit A.1

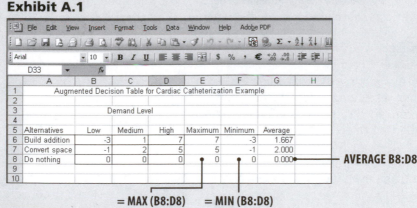

conditions, each based on a different philosophy about what constitutes a good choice. We shall consider four: maximax, maximin, equal likelihood, and minimax regret.

MAXIMAX PROCEDURE

Maximax

An optimistic approach that assumes that no matter what alternative we choose, "nature" will smile favorably on us and choose the state that will benefit us the most.

The **maximax** procedure (called the minimin procedure if the payoffs are costs or losses rather than profits or gains) is an optimistic approach. It assumes that no matter what alternative we choose, "nature" will smile favorably on us and choose the state of nature that will benefit us the most (or hurt us the least). Thus, we choose the alternative with the largest maximum gain (or the smallest minimum loss).

MAXIMIN PROCEDURE

Maximin

A pessimistic approach that assumes that no matter what alternative we choose, "nature" will choose the state that benefits us the least.

The **maximin** procedure (called the minimax procedure if the payoffs are costs or losses) is a pessimistic approach. It assumes that, no matter what alternative we choose, "nature" will choose the state of nature that benefits us the least (or hurts us the most). Thus, we choose the alternative with the largest minimum gain (or the smallest maximum loss). In fact, if "nature" is a competitor who gets to choose his alternative after we have chosen ours, this could be a very good strategy. (This gets into an area called game theory, which we will not discuss.)

Example A.3

Find the maximin solution to Cheryl Sanders's cardiac catheterization service problem described in Example A.1.

Solution:

From Exhibit A.1, the minimum payoffs for the alternatives are:

Build addition:	−3
Convert space:	−1
Do nothing:	0

The largest minimum payoff is 0, so the "maximin" decision is to do nothing.

Equal likelihood

A procedure based on the assumption that if we cannot determine the relative likelihood of the states of nature, then it is rational to presume that they are equally likely.

EQUAL LIKELIHOOD PROCEDURE

One criticism of the maximax and maximin strategies is that they focus on only one payoff for each alternative, ignoring all other states of nature and their payoffs. The **equal likelihood procedure** is based on the assumption that if we cannot determine the relative likelihood of the states of nature, then it is rational to presume that they are

Example A.4

Find the equal likelihood solution to Cheryl Sanders's cardiac catheterization service problem described in Example A.1.

Solution:

From Exhibit A.1, the averages of the rows of the payoff table are:

Build addition:	1.667
Convert space:	2.000
Do nothing:	0

The largest average payoff is 2.0, so the "equal likelihood" decision is to convert space.

equally likely. If this is the case, then we should choose the alternative with the largest average payoff (or the smallest average payoff for losses).

MINIMAX REGRET PROCEDURE

We have all had the experience of making a decision and then, after observing the result, wishing that we had made another choice instead, so that our payoff would have been better (or less bad). That is the concept behind the **minimax regret** procedure: We choose the alternative that will yield the smallest possible maximum regret. The procedure has two steps:

1. Construct a regret table by subtracting each payoff from the maximum payoff in its column. (For a loss table, subtract the smallest loss in each column from each entry in its column.)

2. Apply the minimax procedure to the regret table: Find the maximum regret in each row; then choose the alternative with the smallest maximum regret.

Minimax regret

The approach in which we choose the alternative that will yield the smallest possible maximum regret.

Example A.5

Find the minimax regret solution to Cheryl Sanders's cardiac catheterization service problem described in Example A-1.

Solution:

Step 1: Construct the regret table from the payoff table in Table A.1. As shown in Exhibit A.2, this is done in two steps. First, as shown in Exhibit A.2a, find the maximum entry in each column of the

payoff table. Second, as shown in Exhibit A.2b, each payoff table entry is subtracted from the maximum in its column to get the regret table.

Step 2: Find the maximum regret for each alternative, as shown to the right of the regret table in Figure A.2b. The alternative with the smallest maximum regret is to convert space, with a maximum regret of 2.

Exhibit A.2

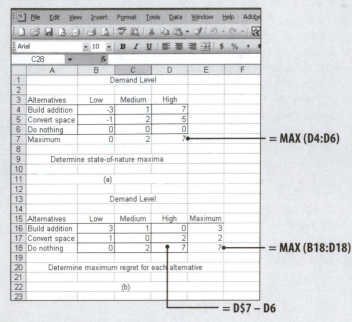

Decision Making Under Risk

There are two basic approaches to decision making under risk: (1) maximizing expected gain or minimizing expected loss, and (2) minimizing expected regret.

MAXIMIZING EXPECTED GAIN

Under some reasonable assumptions about the characteristics of a rational decision maker, it can be shown that when probabilities for the states of nature are known, the alternative that maximizes the expected gain (or minimizes the expected loss) is the appropriate decision. To determine the expected value of a decision alternative, multiply that alternative's payoff under each different state of nature by that state of nature's probability and sum the resulting products.

MINIMIZING EXPECTED REGRET

As an alternative to using the payoff table to maximize the expected gain (or minimize the expected loss), we can choose the alternative that minimizes the expected regret. As shown in Examples A.6 and A.7, the two approaches lead to the same decision.

Comparing the expected regrets found in Example A.7 with the expected payoffs in Example A.6, we see that, for each pair of alternatives, the difference between the values of the expected gains and the difference between the values of the expected regrets are identical. For example, the difference between the expected gains for "build addition" and "convert space" is $1.7 - .8 = .9$. The difference between the expected regrets for the same pair is $1.3 - .4 = .9$. This finding is not specific to this particular example, but is a general result.

Example A.6

(Refer to Example A.1)

Cheryl Sanders has gone back to the hospital's marketing department to get some additional information about the relative likelihood of the different levels of demand for the proposed cardiac catheterization service. After review of their marketing research, the department gives Cheryl the following probability estimates: P(low) = .2, P(medium) = .7, P(high) = .1. Using these probabilities, determine which alternative maximizes the expected value return to the hospital.

Solution:

The projected returns are given by the rows of Table A.1. The expected returns for the three alternatives are:

Build addition: $.2(-3) + .7(1) + .1(7)$
$= -.6 + .7 + .7 = .8$

Convert space: $.2(-1) + .7(2) + .1(5)$
$= -.2 + 1.4 + .5 = 1.7$

Do nothing: $.2(0) + .7(0) + .1(0) = 0$

The alternative with the highest expected payoff is to *convert space*. Exhibit A.3 shows the Excel computation of the expected values.

Exhibit A.3

	A	B	C	D	E	F
1			Demand Level			
2						
3	Alternatives	Low	Medium	High	Expected Payoff	
4	Build addition	-3	1	7	0.8	
5	Convert space	-1	2	5	1.7	
6	Do nothing	0	0	0	0	
7	Probabilities	0.2	0.7	0.1		
8						
9						

= SUMPRODUCT (B$7, B6:D6)

(Refer to Example A.1)

The regret matrix for the cardiac catheterization lab decision problem was developed in Example A.5. Determine which decision alternative minimizes the hospital management's expected regret.

Solution:

Using the regret matrix from Exhibit A.2b and the probabilities given in Example A.6, the expected regrets for the three decision alternatives are:

Build addition: $.2(3) + .7(1) + .1(0)$
$= .6 + .7 + 0 = 1.3$
Convert space: $.2(1) + .7(0) + .1(2)$
$= .2 + 0 + .2 = .4$
Do nothing: $.2(0) + .7(2) + .1(7)$
$= 0 + 1.4 + .7 = 2.1$

The alternative with the lowest expected regret is to *convert space*.

THE EXPECTED VALUE OF PERFECT INFORMATION

If, before having to make a final decision, we could find out exactly what the state of nature was going to be, we could improve the quality of the decision. The **expected value of perfect information (EVPI)** is a measure of the expected current worth to the decision maker of being able to find out, just before having to make the decision, what the state of nature will be. It combines the current assessments of the probabilities of the states of nature with the improved value of knowing the state of nature. Thus the EVPI is computed as the difference between the expected value of making the decision with perfect information (EWPI), given by the weighted combination of the best payoffs for each state of nature, and the expected value of the best decision with current information.

Note that the expected value of perfect information in Example A.8 is exactly the same as the expected regret from Example A.7. Given that EVPI and expected regret are both computed by comparing, for each state of nature, the value of a specific

Expected value of perfect information (EVPI)

A measure of the expected current worth to the decision maker of being able to find out, just before having to make the decision, what the state of nature will be.

(Refer to Example A.1)

Assuming it would be possible to determine the demand level for the cardiac catheterization service before making a final decision about whether to introduce the service and, if so, how large a unit to build, determine the current expected value of having this perfect information.

Solution:

The best decisions for each state of nature (demand level) and their values, as given in Exhibit A.1, are:

Demand	Best Decision	Value
Low	Do nothing	0
Medium	Convert space	2
High	Build addition	7

Using the probabilities of the demand levels given in Example A.6, the expected value with perfect information (EWPI) is:

$$EWPI = .2(0) + .7(2) + .1(7) = 0 + 1.4 + .7 = 2.1$$

The best decision without having perfect information, as found in Example A.6, is to convert space, which has an expected value of 1.7. Thus, the expected value of perfect information is:

$$EVPI = EWPI - E(\text{best decision}) = 2.1 - 1.7 = .4$$

That is, the hospital could increase its expected net present value by $.4 million if it were able to find out what the demand for this new service would be before committing to whether and how to provide it.

decision with the value of the best decision for that state of nature, this result is not an accident. It will always be the case.

Because it is never possible (at least legally) to get perfect information before having to make a decision, the expected value of perfect information is useful mainly as an upper bound on the expected value of sample or imperfect information (such as market surveys or economic forecasts) which is often available before a final decision musts be made.

Decision Trees: An Alternative to Payoff Tables

An alternative to using a payoff to compute the expected values of decision alternatives is to use a **decision tree**.

THE STRUCTURE OF DECISION TREES

As shown in Figure A.1, a decision tree consists of two or more stages or levels, shown in time order from left to right.

Nodes and Branches

Each level of a decision tree consists of nodes (the squares and circles) and branches, which represent alternatives. The square nodes represent decision points; each branch from a decision node represents one of the decision alternatives available at that point. The circles, or **chance nodes**, represent problem features that are determined by chance or probability, such as the states of nature.

Figure A.1 is actually the decision tree for Cheryl Sanders' problem of whether to propose starting a cardiac catheterization service and, if so, how large a unit to build. The nodes have been numbered to facilitate the description of the tree.

▶ Node 1 is the decision node. There are three alternatives, represented by the three branches: 1) Build an addition, 2) Convert existing space, 3) Do nothing.

Decision tree

An alternative to using a payoff to compute the expected values of decision alternatives, which consists of two or more stages or levels, shown in time order from left to right.

Chance node

Problem features that are determined by chance or probability, such as the states of nature.

Figure A.1

Decision tree for cardiac catheterization service proposal

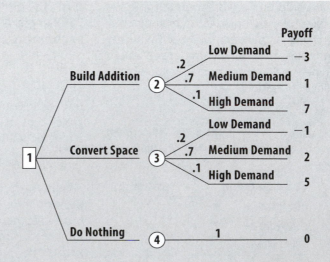

▶ Node 2 is a chance node representing the possible states of nature that might follow a decision to build an addition. There are three possibilities: 1) Low demand, which has a probability of .2; 2) Medium demand, which has a probability of .7; and 3) High demand, which has a probability of .1. Notice that each state of nature's probability has been written next to its branch.

▶ Node 3 is another chance node, representing the possible states of nature that might follow a decision to convert existing space. The branching is identical to the one for Node 2.

▶ Node 4 is the chance node that represents what might happen after a decision to do nothing. While it could have branches identical to those for Nodes 2 and 3, it is simpler to represent this way. That is, with probability 1, nothing is going to happen, because no action is being taken.

Paths and Payoffs

A connected series of branches that starts at the extreme left side of the tree (Node 1) and goes through all levels of the tree is called a **path**. Each path represents one of the

Path

A connected series of branches that starts at the extreme left side of the tree and goes through all levels of the tree.

Use the process of averaging out and folding back to analyze the decision tree shown in Figure A.1. Determine which decision alternative maximizes the expected return for the cardiac catheterization decision problem described in Example A.1.

Solution:

The first round of averaging out consists of replacing each chance branching in the right-most level of the tree by its expected value:

▶ The chance branching from Node 2 is replaced by its expected value:

$$.2(-3) + .7(1) + .1(7) = -.6 + .7 + .7 = .8$$

▶ The chance branching from Node 3 is replaced by its expected value:

$$.2(-1) + .7(2) + .1(5) = -.2 + 1.4 + .5 = 1.7$$

▶ The chance branching from Node 4 is replaced by its expected value, which is 0.

The result of this first round of averaging out is the reduced tree shown in Figure A.2a, in which each second-level chance branching has been replaced by its expected value.

We now back up one level in the tree (folding back). In the second round of "averaging out," Node 1, which is in the new right-most level of the tree of the

reduced tree shown in Figure A.2a, is replaced by the value of the best alternative, which is 1.7 for "Convert space." To show this, the value of the alternative chosen has been written above the decision node and the branches not chosen have been marked out with slashes as shown in Figure A.2(b).

Because the tree now has only one decision node, we can readily see that the decision strategy that maximizes the expected return to the hospital over the planning horizon is: Convert space for an expected net present value of $1.7 million.

Figure A.2

Analysis of cardiac catheterization service proposal decision tree

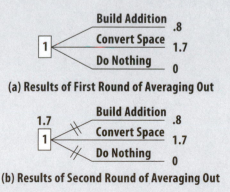

(a) Results of First Round of Averaging Out

(b) Results of Second Round of Averaging Out

possible sequences of decisions and chance results for the problem represented by the tree. For example, "Build addition" from Node 1 and "Medium demand" from Node 2 is one possible path or decision alternative and demand level sequence.

At the extreme right edge of the tree is given the net payoff for each of these possible paths, as given originally in the payoff table in Table A.1. For example, building an addition and experiencing medium demand for the service will result in a net present value of $1 million.

ANALYZING A DECISION TREE

The standard approach to analyzing a decision tree is to choose on the basis of expected value. The procedure for doing this is called **averaging out** and **folding back**.

Averaging out means replacing each branching by a single number. For a chance branching, the number used is the expected value, which is found by multiplying the probability of each branch by the value at its right end and summing. For a decision branching, the number used is the value of the best alternative in the branching.

Folding back means that this process starts at the right hand edge of the tree and proceeds back to the start of the tree, working from right to left.

In practice, we would consolidate the entire analysis process into a single decision tree rather than redrawing successively smaller trees after each round of averaging out and folding back. To do this, the result of each averaging out is written above the node to which it applies, with, as suggested in Example A.9, the decision alternatives not chosen being marked out with slashes. The result of applying this summarization process to the analysis in Example A.9 is shown in the Figure A.3, with the averaging out results being shown in red.

MULTISTAGE DECISION TREES

While we can certainly use a decision tree to analyze a one-decision problem, as just illustrated for Cheryl Sanders's cardiac catheterization service proposal, we really will

Averaging out

The procedure for analyzing a decision tree in which each branch is replaced by a single number.

Folding back

The procedure for analyzing a decision tree in which the process starts at the right hand edge of the tree and proceeds back to the start of the tree, working from right to left.

Figure A.3

Analyzed decision tree for cardiac catheterization service proposal

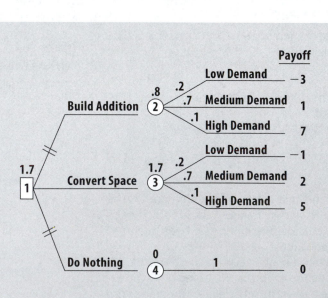

not gain anything we could not get from a payoff table analysis. The real benefit of using a decision tree becomes apparent in more complicated problems with multiple levels of decisions or states of nature, particularly if the decision alternatives, the states of nature, or their probabilities depend on what precedes them in the tree. While we could still use payoff tables to analyze these types of problems, structuring the tables would be difficult. A tree shows the structure and relationships in such a problem much better than a table does.

OTHER APPROACHES TO ANALYZING A DECISION TREE

While expected value analysis is the standard approach to analyzing a decision tree, it is not the only method possible. Two alternative approaches are **risk analysis**, which recognizes the various possible outcomes and their probabilities, and **extreme case analysis**, which, like the maximax and maximin strategies, takes either an optimistic or pessimistic view rather than working with probabilities. Explanations of both approaches follow.

Risk Analysis

A risk analysis approach to analyzing a decision tree recognizes each possible decision combination and the set of possible payoffs and their probabilities. These are then converted into a cumulative probability distribution and graphed for comparison purposes.

Risk analysis

An evaluation of the various possible outcomes and their probabilities.

Extreme case analysis

This is like the maximax *and* maximin *strategies which takes either an optimistic or pessimistic view rather than working with probabilities.*

Example A.10

Fred Silverton has just returned from a week-long trip to China, where he was part of a team sent by his company to explore a joint venture with a Chinese company to manufacture and market consumer electronics in China and Southeast Asia. Part of the decision about whether and how to enter into the arrangement is the decision about the size of the facility to build. The two alternatives discussed were (1) to build a large plant initially or (2) to build a small plant and then, if warranted, expand later or, if business is not good enough, sell out to the Chinese partner.

The possible decisions, along with preliminary estimates of the sales levels, their probabilities, and the resulting net present values of the different combinations are shown in the decision tree in Figure A.4. Notice two particular features of this tree:

▶ It is possible to have two or more successive chance nodes, as in the "High" result of Node 2 (sales level during the first two years) being followed by Node 4 rather than a decision. (Technically, there is a decision to "stay" or "sell

out," but the decision is obvious and is not included in the analysis.)

▶ The probabilities of the states of nature for Nodes 4, 8, 9, 10, and 11, all of which deal with the sales level during years 3–5, depend on the sales level during the first 2 years. That is, the later years' sales probabilities are conditional on the earlier years' results.

Determine what Fred Silverton's strategy should be. That is, determine whether they should initially build a large or small plant and, subsequently, what to do after the end of the first 2 years.

Solution:

The averaging out and folding back analysis of this decision is shown in red on the tree in Figure A.4. The best strategy is to build a large plant (Node 1 choice) and, whether the first 2 years' sales are high or low (Node 4), to stay with the project. The overall expected net present value from following this strategy is $20.0 million.

(continued)

Example A.10

(*continued*)

Figure A.4

Decision tree for Chinese joint venture proposal

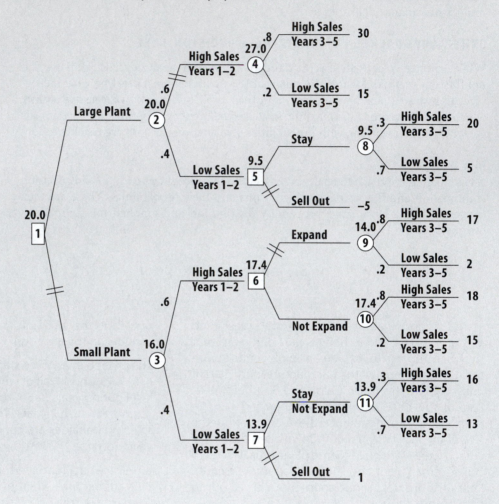

Extreme case analysis

This approach combines the "averaging out and folding back" approach described for expected value analysis with the procedures used earlier for decision making under certainty. The folding back part is the same, but in averaging out, rather than replacing a chance branching by its expected value, instead use the highest branch value (for the "best case" analysis) or use the lowest branch value (for the "worst case" analysis).

The "worst case" analysis will be left for the problems.

Refer back to the decision tree in Figure A.1. Construct cumulative probability distributions for the payoffs for the three decision alternatives.

Solution:

"Build addition" has possible payoffs of −3, with probability .2, 1 with probability .7, and 7, with probability .1. The cumulative probability distribution for "Build addition" is, therefore:

Cumulative Value	Probability
−3	.2
1	.9
1.0	

Similarly, the cumulative probability distributions for the alternatives "Convert space" and "Do nothing" are:

Convert space		Do nothing	
Value	Cumulative Probability	Value	Cumulative Probability
−1	.2	0	1.0
2	.9		
5	1.0		

Figure A.5 shows graphs of these three cumulative probability distributions. The decision maker can choose among the three alternatives by comparing the cumulative distributions on whatever basis he or she is most comfortable with.

Figure A.5
Risk analysis distributions

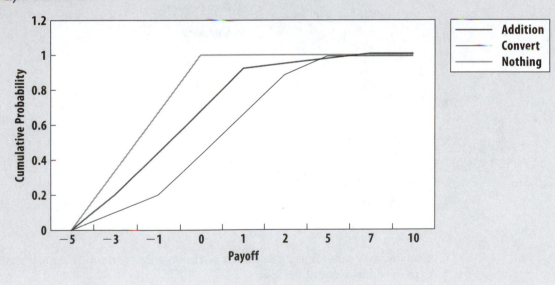

Utility: An Alternative to Dollar Value

In some decisions money is not an appropriate measure of the quality of the various outcomes. For example, how could you put a dollar value on losing your health or winning the top international award in your field? In other cases, the dollar value of an outcome may have implications beyond its monetary significance. A big loss, for

Example A.12

Refer back to Figure A.1. Perform a "best case" analysis on the cardiac catheterization service problem.

Solution:

The results of averaging out and folding back for a "best case" analysis are shown in red in the tree diagram in Figure A.6. The probability values from Figure A.1 have been eliminated since they are not relevant for a "best case" analysis.

In the first round of "averaging out":

▶ The branching from Node 2 is replaced by 7, the value for High demand.

▶ The branching from Node 3 is replaced by 5, the value for High demand.

▶ The branching from Node 4 is replaced by 0, which is the only possible payoff.

The second round of averaging out uses the results from the first round. Because Node 1 is a decision node, its branching is replaced with the value of the alternative chosen. Given that we are following a maximax or "best case" approach, that alternative is "Build addition," with value 7.

Figure A.6
Decision tree for cardiac catheterization proposal, using "best case" analysis

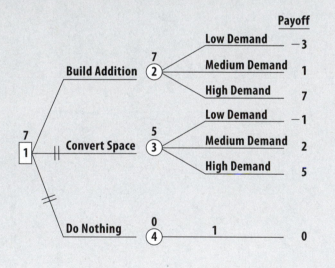

example, may result in the bankruptcy of the organization, which is more significant than the dollar value of the loss.

When dollar value alone is not an adequate measure of the value of an outcome, an alternative measure, utility, may be used. How to determine values for a utility function for a given situation is outside the scope of this supplement. However, a fairly complete discussion may be found in any text on decision theory, such as Howard Raiffa's *Decision Analysis: Introductory Lectures on Choices Under Uncertainty* (Addison-Wesley, 1970). Making decisions based on utility, however, is no different from making decisions based on money, as described in this supplement.

SUMMARY

All decision problems have three basic components: decision alternatives, implementation environments or states of nature, and a payoff function that gives the gain or loss for each alternative/state-of-nature combination.

In decision making under uncertainty, we assume that these three components are all that are known. A number of procedures based on different philosophies of what constitutes a good approach—maximax, maximin, equal likelihood, and minimax regret—were presented and illustrated.

Maximization of expected value or minimization of expected cost is the standard procedure for decision making under risk, in which probabilities for the states of nature are known in addition to the three basic components described.

An alternative to using payoff tables for decision making under risk is the decision tree, in which branchings represent either the decision alternatives or the states of nature relevant at a given point in the process. Decision trees are more flexible than payoff tables and can be more easily used to represent multistage decision problems and situations in which the probabilities of the states of nature depend on what has happened up to that point in the tree. The standard analysis approach for a decision tree with probabilities is averaging out and folding back, in which, starting at the right-most side of the tree, each branching is replaced by a single number—the expected value of a chance branching or the value of the alternative chosen in a decision branching. Two other possible approaches to analyzing a decision tree were also presented: risk analysis and best case or worst case analysis.

KEY TERMS

Averaging out, 794
Chance node, 792
Decision alternative, 786
Decision making under certainty, 787
Decision making under risk, 787
Decision making under uncertainty, 787
Decision tree, 792

Equal likelihood procedure, 788
Expected value of perfect
    information, 791
Extreme case analysis, 795
Folding back, 794
Maximax, 788
Maximin, 788

Minimax regret, 789
Path, 793
Payoff function, 786
Risk analysis, 795
States of nature, 786

SOLVED PROBLEMS

1. A high school band parents organization operates a Christmas tree lot every year to raise funds. Trees are bought in batches of 100 for $1000 and sold for $20 each. Leftover trees are taken away by a landscaping company (at no cost or revenue to the band) to be shredded for mulch. Based on past experience, the organization estimates that they can sell either three, four, five, or six batches of trees.

    a) Find the maximax, maximin, equally likely, and minimax regret decisions based on profits.

    b) Based on prior years' experience, the organization estimates that there is a 10% chance of selling three batches, a 30% chance of selling four batches, a 40% chance of selling five batches, and a 20% chance of selling six batches. Based on these probability estimates, determine the number of batches to buy to maximize expected profits.

Solution:

a) First, develop a profit payoff table as shown in Table A.2. The table entries are determined as follows:

Profit = Revenue − Cost = 2000(sold) − 1000(bought), so: If demand < bought, profit = 2000(demand) − 1000(bought). If demand > bought, profit = (2000 − 1000)(bought).

Table A.2
Payoff Table for Solved Problem 1

	Demand (Batches)			
Bought (Batches)	**3**	**4**	**5**	**6**
3	3000	3000	3000	3000
4	2000	4000	4000	4000
5	1000	3000	5000	5000
6	0	2000	4000	6000

The maximum, minimum, and average profits for the alternatives are shown in Exhibit A.4a.

Maximax: The largest maximum profit is $6000 from stocking six batches.

Maximin: The largest minimum profit is $3000 from stocking three batches.

Equally likely: The largest average profit is $3500 from stocking either four or five batches.

Minimax regret: The regret matrix and the maximum regret for each possible stocking level are shown in Exhibit A.4b. The smallest maximum regret is $2000 from stocking either four or five batches.

b) The expected values of the different possible stocking levels are:

Stock 3: .1(3000) + .3(3000) + .4(3000) + .2(3000) = 3000

Stock 4: .1(2000) + .3(4000) + .4(4000) + .2(4000) = 3800

Stock 5: .1(1000) + .3(3000) + .4(5000) + .2(5000) = 4000

Stock 6: .1(0) + .3(2000) + .4(4000) + .2(6000) = 3400

The stocking level that maximizes expected profits is five batches for an expected profit of $4000.

2. A resort development company has the opportunity to buy all or a portion of the acreage surrounding a lake for development. They must decide the size of the development for which they should buy land and put in roads and utilities. The company's owners are considering either a small or large

Exhibit A.4

	Demand (batches)						
Bought	3	4	5	6	Maximum	Minimum	Average
3	3000	3000	3000	3000	3000	3000	3000
4	2000	4000	4000	4000	4000	2000	3500
5	1000	3000	5000	5000	5000	1000	3500
6	0	2000	4000	6000	6000	0	3000
Maximum	3000	4000	5000	6000			

(a)

Regret Table:

	Demand Level				
Bought	3	4	5	6	Maximum
3	0	1000	2000	3000	3000
4	1000	0	1000	2000	2000
5	2000	1000	0	1000	2000
6	3000	2000	1000	0	3000

Determine maximum regret for each alternative

(b)

development. Similarly, they have identified two general levels of market acceptance of their project: low or high.

Table A.3
Payoff Table for Lakeside Development Problem

Size of Development	Acceptance Level	
	Low	High
Small	5	7.5
Large	−5	25

Estimates of the cost of land, road development, and utility installation for the different development sizes and of how many lots would be sold for each market acceptance level result in the profit estimates (in millions of dollars) for each combination of size and acceptance level are shown in Table A.3.

a) Assuming that the company can not make probability estimates for the different market acceptance levels, determine the appropriate decisions with the maximax, maximin, equally likely, and minimax regret procedures.

b) Using some basic market research, the owners estimate that the probabilities of the different levels of acceptance are P(Low) = .6 and P(High) = .4. Using these probabilities, find the alternative that maximizes expected profits and the expected value of perfect information.

c) Construct and analyze a decision tree using the expected profit criterion.

d) The developers' chief financial officer (CFO) has proposed that the company consider adopting a two-stage development approach. Under this approach the company will initially buy enough property for a small development and also purchase a 3-year option on the rest of the property. At the end of the three years the company can, if it seems warranted, then buy the rest of the property and increase the size of the development. Due to the cost of the option, all final payoffs in Table A.3 will be reduced by 1 ($1,000,000), but the opportunity to take advantage of the initial acceptance results to change the size decision may make up for this reduction.

The CFO believes that the probabilities of the two market acceptance levels during the first three years

will remain as currently estimated: P(Low) = .6 and P(High) = .4. However, he also believes that the probabilities of the final levels of market acceptance can be re-estimated on the basis of the experience during the first 3 years. Specifically, he estimates these probabilities as follows:

P(Low final acceptance|Low initial acceptance) = .8
P(High final acceptance|Low initial acceptance) = .2
P(Low final acceptance|High initial acceptance) = .3
P(High final acceptance|High initial acceptance) = .7

Develop a decision tree to model the CFO's alternative proposal. Analyze this tree to determine whether this two-stage development strategy is preferable to the decision reached in part (c).

Solution:

a) The row maxima, minima, and averages are shown in Exhibit A.5a. From them we can determine that the decisions for the different procedures are:

Maximax: The larger row maximum is 25, so the decision is a large development.

Maximin: The larger row minimum is 5, so the decision is a small development.

Equally likely: The larger row average is 10, which comes from a small development.

The regret matrix and its row maxima are shown in Exhibit A.5b. The alternative with the smallest maximum regret is a large development, with a maximum regret of 10.

Exhibit A.5

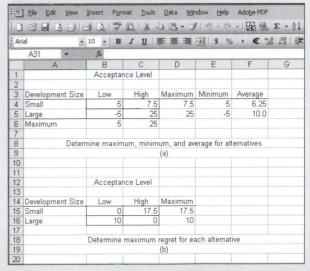

b) The expected profits of the alternatives are:

Alternative	Expected Profit
Small	$.6(5) + .4(7.5) = 6$
Large	$.6(-5) + .4(25) = 7$

The alternative with the higher expected profit is a large development.

Using the highest payoffs for the different states of nature, the expected value with perfect information (EWPI) is:

$$EWPI = .6(5) + .4(25) = 13$$

The expected value of perfect information is:

$$EVPI = EWPI - E(\text{Large development}) = 13 - 7 = 6$$

or $6,000,000.

c) The decision tree and the analysis (in red) are shown in Figure A.7. The averaging out and folding back goes as follows:

Node 2: The expected profits are $.6(5) + .4(7.5) = 6$.

Node 3: The expected profits are $.6(-5) + .4(25) = 7$.

Moving back to the first level:

Node 1: The alternative with the highest expected value is a large development, so mark out (with slashes) the other alternative.

The alternative with the highest expected profit is a large development with expected profit = 7 or $7,000,000.

Figure A.7
Decision tree for basic resort development problem

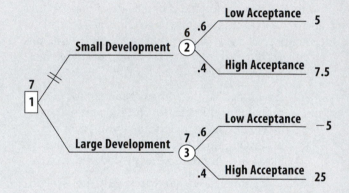

Figure A.8
Decision tree for expanded resort development problem

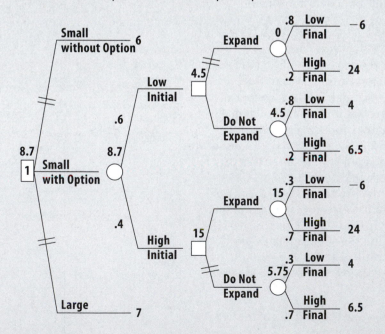

d) The decision tree (with analysis in red) is shown in Figure A.8. The expected payoffs for the two original decision possibilities (small development without an option to expand and large development) are taken from the decision tree in Figure A.7. Based on the analysis shown in Figure A.8, the company should initially build a small development with an option to expand after 3 years. If the initial level of acceptance is low, the company should not expand. If, however, the initial level of acceptance is high, the company should expand. Following this two-stage development strategy increases the expected profit from $7,000,000 for initially adopting a large development, to $8,700,000.

DISCUSSION QUESTIONS

1. Identify the basic components of a decision making problem.

2. Describe the differences among decision making under certainty, uncertainty, and risk.

3. Identify four different procedures for decision making under uncertainty and what the basic concept or philosophy is for each.

4. Describe the basic idea of the expected value of perfect information.

5. Why might using a decision tree be preferable to using a decision table?

6. Describe the process of averaging out and folding back.

PROBLEMS

A-1. A toy company has developed a new toy for the upcoming Christmas season. Because this toy is considerably different from the ones it has manufactured previously, the company will need to develop a new production facility for it. Three facility sizes—small, medium, and large—are under consideration. Given the nature of the toy market, the company is unsure as to what demand level it will encounter. The preliminary analysis is to be based on the demand being low, average, or high. A small amount of subcontracting will be available, so that if the production facility is undersized it will be possible to meet some of the excess demand. The accompanying table shows the estimated profits, in $1000s, of the various facility-size/demand-level combinations.

Payoff Table for Problem A-1

Facility Size	Demand Level		
	Low	Average	High
Small	750	900	900
Medium	350	1100	1300
Large	−250	600	2000

a) Determine the best production facility size using maximax, maximin, equally likely, and minimax regret.

b) The company's initial assessment of the probabilities of the different market sizes is: P(Low) = .5, P(Average) = .3, P(High) = .2. Determine the production facility size that maximizes expected profits and find the expected value of perfect information.

A-2. A publisher has received an unsolicited manuscript of a first novel. The decision is whether to offer the author a contract. Based on an initial reading of the manuscript, the publisher estimates the following profits if a contract is offered: If the sales level is high, profits will be $100,000; if moderate, profits will be $20,000; if low, they will lose $30,000. The publisher estimates the probabilities for the sales level to be: P(High) = .1, P(Moderate) = .4, P(Low) = .5. Determine, based on expected profits, whether the author should be offered a contract or not. Determine the expected value of perfect information.

A-3. A plumbing contractor has the opportunity to bid on a contract to do the plumbing work for a new office building. After reviewing the blueprints and specifications, the contractor estimates that the job will cost $300,000. The possible bids the contractor might make and his estimates of the probability of winning the contract at each bid level are:

Bid	Probability Win
$330,000	.90
$350,000	.75
$375,000	.50
$400,000	.25
$425,000	0

What should the contractor bid if he wishes to maximize his expected profits?

A-4. A developer is planning a new office complex, which may include some retail space. The possible percentages of retail space that the developer is considering are: none, 20%, or 40%. The desirability of the various percentages of retail space depends on the demand for office space. The estimated yearly profits (in $1000s) for the different retail percentages and office space demand levels are given in the accompanying table.

Payoff Table for Problem A-4

Retail Percentage	Office Space Demand		
	Low	Medium	High
None	−100	100	250
20%	150	200	200
40%	300	150	100

a) Determine what the percentage allocation of retail space should be using the maximax, maximin, equally likely, and minimax regret procedures.

b) The developer's assessments of the probabilities of the different office space demand levels are: P(Low) = .3, P(Moderate) = .4, P(High) = .3. Determine the percentage allocation of retail space that maximizes expected yearly profits. Find the expected value of perfect information.

A-5. A recent business school finance graduate has just received an inheritance of $100,000. Trying to decide how she should invest the money, she has identified three possible alternatives: stocks, commodities, and T-bills. The success of any alternative will depend on the performance of the economy over the next year. The accompanying table shows the gain (in $100s) from each investment alternative for each performance level of the economy.

Payoff Table for Problem A-5

Investment Alternatives	Performance of Economy		
	Recession	Stagnant	Growth
Stocks	−10	0	20
Commodities	−50	5	50
T-Bills	7	7	7

a) Determine the best way to invest the money using the maximax, maximin, equally likely, and minimax regret approaches.

b) Her estimates of the probabilities of the different possible performance levels of the economy are: P(Recession) = .1, P(Stagnant) = .6, P(Growth) = .3. Determine how to invest the money to maximize her expected gain. Find the expected value of perfect information.

A-6. Conduct a "worst case" analysis of the decision tree for the cardiac catheterization service proposal in Figure A.1 and Example A.1.

A-7. A hardware store orders snow blowers during the summer for delivery in the fall. Each snow blower costs the store $400 and, if sold prior to or during the winter, sells for $550. The store's manager doesn't want to carry any unsold snow blowers in inventory from one year to the next, so he reduces the price to $350 in the spring in order to get rid of any leftovers. Based on past experience, the store's manager expects that the demand for snow blowers at full price will be between six and ten.

a) Identify the decision alternatives and states of nature and construct a payoff table for the store manager's snow blower stocking problem.

b) Determine the number of snow blowers to stock if the maximax criterion is used.

Repeat for maximin, equally likely, and minimax regret.

c) Based on the long range forecasts for the upcoming winter's weather, the store manager estimates the probabilities of selling different numbers of snow blowers at full price to be: $P(6) = .35$, $P(7) = .30$, $P(8) = .20$, $P(9) = .10$, and $P(10) = .05$. Determine the number of snow blowers to stock to maximize expected profits.

d) Using the same probabilities, find the number of snow blowers to stock to minimize expected regret. Verify that the decision is the same as in part (c).

e) Using the probabilities in part (c), find the expected value of perfect information.

A-8. Dot'z Bakery bakes fresh apple pies each morning for sale that day. A pie costs $2 to make and sells for $4. Any pies left at the end of the day are sold the following day at a discounted price of $1.50. Based on her past experience, the bakery's manager expects to sell between eight and twelve pies per day.

a) Identify the decision alternatives and states of nature and construct a payoff table for the bakery manager's apple pie stocking problem.

b) Determine the number of apple pies to bake if the maximax criterion is used. Repeat for maximin, equally likely, and minimax regret.

c) Based on historical sales records, the bakery manager estimates the probabilities of the different apple pie demand levels as: $P(8) = .1$, $P(9) = .2$, $P(10) = .4$, $P(11) = .2$, $P(12) = .1$. Determine the number of apple pies to bake to maximize expected profits.

d) Using the same probabilities, find the number of apple pies to bake to minimize expected regret. Verify that the decision is the same as in part (c).

e) Using the probabilities in part (c), find the expected value of perfect information.

A-9. Considerable research and a great deal of practical experience show that the production of goods or services is generally subject to learning or experience curve effects. That is, records kept on the operation of many manufacturing and service delivery systems show that the time and cost required to produce a unit of output decrease at a fairly predictable rate as experience with that production increases. Given this predictable improvement, some companies follow a strategy of initially pricing a new product below its production cost as a way of building demand for the product, recognizing that, due to the learning curve effects, the cost will eventually be lower than the sale price, generating profits that will more than compensate for the initial losses.

A company is considering using this type of pricing strategy for a new product it is about to introduce, but is uncertain as to what learning rate to expect and, therefore, what pricing strategy to use. If a low initial price is set based on the assumption of a high rate of improvement and the improvement is slower, then the long-term profits will be lower than anticipated or nonexistent. If, however, a higher initial price is set, then demand would probably be lower and, even if the rate of learning is high, profits will not meet the hoped for levels. Initial assessments of the profit levels under various combinations of pricing and learning rates are summarized in the accompanying table.

Table for Problem A-9

	Rate of Learning		
Pricing Strategy	**Low**	**Moderate**	**High**
Price Low	−10	−3	12
Price Medium	−4	3	10
Price High	1	6	7

a) Determine the pricing strategy to follow if the maximax criterion is used. Repeat for maximin, equally likely, and minimax regret.

b) Based on the company's experience with other new products, the operations manager estimates the probabilities of the different rates of learning to be: $P(\text{Low}) = .2$, $P(\text{Moderate}) = .6$, $P(\text{High}) = .2$. Determine the pricing strategy to follow to maximize expected profits.

c) Using the same probabilities, find the pricing strategy to follow to minimize expected regret. Verify that the decision is the same as in part (c).

d) Using the probabilities in part (c), find the expected value of perfect information.

A-10. Tom Jackson's airline is considering a coupon promotion to increase business. Under this program, the airline will give anyone purchasing a full-fare ticket a coupon worth half off on any future flight. The airline is considering doing this for 2 weeks, a month, or not all. The possible results of undertaking this program are that it will be very successful, moderately successful, or not successful at all in developing new business over the next year after the program is over.

Based on other airline's experience with this type of program, the airline marketing manager estimates the net profits (in millions of dollars) for the various combinations of program times and market responses shown in the accompanying table.

Table for Problem A-10

	Level of Success		
Program Length	Not	Moderate	Very
Month	−5	−1	10
Two Weeks	−2.5	2	7
Do Nothing	0	0	0

a) Determine the amount of time for which to run the promotion if the maximax criterion is used. Repeat for maximin, equally likely, and minimax regret.

b) Again based on other airlines' experience with this type of coupon program, the airline's marketing manager estimates the probabilities of the different levels of program success to be: P(very successful) = .20, P(moderately successful) = .25, P(not successful) = .55. Which alternative should the airline adopt if management wishes to maximize expected net profits from the program? Determine the expected value of perfect information.

A-11. A distributor of greeting cards and related products has the opportunity to participate in the merchandising activities associated with a forthcoming children's movie. Due to the production lead time and the relatively short expected product life, the distributor must make a decision now about how much of this special party pack-

age to order. The distributor's marketing manager estimates that demand for this product will be between 400 and 800 units, in increments of 100 units. A unit, which consists of 1000 party packages, will cost $3000 and sell for $5000 at full price. If demand is too low, the selling price will be cut to $2000 to clear out the excess inventory.

a) Determine the number of units of product to order if the maximax criterion is used. Repeat for maximin, equally likely, and minimax regret.

b) Based on her past experience with similar types of movie-based special products, the marketing manager estimates that the probabilities of the different possible demand levels are: P(400) = .2, P(500) = .4, P(600) = .2, P(700) = .1, and P(800) = .1. Determine the number of units to order to maximize expected profit. Also determine the expected value of perfect information.

c) The manufacturer of the party packages will offer the distributor a discounted cost of $2500 per unit if a minimum of 600 units are ordered. Does the availability of this quantity discount make any difference in the decision about how many units to order if the expected profit criterion is used?

A-12. The management of a company being sued for damages as a result of injuries incurred due to product failure under normal use are consulting with their lawyers to determine how much to offer the plaintiff as a settlement to avoid having to go to trial. The lawyers have suggested taking a low/medium/high offer approach.

In an attempt to get off relatively cheaply, the company could initially offer the plaintiff $100,000, an amount that the lawyers believe would have only a 20%t chance of being accepted. Alternatively, they could offer $150,000, which the lawyers believe would have a 50/50 chance of acceptance, or offer $200,000, which the lawyers believe would definitely be accepted.

If the plaintiff does not accept the initial offer, the company would then make a second, higher offer, which the lawyers believe would have to be higher than a comparable offer made initially to get the same probability of acceptance. Specifically, the lawyers believe that the company would have to offer $175,000 to have a 50/50 chance of acceptance in the second stage and offer $225,000 to be guaranteed of acceptance.

Finally, if the plaintiff accepts neither the first nor the second offer, the lawyers believe that a final offer of $250,000 would definitely be accepted.

a) Determine what strategy the company should follow to minimize the expected cost of the settlement. That is, determine what the initial offer should be and, if it is not accepted, what the second offer should be.

b) Suppose that there is a 30% chance of the plaintiff accepting an initial offer of $100,000 (with no other factors changing.) Would this affect the strategy that minimizes the expected cost?

c) Determine the minimum probability of acceptance of an initial offer of $100,000 that would make the strategy starting with that amount optimal.

A-13. The city manager of Bridgeport is developing a recommendation to the city council on when to undertake repairs needed on one of the main bridges crossing the river that runs through the middle of town. The city engineer has informed her that the bridge is deteriorating at a rate that will make major repairs necessary sometime within the next three years.

If the repairs are done this year, the cost is estimated to be $1.2 million. If the repairs are delayed until next year and the condition of the bridge does not get significantly worse, then inflation and increased minor deterioration are estimated to raise the cost by 10%. If, however, there is significant additional deterioration, which is a function of the severity of the winter, the repairs will have to be done and the cost will increase to $1.8 million. At this point the weather service to which the city subscribes estimates only a 20% chance that the winter will be severe.

If the upcoming winter is not severe, then the city will again have the option of delaying the repairs for another year. Again, if the following winter is not severe, inflation and normal increased deterioration will raise the cost by an ad-

ditional 10% over the cost of repair in the second year. If the winter between the second and third years is severe, the added deterioration to the bridge will raise the cost to $2.4 million. Normal weather patterns suggest that there is a 50/50 chance of a severe winter 2 years from now.

If this were all there were to the decision, the city manager would not have a problem. Because the cost keeps going up, regardless of how severe the winter is, the repairs should be done this year. However, the city manager has been informed by the local state representative that there is a possibility that the city could get a $600,000 grant from the state that would help pay for the repairs, thus reducing the cost to the city. While the grant will not be available for the current year, the representative estimates a 60% chance that the grant will be available in the second year. Furthermore, if the city does not get a grant in year 2, there is a 75% chance they will get one in year 3.

a) Utilizing this information, develop a recommendation for the city manager that will minimize the expected cost to the city of repairing the bridge.

b) Changing nothing else, what is the minimum probability of getting a grant in year 3 (given that one had not be received in year 2) that would make delaying the repair to year 3 (if possible) the optimal strategy.

A-14. The Pittsburgh Steelers have just won the AFC title and the owner of a sports specialty store in Pittsburgh has to decide how many of the special "AFC Champions" T-shirts he should order. The T-shirt manufacturer will only sell the shirts in cases of 100 at $1000 per case. The shirts will be priced for sale at $15 each, with any leftover by the time of the Super Bowl (which will be in two weeks) being sold on the discount table at $6 each. To simplify the analysis, assume that demand for the T-shirts is in whole cases. The sports store owner believes that his store will sell between one and three cases of shirts.

a) Determine the number of cases of shirts the store owner should order if the maximax criterion is used. Repeat for maximin, equally likely, and minimax regret.

b) Based on T-shirt sales during previous Steeler appearances in the Super Bowl, the store owner estimates the probabilities of the different demand levels as: $P(1) = .12$, $P(2) = .48$, $P(3) = .40$. Determine the number of cases of T-shirts to order to maximize expected profits.

c) Using the same probabilities, find the number of cases of T-shirts to order to minimize expected regret. Verify that the decision is the same as in part (b).

d) Using the probabilities in part (b), find the expected value of perfect information.

A-15. (Continuation of Problem A-14.) To provide some protection against getting stuck with too many unsold T-shirts, the store owner has asked the T-shirt producer about the possibility of buying some shirts now and, if desired, more a week later. The producer says he is willing to do this, but, because he will have to set his equipment up to produce a second batch later, the reorder will cost $1200 per case rather than $1000.

The store owner believes that during the first week there is a 60% chance that there will be demand for one case of shirts and a 40% chance of demand for two cases. He also believes that the first week's demand will be a good indication of what the demand will be in the second week. Specifically, he estimates the second week's demand (in cases) to be:

If the first week's demand is for one case:

P(2nd week's demand = 0) = .2

P(2nd week's demand = 1) = .6

P(2nd week's demand = 2) = .2

If the first week's demand is for two cases:

P(2nd week's demand = 0) = .3

P(2nd week's demand = 1) = .7

a) Using a decision tree, determine the ordering strategy that will maximize the store owner's expected profit.

b) Compare the expected profit from following the optimal two-stage ordering strategy developed in part (a) with the expected profit if all shirts have to be ordered initially, as determined in part (b) of Problem A-14.

B

Supplement B: Mathematical Optimization

Supplement Outline

Supplement B: Mathematical Optimization   810

    Linear Programming   810

    The Transportation Model   820

Summary   826

Key Terms   826

Solved Problems   826

Discussion Questions   830

Problems   830

Supplement B: Mathematical Optimization

Any decision-making situation involves two basic issues: What are we making decisions about, and How do we know that one decision alternative is better than another? Of increasing importance in management decision making is the use of mathematical models as part of the process of organizing data, generating decision alternatives, and evaluating those alternatives.

One particular type of mathematical model that has proven itself useful over and over again is mathematical programming. In this model type, values of one or more decision variables are chosen to maximize or minimize the value of an **objective function**, a mathematical expression that states how the variables contribute to achieving the decision maker's objective. Many types of mathematical programming models exist, some more useful in practice than others. In this supplement we will consider two: linear programming, which is an extremely powerful and widely used general model; and the transportation model, a special case of the linear programming model that has particular relevance to the facility location decision.

Linear Programming

Linear programming (LP) is a special type of mathematical programming model. It is used to determine the values of decision variables that will maximize or minimize the value of a linear objective function, subject to a set of linear equation or inequality constraints. A mathematical expression is linear if it is the sum of terms, each of which is a constant times a variable. For example, $5X + 3Y$ is a linear expression, but $3X^2 + 4XY - 6/Y$ is not, because it includes a square, a product, and a quotient.

While restricting both the objective function and the constraints to linear expressions may seem to limit the usefulness of linear programming, that is not the case. The relationships in many problems are sufficiently close to being linear that linear programming has been used extensively and profitably in practically every functional area of business.

A small-scale example of a very popular type of application, the product mix problem, will be used to illustrate the basic ideas of linear programming. In this application, the problem is to determine how many of each of several products to make so as to maximize their total contribution to profit and overhead, without over-using limited resources.

MODEL FORMULATION

Building a linear programming model begins with defining decision variables and formulating the objective function that is to be maximized or minimized. In addition, the constraints that limit the decision maker's freedom to choose values for the decision variables must also be formulated.

GRAPHICAL SOLUTION

When a linear programming problem has only two decision variables, we can solve it graphically. This is obviously not important for solving realistic problems, but the graph helps us to understand some of the basic ideas associated with the solution process and the solution.

Objective function

A mathematical expression that states how the variables contribute to achieving the decision maker's objective.

Linear programming (LP)

A special type of mathematical programming model used to determine the values of decision variables that will maximize or minimize the value of a linear objective function, subject to a set of linear equation or inequality constraints.

The furniture company for which Luis Flores works has introduced a new, higher-quality line of wooden office furniture, which has proven to be so popular that the company can sell all that it can produce. Unfortunately, the special type of wood used for this line is in limited supply, as are the special skills required for its manufacture. But the profit contribution on this line of furniture is higher than it is on the company's other lines. Management would like to maximize the line's profit contribution by producing the best possible combination of the two products in the line: desks and conference tables. Profit contributions and resource usage for the two products in the line are as follows: Each desk requires 3 units of wood, 4 hours of assembly time, and 4 hours of finishing time, and returns $110 to profit and overhead. Each table requires 2 units of wood, 2 hours of assembly time, and 6 hours of finishing time, and returns $160 to profit and overhead. Ten units of wood, 15 hours of assembly time, and 24 hours of finishing time are available per day.

Formulate a linear programming model to determine how many desks and conference tables Luis's company should produce each day.

Solution:

First, define the decision variables as:

D = the number of desks to produce each day
T = the number of conference tables to produce each day

The objective function to be maximized is total contribution to profit, so:

Maximize $110D + 160T$

Three resources are available only in limited supply: wood, assembly time, and finishing time. Set up a constraint for each, stating that the amount of resource used will be no more than the amount available.

Wood: $3D + 2T \leq 10$

Assembly: $4D + 2T \leq 15$

Finishing: $4D + 6T \leq 24$

To illustrate the rationale of these constraints, let us consider the Wood constraint in detail: Each desk produced requires 3 units of wood; thus, the total amount of wood used in making D desks is 3D units. Similarly, each table produced requires 2 units of wood, so the total amount of wood used in making T tables is 2T units. Adding these together, the total amount of wood used in producing D desks and T tales is $3D + 2T$ units. Because only 10 units of wood are available, the company must choose values for D and T that will result in $3D + 2T \leq 10$.

The reasoning behind the assembly and finishing constraints is similar.

Finally, producing negative quantities of these two products obviously makes no sense, so add two non-negativity constraints:

$D \geq 0, T \geq 0$

Solve the problem in Example B.1 graphically.

Solution:

First, set up a two-dimensional solution space with variable axes at right angles to one another, as in Figure B.1. Because the decision variables must have non-negative values, we only need to concern ourselves with the upper-right-hand or non-negative quadrant of the space, which is shown by leaving only that area unshaded.

The next step is to graph each of the constraints, which is done in the first three panels of Figure B.2. To graph an inequality constraint, first graph the equation and then shade the part of the space that does not satisfy the inequality. For example, in Figure B.2a, for the wood constraint, graph the line

(continued)

Example B.2

(continued)

Figure B.1
Two-dimensional solution space with right-angle axes

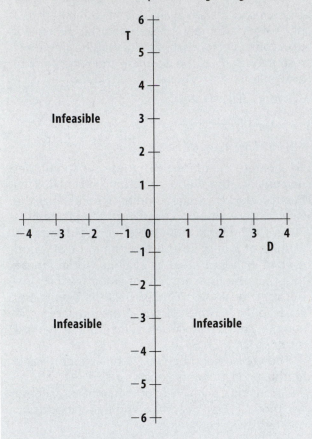

Figure B.2
(a) Wood constraint

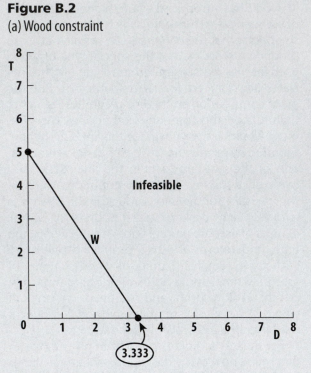

Figure B.2
(b) Assembly constraint

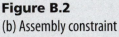

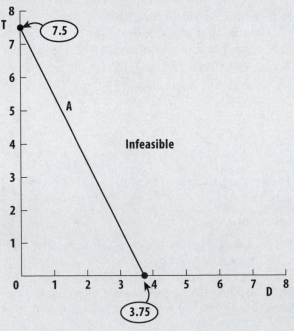

for the equation $3D + 2T = 10$. To determine where the line crosses the D axis, set $T = 0$ and solve the equation to get $D = 3.333$. To determine where the line crosses the T axis, set $D = 0$ and solve the equation to get $T = 5.0$. Next, determine which side of the line satisfies the inequality $3D + 2T < 10$. The easiest way to do this is to check whether the origin, where $D = T = 0$, satisfies the inequality. It does, so all the points on the line and in the space below it satisfy the constraint, and all the points above the line do not. Shade the area above the line, as in Figure B.2a, to show that those points do not satisfy the constraint. Parts (b) and (c) of Figure B.2 are done the same way.

Figure B.2

(c) Finishing constraint

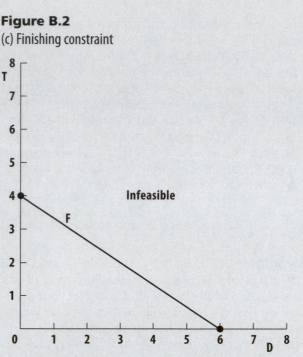

Figure B.2

(d) Feasible set

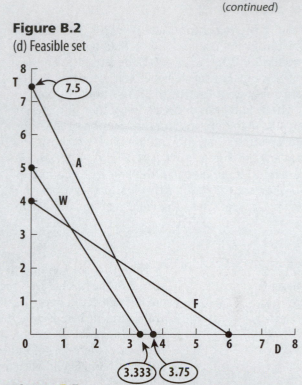

Because the solution must satisfy all the constraints, all three lines should actually be drawn on the same graph. The three individual constraints are combined into one graph in Figure B.2d. The unshaded part of that diagram, along with its edges, represents the **feasible set** for the problem—that is, the set of points that satisfy all the constraints.

The next step is to use the objective function to identify which feasible solution is optimal. Because the objective function is not an equation or an inequality, it cannot be graphed. However, if we set the objective function equal to a specific number, we can graph that equation. Figure B.3 shows the feasible set along with three possible objective function lines. The line closest to the origin, labeled 320, represents the equation $110D + 160T = 320$. Any point on that line represents a solution that gives a total profit contribution of $320. Because the line lies within the feasible set (unshaded area), we know that it is possible to

Figure B.3

Feasible set with representative objective function lines

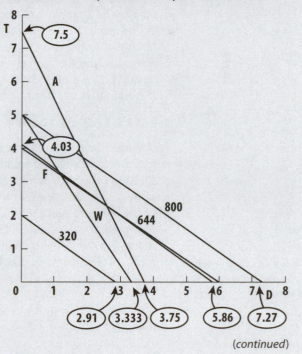

(continued)

Example B.2

(*continued*)

attain a profit contribution of $320. The line furthest from the origin, labeled 800, represents the equation $110D + 160T = 800$. Because this line lies entirely outside the feasible set, we know that a total profit contribution of $800 is not possible.

These two lines show us two other things that are crucial to determining the location of the optimal solution. First, they are parallel, which means that any other line $110D + 160T =$ number will be parallel to them. Second, the line with the higher number on the right side lies further from the origin. To maximize the value of the objective function, we must find a line that is between and parallel to these two, as far from the origin as possible, but still passes through some part of the feasible set. That line is the third line on the graph, labeled 644. The point where that line passes through a corner of the feasible set, at the intersection of the W (wood) and F (finishing) equation lines, is the of the optimal solution to the problem. Solving the W and F equations simultaneously gives the optimal solution: $D = 1.2, T = 3.2$, which gives a profit contribution of $644.[1]

Feasible set

The set of points that satisfy all the constraints.

Note that the solution to the problem in Example B.2 is that it is located at a corner of the feasible set—that is, at a point where two constraint lines cross. (There are five constraint lines: the two axes plus the lines labeled W, A, and F.) This is a general result: If there is an optimal solution (and there will always be one, as long as there is a feasible solution), then there will be one at a corner of the feasible set. In some cases there may be more than one optimal corner solution; if so, they will be at adjacent corners and all points on the line connecting them will also be optimal solutions.

Note also that in the solution to this problem, the variable values are not integers. For purposes of actually using a linear programming problem's solution, this may or may not be a problem. Obviously, Luis Flores's company can not make fractional units of furniture, so the optimal solution can not be implemented. In other problems, fractional units will make sense. Although linear programming does not always yield integer values for the variables, an extension of linear programming, called integer linear programming (IP), does. Many LP computer packages can solve IP problems, although they will be more restricted in size and will take longer to solve.

USING EXCEL'S SOLVER

Solver

Solver is a feature of Microsoft's Excel that can be used to solve linear programing problems

If a linear programming model includes more than two decision variables, then a systematic, computerized solution procedure is needed. The standard computerized LP solution procedure is a variation of the Simplex Method, in which the search for the optimal solution starts at the origin and follows a path from corner to adjacent corner of the solution space until it reaches a corner that it recognizes as being optimal. At that point it stops. Excel's Solver uses a different search procedure, a variation on a more general procedure that can also be used with nonlinear mathematical programming problems (such as those considered above for the single facility location problem).

Using Solver to solve a linear programming problem is a straight forward procedure. First, set the problem up in a spreadsheet. Next, select *Tools* from the menu, select *Solver* from the pull-down menu, and fill in the dialog box. In addition to identifying

---

[1] Verify that the solution $D = 1.2$ and $T = 3.2$ is a feasible solution and does give a total profit contribution of 644 by substituting those values into the three constraints and the objective function.

Use Excel's Solver to solve the LP model in Example B.1. Determine how many desks and conference tables to produce and what the total profit contribution will be. Also determine how much of each resource is used and how much is left over.

Solution:

First set up a spreadsheet, as shown in Exhibit B.1. Columns C and D correspond to the two products, with the changing cells (decision variables) for Desks in cell C5 and for Tables in cell D5. The products' profit contributions are shown in row 8. Rows 15 through 17 contain the resource information, with the amounts used per unit of product in columns C and D of those rows. The total amount of each resource used by the solution in cells C5 and D5 is shown in a cell in column E. Cell E15 shows the amount of Wood used by the solution in cells C5 and D5. The formula in cell E15 is = SUMPRODUCT($C$5:$D$5,C15:D15), which translates into 3 × DESKS + 2 × TABLES. This formula is then copied into E16 and E17, so that cell E16 shows the amount of assembly time used and cell E17 shows the amount of finishing time used. The available

amounts of the resources are given in F15 through F17. Finally, the total contribution to profit and overhead is given in the Target cell F6, the formula for which is =SUMPRODUCT(C5:D5,C8:D8).

Next, click on *Tools* on the menu bar and select *Solver*. The results of filling in the Solver dialog box are in Exhibit B.2. The top part should be obvious. The target cell is F6, where the formula for the total profit contribution is located, and the changing cells are C5 and D5, where the values for the amounts of desks and tables to produce appear. The Constraints box is filled in as follows: Click *Add*. Then click in the left panel, mark E15:E17, select <= from the relationship box, click in the right panel, and mark F15:F17. Doing this sets up the three resource constraints. To include the non-negativity constraints, click *Add* again. Then click in the left panel, mark C5:D5 (the changing cells), select >= from the relationship box, click in the right panel, and type 0.

You are now ready to solve the problem. Click on *Options,* check *Assume Linear Model,* click *OK,* and click *Solve.* In the Solver Results box, mark *Keep Solver Solution* and select the *Answer* and *Sensitivity* reports; click OK. The resulting spreadsheet is shown in Exhibit B.3, which gives the optimal solution, as does the Answer report shown in

Exhibit B.1

	A	B	C	D	E	F	G
	F6			=SUMPRODUCT(C5:D5,C8:D8)			
1	OFFICE FURNITURE PRODUCT MIX PROBLEM						
2							
3	Product:		Desks	Tables			
4						PROFIT:	
5	Quantity to Produce:		0	0			
6						$0.00	
7							
8	Profit per Unit:		$110	$160			
9							
10			Product Resource Requirements				
11	--------------						
12	Resources:		Quantity Required:		Total	Amount	
13			Desks	Tables	Usage	Available	
14							
15	Wood		3	2	0	10	
16	Assembly Time		4	2	0	15	
17	Finishing Time		4	6	0	24	
18							
19							

Exhibit B.2

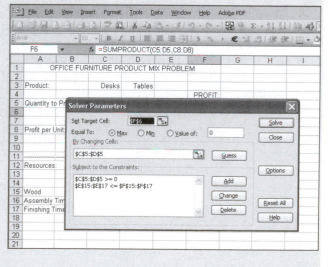

(continued)

Example B.3

(continued)

Exhibit B.4. The optimal solution, which yields a total profit contribution of $644, is to produce 1.2 desks and 3.2 tables. In Exhibit B.4 we see that this solution uses all 10 units of wood, so that the amount of wood left over (the slack for wood) is 0. Further, the amount of assembly time used is 11.2 hours, with assembly time slack = 3.8 hours, and the amount of finishing time used is 24 hours, with finishing time slack = 0 hours.

Exhibit B.3

	A	B	C	D	E	F	G
1	OFFICE FURNITURE PRODUCT MIX PROBLEM						
3	Product:		Desks	Tables			
4						PROFIT:	
5	Quantity to Produce:		1.2	3.2			
6						$644.00	
8	Profit per Unit:		$110	$160			
10				Product Resource Requirements			
12	Resources:		Quantity Required:		Total	Amount	
13			Desks	Tables	Usage	Available	
15	Wood		3	2	10	10	
16	Assembly Time		4	2	11.2	15	
17	Finishing Time		4	6	24	24	

F6 = SUMPRODUCT(C5:D5,C8:D8)

Exhibit B.4

Target Cell (Max)

Cell	Name	Original Value	Final Value
$F$6	PROFIT:	$0.00	$644.00

Adjustable Cells

Cell	Name	Original Value	Final Value
$C$5	DESKS	0	1.2
$D$5	TABLES	0	3.2

Constraints

Cell	Name	Cell Value	Formula	Status	Slack
$E$15	Wood Usage	10	$E$15<=$F$15	Binding	0
$E$16	Assembly Time Usage	11.2	$E$16<=$F$16	Not Binding	3.8
$E$17	Finishing Time Usage	24	$E$17<=$F$17	Binding	0
$C$5	DESKS	1.2	$C$5>=0	Not Binding	1.2
$D$5	TABLES	3.2	$D$5>=0	Not Binding	3.2

the target cell and the changing cells, you must also fill in *the constraints box*. This is done by clicking on the *Add* button next to it and marking a constraint, repeating the process as many times as necessary. Once the dialog box is complete, click on the *Options* button and check *Assume Linear Model*. Click *OK* and then click *Solve*. When the Solver Results box appears, mark the reports you wish to receive and click *OK*.

SHADOW PRICES AND SENSITIVITY ANALYSIS

While all the numbers in a linear programming model are treated as though they are exact and known for certain, that is often not the case in reality; they are only estimates or may change over time. As is the case for any decision model, we are interested in knowing how much these numbers can change without changing the solution, and what the implications of changing any of these numbers would be. That is, we are interested in the **sensitivity** of the solution to the numbers used. Thus we will be looking at three questions:

1. How much can we change a decision variable's objective function coefficient value before it would change the solution?

2. How would changing the limit (right-hand-side value) of a constraint affect the value of the objective function?

3. By how much can we change that limit and still have the same effect?

OBJECTIVE FUNCTION SENSITIVITY

Looking at the graph for the furniture problem (Example B.1) in Figure B.3, it should be obvious that if we make the objective function line slightly flatter or steeper, we will still get the same feasible set corner as the optimal solution. The objective function line will become flatter if we decrease the coefficient of D (desks) to less than $110 or increase the coefficient of T (tables) to more than $160. Similarly, the objective function line will become steeper if we do the opposite—increase the coefficient of D or decrease the coefficient of T.

Looking more closely at Figure B.3, we can see that the maximum amount by which we can flatten the objective function line and still get the same optimal solution is to make it coincide with line F. If the objective function line gets any flatter than line F, the location of the optimal solution will shift to the point where line F crosses the vertical axis, and the new optimal solution will be D = 0 and T = 4. In the same way, we can also see that the steepest we can make the objective function line and still get the same optimal solution is to make it coincide with line W. If the objective function line gets any steeper than line W, the location of the optimal solution will shift to the point where line W crosses the horizontal axis, and the new optimal solution will be D = 3.333 and T = 0.

The slope of a straight line (that is, how flat or steep it is) is determined by the ratio of the coefficients of its two variables. Assuming that we do not change the objective function coefficient of T (keeping it at $160), the smallest we can make the coefficient of D without making the objective function line flatter than line F is $106.667—a (maximum) decrease of $3.333 from the current value of $110. Similarly, the largest we can make the coefficient of D without making the objective function line steeper than line W is $240—a (maximum) increase of $130 from $110. These maximum decrease and increase values may be found in the Desks line of the Sensitivity Report from Solver shown in Exhibit B.5. Thus the **insensitivity range** for the desks objective function coefficient is $106.667 to $240. As long as the profit contribution of a table stays at $160, the profit contribution of a desk can be

Sensitivity

The likelihood of a decision outcome to change based upon the assumed value of a variable.

Insensitivity range

The range of assumed values a decision variable have without changing the decision outcome.

Exhibit B.5

Adjustable Cells

Cell	Name	Final Value	Reduced Cost	Objective Coefficient	Allowable Increase	Allowable Decrease
$C$5	DESKS	1.2	0	110	130	3.333333333
$D$5	TABLES	3.2	0	160	5	86.66666667

Constraints

Cell	Name	Final Value	Shadow Price	Constraint R.H. Side	Allowable Increase	Allowable Decrease
$E$15	Wood Usage	10	2	10	2.375	2
$E$16	Assembly Time Usage	11.2	0	15	1E+30	3.8
$E$17	Finishing Time Usage	24	26	24	6	10.66666667

anywhere in this range and the optimal solution will still be to produce 1.2 desks and 3.2 tables. The total profit contribution will, of course, change to reflect the new unit contributions.

We can apply exactly the same analysis to the Tables line in Exhibit B.5. Assuming we keep the objective function coefficient of D at $110, the maximum amount by which we can decrease the coefficient of T (from $160) without making the objective function line steeper than line W is $86.667, to $73.333. Similarly, the maximum amount by which we can increase the coefficient of T without making the objective function line flatter than line F is $5, to $165. Thus, the insensitivity range for the desks objective function coefficient is $73.333 to $165. As long as the profit contribution of a desk stays at $110, the profit contribution of a table can be anywhere in this range, and the optimal solution will still be to produce 1.2 desks and 3.2 tables.

CHANGING A CONSTRAINT'S LIMIT: THE SHADOW PRICE

Looking again at the graph for the furniture problem in Figure B.3, it should be obvious that changing a constraint's limit or right-hand side, which will move that constraint's equation line, may or may not make any difference in the solution, depending on which line is moved.

Because the location of the current optimal solution is the point where the W and F constraint lines cross, moving either of those lines by changing the amount of either wood or finishing time available will lead to a new optimal solution. This new optimal solution will have a different objective function value. The value will be better if the change in the constraint increases the size of the feasible set, so that a new, better solution can be found; it will be worse if the change reduces the size of the feasible set, so that the previously optimal solution is eliminated.

On the other hand, the current optimal solution is well inside the feasible area for the assembly time constraint (there is assembly time slack), so moving line A in toward the origin a little (by reducing the available assembly time slightly) or moving line A away from the origin (by increasing the available assembly time) will not make a new optimal solution necessary. Because the optimal solution will not change, the objective function value will not change either.

The change in the value of the objective function that results from a one-unit change in the right-hand side of a constraint (while holding everything else constant) is called the constraint's **shadow price**, marginal cost, or marginal value. The shadow price of a constraint is very useful because it tells us the maximum amount we should be willing to pay for a resource, over and above the price used in determining the objective function coefficient values, either to get an additional unit of that resource or to avoid losing one.

Graphically, the shadow price can be found by regraphing the problem with the new constraint line given by the new value of the resource's availability, resolving the problem, and computing the amount by which the objective function value has changed. Within limits, we would find that the change is exactly the same (although of opposite sign) whether the right-hand side of the constraint is increased or decreased.

If Excel's Solver is used to solve the model, the shadow price can be found in the "Constraints" section of the Sensitivity Report. For example, in Exhibit B.5 the shadow price for wood is $2 per unit; the shadow price for finishing time is $26 per hour. The shadow price for assembly time is 0 because changing the location of line A slightly will not change the optimal solution or the objective function value.

Shadow price

The change in the value of the objective function that results from a one-unit change in the right hand side of a constraint.

CHANGING A CONSTRAINT'S LIMIT: THE RANGE

While increasing the amount of wood available from 10 units to 11 would increase the total profit contribution by $2 (from $644 to $646), and a second increase from 11 units to 12 would further increase the total profit contribution by an additional $2 (to $648), a third increase from 12 units to 13 would not raise the total profit contribution to $650. The graph in Figure B.4 makes the reason clear: There is not enough assembly time to take full advantage of that thirteenth unit of wood. In fact, given that there are only 15 hours of assembly time available, the maximum amount of wood that could be used by the optimal solution when 13 units of wood are available (D = 2.625 and T = 2.25, for a profit of $648.75) is only 12.375 units. Thus the maximum increase in the amount of available Wood for which the shadow price will be $2 is 12.375 − 10 = 2.375 units. Similarly, by moving the W line closer to the origin, we find that the maximum decrease in the amount of available wood for which the shadow price would be $2 per unit is 2 units (from 10 down to 8).

Just as the shadow price for a constraint can be found in Solver's Sensitivity Report, so also is the range within which that shadow price holds. Referring to the "Allowable Increase" and "Allowable Decrease" columns in Exhibit B.5, the range for the wood constraint goes from a minimum of 10 − 2 = 8 units to a maximum of 10 + 2.375 = 12.375 units. Assuming nothing else changes, any change in the amount of wood available within that range will have a marginal value of $2 per unit. The results for the finishing time constraint are determined in the same way.

The situation with the assembly time constraint is a little different. Because only 11.2 of the 15 available assembly time hours are actually being used by the current solution, a reduction in the available assembly time to that level will have no effect on the objective function value (the shadow price will be 0). Thus, the maximum reduction for a constraint with slack is equal to the amount of slack, in this case, 3.8 hours, for a lower limit of 11.2 hours. Increasing the amount of assembly time available will have

Figure B.4

Furniture problem with wood = 13

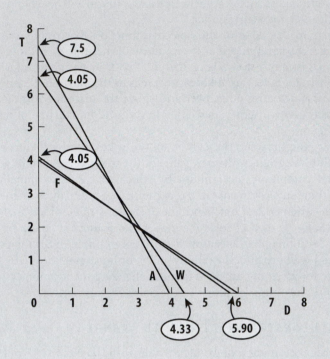

Example B.4

(Refer to Example B.1)

Luis Flores's company would like to increase the production of the new office furniture line and the profit contribution from it. While the supplier cannot provide additional wood in the near future, employees can be asked to work overtime. What is the maximum amount the company should pay for overtime in the two departments, and how much overtime should be worked in each?

Solution:

From the Sensitivity Report in Exhibit B.5, we find that there is already slack in the assembly time constraint, with a shadow price of 0, working any overtime in assembly makes no sense. For finishing time, the shadow price is $26 within a range of 13.333 (24 − 10.667) to 30 (24 + 6) hours. Thus paying an overtime premium of up to $26 per hour for a maximum of 6 additional hours of finishing time would make sense.

no effect at all, other than to increase the slack on a one for one basis. Thus the upper limit for the assembly time constraint's range is ∞.[2]

The Transportation Model

Many companies produce the same product at several factories and distribute it through a number of different warehouses. In such systems a basic problem is to

---

[2] Excel shows ∞ as 1E+30, a very large number (1 followed by 30 zeros).

determine how much of the product to ship from each of the factories to each of the warehouses. The **transportation model** is a special type of linear programming model that can be useful in solving this type of problem.

The basic structure of a transportation model is as follows: A given product is available in specific limited quantities at each of a number of sources (for example, factories) and is required in specified amounts at each of a number of destinations (for example, warehouses). The cost of shipping a unit from each source to each destination is known and is the same for every unit shipped on that route. The problem is to determine how much to ship from each source to each destination so as to minimize the total shipping cost.

Transportation model

A special type of linear programming model.

MODEL FORMULATION

Because of the relatively simple nature of the problem, a special format—called a **transportation tableau**—is used to summarize the information for a transportation model. A transportation tableau is a matrix with a row for each source and a column for each destination. In each cell of the matrix is written the cost of shipping a unit from the row's source to the destination's column. To the right of each row is written the availability at that row's source. At the bottom of each column is written the requirement at that column's destination.

Transportation tableau

A special format used to summarize the information for a transportation model.

Example B.5

Fred Silverton's company produces cell phones at three plants in the Southwest (SW), Midwest (MW), and Southeast (SE). The Southwest plant has a capacity of 100,000 units per month, while each of the other two plants has a capacity of 150,000 units per month. The products are distributed nationally through warehouses in California, which has monthly demand of 70,000 units, Texas (40,000), Michigan (50,000), North Carolina (70,000), and Pennsylvania (90,000). The cost (in $100s) of shipping 1000 units from each plant to each warehouse is given in Table B.1. Formulate a transportation tableau to summarize the information about the production and distribution of cell phones in Fred's company.

Solution:

There are three sources (SW, MW, and SE) and five destinations (CA, TX, MI, NC, and PA), so we need a three-by-five matrix, as shown in Figure B.5. The plants' capacities, in thousands of units, appear along the right edge of the matrix. The warehouses' requirements, also in thousands of units, appear along the bottom edge of the matrix. The unit costs from Table B.1 appear in the squares in the upper-right corner of each cell of the matrix.

Figure B.5

Transportation tableau for example D.3

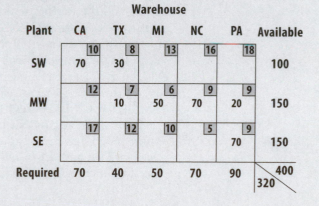

Table B.1

Unit Transportation Costs for Example B.3

Plant	Warehouse				
	CA	TX	MI	NC	PA
SW	10	8	13	16	18
MW	12	7	6	9	9
SE	17	12	10	5	9

If the total units available at the sources equals the total units required at the destinations, a transportation model is said to be balanced. The model in Example B.2 is unbalanced because the total units available (400) is more than the total units required (320). If we wished, we could transform the tableau in Figure B.5 into a balanced tableau by adding a sixth column, called a Dummy destination, that would absorb the excess supply of 80 units. The costs for that column would all be 0 because "shipping" from a real source to the Dummy destination actually means not actually producing and shipping those units. (Similarly, if the total units available at the sources were less than the total units required at the destinations, then we could add a Dummy source to provide the shortage, again with 0 costs. "Shipping" from the Dummy source to a real destination would then represent failing to meet demand.) We will not include the Dummy destination here because it is not needed for our solution procedure.[3]

MODEL SOLUTION

To solve a transportation model, we must assign values to the cells of the transportation tableau (the source/destination shipments) that meet the following two criteria:

1. The sum of the values assigned to a row is equal to the row's availability (less than or equal to if total supply exceeds total demand).

2. The sum of the values assigned to a column is equal to the column's requirements (less than or equal to if total demand exceeds total supply).

The red values in the cells in Figure B.5 constitute a solution to the problem in Example B.5. By multiplying each shipment by its unit cost and summing we get a total cost of $2750. As we shall soon see, however, this solution is not optimal.

While it is possible to find an optimal solution to a relatively small transportation model like the one in Example B.5 by hand, the work can become tedious. We will instead solve this problem using Excel's Solver.

The first step in using Solver to find an optimal solution is to set up a spreadsheet that contains the relevant information and spaces for the solution. Instead of the tableau in Figure B.5, in which both the unit shipping costs and the shipping amounts were entered into the same cell, we will use two matrices, one for the costs and one for the shipments. The spreadsheet in Exhibit B.6 contains the information for the problem in Example B.5. The unit cost matrix, taken from Table B.1, is in B6:F8, with the plant names in column A and the warehouse names in row 5. The shipment matrix, which will be the changing cells for Solver, is in B13:F15, with the plant names in column A and the warehouse names in row 12. The total amounts shipped from the plants will be shown in G13:G15; each is the sum of the shipment cells on its left. The units available are shown in the cells next to these in H13:H15. The total amounts shipped to the warehouses will be shown in B16:F16; each is the sum of the shipment cells above it. The requirements are shown below them in B17:F17. Finally, the total cost, which will be the target cell for Solver, is shown in B19. The formula in that cell is = SUMPRODUCT(B6:F8,B13:F15).

Once the spreadsheet has been set up, the procedure for using Solver to get the optimal solution is basically the same as for a regular LP problem, as described earlier. Click on *Tools* and *Solver* and fill in the dialog box, identifying the target cell (the objective function), the changing cells (the decision variables), and the constraints.

[3] However, you will find it included in many software packages for solving transportation models.

Exhibit B.6

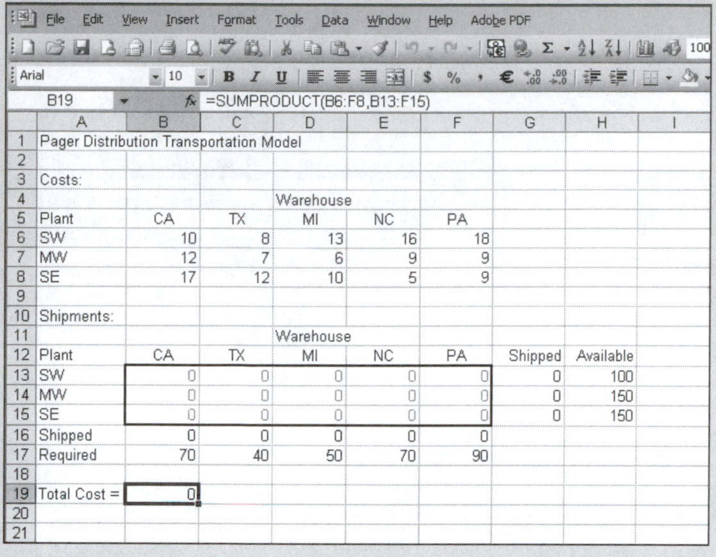

Example B.6

(Refer to Example B.5)

Use Excel's Solver to determine the optimal distribution pattern for cell phones at Fred Silverton's company.

Solution:

The completed dialog box for the problem in the spreadsheet in Exhibit B.6 is shown in Exhibit B.7. The target cell is B19, the total cost. The changing cells are B13:F15, the shipment matrix. There are three sets of constraints:

1. Do not ship more units from a source than are available there. This constraint is handled by specifying that G13:G15 <=H13:H15.

2. Ship to each destination the number of units required there. This constraint is handled by specifying that B16:F16 = B17:F17.

3. All variables must be non-negative. This constraint is handled by specifying that B13:F15 >= 0.

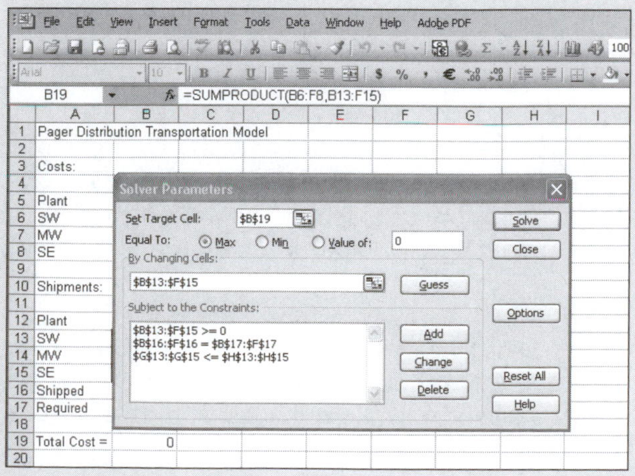

Once the dialog box has been filled in, click *Options*, check *Assume Linear Model,* and click *OK*; then click *Solve*. Choose the Solver Reports desired (*Solution* and *Sensitivity*) and click *OK*.

The solution is shown in Exhibit B.8. The optimal solution, which has a cost of $2440, calls for shipping 70 (thousand) units from SW to CA, 40 from MW to TX, 50 from MW to MI, 10 from MW to PA, 70 from SE to NC, and 80 from SE to PA. Note that all warehouses will receive their full requirements. The SE plant will be utilized to its full capacity, but the SW plant will use only 70 of its 100-unit capacity and the MW plant only 100 of its 150-unit capacity.

Exhibit B.7

(continued)

Example B.6

(continued)

Exhibit B.8

	A	B	C	D	E	F	G	H	I
1	Pager Distribution Transportation Model								
2									
3	Costs:								
4				Warehouse					
5	Plant	CA	TX	MI	NC	PA			
6	SW	10	8	13	16	18			
7	MW	12	7	6	9	9			
8	SE	17	12	10	5	9			
9									
10	Shipments:								
11				Warehouse					
12	Plant	CA	TX	MI	NC	PA	Shipped	Available	
13	SW	70	0	0	0	0	70	100	
14	MW	0	40	50	0	10	100	150	
15	SE	0	0	0	70	80	150	150	
16	Shipped	70	40	50	70	90			
17	Required	70	40	50	70	90			
18									
19	Total Cost =	2440							
20									

Cell B19: =SUMPRODUCT(B6:F8,B13:F15)

SENSITIVITY ANALYSIS

Because a transportation model is a special type of linear programming model, the same sensitivity analysis information is available. In particular, we can find, for each source/destination combination, the range within which its unit cost can vary without changing the optimal shipping pattern. For each unused combination, we can find the reduced cost, the amount by which the unit cost would have to be reduced before that route should be used. In addition, we can find, for each source and destination constraint, the shadow price and the range within which that shadow price holds. For a source, the shadow price indicates by how much the total cost would decrease (increase) if one more (less) unit were available at that source. For a destination, the shadow price indicates by how much the total cost would increase (decrease) if one more (less) unit were required at that destination.

Example B.7

(Refer to Example B.6)

Fred Silverton's company's management is interested in the following two questions: (1) Management will shortly be negotiating a new contract with the trucking company that makes deliveries from the Southwest plant. By how much would the unit cost for shipments to California have to increase before it would change the shipping pattern? (2) Management is considering increasing the capacity of one or more of its pager plants. Which plant, if any, should have its capacity increased?

Solution:

The Sensitivity Report for the problem in Example B.6 is shown in Exhibit B.9. The answers to both questions can be obtained from that output.

(continued)

Exhibit B.9
Adjustable Cells

Cell	Name	Final Value	Reduced Cost	Objective Coefficient	Allowable Increase	Allowable Decrease
$B$13	SW CA	70	0	10	2.000000001	1E+30
$C$13	SW TX	0	0.999999998	7.999999998	1E+30	0.999999998
$D$13	SW MI	0	6.999999999	13	1E+30	6.999999999
$E$13	SW NC	0	11	16	1E+30	11
$F$13	SW PA	0	9	18	1E+30	9
$B$14	MW CA	0	2.000000001	12	1E+30	2.000000001
$C$14	MW TX	40	0	7	0.999999998	1E+30
$D$14	MW MI	50	0	6	4.000000002	1E+30
$E$14	MW NC	0	4	9	1E+30	4
$F$14	MW PA	10	0	9	4	0
$B$15	SE CA	0	6.999999998	17	1E+30	6.999999998
$C$15	SE TX	0	4.999999997	12	1E+30	4.999999997
$D$15	SE MI	0	4.000000002	10	1E+30	4.000000002
$E$15	SE NC	70	0	5	4	1E+30
$F$15	SE PA	80	0	9	0	4

Constraints

Cell	Name	Final Value	Shadow Price	Constraint R.H. Side	Allowable Increase	Allowable Decrease
$B$16	Shipped CA	70	10	70	30	70
$C$16	Shipped TX	40	7	40	50	40
$D$16	Shipped MI	50	6	50	50	50
$E$16	Shipped NC	70	5	70	50	10
$F$16	Shipped PA	90	9	90	50	10
$G$13	SW Shipped	70	0	100	1E+30	30
$G$14	MW Shipped	100	0	150	1E+30	50
$G$15	SE Shipped	150	0	150	10	50

1. In the Adjustable Cells portion of the Sensitivity Report, the maximum amount by which the objective coefficient of cell B13 (the SW/CA shipment variable) can be increased without changing the currently optimal shipping pattern is $2, to a total of $12. If the unit cost increases to more than $12, the optimal solution will be different.

2. The Constraints portion of the Sensitivity Report shows that neither the SW or MW plant is using all of its existing capacity, so neither should have its capacity increased. Although the SE plant is operating at full capacity, its shadow price is 0 within the range of $150 - 50 = 100$ to $150 + 10 = 160$. Thus, there is no economic rationale for increasing the capacity at the southeast plant either.

S U M M A R Y

Any decision-making situation involves two basic issues: What are we making decisions about, and How do we know that one decision alternative is better than another? One useful approach to answering these questions is mathematical programming. Decision variables are defined and an objective function is used to decide which combination of decision variable values is best. We considered three types of mathematical programming models: the single facility location problem, linear programming, and the transportation model, all of which are readily solved with Excel's Solver.

In the single facility location problem the decision variables are the coordinates of a single new facility that will interact with a group of existing facilities. The objective function is the cost of making shipments between the new facility and the existing ones. One of three ways of measuring distance is typically used: (1) the length of the straight line connecting two points, (2) the square of the length of that straight line, or (3) the sum of the two right-angle sides of the triangle for which the straight line is the hypotenuse.

Linear programming is widely used in all functional areas of business. The problem is to determine the

values for the decision variables that maximize or minimize the value of a linear objective function while satisfying a set of linear constraints. While problems with only two variables can be solved graphically, solving realistic problems requires the use of a computer package. In addition to providing the optimal values of the decision variables, the computer package will also provide sensitivity analysis information. Shadow prices for the constraints indicate the marginal values or costs for changes in the amounts of resources or other constraints in the problem. The sensitivity analysis also shows the range for which that shadow price holds and the range within which a variable's objective function coefficient can change without changing the optimal solution.

The transportation model is a special type of linear programming model. In its classic form, the problem is to determine how much of an item to ship from each of the sources at which it is available in limited quantities to each of the destinations at which it is required in specified amounts. Because a transportation model is a type of linear programming model, all the same sensitivity analysis information is available from the solution.

K E Y   T E R M S

Feasible set, 813

Insensitivity range, 817

Linear programming (LP), 810

Objective function, 810

Sensitivity, 817

Shadow price, 819

Solver, 814

Transportation model, 821

Transportation tableau, 821

S O L V E D   P R O B L E M S

1. Tom Tucker's Turkeys is a scientifically managed turkey farm. Tom knows that the nutritional qualities of the turkey feed he uses are important for the proper development of his birds and that the qualities needed vary with the age of the birds. Tom currently has a flock that is 6 weeks old. He knows that, for birds of this age, it is important that each gets a minimum of 12 units of protein, 6 units of carbohydrate, and 2.5 units of vitamin A per day. Tom's feed supplier carries two brands of turkey

feed. An ounce of Torina's costs 0.5 cents and provides 2 units of protein, 1.5 units of carbohydrates, and 0.5 units of vitamin A. An ounce of Schow's costs 0.6 cents and provides 4 units of protein, 1 unit of carbohydrates, and 0.5 units of vitamin A.

a) How much of each type of turkey feed should Tom give to each 6-week-old turkey if he wants to minimize the cost of meeting the nutritional requirements? Solve graphically and with the computer.

b) Suppose Tom wanted to increase the amount of protein each turkey was getting. How much would a 1-unit increase in the protein requirement add to the daily cost of feeding a turkey? For how large an increase would this be true? Repeat for carbohydrates and vitamin A.

c) The feed dealer has told Tom that the price of Torina's will be going up, but he does not know by how much. How much would the price of Torina's have to increase before Tom would change the feed mix for 6-week-old turkeys?

Solution:

Start by developing a linear programming model to plan how to mix the two brands of turkey feed to meet the nutritional requirements at minimum cost. Define:

T = the number of ounces of Torina's to feed each turkey

S = the number of ounces of Schow's to feed each turkey

The objective is to minimize the cost of feeding a turkey, so:
Minimize $0.5T + 0.6S$

There are three types of nutritional requirements: protein, carbohydrates, and vitamin A.

Protein:	$2T + 4S \geq 12$
Carbohydrates:	$1.5T + 1.0S \geq 6$
Vitamin A:	$0.5T + 0.5S \geq 2.5$

We also have non-negativity constraints because negative amounts of feed make no sense:

$T, S >= 0$

a) The graph of the problem is shown in Figure B.6. Note that the feasible set is outside the set of sloped lines and that, since the objective function is to be minimized, we want to bring it as close to the origin as possible. The optimal solution is at the intersection of the protein (line P) and vitamin A (line A) constraints. The solution is to use 4 ounces of Torina's and 1 ounce of Schow's at a cost of 2.6 cents per turkey. The same solution is shown in the Excel Solver spreadsheet in Exhibit B.10.

b) From the Protein line in the Constraints section of the Sensitivity Report in Exhibit B.11,

Figure B.6
Graphical solution for solved problem 1

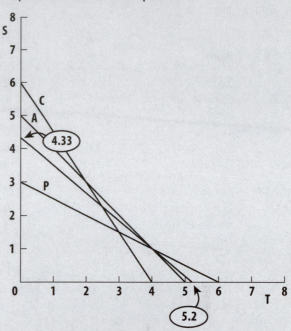

Exhibit B.10

we find that the protein constraint is being met exactly and has a shadow price of 0.05, with a range of $12 - 2 = 10$ to $12 + 4 = 16$. Thus, increasing the protein requirement will add 0.05 cents per day to the cost per turkey for up

Exhibit B.11

Adjustable Cells

Cell	Name	Final Value	Reduced Cost	Objective Coefficient	Allowable Increase	Allowable Decrease
$C$5	Torina	4	0	0.5	0.1	0.2
$D$5	Schow	1	0	0.6	0.4	0.1

Constraints

Cell	Name	Final Value	Shadow Price	Constraint R.H. Side	Allowable Increase	Allowable Decrease
$E$15	Protein Provided	12	0.05	12	4	2
$E$16	Carbohydrates Provided	7	0	6	1	1E+30
$E$17	Vitamin A Provided	2.5	0.8	2.5	0.5	0.25

to 4 additional units of protein. Similarly, from the Carbohydrates line in the Sensitivity Report we find that the amount of carbohydrates in the diet is 7, which is 1 higher than required, and the shadow price is 0 in a range of $(-\infty)$ to $6 + 1 = 7$. Thus, increasing the carbohydrate requirement up to 7 units per day will not increase the cost at all. From the Vitamin A line in the Sensitivity Report, we find that the vitamin A constraint is met exactly and has a shadow price of 0.8 within a range of $2.5 - 0.25 = 2.25$ to $2.5 + 0.5 = 3.0$. Thus, increasing the vitamin A requirement will add 0.8 cents per day to the cost per turkey for up to an additional 0.5 unit of vitamin A.

c) From the Torina's line in the Adjustable Cells section of the Sensitivity Report in Exhibit B.11, we find that the insensitivity range for

Torina's is $0.5 - 0.2 = 0.3$ to $0.5 + 0.1 = 0.6$. Thus, assuming that the price of Schow's remains constant, the turkey feed mix will stay the same as long as the price of Torina's does not increase to more than 0.6 cents per ounce.

2. Worldwide Chemicals produces a variety of products at plants located all over the world and, similarly, sells them in markets all over the world. One particular chemical is produced at plants located in the United States, China, and South Africa. All three plants have excess capacity beyond the amounts needed to satisfy the demands in their local markets. This extra production can be sold through distributors located in Italy, India, and Argentina. Table B.2 gives the production costs and excess capacities at the three plants, the selling prices and maximum sales amounts at the three

Table B.2

Plant Location	Distributor Location			Capacity (tons)	Production Cost
	Italy	India	Argentina		
United States	$20	$30	$16	1000	$60
China	$24	$10	$30	600	$45
South Africa	$15	$8	$12	500	$50
Demand (tons)	800	700	300		
Selling Price	$82	$60	$70		

distributors, and the costs of shipping from the production plants to the distributorships. All costs and revenues are for tons, which is the unit of measure of capacity and demand, and have been converted to dollars at the current exchange rates.

a) Determine an optimal production and distribution plan if Worldwide Chemicals believes that it is important to meet all the demands at the distributorships.

b) Suppose Worldwide Chemicals is willing to treat the demand values as maximums rather than requirements. How does this change the production and distribution plan?

Solution:

a) This can be modeled as a transportation model in which the objective function is to be maximized. The first step is to compute the profit for each plant/distributor combination as Profit = Selling Price at Distributor − Production Cost at Source Plant − Transportation Cost from Plant to Distributor. For example the United States/Italy combination profit is $82 − 60 − 20 = 2$.

Once the profits per ton have been computed, a spreadsheet can be set up, such as the one in Exhibit B.12, which contains the solution to part (a). The profits per ton are in B6:D8, the

changing cells are B14:D16, and the target cell is B20, which is the total profit. The constraints specify that B14:D16 >= 0, E14:E16 <= F14:F16, and B17:D17 = B16:D18. The solution, which has a total profit of $9000, calls for shipping 400 tons from the United States to Italy, 300 tons from the United States to Argentina, 600 tons from China to India, 400 tons from South Africa to Italy, and 100 tons from South Africa to India. As required, all the distributors' demand are met. China and South Africa use all their capacity and the United States uses 700 of the 1000 tons of capacity available.

b) The spreadsheet for part (b) is exactly the same as for part (a). The Solver dialog box is exactly the same also except that B17:D17 <= B18:D18 in the constraints. The solution is given in Exhibit B.13, which shows that a total profit of $13,900 can be achieved by not using any of the capacity at the United States plant and not filling any of the demand at Argentina and only part of the demand at Italy. The optimal shipment pattern calls for shipping 300 tons from China to Italy, 300 tons from China to India, and 500 tons from South Africa to Italy. Not satisfying all the potential demand increases the total profit by $4900 or 54%.

Exhibit B.12

	A	B	C	D	E	F	G
1	Worldwide Chemicals						
2							
3	Profits per Ton:						
4			Distributor				
5	Plant:	Italy	India	Argentina			
6	United States	2	-30	-6			
7	China	13	5	-5			
8	South Africa	17	2	8			
9							
10							
11	Profits per Ton:						
12			Distributor		Amount		
13	Plant:	Italy	India	Argentina	Shipped	Capacity	
14	United States	400	0	300	700	1000	
15	China	0	600	0	600	600	
16	South Africa	400	100	0	500	500	
17	Amount Shipped	800	700	300			
18	Demand	800	700	300			
19							
20	Total Profit:	9000					
21							

B20 = SUMPRODUCT(B6:D8,B14:D16)

Exhibit B.13

	A	B	C	D	E	F	G
1	Worldwide Chemicals						
2							
3	Profits per Ton:						
4			Distributor				
5	Plant:	Italy	India	Argentina			
6	United States	2	-30	-6			
7	China	13	5	-5			
8	South Africa	17	2	8			
9							
10							
11	Profits per Ton:						
12			Distributor		Amount		
13	Plant:	Italy	India	Argentina	Shipped	Capacity	
14	United States	0	0	0	0	1000	
15	China	300	300	0	600	600	
16	South Africa	500	0	0	500	500	
17	Amount Shipped	800	300	0			
18	Demand	800	700	300			
19							
20	Total Profit:	13900					
21							

B20 = SUMPRODUCT(B6:D8,B14:D16)

DISCUSSION QUESTIONS

1. What distinguishes linear programming from other forms of mathematical programming?

2. What are the characteristics of a linear expression?

3. What does the slack variable for a resource constraint tell us?

4. What does a shadow price of a resource constraint in a linear programming model tell us?

5. Why is the shadow price 0 for a constraint with slack?

6. How does graphically solving a maximization LP problem differ from solving a minimization LP problem?

7. What are the basic components of a transportation model?

8. What is the difference between a balanced and an unbalanced transportation model?

9. Why is the transportation model a special type of linear programming?

PROBLEMS

B-1. The taxi drivers for the Yellow Checker Cab Company start their shifts at the company's central garage before driving to one of the city's six districts to look for passengers. At the end of their shifts they return to the garage from wherever they ended their final trips. The current location of the garage has been sold to a developer who will be putting up a new office complex, so the cab company needs to find a new location for their garage. Records kept on the numbers of start-of-shift and end-of-shift trips per month between the garage and the different districts and the locations of the centers of the districts are given in the table.

District	X	Y	Trips
1	27	75	160
2	50	80	370
3	65	52	130
4	50	30	210
5	22	30	80
6	42	53	250

a) Determine the optimal location of the new garage for each of the three distance measures discussed.

b) Compare the three solutions with respect to each of the three cost measures.

B-2. Nature's Bakery makes two types of oatmeal cookies: regular and oatmeal with raisins. One hundred packages of regular oatmeal cookies uses 1000 ounces of oatmeal and contributes $150 to profit and overhead. One hundred packages of oatmeal with raisins cookies uses 700 ounces of oatmeal and 300 ounces of raisins and contributes $175 to profit and overhead. There is sufficient oven time to bake 12,000 packages of either type of cookie or any combination. There are 100,000 ounces of oatmeal and 27,000 ounces of raisins available for use in making cookies. Formulate a linear programming model to help the bakery determine how many packages of each type of cookie to produce.

B-3. Using the information and the model developed for problem B-2;

a) Solve the model developed in Problem B-2 graphically.

b) Solve the model with a computer package.

c) Determine how much oatmeal, raisins, and oven time is used by the solution and how much of each is left over.

d) By how much would the price (and profit contribution) of regular oatmeal cookies have to change before the optimal solution would change?

e) The bakery has the opportunity to purchase additional raisins for $50 per thousand ounces more than what they are currently paying. Should the bakery buy additional raisins at this price and, if so, how many should they buy?

B-4. Pet Supplies Company produces 16-ounce cans of dog food by combining meat by-products, which cost $.60 per pound, and chicken by-products, which cost $.35 per pound. Meat by-products are 60% protein and 30%t fat by weight, while chicken by-products are 40% protein and 10% fat by weight. To meet customer expectations, the final product should contain at least 50% protein and between 15 and 25% fat by weight. Formulate a linear programming model to be used to determine what the composition of the dog food ought to be.

B-5. Using the information and the model developed for problem B-4;

a) Solve the model developed in Problem B-5 graphically.

b) Solve the model with a computer package.

c) Determine what the actual protein and fat content of the dog food are and how far from the minimum or maximum limits these quality characteristics are.

d) By how much can the cost of chicken by-products change before the optimal solution would change?

e) Suppose that the company could reduce the amount of meat and chicken by-products in the dog food mixture, replacing the amount of by-products removed with a filler with no nutritional characteristics. Would this make any difference in the optimal solution?

B-6. WeHaul Trucking is planning its truck purchases for the coming year. $600,000 has been allocated for the purchase of additional trucks, of which three sizes are available. A large truck costs $150,000 and will return the equivalent of $15,000 per year to profit and overhead. A medium-sized truck costs $90,000 and will return the equivalent of $12,000 per year. A small truck costs $50,000 and will return the equivalent of $6000 per year. WeHaul has

maintenance capacity to service either four large trucks, five medium-sized trucks, or eight small trucks, or some equivalent combination. WeHaul believes that they will be able to hire a maximum of seven new drivers for these added trucks. Formulate a linear programming model to be used for determining how many of each size of truck to purchase. (Hint: For maintenance, think in terms of the capacity for large trucks.)

B-7. Using the information and the model developed for problem B-6;

a) Solve the model with a computer.

b) Determine how much of the budget will be used and how much will be left over. Do the same for the maintenance capacity and the number of drivers to be hired.

c) Suppose the budget for purchasing trucks could be increased. By how much would the equivalent annual returns increase for each additional $1000 of budget? For how big an increase would this be true? What if the budget had to be decreased? Answer the same questions.

B-8. Eastman Paper Products produces commercial wrapping paper in 60-inch-wide rolls. A roll is then run through a slitting machine which slices it into narrower rolls for sale. Any extra width from this cutting operation is called trim loss and is considered scrap. For example, if a 60-inch roll is cut into three 18-inch rolls, there will be 6 inches of trim loss. The marketing department presently has orders for 300 12-inch-wide rolls, 400 18-inch-wide rolls, 250 24-inch-wide rolls, and 150 30-inch-wide rolls.

a) List all the ways in which a 60-inch-wide roll can be cut into some combination of narrower rolls without leaving enough left to cut another narrower roll.

Determine the trim loss for each cutting combination.

b) Develop a linear programming model to help Eastman's production department determine how to cut the 60-inch-wide rolls up if their objective is to minimize the total amount of trim loss.

c) Solve the model with a computer.

d) Determine how much trim loss there will be, how many total rolls will be cut, and how many rolls of each smaller size will be produced.

B-9. a) Revise the model in Problem B-8 to recognize the alternative objective of minimizing the total rolls cut.

b) Solve the model with a computer.

c) Determine how much trim loss there will be, how many total rolls will be cut, and how many rolls of each smaller size will be produced.

d) Compare your results from Problems B-8 and B-9.

B-10. The Chesterfield County Police Department wants to provide sufficient police coverage to meet expected needs, but also wants to use the smallest number of personnel possible to control costs. Records kept on the number of officers required by time of day, for 4-hour time blocks, indicate the minimum staffing given in the table.

Period	Time Period	Police Required
1	Midnight–4 a.m.	6
2	4 a.m.–8 a.m.	10
3	8 a.m.–Noon	14
4	Noon–4 p.m.	8
5	4 p.m.–8 p.m.	12
6	8 p.m.–Midnight	9

Assume that a police officer works for 8 consecutive hours and can start at the beginning of any of the six time periods. Further assume that the number of police required each day has the same pattern, so that this is a rolling pattern.

a) Formulate a linear programming model with the objective of minimizing the total number of police needed.

b) Solve the model on a computer.

B-11. Assume now that any police officer in the Chesterfield County Police Department (Problem B-10) can (and is willing to) work 12 straight hours, the extra 4-hour period being paid at time and a half.

a) Reformulate the linear programming model in Problem B-10 to add this additional consideration. The objective should be to minimize total cost. (Hint: The actual cost is not necessary; you can use relative cost.)

b) Solve the model on a computer.

c) Compare the solution found here with the one found in Problem B-10 with no overtime.

B-12. A wholesale distribution company is building a new warehouse, but needs additional space before it will be completed in six months. Space is available for lease in a commercial warehouse on the following terms for 1000-square-foot sections: A 1-month lease will cost $180; a 3-month lease will cost $480; a 6-month lease will cost $900. The monthly requirements (in 1000s of square feet) are given in the table.

Month	Space Required
1	8
2	6
3	3
4	5
5	6
6	4

a) Formulate a model to determine how to rent space at minimum cost.

b) Solve the model on a computer.

c) Are there any months in which there is extra space?

B-13. Nuts2U buys mixed nuts in large quantities and re-blends them to give new mixtures, which it packages in 1-pound containers. There are currently three mixtures available for purchase: Mix A costs $5 per pound and contains 30% peanuts, 30% cashews, 20% hazelnuts, and 20% almonds. Mix B costs $7 per pound and contains 20% peanuts, 50% cashews, and 30% hazelnuts. Mix C costs $3 per pound and contains 70% peanuts, 20% cashews, and 10% almonds. There are currently 100 pounds of Mix A, 70 pounds of Mix B, and 150 pounds of Mix C available for purchase by Nuts2U.

Nuts2U also sells two blends. The Regular Blend sells for $5.50 per pound and contains at least 25% cashews and no more than 40% peanuts. There may be any amounts of hazelnuts and almonds. The Superior Blend sells for $6.50 per pound and must contain no more than 30% peanuts and at least 20% hazelnuts and almonds combined. The rest can be cashews.

a) Formulate a linear programming model to determine how Nuts2U should proceed with production. (Hint: How much Mix A is used in making the Regular Blend?)

b) Solve the model with a computer.

c) How much of each available mix should be bought? How much of each blend Nuts2U sells should be made?

d) What are the actual percentages of the different kinds of nuts in the products sold?

B-14. A truck rental company has offices in eight cities. The numbers of trucks currently available in each city and the number the company wants to have in each city are given in the first table.

City	Have	Want
Adams	12	8
Beaver	7	9
Coaltown	8	10
Dexter	10	7
Edgartown	6	8
Fulton	5	9
Grandview	11	7
Hanover	4	4

The distances between the cities are given in the second table.

a) Set up a transportation model to determine how to relocate trucks from where they are located to where they are wanted while minimizing the total distance traveled.

b) Solve the model on a computer.

B-15. The Delicious Apple Company has orchards in Red City, Golden, and Macville. Estimated amounts of apples to be available from the three orchards are: Red City, 15,000 bushels; Golden, 12,000 bushels; and Macville, 9000 bushels. Apple Products Company wants to buy 10,000 bushels, for which it will pay $2.90 a bushel. Fruit Processors, Inc. is interested in buying up to 12,000 bushels at $3.20 a bushel. Extragood Fruit Company will buy up to 18,000 bushels at $3.10 per bushel. Because the total amount the potential buyers want exceeds what Delicious Apple expects to be able to provide, Delicious would like to distribute its apples to the buyers so as to maximize its profits after recognizing the different selling prices and the costs of shipping from the orchards to the buyers' processing plants, which are given in the table.

| From Orchard | To Customer | | |
	Apple Products	Fruit Processors	Extragood Fruit
Red City	.55	.65	.45
Golden	.35	.45	.55
Macville	.45	.45	.85

Second Table for Problem B-14

| | To | | | | | | | |
From	Adams	Beaver	Coaltown	Dexter	Edgartown	Fulton	Grandview	Hanover
Adams	0	16	20	20	32	42	50	60
Beaver	16	0	26	14	16	28	40	45
Coaltown	20	26	0	36	20	18	24	40
Dexter	20	14	36	0	30	22	30	32
Edgartown	32	16	20	30	0	36	50	18
Fulton	42	28	18	22	36	0	40	15
Grandview	50	40	24	30	50	40	0	21
Hanover	60	45	40	32	18	15	21	0

a) Formulate a transportation model to determine how to allocate the available apples to the buyers so as to maximize net profits.

b) Solve the model on a computer.

B-16. Schwimmer Bicycles needs to develop a production plan for the next 3 months. Because employee turnover is very low and it will not be possible to hire and train additional employees during that time horizon, Schwimmer's production manager knows basically how many bicycles can be produced each month, on either regular or overtime, as given in the table. The production requirements for the three months are also given in the table.

Month	Regular Capacity	Overtime Capacity	Demand
1	250	50	240
2	300	60	320
3	275	55	330

Regular-time production of a bicycle costs $80, with overtime production costing $100. A bicycle can be carried in inventory for a monthly cost of 5% of the production cost.

a) Formulate a transportation model to determine the production plan.

b) Solve the model on a computer.

B-17. Patterson Manufacturing currently operates two factories that supply four distribution warehouses. Production costs $5 per unit at the factory in Austin, which has a capacity of 50,000 units a month, and $5.50 per unit at the factory in Boston, which has a capacity of 75,000 units per month. The warehouses are located in Los Angeles, Kansas City, Jacksonville, and Philadelphia.

Expected growth in demand at the warehouses means that, within another 2 years, the two existing factories will not be able to meet all the warehouse demands, which are expected to be 40,000 units per month at Los Angeles, 30,000 at Kansas City, 40,000 at Jacksonville, and 50,000 at Philadelphia. To allow for additional growth in demand, a new factory capable of producing 50,000 units per month will be opened. Two locations are under consideration, Nashville and Topeka. A factory in Nashville would have fixed costs of $60,000 per month and a unit production cost of $4.75 per unit. A factory in Topeka would have fixed costs of $50,000 and a unit production cost of $5.10 per unit. Transportation costs per unit between each of the existing and proposed factories and the warehouses are given in the table.

Table for Problem B-17

	To Warehouse			
From Factory	Los Angeles	Kansas City	Jacksonville	Philadelphia
Austin	.50	.60	.80	1.00
Boston	1.10	.70	.60	.35
Nashville	.80	.45	.25	.45
Topeka	.50	.20	.60	.85

Use transportation models to determine whether the new factory should be opened in Nashville or Topeka.

C

Supplement C: Queuing Analysis

Supplement Outline

Supplement C: Queuing Analysis   836

   The Components of a Queuing System   836

   Transient and Steady-State Behavior   838

   The Basic Single-Server Model (M/M/1)   838

   The Multiple-Server Exponential Service Time Model (M/M/S)   840

   Finite Queue Models   844

   Finite Population Models   844

   Designing Queuing Systems   845

Summary   848

Key Terms   848

Solved Problems   848

Discussion Questions   850

Problems   850

Supplement C: Queuing Analysis

Have you ever wondered why the ticket agent at the airline desk can be just sitting there a good part of the day but always have a line when you are late for a plane? Even though, *on average*, the capacity of a service system may be greater than the demands placed on it, a **queue** or waiting line forms whenever the current demand for service exceeds the server's current capacity to provide it. Thus, while, over the course of the day, the customer service agent at the airline check-in counter has plenty of time to sell tickets and check baggage for all the customers who will be flying that day, the random ebbs and flows of customer arrivals will cause a line to form at times and the agent to be idle at other times.

Given the pervasiveness of queues in all sorts of businesses, from the line of movie- or concert-goers waiting to buy tickets to the calls on hold or getting a busy signal at a catalog call-in center to the jobs waiting to be processed at a machine center in a factory, structuring a queuing system to provide an optimal, or at least reasonable, balance between customer inconvenience or waiting costs and operational efficiency is a significant design problem for most businesses.

The Components of a Queuing System

As shown in Figure C.1, a queuing system has three basic components: the calling population, the queue or queues, and the service facility. To understand the issues in designing queuing systems and evaluating their performance, we will look at the important characteristics of each.

THE CALLING POPULATION

The **calling population**, or source, is the set of potential customers for the service. **Customers** can be people, like airline passengers who will be checking in, or things, such as jobs waiting to be processed on a machine. The most important characteristic of the calling population is its size, which may be either finite or infinite. A population is

Queue

A sequence of jobs or customers waiting to be processed by a server.

Calling population

A component of the calling system that is the source of potential customers for the services.

Customer

Any individual or group that uses the output of a process.

Figure C.1

General structure of a queuing system

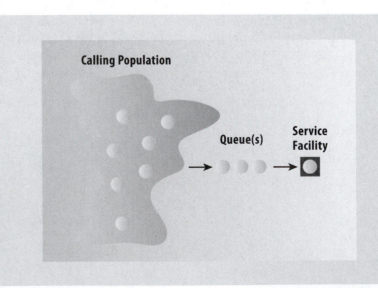

finite if the number of customer is relatively small, such as the five machines an operator is responsible for. A population is considered to be **infinite** if it is large enough that the number of customers already receiving or waiting for service does not affect the rate at which additional customers arrive to get service.

A second important structural characteristic of the calling population is its composition, which refers to the classes or types of customers making up the population. Unless an airline has separate check-in counters for its first-class and coach passengers, there will be only one class of customers. On the other hand, a hospital emergency room has at least three types of arrivals: those with relatively minor problems, those with serious injuries or illnesses, and those in life-threatening situations.

Besides these structural characteristics, the calling population has a number of relevant operating characteristics. The most important is the customer arrival rate or, if there are multiple customer classes, rates. The **arrival rate**, which we will represent by the Greek letter λ (lambda), is the average number of customers arriving for service per time period. The average time between arrivals is then $1/\lambda$.

Two other operating characteristics that may be important are balking and group arrivals. **Balking** is the refusal of an arriving customer to join the queue and wait for service. If customers arrive in groups rather than singly (such as, for example, at most good restaurants), then the distribution of group sizes is important.

THE QUEUE OR QUEUES

Assuming the arriving customer stays (does not balk) and there is no server available, it joins the (or a) queue. The most basic characteristic is the number. If there are multiple queues, then the issue of differentiation arises: Is there a queue for each type of customer or one for each server? A second important structural characteristic is the maximum queue length. In most cases we assume that there is no maximum length. However, an airline reservation system or catalog 800-number has a specific number of telephone lines, some with operators and others (the queue) having customers on hold; when all lines are occupied by callers, any more arriving calls get a busy signal and are turned away (are rejected in queuing terminology).

The most important operating characteristic of the queue(s) is the **queue discipline**, the rule used to determine which waiting customer is served next. In many situations the "fair" rule of first come, first served is used, but in other cases it makes more sense to use some other priority rule. For example, in a job shop popular rules are "do the shortest available job" (good for minimizing inventories), "do the job with the earliest due date" (good for minimizing tardy jobs), and "do the job for our best customer" (good for customer relations).

Other queue operating characteristics that may become important if customers have to wait long times are reneging and jockeying. Similar to balking, **reneging** occurs when a customer initially joins the queue but leaves before receiving service. **Jockeying** or line switching occurs when a customer leaves one queue to join another in the expectation that he or she will get served more quickly (but it never seems to work, does it?).

THE SERVICE FACILITY

Eventually, the waiting customer moves into the **service facility**, the system that actually delivers the service requested or needed. The basic structural characteristics are the number of servers and their configuration. If there are multiple servers, they may be identical or different. If different, they may service different types of customers, provide different parts of the service, or provide the same service at different rates. Multiple servers may be configured in parallel (next to one another) or in a series

Finite

A situation where the number of customers is relatively small.

Infinite

The state at which a population is large enough that the number of customers already receiving or waiting for service does not affect the rate at which additional customers arrive to get service.

Arrival rate

The average number of customers arriving for service per time period.

Balking

The refusal of an arriving customer to join the queue and wait for service.

Queue discipline

The rule used to determine which waiting customer is served next.

Reneging

A situation when a customer initially joins the queue but leaves before receiving the service.

Jockeying

A situation where a customer leaves one queue to join another in the expectation that he or she will get served more quickly.

Service facility

The system that actually delivers the service requested or needed.

Channel

Each parallel server or series of servers through which a customer might pass.

Service rate

The average number of customers that a server could process in a time period if there were always another customer available.

Batch service

Where multiple jobs or customers are processed simultaneously by a single server.

Transient behavior

An unstable queue that exhibits a pattern of growth or decline.

Steady-state behavior

A state when the arrival rate changes or the number of servers changes.

(following one another). Each parallel server or series of servers through which a customer might pass is called a **channel**.

The most important operating characteristic of the service facility is the **service rate**, the average number of customers that a server could process in a time period if there were always another customer available. We will represent the service rate by the Greek letter μ (mu), so that the average service time is $1/\mu$. While we usually assume that a server handles one customer at a time, in some cases there may be **batch service**, meaning that multiple customers are processed simultaneously (think of a roller coaster or a kiln in a pottery).

Transient and Steady-State Behavior

As a queuing system operates over time, it passes back and forth through two types of conditions: transient and steady-state behavior. **Transient** behavior is unstable. The length of a queue exhibits a pattern of growth or decline. Waiting times get longer or shorter. Transient behavior occurs whenever the arrival rate changes or the number of servers changes. **Steady-state** behavior is stable. This does not mean that the queue length and waiting time are constant, but that they fluctuate to some extent around constant average levels. Steady-state behavior will occur, in most cases, after a system has operated with constant arrival and service rates for some period of time.

While theoretical models can be developed to describe the transient behavior of some queuing systems (and simulation can be used for others), it is very difficult, requiring sophisticated mathematical techniques. The models to be discussed and illustrated here are for steady-state behavior.

The Basic Single-Server Model[1]

The most basic queuing model is the basic single-server model, which makes the following assumptions:

1. The calling population is infinite, with only one class of customers.

2. The number of arrivals per time period has a Poisson distribution with rate λ or, equivalently, the time between arrivals has an exponential distribution with average time $1/\lambda$.

3. Service time has an exponential distribution with rate μ or average time $1\backslash\mu$.

4. There are one server and one queue, which has no maximum length.

5. The queue discipline is first come, first served.

6. There is no balking or reneging.

Given the arrival rate λ and the service rate μ, the equations for the steady-state performance measures for this type of system are given in Table C.1. Looking at these equations, it is obvious that the customer arrival rate must be less than the service rate for this type of system to reach steady-state behavior.

---

[1] M/M/1 is an example of the short form of *Kendall's notation*, the standard notation used for describing queuing models. The short form of Kendall's notation is A/B/C in which A stands for the arrival distribution, B standards for the service time distribution, and C is the number of parallel service channels. For both A and B, the following symbols are used for the different distributions: M (Markov) means that the time has an exponential distribution or the number has a Poisson distribution; D stands for deterministic; G stands for general; and E_k stands for Erlang with parameter value k. It is not necessary to use Kendall's notation to describe a queuing system; it has only been used here to make it easier for you to select the appropriate alternative when using the software.

Table C.1

Steady-State Performance Measures for the Basic Queuing Model (M/M/1)

- $\rho = \lambda/\mu$ is the utilization rate or the probability that the server is busy and that an arriving customer will have to wait

- $P(0) = 1 - \rho$ is the probability that the queuing system is empty, with no one receiving or waiting for service

- $P(n) = \rho^n(1 - \rho)$ is the probability that there are n customers in the system, receiving or waiting for service

- $L_q = \dfrac{\lambda^2}{\mu(\mu-\lambda)} = \dfrac{\rho^2}{1-\rho}$ is the mean length of the queue

- $L = \dfrac{\lambda}{\mu-\lambda} = \dfrac{\rho}{1-\rho} = L_q + \rho$ is the mean number of customers in the system, receiving or waiting for service

- $W_q = \dfrac{L_q}{\lambda} = \dfrac{\lambda}{\mu(\mu-\lambda)}$ is the mean time a customer must wait before being served

- $W = \dfrac{L}{\lambda} = W_q + \dfrac{1}{\mu} = \dfrac{1}{\mu-\lambda}$ is the mean time that a customer spends in the system, waiting for or receiving service

Example C.1

Between noon and 2 p.m. passengers arrive at the check-in counter for Tom Jackson's airline at the Flagstaff airport at a rate of $\lambda = 20$ per hour, the actual number of arrivals being Poisson distributed. The single customer service representative takes an average of 2.4 minutes to check a passenger in, for a service rate of $\mu = 25$ per hour, the actual service time having an exponential distribution. (We must be careful to express the arrival rate λ and the service rate μ for the same time period.) Determine the values of the percentage of time the customer service agent is busy, the average number of customers waiting to check in, the average number of customers at the check-in counter, the average amount of time a passenger waits to check in, and the average amount of time a passenger spends at the check-in counter.

Solution:

Because passengers arrive randomly and the amount of time needed to process the passengers varies greatly, with most passengers requiring very little time and a few passengers taking a very long time, exponential distributions are appropriate for the inter-arrival and check-in times. There is a single customer service agent on duty, so the basic M/M/1 queuing model is appropriate for this situation.

Based on the timing information (parameter values) given, the average values of the queuing system performance characteristics (using the equations in Table C.1) are:

▶ The customer service agent is busy $\rho = \lambda\mu = .80$ or 80% of the time, so 80% of arriving passengers have to wait to check in.

(continued)

Example C.1

(continued)

▶ There is an average of $L_q = \dfrac{\lambda^2}{\mu(\mu-\lambda)}$

$= \dfrac{20^2}{25(25-20)} = 3.2$ passengers waiting to

check in at any given time.

▶ There is an average of $L = \dfrac{\lambda}{\mu-\lambda} = \dfrac{20}{25-20} = 4.0$

passengers at the check-in counter at any given time.

▶ A passenger waits for an average of $W_q =$

$\dfrac{\lambda}{\mu(\mu-\lambda)} = \dfrac{20}{25(25-20)} = .16$ hours or 9.6

minutes to check in.

▶ A passenger spends an average of $W =$

$\dfrac{1}{\mu-\lambda} = \dfrac{1}{25-20} = .20$ hours or 12 minutes

at the check-in counter.

ADDITIONAL SINGLE-SERVER QUEUING MODELS

While the basic single-server queuing model described above has proven to be quite useful in practice, there are many situations in which the assumption of exponentially distributed service times is not even a reasonable approximation to reality. Two other single-server models, both of which assume Poisson arrivals but allow for other types of service time distributions, are the general service time distribution model (M/G/1 in Kendall's notation) and the constant or deterministic service-time model (M/D/1). The performance equations for these two models are given in Tables C.2 and C.3 respectively.

The Multiple-Server Exponential Service Time Model (M/M/S)

The conditions for applying this model are identical to those given above for the basic single-server model, except that there are S parallel, identical servers, each of which is called a channel. All arriving customers wait in a single line. When a customer reaches

Table C.2

Steady-State Performance Measures for the Single-Server General Service Time Queuing Model (M/G/1)

The basic equation for this model, which is for the mean length of the queue, L_q, is the Pollaczek-Kinchine equation:

- $L_q = \dfrac{\lambda^2\sigma^2 + \rho^2}{2(1-\rho)}$, where $\rho = \lambda/\mu$ and σ is the standard deviation of the service time

- $L = L_q + \rho$

- $W_q = L_q/\lambda$

- $W = L/\lambda = W_q + 1/\mu$

Table C.3

Steady-State Performance Measures for the Single-Server Deterministic Service Time Queuing Model (M/D/1)

As in Tables C.1 and C.2, $\rho = \lambda/\mu$. Setting $\sigma = 0$ in the equation for L_q in Table C.3, we get:

- $L_q = \dfrac{\rho^2}{2(1-\rho)}$

The equations for the other performance measures are the same as in Table C.2.

- $L = L_q + \rho$
- $W_q = L_q/\lambda$
- $W = L/\lambda = W_q + 1/\mu$

the head of the line, it goes to the first available server. (Think of the way most bank lobbies are set up, as contrasted with the way most supermarkets are set up.)

The formulas for the steady-state performance characteristics of a multiple-server exponential service time model, given in Table C.4, are more complicated that those for the single-server model. The first step is to find the value of $P(0)$, the probability that the system is completely empty, from the equation given or, alternatively, by looking it up in Table C.5. To use this table, first find the value of ρ, using this to determine the row of the table to use. The number of servers, S, determines the column to use. For example, if $\lambda = 2$, $\mu = 1$, and $S = 4$, so that $\rho = .50$, the value of $P(0)$, found in the ".50" row and "4" column of Table C.5, is .1304. That is, the system will be completely empty just over 13% of the time.

Example C.2

Harry's Truck Stop has a single diesel pump. Trucks arrive for fuel on an average of three per hour or 0.05 per minute, Poisson distributed. The time to fill a truck's tank averages 12 minutes, with a standard deviation of 2 minutes. Determine the values for the percentage of time that the pump will be in use, the average number of trucks waiting to use the pump, the average number of trucks at the station, the average amount of time a truck waits to use the pump, and the average amount of time a truck spends at the station.

Solution:

Using a general service time distribution (M/G/1) model and using 1 minute as the basic unit of time, we have $\lambda = .05$ and $\mu = 1\backslash 12 = .08333$. By using the equations in Table C.2, we determine that:

▶ The pump will be in use $\rho = \lambda/\mu = .05/.08333 = .6$ or 60% of the time.

▶ There will be an average of $L_q = \dfrac{\lambda^2\sigma^2 + \rho^2}{2(1-\rho)} = \dfrac{(.05)^2(2)^2 + (.6)^2}{2(1-.6)} = \dfrac{.37}{.8} = 0.4625$ trucks waiting to use the pump.

▶ There will be an average of $L = L_q + \rho = 0.4625 + .6 = 1.0625$ trucks using or waiting for the pump.

▶ A truck will wait an average of $W_q = L_q/\lambda = 0.4625/.05 = 9.25$ minutes before using the pump.

▶ A truck will spend an average of $L = L/\lambda = 1.0625/.05 = 21.25$ minutes waiting for or using the pump.

Table C.4

Steady-State
Performance Measures
for the Multiple-Server
Exponential Service Time
Model (M/M/S)

- $P(0) = \dfrac{1}{\displaystyle\sum_{j=0}^{S-1}\dfrac{(S\rho)^j}{j!} + \dfrac{(S\rho)^s}{S!(1-\rho)}}$,

where $\rho = \lambda/S\mu$ is the percentage utilization of each server, which must be less than 1.0. This means that λ must be less than $S\mu$, the aggregate service capacity of the system.

- $P(n) = \dfrac{(S\rho)^n}{n!}\,P(0)$ for $0 \le n \le S$

- $P(n) = \dfrac{(S\rho)^n}{S!S^{n-S}}\,P(0)$ for $n > S$

- $P(\text{system busy}) = P(n \ge S) = \dfrac{(S\rho)^s\,P(0)}{S!(1-\rho)}$

- $L_q = \dfrac{\rho(S\rho)^s\,P(0)}{S!(1-\rho)^2} = \left(\dfrac{\rho}{1-\rho}\right)P(\text{system busy})$

- $L = L_q + S\rho = L_q + \lambda/\mu$

- $W_q = L_q/\lambda$

- $W = L/\lambda = W_q + 1/\mu$

Table C.5

Steady-State
Performance Measures
for the Single-Server
Finite Queue Model

- $P(0) = \dfrac{1-\rho}{1-\rho^{K+1}}$ for $\rho = \lambda/\mu \ne 1$

- $P(0) = \dfrac{1}{K+1}$ for $\rho = 1$

- $P(n) = \rho^n P(0)$ for $n \le K$

- $P(K) = P(\text{rejection}) = P(\text{lost call}) = \rho^K P(0)$

- $L = \dfrac{\rho}{1-\rho} - \dfrac{(K+1)\rho^{K+1}}{1-\rho^{K+1}}$ for $\rho \ne 1$

- $L = \dfrac{K}{2}$ for $\rho = 1$

- $L_q = L - (1 - P(0))$

- $W_q = \dfrac{L_q}{\lambda(1 - P(K))}$

- $W = W_q + \dfrac{1}{\mu}$

Example C.3

A gas station has an single-stall automatic car wash that takes exactly 2.4 minutes to wash a car, so the service rate is $\mu = 25$ per hour. Cars arrive to use the car wash on an average of one every 3 minutes, Poisson distributed, for an arrival rate of $\lambda =$ twenty per hour. Determine the percentage of time the car wash is busy, the average number of cars waiting to use the car wash, the average number of cars at the car wash, the average amount of time a car waits before being washed, and the average amount of time a car spends at the car wash.

Solution:

This is a deterministic service time (M/D/1) example. From the equations in Table C.3, we determine that:

▶ The car wash will be busy $\rho = \lambda/\mu = 20/25 = .8$ or 80% of the time.

▶ There will be an average of $L_q = \dfrac{\rho^2}{2(1-\rho)} =$

$\dfrac{(.80)^2}{2(1-.8)} = \dfrac{.64}{.4} = 1.6$ cars waiting to use the car wash.

▶ There will be an average of $L = L_q = 1.6 + .8 = 2.4$ cars using or waiting for the car wash.

▶ A car will wait on average $W_q = L_q/\lambda = 1.6/20 = .08$ hours or 4.8 minutes before using the car wash.

▶ A car will spend an average of $W = L/\lambda = 2.4/20 = .12$ hours or 7.2 minutes waiting for or using the car wash.

Note that while ρ, the percentage utilization, for the car wash is exactly the same as at the airline check-in counter in Example C.1, which has the same arrival and service rates, the values for the "waiting" performance measures (L_q and W_q) are exactly half of those in Example C.1. This example should make it obvious that it is service time variability that accounts for much of the waiting in a queuing system.

Example C.4

While the number of passengers on Tom Jackson's airline is low enough between noon and 2 p.m. that one customer service agent can keep up with the check-ins (see Example C.1), the airline operates more flights during the early morning and late afternoon hours as business travelers leave to get to their appointments in other cities and return home at the end of their trips. Between 5 p.m. and 7 p.m., passengers arrive for check-in at the check-in counter for Tom Jackson's airline at the Flagstaff airport at a rate of seventy per hour. Determine the minimum number of agents that must be on duty for the system to reach steady-state conditions and the values of the standard queuing performance measures with that number of agents.

Solution:

Because each passenger requires an average of 2.4 minutes to check in ($\mu = 25$ per hour),

having only one agent on duty is not an option. The line would grow longer and longer, with many unhappy passengers. To be able to reach steady state conditions, the total service capacity ($S\mu$) must be greater than the arrival rate (λ). Thus, based on $\lambda < S\mu$ or $70 < 25S$, a minimum of $S = 3$ agents is required.

We see that, with $S = 3$ agents, the servers are busy $\rho = 93.33\%$ of the time, there is an average of $L_q = 12.27$ passengers waiting to check in, and that those passengers wait for an average of $W_q = .175$ hours or 10.5 minutes. Also, there is an average of $L = 15.07$ total passengers at the check-in counter, and those passengers are there for an average of $W = .215$ hours or 12.9 minutes.

Example C.5

Tom Jackson's airline operates a telephone information and reservation service with a single operator who controls three telephone lines. Two calls can be placed on hold while the operator speaks to a third customer. Additional callers receive a busy signal. Calls come in on an average of one every 2 minutes, Poisson distributed ($\lambda = 0.5$ per minute). Service requires an average of 1.5 minutes, exponentially distributed ($\mu = .6667$ per minute). Determine the values of the standard queuing performance measures for this system.

Solution:

The operating characteristics of this system, which has $\rho = \lambda/\mu = .5/.6667 = .75$, are:

▶ The operator is idle and no one is waiting $P(0) = .3657$ or 36.57% of the time.

▶ The probability that a caller will receive a busy signal and be rejected or lost is $P(K) = P(3) = .1543$.

▶ The mean number of callers in the system, either on hold or speaking to the operator is $L = 1.149$.

▶ The mean number of callers on hold is $L_q = .515$.

▶ The mean time a caller spends on hold is $W_q = 1.218$ minutes.

▶ The mean time a caller spends on the phone, either on hold or speaking to the operator, is $W = 2.718$ minutes.

Finite Queue Models

The models discussed so far all assume that there is no limit to how long the queue may become. In some cases, however, there will be a maximum allowable number of waiting customers due to physical constraints or policy limitations. If this is the case, then any customers arriving when the queue is full will be turned away (**rejection** in queuing terminology) and, as a result, their business may be lost.

Rejection

In a finite queue model, turning away customers arriving when the queue is full.

The conditions for applying this model are identical to those for the multiple single-server model (M/M/S) discussed above, except there is a maximum of K customers in the system at any time, S of which would be in service and the rest in the queue, which has a maximum length of K-S. The equations for the steady-state operating characteristics for the single-server system with a finite queue are given in Table C.5.[2]

Finite Population Models

In some cases the calling population is so small that you cannot assume that it is infinite. In such cases a finite population model must be used. The model given here assumes:

1. Each of the N population members has a Poisson arrival rate of λ per period when not in the queue or receiving service.

2. Each server has a service rate of μ per period, the actual service time having an exponential distribution.

3. The queue discipline for the single queue is first come, first served.

4. There is no balking or reneging.

[2] The equations for the comparable multiple-server model are more complicated and are not given here. That model is, however, available in many software packages, including Excelpom.

Example C.6

A repairperson maintains three machines. Each machine operates for an average of 4 hours before breaking down, the number of failures per operating hour per machine having a Poisson distribution. It takes the repairperson an average of 1 hour to repair a machine, the repair time having an exponential distribution. Determine the values of the standard queuing performance measures for this system.

Solution:

With $N = 3$ machines, $\lambda = 0.25$ breakdowns per operating hour per machine, and $\mu = 1$ repair per hour, the steady-state operating characteristics for this system are:

▶ $P(0) = .4507$ is the probability that all machines are working, so the repairperson is idle 45% of the time and busy 55% of the time.

▶ The mean number of machines not operating is $L = .8028$, so the mean number of machines operating is $N - L = 2.1972$.

▶ The mean time a machine is not operating is $W = 1.4615$ hours.

▶ The mean time a machine waits to be repaired is $W_q = .4615$ hours.

▶ The mean number of machines waiting to be repaired is $L_q = .2535$.

5. The equations for the steady-state operating characteristics are given in Table C.6.[3]

Designing Queuing Systems

Designing a queuing system involves choosing one or more system characteristics that you can control. Examples of such characteristics include: the rate of service, the number of servers, the number of queues, the maximum queue length, the size of a finite population, and the service discipline.

The two basic approaches to designing a queuing system are:

1. Design to meet a performance standard

2. Design to minimize the combined cost of providing service and of not providing enough service

DESIGN TO MEET A SERVICE STANDARD

While it is generally possible to determine the cost of providing a specific level of service capacity, it is often not possible to readily determine the costs incurred as a result of customers having to wait or being rejected for service. In such cases, management might specify one or more service performance standards to be met. The objective is then to determine the least expensive system that will meet those performance standards. An example would be the determination of the number and location of ambulances so as to be able to answer 90% of all calls within a specified time, such as 10 minutes.

DESIGN TO MINIMIZE TOTAL SYSTEM COST

The total cost of a queuing system consists of: (1) the cost of providing service capacity, and (2) the cost of not providing enough capacity. The cost of providing

---

[3] As with the finite queue model just discussed, the equations for the multiple-server version of this model are more complicated and are not given here. However, that model is available in many software packages, including Excelpom.

Table C.6

Steady-State Performance Measures for the Single-Server Finite Population Model

- $P(0) = \dfrac{1}{\displaystyle\sum_{i=0}^{N} \dfrac{N!}{(N-i)!} \rho^{i}}$ where $\rho = \lambda/\mu$

- $P(n) = \dfrac{N!}{(N-n)!} \rho^{n} P(0)$ for $n \leq N$

- $L = N - \dfrac{1}{\rho}(1 - P(0))$

- $\lambda_{e} = \lambda(N - L)$ is the effective arrival rate, recognizing that, on average, there are only $N - L$ population members available to call for service.

- $W = L/\lambda_{e}$

- $W_{q} = W - 1/\mu$

- $L_{q} = \lambda_{e} W_{q}$

capacity usually consists of the costs of servers and the cost of queue spaces. The cost of not providing enough capacity typically includes the costs of customers having to wait, which may include the cost of their lost business in the future, and the cost of lost current customers due to balking, reneging, or rejection. Assuming these costs can be determined, the two types of costs can be added together, as shown in Figure C.2, and an optimal service capacity can be determined.

Figure C.2

Determining the optimal service capacity

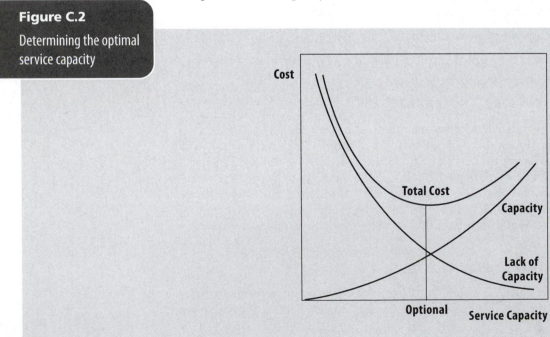

Example C.7

(Refer to Example C.4)

During the evening busy period, passengers for Tom Jackson's airline at the Flagstaff airport have to wait for an average of .175 hours or 10.5 minutes to check in when there are S = 3 agents on duty. Airline management would like to reduce the average waiting time for check-in to no more than 5 minutes. How many agents would have to be on duty to meet this service standard?

Solution:

In Example C.4 we determined that, during the evening busy period, $\lambda = 70$ per hour and $\mu = 25$ per hour. We see that with S = 4 agents the average time spent in the queue is $W_q = 0.014$ hours or 0.86 minutes. Because this is less than the desired service standard of no more than 5 minutes, four agents will be sufficient.

Example C.8

(Refer to Examples C.4 and C.7)

The cost of having a customer service agent on duty at the Flagstaff airport during the evening busy period is $25 per hour. Tom Jackson's airline's management estimates that the cost of making a passenger wait to check in is $50 per hour. How many agents should be on duty during this time to minimize the total cost of the system?

Solution:

We assume that there is no cost of providing waiting spaces (arriving passengers simply queue up in the lobby area), so the cost of providing service capacity is simply the cost of the agents who are on duty:

Cost of service capacity = $C_s S$ = $25S per hour

We assume that there will be no current loss of business due to balking or reneging and, with no limit to the length of the queue, there will be no rejection, so the cost of not providing sufficient capacity is simply the waiting cost for the customers in the system:

Cost of insufficient capacity = $C_w L$
 = $50L per hour

Thus the total cost per hour of operating the system is:

Total cost = $25S + $50L

The minimum total cost can be found by determining the total cost for various values of S and comparing them.

▶ S = 3: In Example C.4 we determined that with S = 3, L = 15.0735. The total cost per hour for operating the check-in counter with S = 3 agents is:

Total Cost = $25S + $50L = $25(3) + $50(15.0735) = $75 + $753.68 = $828.68

▶ S = 4: With S = 4, L = 3.80019. The total cost per hour for operating the check-in counter with S = 4 agents is:

Total Cost = $25(4) + $50(3.80019) = $100 + $190.01 = $290.01

▶ S = 5: With S = 5, L = 3.0412. The total cost per hour for operating the check-in counter with S = 5 agents is:

Total Cost = $25(5) + $50(3.0412) = $125 + $152.06 = $277.06

S ≥ 6: Referring to the equations in Table C.4, we see that the equation for L consists of two terms: L_q, which depends on the value of S, and λ/μ, which does not. In this example, $\lambda/\mu = 70/25 = 2.8$. Thus, no matter how much an additional agent reduces L_q, L cannot be less than 2.8 and the waiting cost component of total cost cannot be reduced below $50(2.8) = $140. Thus there is no point in adding a sixth agent, since doing so will add an additional $25 to the capacity cost while reducing the waiting cost by no more than $152.06 − $140 = $12.06. The optimal number of agents on duty during the evening busy period is, therefore, five.

SUMMARY

A queue is a waiting line. Queues form whenever the current demand for service exceeds the server's current capacity to provide service. The usual objective of queuing analysis is to design an efficient system that balances operational efficiency and customer inconvenience.

The queuing models given in this supplement provide equations for the steady-state operating characteristics of queuing systems that have Poisson arrivals and one of several different service time distributions. Models are given for the basic exponential service

model and its multiple-server extension. Models are also given for single-server models with general or deterministic service times and for exponential service times when there is a finite population or a finite maximum queue length. The operating characteristic values derived from these models can be used to design queuing systems to either meet a specified service standard or minimize the total cost of operating the system, that total cost being the sum of the cost of providing capacity and the cost of providing insufficient capacity.

KEY TERMS

Arrival rate, 837
Balking, 837
Batch service, 838
Calling population, 836
Channel, 838
Customer, 836

Finite population, 837
Infinite population, 837
Jockeying, 837
Queue, 836
Queue discipline, 837
Rejection, 844

Reneging, 837
Service facility, 837
Service rate, 838
Steady-state behavior, 838
Transient behavior, 838

SOLVED PROBLEMS

1. Luis Flores's furniture factory has a three-bay shipping/receiving dock. Trucks arrive to be loaded or unloaded on an average of one every 3 hours, Poisson distributed. It takes a dock crew an average of 2 hours to load or unload a truck, the time being exponentially distributed. The dock manager needs to decide how many of the bays to staff if a dock crew costs $40 an hour and the waiting costs for a truck are $150 an hour.

Solution:

Because (λ = .3333 per hour and (μ = .5 per hour, we have $\lambda < \mu$, so the minimum number of bays to staff is one. The maximum, of course, is three, the number of bays. We can use, as appropriate, the basic single-server (M/M/1) or multiple-server (M/M/S) exponential service time model to determine the steady-state operating characteristics of the system. Because we can expect no balking, reneging, or rejection, the only costs that are

relevant are the cost of servers (dock crews) and the waiting costs for the trucks in the system. The cost to be minimized is, then:

Total Cost = $C_sS + C_wL$

▶ $S = 1$: Using the equation for L from Table C.1,

$$L = \frac{\lambda}{\mu - \lambda} = \frac{.333}{.5 - .3333} = 2.0.$$

The total cost per hour is, then:

Total Cost = $40(1) + $150(2.0) = $40 + $300 = $340

▶ $S = 2$: Using the equations in Table C.4 or software, we find that L = .75 and the total cost per hour is:

Total Cost = $40(2) + $150(.75) = $80 + $112.50 = $192.50

- $S = 3$: Using the equations in Table C.4 or software, we find that $L = .676$ and the total cost per hour is:

Total Cost $= \$40(3) + \$150(.676) =$ $\$120 + \$101.39 = \$221.39$

Because the total cost per hour with two crews ($192.50) is less than the cost with either one crew ($340) or three crews ($221.39), the optimal number of bays to staff is two.

2. (See Example C.5.) Because Tom Jackson's airline does not participate in any of the computerized reservation systems used by the major airlines due to their cost, it depends for its business solely on potential customers walking up to its airport check-in counters or calling its telephone reservation system to book a flight. Management's concern is that a caller who cannot get through to the reservation number may call one of the airline's competitors and the business will be lost. They estimate that each lost call costs the airline an average of $40. Increasing the number of telephone lines into the reservation number would obviously reduce the frequency of lost calls; the hourly cost of an additional telephone line would be $6. Management is also concerned that making callers wait on hold for too long will reduce the number of tickets sold. The average cost of each hour of waiting is estimated to be $20. How many reservation phone lines should the airline maintain to minimize the total cost of operating the reservation system?

Solution:

The problem is to determine the maximum size of a finite queue system in order to minimize the total cost of providing service capacity (the number of lines for answering or holding calls) and of having insufficient capacity (the cost of waiting plus the cost of the lost calls). The total cost per hour is, then:

- Total Cost $= C_s$(Lines) $+ C_w$(Average Number in the System) $+ C_l$(Lost Calls) $= \$6(K) + \$20(L) + \$40(\lambda P(K))$

From Example C.5, we have $\lambda = 0.5$ per minute or thirty per hour and $\mu = 40$ per hour, so $\rho = \lambda/\mu = .75$. Solve by trying different values for K.

$K = 3$: $L = 1.149$ and $P(K) = P(3) = .1543$. Thus:

Total Cost $= \$6(3) + \$20(1.149) +$ $\$40(30(.1543)) = \$18 + \$22.98 + \$185.16$ $= \$226.14$

$K = 4$: Using the equations in Table C.6, we find that

$$L = \frac{\rho}{1-\rho} - \frac{(K+1)\rho^{K+1}}{1-\rho^{K+1}} = \frac{.75}{.25} - \frac{(5)(.75)^5}{1-(.75)^5}$$

$$= 3 - 1.5557 = 1.4443, \quad P(0) = \frac{1-\rho}{1-\rho^{K+1}}$$

$$= \frac{1-.75}{1-(.75)^5} = .3278, \text{ and } P(K) = P(4) = \rho^K P(0)$$

$$= (.75)^4(.3278) = .1037.$$

Thus:

Total Cost $= \$6(4) + \$20(1.4443)$ $+ \$40(30(.1037)) = \$24 + \$28.89 + \$124.44$ $= \$177.33$

$K = 5$: Using software or the same equations used for $K = 4$, we find that $L = 1.7007$ and $P(K) = P(5) = .0722$. Thus:

Total Cost $= \$6(5) + \$20(1.7007)$ $+ \$40(30(.0722)) = \$30 + \$30.01 + \$86.64$ $= \$150.65$

$K = 6$: $L = 1.9217$ and $P(K) = P(6) = .0513$. Thus:

Total Cost $= \$6(6) + \$20(1.9217)$ $+ \$40(30(.0513)) = \$36 + \$38.43 + \$61.56$ $= \$135.99$

$K = 7$: $L = 2.110$ and $P(K) = P(7) = .0371$. Thus:

Total Cost $= \$6(7) + \$20(2.110) +$ $\$40(30(.0371)) = \$42 + \$42.20 + \$44.52$ $= \$128.72$

$K = 8$: $L = 2.2694$ and $P(K) = P(8) = .0271$. Thus:

Total Cost $= \$6(8) + \$20(2.2694)$ $+ \$40(30(.0271)) = \$48 + \$45.39 + \$32.52$ $= \$125.91$

$K = 9$: $L = 2.4033$ and $P(K) = P(9) = .0199$. Thus:

Total Cost $= \$6(9) + \$20(2.4033)$ $+ \$40(30(.0199)) = \$54 + \$48.07 + \$23.88$ $= \$125.95$

Thus, with a single operator, the optimal number of phone lines to have for the reservation system is $K = 8$.

DISCUSSION QUESTIONS

1. What are the basic components of a queuing system and the most important characteristics of each?

2. Explain the difference between a finite and infinite calling population. Why is it important?

3. Why may a first-come, first-served queue discipline not be the best one to use in all situations?

4. What are three significantly different real-world queuing systems? What is each one's basic components and characteristics?

5. Distinguish among the single-server models discussed in this chapter supplement. Why are their differences important in selecting a model to use?

6. What are the differences between servers in parallel and servers in series?

7. What are the different approaches to designing a queuing system? Give examples of when each approach might be appropriate.

8. What cost trade-offs need to be considered in designing a queuing system to minimize costs? Give examples of each type of cost.

9. Why must the arrival rate be less than the service rate in a basic single-server queuing system, but not in a single-server system with a finite queue or a finite population?

10. Why do queues form in service systems even if the arrival rate is less than the service rate?

PROBLEMS

C-1. The local BurgerBox fast food restaurant has a drive-up window. During lunch, customers arrive on an average of one per minute. Service takes an average of 40 seconds, exponentially distributed. What percentage of customers will have to wait to receive service? On average, how long is the line and how long will a customer spend at the restaurant's drive-up window?

C-2. The BurgerBox manager (Problem C-1) believes that, to remain competitive with other fast-food restaurants, a drive-up customer should not have to wait, on average, more than 1 minute. How long, on average, should service take to meet this standard?

C-3. A law firm has two lawyers, each of whom has a secretary. Each lawyer generates documents to be typed at a rate of two per hour. Each secretary takes an average of 20 minutes, exponentially distributed, to type a document. The lawyers are considering changing to a pool arrangement in which both secretaries would work for both lawyers, with the first available secretary doing the next required job. Compare the two arrangements to determine which would be more efficient.

C-4. The Biltmore Towers apartment building is considering building a tennis court. Based on a survey of the residents, on the weekends an average of nine groups per 12-hour day will want to use the court. The residents proposed that playing time be limited to 1 hour, with no reservations. All survey respondents indicated that they would use the full hour. Determine the percentage of court utilization, the average number of groups waiting to use the court, and the average length of time a group will have to wait. Assume there will be no balking or reneging.

C-5. The local TexOK service station has a single mechanic. Service jobs arrive at a rate of one per hour. The probability distribution of service time has a mean of 45 minutes and a standard deviation of 30 minutes. Determine the percentage of time the mechanic is busy, the average number of cars waiting for service, and the average time a car spends at the service station.

C-6. Patients arrive at a medical clinic on Saturday mornings at a rate of one every 10 minutes. The time required for a doctor to take care of a patient is exponentially distributed with an average of 20 minutes. Patients are seen on a first-come, first-served basis by the first available doctor. How many doctors should be on duty on Saturday mornings if the clinic management wants patients to wait no more than 15 minutes on average before being seen by a doctor?

C-7. A small grocery store has a single checkout line. On Saturdays, customers arrive at the checkout on an average of one every 8 minutes. The cashier takes an average of 6 minutes to process a single customer, exponentially distributed. The store's owner believes that the amount of time that a customer has to wait hurts his business; he estimates that waiting time costs him $20 per hour in lost business. In order to speed up service, the owner is considering hiring a teenager to bag the groceries at $6 per hour. With the addition of the bagger, the cashier will be able to process a customer in an average of 4.5 minutes. Should the bagger be hired?

C-8. The Benelux Manufacturing Co. uses a large number of identical machines for one part of its manufacturing process. These machines carry out their operation automatically. However, they occasionally jam up. This happens on an average of once every 5 minutes per machine, following a Poisson process. Clearing a jammed machine is usually fast, taking an average of 30 seconds, exponentially distributed.

The machines are grouped into small areas, with one operator responsible for all the machines in an area. If there are five machines in an area, what is the average number of machines not in production (jammed and either being cleared or waiting) at any given moment? What is the average amount of time a jammed machine must wait to be cleared? What percentage of the time is the operator busy?

C-9. (Refer to Problem C.8) Assume that an operating machine makes a net contribution to profit and overhead of $75 per hour and that the cost of an operator is $18 per hour, including fringe benefits. How many machines should an operator be responsible for?

C-10. A financial analysis group consists of five analysts, each of whom requires the use of a computer terminal connected to a specialized data base an average of once per hour for an

average of 10 minutes at a time, exponentially distributed. At present the analysts share a single terminal. Because of the time lost waiting to use the terminal, the analysts have requested a second terminal. A terminal costs $6 per hour. An analyst is paid $25 per hour, including fringe benefits. Should a second terminal be installed? (Note: This problem requires access to a computer package for solution.)

C-11. The laboratory at Cheryl Sanders' hospital receives test requests at a rate of fifteen per hour, Poisson distributed, during normal working hours (8 a.m. to 4 p.m.). Each of the two lab technicians can handle an average of eight tests per hour, the time per test being exponentially distributed.

a) Determine the percentage of time the technicians are busy, the probability that both technicians are idle at the same time, the average number of tests waiting to be processed, the average amount of time a test waits to be processed, and the average time a test spends at the lab.

b) Determine how many lab technicians are required if Cheryl Sanders wants tests completed in an average of 45 minutes from the time they reach the lab.

C-12. An office that operates 8 hours per day, 240 days per year has a single copying machine. Secretaries arrive at the machine to make copies at a rate of ten per hour, Poisson distributed. The time to complete a copy job is exponentially distributed, with an average of 5 minutes. The copying machine costs $750 per month plus $0.04 per copy. A secretary is paid an average of $12.50 per hour, including fringe benefits.

a) Determine the percentage of time the machine is in use, the average number of secretaries waiting to use the machine (assume no balking or reneging), the average time a secretary waits to use the machine, and the average time a secretary spends at the machine per visit.

b) Given the information presented, would it make sense for the company to add a second, identical copying machine? If so, would three machines make sense?

c) As an alternative to adding one or more additional machines identical to the current one, the office manager has proposed replacing the existing machine with a new one that would take an average of 4 minutes per job and cost $1000 per month plus $0.04 per copy. Compare this alternative to your decision from part (b).

C-13. Passengers arrive at the security screening device at an airport in a Poisson manner at a rate of six per minute. The time for screening has a mean of 6 seconds and a standard deviation of three seconds.

a) Determine the percentage of time the screening device is in use, the average number of passengers waiting to go through the device, the average time a passenger waits to for the device, and the average time a passenger spends at the device.

b) The airport's policy is to open a second screening device when the average number of passengers waiting in line to be screened reaches four. What arrival rate triggers the opening of a second screening device?

C-14. Customers at Moore's Cafeteria arrive, collect their food, and go to a cashier to pay for their food before eating, waiting in a single line for the first available cashier. Customers arrive at the cashiers in a Poisson manner, the rate depending on the time of day. During the breakfast hours, customers arrive at a rate of nine per minute; during the lunch hours the arrival rate is fifteen per minute; during the dinner hours the arrival rate is twelve per minute. Regardless of which meal time it is, the cashier takes an average of 20 seconds to process a customer, the actual time having an exponential distribution. Determine the number of cashiers to have on duty during each meal time if the cafeteria's management wants the average number of customers waiting to check out to be no more than three? To be no more than two?

C-15. The Yelo-Chek Cab Company has a fleet of twenty cabs, which are evenly divided between two garages, each of which has a mechanic. A cab requires servicing of some type on an average of once every eight days, Poisson distributed. The time a mechanic needs to service a cab is exponentially distributed with a mean of half a day. The cab company's owner is considering the possibility of closing the two existing garages and consolidating operations in a single garage. If this is done, the two mechanics will work separately, but the work needed on any of the cabs would be done by the first available mechanic. Compare the existing and proposed systems and recommend which option would be preferable.

Glossary

5 Ws and H A set of questions that can help identify the root cause of a problem.

ABC inventory analysis A form of Pareto analysis, which is based on the rule that 20% of the items in inventory will account for 80% of the value of inventory.

Acceptable quality level (AQL) The proportion of non-conforming items acceptable in a batch. This is the level of quality the customer would only expect to be rejected very infrequently (recognizing the limitations of a supplier's process, the limitations of acceptance sampling, and the cost of obtaining higher levels of quality).

Acceptance sampling A tool that uses information gained from a sample of finished items to determine whether or not to accept the entire batch from which the sample was taken.

Activity-based costing (ABC) A managerial accounting method that allocates the costs to the product-service bundle based on overhead activities performed and aesthetics of the product-service bundle.

Activity-on-arrow A useful aid for understanding the relationships among the activities in a project.

Activity-on-node A useful aid for adequately understanding the relationships among activities to aide in illustrating ideas.

Additive seasonal index The expected difference between the value of a time series and the value, as called for by any trend and cyclic components.

Aggregate plan The ways in which existing resources will be used to meet expected levels of demand for product groups over the immediate range.

Andon boards A large electronic sign that provides real-time operational performance and system status information.

Appraisal costs Expenditures associated with the inspection and testing of materials and services at any point in a value-adding process.

Arrival rate The average number of customers arriving for service per time period.

Assemblers Anything that brings together a variety of different parts, resulting in converging material flows.

Assemble-to-order A combination of the make-to-stock and make-to-order approaches. The production of customer orders are scheduled using components and subassemblies that have been made to stock.

Assembly buffer A collection of work placed wherever material flows that doesn't include the bottleneck join work that has been through the bottleneck.

Assignment rule A procedure that forms the basis for choosing an elemental task for assignment to a workstation.

Asynchronous value-adding systems Systems that allow separate value-adding activities to be scheduled independently.

Attribute measures Measurements of physical and dimensional characteristics in categories.

Automated Data Collection (ADC) Critical components of SCM coordination, accomplished through point-of-sale systems and other types of bar code scanners.

Automated Guided Vehicle (AGV) A tool used to transport materials without a human driver.

Automated storage and retrieval system (AS/RS) A resource that will place materials into a physical inventory location, maintain a record of their location, and return them when needed.

Autonomy The extent to which a worker is free to do a job on her or his own.

Average fixed cost The fixed cost per unit of the product-service bundle.

Average unit cost The sum of the average fixed cost and the average variable cost.

Average variable cost The variable cost per unit.

Averaging out The procedure for analyzing a decision tree in which each branch is replaced by a single number.

Backlog An amount of unmet demand.

Backward infinite scheduling approach A process where managers start with the time they must arrive at the bottleneck and work backward in time.

Backward scheduling A process where companies determine when a stock of outputs will be needed, then place orders on the master schedule so as to ensure the availability of outputs by that time. In MTS companies, planners typically use this to develop the master schedule.

Balanced scorecard Information about performance in key categories.

Baldrige Award The United States' national quality award believed to have played a significant role in promoting quality management practices. Named after Malcolm Baldrige, U.S. Secretary of Commerce from 1981 to 1987, whose managerial excellence is credited with long-term improvements in the efficiency and effectiveness of the U.S. government.

Balking The refusal of an arriving customer to join the queue and wait for service.

Basic producers Producers which use natural resources such as iron ore, oil, wheat, and minerals as inputs. Their outputs are basic materials such as rolled steel, flour and plastic powders.

Batch process A manufacturing system that produces groups of items that are essentially identical, called production lots or batches.

Batch service Where multiple jobs or customers are processed simultaneously by a single server.

Best operating level (BOL) The volume, or scale of operations, at which the average total cost per unit is minimized.

Bill of materials A list indicating what parts and subassemblies go into independent demand items.

Bottleneck Any resource that has insufficient capacity to satisfy requirements.

Bottleneck buffer Work that is waiting to be processed at the bottleneck.

Brainstorming A well-known technique used to generate an extensive list of ideas pertinent to a particular problem.

Brand equity The general perception of value associated with an organization's product service bundle.

Bullwhip effect The tendency of small variations in demand to become larger as their implications are transmitted backward through a supply chain.

Business process An administrative decision-making process that is used to help an organization to leverage its resources toward accomplishing its objectives.

Business process reengineering (BPR) A "blow it up and start over from scratch" improvement technique frequently used to reinvent processes that are weak because they span functional boundaries in hierarchical organization charts but aren't coordinated across these boundaries.

Business strategy The set of decisions that answer the question, "How will we compete in this business?"

Calling population A component of the calling system that is the source of potential customers for the services.

Capacity requirements planning (CRP) Alerts managers to capacity shortages resulting from schedules based on the orders planned by MRP systems.

Capacity strategy The set of long-term decisions a firm makes about the size of its plants and equipment.

Capacity The maximum rate of output from a process.

Capacity utilization The ratio of capacity used during a fixed period of time to the available capacity during that same time period.

Causal models Causal Models that estimate the value of the -dependent variable on the basis of the independent variables.

Cause and effect diagrams (fishbone charts) Charts which categorize the potential reasons for a situation that is observed.

Cellular layout Layout in which a facility is made up of value-adding cells.

Center of gravity method A mathematical technique that gives decision makers a rough idea of the most suitable location for a new facility.

Chance node Problem features that are determined by chance or probability, such as the states of nature.

Channel Each parallel server or series of servers through which a customer might pass.

Chase demand strategy The process where demand is met by matching planned monthly production with forecasted demand, while the inventory account is held constant.

Check sheets Much like a checklist, a checksheet is more oriented toward collecting data and less oriented toward guiding activity.

Checklists A guide to accomplishing a task.

Closed loop MRP users Companies that adjust their master schedules because there are so many material requirements in a given week that it is not possible to load all the work on existing resources and vendors, said to have a what-if? capability.

Closed loop planning A process in which information from your detailed capacity planning is used to level (and insure the feasibility of) the master schedule.

Common cause variation (or random variation) The natural variation inherent in any system.

Competitive clustering An approach used by motels and automobile dealerships to locate themselves close to competitors.

Competitive priority A defined emphasis that a business chooses to pursue and which should be supported by the decisions it makes.

Computer-aided design (CAD) An approach that uses computer software and hardware applications to generate digitized models representing a product's structural characteristics and physical dimensions.

Computer-integrated manufacturing (CIM) The process which combines automated process and material handling technologies with other computer-based manufacturing technologies, so that computers everywhere in the company can "talk" to one another.

Computerized numerical control (CNC) A piece of equipment that has been outfitted with a computer that can store part programs.

Concurrent engineering An approach to product-service design in which the concerns of more than one function are considered simultaneously.

Conglomerate (or unrelated) diversification Decision-making pattern in which an organization owns a wide variety of unrelated business ventures.

Consumer's risk The risk of making a type II error, represented by the Greek letter (beta).

Continuous improvement The process of making localized, incremental improvements using the techniques of business process analysis.

Continuous-flow processes Repetitive non-discrete manufacturing systems.

Control A situation where common cause variation is the only type of variation present in a system or process. In this case, management need not take any special action.

Control charts Statistical tools that allow decision makers to distinguish processes that are in control from those that are out of control.

Control limit A value used to distinguish between commonly expected and unusual values for a sample statistic.

Converters Devices which use basic materials as their inputs and add value by cutting and blending them in various ways.

Corporate strategy A set of decisions that answer the question, "What business are we in?"

Cost-volume break-even analysis (CVBA) A capital investment justification tool that is well suited to modeling the costs associated with fixed automation. It may also be used to justify a new product-service bundle or a change to an existing one.

Cost-volume-flexibility break-even analysis (CVFBA) A tool that can be used to evaluate the economic tradeoffs in technology investments that may pay off through economies of scope.

Countermeasures matrix A tool that provides a way of ranking a variety of possible solutions on a variety of criteria such as effectiveness, feasibility, safety, environmental impact, and cost.

Crash time, Crash cost A higher, faster way will require either additional resources or a different, more expensive way of doing the activity.

Crashing Finding a way to complete an activity more quickly than expected.

Critical activities Those activities on which the scheduled completion of the projects depends.

Critical path method (CPM) A network modeling approach to time management that doesn't allow the expected duration of any activity to be expressed as a probability expression.

Critical path The longest path a project will take to complete its way through its network.

Current budget shortfall The monetary difference between the cumulative cost and the expected cost.

Customer Any individual or group that uses the output of a process.

Customer involvement The customer's role in creating or customizing a particular product-service bundle.

Customer quality The portion of the market that matches the customer profile for which a product-service bundle is designed. It indicates how hard a company will have to work to get customers.

Customer quantity An indicator of market size, stated in terms of the total number of buyers—for example, number of households, number of individuals in a particular demographic category, or number of companies that use a product-service bundle.

Customer value The spending potential of a spending unit such as average household expenditure, average disposable income, and average production volume (for industrial customers).

Customer-driven team structure A business philosophy that states projects come and go, but the type of customer remains largely the same.

Cycle counting A periodic audit of inventory quantities to ensure accuracy.

Cycle time On an assembly line, the time allowed for each workstation to complete its portion of the work on one unit of output.

Cyclic effects Changes in the economy as it moves through the phases of growth and decline in the business cycle, a process that takes several years.

Decision alternatives The set of definable alternatives from which the decision maker must choose.

Decision making under certainty A basic type of decision problem where decision makers have the payoff table, but no information on the relative likelihood of the states of nature. In principle, the analysis is simple: Choose the alternative with

the best payoff. In practice, it is not always that easy, since an "alternative" may actually represent the values for many decision variables.

Decision making under risk A basic type of decision problem where the state of nature is known, so the payoff table has only one column. In principle, the analysis is simple: Choose the alternative with the best payoff.

Decision making under uncertainty A basic type of decision problem where decision makers have the payoff table, but no information on the relative likelihood of the states of nature.

Decision tree An alternative to using a payoff to compute the expected values of decision alternatives, which consists of two or more stages or levels, shown in time order from left to right.

Decreasing returns to scale A situation where variable costs may begin to rise due to problems associated with higher volumes.

Delphi method An approach to generating forecasts from expert opinion in which the forecaster uses a series of surveys to develop a consensus on a subject.

Demand during lead time (DDLT) A variety of ways to develop a probability distribution.

Demand rate The amount of inventory used in a given time period.

Dependent activities Those activities that must be completed in a particular sequence.

Dependent demand inventory The material that goes into the things the firm sells.

Deseasonalize The process of removing seasonality by dividing the actual value by the appropriate seasonal index.

Design for disassembly (DFD) A strategy that explicitly builds parts and component recovery considerations into design decisions.

Design for environment A product development approach that broadens the concept of design for manufacturability even further to include the environmental impact of a design, from the extraction of raw materials to their disposal. This strategy is based on the concept of sustainability.

Design for manufacturability (DFM) A product development approach that explicitly considers the effectiveness with which an item can be made during the initial development of the product-service design. It is based on the belief that the cost of developing and running the value-adding system is as important as the functionality.

Design for procurement The explicit consideration of component parts supply during the initial development of a product-service design.

Discrete processes A method of producing products that can be counted in integer units and are functional only in their completed form.

Diseconomy of scale An economic disadvantage associated with operating at higher volumes.

Dispatching decisions The choices which determine the sequence in which that work will be completed.

Dispatching The process of sequencing jobs through a work center.

Distributed numerical control (DNC) The use of a group of networked CNC machines that run from a common server.

Drum-buffer-rope (DBR) system The most detailed level of scheduling, in which managers must decide who should do what and with which resource.

Dummy activities or milestones Less than brief activities.

Early-finish time (EF) The time at which something will finish if it starts at its early start time and is completed in the estimated time.

Early-start time (ES) The earliest time at which something can begin if all activities preceding it start as early as possible and are completed in their estimated times.

Earned value A situation where the value of the completed work is less than the budgeted expense.

Earned value analysis Analysis of project progress and expenditures relative to project targets.

E-commerce The integrated set of computer technologies that enable consumers and businesses to conduct business over electronic networks.

Economic order quantity The cost-minimizing order quantity, which is the amount that perfectly balances annual ordering costs and annual holding costs.

Economic production quantity (EPQ) The cost-minimizing production order quantity.

Economy of scale The economic advantage that is often associated with the ability to operate at higher volumes.

Economy of scope An economic advantage obtained through process flexibility.

Electronic data interchange (EDI) A method of transferring business information such as demand, price, available capacity, and the anticipated delivery date between suppliers and customers via a predetermined protocol.

Elemental task Operations that cannot be divided, because of technical reasons or managerial preference.

Employee involvement (EI) A formal approach to creating a spirit of teamwork that will lead to widespread process improvements.

Enterprise Resources Planning (ERP) Systems Software packages that integrate decision support programs for the various functional areas with a common database. They allow companies to access the schedules of their downstream suppliers and schedule their own operations so that they are making what will be needed rather than what they think will be needed.

Equal likelihood A procedure based on the assumption that if we cannot determine the relative likelihood of the states of nature, then it is rational to presume that they are equally likely.

Equal likelihood procedure A procedure based on the assumption that if we cannot determine the relative likelihood of the states of nature, then it is rational to presume that they are equally likely.

Expected value of perfect information (EVPI) A measure of the expected current worth to the decision maker of being able to find out, just before having to make the decision, what the state of nature will be.

Expediting A process of walking a job through a facility overriding local scheduling decisions at each point on the route in order to give it top priority.

External customer A customer who exists outside of the organization.

External failure costs Expenditures associated with items that are not fit for use but have nevertheless been transferred to the customer.

Extreme case analysis This is like the *maximax* and *maximin* strategies which takes either an optimistic or pessimistic view rather than working with probabilities.

Fabricators Tools which use the material that is provided by converters to create parts for assembly operations.

Facilitating goods Goods that allow for the transfer of a service's value to the customer.

Facilitating services Services that allow the customer to enjoy the benefits of the good's intended use.

Facilitators Managers that support the teams' efforts and respond to workers' suggestions for improvement.

Facility-level flexibility The flexibility of a system that is referred to as a whole.

Feasible set The set of points that satisfy all the constraints.

Feedback The extent to which a worker is informed about her or his fellow employees, customers, community members, and so on.

Fill rate The percentage of demand filled from stock.

Finite A situation where the number of customers is relatively small.

Finite loading The process which limits the amount of work that is released to a given work center on the basis of capacity considerations.

Finite population A situation where the number of customers is relatively small.

Fixed costs The costs of inputs to the product-service bundle that cannot be changed over the short run.

Fixed-position layout A layout in which value-adding resources travel to the customer, but materials do not travel through a value-adding system.

Fixed-position layout Layout in which a project produces large deliverables, so the material, equipment, and other resources are brought to a central location.

Flexibility The system's ability to respond to uncertainty and variability in the business environment.

Flexible automation A variable process capable of controlling equipment that produces a variety of goods, making the discussion of the value-adding system's flexibility much more complex than it once was.

Flexible manufacturing system (FMS) An automated manufacturing cell—a group of interconnected, numerically controlled machines with automated material-handling capabilities and a shared control system.

Flow time The time a job will require to complete the sequence of activities needed.

Flowcharts Tools that are especially effective in describing a process by graphically depicting all of the steps in the process in sequence.

Folding back The procedure for analyzing a decision tree in which the process starts at the right hand edge of the tree and proceeds back to the start of the tree, working from right to left.

Forecast accuracy A measurement of the selection and use of a forecast model.

Forward finite scheduling approach A process where managers start with the current jobs waiting at the bottleneck and assign time to them—from the present onward—based on their priorities.

Forward scheduling When customers are particularly time sensitive, the master scheduler will usually attempt to add the order as early as possible in the hope that it can be completed within a satisfactory period.

Freeze window A fixed period of time at the beginning of the schedule for which the master schedule is final and not subject to revision.

Functional layout A layout in which value-adding resources are arranged in groups based on what they do.

Gantt chart Bar graphs that show a resource's scheduled area and available time. By displaying the planned timing of activities on a time line, team members recognize what activities are really critical and how well they are keeping up with their project's schedule.

Geographic boundaries The lines of demarcation that allow spatial data to be categorized.

Geographic information system (GIS) A software tool that is used to improve spatially oriented decisions.

Global positioning system (GPS) A highly-effective mechanism for location identification.

Globalization The expanding geographic scope of a firm's value-adding system beyond regional, national, and international levels toward a worldwide multinational scale.

Group technology (GT) An engineering and manufacturing strategy for product and process design based on the development and exploitation of commonalities among parts, equipment, or processes.

Hard automation The automation of dedicated equipment which adds very specialized capabilities to equipment.

Hierarchical team structure A business philosophy that states the team might remain largely the same as projects come and go. Project workers report to the same project manager, who would in turn report to a senior manager, probably the regional director.

Histograms A bar chart that presents a frequency distribution.

Hollow corporation A company that does not actually add value to the items it sells, but interacts with a network of supplying companies to sell their products.

Hybrid layouts Layout in which one facility has multiple purposes.

Increasing returns to scale When operating at low volumes, the average unit cost of producing $(n + 1)$ units is lower than the average unit cost of producing (n) units, increasing returns to scale.

Independent demand inventory Inventory that is addressed by the master schedule is preferred because it is material that the firm produces for sale.

Infinite loading A process which allows planners to assign jobs to work centers regardless of their available capacity.

Infinite population The state at which a population is large enough that the number of customers already receiving or waiting for service does not affect the rate at which additional customers arrive to get service.

Infinite The state at which a population is large enough that the number of customers already receiving or waiting for service does not affect the rate at which additional customers arrive to get service.

Infrastructural decisions Choices which determine the procedures, systems, and policies that coordinate the firm's operations. These decisions are more easily reversed or changed than "bricks and mortar" decisions.

In-plant supplier Suppliers who are provided office space and support on-site at a facility they service.

Input/output control A system that monitors the work assigned to a resource (input) and the work completed by a resource (output).

Insensitivity range The range of assumed values a decision variable have without changing the decision outcome.

Inside exchange of die (IED) Activities that can be done only while a machine is stopped.

Inspection error A mistake that occurs when the measurement applied to the sample is observed, recorded, or interpreted incorrectly.

Inspection The process of comparing the characteristics of a product or service with the characteristics that define its acceptability.

Integrated supply A distributor offers to provide a high level of service on an entire line of products at agreed-upon prices in exchange for a guarantee that they will receive all of the distribution business in that product line.

Internal customers Customers who exist within the organization.

Internal failure costs Expenditures associated with products, subassemblies, or components that are not fit for use and have not yet been transferred to the customer.

Inventory All the money invested in purchasing items the system intends to sell. It is generally desirable to reduce inventory.

Inventory status file (ISF) A record which indicates particulars such as inventory on hand, required lead-time, lot size, vendor, and so forth.

ISO 9000 standards A series of uniform quality standards, covering requirements for design, development, production, installation, servicing, and manufacturing.

Job enlargement Adds skill variety through the addition of new tasks.

Job enrichment Adds task significance and enhances autonomy by combining various jobs.

Job rotation Adds skill variety by moving workers through a series of different paths.

Job shop A production process that is designed to produce small volumes of highly customized products.

Job specialization The process of dividing work according to the type of skill or knowledge required for its completion.

Job-contained feedback channels Private, timely, and accurate data provided on job performance.

Jockeying A situation where a customer leaves one queue to join another in the expectation that he or she will get served more quickly.

Just-in-time (JIT) A system largely developed to enhance productivity and reduce cost by removing waste from production.

Kaizen A Japanese term that can be translated roughly as "continuous improvement." The Kaizen workshop was developed at Toyota in the 1950s to promote active ongoing, continuous improvement. Recently, the technique has been gaining recognition in the United States as a valuable approach to improving operations.

Kanban system A signal that something needs to be done.

Kieretsu A group of companies that cooperate with one another.

Late-finish time (LF) The latest time by which something must be completed if the end of the project is not to be delayed beyond its desired completion time.

Late-start time (LS) The time by which something must start if it is to be completed in its expected time and is to be finished by its late finish time.

Law of diminishing returns A facility cannot produce increasing returns to scale indefinitely.

Lead time The duration between placing and receiving an order.

Lean manufacturing A commonly used synonym for JIT.

Lean production An approach to managing operations without massive buffers of inventory which is becoming much more common.

Lean production An approach to managing operations without massive buffers of inventory which is becoming much more common.

Learning curves A graph of the time required to produce a unit of an item over time.

Learning rate The percentage reduction in the time required to produce one unit each time production doubles.

Leitstands A recent development in computerized graphical interfaces which allows operations managers to schedule work centers and display multiple resource charts electronically.

Level master schedule A schedule in which the same mix of product-service bundles is created repeatedly over the period for which the master schedule has been frozen.

Level production strategy A process where demand is met by altering only the inventory account.

Life-cycle analysis A tool used by designers in an attempt to determine the environmental impact of a product from cradle to grave.

Line balancing A procedure that can be used to optimize the assignment of tasks to work centers.

Linear programming (LP) A special type of mathematical programming model used to determine the values of decision variables that will maximize or minimize the value of a linear objective function, subject to a set of linear equation or inequality constraints.

Loading decisions Choices made to help assign work to resources.

Loading Information that can be used by MRP planners to allocate both purchase orders and internal shop orders to specific operational resources.

Logistics A function responsible for managing the flow and storage of materials.

Lot tolerance percent defective (LTPD) The level of quality that the customer would expect the sampling plan to very infrequently accept (recognizing that such a failure rate could disrupt production schedules, damage other inventory, and otherwise harm the product's quality). This is sometimes called the rejectable quality level.

Machine-level flexibility Flexibility that originates from equipment.

Make span The total processing time for all the jobs that have been loaded on the work area.

Make-to-order A policy where managers have purchase orders in hand when they are planning, so they know the demand for products and services at least as far forward as their processing lead times. They do not actually start the production process until the customer places an order.

Make-to-stock A policy where a company wants to allow for immediate product availability by building inventories of finished product based on forecasted customer demand. The entire schedule is based on forecasted demand figures.

Management science (MS) The current term for operations research.

Manufacturing Resources Planning (MRP II) A broad information system for manufacturing environments.

Marginal cost The cost of providing one additional unit of the product-service bundle.

Mass services A service-intensive process with high labor intensity and low customization.

Master schedule A detailed description of the product-service bundles scheduled to be completed over the near term.

Material requirements planning (MRP) A system needed to identify the quantity and timing of materials required for individual orders and track the progress of those offers through each part of the value-adding system. This is the most-widely-applied computerized production management planning.

Material requirements planning (MRP) A system needed to identify the quantity and timing of materials required for individual orders and to track the progress of those offers through each part of the value-adding system.

Matrix structure The business theory that states employees may be assigned to one or more projects at a given time, but their home department will remain the same.

Maximax An optimistic approach that assumes that no matter what alternative we choose, "nature" will smile favorably on us and choose the state that will benefit us the most. Thus, we choose the alternative with the largest maximum gain.

Maximin A pessimistic approach that assumes that no matter what alternative we choose, "nature" will choose the state that benefits us the least. Thus, we choose the alternative with the largest minimum gain.

Maximum cycle time The market rate of consumption.

Mean absolute deviation (MAD) A measure of forecast accuracy that tells about the average magnitude of error terms.

Mean absolute percentage error (MAPE) A measure of forecast accuracy.

Mean forecast error (MFE) A measure of forecast accuracy that gives the average error term.

Mean squared error (MSE) A measure of forecast accuracy which is analogous to a sample variance in basic statistics.

Minimax regret The approach in which we choose the alternative that will yield the smallest possible maximum regret.

Minimum cycle time The largest elemental task's duration.

Modular design An approach that allows designers to consider an item's components or subsystems independently.

Multiple-factor rating systems A comparison of the attractiveness of several locations on the basis of more than one criteria.

Multiplicative seasonal index The expected ratio of the value of a time series in the period for which the index applies to the value as called for by any trend and cyclic components.

Noncritical activities A situation where the start of finish dates can be delayed without delaying the completion of the project.

Normal time, Normal cost Generally, the best ways of doing an activity.

Numerical control (NC) A machine that can be programmed to operate automatically using coded instructions.

Objective function A mathematical expression that states how the variables contribute to achieving the decision maker's objective.

Operating characteristics (OC) curve A representation of the probability of acceptance of lots of various quality levels.

Operating expense The money the system spends in converting inventory to throughput. It is generally desirable to reduce operating expense.

Operations management (OM) The administration of processes that transform inputs of labor, capital, and materials into output bundles of products and services that are valued by customers.

Operations research (OR) Much of the early development of OR involved refining the operation of radar, estimating war losses, and forecasting enemy strength. Today, operations research is also known as management science (MS).

Operations strategy The set of decisions made in a firm's operations management.

Order-qualifying criteria The process of devising a business strategy to gain a sustainable competitive advantage in the marketplace.

Order-winning criteria Gaining the consideration to win their business.

Original equipment manufacturers Companies that manufacture components and/or products for sale under some other company's name.

Outside exchange of die (OED) Activities in which the next die is ready for use prior to the start of a setup.

Outsourcing The process of contracting with a third party to provide some aspect of the product-service bundle.

Paradigm A way of thinking, a pattern or model that serves as an example.

Parallel (independent) activities Tasks that can be conducted spontaneously.

Pareto charts Bar charts used to distinguish "the vital few from the trivial many." They are based on the Pareto principle, also known as the "80/20 rule."

Path A connected series of branches that starts at the extreme left side of the tree and goes through all levels of the tree.

Payoff function A tool which specifies what that outcome is for every possible alternative/state-of-nature combination. It may be given either as an equation or, when the possible decision alternatives and states of nature are relatively limited, as a payoff table or matrix.

P-D-C-A cycle A set of steps to be repeated in the pursuit of continuous improvement.

Peak demand strategy A situation where capacity is varied to meet the highest level of demand at particular times.

Point of sale (POS) data Information that is captured when the customer actually makes a purchase. It is even more valuable than primary research because it indicates what customers do, not just what they say they do.

Poka yoke The Japanese term for "failproof." For example, a device used at the Cummins Engine Company makes sure the correct transmission is placed in the company's midrange diesel engines.

Postponement A strategy that delays the customization of the product service bundle as long as possible.

Precedence diagram A schematic drawing that shows the order and duration of the required tasks.

Precedence table A complete enumeration of the project's activities and their sequential relationships.

Prevention costs Expenses accrued in efforts to prevent failure and appraisal costs.

Primary research A process which involves managers in gathering the specific information they need about past and potential customers.

Priority rules dispatching rules, sequencing rules Rules used to assign priorities to jobs.

Process (or functional) layout A layout in which value-adding resources are arranged in groups based on what they do.

Process capability The ability of a process to meet specifications is measured by comparing the variation in the process with the allowance for variation provided by the specifications.

Process life cycle (PSLC) As the market continues to decline and volumes drop, the large facilities may be replaced with smaller facilities that have higher variable costs but lower fixed costs (such as batch processes and job shops).

Process map A system overview, which identifies suppliers, outputs, key deliverables, key material flows, key information flows, and feedback loops.

Process-oriented (functional) layout Layout in which all equipment of similar function or type is grouped together in departments or sections.

Producer's risk The risk of making type I errors.

Product layout A layout in which the value-adding resources are arranged in the order in which materials or customers must flow to complete the product-service bundle.

Product simplification A design (or redesign) strategy that improves the manufacturability, serviceability, or reliability of a product or service by reducing the complexity of its design.

Production batch size The number of items a resource is asked to process with one setup.

Production lead time The total time a unit spends on the line.

Productivity The relationship between output and input for any process.

Product-oriented layout Layout employed by repetitive and continuous-flow manufacturing.

Product-service bundle The total value of the purchase, usually including a "bundle" of goods and services.

Professional services A service-intensive process with high labor intensity and high customization.

Program evaluation and review technique (PERT) A network modeling approach of time management that allows the expected duration of any activity to be expressed as a probability distribution.

Project A set of tasks that is completed only once to create a unique product-service bundle.

Project A set of tasks that is completed only once.

Project activities A basic work unit that's related in various ways to other activities in the project.

Project delay The amount of time the project is running behind schedule.

Pull scheduling A system in which work is pulled through the value-adding system by signals from end users.

Purchasing The business function responsible for managing the acquisition of the materials used by an organization.

QI story A structured process that allows a group to use both numeric and subjective data to solve problems.

Qualitative forecasting A planning method based on the subjective assessments of individuals, working separately or in groups, rather than on formal equations.

Quality function deployment (QFD) A design methodology that is used to integrate customer expectations with decisions made throughout the product design process.

Quantitative forecasting A method of using one or more equations to turn a set of numerical or categorical inputs into a forecast of a value or set of values for one or more variables.

Queue A sequence of jobs or customers waiting to be processed by a server.

Queue discipline The rule used to determine which waiting customer is served next.

Radio frequency identification (RFID) Devices that work by placing small microchip-based tags and transponders on items, so their location and quantities can be immediately verified.

Randomness A situation where all other factors that cause the actual observed value of a variable differ from that predicted by the trend, cyclic, and seasonal effects.

Rejection In a finite queue model, turning away customers arriving when the queue is full.

Related diversification Decision-making pattern in which an organization seeks to coordinate the activities of the companies they own.

Reneging A situation when a customer initially joins the queue but leaves before receiving the service.

Reorder point The product of the demand per day and the lead-time in days. An order should be placed when the amount of inventory available for use during lead time exactly equals the amount that will be required during the lead time.

Repetitive process A process that produces standardized outputs from standardized inputs using dedicated equipment.

Risk analysis An evaluation of the various possible outcomes and their probabilities, and extreme case analysis, which, like the maximax and maximin strategies, takes either an optimistic or pessimistic view rather than working with probabilities.

Rolling planning horizon A planning period whose beginning and endpoints slide forward with the passage of time.

Root mean squared error (RMSE) A basis for a forecast interval.

Rough-cut capacity planning A planning method where the feasibility of master schedules must be verified.

Run charts Graphs which document the value of a particular variable over time. Like a control chart, they allow a business to track process changes over time.

Safety stock Extra inventory that is held to reduce the chance of a stockout.

Sampling distribution The probability that a particular sample statistic will take on a given value if common cause variation is the only type of variation present in the system.

Sampling error A situation where a sample is biased, or unrepresentative of the batch.

Saturation marketing An approach (used by Au Bon Pain, a croissant sandwich restaurant chain and others) that segments high-density urban areas into small, focused markets such as shopping malls and office buildings.

Scatter diagrams Used to pictorially present the underlying relationships between variables.

Scenario planning A forecasting method where long-term planners deal with uncertainty by preparing for a variety of possible situations.

Scheduled value shortfall The difference between the budgeted cost to date and the earned value to date. This represents a variance from projected costs, which is behind schedule.

Seasonality Any regular pattern recurring within a time period no more than a year.

Sensitivity The likelihood of a decision outcome to change based upon the assumed value of a variable.

Sensitivity analysis A special type of linear programming model for finding each source destination. Decision makers need to know how much a model's assumptions could change without changing the optimal solution.

Service blueprint A visual diagram—usually a flowchart—that depicts all of the activities in the service delivery process.

Service facility The system that actually delivers the service requested or needed.

Service factory A service-intensive process with low labor intensity and low customization.

Service level The measure of how well an inventory system meets demand.

Service rate The average number of customers that a server could process in a time period if there were always another customer available.

Service recovery The process of converting a customer who is dissatisfied with a service into one who is satisfied.

Service shops A service-intensive process with low labor intensity and high customization.

Shadow price The change in the value of the objective function that results from a one-unit change in the right hand side of a constraint.

Shipping buffer An inventory of finished work used to enhance the probability of correctly-timed shipments.

Silo effect The phenomenon in which organizational barriers prohibit communication among functions.

Simple exponential smoothing (SES) A popular item series model for averaging when there is no seasonality by forecasting the value for next period simply by estimating the height of the horizontal line around which the actual values are randomly scattered.

Simple moving average (SMA) Forecasts the value for the next period simply by estimating the height or level of the horizontal line around which the actual values are randomly scattered.

Simplified systematic layout planning (SSLP) A tool used to develop process-oriented layouts in service organizations and other settings where the need for proximity between departments is influenced by a number of qualitative factors.

Single minute exchange of die system (SMED) Shingo system for quick setups.

Six-sigma programs A management approach that involves employees in improvement project teams seeking to create essentially error-free processes.

Skill variety The extent to which a job includes different activities requiring different skills and talents.

Slack time The duration that an activity can be delayed without delaying the project's completion.

Smoothing constant A number between 0 and 1.

Sole source logistics provider A supplier that handles all aspects of a company's particular need.

Sole sourcing A practice whereby a company commits to buy all of a particular type of services or goods from one vendor.

Solver Solver is a feature of Microsoft's Excel that can be used to solve linear programing problems.

Spatial data warehouse A database including geographic information that can be accessed by users of a client-server computer system.

Special cause variation (or assignable variation) Unlike common cause variation, the presence usually reflects a significant change in the system.

Specification An instruction set that defines the boundary between that which is acceptable and that which is not.

Specification limit The minimum level of conformance to a design target required for an item to be acceptable.

States of nature Aspects of the decision situation over which the decision maker does not have direct control.

Statistical process control (SPC) When processes are monitored and adjusted on the basis of sample data.

Steady-state behavior A state when the arrival rate changes or the number of servers changes.

Strategy A set of actual decisions made by an organization over time.

Stratification A way of breaking data down by category. When data has been aggregated, it often loses its usefulness.

Structural decisions Choices which establish the design, or "bricks and mortar," of the value-adding system. They typically have long-term significance, because they are not easily changed.

Structural variation Changes caused by patterns in the system.

Stocking level The amount of stock available.

Stock-out A zero inventory balance.

Sunk cost The money that has been spent on a project.

Supplier certification A practice of requiring suppliers to document certain characteristics in order to obtain business.

Supply chain management (SCM) The configuration, coordination, and improvement of a sequentially-related set of operations.

Supply-chain configuration The relationships between value-adding activities, both within and outside of the company.

Supply-chain management (SCM) The configuration, coordination, and improvement of a sequentially-related set of operations.

Sustainability Encourages companies to meet the needs of today's consumer without compromising the ability of future generations to meet their needs.

Synchronous value-adding systems Systems whose effective management, because of the presence of a bottleneck, requires that the timing of value-adding activities be coordinated (or synchronized) throughout the system.

Syndicated data Information found in existing databases which provides demographic information about the lifestyles, needs, and expectations of potential customers.

Synergy A condition that makes a combined total worth more than the sum of its individual parts.

System nervousness A problem-causing fluctuation in the material plan.

Taguchi methods Statistical studies that can be used to ensure that product design specifications are wide (or narrow) enough to accommodate likely levels of process variability.

Takt time The rate at which material is used by the customer's value-adding system.

Tampering When managers respond to a common cause variation by taking some special action, which introduces more variation into the system.

Task identity The extent to which a job requires the completion of a recognizable product-service bundle.

Task significance The extent to which a job impacts other people.

Technology selection A variety of issues, including the degree and type of automation and the supplier of the equipment.

Testing The measurement of the performance of complex assemblies and service systems.

Theory of constraints A general approach that can be used to synchronize such value-adding systems containing bottlenecks.

Throughput The rate at which the system generates money through sales.

Time and motion studies Job standards are determined by breaking a task down into its basic movements and measuring the time required to complete those movements.

Time series Models based on extrapolating the historical pattern for the variable of interest into the future.

Time-cost trade-off A procedure for determining how best to trade off increased activity costs for reduced project time.

Total cost overrun When a current budget shortfall and a scheduled value shortfall compromise together.

Total cost The sum of all the fixed and variable costs for a facility over a given period.

Total productive maintenance (TPM) An approach that stresses the idea that workers should maintain their own equipment.

Total quality control (TQC) An approach to ensuring that products conform to specifications that utilizes employees from all functional areas in addition to support from a quality control department.

Total quality management (TQM) A system of management based on a commitment to the customer's total satisfaction, understanding and improving the organization's processes, employee involvement, and data-based decision making.

Trade area analysis Determines the impact of one facility on the business of others. It is especially important for service.

Transfer batch size The number of items that are moved from one resource to the next on a material routing.

Transformation (conversion) process The core set of operations used by a company to provide the primary goods and services that they sell to customers.

Transient behavior An unstable queue that exhibits a pattern of growth or decline.

Transportation model A special type of linear programming model.

Transportation tableau (transportation matrix) A special format used to summarize the information for a transportation model.

Transportation tableau A special format used to summarize the information for a transportation model.

Trends Refers to a general pattern of change over time.

Type I error When a lot that should be accepted is rejected.

Type II error When a lot that should be rejected is accepted.

Utilization of the line The average utilization of workstations on the line.

Value-adding system An organized group of interrelated activities and/or processes that creates the product-service bundle and thereby adds the value required by customers. It includes an organization's managerial infrastructure and the physical processes it uses; traditiona traditionally referred to as the service delivery system in service organizations and in manufacturing as the manufacturing process.

Variable costs The costs of inputs to the product-service bundle that vary with the number of units (or volume) produced or served.

Variable measures Measurements of physical and dimensional characteristics on a continuous scale.

Vendor managed inventory A concept whereby the logistics provider or material supplier keeps track of the materials that are bought by a customer on a regular basis.

Vertical integration The decision to expand a firm's value-adding process ownership into activities provided by suppliers or customers.

Weight-added operations The use of converging material flows to produce items that are much more costly to transport than the supplies from which they are made.

Weight-reduced operations The use of diverging material flows to stratify objects according to their market value.

Work breakdown structure (WBS) A top-down view of the tasks included in a project.

Work sampling Research gathered through the process of timing workers with a stopwatch as they performed the various tasks that made up their jobs.

Work standard A defined procedure for the completion of a task including a clearly stated task duration.

Worker soldiering The social pressure to perform your work in a particular way.

Workstation utilization The ratio of the time a workstation requires to complete its assigned tasks to the cycle time.

Yield management system A service-orientated system that performs a function similar to materials requirement planning.

Index

A

ABC (activity-based costing), 278, 609, 698
ABC inventory analysis, 587–588
Abercrombie & FItch, 466–467
ABN Amro Bank, 567
Acceptable quality level (AQL), 138
Acceptance sampling, 134–140
  error, risk, and tolerance levels, 136–140
  sampling plans, 135–136
Accounting, integrating with:
  aggregate planning, 531, 532
  capacity and location decisions, 343, 344
  facility layout decisions, 406
  forecasting, 490
  job design decisions, 460
  just-in-time (JIT) systems, 627, 628
  materials requirements planning, 728
  operations management, 70
  operations strategy, 36, 47
  process design choices, 296
  product service bundle design, 254
  project management, 192
  quality management, 116
  supply chain coordination, 574
  synchronous planning and control system, 678, 680
Activity-based costing (ABC), 278, 609, 698
Activity-on-arrow (AOA), 209, 210
Activity-on-node (AON), 209–210, 221
Activity timing, 226
Addiction, costs of, 470–471
Additive seasonal index, 507
Adjacency requirements, 420, 421–422, 424, 426–428
A-E-I-O-U-X taxonomy, 420
Aggregate plan, 534
Aggregate planning, 527–568, 575
  chase demand strategy, 542, 545–546, 547
  cut and try method, 554
  e-commerce, 555
  Fonterra Co-operative Group Ltd., 537
  integration with other functions, 531–533
  for intermediate term, 533–538

level production strategy, 542, 543–545
mixed strategies, 548–551, 552
optimizing methods, 551–553
peak demand strategy, 542, 546–548, 550
resizing workforce in Netherlands and U.S., 567–568
in service environments, 540–542
service supply management, 541–542
variables, 538–542
Air traffic controllers, 687
"Always on" executive, 525–526
AMD, 454
American Airlines, 16–17, 482, 750
American National Standards Institute (ANSI), 130
American Production and Inventory Control Society (APICS), 25
American Society for Quality Control (ASQC), 130
America Online (AOL), 346
AMR Corp., 482
Analytic approach, 120–121
Andon board, 659
Appraisal costs, 127
Arpey, Gerhard, 17
Arrival rate, 837
ARTIMIS, 721–722
Assemblers, 82
Assemble-to-order, 55, 538, 539
Assembly buffer, 704
Assignable variation, 141
Assignment rule, 435
Association for Quality and Participation (AQP), 475
Asynchronous value-adding systems, 677
Attribute control charts, 144
Attribute measures, 133
Au Bon Pain, 477
Automated Data Collection (ADC) devices, 91
Automated Guided Vehicle (AGV), 310
Automated storage and retrieval system (AS/RS), 309
Automobile industry, supply chain management, 76–79
Autonomy, 465
Average fixed cost, 355
Average unit cost, 355
Average variable cost, 355

B

Baan, 608
Backlog, 539
Backward infinite scheduling, 694
Backward scheduling, 582
Backward vertical integration, 82
Balanced capacity strategy, 348
Balanced scorecard, 698
Baldrige, Malcolm, 130
Baldrige Award, 115, 130, 134
Balking, 837
Bar code technology, 309
Barrett, Colleen, 481
Basic fixed order quantity model, 589–592
Basic producers, 81
Basic single-server model (M/M/1), 838–840
Batch processes, 52, 316–320
Best operating level (BOL), 357
Bhopal, India chemical plant disaster, 60
Bias, 503
Big MRP, 730
Bill of materials, 734, 735
Birkins, Rodney Jr., 669–670
Birmingham, Fletcher, 652
Bishop, Bill, 288–289
Blueprinting, 660
Boeing, 275, 366, 533
Bose Corporation, 653
Bottleneck, 676. *See also* Synchronous planning and control system
Bottleneck buffer, 703–704
Bradley, David, 63
Brainstorming, 165
Brand equity, 17–18
Brand image, 405
Break-even analysis, 279–280, 356
Breakthrough sequence, 127, 129, 141
Bridgestone/Firestone, 62
Brownfield site, 83
Buffer management situations, 707
Bullwhip effect, 95
Business process, 9
Business process reengineering (BPR), 23, 320–329
  vs. continuous improvement, 322
  designing future process, 328
  document current process, 325–327

Business process reengineering (BPR)
(*continued*)
implementation plan development, 328
implement the plan, 328–329
measure/evaluate/report, 329
organize and educate, 324
prioritizing processes for, 323–324
reengineering algorithm, 322–329
reengineering principles, 329
vision for future process, 327
Business to business (B2B), 24
Business to consumer (B2C), 24

C

CAD/CAM system, 275–276
Cadillac, 18, 649–650
Calling population, 836–837
Capability indexes, 155–159
Capacity, 344
Capacity cushion strategy, 346–347
Capacity decisions, 342–363
capacity strategy, 345–348
capacity utilization, 348–350
economies of capacity decisions, 353–363
integration with other functions, 342–343
learning curves and capacity requirements, 352–353
long-term forecasting, 350–352
Capacity imbalances, 643–644
Capacity requirements planning (CRP), 733
Careers, 25
Carnival Cruise Line, 418–419
Cascading houses of quality, 272
Case studies
ARTIMIS, 721–722
Cisco Systems supply chain blunder, 107–108
data, 525
Delta Air Lines, 327–328
Goodyear/Michelin/Firestone, 62–63
Intel, 453–454
J.C. Penney, 669–670
Mitchellace, Inc., 27–29
NASA, 185–186
Palmer Johnson, 398–399
Southwest Airlines, 481–482
Varion Semiconductor, 780–781
Wilson U.S. Open Tournament Select, 288–289
Cash flow analysis, 304
Causal models, 495
Cause-and-effect diagrams, 163, 167

c-chart, 147–152
Celestica (CLS), 107
Cellular layout, 410–411
Census geography, 373
Center for Business Practices (CBP), 198
Center of gravity method, 374–377
Central limit theorem, 142
Certification in production and inventory management (CPIM), 25
Certified Quality Engineer (CQE), 115
Chambers, John, 107
Chance node, 792
Channel, 838, 840
Channel assembly, 85
Chardon Rubber Co., 652
Chase, Richard, 276
Chase demand strategy, 542, 545–546, 547
Checklists, 162, 164
Checksheets, 163, 164–165
Chrysler, 44, 46, 99, 415
Cisco, 77
Clean Air Act, 59
Clean Water Act, 59
Closed loop MRP users, 733–734
Closed loop planning, 581
Coca-Cola, 18, 645–646
Collaborative planning, forecasting, and replenishment (CPFR), 490–491, 492, 646
Collective bargaining agreements, 300
Collins, Francis S., 204
Common cause variation, 140
Communication, cross-functional, 44, 45
Communication management, 200
Communications networks, 22
Competition, global, 252
Competitive advantage, 34, 41
Competitive analysis, 273, 274
Competitive clustering, 370
Competitive priority, 42
Complementary products and services, 541
Comprehensive Environmental Response, Compensation, and Liability Act (CERCLA), 59
Computer-aided design, 275–276
Computer-aided manufacturing (CAM) system, 275–276
Computer-integrated manufacturing, 312
Computerized numerical control (CNC), 308–309
Computer simulations, 380–385
Computing technologies, 21
Concurrent engineering, 258, 260, 262–264
Condit, Phil, 366

Configuration strategies, 80–86
outsourcing, 84–86
vertical integration, 80–84
Conglomerate diversification, 38–39
Congressional districts, 373
Consensus forecast, 351
Constant service–time model, 840
Constraints theory, 206
Consumer's risk, 137
Continental AG, 63
Continuous-flow processes, 53, 316–320
Continuous improvement, 321, 322
Continuous improvement teams, 660
Contract management, 200
Control, 141
Control charts, 20, 143, 149, 164, 168
Control choices, 54–55
Control limit, 143
Conversion process, 5
Converters, 81
Copy Exactly (Intel), 453
Corning, 107
Corporate strategy, 38–41
Cost management, 200
Cost-volume break-even analysis (CVBA), 294, 306
Cost-volume-flexibility break-even analysis (CVFBA), 294, 312–316
Council for Supply Chain Management Professionals, 25
Countermeasures matrix, 166, 168
Counterseasonal products and services, 541
CPM (critical path method), 206, 207, 209–218
Crandall, Robert, 16–17
Crash cost, 218
Crashing, 206
Crash time, 218
Critical activities, 205–206
Critical Chain Project Management, 206
Critical path, 206, 215–216
Critical path method (CPM), 206, 207
computations with Excel, 217
critical path, 215–216
early start and finish times, 212–213
late start and finish times, 213
slack or float, 214–215
Critical ratio, 755
CRM (customer relationship management), 268–269
Crosby, Philip, 128–129
Crosby Quality College, 129
Cross-functional communication, 44, 45
Cross-function management, 23
Cummins Engine Company, 160
Cumulative standardized normal distribution, Appendix pp. 1–2

Current budget shortfall, 202
Customer, 15, 836
Customer-driven team structure, 195, 197
Customer-focused business strategy, 43
Customer involvement, in value-adding system, 294, 297, 300–303
Customer quality, 365
Customer quantity, 365
Customer relationship management (CRM), 268–269
Customers
  repeat, 122
  segmenting based on service needs, 95
Customer satisfaction, 15–18
  American Airlines, 16–17
  brand equity, 17–18
  business strategy, 43
  facility layout and, 414
  financial advisors, 596
  General Motors, 631
  quality management and, 117
  reactive response vs. proactive solutions, 122–123
  Rogue Ales, 58
  Toshiba Toner Products Division (TPD), 94
Customer value, 365
Cut and try method, 554
Cycle counting, 588
Cycle of failure, 477
Cycle time, 430–431
Cyclic effects, 495–497

D

Daimler-Chrysler Corporation, 44, 46, 91, 99, 169, 301
Damon Holdings Inc., 670
Data-based decision making, 119
DBR system, 693–694, 702–709
Decision alternatives, 786
Decision analysis, 786–798
  components of a decision problem, 786
  decision making under risk, 787, 790–792
  decision making under uncertainty, 787–789
  decision trees, 792–797
  types of decision problems, 787
  utility, 797–798
Decision making, 38
Decision making under certainty, 787
Decision making under risk, 787
Decision making under uncertainty, 787

Decision tree, 792–797
  analyzing, 794
  multistage decision trees, 794–795
  risk analysis, 795
Decreasing returns to scale, 356, 357
Dell, 539
Delphi method, 351, 568
Delta Air Lines, 327–328
Delta Faucet, 492
Demand cushion strategy, 347
Demand during lead time (DDLT), 599
Demand forecasts, 95
Demand-pull scheduling, 661–662
Demand rate, 592
Deming, W. Edwards, 22, 125–127, 443
  fourteen-point philosophy, 126, 127
Deming chain reaction, 125
Deming cycle, 125
Dependent activities, 207
Dependent demand inventory, 582
Deseasonalize, 510, 512
Design for disassembly (DFD), 264
Design for environment (DFE), 264
Design for manufacturability (DFM), 262
Design for procurement (DFP), 263–264
Detection processes, 132–155
  acceptance sampling, 134–140
  statistical process control, 140–155
Deterministic approaches, 536
Deterministic service-time model, 840
Differential pricing, 541
Direct numerical control, 309
Discrete processes, 53
Discrimination, 466
Diseconomy of scale, 358
Dispatching, 754–755
Dispatching decisions, 577
Dispatching rules, 755
Distributed numerical control (DNC), 309
Distribution network reliability, 303
Divisionalization, 39, 41
Division of labor, 18, 458
"Dot-com bubble," 350
Double sampling plan, 135–136
Drug addiction, 470–471
Drum-buffer-rope (DBR) system, 693–694, 702–709
Dummy activities, 208

E

Earliest due date, 755
Early finish time (EF), 212–213
Early start time (ES), 212–213

Earned value, 202
Earned value analysis, 203
eBay, 24
E-commerce, 23–24, 42, 370, 555
Economic Control of Quality of Manufactured Product (Shewhart), 20
Economic order quantity (EOQ), 592
Economic production quantity (EPQ), 602
Economy of scale, 278, 306, 358
Economy of scope, 278, 307–308
Education Society for Resource Professionals, 25
eHub, 108
80/20 rule, 167–168
Electronic Data Interchange (EDI), 78–79, 609, 752
Electronic Data Systems, 567
Elemental tasks, 434
Emergency Planning and Community Right to Know Act, 59
Employee
  absenteeism and turnover, 475, 660
  cross-training, 660
Employee involvement (EI) programs, 55, 472–477
  total quality management and, 118–119
Employers of choice, 475
Engineering, integrating with:
  aggregate planning, 533
  capacity and location decisions, 343, 345
  facility layout decisions, 407
  forecasting, 491
  job design decisions, 461
  just-in-time (JIT) systems, 629
  materials requirements planning, 729
  operations management, 71
  operations strategy, 37, 47
  process design, 295, 297
  product service bundle design, 254
  project management, 192, 193
  quality management, 115, 117
  supply chain coordination, 575
  synchronous planning and control system, 679, 680
Enterprise resources planning (ERP) systems, 24, 79, 92, 606–609, 730
Environmental Protection Agency, 59
Environmental quality, 23, 59–60
Environmental remediation costs, 365
EOQ, 592
Equal Employment Opportunity Commission (EEOC), 466
Equal likelihood procedure, 788–789
Equipment updating, 661

Ergonomics, 471
Estimating trend, 506–507
Excel, 217, 814–817
Excitement characteristics, 270
Expected characteristics, 270
Expected value of perfect information (EVPI), 791
Expediting, 734
Exponential smoothing, 501, 502
External customer, 15
External failure costs, 127
Extreme case analysis, 795, 796
Exxon *Valdez*, 60

F

Fabricators, 81–82
Facilitating goods, 8, 9
Facilitating services, 8
Facilitators, 473
Facility capacity/location choices, 48
Facility layout decisions, 401–454, 661
    A-E-I-O-U-X taxonomy, 420
    case study: Intel, 453–454
    cellular layout, 410–411
    Chrysler Group, 415
    competitiveness and, 412–413
    considerations, 416–417
    distance- and load-based tools, 423–430
    fixed-position layout, 406–408
    hybrid layout, 411–412
    integration with other functions, 405–406
    line balancing, 430
    Miami University (Ohio) recreation center, 420
    process layout, 410, 417
    product layout, 408–410
    simplified systematic layout planning (SSLP), 417–423
Facility-level flexibility, 300
Facility strategy, 361–362
Fail-proofing methods, 160–161
FAK (freight all kinds) shipment designations, 92
Feasible set, 813–814
Feedback, 467
Feigenbaum, Armand, 22, 113, 114
Fill rate, 599
Finance, integrating with:
    aggregate planning, 531, 532
    capacity and location decisions, 344
    facility layout decisions, 406
    forecasting, 490
    job design decisions, 460

just-in-time (JIT) systems, 627, 628
    materials requirements planning, 728
    operations management, 70
    operations strategy, 36, 47
    process design choices, 295, 296
    product service bundle design, 254
    project management, 191, 192
    quality management, 116
    supply chain coordination, 574
    synchronous planning and control system, 677, 678, 679
Fine, Charles, 85
Finite, 837
Finite loading, 753
Finite population models, 844–845
Finite queue models, 844
First come, first served, 755
Fishbone charts, 163, 167
5 Ws and and H, 167
Fixed costs, 353–354
Fixed interval models, 603–605
Fixed order quantity
    basic model, 589–592
    noninstantaneous replenishment, 602–603
    price discounts, 592–595
    variable demand/lead times, 595–602
Fixed-position layout, 52, 406–408
Flexibility, 293, 297, 298–300
Flexible automation, 300, 319
Flexible manufacturing, 301
Flexible manufacturing system, 310, 311
Flextronics (FLEX), 107
Float, 214
Flores, Luis, 4, 5
Florida Power and Light, 660
Flowcharts, 164, 168
Flow time, 757
Fonterra Co-operative Group Ltd., 537
Ford, Henry, 82
Ford Motor Company, 62, 70, 414, 473
    quality management, 121
    suppliers, 83
Forecasting, 485–526
    accuracy, 503–507
    case study: data, 525–526
    forecast errors, 488
    forecasting for planning and control, 489–494
    integration with other functions, 488–489
    more than one period ahead, 501
    qualitative models, 494
    quantitative models, 494
    randomness, 497
    seasonal indexes, 507–514
    seasonality, 497, 502
    short-term, 498–502

simple exponential smoothing, 501
    simple moving average (SMA), 498, 500–501
    time-series components, 495–498
    time-series models, 495
    True Value, 492
Forward finite scheduling, 694
Forward scheduling, 582
Forward vertical integration, 82
Freeze window, 574
Freight All Kinds (FAK) shipment designations, 92
Functional integration, 59
Functional layout, 52, 410
"Functional silos," 12
Functional strategies, 44–46

G

Gantt chart, 166, 168, 209, 759, 762
Garton, Dan, 16
General Electric (GE), 38–39
General Motors (GM), 63, 70, 99, 367, 568, 631
General service time distribution model (M/G/1), 840
Generic house of quality, 271
Geographic boundaries, 372–373
Geographic information systems (GIS), 372–374
Georgia Pacific, 535
Gilbreth, Frank, 462
Gilbreth, Lillian, 20, 462
Global competition, 252
Globalization, 22–23
Global location considerations, 364–365
Global positioning system (GPS), 372
Glossary, 853–862
Goal, The (Goldratt), 694
Goldratt, Eliyahu, 206, 694, 696
Goodman, Susan, 482
Goodyear Tire & Rubber Co., 62–63
Grammel, Mike, 652
Gross requirements, 736
Groupe Michelin, 62–63
Group technology, 265, 310, 311
Gryna, Frank, 138

H

Hackman, J.R., 465
Hallowell, Edward M., 525
Hammer, Michael, 329
Hampton Inn, 268–269
Handfield, R.B., 95

Hankook Tire, 63
Hanna, M.D., 60
Hard automation, 299
Harley-Davidson, 410–411
"Hawthorne Studies," 20
Henson, Gary, 301
Heskett, J.L., 475
Hierarchical engineering, 262–264
Hierarchical team structure, 195, 196
Highway infrastructure, 374
Hillary Step, 691
Histograms, 168
History of OM, 18–22
    functionalization, 21
    industrial psychology/sociology, 20
    Industrial Revolution, 18–19
    Just-in-time (JIT), 22
    management science, 21
    material requirements planning
        (MRP), 21–22
    scientific management, 19–20
    statistical control of quality, 20–21
Hockey stick syndrome, 695–696
Holistic approach, 120–121
Hollow corporation, 82
Honda of America, 411, 474–475
Hows, 271
Human behavior, 20
Human Genome Project, 204
Human resources, integrating with:
    aggregate planning, 531–532, 533
    facility layout decisions, 407
    forecasting, 491
    job design decisions, 459, 461
    just-in-time (JIT) systems, 629
    location decisions, 343, 345
    materials requirements planning,
        727, 729
    operations management, 71
    operations strategy, 37, 47
    process design choices, 295, 297
    project management, 192, 193
    quality management, 115, 117
    supply chain coordination, 575
    synchronous planning and control
        system, 679, 680
Human resources management, 200
Hybrid layout, 411–412
Hybrid service processes, 51–52
HyKo Products, 492

I

IBM, 138
Increasing returns to scale, 356
Independent activities, 207

Industrial psychology, 20
Industrial revolution, 18–19
Industrial sociology, 20
Infineon, 621
Infinite, 837
Infinite loading, 754
Information system, and process
    design, 295
Information technology, 306–307
Infrastructure decisions, 34–35, 46,
    53–56
    maintenance management
        choices, 55
    production planning/control
        choices, 54–55
    quality assurance choices, 55
    supervisory policy choices, 55
    total productive maintenance
        (TPM), 56
Infrastructure inertia, 643
Innovation, 85–86
In-plant supplier, 653
Input/output control, 753
Insensitivity range, 817
Inside exchange of die (IED), 650
Inspection, 133
Inspection error, 136, 137
Institute for Supply Management, 25
Integrated supply, 90
Intel, 107, 453–454, 535
Intel Corporation, 132
Intermarine, 398
Intermediate-range forecasts, 493
Intermediate term operational
    plans, 530
Internal customer, 15
Internal exchange of die (IED), 686
Internal failure costs, 127
Internal rate of return (IRR), 304
International Human Genome
    Sequencing Consortium, 204
Into Thin Air: A Personal Account of
    the Mt. Everest Disaster
    (Krakauer), 691
Inventory, 573–574, 696
    just-in-time (JIT) systems, 637–644
Kanban systems, 656–660
    safety stock, 642–644
Inventory management, 582–587
    ABC inventory analysis, 587–588
    finding correct inventory level,
        584–587
    negative aspects of inventory, 582–583
    positive aspects of inventory, 583–584
    RFID systems, 621
    video and DVD rentals, 585
Inventory status file (ISF), 734, 735
Ishikawa, Kaoru, 124

ISO 9000 certification, 115, 130–132
ISO 9000 standards, 90–91, 131–132
ISO 14000 standards, 91

J

Jackson, Tom, 2–3
J.C. Penney, 669–670
J.D. Edwards, 608
JDS Uniphase, 107
Jergens, 749
Job-contained feedback channels, 469
Job design, 455–483
    case study: Southwest Airlines,
        481–482
    competitive priorities, 477–479
    employee involvement (EI), 472
    integration with other functions,
        459–461
    job specialization, 465
    motivation potential, 465, 468–469
    skill set specialization, 465
    socio-technical systems theory,
        469–472
    standard procedure, 464
    standard times, 462
    task familiarity, 464
    teamwork, encouraging, 472–474
    work standards approaches,
        461–465
Job enlargement, 469
Job enrichment, 469
Job rotation, 469
Job shop, 52, 316, 318
Job specialization, 458, 465
Jockeying, 837
Joiner, Brian, 122
J.P. Morgan Securities, 63
Juran, Joseph M., 22, 127, 138
Juran Institute, 127
Just-in-time (JIT) systems, 22, 73
    applicability of JIT and lean thinking,
        633–635
    case study: J.C. Penney, 669–670
    continuous improvement, 635
    employee involvement, 635
    impact of JIT and lean systems,
        632–633
    integration with other systems,
        627–630
    inventory perspectives, 637–644
    Kanban systems, 654–660
    level scheduling, 636–637
    material planning, 648–654
    and MRP systems combined, 748–749
    and MRP systems compared, 727

Just-in-time (JIT) systems (*continued*)
scheduling and capacity management, 635–648
supply chain and e-commerce considerations, 644–645, 647

K

Kaizen, 169, 323
Kanban, 749
Kanban system, 654–660
Kano model, 266–271
Kaplan, Robert, 698
Kasparov, Gary, 751
Kawasaki, 749
Keating, Kerry, 27–29
Khumawala, B., 749
Kieretsu, 653
Kiwi, 28
Krakauer, Jon, 691
Kumho Industrial Co., 63

L

Landmarks, 374
LaSorda, Tom, 415
Late finish time (LF), 214
Late start time (LS), 214
Law of diminishing returns, 356–357
Lax, Charles, 525
Lead time, 590–591, 592
Lean manufacturing, 632
Lean production, 22, 73
Lean systems, 632–633, 660–662
Lean thinking, 633–635. *See also* Just-in-time (JIT) systems
Learning curves, 352–353
Learning rate, 352
Lee, Harry, 669–670
Leitstands, 762
Less-than-truckload (LTL), 609
Leveling demand, 661
Level master schedule, 636–637
Level production strategy, 542, 543–545
Life-cycle analysis, 264
Life cycles, of products, 253, 256
Linear decision rule (LDR) models, 551
Linear programming, 810–820
Excel's Solver, 814–817
feasible set, 813
graphical solution, 810–814
model formulation, 810
objective function sensitivity, 817–818
range, 819–820
sensitivity analysis, 817

shadow price, 818–819
shadow prices, 817
Linear programming (LP) models, 553
Line balancing, 430, 434
Loading, 733
Loading decisions, 577
Local priority rules, 754–758
Location decisions, 363–385
Boeing, 366
case study: yacht building and repair business, 398–399
center of gravity method, 374–377
decision-making tools, 371–385
Dublin, Ohio fire department, 370
geographic information systems (GIS), 372–374
locating near suppliers/customers, 367–371
location decision hierarchy, 363–367
mathematical modeling/computer simulations, 380–385
multiple-factor rating systems, 377–380
supply chain management and collocation, 371
trade area analysis, 377, 379
Logistics, 73–75, 79, 95
Longest processing time, 756
Longest task time rule, 435, 440–441
Long-range forecasts, 488, 493
Long-run average cost (LRAC) curve, 360–361
Long-term forecasting, 350–352, 530
Lot tolerance percent defective (LTPD), 138
Low-level-coded BOMs, 737
L.R. Nelson, 492

M

Machine-level flexibility, 300
Macro-process map, 326
Magna Steyr, 79
Maier, John, 58
Maintenance management choices, 55
Make or buy choices, 48
Make span, 757
Make-to-order, 54, 538, 572, 732
Make-to-stock, 55, 538, 572
Malcolm Baldrige National Quality Award, 115, 130, 134
Management challenges, in service-intensive operations, 50
Management information systems, integration with:
aggregate planning, 533
facility layout decisions, 407
forecasting, 491

job design decisions, 461
just-in-time (JIT) systems, 629
materials requirements planning, 729, 730
operations management, 71
operations strategy, 37, 47
process design, 297
product service bundle design, 254
project management, 193
quality management, 115, 117
supply chain coordination, 573, 575
synchronous planning and control system, 677, 679, 680
Management science (MS), 21
Managerial processes, BPR and, 321
Manco, Black and Decker, 492
Manufacturing operations, 6
Manufacturing resources planning (MRP), 730
Manugistics, 646
Marginal cost, 356
Marketing, integration with:
aggregate planning, 533
facility layout decisions, 407
forecasting, 491
job design decisions, 461
just-in-time (JIT) systems, 627, 629
location choices and, 343, 345
materials requirements planning, 727–728, 729
operations management, 71
operations strategy, 37, 47
process design, 294–295, 297
product service bundle design, 254
project management, 192, 193
quality management, 115, 117
supply chain coordination, 575
synchronous planning and control system, 677, 679, 680
Mass services, 51
Master schedule, 534
Master scheduling, 572, 573–580
Material planning, 648–654
lot sizes/setup time, 648–651
outside suppliers and logistical issues, 651–654
Materials requirements planning (MRP), 21–22, 723–781
case study: Varian Semiconductor, 780–781
choosing a system, 748
detailed scheduling, 753–762
example (Bonnie's Candle Shop), 737–743
expediting orders, 748
Gantt charts, 759, 762
integrating with other functions, 727–730

JIT/TOC and, 748–749
managing MRP systems, 743–748
master schedule to material plan, 739–742
overview, 733–734
product structure, 737–739
reducing lumpiness and lead time, 742–743
service operations, 749
supply chain impact, 752–753
system logic, 735–737
where used, 731–733
yield management systems, 726, 750, 752
Mathematical modeling, 21, 380–385
Mathematical optimization, 809–826
linear programming, 810–820
transportation model, 820–825
Matrix structure, 194–195
Maximax procedure, 787
Maximin procedure, 788
Maximum cycle time, 431
Mayo, Elton, 20
Mazak, 411
McColl, Hugh, 307
McDonald's, 43, 586
Mean absolute deviation (MAD), 503, 505, 585
Mean absolute percentage error (MAPE), 503, 505
Mean forecast error (MFE), 503, 506, 585
Mean squared error (MSE), 503–504, 585
Media geography, 374
Miami University (Ohio) recreation center, 420
Michelin, Edouard, 62
Michelin tires, 62–63
Micro-process map, 326
Microsoft's Excel, 217
Milestones, 208
Minimax procedure, 788
Minimax regret procedure, 789
Minimin procedure, 787
Minimum cycle time, 435
Minimum slack, 755
Mission statement, 42
Mitchellace case study, 27–28
Modular design, 265–266
Mondrian Hotel, 466
Monotonic increasing/decreasing, 594
Montgomery, Bob, 262
Motion studies, 458, 462
Motivating potential score (MPS), 468
Mt. Everest, 691
Moving average, 500–501, 502
MRP II, 730

Multi-plant strategies, 362
Multiple-factor rating systems, 377–380
Multiple-server exponential service time model (M/M/S), 840
Multiplicative seasonal index, 509–510
Multistage decision trees, 794–795
Münsterberg, Hugo, 20

N

NASA (National Aeronautics and Space Administration), 185–186, 244
National Football League (NFL) franchises, 363
National Institute for Standards and Technology (NIST), 130
National Institute of Drug Abuse, 471
NatSteel Electronics Ltd., 84
Net present value (NPV), 304
Net requirements, 737
Network modeling approaches, 206–209
Nevin, Jack, 77
Newman, R.W., 60
New product costing, 727
Nichols, E.L., 95
Nike, 18
Nodes, 792–793
Noncritical activities, 206
Normal cost, 218
Normal time, 218
np-chart, 147
Numerical control (NC), 307–308

O

Objective function, 810
Obsolescent manufacturing plants, environmental liabilities and, 264
Ohno, Taiichi, 630
Oldham, G.R., 465
Operating characteristics (OC) curve, 139
Operating expense, 696
Operational complexity/uncertainty, 643
Operations management (OM), 4–6
careers, 25
customer satisfaction, 6–9, 15–17
history, 18–22
impact of functional areas on competitive priorities, 47
integrating across business functions, 10–14
measuring effectiveness of, 14–18
scope of, 9–10
time line, 19

Operations research (OR), 21
Operations strategy, 31–63, 46
alignment of operational decisions, 46–56
business strategy, 41–44
case study: Goodyear/Michelin/Firestone, 62–63
corporate strategy, 38–41
cross-functionality, 35–36
decision auditing, 56
environmental excellence and, 59–60
functional strategies, 44–46, 59
infrastructural decisions, 53–56
strategic integration of operational decisions, 57, 59
structural decisions, 46, 48–53
Optimal order quantities, 609–611
Optimized Production Technology, 694
Optimizing methods, 551–553
Oracle, 608
Order-qualifying criteria, 42, 318
Order-winning criteria, 42, 318
Organizational behavior, 20
Organizational chart, 13
Original equipment manufacturers (OEM), 82
Outside exchange of die (OED), 650, 686
Outsourcing, 84–86, 198, 303
OWL (Overwhelmingly Large Telescope), 244

P

Pacific Rim economies, 84
Palmer Johnson, 398–399
Panama Canal, 699
Paradigm, 119
Parallel activities, 207
Pareto analysis, 587
Pareto charts, 163, 167–168
Pareto principle, 167–168
Park Plaza Hospital (Houston, TX), 749
Partner Interface Process (PIP), 108
Part-period balancing, 737
Part-periods, 737
Path, 793–794
Payoff function, 786
p-chart, 144–147, 148
P-D-C-A cycle, 125–127
Peak demand strategy, 542, 546–548, 550
PeopleSoft, 608
Periodic review models, 603–605
PERT (program evaluation and review technique), 206

PERT (program evaluation and review
      technique) (*continued*)
   analyzing networks, 209–218
   computations using Excel, 217
   for political campaign, 210
   probability in, 223–226
Peterson, Robert, 269
Phillips Electronics, 567
Physical geography, 372–373
PinkRoccade, 567
Planned order receipts, 737
Planned order releases, 737
PMBOK, 190, 199, 200–201
PM Solutions, 198
Poka yoke, 160
Postal geography, 374
Postponement, 97
Powerski™ Jetboard™, 262–263
Precedence diagram, 435
Precedence table, 207, 208
Preferred Quality Supplier (PQS)
      award, 132
Prevention costs, 127
Prevention processes, 155–161
   capability indexes, 155–159
   fail-proofing methods, 160–161
   process capability, 155
   six-sigma programs, 159–160
Primary research, 371–372
Priority rules, 754–758
Probabilistic approaches, 536, 732
Process capability, 155, 157–158
Process choice, 316–320
Process design factors, 297–316
   customer involvement, 297, 300–303
   flexibility, 297, 298–300
   supply chain configuration, 297, 303
   technology selection, 298, 304–316
Process layout, 410
Process life cycle, 361
Process map, 325–326
Process-oriented layout, 52
Procter & Gamble, 39, 96–97
Procurement, 75
Procurement management, 200
Producer's risk, 136, 137
Product costing methods, 278–280
   activity-based costing (ABC), 278
   break-even analysis, 279–280
Production batch size, 708
Production lead time, 431
Production management, 21
Production/operations management
      (POM), 21
Production planning choices, 54–55
Productivity, 14–15
Product layout, 408–410
Product life cycles, 253, 256, 361

Product-oriented layout, 53
Product service bundle design process, 8,
      247–289
   case study: Wilson tennis balls,
      288–289
   computer-aided design, 275–276
   concurrent engineering vs.
      sequential/hierarchical
      engineering, 262–264
   cross-functional teams and, 257–262
   decision-making tools, 252
   defined tasks, 251, 253–257
   functional involvement profile for,
      260–261
   group technology, 265
   integrating with other functions, 251,
      252–253
   JIT systems and, 635
   Kano model, 266–271
   modern concurrent engineering
      approach, 260
   modular design, 265–266
   new product introduction vs. process
      choice, 258
   Powerski™ Jetboard™, 262–263
   product costing methods, 278–280
   product simplification, 266
   quality function deployment,
      271–275
   service blueprinting, 276–278
   team-based approach, 252
   tools, 266–280
   traditional sequential approach, 259
Product simplification, 266
Professional services, 51
Pro forma statements, 488
Program evaluation and review
      technique (PERT), 206
Project, 190
Project activities, 207
Project crashing, 218–226
Project delay, 203
Project integration management, 200
Project management, 187–245
   case study: Project Scope, 244–245
   Human Genome Project, 204
   hypothetical matrix, 195
   integrating with other functions,
      191–194
   life cycle, 199–205
   network modeling approaches,
      206–209
   organizational structure, 194–199
   outsourcing, 198
   planning, scheduling, and control,
      205–26
   PMBOK, 190, 199, 200–201
   process, 194

   project cost projection, 202–203
   time-cost trade-offs or project
      crashing, 218–226
Project management body of
      knowledge (PMBOK), 190,
      199, 200–201
Project Management Institute (PMI), 199
Projects, 52
Project Scope, 244–245
Pull and push scheduling system, 703
Pull scheduling system, 654–655
Purchasing, 75–76

Q

QI story, 161–169, 473
Qualitative forecasting model, 494
Quality assurance choices, 55
Quality function deployment, 270,
      271–275
   competitive and technical analysis,
      273, 274
   design targets, 273–275
Quality improvement story, 473
Quality management, 200. *See also* Total
      quality management (TQM)
   acceptance sampling, 134–140
   cross-functionally integrating OM,
      115, 116–117
   cross-functional quality improvement
      teams, 169–170
   detection processes, 132–155
   improvement processes, 161–170
   Intel Corp., 132
   "Kaizen workshop," 169
   prevention processes, 155–161
   QI story, 161–169
   quality system effectiveness measure-
      ment processes, 130–132
   Ritz-Carlton Hotels, 134
   statistical process control, 140–155
   total quality management (TQM),
      115–116
Quality-of-work-life, 697
Quality system assessment processes, 115
Quantitative forecasting models, 494
Queue discipline, 837
Queuing analysis, 836–852
   basic single-server model (M/M/1),
      838–840
   calling population, 836–838
   designing queuing systems, 845–846
   finite population models, 844–845
   finite queue models, 844
   multiple-server exponential service
      time model (M/M/S), 840

queue, 837
service facility, 837–837
steady-state behavior, 838
transient behavior, 838

R

Radio frequency identification (RFID) systems, 91–92, 96, 97, 309, 585, 621
Randomness, 497
Random variation, 140
Ratey, John, 525
RCA, 82
R-chart, 153–155
Redhook Ale, 408, 409
Rejectable quality level, 138
Rejection, 844
Related diversification, 39, 41
Relationship management, 90–91
Reneging, 837
Reorder point, 589
Repetitive process, 53, 316–320
Request for proposals (RFP), 199
Research and development (R&D) projects, 203
Reservation systems, 541
Resource activation, 697
Resource Conservation and Recovery Act, 59
Reverse engineering, 273
RFID systems, 91–92, 96, 97, 309, 585, 621
Richardi, Ralph, 16
Risk analysis, 795
Risk management, 200
Ritz-Carlton Hotels, 134
Rogue Ales, 58
Rolling planning horizon, 535
Root mean squared error (RMSE), 504
Roppolo, Stephen J., 466–467
Roughgarden, Trish, 453
Rules of runs, 143–144, 145
Run charts, 165, 168

S

SABRE (American Airlines), 750
Safety, 471
Safety stock, 598, 600, 606, 642–644, 705
Sampling distributions, 141–143
Sampling error, 136, 137
Sampling plans, 135–136
Sanders, Cheryl, 3, 17
SAP, 607

Sasser, W.E., 475
Saturation marketing, 370
Saturn Corporation, 367, 536
Scamell, R., 749
Scatter diagrams, 165, 168
Scenario planning, 351
Scheduled receipts, 736
Scheduled value shortfall, 203
Scheduling, in an MRP environment, 753–762
  Gantt charts, 759, 762
  local priority rules, 754–758
Schlesinger, L.A., 475
Schmid, Guenter, 621
Scholtes, Peter, 122
Schrager, Ian, 466
Scientific management, 19–20
Scope management, 200
Search decision rule (SDR) models, 553
Sears Auto Center, 63
Seasonal indexes, 507–514
Seasonality, 497, 502, 512
Segmenting customers strategy, 540–541
Sensitivity analysis, 381, 817
Sequencing rules, 755
Sequential engineering, 262–264
Sequential sampling, 136
Service blueprinting, 276–278
Service facility, 837–838
Service factory, 50
Service level, 598
Service operations, 6
Service process matrix, 48–50
Service profit chain, 475–477
Service rate, 838
Service recovery, 123, 661
Service shops, 51
Service standard design, 845
Service supply management, 541–542
Shadow prices, 817, 818–819
Shewhart, Walter, 20, 144
Shewhart cycle, 125
Shingo, Shigeo, 160, 630
Shipping buffer, 705
Shortest processing time (SPT), 755, 758
Short-run average cost (SRAC) curves, 360–361
Short-term forecasts, 488, 493–494, 498–502
Short-term scheduling, 536
Silo effect, 44
Silverton, Fred, 3–4
Simple exponential smoothing (SES), 498, 501
Simple moving average (SMA), 498, 500–501
Simplified systematic layout planning (SSLP), 417, 420–423

Sinclair, Chuck, 62
Singapore-based firms, 84
Single-minute exchange of dies (SMED) system, 474, 650, 686
Single sampling, 135
Six-sigma programs, 159–160
Skill set stratification, 465
Skill variety, 465
Skinner, Wickham, 56
Slack, 214, 216
Slack time, 205–206
Smith, Adam, 18, 458
Smoothing constant, 501
Social responsibility, 59–60
Social system, 469
Solectron (SLR), 85, 107
Sole source logistics provider, 653
Sole sourcing, 90
Solver (Excel), 814–817
Southwest Airlines, 16
Spatial data warehouse, 372
Special cause variation, 141
Specification, 121
Specification limit, 152–153, 157
Standard times, 462
Starbucks Coffee, 370
States of nature, 786
Statistical process control (SPC), 140–155
  by attribute, 144
  c-chart, 147–152
  central limit theorem, 143–143
  control charts and rules of run, 143–144
  np-chart, 147
  p-chart, 144–147
  sampling distributions, 141–143
  types of variation in a system, 140–141
  by variable, 152–155
Steady-state behavior, 838
Steinberg, E., 749
Stempler, David, 337
Stocking level, 605
Stockless purchasing, 85
Stock-out, 596
Stone, Edward, 185
Strategic decision hierarchy, 38–46
  business strategy, 41–44
  corporate strategy, 38–41
  functional strategies, 44–46
  without cross-functional communication, 40
Strategic planning, 35–36
Strategic sourcing, 97
Strategy, 36–37
Strategy formulation process, 39
Stratification, 168
Stratified pareto chart, 166

Structural decisions, 34, 46, 48–53
    facility capacity/location choices, 48
    hybrid service processes, 51–52
    make or buy choices, 48
    process type/process layout choices,
        52–53
    service process type choices, 49–50
    technological mix choices, 48–49
Structural variation, 141
Sunk cost, 203
Superfund Amendments and Reautho-
    rization Act (SARA), 59
Supervisory policy choices, 55
Supplier certification, 90
Supplier Continuous Quality Improve-
    ment (SCQI) award, 132
Supplier Cost Reduction (SCORE)
    program (DaimlerChrysler), 91
Supply chain configuration, 294,
    297, 303
Supply chain coordination, 569–622.
        See also Inventory management
    integrating with other functions,
        572–573
    master scheduling, 573–580
    rough-cut capacity planning,
        581–582
Supply chain management (SCM), 5,
    25–26, 65–108, 371, 555. See also
        Supply Chain Operating Refer-
        ence (SCOR) Model
    automobile industry, 76–79
    case study: Cisco Systems, 107–8
    channel-spanning performance
        measures, 98
    configuration strategies, 80–86
    coordination strategies, 90–101
    cost reductions, 98–101
    decisions, 73–90
    defined, 68
    E-commerce, 91–93
    as education major, 77
    enterprise resources planning systems,
        606–609
    evolution of, 69–73
    improvement principles, 93–98
    integrating across functions, 69, 70
    logistics, 73–75
    outsourcing, 84–86
    performance measures for competitive
        agendas, 99
    purchasing, 75–76
    relationship management, 90–91
    reversal of coordination approach, 92
    river metaphor, 72
    scope of, 9–10
    technology strategy, 97–98
    vertical integration, 80–84

Supply Chain Operating Reference
        (SCOR) Model, 86–90, 580
    business relationships represented, 89
    core management processes,
        86–87, 88
    management processes in, 86
Supply uncertainty, 642
Sustainability, 264
Synchronous planning and control
        system, 673–722
    applicability of, 690–694
    case study: ARTIMIS, 721–722
    cost accounting, 697–698
    drum-buffer-rope (DBR) system,
        693–694, 702–709
    integrating with other functions,
        677–681
    management process, 698–700
    and MRP compared, 727
    performance measures/capacity
        issues, 695–697
    screen printing operation, 681–689
    simple synchronous value-adding
        system, 681–689
    supply chain and, 700–702
Synchronous value-adding
        systems, 676
Syndicated data, 371
Synergy, 37
System nervousness, 748

T

Table top experiments, 464
Taco Bell, 43
Taguchi methods, 263
Takt time, 635
TAL Apparel Ltd., 669–670
Tampering, 141
Target stores, 661
Task identity, 465
Task significance, 465
Taylor, Frederick W., 19, 461–462
Taylor system (Taylorism), 19
Teamwork, 472–474
Technical analysis, 273, 274
Technical system, 469
Technological mix choices, 48–49
Technology, and value-adding
        system, 294
Technology selection, 298, 304–315
    cost-volume break-even analysis, 306
    fixed automation for economies of
        scale, 306
    flexible automation for economies of
        scope, 307–308

Telephone service geography, 374
Temporary workers, 477
Testing, 133
Theory of constraints (TOC), 690,
        692–695
    and MRP combined, 748–749
Throughput, 696
TIGER streets, 373
Time-cost trade-off, 218–226
    patterns, 219
    probability in PERT networks,
        223–226
Time management, 200
Time-series components, 495–498
Time-series forecasting methods, 488
Time-series forecasting models, 495
Time studies, 458, 462
Time study, 19–20
Tobias, Andrew, 596
Total cost, 354
Total cost overrun, 203
Total productive maintenance (TPM), 56
Total quality management (TQM), 22,
        114, 115–119, 115–129, 473
    acceptability vs. desirability, 121
    analytic vs. holistic thinking, 120–121
    Baldrige Award, 130
    class vs. team thinking, 124
    competitive sourcing vs. supply chain
        management, 123–124
    fundamental commitments, 115–19
    reactive response vs. proactive
        solutions, 122–123
    shifting management paradigms,
        119–124
    short-term performance vs. long-term
        market share, 121–122
    U.S. leaders of quality movement,
        124–129
Total system cost minimization, 845–846
Toxic Substances Control Act, 59
Toyoda, Eiji, 630
Toyota, 26, 169, 323, 630
Toyota Production System, 630, 632
Trade area analysis, 377, 379
Transfer batch size, 708
Transformation process, 5
Transient behavior, 838
Transportation matrix, 384
Transportation model, 384, 820–825
    formulation, 821
    model solution, 822–823
    sensitivity analysis, 824–825
Transportation tableau, 384, 821
Trends, 22–26, 495, 496
    cross-function management, 23
    in customer preference, 488
    e-commerce, 23–24

environmental quality, 23
estimating trend, 506–507
globalization, 22–23
TrueValue, 491, 492
Type I error, 136, 137
Type II error, 137

U

Unions, 463, 475
United Airlines, 751
Universal quality standards, 90
Unrelated diversification, 38–39
Utility, 797–798
Utility infrastructure, 374
Utilization of the line, 431

V

Valleyfair Amusement Park "Wild Thing," 276
Value-adding activities, 7
Value-adding system, 9, 10
  business process reengineering, 320–329
  case study: Delta Air Lines, 337–338
  competitive considerations, 293–294
  customer involvement, 294, 297, 300–303
  DaimlerChrysler, 301
  flexibility, 293, 297, 298–300

integration with other functions, 294–295
process choice, 316–320
process design factors, 297–316
supply chain configuration, 294, 297, 303
technology selection, 294, 298, 304–316
Toyota, 323
Value-adding system, designing, 291–338
Variable costs, 354
Variable measures, 133
Varion Semiconductor, 780–781
Vendor managed inventory, 85
Venture Manufacturing Ltd., 84
Vertical integration, 80–84, 303

W

Wai-Chan Chan, 669
Wal-Mart, 63, 79, 96
Ward, Mona, 94
Weight-added operations, 367
Weight-reduced operations, 367
Weiler, Edward, 185
Wendy's, 586
Western Electric Company, 20
Weyerhauser, 535
White, Jim, 780
Wieber, David, 77
Work breakdown structure (WBS), 206–207

Worker safety, 471
Worker's compensation, 29
Worker soldiering, 461
Work in Northeast Ohio Council, 652
Work-in-process (WIP) characteristics, 644
Work sampling, 462–463
Work standard, 462–463
Workstation utilization, 431
WriteSharp, 273–274

X

X-chart, 153–155, 156
Xerox, 17
Xilinx, 107
XML technology, 108

Y

Yellow Freight, 653
Yield management systems, 726, 750, 752

Z

ZanDan, Peter, 269